APA Handbook of

Counseling
Psychology

APA Handbooks in Psychology

APA Handbook of
Counseling
Psychology

VOLUME 1

Theories, Research, and Methods

Nadya A. Fouad, *Editor-in-Chief*

Jean A. Carter and Linda M. Subich, *Associate Editors*

American Psychological Association • Washington, DC

Published by
American Psychological Association
750 First Street, NE
Washington, DC 20002-4242
www.apa.org

To order
APA Order Department
P.O. Box 92984
Washington, DC 20090-2984
Tel: (800) 374-2721; Direct: (202) 336-5510
Fax: (202) 336-5502; TDD/TTY: (202) 336-6123
Online: www.apa.org/pubs/books/
E-mail: order@apa.org

In the U.K., Europe, Africa, and the Middle East, copies may be ordered from
American Psychological Association
3 Henrietta Street
Covent Garden, London
WC2E 8LU England

AMERICAN PSYCHOLOGICAL ASSOCIATION STAFF
Gary R. VandenBos, PhD, *Publisher*
Julia Frank-McNeil, *Senior Director, APA Books*
Theodore J. Baroody, *Director, Reference, APA Books*
Lisa T. Corry and Kristen Knight, *Project Editors, APA Books*

Typeset in Berkeley by Cenveo Publisher Services, Columbia, MD

Printer: Maple-Vail Books, York, PA
Cover Designer: Naylor Design, Washington, DC

Library of Congress Cataloging-in-Publication Data

APA handbook of counseling psychology / Nadya A. Fouad, editor-in-chief,
Jean A. Carter and Linda M. Subich, associate editors.
    p. cm. — (APA Handbooks in psychology)
  Includes bibliographical references and index.
  ISBN-13: 978-1-4338-1107-4
  ISBN-10: 1-4338-1107-3
  1. Counseling psychology--Handbooks, manuals, etc. I. Fouad, Nadya A.
II. Carter, Jean A. III. Subich, Linda Mezydlo, 1956– IV. Title:
Handbook of counseling psychology.
  BF636.6.A63   2012
  158.3—dc23
                    2011042148

British Library Cataloguing-in-Publication Data
A CIP record is available from the British Library.

Printed in the United States of America
First Edition

DOI: 10.1037/13754-000

We dedicate these volumes to the phenomenal and generous scholars who agreed to contribute to this handbook. We also recognize the many Society of Counseling Psychology colleagues and friends who have shaped our lives and careers, preparing us to be a part of this important project. In particular, it was a gift to be able to work in this collaborative team in which we could offer each other wonderful support and friendship throughout the process.

—*Nadya A. Fouad, Linda M. Subich, and Jean A. Carter*

I dedicate this to my family: my husband Bob; my children Nick, Erin, Andrew, and Patrick; and our newest member, our grandson Nolan Leitheiser. Their love and support made this project possible.

—*Nadya A. Fouad*

I dedicate this to my husband Carl and my son Stefan for their love and unwavering support.

—*Linda M. Subich*

I dedicate this to my husband Dean; my children Phil, Chuck, Brett, Catherine, Bill, and Marie; and grandchildren Nick, Daniel, Chuckie, Vincent, Victoria, Eleanor, and Josephine. Their love and support have been immeasurable.

—*Jean A. Carter*

Contents

Volume 1. Theories, Research, and Methods

Editorial Board

About the Editor-in-Chief

Nadya A. Fouad, PhD, ABPP, is University Distinguished Professor and chair in the Department of Educational Psychology at the University of Wisconsin–Milwaukee. Her primary areas of interest are career development of women and of racial and ethnic minorities, cross-cultural vocational assessment, interest measurement, cross-cultural counseling, and race and ethnicity. She is the director of research for the Center for the Study of the Workplace (http://www.studyofwork.com).

Dr. Fouad is editor of *The Counseling Psychologist* and has served on the editorial boards of the *Journal of Vocational Behavior, Journal of Career Assessment, Journal of Counseling Psychology,* and *Career Development Quarterly.* Dr. Fouad is past president of the Society of Counseling Psychology (Division 17) of the American Psychological Association (APA), past chair of Council of Counseling Psychology Training Programs, and past chair of the Board of Educational Affairs of the APA, and chair of the APA Ethics Committee. She cochaired the Multicultural Guidelines Writing Team (Joint Divisions 17 and 45), which culminated in adoption of the Multicultural Guidelines as APA policy in August 2002. Dr. Fouad earned her doctorate in counseling psychology at the University of Minnesota.

Dr. Fouad and her coauthor Romila Singh have recently completed the 1st year of a National Science Foundation–funded study to understand the barriers and supports for more than 5,000 women with engineering degrees who did or did not persist in engineering careers. In addition, Dr. Fouad has an active research team that focuses on career development and cultural competence.

Among the recognitions for Dr. Fouad's research and contributions are the following: the Paul Nelson Award (2010), the APA Award for Distinguished Contributions to Education and Training (2009), the Janet E. Helms Award for Mentoring and Scholarship (2009), the School of Education Faculty Research Award (2007), the APA Division 17 John Holland Award for Outstanding Achievement in Career and Personality Research (2003), and the Distinguished Service Award, Academy of Counseling Psychology (2001).

Contributors

Elizabeth M. Abrams, Doctoral Candidate, Department of Educational Psychology, University of Utah, Salt Lake City

Etiony Aldarondo, PhD, Department of Educational and Psychological Studies, University of Miami, Coral Gables, FL

Douglas W. Bermingham, Doctoral Candidate, Department of Educational Psychology, University of Utah, Salt Lake City

Lydia P. Buki, PhD, Department of Kinesiology and Community Health, University of Illinois at Urbana–Champaign

Angela Byars-Winston, PhD, UW Center for Women's Health Research, School of Medicine and Public Health, University of Wisconsin–Madison

Linda F. Campbell, PhD, Department of Counseling and Human Development Services, University of Georgia, Athens

Todd C. Campbell, PhD, The Bridge Health Clinics and Research Centers, Inc., Milwaukee, WI

Walter L. Campbell, MS, Department of Counseling and Educational Psychology, Indiana University, Bloomington

Robert P. Carnicella, MS, Department of Educational and Counseling Psychology, University at Albany, State University of New York

Jean A. Carter, PhD, Washington Psychological Center, P.C., Washington, DC

Carrie L. Castañeda-Sound, PhD, Graduate School of Education and Psychology, Pepperdine University, Malibu, CA

Aaronson Chew, Doctoral Candidate, Department of Counseling Psychology, University of Wisconsin–Madison

Krista M. Chronister, PhD, Department of Counseling Psychology and Human Resources, University of Oregon, Eugene

Y. Barry Chung, PhD, Department of Counseling and Applied Educational Psychology, Northeastern University, Boston, MA

Kathleen Chwalisz, PhD, Department of Psychology, Southern Illinois University, Carbondale

Collie W. Conoley, PhD, Department of Counseling, Clinical and School Psychology, University of California, Santa Barbara

Stephen W. Cook, PhD, Department of Psychology, Texas Tech University, Lubbock

Stewart E. Cooper, PhD, Department of Psychology, Valparaiso University, Valparaiso, IN

Don E. Davis, MA, Department of Psychology, Virginia Commonwealth University, Richmond

Edward A. Delgado-Romero, PhD, Department of Counseling and Human Development Services, University of Georgia, Athens

Lance S. Dixon, Doctoral Candidate, Department of Psychology, Texas Tech University, Lubbock

Darnell Durrah, Doctoral Candidate, Department of Counselor Education and Counseling Psychology, Marquette University, Milwaukee, WI

Carolyn Zerbe Enns, PhD, Department of Psychology, Cornell College, Mt. Vernon, IA

Dorothy L. Espelage, PhD, Department of Educational Psychology, University of Illinois at Urbana–Champaign

Christine E. Even, PhD, Counseling Center, University of Missouri–Columbia

Shawn Ezrapour, MA, Department of Applied Psychology, New York University, New York

Nadya A. Fouad, PhD, Department of Educational Psychology, University of Wisconsin–Milwaukee

Linda Forrest, PhD, Center on Diversity and Community, University of Oregon, Eugene

Myrna L. Friedlander, PhD, Department of Educational and Counseling Psychology, University at Albany, State University of New York

Hiroko Fukui, MA, Department of Applied Psychology, New York University, New York

Dale R. Fuqua, PhD, Department of Educational Studies, Oklahoma State University, Stillwater

Carol D. Goodheart, EdD, Independent Practice, Princeton, NJ

David B. Guion, Doctoral Candidate, Department of Psychology, Virginia Commonwealth University, Richmond

Douglas C. Haldeman, PhD, Independent Practice, Seattle, WA

Mary J. Heppner, PhD, Educational, School, and Counseling Psychology, College of Education, University of Missouri–Columbia

Puncky Paul Heppner, PhD, Educational, School, and Counseling Psychology, College of Education, University of Missouri–Columbia

Robert D. Hill, PhD, Department of Educational Psychology, University of Utah, Salt Lake City

Joshua N. Hook, PhD, Department of Psychology, University of North Texas, Denton

William T. Hoyt, PhD, Department of Counseling Psychology, University of Wisconsin–Madison

LaRae M. Jome, PhD, Department of Educational and Counseling Psychology, University at Albany, State University of New York

Cindy L. Juntunen, PhD, Department of Counseling Psychology and Community Services, University of North Dakota, Grand Forks

Neeta Kantamneni, PhD, Department of Educational Psychology, University of Nebraska–Lincoln

Maureen E. Kenny, PhD, Department of Counseling, Developmental, and Educational Psychology, Lynch School of Education, Boston College, Chestnut Hill, MA

Julie Koch, PhD, School of Applied Health and Educational Psychology, Oklahoma State University, Stillwater

Kwong-Liem Karl Kwan, PhD, Department of Counseling, San Francisco State University, San Francisco, CA

Jessica E. Lambert, PhD, Trauma, Health and Hazards Center, University of Colorado at Colorado Springs

Richard T. Lapan, PhD, Department of Student Development and Pupil Personnel Services, School of Education, University of Massachusetts at Amherst

Michael Y. Lau, PhD, Department of Counseling and Clinical Psychology, Teachers College, Columbia University, New York, NY

Jioni A. Lewis, Doctoral Candidate, Department of Educational Psychology, University of Illinois at Urbana–Champaign

Cara S. Maffini, Doctoral Candidate, Department of Counseling and Educational Psychology, Indiana University, Bloomington

Brent Mallinckrodt, PhD, Department of Psychology, University of Tennessee–Knoxville

Susan Mao, EdM, Department of Counseling and Clinical Psychology, Teachers College, Columbia University, New York, NY

Elizabeth Markle, Doctoral Candidate, Department of Counseling and Applied Educational Psychology, Northeastern University, Boston, MA

Petra J. McGuire, Doctoral Candidate, Department of Psychology, Texas Tech University, Lubbock

Brian W. McNeill, PhD, Department of Educational Leadership and Counseling Psychology, Washington State University, Pullman

Michael Mobley, PhD, Department of Educational Psychology, Rutgers, The State University of New Jersey, New Brunswick

Lauren B. Moffitt, PhD, Department of Psychology, University of Tennessee, Knoxville

Melissa L. Morgan, PhD, Department of Counseling, Clinical and School Psychology, University of California, Santa Barbara

Susan L. Morrow, PhD, Department of Educational Psychology, University of Utah, Salt Lake City

Helen A. Neville, PhD, Department of Educational Psychology, University of Illinois at Urbana–Champaign

Jody L. Newman, PhD, Department of Educational Psychology, University of Oklahoma, Norman

Mineko Anne Onoue, Doctoral Student, Department of Applied Psychology, New York University, New York

Margaret E. Pierce, EdD, Department of Student Development, School of Education, University of Massachusetts, Amherst

Alex L. Pieterse, PhD, Department of Educational and Counseling Psychology, University at Albany, State University of New York

Megan K. Polanin, MA, School of Education, Counseling Psychology, Loyola University Chicago, Chicago, IL

V. Paul Poteat, PhD, Department of Counseling, Developmental and Educational Psychology, Lynch School of Education, Boston College, Chestnut Hill, MA

Stephen M. Quintana, PhD, Department of Counseling Psychology, University of Wisconsin–Madison

Christine Robitschek, PhD, Department of Psychology, Texas Tech University, Lubbock

John L. Romano, PhD, Department of Educational Psychology, University of Minnesota, Minneapolis

Michael J. Scheel, PhD, Department of Educational Psychology, University of Nebraska–Lincoln

Gwynneth Schell, Doctoral Candidate, Department of Counseling Psychology, University of Wisconsin–Madison

Melissa Selem, Doctoral Candidate, Department of Kinesiology and Community Health, University of Illinois at Urbana–Champaign

Victoria A. Shivy, PhD, Department of Psychology, Virginia Commonwealth University, Richmond

Sandra L. Shullman, PhD, Managing Partner, Columbus Office, Executive Development Group, LLC, Columbus, OH

Elizabeth A. Skowron, PhD, Department of Counseling Psychology, The Pennsylvania State University, University Park

Laura Smith, PhD, Department of Counseling and Clinical Psychology, Teachers College, Columbia University, New York, NY

Lisa B. Spanierman, PhD, Department of Educational and Counseling Psychology, McGill University, Montreal, Quebec, Canada

Cynthia C. Spering, PhD, Department of Psychology and Counseling, Northeastern State University, Tahlequah, OK

Cal D. Stoltenberg, PhD, Department of Educational Psychology, University of Oklahoma, Norman

Linda M. Subich, PhD, Buchtel College of Arts and Sciences, University of Akron, Akron, OH

Lisa A. Suzuki, PhD, Department of Applied Psychology, New York University, New York

Jane L. Swanson, PhD, Department of Psychology, Southern Illinois University, Carbondale

Dawn M. Szymanski, PhD, Department of Psychology, University of Tennessee, Knoxville

Rebecca L. Toporek, PhD, Department of Counseling, San Francisco State University, San Francisco, CA

Sherri Turner, PhD, Department of Educational Psychology, University of Minnesota, Minneapolis

Tammi Vacha-Haase, PhD, Department of Psychology, Colorado State University, Fort Collins

Elizabeth M. Vera, PhD, School of Education, Loyola University Chicago, Chicago, IL

David L. Vogel, PhD, LP, Department of Psychology, Iowa State University, Ames

Lynn Y. Walsh-Blair, Doctoral Candidate, Department of Counseling, Developmental, and Educational Psychology, Lynch School of Education, Boston College, Chestnut Hill, MA

Kenneth T. Wang, PhD, Educational, School, and Counseling Psychology, College of Education, University of Missouri–Columbia

Li-Fei Wang, PhD, National Taiwan Normal University, Taipei

Stephen R. Wester, PhD, LP, Department of Educational Psychology, University of Wisconsin–Milwaukee

Susan C. Whiston, PhD, Department of Counseling and Educational Psychology, Indiana University, Bloomington

Robert A. Williams, PhD, Department of Counseling, San Francisco State University, San Francisco, CA

Petra Woehrle, Doctoral Candidate, Department of Counseling Psychology, The Pennsylvania State University, University Park

Y. Joel Wong, PhD, Department of Counseling and Educational Psychology, Indiana University, Bloomington

Everett L. Worthington Jr., PhD, Department of Psychology, Virginia Commonwealth University, Richmond

Oksana Yakushko, PhD, Pacifica Graduate Institute, Carpinteria, CA

Series Preface

The *APA Handbook of Counseling Psychology* is the sixth publication to be released in the American Psychological Association's *APA Handbooks in Psychology*™ series, instituted in 2010. The series includes multiple two- and three-volume sets focused on core subfields. Additionally, some single-volume handbooks on highly focused content areas within core subfields will be released in coming years.

The five previously released sets are as follows:

- *APA Handbook of Industrial and Organizational Psychology*—three volumes; Sheldon Zedeck, editor-in-chief
- *APA Handbook of Ethics in Psychology*—two volumes; Samuel J. Knapp, editor-in-chief
- *APA Educational Psychology Handbook*—three volumes; Karen R. Harris, Steve Graham, and Tim Urdan, editors-in-chief
- *APA Handbook of Research Methods in Psychology*—three volumes; Harris Cooper, editor-in-chief
- *APA Addiction Syndrome Handbook*—two volumes; Howard J. Shaffer, editor-in-chief

Each set is primarily formulated to address the reference interests and needs of researchers, clinicians, and practitioners in psychology and allied behavioral fields. Each also targets graduate students in psychology who require well-organized, detailed supplementary texts, not only for "filling in" their own specialty areas but also for gaining sound familiarity with other established specialties and emerging trends across the breadth of psychology. Moreover, many of the sets will bear strong interest for professionals in pertinent complementary fields (i.e., depending on content area), be they corporate executives and human resources personnel; doctors, psychiatrists, and other health personnel; teachers and school administrators; or cultural diversity and pastoral counselors, legal professionals, and so forth.

Under the direction of small and select editorial boards consisting of top scholars in the field, with chapters authored by both senior and rising researchers and practitioners, each reference set is committed to a steady focus on best science and best practice. Coverage converges on what is currently known in the particular subject area (including basic historical reviews) and the identification of the most pertinent sources of information in both core and evolving literature. Volumes and chapters alike pinpoint practical issues; probe unresolved and controversial topics; and present future theoretical, research, and practice trends. The editors provide clear guidance to the "dialogue" among chapters, with internal cross-referencing that demonstrates a robust integration of topics to lead the user to a clearer understanding of the complex interrelationships within each field.

With the imprimatur of the largest scientific and professional organization representing psychology in the United States and the largest association of psychologists in the world, and with content edited and authored by some of its most respected members, the *APA Handbooks in Psychology* series will be the indispensable and authoritative reference resource for researchers, instructors, practitioners, and field leaders alike.

Gary R. VandenBos, PhD
APA Publisher

Introduction

Counseling psychology is characterized by its long roots in vocational psychology, prevention, primary interventions, advocacy, and an emphasis on individual differences. The field is distinguished by philosophical approaches that emphasize human strengths and healthy functioning and a keen appreciation for individual differences. Over the years, this approach has led to emerging emphases on prevention, cultural context, dimensions of diversity, the role of work in people's lives, social justice, and advocacy, resulting in expanded roles for counseling psychologists in new settings, contexts, and with new populations. The two volumes in this handbook will highlight the research and practices in counseling psychology's traditional areas as well as in new and emerging areas.

Counseling psychology as a specialty grew from a number of influences, including early career guidance work in the 1900s, assessment work with soldiers in World Wars I and II, advocacy work during the Great Depression, working with returning veterans in the 1940s and 1950s, focusing on hygiology rather than pathology in the 1950s and 1960s, and advocacy work throughout the 1960s and 1970s to promote vocational choice as an avenue for equality. Therapeutic interventions flowed from this early focus on advocacy, prevention, and strengths, emphasizing normal developmental concerns and approaches. More recently, the strands of individual differences, advocacy, prevention, vocational psychology, and developmental approaches have led to attempts to understand the way that gender, race, ethnicity, disability, religion, and social class shape behavior. Counseling psychologists have begun to extend their strengths-based approach beyond the traditional areas of vocational psychology, psychotherapy, and prevention to new settings, such as in schools and hospitals, and new populations, such as children and elderly people. Philosophical emphases on development have led to significant work to help us understand supervision and its role in training.

THE TWO VOLUMES OF THE *APA HANDBOOK OF COUNSELING PSYCHOLOGY*

The chapters in this handbook encompass both traditional and emerging areas in counseling psychology. The associate editors (Linda M. Subich for Volume 1 and Jean A. Carter for Volume 2) and I had three goals for shaping the two volumes of the handbook. We first sought to ensure that we encompassed the traditional areas of counseling psychology as well as incorporating the evolution in the specialty. Second, we endeavored to capture the new and emerging areas of practice settings, populations, and perspectives. Finally, we wanted to consult with well-respected counseling psychology scholars to ensure the breadth of topics to be included in the handbook as well as the scope of the chapters and to garner suggestions for authors who could write for the handbook. Volume 1 was designed to include traditional areas that are covered in handbooks, providing a strong foundation in theories and research in counseling psychology, and Volume 2 focused on both historic and evolving applications.

To address our first goal, we began developing topics for the two volumes by reviewing the content domains defined as counseling psychology's unique areas that were outlined in the Petition for Recognition for the Specialty to the American Psychological Association (APA) Commission on Recognition on Specialties and Proficiencies in Psychology (CRSSP), which were approved in 2005. The following were outlined in the CRSSP petition:

- Professional Issues in Counseling Psychology: knowledge of the history, philosophy of counseling psychology, and specialty guidelines for the provision of counseling psychology services
- Theories and Techniques of Counseling Psychology: integration of theory, research, and practice in the activities of counseling psychologists, efficacy of counseling psychology interventions, and awareness of and appreciation for evidence-based treatments, including research on the process of counseling and the outcomes of counseling processes
- Legal and Ethical Issues: legal and ethical aspects of the profession
- Individual and Cultural Diversity: individual and cultural diversity, broadly defined to include gender, race, ethnicity, social class, religion and spirituality, ability and disability, and sexual orientation
- Psychological Assessment, Diagnosis, and Appraisal: psychometrics, diagnoses from a counseling psychology perspective, and the integration of test and nontest sources of client information
- Vocational Behavior and Career Development: vocational behavior, career development, and expertise in related interventions
- Consultation: consultation for individuals, groups, and organizations, providing preventive and educational interventions, and working with organizations
- Program Evaluation: intervention evaluation and accountability
- Supervision and Training: theory, research, and practice in supervision and training

Our second goal was accomplished by including chapters on the application of counseling psychology research to practice and policy in new settings (correctional facilities, schools, and hospitals), new populations (elderly people, low income), and new areas of growth for counseling psychologists (health psychology, working with the homeless). We wanted chapters that emphasized the growing application or policy implications of our traditional areas of scholarship, such as the relationship between work and mental health, health care disparities, and the ethical implications of social justice work.

Finally, to address our third goal, we drew on recommendations from consulting scholars in counseling psychology to identify (a) general areas to include in the handbook, (b) the scope of each chapter, and (c) potential authors for those chapters. Their comments were integrated and conveyed to authors who agreed to write each chapter. We are grateful for the time these scholars spent on this task and appreciative of their contributions to the handbook. Consulting editors were Y. Barry Chung, Ruth E. Fassinger, Puncky Paul Heppner, Andy Horne, Brent Mallinckrodt, Michael Mobley, Steve Quintana, Elizabeth M. Vera, and Mary O'Leary Wiley.

Our target audience for the handbook includes graduate students and established and developing researchers and practitioners. We envisioned, furthermore, that students in counseling psychology would find essential content in these two volumes. Students in other areas of psychology would find the material valuable as a supplementary text, enhancing their own specialty areas, and gaining a sound familiarity with major specialties across the field. We also envisioned the chapters as useful in providing updated research and applications for counseling psychology researchers and practitioners, as well as professionals in complementary fields such as social work and behavioral health specialties. The strong emphasis on emerging and developing areas leads the reader toward counseling psychology's future.

ORGANIZATION AND CONTENT OF THE HANDBOOK

The chapters in the handbook are organized in two volumes. The first volume focuses on theories and relevant research, and the second volume emphasizes applications and policy implications for these theories. In some cases, general topical areas may appear in both volumes. For example, Volume 1 includes chapters that review theories and research in vocational psychology (Juntunen & Even, Chapter 9) and research on work-related decisions (Jome & Carnicella, Chapter 10); Volume 2 includes chapters on work–family balance (Whiston, Campbell, & Maffini, Chapter 4) and work and mental health (Swanson, Chapter 1). Volume 1 includes a chapter on theories and research on religion and spirituality (Cook, Dixon, & McGuire, Chapter 19), and Volume 2 includes a chapter (Hook, Worthington, & Davis, Chapter 17) on the benefits and challenges of incorporating religion and spirituality into counseling and advocacy practices.

All authors were asked to review key and relevant research, to outline and critically evaluate what is known in each area as well as what is not known, and to indicate areas where more research or attention is needed. Chapters are not intended to be exhaustive reviews but rather to highlight the key literature that has moved each area forward and to provide a guide to readers of what is next needed to enhance counseling psychology.

VOLUME 1: THEORIES, RESEARCH, AND METHODS

Part I: Counseling Psychology Foundations

Volume 1 has 20 chapters, divided into three sections. The first section, Counseling Psychology Foundations, includes seven chapters that offer the reader a primer on the field and its essential domains. In the first chapter, Delgado-Romero, Lau, and Shullman review the critical developments in the field of counseling psychology over the past 10 years. Beginning with a perspective on the field as exemplified by Melba J. T. Vasquez's presidency of the APA, they trace the field's core values, the organization of the Society of Counseling Psychology, its strengths and accomplishments, and contemporary challenges to the organization. They present an overview of science and research accomplishments of, and challenges faced by, counseling psychologists, discuss trends in education and training for counseling psychology, and conclude with a number of future challenges to counseling psychology as a profession. Their broad sweep foreshadows many of the points raised by the authors in the other chapters across the two volumes.

In Chapter 2, Friedlander, Pieterse, and Lambert provide both historical and contemporary perspectives on major classes of theories of psychotherapy. They trace the evolution of psychoanalytic theory, humanistic theory, cognitive behavioral theory, and family systems theory, providing readers with the historical context for the development of the theory, the classic early forms of each theory and the later developments of the theory. They end the chapter with a review of the integrationist model from both the contextual and the common factors approaches, showing how counseling psychology perspectives are compatible with this approach and speculating on its future evolution.

Chapters 3 and 4 focus on counseling psychology research foundations. In Chapter 3, Hoyt and Mallinckrodt approach their chapter on quantitative foundations from their perspectives as associate editor and editor, respectively, of the *Journal of Counseling Psychology*. With a goal of improving the quality of research (and subsequent publication of that research), Hoyt and Mallinckrodt argue for theory-based research, provide recommendations for conducting literature reviews, and give suggestions to improve methodology and analyzing and reporting results. Their chapter represents a distillation of collective research expertise accrued over two distinguished careers. In Chapter 4, Morrow, Castañeda-Sound, and Abrams argue that counseling psychologists need to be aware of the advances in qualitative research in other disciplines. They ground the chapter in the philosophical foundations of qualitative inquiry; review content analyses of qualitative studies in counseling psychology over the past decade; and present readers with an overview of several qualitative designs, such as phenomenology, grounded theory, consensual qualitative research, and participatory action research. They end their chapter with a review of several social justice and multicultural issues in conducting qualitative research and provide a series of practical recommendations to those wanting to use qualitative methodologies and publish their work.

In Chapter 5, Forrest and Campbell provide a comprehensive summary of the trends and challenges in training counseling psychologists. They emphasize developments in multicultural education and training and the shift to competency-based education in professional psychology as well as highlighting counseling psychologists' roles in these large movements. The chapter captures many of the emerging trends in the field, including the growing push toward internationalization, the focus on evidence-based training, the expanding roles in behavioral and integrated health care, the challenges in the interface between doctoral training and master's degree programs, and the controversies over accreditation of master's programs, and, finally, the need for counseling psychologists to be more involved in public policy advocacy. Drawing from their review of the literature and their extensive experience in the profession, Forrest and Campbell offer a number of recommendations throughout the chapter, and finish with a set of general recommendations for the field.

The final two chapters in this section also focus on counseling psychology foundations. Carter and Goodheart's Chapter 6 on interventions lays a foundation for many of the interventions discussed in Volume 2. Rather than a traditional review of various interventions that are tied, for example, to the theories outlined by Friedlander, Pieterse, and Lambert in Chapter 2, they discuss the need for evidence-based practices, trace the history of the debate over how researchers and practitioners approach evidence-based practices, and discuss the different epistemologies of knowing. They also provide readers with an overview of the APA's policy on evidence-based practices, counseling psychology's contribution to that task force (both authors served on the task force, one as chair and one as a member), and counseling psychology principles related to evidence-based practices. Finally, Carter and Goodheart discuss the challenges in ensuring evidence-based practices are culturally appropriate and offer informed speculation about what the future holds for evidence-based practice in psychology.

In Chapter 7, Suzuki, Onoue, Fukui, and Ezrapour also focus on multicultural considerations in their discussion of appropriate assessment models. They focus on how counseling psychologists can assess clients' optimal functioning, and they provide an overview of the controversies in assessment (such as bias, high-stakes testing, and use of technology). In subsequent sections of their chapter, the authors review research on best practices in gathering background information, selecting appropriate measures, and administering tests and surveys to clients. Finally, they review various contextual variables and test-related variables that may influence the assessment process and conclude with their recommendations for best practices.

Part II: Theories and Research

The second section of Volume 1 consists of chapters that review the research and theoretical developments in traditional counseling psychology areas, such as process and outcome in psychotherapy, vocational psychology, positive psychology, prevention, and supervision.

In Chapter 8, Scheel and Conoley review the research in psychotherapy processes and outcomes from both a contextual model (as a framework for psychotherapy) and common factors approach (as the process). They review research on factors common across therapeutic modalities in four areas: client, therapist, relationship, and treatment adherence. In this review, the authors take care to highlight strength-based approaches. Turning to the research on outcomes of therapy, the authors examine how outcome research is conducted and recommend various strategies for how to conduct effective outcome research, including recommendations for outcome measurement as a tool to improve therapy effectiveness. The chapter ends with an extensive list of suggestions for future research in this area.

Chapters 9 and 10 focus on different aspects of vocational psychology. In Chapter 9, Juntunen and Even briefly trace the development of theory in vocational psychology. They then review the major theories in vocational psychology and the research that supports the major tenets of the theories. They also provide an overview of emerging theoretical perspectives in vocational psychology, such as the relational cultural paradigm, psychology of working, and the trilateral model of adaptive career decision making. They end with a call for vocational psychologists to demonstrate the centrality of their work to optimal human functioning.

In Chapter 10, Jome and Carnicella emphasize the various decision points related to work, including work-related decisions across the life span, moving from adolescents and initial work and schooling-related decisions, through decisions for working adults and those contemplating or moving into retirement. The authors review and critique the research on various decision points, such as the transition from school to work, decisions to return to school after entering the workforce, or decisions after a layoff. They end each section with recommendations to strengthen the research in that area and provide suggestions for further research. The chapter ends with the authors' summative comments in this regard.

Chapters 11, 12, and 13 include critical reviews of the theory and research in supervision, positive psychology, and prevention, respectively, all areas closely identified with the field of counseling psychology. In Chapter 11, Stoltenberg and McNeill present two models of supervision developed by counseling psychologists (i.e., the interpersonal approach and the integrative developmental model) and review research on the factors that have been found to be common across models. They then critique the literature on supervision processes, characteristics of supervisees and supervisors, culture and context in supervision, and ethical and legal concerns related to supervision. The chapter ends with a discussion of the competency movement as it relates to supervision and the authors offer their thoughts on future directions for supervision research.

In Chapter 12, Robitschek and Spering provide an overview of positive psychology, starting with an analysis of reasons for counseling psychology's lack of contribution to the overall positive psychology movement. They then review research on two types of well-being (feeling well and doing well) and the research on multidimensional aspects of positive psychology, cultural issues, and best practices for the study of positive psychology. They end by challenging the field to become a stronger contributor to positive psychology. In Chapter 13, Romano, Koch, and Wong also review counseling psychology's contribution to an area that has a long history and literature in broad areas of psychology. Their chapter reviews the role of prevention in counseling and provides an overview of the definition of prevention, models of prevention, and theories that have informed prevention applications. The authors offer a review of the research in three areas of specific interest to counseling psychologists: promoting academic achievement and reducing academic disparities across racial and ethnic and socioeconomic groups, preventing racism and racial prejudice, and preventing suicide.

Part III: Contextual Factors

The remaining seven chapters in Volume 1 focus on theory and research specific to contextual factors that shape individuals' functioning and worldviews. Although these contextual factors overlap and intersect in people's lives, authors were asked to focus their review of theory and research on one particular area. The areas covered include gender, race, sexual orientation, age, religion and spirituality, and social class.

Two chapters focus on gender. In Chapter 14, Wester and Vogel review the evolution of a psychology that focuses solely on the experiences of men, critiquing the research in the psychology of men and masculinity over the past two decades. They organize their critique around research that focuses on global traits (essentialist research) or research that is more contextual, focusing on how a man's definition of his masculinity fits with various situational demands (constructivist research). Their chapter includes implications for counseling men as well as a series of useful suggestions for future research. In Chapter 15, Enns reviews and critiques research on the psychology of women, including sexism and models of social identity, and then focuses on social constructionism, intersectionality, and social power as core themes within contemporary gender theory. She provides readers with an overview of four different theoretical perspectives on gender and power, and highlights the importance of the multiple contexts of people's lives by reviewing research on intersections between gender and other identities. She, too, ends her chapter with well-conceived recommendations for counseling and research with women.

Chapters 16 and 17 review theory and research related to sexual orientation and race/ethnicity, respectively. In Chapter 16, Chung, Szymanski, and Markle provide an overview of the social and political context of lesbian, gay, bisexual, and transgender (LGBT) issues, including public attitudes and policies and research on attitudes of mental health professionals toward LGBT clients. They offer definitions of sexual orientation and the nature of sexual orientation, concluding the latter discussion with a review of the research on conversion therapy. Following a discussion of sexual identity development; and the effects of discrimination and oppression, they present a review of issues that may present particular challenges to LGBT clients, including parenting and vocational development; discuss differences across cultural groups; and conclude with implications for counseling psychology education and training, practice, research, and advocacy.

Quintana, Chew, and Schell take a slightly different approach in Chapter 17, arguing that counseling psychologists can contribute to a psychological science of diversity but that the field needs to move beyond debates and arguments about definitions. They identify common themes underlying theories of race and ethnicity, such as cultural orientations and racial socialization. They review research on ethnic and racial identity development, highlighting the contributions of this research and pointing out two major concerns with the literature. The authors provide readers with an overview of research on discrimination, acculturation and acculturative stress, and the counseling implications of this research. They finish the chapter with a presentation of challenges to a psychological science of diversity and suggestions for further research.

Chapters 18, 19, and 20 represent newer areas of contextually focused research for counseling psychologists. In Chapter 18, Vacha-Haase, Hill, and Bermingham argue that counseling psychology's core values provide an ideal fit for the expanding research and practice work with elderly people. In this chapter, they begin with definitions of aging and review theories of aging that focus on the strengths gained as individuals age, including Erikson's psychosocial model of development, continuity theory, selective optimization with compensation, and positive aging. Similar to the other chapters in this section, they then review intersections of aging and other identity dimensions, including gender, race and ethnicity, and sexual orientation. Their final section highlights the importance of including an emphasis on aging in other areas of counseling psychology, including vocational psychology.

Cook, Dixon, and McGuire also argue that counseling psychology needs to expand its perspective on cultural diversity, although their focus is on the role of religiousness and spirituality as a contextual factor. In Chapter 19, they discuss the challenges of defining and measuring religiousness and spirituality and how these constructs differ. They critique and review models of religious and spiritual development, and review the literature on individuals' image of God and attachment to God. The research on religion and spirituality and its relationship to health, particularly to mental health, is presented and critiqued next, including a review of the role of religion in adverse mental health outcomes. Finally, the authors provide readers with a review of the research on religious coping, prayer, and mental health.

In Chapter 20, the final chapter in Volume 1, Smith and Mao review the research on social class in counseling psychology. They begin with a primer on social stratification theory and measurement, and argue against the use of proxy variables (such as income) in assessing social class. They go on to provide a typology of social class and then review the research on the effects of classism. The implications of social class are viewed through two prisms: social class and well-being (for middle and upper classes) and social class and negative effects for those of poor and working-class individuals. The authors review the research on the social class of mental health providers and potential influences on their work with individuals of lower social class. The chapter ends with a discussion of social exclusion theory and a call to counseling psychologists to work against economic injustice.

VOLUME 2: PRACTICE, INTERVENTIONS, AND APPLICATIONS

As we noted, the second volume focuses on the applications and policy implications of the major areas of theory and research in counseling psychology. We have divided 22 chapters into five major sections: Work and Education, Community and Family, Health, Social Justice, and New Directions: Settings and Populations.

Part I: Work and Education

The first section in Volume 2 focuses on applications related to work and education. In Chapter 1, Swanson examines the integration between work and psychological health.

Swanson begins by noting that although much is known about work and about psychological health, there are substantive gaps in our knowledge about how each influences the other. She begins with definitions of each, then reviews and critiques the literature on the effect of employment status on mental health, as well as on research on the intersection of work and psychological health, such as occupational well-being, satisfaction with work and overall life. She discusses how the intersections between work and psychological health are addressed in counseling, and ends with a call for more research in such areas as the ways in which poor psychological health impedes employment, and how to increase the benefits of the intersection between work and psychological health.

In Chapter 2, Kenny and Walsh-Blair discuss academic achievement in the United States, arguing that counseling psychologists need to understand the factors related to gaps in achievement for various groups. They begin with a review on various factors related to education achievement and research that has examined psychological contributions to the differences among groups in education achievement. They term this the *opportunity gap*, rather than *achievement gap*, referring to the gaps in opportunities for education advancement provided for various groups. They review theories of motivation that may help to inform intervention and the effectiveness of intervention strategies at a variety of levels (e.g., individual, school, community, systemic). They argue that this research can form a base from which counseling psychologists can be strong advocates to ameliorate the opportunity gaps in educational achievement.

Lapan, Turner, and Pierce also focus on opportunity gaps in Chapter 3, but their focus is on preparing students to be ready to enter college or work. They, too, argue that counseling psychologists are uniquely positioned to be social justice advocates who are informed by research in educational development and vocational psychology. Their chapter begins with an overview of concerns about the college and career readiness of adolescents in the United States. They provide readers with an overview of research on theory and interventions in college and career readiness. Finally, they provide recommendations for a national policy to help adolescents be ready for college or a career prior to high school graduation.

In Chapter 4, Whiston, Campbell, and Maffini pull together research and practices from a variety of disciplines related to balancing work and family. They review both the theory and research related to work and family conflicts as well as ways that work and family facilitate each other, and review theories that focus on how work and family can be balanced. Consistent with counseling psychology's contextual focus, they provide a review of research that focuses on work-family interface across racial and ethnic groups. They conclude the chapter with implications for counseling interventions as well as suggestions for future research.

Part II: Community and Family

The second section in Volume 2 focuses on counseling psychology research and theory applied to various areas of the community and to the family.

In Chapter 5, Haldeman addresses the definition of family, suggesting that the traditional notion of a nuclear family (composed of mother, father, and two biological children) is not an accurate reflection of reality for most of the U.S. population. He begins with a historical context for the changes in the function of the family in the community and the changes in gender roles within the family over the past century. He discusses research on same-sex families as well as research specific to families who immigrate to the United States, tracing similarities and differences among families who fit the description of the evolving family. He concludes the chapter with a series of case studies elucidating his points.

Chapters 6, 7, and 8 discuss the need for counseling psychologists to understand and be able to intervene when violence hits various parts of a community. In Chapter 6, Chronister and Aldarondo outline the research and best practices in working with partner violence. They provide an overview of the scope of partner violence in the United States and outline the enormous costs of partner violence—not only to the victim but also to the community. They highlight research on community interventions to help both victims of abuse and their batterers. They conclude with a review of interventions focused on couples and families, as well as the effectiveness of individual interventions. In Chapter 7, Skowron and Woehrle focus exclusively on the maltreatment of children, including an overview of the scope of the problem in the United States and the ways that child maltreatment is tracked. They summarize research on the negative effects of maltreatment on children's development and factors that put children at risk for maltreatment. They provide a review of evidence-based approaches to help prevent and treat child maltreatment.

In Chapter 8, Vera and Polanin discuss the causes, effects, and prevalence of community-wide violence. They provide evidence that supports their argument that some groups are overrepresented among the statistics documenting prevalence, perhaps due to the way that data have been collected. They present research on the psychological effects of being exposed to violence, as well as on moderators of the effects, such as social support. Finally, they present model prevention and advocacy programs and issue a call for counseling psychologists to play a role in preventing community violence.

Part III: Health

Two chapters in Volume 2 focus on counseling psychology and health. Chapter 9 provides an overview of counseling psychologists' roles in health-related research and interventions. Chwalisz summarizes the research conducted by counseling health psychologists in various areas. She highlights counseling psychology's role in promoting a healthy United States and identifies several themes in counseling psychologists' contributions. These include research on stress and resilience; cultural issues on health and health disparities (expanded on in Chapter 10); prevention, intervention, and remediation; and promoting healthy behaviors. She then focuses on counseling psychologists' contributions to health promotion at the primary, secondary, and tertiary levels of intervention, with a particular focus on contributions to the research and interventions on eating and health.

In Chapter 10, Buki and Selem focus specifically on health care disparities, outlining the critical need for counseling psychologists to work to understand and ameliorate those differences. They provide readers with an overview of the major areas of health disparities, including psychosocial determinants of those disparities. They highlight the research on disparities for marginalized groups, including racial and ethnic groups, LGBT individuals, and individuals with disabilities. They close with a discussion of opportunities for counseling psychologists to provide interventions that address health care disparities.

Part IV: Social Justice

Volume 2 has five chapters that focus on counseling psychology's emphasis on social justice. Byars-Winston, Kantamneni, and Mobley address the social justice issues related to economic disparities in Chapter 11, first examining the trends in economic disparities. They review theories of social stratification by economic class and review literature related to mental health effects resulting from economic disparities. They finish with a call to counseling psychologists to provide interventions in vocational psychology, health care, and urban schools, providing ideas for specific interventions in each area. Campbell and Durrah extend the discussion to economic disparities with their focus on the homeless in Chapter 12. They first define homelessness and describe the prevalence of homelessness across the United States. Calling homelessness an "unnatural disaster" (i.e., not caused by nature), they highlight the various factors that contribute to homelessness, including being a veteran, being a victim of domestic violence or human trafficking, or suffering from mental illness or chronic physical illness. They then call on counseling psychologists to play a role in helping to find sustainable and affordable housing for all.

The authors of Chapter 13 examine the relationship between ethics and social justice. Toporek, Kwan, and Williams first distinguish socially just ethics from ethical social justice and discuss the implications for each within the practice, research, and training domains of counseling psychology. They discuss many aspects of social justice in clinical and vocational practice, including assessment, practice, and diagnosis and aspects of interventions, such as language, power, values, and treatment outcomes. In discussing social justice in counseling psychology research, they focus on encouraging researchers to carefully consider the assumptions behind their research and to be careful to respect participants and the communities in which they reside. In keeping with their focus on advocacy competencies, they discuss the importance of social justice in practicing at a systems level, helping to advocate for clients at a more institutional or community level. Finally, they discuss the implications of social justice training for trainees, at the programmatic and curricular levels, and for community partners. Their chapter ends with a set of recommendations for ethical practice, research, and training.

The authors of Chapters 14 and 15 focus on the social justice issues related to racism and heterosexism, respectively. In Chapter 14, Neville, Spanierman, and Lewis present their expanded model of psychological racism. This model first outlines various types of racism, including cultural, institutional, and individual racism, and the negative outcomes of racism, such as mental and physical health disparities and psychological costs. The model also includes antiracism actions that psychologists can take at the individual, group, and interpersonal levels. In Chapter 15, Szymanski and Moffitt provide readers with an overview and critique of the research on external and internalized sexism and heterosexism, including when these are experienced as multiple oppressions. Their review of research on multiple oppressions includes literature from the perspective that experiencing discrimination as a member of more than one marginalized group can be additive, multiplicative or fused, and the psychological consequences of each viewpoint. They conclude the chapter with suggested interventions for those who perpetrate sexism and heterosexism as well as interventions for those who are their victims.

Part V: New Directions—Settings and Populations

The final section of Volume 2 is the largest, with seven chapters, chosen to represent applications in new areas for counseling psychologists. We labeled this as "New Directions—Settings and Populations" to encompass areas that are emergent for counseling psychologists. These include new populations (elderly people, immigrants), new areas of context (religion and spirituality, international competence), and new settings (correctional facilities, organizations, or schools).

In Chapter 16, Shivy and Guion encourage counseling psychologists to be familiar with the various issues in working with offenders. They provide an overview of the correctional system and the mental health needs of offenders, including the barriers to transitioning out of correctional facilities. They note that many counseling psychologists may have clients who have been part of the correctional system. They also advocate that counseling psychologists are uniquely qualified to help create vocational interventions to assist in postcorrectional transitions.

In Chapter 17, Hook, Worthington, and Davis urge counseling psychologists to be more informed and prepared to incorporate their clients' religion or spiritual perspectives into their clinical work. They note the importance of clinicians' awareness of their own religious and spiritual awareness and then discuss how to integrate religion and spirituality into their counseling. They conclude the chapter with guidelines for reaching out and working with pastors, imams, rabbis, priests, and other religious leaders in the community.

Heppner, Wang, Heppner, and Wang propose in Chapter 18 that counseling psychologists need to develop international competence. They argue that counseling psychologists are increasingly involved in international work, that their clients or students may be from other countries, and that it is critical that counseling psychologists extend their multicultural competence to international competence. Their chapter presents the cross-national cultural competence model, highlighting specific competencies in developing cross-national awareness, knowledge, and skills. The authors conclude the chapter with guidelines for educational programs and for the field to foster a climate that supports the development of the cross-national competencies.

Yakushko and Morgan also encourage cross-national competence in Chapter 19, although their focus is on providing counseling psychologists with the background and knowledge to appropriately serve immigrants. They trace the history of immigration to the United States for various groups and review the research on the stressors and psychological consequences of immigration. They also review challenges and barriers for both documented and undocumented immigrants, and they summarize the research on immigrant individuals' resilience and strength. Their chapter concludes with a review of mental health services for immigrants and recommendations for counseling psychologists in practice.

In Chapter 20, Vacha-Haase notes the growing need for mental health services for elderly people and advocates for counseling psychologists to be prepared to effectively offer those services. She provides readers with a review of the clinical issues experienced by older adults as well as research on various types of therapy that have been evaluated with elderly people. She also addresses the challenges likely to be faced by elderly clients. She concludes with a focus on the practical issues of providing therapy to elderly clients and working with Medicare requirements, particularly focusing on medical necessity as a requirement for reimbursement.

The last two chapters in Volume 2 highlight developing areas of practice and research for counseling psychologists. In Chapter 21, Cooper, Newman, and Fuqua present the role that counseling psychologists can play as consultants in organizational level interventions. They provide an overview of the various definitions and models of consultation and discuss the consulting relationship and consulting processes in depth. They caution counseling psychologists to ensure that they have developed specific competencies in consulting before engaging in such roles that may seem an extension of counseling, such as executive coaching. They finish the chapter with a review of multicultural considerations and a review of ethical practice and development of competence. In Chapter 22, Espelage and Poteat provide readers with an overview of the challenges encountered by teachers and counselors in schools, including students' mental health concerns. They evaluate models of intervention in schools and review the research on school bullying. They highlight the potential role for counseling psychologists in schools and ways that counseling psychologists' core values and skills can be used in helping U.S. schools. Finally, they provide a set of recommendations for conducting collaborative research in schools.

ACKNOWLEDGMENTS

We extend our deep appreciation to the consulting editors who provided feedback and helped to guide the development of the content of the handbook. They gave generously of their time, and we are very grateful for their help and guidance. We are also very grateful for the dedication and commitment of our authors, who were gracious in accepting our feedback and in providing yet one more revision. Their collective dedication to the field is clear in their willingness to write and rewrite their chapters, to meet deadlines, and to help us realize our vision of how the handbook could both review what we know and make recommendations about what we need to know. The core values of counseling psychology come through strongly in these 42 chapters as the authors focused on strengths and on context and attended to many aspects of diversity as they addressed their various topics. We are indeed privileged to work with such an outstanding group of scholars.

We are indebted to the help and assistance of the APA Books reference director and staff for their invaluable contributions to this handbook. Ted Baroody, Kristen Knight, and Lisa Corry were wonderful colleagues, helped us keep on track, sent authors (and us) gentle reminders of deadlines, and in general made the process pleasant. Their responsiveness and dedication to the book is very much appreciated.

Finally, as editor-in-chief, I thank the two associate editors, Linda M. Subich for Volume 1 and Jean A. Carter for Volume 2, for making this such a marvelous venture. Together, we formed a vision for the two volumes, identified the final list of authors, and talked every other week as we began to realize the vision in providing feedback to authors. This project would not have been nearly as much fun to do without the friendship and wonderful working relationship the three of us have together. I owe them my deepest thanks and gratitude for their willingness to work on this handbook along with the many other commitments and obligations in their lives.

Nadya A. Fouad
Editor-in-Chief

PART I

COUNSELING PSYCHOLOGY FOUNDATIONS

THE SOCIETY OF COUNSELING PSYCHOLOGY: HISTORICAL VALUES, THEMES, AND PATTERNS VIEWED FROM THE AMERICAN PSYCHOLOGICAL ASSOCIATION PRESIDENTIAL PODIUM

Edward A. Delgado-Romero, Michael Y. Lau, and Sandra L. Shullman

When Melba J. T. Vasquez took the podium in Washington, DC, in August 2011 at the 119th convention of the American Psychological Association (APA), history was made. Vasquez was the first Latina and the first woman of color to assume the presidency of the oldest and largest psychological association in the United States. Vasquez's first ballot election to the APA presidency was remarkable in many ways. She was the second consecutive counseling psychologist (after Carol Goodheart) and fourth ever (after Leona Tyler, Richard Suinn, and Carol Goodheart) to be elected president. Vasquez was a former president of the Society of Counseling Psychology (SCP) and had provided leadership in women's issues, state psychological association work, and ethnic minority issues and events (such as being one of the cofounders of the National Multicultural Summit and Conference; Sue, Bingham, Porche-Burke, & Vasquez, 1999). Her success and career mirrored the expanding success of SCP and many of the themes shaping its recent history: She was a strong feminist and culturally sensitive leader, and her research and practice interests spanned a wide range of areas covering ethics, ethnic minority issues, and workplace harassment. From her APA presidential podium in 2011, she presented a program that featured an emphasis on immigration, racism, and educational disparities;

themes she had both personal and professional experience with as a counseling psychologist (Vasquez, 2001).

We begin this chapter with Vasquez's professional life and ascension to APA presidency as a helpful reference in our review of the history of the field of counseling psychology as focused and reflected by SCP. We propose that Vasquez's accomplishments and professional roles and activities reflect the historical roots of counseling psychology and its dynamic development into the profession and specialty that it is in the 21st century. A number of counseling psychologists have described much of this history (Meara & Myers, 1998; Whiteley, 1984), and we attempt not to replicate a comprehensive review. Rather, like others have (e.g., Heppner, Casas, Carter, & Stone, 2000), we review recent developments of counseling psychology and provide an understanding of these in the context of persisting and emerging issues within the profession.

In the following sections of the chapter, we examine the history and current status of counseling psychology from four perspectives: (a) core values, (b) organization, (c) science and research, and (d) training and education. Although this is a chapter on the history of counseling psychology, we primarily ground our review and analysis in the recent

The authors acknowledge the assistance of Andrew Scott Gibson in the preparation of this chapter.

DOI: 10.1037/13754-001
APA Handbook of Counseling Psychology: Vol. 1. Theories, Research, and Methods, Nadya A. Fouad (Editor-in-Chief)

developments of the profession in the first decade of the 21st century. Also as a chapter in the *APA Handbook of Counseling Psychology*, the emphasis of our historical review and analysis is primarily on APA and SCP. Although there are some limitations in generalizing beyond the structures of APA and SCP, we believe that the substantial historical and current influences of these organizational structures justify their focus. Finally, we aim to give voice to those who are often marginalized or omitted and offer suggestions to continue counseling psychology's inclusion of these perspectives into our history.

PERSPECTIVE: CORE VALUES

We begin by briefly sketching the emergence of counseling psychology as a discipline and highlighting core values that have come to define it. This is not only to acknowledge the historical roots of counseling psychology but also to frame a central lens upon which to understand the history and future trajectory of the discipline. Although counseling psychology has evolved in a number of ways over the years, a set of core values continues to define its identity and professional activities. Returning to our reference of Vasquez's career, we see that although she may not fit the traditional roles of counseling psychologists, her identity and underlying mission have been guided by core counseling psychology values rooted in its historical emergence.

The emergence of the vocational guidance movement, mental health movement, individual differences and psychometric movement, and counseling and psychotherapy from nonmedical and nonpsychoanalytic perspectives (e.g., client-centered theoretical orientation), and the influence of social and historical events (e.g., educational and counseling needs of veterans after World War II) were formative forces in shaping counseling psychology (Watkins, 1983; Whiteley, 1984). Counseling psychology began to adopt a distinct professional identity when it first formed as a division within APA in the mid-1940s (Munley, Duncan, McDonnell, & Sauer, 2004; Whiteley, 1984). A series of national conferences and definitional and training statements further solidified the core identities and activities of the

profession (APA, Division of Counseling and Guidance, Committee on Counselor Training, 1952a, 1952b; APA, Division of Counseling and Guidance, Committee on Definition, 1956), and this tradition has continued into the present. Although the training, research, and applied practices of the profession are often similar to those of other specialties in psychology (e.g., clinical psychology; Brems & Johnson, 1996; Watkins, 1983; Watkins, Lopez, Campbell, & Himmell, 1986), unique core values and guiding principles of counseling psychology provide a more distinct perspective of the identity of counseling psychologists both individually and as a professional group.

A number of counseling psychologists have attempted to derive the core values of the profession and specialty (see Exhibit 1.1; Howard, 1992; Packard, 2009). Several unifying themes (see also Gelso & Fretz, 1991) emerge from reviewing these unique counseling psychology values. Alan Ivey, a past president of the SCP, once described counseling psychology as the "most broadly-based applied psychology specialty" (1979, p. 3) and this description is consistent with the first of these overarching themes. Early training standards of counseling psychology (APA, Division of Counseling and Guidance, Committee on Counselor Training, 1952b) and definitions of the profession (APA, Division of Counseling and Guidance, Committee on Definition, 1956) described broad roles and functions for counseling psychologists in conducting psychological, research, administrative, supervisory, training, and public relation activities. The current issues and status of counseling psychology discussed later in the chapter are very much reflective of the broad and inclusive roots of the profession and discipline. A second broad theme concerns a holistic and contextual understanding of the world. The 1952 training standards addressed this in describing one component of doctoral training in counseling psychology focusing on "knowledge of social environment":

> It is assumed that the counseling psychologist must have knowledge of a great many aspects of our social structure. He [sic] should be familiar with the broad

---

Exhibit 1.1.
Core Counseling Psychology Values

Howard (1992)
 1. Respect for individual
 2. Diversity is good
 3. Interpersonal relationships
 4. Satisfactory career
 5. Growth and development
 6. Scientist–practitioner
 7. Ways of intervening
 8. Enhance coping skills
 9. Importance of environment
10. Altruistic orientation
11. Open-mindedness, theoretical pluralism
12. Prevention rather than remediation
13. Mind-body holism

Packard (2009)
 1. Altruism and enhancing welfare of others is foundation to the profession
 2. Facilitating positive relationships is necessary in bringing about change in those seeking help
 3. Science and practice integration is essential
 4. Focus of healthy and optimal development and growth across the lifespan
 5. Holistic view of person's social and cultural environment and emphasis on strength, resilience, and positive coping
 6. Respect of human dignity for all, and inclusion and celebration of human diversity
 7. Belief in social justice and social advocacy
 8. Value of collaboration and multidisciplinary practice and research involving domestic and international colleagues
 9. Focus on strengths and coping in the context of remedial work with those who seek help

---

problems of social structure and organization, with cultural conditions, and with the heterogeneity of subgroup patterns within our culture. (APA, Division of Counseling and Guidance, Committee on Counselor Training, 1952b, p. 178)

As an extension of the appreciation for holistic and contextual understandings of the world, other value themes that have evolved include the acceptance and celebration of diversity and the focus on strengths and prevention. In other words, counseling psychology is oriented toward accepting the individuals we serve as they are and facilitating positive growth and development by helping them make use of available resources. Although not as explicit in the early history of counseling psychology, social justice and advocacy became natural extensions of the thematic values that have been at the root of counseling psychology. Early evidence of this can be found in the Division 17 Committee on Definition (APA, Division of Counseling and Guidance, Committee on Definition, 1956) report that stated the following:

At the present time, the specialty of counseling psychology is approaching a state of balance among emphases upon contributions to (a) the development of an individual's inner life through concern with his [sic] motivations and emotions,

(b) the individual's achievement of harmony with his [sic] environment through helping him [sic] to develop the resources that he [sic] must bring to this task (e.g., by assisting him [sic] to make effective use of appropriate community resources), and (c) the influencing of society to recognize individual differences and to encourage the fullest development of all persons within it. (p. 283)

Returning to Vasquez, we note the tremendously broad areas her research and practice has encompassed, and her strong commitment to the diversity and social justice values that has emerged from traditional identities and values of counseling psychology as evidence of the themes raised in this section.

Counseling psychology values reveal the common core that binds together the historical development of the discipline. As a discipline that is broadly conceived and guided less by rigid disciplinary boundaries and more by core flexible values, Vasquez's successful reach into diverse research and practice areas may remind counseling psychologists of historical struggles with the core and changing roles and identities of the profession. Increasingly, we see that counseling psychologists are infusing into research and practice arenas typically occupied by other specialties (e.g., clinical psychology, health psychology). Rather than seeing this as diffusion and loss of distinct counseling psychology identity, we might see foundational core values of counseling psychology as naturally guiding counseling psychologists to influence these new research and practice areas. In the subsequent sections, we view counseling psychology from the perspectives of organizational, science and research, and training and education matters. These perspectives will reveal the persistent influences of these core counseling psychology values in shaping the current and future status of the discipline

PERSPECTIVE: ORGANIZATION

A discipline can be defined in part by its members and organizational structures. In this section, we examine the membership of the SCP of the APA as a reflection of the status of the discipline and the interests and activities of counseling psychologists. We focus on under-represented groups within SCP and APA to highlight historical and current commitments to organizational diversity. Furthermore, SCP's organizational structure is another dimension of analysis. Historical and more recent changes with the sections and groups within SCP reveal underlying values of the discipline and the emerging interests and future direction of counseling psychology.

SCP Membership

Who are counseling psychologists and what professional structures define their organization? The main professional organization for counseling psychologists is the SCP Division 17 of APA. SCP and the larger APA have played important historical and continuing roles in shaping the definition, practice, research, and training requirements of counseling psychologists in the United States (e.g., APA, Division of Counseling and Guidance, Committee on Counselor Training, 1952b; Mintz & Bieschke, 2009).

By most measures, the SCP has experienced significant and unprecedented success as an organization. Both the divisional SCP journal, *The Counseling Psychologist* (*TCP*) and the APA counseling psychology journal, *Journal of Counseling Psychology* (*JCP*) are ranked among the top journals in applied

psychology. SCP was one of the founding divisions of the National Multicultural Summit and Conference in 1999 (Sue et al., 1999). Reflective of the core values we described in the previous section, SCP has been consistently engaged as one of the 10 "divisions for social justice" in APA, and has coauthored important guidelines such as the Guidelines for Psychological Practice with Girls and Women (APA, 2007) and the Multicultural Guidelines and the Guidelines on Multicultural Education, Training, Research, Practice, and Organizational Change for Psychologists (APA, 2003). SCP leadership has proven to be an excellent training ground for involvement in APA as SCP members can be found throughout APA governance in roles such as president, chairs of boards and committees, members of the APA board of directors, and on significant task forces and initiatives.

SCP is a large division within APA and data (APA, 2010a, 2010b) indicates that as of 2009 there were 2,209 members of SCP (52% men and 48% women), making SCP the ninth largest division in APA. The average age of an SCP member was 57.4 years and the self-reported racial breakdown of members was: 0.4% American Indian, 4.1% Asian, 3.2% Hispanic, 4.8% Black, 74.8% White, 1% multiracial, and 11.7% unspecified. A comparison of the SCP membership to the overall membership ($n = 97,210$) of APA suggests that the average SCP member is almost 4 years older than the average APA member (APA, 2010a). In every racial minority category SCP has a higher proportion of ethnic minority members than in the overall APA membership. In decreasing order, members were most likely to be found in the following regions: East North Central, South Atlantic, Middle Atlantic, Pacific, and West North Central.

SCP members were overwhelmingly doctoral degree holders (84%), licensed as psychologists (68%), and most likely to work in university settings, human services, and independent practice. The current major field of members was counseling psychology (70%) with 9% of the members listing clinical psychology as their major field. SCP members reported that their primary work activities were mental health services (59%), education (60.5%), management or administration (51%), and research

(47%). In terms of memberships in other divisions, the top five divisions that SCP members belonged to (in order) were Division 35 (Society for Psychology of Women), Division 29 (Psychotherapy), Division 45 (Society for the Psychological Study of Ethnic Minority Issues), Division 42 (Psychologists in Independent Practice), and Division 44 (Society for the Psychological Study of Lesbian, Gay, Bisexual, and Transgender Issues). In addition, counseling psychologists were instrumental in the founding and maintenance of other divisions such as Division 13 (Society of Consulting Psychology), Division 51 (Society for the Psychological Study of Men and Masculinity), and Division 52 (International Psychology).

SCP Over a 25-Year Period: Changes and Stability

Table 1.1 presents selected demographic characteristics of SCP members from 1985, 1999, and 2009 and illustrates changes over a 25-year period. The data were acquired from the APA Division Services Office and originally were compiled from the APA directory by the APA Office of Demographic, Employment and Educational Research (which no longer exists). Data were only available as far back as 1985 (S. Jordan, personal communication, October 6, 2010). We examined these data to understand both the stability of and change in the demographics of SCP. We note that Goodyear et al. (2008) and Munley, Pate, and Duncan (2008) also compiled information about SCP members, both currently and historically, using questionnaires (Goodyear et al., 2008) and the APA Directory (Munley et al., 2008).

Looking over this 25-year period, one can see some marked changes in the membership of SCP. Perhaps most noticeable is the increase in the proportion of women, from 23.9% in 1985 to almost half of the membership by 2009. It is also noteworthy

TABLE 1.1

Selected Demographics, Society of Counseling Psychology 1985, 1999, and 2009

Demographic	1985	1999	2009
Members (*n*)	2,586	2,893	2,209
Gender			
Men	76.1%	60.5%	52.3%
Women	23.9%	39.5%	47.5%
Race/ethnicity			
American Indian	0.0%	0.4%	0.4%
Asian	0.5%	1.7%	4.1%
Hispanic	0.5%	2.1%	3.2%
Black	1.3%	2.9%	4.8%
White	66.7%	81.8%	74.8%
Multiracial/ethnic	—	0.0%	1.0%
Other	—	0.1%	—
Not specified	30.9%	10.9%	11.7%
Mean age	51.12 years	55 years	57.4 years
Top 5 regions (in order)	East North Central	East North Central	East North Central
	Middle Atlantic	Middle Atlantic (t)	South Atlantic
	South Atlantic	South Atlantic (t)	Middle Atlantic
	Pacific	Pacific	Pacific
	West North Central	West South Central	West North Central
Top 5 divisions (in order)	Psychotherapy (29)	Psychotherapy (29)	Women (35)
	Independent Practice (42)	Women (35)	Psychotherapy (29)
	Clinical (12)	Independent Practice (42)	Ethnic Minority Issues (45)
	Women (35)	Family Psychology (43)	Independent Practice (42)
	Educational (15)	Clinical (12)	Lesbian, Gay, Bisexual, and Transgender Issues (44)

Note. Data from American Psychological Association Division Services Office. Dashes indicate that data were not available. (t) = tie.

to see the numbers of ethnic minority SCP members increase from very few (2.3% total) in 1985 to 13.5% in 2009. By 2009, SCP was one of the divisions with the highest percentage of members of color, with only Divisions 45 (Society for the Psychological Study of Ethnic Minority Issues—67.7%) and 52 (International Psychology—15.1%) having a higher percentage of ethnic minority members. This is not surprising given the core values and strong organizational commitment of the discipline on diversity and supporting minority issues.

One significant concern is the 24% decline in SCP membership from 1999 to 2009. This is a continuation of a trend that has existed since membership peaked at 3,390 in 1994, with consistent declines since that time. In contrast, overall membership in APA itself since 1994 has actually increased by approximately 18,000 members, although most divisions report declines in membership. The shrinking of the SCP membership relative to overall APA membership and relative to the number of non-SCP counseling psychologists has implications for the influence of counseling psychology in APA activities on multiple levels (e.g., allotted conference time, governance). Munley et al. (2008) found that 67.8% of counseling psychologists who did not belong to SCP, also did not belong to any other division in APA. These psychologists may choose to identify generally or with another role or specialty. Goodyear et al. (2008) estimated that in 2005 "only 27% of counseling psychologists who are members and fellows belong to SCP" (p. 222) and APA estimated that number to be around 15% in 2009. The numbers of APA members who have a doctorate in the fields of counseling (85%), clinical (92%), and school (80%) and who do not belong to their respective division is high. So this may well be an applied psychology issue generally.

Another trend that is notable is the fact that SCP members are getting older, with an increase in average age of membership from 51.1 years to 57.4 years over the 25-year span. In 2009, only 4.2% of members were under age 34, whereas 25.8% of members were over the age of 65. By contrast, the 1999 data show 9.5% of members under age 34 and 19.5% over age 65. To provide a slightly different context, we note that of the eight divisions larger than SCP, five

had higher average ages, and only three had lower average ages (Industrial–Organizational Psychology, Health Psychology, and Clinical Neuropsychology). Thus, SCP seems to be faring better than most APA divisions in terms of overall numbers, yet we see a looming membership challenge if younger people do not continue to join SCP. Indeed, Goodyear et al. (2008) estimated there are 500 counseling psychology graduates a year, yet SCP membership is not reflecting a continued infusion of new graduates proportional to this graduation rate. Munley et al. (2008) examined data from the APA directory in 2003 and found that 356 counseling psychologists under the age of 34 were members of APA but not of SCP. Munley et al. also found that nearly 68% of non-SCP counseling psychologists did not belong to any division in APA. An interesting point is that young counseling psychologists do not appear to be joining any divisions at all, not just SCP. Is there a shift in professional identity occurring in the newer generations of counseling psychologists? This membership issue also raises again the question of whether SCP is adequately addressing the membership needs of early career counseling psychologists or those who primarily practice as counseling psychologists.

Examining the 2009 data, it is clear that membership in other divisions of APA by SCP members reflects the intensified focus on the setting of private practice and the issues of women, ethnic minorities, and LGBT clients and professionals. Over the past 25 years, SCP members have consistently also been members of Divisions 29 (Psychotherapy), 35 (Society for the Psychology of Women), and 42 (Psychologists in Independent Practice). In 2009 Divisions 44 (Society for the Psychological Study of Lesbian, Gay, Bisexual, and Transgender Issues) and 45 (Society for the Psychological Study of Ethnic Minority Issues) replaced divisions dealing with clinical (Division 12) and family (Division 43) psychology as a top five common divison. From 1985 to 2009, the percentage of SCP members who also belonged to Division 12 (Society of Clinical Psychology) fell by half, which is no doubt a reflection of the continuing distinction between these specialties at the organizational level. Munley et al. (2008) pointed out that non-SCP counseling psychologists, although tending not to belong to any other division by a wide margin, were members of Psychologists in Independent Practice, Psychotherapy, Society for the Psychology of Women, Clinical Neuropsychology, and Society for Family Psychology when they joined divisions.

The membership data presented, although not representative of all counseling psychologists, provides a glimpse into the diversity of its members and the overlapping professional interests with diverse profession and diversity-based organizations. This is not surprising given the core guiding principles of counseling psychology examined earlier. Membership data over the past 25 years also suggest a possible weakening of affiliation with SCP by counseling psychologists. There are a number of possible explanations for this. One of them is consistent with our view that emerging from a broad-based and diversity focused set of values, counseling psychology risks developing into broader and more diffused areas at the expense of a coherent identity and role.

Values Enacted in SCP Membership

As mentioned, diversity is a long-held value of counseling psychologists and this can be operationalized by examining the status and numbers of ethnic minority and LGBT SCP members. Data indicate that the number of ethnic minority SCP members has risen dramatically, and SCP has a reputation for inclusiveness and progressive thinking (Bidell, Ragen, Broach, & Carrillo, 2007; Moradi & Neimeyer, 2005). Until the election of Rosie Phillips Bingham in 1997, however, there had not been an SCP president of color. Since that time there have been several SCP presidents who were persons of color (e.g., Nadya Fouad, Melba Vasquez, Derald Wing Sue, William Parham, Janet Helms, Tanya Israel, and Y. Barry Chung). SCP has been instrumental in APA in addressing ethnic minority issues in such areas as the APA multicultural guidelines (APA, 2003). One area in which there has been relatively little attention has been the role of counseling psychologists in the development and operation of ethnic minority psychological associations (EMPAs) and ethnic minority sections and subgroups. The five U.S. national ethnic minority psychological associations currently recognized by the APA include the Asian American Psychological Association (AAPA), the Association of Black Psychologists (ABPsi), the

National Latina/o Psychological Association (NLPA), the Society of Indian Psychologists (SIP), and APA Division 45 (Society for the Psychological Study of Ethnic Minority Issues). These associations, in partnership with APA, meet regularly to set an agenda for ethnic minority issues in psychology.

Counseling psychologists in general have played important and significant roles in the creation (e.g., Vasquez was one of the founders of Division 45 and NLPA), leadership (e.g., there have been counseling psychology presidents in every EMPA), and day-to-day operations of the EMPAs. The history of ethnic minority psychology has evolved largely separately from the history of counseling psychology (see special issue by Leong, 2009). During her SCP presidency, Linda Forrest used some of her presidential programming hours at the 2008 International Counseling Psychology Conference to organize a symposium focused on the role of counseling psychologists in the EMPAs (Forrest et al., 2008). Present at the symposium were four counseling psychologists who were current or past presidents of the EMPAs. As a result of that collaboration, a project emerged to highlight the role that counseling psychologists have played in the EMPAs and ways to formalize and advance collaborations between the EMPAs and SCP. It became clear that counseling psychologists of color who attempted to negotiate their professional identity across one or more EMPAs and SCP often felt torn between the groups and about where to allocate resources. Given that each EMPA holds conferences, three have journals (with NLPA starting a journal in 2012), and there is a separate membership fee for each group, the potential for ethnic minority counseling psychologists to be spread thin is a possibility and may contribute to the identity diffusion mentioned earlier in the chapter.

The issues facing gay, lesbian, bisexual, transgender, questioning, and queer counseling psychologists are somewhat similar to those facing ethnic minorities. Several groups focus on LGBT issues, such as the Division 17 Section on Lesbian, Gay, Bisexual, and Transgender Issues (SLGBT); Division 44 (Society for the Psychological Study of Lesbian, Gay, Bisexual, and Transgender Issues) in APA; the Association for Lesbian, Gay, Bisexual and Transgender Issues in Counseling (ALGBTIC) in the

American Counseling Association (ACA); and several national advocacy and support groups. LGBT counseling psychologists also face unique issues as they try to negotiate a society in which oppression on the basis of sexual orientation is the norm. Hate crimes and legislative attempts to block the rights of sexual minorities have marked the past decade in particular. These social issues are not isolated from professional life. For example, there was controversy when it was discovered that one of the APA headquarter hotels during the 2010 convention in San Diego was owned by Doug Manchester, who politically and financially supported the anti–gay marriage initiative in California known as Proposition 8. APA used the occasion to raise awareness about LGBT issues but honored their contract (Munsey, 2010). Twelve divisions, including SCP, took a position on the matter (Westefeld, 2010). This issue illustrates the personal and professional discrimination that LGBT counseling psychologists may face in the United States. Research has indicated that there are negative psychological outcomes for LGBT people and their families when faced with discrimination such as marriage amendments (Arm, Horne & Levitt, 2009; Levitt et al., 2009; Rostosky, Riggle, Horne, & Miller, 2009). LGBT counseling psychologists also face these negative outcomes alongside clients and the LGBT community in general.

It is harder to accurately document the history of LGBT leaders and pioneers in counseling psychology because LGBT status is something that an individual may choose to keep private or this aspect of identity may be overlooked by others (Fassinger, Shullman, & Stevenson, 2010). There is hope that the personal stories of LGBT counseling psychologists and allies (e.g., Croteau, Lark, Lidderdale, & Chung, 2005) may help break through this barrier so a fuller account of the influence of LGBT and individuals on the development of SCP can be shared in a future history of counseling psychology.

Although counseling psychologists are used to managing multiple demands, identity conflicts may escalate when competing priorities include a personal (e.g., ethnic minority, gender, sexual orientation) component in the case of ethnic minority, LGBT, and women counseling psychologists (and those who have multiple identifications across those

groups). What can SCP do to address this tension in terms of the history of SCP, current climate in SCP, and going forward? In addition to the stress and decision making of counseling psychologists who are members of underrepresented groups, there are also generations of counseling graduate students who are looking for guidance and mentorship in their professional development (the whole notion of being a role model). Thus, it is important that counseling psychologists who are members of under-represented or oppressed groups encounter a supportive environment in which multiple demands are acknowledged. Awareness of the unique stressors of minority (in all aspects) counseling psychologists and the potential impact on their work, should be a focus of the future.

SCP Structure

The diversity of professional interests within SCP is also gleaned from the structure of the organization. As part of a historic change by SCP leadership in the early 1990s, several structural changes were made to the SCP leadership structure with the goal of helping SCP relate more effectively to APA and make SCP more responsive to younger and underrepresented members (Heppner et al., 2000). In 1992, the executive board structure of SCP was reorganized and vice presidents were created to parallel the structure of APA. New structures within SCP were sections, special interest groups (SIGs), and special task groups (STGs). Sections are formal organizations and SIGs are informal groups formed around a topic. These organizational structures provide a view into the proliferation of counseling psychology into emerging practice and scholarly arenas. The specific areas of focus in each of these organizational structures reflect the deep values rooted in the foundation of counseling psychology— a broad-based specialty interested in the holistic, diverse, and contextual understanding of people and the world.

In 2010, the SCP had 13 sections: Advancement of Women; Animal Human Interaction: Research and Practice; Counseling Health Psychology; Ethnic and Racial Diversity; Independent Practice; International; Lesbian, Gay, Bisexual, and Transgender Issues; Prevention; Positive Psychology; Promotion of Psychotherapy Science; Supervision and Training; University Counseling Centers; and Vocational Psychology. The sections are headed by a chair of section chairs to facilitate communication between the sections and with the SCP executive committee. In addition, students organized a group called Student Affiliates of Seventeen.

In 2010, the SCP had nine SIGs: Adoption Research and Practice; Couples and Families; Faculty at 4-Year Colleges; Hypnosis; Men, Masculinity, and Men's Studies; Older Adults and Aging; Organizational Counseling; Religious and Special Issues; and Rural Practice and Scholarship. Although less formalized in structure and its relationship to the division, special interest groups nevertheless represent the substantive concerns of members not already addressed within the sectional structure.

Establishing a section or SIG is a straightforward and clear process. What is not clear is the individual and collective history of the sections and SIGs and how they have affected the retention, leadership pool, and impact of SCP. The authors of this chapter have extensive involvement with the organizational structure of SCP and believe that the reorganization produced a more responsive, progressive, and inclusive SCP. Very little has been written about the impact of the structural changes, however. A history and summative impact of the sections and SIGs should be undertaken to see whether the goals set forth in the early 1990s (Heppner et al., 2000) were accomplished. We have suggested that the existence of these structures is a natural extension of the guiding values and principles of counseling psychology, and therefore, there is a need for greater understanding of the development and contributions.

One concern is that the accomplishments of the subgroups within SCP might go unrecognized if not recorded. For example, in the 1990s the Section on the Advancement of Women (SAW), the Section on Ethnic and Racial Diversity (SERD), and the Section on Lesbian, Gay, Bisexual, and Transgender Issues (SGLBT) formed a multiyear discussion group called "More Pie" (Fouad, Gerstein, & Toporek, 2006) that eventually resulted in the publication of *The Handbook of Social Justice in Counseling Psychology* (Toporek, Gerstein, Fouad, Roysircar, & Israel, 2006). This collaboration between diverse interest

groups of SCP resulted in crystallizing and focusing an emphasis on social justice for the entire profession. Surely this is what was envisioned by SCP presidents such as Naomi Meara, Mike Patton, and Bruce Fretz from 1988 to 1992 (Heppner et al., 2000). Eighteen years later, these structures are ingrained into the fabric of SCP. We wonder about the scope of impact of the structural changes in SCP and, in particular, we would like to see a history and analysis of the impact of the sections. Which sections have thrived and how has participation in the section structure enhanced or fragmented SCP? What leaders have emerged out of the sections and what impact have they had on SCP and APA? Has the reorganization of the early 1990s met its goals? Should there be new goals for the future?

In particular, we believe that the impact of sections and SIGs that address underrepresented population issues (e.g., SAW, SERD, SGLBT), those that represent traditional strengths of counseling psychology (e.g., vocational, supervision), and those that represent emerging interests (e.g., aging, health) on enhancing intra- and interdivision interests need to be better understood. These structures mirror many interest groups that are also available outside of SCP and that relationship has not yet been examined to our knowledge. For example, one might be a member of SAW and Division 35, with each focusing on women in a different arena and both with officers, awards, and specialized programming at conferences. What unique advantages do the interest groups within SCP provide, and do they enhance or detract from parallel structures in APA? How are they tied to SCP goals, such as retention of members? Finally, several of the sections, in particular SAW, SERD, and SGLBT, have been successful at mentoring future leaders of SCP. What are they doing right that the field can learn from? How can we preserve the history and influence of the sections? These are unanswered questions that are relevant to understanding the historical and future impact of organizational structures within SCP on counseling psychology. The answers we find will also help the profession to better understand the future development of counseling psychology, as core values continue to guide the specialty to practice and research diverse content areas.

PERSPECTIVE: SCIENCE AND RESEARCH

Counseling psychology research and scholarly activities is a dimension of the discipline that reveals important developments in its knowledge base and intellectual interests. The rest of the handbook will more comprehensively cover research topics within contemporary counseling psychology. In this section, we focus on a number of perspectives that reveal some historical and emerging issues within the discipline. We first look at *TCP* as an important outlet for publication of counseling psychology research. Next we explore historical developments of counseling psychology national and regional conferences.

The Counseling Psychologist

The values of counseling psychology have been reflected, examined, and debated in the flagship journal of SCP. *TCP* was first published in the spring of 1969. The founding editor John Whiteley stated in his introduction to the new journal stated that:

> [*TCP*'s] purpose is twofold: 1) to serve as a vehicle for critical analysis and commentary on major professional problems; 2) to offer a forum for communication of matters of professional concern to the membership of the Division. . . . The usual format. . . will involve a major treatise on a problem followed by a critical analysis by eight or so prominent scholars or practitioners. (1969, p. III)

From the beginning, *TCP* distinguished itself from other journals by the major contribution format (what Whiteley referred to as the "major treatise"). The major contribution consists of one or more articles centered on a specific topic, followed by reactions from selected respondents and a rejoinder from the initial authors. The major contribution offered depth that was not possible in journals with restrictive page counts and also provided scholarly interaction in the same issue. Flores, Rooney, Heppner, Douglas, and Wei (1999) conducted a trend analysis of major contributions from 1986 to 1996. They provided empirical evidence (e.g., citations) of the impact of major contributions and ranked the top cited major contributions to that point. Table 1.2 lists the major contributions from 1969 to 2009.

TABLE 1.2

The Counseling Psychologist: Major Contributions and Themes, 1969–2009

Year	Major contribution title
2009	Counseling Chinese—Indigenous and Multicultural Perspectives
	Contextual Factors in Training and practice
	Counseling Psychology Model Training Values Statement Addressing Diversity
	Current Issues in Training
	Meta-Analysis of Clinical Judgment
	Research on Asians and Asian Americans
	Multiculturalism and Social Justice
2008	New Frontiers in Multiculturalism
	Research and Assessment in Counseling Women
	Internalized Heterosexism
	Men's Gender Role Conflict: 25-year Research Summary
	International Forum
	HIV and Vocational Psychology
2007	Culturally Relevant Prevention
	Culturally Sensitive Health Care
	Best Practice Guidelines on Prevention
	Qualitative Issues and Analyses in Counseling Psychology: Part IV
	Qualitative Issues and Analyses in Counseling Psychology: Part III
	Race-Based Traumatic Stress
2006	Quantitative Issues and Analyses In Counseling Psychology: Part II
	Quantitative Issues and Analyses in Counseling Psychology: Part I
	Emerging Issues in Counseling Psychology: Research and Practice
	Clinical Judgment or Mathematical Formulas: A Debate About Accuracy
	Positive Aspects of Human Functioning: A Cornerstone of Counseling Psychology
	Strength-Based Counseling for Youth
2005	Online Counseling: Challenges for the Information Era
	Academic Training in Counseling Psychology
	Perspectives on Race in Counseling Psychology Practice, Training, and Research
	Perspectives on Research in Counseling Psychology
	Vocational Psychology: A Proposal to Move Toward Social Justice
	Practice/Science Integration
2004	Integrating Psychology and Social Justice: A Training Model
	Religious Beliefs and Sexual Orientation
	Career Decisions and Family of Origin: Implications for Vocational Counseling
	Problem Solving and Human Adjustment

(Continued)

TABLE 1.2 *(Continued)*

The Counseling Psychologist: Major Contributions and Themes, 1969–2009

Year	Major contribution title
	Counseling Psychology and School Counseling
	The Fourth National Counseling Psychology Conference: Houston, 2001
2003	Counseling Psychology and Adoption
	Evidence-Based Scientist–Practitioner Training
	Internationalization of Counseling Psychology
	Social Justice and Multicultural Competence in Counseling Psychology
	Work-Oriented Midcareer Development Model
	Building a Bridge From the Past to the Future
2002	Reinvigorating Vocational Psychology
	Counseling Psychology and Schools
	Heterosexual Identity
	Client Perspectives on Multicultural Counseling Competence
	Empirically Supported Interventions
	Feminist Identity Development
2001	Multidimensional Facets of Cultural Competence
	Eating Disorders
	Multicultural Psychology: Creating a Contextual Framework
	Legacies and Traditions in Counseling Psychology
	Work and Relationships
	Current Directions in Chicana/o Psychology
2000	Prevention in Counseling Psychology
	Counseling Psychology Training
	Suicide
	Legacies and Traditions in Counseling Psychology
	Ethical Issues in Managed Care
	Globalization of Counseling Psychology
1999	Invisibility Syndrome
	Trainee Impairment
	Advanced Quantitative Method II
	Advanced Quantitative Methods
	Racism and Psychological Health
	30 Years of *The Counseling Psychologist*
1998	Multicultural Assessment
	Lesbian, Gay, and Bisexual Affirmative Training
	Reconceptualizing Multicultural Counseling
	Male Reference Group Identity Dependence
	Social Cognitive Model of Counselor Training
	Multicultural Training
1997	Consensual Qualitative Research
	School-to-Work Transition
	Social-Counseling Interface: Impediments and Solutions
	Research Training Environments
1996	Wellness
	Adolescence
	Multicultural Challenges: Theory, Evaluation, and Training
	Ethics

TABLE 1.2 *(Continued)*

The Counseling Psychologist: Major Contributions and Themes, 1969–2009

Year	Major contribution title
1995	Social Psychology Applications
	Attachment Theory
	Delayed Memory Debate
	Culture and Counseling
1994	Wife Abuse
	Counseling With Children
	Multicultural Training
	The Counseling Relationship
1993	Ecocounseling Psychology
	Sports Psychology
	White American Researchers and Multicultural Counseling
	Feminist Counseling and Therapy
1992	Counseling Psychologists and Neuropsychologists
	Toward Science-Practice Integration in Brief Counseling and Therapy
	Major Social Theories of Aging and Implications
	New and Early Professionals
1991	Counseling the HIV-Infected Client
	Counseling Psychology and Health Applications
	Counseling Lesbian Women and Gay Men
	Counseling International Students
1990	Counseling Centers of the 1990s
	Systematic Training
	Testing and Assessment
	Group Therapy
1989	Religious Faith Across the Life Span
	Interactional Counseling
	Psychological Nigrescence
	Alternative Research Paradigms
1988	Victimization
	Third National Conference for Counseling Psychology: Planning the Future
	Cognitive Approaches
	Cognitive-Behavioral Treatments of Anxiety
1987	*The Counseling Psychologist*: A Retrospective
	Personal Problem Solving
	Internship
	Dual-Career Families in Perspective
1986	Stress Counseling
	Adaptive Counseling and Therapy
	Paradoxical Interventions
	Research Training in Counseling Psychology
1985	Cross-Cultural Counseling
	Consultation
	The Relationship in Counseling and Psychotherapy
	Counseling for Health
1984	Career Development of Women
	Ethical Decision Making in Counseling Psychology

(Continued)

TABLE 1.2 (*Continued*)

The Counseling Psychologist: Major Contributions and Themes, 1969–2009

Year	Major contribution title
	Counseling Psychology and Aging
	Counseling Psychology: A Historical Perspective
1983	Computer Assisted Counseling
	Family Counseling Psychology
	Counseling Psychology in the Justice System
	Supervision in Counseling II
1982	Research in Counseling Psychology II
	Business and Industry
	Counseling Psychology: The Next Decade
	Supervision in Counseling
1981	Parenting Counseling
	Leisure Counseling
	Adult Transitions
	Professional Certification in Counseling Psychology
1980	Counseling Psychology in the Year 2000 A.D.
1979	Research in Counseling Psychology
	Ego and Self
	Counseling Women III
1978	Counseling Men
	The Behavior Therapies—Circa 1978
1977	Professional Identify
	Rational-Emotive Therapy
	Developmental Counseling Psychology
1976	Career Counseling II
	Counseling Women II
	Counseling Adults
1975	Assertion Training
	Marriage and Family Counseling
	Carl Rogers on Empathy
	Sex Counseling
1974	Gestalt Therapy
	Career Counseling
1973	The Healthy Personality
	Counseling Women
1972	New Directions in Training, Part 2
	New Directions in Training, Part 1
	Integrity Group Therapy
1971	Individual Psychology
	Deliberate Psychological Education
	Existential Counseling
1970	Encounter Groups
	Black Students in Higher Education
1969	Behavioral Counseling
	Student Unrest
	Client-Centered Therapy
	Vocational Development Theory

Note. Articles are presented in reverse chronological order by year and within each year.

We grouped the major contributions by topical themes (see Table 1.3). In addition, we presented the data in 5-year intervals to get a sense of the stability or novelty of the general themes. The most common theme was those major contributions related to aspects of practice. Contributions on multiculturalism and social justice were the next most common theme, followed by research and theory and training. For the most part, themes were remarkably consistent across years, with the exception of multiculturalism and social justice, which went from two major contributions in the first time span to 14 in the most recent.

In addition to the major contributions and reactions to those contributions, the content of *TCP* has also included theoretical and research articles, awards and presidential addresses, and the proceedings of the Division 17 Executive Board.[1] There have also been regular forums such as Legacies and Traditions, Around the Winter Roundtable, and the Professional, Scientific, International, Comments, and In Memoriam Forums. Thus, *TCP* has aspired to balance honoring the history and legacy of counseling psychology, while simultaneously pushing the boundaries of that legacy. The current editor of *TCP*, Nadya Fouad, in her introduction to her editorial term, stated that

> I have always viewed *TCP* as a journal that helps to define both the boundaries as well as the center of counseling psychology. I challenge authors to consider submitting articles that both push the limits of our field to new settings, populations and concerns as well as articles that are updated statements of our traditional settings, populations and concerns. (Fouad, 2008, p. 5)

This statement by Fouad captures the challenge and opportunity that has faced editors of *TCP* (John Whiteley, 1969–1984; Bruce Fretz, 1985–1990; Gerald Stone, 1991–1996; P. Paul Heppner, 1997–2002; Robert T. Carter, 2003–2007; and Nadya A. Fouad, 2008–current)—that is, defining the core of the specialty while at the same time pushing the boundaries of what the specialty might be. Without

[1]With the availability of other forms of mass communication such as the SCP website (http://www.div17.org) and electronic mail, the proceedings of SCP will no longer be in the journal.

TABLE 1.3

Number of *The Counseling Psychologist* (*TCP*) Contributions by Category

Year	Counseling practice	Multicultural/ social justice	Research and theory	Counselor training	Future directions	Gender issues	Professional focus	Special topics	*TCP* history/ self-reflection
2005–2009	15	14	9	4	2	2	0	0	0
2000–2004	15	12	2	3	3	0	1	0	0
1995–1999	5	9	7	5	1	1	0	0	1
1990–1994	12	7	1	1	0	0	2	3	0
1985–1989	11	3	4	1	0	0	1	0	1
1980–1984	5	4	2	2	3	0	2	0	0
1975–1979	5	3	6	0	0	3	1	0	0
1969–1974	9	2	3	2	0	1	0	0	0
Total	77	54	34	18	9	7	7	3	2

a center, counseling psychology disintegrates into a series of tenuously related subspecialties. If the center is too strong and impermeable, then the specialty grows stagnant and discourages innovation. Core counseling psychology values that embrace openness and broadening of the concerns of the specialty, in effect, also begin to weaken what defines the profession.

While other professional fields face declining or increasingly expensive journal space, *TCP* has seen a proliferation of both print and electronic journals. This proliferation, coupled with (a) the increased number of volumes published in *TCP* and (b) the number of conferences that cater to counseling psychologists, means that there are more outlets for counseling psychology students and members. For example, the following journals that may cater to counseling psychologists have begun publication since 2000: *Training and Education in Professional Psychology* (2006); *Asian American Journal of Psychology* (2009); *Journal of Diversity in Higher Education* (2008); *Psychology of Men and Masculinity* (2000); *Psychological Trauma: Theory, Research, Practice and Policy* (2008); *Psychology of Religion and Spirituality* (2008); and *Psychology of Violence* (2010). There are also many choices for conferences, including divisional conferences (e.g., Division 45 hosted an inaugural conference in 2010 and plans to have conferences biennially), regional conferences, state conferences, topical conferences (e.g., Boston College Diversity Challenge), ethnic

minority psychological association conferences, and the National Multicultural Summit and Conference. Therefore, although this may point to the health of the profession, one may worry about a watering down effect of counseling psychology scholarship (i.e., with so many outlets, counseling psychology research may be spread thin), the effect on the major journals, and attendance at APA annual conventions. In an era of shrinking library budgets and diminishing travel funding, is this too much of a good thing? Finally, with so many outlets and specialty conferences available, does this contribute to the diffusion of the identity of counseling psychologists?

TCP is a helpful lens through which to view the scholarship of counseling psychology. Our review suggests that it continues to be an influential outlet for research and scholarship for counseling psychologists. The thematic topics of the major contributions have been both stable and shifting, and these reflect the core interests of counseling psychology as well as a growth of developing areas (e.g., multicultural issues) in recent decades. We believe that core counseling psychology values and identities are at the root of these developments and both contribute not only to a pushing of limits into new research and practice areas but also to a diffusion of core interests that bind traditional counseling psychology. We see this growing tension surface throughout the historical development of the discipline.

The values and direction of the field are not something that is only determined by editors or executive boards. From time to time, a need arose for counseling psychologists to come together distinct from the APA conference and focus on issues of definition and values. These meetings have been collectively known as the national (now international) conferences of counseling psychology.

National and International Conferences

Counseling psychology as an applied specialty took shape in the past century from the diverse number of influences that include vocational guidance, mental health movement, developments in psychometrics, nonmedical and nonpsychoanalytic perspectives on psychotherapy, and social and economic forces of the early 1900s (Watkins, 1983; Whiteley, 1984). With the formation of a separate division within the APA, counseling psychology gained a distinct professional identity and organizational structure. By the early 1950s, the division had gone through a series of name changes, at one point or another being known by one of five names, including the Division of Personnel Psychologists and the Division of Counseling and Guidance Psychologists (Whiteley, 1984). As a natural progression of this early history, one of the notable features of counseling psychology in the 1950s and 1960s was a struggle with the definition and professional identity of the field. A series of national conferences demonstrated efforts and progress in shaping the roles and identities of counseling psychology.

The first two national conferences, in 1951 and 1964, reflected the identity and definitional struggles of the early years of the profession. The 1951 Northwestern Conference was organized at a time when counseling psychology was beginning to shape its public and private identities (Munley et al., 2004). One of the core tasks of the conference was delineating the roles and functions of counseling psychology and also the content areas associated with appropriate practical and research training. As a consequence of the conference, the Committee on Counselor Training of Division 17 published recommended standards for training of doctoral-level counseling psychologists in 1952 (APA, Division of Counseling and Guidance, Committee on Counselor

Training, 1952a, 1952b). Subsequently, continued work later in the decade resulted in one of the first official definitions of counseling psychology specialty by the Division 17 Committee on Definition (APA, Division of Counseling and Guidance, Committee on Definition, 1956).

The Greyston Conference in 1964 resulted in discussions and articulation of a number of issues related to (a) roles and functions of counseling psychologists, (b) content of professional training, (c) organizational matters related to practical training, and (d) unity and diversity of the profession (Thompson & Super, 1964). What came out of the conference largely reaffirmed the functions and values of counseling psychology articulated in the Northwestern Conference. Moreover, there was a growing attention to counseling psychology addressing and meeting the needs of research and practice areas that have come to define the strengths of current-day counseling psychology. Thompson and Super (1964) foresaw issues related to, "domestic and international social issues, such as unemployment, educational handicaps, retraining, undeveloped and underprivileged populations, and delinquency" (p. 13) becoming more important and crucial to the work of counseling psychologists, whereas Samler (1964) pushed for proactive involvement in affecting social change. It is clear that the first two national conferences made more concrete the core values emerging from the early history of counseling psychology.

As the Northwestern and Greyston conferences strengthened the core identity of the specialty (Whiteley, 1984), the 1970s and 1980s saw the increasing call for counseling psychology to incorporate diversity issues into its identity. Division 17 President Allen Ivey reaffirmed three traditional values of counseling psychology (i.e., diversity in approach to profession, commitment to person–environment considerations, and focus on positive and normal development) and called for the addition of a fourth focusing on diversity and sociocultural factors:

A broadly-based counseling psychology which seeks to foster human development in a person-environmental perspective, of necessity, must consider cultural factors of primary importance in any treatment plan, community intervention, or multi-faceted program of assistance. Issues of ageism, sexism, racism, and other forms of conscious and unconscious oppression are antithetical to the goals of counseling psychology. (1979, p. 6)

Efforts to address this fourth core value of counseling psychology became increasingly evident throughout the 1980s and 1990s, and these efforts were reflected in the next three national counseling psychology conferences: the Atlanta Conference in 1987, the Houston Conference in 2001, and the International Counseling Psychology Conference held in Chicago in 2008. The third national conference held in 1986 in Atlanta focused on five major areas of public image: professional practice in various settings, training and accreditation, research, and organizational and political issues in counseling psychology (Weissberg et al., 1988). A review of the reports by the five work groups suggests continued themes of affirming the broad and inclusive nature of the division and profession and the growing attendance to diversity issues. In both training and practice, for example, counseling psychology was called to affect positive change against individual and institutional oppression (Kagan et al., 1988). For the first time in a national conference, attendees also expressed concerns for a lack of support and representation of underserved and under-represented groups within the organization (Brammer et al., 1988). This lack of support and representation contributed to a negative image of the profession (Zytowski, Casas, Gilbert, Lent, & Simon, 1988).

Social justice and social advocacy took center stage in the 2001 Houston conference. The conference theme, "Counseling Psychologists: Making a Difference," was consistent with the overall aims of the conference to implement a more proactive agenda for the profession and to better prepare counseling psychologists to address diversification of their professional roles (Fouad et al., 2004). In advocating social justice and social advocacy within counseling psychology, social action groups (SAGs) were an important component of the conference. SAGs addressed a number of issues, including

racism and the disparity between the poor/working class and the rich that resulted in a series of recommendations pushing for changes both within and outside of the profession (Fouad et al., 2004). Political advocacy training, focusing on social justice issues, was also part of the conference program.

As issues of diversity and social justice grew stronger roots in the discussions within counseling psychology, there was growing attention to the globalization of human culture, generally, and the implications for the practice of counseling psychology (Douce, 2004; Heppner, 2006). The International Counseling Psychology Conference came together as one of the presidential projects of Linda Forrest and was held in Chicago in 2008 with more than 1,400 attendees (Forrest, 2010). The 4-day conference consisted of keynote addresses from scholars representing five countries (Argentina, Portugal, Taiwan, South Africa, and the United States), and five continents (Africa, Asia, Europe, North America, and South America) and featured awards, symposia, paper presentations, roundtables, and posters (SCP, 2008). More than 20 workgroups met to discuss a range of topics, many of which focused on international issues, such as "Advancement and Enrichment of Counseling Psychology in International Settings" and "Cross Border Collaboration in North American Counseling Psychology" (SCP, 2008).

In her presidential address and reflection of the ICPC, Forrest (2010) made a case that issues related to training, professional competencies, and identity of counseling psychologists within the United States become more complex when we think internationally and more globally. Viewing counseling psychology outside of a U.S. context challenges domestic counseling psychologists to be aware of power dynamics and our openness to the bidirectional nature of interacting with our international colleagues (e.g., questions of "exporting knowledge" for the benefit of those outside of the United States vs. fair exchange of ideas and knowledge as equals). Although the Houston Conference "expressly did not have a goal to clarify the identity of counseling psychology" (Fouad et al., 2004, p. 60), acknowledging that the specialty had reached a level of resolution on issues of identity, the internationalization of counseling psychology again raises important issues of definition and core values, knowledge, and skills particular to the discipline. The defining values of counseling psychology (e.g., openness, value for diversity, social activism) provide guidance as we struggle through these issues, and given these unifying and unique perspectives, counseling psychology can and should play a leadership role in the internationalization of psychology more generally.

Even though these conferences provided a venue for counseling psychologists to discuss both international and national perspectives, the regional, state, and local issues of counseling psychology in particular was not always addressed adequately. Therefore, regional conferences were held to address issues facing a smaller subset of counseling psychologists.

PERSPECTIVE: REGIONAL CONFERENCES

APA has a regional structure, but some counseling psychologists found these regional meetings inadequate for the purposes of the specialty of counseling psychology. Delgado-Romero, Bowman, and Gerstein (2006) reviewed the history of regional conferences in Division 17. Although there were sporadic and isolated regional gatherings of counseling psychologists before 1987, the first national attempt to institute a regional conference system (similar to the regional psychological associations) began at the Third National Counseling Psychology Conference held in Atlanta, Georgia, in 1987. At that conference president-elect Jim Hurst proposed a regional conference system that would ideally address declining membership and give graduate students and new professionals a way to participate in the leadership of the division. Ten regional conferences were held in 1988. After that year, regions met only sporadically, if at all, with the exception of the Great Lakes Regional Conference. The Great Lakes region has been the only region that has met annually as suggested and is now in its 22nd year.

Delgado-Romero et al. (2006) pointed out that regional conferences meet needs (e.g., recruitment, retention, and involvement) that are consistently identified as issues by Division 17 presidents and they recommended that the division move toward reinvigorating regional conferences on a national level. As of 2010, only the Southeastern region had

responded by hosting conferences in 2008 and 2010. Perhaps regional needs are being met through regional APA state organizations or through other events, structures, or systems. What is the relative cost and benefit of hosting regional conferences? Could an active regional system advance a national agenda?

Other regionally based organizations have met with frequency. For example the Big 10 Counseling Center Conference has met for almost two decades, and the Dennis H. May Conference on Diversity Issues and the Role of Counseling Centers at the University of Illinois has been meeting since 1991. Furthermore, the Diversity Challenge at Boston College has been meeting since 2001, and the Winter Roundtable on Cultural Psychology and Education had its 28th meeting in 2011. These conferences, along with the Great Lakes Regional Counseling Psychology Conference indicate that the Midwest and Northeastern regions of Counseling Psychology have active regional systems that seem to be addressing regional needs. The relatively weak support for more localized and regional conferences can be because of a number or reasons. On a national level, we have seen counseling psychology wrestle with core identity issues in early national conferences. What has been reaffirmed by discussions in these conferences is not a set of rigid practice and scholarly areas representing the focus of counseling psychology. Rather, and returning to the notion of core values of the specialty, counseling psychologists have consistently developed and elaborated on guiding principles and standards that are applicable in increasingly broad and diverse areas. A consequence of this may be the lack of identification as counseling psychologists at the local level, as counseling psychologists increasingly practice in areas outside of the traditional bounds of counseling psychology. Moreover, larger core value and interests areas are better addressed at national and international levels or regional conferences focused on these central values and interests (e.g., diversity at the Winter Roundtable on Cultural Psychology or Boston College Diversity Challenge).

PERSPECTIVE: TRAINING AND EDUCATION

In terms of academic training programs in 2010, there were 66 academic training programs in counseling psychology. In addition, the student bodies were diverse (70% women, 29% ethnic and racial minorities, 8% international; Norcross, Evans, & Ellis, 2010). Norcross et al. (2010) stated that "the research driven portrait of doctoral training in counseling psychology is of highly competitive, multiculturally diverse, and theoretically pluralistic programs" (p. 257). Both Norcross et al. and Neimeyer, Saferstein, and Rice (2005) provided outcome measures in the context of training models, emphasizing that the training model was one of the most important factors in outcome. Beyond academic training programs, there is a vibrant group of training (practicum, internship, and postdoctoral) and practice organizations, such as counseling centers (organized under Association of Counseling Center Training Agencies and accredited through APA or the Association of Psychological Postdoctoral and Internship Centers), that contribute to the richness of counseling psychology.

Professional Identity

A key to identity issues entails focusing on both what counseling psychology defines itself as and what it defines itself as not. In the history of counseling psychology, the main identity struggle has been definitional—how to define the profession, particularly in light of the existence of clinical psychology (Watkins, 1983; Watkins et al., 1987; Whiteley, 1984). By the 1990s, counseling psychology in general seemed to have resolved some of these identity issues as part of the maturation of the specialty (Fouad et al., 2004; Heppner et al., 2000). In terms of SCP, through several strategic planning initiatives SCP reflected a clearer sense of identity focused on multiculturalism, social justice initiatives, vocational issues, supervision, and positive–developmental psychology—mirroring central tenets spanning the historical development counseling psychology. This overall focus on the identity of counseling as emanating from the core values and worldview of counseling psychologists led to a clearer definition of the field in its own right.

Challenges to identity have continued to arise in familiar and new places that include counselor educators, professional schools of psychology, the American Psychological Society, and program closure. Heppner et al. (2000) described how the profession of counseling psychology had grown distinct from the profession of counselor education and, in particular, the American Counseling Association. This trend intensified in the 2000s as counselor educators through the Council for Accreditation of Counseling and Related Educational Programs (CACREP) began defining their field and restricting counselor education programs to hiring counselor educators (CACREP graduates) as faculty. This decision crystallized a growing rift between counselor education and counseling psychology.

Given that APA defines psychology as a doctoral profession, the issue of master's level training uniquely affects counseling psychology practice and training compared with other applied psychological fields. Some counseling psychology programs are dependent on the revenue generated from terminal master's programs and are concerned about unaccredited programs and how competition from these programs may negatively impact the financial bottom line of their own programs. Clearly, as CACREP and APA policies conflict we may see programs having to choose between the two organizations, if not immediately at least in terms of future hires. Within SCP, there is recent movement to consider solutions to this issue, including investigating alternative master's credentialing (Chung, 2010).

The rise of professional schools offering a doctorate in psychology changed the training and education landscape significantly. On the basis of the professional applied clinical degrees found in other professions, the doctor of psychology (PsyD) is distinct from the doctor of philosophy (PhD) or education doctorate (EdD) traditionally earned by counseling psychologists. The PsyD usually is awarded on the basis of the practitioner–scholar model of training (as opposed to the scientist–practitioner) and is an applied degree. The majority of PsyD programs offer clinical psychology specialization, although two (i.e., Our Lady of the Lake University and the University of St. Thomas) offer the PsyD in counseling psychology.[2] The impact of

---

[2]Accredited in 1995 as a PsyD program, the University of Northern Colorado is a PhD program in counseling psychology as of 2010.

the growing number of PsyD students has been directly felt by counseling psychology programs, perhaps most acutely in the supply–demand problem in internship training. Miville, Adams, and Juntunen (2007) found that counseling psychology training directors believe that the large number of PsyD students has resulted in a supply and demand problem (because of not limiting admissions; see Boggs & Douce, 2000) with the increase of internship applicants and a lagging growth of internship positions. This issue leads to a perceived need for increased practicum hours to stay competitive for internship positions (Parent & Williamson, 2010; Rodolfa, Owen, & Clark, 2007; Stedman, 2007), which is felt by programs as they try to maintain their scientist-practitioner training model.

The Association for Psychological Science (formerly the American Psychological Society; APS) was formed in 1988 in reaction to the growing impact of practitioners in the APA. Its stated purpose was to "advance scientific psychology and its representation as a science on the national level" (http://www.psychologicalscience.org). In 2010, APS claimed more than 20,000 members. APS created the Psychological Clinical Science Accreditation System (PCSAS) in 2007 and accredited its first program in psychological clinical science in 2009. The PCSAS accreditation model was envisioned to become an alternative to APA accreditation (Baker, McFall, & Shoham, 2008). The accreditation was limited to psychology programs in nonprofit, research-intensive universities and, as such, would likely exclude many counseling psychology training programs. The development of APS and their initial move into accreditation, however, could affect the future of both APA and SCP. Drawing from the thematic values raised earlier, the broad-based value of integrating science and practice may be a reason that counseling psychology has not been more involved in APS or PCSAS. In the face of developments that increasingly highlight the recurring tensions between science and practice, counseling psychologists need to be involved in these discussions, as they challenge the integrative core identities and values that have come to define the specialty.

One of the most noticeable and startling trends for counseling psychology has been the relatively recent elimination of a number of strong counseling psychology programs in research universities. For example, in August 2010, alumni of the University of Notre Dame Counseling Psychology Program were informed that the program was being completely phased out in favor of a new clinical psychology program (Merluzzi, personal communication). Notre Dame's program had been continuously accredited since 1972. With the program at Temple University closing in 2011 (accredited since 1973), the program at Indiana State University being phased out (accredited since 1980), and the program at the University of Illinois Urbana–Champaign (accredited since 1985) not accepting applications for 2011–2012, the number of open accredited programs accepting students contracted to 62 (down from a high of 73; Goodyear et al., 2008).[3] Several more programs were potentially at risk because of the negative economic climate or a lack of faculty. As we wrote this chapter, the faculty of the counseling psychology program at Pennsylvania State University informed the SCP Listserv that their program had ceased admissions and is planned for closure.

Programs that were influential during the history of counseling psychology, such as the Ohio State University (OSU), Michigan State University, and Stanford University have all closed in the recent decades. Although some active counseling psychology faculty still remain at these institutions, these institutions no longer train counseling psychologists. If one considers the substantial role that these programs played in the history of counseling psychology for more than 50 years, not having a counseling psychology program at schools such as OSU seems unthinkable. OSU was one of the so-called MOMM group of universities (Maryland, Missouri, and Minnesota being the others) cited as being the most influential in the history of counseling psychology (Horan & Erickson, 1991).

In 2005, Blustein, Goodyear, Perry, and Cypers reviewed the history of accredited programs in counseling psychology. They noted trends over time and the fact that counseling psychology program

---

[3]In October 2010, two counseling psychology programs were under review for initial accreditation by the Committee on Accreditation: Carlow University and Cleveland State University.

losses were proportionally higher than either school or clinical psychology. Blustein et al. (2005) noted that there was a trend toward combining professional and scientific programs. They also examined the institutional context of counseling psychology programs (psychology vs. education) and pointed out the vulnerabilities inherent in each context. They include a full list of program closures to 2005. Do the program closures at Notre Dame, Indiana State, and Penn State portend a new era of program closures, or are these closures part of the general process described by Blustein et al.?

These recent developments in counseling psychology raise a number of questions. What might have the profession looked like with a stronger national presence and operating programs in California (the most populous U.S. state where a single accredited joint program at the University of California–Santa Barbara exists)? Given that the program losses were mainly at research-intensive universities, counseling psychology would have a stronger institutional research context. Taking a broader view, we believe that emergent issues with accreditation and program closures may be a consequence of the trajectory of counseling psychology's development in the past few decades. Counseling psychology is increasingly defined not by traditional boundaries of practice and scholarly interest areas, but by foundational values and principles that are infused in increasingly broad and varied contexts. That is to say, it is more difficult to say *what* counseling psychology does or is than *how* counseling psychology approaches the study of psychology. There are a number of consequences to this. First, counseling psychology may struggle to find a strong public image and identity that is readily understood by other psychologists and the larger public. This has implications for the maintenance and strengthening of graduate and other training programs. Second, counseling psychology, not bounded by rigid practice and scholarly boundaries, is found in broadening and diverse work settings typical of other specialties and professions (e.g., clinical health psychology; Nicholas & Stern, 2011). Although we believe that the proliferation of counseling psychology practice and scholarly interests is a healthy extension of our core values, it is important to maintain strong education and training programs to support new generations of counseling psychologists. As such, we believe that SCP should examine the issue of program closures in greater depth. What are the risk factors for program closure? What programs might be at such risk, and what might be done about it? How can we separate local politics from general program dynamics that might indicate a looming issue? We imagine a comprehensive postmortem of a closed program that would examine the role and perspectives of administrators, faculty, students, and alumni about the program closing. Such a process, conducted publically, might also provide some closure for the many people affected and provide some insight into dynamics that could affect all programs. What systemic and local strategies might be employed to prevent program closure or, better yet, actually strengthen or expand programs?

FUTURE CHALLENGES

In their conclusionary remarks on the history of counseling psychology from 1979 to 1998, Heppner et al. (2000) put forth 10 challenges that counseling psychology face in the future. It has only been a short time since their reflection, and here we selectively review and update the developments of these challenges as a way of pulling together the issues we have raised.

1. Heppner et al. (2000) argued for organizational counseling psychology to collaborate and interface with groups within and outside of the profession. Since the reorganization of the 1990s, SCP has maintained a strong internal structure and has continued to work collaboratively with other APA divisions and structures as well as non-APA counseling psychology organizations. Since Heppner et al.'s call, continued collaboration with Divisions 35, 44, and 45 to host the Multicultural Summit and Conference biennially, and cohosting the International Counseling Psychology Conference with the Council for Counseling Psychology Training Programs (CCPTP) and Association of Counseling Center Training Agencies (ACCTA), are both evidence of the value of collaboration. Also, advocacy with

divisions within APA, and EMPAs to push for EMPA voting seats on APA's Council of Representatives also demonstrate continued efforts to work collaboratively with organized psychology.

2. Heppner et al. (2000) recognized the success of counseling psychology research and called for continued efforts to ensure that research activities more directly affect broader practical and social policy agendas. By all accounts, counseling psychology has continued to maintain an active and vibrant research agenda. Both *JCP* and *TCP* and other, non-APA, journals, such as the *Journal of Counseling and Development* and the *Journal of Multicultural Counseling and Development*, indicate lively and productive research activities within the field. A number of research areas have seen continued growth in counseling psychology. Notably from our review, interests in multiculturalism and social justice have become quite prominent in the research and practice activities of counseling psychologists. This is consistent with Heppner et al.'s (2000) call for further integration of cultural diversity into counseling psychology and is reflected in SCP's ability to attract a high proportion of ethnic minority psychologists into it membership, and the publication trends of multicultural scholarship within counseling psychology and by counseling psychologists (e.g., Lau, Cisco, & Delgado-Romero, 2008). For example, both in terms of national debates at conferences (Fouad et al., 2004) and scholarly work (Fouad et al., 2006; L. Smith 2008; Speight & Vera, 2008), the role that social justice and advocacy plays is increasingly evident. Addressing multicultural issues concerning race, ethnicity, gender, and sexual orientation has grown to be a strength in counseling. Scholarship and discussions within the specialty, however, are increasingly voicing a need to address other personal and cultural identities lacking much attention. Among these include social class (L. Smith, 2008), disability (Henwood & Pope-Davis, 1994), religion and spirituality (Constantine, 1999; Frazier & Hansen, 2009), and indigenous perspectives (Mohatt, 2010). Also, attention to traditional strengths in counseling psychology can at times

be inconsistent (e.g., LGBT issues; N. G. Smith, 2009). The growing interest in these areas is again not surprising given the traditional interests and values of the discipline. We believe that counseling psychologists should continue to play a central role in influencing the research and practice agendas of psychology and related disciplines. The expansion of counseling psychologists into diverse disciplines will facilitate this important task.

3. Although counseling psychology remains a strong and vibrant discipline, there has been a loosening of traditional bonds that tied the discipline together (e.g., vocational psychology). Heppner et al. (2000) raised this issue when pointing out the challenge of maintaining unity in a diversifying discipline. Driven by forces rooted in historical emergence and traditional values of the discipline, this challenge has been coupled with increasing expansion into diverse activities of research and practice. Counseling psychology, for example, can and has contributed to efforts to address a number of manmade and natural tragedies in the past decade. Examples of such tragedies include responses to terrorism (the September 11, 2001 terrorist attacks in the United States), national tragedies such as the shootings at Virginia Tech University (Flynn & Heitzmann, 2008), and natural disasters both domestically and abroad (e.g., Hurricane Katrina in 2005; devastating earthquakes in Haiti in 2010). Soon after Hurricane Katrina hit in 2005, SCP was involved in setting up a Hurricane Relief and Disaster Response Special Task Group that provided direct assistance to students affected by the disaster and facilitated discussion with affiliated organizations (e.g., APA, CCPTP, American Red Cross) to assist in relief efforts (Gerstein & Lent, 2005). The Iraq and Afghanistan wars have also made the issues of veterans and military families a priority for counseling psychologists. A consequence of these wars was the growth of the Veterans Administration (VA) hospital system and an increased need for counseling psychologists within the VA system (Danish & Antonides, 2009). The skills and knowledge of counseling

psychologists are well suited for these crises and large-scale disasters because of our tradition of social justice commitment and training in addressing the needs of clients beyond immediate psychological issues (e.g., vocational, family, and racial–ethnic issues).

4. There is tremendous diversity in the members associated with SCP, but the membership also appears to be aging with fewer and fewer early career and younger counseling psychologists joining the organization as members. Within SCP, there has been a proliferation of sections and groups that although they accurately reflect the emergence of valuable interests within the organization also may fragment the membership. SCP members' overlapping membership with other APA divisions also suggests the diversity and interdisciplinary nature of their professional interests. Heppner et al. (2000) anticipated this tension when they highlighted the need for the discipline to maintain unity in the face of diversification, and we believe this will be a persistent challenge for counseling psychology in the near future. They were also concerned with broadening member involvement in the profession beyond traditional core groups. Within SCP, there have been recent efforts to address this issue and the steading aging of SCP membership. The 2011–2012 SCP president, Barry Chung, initiated a Leadership Academy as one of his presidential initiatives to bring in and train new generation of SCP leaders.

5. Another recent strength area of counseling psychology is in the internationalization of our research and practice interests. The planning of the International Counseling Psychology Conference was a strong statement of counseling psychologists' interest in collaborating and learning from our international colleagues (Forrest, 2010). As such, we echo Heppner et al.'s (2000) challenge for counseling psychology to sustain meaningful collaborations on international and cultural diversity issues.

6. Related to the expansion into new practice areas for counseling psychologists is the need for increased accountability and monitoring of competencies. The movement is toward competency-based

assessment and training (Forrest, Elman, & Shen Miller 2008; Gilfoyle, 2008; Hatcher & Lassiter, 2007; McCutcheon, 2008; Nelson, 2007; Wester, Christianson, Fouad, & Santiago-Rivera, 2008) with an emphasis on diversity competence (Forrest, 2010; Miller, Forrest, & Elman, 2009; Miville et al., 2009). In 2000, Heppner et al. noted that one of the challenges was the gap between training and practice, especially in areas such as health. Counseling psychologists are also finding themselves expanding into practice areas outside of the traditional boundaries of the profession (e.g., business consulting, executive coaching) and in some cases reinvigorating their practice in dormant practices (e.g., educational consultation, career counseling). As such, we continue to echo Heppner et al.'s (2000) call to attend to the training needs of practicing counseling psychologists in diverse arenas.

7. Notable across these observations is the prominence of counseling psychology values and viewpoints in affecting the changes seen in the discipline. Counseling psychology emerged as a broad-based discipline that was rooted in commitment to contextual and strength-based views of those we study and serve. The growth of movements in multiculturalism and diversity, internationalism, and social advocacy across research, practice, and training were natural developments from these strong historical roots. On the one hand, these values define and shape the historical identity of counseling psychology. But on the other hand, this has resulted in an increasingly diversified discipline that lacks a clear public image. There is an inherent tension in core counseling psychology values expansively pushing the discipline outside of its traditional boundaries and the need to retain clear and traditional boundaries for self-identification purposes. The challenges of the nature and structure of training programs (e.g., PhD vs. PsyD or master's level programs) and the dissolution of counseling psychology programs more generally may be a symptom of this tension. Consequently, a challenge for counseling psychology is to deal with this tension in way that maintains the vibrancy and dynamic nature of the discipline. We posit that a subscription to traditional and prevailing

counseling psychology values and perspectives may be the binding force that holds the diverse members and activities in a coherent and effective manner. Counseling psychologists are not defined by *what* they do and *where* they work as much as *how* they conceptualize the work and the values of psychology.

CONCLUSION

Counseling psychology has a long history of self-reflection and contemplation about the profession's future (Whiteley, 1980). In the first issue of *TCP* in 1969, Donald Super speculated about vocational development theory in 1988. Similarly, in 1988, Rude, Weissberg, and Gazda looked into the future on the basis of the themes of the Third National Conference, and Carter (2003) speculated about the role of *TCP* in bridging the past to the new millennium.

Underlying these historic efforts is an attempt to answer two questions: "Who are we?" and "What are we to become?" These are fundamental questions for counseling psychology as a specialty in psychology and for SCP as a professional organization. For many years, the question was answered in relation to the distinction between counseling psychology and related fields (e.g., counselor education and clinical psychology). Historically, there are several pillars of counseling psychology that seem to have eroded in terms of what counseling psychologists currently do (e.g., vocational psychology and prevention; see Goodyear et al., 2008) and how counseling psychologists affiliate and identify (e.g., the fact that the majority of counseling psychologists do not belong to SCP; Forrest, 2008). At the same time, fundamental values of openness, contextualized understandings of the world, and commitment to diversity and social advocacy weave a common thread over the activities and identity of counseling psychology.

We have viewed the history of counseling psychology to date utilizing a variety of perspectives: core values, organization, science and research, and training and education. We have tried to make sense of (and admire) patterns in counseling psychology history and watched as SCP expanded, contracted, and went through different iterations. The task of

writing a chapter on the history of counseling psychology is complex for many reasons. For one, many existing scholars have produced both thorough and highly instructive reviews of the specialty's past (Baker & Subich, 2008; Heppner et al., 2000; Munley et al., 2004; Whiteley, 1984). Moreover, as counseling psychology has developed over the years, determining what constitutes the history of counseling psychology or the activities and accomplishments of counseling psychologists has become an increasingly difficult undertaking. Our approach in this chapter, we believe, demonstrates this observation. By examining both contemporary and historical viewpoints of counseling psychology through shifting lens and multiple perspectives, we observe that a critical juncture is beginning to emerge for counseling psychology. The critical juncture is characterized by a strong core of values and identities that trace our roots to the historical birth of the profession and by a diffusing sense of what constitutes the image of counseling psychology.

Clear thematic values emanate from our review of the history. Our identity and work has been consistently defined by a proactive commitment to an open and accepting approach to understanding the complex interactions of individuals within their environments, with the goals of improving lives and facilitating social change. At the same time, these driving forces and guiding principles have resulted in an ever-expanding proliferation of counseling psychology interests, approaches, and practice settings. Heppner et al. (2000) alluded to this when they expressed concern about maintaining unity for a profession becoming increasingly diversified and varied.

What are important considerations for the future of counseling psychology at this critical juncture? There is a risk, as alluded to by previous historians (Heppner et al., 2000), of professional dissolution through disunity. Drawing from our disciplinary roots of searching for strengths and positives, our assessment of the future remains a positive one. As we have seen, there are a number of venues and opportunities for counseling psychology to continue to speak with a unified voice. Although we see counseling psychologists engaging in professional activities that are increasingly disparate and evolving, we also see a return to some of the roles and settings that have characterized our traditional identity. One way to look at the future of counseling psychology is to return to the thematic values that have been unyielding in shaping the unique contributions of the specialty to psychology and society. Can we (or should we) consider counseling psychology less and less like a specialty or profession, and more and more like a set of strong, ubiquitous, guiding values and competencies that radiate throughout the science and practice of psychology? What are the risks and ramifications for maintaining a distinct professional entity in the way that we have historically? Is there any other helpful mechanism to ensure that such values and competencies are maintained and enhanced throughout psychology with losing the identity of counseling psychology?

We return to the present day as many counseling psychologists balance optimism and pessimism about the future of the profession and the country in general. Perhaps one of the most tangible points of pride and optimism is the success of SCP and its members and programs. APA president Carol Goodheart and her successor Melba Vasquez personify this success. Both are counseling psychologists who represent a broad constituency and have successfully built a political coalition on the basis of their training as counseling psychologists. Both embody the values of counseling psychology and continue the growth of the logical outcomes of many efforts by SCP leaders in the past. Vasquez illustrates deep ties to SCP. She was a former president of both Division 17 (Society of Counseling Psychology) and Division 35 (Society for the Psychology of Women). Vasquez had been the president of a state psychological association (Texas), a founding member of the Society for the Psychological Study of Ethnic Minority Psychology (Division 45) and an APA Council representative for Divisions 17, 35, and 42 (Psychologists in Independent Practice). A fellow of eight APA divisions, Vasquez began her career in a university counseling center and transitioned to private practice, all the while actively contributing to the professional literature. She was also one of the founders of the National Multicultural Summit and Conference in 1999 (Sue et al., 1999). Vasquez's career path and accomplishments present a concrete, illustrative individual career example reflecting the historical development of counseling psychology and SCP in more recent years. In acknowledging her diverse background and interests, we also see a similar shift in the identity and structure of counseling psychology and SCP. In recent decades, there has been a loosening of bonds that traditionally define counseling psychology and an increasing proliferation of counseling psychology into diverse research and practice areas. All the while, multiculturalism, diversity, and social justice have permeated these growth areas. With a complex and shifting professional identity, there is a risk of counseling psychology and SCP losing a coherent and stable public and self-image. We believe, however, that our review has also highlighted deep roots and values that are at the core of recent developments of the discipline. Vasquez is representative of this changing and ever-diffusing identity that at the center is very much held together by core commitments and values. It is this core that we believe will represent counseling psychology as we see counseling psychologists engage in ever-expansive roles and activities in diverse settings. In 2011, as Vasquez addressed APA from her presidential podium, there were many reasons to have optimism for the future and also a feeling of pride in the values that led the SCP to that moment.

In reflecting on "Who are we?" and "Who are we to become?" we look to Schwebel's (1980) words when predicting the status of counseling psychology in the year 2000:

> Counseling Psychology will probably still be around in 2000 A.D. at least in the person of those who continue to do what has been most closely associated with our field in the past and who wish to identify themselves as counseling psychologists. However, how we choose to identify ourselves and whether the field exists by this or any other name, are rather inconsequential matters. What is important is that psychologists should be serving our society, our communities, and our clientele well, drawing on the advances in science and applying them much more on a macro- rather than micro-level. (p. 59)

Schwebel (1980) certainly anticipated the issues that have been raised in this chapter regarding the diversification of counseling psychology research and practice. We believe that the future identity of counseling psychology will be determined less by traditional markers of professional activities and research focus, and more by foundational values and goals that are realized in increasingly diverse and varied contexts. The consequential matter, as Schwebel would argue, is for these values and goals to guide counseling psychologists in serving the greater good of individuals and society on multiple levels. Perhaps after all these years, counseling psychology has continued and will continue to carry core values consistent with disciplinary resilience for all of psychology.

References

American Psychological Association. (2003). Guidelines on multicultural education, training, research, practice and organizational change for psychologists. *American Psychologist, 58*, 377–402. doi:10.1037/0003-066X.58.5.377

American Psychological Association. (2007). Guidelines for psychological practice with girls and women. *American Psychologist, 62*, 949–979. doi:10.1037/0003-066X.62.9.949

American Psychological Association. (2010a). *Demographic characteristics of APA members by membership status, 2009*. Retrieved from http://www.apa.org/workforce/publications/09-member/table-01.pdf

American Psychological Association. (2010b). *2009 Membership statistics for Division 17*. Retrieved from http://www.apa.org/about/division/div17-2009.aspx

American Psychological Association Division of Counseling and Guidance, Committee on Counselor Training. (1952a). The practicum training of counseling psychologists. *American Psychologist, 7*, 175–181.

American Psychological Association Division of Counseling and Guidance, Committee on Counselor Training. (1952b). Recommended standards for training counseling psychologists at the doctoral level. *American Psychologist, 7*, 182–188.

American Psychological Association Division of Counseling and Guidance, Committee on Definition. (1956). Counseling psychology as a specialty. *American Psychologist, 11*, 282–285. doi:10.1037/h0044771

Arm, J. R., Horne, S. G., & Levitt, H. M. (2009). Negotiating connection to GLBT experience: Family members' experience of anti-GLBT movements and policies. *Journal of Counseling Psychology, 56*, 82–96. doi:10.1037/a0012813

Baker, D. B., & Subich, L. M. (2008). Counseling psychology: Historical perspectives. In W. B. Walsh (Ed.), *The biennial review of counseling psychology* (Vol. 1, pp. 1–26). New York, NY: Routledge.

Baker, T. B., McFall, R. M., & Shoham, V. (2008). Current status and future prospects of clinical psychology: Toward a scientifically principled approach to mental and behavioral health care. *Psychological Science in the Public Interest, 9*, 67–103.

Bidell, M. P., Ragen, J. K., Broach, C. D., & Carrillo, E. A. (2007). First impressions: A multicultural content analysis of professional psychology program web sites. *Training and Education in Professional Psychology, 1*, 204–214. doi:10.1037/1931-3918.1.3.204

Blustein, D. L., Goodyear, R. K., Perry, J. C., & Cypers, S. (2005). The shifting sands of Counseling Psychology programs institutional contexts: An environmental scan and revitalizing strategies. *The Counseling Psychologist, 33*, 610–634. doi:10.1177/0011000005277820

Boggs, K. R., & Douce, L. A. (2000). Current status and anticipated changes in psychology internships: Effects on counseling psychology training. *The Counseling Psychologist, 28*, 672–686. doi:10.1177/0011000000285005

Brammer, L., Alcorn, J., Birk, J., Gazda, G., Hurst, J., LaFromboise, T., . . . Scott, N. (1988). Organizational and political issues in counseling psychology: Recommendations for change. *The Counseling Psychologist, 16*, 407–422.

Brems, C., & Johnson, M. E. (1996). Comparison of Ph. D. programs in clinical and counseling psychology. *The Journal of Psychology, 130*, 485–498. doi:10.1080/00223980.1996.9915016

Carter, R. T. (2003). *The Counseling Psychologist* in the new millennium: Building a bridge from the past to the future. *The Counseling Psychologist, 31*, 5–15. doi:10.1177/0011000002239395

Chung, Y. B. (2010). Vice president for education and training report. *American Psychological Association Society of Counseling Psychology Newsletter, XXXI*(1), 3.

Constantine, M. G. (1999). Spiritual and religious issues in counseling racial and ethnic minority populations: An introduction to the special issue. *Journal of Multicultural Counseling and Development, 27*, 179–181.

Croteau, J. M., Lark, J. S., Lidderdale, M. A., & Chung, Y. B. (2009). *Deconstructing heterosexism in the counseling professions: A narrative approach*. Thousand Oaks, CA: Sage.

Danish, S. J., & Antonides, B. J. (2009). What counseling psychologists can do to help returning veterans. *The Counseling Psychologist, 37*, 1076–1089. doi:10.1177/0011000009338303

Delgado-Romero, E. A., Bowman, S., & Gerstein, L. (2006). 18 years of the Great Lakes Regional Counseling Psychology Conference: Revisiting the need for regional conferences. *The Counseling Psychologist, 34*, 420–438. doi:10.1177/0011000005282834

Douce, L. A. (2004). Globalization of counseling psychology. *The Counseling Psychologist, 32*, 142–152. doi:10.1177/0011000003260009

Fassinger, R. E., Shullman, S. L., & Stevenson, M. R. (2010). Toward an affirmative lesbian, gay, bisexual and transgender leadership paradigm. *American Psychologist, 65*, 201–215. doi:10.1037/a0018597

Flores, L. Y., Rooney, S. C., Heppner, P. P., Douglas, L., & Wei, M. F. (1999). Trend analyses of major contributions in *The Counseling Psychologist* cited between 1986–1996: Impact and implications. *The Counseling Psychologist, 27*, 73–95. doi:10.1177/0011000099271006

Flynn, C., & Heitzmann, D. (2008). Tragedy at Virginia Tech: Trauma and its aftermath. *The Counseling Psychologist, 36*, 479–489. doi:10.1177/0011000008314787

Forrest, L. M. (2008). The ever evolving identity of counseling psychologists: Musings of the Society of Counseling Psychology President. *The Counseling Psychologist, 36*, 281–289. doi:10.1177/0011000007313552

Forrest, L. M. (2010). Linking international psychology, professional competence, and leadership: Counseling psychologists as learning partners. *The Counseling Psychologist, 38*, 96–120. doi:10.1177/0011000009350585

Forrest, L. M., Alvarez, A., White, J., Delgado-Romero, E. A., Casas, M., & LaFromboise, T. D. (2008). *Learn more about the five ethnic minority psychological associations.* Symposium presented at the 2008 International Counseling Psychology Conference, Chicago, IL.

Forrest, L. M., Elman, N. S., & Shen Miller, D. S. (2008). Psychology trainees with competence problems: From individual to ecological conceptualizations. *Training and Education in Professional Psychology, 2*, 183–192. doi:10.1037/1931-3918.2.4.183

Fouad, N. A., Gerstein, L. H., & Toporek, R. L. (2006). Social justice and counseling psychology in context. In R. L. Toporek, L. H. Gerstein, N. A. Fouad, G. Roysircar, & T. Israel (Eds.), *Social justice in counseling psychology: Leadership, vision and action* (pp. 1–16). Thousand Oaks, CA: Sage.

Fouad, N. A. (2008). Editor's introduction: Vision for the future of *TCP*. *The Counseling Psychologist, 36*, 5–7.

Fouad, N. A., McPherson, R. H., Gerstein, L., Blustein, D. L., Ellman, N., Helledy, K. I., & Metz, A. J. (2004). Houston, 2001: Context and legacy. *The Counseling Psychologist, 32*, 15–77. doi:10.1177/0011000003259943

Frazier, R. E., & Hansen, N. D. (2009). Religious/spiritual psychotherapy behaviors: Do we do what we believe to be important? *Professional Psychology: Research and Practice, 40*, 81–87. doi:10.1037/a0011671

Gelso, C. J., & Fretz, B. R. (1991). *Counseling psychology.* New York, NY: Harcourt.

Gerstein, L., & Lent, B. (2005). Hurricane relief efforts. *American Psychological Association Society for Counseling Psychology Newsletter, XXVII*(1), 13.

Gilfoyle, N. (2008). The legal exosystem: Risk management in addressing student competence problems in professional psychology training. *Training and Education in Professional Psychology, 2*, 202–209. doi:10.1037/1931-3918.2.4.202

Goodyear, R. K., Murdock, N., Lichtenberg, J. W., McPhersen, R., Koetting, K., & Petren, S. (2008). Stability and change in counseling psychologists' identities, roles, functions, and career satisfaction across 15 years. *The Counseling Psychologist, 36*, 220–249. doi:10.1177/0011000007309481

Hatcher, R. L., & Lassiter, K. D. (2007). Initial training in professional psychology: The practicum competencies outline. *Training and Education in Professional Psychology, 1*, 49–63. doi:10.1037/1931-3918.1.1.49

Henwood, P. G., & Pope-Davis, D. B. (1994). Disability as cultural diversity: Counseling the hearing impaired. *The Counseling Psychologist, 22*, 489–503. doi:10.1177/0011000094223011

Heppner, P. P. (2006). Benefits and challenges of becoming a cross-culturally competent counseling psychologists. *The Counseling Psychologist, 34*, 147–172. doi:10.1177/0011000005282832

Heppner, P. P., Casas, J. M., Carter, J., & Stone, G. L. (2000). The maturation of counseling psychology: Multifaceted perspectives, 1978–1998. In S. D. Brown & R. W. Lent (Eds.), *Handbook of counseling psychology* (3rd ed., pp. 3–49). New York, NY: Wiley.

Horan, J. J., & Erickson, C. D. (1991). Fellowship behavior in Division 17 and the MOMM Cartel. *The Counseling Psychologist, 19*, 253–259. doi:10.1177/0011000091192011

Howard, G. S. (1992). Behold our creation! What counseling psychology has become and might yet become. *Journal of Counseling Psychology, 39*, 419–442. doi:10.1037/0022-0167.39.4.419

Ivey, A. E. (1979). Counseling psychology—The most broadly-based applied psychology specialty. *The*

Counseling Psychologist, 8, 3–6. doi:10.1177/0011 00007900800302

Kagan, N., Armsworth, M. W., Altmaier, E. M., Dowd, E. T., Hansen, J. C., Mills, D. H., . . . Vasquez, M. J. T. (1988). Professional practice of counseling psychology in various settings. *The Counseling Psychologist, 16*, 347–365.

Lau, M. Y., Cisco, H. C., & Delgado-Romero, E. A. (2008). Individual and Institutional research productivity in multicultural psychology. *Journal of Multicultural Counseling and Development, 36*, 194–205.

Leong, F. T. L. (2009). Guest editor's introduction: History of racial and ethnic minority psychology. *Cultural Diversity and Ethnic Minority Psychology, 15*, 315–316. doi:10.1037/a0017556

Levitt, H. M., Ovrebo, E., Anderson-Cleveland, M. B., Leone, C., Jeong, J. Y., Arm, J. R., . . . Horne, S. G. (2009). Balancing dangers: GLBT experience in a time of anti-GLBT legislation. *Journal of Counseling Psychology, 56*, 67–81. doi:10.1037/a0012988

McCutcheon, S. (2008). Addressing problems of insufficient competence during the internship year. *Training and Education in Professional Psychology, 2*, 210–214. doi:10.1037/a0013535

Meara, N. M., & Myers, R. A. (1998). A history of Division 17 (Counseling Psychology): Establishing stability amid change. In D. A. Dewsbury (Ed.), *Unification through division: Histories of divisions of the American Psychological Association* (Vol. 3, pp. 9–41). Washington, DC: American Psychological Association.

Miller, D. S., Forrest, L., & Elman, N. S. (2009). Training directors' conceptualizations of the intersections of diversity and trainee competence problems: A preliminary analysis. *The Counseling Psychologist, 37*, 482–518. doi:10.1177/0011000008316656

Mintz, L. B., & Bieschke, K. J. (2009). Counseling psychology model training values statement addressing diversity: Development and introduction to the major contribution. *The Counseling Psychologist, 37*, 634–640. doi:10.1177/0011000009331923

Miville, M. L., Adams, E. M., & Juntunen, C. L. (2007). Counseling psychology perspectives on the predoctoral internship supply-demand imbalance: Strategies for problem definition and resolution. *Training and Education in Professional Psychology, 1*, 258–266. doi:10.1037/1931-3918.1.4.258

Miville, M. L., Duan, C., Nutt, R., Waehler, C., Suzuki, L., Pistole, C., . . . Corpus, B. (2009). Integrating practice guidelines into professional training: Implications for diversity competence. *The Counseling Psychologist, 37*, 519–563. doi:10.1177/0011000008323651

Mohatt, G. V. (2010). Moving toward an indigenous psychotherapy. *The Counseling Psychologist, 38*, 236–242. doi:10.1177/0011000009345532

Moradi, B., & Neimeyer, G. J. (2005). Diversity in the ivory white tower: A longitudinal look at faculty race/ethnicity in counseling psychology academic training programs. *The Counseling Psychologist, 33*, 655–675. doi:10.1177/0011000005277823

Munley, P. H., Duncan, L. E., McDonnell, K. A., & Sauer, E. M. (2004). Counseling psychology in the United States of America. *Counseling Psychology Quarterly, 17*, 247–271. doi:10.1080/09515070412331317602

Munley, P. H., Pate, W. E., & Duncan, L. E. (2008). Demographic, educational, employment and professional characteristics of counseling psychologists. *The Counseling Psychologist, 36*, 250–280. doi:10.1177/0011000006296915

Munsey, C. (2010). Psychology's case for same-sex marriage. *Monitor on Psychology, 41*, 46.

Neimeyer, G. J., Saferstein, J., & Rice, K. G. (2005). Does the model matter? The relationship between science-practice emphasis and outcomes in academic training programs in counseling psychology. *The Counseling Psychologist, 33*, 635–654. doi:10.1177/0011000005277821

Nelson, P. D. (2007). Striving for competence in the assessment of competence: Psychology's professional education and credentialing journey of public accountability. *Training and Education in Professional Psychology, 1*, 3–12. doi:10.1037/1931-3918.1.1.3

Nicholas, D. R., & Stern, M. (2011). Counseling psychology in clinical health psychology: The impact of specialty perspective. *Professional Psychology: Research and Practice, 42*, 331–337. doi:10.1037/a0024197

Norcross, J. C., Evans, K. L., & Ellis, J. L. (2010). The model does matter II: Admissions and training in APA–accredited counseling psychology programs. *The Counseling Psychologist, 38*, 257–268. doi:10.1177/0011000009339342

Packard, T. (2009). The 2008 Leona Tyler Award address: Core values that distinguish Counseling Psychology: Personal and professional perspectives. *The Counseling Psychologist, 37*, 610–624. doi:10.1177/0011000009333986

Parent, M. C., & Williamson, J. B. (2010). Program disparities in unmatched internship applicants. *Training and Education in Professional Psychology, 4*, 116–120. doi:10.1037/a0018216

Rodolfa, E. R., Owen, J. J., & Clark, S. (2007). Practicum training hours: Fact and fantasy. *Training and Education in Professional Psychology, 1*, 64–73. doi:10.1037/1931-3918.1.1.64

Rostosky, S. S., Riggle, E. D. B., Horne, S. G., & Miller, A. D. (2009). Marriage amendments and psychological distress in lesbian, gay, and bisexual (LGB) adults. *Journal of Counseling Psychology, 56*, 56–66. doi:10.1037/a0013609

Rude, S. S., Weissberg, M., & Gazda, G. M. (1988). Looking into the future: Themes from the Third National Conference for Counseling Psychology. *The Counseling Psychologist, 16*, 423–430. doi:10.1177/0011000088163008

Samler, J. (1964). Where do counseling psychologists work? What do they do? What should they do? In A. S. Thompson & D. E. Super (Eds.), *The professional preparation of counseling psychologists* (pp. 43–67). New York, NY: Columbia University, Teachers College Press.

Schwebel, M. (1980). Epilogue: 2000 A.D. *The Counseling Psychologist, 8*, 59–60. doi:10.1177/001100008000 800419

Smith, L. (2008). Positioning classism within counseling psychology's social justice agenda. *The Counseling Psychologist, 36*, 895–924. doi:10.1177/001100000 7309861

Smith, L. (2009). Enhancing training and practice in the context of poverty. *Training and Education in Professional Psychology, 3*, 84–93. doi:10.1037/a0014459

Smith, N. G. (2009). Productivity in lesbian, gay, bisexual, and transgender scholarship in counseling psychology: Institutional and individual ratings for 1990 through 2008. *The Counseling Psychologist, 38*, 50–68. doi:10.1177/0011000009345533

Society of Counseling Psychology. (2008). *2008 International Counseling Psychology Conference Program.* Chicago, IL: Author.

Speight, S. L., & Vera, E. M. (2008). Social justice and counseling psychology: A challenge to the profession. In S. D. Brown & R. W. Lent (Eds.), *Handbook of counseling psychology* (4th ed., pp. 54–67). New York, NY: Wiley.

Stedman, J. M. (2007). What we know about predoctoral internship training: A 10-year update. *Training and Education in Professional Psychology, 1*, 74–88. doi:10.1037/1931-3918.1.1.74

Sue, D. W., Bingham, R. P., Porche-Burke, L., & Vasquez, M. (1999). The diversification of psychology: A multicultural revolution. *American Psychologist, 54*, 1061–1069. doi:10.1037/0003-066X.54.12.1061

Thompson, S. D., & Super, D. E. (Eds.). (1964). *The professional preparation of counseling psychologists: Report of the 1964 Greyston Conference.* New York, NY: Teachers College, Columbia University.

Toporek, R. L., Gerstein, L. H., Fouad, N. A., Roysircar, G., & Israel, T. (Eds.). (2006). *Social justice in counseling psychology: Leadership, vision, and action.* Thousand Oaks, CA: Sage.

Vasquez, M. J. T. (2001). Reflections on unearned advantages, unearned disadvantages, and empowering experiences. In J. G. Ponterotto, J. M. Casas, L. A. Suzuki, & C. M. Alexander (Eds.), *Handbook of multicultural counseling* (2nd ed., pp. 64–77). Thousand Oaks, CA: Sage.

Watkins, C. E. (1983). Counseling psychology versus clinical psychology: Further explorations on a theme or once more around the "identity" maypole with gusto. *The Counseling Psychologist, 11*, 76–92. doi:10.1177/0011000083114012

Watkins, C. E., Lopez, F. G., Campbell, V. L., & Himmell, C. D. (1986). Counseling psychology and clinical psychology: Some preliminary comparative data. *American Psychologist, 41*, 581–582. doi:10.1037/0003-066X.41.5.581

Watkins, C. E., Schneider, L. J., Cox, J. H., & Reinberg, J. A. (1987). Clinical and counseling psychology: On similarities and differences revisited. *Professional Psychology: Research and Practice, 18*, 530–535. doi:10.1037/0735-7028.18.5.530

Weissberg, M., Rude, S. S., Gazda, G. M., Bozarth, J. D., McDougal, K. S., Slavit, M. R., . . . Walsh, D. J. (1988). An overview of the third national conference for counseling psychology: Planning the future. *The Counseling Psychologist, 16*, 325–331.

Westefeld, J. (2010). President's report. *American Psychological Association Society of Counseling Psychology Newsletter, XXXI*(1), 1–7.

Wester, S. R., Christianson, H. F., Fouad, N. A., & Santiago-Rivera, A. L. (2008). Information processing as problem solving: A collaborative approach to dealing with students exhibiting insufficient competence. *Training and Education in Professional Psychology, 2*, 193–201. doi:10.1037/1931-3918.2.4.193

Whiteley, J. M. (1969). Editor's introduction to The Counseling Psychologist. *The Counseling Psychologist, 1*, III. doi:10.1177/001100006900 100114

Whiteley, J. M. (1980). The future of counseling psychology: Introduction. *The Counseling Psychologist, 8*, 2. doi:10.1177/001100008000800401

Whiteley, J. M. (1984). Counseling psychology: A historical perspective. *The Counseling Psychologist, 12*, 3–109. doi:10.1177/0011000084121001

Zytowski, D. G., Casas, J. M., Gilbert, L. A., Lent, R. W., & Simon, N. P. (1988). Counseling psychology's public image. *The Counseling Psychologist, 16*, 332–346.

CHAPTER 2

THE EVOLUTION OF THEORY IN COUNSELING PSYCHOLOGY

Myrna L. Friedlander, Alex L. Pieterse, and Jessica E. Lambert

Social psychologist Kurt Lewin is credited with the maxim, "There is nothing so practical as a good theory." In this chapter, we begin by summarizing the four major classes of theory in counseling and psychotherapy[1]: psychoanalytic–psychodynamic, humanistic–experiential, cognitive–behavioral, and family systems. The predominant theories within each class are described and compared in their historical contexts, that is, the scientific, social, philosophic, and economic forces that contributed to their emergence and evolution. In each description, we highlight the conceptualization of emotional distress, the therapist's role, the primary therapeutic strategies and interventions, and the expected treatment outcomes.

Although a therapist's theoretical preference is largely a matter of worldview, training, and technical skill, choice of strategy with any specific client should be determined not only by preference but also by a multitude of interacting factors. Moreover, any approach that effectively targets one aspect of human functioning—be it emotion, cognition, or behavior—is likely to have reverberating effects on the other two aspects of functioning. Consequently, the remainder of this chapter addresses integrationist psychotherapy, which privileges contextual factors and factors that are common across theoretical orientations. The contextual and common factors we highlight in this chapter reflect the classic underpinnings of counseling psychology as a professional specialty and 70 years of scholarship in our field: (a) conceptualizing presenting concerns as problems

in living or person–environment fit rather than as mental disorders, (b) considering client characteristics as moderators of treatment choice and content, (c) focusing on development and resilience, and (d) viewing the therapeutic relationship as the primary agent of change. In discussing these four broad factors, we explain how each one contributes to the dialogue in our field about the present and future evolution of integrationist psychotherapy.

PSYCHOANALYTIC AND PSYCHODYNAMIC THERAPY

Historical Context

As eloquently documented in Henri Ellenberger's book, *The Discovery of the Unconscious* (1990), the origins of psychoanalysis can be traced to traditional healing methods in primitive cultures; to early philosophies on the soul and the nature of disease; to religious views on possession, exorcism, and ceremonial healing; and to the rise of modern science in the 18th century. As a curative method, psychoanalysis began in the 1880s with physicians Jean-Martin Charcot and Josef Breuer, who used hypnosis to treat hysterical patients. Neurologist Sigmund Freud, after taking over Breuer's failed treatment of "Anna O.," discovered that patients seemed to recover after recalling early traumas. Realizing, however, that long-lasting change required a different method, Freud began a lengthy and painful self-analysis, the goal of which was to study the unconscious

---

[1]The terms *counseling* and *psychotherapy* are used interchangeably in this chapter.

DOI: 10.1037/13754-002
APA Handbook of Counseling Psychology: Vol. 1. Theories, Research, and Methods, Nadya A. Fouad (Editor-in-Chief)

systematically (as well as to address his own neu-rotic[2] tendencies).

Freud's most influential legacy is a theoretical understanding of the psyche, which began with his book *The Interpretation of Dreams* (1913). Freud's work rapidly attracted the attention of many schol-ars, including William James, who accurately foretold that psychoanalysis would shape psycho-logical thought in the 20th century. Of primary importance were Freud's (a) topographic (conscious vs. unconscious functioning), (b) dynamic (conflict between instincts and defenses), (c) developmental (oral, anal, phallic, latency, and genital stages), (d) economic (distribution and transformation of psychic energy), (e) structural (functions of the id, ego, and superego), and (f) adaptive models of personality.

In the early 1900s, Freud developed the central tenets of psychoanalysis (e.g., unconscious motiva-tion, repression, resistance, and transference) directly from his clinical observations. It is widely believed that Freud began sitting behind patients as they lay prone on a couch at the suggestion of his wife, after Freud complained that his patients (called *analysands*) stared at him uncomfortably. Although traditional (or *orthodox*) analysis is con-ducted *on the couch* 4 days a week, typically lasting for years, Freud often worked with people in other ways. Freud's approach to treatment evolved over the early years, as thoroughly documented in the 24-volume *Standard Edition of the Complete Psycho-logical Works of Sigmund Freud,* translated and edited by James Strachey and Anna Freud (Strachey, Freud, Strachey, & Tyson, 1953–1974).

Between 1910 and 1920, Freud revised his view that repressed childhood sexual trauma causes neu-rotic symptoms, having noticed that some hysterical and obsessive patients had no such early memories. Instead, Freud posited that neurosis arises from a child's dreams and fantasies of incest (the classic Oedipus complex).[3] Other influential analysts, most notably Alfred Adler and Carl Jung, repudiated Freud's sexual explanation of neurosis in favor of

theories of the total personality. By the 1930s, the focus in psychoanalysis had moved from under-standing psychopathology to a focus on practice, and the treatment emphasis had changed from recalling past trauma to understanding the patient's transference to the analyst.

Influenced by the anthropological study of com-parative cultures in the 1930s, several important analysts in Europe (Otto Rank, Wilhelm Reich, Sán-dor Ferenczi) and the United States (Karen Horney, Eric Fromm, Harry Stack Sullivan) took issue with several of Freud's central tenets, particularly the Oedipus complex. Through experimentation, psy-choanalysis became a more active treatment that took into account a patient's *character defenses* and current life situation; the goal became insight into the present, aided by memories of the past.

Psychoanalysis was profoundly influenced by the rise of Nazism and the flight of many early analysts from Germany, Austria, and Hungary. By the 1950s, the British psychoanalytic community was flourish-ing and eventually became known for developing object relations therapy. In the United States as well, psychoanalysis had a strong foothold in medicine after World War II, when the analytic method was widely used to treat war veterans. Whereas in Europe many analysts were lay people, the Ameri-can Psychoanalytic Association limited training in analysis to physicians until a class-action antitrust lawsuit, filed in 1985, eventually opened the door for other mental health professionals to learn about and conduct psychoanalysis.

Classic Models

Freudian psychoanalysis. In traditional analysis, emotional disturbance is said to be maintained by unconscious dynamics between instincts (particu-larly sexual and aggressive drives) and defenses (e.g., denial, intellectualization, disavowed affect, projection). The analyst takes a neutral, observing, and authoritative role, operating as a blank screen onto which the patient projects fantasies. The fun-damental technique is interpretation of the patient's

---

[2]The term *neurosis* was commonly used to refer to anxiety and depression until the 1980s.

[3]By the late 1980s, the revised view of sexual trauma was discredited, following heated debate on the topic when Freud's personal letters were opened to the public (Malcolm, 1984). It was alleged that Freud suppressed the truth about incest because children's sexuality was not palatable in European Victorian society (Masson, 1984).

free associations, which analysts call *the royal road to the unconscious*. The memories, dreams, and fantasies that arise during free association are interpreted by the analyst to discover the origin of a patient's symptoms. By focusing on the patient's resistance and transference to the analyst, repressed memories are uncovered and the patient gains insight, eliminating the need for symptoms. Behavior is not typically a focus of treatment; modification of behavior is seen as ultimately constraining the achievement of deep personality change. At present, classic on-the-couch psychoanalysis is used primarily for the training of psychoanalysts.

Adlerian psychology. In 1911, Adler was the first of Freud's students to disassociate himself from the Vienna Psychoanalytical Society. Critical of Freud's exclusive focus on sexuality, Adler (1929; Ansbacher & Ansbacher, 1964) called his new approach *individual psychology* to emphasize the total person. His best known theoretical formulation has to do with feelings of inferiority that arise from social status and discrimination, birth order, or physical problems, which stimulate a person to strive for superiority.

In terms of treatment, Adler's approach foreshadowed humanistic psychology in its emphasis on the client's growth process and on the therapist as active, caring, and authentic. In traditional Adlerian therapy, the focus is on conscious processes and an analysis of the client's lifestyle through dreams, memories, and fantasies. In contrast to classic analysis, the primary strategy involves connecting past, present, and future and raising the client's *social interest* (i.e., altruistic behavior toward others). Although most therapy from this perspective is individual, Dreikurs (1950, 1959) initiated Adlerian group therapy and multiple therapy (several therapists working together with a single client).

Jungian analysis. In 1913, Carl Jung was the second analyst to break away from Freudian orthodoxy. With his background in literature, religion, and philosophy, Jung was more interested in culture than in developmental processes or drive theory. Jung's major contribution was his theory of the "collective unconscious," his *anima* and *animus* concepts, and his delineation of character types (e.g., introverts

and extraverts). Jung (1954) developed an extensive interpretation of dream symbols as indicators of a patient's life goals. Unlike Freud, who saw dreams as unconscious wishes struggling for expression, Jung viewed dreams as projections, that is, reflections of dilemmas that the dreamer is seeking to resolve.

In terms of treatment, like the Adlerian approach, Jungian therapy has little to do with instinctual drives and is more future oriented than classic analysis. Interpretation of dreams requires a partnership in which not only the client but also the therapist free associates to various elements of the dream. By identifying universal mythic themes, the "unconscious wisdom of the ages" becomes clarified for both client and therapist.

Other influential early models. Elaborating on Freud's concept of the ego, Heinz Hartmann (1964) viewed the ego as a growing, organizing function of the psyche that interacts in developmentally predictable ways with the environment. Central to ego psychology is the notion of *adaptation*, which refers to reciprocity between person and environment. Hartmann used his knowledge about learning and social relations to expand psychoanalysis to account for the adaptive functions of defense mechanisms. Psychosis, for example, was seen as a way for the ego to defend against intolerable anxiety (Wachtel, 1977).

Ego psychologists had little impact on theories of neurosis or analytic technique (Wachtel, 1977). Rather, ego psychology foreshadowed the more elaborated approach to psychoanalysis, object relations therapy. The term *object* was first used by Freud to refer to the target of a person's impulses or instinctual drives; the term was later expanded to refer more generally to interpersonal relations. British theorist Melanie Klein (1932/1975), the first object relations theorist, began her career by analyzing her own son. Later, mourning his death, she broke with Freudian tradition in adapting psychoanalysis to children. Central to Klein's theory were the *death instinct*, the *infantile depressive position* (passivity due to the child's fear of losing the "good object"), and a focus on erogenous body parts (e.g., the male child's fear of castration and ambivalent feelings toward the mother's breast).

Two other early object relations theorists, Fairbairn (1952) and Winnicott (1953; Winnicott, Shepherd, & Davis, 1989), agreed with Klein about internal objects being mental representations but went further by emphasizing the actual (i.e., not fantasized) relationship between child and caretaker. Winnicott's term *good enough mother* reflects the caretaker's reliability in meeting the infant's needs for sustenance and socioemotional development.

By extension, analysts need to be "good enough," that is, providing a safe holding environment to contain their clients' strong emotions. Early object relations therapy, like classic analysis, focused on dreams, wishes, and memories. Later, theorists in the United States (notably Edith Jacobson, Margaret Mahler, and Otto Kernberg) emphasized clients' developmental needs. In treatment, the therapist plays a quasiparental role, providing the client with a secure base from which to tolerate and experience separation so as, eventually, to become fully individuated.

Interpersonal psychoanalysts Harry Stack Sullivan, Frieda Fromm-Reichmann, Eric Fromm, and Clara Thompson, among others, embraced the ego psychology notion that social relationships can create and perpetuate emotional disturbance. These analysts were known for bringing the focus on social relations directly into the consulting room, by encouraging therapists to play an active role in reversing neurosis (Wachtel, 1977). Sullivan, a U.S.-born analyst who is considered the father of interpersonal psychoanalysis, was the first scholar since Freud to offer a systematic theory of personality development. Sullivan's (1953) *theory of reciprocal relations* prompted a large body of empirical research not only on the process of psychotherapy but also on basic interpersonal relationships.

In terms of treatment, Sullivan and other interpersonal analysts decried the Freudian blank screen, emphasizing instead the human influence of the therapist. In Sullivan's approach, therapists are participant observers who use their personal reactions to help clients understand their distorted views of others. Thus the concept of countertransference evolved to an interpersonal view of the therapist's role. Like Freudian analysis, interpersonal analysis relies heavily on insight as the primary mechanism of therapeutic change. Sullivan also advocated giving clients "something to do"

(akin to homework) between sessions—not as advice but rather to consolidate the progress already achieved in therapy (Wachtel, 1977).

Later Developments

Heinz Kohut (1971, 1984), a long-time member of the Chicago Institute for Psychoanalysis, rejected Freudian orthodoxy late in his career, when he concluded that narcissistic clients, in particular, could not be cured through classic analytic technique. Kohut's *self psychology* is similar to object relations and interpersonal theories in its focus on relationships (rather than instincts) but differs in both strategy and technique. According to self psychologists, disorders of the self are not equivalent to neurosis. Rather, fundamental deficits in the self come about when a child develops defenses and other strategies to compensate for neglectful, abusive, or highly narcissistic parenting.

Using this approach, therapists rely on *vicarious introspection* to become *empathically attuned* to the client's inner world. Unlike Rogerian therapy, however, empathy is not communicated through reflection of feeling but rather through interpretation of the transference. Transferential issues generally take one of two forms: mirroring (seeking the therapist's confirmation, love, and recognition) and idealizing (seeking to merge with the idealized therapist). Consequently, interpretations focus on the client's reaction to the therapist's failure to meet unrealistic demands for mirroring and idealizing. Gradually, the client internalizes qualities of the therapist that build ego functioning and result in a more cohesive, less grandiose self.

In the 1970s, in response to (a) the popularity of cognitive–behavioral, group, and family therapy; (b) the increased use of psychotropic medications; and (c) the economic necessity to provide less lengthy treatment, three international congresses were held, the purpose of which was to delineate the requirements for brief psychotherapy. Time-limited analysis actually dated from the mid-1940s, however, when Franz Alexander advocated tailoring treatment to various disorders and using specific selection criteria to work only with patients who had a high level of ego functioning and a strong motivation to change, who responded well to interpretation, and who were willing and able to be fully engaged in the therapeutic process.

Several theorists in the United Kingdom (e.g., David Malan), the United States (e.g., Sheldon Cashdan, Lester Luborsky, James Mann, Peter Sifneos, and Hans Strupp), and Quebec, Canada (Habib Davanloo) developed various *brief psychodynamic* approaches that require roughly 12 to 40 sessions. Like Alexander, therapists working within these models use specific selection criteria and are highly active. In some approaches, the focus is narrowly defined, that is, Oedipal issues (Sifneos, 1979), whereas in other approaches the focus is a particular emotional disorder (e.g., anxiety or depression) or the client's *cyclical maladaptive pattern* in relationships (Strupp & Binder, 1984). In interpersonal psychotherapy (IPT; Klerman, Weissman, Rounsaville, & Chevron, 1984), derived from Sullivan's interpersonal psychoanalysis as a research-based therapy for depression, IPT strategies and interventions target the primary cause of a client's major depression—grief, a role transition, an interpersonal role dispute, or a deficit in social skills.

Some of the brief approaches stayed closer to classic psychoanalysis than others. Davanloo (1980) and Sifneos (1979), for example, interpreted anxiety and character pathology in terms of the client's conflicts between impulses and defenses. Other approaches (e.g., Strupp & Binder, 1984) are more akin to interpersonal analysis, focusing on how a client's relational difficulties are recreated with the therapist. Still other approaches (e.g., IPT), although interpersonal in focus, are more concerned with clients' symptoms, assets, social roles, and coping mechanisms than with unconscious processes or the childhood origin of emotional disturbance.

In the late 1980s, influenced by interpersonal analysis and object relations theory, U.S. analyst Steven Mitchell (1988) developed what is now called *relational psychoanalysis*. In this contemporary form of analysis, personality is said to evolve from relations with early caregivers, and the dynamic tension between instincts and defenses cannot be separated out from relational expectancies on the basis of childhood experience. Theoretically, people are motivated to meet their needs by recreating these early relationships, even those that were neglectful.

The analyst's empathic attunement to the client and an authentic exploration of the therapeutic relationship are the crux of this form of treatment.

HUMANISTIC AND EXPERIENTIAL THERAPY

Historical Context

Humanistic psychology reflects traditional American values of individualism and self-reliance, values that came naturally to Carl Rogers, who was born into a hard-working, Protestant farm family. Rogers's (1942, 1980) humanistic approach was influenced by educators Dewey and Kilpatrick, existential thinkers Buber and Kierkegaard, field theorist Kurt Lewin, and psychoanalyst Otto Rank. Beginning his career in child guidance work with extensive psychodiagnostic testing, Rogers became disenchanted with objective assessment. In creating the *nondirective technique* (as it was originally called), he took issue with the two treatment approaches that prevailed at the time, psychoanalysis and directive counseling, which Rogers saw as not respecting the client's unique perspective. Rogers came to embrace Rank's view that clients have an innate motivation to grow and become healthy, and that the optimal therapeutic role is relational rather than technical. In 1951, the newly termed *client-centered therapy* shifted the focus from how psychotherapy produces change to how individuals *self-actualize*, that is, move toward optimal growth.

Humanistic psychology came into prominence during U.S. President Lyndon Johnson's Great Society era in the 1960s, when psychiatric patients were being moved from large institutions into the community and when the American public was embracing values of liberalism (e.g., civil rights, the antiwar and women's movements, gay rights, and so on). Reflecting these values, the Rogerian approach became less identified with psychotherapy and more identified with personal growth and development. As applied to human relations training (in schools, businesses, medical agencies, and volunteer settings), which became popular in the 1970s, Rogers's approach is called *person-centered therapy way of being* (Rogers, 1980).

Experiential therapy began with a classically trained German analyst, Fritz Perls, who became intrigued with the Gestalt theories of perception that were in vogue in the early 20th century. Although Perls was heavily influenced by Freud, Jung, and Reich, he became drawn to the idea that human experience cannot be reduced to component parts but rather must be understood as *Gestalts* or unified wholes. Fleeing the Nazis to Amsterdam, South Africa, and eventually the United States, Perls wrote several influential books on Gestalt psychotherapy (e.g., Perls, 1969; Perls, Hefferline, & Goodman, 1951) that met with widespread American interest. By the 1960s, major Gestalt training institutes were located in more than 15 U.S. cities.

Classic Models

Client-centered therapy. Rogerian therapy is best known for its emphasis on the therapeutic relationship as the agent of healing. Client-centered therapists provide three basic attitudes—genuineness or congruence, empathic understanding, and unconditional positive regard—that function as a catalyst to change. When the therapist's nonpossessive caring and acceptance are seen as contradicting the client's introjected low self-worth, the client becomes motivated to engage in a process of deep personality change. Although many writers questioned Rogers's claim that these three attitudes are both "necessary and sufficient" for change to occur, the "necessary" aspect is widely acknowledged by therapists of all orientations.

Eschewing psychodiagnostic testing and the medical model of psychopathology, client-centered therapists see their role as more akin to a companion than an all-knowing expert. The primary strategy is empathic listening, which involves clarifying and reflecting the client's feelings, thereby communicating acceptance of the whole person. Over time, as the client comes to feel "prized" by the therapist, the self is viewed more congruently and the client is better able to envision functioning fully in life (Rogers, 1951).

Gestalt therapy. From a Gestalt perspective, maladaptive behavior reflects a lack of awareness, a lack of personal responsibility, poor contact with the environment, disowning of personal needs, and "split" dimensions of the self. As in client-centered

therapy, self-actualization is the goal of Gestalt treatment, but it is not future-directed. Rather, the aim is for clients to be freed to be who they are, not who they are to become. Therapy involves a process of discovery, accommodation, and assimilation. Eventually, integration occurs through balancing the conflicting inner forces that sustain the maladaptive behavior (Perls et al., 1951).

In terms of strategy, Gestalt therapists provide a *here-and-now* environment for self-discovery, growth, and recovery of the disowned aspects of the self. *Completing Gestalts* requires raising the client's figure–ground awareness, which is said to be curative in and of itself (Perls et al., 1951). Seeing themselves as tools, therapists create experiments using, for example, role rehearsal, playing out projections, dramatizing memories, or frustrating clients to promote responsibility. The best known technique is two-chair work, in which the client literally moves from one chair to another, giving voice to the *topdog* (critical, blaming) and *underdog* (helpless) aspects of the self. This dialogue continues until a sense of integration is achieved, that is, the topdog becomes more accepting and the underdog becomes more assertive.

Another common Gestalt technique is *dreamwork*, a technique that was influenced by Carl Jung's view of dream details as projections. In a group format, one client assumes the *hot seat* and *casts* various other group members as aspects from his or her dream. Then, by literally joining the cast, the client theatrically *increases contact* and gains a new awareness of important people or issues in his or her life (Perls, 1969).

Other influential early models. Existential theorists Rollo May, Victor Frankl, Irvin Yalom, and Eugene Gendlin were also influenced by philosophers and literary authors in the early 1900s. In terms of an existential approach to treatment, the major influences were Rank and Rogers, along with others who saw affective experiencing as the way to treat the whole person. Rollo May (1961), founder of existential therapy in the United States, emphasized responsibility in the face of forces that compel people to avoid life or to live a marginalized existence. Existential therapy was popularized by Viktor Frankl's (1963) influential book, *Man's*

Search for Meaning, which describes his experience in a concentration camp during the Holocaust, and by Yalom's (1981) classic work, *Existential Psychotherapy,* which highlights four central human concerns to be addressed in therapy: death, freedom, isolation, and meaninglessness.

Later Developments

The predominant contemporary approaches within this class of theory are emotion-focused therapy (EFT; Greenberg, 2002; Greenberg, Rice, & Elliott, 1993), also called *process-experiential therapy,* and *motivational interviewing* (e.g., Miller & Rollnick, 2002). In common with early humanistic and existential theories, EFT rests on the assumption that humans have a unique capacity to be self-reflectively aware and to symbolize meaning and emotion linguistically. EFT theorists integrated the Rogerian emphasis on relationship and the Gestalt emphasis on deepening feelings with contemporary theories of cognitive–affective functioning and research on change processes in humanistic psychotherapy.

Like Rogers (1942, 1951) and Perls et al. (1951), Greenberg et al. (1993) viewed dysfunction not as prompted by unconscious motivation or repressed emotion but rather by a person's lack of awareness and misconstrual of experience. Theoretically, dysfunction can occur either by restricted or distorted symbolization of emotion or by reliance on primary or secondary emotional responses that are maladaptive. The goal of treatment is for the client to "reorganize experience and construct new emotional meanings" (Greenberg et al., 1993, p. 6).

EFT therapists play an active role in the therapy process by focusing the client's attention on elements of experience that are out of awareness and helping the client symbolize the experience, thereby creating new schemes that allow incoming information to be processed. By joining in the client's phenomenal world with an attitude of tentativeness, EFT therapists identify markers of emotional difficulties. The major strategies are both relational (empathic attunement and affirmation, facilitation of collaboration and an affective bond) and task oriented (emotional processing, promoting growth, and completion of therapy tasks). The primary interventions include experiential focusing and two-chair work (for integrating internal "splits" and for resolving painful "unfinished business" with significant others).

Motivational interviewing (MI; Miller & Rollnick, 2002) is a directive, humanistic approach that is widely used in work with substance abusers. As a treatment method rather than an explanatory theory, MI's major tenet is that motivation for change comes from within the client. More like a partner than a coach, MI therapists focus on resolving the client's ambivalence about change. Avoiding confrontation and argumentation, the traditional techniques used with problem drinkers and drug addicts, MI therapists rely on reflective listening, acceptance, and affirmation, all the while neutrally directing clients to examine the basis of their ambivalence. Resistance is seen not as a personality trait but rather as a sign that the therapist has misjudged the client's readiness for change.

COGNITIVE–BEHAVIORAL THERAPY

Historical Context

By the 1950s, there was growing dissatisfaction with psychoanalysis, the long-term institutionalization of psychiatric patients, and the medical model of disease. Psychoanalysis was criticized for its scientific inadequacy, that is, its lack of testable hypotheses and its assumption that symptoms are invariably expressions of underlying neurosis. In a seminal challenge to the efficacy of psychoanalysis, British researcher Hans Eysenck (1952) argued that several outcome studies and case reports favored a learning approach to treatment.

Behaviorism was first seen as a revolt, whose aim was to move away from the "mentalism" of psychoanalysis and establish the scientific basis of psychology. Although behaviorists agreed with Freud that fear, or anxiety, is the origin of neurosis (Wolpe, 1987), the transition from basic research on learning to applied psychotherapy was a gradual one. Behavior modification evolved from experimental animal studies (e.g., Pavlov in Russia and Thorndike in the United States); to the conditioning and deconditioning of emotions in humans (recall baby Albert and the white rat); to the application of learning principles to personality (Dollard & Miller, 1950), social interactions (Rotter, 1954), and the treatment of neurosis (Wolpe, 1958).

In 1953, B. F. Skinner's influential book, *Science and Human Behavior*, took psychoanalysis to task, and in 1958, Arnold Lazarus introduced the term *behavior therapy* to refer to objective, laboratory-based treatment. By the 1960s, classical and operant conditioning models were being used in the treatment of emotional disorders; techniques included voluntary practice, thought stopping, aversive conditioning, and autohypnosis. Token economies were introduced in residential facilities and psychiatric hospitals, and basic research had demonstrated that operant methods could actually modify psychotic behavior (Lindsley, 1963; Skinner, 1957).

Behavior therapy was scornfully criticized for its simple, mechanistic techniques and for lacking a theory of personality—not only by analysts but also by theorists within its own ranks (Wolpe, 1987). A seminal article (Breger & McGaugh, 1965) challenged the assumption that learning principles could fully explain human behavior. Bandura (1969) argued that learning through observation requires symbolic representation as well as imaginal and verbal coding; even radical behaviorists acknowledged that cognitively based neurotic fear could be corrected verbally as well as behaviorally (Wolpe, 1987). Aaron Beck (1976) theorized that dysfunctional cognitive processing accounts for depression more so than anger turned inward, that is, the classic psychoanalytic view. These various influences, along with basic research in cognitive psychology, gave rise to cognitive therapy. Originally seen as diametrically opposed to behavior modification, cognitive therapy eventually became an accepted treatment, so that by the late 1980s the preferred term was *cognitive–behavioral therapy* (CBT).

Classic Models

Behavior modification. The basic assumption in behavior modification is that because maladaptive behavior is learned, it can be unlearned. The original cause of the maladaptive behavior is of less consequence than the conditions under which it is currently displayed. The therapist takes an active role, first, in developing a functional analysis of the problematic behavior and, second, in selecting specific classical (e.g., covert conditioning) or operant techniques (e.g., shaping, contingency contacting) that target the behavior to be modified (Kanfer & Phillips, 1970).

Exposing the client to the feared object or situation (in guided imagery or in a controlled therapeutic environment) is the primary intervention. Contemporary exposure therapy, which evolved from Wolpe's (1958) classic systematic desensitization technique, is commonly used to treat anxiety, phobias, and post-traumatic stress. According to Wolpe, anxiety and relaxation compete with each other. If a feared situation typically elicits an anxiety response, relaxation in the face of the feared situation will elicit a new response, and the original fear reaction will be weakened. Exposure with response prevention can be gradual or achieved through *flooding* (prolonged exposure). Other common applications of behavior modification include self-control therapy, aversion therapy, assertiveness and social skills training, sex therapy, counseling to prevent and recover from illness, behavioral couples therapy, and parent management training.

Rational–emotive behavior therapy. Influenced by Adler's notion that behavior springs from ideas as well as by Eastern religions and early Stoic philosophers, psychoanalyst Albert Ellis (1962) was drawn to Epictetus's maxim, "Men are disturbed not by things, but by the view which they take of them" (Ellis & Whiteley, 1979, p. 190). In rational-emotive therapy, later renamed *rational–emotive behavior therapy* (REBT), neurosis is said to result from faulty or irrational thought patterns, inappropriate feelings, and dysfunctional behavior. Whether or not these patterns arose in childhood is considered irrelevant because people continually "reindoctrinate" themselves with erroneous, perfectionistic beliefs about the self and others. Deep psychological change is brought about by *cognitive restructuring*, the goal of which is to substantially modify clients' idiosyncratic views of reality by challenging their beliefs and implicit self-statements (e.g., "I must be universally loved" and "It is a catastrophe if I fail").

Thus, rational-emotive behavior therapists are highly active and confrontive, employing various techniques to dramatize how perfectionism (*shoulds* and *musts*) invariably leads to frustration, anxiety, and dysfunction. Regardless of clients' stated feelings, rational-emotive behavior therapists refocus them on the ideas that prompted the feelings. The most common technique is analysis of the A-B-C chain of events, where A = the Activating event (i.e., stimulus), B = the implicit (mediating) Belief, and C = the emotional Consequence. To reinforce in-session disputation of irrational beliefs, therapists routinely give clients *homework assignments* that involve specific and challenging tasks. Since its inception with individual clients, REBT expanded to include group and family work, incorporating more evocative, abreactive elements.

Beck's cognitive therapy.   From his psychoanalytic training, Aaron T. Beck (1976) recognized that thought processes that seem illogical to others may be highly rational to the client because of his or her unique background. In Beck's view, anxiety derives from affective, physiological, and motor appraisals of danger, whereas depression arises from enduring cognitive schemas that make some people particularly vulnerable to this disorder. Whereas biased information processing is at the root of most emotional disorders, depression is characterized by a negative view of self, the world, and the future (known as the *cognitive triad*). The major tenet of cognitive therapy is that a person's response to another reflects a subjective interpretation of the other's intentions and behavior. Like REBT, the primary strategy is to correct maladaptive self-verbalizations. Unlike REBT, however, the emphasis is on challenging underlying thought patterns rather than belief content. Therapy relies on *collaborative empiricism*—through Socratic questioning, clients are empowered to evaluate the evidence that confirms or disconfirms their cognitions. The client–therapist partnership involves discovering and modifying clients' assumptions and *automatic thoughts*, particularly those based on *arbitrary inferences*, that is, distorted core beliefs about the self and the social world. Behavioral techniques include role rehearsal, exposure, experimentation, and stepwise activities to improve mastery and pleasure. Expected treatment outcomes are client engagement, improved reality testing, and emotional change.

Personal construct therapy.   George Kelly's (1955) personal construct theory is considered both a cognitive and a phenomenological approach to treatment. This method, which currently has more adherents in the United Kingdom than in the United States, began as a comprehensive theory of personality, with implications for therapeutic practice. According to Kelly, emotional disorders, which are manifested as *complaints*, can be directly traced to an individual's *personal construal system*. *Constructs* refer to how some people or objects are viewed as alike yet different from other people or objects (e.g., strong vs. weak, beautiful vs. ugly, generous vs. stingy). Another important concept, the *fundamental postulate*, refers to how an individual's construal patterns influence the way he or she anticipates events.

The therapist's role is to accept and work within the client's construal system to gradually reconstruct it. By collaborating with the client to reexamine critical life experiences, a shift can be made in how complaints are perceived. The primary strategy involves confronting the client with new experiences that challenge his or her existing construal structure. One classic intervention is to have the client design and rehearse a new social role to test the limits of his or her personal constructions. For example, a woman who describes herself as *shy* may be directed to write a sketch about herself as *outgoing* and then to enact the outgoing role in various actual social situations, reporting back to the therapist on the results of her "experiment."

Other influential early models.   Albert Bandura (1969) applied his experimental research on observational learning (in reducing snake phobias) to more general coping skills training. A similar approach was developed by Donald Meichenbaum (1977), who used self-instructional training (in *positive self-talk*) to reduce anxiety related to test taking, public speaking, and other fear-provoking situations. In contrast to Ellis (1962) and Beck (1976), who focused on challenging erroneous thoughts and assumptions, Bandura and Meichenbaum used deliberate self-instruction to guide and shape new, more adaptive performance.

Reality therapy was developed by yet another traditional analyst, William Glasser (1965), who based his approach on control theory, a model of brain functioning. Like rational-emotive behavior therapists, reality therapists reject the notion that emotional disorders are caused by environmental stressors. More similar to Meichenbaum's (1977) self-instructional training, reality therapy holds that behavior is a choice and that clients can make rational decisions to satisfy their basic and social needs.

Arnold Lazarus (1967) introduced the term *technical eclecticism* to refer to selecting therapeutic strategies and techniques from different theories that have been shown through research to be maximally effective. In Lazarus's (1967) eclectic multimodal behavior therapy, the therapist first assesses the client's BASIC ID, an acronym that refers to Behavior, Affect, Sensation, Imagery, Cognition, Interpersonal relations, and need for Drug therapy. On the basis of this comprehensive assessment, the therapist selects specific interventions to target the client's major issues and dysfunctional behavior patterns.

Later Developments

Foreshadowed by George Kelly's (1955) personal construct theory, the social constructionist (or *constructivist*) approach to psychotherapy took hold in the late 1980s and early 1990s. Constructivists reject the positivist view (of the physical sciences) that social organisms are akin to machines that can break down and be repaired through a process of locating and analyzing the cause (White & Epston, 1990). Rather, constructivism reflects the philosophic view of reality as interpersonally constructed rather than as immutable truth. This postmodern view actually dates from the 18th-century philosopher Immanuel Kant, who argued that knowledge is a product of how imagination is organized in the mind (Nichols & Schwartz, 2007). Leading constructivist therapists include Mahoney (1991); Efran, Lukens, and Lukens (1990); and family therapists White and Epston (1990), among others.

From a social construction perspective, because all personal beliefs are fluid and context dependent, some ways of construing a life story are more adaptive than others (White & Epston, 1990). For example, whether it is true or not, seeing one's alcoholism as a disease rather than as a moral failure stimulates motivation for change. Therapeutic technique is eschewed in favor of appreciation for the human potential for self-correction. Treatment is collaborative, guided by a

discussion of differences, novel ways of viewing behavior and events, and reflexivity (self-observation), particularly how meaning is interpersonally construed within discourse.

Two other influential contemporary approaches, acceptance and commitment therapy (ACT: Hayes, Strosahl, & Wilson, 1999) and dialectical behavior therapy (DBT; Linehan, 1993), are highly pragmatic yet based in Eastern principles of mindfulness. ACT is an active method that teaches clients to balance acceptance and change. As in Gestalt therapy, clients are taught to stay in the present moment and to accept, rather than struggle against, problematic thoughts and feelings. The goal is to develop a transcendant sense of self to make choices that reflect one's core values. Similarly, DBT is an active approach that integrates mindfulness meditation (from Buddhist philosophy) with standard CBT interventions. Originally developed to treat severely suicidal adults with borderline personality disorder, DBT is currently being used to work with adolescents, couples, clients with eating disorders, and survivors of sexual abuse.

FAMILY SYSTEMS THERAPY

Historical Context

Influenced by psychoanalytic group therapy, several early pioneers began experimenting with family group therapy (Bell, 1961) in psychiatric hospitals, having noticed that many patients would relapse after a brief home visit. Even more curiously, when the patient improved, another family member would often become dysfunctional (Nichols & Schwartz, 2007).

Psychiatrists were not the first to view mental illness contextually, however. From the early 1900s, social workers made home visits and described their cases in terms of concentric levels of influence (i.e., individual, couple, family, community). Therapists in child guidance centers, inspired by the work of Adler, began working with parents to reduce the family's contribution to children's emotional problems (Nichols & Schwartz, 2007).

Arguably the most important contributions to the development of family systems therapy arose from basic research. Studying the families of schizophrenics at the National Institute of Mental Health, Lyman

Wynne developed the concept of *communication deviance* to explain how a thought disorder is transmitted behaviorally within the family (Nichols & Schwartz, 2007). Around the same time, an interdisciplinary group of scientists and psychiatrists at the Veterans Administration in Palo Alto, California, were applying anthropological and communication research to the understanding of schizophrenia among young adults. In their *double-bind theory* (Bateson, Jackson, Haley, & Weakland, 1956), psychosis was explained as a rational response to parental messages that were inherently contradictory and blaming. Theoretically, when these punitive paradoxical messages are repeated over a long period of time, and escape is forbidden, the child begins responding to any aspect of the message with intense panic or rage, which—to an outsider—seems insane. This theory, although subsequently discredited, gave clinicians hope that changing family interaction patterns could potentially cure mental illness.

Another radical explanation for emotional disturbance arose from general systems theory and cybernetics in the fields of engineering, physics, and mathematics (Nichols & Schwartz, 2007). From this perspective, whether human or machine, a *system* has parts that interlock and function as an organized unit, and the breakdown of any significant part affects the functioning of the entire entity. Conversely, how the unit operates as a whole affects the functioning of each of its parts. Extrapolating from cybernetics, psychiatrist Don Jackson (1957) began viewing families as akin to machines, with feedback loops that either keep the system stable through self-regulation (called *homeostasis*) or by evolving to a new state (called *second-order change*). According to Jackson, although emotional disorders seem to be located within individuals, they are actually expressions of family dysregulation. A fundamental, second-order change in the family's operations can thereby influence an individual's emotional health—for better or worse.

Classic Models

Structural family therapy. Among the early family systems theories, Salvador Minuchin's (1974; Minuchin & Fishman, 1981) structural approach most closely reflects the principles of general systems

theory. According to Minuchin, as in nonhuman systems, a family member's impairment reflects a dysfunctional family system. When the parent(s) do not function as executives (i.e., when the children have too much power), when boundaries between people are either too diffuse (*enmeshed*) or rigid (*disengaged*), or when a parent forms a coalition with a child against the other parent, individual family members cannot function with maximum effectiveness. In other words, an individual's emotional distress is invariably located within a dysfunctional family structure, which is maintained homeostatically through repetitive patterns of interaction that prevent family members from achieving optimal psychosocial functioning (Minuchin, 1974).

Structural therapists begin by *joining* with the family to observe the interactional structures that sustain the presenting problem. Highly active therapeutic work involves staging in-session enactments to restore parental authority, challenge enmeshed or rigid boundaries, and interrupt intergenerational coalitions. By restructuring the family's communication and behavior patterns, marital distress will no longer be detoured to a child, and all subsystems (parental, sibling) will be free to achieve optimal functioning (Minuchin & Fishman, 1981).

Strategic and brief problem-focused therapy. Members of the Mental Research Institute group in California (Haley, 1963; Jackson, 1957, 1965; Watzlawick, Weakland, & Fisch, 1974) and the Milan associates in Italy (Selvini Palazzoli, Boscolo, Cecchin, & Prata, 1978) also based their respective therapy approaches on cybernetic principles. Like Minuchin (1974), these theorists eschewed cognition and emotion, focusing rather on the covert rules of behavior that keep individuals and families stuck in dysfunctional patterns of operation (Madanes, 1981). That is, paradoxically, family members' attempted solutions to a problem (*negative feedback loops*) are what actually maintain the problem. In the classic pursue–distance cycle, for example, the more one partner cajoles, threatens, or begs for closeness, the more the other partner distances. Distancing prompts even more frantic cajoling, threatening, and begging for closeness. The remedy is creation of a *positive feedback loop* in which behavioral shifts build on each other so that eventually the destructive reciprocity is disrupted.

Like structural therapists, strategic and problem-focused therapists play an active role in restructuring family interactions, and little attention is paid to helping clients understand the systemic cause of their distress. Rather, *rituals*, *ordeals*, and *therapeutic double binds* are prescribed to disrupt vicious cycles of *problem-maintaining solutions*. Fundamental strategies include *circular questioning*, that is, asking each family member in turn to reflect on the relationships of other family members, and the use of consulting or reflecting teams. Observing the session from behind a one-way mirror, the team relies on authoritative power to deliver creative interventions, the purpose of which is to move the family toward second-order change.

Bowen's family systems theory. Psychoanalyst Murray Bowen (1976; Kerr & Bowen, 1988) began hospitalizing entire families to study the system's contribution to severe emotional disorders. In contrast to structural and strategic theories, Bowen's family systems theory attempts to explain the development of family dysfunction. The central construct, *differentiation of self*, refers to how well a person is able to separate and balance (a) thinking versus feeling (on an intrapsychic level) and (b) autonomy versus togetherness (on an interpersonal level). Poorly differentiated people either fuse with or reactively distance from others (particularly other family members) and form emotional triangles to reduce anxiety and stabilize immature relationships. According to Bowen, these family dynamics are transmitted or projected through the generations by repetitive behavioral patterns. The child in the family who receives the most emotional attention from the parents for any reason (physical or learning problems, birth order, or simply by resembling some other family member) becomes the least differentiated offspring. Because people choose mates who function at a similar level of differentiation, when the adult child marries, his or her children's differentiation levels are constrained by the parents' immaturity. Over multiple generations, serious emotional disturbance is unavoidable (Bowen, 1976).

In contrast to structural and strategic therapy, Bowenian therapists value insight over action.

Therapists remain as neutral as possible to reduce the family's level of anxiety. Therapists typically work with the most differentiated family member, the one most capable of detriangulation. A standard intervention is the creation of a genogram, an emotional family tree, that helps clients discover the covert multigenerational forces that underlie and sustain the current emotional distress. Theoretically, raising the differentiation level of one or more key family members will raise the entire family's level of functioning (Kerr & Bowen, 1988).

Other influential early approaches. Not all of the early family theorists embraced systems thinking. Some therapists remained closer to their roots in psychoanalysis, humanistic, or behavior therapy. Prominent among the analysts were Nathan Ackerman (1958) and Ivan Boszormenyi-Nagy and Spark (1973). Experiential therapists Carl Whitaker (1975) and Virginia Satir (1964) were other highly influential family theorists. Behavior therapists like Patterson (1971) and Stuart (1969) applied learning principles to help parents manage their children's misbehavior and to teach one spouse to help the other overcome emotional distress.

Later Developments
By the 1980s, the predominant approach to couples work was behavioral marital therapy (Jacobson & Margolin, 1979). For families, the major approaches were structural-strategic therapy (Haley, 1976; Minuchin & Fishman, 1981), functional family therapy (Alexander & Parsons, 1982), and parent management training (Patterson, 1982).

Criticizing structural-strategic therapists for being paternalistic, mechanistic, and noncollaborative, feminist authors (e.g., Luepnitz, 1988) helped move the field in a different direction, so that by the 1990s, the predominantly systemic focus of the early theorists had declined. Reflecting the postmodern view that was also being embraced by cognitive therapists, constructivist (e.g., White & Epston, 1990), and solution-focused (e.g., de Shazer, 1985) family therapists helped people "re-author" their personal stories to struggle against self-defeating life scripts and work toward a more hopeful, symptom-free future. Cognitive theorists Epstein and Baucom

(1989) developed cognitive–behavioral marital therapy, and behavior therapists Jacobson and Christensen (1998), having recognized that many couples cannot change longstanding, rigid interaction patterns, created integrative couple therapy, the goal of which is to move partners toward mutual acceptance of each other's limitations. Greenberg and Johnson (1988) developed EFT for couples, an approach that was heavily influenced by experiential therapy, systems thinking, and attachment theory. Shifts within psychoanalysis prompted the development of psychodynamically oriented couple and family therapy (e.g., Scharff & Scharff, 1987).

In contemporary family therapy, the boundaries between theories have become blurred, and integrative approaches are now in the forefront of the field (Nichols & Schwartz, 2007). Moreover, in contrast to the classic view that individual dysfunction—regardless of its nature—is symptomatic of family dysfunction, most present-day family therapy approaches target specific emotional and behavioral problems, for example, alcohol and substance abuse, depression, conduct disorder, juvenile offending, bipolar disorder, schizophrenia, and anorexia nervosa, among others (for a review of contemporary theories, see Friedlander & Diamond, 2011).

THE INTEGRATIONIST MOVEMENT

In the late 20th century, growing interest in psychotherapy integration (e.g., Goldfried, 1980) led to the creation of an international organization, Society for the Exploration of Psychotherapy Integration. The notion of integration has a lengthier history, however, beginning with Dollard and Miller's (1950) comparative analysis of psychoanalysis and behaviorism, Frank's (1961) book *Persuasion and Healing,* which described curative factors in healing across cultures, and Lazarus's (1967, 1976) technical eclecticism and multimodal behavior therapy. The impetus for integration came from the recognition, by proponents of the major theories, that the change process is highly complex, that many theories had shortcomings, and that mutual respect and rapprochement would advance the field more than the acrimonious debates that characterized the early 20th century (Castonguay, Reid, Halperin, & Goldfried, 2003, p. 327).

On the scientific front, researchers demonstrated that the fundamental tenets of one theory also explain client change from other theoretical perspectives. For example, operant conditioning, the hallmark of CBT, was found to occur in both humanistic and psychodynamic therapies (Castonguay et al., 2003). The creation of meta-analysis was also influential in furthering integrationist psychotherapy by giving researchers a statistical method to answer the question, "Which therapy works best?" Conclusions from many meta-analyses, dating from Smith, Glass, and Miller's (1980) seminal study, indicate that (a) the majority of clients benefit from psychotherapy in both the short and long term, and (b) differences in efficacy are less due to specific treatment approach and more due to common (Castonguay et al., 2003) and contextual factors (Wampold, 2001), such as client characteristics and the quality of the therapeutic relationship.

Yet how can success rates be similar across widely divergent therapy approaches? The explanations offered for this apparent paradox (Stiles, Shapiro, & Elliott, 1986) have made such good sense to clinicians that most present-day therapists describe themselves as eclectic or integrationist (Norcross & Prochaska, 1988). One explanation is that good therapy is responsive to each client's unique characteristics and life circumstances (Stiles et al., 1986). That is, skillful therapists vary their interpersonal approach and technique to be maximally effective with different clients and different social contexts. Second, the change factors that most account for psychological healing are common across theories (e.g., the therapeutic relationship, client involvement). Third, because humans function as integrated cognitive, behavioral, and affective systems, when one aspect of functioning improves, the other aspects tend to improve. Thus successful therapy can follow any one of several pathways to health.

Since its introduction in the literature, the term *psychotherapy integration* has come to have varied meanings, alternately referring to (a) eclecticism (Castonguay et al., 2003), that is, applying diverse techniques without concern for their theoretical compatibility; (b) combining two theories into a new approach, for example, Safran's (1998) interpersonal–cognitive therapy; (c) alternating individual, couple, and family formats on the basis of how treatment is progressing (e.g., Pinsof, 1995); (d) describing transtheoretical stages of change (e.g., Prochaska & DiClemente, 1984); (e) delineating empirically based change principles on the basis of client characteristics and social contexts (e.g., Beutler & Harwood, 2000; Castonguay & Beutler, 2006; Goldfried, 1980); and (f) identifying relationship processes that are common across theories (e.g., Norcross, 2002). Thus, it is not a trivial question to ask a therapist who claims to use an integrative approach: "Just what do you mean by that?"

In the next sections, we discuss psychotherapy integration from the contextual and common factors perspective. Our aim is to show how several traditional and contemporary emphases of counseling psychologists are compatible with this perspective. We begin by providing a focused summary of three contextual factors that should guide theory selection and implementation: (a) clients' problems in living, (b) clients' individual characteristics, and (c) clients' developmental histories and coping mechanisms. This section concludes with a summary of the most critical common change agent in psychotherapy: the therapeutic relationship.

Problems in Living as Contextual Factors

In the early 20th century, clinical psychologists were primarily concerned with psychodiagnostic assessment, reflecting the prevailing medical model of diagnosis and treatment. Early counseling psychologists, however, focused on helping people who had a developmental or a situational need for vocational guidance, that is, adolescents who were making occupational choices and veterans returning from World War II (Gelso & Fretz, 1992). Occupational decision making necessitates consideration of the fit between person and environment. Thus, from the dawn of our professional specialty, counseling psychologists were more concerned with adapting theory and technique to a client's situational problems than with selecting a treatment approach solely on the basis of symptomatology.

Responding differentially to each client's unique circumstances is central to integrationist psychotherapy. That is, rather than applying a preferred approach to all clients, or even to all clients with the same symptoms (e.g., depression, anxiety), integrationists first consider how each client's specific life problems affect treatment choice. In the clinical and research literature, optimal theoretical approaches have been identified for many common problems, including career indecision, test anxiety, anger, infertility, parenting problems, adjustment to divorce, and so on. To illustrate, the following sections summarize the literature on psychotherapy (a) for recovering from trauma and (b) for coping with acculturative stress.

Recovery from trauma.   Experiencing sexual abuse, intimate partner violence, combat trauma or violent crime may result in posttraumatic stress disorder (PTSD), a potentially chronic and debilitating disorder. Regardless of whether a trauma survivor meets diagnostic criteria for PTSD, however, he or she is likely to experience myriad problems in living, including adjustment problems, interpersonal concerns, a decreased sense of well-being, and difficulties coping with thoughts and feelings associated with the trauma (e.g., guilt, shame).

From an integrationist perspective, there are multiple pathways to recovery from trauma. Various theoretical approaches can be effective (see Foa, Keane, Friedman, & Cohen, 2009, for a review). Some approaches focus primarily on symptom relief or, more extensively, on overall functioning and development. CBT is commonly used to relieve symptoms of reexperiencing and avoidance (e.g., Cahill, Rothbaum, Resick, & Follette, 2009), alone or in combination with various somatic interventions, such as eye movement desensitization and reprocessing (Shapiro, 1989). The more structured, behavioral approaches include exposure (to eliminate classically conditioned emotional responses) and contingency management (to modify behaviors contributing to symptom maintenance). Approaches that incorporate a cognitive focus emphasize the survivor's belief system about the self and the world (Resnick & Schnicke, 1993), with the goal of modifying maladaptive thoughts that maintain the trauma-related symptoms.

Although many clients benefit substantially from therapy that focuses solely on symptom reduction, a psychodynamic approach may be more useful for clients who can benefit from exploration and working through trauma-related interpersonal difficulties (e.g., Kudler, 2007). Informed by classical psychoanalysis, self-psychology, object relations, and interpersonal psychotherapy, these approaches involve exploring how the client's relationships and sense of self were disrupted by the trauma, the goal being to promote insight and enhance ego strength (Horowitz, 2003).

Effective trauma therapy requires consideration of various contextual factors, such as the client's economic resources, extent of social support, and level of family functioning. There is a growing recognition of the need to provide culturally sensitive therapy to trauma survivors from diverse backgrounds because culture influences how traumatic events are interpreted and understood and how individuals experience and express psychological distress (Stamm & Friedman, 2000). Additionally, most approaches to trauma treatment acknowledge the essential role of the therapeutic relationship because many survivors, particularly those with complex trauma histories, have longstanding relational difficulties and a deep sense of shame or guilt (Herman, 1992). These difficulties, when coupled with experiential avoidance, often interfere with engagement and retention in treatment.

Race-related and acculturative stress. Another contextual factor that influences treatment selection is person–environment fit. Clients who feel alienated from mainstream society by virtue of their minority group status can present with myriad psychological symptoms. Although the fact that racism is associated with emotional distress is no longer in dispute (Carter, 2007), precisely how racism translates to psychological stress has yet to be understood. Race-related distress includes confusion, trauma, fatigue, and anticipatory stress responses (Utsey, Bolden, & Brown, 2001). Acculturative stress, that is, stress reactions that are elicited when people of color, immigrants, and refugees come in contact with a new culture, includes experiences of depression, anxiety, marginalization, and alienation (Short et al., 2009).

From an integrationist perspective, treatment of these kinds of stress reactions demands considerably more than a focus on symptoms. Contemporary theorists believe that "culture should be a primary, not secondary consideration in the development and implementation of mental health interventions" (Smith, 2009, p. 448). Some authors have modified existing theories (e.g., CBT, family systems) to help clients experiencing acculturative stress adjust to U.S. culture or to reduce acculturative conflict within the family (e.g., Arredondo, 2004). Regardless of treatment approach, many authors (e.g., Utsey & Gernat, 2002) urge psychotherapists to empower clients to challenge the social systems that are associated with oppression.

From a multicultural counseling perspective (D. W. Sue & Sue, 2007), common factors like a strong emotional bond and goal consensus are important vehicles of change for clients experiencing race-related stress. For these factors to be maximally effective, however, therapists need to understand each client within the client's social context and intervene in a way that is congruent with the client's worldview (Ivey & Brooks-Harris, 2005).

Client Characteristics as Contextual Factors

The basic dilemma for therapists is reflected in Gordon Paul's (1967) classic litany: "*What* treatment, by *whom*, is effective for *this* individual, with *that* specific problem, and under *which* set of circumstances?" (p. 11). Indeed, this question is at the heart of therapist responsiveness. In the past two decades, researchers have made great strides in identifying client factors that should be taken into account in treatment selection. These moderators of therapy success include personality style (e.g., reactance, openness to experience, extraversion, conscientiousness), demographics (e.g., gender, age, race or ethnicity, sexual orientation, religion, socioeconomic status [SES]), and other contributing characteristics (e.g., level of family functioning, severity of depression, comorbidity). The factors we selected to review in this section are only some of the many potential client moderators of treatment selection.

Gender. Gender—that is, the culturally determined roles, behaviors, and activities considered appropriate for men and women (Worell & Remer,

1992)—shapes self-concept, communication style, and interpersonal behavior. Although research shows no consistent differences in treatment outcomes for men versus women (Clarkin & Levy, 2004), gender apparently influences clients' attitudes toward help seeking, preference for treatment modality, and in-therapy behavior (e.g., degree of emotional disclosure; Good, Thompson, & Braithwaite, 2005). Selecting a gender-sensitive approach involves considering each client's sociocultural context (race, SES, sexual orientation, religion) as well as his or her unique experiences and concerns.

Men are generally less likely than women to seek therapy because of male gender role norms (e.g., self-reliance, stoicism) and the stigma associated with help seeking (Addis & Mahalik, 2003; Good & Robertson, 2010). Because of socialization, many male clients struggle with showing vulnerability, disclosing emotions, and forming a bond with the therapist, tasks that are central to psychotherapy (Good et al., 2005). Thus, regardless of the theoretical approach, effective treatment with male clients requires therapists to be aware of, normalize, and empathize with these conflicts if they arise, for example, by helping the client clarify and evaluate beliefs about masculinity (e.g., "men should always be strong") that may be contributing to the presenting problem or to fully engaging in treatment (Mahalik, 1999). Although interventions from various theories can be tailored to men and their unique concerns, some men are most comfortable with an active, problem-solving approach. (See Brooks, 2010, for an application of Prochaska and DiClemente's [1984] transtheoretical model of change to working with men.)

Beginning in the 1970s, feminist authors brought to light women's unique mental health concerns, including higher rates of depression and interpersonal victimization than men, and the negative impact of traditional gender role expectations (e.g., Brown & Gilligan, 1992). Because of socialization, many women struggle with issues related to competence, self-worth, and body image. Consequently, therapists must be sensitive to how female socialization, bias, discrimination, and violence may have contributed to a client's poor self-esteem and mental health problems. Although interventions from various theoretical perspectives are likely to be effective with women, therapists should be aware of theory-based gender bias that equates mental health with traditional, European American, masculine characteristics, that is, autonomy and individualism (American Psychological Association, 2007). According to feminist scholars (e.g., Jordan, 2008), fostering women's well-being and mental health requires enhancing their relationships and connectedness with others, goals that can be achieved through CBT as well as with family systems, emotion-focused, and psychoanalytic approaches.

Minority group status. Although initially conceptualized in racial or ethnic terms, minority group status currently refers to a range of cultural, racial, sexual, and religious groups who do not represent the dominant social groups in the United States. Briefly, research indicates that the psychological lives of people from social minority groups are often shaped by experiences of prejudice and discrimination, which can engender a range of symptoms, including anxiety, depression, hypervigilance, and anger as well as hypertension and other stress-induced medical conditions (Pascoe & Richman, 2009).

Examining the impact of minority group status on the therapeutic process, authors (e.g., Zane, Nagayama Hall, Sue, Young, & Nunez, 2004) identified the most influential factors: ethnic or racial and sexual identity (and client–therapist match), underutilization of services and length of treatment, cultural mistrust, and worldview. Issues of identity are particularly salient for individuals from racial or ethnic and sexual minority groups (Helms & Cook, 1999; McCarn & Fassinger, 1996). Ethnic and racial matching for clients of color has long had intuitive appeal for fostering greater compliance, engagement, and retention in therapy. Research findings are inconclusive, however, and meta-analyses suggest that ethnic match does not predict premature dropout (Maramba & Nagayama Hall, 2002). Rather, similarity in value systems and in identity status (i.e., from preencounter to integration; Helms & Cook, 1999) may be more influential than demographic factors alone (Liu & Pope-Davis, 2005).

Regardless of the therapist's theoretical approach, treatment may be impeded when the client's racial identity status is more highly developed than that of the therapist; conversely, the therapist's ability to facilitate the client's identity development depends on the therapist's own racial identity status. Similarly, lesbian, gay, and bisexual clients are more likely to engage in treatment with therapists who are knowledgeable about sexual minority identity and to avoid therapists who demonstrate heterocentric attitudes (Burckell & Goldfried, 2006).

Irrespective of theoretical orientation, it is critically important for therapists to appreciate the history associated with their clients' social groups. Because oppression and discrimination characterize the life experiences of people from racial or ethnic and sexual minority groups, clients from these groups are often hesitant to seek help or interact with therapists from the dominant cultural groups. The notion of cultural mistrust, initially conceived within racial terms (e.g., Terrell, Taylor, Menzise, & Barrett, 2009) and shown to be associated with negative outcomes for African American clients (Whaley, 2001), is likely to apply to clients from other minority groups as well. Therapists are most effective when they openly and nondefensively explore experiences of oppression with their minority group clients. With Black American adolescent males, for example, discussion of culturally relevant themes (e.g. racism, respect, boyhood-to-manhood transitions) was shown to facilitate greater engagement and a stronger therapeutic alliance (Jackson-Gilfort, Liddle, Tejeda, & Dakof, 2001).

Evidence is accumulating about efficacy rates for various therapeutic approaches with different racial and ethnic groups (Comas-Díaz, 2006). For example, findings indicate that IPT is effective for reducing depression among African Americans (Brown, Schulberg, Sacco, Perel, & Houck, 1999), and CBT has been shown to reduce panic symptoms among Latinos/as (Sanderson, Rue, & Wetzler, 1998). Authors are increasingly making specific treatment recommendations for clients from different racial and ethnic groups. Organista (2006), for example, proposed that with Latinos/as, the cultural values of *personalismo* and *confianza* suggest that a nonconfrontational response to client anger is likely to be more effective than setting limits. According to Organista, CBT may be the optimal approach for most Latinos/as because of its educative, problem-solving approach, use of homework, and other prescriptive techniques.

Although the empirical findings are promising, individuals from racial and ethnic minority groups remain underrepresented in evidenced-based therapy research (S. Sue, Zane, Nagayama Hall, & Berger, 2009). Furthermore, the literature has been criticized for not attending to within-group variability and failing to address important race- and culture-specific factors, including racism, cultural worldview, and ethnic identity (Comas-Díaz, 2006; D. W. Sue & Sue, 2007). Indeed, although several empirically supported treatments show promise for clients from various racial and ethnic minority groups, researchers rarely include important moderating factors, for example, level of acculturation and intersecting identity statuses (Pieterse & Miller, 2009).

When cultural factors are taken into account, outcome studies reveal that therapists' responsiveness to a client's cultural style and recognition of the client's cultural value system are key ingredients (Griner & Smith, 2006; S. Sue et al., 2009). Recently Comas-Díaz (2011) identified the core contribution of attending to the client's cultural and sociopolitical context when applying any therapeutic modality. Comas-Díaz's integrative approach highlights the anchoring role of the therapeutic relationship. That is, to be optimally therapeutic, therapists should be aware of and continually monitor the power dynamics in the relationship as well as their own cultural sensitivity, cultural empathy, and reflexion–flexibility.

Development and Resilience as Contextual Factors

Although the term *positive psychology* (e.g., Seligman, 1991) was coined to prompt theory and research on optimism, happiness, and general well-being, for more than 70 years counseling psychologists have emphasized these very concepts. In promoting well-being, counseling psychologists traditionally take into account their clients' developmental histories, strengths, coping mechanisms, and level of resilience (Gelso & Fretz, 1992), contextual factors to which therapists must be responsive. In the sections that follow, we review contemporary literature on one developmental factor (attachment style) and one source of coping–resilience (spirituality) that require consideration in treatment selection and adaptation.

Attachment style. According to Bowlby (1969), children develop schemas of self and others (i.e., attachment styles) that guide how they perceive, feel, and behave in social relationships throughout life. Children whose caregivers are relatively responsive and sensitive to their needs are likely to develop a secure attachment style. As adults, they are comfortable with intimacy and respond to interpersonal conflict adaptively (Mikulincer & Shaver, 2007). Conversely, children whose caregivers are chronically unavailable tend to develop an insecure attachment style, either anxious or avoidant. As adults, anxious individuals struggle with fears of abandonment, easily become overwhelmed with emotion, and tend to ruminate and be hypervigilant when distressed; avoidant individuals exhibit excessive striving toward self-reliance, have difficulties with intimacy, and tend to respond to stress by suppressing their thoughts and feelings (Berlin, Cassidy, & Appleyard, 2008).

Adult attachment style is said to influence a client's level of emotional disclosure, degree of responsiveness to interventions, and ability to form and maintain a working therapeutic relationship (Mikulincer & Shaver, 2007). Clients with attachment anxiety tend to present with dysregulated affect, low self-worth, a history of enmeshed relationships, and fears of rejection or abandonment; in therapy, they demonstrate heightened emotional distress, poor boundaries, and excessive dependency on the therapist (Mikulincer & Shaver, 2007). CBT can be used to help these clients regulate their emotions and modify maladaptive cognitions and attribution styles (Newman, Castonguay, Fisher, & Borkovec, 2010). Clients with attachment avoidance may be helped by emotion-focused or interpersonal therapy, inasmuch as they tend to present as emotionally distant, minimize their distress, and have difficulties articulating feelings, particularly in relation to significant others. With highly avoidant clients who find it

difficult to engage in emotive therapy, therapists can explore their emotional avoidance and teach them how to access and express feelings in interpersonal situations (Newman et al., 2010). In EFT couples therapy, maladaptive pursue–distance patterns can be disrupted by encouraging avoidant partners to take a more active role in the relationship and highly anxious partners to learn more effective strategies for expressing personal needs (Johnson, 2003).

Spirituality. Research generally supports the connection between spiritual coping and psychological well-being. For many people, spiritual or religious beliefs provide meaning in life, especially in times of personal crisis. Spiritual coping has been associated with various mental health outcomes, for example, lower rates of depression and anxiety (see Ano & Vasconcelles, 2005, for a review), by providing comfort, a meaning-making framework, a sense of mastery, a supportive community, and an avenue for personal growth (Pargament, Konig, & Perez, 2000).

In the past 10 years, there has been a burgeoning clinical literature on integrating spirituality and psychotherapy (e.g., Miller, 2003; Sperry & Shafranske, 2005). Indeed, given the central role of religion in many people's lives, a number of authors view this integration as essential for culturally sensitive treatment (e.g., Bhui, King, Dein, & O'Connor, 2008). There is a growing consensus about the need to ask clients about the role of spirituality in their lives, the meaning derived from spiritual beliefs, and the degree to which these beliefs or participation in a religious community helped them manage past difficulties (Abu Riaya & Pargament, 2010).

The nature and extent of a client's spirituality is said be important in selecting an appropriate theoretical approach. For example, clients with substance abuse problems for whom spirituality is not relevant may prefer motivational interviewing (Miller & Rollnick, 2002) over participation in Alcoholics or Narcotics Anonymous. On the other hand, clients for whom spirituality is important may be helped by an approach that is compatible with this worldview. Within a CBT framework, for example, these clients can be encouraged to join a faith community, seek adjunctive support from their religious leaders, read spiritual tracts on a regular basis, write in journals, and so on (Miller, 2003). Other compatible approaches include narrative (e.g., White & Epston, 1990) and existential psychotherapy (Yalom, 1981), which explicitly focus on meaning making, and theoretical orientations that integrate meditational practice into therapy, for example, ACT (Hayes et al., 1999) or DBT (Linehan, 1993).

The Therapeutic Relationship Factor as a Common Factor

Central to integrationism is the notion, substantiated by comprehensive literature reviews and meta-analyses (e.g., Norcross, 2002; Wampold, 2001), that various common factors, particularly the therapeutic relationship, account for change more than a therapist's choice of theoretical approach. The vast theoretical and empirical literature on the therapeutic relationship was initiated by three counseling psychologists, the first of whom was Stanley Strong (1968), who described how therapists enhance their interpersonal *power* to motivate clients to change. Second was Edward Bordin (1979), who expanded and defined the psychoanalytic concept *working alliance* (also called *therapeutic alliance*) in terms that made it relevant to all therapeutic approaches. Third and most recently, Charles Gelso (2002) expanded yet another aspect of the therapeutic relationship, the *real relationship*. Each of these important contributions cannot be overemphasized because therapy success—regardless of theoretical approach—is substantially influenced by the strength and quality of the client–therapist relationship (Norcross, 2002; Wampold, 2001).

Social influence theory. The first common factors model of counseling and psychotherapy to be conceptualized and studied empirically was Strong's (1968; Strong & Claiborn, 1982; Strong & Matross, 1973) social influence theory. Applying Frank's (1961) cross-cultural view of curative factors in healing with experimental social psychology, Strong and colleagues argued that successful therapeutic interactions are essentially persuasive encounters in which one individual uses his or her credibility to help another individual give up symptoms and move toward functional change. According to the

model, when three interrelated personal characteristics of therapists—expertness, attractiveness, and trustworthiness—are maximized, clients are more likely to reduce their opposition to therapeutic suggestion and their resistance to personal change. Strong's revolutionary ideas provided a model for the experimental study of psychotherapy processes. Moreover, by emphasizing common factors (therapist credibility, client attitudes, and principles that underlie change), Strong's theory foreshadowed the current trend toward integrationism.

For more than 2 decades, a tremendous amount of empirical research was conducted on the social influence model (for a review, see Corrigan, Dell, & Schmidt, 1980), focusing primarily on client perceptions of therapist characteristics. The second stage in the model, the dynamics of influence, received relatively less attention from researchers, possibly because the social influence perspective came to be overshadowed by the burgeoning scholarship on the working alliance.

Working alliance. Although the working alliance has its seeds in Freud's writings about the importance of patient collaboration in psychoanalysis, recognition of the alliance as an important transtheoretical construct began with Bordin's (1979) seminal article. Bordin defined the alliance as composed of three interrelated components: a trusting emotional bond and client–therapist agreement on the goals and tasks of therapy. Recent authors expanded this definition for work with couples and families by including two aspects of the alliance that are unique to conjoint therapy—the extent to which family members feel safe with one another in a therapeutic context, and the degree to which they share a sense of purpose about the problems, goals, purpose, and value of therapy (Friedlander, Escudero, & Heatherington, 2006).

Operationalized by numerous self-report and observational measures, the working alliance has been the subject of literally thousands of research investigations. Results of comprehensive meta-analyses indicate that a strong alliance—regardless of theoretical approach—is predictive of greater success in both individual (Horvath, Del Re, Flückiger, & Symonds, 2011) and conjoint psychotherapy

(Friedlander, Escudero, Heatherington, & Diamond, 2011). Although there is some controversy about whether the alliance is a forerunner or a by-product of therapy outcome, research indicates that the client's view of the alliance, particularly early in treatment, is critically important (Horvath & Bedi, 2002). Moving forward, current researchers are hoping to delineate the kinds of therapeutic strategies and interventions that optimally develop and sustain a strong working relationship between therapist and client(s).

Real relationship. A relatively new construct within the psychotherapy research literature, the *real relationship* is defined as the part of the therapeutic relationship that does not reflect transferential or countertransferential processes; rather, it is marked by genuine, authentic and reality-based interactions between client and therapist (Gelso, 2009; Gelso & Carter, 1994). Building on earlier writings of psychoanalyst Ralph Greenson (1967), Gelso (2009) added the concepts of valence (quality of attitudes and feelings) and magnitude to explain how the real relationship influences the therapeutic process. Although there is some empirical support for the construct (Fuertes et al., 2007; Marmarosh et al., 2009), an ongoing, central critique surrounds the definition of the term *real* and its distinction from other aspects of the therapeutic relationship (Horvath, 2009). Additionally, because Gelso's conceptualization is highly informed by the construct of transference, it may have maximal utility for psychodynamically informed therapies (Greenberg, 1994).

THE FUTURE OF THEORY IN COUNSELING AND PSYCHOTHERAPY

Our aim in this chapter has been to show that theories of counseling and psychotherapy did not spring full blown from the minds of great thinkers. Rather, each theorist built on what others had observed or demonstrated. Freud expanded on Charcot's and Breuer's work with hypnosis, and Rogers expanded on the neo-Freudians' active focus on relationship. Perls developed Gestalt therapy from theory and research on perception. CBT arose from experimental studies on learning. Family therapy evolved from

clinical observation and basic research in anthropology, communication, physics, engineering, and mathematics. Integrationist psychotherapy resulted from mounting research evidence for (a) similar success rates across bona fide approaches and (b) the central importance of common and contextual factors.

Now that we are in the second decade of the 21st century, we should keep in mind that theories are a product of the social and philosophic contexts of their time. Psychoanalysis was influenced by Victorian mores about sexuality; humanistic theories were influenced by existential philosophy; and newer theories were influenced by late-20th-century interest in feminism, liberalism, cultural diversity, postmodernism, and Eastern philosophies. Contemporary clinical practice has been affected by global immigration, the need for health care cost containment, and the technological revolution—three influences on the present and future evolution of theory development and implementation.

First, because global travel is far more accessible today than it was even 50 years ago, Western societies have witnessed rapid population shifts. Consequently, therapists are of necessity developing competencies for working with clients from highly diverse backgrounds. The theories summarized earlier were, with few exceptions, created by European and American men, and the individualistic value orientation in these theories is quite apparent. Scholars are carefully scrutinizing these theories for their cultural sensitivity and developing or modifying treatments for clients who immigrated to Western countries from highly collectivist societies.

Second, the rising cost of health care has increasingly placed clinical decision making in the hands of economists and third-party policy makers (Baker, McFall, & Shoham, 2008). For the past 20 years, therapists have been guided in their choice of treatment strategy more by empirical evidence than by theoretical preference. Thus, it is critically important to develop interventions that are responsive to various client populations and, in terms of research, to continue teasing out the contextual factors that critically moderate treatment success.

Third, the technological revolution has not only affected global communication and the speed, processing, and exchange of information but also has led to amazing discoveries about brain functioning and behavior. Medical technology has made it possible to diagnose posttraumatic stress from brain imaging (Bremner, 2002); to study changes in the brain pre- and posttherapy (e.g., Linden, 2006); and to treat clients with attention deficits, psychosomatic problems, and emotional dysregulation with neurofeedback machines (e.g., Masterpasqua & Healey, 2003). Virtual support groups and personal counseling (even dream analysis) are available on the Internet, and many therapists regularly communicate with their clients by e-mail or interactive voice messaging (Newman, 2004). Through telepsychology, clinicians are able to assess and make treatment recommendations for clients at a distance who are interviewed on camera. Researchers around the world are collaborating with practitioners in gathering, analyzing, and sharing enormous data files on effective and ineffective treatments. Highly sophisticated statistical models, which can only be analyzed by computers, are making it possible to tease apart the interactive effects of client factors, therapist factors, and factors related to the clinical setting and passage of time (e.g., Percevic, Lambert, & Kordy, 2006).

So where is the field headed? We surmise that the integrationist perspective will continue to grow and that the four major systems of therapy will be improved on the basis of research that emphasizes common and contextual factors with diverse client populations. Integrationism is not a new school or theory, however, to which all therapists are likely to subscribe. Rather, the objective of integration is to deepen our understanding of the therapeutic change process by recognizing the contributions of diverse theoretical orientations and by fostering closer ties between practice and basic theory and research in related disciplines, such as psychopathology and neurobiology (Castonguay, 2010).

As the divide between research and clinical practice narrows, integrationist psychotherapy is likely to become the gold standard, even though it is not inherently superior to "pure" therapy approaches (Castonguay, 2010). Already treatment selection has become less a matter of therapist preference and more a matter of identifying and applying empirically based principles of change. Nonetheless,

psychotherapy remains a highly personal and intimate endeavor. Our challenge as therapists, now and in the future, is to integrate clinical sensitivity with research evidence so as to be maximally responsive to highly diverse clients.

References

Abu Riaya, H., & Pargament, K. I. (2010). Religiously integrated psychotherapy with Muslim clients: From research to practice. *Professional Psychology: Research and Practice, 41*, 181–188. doi:10.1037/a0017988

Ackerman, N. W. (1958). *The psychodynamics of family life.* New York, NY: Basic Books.

Addis, M. E., & Mahalik, J. R. (2003). Men, masculinity, and the context of help seeking. *American Psychologist, 58*, 5–14. doi:10.1037/0003-066X.58.1.5

Adler, A. (1929). *The case of Miss R. The interpretation of a life study.* New York, NY: Greenberg.

Alexander, J., & Parsons, B. (1982). *Functional family therapy.* Monterey, CA: Brooks/Cole. doi:10.1037/11621-000

American Psychological Association. (2007). Guidelines for psychological practice with girls and women. *American Psychologist, 62*, 949–979. doi:10.1037/0003-066X.62.9.949

Ano, G. G., & Vasconcelles, E. B. (2005). Religious coping and psychological adjustment to stress: A meta-analysis. *Journal of Clinical Psychology, 61*, 461–480. doi:10.1002/jclp.20049

Ansbacher, H. L., & Ansbacher, R. (Eds.). (1964). *The individual psychology of Alfred Adler.* New York, NY: Harper Torchbooks.

Arredondo, P. (2004). Immigration and transition: Implications for racial-cultural counseling and clinical practice. In R. T. Carter (Ed.), *Handbook of racial-cultural psychology and counseling* (pp. 392–409). New York, NY: Wiley.

Baker, T. B., McFall, R. M., & Shoham, V. (2008). Current status and future prospects of clinical psychology: Toward a scientifically principled approach to mental and behavioral health care. *Psychological Science in the Public Interest, 9*, 67–103.

Bandura, A. (1969). *Principles of behavior modification.* New York, NY: Holt, Rinhart & Winston.

Bateson, G., Jackson, D. D., Haley, J., & Weakland, J. (1956). Toward a theory of schizophrenia. *Behavioral Science, 1*, 251–264. doi:10.1002/bs.3830010402

Beck, A. T. (1976). *Cognitive therapy and the emotional disorders.* New York, NY: International Universities Press.

Bell, J. E. (1961). *Family group therapy* (Public Health Monograph No. 64). Washington, DC: U.S. Government Printing Office.

Berlin, L. J., Cassidy, J., & Appleyard, K. (2008). Influence of attachment on other relationships. In J. Cassidy & P. R. Shaver (Eds.), *Handbook of attachment: Theory, research, and clinical applications* (2nd ed., pp. 333–347). New York, NY: Guilford Press.

Beutler, L. E., & Harwood, T. M. (2000). *Prescriptive psychotherapy: A practical guide to systematic treatment selection.* New York, NY: Oxford University Press.

Bhui, K., King, M., Dein, S., & O'Connor, W. (2008). Ethnicity and religious coping with mental distress. *Journal of Mental Health, 17,* 141–151. doi:10.1080/09638230701498408

Bordin, E. S. (1979). The generalizability of the psychoanalytic concept of the working alliance. *Psychotherapy: Theory, Research, Practice, Training, 16,* 252–260. doi:10.1037/h0085885

Boszormenyi-Nagy, I., & Spark, G. L. (1973). *Invisible loyalties: Reciprocity in intergenerational family therapy.* New York, NY: Harper & Row.

Bowen, M. (1976). Theory in the practice of psychotherapy. In P. J. Guerin (Ed.), *Family therapy: Theory and practice* (pp. 42–90). New York, NY: Gardner Press.

Bowlby, J. (1969). *Attachment and loss: Vol. 1. Attachment.* New York, NY: Basic Books.

Breger, L., & McGaugh, J. L. (1965). Critique and reformulation of "learning-theory" approaches to psychotherapy and neurosis. *Psychological Bulletin, 63,* 338–358.

Bremner, D. (2002). *Does stress damage the brain? Understanding trauma disorders from a mind-body perspective.* New York, NY: Norton.

Brooks, G. R. (2010). *Beyond the crisis of masculinity: A transtheoretical model for male-friendly therapy.* Washington, DC: American Psychological Association. doi:10.1037/12073-000

Brown, L. M., & Gilligan, C. (1992). *Meeting at the crossroads: Women's psychology and girls' development.* Cambridge, MA: Harvard University Press.

Brown, C., Schulberg, H. C., Sacco, D., Perel, J. M., & Houck, P. R. (1999). Effectiveness of treatments for major depression in primary medical care practice: a post hoc analysis of outcomes for African American and White patients. *Journal of Affective Disorders, 53,* 185–192.

Burckell, L. A., & Goldfried, M. R. (2006). Therapist qualities preferred by sexual-minority individuals. *Psychotherapy: Theory, Research, Practice, Training, 43,* 32–49.

Cahill, S. P., Rothbaum, B. O., Resick, P. A., & Follette, V. M. (2009). Cognitive-behavioral therapy for adults. In E. B. Foa, T. M Keane, & M. J. Friedman (Eds.), *Effective treatments for PTSD: Practice guidelines from the International Society for Traumatic Stress Studies* (2nd ed., pp. 139–222). New York, NY: Guilford Press.

Carter, R. T. (2007). Racism and psychological and emotional injury: Recognizing and assessing race-based traumatic stress. *The Counseling Psychologist, 35,* 13–105.

Castonguay, L. G. (2010, June). *A promising dawn: Integrative connections in psychotherapy.* Presidential address, annual conference of the Society for Psychotherapy Research, Monterey, CA.

Castonguay, L. G., & Beutler, L. E. (Eds.). (2006). *Principles of therapeutic change that work.* New York, NY: Oxford University Press.

Castonguay, L. G., Reid, J. J., Halperin, G. S., & Goldfried, M. R. (2003). Psychotherapy integration. In G. Stricker & T. A. Widiger (Eds.), *Comprehensive handbook of psychology: Vol. 8. Clinical psychology* (pp. 327–345). New York, NY: Wiley.

Clarkin, J. F., & Levy, K. N. (2004). The influence of client variable on psychotherapy. In M. J. Lambert (Ed.), *Bergin and Garfield's handbook of psychotherapy* (pp. 194–226). New York, NY: Wiley.

Comas-Díaz, L. (2006). Cultural variation in the therapeutic relationship. In C. D. Goodheart, A. E. Kadzin, & R. J. Sternberg (Eds.), *Evidence-based psychotherapy: Where practice and research meet* (pp. 81–105). Washington, DC: American Psychological Association.

Comas-Díaz, L. (2011). Multicultural approaches to psychotherapy. In J. Norcross, G. VandenBos, & D. K. Freeheim (Eds.), *History in psychotherapy: Continuity and change* (2nd ed., pp. 243–267). Washington, DC: American Psychological Association. doi:10.1037/12353-008

Corrigan, J. D., Dell, D. M., & Schmidt, L. D. (1980). Counseling as a social influence process: A review. *Journal of Counseling Psychology, 27,* 395–441. doi:10.1037/0022-0167.27.4.395

Davanloo, H. (1980). *Short-term dynamic psychotherapy.* Northvale, NJ: Jason Aronson.

de Shazer, S. (1985). *Keys to solutions in brief therapy.* New York, NY: Norton.

Dollard, J., & Miller, N. E. (1950). *Personality and psychotherapy.* New York, NY: McGraw-Hill.

Dreikurs, R. (1950). Techniques and dynamics of multiple psychotherapy. *Psychiatric Quarterly, 24,* 788–799. doi:10.1007/BF02229835

Dreikurs, R. (1959). Early experiments with group psychotherapy. *American Journal of Psychotherapy, 13,* 882–891.

Efran, J. S., Lukens, M. D., & Lukens, R. J. (1990). *Language, structure, and change: Frameworks of meaning in psychotherapy.* New York, NY: Norton.

Ellenberger, H. (1990). *The discovery of the unconscious.* New York, NY: Basic Books.

Ellis, A. (1962). *Reason and emotion in psychotherapy.* New York, NY: Lyle Stuart.

Ellis, A., & Whiteley, J. M. (1979). *Theoretical and empirical foundations of rational–emotive therapy.* Monterey, CA: Brooks/Cole.

Epstein, N., & Baucom, D. H. (1989). Cognitive-behavioral marital therapy. In A. Freeman, K. M. Simon, L. E. Beutler, & H. Arkowitz (Eds.), *Comprehensive handbook of cognitive therapy* (pp. 491–513). New York, NY: Plenum Press.

Eysenck, H. J. (1952). The effects of psychotherapy: An evaluation. *Journal of Consulting Psychology, 16,* 319–324. doi:10.1037/h0063633

Fairbairn, W. R. D. (1952). *Psychoanalytic studies of the personality.* London, England: Tavistock.

Foa, E. B., Keane, T. M., Friedman, M. J., & Cohen, J. A. (Eds.). (2009). *Effective treatments for PTSD: Practice guidelines from the International Society for Traumatic Stress Studies* (2nd ed.). New York, NY: Guilford Press.

Frank, J. (1961). *Persuasion and healing.* Baltimore, MD: Johns Hopkins University Press.

Frankl, V. (1963). *Man's search for meaning: An introduction to logotherapy.* New York, NY: Pocket Books.

Freud, S. (1913). *The interpretations of dreams.* New York, NY: Macmillan. doi:10.1037/10561-000

Friedlander, M. L., & Diamond, G. M. (2011). Couple and family therapy. In E. Altmaier & J. Hansen (Eds.), *Oxford handbook of counseling psychology* (pp. 647–675). New York, NY: Oxford University Press.

Friedlander, M. L., Escudero, V., & Heatherington, L. (2006). *Therapeutic alliances with couples and families: An empirically informed guide to practice.* Washington, DC: American Psychological Association. doi:10.1037/11410-000

Friedlander, M. L., Escudero, V., & Heatherington, L., & Diamond, G. M. (2011). Alliance in couple and family therapy. *Psychotherapy: Theory, Research, Practice, Training, 48,* 25–33.

Fuertes, J., Mislowack, A., Brown, S., Gur-Arie, S., Wilkinson, S., & Gelso, C. (2007). Correlates of the real relationship in psychotherapy: A study of dyads. *Psychotherapy Research, 17,* 423–430.

Gelso, C. J. (2002). Real relationship: The "something more" of psychotherapy. *Journal of Contemporary Psychotherapy, 32,* 35–40. doi:10.1023/A:1015531228504

Gelso, C. J. (2009). The real relationship in a postmodern world: Theoretical and empirical explorations. *Psychotherapy Research, 19,* 253–264. doi:10.1080/10503300802389242

Gelso, C. J., & Carter, J. A. (1994). Components of the psychotherapy relationship: Their interaction and unfolding during treatment. *Journal of Counseling Psychology, 41,* 296–306.

Gelso, C. J., & Fretz, B. (1992). *Counseling psychology.* New York, NY: Harcourt Brace Jovanovich.

Glasser, W. (1965). *Reality therapy.* New York, NY: Harper Collins.

Goldfried, M. R. (1980). Toward the delineation of therapeutic change principles. *American Psychologist, 35,* 991–999. doi:10.1037/0003-066X.35.11.991

Good, G. E., & Robertson, J. M. (2010). To accept a pilot? Addressing men's ambivalence and altering their expectancies about therapy. *Psychotherapy: Theory, Research, and Practice, 47,* 306–315. doi:10.1037/a0021162

Good, G. E., Thompson, D. A., & Brathwaite, A. D. (2005). Men and therapy: Critical concepts, theoretical frameworks, and research recommendations. *Journal of Clinical Psychology, 61,* 699–711. doi:10.1002/jclp.20104

Greenberg, L. S. (1994). What is "real" in the relationship? Comment on Gelso and Carter (1994). *Journal of Counseling Psychology, 41,* 307–309.

Greenberg, L. S. (2002). *Emotion-focused therapy: Coaching clients to work through their feelings.* Washington, DC: American Psychological Association. doi:10.1037/10447-000

Greenberg, L. S., & Johnson, S. M. (1988). *Emotionally focused therapy for couples.* New York, NY: Guilford Press.

Greenberg, L. S., Rice, L. N., & Elliott, R. (1993). *Facilitating emotional change: The moment by moment process.* New York, NY: Guilford Press.

Greenson, R. R. (1967). *The technique and practice of psychoanalysis* (Vol. 1). New York, NY: International Universities Press.

Griner, D., & Smith, T. B. (2006). Culturally adapted mental health intervention: A meta-analytic review. *Psychotherapy: Theory, Research, Practice, Training, 43,* 531–548. doi:10.1037/0033-3204.43.4.531

Haley, J. (1963). *Strategies of psychotherapy.* New York, NY: Grune & Stratton.

Haley, J. (1976). *Problem-solving therapy.* San Francisco, CA: Jossey-Bass.

Hartmann, H. (1964). *Essays on ego psychology.* New York, NY: International Universities Press.

Hayes, S. C., Strosahl, K., & Wilson, K. G. (1999). *Acceptance and commitment therapy: An experimental approach to behavior change.* New York, NY: Guilford Press.

Helms, J. E., & Cook, D. A. (1999). *Using race and culture in counseling and psychotherapy: Theory and process.* Needham Heights, MA: Allyn & Bacon.

Herman, J. L. (1992). *Trauma and recovery: The aftermath of violence from domestic abuse to political terror.* New York, NY: Basic Books.

Horowitz, M. J. (2003). *Treatment of stress response syndromes.* Arlington, VA: American Psychiatric Press.

Horvath, A. O. (2009). How real is the "real relationship"? *Psychotherapy Research, 19,* 273–277. doi:10.1080/10503300802592506

Horvath, A. O., & Bedi, R. P. (2002). The alliance. In J. C. Norcross (Ed.), *Psychotherapy relationships that work: Therapist contributions and responsiveness to patients* (pp. 37–69). New York, NY: Oxford University Press.

Horvath, A. O., Del Re, C., Flückiger, C., & Symonds, D. (2011). Alliance in individual psychotherapy. *Psychotherapy: Theory, Research, Practice, Training, 48,* 9–16.

Ivey, A. E., & Brooks-Harris, J. E. (2005). Integrative psychotherapy with culturally diverse clients. In J. C. Norcross & M. R. Goldfried (Eds.), *Handbook of psychotherapy integration* (2nd ed., pp. 321–339). New York, NY: Oxford University Press.

Jackson, D. D. (1957). The question of family homeostasis. *The Psychiatric Quarterly Supplement, 31,* 79–90.

Jackson, D. D. (1965). Family rules: The marital quid pro quo. *Archives of General Psychiatry, 12,* 589–594.

Jackson-Gilfort, A., Liddle, H. A., Tejeda, M. J., & Dakof, G. A. (2001). Facilitating engagement of African American male adolescents in family therapy: A cultural theme process study. *Journal of Black Psychology, 27,* 321–340. doi:10.1177/009579840 1027003005

Jacobson, N. S., & Christensen, A. (1998). *Acceptance and change in couple therapy: A therapist's guide to transforming relationships.* New York, NY: Norton.

Jacobson, N. S., & Margolin, A. (1979). *Marital therapy: Strategies based on social learning and behavior exchange principles.* New York, NY: Brunner/Mazel.

Johnson, S. M. (2003). Attachment theory: A guide for couple therapy. In S. M. Johnson & V. E. Whiffen (Eds.), *Attachment processes in couple and family therapy* (pp. 103–123). New York, NY: Guilford Press.

Jordan, J. V. (2008). Recent developments in relational-cultural theory. *Women and Therapy, 31,* 1–4. doi:10.1080/02703140802145540

Jung, C. G. (1954). *The practice of psychotherapy.* New York, NY: Pantheon.

Kanfer, F. H., & Phillips, J. S. (1970). *Learning foundations of behavior therapy.* New York, NY: Wiley.

Kelly, G. A. (1955). *The psychology of personal constructs.* New York, NY: Norton.

Kerr, M., & Bowen, M. (1988). *Family evaluation.* New York, NY: Norton.

Klein, M. (1932/1975). *The psychoanalysis of children.* (A. Strachey, Trans.). New York, NY: Delacorte Press.

Klerman, G. L., Weissman, M. M., Rounsaville, B. J., & Chevron, E. S. (1984). *Interpersonal psychotherapy of depression.* New York, NY: Basic Books.

Kohut, H. (1971). *The analysis of the self.* New York, NY: International Universities Press.

Kohut, H. (1984). *How does analysis cure?* Chicago, IL: University of Chicago Press.

Kudler, H. (2007). The need for psychodynamic principles in outreach to new combat veterans and their families. *Journal of the American Academy of Psychoanalysis and Dynamic Psychiatry, 35,* 39–50. doi:10.1521/jaap.2007.35.1.39

Lazarus, A. A. (1967). In support of technical eclecticism. *Psychological Reports, 21,* 415–416. doi:10.2466/pr0.1967.21.2.415

Lazarus, A. A. (1976). *Multimodal behavior therapy.* New York, NY: Springer.

Linden, D. E. J. (2006). How psychotherapy changes the brain—the contribution of functional neuroimaging. *Molecular Psychiatry, 11,* 528–538. doi:10.1038/sj.mp.4001816

Lindsley, O. R. (1963). Direct measurement and functional definition of vocal hallucinatory symptoms. *Journal of Nervous and Mental Disease, 136,* 293–297. doi:10.1097/00005053-196303000-00013

Linehan, M. M. (1993). *Cognitive behavioral treatment of borderline personality disorder.* New York, NY: Guilford Press.

Liu, W. M., & Pope-Davis, D. B. (2005). The working alliance, therapy ruptures and impasses, and counseling competence: Implications for counselor training and education. In R. T. Carter (Ed.), *The handbook of racial-cultural psychology and counseling* (Vol. 2, pp. 148–167). Hoboken, NJ: Wiley.

Luepnitz, D. (1988). *The family interpreted: Feminist theory in clinical practice.* New York, NY: Basic Books.

Madanes, C. (1981). *Strategic family therapy.* San Francisco, CA: Jossey Bass.

Mahalik, J. R. (1999). Interpersonal psychotherapy with men who experience gender role conflict. *Professional Psychology: Research and Practice, 30,* 5–13. doi:10.1037/0735-7028.30.1.5

Mahoney, M. J. (1991). *Human change processes.* New York, NY: Basic Books.

Malcolm, J. (1984). *In the Freud archives.* New York, NY: Knopf.

Maramba, G. G., & Nagayama Hall, G. C. (2002). Meta-analyses of ethnic match as a predictor of dropout, utilization, and level of functioning. *Cultural Diversity and Ethnic Minority Psychology, 8,* 290–297.

Marmarosh, C. L., Gelso, C. J., Markin, R. D., Majors, R., Mallery, C., & Choi, J. (2009). The real relationship in psychotherapy: Relationships to adult attachments, working alliance, transference, and therapy outcome. *Journal of Counseling Psychology, 56*, 337–350. doi:10.1037/a0015169

Masson, J. M. (1984). *The assault on truth: Freud's suppression of the seduction theory.* New York, NY: Farrar, Straus and Giroux.

Masterpasqua, F., & Healey, K. N. (2003). Neurofeedback in psychological practice. *Professional Psychology: Research and Practice, 34*, 652–656. doi:10.1037/0735-7028.34.6.652

May, R. (1961). *Existential psychology.* New York, NY: Random House.

McCarn, S. R., & Fassinger, R. E. (1996). Revisioning sexual minority identity formation: A new model of lesbian identity and its implications. *The Counseling Psychologist, 24*, 508–534.

Meichenbaum, D. (1977). *Cognitive behavior modification.* New York, NY: Plenum Press.

Mikulincer, M., & Shaver, P. R. (2007). *Attachment in adulthood: Structure, dynamic and change.* New York, NY: Guilford Press.

Miller, G. R. (2003). *Incorporating spirituality in counseling and psychotherapy: Theory and technique.* New York, NY: Wiley.

Miller, W. R., & Rollnick, S. (2002). *Motivational interviewing: Preparing people to change.* New York, NY: Guilford Press.

Minuchin, S. (1974). *Families and family therapy.* Cambridge, MA: Harvard University Press.

Minuchin, S., & Fishman, H. C. (1981). *Family therapy techniques.* Cambridge, MA: Harvard University Press.

Mitchell, S. (1988). *Relational concepts in psychoanalysis: An integration.* Cambridge, MA: Harvard University Press.

Newman, M. G. (2004). Technology in psychotherapy: An introduction. *Journal of Clinical Psychology, 60*, 141–145.

Newman, M. G., Castonguay, L. G., Fisher, A. J., & Borkovec, T. D. (2010, June). *A randomized controlled trial of interpersonal and emotional processing focused treatment in generalized anxiety disorder.* Paper presented at the annual meeting of the Society for Psychotherapy Research, Monterey, CA.

Nichols, M. P., & Schwartz, R. C. (2007). *Family therapy: Concepts and methods* (7th ed.). Boston, MA: Pearson Education.

Norcross, J. C. (Ed.). (2002). *Psychotherapy relationships that work: Therapist contributions and responsiveness to patients.* New York, NY: Oxford University Press.

Norcross, J. C., & Prochaska, J. O. (1988). A study of eclectic (and integrative) views revisited. *Professional Psychology: Research and Practice, 19*, 170–174. doi:10.1037/0735-7028.19.2.170

Organista, K. C. (2006). Cognitive–behavioral therapy with Latinos and Latinas. In P. A. Hays & S. Y. Iwamasa (Eds.), *Culturally responsive cognitive–behavioral therapy: Assessment, practice, and supervision* (pp. 73–96). Washington, DC: American Psychological Association. doi:10.1037/11433-003

Pargament, K. I., Konig, H. G., & Perez, L. M. (2000). The many methods of religious coping: Development and initial validation of the RCOPE. *Journal of Clinical Psychology, 56*, 519–543. doi:10.1002/(SICI)1097-4679(200004)56:4<519::AID-JCLP6>3.0.CO;2-1

Pascoe, E. A., & Richman, L. S. (2009). Perceived discrimination and health: A meta-analytic review. *Psychological Bulletin, 135*, 531–554.

Patterson, G. R. (1971). *Families: Application of social learning theory to family life.* Champaign, IL: Research Press.

Patterson, G. R. (1982). *Coercive family process.* Eugene, OR: Castalia.

Paul, G. L. (1967). Strategies in outcome research in psychotherapy. *Journal of Consulting Psychology, 31*, 109–118. doi:10.1037/h0024436

Percevic, R., Lambert, M. J., & Kordy, H. (2006). What is the predictive value of responses to psychotherapy for its future course? Empirical explorations and consequences for outcome monitoring. *Psychotherapy Research, 16*, 364–373. doi:10.1080/10503300500485524

Perls, F. (1969). *Gestalt therapy verbatim.* Moab, UT: Real People Press.

Perls, F., Hefferline, R., & Goodman, P. (1951). *Gestalt therapy.* New York, NY: Bantam Books.

Pieterse, A. L., & Miller, M. J. (2009). Current considerations in the assessment of adults: A review and extension of culturally inclusive models. In J. Ponterotto, L. A. Suzuki, C. Alexander, & J. M. Cases (Eds.), *Handbook of multicultural counseling* (3rd ed., pp. 649–666). Thousand Oaks, CA: Sage.

Pinsof, W. M. (1995). *Integrative problem-centered therapy: A synthesis of biological, individual, and family therapy.* New York, NY: Basic Books.

Prochaska, J. O., & DiClemente, C. C. (1984). *The transtheoretical approach: Crossing traditional boundaries of therapy.* Homewood, IL: Dow Jones-Irwin.

Resnick, P. A., & Schnicke, M. K. (1993). *Cognitive processing therapy for rape victims: A treatment manual.* Newbury Park, CA: Sage.

Rogers, C. R. (1942). *Counseling and psychotherapy.* Boston, MA: Houghton Mifflin.

Rogers, C. R. (1951). *Client-centered therapy: Its current practice, implications and theory.* Boston, MA: Houghton Mifflin.

Rogers, C. R. (1980). *A way of being.* Boston, MA: Houghton Mifflin.

Rotter, J. B. (1954). *Social learning and clinical psychology.* New York, NY: Prentice-Hall.

Safran, J. (1998). *Widening the scope of cognitive therapy: The therapeutic relationship, emotion, and the process of change.* Northvale, NJ: Jason Aronson.

Sanderson, W. C., Rue, P. J., & Wetzler, S. (1998). The generalization of cognitive behavior therapy for panic disorder. *Journal of Cognitive Psychotherapy, 12,* 323–330.

Satir, V. (1964). *Conjoint family therapy.* Palo Alto, CA: Science and Behavior Books.

Scharff, D., & Scharff, J. (1987). *Object relations family therapy.* New York, NY: Jason Aronson.

Seligman, M. (1991). *Learned optimism.* New York, NY: Knopf.

Selvini Palazzoli, M., Boscolo, L., Cecchin, G., & Prata, G. (1978). *Paradox and counterparadox.* New York, NY: Jason Aronson.

Shapiro, F. (1989). Eye movement desensitization: A new treatment for post-traumatic stress disorder. *Journal of Behavior Therapy and Experimental Psychiatry, 20,* 211–217.

Short, E. L., Suzuki, L., Prendes-Lintel, M., Prendes-Lintel Furr, G., Madabhusim, S., & Mapel, G. (2009). Counseling immigrants and refugees. In J. G. Ponterotto, J. Manuel Casa, L. A. Suzuji, & C. M. Alexander (Eds.), *Handbook of multicultural counseling* (3rd ed., pp. 201–211). Thousand Oaks, CA: Sage.

Sifneos, P. E. (1979). *Short-term dynamic psychotherapy.* New York, NY: Plenum Press.

Skinner, B. F. (1953). *Science and human behavior.* New York, NY: Macmillan.

Skinner, B. F. (1957). *Verbal behavior.* New York, NY: Appleton-Century-Crofts. doi:10.1037/11256-000

Smith, M. L., Glass, G. V., & Miller, T. I. (1980). *The benefits of psychotherapy.* Baltimore, MD: Johns Hopkins University Press.

Smith, T. B. (2009). Culturally congruent practices in counseling and psychotherapy. In J. G. Ponterotto, J. M. Casas, L. A. Suzuki., & C. M. Alexander (Eds.), *Handbook of multicultural counseling* (3rd ed., pp. 439–450). Thousand Oaks, CA: Sage.

Sperry, L., & Shafranske, E. P. (Eds.). (2005). *Spiritually oriented psychotherapy.* Washington, DC: American Psychological Association.

Stamm, B. H., & Friedman, M. J. (2000). Cultural diversity in the appraisal and expression of trauma. In A. Y. Shalev, R. Yehuda, & A. C. McFarlane (Eds.), *International handbook of human response to trauma* (pp. 69–85). New York, NY: Kluwer. doi:10.1007/978-1-4615-4177-6_5

Stiles, W. B., Shapiro, D. A., & Elliott, R. (1986). Are all psychotherapies equivalent? *American Psychologist, 41,* 165–180. doi:10.1037/0003-066X.41.2.165

Strachey, J., Freud, A., Strachey, A., & Tyson, A. (Eds.). (1953–1974). *Standard edition of the complete psychological works of Sigmund Freud.* London, England: Hogarth Press.

Strong, S. R. (1968). Counseling: An interpersonal influence process. *Journal of Counseling Psychology, 15,* 215–224. doi:10.1037/h0020229

Strong, S. R., & Claiborn, C. (1982). *Change through interaction: Social psychological processes of counseling and psychotherapy.* New York, NY: Wiley.

Strong, S. R., & Matross, R. (1973). Change processes in counseling and psychotherapy. *Journal of Counseling Psychology, 20,* 25–37. doi:10.1037/h0034055

Strupp, H. H., & Binder, J. L. (1984). *Psychotherapy in a new key: A guide to time-limited dynamic psychotherapy.* New York, NY: Basic Books.

Stuart, R. B. (1969). An operant-interpersonal treatment for marital discord. *Journal of Consulting and Clinical Psychology, 33,* 675–682. doi:10.1037/h0028475

Sue, D. W., & Sue, D. (2007). *Counseling the culturally diverse* (5th ed.). Hoboken, NJ: Wiley.

Sue, S., Zane, N., Nagayama Hall, G. C., & Berger, L. K. (2009). The case for cultural competency in psychotherapeutic interventions. *Annual Review of Psychology, 60,* 525–548. doi:10.1146/annurev.psych.60.110707.163651

Sullivan, H. S. (1953). *The interpersonal theory of psychiatry.* New York, NY: Norton.

Terrell, F., Taylor, J. Menzise, J., & Barrett, R. (2009). Cultural mistrust. In H. A. Neville, B. M. Tynes, & S. O. Utsey (Eds.), *Handbook of African American psychology* (pp. 299–310). Thousand Oaks, CA: Sage.

Utsey, S. O., Bolden, M. A., & Brown, A. L. (2001). Visions of revolution from the spirit of Frantz Fanon: A psychology of liberation for counseling African Americans confronting societal racism and oppression. In J. G. Ponterotto, J. M. Casas, L. A. Suzuki, & C. M. Alexander (Eds.), *Handbook of multicultural counseling* (2nd ed., pp. 290–310). Thousand Oaks, CA: Sage.

Utsey, S. O., & Gernat, C. A. (2002). White racial identity attitudes and the ego defense mechanisms used by White counselor trainees in racially provocative counseling situations. *Journal of Counseling and Development, 80,* 475–483.

Wachtel, P. L. (1977). *Psychoanalysis and behavior therapy*. New York, NY: Basic Books.

Wampold, B. E. (2001). *The great psychotherapy debate*. New York, NY: Erlbaum.

Watzlawick, P., Weakland, J., & Fisch, R. (1974). *Change: Principles of problem formation and problem resolution*. New York, NY: Norton.

Whaley, A. L. (2001). Cultural mistrust and mental health services for African Americans: A review and meta-analysis. *The Counseling Psychologist, 29*, 513–531. doi:10.1177/0011000001294003

Whitaker, C. A. (1975). Psychotherapy of the absurd: With a special emphasis on the psychotherapy of aggression. *Family Process, 14*, 1–16. doi:10.1111/j.1545-5300.1975.00001.x

White, M., & Epston, D. (1990). *Narrative means to therapeutic ends*. New York, NY: Norton.

Winnicott, C., Shepherd, R., & Davis, M. (1989). *D. W. Winnicott: Psycho-analytic explorations*. Cambridge, MA: Harvard University Press.

Winnicott, D. W. (1953). Transitional objects and transitional phenomena. *The International Journal of Psychoanalysis, 34*, 89–97.

Wolpe, J. (1958). *Psychotherapy by reciprocal inhibition*. Stanford, CA: Stanford University Press.

Wolpe, J. (1987). The promotion of scientific psychotherapy: A long voyage. In J. K. Zeig (Ed.), *The evolution of psychotherapy* (pp. 133–148). New York, NY: Brunner/Mazel.

Worell, J., & Remer, P. (1992). *Feminist perspective in therapy: An empowerment model for women*. New York, NY: Wiley.

Yalom, I. (1981). *Existential psychotherapy*. New York, NY: Basic Books.

Zane, N., Nagayama Hall, G. C., Sue, S., Young, K., & Nunez, J. (2004). Research on psychotherapy with culturally diverse populations. In M. J. Lambert (Ed.), *Bergin and Garfield's handbook of psychotherapy and behavior change* (5th ed., pp. 767–805). New York, NY: Wiley.

CHAPTER 3

IMPROVING THE QUALITY OF RESEARCH IN COUNSELING PSYCHOLOGY: CONCEPTUAL AND METHODOLOGICAL ISSUES

William T. Hoyt and Brent Mallinckrodt

As associate editor and editor of the *Journal of Counseling Psychology (JCP)*, now in the last year of our editorial terms, we have made editorial decisions for more than 760 newly submitted manuscripts and 400 revised manuscripts submitted to the journal. As we evaluate the empirical and theoretical contributions of these manuscripts, we are frequently impressed and delighted by the creativity and rigor of the work we are entrusted to review. We also frequently experience a profound sense of loss when a study falls short of the standards we believe are necessary for publication, especially when it is evident that the researchers have expended a great deal of effort and when—had only a few choices been executed differently—this great effort might well have led to a more fruitful contribution to the literature. Many times we have wished it were somehow possible to transmit a decision letter back in time to the point at which a study was still in the planning stage, so that we could advise a research team to avoid decisions that subsequently prevented us from accepting their study for publication. We envision this chapter as just such a communication. In preparing to write it, we polled all current members of the *JCP* editorial board as well as several experts who had served for many years but are no longer on the board. We asked essentially, "What would you like to be able to tell researchers to help them avoid choices that you have frequently seen prevent a study from making the high level of contribution to

the literature we require of articles published in *JCP*?" We have been able to incorporate many of the wide range of responses into this chapter.

Our goal is to provide suggestions for current and future investigators about how to plan and execute research that will be more likely to have an impact on the field (and thus more likely to be judged as making a substantive contribution when reviewed for publication). Ultimately, we hope that attention to the principles and perspectives articulated here will strengthen the research contribution of counseling psychology as a discipline and enhance the impact of our specialty's unique perspectives and methods on the broader field. Although we primarily consider quantitative research that emphasizes theory testing, some of what we have to say will also have relevance to qualitative scholarship, to the extent that such investigations serve the goal of theory development. As will be seen, we value qualitative research and believe that this set of methods has a place in a theory-driven science of psychology. But space limitations do not allow us to thoroughly address the often quite different considerations governing judgments about the quality of qualitative research. Moreover, we make an effort here to provide guidance that reflects not merely our own preferences but a consensus among methodologists. Whereas such a consensus often exists regarding aspects of quantitative work (and we have consulted both members of *JCP*'s

We are grateful to many members of *JCP*'s editorial board who contributed suggestions for this chapter, and especially to Rene Dawis, Jef Kahn, Matt Martens, Kris Preacher, and Terry Tracey, who provided detailed comments on an initial version, averting some important omissions and helping us fine-tune our recommendations in many areas.

DOI: 10.1037/13754-003
APA Handbook of Counseling Psychology: Vol. 1. Theories, Research, and Methods, Nadya A. Fouad (Editor-in-Chief)

editorial board and a group of eminent methodologists in counseling psychology to reassure ourselves that our recommendations are noncontroversial), we believe that consensus about criteria for evaluating qualitative research is still emerging in our field.

Reviewers and editors distinguish between two types of concerns when evaluating a manuscript. The first are *fixable flaws* that have a good chance of being addressed in a revision, even if doing so might require considerable effort. The second are *fatal flaws* that in the opinion of the reviewer or action editor seriously limit the potential contribution of the manuscript and cannot be addressed through revision. For example, a fixable flaw might be the decision to combine male and female participants into the same analysis. If the data do not support this decision, it is usually possible to examine both groups separately in a revised manuscript. The following actual example of a fatal flaw is particularly memorable because the study involved an extraordinary amount of effort and the research topic was especially promising. (We will not mention the specific research hypotheses to protect the identity of the researchers.) In this study, a team of coders was laboriously trained to a high level of accuracy to rate a specific therapist behavior X and a specific set of potential client reactions Y. A fairly large sample of session videotapes was gathered. Each member of the four-member rating team worked independently to rate three quarters of the sessions. An individual team member provided ratings of both X and Y variables in a given session, however, thus confounding the two ratings. The problem was compounded because raters were aware of the study hypotheses. Because there was no way to untangle this confound, it represented a fatal flaw that prevented an otherwise promising study from being published. (Actually, in this example, the action editor nevertheless invited a revision, contingent on the researchers' willingness to train a new team of raters to provide independent evaluations of either X or Y.) In this chapter, we give special emphasis to fatal flaws because of their implications for a study's chances of being published.

We believe it is also helpful for researchers, especially those near the beginning of their careers, to understand the process an action editor uses to arrive at a decision. Generally, editors and reviewers use two broad criteria to evaluate manuscripts. The first criterion is methodological and is the easier of the two to apply. Did the authors make use of a research design and statistical methods appropriate to their research question? Did they follow recommended procedures in implementing these methods? Were the measures or procedures used by the researchers to operationalize key constructs shown to have adequate reliability and construct validity? Were the authors aware of the limitations of their research design, and did they give due consideration to plausible alternative explanations in discussing their findings?

Methodological considerations are crucial for evaluating the contribution of the manuscript. Science is a cumulative enterprise, and studies using sound measures and procedures (and providing a clear description of these measures and procedures) yield findings that are both interpretable and replicable. However, judgments about methodological quality serve largely as negative indicators in decisions about scientific merit: Poor measurement techniques or analytic methods can constitute a fatal flaw even if other elements of a manuscript (e.g., persuasive literature review, useful research question, important implications for theory or practice) are strong.

Unfortunately, following sound research methods does not guarantee that a study will make an important contribution to the field. In a highly competitive journal such as *JCP*, many more methodologically sound manuscripts are reviewed each year than can be published. Thus, editors and reviewers must base judgments in large part on a second criterion, which is the *substantive contribution* of the study to the field. Studies can make a substantive contribution because they advance a new or established theoretical framework or because they have important implications for practice, or both.

Judgments about a study's substantive contribution are inherently subjective, and for this reason, editors and reviewers often prefer to focus their decision letters to authors on methodological issues, especially if the decision is not to publish the study. Because there tends to be less room for disagreement about these issues, action editors are naturally inclined to rely on these factors in supporting their decision. It is much more difficult to tell an author, in essence "Apart from any methodological considerations, I just do not think this study makes an important enough contribution to publish in *JCP*." This tendency can have an unfortunate consequence, however, in that it may send the message that technical sophistication is the main or only consideration that determines the worth of a scientific investigation.

In this chapter, we include selected recommendations about methodological quality and a few points concerning manuscript preparation that we have observed are frequently occurring problems. Our main emphasis is on the second, substantive dimension of the evaluation of research quality and the effective use of methods and measurement in the service of this substantive contribution. There are two reasons for this focus. First, a wealth of resources is currently available to advise authors about methodological best practices. These include research methods texts (e.g., Heppner, Wampold, & Kivlighan, 2008; Shadish, Cook, & Campbell, 2002), and quantitative methods guides such as Hancock and Mueller's (2010) *The Reviewer's Guide to Quantitative Methods in the Social Sciences,* which provides a concise guide to best practices for all common and many advanced statistical methods. In addition, entire journals are devoted to research methods (e.g., *Psychological Methods*) as well as special issues of journals such as *The Counseling Psychologist* and *JCP*, and individual articles to apprise readers of suggested best practices. Second, appraisals of the substantive contribution of a given research investigation are, in effect, the editor's effort to predict the long-term impact that a manuscript will have on the field. By making explicit the considerations that ground such appraisals, we hope both to demystify this important aspect of the evaluation process and to provide guidance for experienced and aspiring researchers about how to improve the publishability and utility of their scientific work.

The general organization of this chapter will follow the sequence of steps most researchers follow when proceeding from general interest in a broad area to a manuscript accepted for publication. We begin with a basic orientation to the philosophy of science that argues for scientific inquiry as an ongoing process of theory development and theory testing, rather than simple gathering of facts about the world. Given this context, we discuss conceptualization of research questions as simple or elaborate models of causal relations among variables. We offer suggestions for constructing literature reviews that provide strong theoretical grounding for such models and then consider implications of this theory-testing approach for research design. We pay particular attention to the design of studies using correlational data. Although we believe that experimental methods are an essential tool of scientific inquiry (and could be employed more frequently than they currently are in our field), we also recognize the growing interest among counseling psychology researchers in the effects of personal characteristics (e.g., ethnic identity, self-efficacy, body image, perfectionism, attachment styles) and relational attributes (e.g., perceptions of parents, therapeutic alliance; communication style in couples) that must be measured rather than experimentally manipulated.

We then make recommendations about choosing measures to operationalize the variables for a study and about documenting the reliability and validity of these variables. Finally, we describe some considerations for data analysis, including presentation and interpretation of findings. We pay special attention to analytic techniques, such as multiple regression and structural equation modeling (SEM), because the majority of studies published in *JCP* and other counseling psychology journals in recent years have used these techniques to study hypothesized causal relations among measured (as opposed to experimentally manipulated) variables. Finally, we offer some suggestions about tools for effectively implementing the recommended data analysis and reporting practices.

HIGH-IMPACT RESEARCH IS THEORY-DRIVEN RESEARCH

The research enterprise should begin with developing a carefully considered research idea. The brief word *idea* hardly does justice to the complexity of the activity, and it is precisely in this complexity that the seeds of fatal flaws to publication are first sown. Most seasoned faculty advisors have experienced an eager novice student who, when first discussing a research idea, excitedly describes a plan to explore the connection between two or more "really cool variables." We by no means disparage the enthusiasm that arises from what may be primarily an aesthetic perception of the connection between two or more constructs. On the contrary, we believe that such intuitions may often be the seeds of a fruitful dissertation or even a productive program of research. But an important step in converting these germinal ideas into a developed research plan is to familiarize oneself with relevant theory and research, and to consider how the idea can be developed into a coherent contribution to the existing literature. Recent research has documented the growth and decline of specific areas of research interest in the field of counseling psychology. Areas like *human sex differences* that accounted for more than 30% of all articles published in *JCP* during the late 1970s, now account for fewer than 2%, whereas other areas such as *ethnic identity* and *well-being* have more than doubled in publication frequency over the past 10 years (Mallinckrodt, 2011). These changes underscore the importance of staying abreast of recent developments and changing trends in the literature.

A research idea developed without giving careful consideration to existing theory and previous empirical findings is analogous to a house built on a shaky foundation—with a journal's 80% rejection rate playing the role of gale force winds in this scenario. Under this kind of intense scrutiny, a research plan can quickly collapse when it becomes apparent there are critical gaps (key constructs have been omitted), constructs are poorly operationalized, or post hoc it is impossible to build a coherent causal model of relationships between the constructs that were so compelling in the initial stages of the project. Even a methodologically sophisticated, impeccably executed research plan, if it was developed without sufficient attention to theory, is like a solidly built house on a foundation of crumbling stone.

We do not mean to suggest that researchers must always find a single, all-encompassing theory to serve as the basis of their work. On the contrary,

some of the most fruitful research combines principles derived from two or more general theories into a new model for understanding behavior or experiences in the domain of interest. Furthermore, it is not the case that theories published in scholarly journals constitute the only firm foundation for research. Clinical or even personal experience, coupled with a keen sense of curiosity and observation skills, can provide important initial insights that are the foundation of useful theories. A possible next step is elaboration through more systematic qualitative investigations. What is critical is that researchers not neglect the task of theory development as the basis for generating meaningful research hypotheses (Wampold, Davis, & Good, 1990) and that they not ignore existing theory and research findings that could inform their research questions or research methods or both.

To avoid these fatal flaws, it is vital that researchers give careful thought to the scientific foundations of the project at the *idea stage*, when their interests are transformed into a concrete plan for research. Qualitative researchers must consider the importance to the field of the phenomena they seek to describe, or the theoretical model they hope to develop. Quantitative researchers must ask whether their hypotheses derive from a coherent theory of the phenomena under investigation. How will the findings of this study contribute to our confidence in or doubts about this theory and its relevance to practice? If scientific research is a procedure for developing and testing theories about the world, then the contribution of a study cannot be evaluated without due consideration of its theoretical basis and implications. To provide a context for this perspective, we offer a brief overview of recent debates about philosophy of science in counseling psychology and in psychology.

Challenges to Traditional Scientific Methods in Counseling Psychology

Interest in philosophy of science in counseling psychology may have peaked in the decade of the 1980s, starting with Gelso's (1979) major contribution in *The Counseling Psychologist*. Gelso's candid reflections on limitations and challenges of conventional research methods, including important observations concerning the trade-offs between internal and external validity, termed the *bubble hypothesis*, led naturally to the question of whether conceptions of scientific praxis derived from the physical sciences were adequate or appropriate for what Howard (1986) later termed a *human science*. Limitations of traditional scientific methods were further explored in a special section of *JCP* in 1984. Hoshmand (1989) appeared to have captured the spirit of the decade with her resounding critique of what she termed the *received view* of the nature and purpose of scientific inquiry, and her overview of alternative research paradigms—also published as a major contribution in *The Counseling Psychologist*.

These explorations of the philosophical foundations of scientific inquiry were motivated by widespread dissatisfaction with the utility of research for practice, and an earnest desire to enhance the perceived relevance of research in accordance with the ideals of the Boulder (scientist–practitioner) model (Heppner et al., 1992; Hoshmand & Polkinghorne, 1992). One outcome of these reflections has been the flourishing of qualitative inquiry in counseling psychology, in comparison with other fields of psychology (e.g., Kidd, 2002), and a surge of interest among counseling psychologists in methods and philosophical paradigms for qualitative scholarship (Haverkamp, Morrow, & Ponterotto, 2005; Hill, Thompson, & Williams, 1997; Hoshmand, 1989; Hoyt & Bhati, 2007).

A second outcome has been continuing discussion of the relative merits of *laboratory* research (i.e., experimental studies conducted in nonclinic settings, often with volunteer clients, to facilitate random assignment of participants to study conditions and controlled measurement of study variables) and *field* research (i.e., studies of counselors and clients in real-life clinical settings, which enhances generalizability of findings, usually at the cost of some researcher control over the process of data collection) to advance scientific knowledge about psychotherapy processes and outcomes (Heppner et al., 2008, Chapter 4). Doubts about the generalizability of findings from laboratory analog studies led to the decline of this research design in counseling psychology, and in psychotherapy research generally, although there is an emerging consensus that all

forms of data have both strengths and limitations as a foundation for scientific practice, and therefore it is desirable to consult multiple forms of evidence in establishing a scientific foundation for practice (American Psychological Association [APA] Presidential Task Force on Evidence-Based Practice, 2006).

Unificationist View: Role of Theory in Science

Forsyth and Strong (1986) offered an alternative diagnosis of the problems with psychotherapy research. These problems did not reflect the failure of traditional scientific methods but rather a failure to apply these methods in the service of theory-driven science. By situating psychotherapy research in the context of the larger effort to construct useful theories of human behavior, Forsyth and Strong argued, basic and applied researchers can find common ground, and field research, laboratory research, and even research in other disciplines related to the science of human behavior can all contribute to creating theories of behavior and behavior change that are empirically grounded and practically useful.

Forsyth and Strong (1986) contrasted theory-driven research with *technological* and *fact-finding* research. Technological research focuses on narrow questions of what works for whom in a given setting, without a guiding theoretical framework.

> Graduate training in clinical and counseling psychology focuses on the technology of collecting and analyzing data, with a special emphasis on applying findings to therapy, whereas the vital and creative steps of generating transituational propositions from observed relationships are bypassed. Technicians are being trained rather than scientists, and the products of their situationally limited work are of little value to practitioners. (p. 117)

Forsyth and Strong (1986) noted that another way that psychotherapy researchers can be led astray is to confuse the importance of empirical validation of scientific theories with an archaic notion that scientists are primarily fact finders, and therefore must put aside all preconceptions and allow the facts to speak for themselves. Researchers who simply seek to accumulate new facts in a research area, without an overarching theory to help them know where to look, may find that they have many disparate findings but little in the way of coherent narrative to show for their efforts. The problem, according to Forsyth and Strong, is that "because of their mutability and situational specificity, facts are of little long-lasting value in science" (p. 115). Programs of research will yield cumulative knowledge to the extent that they are developed to test and extend theories of human behavior. "Science depends upon theory as much as it depends upon data" (p. 117).

The view of science as a theory-testing enterprise articulated by Forsyth and Strong (1986) parallels developments in philosophy of science and in the methodological literature in psychology during the middle decades of the 20th century. Early behaviorists (Watson, 1913) were influenced by the logical positivist view that science is primarily an inductive enterprise and warned that theorizing about any variable that could not be directly observed and objectively measured undermined the scientific basis of psychology. By the 1950s, however, this was seen to be a shaky foundation for a science of human behavior, precisely because many important causes of behavior reside within the person doing the behaving, and therefore are not directly observable. Measurement theorists (e.g., Campbell & Fiske, 1959; Cronbach & Meehl, 1955) began to grapple with the difficulties of providing validity evidence for measures of unobservable (latent) variables, and methodologists (Campbell & Stanley, 1963; Kenny, 1979; Shadish et al., 2002) elaborated the logic of inference in research designs used to test causal theories about relations among variables when experimental manipulation is not an option. This emerging perspective on the role of science for studying internal processes (thoughts, motives, feelings) as well as observable behaviors was termed *postpositivism* (Campbell, 1984/1999) and emphasized that the elaboration of empirically based psychological theories goes hand in hand with the development and validation of procedures for measuring the latent constructs from which these theories are constructed (Cronbach & Meehl, 1955).

Summary

Thus, the unificationist perspective articulated by Forsyth and Strong (1986) aligns well with the emerging postpositivist program that propelled the movement away from strict behaviorism in psychology in the second half of the 20th century. To contribute to a cumulative scientific understanding of human behavior, studies should be grounded in a strong theory about the behaviors or relations in question and should address the evidence for validity of measures (always a work in progress, in postpositivist inquiry) used to operationalize key theoretical constructs. A range of different types of evidence (e.g., basic research on human cognitive and affective processes, research on physiological and evolutionary perspectives on human behavior, social psychological studies of relational processes as well as both laboratory and field inquiries directly relevant to psychotherapy process and outcome) can contribute to theories of behavior and behavior change with practical utility for planning and delivering psychological interventions. Because a range of evidence is required, and only a multiplicity of research methods can generate that evidence, we believe it is quite counterproductive for editorial decision makers to favor one set of research methods per se over others. Rather, the key question is whether the method selected is a reasonable choice for generating this particular type of evidence.

With respect to our goals in this chapter, the postpositivist approach suggests that studies are likely to make a useful contribution to the literature if they (a) articulate and defend a developed or developing theory about the processes leading to the outcome of interest, (b) consider carefully the strengths and limitations of measurement procedures proposed to operationalize key constructs (and ideally use more than one measurement procedure when feasible), (c) critically evaluate the research design as a test of the theoretical propositions, (d) take steps (e.g., longitudinal measurement to strengthen the basis for causal inferences; controlling for extraneous variables that would otherwise provide plausible alternative explanations for associations observed in the model) to strengthen the links between findings and theory, and (e) give due consideration to both expected and unexpected findings and their implications for both developing theory and the application of this theory in the real world.

A final question that might be asked about the postpositivist approach to scientific inquiry concerns the role of qualitative methods, which have elicited considerable interest among counseling psychologists over the past 30 years. If scientific research is about theory testing, is there a place for qualitative inquiry, particularly given that such investigations aim to provide detailed (*thick*) descriptions of the experience of one or a few participants and not generalizable knowledge about universal principles of human behavior (Morrow & Smith, 2000)? A common response from qualitative methodologists has been that qualitative researchers subscribe to a different scientific paradigm (e.g., Haverkamp et al., 2005; Hoshmand, 1989) and that therefore positivist and postpositivist standards are not relevant for evaluating qualitative research.

We agree that different standards are clearly needed for the evaluation of qualitative and quantitative investigations. We worry, however, that the emphasis on qualitative and quantitative research as essentially separate endeavors—although perhaps initially needed to establish a firm grounding for qualitative inquiry in a discipline with dominant quantitative traditions—can also have some negative consequences. One challenge for reviewers of qualitative studies is that the usual methodological criteria do not apply and proposed methodological standards for qualitative inquiry (e.g., Guba, 1981) that are largely adapted from criteria for quantitative methods may not be good indicators of the quality of qualitative investigations (Hoyt & Bhati, 2007). Additionally, if qualitative inquiry is viewed as an entirely separate pursuit from theory-testing quantitative research, then any alliance between these two approaches is necessarily uneasy, and it is difficult to provide a justification for publishing the two types of scholarship side by side in the same journals. However, qualitative methodologists correctly assert that if alternative methods are relegated only to separate, specialized journals, this may imply to high-stakes evaluators (e.g., tenure committees) that this a second-class form of scholarship and does not rise to the level needed for publication in the established outlets for the discipline.

We believe that the unificationist perspective articulated by Forsyth and Strong (1986) can provide useful guidance about the contributions of both quantitative and qualitative scholarship in a theory-driven science of human behavior. If science is driven by theory (and the outcome of well-conducted research programs is the development of informative and applicable theories), then research training needs to encompass the process of theory development as well as addressing sound research methods. Strong (1991) described what he called the *cycle of science*, which proceeds from the *context of discovery*, or theory generation, to the *context of testing*, or empirical examination of theory-derived hypotheses. The findings of these empirical investigations then suggest further elaborations or modifications of the theory (new discovery), which suggest new empirical studies (further testing), and so on.

Strong (1991) suggested that researchers and research training practices need to focus more on the context of discovery—on the sources of scientific theories and the process of theory elaboration and modification in response to empirical findings. We suggest that the cycle of science provides one promising account of the role of qualitative methods within a postpositivist, theory-derived science of psychology. As noted by the APA Presidential Task Force on Evidence-Based Practice (2006), multiple forms of evidence can contribute to evidence-based psychological practice as long as practitioners are mindful that different forms of evidence have different uses. We suggest that systematic qualitative scholarship (as well as other qualitative sources of information, including clinical observation and general life experience) are fertile grounds for theory development and elaboration and that they fit comfortably within the context of discovery in theory-driven science.

LITERATURE REVIEWS GROUND THE RESEARCH HYPOTHESES

After careful development of a research plan that maximizes the potential scientific contribution of a study, the chief purpose of the abstract and introduction is to persuasively (but dispassionately) communicate this formulation to readers. One important goal of the introduction is to provide a review of literature to demonstrate that the research question has not been adequately addressed in previously published studies. It is crucial to go beyond this, however, and make a case for the importance of the theory underlying the study and for the research hypotheses as a reasonable test of that theory. A rationale amounting to essentially "no one has done this before" is never sufficient. (Upon reading an introduction that rested its case on this argument, a *JCP* reviewer responded, "perhaps there was a good reason!")

A successful review of literature makes a cogent argument, usually on the basis of both theory (perhaps derived from clinical observations or suggested by previous qualitative inquiries) and past research, for a set of causal relations among constructs, usually for a particular setting or population. In an applied journal such as *JCP*, it is useful to point out how this theory is relevant to practice (e.g., case conceptualization, intervention design). The study introduction is a literature review with a purpose. The author's job is not to tell all that is known about the research area, but to construct a coherent summary of past theory and research that logically demonstrates the importance of the research hypotheses for the study.

Reporting Past Findings

The fact that the literature review is motivated by the need to ground the study is not meant to imply that one should ignore past findings that might tend to contradict one's preferred theory. To the contrary, a hallmark of scientific inquiry is the careful consideration of all available evidence. (And remember that reviewers will be selected from among experts in the research area, so that glaring omissions in your literature review will likely not go unnoticed.)

When there are contradictions in past research findings, this can pose both challenges and opportunities for your study. The least effective approach to apparent discrepancies in the literature is simply to describe conflicting findings and summarize by stating that past findings are mixed. Although this approach acknowledges potentially disparate findings (which is a good thing), it is minimally informative for readers new to the area and provides no rationale to support the choices made in your study.

When researchers are faced with apparently conflicting findings, we suggest two considerations derived from meta-analytic thinking about integrating findings across studies: (a) Compare effect sizes, not only *p* values, from past studies, and (b) consider differences in study characteristics (e.g., research design, measurement procedures, population, settings) that might account for differences in findings.

APA's Task Force on Statistical Inference (TFSI; Wilkinson & TFSI, 1999) articulated the methodological consensus that *effect sizes*, which quantify the strength of associations among variables, represent the most precise summaries of study findings, and that investigators should report effect sizes and confidence intervals (CI) for tests of all major hypotheses. This recommendation was incorporated into the sixth edition of the *Publication Manual of the American Psychological Association* (APA, 2010). Effect sizes derived from regression and correlation analyses include the correlation coefficient (r), the unstandardized regression coefficient (B), and the standardized regression coefficient (β). Effect sizes for group comparison analyses (e.g., *t* test, *F* test) include ω^2 and η^2, but the most readily interpretable effect size is usually the standardized mean difference, or Cohen's *d* (J. Cohen, 1988).

As Schmidt (1992) noted, effect sizes are important not only for reporting findings from original studies but also for drawing cumulative conclusions from past literature—for addressing the question, "What do data really mean?" (p. 1173). A simple thought experiment illustrates the importance of this insight. Imagine that you are reviewing a research literature in which you are able to locate only two studies, and they come to discrepant conclusions. Study A ($N = 200$) finds a significant difference between two groups on the outcome variable, whereas Study B ($N = 40$) does not. Your conclusion, on the basis of the *p*-values alone, must be that findings examining this group difference are mixed—one study rejected the null hypothesis ($p < .05$), but the other failed to reject ($p > .05$). When you look carefully at the research reports, however, you find that both studies followed the recommended practice and reported Cohen's *d* for the group comparison—and $d = 0.32$ (indicating a small-to-medium difference between groups) in both studies. Thus, the two studies found exactly the same group difference (perfect replication), and the apparent discrepancy was simply due to the difference in sample sizes. (Study A had sufficient statistical power to reject H_0, whereas Study B did not.) Clearly, if you relied on the p values (i.e., conclusions of the significance tests) to summarize the findings in this literature, your summary would be misleading. By examining the effect sizes, we can see that the findings are consistent across studies.

Thus, one obvious explanation to consider for apparent inconsistencies in the findings of past studies is artifactual. Inconsistencies can arise when we focus only on results of significance tests, simply because sample size (and therefore statistical power) differs among studies. Even when the effect sizes themselves differ (as is typically the case), one should consider whether these differences are greater than would be expected because of sampling error (Schmidt, 1992).

In recommending that you report effect sizes (as well as the results of the significance tests) for previous studies in your literature review, we are not suggesting that a meta-analysis of all past literature is needed every time one wants to conduct a new study in a research area. But simply reporting effect sizes—for example, "X and Y were significantly and moderately correlated ($r = .29, N = 72$)" instead of "X and Y were found to be related"—can be useful for making predictions about the likely magnitude of the associations between variables in your data, which assists with planning for your study (e.g., determining sample size through power analysis) and provides a benchmark for interpreting your findings in the discussion section. This practice can also prevent problems caused by misinterpreting artifactual "differences" among findings of previous studies, as just noted. Effect sizes are readily available for studies reporting regression coefficients and correlation coefficients. Older studies reporting group comparisons often did not report effect sizes, although tools for computing those effect sizes from study data (e.g., Del Re, 2010) can make this process fairly painless and will be briefly described at the end of this chapter.

After examining effect sizes from prior studies, if you find meaningful patterns of differences, readers will be interested in your speculations about possible explanations of these differences. In meta-analysis, this is referred to as the question of *moderators* of the X–Y association—study characteristics that help to predict when (i.e., in what settings or populations; using what measures or research designs) X and Y are likely to be strongly as opposed to weakly or only modestly related. Although such inferences in the context of a narrative literature review are necessarily speculative, they may suggest directions for your own study or for future research in the area, to better understand the generalizability of observed effect sizes. Even speculative explanations for observed variation in study findings are much more useful to readers, and make a stronger contribution to the literature, than a simple list of contradictory results from past research with a summary that findings have been mixed.

Although it is almost always desirable to scrutinize prior research in an area to look for patterns (i.e., possible moderator variables), it is important to keep in mind what may be the most likely explanation for variation in study effect sizes, which is *sampling error*. Sampling theory predicts that if a large number of replicated studies are conducted in a given research area, there will be variability in the obtained effect sizes because of sampling error, but the average effect size across all studies will converge on the population value. For example, if the correlation between X and Y in the population is $r = .30$, and many samples of size $N = 60$ are drawn from this population, sampling theory predicts that 95% of the study effect sizes will fall between $r = .05$ and $r = .52$. This means that if only a handful of studies ($N = 60$) addressing this research question have been conducted, it would not be at all unusual for some of them to find relatively weak effect sizes (say, $r = .20$) and others relatively strong effect sizes (say, $r = .40$), and no explanation is needed for this variation other than sampling error. Even with a moderate to large $N = 120$, the 95% CI for the sampling distribution around $r = .30$ is [.13, .46]. Thus, one should be cautious about concluding that even relatively large differences in findings reflect some substantive difference between studies, especially when sample sizes are small or moderate. Indeed, the first question asked by meta-analysts before searching for moderators to explain variation in study effect sizes is whether the observed variation is significantly greater than would be expected because of chance (sampling error) alone.

Correlational Data and Causal Theories

We can all recall learning in our introductory research design classes that correlation does not imply causation. If hem lengths decrease as stock prices increase, this is not a basis for concluding that shorter skirts cause a buying frenzy. Other possible explanations for this association include causation in the opposite direction (e.g., a "hot" economy has an effect on cultural tastes and therefore on the fashion industry) or joint causation by a third variable (e.g., Alan Greenspan's "irrational exuberance"), with no causal connection at all between skirts and stocks—a relation termed *spurious* by statisticians (Cohen, Cohen, West, & Aiken, 2003). Thus, research design texts hold up the randomized experiment as the gold standard for causal inference and caution against drawing causal conclusions when examining correlational associations among measured (as opposed to manipulated) variables.

Given this background, researchers may feel justifiably reluctant to assert that they are testing causal hypotheses using correlational data. We endorse this scruple. At the same time, because effective correlational research, like effective experimental research, is theory driven, it is important to acknowledge that in general the research hypotheses are derived from causal theories about the relations among constructs and to be explicit about the rationale for the underlying theory.

In his classic text, *Correlation and Causality*, Kenny (1979) explained the basis for causal inferences from correlational data as follows:

1. Statistical inferences are based on (a) a set of assumptions about how the data were generated (the *model*) and (b) procedures for summarizing the observed relations among variables (the *statistical methods*).
2. Inferences from statistics to population parameters are inherently probabilistic (e.g., one concludes in rejecting H_0 that there is only a small probability that the observed data could have been sampled from a population in which H_0 is true), so that even in experimental studies, statistical inferences should not be treated as *proof* of the research hypothesis.
3. What is tested by the statistical methods is the fit of the data to the model. The model itself is an assumption that is not tested by statistical analysis.

For example, Kahn and Garrison (2009) wished to test a mediational theory about the relationship between depression (X) and emotional self-disclosure (Y). They proposed that the relation between these two constructs is negative (higher scores on depression tend to be associated with lower scores on disclosure, and vice versa) and is mediated by a third variable, emotional avoidance (M). They collected data on these three variables in a sample of college students ($N = 853$) and analyzed them using a mediational model. That is, they assumed that correlations among the three variables could be explained by the underlying causal relations among the three variables ($X \rightarrow M \rightarrow Y$). They found that the data fit the model adequately and concluded that there was support for the mediational model.

According to Kenny (1979), this type of evidence is grounds for making causal inferences so long as these inferences are understood to be contingent on the model being evaluated. In essence, this inference could be stated explicitly as follows: *The patterns of associations in the data conform to the predictions of the assumed (mediational) model.* As Kenny noted, the strength of the inference is necessarily different for confirmatory, as compared with disconfirmatory, findings:

> Especially for correlational inference, disconfirmation is usually more convincing than confirmation. A disconfirmation implies that the data are not compatible with the hypothesis. A confirmation shows the opposite that the data are compatible with the hypothesis. But the data also normally confirm a host of alternative inferences. . . . Confirmatory evidence is strong then, only if there are no plausible rival explanations of an effect. (p. 2)

To strengthen the inferences made from correlational studies, then, it is necessary to rule out *plausible rival explanations* for the observed pattern of relations. To take a basic example, the correlation between depression (X) and emotional avoidance (M) can come about because depression causes emotional avoidance, as proposed by Kahn and Garrison (2009), but might also arise because of causation in the opposite direction, that is, people who avoid their emotions tend to become more depressed. To render this possible explanation for their findings less plausible, Kahn and Garrison argued for their preferred explanation on theoretical grounds (citing Campbell-Sills & Barlow's 2007 emotion dysregulation theory of emotional disorders) and also on empirical grounds (citing Gross & John's 2003 experimental study showing that induced negative affect led to decreased emotional expression). Providing both theoretical and empirical support for the assumed causal model in the review of literature strengthened the basis for causal inferences from Kahn and Garrison's confirmatory findings by ruling out (or at least rendering less plausible) one possible alternative explanation for the observed findings.

Kenny (1979) described two additional ways to strengthen the basis for causal conclusions from correlational data sets. To provide a strong basis for the conclusion that X causes Y, it is necessary to provide evidence not only that an association (e.g., a correlation) exists between X and Y but also that (a) X precedes Y in time and (b) the association between X and Y is not spurious (i.e., it does not result because both X and Y are the effects of a third variable Z).

Of these two considerations, ruling out spuriousness is by far the more challenging for researchers in the social sciences, generally, and in counseling psychology, in particular. In the causal modeling literature, this is described as the problem of *model specification*. To satisfy yourself and your reviewers that the observed correlation between X and Y represents a causal association between these two variables, it is necessary to provide a fairly detailed analysis of the two constructs and to consider which third variables are candidates to explain the observed (or expected) association. The potential contribution of your study can be greatly increased by selectively including one or more exogenous variables that may plausibly explain the covariation between X and Y. If X and Y are still significantly associated even when controlling for this potential confound, then the third variable does not (completely) account for the X–Y association, which provides a stronger basis for inferring a causal relation between X and Y.

A well-known debate in developmental psychology exemplifies concerns about spuriousness in the testing of causal hypotheses using correlational data. Harris (1998) reviewed an extensive literature linking parenting style (often categorized as permissive, authoritative, or authoritarian) to children's behavior problems. Harris pointed out that an obvious third variable that should be ruled out to strengthen the support for the causal theory underlying these studies (i.e., that poor parenting causes negative outcomes for the child) is heredity. Essentially, the theory posits that ineffective parental behavior leads to ineffective behavior for the child, but an alternative explanation for this correlation is that parents and children share a genetic predisposition to effective or ineffective behavior. Harris reviewed evidence from twin and sibling studies showing that heritability explains significant proportions of variance in behaviors similar to those measured in parenting style research and that shared environment (which would include parenting style if parents adopt the same style with both siblings) consistently accounts for little or no variance. This argument places the burden of proof on researchers wishing to demonstrate the effects of parenting style to rule out this plausible rival explanation for their findings, by designing studies that control for genetic influences to provide support for the causal link between parenting behaviors and children's behaviors.

Kenny's (1979) other consideration, time precedence, can be addressed by conducting longitudinal studies that measure putative causal variables at an earlier time point and putative effects later. If X is measured at Time 1 and Y at Time 2, it is less plausible to claim that a correlation between the two reflects the effect of Y on X. For example, studies of the effects of working alliance on outcomes in psychotherapy typically measure working alliance relatively early in the therapeutic relationship and use this score to predict outcomes at the end of therapy.

Because of the time precedence of working alliance, it seems plausible to claim that working alliance causes outcomes and not vice versa. (Note that it is logically possible that even this correlation arises because outcomes cause working alliance: End-of-treatment outcomes are likely to be related to intermediate outcomes—improvement in symptoms early in treatment—and such early improvement may affect the working alliance between client and therapist. Campbell & Kenny, 1999, described cross-lagged panel designs intended to address this potential alternative explanation for cross-temporal correlational findings.)

In most areas of psychological research, this type of longitudinal data collection is feasible to strengthen the basis for causal inferences from correlational data. However, it is rarely used in tests of mediation models, which greatly weakens the types of inferences that can be made on the basis of statistical tests of mediation (Judd & Kenny, 2010; Maxwell & Cole, 2007). Although Kahn and Garrison (2009) used concurrent data for their mediational analysis in Study 1, they recognized this limitation and conducted Study 2 in which the measurement of depression (X) preceded the measurement of emotional avoidance (M) and emotional self-disclosure (Y) related to a specific unpleasant event. In Study 2, then, there was a stronger basis for concluding that X–M and X–Y associations reflected the effects of depression (X) on the emotion regulation variables. In this second study, depression predicted both emotional avoidance (related to the unpleasant event) and emotional self-disclosure (also related to this event), although the test of $X \rightarrow M \rightarrow Y$ mediation was not significant. Kahn and Garrison's work provided an example of a multistudy effort that used individual components to test hypotheses while also ruling out leading rival explanations for key findings. Thus, the components are synergistic, with each study enhancing the other's contribution to the literature.

Summary

The literature review provides the theoretical grounding for your research hypotheses and situates your study within the existing literature in the area. We suggest you think about the introduction of your manuscript as the foundation upon which you build the edifice of your method, results, and discussion. Both the foundation and the building (i.e., the study) that you construct upon it must be strong enough to remain standing when the metaphoric winds of an 80% rejection rate have blown down four out of five houses around you. Be sure to review relevant prior research in the area, with special attention to apparently discrepant findings. Discrepancies should be evaluated on the basis of study effect sizes, not just the *p*-values (significance tests), as the latter are a joint function of effect size and sample size. Use the introduction to persuade readers that the study you have conducted provides a well-considered test of a theory important to the field.

Another function of the literature review is to strengthen the basis for making causal inferences from your findings, especially when the data to be presented are correlational rather than experimental. In this case, it is important to provide a justification on the basis of theory and prior research for each hypothesized causal path (e.g., to explain why it is plausible to assume that X causes Y and not vice versa). It is also important to give some thought to whether there is reason to believe that the X–Y association is spurious (i.e., that the association is not one of cause–effect, but rather is a result of joint causation of X and Y by a third variable, Z). It may be important in the introduction to the study to render such possible rival explanations less plausible by reference to prior empirical findings or theory (although such arguments may also be made in the discussion section). More important, when plausible alternative explanations (such as a candidate for a third variable Z) exist, it may be important to measure Z in your study, to show that the X–Y association persists when Z is statistically controlled.

In general, the manuscript introduction will provide the strongest theoretical foundation for the study if the authors ground the research hypotheses in a theoretical framework (with due attention to past research) and attend to the complexities of drawing causal inferences from the type of data (often correlational data) that will be described in the Method section.

OPERATIONALIZING CONSTRUCTS: THE METHOD–INSTRUMENTS SECTION

We have discussed some of the implications of a theory-driven approach to science for developing effective research procedures. A thorough review of the literature may suggest important confounding (*third* or *exogenous*) variables that should be included as statistical controls to strengthen the basis for causal inferences, especially when the data to be collected are correlational. Longitudinal data collection can also help to rule out a pervasive ambiguity present when two variables are measured concurrently (i.e., does *X* really cause *Y* or is it equally plausible to claim that *Y* causes *X*?). Failure to incorporate these design elements can constitute a fatal flaw in that it compromises the interpretation of study findings, particularly when there is no strong theoretical or empirical argument in support of the proposed causal model.

Once researchers have introduced theory-based research hypotheses and determined which variables should be measured, a significant step in the development of the research plan is the choice of measurement procedures used to operationalize these constructs in the study. In this section, we introduce two important and related considerations that are relevant to this decision: (a) evidence for construct validity and (b) the importance of multimodal measurement to rule out method covariance as a pervasive alternative explanation for observed correlations. We also offer advice about the content of the measures subsection of the method section, to address reviewers' and readers' questions about construct validity. Finally, we conclude with some miscellaneous observations about other issues related to the research plan that can strengthen or weaken the contribution of the study.

Construct Validity and Selection of Measures

A critical challenge for researchers in counseling psychology, and many other psychological disciplines, is that so many of the constructs we are interested in understanding are not directly observable or measurable. For example, we are interested in knowing the effects of psychotherapeutic intervention on psychological symptoms (e.g., depression) or psychological well-being, but no objective measures of these outcomes are available. Thus, researchers may consult one or more sources of information, including the client himself or herself, the therapist providing the intervention, acquaintances of the client (e.g., spouse, parent), and independent trained observers (Schulte, 1997). Each of these potential sources has a unique perspective on the person and the characteristic to be measured, and it is often possible to find standardized measures designed for use by each (so that there is some evidence that the scores derived from the measure constitute a reliable and valid index of the construct of interest).

If measures from different sources showed strong agreement, then decisions about which sources to include would not be too consequential for study findings. Studies including measures of the same psychotherapy process or outcome variables from different sources often find only modest agreement (Lambert & Hill, 1994), however, so that study results are likely to vary depending on which sources are selected. In addition, researchers who elect to use self-report measures (the most common data source in counseling psychology research) are often faced with a choice among numerous existing measures. Thus, the decision about how to translate theoretical constructs into data collection procedures is a complex one, and it is desirable to have a rational basis for making choices among different possible measures. For this purpose, investigators are advised to seek out (and report in the Method section) evidence for the *construct validity* of scores derived from a measure for their intended use in the study (Messick, 1989).

Cronbach and Meehl (1955) defined inquiries in construct validity as attempts to answer the question, "What constructs account for variance in test performance?" (p. 282). Implicit in this formulation is the notion that respondents score high or low on psychological measures (tests) for a variety of reasons. It is to be hoped that one source of variance is related to the person's actual standing on the targeted construct. But many other factors, including measurement error, systematic response biases, transient mood states, and test-related motives (e.g., test anxiety; desire to make a good impression), also partially determine where each person's score falls within the distribution of scores in the sample. To put the matter succinctly, not all score variance is true score variance, and it is important for users of the measure to be aware of evidence about what other factors contribute and to what extent. Although various types of evidence (e.g., judgments about appropriateness of item content; predictive or criterion-related validity findings) may inform our evaluations of construct validity, there is a growing consensus among methodologists that, fundamentally, "*all* validation is construct validation" (Cronbach, 1984, p. 126).

One implication of this perspective is that, like the development of a research question, the selection of appropriate measurement procedures must be theory driven. It is emphatically not sufficient to choose a measure simply because it has the right name, or even because others have used it before for a similar purpose. Because choice of measures is so consequential for study findings and for the intended inferences based on these findings, it behooves researchers to familiarize themselves with previous applications of the scale and to evaluate available evidence with an eye toward establishing (a) that the scale does indeed measure the intended construct and (b) what artifacts (e.g., measurement error) and potential confounds (e.g., systematic variance because of socially desirable responding; reactivity) also contribute to score variance. Hoyt, Warbasse, and Chu (2006), in a primer on construct validation, provided a relatively detailed analysis of findings using self-report measures of multicultural competence, to illustrate how a careful analysis of construct validity could be informative for future users of these measures and could suggest further directions for research and theory development related to the underlying construct.

Although reliability and validity are treated as separate features of a measurement procedure in classic psychometric texts (e.g., Crocker & Algina, 1986), it can be argued that this approach is mainly for convenience of exposition and that reliability evidence is just another form of evidence for construct validity. Indeed, this is the perspective taken by generalizability theory, which examines multiple facets that contribute to score variance, and it does not make a sharp distinction between facets traditionally classified as measurement error (e.g., variance in scores attributable to the selection of the item set or to the testing occasion) and those that might be considered to reflect substantive effects (e.g., setting or contextual variance; Cronbach, Gleser, Nanda, & Rajaratnam, 1972). Nonetheless, reliability of scores is generally established by reporting one or more established *reliability coefficients,* whereas validity evidence requires a more complex argument relating to the theory of the construct (what Cronbach & Meehl, 1955, referred to as its *nomological network*) and available empirical findings involving the chosen measurement procedure. Thus, although reliability evidence and validity evidence are both relevant to establishing construct validity of scores, procedures for reporting these two types of evidence are distinct.

Documenting evidence of score reliability.
Reliability coefficients quantify the proportion of variance that is consistent across replicated measurements. Conventionally a reliability coefficient of $r_{XX} = .80$ would be interpreted as indicating that 80% of the variance in scores was replicable (usually called *true score*) variance, and $1 - r_{XX} = .20$ reflects the proportion of score variance attributable to the form of measurement error that was the focus of the reliability study.

One aspect of score reliability that is often overlooked is that a single reliability coefficient does not usually reflect all of the types of error that are relevant to the research design. So Cronbach's *alpha*, the most commonly reported coefficient of reliability, estimates the proportion of variance that is consistent over items. Another familiar reliability index is the *test–retest reliability coefficient*, which is the correlation between scores on the same measure administered on two separate testing occasions. Schmidt, Le, and Ilies (2003) demonstrated that these two coefficients (which they called coefficients of *equivalence* and *stability*, or CE and CS, respectively) quantify the contributions of different types of systematic error variance and noted that frequently both sources of error are relevant to the research application of a measure. (This is because many of the constructs we study are theorized to be stable over time and should also not vary much over equivalent sets of items.)

Given that coefficient alpha can be computed whenever a multi-item measure is administered to a sample of respondents, whereas an estimate of test–retest reliability is more costly to obtain, it is not uncommon for authors of research reports to provide evidence of the former but not the latter. To see how problematic this is, Schmidt et al. (2003) computed both alpha and a combined reliability estimate called the *coefficient of equivalence and stability* (CES; Cronbach, 1947) in a data set ($N = 235$ undergraduate research participants), including diverse measures of personality, intellectual functioning, and positive and negative affect, with replicated measurement over a 1-week interval.

Schmidt et al. (2003) found that for all but one construct (Openness to Experience, one dimension of the five-factor model of personality), investigators who consult only coefficient alpha to determine score reliability overestimate the reliability of scores by between 2% and 18%. The largest differences between alpha and CES were for measures of positive and negative affect (18% and 14%, respectively) and Neuroticism (11%), which suggests that measures of trait affect are likely to be more unstable than measures of personality traits, even over a relatively short retest interval.

There are measurement applications in which one or both of these two most commonly considered sources of error may not be considered relevant. Although test–retest reliability coefficients of $r_{XX} = .80$ are considered desirable in many applications, the appropriate magnitude of this reliability coefficient depends on the nature of the construct. By definition, psychological *states* are more transient than *traits,* and instruments designed to measure states are therefore expected to have more modest test–retest coefficients. Indeed, a test–retest coefficient (e.g., over a 4-week interval) of $r_{XX} = .80$ for a measure of mood states (expected to be relatively transient) is evidence *against* the construct validity of the scale.

By the same token, measures of many constructs treat the items as indicators caused by an underlying (latent) characteristic. For example, a person's performance on items or subtests of an intelligence quotient test is presumed to be caused by the underlying trait (intelligence). Bollen and Lennox (1991) referred to this type of item as an *effects indicator* because item scores reflect the effects of the latent construct on behavior (e.g., test performance; responses to items reflecting attitudes, thoughts, or feelings). When measures are composites of effects indicators, item intercorrelations are expected to be moderate or even high, and a high coefficient alpha (e.g., $r_{XX} = .80$) for the scale scores is desirable.

Another type of indicator that is used in some measures of psychological characteristics is the *causal indicator.* Causal indicators are theorized to cause the latent construct, rather than the other way around (Bollen & Lennox, 1991). For example, measures of psychological stress may include a list of stressors (e.g., work transition, death of a loved one, recent relocation), each of which creates stress for the individual, and the sum of these stressful life events may be taken as an index of current life stress. Conceptually, we expect that few individuals have experienced nearly all of these events. Thus, measures composed of causal indicators frequently show relatively low intercorrelations between items and (therefore) relatively weak internal consistency reliability. Because weak internal consistency is expected for such measures, a low coefficient alpha (e.g., $r_{XX} = .50$) may not be a fatal flaw, provided that there is evidence of construct validity (Bollen & Lennox, 1991). Low internal consistency reliability (alpha), although expected on the basis of the measure design, will still attenuate the correlation between scores on causal indicator measures and scores on measures of related constructs (Schmitt, 1996; see also Schmidt & Hunter, 1996).

Researchers selecting measures for a study should be aware that a single reliability coefficient is generally not an adequate index of the proportion of variance in scores that is attributable to measurement error, because often only one source of error is taken into account in the design of the reliability study. Investigators should think carefully about what sources of error are likely to contribute to score variance and to report reliability coefficients reflecting each of these sources of variance. When more than two sources of error are relevant to the measurement procedure, it is advantageous to use generalizability theory (Hoyt & Melby, 1999;

Shavelson & Webb, 1991) to quantify the proportion of replicable variance in scores. Having a single reliability (or generalizability) coefficient is advantageous for understanding the likely effect of measurement error on study results, which is generally to attenuate effect sizes (Cohen et al., 2003; Hoyt et al., 2006; Schmidt & Hunter, 1996). It is important to be able to take this fact into account when interpreting study findings.

Documenting evidence of construct validity.
When writing the Measures subsection of the Method section, you should report evidence for both reliability and validity of each measure. Because readers will not have easy access to the item content of your scales, you should provide one or two example items from each scale, to help readers assess content validity. (You should also report how you computed scale scores—i.e., mean of items, sum of items, or some other procedure—to assist with interpretation of mean differences, regression coefficients, and other unstandardized effect size measures.) Evidence of score reliability from past studies should include coefficients relevant to the sources of error that are important for your study (usually both time and items are relevant as sources of measurement error) and that say enough about the sample (including the sample size, and the retest interval, for CS) to enable readers to judge whether these past findings are likely to generalize to the present application of the measure. Only report coefficients for the scales you will use in your analyses. (For example, if you will analyze subscale scores, report coefficients for subscales and not the total score.) For multi-item scales, always report Cronbach's alpha (CE) for your sample.

Presentation of validity evidence is more complicated because construct validity cannot be summarized with a single index but rather is based on a careful review of the empirical findings for the scale, to see whether it performs as predicted by theory about the underlying construct. As discussed for literature reviews generally, you should report effect sizes for past studies as well as whether these effect sizes differed significantly from zero. And it is important to briefly describe the sample (and certainly the sample size) so that readers can judge the

likely generalizability of these findings to your population of interest. In describing the psychometric properties of a measure, it is important to remember that reliability and validity are not intrinsic properties of an instrument (Wilkinson & TFSI, 1999); rather they are a joint function of a particular measure, the assessment context, and the specific sample. Although not a fatal flaw, one of the most frequent requests for revisions we make is to ask authors to add a brief description in their method/ instruments section such as "in a sample of 40 counseling center clients" or "in a sample of 110 college undergraduates" to the reports of psychometric data they glean from previous research.

It is helpful to consider evidence for both *convergent* and *discriminant* validity (Hoyt et al., 2006) to demonstrate both overlap with other measures of similar constructs and limited overlap with constructs that are related but conceptually distinct. For a frequently used scale, you will not be able to summarize all available evidence, so you will need to be selective and emphasize the points you think are most persuasive in establishing that scores on this scale reflect the target construct.

Instrument Development Studies

Concerns about validity have special importance in studies specifically designed to develop a new instrument. Such research holds the promise of making a particularly valuable contribution to the field, especially when the underlying construct is of great interest and no standardized measure is yet available. A wealth of useful resources is available to guide researchers who plan to develop a new instrument (e.g., Clark & Watson, 1995; Worthington & Whittaker, 2006). Given our space limitations in this chapter, we only wish to call readers' attention to the earliest stage of this process—the definition of the construct and generation of items to be administered in the development of the measure. Errors at the data analysis stage of measurement development are fixable, because researchers can always reanalyze their data and report a new set of results. But problems with the item pool constitute a fatal flaw and will likely result in the rejection of a manuscript even if the data analyses are skillfully done.

Essentially, the question editors and reviewers must ask is whether the initial pool contained a sufficient number of items to tap each critical aspect of the overarching construct, or whether the pool was constricted by the researchers' potentially limited perspective of the construct. The consequences of publishing a measure that omits an important component of the construct are especially damaging for future research because experience has shown that measures are rarely expanded after their initial publication. The researchers who develop the first measure of a construct have a tremendous influence on the scholarly community for many years to come. Because future measures will tend to be validated in part by examination of their correlations with existing measures, the initial operationalization of a construct becomes foundational in establishing the meaning of that construct going forward.

Like so many other editorial decisions, judgments about the sufficiency of an initial item pool involve a considerable degree of subjectivity. Generally, reviewers will have more confidence in an initial item pool if it contains considerably more items than the eventual measure. Reviewers will have more confidence in item pools generated by a panel of five to six experts rather than one to two researchers. *Expertise* can be defined as first-hand experience with the construct. It is particularly important for researchers to seek out such experts if they have no direct experience of the construct themselves. For example, a team of heterosexual researchers interested in developing a scale of lesbian, gay, bisexual, and transgendered experience of microaggressions would be well advised to recruit a panel of sexual minority men and women to generate the initial item pool. Focus group methods (e.g., Constantine, 2007) may be especially effective in generating a broadly representative initial item pool and can assist the researcher in generating items in the natural idiom of the target group.

Benefits of Multimodal Measurement

Measurement theorists have long encouraged the use of data from multiple sources to strengthen the basis for causal inferences based on correlational evidence. This approach has been referred to as *multiple operationalism* (Shadish et al., 2002), *critical*

multiplism (Houts, Cook, & Shadish, 1986), avoidance of *monomethod measurement* (Heppner et al., 2008), and addressing the problem of *shared method variance* (Campbell & Fiske, 1959).

In their classic paper on the multitrait–multimethod matrix, Campbell and Fiske (1959) advanced the idea that psychological measures are "trait–method units" (p. 84) and that variance in scores necessarily includes both trait variance and method variance. The disturbing implication of this analysis is that *covariance* between measures of different traits, but using the same measurement method, reflects both *trait covariance* and *method covariance*. For example, if a correlation of $r = -.35$ is obtained between scores on measures of trait neuroticism and trait forgiveness, we would like to infer that this effect size reflects the magnitude of association between the underlying constructs (or *traits*)—although attenuated somewhat because of the inevitable presence of measurement error. But if both sets of scores are based on the same measurement method (e.g., a self-report questionnaire), then this correlation is likely to be inflated to an unknown degree by shared method variance. In the absence of data from different sources, there is no empirical basis for conclusions about the extent to which the score correlation reflects the predicted association between constructs as opposed to the expected covariation attributable to monomethod bias.

This problem is pervasive in counseling psychology research, as demonstrated by Hoyt et al.'s (2006) survey of the 2004 volume of the *JCP*. These authors found that of 32 articles reporting primarily quantitative results, 29 (91%) employed monomethod measurement—all measures were derived from the same source (usually participant self-reports). Findings for these studies, which varied from relatively basic analyses of one or two predictors and a single criterion to complex structural models based on intercorrelations among many measured variables, are difficult to interpret when one recognizes that all of these correlations are based partly on trait covariance and partly on method covariance. Empirical evidence indicates that the correlations attributable primarily to common measurement methods (what Campbell & Fiske, 1959, called *heterotrait–monomethod* correlations) can be substantially larger than convergent validity correlations between multimodal measures of the same trait (so-called *monotrait–heteromethod* correlations; Campbell & Fiske, 1959; for a similar finding in variables assessing psychotherapy outcomes, see Pilkonis, Imber, Lewis, & Rubinsky, 1984).

To illustrate the problem, suppose a researcher collected ratings of therapists' empathy and quality of the working alliance from clients (E_c and W_c) and from trained observers (E_o and W_o). A basic requirement of this research design is that ratings of the same construct from different data sources should be more highly correlated than ratings of different constructs from the same source—for example, $r(E_c, E_o) > r(E_c, W_c)$. Collecting data from multiple perspectives allows researchers to test this assumption and helps to rule out the rival hypothesis that an observed association between empathy and working alliance is due primarily to common method variance. Because of potential monomethod bias, there are serious questions about how much can be learned from studies that consist only of analyzing correlations among self-report questionnaires, even when the analyses are technically sophisticated (e.g., structural equation models; multilevel models).

Although we have not repeated this analysis with more recent volumes of *JCP*, it is unlikely that this situation has changed dramatically since 2004. Monomethod studies are so predominant among manuscripts submitted to *JCP* that the occasional study that uses multimodal measurement really stands out. The fact that authors of these studies can state with confidence that observed effect sizes reflect trait correlations (uncontaminated by method covariance) puts them on a much stronger footing to arrive at implications for theory and practice. Although it is certainly possible that such manuscripts contain other fatal flaws that would result in a decision to reject, other considerations being equal, a study employing multimodal measurement generally does a better job of ruling out method covariance as a plausible explanation for observed associations. Thus, it is much more likely to be evaluated as making a substantive contribution than a similar study using only a single measurement method.

The continued allegiance to monomethod measurement in counseling psychology (and in psychology generally) is partly attributable to researchers' lack of awareness of the problems this practice poses for interpretation of findings and is doubtless also partly due to inertia. (If researchers select measures on the basis of what has been popular in previous research in the area, and if self-reports have been popular because they are easy to develop and administer, then the practice of monomethod measurement will to some extent be self-perpetuating.) Researchers may reason that because they want to study internal states (e.g., attitudes, feelings), self-reports are the natural measurement method—or may be unaware that observer, expert, or peer (e.g., spouse) ratings may be useful sources of information on these characteristics. A final factor that may be relevant is that researchers are familiar with formulaic analyses useful when each construct is operationalized with a single self-report questionnaire, but they are less certain about how to address research hypotheses when multiple measures (using multiple methods) have been collected for some or all constructs. SEM is an especially attractive option when multimodal measures are available and a sample large enough to support these methods can be collected because multiple measures can be treated as indicators of the same latent construct. Hoyt and McCullough (2005) provided an overview of issues of multimodal measurement and illustrative examples of several other types of analysis in addition to SEM that capitalize on the multifaceted data generated in multimodal studies, in the context of research on interpersonal forgiveness.

Summary

Careful selection of measures is a critical element of research design. One important criterion is construct validity, which is a summary judgment based on multiple forms of evidence. The most universally fatal flaw, in terms of an error that is virtually never possible to correct through revision, is a failure to adequately operationalize a key construct. If a measure is not valid for the purpose that the researcher intends *with the selected research population*, not much can be done to salvage the project.

A second consideration is the desirability of multimodal measurement. Even if there is solid evidence for the validity of scores on measures of *X* and *Y* separately, the correlation between these two sets of scores provides ambiguous information about the true association between constructs, if both *X* and *Y* use the same measurement method. When it is possible to measure the same construct by several different methods, or even using a single method per construct but different methods for *X* and *Y*, the researcher is on much firmer ground in interpreting observed effect sizes. In these measurement conditions, the impact of method covariance on effect size estimates is reduced or eliminated.

Method and Procedures

Myriad potential fatal flaws can arise in connection with how a study is executed. These flaws can rarely be addressed in a revision because a bell cannot be unrung. Instead, the question for reviewers becomes one of how seriously the potential contribution of the study has been compromised by less than ideal execution. Even the most experienced researchers benefit from having colleagues review their proposed procedures with an eye to spotting potential problems. It is beyond the scope of this chapter to discuss all of these issues, but we do want to call two important aspects of research procedure to readers' attention.

A priori power analysis. A flaw that is not necessarily fatal, but can be critical for small-sample research, is the failure to conduct a power analysis to determine an appropriate sample size before data collection. Statistical power is the probability of obtaining a statistically significant finding, given that the hypothesized association (e.g., a correlation between two continuous variables; a difference in means between two groups on a designated outcome) exists with a given magnitude in the population (the *population effect size*). An a priori power analysis specifies (a) the likely population effect size; (b) the alpha level, or Type I error rate (usually $\alpha = .05$); and (c) the desired level of statistical power, or 1 minus the desired Type II error rate (often $1 - \beta = .80$) for the study. These three pieces of information are then input into a power calculator or are used to consult appropriate power tables (e.g., Cohen, 1988) to compute the sample size (n^*) needed to obtain the desired power.

When a researcher does not conduct an a priori power analysis, there is a danger that she or he will obtain nonsignificant results despite the fact that the research hypothesis is actually true in the population—simply because the study had too little statistical power to reliably detect the hypothesized effect. In other words, the researcher may make a Type II error, by failing to detect an effect (at statistically significant levels) that is present in the population. Both Type I and Type II errors entail costs to the research community and to those who depend on research results—but Type II errors are much more common (Schmidt, 1992). Type II error represents a missed opportunity for discovery that can be quite costly in social terms to the extent that other researchers rely on the mistaken conclusion and fail to pursue a promising treatment or effect.

Procedures for power analysis of mean differences are well established (e.g., Cohen, 1992), with accepted guidelines for estimating effect sizes even when prior data on the group difference of interest are unavailable. As Maxwell (2000) noted, however, power analysis for regression models (or for path coefficients in structural equations models) can be less intuitive, because the most tractable effect size metric (f^2; Cohen, 1988) may be difficult to estimate with confidence in many research contexts. Another pitfall of power analysis in multiple regression is that investigators sometimes base their sample size calculations on an estimate of the multiple R^2 for the full set of predictors. This value may indeed be readily estimated, but it will yield incorrect sample sizes (and usually inflated estimates of statistical power) when the research hypothesis involves the effect size for a single predictor (i.e., involves *B* or β rather than R^2).

Maxwell (2000) proposed several alternative methods to conduct power analyses by estimating correlations among predictors and criterion variables—an exercise that is generally more susceptible of either rational or empirical justification than is the case with estimates of f^2. Computerized assistance for these procedures is not available through most commercial power calculators but has been implemented by Kelley (2007), as briefly described at the end of this chapter.

Manipulation checks. The omission of a manipulation check in an experimental study can be a fatal flaw that calls the validity of the manipulated variable into question. Experimental studies are rare in counseling psychology, and they tend to be either treatment outcome studies or analogue studies of counseling. In any experimental study, it is important to document that the treatment conditions differed as planned. For studies of treatment efficacy, adherence ratings are used to demonstrate that the treatment was implemented as planned. (As Wampold, 2001, noted, additional design features are needed to establish that treatment effects are due to specific ingredients, but this is a separate issue.) In analogue studies, the manipulation may seem obvious to the researcher, but here also a manipulation check is needed. For example, Mallinckrodt and Helms (1986) portrayed counselors with and without a disability via videotape to undergraduate raters, but they made a serious error in not asking whether the raters perceived that the counselor was disabled. It is not the manipulation per se, but the subjects' perceptions of it that produces the effect. Researchers should document these perceptual differences empirically.

Designs that go beyond a dichotomous manipulation check to assess the quality of perceptions or intensity of reactions permit even stronger inferences about causality. For example, in an analogue study of the effects of cultural broaching statements, undergraduate raters could be assigned to two conditions in which a simulated first session is portrayed. The conditions would be identical except that in one the counselor initiates a discussion of her cultural differences with the client, whereas this discussion is skillfully edited out of a duplicate tape used for the other condition. Minimally the researchers should ask subjects in both conditions, after they have completed all ratings of the counselor and cannot go back to alter their responses, a yes–no manipulation check question about whether the counselor discussed her own culture. But consider the advantages of going a step further to ask two or three questions about the extent that subjects perceived the counselor to have discussed her culture, and if so, the degree to which they felt the discussion was appropriate. Doing so would allow

more nuanced analyses of overall group differences. In such a design, the variable assessing the intensity of the manipulation can be examined as a moderator of the hypothesized effect. Participants who view the cultural broaching session are likely to differ regarding the extent to which they perceive this component of the session as valuable or as competently executed by the counselor, and these differences can be included as a predictor of outcomes. Again, the point is that perceptions are important in determining participants' responses to experimental stimuli, and researchers using experimental designs should measure these perceptions and even analyze them as appropriate.

Order effects. Order effects can have a considerable influence on participant responses when researchers use a survey methodology (Schwarz, 1999). Much of the research on this issue has focused on the ordering of items within a questionnaire (and suggests that researchers relying on validity evidence from previous investigations are well advised to maintain the wording and ordering of items that was used in these prior studies). Logically, the same concerns apply when multiple questionnaires are administered. If the order of administration affects the observed correlations between measures, then order effects constitute a plausible rival hypothesis for these correlations. Naturally, there is no way to determine whether this is a problem if all participants complete the questionnaires in the same order. Thus, one way to improve the quality of survey research is to administer the questionnaires in different orders. (For example, there could be three sets of packets, each presenting the surveys in a different order, with participants randomly assigned to receive one of the three orderings.) Then, in the analysis, one can check for order effects and control for them as needed.

ANALYZING AND REPORTING STUDY RESULTS

An effective results section is organized as a narrative that tells the story of how data were analyzed and what was learned relevant to each of the research hypotheses. It should be clear to readers what the purpose of each analysis is and how it addresses the corresponding research question. The *Publication Manual of the American Psychological Association* (APA, 2010) states that effect sizes should routinely be reported for tests of the major findings and that CIs for these effect sizes should be reported "whenever possible" (p. 34). Effect sizes and CIs enhance the contribution of the study by focusing interpretation on the estimate of the strength of association between variables (rather than the significance test) and the precision of this estimate. Post hoc analyses may sometimes be useful to rule out plausible rival explanations for observed associations (see the earlier section Correlational Data and Causal Theories) or to clarify unexpected findings. Unplanned analyses should be identified as exploratory.

In previous sections, we have introduced the idea of using correlational and regression analyses to test causal models of relations among variables. Multiple regression is a flexible data analytic strategy (Cohen et al., 2003) that offers a variety of techniques such as simultaneous regression and hierarchical regression analyses, tests of mediational models, and tests of moderator (statistical interaction) hypotheses (Frazier, Tix, & Barron, 2004; Hoyt, Imel, & Chan, 2008). We have more to say about reporting and interpreting findings from regression analyses in the section Resources for Researchers later in this chapter. We begin this section with an overview of an even more flexible set of techniques developed for model testing—*SEM*, also known as *causal modeling* and *latent variable modeling*. Structural equation models are seen with increasing frequency in manuscripts submitted to *JCP* and can be an effective means to conduct the type of theory-driven research advocated in this chapter. Our focus here will be commonly encountered pitfalls that render these models less useful, and in some cases uninterpretable, and recommendations for more effective use of these techniques. Following this discussion, we will present general suggestions for planning and executing data analyses and writing effective Results sections.

Structural Equation Modeling: Some Concerns and Suggestions

We have argued that theory-driven research ideally consists of tests of theory-derived models that specify causal relations among variables. For relatively simple models, multiple regression is often the natural data analytic technique (especially when one or more of the predictor variables in the model are continuous rather than categorical). As theory and research in an area become better established, it becomes possible to specify more complex models, often with multiple dependent (*endogenous*) variables. These variables can be tested piecemeal using regression techniques (see Kenny, 1979), but this is cumbersome and provides tests of individual paths but not of the overall fit of the theoretical model to the data-derived covariance matrix. The provision of indexes of model fit makes SEM an appealing approach in such cases. In addition, SEM allows investigators to include multiple indicators of each latent construct in the model, which reduces the impact of measurement error on the estimated path coefficients.

The use of SEM in manuscripts submitted to and published in *JCP* appears to be on the rise, reflecting researchers' increased awareness of the value of this technique and possibly also the advent of software packages that allow investigators to specify and analyze SEMs via a mouse-and-menu interface rather than the more burdensome process of specifying the model matrixes directly. Although these developments are positive on balance, some methodologists have cautioned that "the move toward more user-friendly software implicitly creates the danger of individuals using the tools without clearly understanding their purposes and limitations" (Mueller, 1997, p. 354). Our goal in this section is to call readers' attention to some of the common pitfalls that lead reviewers to question the value of SEM-based findings and to point to recommended practices from methodologists seeking to improve the quality of published SEM investigations.

Importance of a theory-derived model.   We have emphasized the value of theory-derived research hypotheses (including justification of the posited causal relations on the basis of theory and past research, and attention to potential exogenous variables that pose a challenge to causal interpretation of observed associations between model variables) regardless of the type of analysis that is planned.

Researchers using SEM should be especially attentive to theoretical grounding, because they are typically testing relatively complex models that may imply a large number of hypotheses about which variables in the model are related to one another, which variable in each pair is the cause and which the effect, and (often overlooked) which pairs of variables are unrelated when other predictors of the effect variable are controlled.

For example, consider a relatively simple causal model involving four variables. There are six possible pairs of relationships among four variables. Perhaps the researcher believes that four of these paths are statistically significant. For each such posited path, one should consider the direction of causation and provide a compelling rationale for this. (When the direction of causation between two variables is unknown or unimportant, the relation can be represented by a two-headed arrow to indicate this.) The two omitted paths from this model also entail strong assumptions, namely, that the two variables share no variance once variance attributed to the remaining variables in the model is controlled. (Full mediation, as described by Baron & Kenny, 1986, is a special case of this situation involving a three-variable model.)

Failing to justify the specified paths (and also omitted paths) will produce results that are difficult to interpret regardless of whether the proposed model fits the data. As Judd and Kenny (2010, p. 118) noted, statistical software packages will dutifully test models that are conceptually nonsensical (they offered as an example a mediational model specifying gender as the mediator variable in a putative causal association between height and weight) and will offer results that either support or contradict it. But if the model being tested is not theoretically justified, then either supportive or contradictory findings are at best meaningless and at worst misleading.

To remind researchers of the fundamental importance of model specification in SEM, MacCallum, Wegener, Uchino, and Fabrigar (1993) presented a careful review of the problem of alternative models:

> For any given model, there will generally be alternative models, represented by different patterns of relations among the variables, that are indistinguishable from the original model in terms of goodness of fit to sample data. . . . Equivalent models cannot be distinguished in terms of goodness of fit. Rather, such models can be distinguished only in terms of other criteria such as interpretability of parameter estimates and meaningfulness of the model. (p. 185)

MacCallum et al.'s (1993) paper included illustrative reanalyses of published SEMs to show how reconfiguration of the structural model (following guidelines specified in the article to guarantee identical fit) produces multiple, identically well-fitting alternative models with different path coefficients and different implications about the network of causal relations among the variables. We believe that anyone who studies these examples will emerge with both greater motivation and an enhanced ability to think through the process of model justification in his or her own research. Unfortunately, too few researchers seem to have absorbed this lesson, to the detriment of published SEM studies. Writing almost 10 years later, McDonald and Ho (2002) lamented that fewer than 10% of the SEM studies they reviewed gave any attention to the existence of equivalent models, adding "further evidence . . . of persistent neglect of this question" (p. 77; see also Martens, 2005).

Selection of indicators. SEMs can be thought of as embodying two separate components: a *measurement model* specifying which of the observed variables load on (or serve as *indicators* of) each latent construct, and a *path model*, which depicts the theorized causal relations among these constructs (Anderson & Gerbing, 1988; McDonald & Ho, 2002, reserved the related term, *structural m odel* to refer to the full model resulting from combining measurement and path models). By representing each construct in the model as the common factor of its set of indicators (a confirmatory factor analysis procedure), investigators (a) obtain a test of the fit of this proposed measurement model and (b) reduce the impact of measurement error on the path coefficients in the path model. Thus, SEM represents one approach to addressing measurement error as a pervasive confound in psychological research, and the considerations of construct validity described with reference to the selection of measures for any quantitative investigation are even more important when selecting indicator variables for constructs in SEM.

If one purpose of latent variable modeling is to control for the effects of measurement error, investigators planning an SEM-based study should ask what sources of error are relevant to the constructs in the model. We have suggested, for example, that time (i.e., measurement occasion) and items are two sources of error relevant to the assessment of most psychological constructs. If raters are involved in deriving scores (as an alternative to self-reports), then two forms of rater bias will generally contribute to score variance (Hoyt, 2000). Although proponents of SEM have sometimes made rather sweeping claims that causal relations in latent variable models are estimated free of attenuation due to measurement error, DeShon (1998) noted that such claims are warranted only if indicators are judiciously chosen to control for the types of measurement error that are relevant to the indicator measures:

> It is certainly true that SEM can estimate relationships among latent variables that account for the measurement error present in the indicators of the latent variables. However, this does not imply that SEM is capable of providing estimates of the relationships among latent variables that correct for all sources of measurement error. There are multiple sources of error in most measurement systems, and applications of SEM rarely account for more than a single source of error. Hence, the parameter estimates in a structural equation model may be severely biased by unassessed sources of measurement error. (pp. 412–413)

For example, it is common for SEM studies published in *JCP* to include as multiple indicators three different self-report measures of the latent construct (or even three different *item parcels* derived from a single self-report measure of that construct). Because these indicators include different items, this

measurement procedure controls for the effects of item-based errors (i.e., measurement error resulting from item inconsistency, which is the error assessed by coefficient alpha). Specific variance because of item content is omitted from the common factor used to represent the latent construct in the SEM, and thus it does not attenuate the association of this construct with other variables in the model. If all three indicators were measured on the same occasion (as is generally the case in such studies), then they still share occasion-specific error. That is, if scores on one indicator are higher or lower because of the time of measurement (e.g., some participants were in a good mood on the day of research participation, whereas others were not), then the same is likely true of the other indicators because these questionnaires were completed on the same testing occasion. This means that occasion-specific variance (i.e., error variance because of temporal instability, as assessed by the coefficient of stability or CS) is shared by all indicators in the set. Shared variance becomes part of the common factor that represents the construct in the SEM, and it attenuates estimates of causal relations with any other variable in the model that was measured at a different time point. (When all variables in the model are measured concurrently, occasion-specific variance is shared between constructs as well as within constructs and has the potential to inflate estimates of path coefficients.)

Thus, it is accurate but incomplete to say that SEM controls for the effects of measurement error. A more precise statement is that *SEM controls for any source of measurement error that varies among the indicators for a given construct*. To control for item-specific variance, then, we should choose indicators that include different items. To control for temporal–instability variance, we should choose indicators that are measured at different time points. In addition, SEM provides a unique opportunity to reduce the pervasive confounding of substantive associations by personal response sets when self-report measures are correlated with other self-report measures (see the section Benefits of Multimodal Measurement). When at least one indicator for each construct is measured by some method other than self-report (e.g., acquaintance ratings, observer ratings, task performance), then personal response biases are not shared by all indicators, do not become part of the common factor that represents the construct, and therefore do not confound the estimates of the path coefficients between variables.

Our purpose in this section has been to call attention to the consequentiality of the choice of indicators for constructs to be modeled in SEM. From a purely statistical perspective, researchers may be more focused on the number of indicators: "Do I need two or three indicators per construct for model identification?" and "Where can I find a reliable third indicator of X?" We wish to emphasize that as important as these statistical considerations are, one should pay at least as much attention to the quality as to the quantity of indicators of latent constructs. To fully capitalize on the virtues of SEM in controlling for the effects of measurement error and other sources of nuisance variance, one can select indicators that do not share this source of variance. For example, if depression is modeled by both a self-report measure and a rating by a trained interviewer, then any variance in the former scores attributable to impression management biases do not contribute to the common factor variance (because they are not shared with the interviewer–report indicator) that represents the construct in the SEM.

Thus, a thoughtful choice of indicator variables, on the basis of an analysis of construct validity (in Cronbach & Meehl's, 1955, sense of a concern about "what constructs account for variance in test performance," p. 282), can greatly enhance the contribution of an SEM study to our understanding of relations among latent variables (Quintana & Maxwell, 1999).

Primacy of the path model. Numerous articles have been written specifically to improve data analysis and reporting of SEMs in counseling psychology research (e.g., Martens, 2005; Quintana & Maxwell, 1999; Weston & Gore, 2006). We will therefore not use space in this chapter to reiterate these conventions. We do, however, wish to call to readers' attention the suggestions of McDonald and Ho (2002) for improving reporting of SEM analyses, both because these suggestions seem particularly a propos for researchers using SEM for theory testing (the

theme of this chapter) and because we believe that researchers in counseling psychology, and in psychology as a whole, have not appreciated the value of McDonald and Ho's recommendations.

A guiding principle of McDonald and Ho's (2002) article is that although both the measurement and path models are important in SEM, it is typically the path model (i.e., the portion of the SEM that specifies a priori predictions about causal relations among the latent variables) that is of immediate interest as a test of theory-derived hypotheses. Given this premise, the authors offer various suggestions about reporting (e.g., depict the measurement model in tabular form so that the indicator variables can be omitted from the path diagram for greater clarity) and analysis. The most important of these, in our view, is the authors' suggestion about providing a specific test for the fit of the path model.

Most researchers reporting SEMs in McDonald and Ho's (2002) review (and also in the review of SEM research in counseling psychology by Martens, 2005) followed the recommendations of Anderson and Gerbing (1988) to conduct a two-step test of model fit. Step 1 is a test of the measurement model (with all paths between latent variables estimated so that they do not detract from model fit). If the measurement model shows satisfactory fit to the data, the analysis proceeds to Step 2, which is a test of the full model (with any paths omitted from the path model fixed to zero rather than freely estimated). Failure to find satisfactory fit at Step 2 can then be confidently attributed to problems with the path model because the measurement model demonstrated acceptable fit at Step 1.

The difficulty with this procedure, according to McDonald and Ho (2002), is that the difference between the degrees of freedom for measurement model and the full structural model can be relatively small, so that there is the potential at Step 2 for a poorly fitting path model to be masked by the good fit of the measurement model (which contributes to acceptable fit for the full model). Their proposed solution is simple and elegant, which is to partition the chi-square statistic (χ^2) for the full model into the χ^2 for the measurement model and the χ^2 for the path model (which, because measurement and structural models are nested, is simply the difference between the χ^2 for Steps 1 and 2). The degrees of freedom (*df*) for this χ^2 is the difference between the *df*s for Steps 1 and 2. The noncentrality parameter (*d*) can be similarly partitioned. This partitioning allows the researcher to compute a well-established index of model fit (root-mean-square error of approximation, or RMSEA) specifically addressing the fit of the path model.

McDonald and Ho (2002) conducted this reanalysis on the 14 studies in their review that provided sufficient information to partition χ^2, *df*, and *d* and that had concluded based on Step 2 of Anderson and Gerbing's (1988) procedure that there was evidence of acceptable fit for the structural model. In almost all of these cases, the path model by itself showed poor fit to the data. The authors concluded,

> If we are willing to rest on the established properties of the RMSEA, the results suggest that in all but a few cases the goodness of fit of the composite structural model, with its large number of degrees of freedom, conceals the badness of fit of the path model, with its much smaller number of degrees of freedom. . . . We tentatively conclude that in the majority of studies for which the measurement model information is available, the goodness of approximation of the path model may be unacceptable, contrary to the published conclusions. By extrapolation, this may be true of those studies for which this information is not available. (p. 75)

McDonald and Ho's (2002) survey of SEM studies encompassed a variety of basic and applied journals, including *JCP*, from a relatively narrow time interval (1995–1997). Nonetheless, the consistency of their findings raises concerns about whether researchers using SEM are looking in the wrong place for evidence to support the fit of the path model (i.e., the hypothesized causal relations among constructs) to the data. These findings also suggest that it may be common for researchers to accept a path model on the basis of evidence of the fit for the full structural model (as recommended by Anderson & Gerbing, 1988, Step 2), when in reality, the fit of

the path model is relatively poor. To the extent that SEM is used in the service of testing complex theories about networks of constructs, it seems desirable to address the fit of the path model using methods described by McDonald and Ho. On the basis of their findings for published SEM studies, there is some doubt about adequate specification of path models in many research areas and cause for renewed concern about the careful theoretical justification of both included and omitted paths in these models, as described in the earlier section Importance of a Theory-Derived Model.

Summary. Successful preparation of a manuscript involving SEM requires an added attention to model justification, including a rationale for variables included in the model, explicit consideration of omitted variables that may provide plausible rival explanations for hypothesized causal paths, justification of the assumed direction of causation for included paths, and also a rationale for the omitted paths. In planning for an SEM study, you should be aware of the problem of equivalent models, and explicitly consider alternative models that may provide equally viable explanations for the fit of your preferred model to the data. Equivalent models cannot be ruled out on empirical grounds, so must be rendered implausible by theoretical arguments or other empirical evidence (e.g., measuring putative causal and effect variables at different points in time). Without a strong theoretical argument supporting your preferred model, the contribution of the study can be doubtful.

A number of technical issues relevant to conducting and reporting SEM studies have important implications for the study's contribution to the literature. These include adequate description (preferably accompanied by a figure) of the a priori measurement and path models, reporting of descriptive statistics (i.e., correlation matrix, means, and *SD*s), criteria for interpreting model fit indexes, and especially the thorny problem of model modifications when (as is common) the a priori model does not fit the data acceptably. These issues are important but are well covered elsewhere (e.g., Martens, 2005; Quintana & Maxwell, 1999; Weston & Gore, 2006) and were not considered here. We do call readers' attention to two issues that we consider crucial and that seem to us to be underappreciated by researchers using SEM. We believe that researchers can greatly strengthen the contribution of SEM studies by judicious choice of indicators for the constructs of interest, following the principles outlined in the earlier section on multimodal measurement. Also, we recommend that researchers follow McDonald and Ho's (2002) suggested procedures to specifically examine the fit of the path model, because it is this model that directly tests the underlying theory of causal relations among the variables.

Finally, although we have given considerable space to issues we believe are critical for authors of manuscripts involving SEM, we do not mean to privilege this method over other important approaches to theory-testing analyses. In particular, there are some research areas (e.g., counseling process and outcome research, and most studies involving labor-intensive measurement methods) in which the relatively large sample sizes required for SEM analyses usually are not feasible. For these research applications, standard analysis of variance and regression models are often perfectly adequate. Indeed, APA's Task Force on Statistical Inference encouraged investigators to choose a "minimally sufficient analysis" to address the research question of interest (Wilkinson & TFSI, 1999, p. 598).

Other Data Analysis and Reporting Issues

Before concluding this section, we will briefly take up three other issues that are frequently a focus of revisions that action editors request or, occasionally, that prevent a study from being published.

Combining demographic groups. Before moving to tests of hypotheses, results sections typically begin with one or more preliminary analyses. By far the most frequent of these involves a comparison of male and female participants' mean scores on the variables of interest. Often, if significant differences are not found, this result is offered as a justification to combine data from men in women in subsequent analyses. The pattern of correlations between two variables can be significantly different for men and women, however, even though mean values are virtually identical in both groups. If sex is a variable of substantive interest, this variable can be dummy-coded (e.g., men = 0, women = 1) and a row for participant sex can be included in the correlation matrix. (The coding procedure should be described in the table note for ease of interpretation.) But it is illogical to use a test of mean differences (whether significant or not) as a basis for the decision about whether to analyze data from male and female participants separately. This decision should be made on the basis of the interaction of sex with whatever other predictor variable is being tested in relation to the outcome of interest. Even if this interaction is suspected (i.e., if you believe the strength of the effect differs for men and women), it is almost always preferable to address this question by analyzing data from the full sample and testing the moderator hypothesis directly, then graphing the interaction if it is significant (Frazier et al., 2004; Hoyt et al., 2008).

Verifying statistical assumptions. A class of omission we see frequently in reports of preliminary analyses concerns whether the data satisfy essential assumptions required of the statistical procedures that will be used to test hypotheses. Authors need to show that their data satisfy these assumptions. For example, group comparisons require relative homogeneity of variance across groups. Although many tests are robust with respect to some degree of violation of these requirements, it is incumbent on the researcher to show that critical assumptions about the data have been met sufficiently. The preliminary results section should provide a report of comprehensive data-screening procedures, including an examination of missing data and key statistical assumptions (see Tabachnick & Fidell, 2007, Chapter 4).

In counseling psychology studies, these screening procedures frequently reveal that one or more variables are not normally distributed. A solution we have seen in manuscripts submitted to *JCP* is that researchers use one or more arithmetic transformations with the hope of reducing skew or kurtosis to nonsignificant levels. Tabachnick and Fidell (2007, pp. 86–88) provided an excellent discussion of these methods but pointed out that results based on transformed data can be difficult to interpret.

Wilcox and Keselman (2003) discussed alternative procedures that offer many advantages over arithmetic transformations but that seem to have escaped the attention of many counseling psychology researchers (perhaps because they are not discussed in popular texts such as Tabachnick & Fidell, 2007). We believe that many studies in which data violate assumptions of normality and homoscedasticity could benefit from using what Wilcox and Keselman termed *modern* methods in contrast to *simple* arithmetic transformations. Their simulation studies show that simple methods do not prevent the problems with low statistical power that occur when data are not normally distributed, principally because outliers usually remain after transformation, even if skew is reduced. Significant problems occur even in cases in which scores in each group *are* normally distributed, but variances are significantly different (e.g., heteroscedasticity).

Wilcox and Keselman (2003) pointed out that in many applied research studies the tests for homogeneity of variance are so seriously underpowered that they lead researchers to conclude that variances are equivalent even for levels of differences between groups that seriously compromise conventional tests for mean differences. The modern methods Wilcox and Keselman have advocated using are statistical comparisons based on the *trimmed mean* and *Winsorized variance* (Staudte & Sheather, 1990). In this procedure, a certain proportion of the highest and lowest values (e.g., the top and bottom 20%) are recoded to the highest or lowest value remaining after trimming this proportion. Sample variance is calculated on the basis of these trimmed values. Wilcox and Keselman (2003) presented a convincing case that these methods offer better control of Type I error and higher statistical power than conventional methods under the practical conditions that most applied researchers face, where groups to be compared differ with respect to variance or degree of skew, where the data contain outliers, and when sample sizes are not very large.

Graphical presentation of findings. Competent use of graphs is an important skill for researchers. Graphical presentations of data are important for exploratory purposes (e.g., checking that data conform to distributional assumptions; examining scatterplots to see whether the relation between variables appears linear), and carefully prepared figures can provide readers with both more detail and more memorable representations of key findings than a comparable tabular presentation (Wilkinson & TFSI, 1999). Lane and Sándor (2009) provided very helpful guidelines and illustrations to assist researchers in making effective use of graphs to present findings.

RESOURCES FOR RESEARCHERS

If the proper tools are lacking, any technical task can feel like a thankless effort that results in a fairly amateurish product. Data analysis is no exception. Many tasks that are basic expectations (e.g., reporting effect sizes and CIs) and some that can greatly enhance the presentation of findings (e.g., effective use of graphics) go beyond the functionality routinely provided by commercial statistical software packages. One useful resource that appears to be relatively rarely used by counseling psychologists is the open-source statistical language R (R Development Core Team, 2009).

The R base package is free and may be downloaded from the R project website (http://www.r-project.org), and it provides extensive functionality, from basic statistical functions to fully customizable graphics. As an open-source language, R facilitates innovation and extension of the base system capabilities, and more than 2,600 extension packages (also free and available on the website) have been created to enhance basic capabilities and implement advanced statistical and graphics applications. The base system, as well as all extension packages, include online documentation of all functions, and additional documentation can be downloaded from the website.

We believe that R may be a good option for counseling psychology researchers because it provides access to extensive capabilities within a unified programming environment (i.e., without the need to export results to other software packages for auxiliary hand calculations or to fine-tune default settings on graphics). Two tools that will be useful to researchers for performing tasks described in this chapter are (a) the compute.es package (Del Re, 2010) for computing effect sizes (Cohen's *d*) on the basis of *t* tests or other statistics reported in published studies, and (b) the MBESS package (Kelley, 2008) for computing CIs for both standardized and unstandardized effect sizes from multiple regression analyses (e.g., *B*, β, R^2). In fact, MBESS is the only readily available software of which we are aware that correctly computes CIs for standardized effect sizes. This package also contains useful functions for computing power and precision for multiple regression analyses, as described in Maxwell (2000) and Kelley and Maxwell (2003; see description in Kelley, 2007).

As with any specialized tool, there is a learning curve for R. One consideration is that the R base system is accessed via typed commands (either interactive or batch) rather than a menu-driven interface. The package R-Commander (Fox et al., 2009) provides a menu interface, which can be an aid in learning R syntax. We believe that for counseling psychologists who see research as a major professional role, the initial time investment will be well repaid by access to R's flexible functionality and growing software library. As with any skilled craft, some things just cannot be accomplished without the right tools, and we have been impressed with the wide and expanding variety of applications that R provides within the same toolbox.

CONCLUSION

We hope this chapter has provided useful suggestions to help counseling psychology researchers increase the potential contribution of their work and, thereby, to strengthen the contribution that our field makes to the broader scholarly community. Our focus has been avoiding the most serious fatal flaws and some of the most frequently occurring fixable flaws identified by reviewers of manuscripts submitted to the *JCP* from 2005 to 2010. New authors should note that even flaws that are fixable tend to diminish the prospects of a manuscript submitted for publication. We have heard from reviewers, and we know from our own experience that when a manuscript is poorly written, or omits multiple pieces of information about measures or procedures, or presents inappropriate analyses of data or interpretations of findings, the presence of these

issues, even though fixable in principle, tends to undermine one's confidence that the study has been conducted with sufficient care to yield useful information about the phenomena under investigation. So researchers who attend to both types of flaws before initial submission of the manuscript will both expedite the review process and enhance the probability of a favorable editorial decision.

We offer a succinct summary of our most important recommendations in three checklists, which are included as Appendix 3.1. We fear that one danger of collating such a set of recommendations is that it might seem—especially for relatively novice researchers—like a daunting list of proscriptive do's and don'ts. We have failed in the task we hoped to achieve through writing this chapter if we have given new investigators the impression that the research enterprise is so fraught with the likelihood of failure that it is not worth pursuing. Thus, in closing, we want to step back from looking at specific potential stumbling points along the research path and instead consider the path as a whole and the intended destination.

Two themes that run through the potential pitfalls and recommendations for avoiding them that we have presented in this chapter are (a) thoughtful selection of a meaningful research question and persuasive argumentation for the importance of hypotheses and findings and (b) careful planning to maximize the validity of the investigation, particularly the validity of the tools and procedures you choose to achieve your goals. We have stressed a theory-driven process of developing research goals as the best means to ensure that they are defined with sufficient precision to allow wise choices about specific tools. The usefulness of a tool or procedure is relative to the purpose of the investigation, with each approach having both strengths and limitations so that no one research design or measurement method is inherently best for all types of inquiry. Thus, an important goal for authors of manuscripts submitted for publication is to argue for the validity (and acknowledge the limitations) of the procedures selected.

Research validity, at its most basic level, is achieving the best match of tools and methods to precisely defined goals. This includes choosing research procedures that strengthen the basis for making causal inferences by reducing the plausibility of alternative explanations for your findings (internal validity) and by sampling procedures that support inferences to the population of interest (external validity). Construct validity is an especially critical consideration, given that the utility of questionnaires, ratings, or experimental manipulations for hypothesis-testing depends on our confidence that these procedures are related to the constructs of the theory that grounds the hypothesis. No study is completely above reproach in any of these areas. Science is a cumulative enterprise, and you should feel free to present your findings as an addition to an existing literature, noting where past research may help to reassure us regarding limitations of the present investigation, and where future research is needed to rule out plausible alternative explanations for your findings.

In this chapter, we hope we have provided some guidance that will improve research validity, but in emphasizing wise selection of well-matched research tools, it is important to keep uppermost in mind that these tasks are always in the service of a higher purpose, which is nothing less than contributing to the welfare of humanity through adding to the store of psychological knowledge. It is true that there are many daunting ways to stumble in this effort, but given all that remains to be discovered and the benefits of those discoveries, we hope that many readers will find the rewards well worth the effort.

APPENDIX 3.1: DO'S AND DON'TS FOR IMPROVING RESEARCH QUALITY

CHECKLIST OF FATAL FLAWS TO AVOID

- At the earliest stages of planning the study, is the basic research idea adequately grounded in theory and existing research?
- Does the manuscript introduction make a convincing case for the importance of the study by presenting the theory-based rationale that guided development of the research idea? In other words, does this study have a solid foundation?
- Although the introduction must necessarily be selective, does it provide a coherent summary of previous research and theory that supports the case for the importance of the study? Does the introduction report effect sizes, with a brief

description of relevant procedures (e.g., nature of the sample) in describing previous findings? If discrepant findings exist, has this been noted in the introduction? Has one or more explanations for the divergence of findings been offered?

- Does each hypothesis or research question described as central to the specific purposes of the study follow logically from the theory and previous research presented in the introduction?
- In correlational studies (which can only provide indirect evidence supporting a causal model), does the proposed model appear to be the most logically plausible? Does the research design include provisions for ruling out important rival hypotheses as explanations for findings?
- Has each construct described in a hypothesis or research question been adequately operationalized? Is the choice of each measure supported by evidence of reliability and validity for the sample used in this study? Have the particular sources of error important to this study been addressed (e.g., evidence of test–retest reliability for measures of relatively stable constructs)?
- In experimental studies, has the manipulation of every independent variable been directly assessed to determine whether the procedures were executed as intended?
- In instrument development studies, have the authors argued persuasively that the conceptual domain was adequately sampled by the initial item pool?
- When using model-testing analyses (e.g., SEM), is the model based on sound theory and past research findings? Is there a clear rationale for included paths (including the direction of causation) and also for excluded paths? What alternative models have been considered and on what basis were they judged to be less plausible than the preferred model?

CHECKLIST OF FEATURES THAT CAN ENHANCE THE CONTRIBUTION OF YOUR STUDY

- Consider using multimodal measurement to avoid the inevitable confounding of substantive and method covariance in monomethod studies.

- When using SEM, select indicators that vary on (and therefore control for) relevant sources of error (e.g., items, measurement method, measurement occasion).

- In experimental studies, consider a manipulation check that assesses the quality of subjects' perceptions or the strength of their reaction. Then consider including this variable in your model.

- Consider that question–order effects are an important potential confound. Many studies can be strengthened by presenting survey components in two or more counterbalanced orders. Considering coding presentation order as a variable and examine possible effects.

- Consider using *robust modern* methods of dealing with data that are not normally distributed or in circumstances when variance is markedly different across groups (i.e., heteroscedasticity).

CHECKLIST OF FIXABLE FLAWS: SAVE TIME AND EFFORT BY AVOIDING THESE PROBLEMS IN THE FIRST VERSION OF YOUR MANUSCRIPT

When describing a measure in the Method section:

- Briefly describe the sample used when citing psychometric data from previous studies.

- Provide one or two example items.

- Explain how you scored the measure, together with what higher scores indicate.

In reporting results:

- Report results of careful data screening.

- Provide evidence that data sufficiently meet statistical requirements of the procedures you use to test hypotheses.

- Report effect sizes and associated confidence intervals.

In SEM studies, is the focus on the path model? Does this demonstrate an acceptable fit even when partitioned away from the measurement portion of the model? When the path model fails to demonstrate adequate fit, what can we learn from model modification indexes about which omitted paths could be freed to improve the fit? What are the implications of these findings for the theory that led to the a priori model?

Are the main findings presented in a form that is easily accessible and readily interpretable? A well-constructed table or graph can add to the impact of the study by providing a clear and memorable summary of the most important results.

References

Anderson, J. C., & Gerbing, D. W. (1988). Structural equation modeling in practice: a review and recommended two-step approach. *Psychological Bulletin, 103*, 411–423. doi:10.1037/0033-2909.103.3.411

American Psychological Association. (2010). *Publication manual of the American Psychological Association* (6th ed.). Washington, DC: Author.

American Psychological Association Presidential Task Force on Evidence-Based Practice. (2006). Evidence-based practice in psychology. *American Psychologist, 61*, 271–285. doi:10.1037/0003-066X.61.4.271

Baron, R. M., & Kenny, D. A. (1986). The moderator–mediator variable distinction in social psychological research: conceptual, strategic, and statistical considerations. *Journal of Personality and Social Psychology, 51*, 1173–1182. doi:10.1037/0022-3514.51.6.1173

Bollen, K., & Lennox, R. (1991). Conventional wisdom on measurement: A structural equation perspective. *Psychological Bulletin, 110*, 305–314. doi:10.1037/0033-2909.110.2.305

Campbell, D. T. (1999). Can we be scientific in applied social science? In D. T. Campbell & M. J. Russo (Eds.), *Social experimentation* (pp. 131–144). Thousand Oaks, CA: Sage. (Original work published 1984)

Campbell, D. T., & Fiske, D. W. (1959). Convergent and discriminant validation by the multitrait–multimethod matrix. *Psychological Bulletin, 56*, 81–105. doi:10.1037/h0046016

Campbell, D. T., & Kenny, D. A. (1999). *A primer on regression artifacts*. New York, NY: Guilford Press.

Campbell, D. T., & Stanley, J. C. (1963). *Experimental and quasi-experimental designs for research*. Dallas, TX: Houghton Mifflin.

Campbell-Sills, L., & Barlow, D. H. (2007). Incorporating emotion regulation into conceptualizations and treatments of anxiety and mood disorders. In J. J. Gross (Ed.), *Handbook of emotion regulation* (pp. 542–559). New York, NY: Guilford Press.

Clark, L. A., & Watson, D. (1995). Constructing validity: Basic issues in objective scale development. *Psychological Assessment, 7*, 309–319. doi:10.1037/1040-3590.7.3.309

Cohen, J. (1988). *Statistical power analysis for the behavioral sciences*. Hillsdale, NJ: Erlbaum.

Cohen, J. (1992). A power primer. *Psychological Bulletin, 112*, 155–159. doi:10.1037/0033-2909.112.1.155

Cohen, J., Cohen, P., West, S. G., & Aiken, L. S. (2003). *Applied multiple regression/correlation analysis for the behavioral sciences* (3rd ed.). Mahwah, NJ: Erlbaum.

Constantine, M. G. (2007). Racial microaggressions against African American clients in cross-racial counseling relationships. *Journal of Counseling Psychology, 54,* 1–16. doi:10.1037/0022-0167.54.1.1

Crocker, L. M., & Algina, J. (1986). *Introduction to classical and modern test theory.* New York, NY: Holt, Rinehart & Winston.

Cronbach, L. J. (1947). Test "reliability": Its meaning and determination. *Psychometrika, 12,* 1–16. doi:10.1007/BF02289289

Cronbach, L. J. (1984). *Essentials of psychological testing* (4th ed.). New York, NY: Harper & Row.

Cronbach, L. J., Gleser, G. C., Nanda, H., & Rajaratnam, N. (1972). *The dependability of behavioral measurements: Theory of generalizability for scores and profiles.* New York, NY: Wiley.

Cronbach, L. J., & Meehl, P. E. (1955). Construct validity in psychological tests. *Psychological Bulletin, 52,* 281–302. doi:10.1037/h0040957

Del Re, A. C. (2010). compute.es: Compute Effect Sizes (R package Version 0.2) [Computer software]. Retrieved from http://CRAN.R-project.org/package=compute.es

DeShon, R. P. (1998). A cautionary note on measurement error corrections in structural equation models. *Psychological Methods, 3,* 412–423. doi:10.1037/1082-989X.3.4.412

Forsyth, D. R., & Strong, S. R. (1986). The scientific study of counseling and psychotherapy: A unificationist view. *American Psychologist, 41,* 113–119. doi:10.1037/0003-066X.41.2.113

Fox, J., Ash, M., Boye, T., Calza, S., Chang, A., Grosjean, P., . . . Wolf, P. (2009). Rcmdr: R Commander (R package Version 1.5–3) [Computer software]. Retrieved from http://CRAN.R-project.org/package=Rcmdr

Frazier, P. A., Tix, A. P., & Barron, K. E. (2004). Testing moderator and mediator effects in counseling psychology research. *Journal of Counseling Psychology, 51,* 115–134. doi:10.1037/0022-0167.51.1.115

Gelso, C. J. (1979). Research in counseling: Methodological and professional issues. *The Counseling Psychologist, 8,* 7–36. doi:10.1177/001100007900800303

Gross, J. J., & John, O. P. (2003). Individual differences in two emotion regulation processes: Implications for affect, relationships, and well-being. *Journal of Personality and Social Psychology, 85,* 348–362. doi:10.1037/0022-3514.85.2.348

Guba, E. G. (1981). Criteria for assessing the trustworthiness of naturalistic inquiries. *Educational Communication and Technology Journal, 29,* 75–91.

Hancock, G., & Mueller, R. O. (2010). *The reviewer's guide to quantitative methods in the social sciences.* New York, NY: Routledge.

Harris, J. R. (1998). *The nurture assumption: Why children turn out the way they do.* New York, NY: Free Press.

Haverkamp, B. E., Morrow, S. L., & Ponterotto, J. G. (2005). A time and place for qualitative and mixed methods in counseling psychology research. *Journal of Counseling Psychology, 52,* 123–125. doi:10.1037/0022-0167.52.2.123

Heppner, P. P., Carter, J. A., Claiborn, C. D., & Brooks, L. (1992). A proposal to integrate science and practice in counseling psychology. *The Counseling Psychologist, 20,* 107–122. doi:10.1177/0011000092201017

Heppner, P. P., Wampold, B. E., & Kivlighan, D. (2008). *Research methods in counseling psychology* (3rd ed.). Belmont, CA: Thomson.

Hill, C. E., Thompson, B. J., & Williams, E. N. (1997). A guide to conducting consensual qualitative research. *The Counseling Psychologist, 25,* 517–572. doi:10.1177/0011000097254001

Hoshmand, L. T. (1989). Alternate research paradigms: A review and teaching proposal. *The Counseling Psychologist, 17,* 3–79. doi:10.1177/0011000089171001

Hoshmand, L. T., & Polkinghorne, D. E. (1992). Redefining the science–practice relationship and professional training. *American Psychologist, 47,* 55–66. doi:10.1037/0003-066X.47.1.55

Houts, A. C., Cook, T. D., & Shadish, W. R. (1986). The person–situation debate: A critical multiplist perspective. *Journal of Personality, 54,* 52–105. doi:10.1111/j.1467-6494.1986.tb00390.x

Howard, G. S. (1986). *Dare we develop a human science?* Notre Dame, IN: Academic Publications.

Hoyt, W. T. (2000). Rater bias in psychological research: When is it a problem and what can we do about it? *Psychological Methods, 5,* 64–86. doi:10.1037/1082-989X.5.1.64

Hoyt, W. T., & Bhati, K. S. (2007). Principles and practices: An empirical examination of qualitative research in the journal of counseling psychology. *Journal of Counseling Psychology, 54,* 201–210. doi:10.1037/0022-0167.54.2.201

Hoyt, W. T., Imel, Z. E., & Chan, F. (2008). Multiple regression and correlation techniques: Recent controversies and best practices. *Rehabilitation Psychology, 53,* 321–339. doi:10.1037/a0013021

Hoyt, W. T., & McCullough, M. E. (2005). Issues in the multimodal measurement of forgiveness. In E. L. Worthington Jr. (Ed.), *Handbook of forgiveness* (pp. 109–123). New York, NY: Routledge.

Hoyt, W. T., & Melby, J. N. (1999). Dependability of measurement in counseling psychology: An introduction to generalizability theory. *The Counseling Psychologist, 27,* 325–352. doi:10.1177/0011000099273003

Hoyt, W. T., Warbasse, R. E., & Chu, E. Y. (2006). Construct validation in counseling psychology research. *The Counseling Psychologist, 34,* 769–805. doi:10.1177/0011000006287389

Judd, C. M., & Kenny, D. A. (2010). Data analysis in social psychology: Recent and recurring issues. In G. Lindzey (Ed.), *Handbook of social psychology* (5th ed., Vol. 1, pp. 115–139). Hoboken, NJ: Wiley.

Kahn, J. H., & Garrison, A. M. (2009). Emotional self-disclosure and emotional avoidance: Relations with symptoms of depression and anxiety. *Journal of Counseling Psychology, 56,* 573–584. doi:10.1037/a0016574

Kelley, K. (2007). Methods for the behavioral, educational, and social sciences: An R package. *Behavior Research Methods, 39,* 979–984. doi:10.3758/BF03192993

Kelley, K. (2008). MBESS: MBESS (R package Version 2.0.0)[Computer software]. Retrieved from http://www.nd.edu/~kkelley

Kelley, K., & Maxwell, S. E. (2003). Sample size for multiple regression: Obtaining regression coefficients that are accurate, not simply significant. *Psychological Methods, 8,* 305–321. doi:10.1037/1082-989X.8.3.305

Kenny, D. A. (1979). *Correlation and causality.* New York, NY: Wiley.

Kidd, S. A. (2002). The role of qualitative research in psychological journals. *Psychological Methods, 7,* 126–138. doi:10.1037/1082-989X.7.1.126

Lambert, M. J., & Hill, C. E. (1994). Assessing psychotherapy outcomes and processes. In S. L. Garfield (Ed.), *Handbook of psychotherapy and behavior change* (4th ed., pp. 72–113). Oxford, England: Wiley.

Lane, D. M., & Sándor, A. (2009). Designing better graphs by including distributional information and integrating words, numbers, and images. *Psychological Methods, 14,* 239–257. doi:10.1037/a0016620

MacCallum, R. C., Wegener, D. T., Uchino, B. N., & Fabrigar, L. R. (1993). The problem of equivalent models in applications of covariance structure analysis. *Psychological Bulletin, 114,* 185–199. doi:10.1037/0033-2909.114.1.185

Mallinckrodt, B. (2011). Addressing the decline in counseling and supervision process and outcome research in the *Journal of Counseling Psychology. The Counseling Psychologist, 39,* 701–704. doi:10.1177/0011000011402837

Mallinckrodt, B., & Helms, J. E. (1986). Effect of disabled counselors' self-disclosures on client perceptions of the counselor. *Journal of Counseling Psychology, 33,* 343–348. doi:10.1037/0022-0167.33.3.343

Martens, M. P. (2005). The use of structural equation modeling in counseling psychology research. *The Counseling Psychologist, 33,* 269–298. doi:10.1177/0011000004272260

Maxwell, S. E. (2000). Sample size and multiple regression analysis. *Psychological Methods, 5,* 434–458. doi:10.1037/1082-989X.5.4.434

Maxwell, S. E., & Cole, D. A. (2007). Bias in cross-sectional analyses of longitudinal mediation. *Psychological Methods, 12,* 23–44. doi:10.1037/1082-989X.12.1.23

McDonald, R. P., & Ho, M. R. (2002). Principles and practice in reporting structural equation analyses. *Psychological Methods, 7,* 64–82. doi:10.1037/1082-989X.7.1.64

Messick, S. (1989). Validity. In R. L. Linn (Ed.), *Educational measurement* (3rd ed., pp. 13–103). Phoenix, AZ: Oryx Press.

Morrow, S. L., & Smith, M. L. (2000). Qualitative research for counseling psychology. In R. W. Lent (Ed.), *Handbook of counseling psychology* (3rd ed., pp. 199–230). Hoboken, NJ: Wiley.

Mueller, R. O. (1997). Structural equation modeling: Back to basics. *Structural Equation Modeling, 4,* 353–369. doi:10.1080/10705519709540081

Pilkonis, P. A., Imber, S. D., Lewis, P., & Rubinsky, P. (1984). A comparative outcome study of individual, group, and conjoint psychotherapy. *Archives of General Psychiatry, 41,* 431–437.

Quintana, S. M., & Maxwell, S. E. (1999). Implications of recent developments in structural equation modeling for counseling psychology. *The Counseling Psychologist, 27,* 485–527. doi:10.1177/0011000099274002

R Development Core Team. (2009). *R: A language and environment for statistical computing.* Vienna, Austria: R Foundation for Statistical Computing. Retrieved from http://www.R-project.org

Schmidt, F. L. (1992). What do data really mean? Research findings, meta-analysis, and cumulative knowledge in psychology. *American Psychologist, 47,* 1173–1181. doi:10.1037/0003-066X.47.10.1173

Schmidt, F. L., & Hunter, J. E. (1996). Measurement error in psychological research: Lessons from 26 research scenarios. *Psychological Methods, 1,* 199–223. doi:10.1037/1082-989X.1.2.199

Schmidt, F. L., Le, H., & Ilies, R. (2003). Beyond alpha: An empirical examination of the effects of different sources of measurement error on reliability estimates for measures of individual-differences constructs. *Psychological Methods, 8*, 206–224. doi:10.1037/1082-989X.8.2.206

Schmitt, N. (1996). Uses and abuses of coefficient alpha. *Psychological Assessment, 8*, 350–353. doi:10.1037/1040-3590.8.4.350

Schulte, D. (1997). Dimensions of outcome measurement. In M. J. Lambert (Ed.), *Measuring patient changes in mood, anxiety, and personality disorders: Toward a core battery* (pp. 57–80). Washington, DC: American Psychological Association. doi:10.1037/10232-002

Schwarz, N. (1999). Self-reports: How the questions shape the answers. *American Psychologist, 54*, 93–105. doi:10.1037/0003-066X.54.2.93

Shadish, W. R., Cook, T. D., & Campbell, D. T. (2002). *Experimental and quasi-experimental designs for generalized causal inference*. Boston, MA: Houghton Mifflin.

Shavelson, R. J., & Webb, N. M. (1991). *Generalizability theory: A primer*. Newbury Park, CA: Sage.

Staudte, R. G., & Sheather, S. J. (1990). *Robust estimation and testing*. New York, NY: Wiley.

Strong, S. R. (1991). Science in counseling psychology: Reply to Gelso (1991) and Patton and Jackson (1991). *Journal of Counseling Psychology, 38*, 217–218. doi:10.1037/0022-0167.38.2.217

Tabachnick, B. G., & Fidell, L. S. (2007). *Using multivariate statistics*. Boston, MA: Pearson.

Wampold, B. E. (2001). *The great psychotherapy debate: Models, methods, and findings*. Mahwah, NJ: Erlbaum.

Wampold, B. E., Davis, B., & Good, R. H., III. (1990). Hypothesis validity of clinical research. *Journal of Consulting and Clinical Psychology, 58*, 360–367. doi:10.1037/0022-006X.58.3.360

Watson, J. B. (1913). Psychology as the behaviorist views it. *Psychological Review, 20*, 158–177. doi:10.1037/h0074428

Weston, R., & Gore, P. A., Jr. (2006). A brief guide to structural equation modeling. *The Counseling Psychologist, 34*, 719–751. doi:10.1177/0011000006286345

Wilcox, R. R., & Keselman, H. J. (2003). Modern robust data analysis methods: Measures of central tendency. *Psychological Methods, 8*, 254–274. doi:10.1037/1082-989X.8.3.254

Wilkinson, L., & Task Force on Statistical Inference. (1999). Statistical methods in psychology journals: Guidelines and explanations. *American Psychologist, 54*, 594–604. doi:10.1037/0003-066X.54.8.594

Worthington, R. L., & Whittaker, T. A. (2006). Scale development research: A content analysis and recommendations for best practices. *The Counseling Psychologist, 34*, 806–838. doi:10.1177/0011000006288127

CHAPTER 4

COUNSELING PSYCHOLOGY RESEARCH METHODS: QUALITATIVE APPROACHES

Susan L. Morrow, Carrie L. Castañeda-Sound, and Elizabeth M. Abrams

Qualitative research methods have gained increasing acceptance and popularity in counseling psychology since early calls (e.g., Hoshmand, 1989; Howard, 1983; Neimeyer & Resnikoff, 1982; Polkinghorne, 1984) for methodological pluralism and alternative research approaches. Although for many years counseling psychology literature was characterized by a handful of methodological guides and research articles, the 1990s saw a serious response to those earlier visions of a multiparadigmatic, multimethod body of inquiry. In 1994, the *Journal of Counseling Psychology* published a special section on qualitative research, in which eight studies using variations on grounded theory approaches were published. Polkinghorne's (1994) reaction to these studies foreshadowed future assessments of the state of the qualitative art and science in counseling psychology. Although he commended the authors on a number of points, notably the rigorous processes used by the investigators to analyze the data, he expressed concern about the limitations of data gathered and the absence of theoretical sampling. These concerns persist in counseling psychology qualitative research in the 21st century.

In 2000, Brown and Lent's third edition of the *Handbook of Counseling Psychology* included a chapter on qualitative research methods (Morrow & Smith, 2000), a comprehensive introduction to qualitative research methods that drew from the larger body of qualitative methodological literature, particularly in education. Given the diversity and comprehensiveness of the qualitative writings in education and the location of many counseling

psychology programs in colleges of education, the educational literature remains an important grounding for our work as counseling psychologists. Our aim in this chapter is to address qualitative research in counseling psychology from the larger perspective of qualitative methodology in education and other disciplines to avoid the encapsulation that might result from too narrow an ideological and methodological base. For this reason, we urge qualitative researchers in counseling psychology to embrace a multiparadigmatic and multidesign approach to conducting, writing, and reviewing qualitative work.

Further milestones in qualitative research included numerous textbooks by counseling psychologists as well as published studies. A key text used by many students of qualitative research has been Creswell's (2007) *Qualitative Inquiry and Research Design: Choosing Among Five Approaches,* now in its second edition. In this text, the author used five published qualitative studies to demonstrate the underlying paradigms and designs of five qualitative approaches to inquiry: narrative, phenomenological, grounded theory, ethnography, and case study. Although not all of these approaches are commonly used by counseling psychology researchers, all have relevance and might be considered more broadly in our field. In addition, this is not a comprehensive list of qualitative designs used in counseling psychology because consensual qualitative research (CQR; Hill, Thompson, & Williams, 1997) is one of the most commonly used qualitative approaches, and participatory action research (PAR;

DOI: 10.1037/13754-004
APA Handbook of Counseling Psychology: Vol. 1. Theories, Research, and Methods, Nadya A. Fouad (Editor-in-Chief)

Kidd & Kral, 2005) is receiving increasing attention as counseling psychologists explore more effective ways of pursuing our multicultural and social justice research agendas.

In 2005 and 2007, respectively, the *Journal of Counseling Psychology* (*JCP*) and *The Counseling Psychologist* (*TCP*) published special issues on qualitative research. *JCP* (Haverkamp, Morrow, & Ponterotto, 2005) addressed foundational elements of qualitative methodology, including qualitative research paradigms (Ponterotto, 2005a), data collection (Polkinghorne, 2005), ethics (Haverkamp, 2005), and trustworthiness (Morrow, 2005). It also contained articles on various research designs, including grounded theory (Fassinger, 2005), phenomenology (Wertz, 2005), narratology (Hoshmand, 2005), PAR (Kidd & Kral, 2005), CQR (Hill et al., 2005), ethnography (Suzuki, Ahluwalia, Mattis, & Quizon, 2005), and action-project method (Young, Valach, & Domene, 2005). Three mixed-method articles were included in this issue, including a conceptual introduction to mixed methods (Hanson, Creswell, Plano Clark, Petska, & Creswell, 2005), ideographic concept mapping (Goodyear, Tracey, Claiborn, Lichtenberg, & Wampold, 2005), and ethnographic decision tree modeling (Beck, 2005). In addition to the individual articles in this journal issue being useful resources for students, the special issue is readily available and has been used as a text in qualitative methods courses in counseling psychology.

In 2007, two special issues of *TCP* (Carter & Morrow, 2007) were dedicated to the best practices in qualitative methods, with articles that complement the *JCP* special issue. These two *TCP* issues include a "comprehensive textbook . . . at the intersection of counseling psychology and qualitative research" (Fine, 2007, p. 460). In this issue, Morrow (2007) addressed the conceptual foundations of qualitative research, followed by the selection and implementation of qualitative research designs (Creswell, Hanson, Plano Clark, & Morales, 2007). Haverkamp and Young (2007) articulated an approach to conducting the literature review in qualitative research and formulating the rationale for a qualitative study. Next, Suzuki, Ahluwalia, Arora, and Mattis (2007) explored strategies for

qualitative data collection, and Yeh and Inman (2007) identified best practices in qualitative data analysis and interpretation. Ponterotto and Grieger (2007) addressed issues of effectively communicating qualitative research, including a special focus on writing qualitative theses and dissertations. Poulin (2007) rounded out the series with her article on teaching qualitative research, and Fine (2007) offered a critical review in which she acknowledged the tensions between counseling psychology, a traditionally postpositivist discipline, and qualitative research traditions that have been grounded more in constructivist and critical traditions. In our opinion, she correctly framed the terrain of qualitatively oriented counseling psychologists as a "borderland" (Anzaldua, 1987) venture–adventure in which we work to resist the inevitable pull of a dominant research paradigm to conform to its standards while educating and stretching "between 'both shores at once,' inventing a language of translation bridging postpositivism to critical, qualitative work" (Fine, 2007, p. 460).

Over the years, counseling psychologists have conducted qualitative research on a wide variety of topics relevant to our field. Ponterotto (2005b) examined qualitative studies that had been published over a 15-year period in the *Journal of Counseling Psychology*. Hoyt and Bhati (2007) built on Ponterotto's work, focusing more specifically on the degree to which these studies reflected the underlying principles of qualitative research in the larger qualitative arena. More recently, Ponterotto, Kuriakose, and Granovskaya (2011) have conducted an investigation of qualitative studies published in North American counseling journals (*Journal of Counseling Psychology, Journal of Counseling and Development,* and *The Counseling Psychologist*) from 1995 through 2006. The findings of these three studies provide an overview of how qualitative research is conducted in counseling and counseling psychology as well as raise questions about the directions that qualitative researchers in our field are going.

The questions raised by these three studies are anchored in an understanding of research paradigms; thus, in this chapter, we first identify the paradigmatic issues that form the foundation of qualitative inquiry. Building on this framework, we describe the current status of the genre by reviewing content analyses of qualitative research in counseling and counseling psychology. Next, we turn our attention to qualitative research designs and modes of inquiry that are relevant to counseling psychology, providing an overview of phenomenology, grounded theory, CQR, PAR, and mixed methods. In keeping with counseling psychology's values and priorities regarding diversity, we address multicultural and social justice issues in qualitative research as well as international and cross-cultural qualitative research. We end the chapter with sections on quality and trustworthiness in qualitative research and writing and on publishing qualitative research in counseling psychology.

PARADIGMATIC UNDERPINNINGS OF QUALITATIVE RESEARCH

Quantitative researchers often scratch their heads in confusion when qualitative researchers insist on discussing paradigms. Those new to the qualitative "culture" (Hoyt & Bhati, 2007) may find qualitative researchers' forays into philosophy of science to be unnecessarily heady. Because the predominant paradigm underpinning quantitative methods has traditionally been positivist or postpositivist, it has not been necessary for conventional researchers to discuss their paradigmatic underpinnings. However, qualitative research is characterized by numerous paradigms and research designs, and failure to understand at least some basic issues across these paradigms leads to unnecessary confusion, such as when a reviewer applies standards of one paradigm to research conducted in another. There are many different philosophical and paradigmatic taxonomies, but one that has been cited frequently in the qualitative research literature was defined by Guba and Lincoln (1994) and articulated for counseling psychologists in *JCP* by Ponterotto (2005a). We have taken some liberties in the brief description of paradigms that follows, partly for simplicity's sake as well as to lend further clarity and expansion. Ponterotto's (2005a) *Primer* is required reading for would-be qualitative researchers.

A paradigm may be viewed as an umbrella containing the researcher's views of reality, how knowledge is acquired, the values that guide the research, the methods used to conduct the research, and the language used to communicate the research process and findings. The paradigms articulated by Ponterotto (2005a) include positivism, postpositivism, constructivism–interpretivism, and critical–ideological. In our brief explanation, we have separated interpretivism and constructivism and have added a pragmatic paradigm.

Although early anthropological qualitative research may be said to have been guided by the values of positivism, qualitative research over time and discipline has largely dismissed positivism as a realistic possibility in the qualitative endeavor. Postpositivists, like positivists, adhere to an objective reality but realize that such a reality can be only imperfectly apprehended. Postpositivist researchers value objectivity as well as maintaining a detached role as researchers.

Ponterotto (2005a), like other theorists, combined constructivism and interpretivism. Others have found it useful to distinguish between the two, however. Viewing postpositivism, interpretivism, and constructivism on a continuum from a more detached and objectivist location to one that is more fully engaged and interactive, one would find interpretivists to be less concerned than postpositivists with detachment or true objectivity but reluctant to engage fully in collaborative meaning-making with participants. A common area of interest among interpretivists and constructivists is the meanings that people make of their life experiences. Although postpositivist qualitative researchers in counseling psychology are interested in these meanings as well, their focus tends to be more on the objective stance of the researcher than the meaning-making process. One area of confusion regarding constructivism relates to whether one is focusing on the internal meaning-making process or a process that is socially constructed.

Critical–ideological theories go further and may be grounded in constructivist—especially social constructivist—perspectives. However, critical–ideological theories are unabashedly political. That is, the goal of such paradigms is to undermine the status quo, using the research process to question power structures in society as well as within the research relationship itself. Typically the researcher–participant interaction is highly interactional and dialogic, and researchers and participants work together for emancipatory ideals.

Denzin and Lincoln (2000) referred to the qualitative researcher as a *bricoleur,* or one who makes use of all the tools at hand to get the job done. Using this model, the "researcher draws on a variety of philosophical positions and methodological tools to accomplish overall research goals" (Ponterotto, 2005b, p. 10). In keeping with this model, a pragmatic approach to paradigm issues may provide maximum flexibility to the researcher, although Ponterotto warned that "if not done carefully, anchoring research in multiple paradigms can serve as cross-purposes and is akin to mixing apples and oranges" (pp. 10–11). Pragmatism centralizes the research question rather than philosophical or methodological issues, and it focuses on what works best to accomplish the research goals (Tashakkori & Teddlie, 2003). A pragmatist paradigm is particularly useful in mixed-method (qualitative–quantitative) studies.

As will become evident, certain research designs appear to be a perfect fit with certain paradigms. It will also become clear, however, that there are appropriate times to ground a particular study and its design in a paradigm that is not traditionally associated with that approach. We recommend that researchers become very familiar with the paradigms and designs they wish to use before attempting too ambitious a *bricolage.* This overview of paradigms is necessarily incomplete given the constraints of space, but it will provide the reader with a working understanding to facilitate comprehension of the goals and findings of the three content analyses described in the next section.

Content Analyses of Published Qualitative Research in Counseling and Counseling Psychology

Ponterotto's (2005b) examination of 49 qualitative and mixed-method studies revealed interesting findings about the status of qualitative research published in *JCP* between 1989 and 2003. To begin, he found that of the 49 studies, 21 could be classified as coming from a constructivist paradigm (for a description of

paradigms and their importance to qualitative research, see Ponterotto, 2005a), nine were postpositivist, 17 were postpositivist–constructivist, and two were constructivist–postpositivist. None fell within a critical–ideological paradigm. Ponterotto found a wide variety of research designs represented across these studies, the most frequently used being CQR, grounded theory, and phenomenology. Numbers of participants ranged from five to 26, with face-to-face interviews accounting for the primary data-gathering strategy. These interviews ranged from 30 minutes to 4 hours, with CQR interviews being the shortest. Other data sources included telephone interviews, psychotherapy transcripts, and written responses to open-ended questions. From 1989 to 1993, *JCP* did not publish any qualitative studies. In 1994, the total number of qualitative articles jumped to eight, all of which appeared in the special issue described above. Then, between 1994 and 2003, the number of qualitative articles ranged from two to five per year. Thus, despite increasing numbers of conceptual and methodological articles and chapters in counseling and counseling psychology, along with several qualitative texts, the number of studies actually published in the journal was small. It should be noted, however, that *JCP* was the leader in psychology journals publishing qualitative studies during that time.

Hoyt and Bhati (2007) expanded on Ponterotto's (2005b) work by examining *JCP* qualitative articles during the same period, using a critical analysis to analyze the extent to which qualitative research in *JCP* reflected the underlying values and principles of the larger qualitative genre. Characterizing the qualitative–quantitative paradigms as different cultures, each with its own "socially transmitted collection of knowledge, habits, and skills" (de Waal, 2001, as cited in Hoyt & Bhati, 2007, p. 202), the authors pointed to the defining features of qualitative inquiry according to Morrow and Smith (2000). These included the focus of inquiry (idiographic, in which the focus is on individual uniqueness vs. the nomothetic focus of quantitative research that values representativeness and generalizability), the research setting (extensive, intensive time in the natural setting of participants), and the researcher's role (the researcher, as the primary instrument of the research, engages in an intensive self-reflective process to examine her or his assumptions and biases and use them appropriately in the investigation). In addition, qualitative research should be judged by standards that emerge from the qualitative genre as well as from the guiding paradigm of the research. Therefore, the imposition of quantitative concepts such as reliability, validity, and generalizability on qualitative research would be as inappropriate as criticizing a quantitative study for not uncovering the deeper meanings clients make of their experiences.

Hoyt and Bhati (2007) conducted a content analysis of the same studies examined by Ponterotto (2005b), coding for attributes that related to the research focus, research setting, and researcher's role as well as for the presentation of results, to understand the extent to which these studies reflected the goals of qualitative research. Their findings revealed some important patterns in the ways qualitative research was conducted over this 15-year period. In contrast to the qualitative principles surrounding the importance of a high level of acquaintance and a collaborative relationship between researchers and participants, the authors found a trend indicating that most of the researchers conducting data analysis (frequently termed *coders* or *auditors* in the literature) had little or no contact with research participants. The modal length of interview was 60 min, and this normally took place in a single interview, in contrast with Polkinghorne's (2005) recommendation that an adequate interview spans at least three meetings to develop rapport and gain in-depth understanding of the participant's experience. The vast majority of researchers (80%) had either no direct contact with participants at all or conducted interviews in artificial settings as opposed to participants' natural environments. A small majority of studies (58%) provided some information about the self-reflective processes of the primary researchers, although the focus was on controlling subjectivity rather than using that subjectivity as an integral part of the researcher–participant relationship and to enhance the quality of the findings as is more prevalent in the larger qualitative research community. Hoyt and Bhati found that there was generally consistency in following the qualitative principle of using the words of participants to support

interpretations made by researchers in studies in *JCP* during this period. An important finding of Hoyt and Bhati's examination of change over time was that there was decreasing fidelity between qualitative principles and published qualitative studies in *JCP* over the span of their analysis. This raises significant questions about the direction of qualitative research in counseling psychology in relation to the larger qualitative genre.

The third study in this series (Ponterotto, Kuriakose, & Granovskaya, 2011), still in progress, intended to learn to what degree "actual qualitative research production matched the mounting conceptual calls for expanded methodologies" (p. 5). This study extended and updated Ponterotto's (2005b) study by expanding the scope of journals to include not only *JCP* but *TCP* and the *Journal of Counseling and Development* (*JCD*) as well over a more recent time frame (1995–2006). For each study, the authors examined the underlying research paradigm, the research design or inquiry approach, procedures for gathering data, participant selection, and the topic of the research. Ponterotto et al. (2011) concluded that over the time span investigated, the field is moving from a predominantly postpositivist, quantitative stance to one that embraces broader paradigmatic and methodological diversity. The most common paradigm underlying qualitative research in the field was constructivism, followed by a combined postpositivist–constructivist paradigm in which postpositivism was the stronger grounding, then constructivist–postpositivist, and finally postpositivist. No evidence was found for an underlying ideological–critical paradigm or a pragmatic approach.

Qualitative Research Designs and Modes of Inquiry

As suggested throughout this chapter, there are numerous approaches to qualitative research. We have identified just a handful of these approaches to give readers an overview of those qualitative research designs or modes of inquiry that have either been most used in counseling psychology or hold particular promise given the values of our discipline. These are phenomenology, grounded theory, CQR, PAR, and mixed method. Excellent resources, already referred to and elaborated in this chapter, are available as how-to guides to conducting research using these approaches; thus, the focus in this chapter will be an update on these designs with particular applicability to counseling psychology in the second decade of the 21st century.

Phenomenology. Perhaps the most complex of qualitative research designs, phenomenology is, foremost, a philosophical tradition with strong links to psychology, particularly existential psychology (Wertz, 2005). Although the philosophical underpinnings are beyond the scope of this chapter, researchers interested in conducting phenomenological research would do well to immerse themselves in the history and philosophy of phenomenology. We view phenomenology as a philosophy, a subparadigm of interpretivism (with an important distinction noted below), and a research design or mode of inquiry.

Wertz (2005) described four basic principles of phenomenology. The first principle is related to the psychological phenomenological attitude, which is that "scientific knowledge begins with a fresh and unbiased description of its subject matter" (p. 167). Husserl (1913/1962) advocated two approaches to ensure this stance, called *epochés*. The first epoché requires the researcher to *bracket*, or set aside, all scientific knowledge about the phenomenon, "suspend[ing] received science, put[ting] it out of play" (Wertz, 2005, p. 168), to have a fresh perspective on the phenomenon. The second epoché brackets the researcher's own "naive" understandings of the phenomenon. The researcher's self-reflection allows the researcher to understand her or his own perspective as well as to develop an empathic understanding of the world of the participants.

The second underlying principle of phenomenology, according to Wertz (2005), is the *intuition of essences* or the *eidetic reduction* of the phenomenon. The researcher engages in a process of examining the phenomenon from every possible angle to understand what are the underlying essences or invariant characteristics of the phenomenon. According to Creswell (2007), "the basic purpose of phenomenology is to reduce individual experiences with a phenomenon to a description of the universal essence" (p. 58). This essence is discovered through a process referred to by Giorgi (1997) as *imaginative variation*,

in which the researcher uses intuition or imagination (viewed here as a rigorous inquiry process) to systematically subject the phenomenon to as many variations as possible to "distinguish essential features from those that are accidental or incidental" (Wertz, 2005, p. 168).

The third principle of phenomenological qualitative research, according to Wertz (2005), is *intentionality and intentional analysis*. Intentionality implies that human consciousness is not separate from the object of its awareness. This concept challenges the traditional Cartesian subject–object dichotomy. Giorgi (1997) asserted that there can be no subject without an object and vice versa.

Finally, Wertz (2005) identified the *life-world* or *lived world* as the fourth principle of phenomenology. This conceptually extends intentionality by viewing the human being as a self, with a unique perspective, imbedded with others in the world (Giorgi, 1997).

Qualitative phenomenological research methods. Grounded in the foregoing principles, the purpose of a phenomenological study is to glean from the data (predominantly interviews) the essence of participants' subjective experiences of the phenomenon of interest. Giorgi (1997) emphasized that phenomenological research aims not to interpret the data, construct meanings, or develop theory, but purely to describe that essence. Moustakas's (1994) approach to psychological phenomenological research emphasizes the core principles of phenomenology in that it makes use of epoché (bracketing) and focuses on descriptions, rather than interpretations, of participants' experiences. We recommend a synthesis of the research methods and strategies suggested by Giorgi (1997), Moustakas (1994), and Wertz (2005). The following procedures characterize a phenomenological study.

■ Identify the phenomenon of interest and articulate the research question or problem. Topics and problems that are most appropriate to a phenomenological approach are those in which a number of people have common or shared experiences of a phenomenon. In counseling psychology, such topics might include client or supervisee experiences of counseling or supervision (e.g.,

Worthen & McNeill, 1996); university counseling center clients' experiences of a campus crisis; or academic climate for graduate students of color.

- Examine one's own knowledge, beliefs, experiences, feelings, biases, and assumptions about the phenomenon. Bringing these perspectives to light helps the researcher to bracket them, providing a cleaner canvas upon which to paint the descriptions of participants' experiences. This examination, epoché, and bracketing should occur throughout the study and writing of the results. Moustakas (1994) recommended that researchers write up their own experiences and the context in which they occurred as part of the results of the study.
- Identify the individuals who have experienced the phenomenon or whose lives "involve a revelatory relationship with the subject matter under investigation" (Wertz, 2005, p. 171).
- Gather data. The main tool for gathering data in a phenomenological study is the in-depth individual interview. However, researchers have also used verbal or written descriptions from the participant's experience, drawings, group discussions, and even descriptions offered by others who have observed the person who has had the experience (Wertz, 2005). Phenomenological interviews tend to be characterized by a small number of global questions to elicit rich descriptions from participants.
- Conduct a phenomenological data analysis. The researcher immerses her- or himself in the data transcripts, highlighting meaning units (sections of text that illustrate participants' experiences of the phenomenon), and then groups these units into clusters of meaning that become themes. Themes and significant statements from the text are then used to write a description of participants' experiences and the context or setting in which the participants had those experiences (Creswell, 2007).
- Write a "composite description" that presents "the 'essence' of the phenomenon" (Creswell, 2007, p. 159).

The philosophical underpinnings of phenomenology are continually evolving, as are the procedures and methods used by phenomenological researchers. It is important that would-be phenomenological researchers give serious study to the history and philosophy of phenomenology as well as become well acquainted with the wide variety of phenomenological research approaches before embarking on a phenomenological investigation. Wertz (2005) suggested that phenomenology was particularly appropriate to counseling psychology research because it engages the "study of subjectivity and the full human person," is able to "capture the richness and complexity of psychological life as it is concretely lived," and brings us "close to the naturally occurring struggles and triumphs of persons" (p. 176).

Grounded theory. Grounded theory has been a favorite qualitative research design among counseling psychologists over time; in addition, it is "probably the most commonly used qualitative method, surpassing ethnography, and it is used internationally" (Morse et al., 2009, p. 9). Because of its emphasis on examining processes, grounded theory is particularly suited to counseling psychology research on therapy process. Sociologists Glaser and Strauss (1967) developed the first systematic approach to grounded theory, also known as the constant comparative method. This approach was further developed by Glaser (1978), Strauss (1987), Corbin and Strauss (1990), and Strauss and Corbin (1990). Glaser brought a postpositivist perspective to this endeavor and gave to grounded theory "dispassionate empiricism, rigorous codified methods, emphasis on emergent discoveries, and its somewhat ambiguous specialized language that echoes quantitative methods" (Charmaz, 2006, p. 7). Strauss's roots were in the Chicago School of Sociology's pragmatist approach, and he "brought notions of human agency, emergent processes, social and subjective meanings, problem-solving practices, and the open-ended study of action to grounded theory" (Charmaz, 2006, p. 7). His pragmatic perspective also supported a more constructivist approach embodied in symbolic interactionism, in which "society, reality, and self are constructed through interaction and thus rely on language and communication . . . and addresses how people create, enact, and change meanings and actions" (Charmaz, 2006, p. 7). Glaser's and

Strauss's point of convergence was in their interest in "fundamental social or social psychological processes within a social setting or a particular experience" (Charmaz, 2006, p. 7). Over time, Glaser's and Strauss's (the latter along with Corbin) paths diverged considerably, resulting in Glaser publicly criticizing Strauss for abandoning the inductive, discovery-oriented approach that formed the heart of the method and claiming that the procedures proposed by Strauss and Corbin "force data and analysis into preconceived categories" (Charmaz, 2006, p. 8), a problem that the first author of this chapter has encountered in her work. Nonetheless, Strauss and Corbin's approach remains an important resource for graduate students worldwide (Charmaz, 2006). Grounded theory has been used congruently within both postpositivist and constructivist paradigms, making it an ideal mode of inquiry for counseling psychologists who favor either paradigm.

Charmaz (2006) studied with and was mentored by both Glaser and Strauss and has brought together the divergent traditions into a constructivist grounded theory. She has preserved the values of early grounded theory and many of the practices that contribute to theoretical sensitivity on the part of the researcher while outlining a clear and usable framework for conducting and analyzing a grounded theory study. Because of the need by graduate students and novice qualitative researchers to have a research method that provides structure while permitting paradigmatic flexibility, Charmaz's approach is increasingly attractive to counseling psychology researchers, teachers, and students. Counseling psychology qualitative methodologists (Creswell, 2007; Fassinger, 2005) have grounded their writing on a synthesis of the Glaser–Strauss–Corbin work and that of Charmaz. Just as we recommend that phenomenologists steep themselves in phenomenological history, philosophy, and methodology before embarking on a phenomenological study, it is essential that grounded theory researchers become familiar with the main body of literature on grounded theory by Glaser and Strauss (separately and together), Strauss and Corbin, and Charmaz as well as newer work on the development of grounded theory that is described later in this chapter (Morse et al., 2009). Although space does not permit us to

expand further than these resources, we also recommend Clarke's (2005) work on situational analysis, an innovative extension of grounded theory using mapping.

Conducting grounded theory research. As both Charmaz (2000) and Fassinger (2005) have written, much of the information available about grounded theory relates to data analysis. Indeed, we too have observed a tendency among some counseling psychology researchers to describe their work as a grounded theory study on the basis of having conducted open, axial, and selective coding (the steps in grounded theory data analysis proposed by Strauss & Corbin, 1990). To the credit of these researchers, and as Polkinghorne (1994) observed, grounded theory studies in counseling psychology are characterized by rigorous data analysis procedures. Many of the core grounded theory processes of data gathering and ensuring trustworthiness of the study are missing in some of this work, however. Two important components of grounded theory research are theoretical memos and constant comparison. Throughout data collection and analysis, the researcher makes preliminary and ongoing analytic notes about interviews, codes, and other ideas that surface during the course of the research. In addition, grounded theory researchers make use of the *constant comparative method,* during which the researcher continually moves from comparing data to other data in the early stages, data to emerging codes, codes to codes, codes to categories, and back again. This process ensures thorough immersion in the data as well as developing an increasingly complex understanding of the data and development of theory.

Grounded theory means that the researcher constructs a theoretical understanding of human processes that is grounded in the data (Charmaz, 2006). Thus, researchers approach the setting with an attitude of wanting to learn about the participants and their context. Although grounded theorists may disagree about whether to be engaged in the literature before conducting a grounded theory study, all agree on the importance of entering the field with an open mind, setting aside preconceptions and assumptions as much as possible.

In grounded theory research, data analysis begins immediately upon gathering early data. We "separate, sort, and synthesize these [early] data through qualitative coding" (Charmaz, 2006, p. 2). The primary reason for early data analysis is that the research design must be flexible and emergent (Morrow & Smith, 2000), and early analysis will point the researcher in new directions to gather the data that will provide the fullest, richest understanding possible. Thus, the researcher does not just gather data and then analyze them; she or he develops a plan for initial data gathering that is intentionally flexible and that may lead in unexpected directions. This is known as *theoretical sampling,* in which the researcher uses the emerging analysis to identify what is not yet known. Starting at the most basic, concrete level of data, the researcher constructs increasing levels of abstraction that will move toward an explanatory theory (Charmaz, 2006).

Although there are varied approaches to analyzing qualitative data, Charmaz (2006) has provided an approach that is quite accessible to new grounded theory researchers but also, along with work by Clarke (2005), Morse et al. (2009), and others, moves grounded theory into the 21st century and into its "second generation" (Morse et al., 2009). Grounded theory analysis is characterized by a process of initial coding, focused coding, axial coding, and theoretical coding. Initial coding stays very close to the data and may be conducted word-by-word, line-by-line, meaning unit–by–meaning unit, or incident-to-incident. Codes are typically short, simple, and precise and remain as close to the words of participants as possible. In focused coding, the researcher uses her or his emerging analytic understandings of the data to bring together the most significant or frequently occurring early codes to form categories. In axial coding (Strauss & Corbin, 1990), the researcher defines the properties and dimensions of each category; this phase of coding is described very clearly by Fassinger (2005). Finally, theoretical coding specifies the relationships among categories and forms the basis for articulating the theory. It is at this level that researchers should be watchful not to adopt specific theoretical schemas (e.g., from Strauss & Corbin, 1990) into which to force their data. This final theoretical step should emerge naturally from those that preceded it.

In many grounded theory investigations in counseling psychology (as well as in other disciplines), "theory" might better be labeled a conceptual model. Charmaz (2006) articulated the confusion surrounding the idea of "theory" in grounded theory. Theory, from a positivist perspective, looks for causes and explanations, emphasizes generalizability and universality, and holds prediction as its goal. In contrast, "interpretive theory calls for the imaginative understanding of the studied phenomenon. This type of theory assumes emergent, multiple realities; indeterminacy; facts and values as linked; truth as provisional; and social life as processual" (Charmaz, 2006, p. 126). It is this latter approach to theory that is at the heart of grounded theory construction. Charmaz (2006) goes further to distinguish between objectivist grounded theory, which originates in a positivist–postpositivist paradigm and "attends to data as real in and of themselves and does not attend to the processes of their production" (p. 131), and constructivist grounded theory, which "places priority on the phenomena of the study and sees both data and analysis as created from shared experiences and relationships with participants" (p. 130). Some of the misunderstandings in the editorial review process or in the dissertation defense stem from the confusion of these two paradigmatic, methodological, and theoretical positions. That is, counseling psychology is still a predominantly postpositivist discipline; thus objectivist standards of research are automatically applied to qualitative research regardless of its underlying paradigm. Charmaz (2006) articulated the movement from a postpositivist to a contemporary, constructivist frame when she wrote, "Neither data nor theories are discovered. Rather, we are part of the world we study and the data we collect. We *construct* our grounded theories through our past and present involvements and interactions with people, perspectives, and research practices" (p. 10).

Consensual qualitative research.   CQR (Hill et al., 1997), one of the most-used qualitative research designs in counseling psychology (along with phenomenology and grounded theory), is the only qualitative approach developed directly from within counseling psychology. Having tried a number of approaches to conducting qualitative research, the authors were frustrated by the vagueness of many modes of inquiry and the difficulty in understanding and implementing the methods. They synthesized aspects of phenomenological, grounded theory, and comprehensive process analysis to "integrate the best features of existing methods and also be rigorous and easy to learn" (Hill et al., 2005, p. 196). Ponterotto et al. (2011) classified CQR within the combined postpositivist–constructivist paradigm. The primary source of data in CQR has traditionally been open-ended, semistructured individual interviews. Some distinguishing characteristics of the method are the use of judges and independent auditors, a consensus process of data analysis by team members, and an analytic process that identifies domains, core ideas, and cross-analyses (Hill et al., 1997, 2005). These authors also recommended that researchers engage in a self-reflective process in which they identify their expectations and biases, making them public "so that readers can evaluate the findings with this knowledge in mind" (Hill et al., 2005, p. 197). They also advised that research team members discuss with each other their biases during the research process to ensure that the analysis is not negatively affected. CQR is conducted by a research team, typically made up of psychologists and graduate students. Emphasis is placed on thoroughly training team members who are new to the method; and the authors recommended attending to issues of unequal power in research teams (Hill et al., 2005).

Conducting CQR. Hill et al. (1997) suggested selecting eight to 15 participants, sampled randomly from a homogeneous population. Originally, the authors recommended developing detailed interview protocols, with several questions and additional probes. Later, reporting that researchers over time had asked an average of 12 questions (mode = 15), they suggested that interview questions be limited to eight to 10 questions for a 1-hour interview, noting that too many questions led to "'thin' questionnaire-like data rather than a rich understanding of individuals' experiences" (Hill et al., 2005, p. 199).

The consensus process of CQR is very well articulated and developed. It "relies on mutual respect, equal involvement, and shared power" (Hill et al., 1997, p. 523) and attempts to balance the need for arriving at a common understanding of the data while still respecting individual viewpoints and worldviews. Team members are encouraged to discuss differences of opinion and the associated feelings openly to enhance the consensus process.

Data analysis begins by deriving a "start list" of domains from the literature, the data, or both. Hill et al. (2005) suggested that a start list derived from the data would reduce preconceived ideas that might arise from the literature. These domains are subsequently used to code the data. Moving to the next level of abstraction, core ideas are constructed that express the words of participants in language that is "concise, clear, and comparable across cases" (Hill et al., 2005, p. 200). Finally, cross-analysis is conducted, in which core ideas are examined across cases and clustered into categories, and frequencies are identified for the core ideas across the sample. Auditors provide detailed feedback throughout the analytic process. Hill et al. suggested that internal auditors might be better able to grasp the complexity but may be biased by their interaction with the data and the team; they recommended at least one external auditor to prevent this problem.

More recently, Hill et al. (2005) have applied CQR to case studies (CQR-C; Jackson, Chui, & Hill, 2006) and to simple qualitative data (e.g., responses to open-ended questions at the end of a survey; consensual qualitative research—modified [CQR-M]; Spangler, Liu, & Hill, 2006). In CQR-C, recordings of counseling sessions make up the primary data. The development of domains is preceded by defining therapeutic events that relate to the phenomenon of interest (Jackson, Chui, & Hill, 2006). This approach emphasizes triangulation, or the use of additional data sources beyond recorded sessions, such as interviewing the counselor and client. The team meets to discuss varying members' interpretations of the data, followed by constructing a case conceptualization. This construction begins with individual team members presenting their conceptualizations, followed by team members querying the presenter. Team members then develop short revised conceptualizations, and the consensus process is used to identify the most pertinent material and develop a consolidated model. CQR-M offers a systematic way to analyze brief responses to open-ended questions often included as part of a survey instrument (Spangler, Liu, & Hill, 2006). In CQR-M, domains and categories emerge from the data. Cross-analysis is not used because of the limited amount of data received from each participant, and auditors are not viewed as necessary.

As with previously described research designs, it is essential that those wishing to conduct CQR ground themselves in the methodological literature. Until recently, information on conducting CQR was limited to two comprehensive journal articles. Hill (2011) has recently published an edited book that will be of value to CQR researchers.

Participatory action research. Action research has been documented in the social sciences and education since the early 20th century (Lewin, 1946). The past several decades have seen many transformations of action research that span political and ideological continua. Recently, Fine (2007) and Smith, Chambers, and Bratini (2009) have called on researchers in counseling psychology to take this vision to the next level by deconstructing traditional approaches to research. This call includes an expansion of our "methodological imagination" to include collaborative, power-sharing, and decolonizing strategies, such as conducting PAR. In this section, we provide resources for building a case for PAR within the field of counseling psychology as a tool for social justice and healing of oppression. Then we will offer advice for graduate students, early career professionals, and experienced quantitative and qualitative researchers who are interested in pursuing this approach to research.

Building a case for PAR. Although currently situated within the context of individual mental health processes, counseling psychology has been moving in a direction toward social justice. In 1991, after more than a decade of multicultural research and practice in psychology, Pedersen declared multiculturalism a "fourth force" in counseling and psychology. Following this declaration has been a flurry of new research in this area as well as a shift from individual awareness of diversity and multicultural issues to a systemic understanding of oppression, privilege, and social justice (Speight & Vera, 2004; Vera & Speight, 2003). However, although

counseling psychology has made a shift toward investigating social justice phenomena, the field has yet to critically analyze power dynamics and social justice concerns *within* the research process. If counseling psychology wants to remain relevant in our understandings of power, privilege, and oppression, then we must turn our attention toward the rapidly changing world of research and the global push toward and acceptance of PAR (Brydon-Miller, 2008; Kindon, Pain, & Kesby, 2007).

PAR is a practical way to go beyond studying social justice topics and infuse social justice action and values of democratic participation into the research design process. To be clear, PAR is not a research design but rather an approach or a worldview to doing research *with* rather than *on* individuals and communities. Fals-Borda and Rahman (1991) wrote, "[PAR] is the implicitly empowering process in which a group of people become aware of the nature of their disenfranchisement, the mechanics through which inequity is perpetuated, and their ability to change their circumstances" (p. 2).

The researcher–researched relationship is critically analyzed and transformed from a top-down power relationship to one that is founded on democratic values and power sharing. The role of researcher is transformed from the traditional notions of the academic researcher who holds power in terms of the design, implementation, interpretation, and write-up of the research, to a model in which traditional research participants are now considered coresearchers and whose input and participation is required throughout the entire research process (Kidd & Kral, 2005). Additionally, there is an underlying belief in the capacity of community members to generate knowledge that adds to the existing literature, to create and take direct action on the basis of their findings, and to reflect on the wisdom of that knowledge through a continual process of *plan–act–observe–reflect* (Herr & Anderson, 2005).

Making a beginning with PAR. PAR is gaining in popularity and validation as a respected and forward-thinking research process, and at the same time, there are few counseling psychologists engaging in and writing about PAR. Thus, it may be challenging for graduate students and professionals to access mentors and training in PAR even though they may identify PAR as their preferred approach to social justice research. In addition, PAR requires more time and energy devoted throughout the entire process and may initially turn off graduate students and advisors from pursuing this type of research because of time constraints around a dissertation project as well as a publish-or-perish environment for academics working toward tenure. Although we do not encourage the continuation of the publish-or-perish environment, we understand that many of us are currently residing within this structural environment and may need assistance in how to conduct PAR within this type of institution.

First, PAR requires us to go beyond the confines of psychology and to begin to think of ourselves as interdisciplinary researchers as we familiarize ourselves with various fields' writings on this social justice approach to research (see Bishop, 2005; Fine et al., 2003; Kemmis & McTaggart, 2005; Lykes, Coquillon, & Rabenstein, 2010; Prilleltensky & Nelson, 2002). Many authors and activists can serve as our initial mentors as we immerse ourselves in this knowledge base and begin to *unlearn* the traditional power dynamics of researcher–participant relations. This also includes educating ourselves on the theoretical foundations of PAR (see Freire, 2003; Lewin, 1946; Martín-Baró, 1994; Memmi, 1965; Norsworthy & Khuankaew, 2006; Smith, Chambers, & Bratini, 2009; Tuhiwai Smith, 1999).

Gathering knowledge from multiple fields' perspectives, underpinnings, and various intersections (e.g., history, education, nursing, community psychology) allows for a deeper and more coherent understanding of PAR. In our review of PAR literature, we noticed many nonfiction and philosophical writings woven into PAR articles to increase the capacity for critical consciousness-raising and for connecting psychology to other disciplines (see hooks, 2009; Mohanty, 2006; Starhawk, 1997). For example, Fine (2007) has encouraged a methodological "border crossing" for research in counseling psychology based on metaphors from Gloria Anzaldua's *Borderlands/la frontera* (1987). Fine supported her article with evidence of *psychopolitical validity* (epistemic subtype; Prilleltensky, 2003) as she engaged in this interdisciplinary dialogue and argued for an integrated theory of power that

includes both psychological and political perspectives. Additionally, she has added to the knowledge base by using rich, thick description and creating dialogue between and across disciplines that are writing about and practicing social justice. Fine established this dialogue in her writing, but we can extend this metaphor to our own communities by creating a PAR discussion group that includes people steeped in various fields and knowledge bases coming together to form a powerful and collaborative think tank.

Timing a PAR project so that a student can graduate or publish in a timely manner is also important, and we provide an example of working through this challenge. The first and third authors (advisor and student, respectively) of this chapter wanted to launch a PAR project together in their own community on the basis of responses from community members' needs and concerns. Instead of waiting for the student to get to the dissertation phase of her graduate work, they launched the PAR project in the student's 1st year of the graduate program. Abrams thus had completed her predissertation research project (in some graduate programs, this is called the *master's thesis project* or the *early research project*) by the time of her entry into the field, along with the relationship-building processes that occur during the beginning phases of a PAR project.

At the commencement of Abrams's dissertation research, this PAR project will have already been under way for more than 2 years, and the community member coresearchers will be deep within the cycle of plan–act–observe–reflect (Herr & Anderson, 2005). Also, because PAR projects look so different from one another, there are always opportunities to write and publish various aspects, joys, and challenges of the work in which a community of researchers is engaged. Thus, each PAR project can elicit many publications in both academic and community literature bases. In fact, the documentation and dissemination of the project may be a social action project in itself and contribute greatly to our understanding of how community-based projects may empower and provide healing to individuals living within those communities. We recommend that a good place to start is for advisors and students to read together the brief but informative and practical book, *The Action Research Dissertation* (Herr & Anderson, 2005).

Finally, PAR may be important in the training of graduate students for increasing multicultural competence and social justice advocacy through the actual practice of building relationships in communities that are based in power sharing, collaboration, mutuality, and solidarity. Students can learn the values of social justice through interdisciplinary readings and dialogues as well as through the experience of engaging with people in a community and in the transformation of social processes and structures. Professionals, community members, and students can learn together how to empower themselves, share their power, and attend to issues of power dynamics in ways that are growth-promoting and healing rather than destructive and oppressive. By attending to these dynamics, students also have the opportunity to actively practice aspirational ethics and work through ethical dilemmas that arise, which may aid in their preparation to be ethical researchers, teachers, and clinicians.

PAR is an approach to research that actively promotes liberation and social justice through the development of social consciousness; the planning and implementation of social action projects; and activities of relationship building, power sharing, collaboration, and reflexivity of not just the content of the research but also the processes. It is our hope that more counseling psychologists take up this forward-thinking approach to social justice work in their activism and writing as well as in the training of graduate students.

Mixed methods. Within both qualitative and quantitative paradigms, *triangulation* is used to enhance the credibility of a study by bringing different lenses to the study of the topic at hand. In qualitative research, triangulation may be achieved by using multiple sources of data, multiple investigators, various theories, or multiple methods (Denzin, 1978). Traditionally, ethnography and case studies have employed both qualitative and quantitative strategies; so, although considered qualitative approaches, these methods often are, in fact, mixed-method approaches. Mixed-method (qualitative–quantitative) research can provide both the depth

and richness of meaning that are possible using qualitative research as well as broader, more generalizable findings from quantitative research. Creswell, Plano Clark, Gutmann, and Hanson (2003) defined mixed-method research as

> the collection or analysis of both quantitative and qualitative data in a single study in which the data are collected concurrently or sequentially, are given a priority, and involve the integration of the data at one or more stages in the process of research. (p. 212)

In addition to triangulation, Greene, Caracelli, and Graham (1989) articulated reasons for conducting mixed-method research, including complementarity (where findings from one method expand on or elaborate the other), development (results from one analytical strand are used to inform or develop the other), initiation (looking for contradictions and paradoxes when results from the two methods are compared), and expansion (where the range and breadth of a study is expanded by using multiple analytical elements for different phases of the research). Other reasons for using mixed methods include achieving a better understanding of a phenomenon by combining quantitative and qualitative findings, using qualitative research to identify constructs that may then be tested qualitatively, using quantitative findings to help identify appropriate participants for a subsequent qualitative investigation, and gathering information about members of marginalized or under-represented groups (Hanson et al., 2005).

The mixed-method researcher has numerous decisions to make and challenges to face. The first involves making decisions about the paradigm or theoretical lens that will undergird the study (Hanson et al., 2005). Paradigm debates abound as to whether it is appropriate to mix paradigms, which may be necessary in a mixed-method study. As noted, Tashakkori and Teddlie (2003) advocated a pragmatist approach to paradigms, particularly when using mixed methods. A second task of the mixed-method researcher is to make decisions about the priority placed on the different methods (whether qualitative and quantitative approaches will be relatively equal in weight or unequal) and issues of timing (whether the qualitative and quantitative data collection will occur concurrently or sequentially; Creswell et al., 2003). Finally, the researcher must carefully plan how she or he will integrate the qualitative and quantitative data.

Several typologies of mixed-method research designs are used across disciplines. One approach, developed by Creswell et al. (2003), articulates six types of designs, three sequential and three concurrent. Within each, the three designs vary according to their paradigmatic bases and whether there is an advocacy–social justice approach associated with the design, whether the priority given to qualitative and quantitative components is equal, when data are analyzed and integrated, and which procedural notations are used to illustrate the approach (Hanson et al., 2005).

Hanson et al. (2005) stressed the importance of clearly stating the research purpose and questions as well as explaining the rationale for using mixed methods. Also, because it is challenging to master both qualitative and quantitative methods, they recommend conducting research in teams, where the strengths of different researchers can be maximized. Finally, they suggested that mixed-method researchers be explicit about indicating mixed-method designs in the titles of their manuscripts and use the developing nomenclature to build a common understanding of mixed-method research.

In addition to the research designs described in this chapter, there are many more, including ethnography, case study, narrative research, and others. We encourage qualitative researchers to explore these designs to find approaches that best fit their research questions to continue to become a more methodologically diverse discipline. This may be particularly important given counseling psychology's multicultural and social justice agendas.

Multicultural and Social Justice Issues in Qualitative Research in Counseling Psychology

Intrinsic to qualitative research is the goal of giving voice to the experience of participants and allowing the complexities of their lives to unfold. This is consistent with culturally sensitive research, which centralizes the cultural context of participants (Choudhuri, 2003, 2005) and aims to dismantle Eurocentric and privileged paradigms. Tillman (2002) insightfully explained, "Culture can be conceptualized and defined differently depending on one's worldview and one's particular needs as a researcher and scholar" (p. 3). As counseling psychology reawakens to a social justice agenda (Speight & Vera, 2008), the definition of culture shifts and is much more dynamic and contextualized. Culture with a social justice frame is nestled within the concepts of power, privilege, and access to resources. Without adequate multicultural competency, however, the researcher may encounter numerous roadblocks and run the risk of an ethical violation.

Counseling psychologists are held accountable by the American Psychological Association's (APA) code of ethics to conduct research within their areas of competence (APA, 2010). Using the principle of *nonmaleficence* (do no harm) as a baseline, critical decision points in multicultural qualitative research can be identified within the study's design (e.g., development of the research question(s), participant recruitment, data collection, data analysis, and the presentation of the results). Haverkamp (2005) eloquently cautioned, "What makes research 'ethical' is not a characteristic of the design or procedures, but of our individual decisions, actions, relationships, and commitments" (p. 147). To conduct ethical multicultural qualitative research, researchers must be mindful of design-related decisions and how we are relating to the individuals and communities under study. This is the first act of social justice in the quest to repair cultural mistrust of researchers resulting from historical injustices committed in the name of research (Schulz, Caldwell, & Foster, 2003).

The APA "Guidelines on Multicultural Education, Training, Research, Practice, and Organizational Change for Psychologists" (APA, 2003) address the first relevant decision point in multicultural qualitative research, which is the development of the research question(s). Qualitative research questions should be examined for inherent biases that frame the study with a deficit perspective (Egharevba, 2001). For example, Villalpando's (2003) longitudinal, multimethod study of students of color on college campuses could have been framed from a deficit perspective had he asked why students of color segregate themselves from the predominately White student body. This type of question would have been in line with the theory of *racial balkanization* (Duster, 1995), which presumes that students of color hanging out together on college campuses are engaging in self-segregation. Instead, using a Latino/a critical race theory paradigm, Villalpando (2003) explored how Chicano/a student peer groups influence each other's "socially conscious values," subsequent career choices, and service to the community.

Participant recruitment is a second decision point. Sampling and recruitment strategies often require that the researcher be clear about the parameters for participation. Demographic characteristics such as racial–ethnic identification, sexual orientation, age, religion, and immigration status can be sensitive issues (Choudhuri, 2005). Using language to describe the study and requirements for inclusion that are jargon free and nonpatronizing is critical. This is a situation in which having an insider's perspective, a research team, or consultants can be very useful. DeBlaere, Brewster, Sarkees, and Moradi (2010) provided a thorough review of the complexity of self-identification for lesbian, gay, and bisexual (LGB) people of color, which reflects the intersectionality of sexual orientation, race and ethnicity, and gender. The authors suggested that researchers become aware of the variety of descriptions across cultures when communicating about self-identification during recruitment. Another example of an issue with recruitment involves immigration-related generational status. Self-identification as a first-generation, 1.5-generation (Kim, Brenner, Liang, & Asay, 2003), or second-generation immigrant can be complicated by a childhood of frequent transnational migration. Also, asking participants to reveal citizenship status without careful consideration of historical context and consequences of answering such a question is an exertion—and possible misuse—of the researcher's power and privilege.

The third decision point involves issues related to data collection. Keeping in mind Haverkamp's (2005) focus on relationship with participants, before entering a community, understanding the

cultural norms and the way these norms can shift will prevent missteps by the researcher. These errors may be due to a lack of knowledge or experience with a community, but also could be due to a misguided sense of the insider's perspective. For example, an unmarried, third-generation, Mexican American qualitative researcher may have very little in common with a Latina mother who recently immigrated from Venezuela. Instead, an Ethiopian male qualitative researcher who recently immigrated to the United States with his family might have a better understanding of the participant's experience. Thus, rather than assuming racial, ethnic, or gender matching will facilitate the relational connection, the researcher should consider markers most salient in participants' lives (i.e., family and immigration status).

Developing interview questions that effectively tap into the participants' experiences requires careful thought. Bowleg's (2008) work about the methodological challenges of *intersectionality* research emphasizes the importance of asking good questions. In her research with Black lesbian women, she avoided the "additive approach (Black + Lesbian + Woman)" (p. 314), and instead focused on intersectionality by asking questions about participants' experiences as Black lesbian women, rather than asking questions with the phrase "race, gender, *and/or* sexual orientation" (p. 316). Godreau (2008) also tackled the power of language by examining the contextual nature of linguistic shifts of racial terminology in Puerto Rico. She explained that "slippery semantics" occur within a conversation when individuals use "multiple racial terms to describe the same individual, the consistent use of binary black/white terminology, or the use of the same racial term to describe different 'types of phenotypes' during a single narrative event" (Godreau, 2008, p. 7). The social negotiation of other- and self-identification is an example of the multicultural complexity that a qualitative researcher must consider when developing the criteria for inclusion as well as during data collection.

Family interviews are another possible method of data collection. Berghauser (2009) shared the difficulties and benefits of this method in her report of the phenomenological experience of challenges and resiliency in same-sex parented families. She conducted interviews with all of the family members at the same time and later reflected on the power of the interview process:

> In several of these interviews, words and facial expressions suggested that this format had opened new conversations among family members, and encouraged the questioning of certain ideas and values held by the family. Since maintaining high levels of daily activity was significant for all of the families; simply sitting as a family and talking about what that means seemed to cement and affirm them as a unique family unit. More plainly, from a social constructionist view, telling others outside the family system about your family would appear to make it all more real and acknowledged. (p. 125)

She also urged researchers conducting family interviews to "acknowledge the privilege of being part of their shared intimacy" (Berghauser, 2009, p. 124).

The final decision point involves data analysis and (re)presentation of participants' stories. Because the researcher is the instrument of data collection, this process requires continuous examination of the researcher's worldview. A major concern in multicultural qualitative research is misinterpreting participants' narratives and, as a result, perpetuating stereotypes. One method for avoiding this scenario is to use a collaborative approach and ask participants to be coresearchers in the analytic process (Morrow & Smith, 1995). With the goal of accurate interpretations, Lyons and Bike (2010) reiterated the value of member checks and added that researchers are fulfilling a "moral responsibility to participants" (p. 422) by doing so. Bilingual researchers who conduct interviews in the participants' native languages may consider leaving participant transcripts in the original language, even conducting the analysis in the participant's language before translating the results into the language of the final audience. Lyons and Bike also suggested supporting interpretations with an abundance of participant quotes. These quotes may appear first in the participant's natural language,

followed by translation to the language of publication. This not only (re)presents the participants' voices, but privileges their words and worldview within the results.

As multicultural qualitative research increasingly gains attention within counseling psychology, the needs of researchers evolve as well. The conflicts between ethical dilemmas and sound qualitative methods (e.g., in-depth interviews) create the need for continued review of the practice of multicultural qualitative research. Martín-Baró (1994) furthered this assertion by suggesting that psychological researchers

> examine our theoretical assumptions, not so much from the standpoint of their intrinsic logic as from their historical logic; that is, in terms of whether they work and are truly effective in the here and now. But on the other hand, it forces us to cast off the veil of lies we move about in, and to look at the truth of our social existence without the ideological crutches of our routine work or of professional inertia. (p. 120)

This statement challenges seasoned qualitative researchers to seek flexibility in shifting methods and paradigms to be congruent with the community under study. Martín-Baró (1994) spoke of professional inertia, which can be applied to multicultural qualitative research. This inertia may be due to a lack of training and exposure to diverse methodologies, or it may be due to professional pressure. We are obliged to examine when we feel safe with a particular methodological approach rather than considering the fit with the community to be studied; otherwise, the voices of the research participants may be lost in this state of inertia, and we may cause more harm than good by presenting their "voices" in inaccurate ways or alienating them from the research process.

International Issues in Qualitative Research in Counseling Psychology

Although the counseling professions as well as the broader field of psychology have been involved in international activities for more than a century, there has been a recent flurry of international activity in counseling psychology that has included (among other projects) the creation of an international section of Division 17 of APA, an international counseling psychology conference, and a new handbook on cross-cultural counseling that includes authors from around the world (for more information, see Gerstein, Heppner, Ægisdottir, Leung, & Norsworthy, 2009). Although this renewed interest in international psychology is exciting and full of promising collaborations, there are also important challenges to consider when engaging in cross-cultural research. In this section, we briefly problematize the exportation of U.S. research methodologies and processes to other countries and cultures. Then we propose international qualitative research practices that value cooperation, nonexploitation, and mutuality and that work toward social change.

Challenges to consider in cross-cultural research. Trimble and Fisher (2006) recounted the history of exploitation of indigenous and international communities in research. They wrote,

> Over the decades, well-intended researchers found their way to Indian and native communities, consorted with tribal leaders and their informants, conducted their research, snapped countless photos, recorded sacred songs, and documented rituals and ceremonies, many of which were forbidden to be witnessed by outsiders; then they left, in many instances never to be heard from again. (p. xvi)

Although this form of data mining is no longer acceptable in anthropology communities, it is still widely practiced in other fields of international research, including psychology. In their chapter on bringing social justice practices to international counseling psychology activities, Norsworthy and Khuankaew (2006) featured "voices from Asia" (p. 423), or stories from people living in Asia who had recently experienced exploitation and oppression from Western professionals coming to their country to "help" but who arrived with only a

Westerner-as-expert framework for helping. The stance of researcher-as-expert is taught and practiced in counseling psychology graduate programs across the United States. Because of the U.S. position of power and privilege in the global village, this attitude is at best not helpful and at worst harmful when engaging in cross-cultural work and relationships. Beyond assuming the general role of the expert, there are additional ethical dilemmas and challenges in exporting U.S. psychology models across borders of cultures and countries. Norsworthy, Heppner, Ægisdottir, Gerstein, and Pedersen (2009) wrote, "We have maintained that the exportation of U.S. psychology and counseling can become an instrument of psychological colonization, particularly in relation to the exportation of U.S. counseling models to non-Western contexts" (p. 78).[1]

There are also methodological challenges to consider in conducting cross-cultural qualitative research. Ægisdottir, Gerstein, Leung, Kwan, and Lonner (2009) described three issues of equivalence across cultures that include *conceptual, functional,* and *linguistic.* In other words, conceptual understandings, functions and operations of the research constructs, and the ways in which these concepts are formed and expressed (written, oral, or performance) may not translate as we expect them to across cultures. For example, the word *gender* in the United States has markedly different historical, social, and political contexts attached to it than to the relatively new word, *gender,* in Thailand (Norsworthy & Khuankaew, 2006). Thus, a well-intentioned U.S. researcher conducting a qualitative interview study about *gender* in Chiang Mai, Thailand, may unknowingly bring U.S. conceptions, functions, and linguistics to the design, implementation, and interpretation of the research. This not only produces wholly inaccurate research but also continues the reign of U.S. imperialism by defining the Thai reality of *gender* through the lens of U.S. history, politics, and social processes.

Possibilities for cross-cultural research. In qualitative research, the concept of *thick description*

[1]Note that in this chapter, we use the term *Western* as it is used by people in South and Southeast Asia to describe people living in Global North countries such as Canada, the United States, and those in Western Europe.

(Geertz, 1973) is prized and considered a method to which to aspire. Ægisdottir et al. (2009) recommended that counseling psychology stands to learn much about thick description in cross-cultural research from the field of anthropology. They wrote,

> Not surprisingly, anthropologists acquire much more revealing and valid information through extended periods of time in the field. This is in sharp contrast to cross-cultural counseling researchers, who often spend a limited time in the field and instead rely on interviews and survey methodology to collect data (pp. 102–103)

They recommended various methods and techniques to use in cross-cultural qualitative research, such as participant observation, unstructured interviews, free listing, and the cultural consensus model by Romney, Weller, and Batchelder (1986).

According to Norsworthy et al. (2009), U.S. counseling psychologists can begin to make a new name for psychology in the international arena in various ways. A first step includes educating oneself about the history of colonialism, U.S. imperialism, and xenophobia as well as liberation, indigenous, feminist, and critical theories. Additionally, they recommended engaging in research that includes participatory action models, power sharing, and collaboration throughout the research process. This may mean unlearning traditional modes of research from a postpositivist paradigm and wrestling with new conceptions of researcher power dynamics and relationships between researcher, participant, and coresearcher. Norsworthy and Khuankaew (2006) shared the importance of cross-cultural counseling psychologists partnering with local communities rather than going directly to the academic institutions in other countries. Additionally, they wrote, "Qualitative methodologies aimed at centering and amplifying the experiences and voices of the research and practice communities as authorities over their own lives serve as liberatory vehicles for groups that have been historically and/or globally devalued and silenced" (p. 439). Finally, Horne and Mathews (2004, 2006) outlined a model of international consultation for counseling psychologists that can be relevant to qualitative researchers who are interested

in preparing themselves for cross-cultural work. This model includes setting a context for collaboration, researcher self-evaluation of biases and values, engagement in power sharing, privileging participant–coresearcher needs and goals, an awareness of the impact of research on participants–coresearchers, a social justice–action component, and a collaborative evaluation process and follow-up contact.

Finally, for those interested in pursuing socially just cross-cultural research, we provide examplars of this challenging yet promising international work. In Norsworthy and Khuankaew (2004), the authors walked through their capacity-building workshop model for working with women who have experienced gender-based violence in Southeast Asia. Lykes and Moane (2009) provided a compelling argument for the use of liberation and feminist psychologies when engaging in research, consultation, or practice in the global village. In fact, the entire Volume 19 of the journal *Feminism and Psychology* includes articles written from around the globe on using liberatory, feminist, and participatory research and consultation practices. Norsworthy and Khuankaew (2006) detailed the joys and challenges along the journey of their own working relationship and friendship across global North–South borders. Last, but certainly not least, Part II of the *International Handbook of Cross-cultural Counseling* (Gerstein et al., 2009) provides outstanding chapters written by counseling professionals, healers, and helpers from various regions of the world. These articles offer examples of grassroots advocacy and social justice movements as well as the historical, social, and political contexts of the counseling, consultation, and helping professions established in those regions.

Quality and Trustworthiness in Qualitative Research

Trustworthiness is the term frequently used by qualitative researchers to describe the "rigor" or "credibility" of a qualitative study. Issues of what constitutes trustworthiness in a qualitative study are complicated by the paradigms that underpin the research. Because most quantitative research is conducted from a postpositivist paradigm, a common language expressing the standards for quality has developed over time so that quantitative researchers need not articulate their paradigm nor explain constructs such as validity, reliability, and generalizability. Qualitative researchers, however, have some common standards and practices across paradigms as well as some that are paradigm-specific (Morrow, 2005). Although it is beyond the scope of this chapter to address particular paradigm-specific standards of trustworthiness, it is important that researchers, dissertation committee members, and reviewers understand the differences among paradigms and apply appropriate standards. Researchers will do well to assess the journals in which they hope to publish to select paradigms that are acceptable to those journals.

Morrow (2005) articulated four overarching criteria for trustworthiness that transcend specific paradigms. The first criterion, social validity, relates closely to the social value of the research we conduct as counseling psychologists who are striving for multicultural competence and who are committed to social justice. The second addresses how researchers deal with subjectivity and reflexivity. Although the purposes of self-reflection vary across paradigms (from bracketing to engaging one's subjectivity), this process is an essential component of trustworthiness in qualitative research. The third component is adequacy of data. Researchers vary in their estimates about how many participants constitute a good study, and concepts such as redundancy of data or theoretical saturation are good guidelines for researchers. The goal of a qualitative study is to have findings that are rich and complex; sufficient data are essential to achieve this goal. Adequacy of interpretation goes hand-in-hand with adequacy of data and involves immersion in the data, a systematic and well-thought-out analytic strategy, and writing that offers a balance of the researcher's interpretation and participants' supporting quotes. Thick description, consisting of not only rich, full, descriptions but also of the context of the research and participants' lives, is an indispensable component of adequate interpretation and of trustworthiness.

WRITING AND PUBLISHING QUALITATIVE RESEARCH IN COUNSELING PSYCHOLOGY

Compared with other social science disciplines whose roots are in positivism–postpositivism,

counseling psychology is a hospitable venue for qualitative researchers to conduct, write, and publish qualitative research. Although we certainly have a way to go to be fully embracing of qualitative research (Ponterotto & Grieger, 2007), both of our major publishing outlets, *TCP* and *JCP*, welcome rigorously conducted and well-written qualitative work. Morrow (2005) and Ponterotto and Grieger (2007) made a number of recommendations for writing and publishing qualitative research. Ponterotto and Grieger argued that the foundation of successful writing and publishing is sufficient training in qualitative methods. Although only a small minority of counseling psychology programs provide this training, the authors recommended pursuing training at conferences as well as taking advantages of the rich variety of qualitative resources available. They also outlined four phases of development for the novice researcher to attain mastery. They further emphasized the importance of having knowledge of philosophy of science, research paradigms, and a variety of research methods.

Many facets of good writing are common to both quantitative and qualitative research approaches. Ponterotto and Grieger (2007) and Elliott, Fischer, and Rennie (1999) suggested seven guidelines to increase publishability of qualitative research. These included owning one's perspective as the researcher, describing research participants in depth and detail, grounding the results in examples, detailing procedures for establishing trustworthiness, presenting results in a coherent manner, specifying whether the goals of the research are general or specific, and resonating with the audience. Ponterotto and Grieger described thick description as "the linchpin of qualitative writing" (p. 416). They further emphasized knowing one's audience and gave guidelines for targeting specific journals and books for publication. They included a special section for graduate students on conducting qualitative research.

A number of valuable resources will assist the qualitative researcher in achieving her or his writing goals. Morrow (2005), in an appendix to her article on trustworthiness, provided an outline for qualitative research proposals that expands on APA Style by including sections unique to qualitative research. Ponterotto and Grieger (2007) gave excellent recommendations for writing qualitative journal articles. In addition, *JCP* (2010) has published *Guidelines for Reviewing Manuscripts for the* Journal of Counseling Psychology, which integrates guidelines that have been developed for reviewing qualitative research. These guidelines are a valuable tool for writing manuscripts for publication for any professional journal.

CONCLUSION

In this chapter, we have identified the current status of qualitative research in counseling psychology. As Ponterotto (2005b, 2005c) and Hoyt and Bhati (2007) suggested, we have made strides in our discipline, but we still have room to grow if we are to respond to the multiple calls for methodological diversity. In particular, graduate training programs should assess their responsibility for adequately educating students in qualitative methods, given that both of our discipline's journals welcome and publish qualitative research. Just as training programs insist that their graduates (including the majority of counseling psychology students who will go on to be practitioners) become intelligent consumers of research, it is imperative that with the increasing numbers of qualitative studies in our field, our students become conversant in qualitative methodologies.

At present, counseling psychology demonstrates some diversity in the paradigms and research designs that are published in our journals. There is a paucity of qualitative research, however, on the basis of critical–ideological paradigms or that use methods such as PAR. This is likely because these paradigms and methods run counter to the predominantly postpositivist, quantitative orientation of our field. Despite the gains that we have made to broaden our research horizons, it may be that those qualitative approaches that are most compatible with the dominant model are more acceptable to the mainstream of counseling psychology. Counseling psychologists are, indeed, conducting qualitative research on the basis of critical–ideological paradigms, particularly in the areas of multiculturalism and social justice. They are also conducting PAR that is published in journals outside of our specific

discipline. It would be helpful to raise questions about institutional barriers (e.g., funding sources; implications for graduation, tenure, and promotion; openness of our journals to alternative paradigms and methods) to publishing in counseling psychology outlets. It is likely that younger, social justice–oriented counseling psychologists who are pursuing alternative approaches lack the institutional power to affect more powerful faculty, funders, and editorial boards. Thus, more conventional qualitative—and quantitative—researchers bear the responsibility to work as allies to open the doors to genuine methodological diversity.

Another barrier to the inclusion of PAR in our methodological repertoire is the likelihood that institutional structures do not reward this more longitudinal approach to research. Qualitative research, in general, takes more time to conduct than does quantitative research; and it requires more space to adequately publish results. PAR, specifically, requires even more time and resources, as entry into the field and building trust in oppressed communities often engage the researcher in a long and challenging journey. Participating with a community in social action is no short-term fix. Counseling psychology researchers have the opportunity to address institutional norms that limit the scope of meaningful research. In addition, we can join with practitioner–activists in the community to conduct community-based research.

Finally, given our commitments to multiculturalism and social justice, we should assess the limitations of our paradigms and designs in responding to the needs of underrepresented, marginalized, and oppressed peoples. Most notably, the predominance of single, short, individual interviews ignores the relational values of many cultural groups. Such interviews may highlight the unequal power held by academic researchers. Despite Polkinghorne's (2005) strong recommendation that interviewers should have at least three meetings with research participants, the pressures of time to graduation and publishing expectations may make researchers shortsighted about creative alternatives to the single-session interview. In addition to multiple-session interviews, focus groups should become a norm for interviewing members of marginalized groups because such groups help to minimize the power of the researcher while providing validation and support for participants. These strategies may help to shift the focus from mere rapport building to building meaningful and empowering research relationships.

In this chapter, we have briefly addressed issues of quality and trustworthiness in qualitative research and noted the importance of applying appropriate standards to qualitative studies from different paradigms. We suggest that education in philosophy of science and scientific paradigms be incorporated into doctoral programs, with an application component so that doctoral trainees can begin to understand the relevance of paradigmatic clarity. Furthermore, we urge research committee members and journal manuscript reviewers to become familiar with the paradigms undergirding qualitative research and to apply appropriate standards in the review process.

Overall, counseling psychology is a leader in psychology as a whole in embracing qualitative research into its scientific repertoire. We believe this reflects our openness as a discipline to diversities of all kinds. It is our hope that counseling psychology will avoid becoming parochial in its approach to alternative paradigms and methods and also that qualitative researchers will reach out beyond disciplinary boundaries to take part in the larger evolution of qualitative research.

References

Ægisdóttir, S., Gerstein, L. H., Leung, S. M. A, Kwan, K. L. K., & Lonner, W. J. (2009). Theoretical and methodological issues when studying culture. In L. H. Gerstein, P. P. Heppner, S. Ægisdóttir, S. M. A. Leung, & K. L. Norsworthy (Eds.), *International handbook of cross-cultural counseling: Cultural assumptions and practices worldwide* (pp. 89–109). Thousand Oaks, CA: Sage.

American Psychological Association. (2003). Guidelines on multicultural education, training, research, practice, and organizational change for psychologists. *American Psychologist, 58*, 377–402. doi:10.1037/0003-066X.58.5.377

American Psychological Association. (2010). *Ethical principles of psychologists and code of conduct (2002, Amended June 1, 2010)*. Retrieved from http://www.apa.org/ethics/code/index.aspx

Anzaldua, G. (1987). La conciencia de la mestiza [Towards a new consciousness]. In G. Anzaldua (Ed.), *Borderlands/la frontera: The new mestiza* (2nd ed., p. 377–389). San Francisco, CA: Aunt Lute.

Beck, K. A. (2005). Ethnographic decision tree modeling: A research method for counseling psychology. *Journal of Counseling Psychology, 52*, 243–249. doi:10.1037/0022-0167.52.2.243

Berghauser, K. (2009). *A phenomenological study of same-sex parented families: Perspectives on relational resiliency and social challenge* (Doctoral dissertation). Available from Proquest Dissertations and Theses database. (ProQuest ID 1852713221)

Bishop, R. (2005). Freeing ourselves from neocolonial domination in research: A Kaupapa Maori approach to creating knowledge. In N. K. Denzin & Y. S. Lincoln (Eds.), *The Sage handbook of qualitative research* (3rd ed., pp. 109–138). Thousand Oaks, CA: Sage.

Bowleg, L. (2008). When Black + lesbian + woman ≠ Black lesbian woman: The methodological challenges of qualitative and quantitative intersectionality research. *Sex Roles, 59*, 312–325. doi:10.1007/s11199-008-9400-z

Brydon-Miller, M. (2008). Ethics and action research: Deepening our commitment to principles of social justice and redefining systems of democratic practice. In P. Reason & H. Bradbury (Eds.), *The Sage handbook of action research: Participative inquiry and practice* (2nd ed., pp. 199–210). Thousand Oaks, CA: Sage.

Carter, R. T., & Morrow, S. L. (2007). Qualitative research: Current and best practices. *The Counseling Psychologist, 35*, 205–208. doi:10.1177/0011000006296913

Charmaz, K. (2000). Grounded theory: Objectivist and constructivist methods. In N. K. Denzin & Y. S. Lincoln (Eds.), *Handbook of qualitative research* (2nd ed., pp. 509–536). Thousand Oaks, CA: Sage.

Charmaz, K. (2006). *Constructing grounded theory: A practical guide through qualitative analysis*. London, England: Sage.

Choudhuri, D. D. (2003). Qualitative research and multicultural counseling competency. In D. Pope-Davis, H. L. K. Coleman, W. M. Liu, & R. L. Toporek (Eds.), *Handbook of multicultural competencies in counseling and psychology* (pp. 267–281). Thousand Oaks, CA: Sage.

Choudhuri, D. D. (2005). Conducting culturally sensitive qualitative research. In M. G. Constantine & D. W. Sue (Eds.), *Strategies for building multicultural competence in mental health and educational settings* (pp. 269–282). Hoboken, NJ: Wiley.

Clarke, A. E. (2005). *Situational analysis: Grounded theory after the postmodern turn*. Thousand Oaks, CA: Sage.

Corbin, J., & Strauss, A. L. (1990). Grounded theory research: Procedures, canons, and evaluative criteria. *Qualitative Sociology, 13,* 3–21. doi:10.1007/BF00988593

Creswell, J. W. (2007). *Qualitative inquiry and research design: Choosing among five approaches.* Thousand Oaks, CA: Sage.

Creswell, J. W., Hanson, W. E., Plano Clark, V. L., & Morales, A. (2007). Qualitative research designs: Selection and implementation. *The Counseling Psychologist, 35,* 236–264. doi:10.1177/0011000006287390

Creswell, J. W., Plano Clark, V. L., Gutmann, M. L., & Hanson, W. E. (2003). Advanced mixed methods research designs. In A. Tashakkori & C. Teddlie (Eds.), *Handbook of mixed methods in social and behavioral research* (pp. 209–240). Thousand Oaks, CA: Sage.

DeBlaere, C., Brewster, M., Sarkees, A., & Moradi, B. (2010). Conducting research with LGB people of color: Methodological challenges and strategies. *The Counseling Psychologist, 38,* 331–362.

Denzin, N. K. (1978). *The research act: A theoretical introduction to sociological methods.* New York, NY: McGraw-Hill.

Denzin, N. K., & Lincoln, Y. S. (2000). Introduction: The discipline and practice of qualitative research. In N. K. Denzin & Y. S. Lincoln (Eds.), *Handbook of qualitative research* (2nd ed., pp. 1–28). Thousand Oaks, CA: Sage.

de Waal, F. (2001). *The ape and the sushi master: Cultural reflections of a primatologist.* New York, NY: Basic Books.

Duster, T. (1995). They're taking over! And other myths about race on campus. In M. Berube & C. Nelson (Eds.), *Higher education under fire: Politics, economics, and the crisis of the humanities* (pp. 276–283). New York, NY: Routledge.

Egharevba, I. (2001). Researching an "other" minority ethnic community: Reflections of a Black female researcher on the intersections of race, gender and other power positions in the research process. *International Journal of Social Research Methodology: Theory and Practice, 4,* 225–241. doi:10.1080/13645570010023760

Elliott, R., Fischer, C. T., & Rennie, D. L. (1999). Evolving guidelines for publication of qualitative research studies in psychology and related fields. *British Journal of Clinical Psychology, 38,* 215–229.

Fals-Borda, O., & Rahman, M. A. (Eds.). (1991). *Action and knowledge: Breaking the monopoly with participatory action research.* New York, NY: Apex.

Fassinger, R. E. (2005). Paradigms, praxis, problems, and promise: Grounded theory in counseling psychology research. *Journal of Counseling Psychology, 52,* 156–166. doi:10.1037/0022-0167.52.2.156

Fine, M. (2007). Expanding the methodological imagination. *The Counseling Psychologist, 35,* 459–473. doi:10.1177/0011000006296172

Fine, M., Torre, M. E., Boudin, K., Bowen, I., Clark, J., Hylton, D., . . . Upegui, D. (2003). Participatory action research: From within and beyond the prison bars. In P. Camic, J. E. Rhodes, & L. Yardley (Eds.), *Qualitative research in psychology: Expanding perspectives in methodology and design* (pp. 173–198). Washington, DC: American Psychological Association. doi:10.1037/10595-010

Freire, P. (2003). *Pedagogy of the oppressed* (30th anniversary edition). New York, NY: Continuum.

Geertz, C. (1973). Thick description: Toward an interpretive theory of culture. In *The interpretation of cultures: Selected essays by Clifford Geertz* (pp. 1–30). New York, NY: Basic.

Gerstein, L. H., Heppner, P. P., Ægisdottir, S., Leung, S. M. A., & Norsworthy, K. L. (Eds.). (2009). *International handbook of cross-cultural counseling: Cultural assumptions and practices worldwide.* Thousand Oaks, CA: Sage.

Giorgi, A. (1997). The theory, practice, and evaluation of the phenomenological method as a qualitative research procedure. *Journal of Phenomenological Psychology, 28,* 235–260. doi:10.1163/156916297X00103

Glaser, B. G. (1978). *Theoretical sensitivity.* Mill Valley, CA: The Sociology Press.

Glaser, B. G., & Strauss, A. L. (1967). *The discovery of grounded theory.* Chicago, IL: Aldine.

Godreau, I. (2008). Slippery semantics: Race talk and everyday uses of racial terminology in Puerto Rico. *Centro Journal, 20,* 5–33.

Goodyear, R. K., Tracey, T. J. G., Claiborn, C. D., Lichtenberg, J. W., & Wampold, B. E. (2005). Ideographic concept mapping in counseling psychology research: Conceptual overview, methodology, and an illustration. *Journal of Counseling Psychology, 52,* 236–242. doi:10.1037/0022-0167.52.2.236

Greene, J. C., Caracelli, V. J., & Graham, W. F. (1989). Toward a conceptual framework for mixed-method evaluation designs. *Educational Evaluation and Policy Analysis, 11,* 255–274.

Guba, E. G., & Lincoln, Y. S. (1994). Competing paradigms in qualitative research. In N. K. Denzin & Y. S. Lincoln (Eds.), *Handbook of qualitative research* (pp. 105–117). Thousand Oaks, CA: Sage.

Hanson, W. E., Creswell, J. W., Plano Clark, V. L., Petska, K. S., & Creswell, J. D. (2005). Mixed methods research designs in counseling psychology. *Journal of Counseling Psychology, 52,* 224–235. doi:10.1037/0022-0167.52.2.224

Haverkamp, B. E. (2005). Ethical perspectives on qualitative research in applied psychology. *Journal of Counseling Psychology, 52*, 146–155. doi:10.1037/0022-0167.52.2.146

Haverkamp, B. E., Morrow, S. L., & Ponterotto, J. G. (2005). A time and place for qualitative and mixed methods in counseling psychology research. *Journal of Counseling Psychology, 52*, 123–125. doi:10.1037/0022-0167.52.2.123

Haverkamp, B. E., & Young, R. A. (2007). Paradigms, purpose, and the role of the literature. *The Counseling Psychologist, 35*, 265–294. doi:10.1177/001100000 6292597

Herr, K., & Anderson, G. L. (2005). *The action research dissertation*. Thousand Oaks, CA: Sage.

Hill, C. E. (2011). *Consensual qualitative research: A practical resource for investigating social science phenomena*. Washington, DC: American Psychological Association.

Hill, C. E., Knox, S., Thompson, B. J., Williams, E. N., Hess, S. A., & Ladany, N. (2005). Consensual qualitative research: An update. *Journal of Counseling Psychology, 52*, 196–205. doi:10.1037/0022-0167. 52.2.196

Hill, C. E., Thompson, B., & Williams, E. N. (1997). A guide to conducting consensual qualitative research. *The Counseling Psychologist, 25*, 517–572. doi:10.1177/0011000097254001

hooks, b. (2010). *Teaching critical thinking: Practical wisdom*. New York, NY: Taylor & Francis.

Horne, S. G., & Mathews, S. S. (2004). Collaborative consultation: International applications of a multicultural feminist approach. *Journal of Multicultural Counseling and Development, 32*, 366–378.

Horne, S. G., & Mathews, S. S. (2006). A social justice approach to international collaborative consultation. In R. L. Toporek, L. H. Gerstein, N. A. Fouad, G. Roysircar-Sodowsky, & T. Israel (Eds.), *Handbook for social justice in counseling psychology: Leadership, vision, and action* (pp. 388–405). Thousand Oaks, CA: Sage.

Hoshmand, L. T. (1989). Alternate research paradigms: A review and teaching proposal. *The Counseling Psychologist, 17*, 3–79. doi:10.1177/00110000 89171001

Hoshmand, L. T. (2005). Narratology, cultural psychology, and counseling research. *Journal of Counseling Psychology, 52*, 178–186. doi:10.1037/0022-0167. 52.2.178

Howard, G. S. (1983). Toward methodological pluralism. *Journal of Counseling Psychology, 30*, 19–21. doi:10.1037/0022-0167.30.1.19

Hoyt, W. T., & Bhati, K. S. (2007). Principles and practices: An empirical examination of qualitative research in the *Journal of Counseling Psychology*. *Journal of Counseling Psychology, 54*, 201–210. doi:10.1037/0022-0167.54.2.201

Husserl, E. (1962). *Ideas: General introduction to pure phenomenology* (W. R. B. Gibson, Trans.). New York, NY: Collier. (Original work published 1913)

Jackson, J., Chui, H., & Hill, C. E. (2006). *The modification of CQR for case study research: An introduction to CQR*. Unpublished manuscript.

Journal of Counseling Psychology. (2010). Guidelines for reviewing manuscripts for the *Journal of Counseling Psychology*. Retrieved from http://www.apa.org/pubs/ journals/features/cou-reviewer-guidelines.pdf

Kemmis, S., & McTaggart, R. (2005). Participatory action research: Communicative action and the public sphere. In N. K. Denzin & Y. S. Lincoln (Eds.), *The Sage handbook of qualitative research* (3rd ed., pp. 559–603). Thousand Oaks, CA: Sage.

Kidd, S. A., & Kral, M. J. (2005). Practicing participatory action research. *Journal of Counseling Psychology, 52*, 187–195. doi:10.1037/0022-0167.52.2.187

Kim, B. S. K., Brenner, B. R., Liang, C. T. H., & Asay, P. A. (2003). A qualitative study of adaptation experiences of 1.5-generation Asian Americans. *Cultural Diversity and Ethnic Minority Psychology, 9*, 156–170. doi:10.1037/1099-9809.9.2.156

Kindon, S., Pain, R., & Kesby, M. (2007). Connecting people, participation and place. In S. Kindon, R. Pain, & M. Kesby (Eds.), *Participatory action research approaches and methods: Connecting people, participation and place* (pp. 1–5). New York, NY: Routledge.

Lewin, K. (1946). Action research and minority problems. *Journal of Social Issues, 2*, 34–46. doi:10.1111/j.1540-4560.1946.tb02295.x

Lykes, M. B., Coquillon, E., & Rabenstein, K. L. (2010). Theoretical and methodological challenges in participatory community-based research. In H. Landrine & N. F. Russo (Eds.), *Handbook of diversity in feminist psychology* (pp. 55–82). New York, NY: Springer.

Lykes, M. B., & Moane, G. (2009). Editors' introduction: Whither feminist liberation psychology? Critical explorations of feminist and liberation psychologies for a globalizing world. *Feminism and Psychology, 19*, 283–297. doi:10.1177/0959353509105620

Lyons, H. Z., & Bike, D. H. (2010). Designing and interpreting research in multicultural counseling. In J. G. Ponterotto, J. M. Casas, L. A. Suzuki, & C. M. Alexander (Eds.), *Handbook of multicultural counseling* (3rd ed., pp. 413–425). Thousand Oaks, CA: Sage.

Martín-Baró, I. (1994). *Writings for a liberation psychology*. Cambridge, MA: Harvard University Press.

Memmi, A. (1965). *The colonizer and the colonized*. Boston, MA: Beacon.

Mohanty, C. T. (2006). *Feminism without borders: Decolonizing theory, practicing solidarity*. Durham, NC: Duke University Press.

Morrow, S. L. (2005). Quality and trustworthiness in counseling psychology. *Journal of Counseling Psychology, 52*, 250–260. doi:10.1037/0022-0167.52.2.250

Morrow, S. L. (2007). Qualitative research in counseling psychology: Conceptual foundations. *The Counseling Psychologist, 35*, 209–235. doi:10.1177/001100000 6286990

Morrow, S. L., & Smith, M. L. (1995). Constructions of survival and coping by women who have survived childhood sexual abuse. *Journal of Counseling Psychology, 42*, 24–33. doi:10.1037/0022-0167.42.1.24

Morrow, S. L., & Smith, M. L. (2000). Qualitative research for counseling psychology. In S. D. Brown & R. W. Lent (Eds.), *Handbook of counseling psychology* (3rd ed., pp. 199–230). New York, NY: Wiley.

Morse, J. M., Stern, P. N., Corbin, J., Bowers, B., Charmaz, K., & Clarke, A. E. (2009). *Developing grounded theory: The second generation*. Walnut Creek, CA: Left Coast Press.

Moustakas, C. (1994). *Phenomenological research methods*. Thousand Oaks, CA: Sage.

Neimeyer, G., & Resnikoff, A. (1982). Qualitative strategies in counseling research. *The Counseling Psychologist, 10*, 75–85. doi:10.1177/0011000082104015

Norsworthy, K. L., Heppner, P. P., Ægisdottir, S., Gerstein, L. H., & Pedersen, P. B. (2009). Exportation of U.S.-based models of counseling and counseling psychology. In L. H. Gerstein, P. P. Heppner, S. Ægisdottir, S. M. A. Leung, & K. L. Norsworthy (Eds.), *International handbook of cross-cultural counseling: Cultural assumptions and practices worldwide* (pp. 69–88). Thousand Oaks, CA: Sage.

Norsworthy, K. L., & Khuankaew, O. (2004). Women of Burma speak out: Workshops to deconstruct gender-based violence and build systems of peace and justice. *Journal for Specialists in Group Work, 29*, 259–283. doi:10.1080/01933920490477011

Norsworthy, K. L., & Khuankaew, O. (2006). Bringing social justice to international practices of counseling psychology. In R. L. Toporek, L. H. Gerstein, N. A. Fouad, G. Roysircar-Sodowsky, & T. Israel (Eds.), *Handbook for social justice in counseling psychology: Leadership, vision, and action* (pp. 421–441). Thousand Oaks, CA: Sage.

Pedersen, P. B. (1991). Multiculturalism as a generic approach to counseling. *Journal of Counseling and Development, 70*, 6–12.

Polkinghorne, D. E. (1984). Further extension of methodological diversity for counseling psychology. *Journal of Counseling Psychology, 31*, 416–429. doi:10.1037/0022-0167.31.4.416

Polkinghorne, D. E. (1994). Reaction to special section on qualitative research in counseling process and outcome. *Journal of Counseling Psychology, 41*, 510–512. doi:10.1037/0022-0167.41.4.510

Polkinghorne, D. E. (2005). Language and meaning: Data collection in qualitative research. *Journal of Counseling Psychology, 52*, 137–145. doi:10.1037/0022-0167.52.2.137

Ponterotto, J. G. (2005a). Qualitative research in counseling psychology: A primer on research paradigms and philosophy of science. *Journal of Counseling Psychology, 52*, 126–136. doi:10.1037/0022-0167.52.2.126

Ponterotto, J. G. (2005b). *Qualitative research in the* Journal of Counseling Psychology, *1989–2003: A paradigmatic and methodological classification*. Unpublished manuscript.

Ponterotto, J. G. (2005c). Qualitative research training in counseling psychology: A survey of directors of training. *Teaching of Psychology, 32*, 60–62.

Ponterotto, J. G., & Grieger, I. (2007). Effectively communicating qualitative research. *The Counseling Psychologist, 35*, 404–430. doi:10.1177/001 1000006287443

Ponterotto, J. G., Kuriakose, G., & Granovskaya, Y. (2011). *A paradigmatic and methodological content analysis of qualitative research published in the* Journal of Counseling Psychology, *the* Journal of Counseling and Development, *and* The Counseling Psychologist *from 1995–2006: Evidence of a paradigm shift in counseling research?* Unpublished manuscript, Fordham University, New York.

Poulin, K. L. (2007). Teaching qualitative research: Lessons from practice. *The Counseling Psychologist, 35*, 431–458. doi:10.1177/0011000006294813

Prilleltensky, I. (2003). Understanding, resisting, and overcoming oppression: Toward psychopolitical validity. *American Journal of Community Psychology, 31*, 195–201. doi:10.1023/A:1023043108210

Prilleltensky, I., & Nelson, G. (2002). *Doing psychology critically: Making a difference in diverse settings*. New York, NY: Palgrave Macmillan.

Romney, A. K., Weller, S. C., & Batchelder, W. H. (1986). Culture as consensus: A theory of culture and informant accuracy. *American Anthropologist, 88*, 313–338. doi:10.1525/aa.1986.88.2.02a00020

Schulz, A., Caldwell, C., & Foster, S. (2003). What are they going to do with the information? Latino/Latina and African American perspectives on the Human Genome Project. *Health Education and Behavior, 30*, 151–169. doi:10.1177/1090198102251026

Smith, L., Chambers, D. A., & Bratini, L. (2009). When oppression is the pathogen: The participatory development of socially just mental health practice. *American Journal of Orthopsychiatry, 79*, 159–168. doi:10.1037/a0015353

Spangler, P. T., Liu, J., & Hill, C. E. (2006). *CQR for simple qualitative data.* Unpublished manuscript.

Speight, S. L., & Vera, E. M. (2004). A social justice agenda: Ready or not? *The Counseling Psychologist, 32*, 109–118. doi:10.1177/0011000003260005

Speight, S. L., & Vera, E. M. (2008). Social justice and counseling psychology: A challenge to the profession. In S. D. Brown & R. W. Lent (Eds.), *Handbook of counseling psychology* (pp. 54–67). Hoboken, NJ: Wiley.

Starhawk, (1997). *Dreaming the dark: Magic, sex, and politics.* Boston, MA: Beacon.

Strauss, A. L. (1987). *Qualitative analysis for social scientists.* New York, NY: Cambridge University Press. doi:10.1017/CBO9780511557842

Strauss, A. L., & Corbin, J. (1990). *Basics of qualitative research: Grounded theory procedures and techniques.* Newbury Park, CA: Sage.

Suzuki, L. A., Ahluwalia, M. K., Arora, A., & Mattis, J. S. (2007). The pond you fish in determines the fish you catch: Exploring strategies for qualitative data collection. *The Counseling Psychologist, 35*, 295–327. doi:10.1177/0011000006290983

Suzuki, L. A., Ahluwalia, M. K., Mattis, J. S., & Quizon, C. A. (2005). Ethnography in counseling psychology research: Possibilities for application. *Journal of Counseling Psychology, 52*, 206–214. doi:10.1037/0022-0167.52.2.206

Tashakkori, A., & Teddlie, C. (2003). *Handbook of mixed methods in social and behavioral research.* Thousand Oaks, CA: Sage.

Tillman, L. C. (2002). Culturally sensitive research approaches: An African-American perspective. *Educational Researcher, 31*(9), 3–12. doi:10.3102/0013189X031009003

Toporek, R. L., & Williams, R. A. (2006). Ethics and professional issues related to the practice of social justice in counseling psychology. In R. L. Toporek, L. H. Gerstein, N. A. Fouad, G. Roysircar-Sodowsky, & T. Israel (Eds.), *Handbook for social justice in counseling psychology: Leadership, vision, and action* (pp. 17–34). Thousand Oaks, CA: Sage.

Trimble, J. E., & Fisher, C. B. (2006). *The handbook of ethical research with ethnocultural populations and communities.* Thousand Oaks, CA: Sage.

Tuhiwai Smith, L. (1999). *Decolonizing methodologies.* New York, NY: Zed.

Vera, E. M., & Speight, S. L. (2003). Multicultural competence, social justice and counseling psychology: Expanding our roles. *The Counseling Psychologist, 31*, 253–272. doi:10.1177/0011000003031003001

Villalpando, O. (2003). Self-segregation or self-preservation? A critical race theory and Latina/o critical theory analysis of a study of Chicana/o college students. *International Journal of Qualitative Studies in Education, 16*, 619–646. doi:10.1080/0951839032000142922

Wertz, F. J. (2005). Phenomenological research methods for counseling psychology. *Journal of Counseling Psychology, 52*, 167–177. doi:10.1037/0022-0167.52.2.167

Worthen, V., & McNeill, B. W. (1996). A phenomenological investigation of "good" supervision events. *Journal of Counseling Psychology, 43*, 25–34. doi:10.1037/0022-0167.43.1.25

Yeh, C. J., & Inman, A. G. (2007). Qualitative data analysis and interpretation in counseling psychology: Strategies for best practices. *The Counseling Psychologist, 35*, 369–403. doi:10.1177/0011000006292596

Young, R. A., Valach, L., & Domene, J. F. (2005). The action-project method in counseling psychology. *Journal of Counseling Psychology, 52*, 215–223. doi:10.1037/0022-0167.52.2.215

APA HANDBOOK OF COUNSELING PSYCHOLOGY; ED. BY
NADYA A. FOUAD.
                              Cloth   1132 P.
WASHINGTON: AMER PSYCHOLOGICAL ASSN, 2012
SER: APA HANDBOOKS IN PSYCHOLOGY.

ED: UNIVERSITY OF WISCONSIN, MILWAUKEE. 2 VOL.
SET. COLLECTION OF NEW ESSAYS.
LCCN 2011-42148
  ISBN 1433811073   **Library PO#** AP-BOOKS

	List	395.00	USD
395 NATIONAL UNIVERSITY LIBRAR	**Disc**	14.0%	
App. Date 8/01/12 SOC-SCI 8214-11	**Net**	339.70	USD

SUBJ: COUNSELING PSYCHOLOGY--HANDBOOKS, MANUALS,
ETC.

CLASS BF636.6   DEWEY# 158.3   LEVEL ADV-AC

YBP Library Services

APA HANDBOOK OF COUNSELING PSYCHOLOGY; ED. BY
NADYA A. FOUAD.
                              Cloth   1132 P.
WASHINGTON: AMER PSYCHOLOGICAL ASSN, 2012
SER: APA HANDBOOKS IN PSYCHOLOGY.

ED: UNIVERSITY OF WISCONSIN, MILWAUKEE. 2 VOL.
SET. COLLECTION OF NEW ESSAYS.
  LCCN 2011-42148
  ISBN 1433811073   **Library PO#** AP-BOOKS

	List	395.00	USD
395 NATIONAL UNIVERSITY LIBRAR	**Disc**	14.0%	
App. Date 8/01/12 SOC-SCI 8214-11	**Net**	339.70	USD

SUBJ: COUNSELING PSYCHOLOGY--HANDBOOKS, MANUALS,
ETC.

CLASS BF636.6   DEWEY# 158.3   LEVEL ADV-AC

CHAPTER 5

EMERGING TRENDS IN COUNSELING PSYCHOLOGY EDUCATION AND TRAINING

Linda Forrest and Linda F. Campbell

According to Goodyear et al. (2000), "during all of its history, the specialty of counseling psychology has evolved constantly in response to changes in the context in which it exists. As the specialty has changed, so too has training" (p. 603). Counseling psychology education and training has been the focus of many articles across the history of counseling psychology (e.g., Meara et al., 1988); however, education and training has not been the focus of a chapter in a counseling psychology–focused handbook until now. In this chapter, we first review important developments and trends over the past decade that have advanced the education and training of counseling psychologists. Within each section, we also describe perceived gaps and offer recommendations that address the challenges we see now and on the horizon. Finally, we conclude the chapter with overarching and systemic recommendations.

In preparation for writing this chapter on education and training, we reviewed the past decade of issues of the major journals in counseling psychology as well as numerous counseling psychology chapters and books with a counseling psychology focus to identify potential subtopics. We also reviewed issues of *Professional Psychology: Research and Practice* and the new American Psychological Association (APA) journal dedicated to education and training, *Training and Education in Professional Psychology*. We paid special attention to major contributions in *The Counseling Psychologist*, especially if the focus of the major contributions had implications for education and training. Because the

Council of Counseling Psychology Training Programs (CCPTP) is the organization within the specialty of counseling psychology devoted to education and training, we also reviewed recent CCPTP conference programs and listserv archives for topics of importance to this chapter. We do not claim that this review has been exhaustive, but we believe that through this process, we have selected topics with the greatest significance to counseling psychology education and training.

Delimiting the most important developments, events, and actions influencing education and training in counseling psychology was not an easy task. We focus the majority of the chapter on two issues that were repeatedly written about over the past decade: (a) diversity and multicultural scholarship and actions and their integration into training programs and (b) the competency movement, a major cultural shift in education and training focused on identifying baseline competencies required to be a professional psychologist and methods for assessing those competencies. Several other topics captured our attention, not so much because of the quantity of coverage they have received but because we deemed them to have important implications for the future of education and training in counseling psychology. Because of space limitations, these topics receive briefer coverage: internationalization in counseling psychology, evidence-based training, behavioral–integrated health care, the sequence of doctoral training, the interface with master's degree programs and accreditation developments, and public policy advocacy. Of necessity, we have paid little

DOI: 10.1037/13754-005
APA Handbook of Counseling Psychology: Vol. 1. Theories, Research, and Methods, Nadya A. Fouad (Editor-in-Chief)

attention to historical events in education and training before 2000.

We have worked to capture the complexity of interlocking and overlapping issues without over-simplifying their coverage. Many of the issues we address in this chapter overlap broadly with professional psychology training in general; in some cases (e.g., multicultural psychology), counseling psychologists have developed models and influenced education and training for all of professional psychology; other changes at the national level (e.g., behavioral health, integrated health care) have evolved with limited input from counseling psychology educators. One of the great transitions of the past decade has been movement from a more isolationist paradigm in which counseling psychology attended to its training issues apart from broader professional psychology training to a more integrated approach. Leaders within the CCPTP and the Society of Counseling Psychology (SCP) understand the importance of being active and involved in national leadership and influencing and shaping the future of professional psychology education and training with counseling psychology philosophy and values. The result has been that counseling psychology education and training has become more mainstream in some critical and important ways. Similarly, counseling psychology educators have been on the forefront and better informed about educational forces and changes at the national level, allowing us to more quickly incorporate these changes into our counseling psychology training programs (e.g., competencies, benchmarks).

MULTICULTURAL EDUCATION AND TRAINING

We begin this review with developments in diversity and multicultural education and training in counseling psychology for three reasons: the breath and depth of attention to diversity issues over the past decade, their importance as a mainstay value and presence in what it means to be a counseling psychologist, and educators' commitment to the development of multicultural competence as a defining priority in the education and training of counseling psychologists. A clear marker of this growth during the past decade is the large number of books published on different aspects and approaches to diversity (e.g., Bieschke, Perez, & DeBord, 2007; Constantine & Sue, 2005; Fouad & Arredondo, 2007; Ponterotto, Casas, Suzuki, & Alexander, 2001, 2009; Pope-Davis, Coleman, Liu, & Toporek, 2003; Ridley, 2005; Roysircar, Sandhu, & Bibbins, 2003; Sue, 2010; Toporek, Gerstein, Fouad, Roysircar, & Israel, 2006). We address six topics under the rubric of multicultural education and training: (a) progress on filling the pipeline, (b) the creation and growth of the National Multicultural Conference and Summit (NMCS), (c) the identification of individual and cultural diversity as one of the foundational competencies in professional psychology, (d) the development and APA approval of myriad diversity-focused guidelines and recommendations for their integration into curriculum and training settings, (e) the development of the "Counseling Psychology Model Training Values Statement Addressing Diversity" (CCPTP, Association of Counseling Center Training Agencies [ACCTA], & SCP, 2009), and (f) the training implications of recent diversity-focused court challenges and rulings.

Progress on Filling the Pipeline

Efforts by counseling psychology programs to recruit and retain a diverse group of students and faculty have shown slow, steady progress. In a 2007 survey of APA-accredited counseling psychology programs (with a 99% response rate), Norcross, Evans, and Ellis (2010) found that the percentage of ethnic minority students had risen to 29% from the 25% reported in 1998. Moradi and Neimeyer (2005) reviewed longitudinal data on ethnic minority faculty members in counseling psychology programs based on the CCPTPs' annual surveys and found "a clear and consistent increase from approximately 7% (in 1981–1982) to 26% (in 2001–2003)" (p. 662). Moradi and Neimeyer compared faculty data with 2002 census data and reported that African American (11%–12%) and Asian American (3%–4%) faculty percentages appear to approximate those of the general population, with Latino/a faculty percentages (6%–9%) being below their levels in the general population (13.5%) and Native American comparisons being difficult to determine because of CCPTP data constraints.

According to Maton, Kohout, Wicherski, Leary, and Vinokurov (2006), the ethnic minority pipeline for students and faculty in the larger discipline of psychology falls short of counseling psychology statistics. Rates of entry into doctoral programs for ethnic minority students have grown from 17% in 1995 to 22% in 2003. Yet during the same time period, those completing a doctorate in psychology remained stagnant at around 14% to 15%, suggesting a substantial attrition rate during doctoral training for students of color. More devastating is the low percentage of ethnic minority faculty (12%) compared with the overall representation of ethnic minorities in the U.S. population (32%) on the basis of 2003 census data (Maton et al., 2006).

The increased presence of many more ethnic minority students and faculty in counseling psychology programs probably is a major reason for the increase in attention to multicultural issues in counseling psychology. Yet, more progress is needed especially for Latino/a and Native Americans, if the percentage of students, faculty, and practitioners are to parallel their demographics numbers in the U.S. population.

Recommendations. To increase the number of Latina/o and Native American faculty in counseling psychology programs to match their overall representation in U.S. population, we recommend a joint recruitment–mentoring initiative between CCPTP and the National Latina/o Psychology Association and the Society of Indian Psychologists. Also the differential recruitment rates of faculty and students of color among psychology specialties provide an ideal comparison bases for a study to determine what factors help or hinder the process and might point to promising practices to improve the psychology pipeline. Increasing evidence indicates that a diverse student body and faculty have benefits that

> transcend the ethnic background of the
> students, so that all students report an
> increased ability to work with members
> of other ethnic groups, an increased
> acceptance of those from other cul-
> tural backgrounds, and an increased

> participation in community-based and
> other civic activities following gradua-
> tion. (Rogers & Molina, 2006, p. 143)

Thus, we recommend that pipeline progress remain a high priority goal for counseling psychology educators.

Growth of the National Multicultural Conference and Summit

The coordinators of the first and second NMCS, Sue, Bingham, Porché-Burke, and Vasquez (1999), are ethnic minority psychologists, three of whom were at the same time in 1999 presidents of APA Divisions 17, 35, and 45. All were trained and identify as counseling psychologists, so from the beginning, the NMCS was influenced by the philosophical commitments and practical dispositions of counseling psychology. The goals for the first conference were to bring

> together some of the most well-known
> multicultural scholars and practitioners
> in the field to (a) examine state-of-the-
> art issues in ethnic minority psychology;
> (b) facilitate difficult dialogues on race,
> gender, and sexual orientation; (c) forge
> multicultural alliances for political action
> and advocacy; and (d) develop strategies
> for multicultural organizational change.
> (Sue et al., 1999, p. 1061)

Since 1999, the NMCS has been held every 2 years, with the seventh NMCS held in January 2011. The conference provides a time and place for diversity-focused synergy in psychology, furthers the development of multicultural scholarship, and keeps attention focused on psychological needs of minority individuals and communities (Bingham, Porché-Burke, James, Sue, & Vasquez, 2002).

Although multicultural education and training was not mentioned as a goal or focus of the first NMCS, the first and subsequent conferences (on the basis of a review of symposia presented) have included programs focused on integrating multicultural scholarship, difficult dialogues, and advocacy into the curriculum as well as symposia on organizational change focused on training policies and practices. Besides these direct influences, the seven conferences have had indirect influences on education and training. The conferences have drawn a large number of students providing them with initial opportunities to present their work on diversity topics in a supportive environment and have created a space for students to participate in difficult dialogues among diverse and marginalized populations. Thoughtfully constructed difficult dialogues have been part of the conference since its inception and represent an experiential learning caldron for both students and faculty about the importance of understanding the intersectionality of diversities (the idea that many individuals embody multiple marginalized positions). Counseling psychologists have been key leaders and facilitators of these difficult dialogues. Preparation and training to lead these difficult dialogues at an NMCS has become more sophisticated with each subsequent conference, so participating faculty and students have been exposed to the increasingly sophisticated strategies for difficult dialogues, which in turn has influenced the curriculum and policies of counseling psychology programs.

Other important consequences of the NMCS have been increased cross-divisional collaborations, increased involvement of APA leadership (both volunteers and staff) at the conference, and the creation of a place at which diversity conflicts can arise and be addressed in a manner that helps psychology become more sophisticated about diversity intersections. The sustained success of the NMCS is best exemplified by the increasing number of APA divisions that sponsor the conference and hold their midyear meetings in conjunction with it, and the establishment of an endowment fund with the dream of creating financial stability for future NMCS. The campaign for the NMCS Legacy Fund seeks to raise $250,000 in pledges that will provide support for the NMCS in perpetuity beginning with the 2015 NMCS.

Recommendations.   Our review of program titles from the last seven NMCS revealed an uneven coverage of education and training topics; thus we recommend at a minimum that the CCPTP work with the NMCS coordinators to develop a program track focused on multicultural education and train-

ing issues and a dissemination plan of the program content to training programs. Ideally, a whole conference could be devoted to education and training issues. Ultimately, we believe that consistent programming focused on multicultural education and training will produce important benefits for psychology (e.g., curriculum and pedagogical innovations, program policy improvements).

Individual and Cultural Diversity Competency

As part of the Competency Conference in 2002 (Kaslow et al., 2004), individual and cultural diversity (ICD) was identified as one of the eight core competencies for professional psychologists. In this section on Multicultural Education and Training, we focus specifically on the ICD competency; the overall competency movement and its significance to education and training is more fully explicated in the next section. The ICD working group at the 2002 conference (a) identified ICD subcompetencies, (b) described the educational and training experiences required to develop ICD competencies, and (c) identified some initial strategies and methods for the assessment of ICD competencies. The article (Daniel, Roysircar, Abeles, & Boyd, 2004) resulting from the ICD working group focused on racism, homophobia, and ageism and within each of these areas addressed two subcompetencies: (a) awareness of assumptions, values, and biases and (b) knowledge of research, assessment, and practice.

Rodolfa et al. (2005) identified the ICD competency as a foundational competency, a building block for all other competencies that is infused in all aspects of being a psychologist. Fouad et al.'s (2009) "Competency Benchmarks" document further delineated the ICD competency. Four essential subcomponents were identified: self as shaped by ICD, others as shaped by ICD, interactions between self and others as shaped by ICD, and applications on the basis of ICD. Each ICD subcomponent and the corresponding behavioral anchors were described at three levels of professional development: readiness for practicum, internship, and entry to practice. The companion article, the "Competency Assessment Toolkit" (Kaslow et al., 2009), described a myriad of assessment tools, including recommendations about which were most appropriate for measuring the ICD essential components.

Identifying the ICD competency as foundational for all psychologists placed competence with diversity issues as central to what it means to be a psychologist and provided the framework for ensuring that graduates of professional psychology programs have a minimal level of multicultural competence. Yet Donovan and Ponce (2009) recommended caution and careful attention to how dominant "sociocultural factors may have influenced the conceptualization and operationalization of the benchmarks . . . [and] may affect how faculty assess trainees from systemically disadvantaged groups" (pp. S48–S49). Other authors have also raised concerns about how faculty multicultural competence might influence judgments and evaluation of trainees' competence (Forrest, Elman, & Shen-Miller, 2008; Shen-Miller, Forrest, & Elman, 2009).

Recommendations. Because dominant cultural values and influences may have inadvertently narrowed our definitions of competence in a manner that disadvantages some cultural groups, we recommend that a team of multicultural experts conduct

a careful analysis of current and future competency documents to ensure that they are broadly culturally inclusive. Full integration of the ICD competency into education and training will make it more likely that all 15 professional competencies represent and are inclusive of many different cultural backgrounds and group identities.

APA Approved Diversity-Focused Guidelines and Implications for Training

During the same time that ICD was identified as a foundational competency for professional psychologists, the APA approved a series of diversity-focused practice guidelines. Together, these documents are aspirational in nature and represent a huge step forward in laying out clear expectations about professional conduct when working with clients from diverse populations. Counseling psychologists have been actively involved as members and chairs of task forces established to develop and move these guidelines through the APA governance system, a complicated and lengthy process that requires strategic and political acumen. Table 5.1 identifies those guidelines that have been approved by APA as well as those in the pipeline.

TABLE 5.1

American Psychological Association (APA) Approved Diversity-Focused Guidelines

Title of document	Population focus	APA approved/ published	Counseling psychologist involvement	Division involvement
Guidelines for psychotherapy with lesbian, gay, and bisexual clients	Lesbian, gay, bisexual	2000 Revised, 2011	Kris Hancock, Cochair Armand Cerbone, Cochair	Division 44
Guidelines on multicultural education, training, research, practice, and organizational change for psychologists	Race/ethnicity	2003	Patricia Arredondo, Cochair Nadya Fouad, Cochair	Divisions 17 and 45
Guidelines for psychological practice with older adults	Older adults	2004	Michael Duffy, Member of Task Force Geoffrey Reed, APA Staff	
Guidelines for psychological practice with girls and women	Girls and women	2007	Carol Zerbe Enns, Tri-Chair Roberta Nutt, Tri-Chair	Divisions 17 and 35
Guidelines for assessment and intervention with persons with disabilities	Individuals with disibilities	2011	Kay Kriegsman, Member	
Guidelines for psychological practice with boys and men	Men and boys	In pipeline	Frederic Rabinowitz, Chair	Divisions 17 and 51

The APA guidelines (approved and in the pipeline) have important implications and challenges for the education and training of counseling psychologists. Space in the curriculum to cover these guidelines may create competing priorities and probably results in uneven coverage of the various guidelines and diverse levels of competence for graduates of counseling psychology programs. To address these concerns, the SCP and CCPTP established a joint Special Task Group (STG) "to explore effective training strategies . . . and develop an integrative approach for teaching the practice guidelines with diverse populations" (Miville et al., 2009, pp. 519–520). This group articulated underlying shared assumptions, ascertained common elements across diversity-focused guidelines, identified an integrated training approach, and outlined desired training outcomes and possible assessment tools. Their brief review of the literature on the guidelines found that much more has been written about the implications for training related to the multicultural (MC) and lesbian, gay, bisexual (LGB) guidelines than others (e.g., aging, girls and women). A survey of training directors (TDs) of counseling psychology programs about their program's coverage of the guidelines found similar results (i.e., 93% of their programs covered the MC guidelines, 88% covered LGB guidelines, 50% covered the aging guidelines, and only 17% the gender guidelines). TDs identified as barriers to an integrative training approach "uneven support among faculty . . . and uneven levels of competence" (Miville et al., 2009, p. 532). Miville et al. (2009) recommended a multidimensional, integrative approach to teaching the diversity guidelines because it matches the real lives of clients' who often belong to multiple and intersecting social identity groups.

Although both APA ethical and accreditation guidelines (APA, 2000a, 2010b) hold psychologists and programs accountable to multiple types of diversity, Miville et al. (2009) were the first to develop an integrative model responsive to all aspects of diversity covered by APA approved guidelines. The integrative training model (ITM) included four stages: understanding the multicultural self, two aspects of understanding others—the broad and general domains common to all minority groups as well as narrow and specific domains that capture unique cultural characteristics of specific minority groups, and finally, intervention strategies. Competency assessment was also critical in all aspects of the integrative model.

We identified numerous benefits associated with the development of the ITM. The four ITM stages closely match the ICD competencies laid out in the "Competency Benchmarks" (Fouad et al., 2009) document, yet Miville et al. (2009) more fully articulated the "understanding others" by dividing it into two components. Both the ITM and ICD component of the "Competency Benchmarks" document moved the APA approved diversity-focused guidelines from policy to implementation by providing guidance for educators and trainers about ways to address multicultural competence as well as its subcompetencies in academic programs and internships, and how to assess these competencies across the training sequence.

Because APA has mandated that approved guidelines be aspirational in nature rather than establish mandatory standards, the APA *Ethical Principles of Psychologists and Code of Conduct* (Ethics Code; 2010b) is the only place within APA where mandatory diversity standards exist. The APA Ethics Code provides only three standards that specifically address diversity issues: nondiscrimination (Standard 3.01), competence when working with diverse populations (Standard 2.01(b)), and attention to language and cultural identities when interpreting assessment results (Standard 9.06). We believe that the lack of mandatory standards in diversity-focused guidelines and very limited coverage of diversity-related issues in the mandatory section of the APA Ethics Code leaves the door open for the delivery of inadequate and harmful services to clients from marginalized populations with no professional consequences for such behaviors.

Recommendations. The next ethics code revision process provides an ideal time to further develop diversity-focused mandatory standards. We recommend a concerted effort by CCPTP and the SCP to identify possible additions to the Standards section of the APA Ethics Code that would strengthen the code's ability to hold psychologists accountable for providing competent services to diverse and marginalized populations. Furthermore, we recommend active participation in the ethics code revision process, including the appointment of counseling psychologists are appointed to the Revision Task Force and submission of comments during the public comment period by individual counseling psychologists and counseling psychology professional groups.

Finally, the ITM creates a holistic framework for diversity training and the development of diversity competence, yet, its significance must be determined through implementation and evaluation. We recommend that CCPTP make this a priority. Several training programs could volunteer to be demonstration sites whose data would provide empirical evidence for the effectiveness of the model. In turn, the ITM could be considered and incorporated into APA diversity-focused guidelines when they are revised.

Model Training Values Statement Addressing Diversity

As counseling psychology programs increased the number of students from under-represented groups, and faculty improved their coverage of multiple forms of diversity and oppression in academic and internship training programs, greater complexity surfaced in the form of cultural clashes and conflicts presenting faculty and supervisors with new and difficult conundrums. Increased attention to multiple forms of diversity meant increased diversity in deeply held personal values, requiring faculty "to examine their own values, the values of the profession, and to define how they will deal with diversity-related values conflicts in training" (Mintz et al., 2009, p. 648). Three counseling psychology professional organizations, the SCP, the CCPTP, and the ACCTA, together developed and approved in 2006 a "Counseling Psychology Model Training Values Statement Addressing Diversity" (CCPTP, ACCTA, & SCP, 2009), a document that provides guidance for trainers and trainees about how to ensure that personal beliefs do not negatively influence client services. The Values Statement (VS) was drafted on the basis of several assumptions. First, clients deserve the highest quality services regardless of their demographic characteristics and social group identities. Second, educational programs have an imperative to develop and graduate psychologists

who meet at least a minimal level of competence to serve a wide cross-section of clients. And, third, trainers must be role models for professional standards that require nondiscriminatory client services. The initial impetus for this statement was a CCPTP listserv discussion responding to a TD's inquiry about how other TDs handled situations in which students with strong religious beliefs refused to see lesbian, gay, bisexual, and transgendered (LGBT) clients. The ensuing discussion resulted in more than 40 responses, a session on this topic at the 2005 CCPTP meeting, and agreement that developing guidance for training communities was needed.

Mintz and Bieschke (2009) oversaw the development of a major contribution to *The Counseling Psychologist* that included the VS, four related articles, and several commentaries. The lead article provided a brief "values" history, articulated "trainers' expressed need for guidance in dealing with these complex and often emotionally charged value clashes in training" (Mintz et al., 2009, p. 644), defined broad transcendent, orienting values, clarified how the VS goes above and beyond other professional documents, and laid out the responsibilities of trainers. A second article focused on how to operationalize the VS (Winterowd, Adams, Miville, & Mintz, 2009), and the final two articles applied the VS to admission decisions (Loewy, Juntunen, & Duan, 2009) and internship settings (Illfelder-Kaye, Lese-Fowler, Bursley, Reyes, & Bieschke, 2009). These authors asserted that trainees cannot opt out from addressing diversity-related conflicts during training and must resolve conflicts in a manner that meets professional standards for competent care to diverse clients. Trainees are not required to change their personal values but must (a) know their biases, (b) understand how bias functions in their work as therapists, (c) work to resolve any biases in a manner consistent with professional ethics, (d) provide care that meets professional standards, and (e) be able to serve a wide variety of clients. The VS also provides guidelines for reducing common diversity clashes that have polarized training cohorts, training environments, and the larger society. Bieschke and Mintz (2009) argued that religious trainees and psychologists could remain true to religious beliefs while also providing ethical and competent service to sexual minorities. Similarly sexual minorities can remain true to their sexual orientation and identity, yet provide competent care to religious clients who believe being LGBT is wrong. The authors of the major contribution (Bieschke & Mintz, 2009; Mintz et al., 2009) described the VS as an articulation of a transcendent value of examining personal beliefs in light of professional standards and keeping clients' welfare as the priority, particularly clients from groups that are marginalized by society.

In our assessment, the VS is a major accomplishment of the past decade and a marker of progress in counseling psychology's growing sophistication about diversity issues. In our judgment, the benefits of the VS are many. First, the VS is philosophically grounded in APA policies (i.e., ethics, accreditation, diversity-focused guidelines), yet offers specific guidance about expectations for both trainers and trainees when personal values conflict with professional standards and what behaviors are expected when value conflicts or clashes occur during training. Second, the VS is consistent with the competency model of education and training and the ICD competency. Third, the VS offers programs and applicants the opportunity to assess fit, provides applicants full disclosure in advance of admissions, and helps programs avoid discriminatory admission practices (Loewy et al., 2009). Fourth, the VS also sets the stage for increased dialogue about diversity and provides clear guidance for trainers about how to manage themselves when diversity conflicts arise during training. Fifth, although the VS was developed by counseling psychologists for counseling psychology trainers and trainees, it has the potential to be applicable to all of professional psychology (Grus, 2009).

Even with these accomplishments associated with the VS, we have identified several gaps that need further attention. One of these is the impact of religious beliefs. Vera (2009) stated, "religion is a source of discomfort for those who train future psychologists . . . [and] there is a great deal of perceived incompetence from both educators and trainees in their ability to work with such issues" (p. 746). Vera also expressed the belief that there is a mixed message within professional psychology if we compare the VS with footnote 4 of Domain D in

the *Guidelines and Principles for Accreditation of Programs in Professional Psychology* (APA, 2000a) that protects the constitutional right of religious-affiliated training programs to admit students with shared religious values. Vera recommended that the field push for greater consistency and work toward integrating the VS in the accreditation guidelines and eliminating footnote 4.

Recommendations. Similar to Vera (2009), we recommend that the VS and articles in the major contribution be shared with the members of the Commission on Accreditation (CoA) to further the discussions about professional psychology's responsibilities when values are in conflict. We also see broader possibilities for counseling psychologists to work to expand the influence of the VS on professional psychology by (a) reaching out to Divisions 12 and 16 to present joint symposia at APA and NMCS, (b) seeking approval of the VS by clinical and school psychology professional organizations, and (c) introducing the VS to the Council of Chairs of Training Councils (CCTC) and APA Board of Educational Affairs (BEA), with the goal of developing a professionwide, shared document that has the potential to become APA policy.

Diversity Challenges and Court Rulings: Implications for Education and Training

Two recent federal district court cases (*Keeton v. Anderson-Wiley et al.*, 2010; *Ward v. Wilbanks et al.*, 2009) reinforced previous court decisions that faculty and academic programs have the right to establish and enforce academic and professional standards required to successfully complete educational programs. In these cases associated with masters in counseling programs at Eastern Michigan University (Schmidt, 2010a) and Augusta State University (Schmidt, 2010b), the students refused to provide counseling to individuals whose sexual orientation was in conflict with their religious beliefs; the faculty established remedial actions; and when the students refused to engage or complete the remediation plan, they were dismissed from the program. Subsequently, both students, with the help of the Alliance Defense Fund (ADF), a coalition of Christian lawyers, sued the universities. The ADF lawyers argued that being forced to comply with the remediation effectively required the students to change their religious beliefs, and the academic programs' attorneys argued that ethical codes (American Counseling Association) and professional standards require counselors to provide services to categories of clients in a nondiscriminatory manner.

Judge Hall, in the Augusta State case, cited evidence submitted by the university that the student was not sanctioned for her religious beliefs but for failing to meet ethical and professional standards established by the training program. Faculty members testified that they did not care about the student's personal religious beliefs or require that she change them; they required only that she agree to counsel people in a nondiscriminatory manner consistent with the standards of the profession, including not imposing her moral viewpoint on clients or attempting to change a client's sexual orientation.

Judge Steeh, in the Eastern Michigan University case, upheld the right of the counseling program to dismiss a master's student who declined to counsel a gay client. The judge found that the university was enforcing a legitimate educational requirement (i.e., students must learn to counsel all kinds of clients in a manner that does not judge them or their values). Judge Steeh stated that he was not endorsing the association's ethics code, but respecting the professional association's right to establish an ethics code and the right of universities and their faculty to include compliance with the ethics code as an academic requirement. Like Judge Steeh, Judge Hall ruled that matters of education policy are correctly left to educators and that is not the role of judges to second-guess faculty decisions.

These court cases, like the VS, provide guidance to faculty responsible for academic programs about how to negotiate value conflicts during training. The right of the faculty to establish and enforce educational and professional standards was affirmed. A critical mainstay was the academic program's clarity in student handbooks and curricular materials about academic requirements that included the need to uphold the ethical standards of the profession as codified in the association's ethics code. Also, important in both of these cases was the opportunity for these students to freely express their religious

beliefs in the classroom during discussions about diversity. At the same time, there was a clear delineation between personal beliefs that could be freely expressed in classrooms and the responsibilities that these same personal beliefs and moral standards must not be enforced on clients because of the potential harm to client well-being. Thus, the court rulings, like the VS recommendations, reinforce the importance of faculty keeping their focus *not* on students' beliefs but on their professional behaviors and performance with clients.

These cases are currently under appeal to their respective federal circuit courts and amicus briefs have been filed. Not only are the courts involved, but recently, House Bill 2565, an act amending Title 15, Chapter 14, Arizona Revised Statutes by adding Article 6, also called the University Students' Religious Liberty Act (2011), was introduced and passed by the Arizona House. The part of the bill that is pertinent to training programs reads,

> A university or community college shall not discipline or discriminate against a student in a counseling, social work or psychology program because the student refuses to counsel a client about goals that conflict with the student's sincerely held religious belief or conviction. (15-1862, E)

The Arizona Senate version of the bill was amended to include "if the student consults with the supervising instructor or professor to determine the proper course of action to avoid harm to the client" (15-1862, E). There were strong lobbying efforts occurring to support the passage of this bill (see Center for Arizona Policy, 2011). Thus, the legal requirements that faculty must meet will not be determined solely by the courts but also may be influenced by state and federal legislation.

Recommendations. CCPTP and individual training programs need to monitor the outcome of these appeals court and legislative decisions that will further inform education and training programs about how best to handle value conflicts that arise during training. During these times of highly contentious court cases and legislative actions, we recommend that faculty collaborate with institutional lawyers to keep them apprised of court rulings as well as obtain their assistance in ensuring that local policies and practices are adequate to protect the program when challenges do arise. Additionally, we encourage programs and the professional organizations to engage in advocacy associated with legislative proposals to ensure that psychology training values and professional ethics are incorporated into state laws addressing faculty responsibilities.

CROSS-SUBTOPIC RECOMMENDATIONS

Thus far in this chapter, we have described the gaps we perceive and recommendations to address those gaps specific to the content of each subsection. Herein we make recommendations that intersect multiple subtopics. Possibilities exist for developing deeper understandings of diversity conflicts through faculty and trainers' discussions of the intersection of the VS with recent and upcoming court rulings. Do precedents set by court cases or other legislation suggest or require any revisions of the VS? We recommend that counseling psychology trainers continue to refine the VS as the legal situation becomes clearer. We also recommend that CCPTP, ACCTA, and SCP leaders encourage APA lawyers to use the VS, especially the philosophy and transcendent values, if they file amicus briefs in future court cases. The VS has the potential to be a useful resource as diversity-focused guidelines are revised and when the APA Ethics Code (2010b) is next updated. Similarly the VS may have implications for the further development of the ICD competency, its essential components (i.e., trainee expectations during diversity conflicts), benchmarks (e.g., developmental markers of trainee behavior when diversity collusions occur) and assessment strategies that are specific to diversity conflicts.

The Competency Movement: A Cultural Shift

Some revolutionary changes such as the impact of computers and electronic communication are adopted even before the public has developed terminology, policies, ethical decision making, and other systems with which to engage the cultural shift. Gladwell (2000) described variations in how innovations are adopted by a population, including those who create the idea, those who innovate and develop the idea, those who are early adopters and want to try out the new idea even though the kinks are not worked out and the price has not come down, and those who are late adopters and want to make sure that when the tires are kicked, they do not go flat. The competency movement has been described as a shift to a culture of competence in professional psychology (Roberts, Borden, Christiansen, & Lopez, 2005). Like other cultural shifts, there has been developmental variations as competency models are being created, investigated, selectively implemented, and then adopted within the professional training community.

Professional competency was defined by Epstein and Hundert (2002) as "the habitual and judicious use of communication, knowledge, technical skills, clinical reasoning, emotions, values, and reflection in daily practice for the benefit of the individual and community being served" (p. 227). According to Fouad et al. (2009), "competence also implies performance at an acceptable level, and presumes integration of multiple competencies" (p. S6).

Why Is the Competency Movement Viewed as a Cultural Shift?

Most cultural shifts occur because internal (e.g., intraprofessional) or external forces (e.g., market forces, legal or regulatory changes) require change to (a) maintain homeostasis or (b) achieve a valued goal. In this section, we describe how the competency movement has acquired the stature of a cultural shift and how counseling psychologists have played leadership roles in this movement.

Internal forces. In 1996, Betsy Altmeier, a counseling psychologist, chaired the CoA through a major revision of its guidelines. CoA adopted the requirement that programs identify their goals and objectives and provide evidence that students attain those desired *outcomes* (i.e., programs must show evidence that students are successfully able to demonstrate the programs' professed education and training goals).

Additionally, training programs have struggled with identification and remediation of trainees with *problems in professional competence* (Elman & Forrest, 2007). The competency movement makes an important contribution toward addressing the complexities present in evaluating clinical skills especially when problems develop. Students who have academic difficulties in coursework that is measured by test scores, written papers, and other conventional means are evaluated often through answers being either right or wrong, or with clear parameters expected for responses. Clinical work is not as quantifiable and often students with clinical competency problems are not accurately evaluated because the measures for clinical evaluation have not been as well developed at this point. Competency evaluation lends itself to richer and more thorough and accurate use and has particular value for those clinical skill-based areas that are best served by nontraditional means of evaluation (e.g., standardized patients, portfolios, objective structured clinical examination [OSCE]). Recommendations for further development of these and other means of evaluation include performance benchmarks, assessment tools to evaluate outcomes, and delineation of best practices in remediation (Carraccio, Wolfsthal, Englander, Ferents, & Martin, 2002).

A third force driving the competency movement is that for some time, psychology has experienced a communication divide between practitioners and researchers. Some researchers thought that practitioners were not incorporating into their practice what is known through empirically supported research. Some practitioners viewed researchers as designing studies in such a way that the findings are not applicable to the realities of professional practice. This schism between researchers and practitioners about criteria for evidence for effective practice was a central concern that inspired the appointment of the 2005 APA Presidential Task Force on Evidence-Based Practice in Psychology (EBPP), which was charged with explicating a shared understanding of *evidence-based practice.*

Counseling psychologists on the task force included Carol Goodheart (Chair), Jean Carter, Ron Levant, and Bruce Wampold. The task force's definition and policy statement adopted by the APA Council of Representatives (APA, 2006a) without change stated that "evidence-based practice in psychology is the integration of the best available research with clinical expertise in the context of patient characteristics, culture, values, and preferences." (p. 1). The acceptance of this definition set a new standard for attaining competence in training and practice in ways that previous standards for trainees' knowledge, skills, and attitudes had not done and required new strategies for assessing competence.

External forces. Shifts in the world outside of professional psychology also contributed to the call for competency, including increasing demands for evidence that psychological treatments are effective, especially from third-party payers. Federal government grantors, endowments, and private funding sources are also raising the bar and requesting evidence of effectiveness to obtain financial support. Consumers are also alert to the information available through media, Internet, and other public sources about professional competence and how to use that information to navigate their choices for psychological services. All of these factors, both internal and external to professional psychology, contributed to an inevitable shift to a culture of competence.

Brief Review of Competency Advancement

A major step forward for competency development occurred in 2002 with the Competencies Conference: Future Directions in Education and Credentialing, sponsored by the Association of Psychology Postdoctoral and Internship Centers (APPIC; Kaslow et al., 2004). Several important outcomes of the Competencies Conference and articles that followed were (a) the identification of 12 core competencies and (b) a three-dimensional "cube" model to represent the competencies that categorized competencies as foundational, functional, and level of development in training (Rodolfa et al., 2005). Three counseling psychologists served on the steering committee for this conference (Linda Forrest, Joyce Illfelder-Kaye, and Melba Vasquez), 12 served as working group leaders (Patricia Arredondo, Kathy Bieschke, Martha Christiansen, Jenny Cornish, Cynthia de las Fuentas, Louise Douce, Nancy Elman, Nadya Fouad, Larry James, Greg Keilin, Emil Rodolfa, and Cal Stoltenberg), and 26% of the participants were counseling psychologists.

In 2003, the APA Task Force on the Assessment of Competency in Professional Psychology (that included counseling psychologist Jim Lichtenberg) delineated the issues associated with the assessment of competencies. In 2006, the Competency Benchmark Work Group proposed by the CCTC to the BEA resulted in a working group to operationalize the competencies and bridge the gap between the cube model and competency-based training. Eleven of the 32 members of the working group were counseling psychologists and included Linda Campbell, Madonna Constantine, Nancy Elman, Linda Forrest, Nadya Fouad (Chair), Marty Heesacker, Michael Madsen, Lee Nelson, Ted Packard, Emil Rodolfa, and Barry Schreier. The Benchmark Work Group identified the essential components of each competency as well as behavioral anchors that would, when performed by trainees, demonstrate adequate performance of the competency at the level and stage being evaluated. Three additional competencies were identified (professionalism, teaching, and advocacy), resulting in 15 competencies. The benchmarks were defined across three developmental levels of training (readiness for practicum, internship, and entry to practice).

The "Competency Benchmarks" document has clear implications for training (Fouad et al., 2009). First, the competency model is meant to identify and evaluate competencies at an individual trainee level rather than the past "group standard," which involved all students taking the same courses in the same sequence. Second, training programs need to be prepared to address trainee and faculty concerns about competency levels for individual students. Third, faculty must identify more effective means for addressing attainment of competence and when not present be prepared to develop appropriate remediations. Last, the developmental benchmarks clarified the expected competencies for students moving to the next level of training and facilitated communication between trainers at different levels of the

training sequence on the basis of shared understandings of competency expectations.

In 2008, the Competency Assessment Toolkit Work Group, supported by the APA BEA, was composed of six members, three of whom were counseling psychologists: Nadya Fouad, Linda Campbell, and Emil Rodolfa. The work group was charged with creating a "toolkit" that would serve as a companion document to the "Competency Benchmarks." The "Competency Assessment Toolkit" (Kaslow et al., 2009) identified methods to assess the foundational and functional competencies delineated in the "Competency Benchmarks" (Fouad et al., 2009) document. The identification of methods was facilitated by the earlier work of the Accreditation Council for Graduate Medical Education and the American Board of Medical Specialties (Andrews & Burruss, 2004). Those methods included in the toolkit were 360-degree evaluations, client–patient process and outcome data, competency evaluation rating forms, live or recorded performance ratings, OSCE (e.g., encounters with standard clients–patients presenting a symptom), portfolios, simulation–role plays, and standardized client–patient interviews. These methods are not exhaustive but represent the methods incorporated into the "Competency Assessment Toolkit."

In 2010, the Work Group to Refine the Benchmarks and Field Test the Relationship Competency was established with Nadya Fouad as chair and Linda Campbell as a member. The Association of State and Provincial Psychology Boards (ASPPB) Foundation funded the work group to further develop the benchmarks at a more practical level and field test the Relationship Competency for accuracy and application to determine the following: Does it identify the relationship problems that emerge for trainees, and does it enable trainers to be alert to early detection of relationship problems? The work group is also developing ways of using the "Competency Benchmarks" (Fouad et al., 2009) document in a more efficient, streamlined, and pragmatic manner with the goal of utility and effectiveness.

Perhaps the most important contributions of the competency efforts from the original competency conference through the "Competency Benchmarks"

(Fouad et al., 2009) document and subsequent initiatives is the way programs are thinking differently about training. What students are able to do as a result of their training is now becoming the focus, and we are using our skills as educators to evaluate these competencies in increasingly sophisticated ways. The movement toward a culture of competency is quite remarkable given the timeframe in which these major advances have occurred, and given resource allocation, financial limitations, and difficulties in synchronizing efforts among multiple professional organizations.

Problems of Professional Competence

Most TDs of academic and internship training programs report having trainees with competence problems (Huprich & Rudd, 2004; Vacha-Haase, Davenport, & Kerewsky, 2004) who "consume inordinate administrative and supervisory time and energy" (Kaslow, Rubin, Forrest, et al., 2007, p. 480). Historically, TDs have responded at the individual trainee–program level with minimal consultation, limited guidance from the scholarly literature, and almost nonexistent national conversation among trainers. In the past decade, educators have dedicated considerable effort to better understand and respond to trainees who are having difficulties meeting standards of professional competence. Increasing attention has been paid to the development of appropriate strategies and program policies to identify, remediate, and where appropriate, dismiss psychology trainees with competence problems, resulting in increased publications on the topic as well as thriving national dialogue.

Historically, *trainee impairment* has been the most common term used. Over the past decade, proposed changes in terminology have improved and clarified faculty and trainers' responsibilities. (Elman & Forrest, 2007; Falender, Collins, & Shafranske, 2005, 2009; Forrest, Elman, Gizara, & Vacha-Haase, 1999). Elman and Forrest (in collaboration with the Working Group on Trainees with Competence) proposed new terminology—*problems with professional competence* or *professional competence problems*—and these terms appear to be taking hold. The new terminology is in "closer alignment with ethical standards (APA, 2010b),

accreditation guidelines and principles (APA, 2000a), and the core competencies movement (Kaslow et al., 2004)" (Elman & Forrest, p. 507). The change to competence terminology assists educators to turn their attention from trainees' psychological or personality problems to a focus on professional performance and functioning and design of remediations that concentrate on professional criteria and interventions to meet professional standards. Professional competence language also avoids legal complications resulting from the use of impairment because the term overlaps with protections offered by the American Disabilities Act (Falender et al., 2005, 2009).

Research on psychology trainees with problems has increased in the past decade. Further data have been gathered about the prevalence of trainee competence problems (Huprich & Rudd, 2004; Vacha-Haase et al., 2004). Limitations associated with personal therapy, the most common form of remediation, have been identified (Elman & Forrest, 2004). Faculty gatekeeping responsibilities have been clarified (Elman & Forrest, 2004; Gaubatz & Vera, 2002, 2006). Aspects of trainers and training environments that make it more difficult to intervene have been identified (Gizara & Forrest, 2004). Studies have confirmed that students are deeply troubled by peers' incompetence, lack confidence that faculty are adequately addressing their peers' competence, are uncertain about their responsibilities to peers with problems, and report that problem peers negatively affect their own education (Oliver, Bernstein, Anderson, Blashfield, & Roberts, 2004; Rosenberg, Getzelman, Arcinue, & Oren, 2005; Shen-Miller et al., 2011).

"Historically, psychologists have conceptualized trainee and psychologist incompetence . . . as a problem that rests in the individual" (Forrest et al., 2008, p. 183). Yet, according to Behnke (2008), "an appropriate understanding of and response to questions regarding a trainee's competence must be based on systemic as well as individual considerations" (p. 215). In the past decade, there has been a substantial shift to a more ecological and systems perspective that sees trainee problems embedded in larger training ecologies (Elman et al., 1999; Forrest et al., 2008). For example, there has been increased attention to better understanding how faculty competence problems, the quality of faculty collegial relationships, healthy training environments, and faculty skill development support or hinder the identification and management of trainees with competence problems (Forrest & Elman, 2010; Forrest, Elman, Huprich, Jacobs, & Kaslow, 2010; Jacobs et al., 2011). As the training ecology has received more attention, communication responsibilities among trainers across levels of training have been clarified (Kaslow, Rubin, Forrest, et al., 2007). Also greater attention has been paid to macro-level ecological factors, such as how culture and diversity may impinge on faculty actions with trainees with competence problems (Shen-Miller et al., 2009). Finally, policies for identification, remediation, and dismissal have been reviewed to determine whether they can withstand institutional and legal challenges and at the same time provide protection for the program as well as the student (Gilfoyle, 2008).

A substantial amount of the work described thus far has been completed by the members of the Trainees with Competence Problem Working Group, originally supported by CCTC and now by the APA Education Directorate, consisting of a cross-section of psychologists (students, trainers, practitioners, regulators, APA staff members) at different levels of the training sequence (academic, internship, and postdoctorate) who identify with different psychology specialties (e.g., counseling, clinical, and health). Group members have been involved in the development of several useful documents to guide trainers and training programs, including (a) a model policy to inform students in advance of the comprehensive nature of evaluation in professional psychology training programs (CCTC, 2004), (b) recommended strategies for communication between academic programs and internships (CCTC, 2007), and (c) a model remediation template (http://www.apa.org/ed/graduate/competency.aspx). In 2007, the Working Group published a comprehensive set of recommendations for recognizing, assessing, and intervening with problems of professional competence that included coverage of definitional issues, preparing the system, self-assessment, remediation, diversity, communication across levels of the system, confidentiality, and

ethical, regulatory, and legal issues (Kaslow, Rubin, Forrest, et al., 2007).

Although the past decade has resulted in substantial improvements in the gatekeeping practices of educators and increased scholarship on trainees with competence problems, important gaps in research and practice need further attention. Other professions, including medicine (Papadikis et al., 2005) and law (Baer & Corneille, 1992), have conducted studies to compare individuals sanctioned by licensing boards to determine whether they had a higher percentage of reports of problems during training than a control comparison group. No such studies exist in professional psychology. Another gap in our training models is the lack of attention and scholarly writing about the contradictory roles in which educators find themselves. These include, for example, providing mentoring and support while also being gatekeepers who uphold professional standards (Johnson et al., 2008) or engaging in informal psychological assessments of students with competence problems when formal psychological assessments conducted by psychologists with arm's-length relationships to the program might be more appropriate (Forrest et al., 2008). Another issue that requires greater attention from trainers and the training community is the development of a more complex, nuanced, and appropriate conceptualization of confidentiality when problems of professional competence are identified (Forrest & Elman, 2005). Client–therapist models of confidentiality applied to trainees with competence problems are too simplistic, may inadvertently support privacy that leans toward secrecy about professional behavior, and limit trainers' options for communicating clearly to other trainees about standards of professional competence. Professionals and professionals-in-training's confidentiality is inherently different from client confidentiality. The development of new conceptual models that identify the limits of confidentiality when applied to trainees with competence problems are needed. Initial attempts to rethink confidentiality within a competence framework (Forrest & Elman, 2005; Kaslow, Rubin, Forrest, et al., 2007) are important steps forward. In summary, we agree with Behnke (2008), who has asserted that much work has been done on problems of professional competence but much work remains.

Recommendations

Systemic perspective. An overarching observation of the context in which the competency movement is evolving is the importance of a systems perspective on assessment rather than individuals assessment. This approach would resolve the mentor–gatekeeper conflict and would also allow us to reflect in a more comprehensive way on training and the importance of coordinated efforts among trainers. Much of the richness of competency evaluation will be lost if we fail to realize these relational and integrated factors.

Facilitating the shift. Facilitating the competency shift will necessitate all major training groups endorsing the model and teaching the model as part of the curriculum, adopting means for assessing competencies, and developing organizational structures to support the maintenance of the shift (Kenkel, 2009). Facilitating the competency shift could also be helped by access to additional resources, such as online evaluation systems. We need to create a culture in which providing trainees feedback on areas of needed development becomes normative, and competency-based assessment is used to guide the education and training plan for each individual trainee and not reserved for those who are failing to meet competency benchmarks. Furthermore, we need to strive to ensure that diversity and all of the multiple facets therein will be an integral part of the development of competency-based training (Donovan & Ponce, 2009). Similarly, a successful shift toward a competency-based model will be reflected by a purposeful focus on the identification of problems of professional competence and the development of effective remediations.

Maintaining the shift. A premise of competency-based education and training is that feedback from assessments not only guides the learner but also informs the program on how it might implement change to enhance education and training. As such, professional psychology should engage in ongoing self-assessment of the shift to competency to determine needs and guide planning for additional

initiatives. Key areas that have only begun to be explored are expanding models such as the competencies benchmark to address competency maintenance and enhancement over the course of one's professional career, working collaboratively to develop interprofessional competency models to reflect the roles that psychologists play in integrated health care teams, and developing competency models for recognized specialties in professional psychology. Competency-based training should not be seen as new but rather as evolving (Schulte & Daly, 2009). We want the current efforts to result in a value-added change rather than an additional regulatory burden. The Competency Benchmarks model should be field tested across programs and purposes. The complete benchmarks may not be applicable in all setting for all purposes, and decisions will need to be made on which elements are necessary for which purposes. According to DeMers (2009), "the unanswered or even unspoken question is who will be the responsible party that develops these guidelines, collects and integrates the results of these early experiments, and ultimately refines or revises the model and toolkit in light of these findings" (p. S68).

Recommendations for counseling psychology. Without taking away from these impressive strides, there are several areas in which we need further work. Counseling psychology competencies that have not yet been incorporated into the competency delineations are vocational, social justice, and prevention competencies. Vocational psychology espouses the importance of understanding the meaning of the role of career and work in identity formation and life-span development. Our work as psychologists whether as practitioners, trainers, or researchers all comes back to the fact that a major force in everyone's life is the quality, context, and meaning of work. A culture of competency cannot be truly comprehensive without the inclusion of competencies to engage with individuals about their work and careers (Fouad & Bynner, 2008).

Prevention, as defined by Albee (2000), is the reduction of future incidences of a disorder or disease. Romano and Hage (2000) have proposed a prevention-based agenda for counseling psychology and have been leaders in developing prevention guidelines with the hope that they will become APA policy. The fact remains that work is still needed to incorporate prevention into a competency model in any meaningful way.

As noted in recent overviews (Toporek et al., 2006), social justice is recognized as a primary value and holds great importance for training, practice, and research in counseling psychology. Social justice is often linked to multiculturalism and focused on responding to systemic inequalities that marginalize and disenfranchise individuals and groups (Vera & Speight, 2003). The training community is currently challenged to define the competencies that trainees must have to be competent in social justice and decide where and how the mastery of this knowledge, skills, and attitudes will be incorporated into the developing continuum of training (Lewis, 2010).

Enormous strides have been made in the development of competencies for professional psychology. When Roberts et al. (2005) identified the phrase *culture of competence*, they also noted that before a culture of competence can be established, the professional community must agree on values and professional habits. By their definition, we are on the way, but we are not there yet.

OTHER CRITICAL EDUCATION AND TRAINING ISSUES

Beyond the two major topics (multicultural education and training, and the competency movement), we have identified six other topics we deem important to cover in this decade review of critical issues in education and training in counseling psychology. We have organized this section into external and internal influences that have affected the education and training of counseling psychologists. External societal changes have required educators to reshape the professional psychology curriculum and have been the impetus to add new content to the curriculum. These changes will be presented first in this section, including (a) the increasingly global nature of the world and the corresponding need for internationalizing education and training, (b) the

increased demand from numerous sources (insurance companies, clients, federal government) to have evidence that practice interventions improve clients' lives, and (c) the delivery of psychological services (behavioral health) within the health care delivery system. Internal to psychology influences on education and training are presented next and are more political in nature, including (a) sequence of training issues, (b) accreditation dynamics, and (c) advocacy to increase federal funds to support psychology education and training.

Internationalization of Education and Training

In an increasingly global world, "more psychological research is being done outside the United States than inside, yet precious little of it is published by APA journals. . . . American psychologists know far less about psychology in other cultures than international psychologists know about us" (Pedersen, 2003, p. 400), making American psychologists vulnerable to *cultural encapsulation*, a term first coined by Wrenn (1962). Lack of information within education and training programs about counseling psychology around the world and limited exposure to the work of scholars from other countries make our graduates vulnerable to believing that counseling psychology is a solely U.S.-based specialty. According to Leung (2003), "counseling psychology programs should not perpetuate the cultural encapsulation of the profession by exposing trainees only to counseling psychology as it is written and practiced in the United States" (p. 415). Such educational practices increase the likelihood of cultural bias being enacted, and creates the potential for U.S.-based counseling psychologists to become further isolated from international colleagues (Forrest, 2010). The good news is that over the past decade there has been substantial growth in the coverage of international issues within counseling psychology. Markers of this growth include (a) the SCP presidential initiatives that have extended the reach of SCP to an international level (Douce, 2004; Forrest, 2010; Heppner, 2006; Nutt, 2007), (b) the 2002 formation within the International Association of Applied Psychology of a counseling psychology division (Division 16), (c) major contributions focused on international topics published in *The Counseling Psychologist* (*TCP*; Leong & Blustein, 2000; Leong & Ponterotto, 2003), (d) the establishment in 2005 of an International Section within the SCP, (e) an increase in publications by non-U.S.-based international scholars in *TCP* (Kwan & Gerstein, 2008), and (f) the 2008 International Counseling Psychology Conference, the first counseling psychology conference to expand to an international platform (Forrest, 2010).

Despite growth on the research and professional organization front (for a summary of developments, see Forrest, 2010; Gerstein, Heppner, Ægisdóttir, Leung, & Norsworthy, 2009), less attention has been paid to international education and training. In 2003, Leong and Ponterotto published a proposal for internationalizing counseling psychology that included eight suggestions to enlarge the international focus in training programs. Their recommendations included the following: (a) Integrate international perspectives into multicultural curriculum, (b) modify admissions criteria to incorporate international travel and study abroad experiences, (c) support international opportunities for graduate students and faculty, (d) require a foreign language competence, (e) support travel to international conferences, (f) support international scholars programs and visiting faculty from other countries, (g) incorporate readings from non-U.S. scholars into the curriculum, and (h) promote internships and externships at local sites (international student centers, immigrant, or refuge centers) and in other countries.

Marsella and Pedersen (2004) proposed "50 ways to internationalize the curriculum" (p. 419) that included recommendations directed toward the APA, psychology departments (e.g., mission, orientation, values, curriculum, extracurricular activities), and universities. The list is too large to enumerate here, but it is rich with creative ways for improving the international nature of education within counseling psychology programs. Similarly, in an article focused on international training, Gerstein and Ægisdóttir (2007) offered numerous suggestions for helping students (a) learn about their cultural biases, (b) create motivation to be interested in international issues, (c) address

practical and methodological challenges in conducting research in other countries, and (d) think about social change when working internationally.

In one of the few empirical studies on international education and training, Turner-Essel and Waehler (2009) surveyed TDs of counseling psychology programs to determine the extent to which Leong and Ponterotto's (2003) suggestions were being implemented. Their findings suggested that many programs include international experience in admission considerations (89%), promote attendance at international conferences (71%), and incorporate international issues within their multicultural framework (70%). TDs described financial (for both faculty and students) and time constraints as major obstacles to internationalizing curriculum and training programs. The results from qualitative interviews further suggested that faculty and student efforts appear to be the foundation upon which international-focused efforts can grow within an academic program. Also, international students and alumni created bridges and linked U.S. programs to faculty in other countries, creating opportunities for collaborations and bilateral exchanges. Turner-Essel and Waehler concluded that there was much interest and greater awareness of international issues in training in 2009 than when Leong and Ponterotto made their training recommendations.

The increased presence of international students in U.S. counseling psychology programs is an important part of the trend toward greater attention to international issues in counseling psychology programs. Forrest (2010) wrote,

> In 2007, 8.2% ($N = 243$ out of 2,890) of the students in U.S.-based APA-accredited counseling psychology programs were international students (Susan Zlotlow, APA Office of Accreditation, personal communication, July 31, 2008) and this number has been trending upward over the past 5 years. (p. 105)

As the percentages increase and a critical mass of international students is reached, it becomes easier for them to speak up about their experiences and issues and to integrate their diverse perspectives into didactic and experiential interactions within training programs. The large presence of international students at the International Counseling Psychology Conference created a tipping point toward an international critical mass. At the conference, international students offered cultural and country-specific knowledge and expertise while they found support for who they are and a professional home in counseling psychology (Forrest, 2008).

Between 2000 and 2004, international issues in counseling journals accounted for only 6% of the publications (Gerstein & Ægisdóttir, 2007). More recently, there has been an increase in publications, mostly because of the *International Handbook on Cross-Cultural Counseling* (Gerstein et al., 2009). Technological developments (e.g., e-mail, Skype, other Internet tools, faster transportation options) have created opportunities for connecting with colleagues, have increased the likelihood of cross-national collaborations, and may partly explain the increased publications about international issues in counseling psychology. These publications have helped create the conceptual and empirical backbone for the development of rich curricula materials. The focus of these publications has been to identify obstacles to improving the coverage of international issues in counseling psychology training—for example, cultural encapsulation, ethnocentric bias, the emphasis on individualism, a global homogenization of counseling that disrupts or ignores indigenous healing practices, the unconscious exportation of U.S.-based psychology without attention to possible negative consequences, and a monolingual context reliant on English as the language of collaboration. More publications devoted to describing how to prepare students for cross-cultural and cross-national teaching, consulting, counseling, and research are needed to advance this work.

A number of complex issues complicate efforts to further international perspectives in counseling psychology education and training. First and foremost are the challenges and limitations imposed by APA accreditation standards and state licensing laws. For example, students who wish to complete their practicum or internship experiences in other countries must consider the consequences of not having an APA-accredited internship and how it may affect their future job options and on their ability to become licensed in the United States. International students who plan to return to their home countries are more focused on receiving training that will be culturally relevant and valid in their home countries. Faculty and program decisions and approval of overseas practicum and internship experiences require attention to equivalency and adequate monitoring and communication between supervisors, sites, and training programs, if the experience is to meet APA accreditation standards. For an international student perspective on these issues, a recent text produced by individuals actively involved in the American Psychological Association of Graduate Students (APAGS; Hasan, Fouad, & Williams-Nickelson, 2008) provides advice about these and many other issues for international students studying psychology in the United States.

Within international education and training across professional psychology, we identified three gaps that need attention. Although the competency movement has resulted in the delineation of 15 professional competencies, including ICD, there is no delineation of how this competency is similar or different from an international competency. According to Leung (2003), "the multicultural movement in counseling psychology has been confined mostly to ethnic and diversity issues within the United States; it has yet to transcend international boundaries" (p. 414). Yet, Ægisdóttir and Gerstein (2007) saw international competence as the new frontier in multicultural training. There have been discussions in the literature about the differences between U.S. multicultural and cross-national counseling (Heppner et al., 2009) as well as differences among multicultural, cross-cultural, and international psychology (Takooshian, 2003). Takooshian asserted that there is little overlap among the authors who write in each of these areas of psychology. Leong and Ponterotto (2003) and Varenne (2003) argued that the multicultural framework is inadequate and unlikely to be useful on an international level. From our perspective, the ICD competency does not adequately address specific competencies required to be a competent psychologist in the international arena. The essential components and benchmarks of an international competency still need to be defined and delineated either within the current ICD competency or as a separate competency. Another gap we identified is that there are no empirical studies about what types of training are effective in developing international competence. Studies of multicultural competencies provide a framework (i.e., developmental stages and recommended training sequences) that might be useful in designing studies about the development of international competence. Because these competencies are not synonymous, care needs to be taken to capture the unique aspects of international competence; cross-national collaborations and studies are necessary to determine the components of an international competency. Outcome studies specifically assessing training interventions that successfully develop international competencies are needed. We also support the continued effort by editors of counseling psychology journals to publish internationally focused scholarship that creates the foundational materials for education on international issues.

Recommendations. At a minimum, individual programs and ideally CCPTP need to develop criteria for international training options (practica and internships) as one step in enhancing the internationalization of U.S.-based education and training. CCPTP should continue to include presentations on international issues at its midyear meetings with the goal of keeping counseling psychology education and training on pace with society's rapid internationalization. More important, we recommend that international issues be considered during the next revision of the accreditation standards and APA Ethics Code (2010b). Incorporating a more global perspective into these documents is a necessary step toward decreasing the cultural encapsulation and isolation of U.S.-based psychology and increasing the international competence of psychologists and U.S.-based training programs.

The Emergence of Evidence-Based Practice

"Evidence-based practice in psychology (EBPP) is the integration of the best available research with clinical expertise in the context of patient characteristics, culture, and preferences" (APA, 2006a, p. 273). The adoption of this definition by the APA

Council of Representatives established the standard for practice in psychology and for the relationship between science and practice in answering the question, "What is evidence?" The values underlying this evidence-based practice definition are rooted in the training model in counseling psychology.

Counseling psychology training model.
According to Stoltenberg et al. (2000), "the scientist–practitioner model is core to the identity of counseling psychology" (p. 629). Counseling psychology training programs strive to attain the integration of science and practice perspectives (Murdock, Alcorn, Heesacker, & Stoltenberg, 1998). With regard to practice, "the scientist role is as important in the moment-by-moment process of clinical activity as it is in conducting controlled empirical studies" (Stoltenberg et al., 2000, p. 631). Practitioners must have critical thinking ability and scientific mindedness to competently develop a case conceptualization, formulate hypotheses, select a treatment plan, and evaluate the effectiveness of the intervention. With regard to research, clinical practice renders vital information that is essential to advancing effective outcomes. The therapeutic alliance, common factors across theoretical approaches, client variables, therapists' stance, and other factors are viewed as critically important in determining research methodology and design.

Does the model matter? Are there differences between scientist–practitioner programs in which students have a primary practice trajectory in contrast to those programs in which students have a research or education track as a career direction? Neimeyer, Saferstein, and Rice (2005) found that in programs that were more scientifically oriented, graduates produced more publications and scholarly presentations. Important similarities were that all programs on average matched 85% of their students for internship placement; however, differences in placement setting did reflect the orientation of programs. Students from programs with a science emphasis were more likely to be matched with counseling centers and Veterans Administrations. Students from programs with a practice orientation tended to be matched with community sites such as hospitals, community mental health settings, and child and family centers. Counseling psychology has continued to appreciate that neither research alone nor practice alone can serve the greater purpose of the profession, which is the dissemination and application of created knowledge.

Counseling psychology and evidence-based practice. As early as 1996, an STG within Division 17 was formed on empirically supported interventions in counseling psychology led by Jim Lichtenberg with the charge of giving consideration to the ideals and values of counseling psychology that included the following types of diversity: settings, service providers, needs and responsiveness of clients–patients, and appropriate empirical methods (Wampold, Lichtenberg, & Waehler, 2002). The charge also requested that any principles developed about empirically supported treatments be consistent with the "traditions, roles, settings, clientele of counseling psychologists, reflect current methodological developments, and be supported by knowledge in counseling psychology" (Wampold et al., 2002, pp. 203–204). The STG concluded that validation of treatments for all persons in all situations is "impossible." Interventions must be selected and administered locally because clients do not present for treatment with unitary and well-clarified problems requiring counseling psychologists to exercise their clinical judgment while being informed by science. Also, clients must have the freedom to choose among validated interventions, and the complexity of client diversity is important. One sees from these principles that this STG reaffirmed the values of counseling psychology and anticipated the criticisms subsequent proposals on empirically supported treatment would receive. Most important, however, the STG served as a precursor to the values and components of the APA evidence-based practice definition.

Counseling psychology's values implemented through training, curriculum, research, clinical skills, and the adherence to the integrated scientist–practitioner model positioned counseling psychologists to readily embrace evidence-based practice. That is to say, 10 years before the APA's adoption of the evidence-based practice definition, the Counseling Psychology STG drew an initial blueprint for

what would become the standard for evidence-based practice.

APA evidence-based practice definition. Components of the APA (2006a) evidence-based practice definition described foundational elements of counseling psychology:

1. The *best available research* is entrenched in counseling psychology training focused on scientific–mindedness, knowledge, and critical thinking.
2. *Clinical expertise* may include assessment, treatment planning, decision making, interpersonal expertise, and continual self-reflection (Wilson et al., 2009). Clinical expertise serves as the point of judgment in matching the best scientific evidence with the client variables to maximize fit. The inclusion of clinical expertise as an equivalent source of evidence cannot be overestimated. Until this recognition, the expertise of the practitioner was not viewed on par with research, resulting in practitioners feeling devalued within the profession.
3. The inclusion of *client characteristics, culture, and preferences* signaled a major shift in perception about factors that contribute to outcome effectiveness. Counseling psychology has had as a mainstay promoting and advocating for the importance of diversity in the context of individual differences and multicultural perspectives (Waehler, Kalodner, Wampold, & Lichtenberg, 2000).

Recommendations. Counseling psychologists working in training and practice settings could and should participate in the dissemination and implementation of the evidence-based practice model. Psychologists for the most part are now familiar with the definition, purpose, and significance of the evidence-based practice components, yet many professionals have not yet incorporated this model into their practice. Thus, we recommend that counseling psychology educators and trainers continue their leadership and modeling of mutual respect for science and practice, and as essential elements together, not as unrelated constructs. Counseling psychologists are well positioned to facilitate the incorporation across the profession of the evidence-based factors into research, practice, education, and training.

Behavioral Health and Integrated Care

Over the past decade, concomitant with rapid changes in the delivery of health care in our society, we have seen an increased number of psychologists working in behavioral health across a wide cross-section of health care settings. Similarly within professional psychology training, great emphasis has been placed on preparing psychologists to work in health care settings. National leadership within professional psychology focused on behavioral health and integrated health care is observable in many ways (e.g., APA Interdivisional Healthcare Committee, APA Integrated Health Care Initiative, APA Presidential Task Force on Achieving Integrated Health Care for an Aging Population, and the revitalization of the Council of Clinical Health Psychology Training Programs [CCHPTP]).

Approximately 60% of all primary care medical visits have major behavioral health components (Cummings, Cummings, & Johnson, 1997) and include depression resulting from injury, chest pain with panic attacks, physical symptoms responsive to behavioral treatment (e.g., asthma), behavioral risk factors for disease (e.g., smoking, weight), psychological presentation of organ disease (e.g., depression with hypothyroidism), and somatic symptoms related to behavioral factors (e.g., poor compliance with treatment regimen; Belar, 2008). The presence of psychologists in interdisciplinary settings, participating in integrated care with behavioral health care expertise, is not only a fast growing arena for psychologists but also critically important to the continued viability and impact of psychology in health care.

Examples of the type of services psychologists provide in health care settings include assessment for organ transplant, teaching medical professionals psychological components to health care, biofeedback for self-management, family interventions for children's diseases such as asthma, stress management in preparation for surgery, and development of treatments for smoking or weight management (Belar, 2008). Collaboration, consultation, and systems competencies are necessary in an interdisciplinary environment in which teamwork, consensus decision making, and effective problem resolution are necessary skills. Just as behavioral change is a primary goal for patients in behavioral health treatment of disease states, prevention is also an important component of psychologists' role in the integrated care model (McDaniel & Fogarty, 2009). Counseling psychologists' focus on strength-based and resilience approaches, optimal functioning, and prevention goals is well suited for primary care as well as psychoeducational and consultative interventions with patients, families, and other health care professionals.

Even though training for counseling psychologists incorporates values and skills with relevance to behavioral health care, several changes need to be made in counseling psychology curriculum and training experiences to better prepare students for this growing area. Of 666 internship programs participating in the 2008 APPIC internship match, 209 (31.3%) had major rotations and 398 (59.7%) had minor rotations in clinical health psychology (APPIC, 2008). Most counseling psychology training programs, however, have not made curricular revisions to include behavioral health training to the same degree as other psychology specialties. Clinical health psychology, in fact, is one of the most common tracks available among accredited doctoral programs in clinical psychology with 75 programs (32% of clinical programs) offering training (APA, 2008). Approximately 12% of counseling psychology programs currently offer training in health psychology, including Ball State University, University of Denver, University of Iowa, University of Miami, and Virginia Commonwealth (Nicholas & Stern, 2011).

Recommendations. For counseling psychology to be part of this growing trend, graduates will need to be prepared to practice in health care settings. This requires doctoral training programs to design and implement health psychology components into the curriculum with attention to knowledge, practice (practicum and internship), and research experiences in behavioral health (disease, health promotion, and wellness) and health care systems. Earlier recommendations for improved preparedness for psychologists entering primary care work settings included (a) targeted continuing education for practicing psychologists who are interesting in working in these arenas, (b) professional development programs for faculty who serve as role models for students interested in primary care, and (c) more interdisciplinary experiences in doctoral and internship training (McDaniel et al., 2004).

We recommend that CCPTP in conjunction with the SCP Health Psychology Section develop a blueprint to integrate health psychology into counseling psychology programs that includes curricula materials, strategies for developing behavioral health practicum training options, and increased attention to preparing students for internships with health psychology major and minor rotations. We believe the ramifications of the growing job market for psychologists within an integrated health care delivery system requires focused attention by counseling psychology educators.

Sequence of Doctoral Education and Training

Three levels of doctoral training—practicum, internship, and postdoctoral training—are reciprocally linked through the developmental and sequential components of learning and knowledge, skill acquisition, competency assessment and evaluation, and levels of outcome expectations. Several challenges and shifts have emerged over the past decade with mostly unintended reciprocal impacts on other levels of training. We describe these changes in this section of the chapter.

Internship imbalance.   During the past several years, positions in internships have grown by 5%, whereas the applicant pool has grown by 20% (J. Baker, McCutcheon, & Keilin, 2007). In recent years, on average, 21% to 25% of students (approximately 840) from APA-accredited doctoral programs were not matched with an internship (APPIC, 2010; Grus, 2011; Rodolfa, Bell, Bieschke, Davis, & Peterson, 2007). The data pertaining to counseling psychology students is tracked both by CCPTP and the APA CoA. In a 10-year review, counseling psychology programs represented 20% of the programs, yet counseling psychology students represented only 11% of the students who participated in the APPIC Match compared with clinical psychology at 80% (APA, 2005; CCPTP, 2005). Counseling psychology students have maintained an 89% placement rate in APA-accredited internships. Given that the average placement rate over the past 5 years has been approximately 78% for all specialties, counseling psychology's current placement rate of 89% (Norcross et al., 2010) to date reflects well on our training programs.

Miville, Adams, and Juntunen (2007) surveyed counseling psychology TDs who rendered opinions on reasons that individual students did not match: self-imposed geographic limitations (61%), interpersonal competency problems (39%), supply-and-demand imbalance (39%), applied only to highly competitive sites (20%), and lack of practicum hours (12%). The TDs' views on the reason for the imbalance were (a) too many students being admitted, (b) psychology does not predetermine admissions numbers across training programs, and (c) psychology has not aggressively developed internship sites. Madson, Hasan, Williams-Nickelson, Kettman, and Van Sickle (2007) summarized graduate students' perspectives on the internship imbalance. Without a doubt, the imbalance problem is complex. Given the resources needed to develop internships, such as money, labor-intensive supervision, office space, curricula, technical support, and administrative structures, this is no simple matter. One recommendation for short-term relief is voluntary restraint in admissions across graduate programs (J. Baker et al., 2007).

The internship imbalance has affected profoundly the practicum training experience. An unintended consequence of the internship imbalance is that students are accumulating high numbers of practicum hours hoping to strengthen their internship applications. The internship experience is meant to be one of advanced training at higher levels of competency development. Yet, internships, with some exceptions, are most often practice-oriented rather than teaching or research focused, resulting in the perception that the more clinical hours students have, the stronger they are as applicants for internships.

The internship imbalance problem raises the question: Do we know if we are training too many psychologists based on the imbalance or is the problem logistical in that for various reasons we simply don't have enough sites and positions for internships? In the announcement that established the APA Center for Psychology Workforce Analysis, Cynthia Belar, Executive Director of the Education Directorate, asserted that "one of the major functions of a disciplinary society should be gathering data on its own discipline, its pipeline, and its graduates" (Munsey, 2007, p. 15). A workforce analysis is an empirical process through which multiple source data are used to identify the number and relevant characteristics of psychology trainees, to identify psychologists currently in the field, and to project the need for psychologists across existing and emerging settings (Grus, 2011; Rozensky, Grus, Belar, Nelson, & Kohout, 2007).

Practicum changes. Practicum is a core component of doctoral training and the first step toward independent competence in psychology (Hatcher & Lassiter, 2007). The practicum experience has evolved over the past decade and developments include Practicum Competencies Outline (Hatcher & Lassiter, 2007), designation as a competency level in the Competency Benchmarks (Fouad et al., 2009), and the development of Guidelines on Practicum Experience for Licensure (ASPPB, 2009). Together these developments give clarity to the foundational importance of practicum in education and training of psychologists. Practicum activities are composed of intervention, assessment, evaluation, research, consultation, advocacy, teaching, and supervision (Lewis, Hatcher, & Pate, 2005). The number of practicum hours needed varies depending on who is asked. Rodolfa, Ko, and Petersen (2004) found that academic and internship TDs expect students to complete on average 1,094 and 1,255 hours, respectively, with 25% being direct hours. The race for more clinical hours and the reality of the internship imbalance has had a negative impact on programs and students: increased stress, time, and costs resulting from nonplacement; increased mentoring and tutoring through the application process; and decreased emphasis on research training as a by-product of the focus on clinical hours. Recommendations to programs and practicum students include (a) completion of the dissertation proposal before internship, (b) feedback sessions on students' internship application, (c) strong encouragement to engage in mock interviews, and (d) application to at least 15 sites (Miville et al., 2007).

These intensive experiences at the practicum level served as one of the reasons that postdoctoral requirements were called into question. Although practicum is the beginning level of clinical skill development, groups within the governance of APA, particularly in the practice community, attested that practicum training had reached a level of quality, intensity, and duration that could serve as the 2nd clinical year requirement. When APA policy changed to recognize this option of the 2nd year of clinical experience being completed before graduation, scrutiny was brought to bear on the quality of the practicum experience.

The ASPPB developed guidelines for the type of practicum experience that would meet the second-year clinical experience requirement for licensure (ASPPB, 2009). Training programs must now consider whether to meet these criteria and whether they benefit students who may not pursue a postdoctoral experience for licensure. Furthermore, the question of whether there is a professional obligation for training programs in jurisdictions that no longer require the postdoctoral experience for licensure has not been resolved. The effect on the postdoctoral requirement of students' compiling hundreds of practicum hours is yet another unintended but highly significant consequence. Students and APA governance groups, particularly those focused on practice issues, have questioned whether practicum had begun to take on the training, skill acquisition, and professional development that raised questions about the necessity for a postdoctoral year of training.

Postdoctoral requirement reconsidered. In the early 2000s, the APA Board of Directors and others in governance became alarmed at several growing concerns, including (a) the unavailability of declared postdoctoral sites (at that time nine states were requiring a postdoctoral experience, whereas not one postdoctoral site was available in any of those states; Kaslow et al., 1992), (b) survey reports of postdoctoral trainees needing to work at multiple sites to accumulate required hours (Hogg, Keen, Barton, & Yardell, 1999), (c) lack of reimbursement from third-party payers for nonlicensed post-doctorates (Clay, 2000), and (d) mounting debt for students. The APA Commission on Education and Training Leading to Licensure was established in 2000 with the charge of deciding the requisite training requirements necessary for licensure. After deliberation, the commission issued this proposal: "A trainee must complete a doctoral degree from an APA or CPA accredited program and two years of organized, supervised, sequential professional training (one of which must be an APA or CPA accredited pre-doctoral internship program" (APA, 2000b, p. 3). At the time, there was no attempt to bring this recommendation to a vote, but rather the commission allowed 5 years for the training community to thoroughly consider and decide on the sequence of training to licensure. Subsequently, in 2005, an APA working group recommended and the APA Council approved that 2 years of supervised professional experience are required. One year is the predoctoral internship; however, the second year may be completed before or subsequent to the granting of the degree (APA, 2006b).

The effect of the reciprocally linked levels of training in psychology has resulted in unintended consequences across training levels. *The internship imbalance* has affected the practicum level by motivating students to seek as many hours as possible. The pursuit of clinical hours may be taking time and credit hours that otherwise would be used for research skill development. Students have increased the number of sites to which they apply, affecting the internship sites by hugely increasing the number of applications they must review. The impact of the expanded number of hours and increasing complexity of practicum training has been partially responsible for the APA policy change of no longer requiring that the second clinical year be postdoctoral. This policy change has affected practicum-level training, particularly in jurisdictions that no longer require a postdoctoral experience, requiring programs to grapple with the decision to meet the ASPPB

practicum requirements or to continue their conventional practicum requirement. Furthermore this policy change has transferred the responsibility for meeting the entry-to-practice competency from the postdoctoral year to the internship year.

An overarching challenge of this reciprocity of effect influences mobility. Students completing internship will need to make a decision about whether to complete a postdoctoral experience. As early career psychologists without any postdoctoral experience, they may not be able to be licensed in jurisdictions that still require a postdoctoral year. The process becomes even more challenging in that some jurisdictions that require a postdoctoral experience are taking the position that early career psychologists cannot choose to do a postdoctoral year if they are already licensed (i.e., they cannot place themselves back into training). All of these challenges are being addressed by professional organizations within the education and training community. The psychology community has many virtues and solid values among which is its commitment to students and to shepherding them through quality training so they may take their places within the profession.

Recommendations.   Counseling psychologists through CCPTP need to participate in initiatives to reduce the internship imbalance, address the burgeoning number of practicum hours, and develop lobbying strategies at the state legislature level. These efforts may take the form of working groups and collaborations with other education and training entities, including the CCTC and the APA BEA. As jurisdictions discontinue the postdoctoral training requirement, we also recommend that a template for practicum as the second clinical year in doctoral training be developed to enhance uniformity in requirements and facilitate mobility of practice.

Impact of Accreditation Developments on Counseling Psychology

Accreditation as the imprimatur of quality in education and professional training has undergone numerous changes over the past decade. Several challenges affect psychology professional training in general and counseling psychology in particular. There has been substantial growth in accredited counseling psychology programs, with the largest growth occurring in the 1980s and 1990s when accredited programs tripled (Heppner, Casas, Carter, & Stone, 2000). Blustein, Goodyear, Perry, and Cypers (2005) summarized the history of accreditation of counseling psychology programs, noting that of counseling psychology programs that have been accredited, approximately a third "have been, or are being, phased out or have been converted to combined-integrated programs" (p. 611), and provided assessment as to why these losses occurred as well as strategies for maintaining healthy counseling psychology programs.

Recently, the most significant challenge appears to be the accreditation of master's training. In 2000, McPherson, Pisecco, Elman, Crosbie-Burnett, and Sayger provided a summary of counseling psychology's ambivalent relationship with master's training. Many doctoral counseling psychology programs are located in colleges of education in proximity to masters in counseling programs, and in some cases, faculty jointly oversee both programs with accreditation by the CoA for the doctoral program and the Council for Accreditation of Counseling and Related Educational Programs (CACREP) for counseling masters. In turn, these accreditations have implications for licensure to practice at both levels.

CACREP's 2009 accreditation changes created particular concern for doctoral programs and faculty that substantially overlap with CACREP-accredited master's programs. CACREP's new standards require that there be at least three core full-time faculty who

> have earned their doctoral degree in counselor education and supervision, preferably from a CACREP-accredited program or have been employed as full-time faculty members in a counselor education program for a minimum of one full academic year before July 1, 2013. (CACREP, 2009, p. 6).

This new requirement means that faculty who are hired after 2012 with degrees in counseling

psychology will not count as part of the core faculty, making it impossible for some master's programs to meet the CACREP accreditation standards after 2013. Complicating this situation was APA's long-standing policy focused on the doctorate as the entry-level degree to professional practice with a concomitant lack of attention to master's training. In 2008, the SCP and the CCPTP established a joint STG on master's programs (chaired by Michael Scheel) and an STG on CACREP accreditation (chaired by Barry Chung) to address the problems and make recommendations to both organizations, the CCTC, and APA.

As of this writing, action in two areas has been unfolding. In October 2010, the BEA passed a draft resolution that articulates a potential new relationship between APA and master's education and training, that recognizes the master's degree as preparation for three possible outcomes: (a) advanced doctoral education, (b) further graduate or professional education in fields other than psychology, and (c) employment in areas for which a master's degree is appropriate (APA, 2010a). The resolution includes for the first time a commitment on APA's part to include master's training as part of its broad K–12 to lifelong learning education and training agenda. When and if this resolution is accepted as APA policy, it will have great significance to the shape of counseling psychology education and training particularly in universities with counselor education programs.

Alongside this effort inside APA, efforts were made to develop a new master's accreditation by working with the Master in Psychology Accreditation Council (MPAC). A draft of common accreditation standards under a new name, Masters in Psychology and Counseling Accrediting Council (MPCAC) was released for public comment in 2011. The new standards would allow counseling psychology master's programs to opt to be accredited under either the MPAC or MPCAC accreditation criteria, thus recognizing that master's programs are located in both psychology departments and colleges of education with strong affiliations with the psychology or counseling profession or both.

The criteria were drafted to allow programs to respond to local university fit, job market, reimbursement, and state licensing issues and determine the best accrediting group. Other benefits of this new accreditation option include the following: (a) as part of the criteria, required cultural competency and the encouragement of a social justice focus; (b) flexible language that allows programs to determine their training goals and objectives; (c) a strong focus on outcome-based measures tied specifically to program goals, much like the APA accreditation guidelines; (d) consistency with the shift to a "culture of competency"; and (e) user-friendly, cost-effective, and with limited bureaucracy in the accreditation structure. If this alternate accreditation process comes into existence it will help stem the tide of the potential narrowing of counselor licensing laws. As of this writing, several CCPTP-member academic programs have volunteered to pilot the new accreditation criteria. Scheel (2011a) provided a description of the issues, history, and recommendations for counseling psychology. We recommend that CCPTP and individual programs continue to monitor these evolving challenges with careful attention to the national trends and local needs.

In addition to CACREP's standards limiting criteria for faculty, there have been efforts to limit counselor licensing laws by requiring that applicants have graduated from a CACREP-accredited program. One state, New Jersey, passed new licensing legislation with CACREP-limiting language and did so without substantial transparency or opportunity for public input. CCPTP committed to (a) writing letters to state-level counselor licensing boards to underscore the benefits of maintaining broadly worded counselor licensing laws that allow for alternate accreditation systems, (b) monitoring closely efforts to change counselor licensing laws, and (c) sending representatives to the American Association of State Counselor Licensing Boards' annual conference (for details of CCPTP action items, see Scheel, 2011b). We recommend that individual training programs pay close attention to legal actions that will affect their state and local programs and participate in national CCPTP efforts to address accreditation and licensing concerns.

While challenges were happening on the master's accreditation front, additional challenges have

arisen in doctoral accreditation. The historically uneasy relationship between clinical scientist programs and the growing number of APA-accredited practitioner-focused programs resulted in the clinical scientist group proposing a new Psychological Clinical Science Accreditation System (PCSAS), "that demands high quality science training as a central feature of doctoral training" (T. B. Baker, McFall, & Shoham, 2008, p. 67). As of this writing, PCSAS has accredited several research-intensive clinical psychology programs. PCSAS has had less immediate impact on counseling psychology programs, probably because most identify as scientist-practitioner programs and there are only a few counseling psychology doctorate programs (Stoltenberg et al., 2000).

Each of these newly proposed accreditation bodies (MPCAC and PCSAS) are in the early stages of development and are not yet recognized by the Council of Higher Education Accreditation (CHEA). In contrast, the APA CoA is a long-standing and established accreditation body recognized by the CHEA and the U.S. Department of Education and continues to be the primary accreditor for professional graduate education in psychology. Over the past decade there have been changes within the CoA. In 2007, the then–Committee on Accreditation became the Commission on Accreditation, expanding its membership from 21 to 32 and now including representatives from previously unrepresented groups. Parallel with the growing emphasis on competencies and the assessment of their outcomes, CoA regularly releases new implementing regulations (IRs). These regulations represent clarification and further delineation of the *Guidelines and Principles for Accreditation of Programs in Professional Psychology* (APA, 2000a), and understanding and complying with these regulations has important consequences for doctoral programs in counseling psychology. Among those IRs in the past few years are regulations clarifying the following: disclosure of outcomes to allow for informed decisions by prospective students, diversity recruitment, education and training, empirically supported procedures and treatments, distance and electronically mediated education, and telesupervision. (Approved IRs are available on the CoA

website at http://www.apa.org/ed/accreditation/
index.aspx.)

Recommendations. We commend CCPTP for
its attention to master's accreditation issues and
its leadership in creating options for programs
struggling to meet newly implemented CACREP
standards. We recommend that CCPTP consider
developing a state-level advocacy network, perhaps
modeled after the Federal Education Advocacy
Coordinators (FEDAC) described in the next section. Statewide coordinators could monitor impending changes in licensing laws and administrative
rules that might limit and jeopardize the professional options for master's program graduates.
Coordinators could keep faculty and practitioners
within the state apprised of opportunities for lobbying and influencing the legislation on rule changes.
Given the regularity with which CoA drafts, releases
for public comment, and approves new IRs, we
recommend that CCPTP and individual programs
(a) stay current on IRs out for public comment;
(b) respond to proposed IRs with the perspectives,
values, and strengths of counseling psychology;
and (c) ensure that their program is consistent with
recently approved IRs, so that programs can be in
compliance and maintain accreditation.

Public Policy and Advocacy

During the past decade, an education and training
focus on public policy advocacy has grown from
tentative initial steps by a few psychologists to a
national network of psychologists involved in lobbying congressional delegations on legislation of
importance to the education and training community. In 2001, the FEDAC was established as a campus-
based nationwide education advocacy grassroots
network to assist the APA Education Directorate
and Public Policy Education staff to gain federal
support for psychology education and training.
FEDAC is organized into 10 regions across the
United States. Regional coordinators are charged
with identifying a local coordinator in every APA-
accredited academic or internship program and are
involved in (a) distributing action alerts to local
coordinators requesting psychologists in their location to write or call their senators and representatives

about a specific action needed, (b) identifying
psychologist constituents for Capitol Hill visits,
(c) assisting in drafting congressional testimony,
and (d) assisting APA staff during Educational
Leadership Conferences in preparing psychologists
for Capitol Hill visits. Many counseling psychologists (e.g., Sherry Benton, Patricia Cole, Linda Forrest, Laura Palmer, Linda Campbell) have been
actively involved as FEDAC regional coordinators.

In addition, many more counseling psychologists have become actively involved in advocacy
dinners, raising money in support of members of
the U.S. Senate and House of Representatives who
have the potential to become champions for psychology education and training. During the past
decade, leaders of counseling psychology from SCP,
CCPTP, and ACCTA have held advocacy dinners at
both the Houston National Counseling Psychology
Conference in 2001, raising $5,530 to support Ted
Strickland (Ohio), at the time a member of the U.S.
House of Representatives, and the International
Counseling Psychology Conference in 2008
raised $24,112 to support Senator Patty Murray
(Washington).

Counseling psychologists have been active supporters of the annual Educational Advocacy Break-
fast at the APA convention and financial supporters
of the Education Advocacy Trust (EdAT), a func-
tionally autonomous, unit within the APA Practice
Organization, a 501(c)(6) organization. The EdAT,
because it is separate from APA, can provide financial and staff support for educational advocacy
events and actions. (For an account of advocacy
efforts, see http://www.apa.org/about/gr/education/
advocacy/index.aspx.)

To date, the major focus of the FEDAC advocacy
efforts has been to seek authorization and funding
for the Graduate Psychology Education (GPE) program, a federally designated program with its own
line in the federal budget. The GPE funds academic
and internship programs that foster interdisciplinary
approaches to health care services to underserved
population. To date, several counseling psychology
programs have received GPE funding (e.g., Boston
College, Colorado State University, New Mexico
State University, Texas Tech University, the University of North Dakota).

One other advocacy effort has resulted in increased federal funding for education and training especially for those who work in university counseling centers. Counseling psychologists working in counseling centers (e.g., Sherry Benton, Louise Douce) were involved in helping the APA public policy staff develop the Campus Care and Counseling Act that was introduced as House Bill 3593. This House Bill was later incorporated into the Garrett Lee Smith Memorial Act (P. L. 108-355) that passed both branches of Congress in 2004. The Garrett Lee Smith Act provides additional funds for campus counseling centers to focus on suicide prevention programs. Subsequent bills have been introduced in Congress to provide additional support for direct mental health services to college students.

Recommendations. Further involvement of counseling psychologists in public policy advocacy efforts is important to continue. Having ongoing relationships working with key APA staff in the Education Directorate and being on the ground floor as APA develops its education advocacy strategies and priorities is critical. Counseling psychologists need to be present when the language of the bills and the criteria for funding are being discussed and established. CCPTP, ACCTA, and SCCP need to ensure that counseling psychologists are interacting with APA public policy staff, are appointed as FEDAC regional and institutional coordinators, and are raising money and attending advocacy dinners. We recommend that (a) CCPTP and ACCTA include advocacy training as part of their annual meetings, and (b) SCP offer advocacy training for students and early career psychologists. Given that advocacy has been identified as a competency in the benchmark documents, curriculum materials on public policy advocacy need to be included in professional seminars, and students should develop and have opportunities to practice advocacy skills as part of their graduate training; APAGS advocacy efforts provide an ideal mechanism for doing so. Given the recent enactment of state laws described in this chapter, faculty and students should be encouraged to participate in state-level advocacy efforts organized by their state psychological association.

NATIONAL PROFESSIONAL ORGANIZATIONS DEVOTED TO EDUCATION AND TRAINING

We conclude with a brief but important section describing national professional organizations that focus on and influence counseling psychology education and training: the CCPTP, the ACCTA, and the SCP vice president for education and training (and his or her advisory board within the SCP).

CCPTP is a national professional organization composed of directors of training of counseling psychology doctoral programs with 72 institutional members and 45 individual members (see http://www.ccptp.org). Since its inception under the early leadership of Bruce Fretz, CCPTP has served as a valuable resource for individual TDs, be they new or seasoned, about the leadership challenges they face. CCPTP with its listserv and annual meetings has created a cohesive space for academic program TDs to explore myriad issues. In the past decade, CCPTP has addressed many of the issues covered in this chapter (e.g., the internship imbalance, multicultural and international education and training, trainee competence problems, implementation of competency-based training, accreditation issues, and public policy advocacy). In recent years CCPTP has interacted more regularly with other training councils (joint training council conferences in 2000 and 2010) and has increased its participation and influence within the CCTC, an organization of 16 training councils and seven other professional organizations in psychology. According to the CCTC website,

> CCTC promotes discussion of professional education of psychologists, develops recommendations to be reviewed and possibly implemented by member organizations, encourages communication between CCTC members and associated organizations, and provides comment to the Board of Educational Affairs (BEA), the Committee on Accreditation (CoA), and other APA Boards and Committees. (CCTC, n.d.)

ACCTA is a national professional organization composed of TDs responsible for internships in university and college counseling centers with 155 members (see https://www.accta.net). Like CCPTP, ACCTA provides resources and support for TDs overseeing internship programs through its listserv and annual conference. ACCTA runs a separate clearinghouse to provide assistance to interns and sites that did not successfully match on the annual match day. ACCTA along with CCPTP has actively worked to solve the internship imbalance problem and keeps its members updated on other critical trends affecting counseling center internship training. Like CCPTP, ACCTA participates in CCTC and other joint efforts with other training councils.

The SCP vice president of education and training and his or her advisory board members work closely with CCPTP and ACCTA to address critical issues in education and training. These organizations and individuals are the identified leaders in education and training within counseling psychology. Many of the initiatives and policies that have had a major impact in education and training were born and developed within these organizations. Similarly, they are a critical force for accomplishing many of the recommendations described in this chapter.

OVERARCHING AND SYSTEMIC RECOMMENDATIONS

In this final section, we address the question, "Where should counseling psychology education and training be heading?" and make overarching and systemic recommendations. Throughout this chapter, we have made section-by-section recommendations. To enact many of these recommendations requires that counseling psychologists be active leaders at the national level where education and training policies are being developed, debated, and approved, most notably within CCTC, the CoA, APA Education Directorate and BEA, FEDAC, Council of Specialties, and national task forces and working groups focused on education and training. Representing counseling psychology at the table and being active and respected leaders have been important components of our success to date. We must be vigilant to ensure that counseling psychologists continue to be nominated, appointed, and elected to leadership positions in the noted organizations.

Yet, there is room for growth. Counseling psychology could have a higher profile and greater impact on professional psychology education and training. To do so requires strategic and tactical planning; it requires us to be more savvy and political in these larger organizations representing multiple specialties in psychology. Thus, an overarching recommendation is that CCPTP (with its organizational partners, ACCTA and SCP, and counseling psychologists who have served on national groups) engage in a comprehensive strategic planning process that charts the next decade for counseling psychology education and training. Such a strategic plan needs to identify key issues internal and external to counseling psychology education and training that need our attention and that establish goals, objectives, tactics, and timetables for each issue identified. Like most strategic planning process, the plan needs to be reviewed and updated on a regular basis (e.g., every 5 years). In this review, we have described numerous places where we believe counseling psychology education and training is ahead of the curve (e.g., guidelines implementation, values statement, evidence-based practice) and has great potential to influence and improve the larger arena of professional psychology education and training. Similarly, we have identified places where we are clearly behind the curve (e.g., behavioral health) and that need our concerted attention. Counseling psychology education and training organizations also need to be thoughtfully responsive and potentially nimble to directional changes that are occurring on the horizon in the broader arena of psychology and society.

What organizational structures are in place to monitor societal and psychology changes, determine their influences, and create the appropriate response within counseling psychology education and training? Many of the recommendations in this chapter may be worthwhile ideas, yet time and effort is limited. Strategic planning processes allow for multiple goals to be reviewed, prioritized, and sequenced for maximum effectiveness. This review and the recommendations herein are an initial starting place. The future of education and training in counseling psychology deserves a systematic and strategic proactive plan on the basis of dialogue across a wide cross-section of counseling psychology leaders.

Most recommendations in this chapter have been addressed to counseling psychologists in leadership positions. Yet we also believe that individual faculty members and students need to pay close attention to the changing national agenda within psychology and to larger societal changes that require a response at the education and training level. Time during faculty meetings should be devoted to discussing national trends. Faculty members should ensure that TDs share the ideas and materials from the CCPTP listserv and conference presentations. Program faculty should be individually or collectively responding during open comment periods on national education and training issues. Students should be informed and current about the unfolding trends in education and training and in professional psychology. Students need to be exposed to a culture that teaches them early in their careers that being actively involved in shaping their professional future involves not just attention to their individual career development but also engagement in influencing the profession and its future.

During the past decade, education and training in counseling psychology has been extraordinarily successful as evidenced by the status and accomplishments described in this chapter. The chapter weaves the story of why education and training in counseling psychology is robust and strong. As we have written this chapter, we have become even more confident about a vibrant future. The essential elements of health for individuals, groups, and organizations are the strengths of counseling psychology: valuing differences, strength-based approaches, social justice and prevention, authentic integration of research and practice, psychology of work, and many others. All of these long-standing traditions of counseling psychology signal the health of the specialty for the foreseeable future and create the platforms for counseling psychology leadership within professional psychology education and training.

References

Ægisdóttir, S., & Gerstein, L. H. (2009). International counseling competencies: A new frontier in multicultural training. In J. G. Ponterotto, J. M. Casas, L. A. Suzuki, & C. M. Alexander (Eds.), *Handbook of multicultural counseling* (3rd ed., pp. 175–188). Thousand Oaks, CA: Sage.

Albee, G. W. (2000). The Boulder model's fatal flaw. *American Psychologist, 55,* 247–248. doi:10.1037/0003-066X.55.2.247

American Psychological Association. (2000a). *Guidelines and principles for accreditation of programs in professional psychology.* Washington, DC: Author.

American Psychological Association. (2000b). *Report of the APA Commission on Education and Training Leading to Licensure in Psychology.* Retrieved from http://www.am.org/cudcp/report_of_the_commission_on_educ.htm

American Psychological Association. (2003). Guidelines on multicultural education, training, research, practice, and organizational change for psychologists. *American Psychologist, 58,* 377–402. doi:10.1037/0003-066X.58.5.377

American Psychological Association. (2004). Guidelines for psychological practice with older adults. *American Psychologist, 59,* 236–260. doi:10.1037/0003-066X.59.4.236

American Psychological Association. (2006a). *Doctorates minimum entry into the practice of psychology.* Retrieved from http://www.apa.org/governance/epm/chapter4b.html#7

American Psychological Association. (2006b). Evidence-based practice in psychology. *American Psychologist, 61,* 271–285. doi:10.1037/0003-066X.61.4.271

American Psychological Association. (2007). Guidelines for psychological practice with girls and women. *American Psychologist, 62,* 949–979. doi:10.1037/0003-066X.62.9.949

American Psychological Association. (2008). *Graduate study in psychology.* Washington, DC: Author.

American Psychological Association. (2010a). *Board of Educational Affairs draft operative policy statement: The master's degree in psychology.* Available upon request from the American Psychological Association, Education Directorate, Washington, DC.

American Psychological Association. (2010b). *Ethical principles of psychologists and code of conduct (2002, Amended June 1, 2010).* Retrieved from http://www.apa.org/ethics/code/index.aspx

American Psychological Association Committee on Accreditation. (2005). *2005 Annual report.* Retrieved from http://www.apa.org/ed/accreditation/about/coa/annual-report-2005.pdf

Andrews, L. B., & Burruss, J. W. (2004). *Core competencies for psychiatric education: Defining, teaching, and assessing resident competence.* Washington, DC: American Psychiatric Publishing.

Association of Psychology Postdoctoral and Internship Centers. (2008). *APPIC program statistics*. Retrieved from http://www.appic.org/directory/4_3_1_directory_Program_Stats.html

Association of Psychology Postdoctoral and Internship Centers. (2010). *Match survey of intern applicants*. Retrieved from http://www.appic.org/match/5_2_2_1_12_match_about_statistics_general_2010.html

Association of State and Provincial Psychology Boards. (2009). *Guidelines on practicum experience for licensure*. Retrieved from http://www.asppb.net/files/public/Final_Prac_Guidelines_1_31_09.pdf

Baer, C., & Corneille, P. (1992). Character and fitness inquiry: From bar admission to professional discipline. *Bar Examiner, 61*, 5–12.

Baker, J., McCutcheon, S., & Keilin, W. G. (2007). The internship supply-demand imbalance: The APPIC perspective. *Training and Education in Professional Psychology, 1*, 287–293. doi:10.1037/1931-3918.1.4.287

Baker, T. B., McFall, R. M., & Shoham, V. (2008). Current status and future prospects of clinical psychology: Toward a scientifically principled approach to mental and behavioral health care. *Psychological Science in the Public Interest, 9*, 67–103.

Behnke, S. H. (2008). Discussion: Toward elaborating and implementing a conceptualization of healthy, safe training environments. *Training and Education in Professional Psychology, 2*, 215–218.

Belar, C. D. (2008). Clinical health psychology: A health care specialty in professional psychology. *Professional Psychology: Research and Practice, 39*, 229–233. doi:10.1037/0735-7028.39.2.229

Bieschke, K. J., & Mintz, L. (2009). Addressing concerns and taking on the third rail. *The Counseling Psychologist, 37*, 772–779. doi:10.1177/0011000009338403

Bieschke, K. J., Perez, R. M., & DeBord, K. A. (Eds.). (2007). *Handbook of counseling and psychotherapy with lesbian, gay, bisexual, and transgender clients* (2nd ed.). Washington, DC: American Psychological Association. doi:10.1037/11482-000

Bingham, R. P., & Porché-Burke, L. James, S., Sue, D. W., & Vasquez, M. J. T. (2002). Introduction: A report on the National Multicultural Conference and Summit II. *Cultural Diversity and Ethnic Minority Psychology, 8*, 75–87.

Blustein, D. L., Goodyear, R. K., Perry, J. C., & Cypers, S. (2005). The shifting sands of counseling psychology programs' institutional contexts: An environmental scan and revitalizing strategies. *The Counseling Psychologist, 33*, 610–634. doi:10.1177/0011000005277820

Carraccio, C., Wolfsthal, S. D., Englander, R., Ferents, K., & Martin, C. (2002). Shifting paradigms: From Flexner to competencies. *Academic Medicine, 77*, 361–367. doi:10.1097/00001888-200205000-00003

Center for Arizona Policy. (2011). *Family issues fact sheet (No. 2011–11): HB 2565 University Students' Religious Liberty Act*. Retrieved from www.azleg.gov/legtext/50leg/1r/bills/hb2565h.pdf

Clay, R. (2000, August). The postdoc trap. *Monitor on Psychology, 31*, 20–26.

Constantine, M. G., & Sue, D. W. (Eds.). (2005). *Strategies for building multicultural competence in mental health and educational settings*. Hoboken, NJ: Wiley.

Council for Accreditation of Counseling and Related Educational Programs. (2009). *2009 Standards*. Retrieved from http://www.cacrep.org/detail/issues.cfm

Council of Chairs of Training Councils. (2004). *The comprehensive evaluation of student-trainee competence in professional psychology programs*. Retrieved from http://www.psychtrainingcouncils.org/documents.html

Council of Chairs of Training Councils. (2007). *Recommendations for communication*. Retrieved from http://www.psychtrainingcouncils.org/documents.html

Council of Chairs of Training Councils. (n.d.) *About CCTC*. Retrieved from http://psychtrainingcouncils.org/about.html

Council of Counseling Psychology Training Programs. (2005). *Annual survey data 2005*. Retrieved from http://www.ccptp.org/resources/surveydata.html

Council of Counseling Psychology Training Programs, Association of Counseling Center Training Agencies, & Society of Counseling Psychology. (2009). Counseling psychology model training values statement addressing diversity. *The Counseling Psychologist, 37*, 641–643. doi:10.1177/0011000009331930

Cummings, N. A., Cummings, J. L., & Johnson, J. N. (1997). Introduction. In N. A. Cummings, J. L. Cummings, & J. N. Johnson (Eds.), *Behavioral health in primary care: A guide for clinical integration* (pp. 21–27). Madison, WI: Psychosocial Press.

Daniel, J. H., Roysircar, G., Abeles, N., & Boyd, C. (2004). Individual and cultural diversity competency: Focus on the therapist. *Journal of Clinical Psychology, 60*, 755–770. doi:10.1002/jclp.20014

DeMers, S. T. (2009). Real progress with significant challenges ahead: Advancing competency assessment in psychology. *Training and Education in Professional Psychology, 3*, S66–S69. doi:10.1037/a0017534

Donovan, R. A., & Ponce, A. N. (2009). Identification and measurement of core competencies in professional psychology: Areas for consideration. *Training and Education in Professional Psychology, 3,* S46–S49. doi:10.1037/a0017302

Douce, L. A. (2004). Globalization of counseling psychology: Presidential address. *The Counseling Psychologist, 32,* 142–152. doi:10.1177/001100000 3260009

Elman, N., & Forrest, L. (2004). Psychotherapy in the remediation of psychology trainees: Exploratory interviews with training directors. *Professional Psychology: Research and Practice, 35,* 123–130. doi:10.1037/0735-7028.35.2.123

Elman, N. S., & Forrest, L. (2007). From trainee impairment to professional competence problems: Seeking new terminology that facilitates effective action. *Professional Psychology: Research and Practice, 38,* 501–509. doi:10.1037/0735-7028.38.5.501

Elman, N., Forrest, L., Vacha-Haase, T., & Gizara, S. (1999). A systems perspective on trainee impairment: Continuing the dialogue. *The Counseling Psychologist, 27,* 712–721. doi:10.1177/0011000099275005

Epstein, R. M., & Hundert, E. M. (2002). Defining and assessing professional competence. *JAMA, 287,* 226–235. doi:10.1001/jama.287.2.226

Falender, C. A., Collins, C. J., & Shafranske, E. P. (2005, November/December). Use of the term "impairment" in psychology supervision. *The California Psychologist,* 21–22.

Falender, C. A., Collins, C. J., & Shafranske, E. P. (2009). "Impairment" and performance issues in clinical supervision: After the 2008 ADA Amendments Act. *Training and Education in Professional Psychology, 3,* 240–249. doi:10.1037/a0017153

Forrest, L. (2008, April). Reflections on the international counseling psychology conference. *Society of Counseling Psychology Newsletter.* Retrieved from http://www.div17.org/pubs_newsletters.html

Forrest, L. (2010). Presidential address: Linking international psychology, professional competence and leadership: Counseling psychologists as learning partners. *The Counseling Psychologist, 38,* 96–120. doi:10.1177/0011000009350585

Forrest, L., & Elman, N. (2005). Psychotherapy for poorly performing trainees: Are there limits to confidentiality? *Psychotherapy Bulletin, 40,* 29–37.

Forrest, L., & Elman, N. S. (2010, January). *Trainees with competence problems: Developing practical skills for unavoidable difficult conversations.* Presentation at the midyear meeting of the Council of Counseling Psychology Training Programs, Orlando, FL.

Forrest, L., Elman, N., Gizara, S., & Vacha-Haase, T. (1999). Trainee impairment: A review of identification, remediation, dismissal, and legal issues. *The Counseling Psychologist, 27,* 627–686. doi:10.1177/0011000099275001

Forrest, L., Elman, N. S., Huprich, S., Jacobs, S., & Kaslow, N. (2010, August). Faculty members' actions with trainees with competence problems. In C. Grus (Chair), *Faculty and peer experiences with students with problems of professional competence.* Symposium presented at the 118th Annual Convention of the American Psychological Association, San Diego, CA.

Forrest, L., Elman, N. S., & Shen-Miller, D. S. (2008). Psychology trainees with competence problems: From individual to ecological conceptualizations. *Training and Education in Professional Psychology, 2,* 183–192. doi:10.1037/1931-3918.2.4.183

Fouad, N. A., & Arredondo, P. (2007). *Becoming culturally oriented: Practical advice for psychologists and educators.* Washington, DC: American Psychological Association. doi:10.1037/11483-000

Fouad, N. A., & Bynner, J. (2008). Work transitions. *American Psychologist, 63,* 241–251. doi:10.1037/ 0003-066X.63.4.241

Fouad. N. A., Grus, C. L., Hatcher, R. L., Kaslow, N. J., Hutchings, P. S., Madson, M. B., . . . Crossman, R. E. (2009). Competency benchmarks: A model for understanding and measuring competence in professional psychology across training levels. *Training and Education in Professional Psychology, 3,* S5–S26.

Garrett Lee Smith Memorial Act, Pub. L. No. 108-355 (2004).

Gaubatz, M. D., & Vera, E. M. (2002). Do formalized gatekeeping procedures increase programs' follow-up with deficient trainees? *Counselor Education and Supervision, 41,* 294–305.

Gaubatz, M. D., & Vera, E. M. (2006). Trainee competence in master's level counseling programs: A comparison of counselor educators' and students' views. *Counselor Education and Supervision, 46,* 32–43.

Gerstein, L. H., & Ægisdóttir, S. (2007). Training international social change agents: Transcending a U.S. counseling paradigm. *Counselor Education and Supervision, 47,* 123–139.

Gerstein, L. H., Heppner, P. P., Ægisdóttir, S., Leung, S. A., & Norsworthy, K. L. (2009). Cross-cultural counseling: History, challenges, and rationale. In L. H. Gerstein, P. P. Heppner, S. Ægisdóttir, S. A. Leung, & K. L. Norsworthy (Eds.), *International handbook of cross-cultural counseling: Cultural assumptions and practices worldwide* (pp. 3–32). Thousand Oaks, CA: Sage.

Gilfoyle, N. (2008). The legal exosystem: Risk management in addressing student competence problems in professional psychology training. *Training and Education in Professional Psychology, 2,* 202–209. doi:10.1037/1931-3918.2.4.202

Gizara, S., & Forrest, L. (2004). Supervisors' experiences of trainee impairment and incompetence at APA-accredited internship sites. *Professional Psychology: Research and Practice, 35*, 131–140. doi:10.1037/0735-7028.35.2.131

Gladwell, M. (2000). *The tipping point.* New York, NY: Little, Brown.

Goodyear, R. K., Cortese, J. R., Guzzardo, C. R., Allison, R. D., Claiborn, C. D., & Packard, T. (2000). Factors, trends, and topics in the evolution of counseling psychology training. *The Counseling Psychologist, 28*, 603–621. doi:10.1177/0011000000285001

Grus, C. L. (2009). Implications of the counseling psychology model training values statement addressing diversity for education and training in professional psychology. *The Counseling Psychologist, 37*, 752–759. doi:10.1177/0011000009334432

Grus, C. L. (2011). Training, credentialing and new roles in clinical psychology: Emerging trends. In D. H. Barlow (Ed.), *The Oxford handbook of clinical psychology* (pp. 150–168). New York, NY: Oxford University Press.

Hasan, N. T., Fouad, N. A., & Williams-Nickelson, C. (2008). *Studying psychology in the United States: Expert guidance for international students.* New York, NY: Kluwer Academic/Plenum.

Hatcher, R. L., & Lassiter, K. D. (2007). Initial training in professional psychology: The practicum competencies outline. *Training and Education in Professional Psychology, 1*, 49–63. doi:10.1037/1931-3918.1.1.49

Heppner, P. P. (2006). The benefits and challenges of becoming a cross-culturally competent counseling psychologist: Presidential address. *The Counseling Psychologist, 34*, 147–172. doi:10.1177/0011000005282832

Heppner, P. P., Ægisdóttir, S., Leung, S. A., Duan, C., Helms, J. E., Gerstein, L. H., & Pedersen, P. B. (2009). The intersection of multicultural and cross-national movements in the United States: A complementary role to promote culturally sensitive research, training, and practice. In L. H. Gerstein, P. P. Heppner, S. Ægisdóttir, S. A. Leung, & K. L. Norsworthy (Eds.), *International handbook of cross-cultural counseling: Cultural assumptions and practices worldwide* (pp. 33–52). Thousand Oaks, CA: Sage.

Heppner, P. P., Casas, J. M., Carter, J., & Stone, G. L. (2000). The maturation of counseling psychology: Multifaceted perspectives, 1978–1998. In S. D. Brown & R.W. Lent (Eds.), *Handbook of counseling psychology* (pp. 3–49). New York, NY: Wiley.

Hogg, A., Keen, B., Barton, J., & Yardell, D. (1999). Between a rock . . . : Postdoctoral supervision in Arizona. *Arizona Psychologist, 19*, 4–10.

Huprich, S. K., & Rudd, M. D. (2004). A national survey of trainee impairment in clinical, counseling, and school psychology doctoral programs and internships. *Journal of Clinical Psychology, 60*, 43–52. doi:10.1002/jclp.10233

Illfelder-Kaye, J., Lese-Fowler, K., Bursley, K., Reyes, E., & Bieschke, K. J. (2009). Implementing the training values statement addressing diversity in university counseling center internships. *The Counseling Psychologist, 37*, 721–743. doi:10.1177/0011000009331947

Jacobs, S. C., Huprich, S. K., Grus, C. L., Cage, E. A., Elman, N. S., Forrest, L., . . . Kaslow, N. J. (2011). Trainees with professional competency problems: Preparing trainers for difficult but necessary conversations. *Training and Education in Professional Psychology, 5*, 175–184.

Johnson, W. B., Elman, N. S., Forrest, L., Robiner, W. N., Rodolfa, E., & Schaffer, J. B. (2008). Addressing professional competence problems in trainees: Some ethical considerations. *Professional Psychology: Research and Practice, 39*, 589–599. doi:10.1037/a0014264

Kaslow, N. J., Borden, K. A., Collins, F. L., Forrest, L., Illfelder-Kaye, J., Nelson, P. D., . . . Willmuth, M. E. (2004). Competencies conference: Future directions in education and credentialing in professional psychology. *Journal of Clinical Psychology, 60*, 99–712.

Kaslow, N. J., Grus, C. L., Campbell, L. F., Fouad, N. A., Hatcher, R. L., & Rodolfa, E. R. (2009). Competency assessment toolkit for professional psychology. *Training and Education in Professional Psychology, 3*, S27–S45. doi:10.1037/a0015833

Kaslow, N. J., McCarthy, S. M., Rogers, J. H., & Summerville, M. B. (1992). Psychology postdoctoral training: A developmental perspective. *Professional Psychology: Research and Practice, 23*, 369–375. doi:10.1037/0735-7028.23.5.369

Kaslow, N. J., Rubin, N. J., Bebeau, M. J., Leigh, I. W., Lichtenberg, J. W., Nelson, P. D., . . . Smith I. L. (2007). Guiding principles and recommendations for the assessment of competence. *Professional Psychology: Research and Practice, 38*, 441–451. doi:10.1037/0735-7028.38.5.441

Kaslow, N. J., Rubin, N. J., Forrest, L. M., Elman, N. S., Van Horne, B. A., Jacobs, S. C., . . . Thorne, B. E. (2007). Recognizing, assessing, and intervening with problems of professional competence. *Professional Psychology: Research and Practice, 38*, 479–492. doi:10.1037/0735-7028.38.5.479

Keeton v. Anderson-Wiley et al., No. 10-13925 (S. D. Ga. 2010).

Kenkel, M. B. (2009). Adopting a competency model for professional psychology: Essential elements and resources. *Training and Education in Professional Psychology, 3*, S59–S62. doi:10.1037/a0017037

Kwan, K. L. K., & Gerstein, L. (2008). Envisioning a counseling psychology of the world. *The Counseling Psychologist, 36*, 182–187. doi:10.1177/0011000007313269

Leong, F. T. L., & Blustein, D. L. (2000). Toward a global vision of counseling psychology. *The Counseling Psychologist, 28*, 5–9. doi:10.1177/0011000000281001

Leong, F. T. L., & Ponterotto, J. G. (2003). A proposal for internationalizing counseling psychology in the United States: Rationale, recommendations, and challenges. *The Counseling Psychologist, 31*, 381–395. doi:10.1177/0011000003031004001

Leung, S. A. (2003). A journey worth traveling: Globalization of counseling psychology. *The Counseling Psychologist, 31*, 412–419. doi:10.1177/0011000003031004004

Lewis, B. L. (2010). Social justice in practicum training: Competencies and developmental implications. *Training and Education in Professional Psychology, 4*, 145–152. doi:10.1037/a0017383

Lewis, B. L., Hatcher, R. L., & Pate, W. E. (2005). The practicum experience: A survey of practicum site coordinators. *Professional Psychology: Research and Practice, 36*, 291–298. doi:10.1037/0735-7028.36.3.291

Loewy, M. I., Juntunen, C. L., & Duan, C. (2009). Application of the counseling psychology model training values statement addressing diversity to the admission process. *The Counseling Psychologist, 37*, 705–720. doi:10.1177/0011000009331942

Madson, M. B., Hasan, N. T., Williams-Nickelson, C., Kettman, J. J., & Van Sickle, K. S. (2007). The internship supply and demand issue: Graduate student's perspectives. *Training and Education in Professional Psychology, 1*, 249–257. doi:10.1037/1931-3918.1.4.249

Marsella, A. J., & Pedersen, P. B. (2004). Internationalizing the counseling psychology curriculum: Toward new values, competencies, and directions. *Counselling Psychology Quarterly, 17*, 413–423. doi:10.1080/09515070412331331246

Maton, K. I., Kohout, J. L., Wicherski, M., Leary, G. E., & Vinokurov, A. (2006). Minority students of color and the psychology graduate pipeline: Disquieting and encouraging trends, 1989–2003. *American Psychologist, 61*, 117–131. doi:10.1037/0003-066X.61.2.117

McDaniel, S. H., & Fogarty, C. T. (2009). What primary care psychology has to offer the patient-centered medical home. *Professional Psychology: Research and Practice, 40*, 483–492. doi:10.1037/a0016751

McDaniel, S. H., Hargrove, D. S., Belar, C. D., Schroeder, C., & Freeman, E. L. (2004). Recommendations for education and training in primary care psychology. In R. H. Frank, S. H. McDaniel, J. H. Bray, & M. Heldring (Eds.), *Primary care psychology* (pp. 63–92). Washington, DC: American Psychological Association. doi:10.1037/10651-004

McPherson, R. H., Pisecco, S., Elman, N. S., Crosbie-Burnett, M., & Sayger, T. V. (2000). Counseling psychology's ambivalent relationship with master's-level training. *The Counseling Psychologist, 28*, 687–700. doi:10.1177/0011000000285006

Meara, N. M., Schmidt, L. D., Carrington, C. H., Davis, K. L., Dixon, D. N., Fretz, B. R., . . . Sunin, R. M. (1988). Training and accreditation in counseling psychology. *The Counseling Psychologist, 16*, 366–384. doi:10.1177/0011000088163005

Mintz, L. B., & Bieschke, K. J. (2009). Counseling psychology model training values statement addressing diversity: Development and introduction to major contribution. *The Counseling Psychologist, 37*, 634–640. doi:10.1177/0011000009331923

Mintz, L. B., Jackson, A. P., Neville, H. A., Illfelder-Kaye, J., Winterowd, C. L., & Loewy, M. I. (2009). The need for a counseling psychology model training values statement addressing diversity. *The Counseling Psychologist, 37*, 644–675.

Miville, M., Adams, E., & Juntunen, C. (2007). Counseling psychology perspectives on the predoctoral internship supply-demand imbalance: Strategies for problem definition and resolution. *Training and Education in Professional Psychology, 1*, 258–266. doi:10.1037/1931-3918.1.4.258

Miville, M., Duan, C., Nutt, R., Waehler, C., Suzuki, L., Pistole, C., . . . Corpus, M. (2009). Integrating practice guidelines into professional training: Implications for diversity competence. *The Counseling Psychologist, 37*, 519–563.

Moradi, B., & Neimeyer, G. J. (2005). Diversity in the ivory white tower: A longitudinal look at faculty race/ethnicity in counseling psychology academic training programs. *The Counseling Psychologist, 33*, 655–675. doi:10.1177/0011000005277823

Munsey, C. (2007). New APA center analyzes psychology employment and training trends. *APA Monitor, 38*, 15.

Murdock, N. L., Alcorn, J., Heesacker, M., & Stoltenberg, C. (1998). Model training program in counseling psychology. *The Counseling Psychologist, 26*, 658–672. doi:10.1177/0011000098264008

Neimeyer, G. J., Saferstein, J., & Rice, K. G. (2005). Does the model matter? The relationship between science-practice emphasis and outcomes in academic training programs in counseling psychology. *The Counseling Psychologist, 33*, 635–654. doi:10.1177/0011000005277821

Nicholas, D. R., & Stern, M. (2011). Counseling psychology in clinical health psychology: The impact of specialty perspective. *Professional Psychology: Research and Practice, 42,* 331–337.

Norcross, J. C., Evans, K. L., & Ellis, J. L. (2010). The model does matter II: Admissions and training in APA-accredited counseling psychology programs. *The Counseling Psychologist, 38,* 257–268. doi:10.1177/0011000009339342

Norcross, J. C., Sayette, M. A., Mayne, T. J., Karg, R. S., & Turkson, M. A. (1998). Selecting a doctoral program in professional psychology: Some comparisons among PhD counseling, PhD clinical, and PsyD clinical psychology programs. *Professional Psychology: Research and Practice, 29,* 609–614. doi:10.1037/0735-7028.29.6.609

Nutt, R. L. (2007). Implications of globalization for training counseling psychology: Presidential address. *The Counseling Psychologist, 35,* 157–171. doi:10.1177/0011000006294671

Oliver, M. N., Bernstein, J. H., Anderson, K. G., Blashfield, R. K., & Roberts, M. C. (2004). An exploratory examination of student attitudes toward "impaired" peers in clinical psychology training programs. *Professional Psychology: Research and Practice, 35,* 141–147. doi:10.1037/0735-7028.35.2.141

Papadikis, M. A., Teherani, A., Banach, M. A., Knettler, T. R., Rattner, S. L., Stern, D. T., . . . Hodgson, C. S. (2005). Disciplinary action by medical boards and prior behavior in medical school. *New England Journal of Medicine, 353,* 2673–2682.

Pedersen, P. (2003). Culturally biased assumptions in counseling psychology. *The Counseling Psychologist, 31,* 396–403. doi:10.1177/0011000003031004002

Ponterotto, J. G., Casas, J. M., Suzuki, L. A., & Alexander, C. A. (Eds.). (2001). *Handbook of multicultural counseling* (2nd ed.). Thousand Oaks, CA: Sage.

Ponterotto, J. G., Casas, J. M., Suzuki, L. A., & Alexander, C. A. (Eds.). (2009). *Handbook of multicultural counseling* (3rd ed.). Thousand Oaks, CA: Sage.

Pope-Davis, D. B., Coleman, H. L. K., Liu, W. M., & Toporek, R. L. (Eds.). (2003). *Handbook of multicultural competencies in counseling and psychology.* Thousand Oaks, CA: Sage.

Ridley, C. R. (2005). *Overcoming unintentional racism in counseling and therapy: A practitioner's guide to intentional intervention* (2nd ed.). Thousand Oaks, CA: Sage.

Roberts, M. C., Borden, K. A., Christiansen, M. D., & Lopez, S. J. (2005). Fostering a culture shift: Assessment of competence in the education and careers of professional psychologists. *Professional Psychology: Research and Practice, 36,* 355–361. doi:10.1037/0735-7028.36.4.355

Rodolfa, E. R., Bell, D. J., Bieschke, K. J., Davis, C., & Peterson, R. L. (2007). The internship match: Understanding the problem-seeking solutions. *Training and Education in Professional Psychology, 1,* 225–228. doi:10.1037/1931-3918.1.4.225

Rodolfa, E. R., Bent, R. J., Eisman, E., Nelson, P. D., Rehm, L., & Ritchie, P. (2005). A cube model for competency development: Implications for psychology educators and regulators. *Professional Psychology: Research and Practice, 36,* 347–354. doi:10.1037/0735-7028.36.4.347

Rodolfa, E. R., Ko, S. F., & Petersen, L. (2004). Psychology training directors' views of trainees' readiness to practice independently. *Professional Psychology: Research and Practice, 35,* 397–404. doi:10.1037/0735-7028.35.4.397

Rogers, M. R., & Molina, L. E. (2006). Exemplary efforts in psychology to recruit and retain graduate students of color. *American Psychologist, 61,* 143–156. doi:10.1037/0003-066X.61.2.143

Romano, J. L., & Hage, S. M. (2000). Prevention and counseling psychology: Revitalizing commitments for the 21st century. *The Counseling Psychologist, 28,* 733–763. doi:10.1177/0011000000286001

Rosenberg, J. I., Getzelman, M. A., Arcinue, F., & Oren, C. Z. (2005). An exploratory look at students' experiences of problematic peers in academic professional psychology programs. *Professional Psychology: Research and Practice, 36,* 665–673. doi:10.1037/0735-7028.36.6.665

Roysircar, G., Sandhu, D. S., & Bibbins, V. E. (Eds.). (2003). *Multicultural competencies: A guidebook of practices.* Alexandria, VA: Association for Multicultural Counseling & Development.

Rozensky, R. H., Grus, C. L., Belar, C. D., Nelson, P. D., & Kohout, J. L. (2007). Using workforce analysis to answer questions related to the internship imbalance and career pipeline in professional psychology. *Training and Education in Professional Psychology, 1,* 238–248. doi:10.1037/1931-3918.1.4.238

Scheel, M. J. (2011a, February). *Counseling psychology and master's level training.* Paper presented at the midwinter meeting of the Council of Counseling Psychology Training Programs, Tamaya, NM. Retrieved from http://www.ccptp.org/resources/2011 conferenceresources.html

Scheel, M. J. (2011b). *New master's accreditation: Summary of roundtable discussions.* Council of Counseling Psychology Training Programs. Retrieved from http://www.ccptp.org/resources/2011conferenceresources.html

Schmidt, P. (2010a, July 22). Augusta State U. is accused of requiring a counseling student to accept homosexuality. *The Chronicle of Higher Education.* Retrieved from http://chronicle.com/article/Augusta-State-U-Is-Accused-of/123650/

Schmidt, P. (2010b, July 27). Federal judge upholds dismissal of counseling student who balked at treating gay clients. *The Chronicle of Higher Education.* Retrieved from http://chronicle.com/article/Judge-Upholds-Dismissal-of/123704/

Schulte, A. C., & Daly, E. J. (2009). Operationalizing and evaluating professional competencies in psychology: Out with the old, in with the new? *Training and Education in Professional Psychology, 3,* S54–S58. doi:10.1037/a0017155

Shen-Miller, D. S., Forrest, L., & Elman, N. S. (2009). Training directors' conceptualization of the intersection of diversity and trainee competence problems: A preliminary analysis. *The Counseling Psychologist, 37,* 482–518. doi:10.1177/0011000008316656

Shen-Miller, D. S., Grus, C. L., Van Sickle, K, S., Schwartz-Mette, R., Cage, E. A., Elman, N. S., . . . Kaslow, N. J. (2011). Trainees' experiences with peers having competence problems: A national survey. *Training and Education in Professional Psychology, 5,* 112–121.

Stoltenberg, C. D., Pace, T. M., Kashubeck-West, S., Biever, J. L., Patterson, T., & Welch, I. D. (2000). Training models in counseling psychology: Scientist-practitioner versus practitioner-scholar. *The Counseling Psychologist, 28,* 622–640. doi:10.1177/0011000000285002

Sue, D. W. (2010). *Microaggressions in everyday life: Race, gender, and sexual orientation.* Hoboken, NJ: Wiley.

Sue, D. W., Bingham, R. P., Porché-Burke, L., & Vasquez, M. (1999). The diversification of psychology: A multicultural revolution. *American Psychologist, 54,* 1061–1069. doi:10.1037/0003-066X.54.12.1061

Takooshian, H. (2003). Counseling psychology's wide new horizon. *The Counseling Psychologist, 31,* 420–426. doi:10.1177/0011000003031004005

Toporek, R., Gerstein, L., Fouad, N., Roysircar, G., & Israel, T. (Eds.). (2006). *Handbook for social justice in counseling psychology: Leadership, vision, and action.* Thousand Oaks, CA: Sage.

Turner-Essel, L., & Waehler, C. (2009). Integrating internationalization in counseling psychology training programs. *The Counseling Psychologist, 37,* 877–901. doi:10.1177/0011000009336149

University Students' Religious Liberty Act, H.R. 2565, 50th Leg., Reg. Sess. (Ariz. 2011).

Vacha-Haase, T., Davenport, D. S., & Kerewsky, S. D. (2004). Problematic students: Gatekeeping practices of academic professional psychology programs. *Professional Psychology: Research and Practice, 35,* 115–122. doi:10.1037/0735-7028.35.2.115

Varenne, H. (2003). On internationalizing counseling psychology: A view from cultural anthropology. *The Counseling Psychologist, 31,* 404–411. doi:10.1177/0011000003031004003

Vera, E. M. (2009). When human rights and cultural values collide: What do we value? *The Counseling Psychologist, 37,* 744–751. doi:10.1177/0011000009333985

Vera, E. M., & Speight, S. L. (2003). Multicultural competence, social justice, and counseling psychology: Expanding our roles. *The Counseling Psychologist, 31,* 253–272. doi:10.1177/0011000003031003001

Waehler, C. A., Kalodner, C. R., Wampold, B. E., & Lichtenberg, J. W. (2000). Empirically supported treatments (ESTs) in perspective: Implications for counseling psychology training. *The Counseling Psychologist, 28,* 657–671. doi:10.1177/0011000000285004

Wampold, B. E., Lichtenberg, J. W., & Waehler, C. A. (2002). Principles of empirically supported interventions in counseling psychology. *The Counseling Psychologist, 30,* 197–217. doi:10.1177/0011000002302001

Ward v. Wilbanks et al., No. 2:2009cv11237 (E. D. Mich. 2009).

Wilson, J. L., Armoutliev, E., Yakunina, E., & Werth, J. L., Jr. (2009). Practicing psychologists' reflections on evidence-based practice in psychology. *Professional Psychology: Research and Practice, 40,* 403–409. doi:10.1037/a0016247

Winterowd, C. L., Adams, E. M., Miville, M. L., & Mintz, L. B. (2009). Operationalizing, instilling, and assessing counseling psychology training values related to diversity in academic programs. *The Counseling Psychologist, 37,* 676–704. doi:10.1177/0011000009331936

Wrenn, G. (1962). The culturally encapsulated counselor. *Harvard Educational Review, 32,* 444–449.

CHAPTER 6

INTERVENTIONS AND EVIDENCE IN COUNSELING PSYCHOLOGY: A VIEW ON EVIDENCE-BASED PRACTICE

Jean A. Carter and Carol D. Goodheart

Typical chapters on interventions in psychology trace particular approaches (e.g., cognitive behavior therapy, interpersonal therapy, psychodynamic psychotherapy), particular targets (e.g., work and careers, interpersonal problems), specific populations, or particular categories of diagnosis (e.g., depression, posttraumatic stress disorder). Murdock's (2008) text on theoretical approaches is an excellent example to which readers may refer. This chapter, however, takes a different approach. It presents the different epistemologies that are the foundation for science–practice integration and how they are applied; models of evidence-based practice and their implications; the American Psychological Association's (APA's) policy on evidence-based practice in psychology (EBPP), including counseling psychology's important contributions to this policy; and the interplay between evidence-based practice and multiculturalism.

SCIENCE–PRACTICE INTEGRATION: USING EVIDENCE IN PRACTICE

EBPP is an integrative approach in which practitioners actively and deliberately use relevant scientific findings to provide effective treatment to clients. It represents the current iteration of the scientist–practitioner model that is foundational for counseling psychology (Chwalisz, 2003) in which both researchers and practitioners emphasize the lively

dynamic of the contributions from both research and practice perspectives. The integration of research and practice perspectives and between implementation of accountability and the use of evidence is not always smooth. Although research and practice within the interventions arena are aimed toward the same goal of best practice for the best outcome for clients, the emphases are different.

DIFFERENCES BETWEEN INTERVENTION RESEARCHERS AND CLINICIANS

Ways of knowing are different for clinicians and researchers. There are between-group differences for clinicians and researchers in worldview, incentives, personality, and the role between researchers and clinicians. First, practice and research are different endeavors with distinct purposes (Goodheart, 2006). The professional interests and objectives, the cultures and constraints of work settings, the work products, the rhythm of daily life, and even the kinds of questions posed differ for practitioners and researchers. There are different values placed on the kinds of evidence each group uses for its work. The presence of differing values affects the orientation toward treatment held by the two groups.

Second, researchers and practitioners differ in personality characteristics. They vary on the underlying continuum of egocentric–sociocentric views of the world, and they hold different epistemological

Portions of this chapter are adapted and reprinted from "The Proper Focus of Evidence-Based Practice in Psychology," by C. D. Goodheart and J. A. Carter, in *Biennial Review of Counseling Psychology* (Vol. 1, Chapter 3, pp. 47–70) by W. B. Walsh (Ed.), 2008, New York, NY: Taylor & Francis. Copyright 2008 by Taylor & Francis Group, LLC, a division of Informa plc. Adapted with permission.

DOI: 10.1037/13754-006
APA Handbook of Counseling Psychology: Vol. 1. Theories, Research, and Methods, Nadya A. Fouad (Editor-in-Chief)

values, such as increasing knowledge versus improving the human condition. They often have differing theoretical orientations, cognitive strengths, and developmental influences (Conway, 1988; Dana, 1987; Frank, 1984; Zachar & Leong, 1992).

Third, role demands for researchers and practitioners differ (Goodheart, 2006). Researchers must show that a treatment works under specified conditions, but clinicians must do all they can to resolve the problem at hand. For the most part, researchers seek efficacy, internal validity, and reliability on the basis of clinical trials, whereas practitioners seek effectiveness, external validity (utility), and feasibility (resources) for the particular problem at the moment. These are broad-stroke differences, and few individual psychologists fit neatly into these categories. Instead, psychologists span a continuum of traits.

Common Ground for Practitioners and Intervention Researchers

Despite these many differences, commonalities offer opportunities for rapprochement among psychologists with epistemological differences. Although significant tensions remain for such issues as reductionism versus contextualism and acceptance versus rejection of the fact–value dichotomy, it is important to move beyond an oppositional approach to these differences (Russo, 2006). The whole really is greater than the sum of its parts. All psychologists are trained in scientific methods and attitudes, regardless of their eventual work setting and focus. All are committed to the improvement of patients' lives through good psychological research and practice. All agree on the high priority of patient care, the need for high-quality professional training, and the importance of the scientific research foundation for practice. All recognize the importance of expertise and sensitivity to patient characteristics, culture, and preferences and tailoring care to the person (Goodheart & Kazdin, 2006).

Researchers attempt to understand the process of psychological interventions; the principles that underlie change; the impact of various characteristics of clients, practitioners, and intervention techniques and processes; and the factors that affect treatment process and outcome. Their primary goal is knowing the principles that lead to reliably

effective services. Practitioners have a primary goal of helping the individual, couple, family, group, or organization in front of them. Although the principles provide an essential backdrop and guidance, each day is a new adventure in which individual characteristics, unique combinations, and life events can bring something unexpected at a moment's notice.

The purposes of the endeavor, the role demands, and the goals are overlapping but not identical. The orientation toward treatment is different. The accumulation of evidence is often different as well. Practitioners live within a context of daily individual differences and try to understand larger principles from that perspective, whereas researchers typically begin with larger principles that they try to understand as a best fit for both groups and individuals.

Diverse Epistemologies

Different perspectives between researchers and clinicians provide a prism through which evidence— its nature, sources, and implications—can be understood and through which we understand what we "know." The different perspectives embodied in the movement toward increasingly solid grounding of psychology's interventions within our extensive body of research evidence (the EBPP movement) has been described as a *culture war* in which applied psychologists with differing worldviews battle over what treatment approaches to use and on what basis those decisions are made (Messer, 2004). Psychologists have a great deal of difficulty agreeing on what approaches to science to attend to and what the translation of science into practice should look like. Stated simply, there is a central tension between those who believe one or the other of the following:

- Best practice entails *starting with a diagnosed disorder* and applying an empirically based treatment package (EBT) with a central emphasis on techniques that have been demonstrated to be efficacious. Other evidence is sought only when an EBT is not available or is not working. This may be characterized as the use of a hierarchical system of treatment, in line with the hierarchy of evidence.

- Best practice entails *starting with the client*, establishing a therapeutic relationship, and developing a treatment plan woven from research evidence on interventions, common factors, human development, psychopathology, individual and group differences, and other relevant research topics. This may be characterized as the use of a heterarchical system, in line with the need for multiple strands of research evidence and clinical information to tailor treatment to a particular client (Goodheart & Kazdin, 2006, p. 8).

Differences in the underlying philosophies of science that guide the work of researchers and clinicians contribute significantly to this tension. It is important to understand these important distinctions to arrive at a rapprochement that advances both science and practice.

What Do We Know and How Do We Know It?

Epistemology is the branch of philosophy that studies the nature of knowledge as well as its structures, sources, and scope. In other words, how do we know what we know? What language do we use to describe it to others? What knowledge do we value? Where do we direct our energies to obtain new knowledge? How do we achieve harmony with psychologists who do not hold the same worldview? And how do we integrate science and clinical wisdom?

Logical positivism—a scientific method of controlled, valid, replicable, and hierarchical evidence—has remained the dominant epistemology for psychology. It leads to advances in psychological treatment on the basis of a hierarchy of scientific evidence. This epistemology assumes that the scientific method of controlled, internally valid, and replicable observation is the best way to understand the world and improve evidence-based practice. The viewpoint has well-described strengths and a logically consistent strategy for the discovery and verification of new knowledge and encourages causal understanding and confidence in scientific findings. It is internally and externally consistent, with considerable validity.

At the same time, it has limitations, and some take exception to the dominance of this epistemology,

especially when relied on in isolation. The limitations of logical positivism have been well-summarized by Morowski (2005, p. 3):

- The choice of quantification as the best way to classify and describe mental life and behavior leads to disregard for qualitative experience and methods.
- The choice of reductionism as the best explanatory mode leads to the neglect of holism, emergence, and a unified gestalt.
- The choice of the positivist scientific method as exclusively sufficient leads to the lack of measurement and integration of other valuable phenomena, such as those embraced by the physical sciences.
- The assumed neutrality of the observer as standing outside the interaction may lead to dehumanizing explanations, limits on knowledge of internal experience and unexamined biases.
- The assumed value-free position of science leads to ignoring the values and beliefs inherent in the choices made during the scientific process.
- The assumption of universal laws of human nature may miss consideration for the dynamic, temporal, and contextual aspects of human nature, and, in particular, the unique combination of characteristics found in individuals.
- The influence of a dominant worldview that may overlook individual, cultural and social differences could alter understandings of what have been assumed to be universal laws.

Is there an alternative that will both challenge and augment the dominant focus on predictability, objectivity, determinism, and statistical regularity? Not surprisingly, alternative constructions that challenge a nondiverse dominant epistemology have come from clinicians, women, ethnic minorities, and qualitative researchers with different worldviews.

Other epistemologies that provide a framework for the pursuit of knowledge relevant to both science and practice (Morowski, 2005) include:

- Radical empiricism (e.g., ecological psychology is an outgrowth of this epistemology that espouses pragmatism, transformation in immediate experience, and engagement)

- Standpoint theories (e.g., these epistemologies rest on a belief in multiple perspectives as equally valid and seek a science not restricted to a singular perspective of human experience; these are integral to the feminist and Black psychology movements as well as to other socioeconomic and historical conditions)
- Constructivism (e.g., role theory, relational psychology, narrative psychology, and self psychology are outgrowths of observations that people construct views of the self and the world through active social processes)
- Dynamic nominalism (e.g., feminist, ethnic minority, lesbian, gay, bisexual, transsexual, and some intervention research assumes a dynamic looping process of human change that in turn changes the human sciences)

These ways of knowing recognize the presence and force of uncertainty, indeterminism, pluralism, plasticity, and complexity in human beings (Morowski, 2005). They are also consistent with counseling psychology's values and emphases and support a multicultural perspective, worldview, way of being, and view of psychological interventions.

As we move science and practice forward, psychology benefits from enlarged epistemological frames of reference. Although all psychologists are trained in the scientific foundations of psychological knowledge and rely on a scientific foundation, the nature of the therapeutic enterprise calls on practitioners to rely on both nomothetic (attempts to discover general laws) and idiographic (attempts to understand a particular individual or event) processes, findings based on both quantitative and qualitative methods, and views based on both scientific and humanistic attitudes. These are psychology's dual heritage (Kimble, 1984; Messer, 2004). Nevertheless, it remains a challenge to integrate the unique strengths of different approaches to knowledge in practical applications. What can guide us in our search for empirical and evidentiary resources to support what is known as EBPP?

THE CURRENT CONTEXT FOR EVIDENCE-BASED PRACTICE

Like our fellow applied specialties, counseling psychology has a long history of commitment to an integrated scientist–practitioner model, although debates about how best to implement such a model persist. The ongoing discussion, deliberation, and debate about the scientist–practitioner model (Chwalisz, 2003) are important, interesting, and engaging and lead to various models of training. In recent years, however, the relationship between science and practice has taken center stage in public considerations of access to services and the utility of those services.

The current emphasis on the integration of scientific inquiry with practice applications arises primarily out of calls for accountability and quality (and the supporting research) along with greater acceptability and accessibility of psychological treatments. Although stigma, doubt, and uncertainty about mental health services and their value persist, a wider view of evidence and research that captures the complexity of effective treatment suggests that an increase, not a decrease in the provision of mental health services is warranted. Early onset of psychological disorders, the value of treatment, and the damaging impact on individuals, families, businesses, and society of untreated (or undertreated) mental health disorders becomes clearer (Reed & Eisman, 2006). Psychology's commitment to the scientist–practitioner model, its empirical foundation, its methodologies, and its results as justification for the applications of psychological principles serve it well within this context. However, defining and implementing evidence-based practice initiatives has not been a simple matter, and organized psychology's efforts to define the proper focus for the integration of evidence and practice have taken various forms. Counseling psychology's integrated scientist–practitioner model has given serious impetus to our leadership within this arena of accountability.

TWO APPROACHES TO EBPP

The two general approaches to bringing evidence and accountability to the daily life of psychological practice are described in the following sections. One begins with a diagnosed disorder and prescribed techniques (often called *empirically validated treatment*, *evidence-based treatment*, or *empirically supported treatment*) that are based on intervention protocols tested in randomized clinical research trials. The other starts with the client and a therapeutic relationship, and is based on broad research evidence from multiple sources (often called *evidence-based practice*).

Disorder or Technique-Focused Approaches

Disorder- and technique focused approaches require the delineation of specific techniques, treaments, or interventions with demonstrated efficacy and/or effectiveness, and they include a requirement for high levels of internal validity, with less emphasis on external validity. They draw on a biopsychosocial approach to science akin to the natural sciences and rest on positivistic empiricism (Hoshmand, 2003). Within this approach, treatments are the focus (rather than the client). Through rigorous methodologies and clear delineation of parameters, psychological treatments can be compared with each other and to alternative treatments (such as psychotropic medications) and effectiveness can be determined. APA Division 12 (Clinical Psychology) has strongly advocated for this approach as primary (Chambless & Ollendick, 2001).

A related approach includes the delineation of treatment guidelines for particular target populations or diagnostic groups. This approach emerges from a focus on client groups with common characteristics and ordinarily with shared diagnoses. Treatment guidelines are based on rigorous and comprehensive research literature reviews of treatment interventions for specific disorders. This approach requires clear delineation of parameters, in this instance focused on diagnosis. The American Psychiatric Association's guidelines follow this approach (http://www.psych.org/psych_pract/treatg/pg/prac_guide.cfm). The APA is undertaking the development of treatment guidelines to ensure that psychological treatment methods and approaches to client problems remain strongly visible within the health care arena and that they are recognized as equally or more effective than

medications for many conditions, with fewer risks of side effects.

Integrative Client-Centered or Relational Approaches

Integrative client-centered or relational approaches involve delineation of procedures or principles for the integration of research evidence into pracice applications. They enlarge the framework for appropriate and necessary research evidence and methodological approaches. It emphasizes common factors and the psychotherapy relationship as well as basic psychological science. This integrative approach prizes multiple strands of research evidence and clinical expertise to enhance outcomes and quality. It requires an understanding of fundamental principles of change and the utility of a variety of techniques that can be integrated within a fluid practice context and tailored to individual patient characteristics. It focuses on a range of factors (including client characteristics and diagnoses) and can embrace multiple techniques and treatment strategies (Carter, 2006). It also assumes that psychologist practitioners can be good consumers of the psychological literature. APA Divisions 32 (Society for Humanistic Psychology), 29 (Psychotherapy; principles of empirically supported relationships; Ackerman et al., 2001; Norcross, 2002); and 17 (Society of Counseling Psychology; principles of empirically supported interventions; Wampold, Lichtenberg, & Waehler, 2002) all reflect this approach in their initiatives around evidence-based practice. Importantly, this approach is intrinsically individualistic, emphasizing complex interplays of individual characteristics, while also acknowledging group characteristics, treatment strategies, and diagnoses.

APA's Policy on EBPP

APA, with its responsibility to represent the breadth of the discipline, recognizes the importance of EBPP issues for accountability, health care policy development, and the health care marketplace. In 2005, APA President Ronald F. Levant appointed a Presidential Task Force (TF) on Evidence-Based Practice to develop policy language and a report containing the rationale and references for the policy recommendation. The policy was approved by the APA

Council of Representatives in 2005 (APA, 2005). Counseling psychologists Ronald Levant (ex officio), Carol Goodheart (Chair), Jean Carter, and Bruce Wampold participated on the TF. The resulting documents were designed to show how evidence should be used to design and offer safe effective services that benefit clients as well as demonstrate to the public and health care systems that psychologists are providing evidence-based services.

The TF began with the Institute of Medicine's (IOM's) definition of evidence-based medicine because it is widely accepted in science and health care practice. Evidence-based medicine is a three-legged stool, as described by the IOM (2001):

> Evidence based [medicine] is the integration of best research evidence with clinical expertise and patient values. Best research evidence refers to clinically relevant research, often from the basic health and medical sciences, but especially from patient centered clinical research. . . . Clinical expertise means the ability to use clinical skills and past experience to rapidly identify each patient's unique health state and diagnosis, individual risks and benefits of potential interventions, and personal values and expectations. Patient values refers to the unique preferences, concerns and expectations that each patient brings to a clinical encounter and that must be integrated into clinical decisions if they are to serve the patient. (p. 147)

The APA TF engaged in considerable dialogue about the nature and streams of evidence emphasized in psychology, appropriate research designs to incorporate both internal and external validity, the role of clinical expertise, and the incorporation of patient characteristics in addition to values as well as many other philosophy of science and feasibility of practice issues. Ultimately, the TF crafted the definition and explication for psychology to reflect sound evidence on therapeutic effectiveness and the vital role played by the therapist and the patient working in a collaborative endeavor undertaken for optimal results. The definition, which closely parallels the one adopted by the IOM, as adopted by the

APA Council of Representatives is as follows: "Evidence Based Practice in Psychology (EBPP) is the integration of the best available research with clinical expertise in the context of patient characteristics, culture and preferences" (APA, 2005, p. 1).

The APA policy expands the third leg of the stool, which refers to patients in a way that is entirely consistent with counseling psychology's values. It paves the way for approaches to EBPP that are applicable to and adaptable for global and multicultural individuals and communities. In fact, one could read the APA definition as strongly supportive of this adaptability.

APA's expanded definition includes patient characteristics, including such variables as level of function and readiness for change, race, ethnicity, gender, sexual orientation, and cultural context, to create a model that is centered in the patient. Patient centeredness implies more than a focus on choice, values, and preferences because patient characteristics are known to moderate the effects of interventions (APA Presidential Task Force on Evidence-Based Practice, 2006). Patient characteristics, in addition to level of pathology, comorbidity, other clinical concerns, and life context (such as socioeconomic status, class, and culture) are particularly salient and important in mental health. Although research on characteristics and context remains sparse, and we do not yet fully know the extent to which cross-diagnostic characteristics (including personality traits) affect the impact of our interventions, these factors must be incorporated into any effective treatment approach or plan. The APA policy takes into account the evolving nature of science, and we expect the evidence to become clearer over time.

Counseling Psychology's Contributions to EBPP

Counseling psychology, throughout its history, has been deeply involved in fostering the integration of science and practice and the purposeful use of evidence in practice. Our specialty within the discipline has made strong contributions to the evidence-based practice movement, both in its contribution to the APA policy and in developing principles that befit the values and approaches inherent to counseling psychology. In undertaking an initiative to delineate an evidence-based practice model appropriate for counseling psychology, a task force appointed by Division 17 (Society of Counseling Psychology) developed principles of evidence-based practice with the goals of

> (a) making counseling psychologists and students more aware of the current empirical status of interventions in counseling psychology, (b) increasing predoctoral and postdoctoral training in psychological interventions that have been supported by empirical research and (c) fostering public understanding and appreciation of empirically supported interventions offered by counseling psychologists. (Wampold et al., 2002)

The outcome was a set of principles for understanding and assessing evidence as a basis for practice. The principles were incorporated in the deliberations and policy statement of the APA Presidential Task Force on Evidence-Based Practice in Psychology. The seven Principles of Empirically Supported Interventions are as follows:

> Principle 1: Level of Specificity Should Be Considered When Evaluating Outcomes.
> Principle 2: Level of Specificity Should Not Be Restricted to Diagnosis.
> Principle 3: Scientific Evidence Needs to Be Examined in Its Entirety and Aggregated Appropriately.
> Principle 4: Evidence for Absolute and Relative Efficacy Needs to Be Presented.
> Principle 5: Causal Attributions for Specific Ingredients Should Be Made Only if the Evidence Is Persuasive.
> Principle 6: Outcomes Should Be Assessed Appropriately and Broadly.
> Principle 7: Outcomes Should Be Assessed Locally and Freedom of Choice Should Be Recognized.

These principles offer guidance to researchers, educators, and practitioners on the development of treatment approaches and the research foundation on which they are based. This model accommodates

the competing tensions of internal and external validity in which experimental rigor and real-world clinical application are both valued. The principles endorsed by the Society of Counseling Psychology are quite useful for understanding and interpreting the empirical foundation for various practice interventions and processes. For example, Principle 7 would suggest that the appropriate outcomes for any given client should be determined within that client's context and on the basis of that client's needs and goals. Principle 2 would suggest that the problems to be addressed, and the assessment of outcome, should not be restricted to those for which diagnostic categories have been created. Clients may face problems that are not adequately captured by diagnosis and those problems may be legitimate emphases for treatment.

Similarly, it may be helpful for counseling psychologists to consider the extent to which evidence-based practice approaches are consistent with the core values and principles of counseling psychology. These core principles (as adapted from Gelso & Fretz, 1986) include the following:

1. A focus on health and adaptation, building upon strengths, as differentiated from an emphasis on psychopathology;
2. A focus on a developmental perspective and a life span approach, which takes into account individual, group and system needs, in order to foster growth;
3. A focus on social and cultural context, in order to enhance individual, group and system environments, interactions and well-being, and an emphasis on multiculturalism and diversity;
4. A focus on brief interventions, in so far as they are effective and meet the needs of the person, group or system;
5. A focus on healthy work relationships, behavior and role fulfillment.

As noted, the two major approaches to evidence-based practice rely on (a) specific interventions or intervention strategies for specific diagnoses and treatment populations (diagnosed disorder) and (b) practice strategies that are relationally grounded and patient centered. Counseling psychologists feature prominently in the latter approach and the principles espoused by the Society of Counseling Psychology are more consistent with the latter approach as well. Many practicing counseling psychologists are integrationists (as are many clinical psychologists), however; they draw on both approaches, depending on the particular clinical circumstance and the problems to be addressed. In delineating the strengths of the patient-centered approach, we do not mean to suggest there is no place for scientifically derived intervention strategies for specific diagnoses. Both approaches contribute to our knowledge base.

Yet, an approach to evidence-based practice that relies *solely* on specific intervention strategies for specific diagnoses and treatment populations is, necessarily, focused on pathology and a medical disease model rather than on a health and adaptation model. A model based on health may be preventive, enhancing, or adaptive to chronic conditions, rather than solely focused on remediation. In addition, a health and adaptation model facilitates a client's positive strivings for growth and her or his recognition of changing needs and perspective across the life span. Furthermore, such an approach recognizes diversity and embraces individual differences as well as complex group identity differences, which are increasingly important in a multicultural nation.

EBPP AND MULTICULTURALISM

The increased attention to and interest in developing culturally appropriate approaches to treatment arise from several interlocking "culture wars." First is accountability. The Surgeon General's report on mental health (U.S. Department of Health and Human Services, 2001) and the President's New Freedom Commission Report (2003) publicized ethnic disparities in mental health on the basis of ineffective or inaccessible treatments. The need for accountability creates a demand for better understanding of treatment adaptations that will result in more effective treatments with better outcomes. The various approaches to evidence-based practice are a partial response to this call for accountability, but we are still faced with a dearth of information about culturally effective treatments. Second are the differences between disorder–technique approaches and

client–relational approaches. The former approach minimizes differences between client groups, whereas the latter emphasizes client individuality. To the extent that the uniqueness of client characteristics as it relates to the therapeutic relationship is emphasized, practitioners and researchers are called on to focus on all characteristics of diversity and the impact on treatment. Third, the meanings of cultural diversity nationally and internationally are increasingly understood and accepted as significant factors in a wide range of human endeavors and relationships, including psychological practice. The first two culture wars have been addressed earlier in this chapter. The third culture war is addressed here. Many resources are available in the area of multiculturalism, societal change, racial, and other identities. The next section provides a brief sketch of how changes in the role of cultural diversity and evolution in evidence-based practice have (and should) go hand in hand.

Applicability of Strategies

Conceptually, approaches that begin with the client are eminently adaptable to individuals, groups, or systems representing varying identities, characteristics, and cultures. There is no requisite need for multiple studies on various population groups to norm each treatment strategy according to the different groups to which it may apply. At the same time, this does not mean that empirical evidence about different population groups is irrelevant. Quite the contrary, evidence about different population groups provides significant grounding for practice applications as that evidence is incorporated into the developing treatment process (see reviews by Bernal et al., 2009; Chwalisz, 2003; Neville & Mobley, 2001; Ponterotto, 1998). Considerable work needs to be done to build a sufficient body of literature to explicate approaches that may be immediately applicable across cultures and those that may require adaptations to suit the needs of particular clients and client groups.

Current empirical evidence is limited for the application of strategies to minority populations that are well-researched on majority populations. This leaves uncertain which treatment strategies apply and what kinds of adaptations are appropriate. The need for additional evidence in this area is urgent, given that more than a third of the U.S. population is composed of ethnic minorities and the proportion is growing (see http://2010.census.gov/2010census/data). We need to know more about which cultures we are reaching effectively and those we are not as well as what adaptations would make strategies culturally appropriate. A growing body of research on human diversity includes culture within psychotherapy (e.g., see the special issue of *Psychotherapy*, titled "Culture, Race and Ethnicity in Psychotherapy," guest edited by Leong & Lopez, 2006). This places psychology in a strong position to find ways to integrate research and clinical expertise with an understanding of the patient characteristics that are essential to EBPP (Zane, Hall, Sue, Young, & Nunez, 2004). Counseling psychology's commitment to multiculturalism and valuing of individual differences is aligned with treatment approaches based on attention to health and adaptation, life-span perspective, diversity, individual and group differences, and role fulfillment.

Addressing Cultural Differences

Historically, cultural differences encountered by minority groups were primarily resolved through assimilation to the dominant culture in such a way that unique or distinguishing characteristics of an individual or a cultural group effectively disappear. The goal from this perspective is for minority groups to become indistinguishable from the dominant culture (Coleman, 1995). To the extent that the characteristics that differentiate minority groups from majority groups do not (or cannot) disappear, individuals or groups are not assimilated into the dominant culture. To the extent that those characteristics recede or disappear, the dominant majority worldview may be treated as *the* worldview, and anything not fitting that view is discounted, diminished, denied or stigmatized, and dismissed. This approach, combined with ease or difficulty of sampling issues (Sue et al., 2006), has led psychotherapy research down a path in which we know much about White YAVIS (young, attractive, verbal, intelligent, and successful) clients and psychotherapy dyads, and little about HOUND (humble, old,

unattractive, nonverbal, and dumb—or those people stereotyped in that way) clients (Comas-Díaz, 2006). Despite its long history, psychotherapy research most frequently has had no report on race or ethnicity of participants or has reported only small percentages of undifferentiated non-Whites (Sue et al., 2006).

This leaves us with little knowledge of for *whom* treatments may work. It also leads to insufficient knowledge of *what* works within an understanding of the role and impact of culture and ethnicity in relationship building, empathic opportunities, communication styles, and goals, to name a few. What are often missing are the uniquely moderating effects that culture, ethnicity, and other diversity variables bring to both process and outcome of treatment (Comas-Díaz, 2006).

Psychology has moved toward a process of recognition and acceptance of a diversity of cultural identification strategies, including mono- and bicultural strategies (Coleman, 1995; LaFromboise, Coleman, & Gerton, 1993). In recent years, both the Society of Counseling Psychology and the APA have affirmed diversity as a core value and a significant area of emphasis in both scholarly and applied areas. This recognition embraces multicultural strategies and infuses a multicultural perspective throughout our endeavors. This embrace is reflected in our approaches to psychotherapy research, our definition of EBPP, and our emerging treatment strategies. In fact, claiming the value of multiculturalism in which both individual and group differences are valued and multiple identities are recognized demands approaches to practice that are appropriate, efficacious, and effective within this context of difference. Our research models and evidence sources that are appropriate to a multicultural perspective may be much more idiographic than nomothetic. Translating research for multiculturally appropriate practice will include asking the right questions in research and practice, understanding which sources of evidence provide the most useful information, emphasizing transfer of training and extension of models, and ensuring proper assessments and matching of treatment with diagnosis, leading to culturally sensitive psychotherapy (Comas-Díaz, 2006; Sue et al., 2006).

La Roche and Christopher (2009) built on Hall's (2001) conceptualization of culturally sensitive psychotherapy. They offered a brief history of the relationship between developments in various versions of evidence-based practice leading to a description of culturally sensitive psychotherapy (CSP) that includes tailoring interventions to cultural characteristics and cultural groups. CSP includes constructs for classification (how characteristics are measured or operationally defined and how individuals are classified into groups), assumptions of unique group characteristics that differentiate groups from one another, and the translation of these unique characteristics into treatment strategies. This final translation step will require an understanding of which treatment factors are universal versus those that are culture specific as well as how the universal and the specific may interact to enhance treatment effectiveness for different cultural groups.

The research and practice literatures continue to expand in ways that build a deeper knowledge of the role of diversity dimensions in individuals' lives and in the process and outcome of psychological treatments. Counseling psychology's commitment to diversity and multiculturalism and its leadership in expanding our knowledge base and evidence-based practice is in the center of this burgeoning literature that will allow for greater availability of effective treatment nationally and internationally.

INTO THE FUTURE . . .

Interventions in psychology have a long history of solid grounding in research paradigms supporting the effectiveness of techniques that are used in the context of a therapeutic relationship. Counseling psychology's approach to evidence-based practice recognizes the epistemological frames that guide the use of multiple streams of evidence and models of research. We have a rich body of literature to guide practitioners as they integrate recent research findings into their practice and to stimulate researchers who are attempting to answer questions that are meaningful for better client outcomes.

As we look to the future, we anticipate the following:

- The research literature will continue to expand, building on foundations that include both intervention-driven and client-driven sources of questions and methodologies appropriate to both.
- Translational research and the translation of research that improves the effectiveness of interventions will receive increasing emphasis and become increasingly available in forms useful to practitioners.
- Approaches to better incorporate multiculturalism in interventions will receive broader attention, and attention to issues of diversity will become the standard for research intended for practice applications.
- Counseling psychology will continue to provide leadership through its lasting commitment to scientist–practitioner integration.
- Counseling psychology will continue to provide leadership through its deep commitment to the value of multiculturalism and diversity and to the building of culturally sensitive approaches to practice.

References

Ackerman, S. J., Benjamin, L. S., Beutler, L. E., Gelso, C. J., Goldfried, M. R., Hill, C., . . . Rainer, J. (2001). Empirically supported therapy relationships: Conclusions and recommendations of the Division 29 Task Force. *Psychotherapy: Theory, Research, Practice, Training, 38*, 495–497. doi:10.1037/0033-3204.38.4.495

American Psychological Association. (2005). *Policy statement on evidence-based practice in psychology.* Retrieved from http://www2.apa.org/practice/ebpstatement.pdf

American Psychological Association Presidential Task Force on Evidence-Based Practice. (2006). Evidence-based practice in psychology. *American Psychologist, 61*, 271–285. doi:10.1037/0003-066X.61.4.271

Bernal, G., Jimenez-Chafey, M. I., & Rodriguez, M. M. D. (2009). Cultural adaptation of treatments: A resource for considering culture in evidence-based practice. *Professional Psychology: Research and Practice, 40*, 361–368. doi:10.1037/a0016401

Carter, J. A. (2006). Theoretical pluralism and technical eclecticism. In C. D. Goodheart, A. E. Kazdin, & R. J. Sternberg (Eds.), *Evidence-based psychotherapy: Where practice and research meet* (pp. 63–80).

Washington, DC: American Psychological Association. doi:10.1037/11423-003

Chambless, D. L., & Ollendick, T. H. (2001). Empirically supported psychological interventions: Controversies and evidence. *Annual Review of Psychology, 52*, 685–716. doi:10.1146/annurev.psych.52.1.685

Chwalisz, K. (2003). Evidence-based practice: A framework for twenty-first-century scientist-practitioner training. *The Counseling Psychologist, 31*, 497–528. doi:10.1177/0011000003256347

Coleman, H. (1995). Strategies for coping with cultural diversity. *The Counseling Psychologist, 23*, 722–740. doi:10.1177/0011000095234011

Comas-Díaz, L. (2006). Cultural variation in the therapeutic relationship. In C. D. Goodheart, A. E. Kazdin, & R. J. Sternberg (Eds.), *Evidence-based psychotherapy: Where practice and research meet* (pp. 81–106). Washington, DC: American Psychological Association. doi:10.1037/11423-004

Conway, J. B. (1988). Differences among clinical psychologists: Scientists, practitioners, and scientist-practitioners. *Professional Psychology: Research and Practice, 19*, 642–655. doi:10.1037/0735-7028.19.6.642

Dana, R. H. (1987). Training for professional psychology: Science, practice, and identity. *Professional Psychology: Research and Practice, 18*, 9–16. doi:10.1037/0735-7028.18.1.9

Frank, G. (1984). The Boulder model: History, rationale, and critique. *Professional Psychology: Research and Practice, 15*, 417–435. doi:10.1037/0735-7028.15.3.417

Gelso, C. J., & Fretz, B. F. (1986). *Introduction to counseling psychology.* New York, NY: Wiley.

Goodheart, C. D. (2006). Evidence, endeavor, and expertise in psychology practice. In C. D. Goodheart, A. E. Kazdin, & R. J. Sternberg (Eds.), *Evidence-based psychotherapy: Where practice and research meet* (pp. 37–61). Washington, DC: American Psychological Association. doi:10.1037/11423-002

Goodheart, C. D., & Carter, J. A. (2008). The proper focus of evidence-based practice in psychology. In W. B. Walsh (Ed.), *Biennial review of counseling psychology* (Vol. 1, pp. 47–70). New York, NY: Taylor & Francis.

Goodheart, C. D., & Kazdin, A. E. (2006). Introduction. In C. D. Goodheart, A. E. Kazdin, & R. J. Sternberg (Eds.), *Evidence-based psychotherapy: Where practice and research meet* (pp. 3–10). Washington, DC: American Psychological Association. doi:10.1037/11423-000

Hall, G. C. N. (2001). Psychotherapy research with ethnic minorities: Empirical, ethical and conceptual issues. *Journal of Consulting and Clinical Psychology, 69*, 502–510. doi:10.1037/0022-006X.69.3.502

Hoshmand, L. T. (2003). Applied epistemology and professional training in a science-based cultural enterprise. *The Counseling Psychologist, 31*, 529–538. doi:10.1177/0011000003256353

Institute of Medicine. (2001). *Crossing the quality chasm: A new health system for the 21st century.* Washington, DC: National Academy of Sciences.

Kimble, G. (1984). Psychology's two cultures. *American Psychologist, 39*, 833–839. doi:10.1037/0003-066X.39.8.833

LaFromboise, T. D., Coleman, H. L. K., & Gerton, J. (1993). Psychological impact of biculturalism: Evidence and theory. *Psychological Bulletin, 114*, 395–412. doi:10.1037/0033-2909.114.3.395

La Roche, M. J., & Christopher, M. S. (2009). Changing paradigms from empirically supported treatment to evidence-based practice: A cultural perspective. *Professional Psychology: Research and Practice, 40*, 396–402. doi:10.1037/a0015240

Leong, F. T. L., & Lopez, S. (Eds.). (2006). Culture, race and ethnicity [Special issue]. *Psychotherapy, 43*(4).

Messer, S. B. (2004). Evidence-based practice: Beyond empirically supported treatments. *Professional Psychology: Research and Practice, 35*, 580–588. doi:10.1037/0735-7028.35.6.580

Morowski, J. G. (2005, September). *Epistemological diversity in the history of modern psychology.* Paper presented at the Education Leadership Conference, American Psychological Association, Arlington, VA.

Murdock, N. L. (2008). *Theories of counseling and psychotherapy: A case approach* (2nd ed.). Englewood Cliffs, NJ: Prentice-Hall.

Neville, H. A., & Mobley, M. (2001). Social identities in contexts: An ecological model of multicultural counseling psychology processes. *The Counseling Psychologist, 29*, 471–486. doi:10.1177/0011000001294001

Norcross, J. C. (Ed.). (2002). *Relationships that work.* New York, NY: Oxford University Press.

Ponterotto, J. G. (1998). Charting a course for research in multicultural counseling training. *The Counseling Psychologist, 26*, 43–68. doi:10.1177/0011000098261004

President's New Freedom Commission on Mental Health. (2003). *Achieving the promise: Transforming mental health care in America.* Retrieved from http://govinfo.library.unt.edu/mentalhealthcommission/reports/FinalReport/toc.html

Reed, G. M., & Eisman, E. J. (2006). Uses and misuses of evidence: Managed care, treatment guidelines, and outcomes measurement in professional practice. In C. D. Goodheart, A. E. Kazdin, & R. J. Sternberg

(Eds.), *Evidence-based psychotherapy: Where practice and research meet* (pp. 13–36). Washington, DC: American Psychological Association. doi:10.1037/11423-001

Russo, N. F. (2006, August). *Clinical wisdom, science, and policy: Lessons from the front lines.* Paper presented at the 114th Annual Convention of the American Psychological Association, New Orleans, LA.

Sue, S., Zane, N., Levant, R. G., Silverstein, L. B., Brown, L. S., Olkin, R., & Taliaferro, G. (2006). How well do both evidence-based practices and treatment as usual satisfactorily address the various dimensions of diversity? In J. C. Norcross, L. E. Beutler, & R. F. Levant, Eds., *Evidence-based practices in mental health: Debate and dialogue on the fundamental questions* (pp. 329–374). Washington, DC: American Psychological Association.

U.S. Department of Health and Human Services. (2001). *Mental health: Culture, race, and ethnicity—a supplement to mental health: A report of the Surgeon General.* Rockville, MD: U.S. Department of Health and Human Services, Substance Abuse and Mental Health Services Administration, Center for Mental Health Services.

Wampold, B. E., Lichtenberg, J. W., & Waehler, C. A. (2002). Principles of empirically supported interventions in counseling psychology. *The Counseling Psychologist, 30,* 197–217. doi:10.1177/0011000002302001

Zachar, P., & Leong, F. T. (1992). A problem of personality: Scientist and practitioner differences in psychology. *Journal of Personality, 60,* 665–667. doi:10.1111/j.1467-6494.1992.tb00925.x

Zane, N., Hall, G. C. N., Sue, S., Young, K., & Nunez, J. (2004). Research on psychotherapy with culturally diverse populations. In M. J. Lambert (Ed.), *Bergin and Garfield's handbook of psychotherapy and behavior change* (pp. 767–804). New York, NY: Wiley.

CHAPTER 7

FOUNDATIONS OF COUNSELING PSYCHOLOGY: ASSESSMENT

Lisa A. Suzuki, Mineko Anne Onoue, Hiroko Fukui, and Shawn Ezrapour

Counseling psychologists are uniquely trained to understand the complexity of psychological assessment. The role definition of counseling psychologists in the Society of Counseling Psychology (n.d.) states that we focus attention on "emotional, social, vocational, educational, health-related, developmental and organizational concerns" of individuals and communities within a multicultural context incorporating a range of practices. As counseling psychologists, our goal is to "help people improve their well-being, alleviate distress and maladjustment, resolve crises, and increase their ability to live more highly functioning lives" (Society of Counseling Psychology, n.d.). Helping clients often includes conducting a comprehensive evaluation to determine the individual's strengths and limitations in the context of their lived experiences. Thus, reaching our goal often entails aspects of psychological assessment, that is, "any activity designed to further the process of accumulating information and forming a judgment about the behavioral, emotional, or social characteristics of an individual" (Sattler & Hoge, 2006, p. 4).

Counseling psychologists are trained to be competent in widely utilized and state-of-the-art assessment practices employing traditional psychological measures (e.g., personality, aptitude, vocational interest). Counseling psychologists are dedicated to understanding individuals within their cultural context focusing on a normative developmental trajectory while attending to the historical, political, economic, cultural, and social environments that affect human functioning. Counseling psychologists understand the importance of clinical diagnosis and trajectories of mental illness, but our goal is to consider these deficits in relation to the whole person from a positive psychological and strengths-based perspective.

The purpose of this chapter is to provide the reader with salient information regarding current theory and research focusing on the assessment of diverse clients from a counseling psychology perspective. To accomplish this, we attempt to identify what is important for counseling psychologists to know about assessment and provide information within our unique disciplinary perspective. The chapter is divided into the following general sections: (a) counseling psychology and the assessment of optimal functioning, (b) controversies in light of the changing landscape of assessment, (c) gathering background information, selecting appropriate measures, and considering test administration, (d) contextual variables affecting the assessment process, (e) test-related variables affecting the assessment process, and (f) an examination of testing exemplars. We conclude with an illustrative case to highlight the issues noted in the preceding sections along with recommendations for best practices.

COUNSELING PSYCHOLOGY AND THE ASSESSMENT OF OPTIMAL FUNCTIONING

The development of positive psychology measures to assess optimal functioning fits well within a

Special thanks to Muninder Ahluwalia and John Kugler for their feedback on previous versions of this chapter.

DOI: 10.1037/13754-007
APA Handbook of Counseling Psychology: Vol. 1. Theories, Research, and Methods, Nadya A. Fouad (Editor-in-Chief)

counseling psychology perspective (S. J. Lopez & Snyder, 2003b; Walsh, 2003). On the basis of their review of the assessment literature in this area, Frazier, Oishi, and Steger (2003) noted that there is no uniformly agreed-on operational definition of optimal human functioning. They identified various constructs that fall within this domain, including autonomy, personal growth, purpose, positive relationships, self-esteem, mastery, happiness, hope, optimism, courage, wisdom, forgiveness, responsibility, nurturance, posttraumatic growth, and tolerance. Despite the importance of these constructs in understanding an individual's strengths, usage of these measures has not extended beyond applications in research settings despite evidence of validity and reliability.

In examining measures of subjective well-being, meaning in life, and posttraumatic growth, Frazier et al. (2003) noted potential limitations in the usage of measures in these areas. These include (a) social desirability, (b) effects of mood and question order, (c) memory biases, and (d) lack of attention to culture and ethnicity. They noted that there is potential for response sets (e.g., social desirability) given the positive valence put upon aspects of positive functioning and feeling states (e.g., happiness, meaning). Other concerns include negative mood states that are likely to affect responses on optimal measures requiring reflection on aspects of positive well-being. Presentation of items may also affect assessment as examinees may link issues embedded in earlier items with those that come later (e.g., dating and life satisfaction). Memory biases may also be in operation as research shows individuals have a tendency to think of themselves as either more consistent over time or more changed over a distinct period of time in their self-assessments (Ross & Conway, 1986).

A major limitation of these scales is the lack of attention paid to culture. Examination of potential differences in understanding cultural aspects of optimal functioning is often missing. For example, Frazier et al. (2003) noted that measures in this area focus primarily on individual conceptualizations of these constructs without considering the impact of collectivistic perspectives.

Given these limitations, it is no wonder that the field of mainstream psychological assessment

remains virtually untouched by developments in the positive psychology domain. It is critical that counseling psychologists advocate for the integration of a strength-based focus and contextual understanding so this important perspective is not lost amid the current emphasis placed on individual pathology and community deficits.

CONTROVERSIES IN ASSESSMENT

A number of controversies have emerged surrounding the usage of psychological tests to assess diverse aspects of human functioning. Some of these are longstanding and others have arisen given the changing landscape of psychological practice. Specific controversies include the challenges of test bias, integrating culture in diagnosis, high-stakes testing, the health care costs of evaluation, and increasing dependence on computer-based assessment practices.

Test Bias

Historically, during the 1960s, one of the great challenges to many assessment tests was charges of test bias. The discussion of bias in psychological testing as a *scientific* issue should concern only the statistical meaning: whether there is systematic error in the measurement of a psychological attribute as a function of membership in one or another cultural or racial subgroup (Reynolds, 1982a, 1982b, cited in Reynolds & Lowe, 2009, p. 333).

Controversies emerged as a result of differential scoring patterns by various racial and ethnic groups. The standard deviation difference in the performance of African Americans and Whites on standardized IQ tests has been a point of contention for more than a century (Reynolds & Lowe, 2009). These problems have been exacerbated because tests are now being transported internationally from one cultural context to another (Greenfield, 1997). Tests are often translated into different languages and renormed on new populations. For example, the Wechsler Intelligence Scale for Children–III has been standardized in 13 different countries including Taiwan, Japan, the Republic of Korea, Greece, Sweden, Germany, and Belgium (Georgas, Weiss, van de Vijver, & Saklofske, 2003).

Test bias has been examined with respect to discrepancies between men and women as well as members of different racial and ethnic groups. Sources of test bias include inappropriate test content, inappropriate standardization samples (e.g., representation), inequitable social consequences, differential predictive validity, and examiner–clinician bias (Malgady, Rogler, & Costantino, 1987; Reynolds & Lowe, 2009). We highlight aspects of these various sources but concentrate our discussion by focusing on the potential role of the examiner–clinician as a source of bias in this section.

Inappropriate test content refers to the finding that members of various racial and ethnic groups may not be exposed to or equally familiar with the content of test items, leading to greater disadvantage in obtaining a correct response. Inappropriate standardization samples are evident when marginalized racial and ethnic groups are not represented adequately in the standardization sample (Valencia & Suzuki, 1997). Although many tests employ census-based representational samples, the overall numbers of particular racial and ethnic group members may be so small as to be insignificant.

Although the preceding sources of bias focus on the tests themselves, the results obtained from such measures introduce additional concerns. For example, usage of tests in education have led to inequitable social consequences translating to students from marginalized racial and ethnic groups being placed in lower ability tracks and special education at disproportionately higher rates, thus affecting future educational and career opportunities. Concerns have been raised that tests may accurately predict outcomes for members of the majority culture but do less well in predicting outcomes (e.g., grade point average) for members of racially and ethnically marginalized groups. Reynolds and Lowe (2009) noted that the issues of education classification, tracking, and social consequences are not solely in the purview of testing and assessment practices as they reflect systemic problems within education.

Examiner–Clinician Bias

In addition to charges of bias regarding the development and usage of measurements, criticisms have also targeted the clinician. Psychologists are embedded within their own cultural context and their own social location, both of which can permeate their decision-making process. Historically, U.S. psychology was firmly rooted in the White European American experience that arguably is still reflected in the assessment process. Potential sources of clinician bias include stereotyping that can affect test administration and lead to inaccurate inferences about the individual being assessed (Dana, 2000).

Clinician bias is often unconscious and may be evidenced in the diagnosis of psychological disorders due to the client's gender, ethnicity, or socioeconomic status (SES; Worell & Robinson, 2009). A number of diagnostic biases have been made by clinicians because of prejudice based on gender or ethnicity. These include judgments of excessive pathology in diagnosis (overpathologizing) or a lack of pathology and no need for diagnosis (Lopez, 1989). In either case, the clinician makes a wrong diagnosis based on the results of an assessment because they do not take into consideration gender or ethnicity.

In addition, individuals from various ethnic groups may be given an "ethnic gloss" that can obscure accurate perception and lead to results that lack depth and generalizability and are based on misrepresentation (Trimble, Helms, & Root, 2003, p. 242). Members of diverse ethnocultural groups are at a risk of being overpathologized by psychologists who may neglect to consider the effects of responding and coping with oppressive and stressful conditions (Sue & Sue, 1972). For example, the Minnesota Multiphasic Personality Inventory–2 (MMPI-2; Butcher, Dahlstrom, Graham, Tellegen, & Kaemmer, 1989), one of the most widely used and accepted personality measures has been found to "pathologize Indigenous worldviews, knowledge, beliefs, and behaviors rather than accurately assess psychopathology" (Hill, Pace, & Robbins, 2010, p. 16). Similar charges have been made against the Rorschach inkblot test (Allen & Dana, 2004). In particular, criticism is directed at what is known as the contemporary standard of practice—Exner's Comprehensive System for the Rorschach (Exner, 2001, 2003)—by a number of researchers (e.g., Ganellen, 2002; Lilienfeld, Wood, & Garb, 2000). In a survey of Rorschach studies, researchers found a lack of normative data for various racial and ethnic groups, including Blacks, Hispanic Americans, and Native Americans (Garb, Wood, Nezworski, Grove, & Stejskal, 2001).

Integrating Culture in Diagnosis

Historically, many ethnic groups have been marginalized and pathologized in the mental health profession through clinical bias in the diagnostic process (Dana, 2008). Knowledge of this history, and the negative impact it has had on various ethnic groups is vitally important given that one of the primary functions of psychological assessment is clinical diagnosis, a process that has yielded racial and ethnic group disparities. Members of marginalized racial and ethnic groups have a much higher incidence of psychotic diagnoses than nonminority populations (Gross, Herbert, Knatterud, & Donner, 1969, cited in Malgady et al., 1987). Data indicate that African Americans are overdiagnosed as schizophrenic and are notably admitted to state psychiatric hospitals at higher rates than White populations (Baker & Bell, 1999; Lawson, Hepler, Holladay, & Cuffel, 1994). These disparities have led to questions regarding the application of criteria and formulation of clinical diagnoses that are assumed to be universal (e.g., *Diagnostic and Statistical Manual of Mental Disorders* [4th ed., text revision; *DSM–IV–TR*], American Psychiatric Association, 2000; Dana, 2008).

In addition, although culture-bound syndromes are now included in the *DSM–IV–TR*, they remain isolated in an appendix (American Psychiatric Association, 2000). Similarly, the *International Classification of Diseases–10* (*ICD-10*; World Health Organization, 1992), developed in consultation with researchers and clinicians in 32 countries, contains an annexed section identifying 12 culture-specific disorders. These disorders do not fit within the established psychiatric classifications and are associated with particular cultural groups. The *ICD-10* notes that some of these syndromes reflect ethnic or exoticized conditions that may be relatively rare in occurrence. The identification and assessment of culture-bound disorders continues to be a controversial process as there remains substantial dissent within the psychological community with regard to their existence (World Health Organization, 1992).

High-Stakes Testing

Usage of test scores to make decisions about education and employment opportunities have become paramount in our society. In the 1980s, high-stakes-testing policies were implemented to raise achievement standards (Bovaird & Römhild, 2010). Nearly all states established education standards and implemented statewide assessment policies. The policies were based on a business model rewarding school communities, teachers, and administrators for high performance. The No Child Left Behind policy mandated high-stakes tests to be administered annually in reading and math for students in the third to eighth grade. Administrators and teachers are held accountable for the achievement of students, with many states providing incentives for high scores and improvement in performance. School report cards made available to the public often include data related to these high-stakes tests. Bovaird and Römhild (2010) noted that school achievement reports have affected communities as parents make housing decisions on the basis of school performance reports, and neighborhoods are rated by achievement test scores, which in turn influence property values.

On the national level, concerns regarding the achievement gap between students from different racial and ethnic groups are often the focus of discourse when test results are released (e.g., group differences on high-stakes testing). This has led to the application of item response theory, and application of differential item functioning (DIF) methods is a way to identify potentially biased test items (Frisby, 2008):

> DIF occurs whenever test takers who are of equal proficiency on the latent trait but are member of different demographic groups (for example, gender or ethnicity) perform differently on an item. Flagged items are then examined, and a subjective determination is made as to whether the DIF effect occurs from construct–irrelevant factors. (Frisby, 2008, pp. 533–534)

An understanding of the various methods employed to examine potential bias like DIF can be helpful in understanding the strengths and limitations of particular measures. A number of texts are available to assist the reader in this process, including *Adapting Educational and Psychological Tests for Cross-Cultural Assessment* (e.g., Hambleton, Merenda, & Spielberger, 2005).

This reliance on test scores as indicative of achievement has spread internationally with the added implication of competition reminiscent of the cold war era (i.e., Sputnik). Recent publication of the 2010 results of the Programme for International Student Assessment (PISA; Organization for Economic Cooperation and Development, 2011) highlighted the major role and credence given to the power of tests in assessing national standards of education. PISA, an internationally standardized assessment, was developed to examine 15-year-old performance in reading, mathematical and scientific literacy, knowledge, and skills needed in adult life. Sixty-five countries participated in 2009 with an additional 9 in 2010. The test data are based on 4,500 to 10,000 students assessed in each country. The results of the 2010 data collection phase were released recently. An article in the *New York Times* quoted the U.S. Secretary of Education Arne Duncan stating

> I know skeptics will want to argue with the results, but we consider them to be accurate, and reliable, and we have to see them as a challenge to get better . . . The United States came in 23rd or 24th in most subjects, we can quibble, or we can face the brutal truth that we're being out-educated. (Dillon, 2010, para. 10)

Of particular note was the finding that average math scores of U.S. students were below those of 30 other countries.

High Cost of Assessment

Although there exist many proponents of psychological testing, the debates over validity, relevance, and importance of psychological tests continue especially in light of the high costs attached to psychological assessments. The cost of a psychological evaluation varies by geographic region and area (e.g., neuropsychological evaluation, educational evaluation), but perusal of various websites yielded a cost

range between $1,500 and $2,500. Some sites noted charges of $150 per hour for an evaluation. Tests, such as the Rorschach and Thematic Apperception Test (TAT), are notoriously time-consuming for clinicians to score and interpret (Groth-Marnat, 2009).

In addition to the cost to the consumer, practitioners and agencies are often strapped with the financial burden of purchasing new measures and recent editions of tests. A number of the most frequently used and most comprehensive measures in the areas of personality and cognitive testing are expensive (e.g., MMPI-2-RF Starter Kit $221/three assessments; MMPI-2-RF Handscoring Starter Kit $450.00/25 assessments; Wechler Adult Intelligence Scale–IV [WAIS-IV] Basic Kit $1,100). Although handscoring may be a cost saver in terms of initial investment, the additional time required will often be passed on to the consumer. In addition to these basic test costs, examiners may feel compelled to invest in software packages to assist them in scoring and interpreting results (e.g., Rorschach Interpretive Assistance Program: Version 5 [RIAP-5] $690).

Managed care policies have dictated changes in clinical assessment stressing the importance of monitoring and documenting progress. This combined with the pressure to increase time efficiency and reduce costs have led to increase in clinician's use of brief, symptom-focused inventories (Groth-Marnat, 2009). Managed care requires psychologists to demonstrate the cost-effectiveness of their services; for assessment, this necessitates evidence that assessment will not only optimize treatment but also increase the speed at which desired outcomes are obtained (Groth-Marnat, 2009).

Concerns have also been raised within the profession regarding the utility of results. Eisman et al. (2000) reported that based on the responses of more than 500 psychologists,

> Critics argue that psychological assessment is time consuming, expensive, and of limited utility in the context of current patterns of care. . . . The practice of routine psychological assessments for all patients, an issue cited by managed care as a factor in skyrocketing health care costs, has all but been eliminated

and is no longer an issue. However, the profession's lack of advocacy in encouraging, implementing, and disseminating research that demonstrates the efficacy and utility of assessment in treatment planning has allowed the pendulum to swing too far in the other direction. (pp. 131–132)

Many practitioners must decide when a full evaluation should be conducted and whether it may be more judicious to engage in other diagnostic strategies. Sometimes one can get the same information just by asking the client questions as can be obtained by engaging in a costly and lengthy test.

Usage of Technology

During recent years, advancements in technology have helped increase the role of computers in the field of psychological assessment. This change in the landscape of assessment has not been without controversy, however. The term *computerized assessment* "encompasses all procedures that involve computer assistance in evaluating educational and behavioral goals" (Ahluwalia, 2008, p. 92). Tools and products that utilize computers in assessment include standardized measure questionnaires, interviews, automated test scoring, analysis and interpretation programs, computer-adaptive testing, and other services. One particular area of controversy is in computer-based testing (CBT), which refers to "the use of computers in test administration, scoring, and interpretation of results" (Ahluwalia, 2008, p. 93). One of the advantages of CBT is that administration, scoring, and interpretation are done more quickly and with less effort than traditional paper-and-pencil tests, making them more cost-effective (Butcher, 1987, cited in Butcher, Perry, & Dean, 2009). Also, CBTs may be helpful to certain groups, for example, by reducing stereotype and discrimination threats associated with test evaluators (Ahluwalia, 2008). CBT interpretations provide objective baseline data integrating scientific empirical findings, streamlining and facilitating the interpretation process, and reducing the "likelihood of biased interpretative statements and human error" (Butcher et al., 2009, p. 173).

Computer adaptive instruments are often "programmed to determine when sufficient information has been collected from the client to estimate the traits or characteristics being assessed" (Butcher et al., 2009, p. 174). Adaptive testing is possible given that items are scored "immediately to assess the difficulty and discrimination levels to determine the next item to be administered" (Butcher et al., 2009, p. 174). This type of precision is not possible using traditional individualized assessment practices. Thus, a major contribution of computer adaptive testing is that participants engage in a much more streamlined process, eliminating "redundant or inappropriate items" and as a "result, test length and time can be significantly reduced" (Butcher et al., 2009, p. 174). Computer technology offers the possibility of remote access to clients through the Internet (Butcher et al., 2009). Use of these methods should be done with caution given that the "development and validation of Internet-based assessment resources has not kept pace with the technological developments" (Butcher et al., 2009, p. 176). In addition, the clinician is unable to monitor the testing environment or observe the client while taking the test. The issue of security of test items is also problematic.

Along with their usefulness, CBTs have also raised red flags. For example, with regard to multicultural populations or people of varying socioeconomic background, Ahluwalia (2008) has argued that "test construction needs to preemptively consider the needs of different groups being served and design tests that will constitute a fair assessment of skills, traits, or something else" (p. 95). The criteria may not be met when using CBTs with people of different ethnicities or of different SES levels. Furthering this claim, Knauss (2001) illuminated the fact that "tests can now be administered, scored, and interpreted without human contact," which means they may not be as individually tailored as paper-and-pencil tests (p. 237). In addition, CBT does not remove the important role of the clinician but rather assists in the process of assessment.

Similar arguments can be made for school CBTs. Park (2005) gave an example of a test that although culturally appropriate, failed to take into account any other differences that may have affected participants' experiences of the implementation or interpretation of the test, such as SES. SES can have an indirect impact on the results of CBTs, for example, influencing students' access to computer resources, which may, in turn, affect how comfortable they are with CBTs and skew the results.

GATHERING BACKGROUND INFORMATION, SELECTING MEASURES, AND CONSIDERATIONS IN TEST ADMINISTRATION

Although the process of assessment has been reviewed in a number of seminal texts (e.g., Groth-Marnat, 2009), we feel it is imperative to highlight the importance of obtaining a broad understanding of the individual's background, attending to the selection of appropriate measures, and making adjustments in test administration. It is critical that problems be understood within the cultural context and life circumstances of the individual being assessed (Flores & Obasi, 2003).

Gathering Background Information

Two resources available to counseling psychologists to obtain a wide array of information beyond the traditional intake interview include the Person-In-Culture Interview (PICI; Berg-Cross & Chinen, 1995) and the Cultural Assessment Interview Protocol (CAIP; Grieger, 2008). The novel aspects of these interviews include attention to cultural expressions of emotion, experiences in community, religious beliefs, spirituality, meaning, cultural identity, acculturation, racial–cultural identity, and experiences with bias.

Although discrimination can be overt, experiences of bias and discrimination are often experienced in subtle forms and can still have devastating effects on individuals. Discrimination and racism is insidious by nature and the counseling psychology literature includes attention to microaggressions (e.g., microassault, microinsult, and microinvalidations) that affect individuals and groups (Sue et al., 2007). Microaggressions are quick encounters with individuals or the environment that "communicate hostile, derogatory or negative racial slights and insults to the target person or group" (Sue et al., 2007, p. 273).

In assessment, understanding a client's experience of systemic and interpersonal microaggressions (if not direct, open discrimination) is important in understanding the potential oppression they have faced and how this may affect assessment processes and inform competent intervention. For example, recent immigrants may be ignored despite being well-educated because of their limited English or may be treated in a condescending way by public officials because of their language accent. Members of visible racial ethnic groups are often identified as being "foreign" and treated as noncitizens. As one client noted, "I don't like New Yorkers, they are so rude and push me on the subway; one person told me to go home." Knowing the particular context of the client before testing is imperative because without this understanding the clinician can misdiagnose, select inappropriate measures, or misinterpret results. In addition to clinical concerns, the microaggressions experienced with professionals may affect the level of trust a client experiences and their engagement in the assessment process.

Selecting Appropriate Measures

A number of tests exist for each psychological domain that may be relevant with respect to an individual's presenting issue of concern. As Greenfield (1997) noted, "tests are not universal instruments: They are specific cultural genres" (p. 1122). Therefore, selecting the most appropriate measure includes attention to a variety of issues, including those related to the individual being evaluated and the tests themselves (Sattler, 1993). As a first step, the test manual should be consulted to determine whether the purposes and applications of the test are in line with the needs of the client. In addition, the manual will include the qualifications needed to administer and interpret the results (e.g., level of training) and should provide procedures that were followed in the development of item content. It behooves the psychologist to understand this process given that inclusion of cultural consultants and "egalitarian, multicultural collaboration in instrument development constitutes a powerful tool to detect and prevent the cross-cultural misunderstandings that undermine validity in cross-cultural ability" (Greenfield, 1997, p. 1117).

Examinee considerations include the following: (a) Does the individual possess the prerequisite skills needed to complete the test? (b) Is the vocabulary and reading level of the instructions and items appropriate for the individual? (c) Are the item presentations and response formats suitable for the individual? (d) What adaptations may be necessary in administering the test and are these allowable based on standardized procedures? (e) Is the test available in the language and dialect of the individual being assessed? and (f) Will the materials and tasks be of interest to the individual being assessed? Test considerations include the following: (a) How recently was the test developed? Is it in need of revision? (b) Are the instructions for administration clearly presented? (c) How reliable and valid is the test and with what populations? (d) Have the test items been reviewed for potential sex, racial, and ethnic bias? (e) Were multiple methods used to examine concurrent test and criterion relationships (e.g., Frazier et al., 2003)? (f) Are the procedures used to derive scores clearly presented along with norming information? and (g) Can the test be administered in a group setting? In addition, the examiner should make use of available recommendations regarding response format. For example, Greenfield (1997) has recommended that multiple-choice formats not be used unless the examinee has "considerable formal education" (p. 1121). Armed with knowledge about these test and examinee considerations and using relevant questions as a guide, the counseling psychologist can engage in the process of test selection.

Administering Tests

Assessment is a process that requires the establishment of a relationship between the examiner and the examinee that is often time limited. As in the case of establishing rapport in therapy, assessment requires that the clinician be sensitive to the client's racial, ethnic, and cultural identities (Sue et al., 2007; Sue & Sue, 2003). Greenfield (1997) wrote,

> For participants from collectivistic cultures, the tester may need to have or to establish a personal relationship with the testee outside the testing situation

before a valid assessment can be done. This strategy prevents discomfort with stranger communication from interfering with the test interview. (p. 1121)

Clients may vary in their formal versus informal interaction style, self-disclosure, eye contact, or comfort with physical proximity (Groth-Marnat, 2009). Understanding and accommodating potentially culture-specific behaviors during test administration may enhance performance. For example, McShane (1989) noted that avoiding direct visual contact with students, accommodating softer levels of speech, and being aware of a tendency for American Indian children to use short, quick responses may enable the evaluator to obtain better estimates of the abilities of American Indian children. It is also important that examiners "develop a flexible language that allows people to define themselves in ways that more accurately reflect their heritage and cultural practices" (McGoldrick, Giordano, & Garcia-Preto, 2005, p. 7).

In addition to these accommodations, after following standardized administration protocols, the examiner may engage in testing-the-limit procedures that may be helpful in obtaining relevant information. The procedures outlined by Sattler and Hoge (2006) provided a summative review of a wide range of testing-the-limit procedures in their discussion of the assessment of children with brain injuries:

> Testing-of-limits may include modifying instructions to involve more or fewer cues, adjusting the pace at which information is presented, modifying the modality of presentation, modifying the starting or discontinuance procedures by administering additional items, adjusting memory demands (e.g., using recognition instead of recall procedures), modifying the response format (e.g., allowing pointing instead of oral responses), adjusting task complexity (e.g., making tasks more concrete), and asking for explanations of responses. (p. 557)

After the test is administered according to its standardization, the examiner may allow additional time for completion of a task, ask the examinee for an oral explanation of a particular response, or provide paper and pencil in cases in which standardization requires that the individual solve problems without these aids. Any deviation from the standardization protocol should be duly noted in the written report of the assessment results.

MEASUREMENT-RELATED VARIABLES AFFECTING THE ASSESSMENT PROCESS

As noted in the preceding section, a number of test-related variables are relevant to the process of assessment. These variables affect not only the selection of tests but also the process of assessment. In this section, we highlight various forms of equivalence: cultural loading and culturally reduced measures.

Equivalence

As the name implies, equivalence in assessment refers to whether different versions of a test (e.g., language) are the same with respect to vital aspects of the measure as applied to individuals from diverse cultural backgrounds. Helms (1992) highlighted various forms of equivalence in relation to cognitive ability testing with Blacks and Whites, including cultural, functional, linguistic, psychometric, testing condition, contextual, and sampling. Shoeb, Weinstein, and Mollica (2007) noted the importance of various forms of equivalence with respect to the assessment of trauma, including content, semantic, technical, and criterion. Equivalence has implications for all domains of psychological testing. With regard to cultural equivalence, Helms (1992) questioned whether culturally conditioned skills exist and whether these vary with respect to measurement procedures. For example, do test-taking strategies, their meaning, and their relationship to predictive criteria differ between groups in response to the same material? In addition, how can the cultural characteristics of these tests best be assessed?

Cultural Loading and Culturally Reduced Measures

A number of efforts were made to create "culture fair" measures, especially in the area of cognitive

ability testing. In particular, the search for measures that would have universal applicability is documented. The conclusion of this work, however, was that all tests are culturally loaded (Sattler, 2008). That is, tests reflect information valued within the cultural context in which the test was developed. Culturally reduced measures have been developed that require either little or no language for the presentation of items or the responses of examinees. Consideration of cultural loading has resulted in the creation of new mechanisms to assist psychologists when making determinations regarding the selection of appropriate measures. For example, Flanagan, Ortiz, and Alfonso (2007) have developed the cross-battery assessment model to enable an examiner to select measures from a range of potential tests examining broad and narrow ability areas. In addition, the culture-language test classifications (McGrew & Flanagan, 1998) consider the cultural loading (cultural specificity) of measures and degree of linguistic demand to assist examiners in selecting appropriate tests and examine test score patterns.

CLIENT-RELATED CONTEXTUAL VARIABLES AFFECTING THE ASSESSMENT PROCESS

A number of important variables must be considered in the assessment process, including those pertaining to the individual being assessed (i.e., culture, language, acculturation, SES, geographic location, gender, and disability status). Over time, availability of technology and widespread dissemination of information has lessened the impact of some of these variables. For example, the influence of geographic location (e.g., urban vs. rural residence) has decreased in many communities given increased access to technology.

Although our discussion addresses each of these variables separately, it is important to note that assessment results are influenced by multiple identities. For example, a number of issues influence the understanding of women's lives, including their sexual orientation, sexual identity, ethnicity, nationality, immigration status, age, and physicality (Worell & Robinson, 2009). In addition, environmental factors, such as advantage and disadvantage on the basis of gender, culture, and SES may affect assessment results (Worell & Robinson, 2009). In the following sections, we address each variable separately, highlighting definitions and implications of these constructs to the process of assessment. In addition, we provide brief descriptions of available measures related to these constructs when relevant.

Culture

Culture has been identified as one of the most "misunderstood constructs" in psychology (Pedersen, 1999, p. 3), and it is believed to have an impact on all psychological phenomenon related to the assessment process. Despite its importance, the operational definition of what constitutes culture has been debated in the literature for decades. Hundreds of definitions have been identified (Kroeber & Kluckhohn, 1963); however, one of the most frequently cited in the social sciences defines *culture* as "a historically transmitted pattern of meanings embodied in symbols, a system of inherited conceptions expressed in symbolic forms by means of which [people] communicate, perpetuate, and develop their knowledge about and attitudes toward life" (Geertz, 1973, p. 89). Cultures are dynamic and change over time (e.g., S. R. Lopez & Guarnaccia, 2000). In addition, individuals often belong to several different cultural groups, simultaneously possessing multiple intersecting identities. In the psychological literature, culture has most often been linked to race, ethnicity, religious belief, social class, gender, sexual orientation, age, disability status, geographic boundary, and language (Goldberger & Veroff, 1995). All of these identities have the potential to affect the process of assessment. Most test content includes items representing "symbolic culture"—that which is shared, including "values, knowledge, and communication" (Greenfield, 1997, p. 1115). Entire volumes have been dedicated to understanding the impact of culture on test performance related to the various domains in psychology (e.g., Suzuki & Ponterotto, 2008).

The field of assessment has been plagued with challenges regarding the usage of various measures with members of different cultural groups. Research in the area of multicultural assessment has generally focused on the performance of different racial and ethnic groups on various measures. As noted, concerns have arisen with respect to test content, translation, language, and clinical diagnoses with regard to specific racial–ethnic populations. A psychologist's willingness to learn more about an individual's cultural background is critical as noted in the section Gathering Background Information. Psychologists must educate themselves to understand the many ways in which a client's cultural identity may affect the assessment process.

Racial Identity and Ethnic Identity

Racial identity and ethnic identity are factors that may affect the process of psychological assessment. Counseling psychologists have contributed to the discourse on the importance of racial and ethnic identity and its measurement over the past 2 decades. *Racial identity* refers to one's perception of a collective or group identity based on a common heritage with a particular racial group (Helms, 1995). *Ethnic identity* refers to aspects of a person's social identity in relation to membership in various social groups taking into consideration the value and emotional significance attached to these memberships (e.g., how a person makes decisions about the role of ethnicity in their lives regardless of their involvement in their ethnic community (Phinney, 1992).

Stressors from cross-cultural interactions may affect assessment outcomes. For example, racial identity has been related to experiences of racism for African American college students (Johnson & Arbona, 2006). Racial identity statuses have also been linked to Black student performance on cognitive ability tests (Helms, 2002, 2004). Higher levels of Black idealization were linked to lower SAT scores. In achievement testing, clinicians must consider whether an individual's racial identity and ethnic identity may play a role in test performance related to stereotype threat. *Stereotype threat* refers to the anxiety associated with fulfilling a negative stereotype about the group to which one belongs (Aronson, 2002; Steele & Aronson, 1995). In achievement testing, African Americans tend to score lower when given a racial cue making salient a particular negative stereotype (Steele & Aronson, 1995). In a study comparing Asians and Latinos on a math tests, Asians who strongly identify as Asian performed better, exhibiting an ethnicity boost or positive stereotype, whereas Latinos highly identified with their group performed worse (Armenta, 2010).

A review of racial identity and ethnic identity measures indicated that the scales vary on a number of dimensions. Some are specifically aimed at a particular racial or ethnic group, whereas others are designed to obtain information from members of multiple racial and ethnic groups, including attention to culture and nationality (Suzuki, Rodriguez, Onoue, & Ahluwalia, 2011).

Reviews of racial identity measures are provided in a number of sources (e.g., Fischer & Moradi, 2001). Racial identity scales were developed on the basis of particular models of identity development focusing primarily on Black and White populations. One of the most popular is Helms's Racial Identity Attitude Scale (Helms & Parham, 1996), which encompasses four nonlinear statuses: preencounter (pro-White majority/anti-Black views), encounter (reevaluation of personal attitudes to race), immersion–emersion (an increase in both pro-Black and anti-White attitudes), and internalization (a bicultural world view, including pro-Black and pro-White views).

Other scales, such as the Revised Multidimensional Inventory of Black Identity (Sellers, Rowley, Chavous, Shelton, & Smith, 1997), measure what are referred to as stable dimensions of African American racial identity: salience (degree of racial identity as relevant to core self-concept at particular moment in time), centrality (race as a core self-concept), ideology (philosophy of an African American way of life), and regard (affective and evaluative judgment of individual's racial group).

Racial identity scales assessing White identity include statuses that move between naiveté about differences between Black and White people to accepting and understanding difference. These statuses include contact (satisfaction with racial status quo, obliviousness to racism), disintegration (racial moral dilemmas, feeling the need to choose between group loyalty and morals), reintegration (idealization of own racial group, intolerance for other groups), pseudoindependence (intellectual commitment to one's own socioracial group; deceptive tolerance of other groups), and autonomy (informed, positive socioracial–group commitment; Helms, 1995; Helms & Carter, 1990).

Ethnic identity scales assess features of identity as specified by the author's definition of ethnic identity. These differing definitions result in a range of qualitative categories assessed by each scale and include such categories as individual differences in group members' retention of cultural characteristics in behavior and ideology, how individuals relate to their ethnic identity group, and internal experience of their ethnic identity (Suzuki, Rodriguez, Onoue, & Ahluwalia, 2011).

In a review of measures of ethnic identity, six out of 13 measures focused on Asian American ethnic identity. The scales focusing on Asian–Asian Americans included the East Asian Ethnic Identity Scale (Barry, 2002), the General Ethnicity Questionnaire (Tsai, Ying, & Lee, 2000), the Scale of Ethnic Experience (Malcarne, Chavira, Fernandez, & Liu, 2006), the Suinn-Lew Asian Self-Identity Acculturation Scale (Suinn, Rickard-Figueroa, Lew, & Vigil, 1987), and the Taiwanese Ethnic Identity Scale (Tsai & Curbow, 2001). The non-Asian/Asian American scales focused on Latino/a, Black, bicultural, and multigroup ethnic identity. It is interesting to consider the strengths and limitations of the range of ethnic identity measures. For example, examining the Asian American scales leads one to consider that Pan-Asian ethnic identity scales imply universality of Asian experience across nationalities, whereas specific measures for Asian groups result in highly specific measures that are applicable only to particular subgroups.

The Multigroup Ethnic Identity Measure (MEIM; Phinney, 1992) and the Ethnic Identity Scale (Umaña-Taylor, Yazedjian, & Bámaca-Gómez, 2004) are two scales that address ethnic identity as a quality measurable across various ethnic groups. The aim of the MEIM was to find commonalities across individuals that could then be applied to many different ethnic groups (Fischer & Moradi, 2001). The MEIM describes ethnic identity in linear stages of development and achievement; these are measured in discrete measurable components: self-identification and ethnicity (committed ethnic identity via identity achievement), ethnic behaviors and practices (related to own ethnicity), and belonging (affirmation from own ethnic group; Phinney, 1992). Phinney (1992) noted that a generalized measure does not address the uniqueness of particular groups. Although the MEIM assesses the role of ethnic identity across groups, it is limited in its description of culture-specific factors (Fischer & Moradi, 2001).

Despite the theoretical importance of racial identity and ethnic identity theory and the number of scales that have been developed to assess these constructs, the application these measures has remained primarily in research and training. The future viability of such measures and their integration into mainstream assessment practice is questionable. In the absence of such test use, the major challenge for counseling psychologists is to ensure that attention to these theoretical constructs remains part of the contextual information used in the assessment of a client's complex identity.

Language

One of the major difficulties in cross-cultural usage of psychological measures is language proficiency. Estimates of the current number of languages spoken in the United States alone stands at approximately 600 (cited in E. C. Lopez, 2010). As noted, all tests are culturally loaded, and one of the ways this is demonstrated is in emphasis placed on language to convey items and tasks to the individual being assessed. Language reflects cultural nuances and affects the measurement of particular constructs including ability. For example, Gladwell (2008) pointed out differences in number naming systems in English and Asian languages. He noted that the English counting system requires children to learn different forms. Asian languages are logical—"Eleven is ten-one. Twelve is ten-two. Twenty-four is two-tens-four and so on" (Gladwell, 2008, p. 229). Thus, Asian children learn to count faster than American children. Gladwell (2008) noted that by the age of 5 "American children are already a *year* behind their Asian counterparts in the most fundamental of math skills" (p. 229).

Faced with limited measurement tools, normed and validated for different ethnocultural groups, clinicians have often relied on translators and interpreters to facilitate the assessment process using English-based tests. Translators generally work with written language, whereas interpreters focus on spoken language (E. C. Lopez, 2010). Given the important role that translators and interpreters play in the development and administration of psychological tests, guidelines have been developed for training and ethical conduct (e.g., National Council on Interpreting in Health Care, 2004). As E. C. Lopez (2010) noted, effective interpreters are proficient in two languages and knowledgeable about cultural and professional context and about ethics (e.g., confidentiality). In addition, they must possess good listening and memory skills and have knowledge of technical aspects of the assessment process and vocabulary pertaining to the test.

In the past, it has been sufficient for test developers to employ back-translation methods, whereby a test is translated from its original form to a target language and then translated back to its original language to ensure linguistic equivalence. However, state-of-the-art practices now use indigenous focus groups, expert reviewers, and racial–ethnic oversampling. An example of the complex nature of cultural adaptation and translation of assessment instruments is noted in the procedures followed by researchers using the Harvard Trauma Questionnaire (Fabri, 2008). This questionnaire has been modified and adapted for use with multiple populations, incorporating ethnographic interviews with local staff and community members, key informants who serve as consultants, and a review process by an expert panel.

Acculturation

Numerous definitions have been identified for the multifaceted and bidimensional construct of acculturation. Acculturation is an "essential component of multicultural assessment" (Rivera, 2008, p. 74). On the basis of her extensive review of the acculturation literature, Rivera noted that

> acculturation generally is viewed as a dynamic process of change and adaptation that individuals undergo as a result of contact with members of a different culture. This change is influenced by the environment the individual resides in as

well as qualities innate to that individual. These changes influence the attitudes, beliefs, values, affect, and behavior of those undergoing the acculturation process. (p. 76)

The process of acculturation affects individuals in psychological and sociocultural ways, with variations of findings depending on how acculturation is defined by researchers (van de Vijver & Phalet, 2004). Acculturation is associated with mental health; the stress of acculturation can lead to distress in areas of physical well-being and psychological health and has social implications as well (Berry, Kim, Minde, & Mok, 1987). The features relevant to psychological testing, as noted by van de Vijver and Phalet (2004), include "feeling well" (psychological adjustment), "performing well," and sociocultural adaptation (p. 223). van de Vijver and Phalet noted that acculturation factors related to achievement testing include attitudes to adaption, length of residence, achievement motivation, extraversion, language mastery, cultural distance, skills, and social contacts. Acculturation factors related to psychological assessment include positive attitudes toward cultural maintenance, social support, continuity in family, continuity in family life, collectivism values, and locus of control.

Measures of acculturation often focus on behavioral (e.g., language, customs, food, music), affective (e.g., feelings about identity), and cognitive (e.g., beliefs about gender role, attitudes, values) aspects of acculturation (Cuéllar, Arnold, & Maldonado, 1995; Rivera, 2008). Zane and Mak (2003; cited in Rivera, 2008) examined 21 measures of acculturation yielding the following thematic areas: language use and preference, social affiliation, daily living habits, cultural traditions, communication style, cultural identity and pride, perceived prejudice and discrimination, generational status, family socialization, and cultural values. In their review of 33 acculturation instruments, Kim and Abreu (2001) noted a number of limitations. One of the most glaring was that despite common acceptance that acculturation is a bidimensional construct, 70% of the scales were based on an *unilinear* (i.e., reflecting a singular process of adjustment toward the mainstream culture)

model (Kim & Abreu, 2001). Rivera (2008) noted that qualitative assessments offer "a broader and more comprehensive understanding of acculturation status and the influence of acculturation in the lives of diverse individuals" (p. 86).

Socioeconomic Status

Contemporary measures of SES focus primarily on occupational position, education, and income. SES has been linked to a number of important psychological and overall health outcomes, including morbidity and mortality rates as well as emotional well-being (Fotso & Kuate-Defo, 2005; Mustard & Frolich, 1995). Despite its importance, however, there is an "absence of good SES data" (Oakes & Rossi, 2003, p. 770). The operationalization and measurement of the SES construct has been elusive. "Prominent scholars have debated the theory, operationalization, and usefulness of SES constructs for about 125 years" (Oakes & Rossi, 2003, p. 770). Occupations of heads of household, examination of small communities in relation to individual social status (i.e., exploring households within social hierarchies), education levels and occupation or occupational status, and indicators of prestige are some of the variables that have been considered in the measurement of SES.

Mustard and Frolich (1995) argued that although there are "a wide range of approaches to the measurement of socioeconomic status," in the context of the assessment of one's health, a correct approach should include "a profile of the social, economic, and physical environment in which the individual works and lives" (p. 45). They include among their measurements of SES housing characteristics, education attainment levels, type of employment, income levels, mobility, and social characteristics (including age and marital status). Similarly, Fotso and Kuate-Defo (2005) noted that the relationship between SES and health is well documented in the international epidemiological, economic, and sociological literature. The authors referenced traditional education, income measures, information on household possessions, and levels of community development as indicators of SES.

Poverty has been linked to environmental factors that may affect test performance. These factors include presence of lead in substandard housing; usage of alcohol during pregnancy, health issues (e.g., poorer dental health, vision, and hearing; asthma), exposure to pollution, inadequate medical care, and little exposure to reading material and language stimulation (Nisbett, 2009). Nisbett (2009) also noted that this lack of resources leads to vitamin and mineral deficiencies, greater exposure to emotional trauma, frequent changes in residence in poorer neighborhoods, poorer quality schools, and less desirable peer groups.

Geographic Location

Although differences in test performance between people from various geographic locations have diminished because of increased access to technology and other resources, concerns continue to be noted related to particular communities. For example, Urquhart Hagie, Gallipo, and Swen (2003) raised concerns regarding performance of students from the Lakota Sioux reservation on standardized tests because of their geographic isolation and limited access to resources. Access to television and other forms of technology may be viewed as too expensive and unavailable. In addition, awareness of national political issues may not be a part of the curriculum given other local priorities.

Gender

Gender differences in test performance have been noted in nearly all psychological domains, including cognitive, personality, and vocational interests (Suzuki & Ahluwalia, 2003). The assumption of gender differences has permeated the literature; however, Hyde (2005) posited the gender similarities hypothesis on the basis of meta-analytic research on psychological gender differences, including the areas of cognition, communication, social and personality, psychological well-being, motor behaviors, and moral reasoning. Her findings indicate that the largest gender differences are in the areas of motor performance (i.e., throwing velocity and throwing distance), measures of sexuality (i.e., incidences of masturbation, attitudes about sex), with moderate differences in aggression. Hyde noted that the size of gender differences may vary with age and context, stating that "it is clear that

gender differences can be created, erased, or reversed depending on the context. . . . These findings provide strong evidence against the differences model and its notions that psychological gender differences are large and stable" (p. 589).

In the past, women have been reported to perform better on tasks in the areas of memory (e.g., long-term memory, recall of literature and foreign languages), perceptual speed, and decoding of nonverbal communication (Cohen & Swerdlik, 1999). Men have been reported to score higher on tasks involving transformations in visual working memory, motor accuracy, general knowledge, fluid reasoning, and verbal analogies (Cohen & Swerdlik, 1999). In light of Hyde's findings, although not specifically pertaining to these particular tasks, gender differences appear suspect and attention to age, context, and other variables need to be considered as part of the interpretation of such findings. In addition, explanations regarding these differences also include socialization and environmental reinforcement and potential physiological factors (i.e., sex differences in brain organization and structural differences in brain anatomy; Kestemberg, Silverman, & Santandreu, 2003).

The most frequently used measures provide information in their technical reports examining gender. With regard to personality assessment, some of the most popular quantitative and projective personality tests have yielded significant gender differences. For example, the MMPI-2 (Butcher et al., 1989) provides different norms for men and women and includes the Gender Role-Masculine (GM) and Gender Role-Feminine (GF) scales (Friedman, Lewak, Nichols, & Webb, 2001). Although the gap between gender groups has decreased in the most recent versions, researchers noted: "The clinician must be sensitive to such gender issues to effectively interpret MMPI-2 code patterns. Although the MMPI-2 is robust enough that it is not likely that these gender issues invalidate interpretation, more research is clearly needed" (Friedman et al., 2001, p. 432). In addition, researchers studying projective measures such as the TAT noted the importance of considering gender differences in responses. As early as 1975, Bellak recommended that different TAT cards be used for men and women because qualitative differences were noted between the stories told by men and those by women.

Gender differences have played a major role in the development of vocational interest inventories. Betz (1993) noted that women and men have different career socialization experiences and treatment in the workplace. For example, men and women score differentially on approximately 25% to 33% of the items in the Strong Interest Inventory (SII; Harmon, Hansen, Borgen, & Hammer, 1994). Men and women in the same occupation also score differently on a number of SII items.

Finding answers to understand the meaning of score differences has been inconclusive at best, and the study of gender differences has often been neglected (Brown, 1990). Explanations related to differences in gender socialization and opportunity barriers have often been cited. Questions of gender bias "evidenced when there is systematic error, related to membership in a particular gender group, in the approximation of a true score" (Suzuki & Ahluwalia, 2003, p. 120) have often been raised in light of discrepancies in scores between males and females. Gender role analysis in clinical assessment requires that the examiner be knowledgeable regarding relationships between gender and other demographic characteristics of the individual (e.g., race, ethnicity, class, and age) that may affect the assessment process (Brown, 1990). In addition, the process calls for the examiner to be aware of their gender biases that may be affecting the process. Using an interview format, the examiner explores these issues by asking the client to talk about the meaning of gender membership and role.

Disability Status

One of the major uses of psychological assessment instruments has been in the determination of disability status. The term disability can refer to traumatic brain injuries, learning disabilities, developmental disability, emotional and behavioral disorders, communication disorders, hearing disabilities, visual impairments and physical disabilities. Each of these impairment categories has implications for testing purposes and scales have been developed to facilitate the diagnosis of psychopathology and learning problems.

Learning disabilities constitute the largest special education category and include difficulties in developing skills in reading, writing, listening, speaking, reasoning, spelling, or math (Groth-Marnat, 2009). In many cases, the role of the clinician in assessing a learning disability is to identify the client's strengths and weaknesses to best recommend future directions of education, therapy, or clinical placement (Groth-Marnat, 2009). It is important for clinicians to note that some learning disorders that cause distress and impairment do not necessarily qualify as a disability; a learning disorder is a more broadly used term than learning disability, which comes from a legal perspective (Mapou, 2009).

Disability conditions affect access to services and opportunities. In cases in which the disability status of the individual is known, the examiner may need to consider alternative testing options to ensure an accurate assessment of the individual's strengths and limitations. For example, for a client who has visual impairments, the WAIS-IV is an inappropriate diagnostic tool because it relies on subtests that require visual synthesis and visual comprehension.

Issues surrounding assessment of individuals with disabilities are most pronounced in the education system. As noted, an increased emphasis on accountability in the school system has highlighted the need for valid assessment techniques of students with disabilities. In particular, the No Child Left Behind legislation of 2002 made it necessary to develop new measures of academic progress in the school setting. Roach and Elliott (2006), however, argued that "many states have struggled to develop alternate assessments that meet federal mandates" because skills and concepts measured by the exam were inappropriate or irrelevant for students with significant disabilities, or the measure was "considered a special education function and therefore only nominally connected to the state's overall assessment system" (pp. 181–182). Furthermore, "alternate assessments are intended to facilitate accountability and curricular access for students with significant disabilities and to motivate special educators to provide standards-based curriculum and instruction to all students" (Roach & Elliott, 2006, p. 193). Any form of alternate assessment that claims to measure the progress of students with cognitive disabilities must be an accurate reflector of what students are studying in their classes, must be aligned to state-level content standards, and must yield scores that can be used for annual yearly progress measures (Roach & Elliott, 2006). Forms of alternate assessment include portfolios, performance tasks, and rating scales (e.g., teacher). Movement toward alternate assessments also include curriculum-based assessment, dynamic assessment, and response to intervention models. In each case, students are tested based on material derived from their course material and provided with a variety of techniques and opportunities to master the material. These assessment features represent a significant deviation from the utilization of standardized tests of achievement.

Lesbian, Gay, Bisexual, and Transgender Identities

The field of psychology has historically underrepresented issues of importance in the assessment of lesbian, gay, bisexual, and transgender (LGBT) populations, focusing on sexual orientation as a form of pathology (Rothblum, 2000). Sexual orientation was removed from the *DSM* in the mid-1970s. A seminal article by Chernin, Holden, and Chandler (1997) highlighted the existence of heterosexist bias in psychological assessment, identifying three types of bias relevant to various assessment instruments: omission bias, connotation bias, and contiguity bias. *Omission bias* "occurs when wording and items refer to concepts and circumstances associated exclusively with heterosexuality" (Chernin et al., p. 69). *Connotation bias* exists when words with negative connotations are associated with members of sexual minority groups. *Contiguity bias* "involves scales that assess homosexuality or bisexuality appearing among those that assess psychopathology" (Chernin et al., p. 70). The potential existence of heterosexist bias should be considered in the process of assessment.

Currently, the APA guidelines address the importance of preparatory work as a competency to work with LGBT clients (American Psychological Association, 2000, 2009, 2010). Despite this attention, there is a noticeable lack of research on LGBT status as it contributes to bias in clinical assessment. This is indicated by a lack of attention to sexual orientation in test norms and few published articles. This dearth of information specifically on the interaction of

sexual orientation and clinical assessment reflects that "heterosexist discourse is supported by silence regarding sexual orientation issues" (Croteau, Bieschke, Fassinger, & Manning, 2008, p. 196).

As a field, counseling psychology has made significant contributions to sexual identity theories and LGBT affirmative psychology; as such, the authors urge clinicians to consider LGBT status as a meaningful contextual factor often silenced, which may affect assessment in clinician bias and test bias that is yet undetected by formal research. In addition, LGBT individuals have complex identities, and they may have many ways in which they define themselves even thought they often are forced to categorize themselves by "check-off boxes" on census-like forms (Israel, 2004, p. 183). LGBT individuals may exhibit stress-related behaviors. As noted by Chernin et al. (1997) "gay men and lesbians experience difficulty responding to items regarding significant others phrased in terms of the other gender" (p. 69). In addition, they report that on the MMPI-2 "references to children from same-sex parental households are overlooked because all items regarding parenting refer to having both a mother and father" (Chernin et al., 1997, p. 71). To competently assess members of the LGBT communities, clinicians need to possess awareness and knowledge of various psychological instruments and skills, as outlined in counselor competencies (Israel, Ketz, Detrie, Burke, & Shulman, 2003).

GUIDELINES AND STANDARDS INFORMING COMPETENT ASSESSMENT PRACTICES

Given the importance of competent assessment practices, counseling psychologists must be aware of the published guidelines and standards that define competency in this area and inform best practices. Guidelines pertaining to assessment practices are noted in the APA's *Ethical Principles of Psychologists and Code of Conduct* (2010); *Guidelines on Multicultural Education, Training, Research, Practice and Organizational Change for Psychologists* (APA, 2002); and the benchmark assessment competencies (Krishnamurthy et al., 2004). In addition, there exist *Standards for Educational and Psychological Testing* (American Educational Research Association [AERA], APA, & the National Council on Measurement and Education [NCME], 1999) endorsed jointly by the APA, AERA, and the NCME. It is critical that counseling psychologists be aware of these documents to insure and advocate for best practices. Although the importance of these guidelines may seem self-evident, ethical substandards (i.e., attempts to disguise and rationalize unethical behavior) and clear breaches in guidelines have been reported (Eyde, Robertson, & Krug, 2010). Lack of knowledge, budgetary constraints, and limited access to resources are just a few of the difficulties that confront counseling psychologists in the field.

Ethical Guidelines

The APA *Ethical Principles of Psychologists and Code of Conduct* (2010) denotes 11 stipulated guidelines for ethical assessment. These guidelines govern the following areas: test basis, use, informed consent process, release of test data, test construction, interpretation of results, qualifications, use of obsolete and outdated test results, use of scoring and interpretation services, explanation of assessment results, and maintenance of test security. Emphasis is placed on ensuring that psychologists are able to clearly substantiate their findings and conclusions. When instruments are used with limited reliability and validity, these limitations must be noted and considered in the veracity of conclusions and recommendations. In particular, reliability and validity should be established for use with members of the population being tested. Usage of interpreters and language considerations are emphasized in the informed consent process and the actual administration of measures. Issues of bias in test construction are addressed as well as the importance of integrating "situational, personal, linguistic, and cultural differences" in interpreting assessment results (APA, 2010).

Multicultural Competencies and Guidelines

In 2002, the APA adopted the *Guidelines on Multicultural Education, Training, Research, Practice and Organizational Change for Psychologists* (APA,

2002). The document contains six guidelines, one of which specifically addresses assessment in practice (Guideline 5). Psychologists are called on to be knowledgeable of a "broad range" of assessment strategies and techniques, data-generating procedures, and standardized instruments. In particular, attention to issues of validity, reliability, and equivalence are noted across various racial and ethnic groups. Examiners should select measures that are adapted to the specific individual or group. The authors note that when this information is unavailable, it behooves the researcher to "use pilot tests and interviews" to determine the "cultural validity" of the measures as "psychologists strive to apply culturally-appropriate skills in clinical and other applied psychological practices" (APA, 2010). The multicultural guidelines also emphasize understanding the limitations of various assessment practices (i.e., instrumentation and diagnostic methods) and the importance of understanding the cultural and linguistic characteristics of the individual being assessed.

Assessment Competencies

In 2002, the *Competencies Conference: Future Directions in Education and Credentialing in Professional Psychology* was held with work groups focusing on eight core areas of psychology, one of which was assessment. Eight core competencies essential to services related to psychological assessment were identified and recommendations for psychologist training were indicated (Krishnamurthy et al., 2004). Again, the call for psychologists to be knowledgeable regarding test theory (e.g., psychometrics), test development practices, and theoretical and empirical foundations of assessment practice were emphasized. In addition, knowledge and assessment skill in multiple areas of cognitive, affective, behavioral, and personality functioning were noted (Krishnamurthy et al., 2004). The purposes of assessment were highlighted, including examination of treatment and intervention outcomes and awareness that assessment can serve as a form of intervention. The importance of understanding the various stages of assessment, the context of relationship, and the importance of collaboration in assessment was also highlighted in the formulation of the *Assessment* of Competency Benchmarks: A Developmental Model for Defining and Measuring Competence in Professional Psychology (Assessment of Competency Benchmarks Work Group, 2007). This document was designed to facilitate discussion and implementation of competency-based approaches to measuring student-learning outcomes related to all areas of psychological, training including assessment.

Standards for Educational and Psychological Testing

A joint undertaking by the AERA, APA, and NCME led to the publication of *The Standards for Educational and Psychological Testing* (AERA, APA, & NCME, 1999), currently being revised. The standards address in a more detailed format issues related to test construction, evaluation, and technical documentation (i.e., validity; reliability; test development and revision; scales, norms, and score comparability; administration, scoring and reporting of data; and supporting documentation for tests), fairness in testing (i.e., test use; rights and responsibilities of test takers; and testing individuals from diverse linguistic backgrounds and individuals with disabilities), and testing application (i.e., responsibilities of test users, psychological and educational assessment; testing in employment settings and credentialing; and program development, evaluation, and public policy).

As noted in the other publications cited in this section, the standards (AERA, APA, & NCME, 1999) emphasize the importance of knowledge and professional judgment in evaluating individuals from diverse ethnocultural backgrounds. The standards also address test developers who are called on to collect validity data for each linguistic subgroup whenever possible and to provide linguistic modifications in the test manuals for appropriate usage. In the case of translated measures, the procedures followed should be accurately described along with empirical evidence to support comparable versions of the measure with adequate reliability and validity indicated. When using interpreters, the standards note that this individual must be proficient in both languages and have knowledge of the assessment process (see the section Language). Knowledge of these standards provides counseling

psychologists with a foundation upon which to advocate for better reporting of test development practices and the importance of addressing contextual variables and indicators of multiple identities to provide greater accuracy in interpretation of test findings.

EXAMINATION OF TESTING EXEMPLARS

Given the information contained in this chapter focusing on guidelines and competencies governing and informing sound assessment practices, we struggled to address exemplars in assessment for counseling psychologists. Our struggle focused on how to best highlight the most frequently used instruments in psychological practice through a counseling psychology perspective. The difficulties stem from the realization that mainstream psychology assessment practices have often not been under the auspices of counseling psychology. For example, vocational assessment is often not highlighted in mainstream psychological assessment texts (e.g., Groth-Marnat, 2009).

The sections that follow highlight various domains of assessment with attention to issues of context and diversity, the mainstays of counseling psychology. In selecting these testing exemplars, we focus on the most frequently used instruments in each domain to increase the usefulness of the material for counseling psychologists. Although in earlier discussion we noted the lack of attention given to vocational and positive psychology in psychological assessment, we include attention to these measures in the hopes that they will become part of the mainstream of assessment in the future.

The areas covered are measures of personality and emotional functioning; vocation; achievement; intelligence; and positive psychology, quality of life, and problem solving. Given the sheer number of available tests, we were unable to provide an exhaustive listing; however, we reference more comprehensive texts and reviews or articles whenever possible to provide the reader with potential sources of additional information. All of the measurement tools identified as exemplars provide attention to validity and reliability as well as other psychometric constructs.

Personality and Emotional Functioning

The domain of personality and emotional functioning assessment contains the largest number of instruments and includes the greatest level of diversity in terms of types of measures (i.e., qualitative and quantitative). A number of "classic" projective measures, including the Rorschach Comprehensive System (Exner, 2001, 2003), TAT (Murray, 1971), Draw-a-Person (Goodenough & Harris, 1950), House–Tree–Person (Buck, Warren, Jolles, Wench, & Hammer, 1946–1993), and the Rotter incomplete sentences blank (Rotter, Lah, & Rafferty, 1992) are frequently used. These projective measures are composed of tasks that are "generally unstructured" resulting in individual responses that "reflect internal needs, emotions, past experiences, thought processes, relational patterns, and various aspects of behavior" (Hilsenroth & Segal, 2004, p. 283). Although originally developed from a psychoanalytic perspective, they are currently used as tools within other theoretical paradigms (Esquivel, Oades-Sese, & Olitzky, 2008). As noted, although these tests were originally developed to utilize more qualitative methods of interpretation (e.g., thematic), alternative scoring systems have evolved leading to quantitative interpretation focusing on the frequency of themes or codes. With regard to the qualitative aspects of these measures, the traditional issues of validity and reliability are limited, particularly given the somewhat-subjective nature of the coding process. That being said, projective tests have continued to be a mainstay of the psychological assessment process for decades given the qualitative information they reveal, which, at times, cannot be accessed through a purely quantitative scale with set items and response options.

Drawing techniques in assessment include the human figure (male and female), family representations (e.g., kinetic family), house, and tree. "The assumption is that drawings both represent conscious mental processes and abilities (cognitive, perceptual motor) and reflect inner subconscious and symbolic expressions of feelings, conflicts and needs" (Esquivel et al., 2008, p. 347). More specifically, drawings provide glimpses into an individual's personality and can provide information regarding reality testing, sex role identification, sexual abuse, and self-esteem.

Utilizing drawings cross-culturally must be done with caution given that visual symbols may take on different meanings in different cultures. For example, the color red may represent blood or anger in one culture but good luck (i.e., for Chinese) in another. Questions may be raised in terms of particular physical features tied to particular groups. The presence of a chimney may indicate warm intimate relations and may also be associated as a phallic symbol (Oster & Gould, 1987). Some individuals may not draw a chimney given their geographic residence in tropical climates. Those living in an urban setting may draw apartment buildings with no chimneys to represent their residence. Esquivel et al. (2008) noted that the examiner must be aware of the influence of the individual's culture when interpreting projective drawings and the interpretation guidelines must be applied appropriately.

Narrative assessment tools include analysis of stories, personal anecdotes, journals, and autobiographies. "Narratives can capture both individual life stories and patterns of meaning within and across cultures" (Esquivel et al., 2008, p. 358). Concerns can arise given that the obtained narratives are often based on the presentation of some visual stimuli, such as in the case of the TAT. Questions concerning the cultural relevance of these visual stimuli have been noted, and relatively newer measures like the Tell-Me-A-Story (Costantino, Malgady, & Rogler, 1988) instrument have been developed and normed on urban children from various backgrounds based on the nature of the figures depicted in the pictures (e.g., Puerto Rican version, Black version, nonminority version). Some of the TAT cards have been useful in research conducted with immigrant and refugee populations (Suárez-Orozco, Suárez-Orozco, & Todorova, 2008).

The Rorschach inkblot test (Rorschach, 1942) remains "one of the most frequently used clinical assessment approaches" (Esquivel et al., 2008, p. 361) despite decades of criticism regarding its subjectivity and potential bias. Exner (2001, 2003) formulated the Comprehensive System, which provides a method of obtaining empirical data (i.e., scoring) based on an individual's responses to the inkblots. The Rorschach is considered to be relatively culture free given the ambiguity of the inkblots. That being said, however, concerns have arisen regarding the usage of the Comprehensive System with diverse cultural groups (Esquivel et al., 2008).

By far the largest number of tests in the category of emotional functioning and personality are quantitative in nature. Most of these instruments are used in the assessment of psychopathology, most notably the MMPI-2 (Butcher et al., 1989) and the Millon Clinical Multiaxial Inventory–III (MCMI-III; Millon, Millon, Davis, & Grossman, 2006). The MMPI-2 is the most frequently researched personality measure with 11,214 citations on PsycINFO. Together, the MMPI-2 and the MCMI-III constitute the "most widely used psychodiagnostic instruments in the United States" (Kwan & Maestas, 2008, p. 425). Despite their frequent usage, concerns have arisen regarding the validity of such instruments with non-White individuals. Kwan and Maestas (2008) provided a review of the usage of these instruments with various ethnocultural populations as they concluded that "empirical questions" (p. 441) remain. Research indicates that these assessment tools may have differential impacts on ethnic and racial populations.

Studies on MMPI-2 assessment with racially and ethnically diverse groups illuminate some of the test's weaknesses and strengths as well as the difficulty in generalizing from a specific study sample (Kwan & Maestas, 2008). Studies mostly compare between groups (e.g., African American and Caucasian groups; Latino and Caucasian) on the basis of race or between a specific racial group and the overall normative sample. Studies have shown significant differences between African Americans and Caucasians across scales (Castro, Gordon, Brown, Anestis, & Joiner, 2008; Greene, 1987; Hall, Bansal, & Lopez, 1999). Native Americans also show different patterns of response in personality assessment than Caucasian Americans with varying explanations of experience and oppression (Hill et al., 2010; Pace et al., 2006; Robin, Greene, Albaugh, Caldwell, & Goldman, 2003). Levels of acculturation and education appear to have a relationship with scores on these measures.

The Sixteen Personality Factor Questionnaire (5th ed.; 16PF; Russell & Karol, 1994), California Personality Inventory–260TM (CPI-260TM; Gough

& Bradley, 2002, 2005), and the Myers-Briggs Type Indicator—Form M (MBTI; Myers, McCaulley, Quenk, & Hammer, 1998) are measures of "normal personality." Strack, Dunaway, and Schulenberg (2008) noted that the measures have been normed on predominantly Caucasian samples and there exists a need for additional norms to enhance their usage with diverse ethnocultural populations. The scales themselves have been translated into a number of different languages (e.g., the 16PF is offered in 30 different language versions). Research has not kept pace with the proliferation of translated versions of various measures, therefore, the need for additional study examining the usage of these instruments with diverse populations continues.

Vocational Measures

Attention to vocational issues and assessment is one of the historical foundations of counseling psychology (Gainor, 2001). The purpose of the measures in this area is to assist individuals in understanding their vocational interests and enhance their thinking about educational and vocational options (Jackson, Holder, & Ramage, 2008). "Vocational assessment in its most ethical and democratic form should broaden the career options available to people and increase their chances of satisfaction and success" (Gainor, 2001, p. 170). Challenges of racial, gender, and class bias have plagued the field given that the theoretical foundations of the field were based on "White, Western, English-speaking, middle-class, linguistic, heterosexual, male perspectives" with little relevance to the lives of "people of color; gay men; lesbians, bisexuals, and transgendered people; women, the poor; or people with disabilities" (Gainor, 2001, p. 171).

In vocational assessment, it is important to take into consideration the social–historical background of the individual being evaluated. Gainor (2001) reported that African Americans have at times been found to score higher on areas of social interest. She hypothesizes that there may be historical reasons for this finding, therefore, results should not lead to a narrowing of career options without further investigation. Gainor emphasized that vocational assessments must be supplemented with data regarding contextual and environmental factors to ensure appropriate vocational and career counseling with diverse racial and ethnic groups.

In a meta-analysis of 16 studies examining career aspirations, perceptions of opportunities and barriers, and tasks related to decision making and exploration, Fouad and Byars-Winston (2005) found support for the recommendation that context and environment be taken into account. Findings indicated that race and ethnicity did not contribute much to differences in career aspirations or decision-making attitudes. They did find, however, that groups differed in their perception of career opportunities and barriers. Cultural minorities may face racism or discrimination limiting their occupational opportunities that in turn affect their career choices. Thus, information gleaned from interest inventories will need to be augmented with discussion regarding opportunities and barriers that the individual may have experienced affecting their vocational interests and choices.

A number of career measures have emerged over the years. Some of the most popular instruments include the Career Assessment Inventory (Johansson, 1984), the Career Development Inventory (CDI; Sundre, 2001), and the SII (Donnay, Morris, Schaubhut, & Thompson, 2005). The Career Assessment Inventory, second vocational edition (Johansson, 1984) reports scores according to six general theme scales (realistic, investigative, artistic, social, enterprising, and conventional) with much more extensive information regarding gender, education, and ethnicity using a self-report, 305-question, Likert-style questionnaire. Similarly the CDI assesses stages of career development as they relate to affective and cognitive development. Greater attempts to address issues of diversity are seen in more recent versions of measures in vocational assessment. For example, the most recent version of the manual for the SII (Donnay et al., 2005) includes a standardization sample of 1,125 women and 1,125 men, reflecting characteristics of the 2000 census.

Achievement Tests

The importance of academic skills in the core areas of reading, math, science, and other subject areas are clearly noted as evidenced by the discourse on high-stakes testing. Some of these tests are linked to tracking in the education system, and the content of many of these tests is based on curriculum content. In addition, an individual's performance on these measures can be compared with national norms. Given the importance relegated to achievement tests in our society, extensive efforts are made in the norming process of schoolwide (group) administered tests. For example, some of the more frequently used achievement measures like the Stanford Achievement Test (10th ed.; Pearson Assessments, 2003) and the Iowa Test of Basic Skills (Hoover, Dunbar, & Frisbie, 2003) are normed yearly on nationally representative samples upward of 170,000 to 250,000 students with attention to issues of public and private schools, geographic region, SES, race, and ethnicity, all reflecting national census data.

Examples of individually administered achievement tests are also available to the examiner. Some of the more popular tests in this area include the Wechsler Individual Achievement Test (3rd ed.; Pearson Education, Inc., 2009), the Wide Range Achievement Test–4 (Wilkinson & Robertson, 2006), and the Woodcock-Johnson III (Woodcock, McGrew, & Mather, 2001). Efforts made to standardize these instruments on nationally representative samples is extensive, ranging from 3,000 to 8,000 students from grades K–12 stratified by age, gender, ethnicity, geographic region, and parental education.

Intelligence Tests

Although many definitions of intelligence are noted in the literature, most focus on cognitive abilities such as abstract reasoning, problem solving, and acquisition of knowledge (Snyderman & Rothman, 1988). Sternberg and Kaufman (1998) noted that culture defines intelligence, as it dictates what is considered intelligent behavior.

Intelligence measures are used in the diagnosis of mental deficiency, determination of educational placement, and job selection (Greenfield, 1997). Of the multitude of measures available in this area, the most popular are the Wechsler scales. Although these tests have gone through multiple revisions, the primary content of the scales (i.e., assessing verbal comprehension and nonverbal reasoning) has been maintained. Similar to achievement tests, concerns have arisen regarding racial and ethnic group differences on these scales. In general, group differences in overall IQ stand at Whites 100, Blacks 85, Hispanics midway between Blacks and Whites, and Asians and Jews somewhere above 100 ("Mainstream Science," 1994). Past literature indicates that Native Americans score at approximately 90 (McShane, 1982). There is growing evidence that the IQ gap between Blacks and Whites is narrowing (Nisbett, 2009). For example, IQ differences between Black and White 12-year-olds dropped from 15 points to 9.5 points over the past 3 decades (Nisbett, 2009).

As noted, charges of test bias were raised and numerous challenges posed regarding the use of these tests with Black, Latino, and American Indian students (Suzuki & Valencia, 1997). Valencia, Suzuki, and Salinas (2001) noted that the majority of empirical studies in this area revealed no significant evidence of bias. The most frequently used measures of intelligence are based on state-of-the-art test development practices, including expert review panels, racial and ethnic oversampling, and so on. In addition, the measures are standardized on representative census data taking into consideration gender, race and ethnicity, region of the country, urban and rural status, parental occupation, SES, and educational level. The Wechsler scales have been translated and renormed in a number of different countries, including those in Europe and Asia.

Positive Psychology, Quality of Life, and Problem-Solving Measures

Most tests cited thus far are usually administered to identify problems or examine the impact of intervention regarding problematic areas for the individual. In the context of studying an individual's limitations, it is crucial to integrate an understanding of their strengths. Positive psychological assessment emphasizes examination of "human strengths, healthy processes, and fulfillments" (S. J. Lopez, Snyder, & Rasmussen, 2003, p. 7) and balances strengths as well as weaknesses. One of the assumptions of positive assessment is that "practitioners must assume that all people and environments are both strong and weak. The reason for the assumption

is simple: People only search for things they believe to exist" (S. J. Lopez et al., 2003, p. 13). In addition, "All people have psychological strengths and the capacity to attain optimal mental health" (S. J. Lopez & Snyder, 2003a, p. 463).

Positive Psychological Assessment (S. J. Lopez & Snyder, 2003b) includes the following assessment constructs: hope, problem-solving appraisal, well-being, optimism, self-efficacy, creativity, wisdom, courage, positive emotions (e.g., self-esteem, romantic love), interpersonal constructs (e.g., empathy, forgiveness), religion and moral judgment, quality of life, optimal human functioning, and environmental assessment. Although mainstream psychological assessment practices continue to be more problem driven, the incorporation of positive measures in a psychological evaluation is noteworthy given the focus of counseling psychology on well-being.

Quality-of-life (QOL) scales encompass an examination of personal well-being within a person's unique context and overall human condition (Verdugo, Schalock, Keither, & Stancliffe, 2005). The authors referenced literature indicating the most frequently cited QOL domains, including interpersonal relations, social inclusion, personal development, physical well-being, self-determination, material well-being, family, recreation and leisure, and environment. They also reported that happiness, well-being, and satisfaction may not be universal and generalizable. Utsey and Bolden (2008) noted, "A major issue in the conceptualization and measurement of QOL, is that both the construct and the existing instrumentation are steeped in a Western cultural epistemological framework and worldview" (p. 300). Utsey and Bolden discussed differences in QOL based on the dichotomy between individualistic and collectivistic cultures.

Problem-solving appraisal has been linked to psychological adjustment, physical health, coping, and vocational adjustment with implications for understanding an individual's strengths, life satisfaction, and well-being. One of the most widely used measures in this area is the Problem-Solving Inventory (PSI; Heppner, 1988), which assesses perceptions of an individual's problem-solving ability and their behaviors and attitudes regarding problem-solving style (Heppner, Witty, & Dixon, 2004). In a seminal review of 20 years of research using the PSI, problem-solving appraisal has been studied in relation to depression, hopelessness and suicidality, anxiety and worry, alcohol use and abuse, eating disorders, childhood adjustment, childhood trauma, coping, help seeking, other physical health indicators, education outcomes, and vocational issues (Heppner et al., 2004).

Although the future of positive psychological assessment is promising, as noted, the measures have not attained deserved status in the psychological assessment literature. For example, core texts in the field of assessment do not include enough attention to positive psychological measures that are steadily growing in number. Many scales remain at a research level but could have important implications for overall assessment. In addition, some constructs, such as courage, have been tied to physiological indicators of fear and stress (S. R. Lopez, O'Byrne, & Petersen, 2003) and empathy-related responses have been associated with changes in heart rate and skin conductance (Zhou, Valiente, & Eisenberg, 2003). Readers interested in finding out more about these measures are referred to *Positive Psychological Assessment: A Handbook of Models and Measures* (S. J. Lopez & Synder, 2003b), which contains not only descriptions of the various measures but also copies of some of the actual scales.

ILLUSTRATIVE CASE EXAMPLE

Throughout this chapter, we have attempted to identify the importance of a counseling psychology perspective in understanding the lives of members of diverse racial and ethnic backgrounds. The limitations of our assessment tools make our focus on context, normative development, and positive strengths an imperative. In this case example, we illustrate the importance of working collaboratively with the client and other stakeholders (e.g., family members) to obtain salient background information. In addition, we integrate the importance of empirical knowledge of the assessment tools to glean the most comprehensive picture of the person being assessed. In this case, we demonstrate how traditional measures can be used effectively given understanding of the individual's life in the context of

their experiences and meaning making. This case is fictitious and does not reflect a particular individual.

Reason for Referral

Karam is a 72-year-old Sikh male who lives in New York City. He was referred for a psychological evaluation given concerns from family members indicating that he has become despondent and reports a number of physical ailments, including headaches and joint pain. The initial diagnosis obtained from his family physician indicates that he is depressed.

Karam's eldest son, Rajveer, who lives nearby accompanied him to the appointment and provided additional information as Karam declined to elaborate and provide details regarding his background. He noted that Karam has become more and more lethargic over the past 2 years since retirement.

Karam recently celebrated his 50th wedding anniversary to Paramdeep. Karam has three children, ages 30 to 42, who are professionally accomplished, all having earned graduate degrees and living independently. All are married with children. Karam expressed pride when stating that he has five grandchildren.

Karam is highly educated, having obtained a doctorate in epidemiology before his immigration to the United States with his family in 1975 at age 35. He worked as an academic for 35 years, teaching at a well-known university until he retired at the age of 70. He currently maintains emeritus status and has served as a guest lecturer in recent years. Upon retirement, he wanted to give back to the community. He began volunteering at a local community center but, without explanation, stopped going after a few weeks.

Karam is in good health and is currently taking a daily multivitamin. He and his wife exercise daily by taking walks or going on the treadmill during bad weather.

What Is Missing?

To begin, if one is not familiar with the background of the individual's community, that is good place to begin. In the case of Karam, it is especially important given his self-identification as a Sikh man. This would include understanding the general circumstances of immigration and the religious group's history in the United States. A great deal of information can be gleaned quickly through journal articles, texts, and Internet sources, but it is always critical to ask for verification from the client.

As noted by Ahluwalia (in press), Sikhs are a minority in India. There are approximately 25 million Sikhs worldwide and approximately 500,000 Sikhs in the United States. The term *Sikh* refers to seekers of truth. The founder of the religion advocated for the unity of humankind and the need to fight against oppression (Singh, 1998). Outward symbols of Sikhism for men and women include *kes* (uncut hair), with men covering their head with a turban and women either using a *chuni* (headscarf) or else not covering their head. Turbans are considered to be private and not to be removed by anyone else other than the wearer (Ahluwalia & Pelletteire, 2010).

Historical context. In 1947, the partition of what is now India and Pakistan led to a mass exodus in which Sikhs and Hindus fled from Pakistan to India, whereas Muslims left India for the Islamic state of Pakistan. The loss of human life during this time period included 1 million Hindu, Sikhs, and Muslims. In 1984, the Indian army attacked the Golden Temple, the most sacred site for Sikhs, and killed a number of innocent members of this community. In retaliation, two Sikh bodyguards killed the prime minister. During the unchecked Delhi riots that followed, Sikhs were targeted and approximately 4,000 were killed.

Moving ahead. Equipped with this information, the psychologist proceeded to talk with Karam about his experiences, asking targeted questions based on the information she had obtained. Karam responded to these questions and engaged in discussion with the examiner around his childhood experiences. He discussed at length his early memories during partition and the violence he observed at the age of 7. Karam became tearful as he recalled the dead bodies and half-naked women that he later learned had been raped. He told the examiner that his wife knew of these incidents, but they had never spoken specifically about these memories with his family because "what good would it do to talk about them?"

After immigrating to the United States, Karam noted that all of his time was spent earning a living to support his family and building a career that has earned him respect. He felt safe in America and felt that he was able to leave those painful memories behind him. Years later, Karam recalled reading about what was happening to his family and community after the attack on the Golden Temple in 1984. "I could not believe what I was reading," he said. Though it was painful to realize what was happening in India, "I felt that I was safe in the U.S."

Karam became agitated when speaking about September 11 and how this event changed how he viewed America:

> My colleagues at the university looked at me kind of funny. Some of them had been my friends for so long but I could sense a change. Some suggested I take the turban off because it seems irrelevant in this era and was just causing difficulty for me. I wanted to ask them, "Do you think I'm a terrorist?" I read about how Sikhs were experiencing overt discrimination, harassment, and violence, but that did not happen to me in that way. After a few weeks, I finally had a talk with some of my colleagues and when I confronted them, they apologized. Life went on but it was never quite the same.

Karam retired in 2009 and started doing volunteer work at the local community center. "I thought it would be a good way to spend my time to give to others. I enjoyed working with young people at the university." Karam expressed disbelief as he noted, "I was so shocked by the ignorance that confronted me there." He went on to describe the racist and cruel things that he was exposed to:

> Someone left me notes saying, "terrorist go home" on my desk. At first, I let it go but then it got worse. One of the youngsters tried to grab my turban and I felt someone try to push me down the stairs. I didn't feel safe there anymore. In fact, I didn't feel safe anywhere.

Karam left the community center after volunteering for only a few months.

The Evaluation

Karam obtained a 145 full scale IQ with nearly all subtest scores in the superior range. A relatively lower subtest score was noted on the Digits Forward/Backward assessing short-term memory and working memory. His motor processing was also relatively slow as noted on the symbol search subtest.

The MMPI-2 revealed elevations on Scales 1 (Hypochondriasis), 2 (Depression), and 4 (Psychopathic Deviate). Karam endorsed specific items that indicated anger directed toward others as well as himself.

On the TAT, themes of anger and sadness were noted as well as a sense of overall frustration. In response to a picture with a boy and a violin, Karam responded.

> The boy must practice the violin so that that he can be a good musician. The best . . . he does this because he wants to be successful. So he practices and practices and becomes the best in his school. His parents are so proud of him. He is able to support his family. He wins awards and people pay him a lot of money to give concerts. People just like to be with him because he is so good.
>
> [How does the story end?]
>
> The boy grows up and the people that he thought were his friends decide that he isn't as good as they thought he was. They move on to focus on other violinists who are younger. When he confronts them for not supporting him, they turn against him and he never plays in a concert again. They were not true friends.

On the Rorschach, Karam's responses were sparse, focusing primarily on form with limited use of other dimensions (e.g., color, movement). He did not respond to the color cards with the exception of one that contained the color red, which he identified as "bloodshed."

The Interpretation

Integrating the background information with the test results provides a snapshot of Karam's life as he

sees it at this current time. What is significant is his recollection of early traumatic events in his life (i.e., partition as a young boy) that he has not spoken about with his family. These memories are becoming more salient given the relatively more recent experiences he has had dealing with racism and discrimination in his workplace (subtle) and at the community center (overt). Working in an academic setting, although more difficult since September 11, sheltered him to some extent from the reports of violence and discrimination against Sikhs in New York City after the terrorist attacks. He was able to confront colleagues that he had known as friends about how they were treating him and received an apology. At the community center, however, he came face to face with overt racism and felt threatened by adolescents who he did not know. Therefore, it was less likely that he could confront them directly given that they had no investment in a relationship with him. Karam experienced his world as unsafe, unpredictable, and unfair. In light of this information, the score elevations on the MMPI-2 and themes derived on the TAT can be understood in light of Karam's experiences. Rather than indicators of psychopathology, they represent more natural outcomes based on his context.

Test scores highlight his superior intelligence with relative losses in short-term memory and working memory because of his feelings of lethargy and depression. His MMPI-2 scores reflect his disappointments, anger, and frustration at himself and those around him. His TAT stories reflect his growing disappointment with the world at large and his acceptance of outcomes in life that are bad despite hard work and initial success. Similarly, Karam's Rorchach responses do not reflect human engagement and his only response to color as "bloodshed" reflects his experiences of trauma especially those he witnessed as a young child. Karam may be engaging in somaticization of his psychological symptoms characterized by joint pain and headaches.

Our goal in presenting this case is to illustrate the importance of context in the interpretation of test results. Historical, political, and economic issues play a vital role in understanding Karam's current situation and making an accurate assessment. Without knowledge of his background and his community's history, the roots of his depression and anger would be difficult to ascertain.

RECOMMENDATIONS FOR BEST PRACTICES FROM A COUNSELING PSYCHOLOGY PERSPECTIVE

This chapter has provided an overview of the foundations of assessment in counseling psychology. Although many of the assessment topics are applicable to all psychological disciplines (e.g., counseling, clinical, school), the goal of understanding individuals from a normative perspective is paramount in counseling psychology. Assisting the individual to achieve a better quality of life, alleviate distress, and combat maladjustment are clearly within the purview of our field. Understanding the complex nature of the assessment process—that is, establishing the relationship with the examinee, identifying and understanding the problem to be addressed in the evaluation, selecting and administering the most appropriate instruments, and finally making sense of the results so that they benefit the individual is the core of our practice. It is critical that counseling psychologists be well trained and competent in the art of assessment as "the goal of any examiner is to be better than the tests he or she uses" (Kaufman, 1990, p. 24). The complexities of the process cannot be underestimated. One must be knowledgeable, shrewd, and astute to fully master this important mainstay of our practice.

The sheer increase in the number of measures currently available to an evaluator has never been higher. Understanding the complex network of variables that can affect the results of any test is critical. Although more sophisticated test development practices (e.g., census-based standardization samples, expert reviews) are now followed with more information provided regarding sampling characteristics (e.g., mean scores and standard deviations by racial and ethnic group), it remains critical that counseling psychologists attend to variables that may affect the assessment process. We have covered a number of these in this chapter (e.g., racial identity, ethnic identity, language, acculturation, SES, disability status, and sexual orientation), but there may be other contextual variables that have yet to be uncovered given

the changing landscape of psychology and necessary globalization (e.g., international) of our practice.

Our discussion has highlighted the limitations of our knowledge base. The continual reliance on standardized measures as indicators of accountability (e.g., high-stakes testing) and gatekeepers of future opportunity is misguided and problematic. Although technology has enabled us to increase the sophistication with which we examine the psychometric properties of our assessment tools, appropriate application in real-life settings is critical. Computerized scoring and report-writing software programs are limited in what background information about the individual can be integrated into the results. The controversies that have evolved surrounding the testing enterprise attest to the challenges of this burgeoning practice. As counseling psychologists, we must continue to advocate for state-of-the-art test development practices and for examination of the role of contextual and test-related variables that can affect the assessment process.

We offer the following as specific recommendations for counseling psychologists engaged in the assessment process:

1. Advocate for greater attention to cultural and contextual factors in the development and restandardization of measures. Issues of cultural validity must be addressed as a part of the test development process.
2. Enter into the assessment process with an understanding of one's own strengths and limitations related to the assessment process with particular clients from diverse backgrounds.
3. Gather comprehensive background information and consider the client's context to ensure relevant interpretation of test results.
4. Question the assumptions underlying the theoretical foundation and cultural loading of measures being considered for usage and their appropriateness with particular clients.
5. Be aware of the strengths and limitations of selected measures in light of the unique circumstances of each client.
6. Be cautious when utilizing computerized administration, scoring, and interpretation programs because they often do not take into

consideration all demographic information and life experiences of the individual being assessed.

7. Ensure that translators and interpreters engaged in the assessment process are adequately trained.

8. Highlight any modifications that were made during the assessment process to provide opportunities for greater understanding of the individual being assessed (e.g., testing-the-limits).

9. Look beyond the findings of high-stakes tests to understand results in context.

10. Allow clients and other stakeholders an opportunity to comment on overall findings, including their perspectives on the assessment process.

References

Ahluwalia, M. K. (in press). Holding my breath: The experience of being Sikh after 9/11. *Traumatology*.

Ahluwalia, M. K. (2008). Multicultural issues in computer-based assessment. In L. A. Suzuki & J. G. Ponterotto (Eds.), *Handbook of multicultural assessment: Clinical, psychological, and educational applications* (3rd ed., pp. 92–106). San Francisco, CA: Sage.

Ahluwalia, M. K., & Pellettiere, L. (2010). Sikh men post 9/11: Misidentification, discrimination, and coping. *Asian American Journal of Psychology, 1*, 303–314. doi:10.1037/a0022156

Allen, J., & Dana, R. H. (2004). Methodological issues in cross-cultural and multicultural Rorschach research. *Journal of Personality Assessment, 82*, 189–206. doi:10.1207/s15327752jpa8202_7

American Educational Research Association, American Psychological Association, & the National Council on Measurement and Education. (1999). *The standards for educational and psychological testing.* Washington, DC: American Educational Research Association.

American Psychiatric Association. (2000). *Diagnostic and statistical manual of mental disorders* (4th ed., text revision). Washington, DC: Author.

American Psychological Association. (2000). Guidelines for psychotherapy with lesbian, gay, and bisexual clients. *American Psychologist, 55*, 1440–1451. doi:10.1037/0003-066X.55.12.1440

American Psychological Association. (2002). *Guidelines on multicultural education, training, research, practice, and organizational change for psychologists.* Washington, DC: Author.

American Psychological Association. (2009). *Guidelines and principles for accreditation of programs in professional psychology.* Retrieved from http://www.apa.org/ed/accreditation/about/policies/guiding-principles.pdf

American Psychological Association. (2010). *Ethical principles of psychologists and code of conduct (2002, Amended June 1, 2010).* Retrieved from http://www.apa.org/ethics/code/index.aspx

Armenta, B. E. (2010). Stereotype boost and stereotype threat effects: The moderating role of ethnic identification. *Cultural Diversity and Ethnic Minority Psychology, 16*, 94–98. doi:10.1037/a0017564

Aronson, J. (2002). *Improving academic achievement: Impact of psychological factors on education* (pp. 279–301). San Diego, CA: Academic Press. doi:10.1016/B978-012064455-1/50017-8

Assessment of Competency Benchmarks Work Group. (2007, June). *Assessment of Competency Benchmarks Work Group: A developmental model for defining and measuring competence in professional psychology.* Retrieved from http://www.psychtrainingcouncils.org/pubs/Competency%20Benchmarks.pdf

Baker, F. M., & Bell, C. C. (1999). Issues in the psychiatric treatment of Blacks. *Psychiatric Services, 50*, 362–368.

Barry, D. T. (2002). An ethnic identity scale for East Asian immigrants. *Journal of Immigrant Health, 4*, 87–94. doi:10.1023/A:1014598509380

Bellak, L. (1975). *The Thematic Apperception Test, the Children's Apperception Test, and the Senior Apperception Technique in clinical use* (3rd ed.). New York, NY: Grune & Stratton.

Berg-Cross, L., & Chinen, R. T. (1995). Multicultural training models and the Person in culture interview. In J. G. Ponterotto, J. M. Casas, L. A. Suzuki, & C. M. Alexander (Eds.), *Handbook of multicultural counseling* (pp. 333–356). Thousand Oaks, CA: Sage.

Berry, J. W., Kim, U., Minde, T., & Mok, D. (1987). Comparative studies of acculturative stress. *The International Migration Review, 21*, 490–511. doi:10.2307/2546607

Betz, N. E. (1993). Issues in the use of ability and interest measures with women. *Journal of Career Assessment, 1*, 217–232. doi:10.1177/106907279300100302

Bovaird, J. A., & Römhild, A. (2010). High Stakes Testing. In C. C. Clauss-Ehlers (Ed.), *Encyclopedia of cross-cultural school psychology* (pp. 504–507). New York, NY: Springer.

Brown, L. S. (1990). Taking account of gender in the clinical assessment interview. *Professional Psychology: Research and Practice, 21*, 12–17. doi:10.1037/0735-7028.21.1.12

Buck, J. N., Warren, W. L., Jolles, I., Wench, S. L., & Hammer, E. F. (1946–1993). *H-T-P: House–Tree–Person projective technique.* Los Angeles, CA: Western Psychological Services.

Butcher, J. N. (1987). Computerized clinical and personality assessment using the MMPI. In J. N. Butcher (Ed.), *Computerized psychological assessment* (pp. 161–197). New York, NY: Basic Books.

Butcher, J. N., Dahlstrom, W. G., Graham, J. R., Tellegen, A., & Kaemmer, B. (1989). *Minnesota Multiphasic Personality Inventory–2 (MMPI-2) manual for administration and scoring.* Minneapolis: University of Minnesota Press.

Butcher, J. N., Perry, J., & Dean, B. L. (2009). Computer-based assessment. In J. N. Butcher (Ed.), *Oxford handbook of clinical and personality assessment* (pp. 163–187). New York, NY: Oxford University Press.

Castro, Y., Gordon, K. H., Brown, J. S., Anestis, J. C., & Joiner, T. E., Jr. (2008). Examination of racial differences on the MMPI-2 clinical and restructures clinical scales in an outpatient sample. *Assessment, 15,* 277–286. doi:10.1177/1073191107312735

Chernin, J., Holden, J. M., & Chandler, C. (1997). Bias in psychological assessment: Heterosexism. *Measurement and Evaluation in Counseling and Development, 30,* 68–76.

Cohen, R. J., & Swerdlik, M. E. (1999). *Psychological testing and assessment: An introduction to tests and measurements* (4th ed.). Mountain View, CA: Mayfield.

Costantino, G., Malgady, R., & Rogler, L. H. (1988). *Tell-me-a-story (TEMAS).* Beverly Hills, CA: Western Psychological Services.

Croteau, J. M., Bieschke, K. J., Fassinger, R. E., & Manning, J. L. (2008). Counseling psychology and sexual orientation: History, selective trends, and future directions. In S. D. Brown & R. W. Lent (Eds.), *Handbook of counseling psychology* (4th ed., pp. 194–211). New York, NY: Wiley.

Cuéllar, L., Arnold, B., & Maldonado, R. (1995). An acculturation scale for Mexican Americans–II: A revision of the original ARSMA scale. *Hispanic Journal of Behavioral Sciences, 17,* 275–304. doi:10.1177/07399863950173001

Dana, R. H. (Ed.). (2000). *Handbook of cross-cultural and multicultural personality assessment.* Mahwah, NJ: Erlbaum.

Dana, R. H. (2008). Clinical diagnoses in multicultural populations. In L. A. Suzuki & J. G. Ponterotto (Eds.), *Handbook of multicultural assessment: Clinical, psychological, and educational applications* (3rd ed., pp. 107–131). San Francisco, CA: Sage.

Dillon, S. (2010, December 7). Top test scores from Shanghai stun educators. *New York Times: Education.* Retrieved from http://www.nytimes.com/2010/12/07/education/07education.html?_r=1

Donnay, D. A. C., Morris, M. L., Schaubhut, N. A., & Thompson, R. C. (2005). *Strong Interest Inventory manual: Research, development and strategies for interpretation.* Mountain View, CA: CPP.

Eisman, E., Dies, R., Finn, S. E., Eyde, L., Kay, G. G., Kubiszyn, T., . . . Moreland, K. (2000). Problems and limitations in the use of psychological assessment in contemporary healthcare delivery. *Professional Psychology: Research and Practice, 31,* 131–140. doi:10.1037/0735-7028.31.2.131

Esquivel, G. B., Oades-Sese, G. V., & Olitzky, S. L. (2008). Multicultural issues in projective assessment. In L. A. Suzuki & J. G. Ponterotto (Eds.), *Handbook of multicultural assessment: Clinical, psychological, and educational applications* (3rd ed., pp. 346–374). San Francisco, CA: Sage.

Exner, J. E. (2001). *A Rorschach workbook for the Comprehensive System* (5th ed.). Asheville, NC: Rorschach Workshops.

Exner, J. E. (2003). *The Rorschach: A Comprehensive System* (4th ed.). Hoboken, NJ: John Wiley.

Eyde, L. D., Robertson, G. J., & Krug, S. E. (2010). *Responsible test use: Case studies for assessing human behavior* (2nd ed.). Washington, DC: American Psychological Association.

Fabri, M. (2008). Cultural adaptation and translation of assessment instruments for diverse populations: The use of the Harvard trauma questionnaire in Rwanda. In L. A. Suzuki & J. G. Ponterotto (Eds.), *Handbook of multicultural assessment: Clinical, psychological, and educational applications* (3rd ed., pp. 195–219). San Francisco, CA: Sage.

Fischer, A. R., & Moradi, B. (2001). Racial and ethnic identity: Recent developments and needed directions. In J. G. Ponterotto, J. M. Casas, L. A. Suzuki, & C. M. Alexander (Eds.), *Handbook of multicultural counseling* (2nd ed., pp. 341–370). Thousand Oaks, CA: Sage.

Flanagan, D. P., Ortiz, S. O., & Alfonso, V. C. (2007). *Essentials of cross-battery assessment* (2nd ed.). San Francisco, CA: Wiley.

Flores, L. Y., & Obasi, E. M. (2003). Positive psychological assessment in an increasingly diverse world. In S. J. Lopez & C. R. Snyder (Eds.), *Positive psychological assessment: A handbook of models and measures* (pp. 41–54). Washington, DC: American Psychological Association. doi:10.1037/10612-003

Fotso, J. C., & Kuate-Defo, K. B. (2005). Measuring socioeconomic status in health research in developing countries: Should we be focusing on households, communities or both? *Social Indicators Research, 72,* 189–237. doi:10.1007/s11205-004-5579-8

Fouad, N. A., & Byars-Winston, A. (2005). Cultural context of career choice: Meta analysis of race/ethnicity differences. *The Career Development Quarterly, 53,* 223–233.

Frazier, P., Oishi, S., & Steger, M. (2003). Assessing optimal human functioning. In W. B. Walsh (Ed.), *Counseling psychology and optimal human functioning* (pp. 251–278). Mahwah, NJ: Erlbaum.

Friedman, A. F., Lewak, R., Nichols, D. S., & Webb, J. T. (2001). *Psychological assessment with the MMPI-2.* Mahwah, NJ: Erlbaum.

Frisby, C. L. (2008). Academic achievement testing for culturally diverse groups. In L. A. Suzuki & J. G. Ponterotto (Eds.), *Handbook of multicultural assessment: Clinical, psychological and educational applications* (2nd ed., pp. 520–541). San Francisco, CA: Jossey-Bass.

Gainor, K. A. (2001). Vocational assessment with culturally diverse populations. In L. A. Suzuki, J. G. Ponterotto, & P. J. Meller (Eds.), *Handbook of multicultural assessment: Clinical, psychological and educational applications* (pp. 169–189). San Francisco, CA: Jossey-Bass.

Ganellen, R. J. (2002). Calming the storm: Contemporary use of the Rorschach. *PsycCRITIQUES, 47,* 325–327. doi:10.1037/001141

Garb, H. N., Wood, J. M., Nezworski, M. T., Grove, W. M., & Stejskal, W. J. (2001). Toward a resolution of the Rorschach controversy. *Psychological Assessment, 13,* 433–448. doi:10.1037/1040-3590.13.4.433

Geertz, C. (1973). *The interpretation of cultures: Selected essays by Clifford Geertz.* New York, NY: Basic Books.

Georgas, I., Weiss, L. G., van de Vijver, F. J. R., & Saklofske, D. H. (Eds.). (2003). *Culture and children's intelligence: Cross cultural analysis of the WISC-III.* New York, NY: Academic Press.

Gladwell, M. (2008). *Outliers: The story of success.* New York, NY: Little, Brown.

Goldberger, N. R., & Veroff, J. B. (Eds.). (1995). *The culture and psychology reader.* New York, NY: NYU Press.

Goodenough, F. L., & Harris, D. B. (1950). Studies in the psychology of children's drawings II: 1928–1949. *Psychological Bulletin, 47,* 369–433. doi:10.1037/h0058368

Gough, H. G., & Bradley, P. (2002). *CPITM manual* (3rd ed.). Mountain View, CA: CPP.

Gough, H. G., & Bradley, P. (2005). *CPI 260TM manual.* Mountain View, CA: CPP.

Greene, R. L. (1987). Ethnicity and MMPI performance: A review. *Journal of Consulting and Clinical Psychology, 55,* 497–512. doi:10.1037/0022-006X.55.4.497

Greenfield, P. M. (1997). You can't take it with you: Why ability assessments don't cross cultures. *American Psychologist, 52),* 1115–1124. doi:10.1037/0003-066X.52.10.1115

Grieger, I. (2008). A cultural assessment framework and interview protocol. In L. A. Suzuki & J. G. Ponterotto (Eds.), *Handbook of multicultural assessment: Clinical, psychological, and educational applications* (3rd ed., pp. 132–161). San Francisco, CA: Sage.

Gross, H. S., Herbert, M. R., Knatterud, G. L., & Donner, L. (1969). The effect of race and sex on the variation of diagnosis and disposition. *Journal of Nervous and Mental Disease, 148,* 638–642.

Groth-Marnat, G. (2009). *Handbook of psychological assessment* (5th ed.). Hoboken, NJ: Wiley.

Hall, G. C. N., Bansal, A., & Lopez, I. R. (1999). Ethnicity and psychopathology: A meta analytic review of 31 years of comparative MMPI/MMPI-2 research. *Psychological Assessment, 11,* 186–197. doi:10.1037/1040-3590.11.2.186

Hambleton, R. K., Merenda, P. F., & Spielberger, C. D. (Eds.). (2005). *Adapting educational and psychological tests for cross-cultural assessment.* Mahwah, NJ: Erlbaum.

Harmon, L. W., Hansen, J. C., Borgen, F. H., & Hammer, A. L. (1994). *Strong Interest Inventory: Applications and technical guide.* Stanford, CA: Stanford University Press.

Helms, J. E. (1992). Why is there no study of cultural equivalence in standardized cognitive ability testing? *American Psychologist, 47,* 1083–1101. doi:10.1037/0003-066X.47.9.1083

Helms, J. E. (1995). An update of Helm's White and people of color racial identity models. In J. G. Ponterotto & J. M. Casas (Eds.), *Handbook of multicultural counseling* (pp. 181–198). Thousand Oaks, CA: Sage.

Helms, J. E. (2002). A remedy for the Black–White score disparity. *American Psychologist, 57,* 303–305. doi:10.1037/0003-066X.57.4.303b

Helms, J. E. (2004). The 2003 Leona Tyler Award Address: Making race a matter of individual differences within groups. *The Counseling Psychologist, 32,* 473–483. doi:10.1177/0011000003262801

Helms, J. S., & Carter, R. T. (1990). Development of the White racial identity attitude inventory. In J. E. Helms (Ed.), *Black and White racial identity: Theory, research and practice* (pp. 67–80). Westport, CT: Greenwood.

Helms, J. S., & Parham, T. A. (1996). The Racial Identity Attitudes Scale. In R. L. Jones (Ed.), *Handbook of tests and measurements for Black populations* (Vol. 1, pp. 167–174). Hampton, VA: Cobb & Henry.

Heppner, P. P. (1988). *The Problem Solving Inventory: Manual.* Palo Alto, CA: Consulting Psychologists Press.

Heppner, P. P., Witty, T. E., & Dixon, W. A. (2004). Problem-solving appraisal and human adjustment:

A review of 20 years of research using the Problem-Solving Inventory. *The Counseling Psychologist, 32,* 344–428. doi:10.1177/0011000003262793

Hill, J. S., Pace, T. M., & Robbins, R. R. (2010). Decolonizing personality assessment and honoring indigenous voices: A critical examination of the MMPI-2. *Cultural Diversity and Ethnic Minority Psychology, 16,* 16–25. doi:10.1037/a0016110

Hoover, H. D., Dunbar, S. B., & Frisbie, D. A. (2003). *Iowa Test of Basic Skills–Form B.* Rolling Meadows, IL: Riverside.

Hyde, J. S. (2005). The gender similarities hypothesis. *American Psychologist, 60,* 581–592. doi:10.1037/0003-066X.60.6.581

Israel, T. (2004). Conversations, not categories: The intersection of biracial and bisexual identities. *Women and Therapy, 27,* 173–184. doi:10.1300/J015v27n01_12

Israel, T., Ketz, K., Detrie, P. M., Burke, M. C., & Shulman, J. L. (2003). Identifying counselor competencies for working with lesbian, gay, and bisexual clients. *Journal of Gay and Lesbian Psychotherapy, 7,* 3–21. doi:10.1300/J236v07n04_02

Jackson, M. A., Holder, A. M. B., & Ramage, M. T. (2008). Culturally competent vocational assessment with at-risk adolescents. In L. A. Suzuki & J. G. Ponterotto (Eds.), *Handbook of multicultural assessment: Clinical, psychological and educational applications* (pp. 273–298). San Francisco, CA: Jossey-Bass.

Johansson, C. B. (1984). *Career Assessment Inventory: The enhanced version.* San Antonio, TX: Pearson.

Johnson, S. C., & Arbona, C. (2006). The relation of ethnic identity, and race-related stress among African American college students. *Journal of Counseling and Development, 47,* 495–507.

Kaufman, A. S. (1990). *Assessing adolescent and adult intelligence.* Needham Heights, MA: Allyn & Bacon.

Kestemberg, L. B., Silverman, M. B. T., & Santandreu, N. G. (2003). Gender differences in neuropsychological functioning. In M. Kopala & M. A. Keitel (Eds.), *Handbook of counseling women* (pp. 86–105). Thousand Oaks, CA: Sage.

Kim, B. S. K., & Abreu, J. M. (2001). Acculturation measurement: Theory, current instruments, and future directions. In J. G. Ponterotto, J. M. Casas, L. A. Suzuki, & C. M. Alexander (Eds.), *Handbook of multicultural counseling* (2nd ed., pp. 394–424). Thousand Oaks, CA: Sage.

Knauss, L. K. (2001). Ethical issues in psychological assessment in school settings. *Journal of Personality Assessment, 77,* 231–241. doi:10.1207/S15327752JPA7702_06

Krishnamurthy, R., VandeCreek, L., Kaslow, N. J., Tazeau, Y. N., Mivile, M. L., Kerns, R., . . . Benton, S. A. (2004). Achieving competency in psychological assessment: Directions for education and training. *Journal of Clinical Psychology, 60,* 725–739. doi:10.1002/jclp.20010

Kroeber, A. L., & Kluckhohn, C. (1963). *Culture: A critical review of concepts and definitions.* Cambridge, MA: Harvard University Press.

Kwan, K. L. K., & Maestas, M. L. (2008). MMPI-2 and MCMI-III performances of non-White people in the United States: What we (don't) know and where we can go from here. In L. A. Suzuki & J. G. Ponterotto (Eds.), *Handbook of multicultural assessment: Clinical, psychological, and educational applications* (3rd ed., pp. 425–446). San Francisco, CA: Sage.

Lawson, W. B., Hepler, N., Holladay, J., & Cuffel, B. (1994). Race as a factor in inpatient and outpatient admissions and diagnosis. *Hospital and Community Psychiatry, 45,* 72–74.

Lilienfeld, S. O., Wood, J. W., & Garb, H. N. (2000). The scientific status of projective techniques. *Psychological Science in the Public Interest, 1,* 27–66.

Lopez, E. C. (2010). Interpreters. In C. C. Clauss-Ehlers (Ed.), *Encyclopedia of cross-cultural school psychology* (pp. 547–553). New York, NY: Springer.

Lopez, S. J., & Snyder, C. R. (2003a). The future of positive psychological assessment: Making a difference. In S. J. Lopez & C. R. Snyder (Eds.), *Positive psychological assessment: A handbook of models and measures* (pp. 461–468). Washington, DC: American Psychological Association. doi:10.1037/10612-029

Lopez, S. J., & Snyder, C. R. (Eds.). (2003b). *Positive psychological assessment: A handbook of models and measures.* Washington, DC: American Psychological Association. doi:10.1037/10612-000

Lopez, S. J., Snyder, C. R., & Rasmussen, H. N. (2003). Striking a vital balance: Developing a complementary focus on human weakness and strength through positive psychological assessment. In S. J. Lopez & C. R. Snyder (Eds.), *Positive psychological assessment: A handbook of models and measures* (pp. 3–20). Washington, DC: American Psychological Association. doi:10.1037/10612-001

Lopez, S. R. (1989). Patient variable biases in clinical judgment: Conceptual overview and methodological considerations. *Psychological Bulletin, 106,* 184–203.

Lopez, S. R., & Guarnaccia, P. J. J. (2000). Cultural psychopathology: Uncovering the social world of mental illness. *Annual Review of Psychology, 51,* 571–598. doi:10.1146/annurev.psych.51.1.571

Lopez, S. R., O'Byrne, K. K., & Petersen, S. (2003). Profiling courage. In S. J. Lopez & C. R. Snyder (Eds.), *Handbook of positive psychological assessment:*

A handbook of models and measures (pp. 185–197). Washington, DC: American Psychological Association. doi:10.1037/10612-012

Mainstream science on intelligence. (1994, December 13). *The Wall Street Journal*, p. A18.

Malcarne, V. L., Chavira, D. A., Fernandez, S., & Liu, P. J. (2006). The Scale of Ethnic Experience: Development and psychometric properties. *Journal of Personality Assessment, 86*, 150–161. doi:10.1207/s15327752jpa8602_04

Malgady, R. G., Rogler, L. H., & Costantino, G. (1987). Ethnocultural and linguistic bias in mental health evaluation of Hispanics. *American Psychologist, 42*, 228–234. doi:10.1037/0003-066X.42.3.228

Mapou, R. I. (2009). *Adult learning disabilities and ADHD: Research informed assessment*. New York, NY: Oxford University Press.

McGoldrick, M., Giordano, J., & Garcia-Preto, N. (2005). *Ethnicity and family therapy*. New York, NY: Guilford Press.

McGrew, K. S., & Flanagan, D. P. (1998). *The Intelligence Test Desk Reference (ITDR): Gf-Gc Cross Battery Assessment*. Boston, MA: Allyn & Bacon.

McShane, D. (1982). A review of scores of American Indian children on the Wechsler Intelligence Scale. *White Cloud Journal of American Indian Mental Health, 2*, 18–22.

McShane, D. (1989, April). *Testing and American Indians, Alaska Natives*. Paper presented at a symposium sponsored by the National Commission on Testing and Public Policy, Albuquerque, NM.

Millon, T., Millon, C., Davis, R., & Grossman, S. (2006). *Millon Clinical Multiaxial Inventory-III manual* (3rd ed.). Minneapolis, MN: National Computer Systems Pearson.

Murray, H. A. (1971). *Thematic Apperception Test*. Cambridge, MA: Harvard Press. (Original work published 1943)

Mustard, C. A., & Frolich, N. (1995). Socioeconomic status and the health of the population. *Medical Care, 33*(12), DS43–DS54.

Myers, I. B., McCaulley, M. H., Quenk, N. L., & Hammer, A. L. (1998). *MBTI manual: A guide to the development and use of the Myers-Briggs Type Indicator* (3rd ed.). Palo Alto, CA: Consulting Psychologists Press.

National Council on Interpreting in Health Care. (2004). *Code of ethics for interpreters in health care*. Retrieved from http://www.ncihc.org/mc/page.do?sitePageID=57768

Nisbett, R. E. (2009). *Intelligence and how to get it: Why schools and cultures count*. New York, NY: Norton.

Oakes, J. M., & Rossi, P. H. (2003). The measurement of SES in health research: Current practice and steps

toward a new approach. *Social Science and Medicine, 56*, 769–784. doi:10.1016/S0277-9536(02)00073-4

Organisation for Economic Co-Operation and Development. (2011). *Programme for international student assessment*. Retrieved from http://www.pisa.occd.org/pages/0,3417%en_32252351_3223509_1_1_1_1.00.html

Oster, G. D., & Gould, P. (1987). *Using drawings in assessment and therapy: A guide for mental health professionals*. New York, NY: Brunner/Mazel.

Pace, T. M., Robbins, R. R., Choney, S. K., Hill, J. S., Lacey, K., & Blair, G. (2006). A cultural-contextual perspective on the validity of the MMPI-2 with American Indians. *Cultural Diversity and Ethnic Minority Psychology, 12*, 320–333. doi:10.1037/1099-9809.12.2.320

Park, J. (2005). Learning in a new computerized testing system. *Journal of Educational Psychology, 97*, 436–443. doi:10.1037/0022-0663.97.3.436

Pearson Education, Inc. (2009). *Wechsler Individual Achievement Test* (3rd ed.). San Antonio, TX: Pearson.

Pearson Assessments. (2003). *Stanford Achievement Test series* (10th ed.). Retrieved from http://www.pearsonassessments.com/HAIWEB/Cultures/en-us/Productdetail.htm?Pid=SAT10C

Pedersen, P. (1999). Culture-centered interventions as a fourth dimension of psychology. In P. Pedersen (Ed.), *Multiculturalism as a fourth force* (pp. 3–18). New York, NY: Sage.

Phinney, J. S. (1992). The multigroup ethnic identity measure: A new scale for use with diverse groups. *Journal of Adolescent Research, 7*, 156–176. doi:10.1177/074355489272003

Reynolds, C. R. (1982a). Construct and predictive bias. In R. A. Berk (Ed.), *Handbook of methods for detecting test bias* (pp. 199–227). Baltimore, MD: Johns Hopkins University Press.

Reynolds, C. R. (1982b). The problem of bias in psychological assessment. In C. R. Reynolds & T. B. Gutkin (Eds.), *The handbook of school psychology* (pp. 178–208). New York, NY: Wiley.

Reynolds, C. R., & Lowe, P. A. (2009). The problem of bias in psychological assessment. In T. B. Gutkin & C. R. Reynolds (Eds.), *The handbook of school psychology* (4th ed., pp. 332–374). Hoboken, NJ: Wiley.

Rivera, L. M. (2008). Aculturation and multicultural assessment: Issues, trends, and practice. In L. A. Suzuki & J. G. Ponterotto (Eds.), *Handbook of multicultural assessment: Clinical, psychological, and educational applications* (3rd ed., pp. 73–91). San Francisco, CA: Jossey-Bass.

Roach, A. T., & Elliott, S. N. (2006). The influence of access to general education curriculum or alternate assessment performance of students with significant cognitive disabilities. *Educational Evaluation and Policy Analysis, 28,* 181–194. doi:10.3102/01623737028002181

Robin, R. W., Greene, R. L., Albaugh, B., Caldwell, A., & Goldman, D. (2003). Use of the MMPI-2 in American Indians: I. Comparability of the MMPI-2 between two tribes and with the MMPI-2 normative group. *Psychological Assessment, 15,* 351–359. doi:10.1037/1040-3590.15.3.351

Rorschach, H. (1942). *Psychodiagnostics: A diagnostic test based on perception* (3rd ed., B. Kronenberg & P. Lemkau, Trans.). Berne, Switzerland: Hans Huber. (Original work published in 1921)

Ross, M., & Conway, M. (1986). Remembering one's own past: The construction of personal histories. In R. M. Sorrentino & E. T. Higgins (Eds.), *Handbook of motivation and cognition: Foundations of social behavior* (pp. 122–144). New York, NY: Wiley.

Rothblum, E. D. (2000). "Somewhere in Des Moines or San Antonio": Historical perspectives on lesbian, gay, and bisexual health. In R. M. Perez, K. A. DeBord, & K. J. Bieschke (Eds.), *Handbook of counseling and psychotherapy with lesbian, gay, and bisexual clients* (pp. 359–382). Washington, DC: American Psychological Association.

Rotter, J. B., Lah, M. I., & Rafferty, J. E. (1992). *Rotter incomplete sentences blank.* San Antonio, TX: The Psychological Corporation.

Russell, M., & Karol, D. (1994). *The 16PF administrator's manual* (5th ed.). Champaign, IL: Institute for Personality and Ability Testing, Inc.

Sattler, J. M. (1993). *Assessment of children* (3rd ed.). San Diego, CA: Author.

Sattler, J. M. (2008). *Assessment of children: Cognitive foundations* (5th ed.). San Diego, CA: Author.

Sattler, J. M., & Hoge, R. D. (2006). *Assessment of children: Behavioral, social, and clinical foundations* (5th ed.). San Diego, CA: Jerome M. Sattler.

Sellers, R. M., Rowley, S. A. J., Chavous, T. M., Shelton, N. J., & Smith, M. A. (1997). Multidimensional inventory of black identity: A preliminary investigation of reliability and construct validity. *Journal of Personality and Social Psychology, 73,* 805–815. doi:10.1037/0022-3514.73.4.805

Shoeb, M., Weinstein, H., & Mollica, R. (2007). The Harvard Trauma Questionnaire: Adapting a cross-cultural instrument for measuring torture, trauma, and posttraumatic stress disorder in Iraqi refugees. *International Journal of Social Psychiatry, 53,* 447–463. doi:10.1177/0020764007078362

Singh, G. (1998). *A history of the Sikh people (1469–1988).* New Delhi, India: Allied.

Snyderman, M., & Rothman, S. (1988). *The IQ controversy: The media and public policy.* New Brunswick, NJ: Transaction Books.

Society of Counseling Psychology. (n.d.) *About counseling psychologists.* Retrieved from http://www.div17.org/students_defining.html

Steele, C. M., & Aronson, J. (1995). Stereotype threat and intellectual test performance of African Americans. *Journal of Personality and Social Psychology, 69,* 797–811. doi:10.1037/0022-3514.69.5.797

Sternberg, R. J., & Kaufman, J. C. (1998). Human abilities. *Annual Review of Psychology, 49,* 479–502. doi:10.1146/annurev.psych.49.1.479

Strack, K. M., Dunaway, M. H., & Schulenberg, S. E. (2008). On the multicultural utility of the 16PF and the CPI-434 in the United States. In L. A. Suzuki & J. G. Ponterotto (Eds.), *Handbook of multicultural assessment: Clinical, psychological and educational applications* (pp. 375–401). San Francisco, CA: Jossey-Bass.

Suárez-Orozco, C., Suárez-Orozco, M., & Todorova, I. (2008). *Learning in a new land: Immigrant students in American society.* Cambridge, MA: Harvard University Press.

Sue, D. W., Capodilupo, C. M., Torino, G. C., Bucceri, J. M., Holder, A. M. B., Nadal, K. L., & Esquilin, M. (2007). Racial microaggressions in everyday life: Implications for clinical practice. *American Psychologist, 62,* 271–286. doi:10.1037/0003-066X.62.4.271

Sue, D. W., & Sue, D. (1972). Ethnic minorities: Resistance to being researched. *Professional Psychology, 3,* 11–17. doi:10.1037/h0021487

Sue, D. W., & Sue, D. (2003). *Counseling the culturally diverse: Theory and practice* (4th ed.). Hoboken, NJ: Wiley.

Suinn, R. M., Rickard-Figueroa, K., Lew, S., & Vigil, P. (1987). The Suinn-Lew Asian self-identity acculturation scale: An initial report. *Educational and Psychological Measurement, 47,* 401–407. doi:10.1177/0013164487472012

Sundre, D. L. (2001). Review of the test instrument Career Development Inventory (CDI). In J. T. Kapes & E. A. Whitfield (Eds.), *A counselor's guide to career assessment instruments* (4th ed., pp. 323–330). Alexandria, VA: National Career Development Association.

Suzuki, L. A., & Ahluwalia, M. K. (2003). Gender issues in personality, cognitive, and vocational assessment of women. In M. Kopala & M. A. Keitel (Eds.), *Handbook of counseling women* (pp. 119–130). Thousand Oaks, CA: Sage.

Suzuki, L. A., & Ponterotto, J. G. (Eds.). (2008). *Handbook of multicultural assessment: Clinical, psychological and educational applications.* San Francisco, CA: Jossey-Bass.

Suzuki, L. A., Rodriguez, K. H., Onoue, A. M., & Ahluwalia, M. K. (2011, January). *Content analysis of racial identity, ethnic identity, and acculturation measures.* Poster presented at the National Multicultural Conference and Summit, Seattle, WA.

Suzuki, L. A., & Valencia, R. R. (1997). Race/ethnicity and measured intelligence: Educational implications. *American Psychologist, 52,* 1103–1114. doi:10.1037/0003-066X.52.10.1103

Trimble, J. E., Helms, J. E., & Root, M. P. P. (2003). Social and psychological perspectives on ethnic and racial identity. In G. Bernal, J. E. Trimble, A. K. Burlew, & F. T. Leong (Eds.), *Handbook of racial and ethnic minority psychology* (pp. 219–275). Thousand Oaks, CA: Sage.

Tsai, G., & Curbow, B. (2001). The development and validation of the Taiwanese Ethnic ID Scale (TEIS): A "derived etic" approach. *Journal of Immigrant Health, 3,* 199–212. doi:10.1023/A:1012279628385

Tsai, J. L., Ying, Y., & Lee, P. A. (2000). The meaning of "being Chinese" and "being American." *Journal of Cross-Cultural Psychology, 31,* 302–332. doi:10.1177/0022022100031003002

Umaña-Taylor, A. J., Yazedjian, A., & Bámaca-Gómez, M. (2004). Developing the ethnic identity scale using Eriksonian and social identity perspectives. *Identity: An International Journal of Theory and Research, 4,* 9–38. doi:10.1207/S1532706XID0401_2

Urquhart Hagie, M. A., Gallipo, P. L., & Swen, L. (2003). Traditional culture versus traditional assessment for American Indian students: An investigation of potential test item bias. *Assessment for Effective Intervention, 29,* 15–25. doi:10.1177/07372477030 2900103

Utsey, S. O., & Bolden, M. A. (2008). Cross-cultural considerations in quality-of-life assessment. In L. A. Suzuki & J. G. Ponterotto (Eds.), *Handbook of multicultural assessment: Clinical, psychological and educational applications* (3rd ed., pp. 299–317). San Francisco, CA: Sage.

Valencia, R. R., & Suzuki, L. A. (1997). *Intelligence testing and minority students: Foundations, performance factors, and assessment issues.* Thousand Oaks, CA: Sage.

Valencia, R. R., Suzuki, L. A., & Salinas, M. F. (2001). Test bias. In R. R. Valencia & L. A. Suzuki (Eds.), *Intelligence testing and minority students: Foundations, performance factors, and assessment issues* (pp. 111–150). Thousand Oaks, CA: Sage.

van de Vijver, F. J. R., & Phalet, K. (2004). Assessment in a multicultural groups: The role of acculturation. *Applied Psychology: An International Review, 53,* 215–236.

Verdugo, M. A., Schalock, R. L., Keither, K. D., & Stancliffe, R. (2005). Quality of life and its measurement: Important principles and guidelines. *Journal of Intellectual Disability Research, 49,* 707–717. doi:10.1111/j.1365-2788.2005.00739.x

Walsh, W. B. (2003). *Counseling psychology and optimal human functioning.* Mahwah, NJ: Erlbaum.

Wilkinson, G. S., & Robertson, G. J. (2006). *Wide Range Achievement Test–4.* Los Angeles, CA: Western Psychological Services.

Woodcock, R. W., McGrew, K. S., & Mather, N. (2001). *Woodcock-Johnson-III.* Rolling Meadows, IL: Riverside.

Worell, J., & Robinson, D. A. (2009). Issues in clinical assessment with women. In J. N. Butcher (Ed.), *Oxford handbook of personality assessment* (pp. 415–431). New York, NY: Oxford University Press.

World Health Organization. (1992). *The ICD-10 classification of mental and behavioural disorders: Clinical description and diagnostic guidelines.* Geneva, Switzerland: Author.

Zane, N., & Mak, W. (2003). Major approaches to the measurement of acculturation among ethnic minority populations: A content analysis and an alternative empirical strategy. In K. M. Chun, P. B. Organista, & G. Marin (Eds.), *Acculturation: Advances in theory, measurement, and applied research* (pp. 39–60). Washington, DC: American Psychological Association.

Zhou, Q., Valiente, C., & Eisenberg, N. (2003). Empathy and its measurement. In S. Lopez & C. R. Snyder (Eds.), *Positive psychological assessment: A handbook of models and measures* (pp. 269–284). Washington, DC: American Psychological Association. doi:10.1037/10612-017

PART II

THEORIES AND RESEARCH

CHAPTER 8

PSYCHOTHERAPY PROCESS AND OUTCOME RESEARCH IN COUNSELING PSYCHOLOGY

Michael J. Scheel and Collie W. Conoley

In writing a review of process and outcome research in counseling psychology, we begin by first establishing parameters that identify process and outcome research within the field of counseling psychology. To this end, we have chosen the contextual–common factors perspective, the integration of cultural context, and a focus on client strengths as three areas oriented toward counseling psychology. The contextual model of therapy organizes our review, best described as a review of the extant literature within the parameters we have designated. The reader will not find, for instance, the inclusion of research examining the effectiveness of specific treatments for a specific diagnostic category because that conceptualization of process and outcome research would fly in the face of a common factors perspective and would be, in our opinion, context stripping.

We start with a description of the contextual model and then move to a four-component common factors framework to cover our review of process and outcome research. Cultural context and a strength orientation are incorporated into our common factors framework, combined with more traditionally thought-of psychotherapy processes like the working alliance and therapist empathy. We end our review with a discussion of research methods and offer suggestions of which roads to take in the future pursuit of psychotherapy research oriented toward the field of counseling psychology.

THE CONTEXTUAL MODEL OF PSYCHOTHERAPY

The character of counseling psychology fits well with the contextual model of psychotherapy. Treatment adjustments are made to fit the context presented by the client, rather than a prescriptive approach devoid of context except for the client's problem. The contextual model and the common factors model are not the same although overlap is evident. The contextual model provides a frame for therapy, whereas common factors are the processes of therapy. Wampold (2001) described the contextual model as a healing context guided by the characteristics of the client. In contrast, he explains the common factors model as referring to a set of elements common to and contributing across specific approaches no matter the client or the context. Each common factor contributes to a piece of the outcome pie in every approach to therapy. The working alliance is an example of a contextually derived common factor. Although the working alliance exists across all treatments, the working alliance depends on the therapist's ability to match treatment to the client's context and the client's openness and ability to accept the alliance.

The contextual model as proposed by Frank and Frank (1991) in their seminal work, *Persuasion and Healing: A Comparative Study of Psychotherapy*, and later emphasized by Wampold (2001, 2007), offers an explanation of contextual psychotherapy as a convergence of the participants, client and therapist. Within a healing setting, the therapist and client

DOI: 10.1037/13754-008
APA Handbook of Counseling Psychology: Vol. 1. Theories, Research, and Methods, Nadya A. Fouad (Editor-in-Chief)

accept the rationale for a particular treatment (i.e., treatment coherency) and the therapeutic strategies embedded within that treatment. The therapist offers new learning in the form of culturally fitting interventions. The client responds through engagement in an emotionally charged and confiding relationship with the therapist. All elements contribute to the development of the therapeutic relationship. Overall, the relationship might be thought of as the product of an interaction of all client and counselor inputs.

The contextual model is primarily differentiated from the medical model (Orlinsky, 2010; Wampold, 2007) by the contextual model fitting the client and the client's context, whereas a medical model treatment fits the diagnosis or problem label. The medical model is decontextualized in that a therapeutic procedure is applied to an emotional or behavioral disorder not the client. Medical model treatment operates under the assumption that an optimal treatment exists for each disorder. In arguing for an alternative to the medical model, Orlinsky (2010) wrote that the most effective form of therapy is "what works." He asserted that what works matches the client's context. The client accepts the approach as something that can be of help, thus the client becomes more hopeful and more motivated to be involved with the treatment. Orlinsky (2010) called the what-works method the alternate paradigm to the medical treatment model. Wampold (2007) stated that the medical model is designed to directly affect the biological system. This orientation assumes a direct effect circumventing contextual mediators. In comparison, he explained that the contextual model's healing practices are "embedded in a healing context, rely on the interaction between the healer and the recipient of the treatment, and involve the interpretation of events and their meaning" (p. 861). Wampold asserted that cultural context and client expectations and preferences, although not ignored entirely in medical model treatment, are not its top priority. Instead, the medical model assumes an outcome based on the influence of a medical or therapeutic procedure.

A flaw in applying the medical model to psychological interventions emerges when identifying the active curative ingredients in an intervention. For example, the curative ingredient in eye movement desensitization and reprocessing (EMDR) for the successful treatment of posttraumatic stress disorder (PTSD) is puzzling. The American Psychological Association (APA) Presidential Task Force on Evidence-Based Practice (APA, 2006) labeled EMDR as possessing strong research but also as controversial (e.g., Devilly & Spence, 1999; Wilson, Becker, & Tinker, 1995). Controversial because although findings in the 1990s showed EMDR to be effective for PTSD, a meta-analysis later demonstrated EMDR to be no more effective than other exposure-based treatments (Davidson & Parker, 2001). The active ingredient in the treatment was thought to be exposure. We posit that even with exposure treatment for PTSD, other active ingredients may be unaccounted for as well, such as a strong working alliance, client readiness, hope and involvement in the change process, and therapist skill and hope for the client.

Greenberg and Watson (2006) asserted that "clinicians need to know the active processes that lead to change, not just the specific steps to follow from a manual" (p. 82). The question of how psychotherapy works is the crucial process research question of the 21st century. Greenberg and Watson argued for a contextual model, stating, "It is not that therapists engage in behaviors that determine therapeutic effects as much as it is how the client responds to those behaviors and what processes the behaviors initiate in the client" (p. 82). Furthermore, Greenberg and Watson promoted context-sensitive process research when stating, "effective treatment is systematically responsive; therapists' and clients' behavior is influenced by emerging contexts, including perceptions of each other's characteristics and behavior" (p. 84). We now turn to a discussion of what is known about common factors in psychotherapy research and treatment.

COMMON FACTORS IN THERAPY PROCESS AND OUTCOME RESEARCH

Common factors, sometimes referred to as *nonspecific ingredients* of therapy, are those contributors to therapy outcomes present in all forms of effective therapy. Through the ages, several giants in the field of psychotherapy, including Rosenzweig (1936), Rogers (1942), Garfield (1957), Frank and Frank (1991), and most recently Wampold (2001) championed the importance of common factors. Several common factors have accumulated strong empirical support. For instance, Greenberg and Watson (2006) pointed out that empathy (Greenberg, Bohart, Elliott, & Watson, 2001), the working alliance (Horvath & Greenberg, 1994), and depth of experiencing (Hendricks, 2002; Orlinsky & Howard, 1986) have all been clearly established as critical common factors for positive outcomes in psychotherapy. Using a contextual lens, we observe that even the application of empathy varies from context to context depending on a myriad of considerations, including the client's culture, attachment and interpersonal history, and current emotional state and cognitive processing capacity.

Categories of Common Factors

We organize this review using four categories of common factors: (a) therapist, (b) client, (c) relationship, and (d) treatment coherency (see Figure 8.1). Each of these categories occurs in all psychotherapies. The four categories subsume the Grencavage and Norcross (1990) groupings with the exception of change processes, which we consider to be outcomes, not a common factor. In our categorization, client factors include beliefs about therapy (e.g., hope; motivation), involvement in therapy, and client dispositions (e.g., symptom severity). Therapist factors include therapist behaviors (e.g., empathy). The relationship factor is best known as the alliance, but our review will include research that broadens this category. Frank and Frank (1991) originally introduced our fourth category, treatment coherency, and we interpret it as involving the matching process in therapy. For example, matching can consist of fitting the rationale of how therapy can be effective so that it is accepted by the client. The therapist may match the client's culture and incorporate the client's theory of how change occurs. Client strengths are included in the treatment coherency category because using the client's strengths matches the client's context.

Client Common Factors

Lambert (1992) produced a pie chart of therapeutic factors that contribute to outcome. The chart includes common factors (30%), techniques (15%), extratherapeutic change (40%), and expectancy or placebo effect (15%). Lambert defined extratherapeutic change as including client factors and client environments that we name *client common factors*. Client factors include client subjective experiences (e.g., problem severity or functional impairment; Norcross, 2010), client behaviors (i.e., involvement, resistance, reactions, disclosures, transference; Hill & Williams, 2000), and client environment or context (e.g., culture). The 40% of the Lambert pie occupied by extratherapeutic change indicates a significant amount of outcome variance due to the client.

In addition, the Lambert pie shows expectancy or placebo effects accounting for 15% of outcome variance. We include expectancy effects with client factors because client expectations for treatment are client beliefs that exist in all types of psychotherapy. For instance, if clients are optimistic about a particular treatment, they are predisposed to positive results. Thus, combining extratherapeutic change and expectancy effects as client common factors theoretically accounts for a sizeable total of 55% of outcome.

Wampold (2001) and Wampold and Serlin (2000) offered compelling arguments that factors common across approaches are more influential to client change than ingredients specific to any one treatment. The working alliance has been found to contribute between 5% (Martin, Garske, & Davis, 2000) and 7% (Horvath & Symonds, 1991) to treatment outcome; therapist effect has been found to contribute between 6% (Luborsky, McLellan, Diguer, Woody, & Seligman, 1997) and 9% (Crits-Christoph et al., 1991); and Wampold and Serlin demonstrated the effect due to specific treatment to be nil or artificial when client, therapist, and relationship factors are considered. Client factors are conspicuously absent from the list of known contributors to outcome. Bohart and Tallman (2010) described client factors as the most neglected of all common factors. Despite a lack of research of client factors, Wampold (2001) broadly affirmed that "variance due to clients is great" (p. 204), and Norcross and Lambert (2006) stated, "We estimate that

Common factors contributing to outcome

Client Factors
    Theorized
        Expectations/hope
        Motivation and autonomy
        Involvement

Therapist Factors
    Demonstrably effective
        Empathy
    Probably effective
        Positive regard
        Congruence/genuine
        Feedback
        Self-disclosure
        Countertransference management
        Quality of relational interpretation

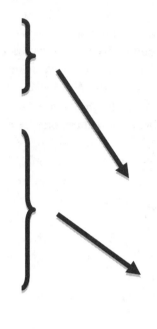

Relationship Factors
    Demonstrably effective
        Working alliance
        Goal consensus and collaboration
    Theorized
        Transference–countertransference style
        Real relationship
        Attachment style

Treatment Coherency
    Theorized
        Cultural competency
        Cultural empathy
        Use of client strengths
        Matching treatment to client beliefs
        Matching cultural characteristics

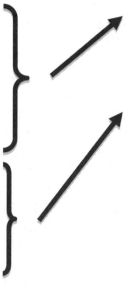

Outcome

FIGURE 8.1. Four component common factors model in relation to outcome. "Demonstrably effective" and "Probably effective" designations based on the report from the APA Division 29 Task Force (Norcross, 2001). The "Theorized" designation is derived from the authors' review of outcome literature.

the patient, including the severity of his or her distress, accounts for approximately 25% to 30% of the total variance" (p. 210). If the estimates are accurate, then client factors are more important to outcome than the working alliance.

Client motivation and autonomy. Ryan, Lynch, Vansteenkiste, and Deci (2011) highlighted client motivation and autonomy as inextricably linked common factors. A client may freely choose (i.e., client volition) to fully participate in therapy, and this volition constitutes client motivation. Ryan et al. (2011) explained that all major psychotherapy approaches possess methods to increase client autonomy and motivation. For instance, in cognitive–behavioral therapy (CBT), therapists persuade or model to promote client beliefs about the efficacy of a proposed intervention (Caprara & Cervone, 2000). In behavioral and cognitive behavioral therapies, transparency increases motivation by fully explaining, providing a compelling rationale, and seeking approval from the client (Antony & Roemer, 2003; Bieling, McCabe, & Antony, 2006). In dynamic forms of therapy, clients are chiefly motivated by the quality of their relationships, and therefore, therapists work through the relationship to explore transference (Greenberg & Mitchell, 1983) as a means to overcome resistance to therapy (Kaner & Prelinger, 2005). In humanistic forms of therapy (i.e., person-centered; existential) motivation is thought to be engendered through trust and positive regard built within the relationship. Authenticity, genuineness, and self-actualization are at the heart of existential therapy, all concepts central to autonomous motivation. Evident from these examples, client motivation and autonomy are held in high regard as desirable process goals across the major forms of psychotherapy.

Zuroff et al. (2007) found support for autonomous motivation as a client common factor in a study comparing CBT, interpersonal therapy, and pharmacotherapy with 95 depressed clients receiving treatment over 16 sessions. The working alliance, client autonomous motivation, and therapist autonomy support were assessed after the third session. At termination, client autonomous motivation was found to be a stronger predictor of outcome than the working alliance.

Results from the Zuroff et al. (2007) study indicated an impressive relationship between client factors and outcome. The significant predictive influence of client autonomous motivation suggests that when a client can freely choose to act collaboratively with a therapist toward the goal of positive change, treatment offers a strong possibility of success. Willing and motivated clients move toward positive differences away from the problem. Conversely, when clients are unwilling or lack volition,

such as is particularly the case in mandated treatment, therapy becomes more difficult. The therapist may be brilliant in the implementation of a specific treatment, but if the client is unwilling, progress will be much harder to achieve. We postulate and results from Zuroff et al. support the premise that progress in therapy is at least partly determined by the event of the therapist winning over the client, increasing motivation for the treatment.

Client involvement.   Bohart and Tallman (2010) emphasized that "clients' active involvement in therapeutic process is critical to success" (p. 83). Clients can actively contribute to processes that lead to improved therapy outcomes. Bohart and Tallman asserted that clients actively work to select the helpful parts of all that therapy offers. Using client diaries, Mackrill (2008) found that clients actively translated parts of their therapy into their own meaning and applied their interpretations in their lives. Clients have their own ideas about what they need (Philips, Werbart, Wennberg, & Schubert, 2007). For example, if a client needs support they find therapist empathy supportive; if insight is needed then empathy is viewed as promoting insight (Bohart & Boyd, 1997).

Whether described as extratherapeutic factors, expectancy factors, or common factors, clearly client factors are important to outcomes in therapy. If clients are choosing to participate, motivated toward any specific treatment and involved in a collaborative therapeutic process, then the chance of therapy success increases.

Therapist Common Factors
Norcross (2010) identified several therapist factors as effective relationship elements recognized through meta-analyses conducted by the APA Division 29 Task Force on Empirically Supported Therapy Relationships (Norcross, 2002). Empathy was the only therapist behavior classified as a "demonstrably effective" (Norcross, 2010, p. 123) element, putting it at the same level of empirical support as the working alliance, cohesion in group therapy, and goal consensus and collaboration. "Probably effective" (Norcross, 2010, p. 123) therapist qualities and behaviors identified by the task force were positive

regard, congruence–genuineness, feedback, self-disclosure, management of countertransference, and quality of relational interpretations (see Figure 8.1).

Empathy.   Rogers (1957) defined *empathy* as "the therapist's sensitive ability and willingness to understand clients' thoughts, feelings, and struggles from their point of view" (p. 98). Empathy, then, holds high status as an effective process at the level of the alliance. Yet, the act of empathy requires great therapeutic skill, requiring the therapist to be attuned to the client. Therapists' intentions to demonstrate empathy to the client are not enough. Clients must also experience the therapist behavior as empathy (Hill & Nutt Williams, 2000; Norcross, 2010). Thus, therapists' empathy behaviors are linked to clients' subjective experiences of empathy. Bachelor and Horvath (1999) emphasized that each client's response to the therapist's intention of empathy is based on the client's unique needs at that moment in that context. In other words, therapist use of empathy must fit with the client's context for empathy to be realized.

"Probably effective" therapist behaviors.   Positive regard is a probably effective therapist behavior. *Positive regard* includes warmth, acceptance, and unconditional caring of the client and the client's experience. Therapists strive to accept clients through empathy and acceptance of client subjective views, acknowledging clients' rights to their perspectives. Positive regard does not mean endorsement of the client's behavior or perspective or judging the client's viewpoint as correct or accurate. Norcross (2010) reported that studies conducted since 1990 show mixed support for positive regard as a facilitative condition. In positive regard's favor, Farber and Lane (2002) found no negative relationships between positive regard and outcome.

Congruence or genuineness constitutes a second probably effective variable. *Congruence* means that the therapist's internal state matches his or her external state (Rogers, 1957). Norcross (2010) identified two parts of congruence, the therapist's personal integration and "the therapist's capacity to communicate his or her personhood to the client" (p. 123). For example, if the therapist is feeling uneasy during a moment of therapy and expresses the feeling of uneasiness verbally or nonverbally to the client, the therapist is demonstrating congruence. Meta-analytic results of studies of congruence show mixed support with 20 of 77 studies showing a positive association with outcome and the rest produced nonsignificant results (Klein, Kolden, Michels, & Chisholm-Stockard, 2002).

Feedback, a third probably effective therapist factor, means providing the client descriptive and evaluative information about the client's behavior (Norcross, 2002). Claiborn, Goodyear, and Horner (2002) found positive results in eight of 11 studies of feedback reviewed. Feedback is facilitative of collaboration with the client, can aid in demonstrating congruence, and when done in a constructive way, can communicate positive regard for the client.

Self-disclosure, a fourth probably effective factor, is the therapist act of revealing something personal to the client (Hill & O'Brien, 1999). Self-disclosure is used to create feelings of similarity between the client and the therapist (Edwards & Murdock, 1994). Although its direct relationship to outcome is unknown, analogue studies demonstrate that self-disclosure is effective in increasing client ratings of helpfulness and enhancing empathy. Self-disclosure may also be related to genuineness by helping the client to see the therapist as a real person in a real relationship (Hill & Williams, 2000).

A fifth probably effective variable, management of countertransference, is important because of the potential for damage to the client and the relationship from countertransference if it is not managed. *Countertransference* is defined as all therapist reactions to a client (Fromm-Reichman, 1950). Therapist lack of awareness of countertransference may lead to negative effects and alternatively, awareness of countertransference may be facilitative of the therapy process (Gelso & Fretz, 2001). Hayes, Riker, and Ingram (1997) pointed out the significance of managing countertransference with more difficult clients who tend to pull strong feelings of a more personal nature from the therapist.

The task force's final probably effective variable, quality of relational interpretations, is the use of new and expanded meanings conveyed to the client about the client's overt behaviors (Hill & O'Brien, 1999). These meanings may result in increased insight or awareness of processes previously outside the client's conscious awareness. Transference interpretations, especially when numerous, have poorer results (Crits-Christoph & Gibbons, 2002; Høglend, 1996; Piper, Joyce, McCallum, & Azim, 1993). Interpretations at a moderate depth show more positive results (Claiborn & Dowd, 1985) as do interpretations of interpersonal dynamics (Luborsky & Crits-Christoph, 1998).

Interestingly, confrontation (not among the probably effective elements) has for the most part produced negative reactions from clients (Hill et al., 1988) and may consequently work against the formation of the working alliance. Confrontation as a therapist behavior is defined as pointing out a contradiction or discrepancy to the client (Hill, 1986). Burke, Arkowitz, and Dunn (2002) found confrontation to be ineffective whereas, in comparison, more supportive motivational interviewing techniques of empathy, rolling with resistance, developing discrepancy, and supporting self-efficacy, yielded positive results. We wonder whether an authentic interpersonal process (i.e., genuineness) used to point out a discrepancy might be helpful while avoiding damage to the relationship.

Therapist effect. Discovering the ingredients of the therapist effect remains a goal for psychotherapy researchers. Psychotherapy studies typically ignore the effect due to therapist (Wampold, 2006). For example, in a hypothetical study of a therapeutic approach, 50 clients are randomly assigned to either receive the treatment or the control condition. Ten therapists are trained to deliver either the treatment or the control through individual therapy. Consequently, the study design possesses a nested variable termed therapist effect. If each therapist sees five clients, each group of five is linked by a common therapist. Too often studies fail to account for the nested effect of therapist by grouping all clients together through the design of the study, thus violating the assumption of independence of measurement. The therapist is the commonality or dependence known as the nested factor.

In reanalyzing data obtained from psychotherapy randomized clinical trials (RCT), Wampold (2006) reported that therapist effect accounts for approximately 8% of outcome variance. Therapist effect is sizeable when compared with the 5% estimate of effect due to the alliance. Further validation of the significance of therapist effect is found in the Wampold and Brown (2005) investigation of 6,146 clients with 586 therapists conducting therapy in natural settings (e.g., private practice; clinics) in which 5% of outcome variance was found to be due to therapist effect. Wampold emphasized, "The relatively large proportion of variability in outcomes due to psychotherapists infers that some psychotherapists consistently produce better outcomes than others; consequently, psychotherapists are a worthy locus of validation" (p. 205). He also included an important caveat in making the point that more difficult clients may affect the effectiveness of a therapist. Thus, psychotherapy research should randomly assign clients to therapist to attempt to account for client effect on therapist.

Although accounting for therapist effect is essential, research has not been able to consistently demonstrate that more static therapist characteristics are related to therapy outcomes. Wampold and Brown (2005) in their large study found that therapist variability was not accounted for by therapist academic degree, therapist experience, therapist and client sex and age, client medication status, or client diagnosis. Blatt, Sanislow, Zuroff, and Pilkonis (1996) reanalyzed data from the National Institute of Mental Health treatment study of depression and found no significant effects for therapist age, sex, race, religion, marital status, experience, and experience with specific therapies used with depression. Huppert et al. (2001) studied CBT treatment for panic disorders and found effectiveness *not* related to therapist age, gender, gender match, or experience with CBT but rather related to overall psychotherapy experience.

What we most clearly know about therapists thus far is that those who successfully adapt therapy to client context will be more effective. This is demonstrated by the consistent positive relationships between outcomes and the quality of the alliance, empathy, goal consensus, and customizing therapy to the client (Norcross, 2002). Each of these variables is more about the therapist showing flexibility in adapting therapy to the client than about years of experience, age, or gender. Further evidence includes the Vocisano et al. (2004) study that therapists who emphasized the therapeutic relationship were more effective. This result is not surprising when considering that the formation of the alliance is related to the contextualized fit between client and therapist. The therapist's level of cultural competence is covered in depth in Chapter 17 of this volume. We review the therapist's use of cultural knowledge in the section Treatment Coherency as a Common Factor later in the chapter.

Relationship Common Factors

Central among all psychotherapy processes may be the constructs included in the relationship between therapist and client (Norcross, 2010). Frank and Frank (1991) included the quality of an emotionally charged and confiding relationship as an essential element of the contextual psychotherapy model. Wampold (2001) reminded us of the centrality of the relationship as a major contributor to outcome as demonstrated through meta-analytic findings that account for 5% of outcome variance. Clients consistently list the relationship as a major reason for a successful experience in psychotherapy (Norcross, 2010). Three of the four elements identified by the Division 29 Task Force as "demonstrably effective," the working alliance, goal consensus and collaboration, and empathy contribute to the quality of the therapeutic relationship. The fourth element, cohesion in group therapy, is a parallel concept to the relationship in individual therapy.

Often, the results of process and outcome studies imply that the relationship is completely accounted for through inclusion of the working alliance. Gelso and colleagues' research over the past 2 decades has helped expand our understanding. Gelso and Carter (1994) broadened the definition of the relationship as "the feelings and attitudes that counseling participants have toward one another, and the manner in which these are expressed" (p. 297). Gelso and Samstag (2008) posited, "Often the relationship has been confused with therapist-offered conditions (e.g., empathy, positive regard, genuineness), whereas these conditions only represent one side of the relationship, the therapist side" (p. 267). They believed that considering the alliance as encompassing

all of the relationship is "too limiting" (p. 267). Gelso and Hayes (1998) presented a multidimensional view of the relationship through the tripartite model of (a) the working alliance (WA), (b) transference–countertransference, and (c) the real relationship (RR). The following is a review of the three relationship dimensions and their influence on outcome. The review begins by examining attachment as a contextual variable influential in the development of the relationship in therapy.

Attachment style. Bowlby (1973, 1980, 1988) introduced *attachment style* as the assumptions, expectations, attributions, and standards about relationships derived during childhood that influence relationships throughout the life span. Working models are constructed from early, significant relationships and relationship experiences that develop by adulthood into affect regulating schemas. Bowlby (1988) hypothesized that more secure attachment styles promote greater exploration in adult relationships. Mallinckrodt, Porter, and Kivlighan (2005) offered two studies in support of this hypothesis through findings in which (a) insecure adult attachments were associated with insecure therapeutic attachments and (b) secure therapeutic attachments were related to greater exploration in therapy as represented by measures of session depth and session smoothness. Their findings also indicated that therapeutic attachment predicted variance not accounted for by the working alliance. Further evidence was found for a significant negative relationship between anxious insecure attachment and the alliance, meaning that alliance development is more difficult with anxiously attached clients. A number of studies of attachment in psychotherapy have demonstrated relationships to the WA (Eames & Roth, 2000; Kanninen, Salo, & Punamaki, 2000; Kivlighan, Patton, & Foote, 1998; Ligiéro & Gelso, 2002; Satterfield & Lyddon, 1995; Sauer, Lopez, & Gormley, 2003), to transference (Woodhouse, Schlosser, Crook, Ligiéro, & Gelso, 2003), and to the therapeutic relationship (Dozier & Tyrell, 1998; F. G. Lopez & Brennan, 2000; Mallinckrodt, Gantt, & Coble, 1995). Client avoidant attachment style has particularly been demonstrated to be negatively correlated with the formation of the RR (Fuertes et al., 2007; Marmarosh et al., 2009). Thus for training and practice, client attachment history and style are salient client characteristics worthy of consideration in the development of the therapeutic relationship.

The WA.   As noted, the therapeutic relationship and the WA, although sometimes used interchangeably, are not synonymous. The tendency to view alliance as the totality of the relationship is probably due to the clear and concise conceptualization of the alliance and the supporting research for the construct. The straightforward concept facilitated the development of an easily applied WA measure for process and outcome research. Bordin (1979, 1994) empirically derived the alliance to be represented by three components: (a) goals agreement, (b) tasks (i.e., techniques, treatments) agreement, and (c) bond (degree of confidence and trust) between therapist and client. Horvath and Greenberg (1989) introduced the working alliance inventory (WAI) on the basis of the Bordin model. The development of the WAI with client, therapist, and observer forms as well as a short form allowed researchers to validly measure the alliance from multiple perspectives. Several approaches have examined processes that contribute to the therapeutic alliance.

Alliance rupture–repair.   Although perhaps inevitable, ruptures in the alliance can slow therapeutic progress or lead to premature client terminations (Gelso & Samstag, 2008). Therefore, rupture–repair strategies involving renegotiations between client and therapist of goals, tasks, and therapy processes are crucial therapy skills to learn and apply. Gelso and Samstag defined a *rupture* as "a negative shift in the alliance over time or as difficulty in stabilizing an alliance" (2008, p. 269). Hostile ruptures are expressed by client withdrawal and client confrontation (Safran, Crocker, McMain, & Murray, 1990). Client tendencies toward deference to the therapist have been found to work against the identification of rupture markers. Rennie (1994) found through a qualitative investigation that clients' deference to their therapists and the need to protect their therapists prevented clients from openly expressing dissatisfaction. Even experienced therapists are not particularly good at recognizing rupture markers (Regan &

Hill, 1992). Rhodes, Hill, Thompson, and Elliott (1994) used a qualitative method with 19 clients who retrospectively recalled major misunderstandings during therapy. Although 11 clients were found to resolve misunderstandings with their therapist during therapy, findings also revealed that five of eight clients with unresolved events in therapy failed to reveal their dissatisfaction until they stopped therapy. The unresolved cases were associated with poor therapeutic relationships.

Unfortunately, repairing alliance ruptures with strategies consistent with the therapeutic approach being employed in a session can be ineffective in repairing the relationship. Piper, Azim, Joyce, and McCallum (1991) found that in CBT, convincing clients they were wrong by addressing cognitive distortions or cognitive errors was not helpful in repairing ruptures, nor was interpreting ruptures as transference in psychodynamic therapy. Safran, Muran, Samstag, and Stevens (2001), in their review of research on the effectiveness of rupture-repair methods, suggested that therapists who take a nondefensive stance rather than showing clients the error of their ways allow the client to feel safe to express negative feelings toward the therapist or about therapy, which may be the more effective method. They also pointed out that research of rupture-repair methods has largely involved small samples and is in its infancy as a line of research.

The WA and outcome.   The client's report of a strong WA is the strongest single process measure predicting therapy outcomes as attested by two decades of meta-analyses (Horvath & Symonds, 1991; Martin, Garske, & Davis, 2000). The alliance–outcome correlation, although relatively small, remains consistent across different modalities and client populations: a .21 correlation in the Horvath and Bedi (2002) meta-analysis ($N = 89$ studies) of adult therapy; .20 in the Shirk and Karver (2003) meta-analysis ($N = 23$ studies) of child and adolescent therapy; .22 in the Horvath and Symonds (1991) study of adult individual therapy; and .26 in the Martin, Garske, and Davis (2000) study of adult individual therapy. In addition, the alliance seems to be independent of early symptom alleviation in its prediction of outcome (Constantino, Arnow, Blasey, & Agras, 2005).

Transference–countertransference. The second component of Gelso and Samstag's (2008) tripartite model of the therapeutic relationship is the transference–countertransference element. Gelso and Samstag differentiated transference from the WA and the RR by its emphasis on distortion and displacement in perceptions of relationships. *Transference* refers to the client's displacement onto the therapist aspects of significant relationships in the client's current or past life experiences (Gelso & Samstag, 2008). Working models can explain the mental representations of the past relationships clients bring into a therapeutic relationship. Previous relationship experiences are carried over into the present relationship, thereby, influencing the nature of the therapeutic relationship. A cognitive–developmental perspective explains reality as both perceived and constructed, and it helps to normalize transference as a typical process involving assimilation and accommodation. New relationship information is mapped onto existing schema (i.e., assimilation). The new information not fitting with existing schemas is accommodated, facilitating the construction of new schema. This process helps explain how the development of a therapeutic relationship affects client change as conceptualized within relationship-oriented therapies such as interpersonal process therapy. For instance, untrusting clients accommodate new information about trusting relationships through experiences in the therapeutic relationship. Thus, clients learn to trust their therapist. Clients then generalize or transfer the new trusting dimension of their constructed working model of relationships onto other important relationships outside of therapy.

Transference and outcome. Transference is unusually difficult to study because of measurement issues inherent in this very complex phenomenon (Gelso & Samstag, 2008). Some question remains as to whether transference is discernable by valid and reliable means of assessment. Despite these measurement challenges, a limited amount of evidence is available for the correspondence between reduction of problem symptoms and reduction

of negative expectations of relationships (Crits-Christoph & Luborsky, 1990; Silberschatz & Curtis, 1993). Gelso et al. (2005) pointed out that therapist-rated negative transference has proven in prior research (Gelso, Kivlighan, Wine, Jones, & Friedman, 1997; Woodhouse et al., 2003), more so than positive transference, to be predictive of psychotherapy process and outcome variables.

Countertransference. Countertransference, or transference by the therapist, is important as a contributor to the therapeutic relationship when considering the collaborative nature of the therapeutic relationship. *Countertransference* can be defined as "the therapist's internal and external reactions that are shaped by the therapist's past and present emotional conflicts and vulnerabilities" (Gelso & Hayes, 2007, p. 25). A broader definition is simply to include all therapist emotional reactions to the client as mentioned in the section on "probably effective" therapist behaviors earlier in this chapter. Using this broader definition, countertransference can be viewed as both a hindrance and an invaluable asset for the therapist's use in therapy (Epstein & Feiner, 1988). On one hand, countertransference reactions can bias therapist perceptions of the client, especially if the reactions are directly related to the therapist's experiences in other relationships that do not relate to the present client. On the other hand, therapist internal reactions toward the client can help in forming hypotheses about the client in other relationships outside of therapy. In a sense, countertransference reactions can be described as what the client "pulls" from the therapist, allowing the therapist to gain insight about others' experiences with the client.

In regard to countertransference as a hindrance, unhelpful therapist reactions are divided into affect, cognition, and behavior. Anxiety is the most common affective reaction when therapists' unresolved issues are tapped (Gelso & Hayes, 2007). Cognitively, memory distortion or inaccurate recall of events in therapy is associated with countertransference (Gelso, Fassinger, Gomez, & Latts, 1995). Behaviorally, therapists tend to avoid or detach from clients through minimization of client feelings, disapproval, changing topics, or acting more impersonal (Gelso & Hayes, 2007; Hayes & Gelso, 2001).

Countertransference and outcome. The association between countertransference and outcome has some research support primarily via indirect evidence of influence on other therapeutic processes. Countertransference has been associated with unhelpful processes in therapy, such as deterioration or rupture of the working alliance (Ligiéro & Gelso, 2002; Rosenberger & Hayes, 2002). Countertransference management (CM) has proven to be facilitative of therapy. CM consists of anxiety management, self-insight, self-integration, empathy, and conceptualizing ability (Van Wagoner, Gelso, Hayes, & Diemer, 1991). CM has a positive relationship with a stronger working alliance (Rosenberger & Hayes, 2002) and with positive outcomes (Gelso, Latts, Gomez, & Fassinger, 2002). In qualitative studies, countertransference demonstrates a negative influence on treatment effectiveness (Gelso, Hill, Mohr, Rochlen, & Zack, 1999; Hill, Nutt-Williams, Heaton, Thompson, & Rhodes, 1996).

The RR. The third element of the tripartite model of the relationship is the RR. Greenson (1967) was first to divide the therapeutic relationship into the WA, transference–countertransference, and the RR. He viewed the WA as a product of therapy, and the RR as fundamental across all types of human relationships. Additionally, he viewed the WA as the collaboration between therapist and client that emerges from the realness and genuineness of the RR. Gelso (2004) defined the RR as "the personal relationship existing between two or more people as reflected in the degree to which each is genuine with the other and perceives the other in ways that befit the other" (p. 6). The RR is thought of as free of transference and lacking the distortions derived from previous relationship experiences (Fuertes et al., 2007; Gelso et al., 2005; Kelley et al., 2009; Marmarosh et al., 2009). It is composed of two dimensions, genuineness and realism. Genuineness is "the ability to be who one truly is, to be nonphony, to be authentic in the here and now" (Gelso, 2002, p. 37). *Genuineness* is a Rogerian (Rogers, 1957) quality we interpret as being present to the other person rather than acting out of some illusion based on an idealized or feared aspect of the relationship. *Realism* is defined as "the experiencing or perceiving of the other in

ways that befit him or her, rather than as projections of wished for or feared others" (Gelso, 2002, p. 37). Realism occurs when the relationship is free of transference (e.g., Gelso et al., 2005; Marmarosh et al., 2009).

Measuring the RR. Measurement of the RR is a daunting task requiring the assessment of therapist and client realistic perceptions (i.e., free of distortions) about the relationship. The measurement challenge is to tease out what is real about the relationship from the WA and transference. Thus far, only therapist and client ratings have been used to measure RR. Gelso et al. (2005) developed and validated the Real Relationship Inventory–Therapist (RRI-T), and Kelley et al. (2009) developed and validated the client version (RRI-C). Both inventories measure the therapist or client perceptions of what is real. Objective truth about what is real is not the goal of either measure. "Such perceptions likely represent some combination of any given rater's representations and the actual reality of the participants and their relationship" (Marmarosh et al., 2009, p. 228). The RR is hypothesized to influence the WA, transference–countertransference, and outcome, and research evidence for these relationships is reviewed next (Marmarosh et al., 2009).

Attachment and the RR. Fitting the hypothesized relationship, Fuertes et al. (2007) found that client avoidant attachment was negatively correlated with the RR. In the Marmarosh et al. (2009) study, attachment anxiety was positively correlated with positive transference and negatively correlated with negative transference. As with the Fuertes et al. study, avoidant attachment was negatively correlated with the RR, and anxious attachment's influence on RR was less clear.

The WA and the RR. The WA and the RR consistently have achieved strong correlations with each other (Fuertes et al., 2007; Gelso et al., 2005). For example, Marmarosh et al. (2009) found correlations of .79 (client-rated WA and client-rated RR), .66 (therapist-rated WA and therapist-rated RR), .35 (therapist-rated WA and client-rated RR), and .14 (client-rated WA and therapist-rated RR). Some variance can be attributed to rater similarity (e.g., therapist-rated WA and therapist-rated RR) versus rater difference (e.g., therapist-rated WA and client-rated RR). Findings from the Marmarosh study, however, demonstrate that therapist-rated RR predicted outcome above and beyond client- or therapist-rated WA. We recommend more research to replicate these findings. Such results lend more strength to the assertion of the multidimensionality of the therapeutic relationship as composed by at least two separate dimensions, WA and RR.

Transference and the RR. Evidence of a negative correlation between therapist-rated negative transference and RR has been replicated between the Gelso et al. (2005) and the Marmarosh et al. (2009) studies. In general, negative transference more than positive transference has been more predictive of therapy process and outcome variables in several studies (Gelso et al., 1997, 2005; Woodhouse et al., 2003).

Outcome and the RR. In the Marmarosh et al. (2009) study, therapist-reported RR predicted symptom reduction. Examining the two components of RR revealed that realism not genuineness accounted for a significant amount of variance in the outcome measure. However, Marmarosh et al. also pointed out that the intercorrelation between realism and genuineness ($r = .63$, $p < .001$) was high, similar to findings in the Fuertes et al. (2007) and Gelso et al. (2005) investigations, making it difficult to differentiate between the two dimensions of RR.

Marmarosh et al. (2009) interpreted their results as indicating that therapists can often predict client outcome on the basis of clients' exhibiting negative transference. These results suggest that clients who exhibit negative transference (e.g., resistance to therapy; defensiveness) would do less well in brief therapy than clients perceived to be more real through the demonstration of more cooperation, hope, and more engagement. Client perceptions of the RR are less predictive of outcome than therapist ratings. This result is similar to studies of the WA in which therapist ratings of WA were more predictive of outcome than client ratings (Baldwin, Wampold, & Imel, 2007; Kramer, Roten, Beretta, Michel, & Despland, 2008).

Treatment Coherency as a Common Factor

We display treatment coherency as a common factor category in Figure 8.1 and list cultural competence, cultural empathy, use of client strengths, matching treatment to client beliefs, and matching cultural characteristics under treatment coherency. Frank and Frank's (1991) description of the coherency factor within their contextual framework is the presentation of a rationale to a client for a treatment that the client believes in or is convinced will be helpful. Wampold (2001) stated that "it is critical that the rationale for the treatment be consistent with the worldview, assumptive base, and attitudes and values of the client or, alternatively, that the therapist assists the client to become in accord with the rationale" (p. 25). We add that both therapist and client have a part in coherency. Therapist and client must match by the therapist presenting a treatment in a way that fits with the client's context, and in turn, the client perceives the rationale as coherent within the client's context.

Matching treatments with client cultures. Imel and Wampold (2008) explained "the multicultural implications of the contextual approach, and its shift in perspective from *what* treatment is provided to *how* treatment is provided are noteworthy" (p. 261). Of paramount importance in the contextual model of therapy is the provision of a compelling framework that resonates with the client. To be compelling, to resonate with the client, a rationale for treatment must be compatible with the client's culture; it must be coherent within the client's culture. The rationale must be "offered in the expected cultural frame of the healing practice" (Imel & Wampold, 2008, p. 261) and be a good fit with the client's beliefs about current levels of distress and about how change can occur for him or her. Thus, the rationale must be consistent with the client's worldview. If not, we hypothesize several negative outcomes, namely, impeded alliance development, alliance ruptures, lack of perceived cultural competence, failure to communicate empathy, premature termination, and, ultimately, poor outcomes.

Fischer, Jome, and Atkinson (1998) offered a model of multicultural counseling and healing that is contextualized and emphasizes common factors applicable across cultures. Their model is based on Frank and Frank's (1991) contextual model of healing. The model provides etic (culturally transcendent) approaches to counseling, such as rapport building, positive regard, and empathy, and emic (culturally specific) approaches. For example, turn-taking may be a culturally specific method with a particular Native American client, and the Fischer et al. model accommodates such types of culturally relevant adaptations. Fischer et al. (1998) described their common factors model as a "skeleton of universal healing factors [that] requires the flesh of cultural knowledge" (p. 525). The model includes four components: the therapeutic relationship, shared worldview, client expectations, and rituals or interventions to heal. The therapeutic relationship is built on role investment, empathic resonance, and mutual affirmation (Orlinsky & Howard, 1986). Within it, the therapist ideally exhibits warmth, genuineness, and empathy (Torrey, 1986). The shared worldview is a joint framework from which both client and counselor operate in therapy. Torrey (1986) explained shared worldview in therapy as including language and thought processes similar to those of the client, understanding of causative forces in the client's world, and classification systems of psychological problems within the client's culture. Client expectations refer to instilling hope in the client. The ritual or intervention corresponds with the client's culture. For instance the use of family, religion, or spirituality may be part of the client's culture. In other words, accommodations are made to match the client's culture so the intervention will be more compelling and coherent to the client.

The examination of culture continues to grow as an important contextual factor in psychotherapy research. Ponterotto (2008) provided a historical map of multicultural counseling research in terms of five historical moments. The 1990s, or the fourth moment in the development of multicultural counseling research, included (a) attention to cultural competence in practice and training; (b) focus on racial identity, acculturation, and worldview in research; and (c) inclusion of nonethnic and nonracial minority groups. The fifth moment has occurred over the past decade with the major themes of (a) international

expansion; (b) intersection of multicultural counseling with other specialties such as positive psychology; (c) inclusion of acculturation, worldview, racial identity, and cultural competence in counseling process and outcome; and (d) moving theory and research from an etic (culturally transcendent) focus to an emic (culturally specific) focus.

Client–therapist similarity. We begin our review of research of the coherency common factor by examining the influence of matching culturally specific factors between therapist and client. A body of client–therapist similarity research exists in which matching of ethnicity, race, gender, and sexual orientation of therapist and client is examined.

Match with gay, lesbian, bisexual, and transgendered clients. We did not find any well-designed studies on matching gay, lesbian, bisexual, and transgendered (GLBT) therapists and clients. Several retrospective studies using samples of opportunity found consistent reports of strong preferences for matching nonheterosexual therapists and clients (e.g., Jones, Botsko, & Gorman, 2003; Liddle, 1996). The GLBT client retrospectives from the 1990s and before reported many therapy problems, underscoring the necessity for increased cultural competence in therapists.

Regrettably the few studies examining therapies without cultural accommodation for gay male clients produced contradictory findings. Antoni et al. (2006) in a CBT RCT study without cultural accommodation for HIV-positive gay men successfully demonstrated depression reduction. In contrast, Carrico et al. (2006) were not successful in reducing depression in a CBT RCT study without cultural accommodation for HIV-positive gay clients. Unfortunately, information about the cultural competence level of the therapists was not revealed. We found only one case study of a therapy that included cultural accommodation. Satterfield and Crabb (2010) reported success in treating a depressed elderly gay man. Specific information about treatment accommodation and therapist competence in studies would reveal whether the matching of culture occurs through therapist competence rather than structure of the intervention. The research in GLBT is sparse, leaving no clear recommendations.

Gender matching between therapist and client.
Although adult female clients tend to prefer female therapists (Fowler, Wagner, Iachini, & Johnson, 1992; Jones, Krupnick, & Kerig, 1987), research fails to support gender matching to improve adult therapy outcome (Cottone, Drucker, & Javier, 2002; Zlotnick, Elkin, & Shea, 1998) or to decrease attrition (Sterling, Gottheil, Weinstein, & Serota, 1998). However, in a meta-analysis, Wintersteen, Mensinger, and Diamond (2005) found reports of higher alliances and lower attrition in substance abuse counseling with female and male adolescent gender matches. Gender mismatched adolescent boys were especially more likely to drop out of therapy.

Therapist–client similarity of race and ethnicity.
The research on matching race and ethnicity of adult client and therapist has been mixed at best and not supported at worst. The few studies matching African American clients and therapists are not supported. Shin et al.'s (2005) meta-analysis evaluating matching of European and African American clients in 10 studies between 1991 and 2001 found that for both groups matching was not significant in enhancing outcome (i.e., overall functioning, service retention, and total number of sessions attended). The Shin et al. meta-analysis supported Maramba and Nagayama Hall's (2002) previous meta-analysis of most of the same research studies. The Gamst, Dana, Der-Karabetian, and Kramer (2004) meta-analysis found no evidence of effectiveness for ethnic or racial matching for Latinos, African Americans, and European Americans in child and adolescent therapy. Findings for matching of adult Latinos and Asian Americans contain mixed results. Wintersteen, Mensinger, and Diamond (2005) found in their meta-analysis that racial and ethnic matches for the adolescents lowered attrition but did not contribute to alliances. The latest studies suggest that language may be the most critical variable in the early promise of ethnic and racial matching for Latinos and Asian Americans (e.g., Gamst et al., 2004; Griner & Smith, 2006; Le Meyer, Zane, Cho, & Takeuchi, 2009).

Beyond language, the inconsistent advantages of race and ethnic matching could be attributed to the treatment adaptation or the cultural competence of the therapist. Griner and Smith (2006) identified 76 culturally adapted intervention studies with outcome measures. Their results supported cultural adaptations and accommodations with the largest effect size associated with interventions focusing on only one cultural group. An example of the successful use of cultural adaptation is found in the use of family-based interventions as a culturally competent skill for working with Hispanic clients. Working with the entire family matches the high value placed on family in Hispanic culture (e.g., Santisteban et al., 2003; Szapocznik et al., 1988; Waldron, Slesnick, Brody, Turner, & Peterson, 2001).

In summary of the research on therapist–client similarity, the most definitive findings suggest attending to the client's primary language (e.g., Griner & Smith, 2006; Le Meyer et al., 2009), socioeconomic status (Wierzbicki & Pekarik, 1993), the sex of client if an adolescent (Wintersteen, Mensinger & Diamond, 2005), and ethnicity or race for culturally appropriate treatment (e.g., Constantino, Malgady & Primavera, 2009; Griner & Smith, 2006)

Cultural competency and treatment coherency.
Constantine and Ladany (2001) provided a multicultural counseling competence model hypothesized to be a set of helping processes common or applicable across cultures. The model was designed in response to Fischer, Jome, and Atkinson's (1998) call for a common factors model of cultural competence, and expands on the original Sue, Arredondo, and McDavis (1992) attitudes and beliefs, knowledge, and skills model of multicultural competence. Six competencies are proposed: (a) counselor self-awareness of multiple cultural identities and racial–cultural socializations, (b) knowledge of multicultural issues, (c) self-efficacy toward multicultural counseling, (d) understanding of unique client variables that affect the individual client's cultural context, (e) an effective working alliance, and (f) multicultural counseling skills.

Several measures of multicultural competence have been developed that either use therapists' perceptions (e.g., Multicultural Awareness–Knowledge–Skills Survey; D'Andrea, Daniels, & Heck, 1991; Multicultural Counseling Inventory; Sodowsky et al., 1994) or observer ratings (e.g., Cross-Cultural

Counseling Inventory—Revised; LaFromboise, Coleman, & Hernandez, 1991) of competence. Although these measures provide important perspectives, several authors have postulated that therapist self-ratings of competence actually measure self-efficacy to engage in multicultural counseling (e.g., Constantine & Ladany, 2001; Ottavi, Pope-Davis, & Dings, 1994). Instead of therapist self-ratings, using clients' judgments of their therapists' cultural competence may provide a more useful subjective reality that has important implications for process and outcome assessment in therapy. Arguably the client's experience is a more parsimonious measure for judging whether the therapist acts within the client's culture. If clients perceive the therapist as lacking multicultural competence, several therapeutic processes may suffer (i.e., therapeutic relationship formation; empathy; client commitment and motivation). Thus, it is crucial to obtain clients' subjective views of therapist competence as a variable in the prediction of therapy outcome.

In a content analysis of 20 years of multicultural counseling competence research, Worthington et al. (2007) observed that relatively little research of processes and outcomes in multicultural counseling with real clients had been conducted, and only a handful of studies had examined client perceptions of multicultural competence. One study cited, Pope-Davis et al. (2002), used a grounded theory design to examine experiences of culturally diverse clients in counseling. Ten therapist–client dyads participated, representing multiple combinations of culture, ethnicity, race, gender, and sexual orientation. The core finding was that client experiences with multicultural counseling depended on clients' needs and their evaluation of how much they believed their counselors had met their needs. Additionally, client needs in therapy were found to dictate the degree of emphasis placed on culture. For instance, one client expressed a strong need to discuss issues and experiences with racism and oppression. The study also demonstrated that counselors who showed interest in client cultures were perceived as being more culturally competent. Clients who identified more with their cultures seemed to prefer racial- or gender-similar counselors. The importance

of therapists' multicultural competence varied from client to client and was not necessarily due to static characteristics such as being a member of an ethnically underrepresented group. Client perceptions of cultural similarity between counselor and client were influential in helping clients believe that therapists could understand their culture. Client perceptions of equity and power in the therapeutic relationship were factors in the development of the alliance and in facilitating client disclosure. It seems, as exemplified by this study, that qualitative research provides a richness and depth needed at this point in the study of multicultural competency.

Constantine's studies (2001, 2002, 2007) were cited by Worthington et al. (2007) as the few examples of multicultural research conducted with real clients. In 2001, Constantine found that ethnic minority counselor trainees received higher ratings of multicultural competence than their White American counterparts, and prior multicultural training predicted observer-rated competence but self-reported competence did not. Then in 2002, Constantine found that satisfaction with therapy ratings for ethnically diverse clients was predicted by their ratings of counselor competence. Finally in 2007, Constantine used structural equation modeling to demonstrate that the working alliance predicted both general competence and cultural competence with 40 African American client–White counselor dyads. This line of research was advanced by Owen, Leach, Wampold, and Rodolfa (2011) in conducting a study with 143 clients and 31 therapists investigating the relationship between client ratings of therapist cultural competence and outcome. Findings did not support "the belief that some therapists generally express more cultural competencies consistently with their clients than other therapists" (Owen et al., 2011, p. 5). Instead, cultural competence was more related to individual client perceptions of their therapist and how therapy was progressing.

These studies fail to provide a clear picture of the influence of multicultural competency on therapy outcomes. Worthington and Dillon (2011) held that 30 years of multicultural counseling research produced only mixed and confusing results concerning the influence of multicultural competence on counseling, and they believed the contradictory findings are due to the need to apply updated theories that include more contemporary concepts, such as microaggressions, in investigations of multicultural competence and outcome.

Cultural competence demonstrated through the therapist matching process. A specific application of therapist cultural competence is therapists matching with clients' problems and goal perceptions. Matching with client goals and problems has been related to heightened session and treatment outcome or failure for counseling dyads (e.g., Withrow, 2008; Zane et al., 2005). Purposeful matching of clients' beliefs about goals and problems require therapist knowledge of the client's culture for acquiring a match and could be considered a cultural accommodation as well as demonstration of cultural competence.

Two emergent concepts: Racial microaggressions and cultural empathy. Racial microaggressions and cultural empathy are juxtaposed in their contributions, at least theoretically, to cultural competency and to treatment coherency. Racial microaggressions in therapy constitute a process that is the epitome of the lack of cultural competency. In comparison, cultural empathy is the essence of the demonstration of cultural competency, matching the client through empathy. Presumably, cultural empathy is a process related to treatment coherency, whereas racial microaggressions are associated with a mismatched, incoherent treatment. Racial microaggressions are posited to cause ruptures in the therapeutic alliance (Sue et al., 2007), and we believe cultural empathy can create a stronger bond between counselor and client. Although both constructs are presented in theoretical writings, more research is needed to explore their relationships to each other as well as to cultural competency, to treatment coherence, and to outcome within multicultural counseling contexts.

Sue et al. (2007) defined *racial microaggressions* as "brief and commonplace daily, verbal, behavioral, or environmental indignities, whether intentional or unintentional, that communicate hostile, derogatory, or negative racial slights and insults toward people of color" (p. 273). They also suggested that microaggressions fall into three categories: microassaults, microinsults, and microinvalidations. The last two categories are hypothesized to occur more often in therapy than microassaults. Microassaults are explicit acts of racial aggression, whereas microinsults and microinvalidations are less overtly apparent. Sue et al. provided examples of microinsults and microinvalidations in therapy. One type of microinsult, *assumption of criminality*, might occur in doing a thorough history for substance abuse with a Native American client. The therapist committing the microaggression demonstrates skepticism for the lack of evidence for a substance abuse hypothesis. Microinvalidations include *denial of racism* that might involve a therapist refusing to acknowledge that race and racial prejudice play a role in the therapist's work with a racially different client. Racial microaggressions take place in cross-racial dyads, but Sue et al. pointed out that microaggressions can occur in several other types of cross-cultural dyads (e.g., gay client–straight counselor; Muslim client–Christian counselor). Microaggression degradations can be subtle and brief, and at an unconscious level sending a negative message attributed to being a member of a racial minority group. Sue et al. offered the opinion that White therapists may be prone to racial microaggressions because of their cultural socialization and may ignorantly view liberal mindedness as giving them immunity to racial microaggressions.

Sue et al. (2007) encouraged research on microaggressions in the context of therapy when stating, "examining how cross-racial dyadic compositions impact the process and outcome of counselor/client interactions would be a tremendous contribution to the field of counseling and clinical psychology" (p. 283). Although a growing body of literature demonstrates the prevalence of racial microaggressions in most types of cross-racial relationships, to date only Constantine's (2007) groundbreaking research has examined microaggressions in therapy. In this investigation, the measurement barrier cited by Sue et al. to studying microaggressions in therapy was overcome by the construction of the 10-item Racial Microaggesssions in Counseling Scale (RMAC). Focus groups composed of former African American clients were employed to generate 12 categories of microaggressions. On the basis of these categories, the RMAC was constructed. In the next stage of the investigation, racial microaggressions, general counselor competence, cultural competence, the working alliance, and satisfaction with counseling were included as variables in testing a path model using perceptions of 40 former African American clients who had terminated from therapy in which they had been seen by 19 White therapists. Findings indicated that (a) microaggressions significantly predicted the working alliance, (b) the working alliance significantly predicted general competence and cultural competence, and (c) microaggressions independently predicted counseling satisfaction.

In a second study of microaggressions having important implications for therapy, Constantine and Sue (2007) generated seven categories of microaggressions through analysis of qualitative interviews with 10 Black supervisees in cross-racial supervisory relationships. They concluded that supervisors tended to have "minimized, dismissed or avoided discussing racial-cultural issues in supervision" (Constantine & Sue, 2007, p. 148). This research indicated the commonplace nature of microaggressions in supervision between White supervisors and Black supervisees. Although this research did not involve therapy with clients, it did support assertions made by Sue et al. (2007) of the proneness of White counselors and psychologists, at least those who also supervise, to minimize or dismiss race as irrelevant. These findings in supervision suggest that only a small jump in reasoning must be made to see microaggressions as prevalent in therapy.

The Constantine (2007) study demonstrated microaggressions' influence on other common factor processes (working alliance; therapist competence). Further empirical connections between microaggressions and client factors (e.g., client expectations; involvement), therapist factors (e.g., empathy; positive regard), and relationship factors (countertransference; alliance ruptures and rupture management) need examination as well. Additionally, deeper and richer understanding of the experiences of clients and therapists, the participants of the microaggression process, should be explored through small sample size and qualitative methods.

Cultural empathy is an intriguing concept that is yet to be included in therapy research. We were unable to find any investigation of cultural empathy's influence on cultural competence, microaggressions, the development of the relationship, or outcomes in therapy. We did discover work by van der Zee and Van Oudenhoven (2000) in which they identified cultural empathy as one of seven components of multicultural effectiveness. They then developed the Multicultural Personality Questionnaire (MPQ) on the basis of the seven components of multicultural effectiveness. Factor analysis of the MPQ produced a five-factor structure consisting of cultural empathy, open-mindedness, emotional stability, social initiative, and flexibility. van der Zee and Van Oudenhoven (2001) defined *cultural empathy*, as reported by Ponterotto (2008), as "the ability to empathize with the thoughts, behaviors, and feelings of culturally diverse individuals" (p. 130). Research using the MPQ that includes cultural empathy could be adapted to the study of cultural competence, microaggressions, the development of the working alliance in cross-cultural counseling, and studies of outcome in culturally diverse counseling situations.

Matching treatments to clients by using client strengths. Strength-oriented therapy fits nicely under the treatment coherency common factors category (see Figure 8.1). The use of client strengths in therapy is a component of all major psychotherapy theory clusters (i.e., cognitive–behavioral; humanistic–experiential; psychoanalytic–psychodynamic) as pointed out by Gelso and Woodhouse (2003) in their examination of positive therapy processes. We posit that therapists who use client strengths are matching therapy with the client's context and must understand clients' cultures to identify their strengths. Focusing on client strengths also falls in line with the identifying characteristics of counseling psychology by emphasizing client assets and successes. The use of client strengths in therapy is depathologizing (i.e., antimedical model), is preventive, emphasizes health and mental health, and can maximize human potential (Gelso & Fretz, 2001; Gelso & Woodhouse, 2003).

Although increased emphasis on client assets in therapy is most recently born out of the positive psychology movement, a strength orientation in humanistic therapies has a long and rich history as a therapeutic process. Rogers (1951, 1957) is perhaps the most well known for the belief in individuals' capacity for growth and self-actualization through facilitative conditions of psychotherapy. Strategic brief therapies also promote methods of using client strengths. Erickson (1962) and Erickson and Rossi (1979) advanced the concept of utilization of client strengths in hypnotherapy; Fisch, Weakland, and Segal (1982) promoted the use of client positions in therapy; de Shazer (1988) described an isomorphic process of interventions mapped onto client strengths. These uses of client strengths in therapy conform to the contextual view of therapy in which treatment is matched to the client, not to the diagnostic label.

Conoley et al. (1994) identified the use of client strengths as a significant predictor of client implementation of homework recommendations along with the fit and difficulty of the recommendation. Thus, matching the client's view of therapy and how it fits for the client shows evidence of contributing to increased engagement through the client's actions. Later, Scheel et al. (1999) continued this line of research and found that client implementation of therapist recommendations was predicted by client acceptability of treatment, measured through the Counselor Recommendation Rating Scale (CRRS). The CRRS is made up of three subscales, client ratings of the fit of treatment, difficulty of the proposed treatment, and the therapist's influence. In the Conoley et al. study, videotapes of therapy sessions were coded to assess the degree of match between the counselor homework recommendation that included a rationale given during the session for doing the homework and the client's context. In the Scheel et al. study, 102 clients at a university counseling center rated their acceptability through the CRRS of their counselors' (*n* = 27) homework recommendations. Acceptability predicted implementation of homework recommendations. Thus, these two studies demonstrated that client treatment acceptability is predictive of clients taking positive actions by implementing homework recommendations, and acceptability was established as the match of the recommended intervention with the client's context.

Methods of using client strengths. Constructivist therapies are concerned with the construction of new meaning and solutions, and they offer a number of positive, strength-oriented processes. Among constructivist approaches, solution-focused therapy (SFT; e.g., DeJong & Berg, 1998) is rich in such techniques as exception finding, the miracle question, complimenting, scaling questions, and compliment-bridging statement–task at the conclusion of a session. Each technique is designed to build on exceptions to the problem or when the problem is less. The focus is on the construction of a future in which a solution has taken the place of the problem and, consequently, the problem is alleviated. In the one review of the effectiveness of SFT, small but consistent positive effects were found in 15 studies, with only four judged as well-controlled investigations (Gingerich & Eisengart, 2000).

An interesting strategy, termed *solution talk* (de Shazer, 1988; Furman & Ahola, 1992; Miller, Duncan, & Hubble, 1997) in SFT and *change talk* in motivational interviewing (Miller & Rose, 2009) is used in constructivist approaches to encourage clients to conceive of and visualize future times free of a client-identified problem. Moyers, Martin, Houck, Christopher, and Tonigan (2009) detected a mediational role of change talk between therapist behavior and outcomes in substance abuse counseling.

Hope theory and broaden-and-build theory.
Historically, positive processes have been introduced through constructivist, strategic, and humanistic approaches, but relatively little scientific evidence is available linking strength-oriented processes and outcomes in therapy. We highlight in this section what is available in theoretical advances and existing research evidence supporting a strength orientation. Two theories, hope theory and broaden-and-build theory, can potentially contribute to the development of positive processes in therapy. The few applications of these theories in therapy also are described.

"Positive expectations for change" by either client or counselor is an essential ingredient in the Frank and Frank (1991) contextual healing model. Positive expectations for change encompass hope and engendering hope and can be classified as a strength-oriented therapeutic process. Frank and Frank emphasized a healing context requiring that therapists address issues of hopelessness or demoralization. Positive strategies theorized to be effective in promoting remoralization focus on client assets (Seligman, Rashid, & Parks, 2006) or the promotion of future aspirations or goals (e.g., Snyder, 2000). Solution-building also is posited to foster hope. "The development of well-formed goals through amplifying answers to the miracle question—encourages clients to develop a detailed vision of what their lives might be like when their problems are solved" (DeJong & Berg, 1998, p. 247). Perhaps the most significant contribution to understanding the promotion of hope is Snyder and colleagues' hope theory and its applications to therapy (Snyder, 2000, 2002; Snyder, Michael, & Cheavens, 1999; Snyder, Parenteau, Shorey, Kahle, & Berg, 2002). Three components make up hope theory: (a) goals, (b) pathways, and (c) agency. Snyder (2002) explained that goals provide targets for mental actions. Pathways are the specific means by which an individual can reach his or her goals. Agency is an individual's perceived capacity to follow the pathway to the goal. Snyder et al. (1991) demonstrated that when impediments to goals are encountered, agency (hope) helps individuals find ways to channel their motivational energy to develop new, effective, alternative pathways to their goals. Conversely, individuals with low hope are more easily discouraged, less resilient. Hope theory applications in therapy and evidence of effectiveness have been demonstrated in group therapy (Cheavens, Feldman, Gum, Michael, & Snyder, 2006; Klausner, Snyder, & Cheavens, 2000) and in relationship enhancement (Worthington et al., 1997). Finding ways to influence hopeless clients is essential within a contextual therapy perspective. The Cheavens et al. (2006) study found that the goals-pathways-agency framework increased agency (i.e., hope), life meanings, and self-esteem in a sample of clients suffering from depression.

The second theory with potential applications for the production of positive processes in therapy is Fredrickson's (2001) broaden-and-build theory of positive emotions. It is based on the premise that positive emotions act to broaden whereas negative emotions serve a focusing function. In psychotherapy literature, the study of unpleasant emotions far exceeds the study of positive emotions, making Fredrickson's theory unique. Within broaden-and-build theory, negative emotions are thought to constrain an individual's attention, facilitating more in-depth exploration of a negative emotion and the important aspects of self related to the negative emotion (e.g., grief and sadness related to the experience of coping with loss). On the other hand, positive emotions are seen as serving a broadening function, increasing options to address problems, opening the way for new solutions, initiating new courses of action, encouraging creative problem solving, and fostering reinterpretations resulting in new beliefs. Fredrickson and Joiner (2002) found support for the broaden-and-build theory in a study using a nonclinical sample of 138 college students in which positive emotions (e.g., hope, joy, optimism) and broadminded coping reciprocally predicted each another. A second study by Fredrickson and Branigan (2003) produced similar results in which positive emotions broadened the focus of attention and increased thought-action sequences in a sample of 104 undergraduates. Although the research supporting broaden-and-build theory currently involves only nonclinical samples, results indicate the potential benefits of fostering positive emotions in therapy as a method of facilitating problem solving, coping, and decision making.

The broaden-and-build theory postulates two change mechanisms related to positive emotions. First, the broadening step includes a person experiencing energy, creativity, openness to new experiences, and social engagement. The second step builds on the first to achieve new resources, knowledge, or relationships. The experiences, in turn, create more positive emotions that fuel a positive escalation in which positive emotions and broadening gain energy in reciprocal fashion. The broadening process replaces the narrowed focus and the negative emotions. In a study of 138 college students, Fredrickson and Joiner (2002) demonstrated the prediction of broadminded coping from positive emotions, and conversely, positive emotions were predicted from broadmindedness. Thus, this study provides an example of the spiraling phenomenon coming from the interaction of positive emotions and broadmindedness. Theory and research on broaden-and-build is now moving into the domain of psychotherapy. Fitzpatrick and Stalikas (2008) theoretically connected the domains of psychotherapy and positive psychology through the broaden-and-build theory and even went so far as to propose that broadening is a common factor. They postulated that the functions of broadening and building are similar to descriptions of how change occurs across different forms of psychotherapy, and positive emotions, long thought of as indicators of change, may have a generative change effect.

Strength-oriented therapy models. Along with broaden-and-build and hope theory, the past 5 years have produced four strength-oriented models of therapy: (a) Smith's (2006) strength-based model, (b) Wong's (2006) strength-centered model, (c) Seligman et al.'s (2006) positive psychotherapy treatment (PPT) model for depression, and (d) Conoley and Conoley's (2008) positive family therapy model. Authors of each model have cited the positive psychology movement as a driving force in moving to strength-oriented approaches. Broaden-and-build (Fredrickson, 2001) and hope (Cheavens, Feldman, Woodward, & Snyder, 2006; Snyder, 2000, 2002; Snyder, Parenteau, Shorey, Kahle, & Berg, 2002) theories have been referenced by S. J. Lopez (2008) as foundations of positive psychotherapies in his review of the interface between positive psychology and counseling psychology. Commonalities exist among these models. Each possesses methods to identify and enhance strengths. The transformation of meaning is promoted through positive reframing and exception finding. Most of the models focus on the future through goals. Positive emotions are encouraged. An action component is present in most through homework or in-session exercises that allow practice and are designed to trigger the broaden-and-build escalation. The promotion of hope is implemented through future focus, goal development, encouragement, and an emphasis on strengths over deficits and problems. Thus far, only Seligman et al. have conducted outcome research

testing their model. Using a manualized approach with severely depressed clients, PPT was found superior to standard treatment for depression that included pharmacotherapy.

Progress in the establishment of strength-oriented approaches can be facilitated through more research. Process research can explore the development of the therapeutic relationship, cultural competence, client motivation and involvement, and therapist strength-engendering processes. Effort should be made to explore processes that are most adaptive with the context of the client and to test the effectiveness of the elements of these technique-rich strength-oriented models. Finally, outcome research must address the overriding question of whether positive emotions and meanings can actualize the second component of broaden-and-build theory—replacement of the negative with positive emotions—and whether goal attainment obviates presenting problems. This question can be answered through empirical tests of the effectiveness of the newly developed strength-oriented therapy models reviewed in this chapter.

RESEARCH METHODS TO STUDY "HOW IS TREATMENT EFFECTIVE?"

Research questions consistent with a contextual model of therapy and salient for counseling psychology involve consideration of contextual influences, and how treatment can be applied effectively when considering those contextual influences. Rather than investigating the effects of a specific treatment, effects due to the match between treatment context and the client are explored. The current state of therapy research in counseling psychology is oriented toward common factors to treatment organized by effects due to client, therapist, and relationship. Wampold (2001, 2007) emphasized the contextual model of therapy with the important component of the model being a coherent treatment explanation that is communicated from therapist to client. Coherence is determined from several contextual factors, including culture, the client's state of demoralization, the client's view of how the problem can be solved, and the current state of the therapeutic relationship. Investigations of effective processes that unfold through the course of treatment inform contextualized practices. Thus, the critical research question in the field in the 21st century is, "How is treatment effective within specific therapeutic contexts?"

Seeking contextual understandings of processes and outcomes in therapy requires a broader view of alternative research designs that go beyond traditional large group methodologies. RCTs in which clients are randomly assigned to a treatment or control conditions are appropriate designs when testing the efficacy of a treatment for a specific disorder. The flaw of RCTs for contextually oriented research in which treatment is oriented to client, not disorder, is the assumption of homogeneity (Greenberg & Watson, 2006; Stiles, 2004). The assumption of homogeneity denies that differences exist among clients in their responses to treatment and that differences exist in how treatments are applied from client to client. In natural settings and even in clinical trials, therapists tend to adapt treatment to individual clients (Greenberg & Watson, 2006). Responsivity is also an issue and must be accounted for. Stiles (2004) defined client responsivity as "behavior that is affected by emerging context, including others' behavior" (pp. 105–106). Greenberg and Watson stated that "effective treatment is systematically responsive; therapist and client's behavior is influenced by emerging contexts, including perceptions of each other's characteristics and behavior" (Stiles, Honos-Webb, & Surko, 1998, p. 84).

Alternatives to Large Group Designs to Answer "How" Questions

Given the significant role in psychological treatment of the responsiveness of clients and therapists to context, alternatives to large sample size research designs are needed to capture the influence of the contextual factors. Qualitative, small sample size, and case study designs provide the means by which context can be considered.

Qualitative design. Qualitative designs allow for in-depth examinations of phenomenon and cases. Hill (2004) explained that qualitative research "provides procedural evidence for judging the effectiveness of therapy" (p. 75). She further explained that when therapists and clients tell their stories of their experiences, we make judgments about the credibility and coherency of their stories and then make judgments about the effectiveness of the therapy that is being portrayed. Other advantages of qualitative over hypothesis testing research include the attractiveness and transferability of qualitative research to therapy. "Having a client tell us about a powerful healing experience with a compassionate therapist is typically far more compelling than learning that the average client's changes were clinically significant" (Hill, 2004, p. 75). A thorough and comprehensive review of qualitative methods can be found in Chapter 4, this volume.

Small sample size and case study designs. Case studies, multiple case studies, and small sample size designs provide other opportunities for contextually rich scientific investigations of therapy. Stiles (2004) explained, "Case studies have some distinct scientific advantages (over hypothesis testing research) for quality control on the complex, nuanced, context-responsive aspects of psychotherapy and psychotherapy theories, and they may be more satisfying to clinicians" (pp. 57–58). A multiple–case study approach can be used to triangulate data by using multiple distinct features to inform us about the phenomenon of interest. When a finding is discrepant with an existing theory, the result can be used to adjust the theory to include the occurrence uncovered through the case study. Case studies can describe the interaction between client and therapist in the application of a certain treatment corresponding to a particular theoretical perspective. Validity and credibility come out of detailed descriptions (e.g., context, sequences, nuances) of observations of the application of theory-derived treatment within a client context that is richly described. When an unexpected response deviates from theory, the findings are used to extend and enrich the theory. Several classic case studies, the case of Dora for psychoanalysis and Little Albert for behaviorism, were noted by Stiles (2004) as particularly compelling in psychotherapy's history.

GROWTH MODELING: A CONTEXTUALIZED TOOL FOR PROCESS AND OUTCOME STUDIES

Multilevel growth modeling, sometimes named *hierarchical linear modeling*, is a useful method in process and outcome research for studies designed to understand how individuals change over time (Bryk & Raudenbush, 1992; Chou, Bentler, & Pentz, 1998; Lawrence & Hancock, 1998). Growth modeling possesses several advantages in comparison with the analysis of variance repeated measures design for the study of growth or change over time. One advantage is the use of nested designs in which, for example, therapist as a random effect can be considered. Another example of a nested effect includes clients grouped by ethnicity or therapists grouped by level of experience. The multiple levels provide a model that in essence depicts multiple contextual variables. Thus, we see growth modeling as able to contextualize studies of change over time.

A second advantage is the ability to adequately address the assumption of independence of measure. The nested design allows for and accounts for dependency. A final advantage is the ability to account for missing data through estimation. Process and outcome therapy research is by nature, messy, in that missing data is common when clients cancel sessions or fail to complete measures before or after a session. Growth modeling allows researchers to compare individual models of therapy with an average model, taking into account the initial level and the rate of change (trajectory of the model), and it assesses individual deviations from what is expected or identifies individual models or model patterns that are inconsistent from what is theorized.

USING OUTCOMES TO MANAGE TREATMENT

A review of process and outcome research and the state of research in counseling psychology would not be complete without including an emerging trend in outcome research, that is, managing treatment through the repeated measurement of outcomes throughout the course of therapy (Lambert & Vermeersch, 2008). Traditionally in psychotherapy treatment, client outcomes are measured at the beginning and at the conclusion of treatment (i.e., pre- and posttreatment). Pre- and postassessments are helpful but limited to gaining general efficacy or effectiveness of treatment. Sometimes a follow-up assessment several months after termination is also included to assess the extent of treatment deterioration. Typically, few outcome data are collected while treatment is under way that would inform researchers and practitioners of the process as it unfolds and that would raise alarms when treatment strategies either do not have an effect or are part of a deterioration process.

Lambert and Vermeersch (2008) explained that the state of outcome assessment is now moving to tracking outcome throughout treatment. Repeated assessment of outcome throughout treatment helps to identify patterns of change. Perhaps more important, repeated monitoring of outcome also provides opportunities to alter or modify treatment on the basis of real-time outcome assessment. Using outcomes as feedback to guide therapy is termed psychotherapy outcome management, and several management systems have been developed. One such system is the Partners for Change Outcome Management System (PCOMS; Miller, Duncan, Sorrell, & Brown, 2005), which uses two brief four-item measures to efficiently collect outcomes repeatedly. The measures are clinically friendly instruments, easily administered, and easily completed. One measure (Outcome Rating Scale [ORS]) assesses outcome and a second measure assesses the alliance (Session Rating Scale [SRS]). The client marks an *X* along a 10-cm line segment for each item, and scoring is simply done by measuring where along the line segment the *X* has been placed. Therapist and client can discuss the results of the assessments each session, thereby introducing the element of feedback to treatment. Reese, Norsworthy, and Rowlands (2009) found in two studies using PCOMS that clients receiving continuous feedback through the course of therapy made significant treatment gains in comparison to clients not receiving feedback.

Lambert and Vermeersch (2008) described a comprehensive management system consisting of the combined use of the Outcome Questionnaire–45 (OQ-45; Lambert et al., 2004), a reliable change index (Jacobson & Truax, 1991) of 14 points or more, a normal functioning cutoff score (63), and a clinical support tool (CST) to guide adjustments to therapy when clients are indicated as Not On Track (NOT) on the basis of change scores and cutoff scores of the OQ-45. Five studies (Harmon et al., 2007; Hawkins, Lambert, Vermeersch, Slade, & Tuttle, 2004; Lambert, Whipple, et al., 2001; Lambert, Whipple, Vermeersch, et al., 2002; Whipple et al., 2003) using this treatment management system demonstrated that ongoing feedback through management systems combined with prescriptive adjustments to treatment (i.e., CST) produced better outcomes with NOT clients. A management system is especially important for the 30% to 40% of clients on average who do not demonstrate change through the course of therapy and the 5% to 15% who get worse (i.e., deteriorate) in therapy (Hansen, Lambert, & Forman, 2002; Lambert & Ogles, 2004). In treatment management systems, when a client is assessed as NOT, the therapist and sometimes the client receive this feedback and a CST is applied to assist in modifying treatment. Thus, treatment is altered for clients who are not making adequate progress at the time when outcome deterioration is detected.

In a combined sample of more than 4,000 clients among the five studies of the use of feedback, "the improved outcomes for the clients in the experimental conditions (use of feedback conditions) are not only statistically significant but possess considerable clinical meaning for the individual client" (Lambert & Vermeersch, 2008, p. 244). These impressive results prompted a recommendation in the evidenced-based practice report published in the *American Psychologist* (APA, 2006) in which the use of feedback was recommended as an evidence-based practice in psychology with NOT clients.

CONCLUSION

Published counseling-related research in the primary journals of counseling psychology has decreased markedly over the past 30 years (Scheel et al., 2011). Several hypotheses have been advanced to explain the reasons for this decline. One hypothesis is

decreased interest in process and outcome research in our field, which may be a consequence of Wampold's (2001) seminal work, *The Great Psychotherapy Debate: Models, Methods, and Findings*, in which the significant influence of common factors on therapy outcomes was established. Perhaps some researchers are searching for new directions to pursue, perceiving that major questions about effectiveness of therapy have been answered. In our review, we encourage a shift toward "How is therapy effective within client contexts?" and away from "What therapies are effective for various disorders?"

A second hypothesis concerning reasons for the decrease in counseling research is related to the growing sophistication of research methodologies requiring significant resources to carry out research with large sample sizes using complex designs. We encourage researchers to diversify methods to contextualize research. The large sample size designs have their place within the landscape of process and outcome research, but small sample size and qualitative designs to more deeply explore "how" questions are also needed.

Our review has indicated several avenues for counseling psychologists to pursue in conducting process and outcome research. We encourage researchers to go deeper in examining the roles of common factors in therapy processes and in the delineation of common factors' contributions to outcome. There is a great need to use research to understand the interaction among common factors, the individual contributions of common factors, and best practices in the promotion of common factors as process tools in therapy. Additionally, identification of other common factors (beyond the working alliance) is encouraged, including culturally oriented types, given that all clients are cultural beings. We purposefully integrated cultural factors into our common factors framework in the hope that research would move to this orientation of regularly considering culture. More concentrated attention to the contributions of cultural factors to outcome is sorely needed. Culturally related process and outcome research is in its infancy, with only a few studies that link culturally appropriate processes to outcome.

Although the working alliance and even therapist common factors are supported through research, less has been studied about client common factors. The majority of what we have presented in this review on client common factors comes from theoretical writings. We also point out that in theory, the bulk of outcome variance may be accounted for by client factors (i.e., up to 55% of outcome variance), yet client common factors do not possess a substantial research base.

Our review also forwards the concept of aligning contextual practice with contextualized research designs. This means broadening our view of acceptable and appropriate research to include diverse methods oriented toward contextualized investigations in addition to more accepted traditional large-group, hypothesis-testing studies.

More studies of strength-oriented practices as processes in therapy would help to catch up with theoretical writings spurred on by the positive psychology movement. As yet, very little evidence is available solidifying the contributions of strength-oriented processes to therapy outcomes. Several process questions about the role of the use of client strengths remain unexplored. The use of client strengths in therapy is theorized to replace client deficits, problems, or negative emotions, yet little research has been conducted to test this premise.

Studies that include multiple and varied observations, including client perspectives about experiences in therapy would mirror the complexity of factors that interact in therapy. Because therapists' intents sometimes do not agree or match with clients' experiences as the recipients of the therapist behavior, both therapist and client subjective experiences are crucial to garner the whole picture. The following list is composed of recommendations for future directions in the study of processes and outcomes in psychotherapy research organized by our beliefs about the needs within the field of counseling psychology: (a) common factors research, (b) culturally contextualized research, (c) strength-oriented processes, and (d) diverse research designs to capture context.

Common Factors Research

1. Comprehensively examine the therapeutic relationship by including the real relationship and transference–countertransference with the alliance.

2. Conduct common factors research to expand the list of evidenced-based common factors as well as examine the interaction among common factors.

3. Acknowledge that we know the least about client common factors and advance research to identify the core client factors. Consider and test client motivation as a core common factor. Core common factors would be those factors that have a designation as "demonstrably effective."

4. Continue to develop and establish hope as a core factor of the contextual model of therapy. Continue to work toward the establishment of a relationship between client hope and outcome.

5. Explore and further develop understanding of the alliance rupture–repair phenomenon in therapy. Continue to explore the connections between transference–countertransference and ruptures. Consider the contribution of the real relationship as a mediator between transference and the alliance.

6. Continue to advance the connections between attachment style and therapeutic relationship. Include avoidant, anxious, and secure attachment in combination with the two components of the real relationship (i.e., genuineness and realness).

7. Include treatment coherency in investigations of common factors. Examine the relationship between matching components of treatment and outcomes.

Culturally Contextualized Research

1. Conduct more research to assess client perspectives and experiences of cultural competence.

2. Explore the relationship among cultural empathy, cultural competence, and racial microaggressions.

3. Conduct more process and outcome research in which cultural variables are linked to outcome.

4. Continue to establish cultural competence as a common factor that influences the therapeutic relationship across all approaches.

5. Develop methods to operationalize racial microaggressions in therapy. Especially seek client experiences of microaggressions. Investigate the microaggression–alliance relationship.

6. Include measures of cultural accommodation in outcome studies to compare the effectiveness of treatments with cultural accommodation and without.

Strength-Oriented Processes

1. Examine the use of client strengths in therapy through process studies.
2. Explore the effectiveness of strength-oriented approaches now available through newly developed strength-oriented models. Look at client experiences of match and coherency when client strengths are used in therapy.
3. Explore the positive emotion–negative emotion relationship. Also explore the question, "Do positive emotions broaden and then replace negative emotions in therapy?"
4. Examine the causal link between goals and hope in therapy.
5. Investigate the influence of therapist strength-oriented practices (identification of strengths, positive reframes, encouragement, capitalization, exception finding) on other common factors (e.g., client hope and motivation, the development of realness, the development of the alliance) and in the alleviation of problem symptoms.
6. Investigate the relationship among strength-oriented approaches, cultural competence, the development of the relationship, and client motivation.

Diverse Research Designs to Capture Context

1. Seek multiple contexts and interactions among contexts (i.e., client, therapist, relationship; Client × Therapist; Client × Relationship; Therapist × Relationship; Client × Therapist × Relationship).
2. Conduct analogue research to test theories, to develop innovative therapeutic practices, and to maximize internal validity and credibility; then expand to naturalistic settings to establish external validity and transferability.
3. Broaden the use of analytic methods to include qualitative, mixed methods, small sample size, and case studies. Continue to conduct rigorous scientific investigations within the parameters of the analytic method employed.
4. Apply research methods to answer research questions about the effectiveness of the match between treatment and client context.
5. Through diverse research methods, identify the mediating effects (e.g. racial microaggressions)

between processes (e.g., development of the working alliance) and outcomes.
6. Explore outcome management systems and the application of therapeutic processes as responses to the identification of NOT clients.

References

American Psychological Association. (2003). Guidelines on multicultural education, training, research, practice, and organizational change for psychologists. *American Psychologist, 58,* 377–402. doi:10.1037/0003-066X.58.5.377

American Psychological Association. (2006). Evidence-based practice in psychology. *American Psychologist, 61,* 271–285. doi:10.1037/0003-066X.61.4.271

Antoni, M. H., Carrico, A. W., Durán, R. E., Spitzer, S., Penedo, F., Ironson, G., . . . Schneiderman, N. (2006). Randomized clinical trial of cognitive behavioral stress management on human immunodeficiency virus viral load in gay men treated with highly active antiretroviral therapy. *Psychosomatic Medicine, 68,* 143–151. doi:10.1097/01.psy.0000195749.60049.63

Antony, M. M., & Roemer, L. (2003). Behavior therapy. In A. S. Gurman & S. Messer (Eds.), *Essential psychotherapies* (pp. 182–223). New York, NY: Guilford Press.

Bachelor, A., & Horvath, A. (1999). The therapeutic relationship. In M. A. Hubble, B. L. Duncan, & S. D. Miller (Eds.), *The heart and soul of change: What works in therapy* (pp. 133–178). Washington, DC: American Psychological Association. doi:10.1037/11132-004

Baldwin, S. A., Wampold, B., & Imel, Z. (2007). Untangling the alliance-outcome correlation: Exploring the relative importance of therapist and patient variability in the alliance. *Journal of Consulting and Clinical Psychology, 75,* 842–852. doi:10.1037/0022-006X.75.6.842

Bieling, P. J., McCabe, R. E., & Antony, M. M. (2006). *Cognitive-behavior therapy in groups.* New York, NY: Guilford Press.

Blatt, S. J., Sanislow, C. A., Zuroff, D. C., & Pilkonis, P. A. (1996). Characteristics of effective therapists: Further analyses of data from the National Institute of Mental Health Treatment of Depression Collaborative Research Program. *Journal of Consulting and Clinical Psychology, 64,* 1276–1284. doi:10.1037/0022-006X.64.6.1276

Bohart, A. C., & Boyd, G. (1997, December). *Clients' construction of the therapy process: A qualitative analysis.* Paper presented at the meeting of the North American Association of the Society for Psychotherapy Research, Tucson, AZ.

Bohart, A. C., & Tallman, K. (2010). Clients: The neglected common factor in psychotherapy. In B. L. Duncan, S. D. Miller, B. E. Wampold, & M. A. Hubble (Eds.), *The heart and soul of change: Delivering what works in therapy* (2nd ed.). Washington, DC: American Psychological Association.

Bordin, E. S. (1979). The generalizability of the psychoanalytic concept of the working alliance. *Psychotherapy: Theory, Research and Practice, 16*, 252–260. doi:10.1037/h0085885

Bordin, E. S. (1994). Theory and research on the therapeutic working alliance: New direction. In A. O. Horvath & L. S. Greenberg (Eds.), *The working alliance: Theory, research, and practice* (pp. 13–37). New York, NY: Wiley.

Bowlby, J. (1973). *Attachment and loss: Vol. 2. Separation.* London, England: Hogarth Press and the Institute of Psychoanalysis.

Bowlby, J. (1980). *Attachment and loss: Vol. 3. Sadness and depression.* New York, NY: Basic Books.

Bowlby, J. (1988). *A secure base: Parent–child attachment and healthy human development.* New York, NY: Basic Books.

Bryk, A. S., & Raudenbush, S. W. (1992). *Hierarchical linear models: Advanced quantitative techniques.* Newbury Park, CA: Sage.

Burke, B. L., Arkowitz, H., & Dunn, C. (2002). The efficacy of motivational interviewing and its adaptations: What we know so far. In W. R. Miller & S. Rollnick (Eds.), *Motivational interviewing: Preparing people for change* (2nd ed., pp. 217–250). New York, NY: Guilford Press.

Caprara, G. V., & Cervone, D. (2000). *Personality: Determinants, dynamics, and potentials.* Cambridge, England: Cambridge University Press. doi:10.1017/CBO9780511812767

Carrico, A. W., Chesney, M. A., Johnson, M. O., Morin, S. F., Neilands, T. B., Remien, R. H., . . . NIMH Healthy Living Project Team. (2009). Randomized controlled trial of a cognitive-behavioral intervention for HIV-positive persons: An investigation of treatment effects on psychosocial adjustment. *AIDS and Behavior, 13*, 555–563. doi:10.1007/s10461-008-9429-6

Cheavens, J. S., Feldman, D. B., Gum, A., Michael, S. T., & Snyder, C. R. (2006). Hope therapy in a community sample: A pilot investigation. *Social Indicators Research, 77*, 61–78. doi:10.1007/s11205-005-5553-0

Cheavens, J. S., Feldman, D. B., Woodward, J. T., & Snyder, C. R. (2006). Hope in cognitive psychotherapies: On working with client strengths. *Journal of Cognitive Psychotherapy, 20*, 135–145.

Chou, C. P., Bentler, P. M., & Pentz, M. A. (1998). Comparisons of two statistical approaches to study growth curves: The multilevel model and the latent curve analysis. *Structural Equation Modeling, 5*, 247–266. doi:10.1080/10705519809540104

Claiborn, C. D., & Dowd, E. D. (1985). Attributional interpretation in counseling: Content versus discrepancy. *Journal of Counseling Psychology, 32*, 188–196. doi:10.1037/0022-0167.32.2.188

Claiborn, C. D., Goodyear, R. K., & Horner, P. A. (2002). Feedback. In J. C. Norcross (Ed.), *Psychotherapy relationships that work* (pp. 217–233). New York, NY: Oxford University Press.

Conoley, C. W., & Conoley, J. C. (2008). *Positive psychology and family therapy: Creative techniques and practical tools for guiding change and enhancing growth.* Hoboken, NJ: Wiley.

Conoley, C. W., Padula, M. A., Payton, D. S., & Daniels, J. A. (1994). Predictors of client implementation of counselor recommendations: Match with problem, difficulty level, and building client strengths. *Journal of Counseling Psychology, 41*, 3–7. doi:10.1037/0022-0167.41.1.3

Constantine, M. G. (2001). Predictors of observer ratings of multicultural counseling competence in Black, Latino, and White American trainees. *Journal of Counseling Psychology, 48*, 456–462. doi:10.1037/0022-0167.48.4.456

Constantine, M. G. (2002). Predictors of satisfaction with counseling: Racial and ethnic minority clients' attitudes toward counseling and ratings of their counselors' general and multicultural counseling competence. *Journal of Counseling Psychology, 49*, 255–263. doi:10.1037/0022-0167.49.2.255

Constantine, M. G. (2007). Racial microaggressions against African American clients in cross-racial counseling relationships. *Journal of Counseling Psychology, 54*, 1–16. doi:10.1037/0022-0167.54.1.1

Constantine, M. G., & Ladany, N. (2001). New visions for defining and assessing multicultural counseling competence. In M. J. Casas, L. A. Suzuki, & C. M. Alexander (Eds.), *Handbook of multicultural counseling* (2nd ed., pp. 482–498). Thousand Oaks, CA: Sage.

Constantine, M. G., & Sue, D. W. (2007). Perceptions of racial microaggressions among Black supervisees in cross-racial dyads. *Journal of Counseling Psychology, 54*, 142–153. doi:10.1037/0022-0167.54.2.142

Constantino, M. J., Arnow, B. A., Blasey, C., & Agras, W. S. (2005). The association between patient characteristics and the therapeutic alliance in cognitive–behavioral and interpersonal therapy for bulimia nervosa. *Journal of Consulting and Clinical Psychology, 73*, 203–211. doi:10.1037/0022-006X.73.2.203

Constantino, G., Malgady, R. G., & Primavera, L. H. (2009). Congruence between culturally competent treatment and cultural needs of older Latinos. *Journal of Consulting and Clinical Psychology, 77*, 941–949. doi:10.1037/a0016341

Cottone, J. G., Drucker, P., & Javier, R. A. (2002). Gender differences in psychotherapy dyads: Changes in psychological symptoms and responsiveness to treatment during 3 months of therapy. *Psychotherapy: Theory, Research, Practice, Training, 39*, 297–308. doi:10.1037/0033-3204.39.4.297

Crits-Christoph, P., Baranackie, K., Kurcias, J. S., Carroll, K., Luborsky, L., McLellan, T., . . . Zitrin, C. (1991). Meta-analysis of therapist effects in psychotherapy outcome studies. *Psychotherapy Research, 1*, 81–91. doi:10.1080/10503309112331335511

Crits-Christoph, P., & Gibbons, M. C. (2002). Relational interpretation. In J. C. Norcross (Ed.), *Psychotherapy relationships that work* (pp. 285–300). New York, NY: Oxford University Press.

Crits-Christoph, P., & Luborsky, L. (1990). The changes in CCRT pervasiveness during psychotherapy. In L. Luborsky & P. Crits-Christoph (Eds.), *Understanding transference: The core conflictual relationship theme method* (pp. 133–146). New York, NY: Basic Books.

D'Andrea, M., Daniels, J., & Heck, R. (1991). Evaluating the impact of multicultural counseling training. *Journal of Counseling and Development, 70*, 143–150.

Davidson, P. R., & Parker, K. C. (2001). Eye movement desensitization and reprocessing (EMDR): A meta-analysis. *Journal of Consulting and Clinical Psychology, 69*, 305–316. doi:10.1037/0022-006X.69.2.305

DeJong, P., & Berg, I. K. (1998). *Interviewing for solutions*. Pacific Grove, CA: Brooks/Cole.

de Shazer, S. (1988). *Clues: Investigation solutions in brief therapy*. New York, NY: Norton.

Devilly, G. J., & Spence, S. H. (1999). The relative efficacy and treatment distress of EMDR and a cognitive behavioral trauma treatment protocol in the amelioration of post traumatic stress disorder. *Journal of Anxiety Disorders, 13*, 131–157. doi:10.1016/S0887-6185(98)00044-9

Dozier, M., & Tyrell, C. (1998). The role of attachment in therapeutic relationships. In J. A. Simpson & W. S. Rholes (Eds.), *Attachment theory and close relationships* (pp. 221–248). New York, NY: Guilford Press.

Eames, V., & Roth, A. (2000). Patient attachment orientation and the earlier working alliance: A study of patient and therapist aspects of alliance quality and ruptures. *Psychotherapy Research, 10*, 421–434. doi:10.1093/ptr/10.4.421

Edwards, C. E., & Murdock, N. L. (1994). Characteristics of therapist self-disclosure in the counseling process. *Journal of Counseling and Development, 72*, 384–389.

Epstein, L., & Feiner, A. H. (1988). Countertransference: The therapist's contribution to treatment. In B. Wolstein (Ed.), *Essential papers on countertransference* (pp. 282–303). New York, NY: New York University Press.

Erickson, M. E. (1962). Basic psychological problems in hypnotic research. In G. Estabrooks (Ed.), *Hypnosis: Current problems* (pp. 207–223). New York, NY: Harper & Row.

Erickson, M. E., & Rossi, E. (1979). *Hypnotherapy: An exploratory casebook*. New York, NY: Irvington.

Farber, B. A., & Lane, J. S. (2002). Positive regard. In J. C. Norcross (Ed.), *Psychotherapy relationships that work* (pp. 175–194). New York, NY: Oxford University Press.

Fisch, R., Weakland, J. H., & Segal, L. (1982). *The tactics of change*. San Francisco, CA: Jossey-Bass.

Fischer, A. R., Jome, L. M., & Atkinson, D. R. (1998). Reconceptualizing multicultural counseling: Universal healing conditions in a culturally specific context. *The Counseling Psychologist, 26*, 525–588. doi:10.1177/0011000098264001

Fitzpatrick, M. R., & Stalikas, A. (2008). Positive emotions as generators of therapeutic change. *Journal of Psychotherapy Integration, 18*, 137–154. doi:10.1037/1053-0479.18.2.137

Fowler, W. E., Wagner, W. G., Iachini, A., & Johnson, J. T. (1992). The impact of sex of psychological examiner on sexually abused girls' preference for and anticipated comfort with male versus female counselors. *Child Study Journal, 22*, 1–10.

Frank, J. D., & Frank, J. B. (1991). *Persuasion and healing: A comparative study of psychotherapy* (3rd ed.). Baltimore, MD: Johns Hopkins University Press.

Fredrickson, B. L. (2001). The role of positive emotions in positive psychology: The broaden-and-build theory of positive emotions. *American Psychologist, 56*, 218–226. doi:10.1037/0003-066X.56.3.218

Fredrickson, B. L., & Branigan, C. (2003). Positive emotions broaden the scope of attention and thought–action repertoires. *Cognition and Emotion, 19*, 313–332. doi:10.1080/02699930441000238

Fredrickson, B. L., & Joiner, T. (2002). Positive emotions trigger upward toward emotional well-being. *Psychological Science, 13*, 172–175. doi:10.1111/1467-9280.00431

Fromm-Reichman, F. (1950). *Principles of intensive psychotherapy*. Chicago, IL: University of Chicago.

Fuertes, J., Mislowack, A., Brown, S., Gur-Aries, S., Wilkinson, S., & Gelso, C. (2007). Correlates of the real relationship in psychotherapy: A study of dyads. *Psychotherapy: Theory, Research, Practice, Training, 17*, 423–430.

Furman, B., & Ahola, T. (1992). *Solution talk: Hosting therapeutic conversations*. New York, NY: Norton.

Gamst, G., Dana, R. H., Der-Karabetian, A., & Kramer, T. (2004). Ethnic match and treatment outcomes for child and adolescent mental health center clients. *Journal of Counseling and Development, 82,* 457–465.

Garfield, S. L. (1957). *Introductory clinical psychology.* New York, NY: Macmillan.

Gelso, C., & Carter, J. (1994). Components of the psychotherapy relationship: Their interaction and unfolding during treatment. *Journal of Counseling Psychology, 41,* 296–306. doi:10.1037/0022-0167.41.3.296

Gelso, C., & Fretz, B. (2001). *Counseling psychology* (2nd ed.). Belmont, CA: Thomson Wadsworth.

Gelso, C. J. (2002). The real relationship: The "something more" of psychotherapy. *Journal of Contemporary Psychotherapy, 32,* 35–40. doi:10.1023/A:1015531228504

Gelso, C. J. (2004, June). *A theory of the real relationship in psychotherapy.* Paper presented at the International Conference of the Society for Psychotherapy Research, Rome, Italy.

Gelso, C. J., Fassinger, R., Gomez, M., & Latts, M. (1995). Countertransference reactions to lesbian clients: The role of homophobia, counselor gender, and countertransfernce management. *Journal of Counseling Psychology, 42,* 356–364. doi:10.1037/0022-0167.42.3.356

Gelso, C. J., & Hayes, J. (1998). *The psychotherapy relationship: Theory, research, and practice.* New York, NY: Wiley.

Gelso, C. J., & Hayes, J. (2007). *Countertransference and the therapists' inner experience. Perils and possibilities.* Hillsdale, NJ: Erlbaum.

Gelso, C. J., Hill, C., Mohr, J., Rochlen, A., & Zack, J. (1999). Describing the face of transference: Psychodynamic therapists' recollections about transference in cases of successful long-term therapy. *Journal of Counseling Psychology, 46,* 257–267. doi:10.1037/0022-0167.46.2.257

Gelso, C. J., Kelley, F. A., Fuertes, J. N., Marmarosh, C., Holmes, S. E., & Costas, C. (2005). Measuring the real relationship in psychotherapy: Initial validation of the Therapist form. *Journal of Counseling Psychology, 52,* 640–649. doi:10.1037/0022-0167.52.4.640

Gelso, C. J., Kivlighan, D. M., Wine, B., Jones, A., & Friedman, S. C. (1997). Transference, insight, and the course of time-limited therapy. *Journal of Counseling Psychology, 44,* 209–217. doi:10.1037/0022-0167.44.2.209

Gelso, C. J., Latts, M. G., Gomez, M., & Fassinger, R. (2002). Countertransference management and therapy outcome: An initial evaluation. *Journal*

of Clinical Psychology, 58, 861–867. doi:10.1002/jclp.2010

Gelso, C. J., & Samstag, L. W. (2008). A tripartite model of the therapeutic relationship. In S. D. Brown & R. W. Lent (Eds.), *Handbook of counseling psychology* (pp. 267–283). Hoboken, NJ: Wiley.

Gelso, C. J., & Woodhouse, S. (2003). Toward a positive psychotherapy: Focus on human strength. In B. W. Walsh (Ed.), *Counseling psychology and optimal human functioning* (pp. 171–197). Mahwah, NJ: Erlbaum.

Gingerich, W. J., & Eisengart, S. (2000). Solution-focused brief therapy: A review of the outcome research. *Family Process, 39,* 477–498. doi:10.1111/j.1545-5300.2000.39408.x

Greenberg, J. P., & Mitchell, S. A. (1983). *Object relations in psychodynamic theory.* Cambridge, MA: Harvard University Press.

Greenberg, L. S., Bohart, A., Elliott, R., & Watson, J. (2001). Empathy. *Psychotherapy: Theory, Research, Practice, Training, 38,* 380–384. doi:10.1037/0033-3204.38.4.380

Greenberg, L. S., & Watson, J. C. (2006). Change process research. In J. C. Norcross, L. E. Beutler, & R. F. Levant (Eds.), *Evidence-based practice in mental health: Debate and dialogue on the fundamental questions* (pp. 81–89). Washington, DC: American Psychological Association.

Greenson, R. R. (1967). *The technique and practice of psychoanalysis* (Vol. 1). New York, NY: International Universities Press.

Grencavage, L. M., & Norcross, J. C. (1990). Where are the commonalities among the therapeutic common factors? *Professional Psychology: Research and Practice, 21,* 372–378. doi:10.1037/0735-7028.21.5.372

Griner, D., & Smith, T. B. (2006). Culturally adapted mental health intervention: A meta-analytic review. *Psychotherapy: Theory, Research, Practice, Training, 43,* 531–548.

Hansen, N. B., Lambert, M. J., & Forman, E. B. (2002). The psychotherapy dose-response effect and its implications for treatment delivery services. *Clinical Psychology: Science and Practice, 9,* 329–343. doi:10.1093/clipsy.9.3.329

Harmon, S. C., Lambert, M. J., Smart, D. W., Hawkins, E. J., Nielsen, S. L., Slade, K., & Lutz, W. (2007). Enhancing outcome for potential treatment failures: Therapist/client feedback and clinical support tools. *Psychotherapy Research, 17,* 379–392. doi:10.1080/10503300600702331

Hawkins, E. J., Lambert, M. J., Vermeersch, D. A., Slade, K., & Tuttle, K. (2004). The effects of providing patient progress information to therapists and patients. *Psychotherapy Research, 14,* 308–327. doi:10.1093/ptr/kph027

Hayes, J. A., & Gelso, C. J. (2001). Clinical implications of research on countertransference: Science informing practice. *Journal of Clinical Psychology/In Session, 57,* 1041–1052.

Hayes, J. A., Riker, J. R., & Ingram, K. M. (1997). Countertransference behavior and management in brief counseling: A field study. *Psychotherapy Research, 7,* 145–153. doi:10.1080/10503309712331331933

Hendricks, M. N. (2002). Focusing-oriented/experiential psychotherapy. In D. Cain & J. Seeman (Eds.), *Humanistic psychotherapies: Handbook of research and practice* (pp. 221–251). Washington, DC: American Psychological Association. doi:10.1037/10439-007

Hill, C. E. (1986). An overview of the Hill counselor and client verbal response modes category systems. In L. Greenberg & W. Pinsof (Eds.), *The psychotherapeutic process: A research handbook* (pp. 131–159). New York, NY: Guilford Press.

Hill, C. E. (2004). Qualitative research. In J. C. Norcross, L. E. Beutler, & R. F. Levant (Eds.), *Evidence-based practices in mental health: Debate and dialogue about the fundamental questions* (pp. 74–81). Washington, DC: American Psychological Association.

Hill, C. E., Helms, J. E., Tichenor, V., Spiegel, S. B., O'Grady, K. E., & Perry, E. S. (1988). The effects of therapist response modes in brief psychotherapy. *Journal of Counseling Psychology, 35,* 222–233. doi:10.1037/0022-0167.35.3.222

Hill, C. E., & Nutt Williams, E. N. (2000). The process of individual therapy. In S. D. Brown & R. W. Lent (Eds.), *Handbook of counseling psychology* (3rd ed., pp. 670–710). New York, NY: Wiley.

Hill, C. E., Nutt-Williams, E., Heaton, K., Thompson, B., & Rhodes, R. (1996). Therapist retrospective recall of impasses in long-term psychotherapy: A qualitative analysis. *Journal of Counseling Psychology, 43,* 207–217. doi:10.1037/0022-0167.43.2.207

Hill, C. E., & O'Brien, K. M. (1999). *Helping skills: Facilitating exploration, insight and action.* Washington, DC: American Psychological Association.

Høglend, P. (1996). Analysis of transference in patients with personality disorders. *Journal of Personality Disorders, 10,* 122–131. doi:10.1521/pedi.1996.10.2.122

Horvath, A., & Greenberg, L. (Eds.). (1994). *The working alliance: Theory, research, and practice.* New York, NY: Wiley.

Horvath, A. O., & Bedi, R. P. (2002). The alliance. In J. C. Norcross (Ed.), *Psychotherapy relationships that work* (pp. 37–69). New York, NY: Oxford University Press.

Horvath, A. O., & Greenberg, L. (1989). Development and validation of the Working Alliance Inventory. *Journal of Counseling Psychology, 36,* 223–233. doi:10.1037/0022-0167.36.2.223

Horvath, A. O., & Symonds, B. D. (1991). Relation between working alliance and outcome in psychotherapy: A meta-analysis. *Journal of Counseling Psychology, 38,* 139–149. doi:10.1037/0022-0167.38.2.139

Huppert, J. D., Butka, L. F., Barlow, D. H., Gorman, J. M., Shear, M. K., & Woods, S. W. (2001). Therapists, therapist variables, and cognitive-behavioral therapy outcomes in a multicenter trial for panic disorder. *Journal of Consulting and Clinical Psychology, 69,* 747–755. doi:10.1037/0022-006X.69.5.747

Imel, Z. E., & Wampold, B. E. (2008). The importance of treatment and the science of common factors in psychotherapy. In S. D. Brown & R. W. Lent (Eds.), *Handbook of counseling psychology* (pp. 249–266). Hoboken, NJ: John.

Jacobson, N. S., & Truax, P. (1991). Clinical significance: A statistical approach to defining meaningful change in psychotherapy research. *Journal of Consulting and Clinical Psychology, 59,* 12–19. doi:10.1037/0022-006X.59.1.12

Jones, E. E., Krupnick, J. L., & Kerig, P. K. (1987). Some gender effects in a brief psychotherapy. *Psychotherapy: Theory, Research, Practice, Training, 24,* 336–352. doi:10.1037/h0085724

Jones, M. A., Botsko, M., & Gorman, B. S. (2003). Predictors of psychotherapeutic benefit of lesbian, gay, and bisexual clients: The effects of sexual orientation matching and other factors. *Psychotherapy: Theory, Research, Practice, Training, 40,* 289–301. doi:10.1037/0033-3204.40.4.289

Kaner, A., & Prelinger, E. (2005). *The craft of psychodynamic psychotherapy.* Lanham, MD: Jason Aronson.

Kanninen, K., Salo, J., & Punamaki, R. L. (2000). Attachment patterns and working alliance in trauma therapy for victims of political violence. *Psychotherapy Research, 10,* 435–449. doi:10.1093/ptr/10.4.435

Kelley, F. A., Gelso, C. J., Fuertes, J., Marmarosh, C., & Lanier, S. (2009). *The development and psychometric investigation of the client version of the Real Relationship Inventory.* Manuscript submitted for publication.

Kivlighan, D. M., Jr., Patton, M. J., & Foote, D. (1998). Moderating effects of client attachment on the counselor experience: Working alliance relationship. *Journal of Counseling Psychology, 45,* 274–278. doi:10.1037/0022-0167.45.3.274

Klausner, E. J., Snyder, C. R., & Cheavens, J. (2000). Teaching hope to a population of older, depressed adults. In G. Williamson (Ed.), *Advances in aging theory and research* (pp. 295–310). New York, NY: Plenum.

Klein, M. G., Kolden, G. G., Michels, J. L., & Chisholm-Stockard, S. (2002). Congruence. In J. C. Norcross

(Ed.), *Psychotherapy relationships that work* (pp. 195–215). New York, NY: Oxford University Press.

Kramer, U., Roten, Y., Beretta, V., Michel, L., & Despland, J. (2008). Patients' and therapists' view of early alliance building in dynamic psychotherapy: Patterns and relation to outcome. *Journal of Counseling Psychology, 55,* 89–95. doi:10.1037/0022-0167.55.1.89

LaFromboise, T. D., Coleman, H. L. K., & Hernandez, A. (1991). Development and factor structure of the Cross-Cultural Counseling Inventory-Revised. *Professional Psychology, Research, Practice, Training, 22,* 380–388. doi:10.1037/0735-7028.22.5.380

Lambert, M. J. (1992). Psychotherapy outcome research: Implications for integrative and eclectic therapists. In J. C. Norcross & M. R. Goldfried (Eds.), *Handbook of psychotherapy and behavior change* (4th ed., pp. 143–189). New York, NY: Wiley.

Lambert, M. J., Morton, J. J., Hatfield, D., Harmon, C., Hamilton, S., Reid, R. C., . . . Burlingame, G. M. (2004). *Administration and scoring manual for the Outcome Questionnaire-45.* Salt Lake City, UT: OQ Measures.

Lambert, M. J., & Ogles, B. M. (2004). The efficacy and effectiveness of psychotherapy. In M. J. Lambert (Ed.), *Bergin and Garfield's handbook of psychotherapy and behavior change* (5th ed., pp. 139–193). Hoboken, NJ: Wiley.

Lambert, M. J., & Vermeersch, D. A. (2008). Measuring and improving psychotherapy outcome in routine practice. In S. D. Brown & R. W. Lent (Eds.), *Handbook of counseling psychology* (4th ed., pp. 233–248). Hoboken, NJ: Wiley.

Lambert, M. J., Whipple, J. L., Smart, D. W., Vermeersch, D. A., Nielsen, S. L., & Hawkins, E. J. (2001). The effects of providing therapists with feedback on client progress during psychotherapy: Are outcomes enhanced? *Psychotherapy Research, 11,* 49–68. doi:10.1080/713663852

Lambert, M. J., Whipple, J. L., Vermeersch, D. A., Smart, D. W., Hawkins, E. J., Nielsen, S. L., & Goates, M. (2002). Enhancing psychotherapy outcomes via providing feedback on client progress: A replication. *Clinical Psychology and Psychotherapy, 9,* 91–103. doi:10.1002/cpp.324

Lawrence, F. R., & Hancock, G. R. (1998). Assessing change over time using latent growth modeling. *Measurement and Evaluation in Counseling and Development, 30,* 211–224.

Le Meyer, O., Zane, N., Cho, Y. I., & Takeuchi, D. T. (2009). Use of specialty mental health services by Asian Americans with psychiatric disorders. *Journal of Consulting and Clinical Psychology, 77,* 1000–1005. doi:10.1037/a0017065

Liddle, B. J. (1996). Therapist sexual orientation, gender, and counseling practices as they relate to

ratings on helpfulness by gay and lesbian clients. *Journal of Counseling Psychology, 43,* 394–401. doi:10.1037/0022-0167.43.4.394

Ligiéro, D., & Gelso, C. J. (2002). Countertransference, attachment, and the working alliance: The therapist's contributions. *Psychotherapy: Theory, Research, Practice, Training, 39,* 3–11. doi:10.1037/0033-3204.39.1.3

Lopez, F. G., & Brennan, K. A. (2000). Dynamic processes underlying adult attachment organization: Toward an attachment theoretical perspective on the healthy and effective self. *Journal of Counseling Psychology, 47,* 283–300. doi:10.1037/0022-0167.47.3.283

Lopez, S. J. (2008). The interface of counseling psychology and positive psychology: Assessing and promoting strengths. In S. D. Brown & R. W. Lent (Eds.), *Handbook of counseling psychology* (4th ed., pp. 86–99). Hoboken, NJ: Wiley.

Luborsky, L., & Crits-Christoph, P. (1998). *Understanding transference: The core conflictual relationship theme method* (2nd ed.). Washington, DC: American Psychological Association. doi:10.1037/10250-000

Luborsky, L., McLellan, A. T., Diguer, L., Woody, G., & Seligman, D. A. (1997). The psychotherapist matters: Comparison of outcomes across twenty-two therapists and seven patient samples. *Clinical Psychology: Science and Practice, 4,* 53–65. doi:10.1111/j.1468-2850.1997.tb00099.x

Mackrill, T. (2008). Exploring psychotherapy clients' independent strategies for change while in therapy. *British Journal of Guidance and Counselling, 36,* 441–453. doi:10.1080/03069880802343837

Mallinckrodt, B., Gantt, D., & Coble, H. (1995). Attachment patterns in the psychotherapy relationship: Development of the Client Attachment to Therapist Scale. *Journal of Counseling Psychology, 42,* 307–317. doi:10.1037/0022-0167.42.3.307

Mallinckrodt, B., Porter, M. J., & Kivlighan, D. M. Jr. (2005). Client attachment to therapist, depth of session exploration, and object relations in brief psychotherapy. *Psychotherapy: Theory, Research, Practice, Training, 42,* 85–100.

Maramba, G. G., & Nagayama Hall, G. C. (2002). Meta-analyses of ethnic match as a predictor of dropout, utilization, and level of functioning. *Cultural Diversity and Ethnic Minority Psychology, 8,* 290–297. doi:10.1037/1099-9809.8.3.290

Marmarosh, C. L., Gelso, C. J., Markin, R. D., Majors, R., Mallory, C., & Choi, J. (2009). The real relationship in psychotherapy: Relationships to adult attachments, working alliance, and therapy outcome. *Journal of Counseling Psychology, 56,* 337–350. doi:10.1037/a0015169

Martin, D. J., Garske, J. P., & Davis, M. K. (2000). Relation of the therapeutic alliance with outcome and other variables: A meta-analytic review. *Journal of Consulting and Clinical Psychology, 68,* 438–450. doi:10.1037/0022-006X.68.3.438

Miller, S., Duncan, B., & Hubble, M. (1997). *Escape from Babel: Toward a unifying language for psychotherapy practice.* New York, NY: Norton.

Miller, S. D., Duncan, B. L., Sorrell, R., & Brown, G. S. (2005). The partners for change outcome system. *Journal of Clinical Psychology, 61,* 199–208.

Miller, W. R., & Rose, G. S. (2009). Toward a theory of motivational interviewing. *American Psychologist, 64,* 527–537. doi:10.1037/a0016830

Moyers, T. B., Martin, T., Houck, J. M., Christopher, P. J., & Tonigan, J. S. (2009). From in-session behaviors to drinking outcomes: A causal chain for motivational interviewing. *Journal of Consulting and Clinical Psychology, 77,* 1113–1124. doi:10.1037/a0017189

Norcross, J. C. (2001). Purposes, processes and products of the Task Force on Empirically Supported Therapy Relationships. *Psychotherapy, 38,* 345–356.

Norcross, J. C. (2002). Empirically supported therapy relationships. In J. C. Norcross (Ed.), *Psychotherapy relationships that work: Therapist contributions and responsiveness to patient needs* (pp. 3–16). New York, NY: Oxford University Press.

Norcross, J. C. (2010). The therapeutic relationship. In B. L. Duncan, S. D. Miller, B. E. Wampold, & M. A. Hubble (Eds.), *The heart and soul of change: Delivering what works in therapy* (2nd ed., pp. 113–141). Washington, DC: American Psychological Association.

Norcross, J. C. (Ed.). (2002). *Psychotherapy relationships that work: Therapist contributions and responsiveness to patient needs.* New York, NY: Oxford University Press.

Norcross, J. C., & Lambert, M. J. (2006). The therapy relationship. In J. C. Norcross, L. E. Beutler, & R. F. Levant (Eds.), *Evidence-based practices in mental health: Debate and dialogue about the fundamental questions* (pp. 208–218). Washington, DC: American Psychological Association.

Orlinsky, D. E. (2010). Foreword. In B. L. Duncan, S. D. Miller, B. E. Wampold, & M. A. Hubble (Eds.), *The heart and soul of change: Delivering what works in therapy* (2nd ed.). Washington, DC: American Psychological Association.

Orlinsky, D. E., & Howard, K. I. (1986). Process and outcome in psychotherapy. In S. Garfield & A. Bergin (Eds.), *Handbook of psychotherapy and behavior change* (3rd ed., pp. 283–330). New York, NY: Wiley.

Ottavi, T. M., Pope-Davis, D. B., & Ding, J. G. (1994). Relationship between White racial identity attitudes and self-reported multicultural counseling competencies. *Journal of Counseling Psychology, 41,* 149–154.

Owen, J., Leach, M. M., Wampold, B., & Rodolfa, E. (2011). Client and therapist variability in clients' perceptions of their therapists' multicultural competencies. *Journal of Counseling Psychology, 58,* 1–9. doi:10.1037/a0021496

Philips, B., Werbart, A., Wennberg, P., & Schubert, J. (2007). Young adults' ideas of cure prior to psychoanalytic psychotherapy. *Journal of Clinical Psychology, 63,* 213–232. doi:10.1002/jclp.20342

Piper, W. E., Azim, H., Joyce, A. S., & McCallum, M. (1991). Transference interpretations, therapeutic alliance, and outcome in short term individual psychotherapy. *Archives of General Psychiatry, 48,* 946–953.

Piper, W. E., Joyce, A. S., McCallum, M., & Azim, H. F. A. (1993). Concentration and correspondence of transference interpretations in short-term psychotherapy. *Journal of Consulting and Clinical Psychology, 61,* 586–595. doi:10.1037/0022-006X.61.4.586

Piper, W. E., Ogrodniczuk, J. S., Joyce, A. S., McCullum, M., Rosie, J. A., O'Kelly, J. G., & Steinberg, P. I. (1999). Prediction of dropping out in time-limited interpretive individual psychotherapy. *Psychotherapy: Theory, Research, Practice, Training, 36,* 114–122. doi:10.1037/h0087787

Ponterotto, J. G. (2008). Theoretical and empirical advances in multicultural counseling and psychotherapy. In S. D. Brown & R. W. Lent (Eds.), *Handbook of counseling psychology* (4th ed., pp. 121–140). Hoboken, NJ: Wiley.

Pope-Davis, D. B., Toporek, R. L., Ortega-Villalobos, L., Ligiéro, D. P., Brittan-Powell, C. S., Liu, W. M., . . . Liang, C. T. H. (2002). Client perspectives of multicultural competence: A qualitative examination. *The Counseling Psychologist, 30,* 355–393. doi:10.1177/0011000002303001

Reese, J. R., Norsworthy, L. A., & Rowlands, S. R. (2009). Does a continuous feedback system improve psychotherapy outcome? *Psychotherapy: Theory, Research, Practice, Training, 46,* 418–431. doi:10.1037/a0017901

Regan, A. M., & Hill, C. E. (1992). Investigation of what clients and counselors do not say in brief therapy. *Journal of Counseling Psychology, 39,* 168–174. doi:10.1037/0022-0167.39.2.168

Rennie, D. L. (1994). Clients' deference in psychotherapy. *Journal of Counseling Psychology, 41,* 427–437. doi:10.1037/0022-0167.41.4.427

Rhodes, R. H., Hill, C. E., Thompson, B. J., & Elliott, R. (1994). Client retrospective recall of resolved and unresolved misunderstanding events.

Journal of Counseling Psychology, 41, 473–483. doi:10.1037/0022-0167.41.4.473

Rogers, C. (1942). *Counseling and psychotherapy.* Boston, MA: Houghton Mifflin.

Rogers, C. R. (1951). *Client-centered therapy.* Boston, MA: Houghton-Mifflin.

Rogers, C. R. (1957). The necessary and sufficient conditions of therapeutic personality change. *Journal of Consulting Psychology, 21,* 95–103. doi:10.1037/h0045357

Rosenberger, E. W., & Hayes, J. A. (2002). Origins, consequences, and management of countertransference: A case study. *Journal of Counseling Psychology, 49,* 221–232. doi:10.1037/0022-0167.49.2.221

Rosenzweig, S. (1936). Some implicit common factors in diverse methods of psychotherapy. *American Journal of Orthopsychiatry, 6,* 412–415. doi:10.1111/j.1939-0025.1936.tb05248.x

Ryan, R., Lynch, M., Vansteenkiste, M., & Deci, E. (2011). Motivation and autonomy in counseling, psychotherapy, and behavior change. *The Counseling Psychologist, 39,* 193–260. doi:10.1177/0011000009359313

Safran, J. D., Crocker, P., McMain, S., & Murray, P. (1990). The therapeutic alliance rupture as a therapy event for empirical investigation. *Psychotherapy: Theory, Research, Practice, Training, 27,* 154–165. doi:10.1037/0033-3204.27.2.154

Safran, J. D., Muran, J. C., Samstag, L. W., & Stevens, C. (2001). Repairing alliance ruptures. *Psychotherapy: Theory, Research, Practice, Training, 38,* 406–412. doi:10.1037/0033-3204.38.4.406

Safran, J. D., Muran, J. C., Samstag, L. W., & Stevens, C. (2002). Repairing alliance ruptures. In J. C. Norcross (Ed.), *Psychotherapy relationships that work* (pp. 235–254). New York, NY: Oxford University Press.

Santisteban, D. A., Coatsworth, J. D., Perez-Vidal, A., Kurtines, W. M., Schwartz, S. J., LaPerriere, A., & Szapocznik, J. (2003). Efficacy of brief strategic family therapy in modifying Hispanic adolescent behavior problems and substance use. *Journal of Family Psychology, 17,* 121–133. doi:10.1037/0893-3200.17.1.121

Satterfield, J. M., & Crabb, R. (2010). Cognitive–behavioral therapy for depression in an older gay man: A clinical case study. *Cognitive and Behavioral Practice, 17,* 45–55. doi:10.1016/j.cbpra.2009.04.008

Satterfield, W. A., & Lyddon, W. J. (1995). Client attachment and perceptions of the working alliance with counselor trainees. *Journal of Counseling Psychology, 42,* 187–189. doi:10.1037/0022-0167.42.2.187

Sauer, E. M., Lopez, F. G., & Gormley, B. (2003). Respective contributions of therapist and client adult attachment orientations to the development of the early working alliance: A preliminary growth modeling study. *Psychotherapy Research, 13,* 371–382.

Scheel, M. J., Berman, M., Friedlander, M. L., Conoley, C. W., Duan, C., & Whiston, S. C. (2011). Whatever happened to counseling in counseling psychology? *The Counseling Psychologist, 39,* 673–692.

Scheel, M. J., Seaman, S., Roach, K., Mullin, T., & Blackwell-Mahoney, K. (1999). Client implementation of therapist recommendations: Predicted by client perception of fit, difficulty of implementation, and therapist influence. *Journal of Counseling Psychology, 46,* 308–316. doi:10.1037/0022-0167.46.3.308

Seligman, M. E. P., Rashid, T., & Parks, A. C. (2006). Positive psychotherapy. *American Psychologist, 61,* 774–788. doi:10.1037/0003-066X.61.8.774

Seligman, M. E. P., Steen, T. A., Park, N., & Peterson, C. (2005). Positive psychology progress: Empirical validation of interventions. *Tidsskrift for Norsk Psykologforening, 42,* 874–884.

Shin, S., Chow, C., Camacho-Gonsalves, T., Levy, R. J., Allen, I. E., & Leff, H. S. (2005). A meta-analytic review of racial–ethnic matching for African American and Caucasian American clients and clinicians. *Journal of Counseling Psychology, 52,* 45–56. doi:10.1037/0022-0167.52.1.45

Shirk, S. R., & Karver, M. (2003). Prediction of treatment outcome from relationship variables in child and adolescent therapy: A meta-analytic review. *Journal of Consulting and Clinical Psychology, 71,* 452–464. doi:10.1037/0022-006X.71.3.452

Silberschatz, G., & Curtis, J. (1993). Measuring the therapist's impact on the patient's therapeutic progress. *Journal of Consulting and Clinical Psychology, 61,* 403–411. doi:10.1037/0022-006X.61.3.403

Smith, E. J. (2006). The strength-based counseling model. *The Counseling Psychologist, 34,* 13–79. doi:10.1177/0011000005277018

Snyder, C. R. (2000). The past and possible futures of hope. *Journal of Social and Clinical Psychology, 19,* 11–28. doi:10.1521/jscp.2000.19.1.11

Snyder, C. R. (2002). Hope theory: Rainbows in the mind. *Psychological Inquiry, 13,* 249–275. doi:10.1207/S15327965PLI1304_01

Snyder, C. R., Harris, C., Anderson, J. R., Holleran, S. A., Irving, L. M., Sigmon, S. T., . . . Harvey, P. (1991). The will and the ways: Development and validation of an individual-differences measure of hope. *Journal of Personality and Social Psychology, 60,* 570–585. doi:10.1037/0022-3514.60.4.570

Snyder, C. R., Michael, S., & Cheavens, J. (1999). Hope as a psychotherapeutic foundation for nonspecific factors, placebos, and expectancies. In M. A. Hubble, B. Duncan, & S. Miller (Eds.), *Heart and soul of change: What works in therapy* (pp. 179–200). Washington, DC: American Psychological Association. doi:10.1037/11132-005

Snyder, C. R., Parenteau, S. C., Shorey, H. S., Kahle, K. E., & Berg, C. (2002). Hope as the underlying process in the psychotherapeutic change process. *International Gestalt Journal, 25,* 11–29.

Sodowsky, G. R., Taffe, R. C., Gutkin, T. B., & Wise, S. L. (1994). Development of the Multicultural Counseling Inventory: A self-report measure of multicultural competencies. *Journal of Counseling Psychology, 41,* 137–148. doi:10.1037/0022-0167. 41.2.137

Sterling, R. C., Gottheil, E., Weinstein, S. P., & Serota, R. (1998). Therapist/patient race and sex matching: Treatment retention and 9-month follow-up outcome. *Addiction, 93,* 1043–1050. doi:10.1046/j.1360-0443.1998.93710439.x

Stiles, W. B. (2004). Dialogue: Convergence and contention. In J. C. Norcross, L. E. Beutler, & R. F. Levant (Eds.), *Evidence-based practices in mental health: Debate and dialogue about the fundamental questions* (pp. 105–107). Washington, DC: American Psychological Association.

Stiles, W. B., Honos-Webb, L., & Surko, M. (1998). Responsiveness in psychotherapy. *Clinical Psychology: Science and Practice, 5,* 439–458. doi:10.1111/j.1468-2850.1998.tb00166.x

Sue, D. W., Arredondo, P., & McDavis, R. J. (1992). Multicultural competencies and standards: A call to the profession. *Journal of Multicultural Counseling and Development, 20,* 115–129.

Sue, D. W., Capodilupo, C. M., Torino, G. C., Bucceri, J. M., Holder, A. M. B., Nadal, K. L., & Esquilin, J. M. (2007). Racial microaggressions in everyday life: Implications for clinical practice. *American Psychologist, 62,* 271–286. doi:10.1037/0003-066X. 62.4.271

Szapocznik, J., Perez-Vidal, A., Brickman, A. L., Foote, F. H., Santisteban, D., Hervis, O., & Kurtines, W. M. (1988). Engaging adolescent drug abusers and their families in treatment: A strategic structural systems approach. *Journal of Consulting and Clinical Psychology, 56,* 552–557. doi:10.1037/0022-006X. 56.4.552

Torrey, E. F. (1986). *Witchdoctors and psychiatrists: The common roots of psychotherapy and its future.* New York, NY: Harper & Row.

van der Zee, K., & Van Oudenhoven, J. P. (2000). The Multicultural Personality Questionnaire: A multidimensional instrument of multicultural effectiveness. *European Journal of Personality, 14,* 291–309. doi:10.1002/1099-0984(200007/08)14:4>291::AID-PER377<3.0.CO;2-6

van der Zee, K., & Van Oudenhoven, J. P. (2001). The Multicultural Personality Questionnaire: Reliability and validity of self- and other ratings of multicultural effectiveness. *Journal of Research in Personality, 35,* 278–288. doi:10.1006/jrpe.2001.2320

Van Wagoner, S., Gelso, C., Hayes, J., & Diemer, R. (1991). Countertransference and the reputedly excellent therapist. *Psychotherapy: Theory, Research, Practice, Training, 28,* 411–421. doi:10.1037/0033-3204.28.3.411

Vocisano, C., Klein, D. F., Arnow, B., Rivera, C., Blalock, J., Rothbaum, B., . . . Thase, M. E. (2004). Therapist variables that predict symptom change in psychotherapy with chronically depressed outpatients. *Psychotherapy: Theory, Research, Practice, Training, 41,* 255–265. doi:10.1037/0033-3204.41.3.255

Waldron, H. B., Slesnick, N., Brody, J. L., Turner, C. W., & Peterson, T. R. (2001). Treatment outcomes for adolescent substance abuse at 4- and 7-month assessments. *Journal of Consulting and Clinical Psychology, 69,* 802–813.

Wampold, B. E. (2001). *The great psychotherapy debate: Models, methods, and findings.* Mahwah, NJ: Erlbaum.

Wampold, B. E. (2006). The psychotherapist. In J. C. Norcross, L. E. Beutler, & R. F. Levant (Eds.), *Evidence-based practice in mental health: Debate and dialogue on the fundamental questions* (pp. 200–208). Washington, DC: American Psychological Association.

Wampold, B. E. (2007, November). Psychotherapy: The humanistic (and effective) treatment. *American Psychologist, 62,* 857–873. doi:10.1037/0003-066X.62.8.857

Wampold, B. E., & Brown, G. (2005). Estimating therapist variability in outcomes attributable to therapists: A naturalistic study of outcomes in managed care. *Journal of Consulting and Clinical Psychology, 73,* 914–923. doi:10.1037/0022-006X.73.5.914

Wampold, B. E., & Serlin, R. C. (2000). The consequences of ignoring a nested factor on measures of effect size in analysis of variance designs. *Psychological Methods, 5,* 425–433. doi:10.1037/1082-989X.5.4.425

Whipple, J. L., Lambert, M. J., Vermeersch, D. A., Smart, D. W., Nielsen, S. L., & Hawkins, E. J. (2003). Improving the effects of psychotherapy: The use of early identification of treatment failure and problem solving strategies in routine practice. *Journal of Counseling Psychology, 50,* 59–68. doi:10.1037/0022-0167.50.1.59

Wierzbicki, M., & Pekarik, G. (1993). A meta-analysis of psychotherapy dropout. *Professional Psychology: Research and Practice, 24,* 190–195. doi:10.1037/0735-7028.24.2.190

Wilson, S. A., Becker, L. A., & Tinker, R. H. (1995). Eye movement desensitization and reprocessing (EMDR) treatment for psychologically traumatized individuals. *Journal of Consulting and Clinical Psychology, 63,* 928–937. doi:10.1037/0022-006X.63.6.928

Wintersteen, M. B., Mensinger, J. L., & Diamond, G. S. (2005). Do gender and racial differences between patient and therapist affect therapeutic alliance and treatment retention in adolescents? *Professional Psychology: Research and Practice, 36,* 400–408. doi:10.1037/0735-7028.36.4.400

Withrow, R. L. (2008). Early intervention with Latino families: Implications for practice. *Journal of Multicultural Counseling and Development, 36,* 245–256. Retrieved from www.csa.com

Wong, Y. J. (2006). Strength-centered therapy: A social constructionist, virtues-based psychotherapy. *Psychotherapy: Theory, Research, Practice, Training, 43,* 133–146. doi:10.1037/0033-3204.43.2.133

Woodhouse, S., Schlosser, R., Crook, R. E., Ligiéro, D., & Gelso, C. J. (2003). Patient attachment to therapist: Relations to transference and patient recollections of parental caregiving. *Journal of Counseling Psychology, 50,* 395–408. doi:10.1037/0022-0167.50.4.395

Worthington, E. L., Jr., Hight, T. L., Ripley, J. S., Perrone, K. M., Kurusu, T. A., & Jones, D. R. (1997). Strategic hope-focused relationship-enhancement counseling with individuals. *Journal of Counseling Psychology, 44,* 381–389. doi:10.1037/0022-0167.44.4.381

Worthington, R. L., & Dillon, F. R. (2011). Deconstructing multicultural counseling competencies research: Comment on Owen, Leach, Wampold, and Rodolfa (2011). *Journal of Counseling Psychology, 58,* 10–15. doi:10.1037/a0022177

Worthington, R. L., Soth-McNett, A. M., & Moreno, M. V. (2007). Multicultural counseling competencies research: A 20-year content analysis. *Journal of Counseling Psychology, 54,* 351–361. doi:10.1037/0022-0167.54.4.351

Zane, N., Sue, S., Chang, J., Huang, L., Huang, J., Lowe, S., . . . Lee, E. (2005). Beyond ethnic match: Effects of client–therapist cognitive match in problem perception, coping orientation, and therapy goals on treatment outcomes. *Journal of Community Psychology, 33,* 569–585. doi:10.1002/jcop.20067

Zlotnick, C., Elkin, I., & Shea, M. T. (1998). Does the gender of a patient or the gender of a therapist affect the treatment of patients with major depression? *Journal of Consulting and Clinical Psychology, 66,* 655–659. doi:10.1037/0022-006X.66.4.655

Zuroff, D. C., Koestner, R., Moskowitz, D. S., McBride, C., Marshall, M., & Bagby, M. (2007). Autonomous motivation for therapy: A new common factor in brief treatments for depression. *Psychotherapy Research, 17,* 137–147. doi:10.1080/10503300600919380

CHAPTER 9

THEORIES OF VOCATIONAL PSYCHOLOGY

Cindy L. Juntunen and Christine E. Even

Vocation and occupation have been important human concerns since ancient times. Work and preparing youth to work are arguably foundational to any organized society because these activities provide the structure and resources necessary to meet social and individual needs. In fact, evidence of attention to vocational development can be found in the writings of Plato, Aristotle, Confucius, and Lao-tzu, many of which addressed such issues as aptitude, interests, and work for the social good (Dumont & Carson, 1995).

Theories of vocational development, on the other hand, have a much shorter history. The 1909 publication of Frank Parsons's *Choosing a Vocation* marked the first theoretical examination of vocation and vocational development. Parsons proposed three basic tenets to making occupational decisions: know yourself, know the expectations and demands of different kinds of work, and know how these two things are related. These three constructs will be apparent in various ways throughout the theories examined in this chapter.

In conjunction with the emerging work in testing by Binet, Munsterberg's early work in industrial–organizational (I-O) psychology, and Spranger's research on personality and work (Herr, 2001), Parsons's ideas generated a swell of interest in identifying individual and work (and workplace) characteristics that would lead to an optimal match or person–environment fit.

DEVELOPMENT AND DEFINITIONS OF VOCATIONAL PSYCHOLOGY

In the first half of the 20th century, much of the work in vocational and career development was occurring outside the profession of psychology. Although industrial–organizational (I-O) psychology had emerged as a specialization with an emphasis on the workplace, the focus on the individual as an active agent in the vocational process was left primarily to guidance and counseling (Herr, 2001).

The 1946 formation of the Division of Counseling Psychology, which included leaders in vocational guidance and psychologists interested in what was then called *personnel psychology* (Super, 1955), provided a foundation for the development of vocational psychology.

Vocation was firmly anchored as relevant to the study of human behavior by Crites (1969), who defined *vocational psychology* as "the study of the individual's vocational behavior and development through the years of choice and adjustment" (p. 23). The emphasis on the study of vocational behavior has spawned several decades' worth of empirically supported vocational assessments, interventions, and theories (Brown & Krane, 2000; Oliver & Spokane, 1988; Whiston, Sexton, & Lasoff, 1998), several of which are reviewed in subsequent sections of this chapter.

Early definitions of *vocation* and *vocational psychology* included an emphasis on the development of vocation and a sequence of development identified as *career* (Super, 1957, 1990), which assumed a lifelong trajectory. Choice, interests, decision making, work values, and person–environment fit were major constructs of study, and they placed an emphasis primarily on the individual whose career was developing. Many of the essential tenets of these

DOI: 10.1037/13754-009
APA Handbook of Counseling Psychology: Vol. 1. Theories, Research, and Methods, Nadya A. Fouad (Editor-in-Chief)

early theories were based on research and application with primarily White and middle-class men, with limited attention paid to social structures that might affect the career trajectory (Fouad, 2007).

In contrast, more recent vocational theories have also addressed the larger systems in which individuals make vocational decisions and have acknowledged that individual choice may not always be the most relevant factor in vocational attainment (Blustein, 2006). This is reflected in a more recent definition of vocational psychology, proposed by Walsh and Savickas (2005), as

> a field, comprised of theory, intervention, and research practices, that is committed to the importance of work and relationships in people's lives, to helping people live healthy and productive lives, and to social justice, especially with respect to providing access to opportunity for those marginalized or disadvantaged due to social locations such as gender, race, and class (p. 59).

Walsh and Savickas's (2005) definition reflected the long history of vocational psychology and vocational theory being responsive to social change. In fact, Herr (2001, 2003) provided numerous examples of vocational psychology both influencing and being responsive to public policy and legislative initiatives. Increasingly, vocational scholars (Blustein, 2006; Fouad, 2007; Fouad & Kantamneni, 2008) have encouraged the field to examine the intersection of multiple dimensions (e.g., race *and* gender *and* social class) of context. Furthermore, the explicit inclusion of the role of work in healthy lives and relationships highlights the centrality of work to psychological well-being, an assertion that has since received robust empirical support (Paul & Moser, 2009).

CHAPTER OVERVIEW

Vocational psychology is in the midst of significant and exciting change (Fouad, 2007). At least partly in response to tremendous changes in the global labor market (Friedman, 2005), the field has changed dramatically in the past 10 to 15 years. These changes are leading to new theoretical perspectives and the

potential for meaningful gains in vocational scholarship, particularly in terms of the relevance of vocation to historically underserved groups.

In reflection of that change, this chapter is presented in two large sections. In the first, established theories of vocational psychology are reviewed. These theories have contributed to the development of counseling interventions and productive lines of scholarship throughout the 20th century. The second major section focuses on three emerging paradigms that have the potential to shape vocational theory, intervention, and research throughout the 21st century. Together, these established and emerging theories reflect the diversity and innovation of vocational psychology, and its application to human well-being across an array of life domains.

ESTABLISHED THEORIES OF VOCATIONAL PSYCHOLOGY

Beginning with the work of Parsons (1909), the desire to better understand how people make vocational decisions has shaped vocational psychology. This motivation is evident in the three major schools of established vocational psychology: person–environment, which is an outgrowth of Parsons's trait-and-factor model; developmental approaches, which introduced the concept of *career* near the middle of the century; and social learning and social cognitive theories, which paid increasing attention to the impact of social forces on personal attributes relevant to career behaviors.

Although each of these schools of vocational psychology examines vocational behavior through a different lens, they do share several common constructs. These include an emphasis on interest as a factor in vocational behavior, the role of relationships in vocational behavior, and attention to barriers to vocational decision making (Fouad, 2007). In addition, these theories focus on the individual and adhere to the underlying assumption that individuals will have some element of choice in their vocational outcomes (Blustein, 2006; Richardson, 1993). As described in the following section, the extensive research base examining the basic propositions of these theories suggests that these constructs and assumptions do hold true for a significant number of people.

PERSON–ENVIRONMENT THEORIES

We are not all alike; there are diversities of
natures among us which are adapted to different
occupations.

—Plato

The traits possessed by a person (*P*) and the factors
required for success in a given workplace environment (*E*) are two major components of vocational
success in person–environment (P-E) theories. A
third major component, central to the P-E theories
is the interaction of the *P* and *E* characteristics,
which will determine the goodness of fit between an
individual and a specific job or area of work. P-E fit
theories, most notably Holland's vocational personalities theory (1959) and the theory of work adjustment (TWA; Dawis & Lofquist, 1984), are anchored
in the psychology of individual differences and as
such focus on the variability between individuals.
Such variability can be expressed through interests,
abilities, values, needs, and approach to work, all
potentially important contributors to the P-E fit.

The emphasis on characteristics and matching
in P-E fit models has contributed to several well-
established and widely used vocational assessments.
Interest inventories such as the *Vocational Preference
Inventory* (Holland, 1985) and the *Self-Directed
Search* (Holland, Fritzsche, & Powell, 1994) grew
out of Holland's practical and accessible theory of
vocational personalities (Spokane & Cruza-Guet,
2005). The TWA project (Dawis & Lofquist, 1984),
with its clear emphasis on the person within the
work environment, has developed measures of work
satisfaction (*Minnesota Satisfaction Questionnaire*;
Weiss, Dawis, England, & Lofquist, 1967) and work
needs or values (*Minnesota Importance Questionnaire*;
Gay, Weiss, Hendel, Dawis, & Lofquist, 1971) that
are widely used in vocational research.

Both of these theories have been supported
through extensive research and are briefly reviewed
in the following sections, with an emphasis on their
current and future role in vocational theory.

Holland's Theory of Vocational Personalities

Fifty years of application and empirical examination
have established Holland's (1959, 1997) theory of

vocational personalities as a generally sound and
useful tool for vocational practitioners and
researchers alike. Given the remarkable legacy left
by Holland, only the highlights of the theory and
its current status can be adequately addressed in
this chapter. For thorough reviews, readers are
referred to Nauta (2010) and Spokane and Cruza-
Guet (2005).

**Major tenets and empirical support of Holland's
theory of vocational personalities.** As the name
implies, Holland's (1959, 1997) theory identifies
characteristics of individual personality types. It also
assigns these personality types to work settings or
occupations. A set of diagnostic indicators can then
be utilized to help the individual find the best P-E
fit. These basic components of the theory require
that the person understand his or her own characteristics and know the characteristics of the world of
work to obtain a good match between the two.

RIASEC personality types. Holland's theory
is most easily recognized by the iconic RIASEC
(Holland, 1959) hexagon that he used to describe
six major vocational personality types. These types
include *realistic* (R), which emphasizes hands-on
and practical work with tools or animals; *investigative* (I), which focuses on interests in science,
analysis, or intellectual inquiry; *artistic* (A), which
represents an orientation toward creativity, sponta-
neity, and originality in expression and ideas; *social*
(S), which reflects interests that include working
with others, often in a helping or cooperative role;
enterprising (E), which also reflects an orientation
toward working with others, in more of a persuasive
or leadership role, and with a preference for competition; and *conventional* (C), which is typified by a
preference for structure, organized information, and
attention to detail.

Most individuals will have interests in more than
one of these areas, and so will end up with a code,
generally made up of three RIASEC categories, that
best describes their vocational personality and
potential best occupational fit. For example, a person with an IAS code will have more investigative,
artistic, and social interests than conventional, realistic, or enterprising interests, and this person is
more likely to find a better fit in occupations that

include investigative, artistic, and or social activities. Similarly, occupations can be typified by RIASEC codes, a system that is widely used in career counseling and job placement centers.

Although there have been modifications to several of Holland's theoretical tenets over the years, these six categories have remained relatively constant and have been integrated into numerous other career assessment instruments used in a variety of settings and across populations (Nauta, 2010). Numerous empirical investigations have further demonstrated that the basic RIASEC structure is valid across cultural (Day & Rounds, 1998; Fouad, 2002) and age (Holland, 1962; Tracey & Rounds, 1993) groups. Tracey and Rounds (1993) also found the RIASEC model to fit equally well for males and females in a meta-analysis, although others (Betz & Schifano, 2000; Fouad, 2002) have continued to identify gender differences, particularly in lower endorsement by women of interests in the "realistic" category.

Diagnostic indicators. The assessment of RIASEC types is augmented by four interpretive diagnostic indicators, which counselors and clients can use to increase the meaningfulness of the vocational personality. The first indicator is *congruence*, which Holland identified as the degree of fit between the individual and the work environment or occupation. Congruence is theoretically predictive of vocational satisfaction (Holland, 1959), although the empirical evidence of this relationship is mixed (Tsabari, Tziner, & Meir, 2005). When congruence is found to be correlated with vocational satisfaction, it is seldom above a small to moderate magnitude (Spokane, Meir, & Catalano, 2000; Tsabari et al., 2005). Furthermore, a recent investigation demonstrated that incongruence (i.e., the lack of fit between personal and occupational codes) did not correlate negatively with overall job satisfaction (Dik, Strife, & Hansen, 2010).

Two diagnostic indicators, consistency and differentiation, have received considerably less empirical attention (Nauta, 2010). *Consistency* refers to the agreement or harmony among the first two codes endorsed by a given individual. A person with adjacent codes, such as RIA or RIE, is expected to have more similar interests and less difficulty making

decisions than a person with inconsistent (or nonadjacent) codes on the hexagon, such as RSA or RSE. A third diagnostic indicator, *differentiation*, also examines the internal organization of an individual's scores, by attending to the degree to which clear and distinct types emerge. An individual with one, two, or three codes that are distinctly higher than the remaining codes is considered more highly differentiated, whereas an individual who scores similarly among all six types is considered nondifferentiated. Individuals who are differentiated are expected to have greater clarity about their vocational interests and therefore improved ability to make decisions.

Together, consistency and differentiation predict the final indicator, *identity*, which refers to the extent to which a person has a clear sense of his or her own goals and interests (Holland, 1997) and the confidence to make good career decisions (Holland, Diager, & Power, 1980). Vocational identity has been investigated more fully than consistency or differentiation, although again with inconsistent results (Nauta, 2010). There may be some relationship between vocational identity and psychological well-being (Strauser, Lustig, & Ciftçi, 2008), an area of inquiry that would benefit from further exploration.

Many opportunities remain to examine variables that may influence the relationships between Holland's diagnostic indicators and vocational outcomes (Nauta, 2010). Given the ongoing empirical attention paid to Holland's work (Betz, 2008), it is likely that future researchers will continue to investigate the complexities of these relationships. Nauta (2010) identified the empirical emphasis on person types, rather than environment types, and noted that expanding research on the nature of work environments would be an interesting expansion of research on Holland's theory. Another potentially rich area of future research would be to assess the application of Holland's tenets in a complex sociocultural context, attending more fully to the larger sociocultural environment in which the P-E fit exists.

Contemporary applicability of Holland's theory of vocational personality. Both Holland's theory and the resulting assessment instruments are notable for being easily used by clients and practitioners while maintaining a significant impact on research in counseling psychology (Nauta, 2010; Spokane & Cruza-Guet, 2005). The applicability of the RIASEC construct is readily apparent in its wide adoption across numerous assessments and occupational category systems.

The potential limitation to Holland's present and future relevance lies in the theory's emphasis on individual choice and interests, and its relative lack of attention to the external and social factors that can mitigate choice. This does not make Holland's theory irrelevant (Nauta, 2010); it does, however, highlight an assumption that personal choice and the development of interests are primary contributors to the P-E fit. This can limit the applicability of Holland's tenets for individuals who have limited access to choice because of such factors as poverty, lack of access to education, or discrimination related to social identities, among numerous other factors.

The value of Holland's assessment tools, the elegance of his major tenets, and the ongoing empirical evaluation of the theory warrant adaptation of the approach to meet the needs of a broader range of individuals, rather than discarding it as irrelevant. Such adaptation can occur by considering the personality types and the P-E fit in the context of the larger social forces that influence individual behavior and the work environment. An ecological perspective, such as that of Bronfenbrenner (1977) places both the individual and the work environment within nested subsystems. These subsystems include (a) the *microsystem*, which consists of the interpersonal interactions that occur in a given setting such as home, school, work, or social group; (b) the *mesosystem*, in which two or more microsystem environments interact, such as the relationship between work and home; (c) the *exosystem*, which consists of social structures and linkages that indirectly affect individuals, such as community resources or neighborhood characteristics; and (d) the *macrosystem*, which is most distal from the individual and includes norms and values of the larger society.

The traditional application of Holland's theory would focus almost exclusively on the microsystem, which is inclusive of the individual and specific environments. A more contextual and contemporary approach would actively and intentionally infuse

influences from the mesosystem (e.g., by acknowledging the need to balance work and family demands), the exosystem (e.g., recognizing that interests and choices may be restricted by the kinds of work available in a given community), and the macrosystem (e.g., being attuned to the potential for global changes in the labor market to shift availability of work that is of interest to an individual). For example, in qualitative interview with American Indians, Juntunen et al. (2001) found that career choices were strongly influenced by family and community factors and that interests did not emerge as a determining factor in any of the interviews conducted. To assume that interests are not important for American Indian clients would overlook the reality that the RIASEC model has been identified as meaningful across cultural groups (Day & Rounds, 1998). A more useful perspective would be to examine the ways in which cultural and community expectations (exosystem variables) can influence the individual's career choice process.

The Minnesota Theory of Work Adjustment

The TWA (Dawis & Lofquist, 1984) emerged from the University of Minnesota's Work Adjustment Project, a federally funded research program that was designed to study how vocational rehabilitation clients adjusted to work. Although TWA is clearly anchored in individual differences psychology, as is Holland's theory, it differs in its focus on the interaction between the person and the environment. Whereas much of Holland's attention was directed to the individual's characteristics, much of the focus of TWA is on the expectations of the work environment (Dawis, 2005) and the individual's ability to meet those expectations.

Major tenets and empirical support of the theory of work adjustment.   The TWA includes a process model and a predictive model, both explored in this section. As a P-E fit theory, with an emphasis on the interaction of *P* and *E*, TWA assumes that (a) the person has requirements or needs that have to be met, many if not most of which are met through the environment; (b) the person has capabilities that enable him or her to meet these requirements; and (c) the person's behavior within the environment is about meeting these requirements (Dawis, 2005). In this constellation, the person and the environment are parallel and complementary. This means that the environment also has requirements, or expectations, and the capabilities to meet these requirements, by offering reinforcers that meet the person's needs.

The relationship between person and environment is assessed on several domains. *Satisfaction* is used to denote the person's satisfaction with the work environment's ability to fulfill his or her requirements. *Satisfactoriness* denotes the environment's satisfaction with the individual's performance. *Maintenance behavior* is the individual's behavior that serves to maintain the P-E interaction, whereas *adjustment behavior* is where the individual changes his or her behavior to change the interaction. *Tenure* is the length of time the person stays within the work environment. Satisfaction, satisfactoriness, and tenure of the individual within a given work environment are the basic indicators of work adjustment (Dawis & Lofquist, 1984).

TWA predictive model. In the basic predictive model, the individual's satisfaction and satisfactoriness are predicted from two correspondence variables: (a) the correspondence of the work environment's reinforcer factors to the person's values and (b) the correspondence of the person's ability to the requirements of the work environment. The person's satisfaction and satisfactoriness then predict the person's tenure within the work environment.

The TWA's expanded predictive model was developed to improve prediction through the inclusion of moderator variables. TWA proposes that the person's satisfactoriness moderates the correlation between the environment's reinforcers to the person's values correspondence and the person's satisfaction. Similarly, the person's satisfaction moderates the correlation between the person's abilities to the work environments correspondence with the person's satisfactoriness. It has been further proposed that style correspondence moderates the prediction of satisfaction and satisfactoriness. According to TWA, four *personality styles* describe how the person typically responds in work: (a) *celerity* is the quickness of the response, (b) *pace* is the intensity of the

response, (c) *rhythm* is the pattern of the response, and (d) *endurance* is the persistence or length of time of the response.

Parallel variables describe the *environment style*. The correspondence between the person's style and environment's style further moderate the prediction of the person's satisfaction and satisfactoriness. The prediction of satisfaction and satisfactoriness is higher for those individuals with a better style correspondence to their work environment, and lower for those with a poorer style correspondence (Dawis, 2005).

According to Dawis (2005), ample evidence suggests that the TWA P-E correspondence variables alone are able to predict work adjustment outcomes with sufficient precision. This assertion has been supported by Saks and Ashforth (1997), who found that participant perceptions of fit (measured as person–job [P-J] and person–organization [P-O] fit) predicted both job satisfaction and intention to stay in the job. Specifically, P-J fit was related to job satisfaction, and both P-J and P-O fit were negatively predictive of intention to quit. Interestingly, only P-O fit was correlated with actual turnover in this longitudinal study. In a later study, Saks and Ashforth (2002) concluded that fit perceptions were also an important link between job search activities and the quality of employment. The authors also noted that career planning was the strongest predictor of P-J fit perceptions, an issue of particular relevance to the practice of vocational psychology.

TWA P-E correspondence variables have also predicted work satisfaction and tenure among diverse groups. In an assessment of the applicability of TWA variables among African American workers (Lyons & O'Brien, 2006), perceptions of fit explained 43% and 17% of the variance of job satisfaction and intention to quit, respectively. Furthermore, these relationships were not moderated by racial climate, supporting the notion that fit perceptions are primary determinants of employment outcomes. These findings were also supported by qualitative interviews with the participants, who referred primarily to TWA values (achievement, altruism, autonomy, comfort, safety, and status) as factors that supported satisfaction at work. Perception of fit appears to also be a strong predictor of job satisfaction among lesbian, gay, and bisexual employees, accounting for 48% of job satisfaction in one study (Lyons, Brenner, & Fassinger, 2005).

The evidence supporting the role of TWA P-E variables makes the predictive model both theoretically and practically useful as it can help people identify work opportunities that will likely bring them satisfaction, satisfactoriness, and tenure. The model fails, however, to explain the work adjustment process, and this led to the development of the process model.

TWA process model. The TWA process model was developed to explain how the person–environment correspondence (PEC) is achieved, maintained, and reachieved, if necessary (Dawis & Lofquist, 1976). The focus of the process model is on adjustment behavior and adjustment style, which consists of four variables: flexibility, activeness, reactiveness, and perseverance. These four variables can be used to describe the process of adjustment for both the individual and the work environment.

The TWA process model describes adjustment as a cycle that starts when either the person or environment becomes dissatisfied and initiates adjustment behavior. *Flexibility* is the degree of discorrespondence that is tolerated before becoming dissatisfied enough to engage in adjustment behavior. Once the individual decides to initiate adjustment behavior, there are two modes of adjustment possible. *Activeness* is the mode of adjustment in which the person attempts to adjust by acting on or changing the environment. An example of this mode of adjustment would be to request a promotion if reward or prestige needs are not being met. *Reactiveness* is the alternate adjustment mode in which the person attempts to adjust by acting on the self rather than the environment. An example of this would be to acquire new skills or better utilize existing ones. The length of time a person will attempt to make adjustments to decrease discorrespondence reflects the person's *perseverence.* Ultimately, the adjustment cycle ends with either the person being satisfied or so dissatisfied as to leave the work environment.

The process model has been the subject of less empirical examination than the predictive model. In one study of senior military leaders, activeness, or the ability to influence the environment to maintain congruence, was offered as a potential explanation for the homogeneity of participants' Myers-Briggs

Type Indicators scores (Gailbreath, Wagner, Moffett, & Hein, 1997). In another study of civilian employees in Australia, partial support for the process model was identified (Griffin & Hesketh, 2003). Specifically, the proactive and reactive factors were found to contribute to career adjustment and adaptability. Theoretically, the TWA process model has implications for working with people who are not experiencing correspondence with their current work environment. Examining the individual's adjustment style patterns and choices in the counseling process can assist individuals in obtaining and maintaining correspondence in their work environments. Additional examination of the process model variables is warranted, however, given the extremely limited extant research.

Contemporary application of the theory of work adjustment. Dawis and Lofquist (1984) have suggested that counseling psychologists can use the TWA to guide three aspects of vocational counseling: career choice counseling, on-the-job career adjustment, and job change counseling. The TWA has implications for career choice counseling interventions as early as childhood. Dawis (2005) stated that "children have to learn about their needs and values much more explicitly, to the same extent that they learn about their skills and abilities" (p. 17). Hence, teachers and counselors are in a prime position to educate children and their parents about self-assessment of their needs, skills, values, and abilities. They can also teach about individual differences as well as environmental differences and explain how an optimal environment is different for each individual.

Perhaps more than most other vocational theories, TWA is particularly useful for on-the-job adjustment counseling and for job-change counseling. TWA provides a framework for analyzing discorrespondence within the work environment and determining possible approaches to solving the problem, whether making adjustments within the existing work environment or seeking a new work environment. Examining approaches to adjustment, including activeness and reactiveness strategies, are useful for on-the-job adjustment counseling. Dawis (2005) stated that analyzing the individual's perception of dissatisfaction is also important, as it may not reflect reality. Assisting the worker to see the situation rationally can provide a comprehensive view of the situation that allows for exploration and adjustment as needed. Choosing a career is another arena in which TWA can be utilized. Knowledge of an individual's needs, values, skills, abilities, and style characteristics can help in choosing a career. These variables can be assessed through the use of several of the previously mentioned measures. For example, the Minnesota Occupational Classification System (Chartrand, Dohm, Dawis, & Lofquist, 1987) can be used to help clients identify occupational possibilities that reinforce their needs and values and make use of their skills and abilities (Dawis, 2005). Career counselors are in a prime position to help individuals' assess not only themselves but also the types of work environments in which they are most likely to find satisfaction and satisfactoriness.

The TWA is applicable across a wide range of ages and developmental levels. According to Harper and Shoffner (2004), the TWA is useful in addressing career development of retirees who want to continue working but need to first explore their career choices before choosing a new occupation. Recently, the TWA has been suggested as a plausible framework for identifying potential career challenges and job satisfaction among lesbian, gay, and bisexual employees. Degges-White and Shoffner (2002) noted that lesbians face particular challenges within each of the four prime components of TWA: satisfaction, PEC, reinforcement value, and ability. They stated that TWA's focus on the individual's interface with the work environment makes the theory particularly applicable to minority populations.

TWA is a robust and thriving vocational theory and has recently been extended beyond the vocational domain through PEC theory (Dawis, 2002; Lofquist & Dawis, 1991). PEC is an extension of the TWA concepts and dynamics into the realm of general counseling. Eggerth (2008) argued that PEC offers a counseling model grounded in TWA concepts that fall within a broader philosophical orientation of positive psychology. Such an extension has the potential to add to the support of TWA tenets and more fully integrate vocational and general counseling, consistent with current trends toward recognizing the reciprocal nature of vocational and other life domains (Blustein, 2008; Fouad, 2007; Juntunen, 2006).

DEVELOPMENTAL THEORIES

There is broad consensus that the development of career interests and aspirations begins in childhood (Hartung, Porfeli, & Vondracek, 2008) and continues throughout life as part of the overall development of individuals (Savickas, 2002). A close examination of the language used in most career theories will reveal at least some reliance on development, although such assumptions are not always adequately tested. Despite the inclusion of terms such as *development* and *sequential* in the initial definitions of vocational psychology (Crites, 1969), extensive longitudinal examination of the vocational process remains limited (Savickas, 2002; Vondracek, 2007).

The developmental theories presented in this section share a common emphasis on the impact of sequential life experiences, including those of childhood, on subsequent vocational development. They vary considerably, however, in the emphasis given to the interaction of the developing individual with his or her social environment or context.

The influence of context on development has been described by Vondracek, Lerner, and Schulenberg (1983) as a dynamic interaction in which both the individual and the social context change interdependently over time. This basic theoretical assumption requires that vocational development be seen as a process in which the individual responds to social context and also creates change in the social context, such that his or her own vocational opportunities are constantly changing and amenable to change by the individual (Vondracek et al., 1983). Earlier developmental theories, such as Super's life-span life-space theory, gave limited attention to the role of context, but as this section will illuminate, that has changed through the evolution of developmental vocational theory.

Super's Life-Span Life-Space Theory
Donald E. Super was motivated to understand *how* people made vocational and career decisions, and how those decisions could become increasingly

effective or congruent over the life span. In response to the early trait-factor (or P-E) theories that focused primarily on the identification and description of individual differences, Super (1957, 1969, 1990) developed the life-span life-space theory that defined developmental vocational or career tasks for each life stage. This innovative model moved the field from vocational guidance to career counseling, and identified career as a valuable area of inquiry for the behavioral sciences (Savickas, 2001).

Major tenets of life-span life-space theory.   Super's (1990) model consisted of 14 propositions about career development, individuals, and the expression of self-concept in career and work situations. The model was typified by the *career rainbow*, a developmental arc that included stages of development across multiple life roles. Together, these stages and roles created a process that would eventually culminate in a career trajectory that was inclusive of childhood exploration and final retirement.

Super (1990) conceptualized individuals as moving through five stages of career development, each of which is broken up into substages and contains key tasks. The first stage, *growth*, occurs throughout early childhood and elementary school, concluding at adolescence. The primary tasks during this stage are curiosity, learning about the world of work, and forming initial attitudes and work habits. Adolescence and early adulthood, those years that extend through the major periods of formal education, are included in the *exploration* stage. The main tasks during exploration include crystallizing areas of interest, developing the ability to make career decisions, and making a choice about a career that fits the individual's interest, values, and abilities. An important characteristic emerging during exploration is that of *career maturity*, which refers to an individual's readiness to make planful career decisions, and relies on having enough knowledge about the work world and of one's own values and interests to make an informed decision (Savickas, 2001; Super, 1957, 1969). The Career Development Inventory (Super, 1973; Super & Thompson, 1979) was developed to measure career maturity.

Once the career choice is made, which Super (1990) assumed would occur during the early 20s,

the young adult identifies a permanent job and begins a long stage of settling into the career path, called *establishment*. The tasks associated with establishment include adjusting to work expectations and performing adequately (Savickas, 2001). Positioning one's self for advancement is also a priority in this stage. Establishment is followed by *maintenance*, a stage in which the decision facing the individual is whether to maintain the status quo or attempt innovation to stay ahead or abreast of advancements in the career field. This is also a time during which individuals may reconsider whether they want to stay in their original field or make changes, either for their own benefit or in response to external forces. The final stage, *disengagement*, includes decreasing workload and preparing for and enjoying retirement.

Contemporary vocational and developmental theorists have criticized the linear and normative nature of Super's stage approach, noting that it fails to acknowledge the interaction between individuals and their environments (Vondracek & Porfeli, 2002). By focusing on the normative tasks that accompany a predictable career trajectory, the life-span life-space theory does not adequately accommodate the numerous variations that a given individual might encounter throughout his or her lifetime, from personal health challenges to global economic crises. Much of the research supporting the development of the life-span life-space career trajectory was based on the work experiences of men and on the work expectations of adolescent boys (Super, 1985). Although Super did eventually incorporate samples of women into his research and also acknowledged the impact of gender in his later international Work Importance Study (WIS; Super & Šverko, 1995), the essential idea of developmental career stages was not tested or modified in response to women's career paths.

Despite these criticisms, Super recognized that people would not necessarily progress exclusively in a linear fashion from one stage to the next. In a process called *recycling* (Super, 1994), individuals whose career interests or situation changed might return to a previous stage and recomplete the tasks associated with that stage on a new career trajectory. For example, a 30-year-old seeking a career change may return to the exploration stage and go through the process of crystallizing a new career decision. Super also modified the idea of career maturity to *career adaptability* for adults, recognizing the need for adults to be able to "cope with developmental and adaptation tasks, while recognizing that the capacity to do so is not curvilinear and that it may be have many peaks and valleys" (Super, Osborne, Walsh, Brown, & Niles, 1992, p. 75).

In addition to career maturity and career adaptability, Super suggested that individual progression through the career development stages is modified by values and role salience. *Values* are defined as an objective sought by the individual, be it a psychological state, material reward, or relationship (Super, 1990). *Role salience* refers to the value placed on one life role relative to the others of five identified life roles: work, community service–citizenship, study, leisure, and homemaking–home and family. Both values and role salience have been the subject of extensive examination through the WIS, led by Super and a team of international colleagues (Super & Šverko, 1995). Their work has resulted in the development of the Values Scale and the Salience Inventory (Super & Šverko, 1995), both well-validated instruments. The WIS has resulted in significant empirical support for the role played by values and for the prominence of values oriented toward self-actualization and self-fulfillment in international samples (Šverko, 2001) as well as evidence of the meaningfulness of role salience across age-groups (Šverko, 2001).

There is also empirical support for the tasks connected to the exploration and establishment stages proposed by Super. In the Career Pattern Study, a longitudinal study of 100 men, Super (1985) found measurable differences in vocational maturity between ninth and 12th grade. Furthermore, 12th-grade predictions of young adult vocational behavior were correlated with levels of job status, job satisfaction, and occupational advancement achieved at age 25. Nevill and Super (1988) also found that career maturity was related to commitment to work among college men and women. A crystallized vocational self-concept has been found to have a mediating effect on the relationship between attachment and separation factors and career indecision among college students, such that students with a crystallized

vocational self-concept had less career indecision (Tokar, Withrow, Hall, & Moradi, 2003). Fewer studies have addressed the developmental tasks of the growth stage, as the vocational development of children continues to be understudied (Porfeli, Hartung, & Vondracek, 2008). Limited empirical attention has also been paid to the maintenance and disengagement stages (Savickas, 2001), although Super's attention to midlife and older adult career development was a fairly novel addition to vocational psychology theory.

Contemporary application of Super's developmental theory. Super turned his attention to application of his theory through the Career Development Assessment and Counseling (C-DAC; Super et al., 1992) approach following the development of instruments to assess values, role salience, career maturity, and career adaptability (Niles, 2001). The C-DAC approach attends to both content and process of career decision making and emphasizes the importance of career adaptability. According to Niles (2001), this approach anticipated the need for more complex responses to a changing labor force.

The C-DAC model is a good example of the integration of empirically supported interventions that has been central to the rigor of vocational psychology theory and intervention. In addition, with its emphasis on preparing to adapt to changing circumstances, it laid important groundwork for contemporary counseling models such as career construction (Savickas, 2005), discussed later in this section.

Gottfredson's Theory of Circumscription and Compromise

Gottfredson's (1981, 1986, 2005) theory of circumscription and compromise also focuses on the career decision-making process within the context of development. The theory has been the subject of limited empirical examination. It is unique, however, in its attention to gender norms and social status, and as such has served an important link between developmental theories and some of the later career theories that are more attuned to sociocultural context.

Major tenets of the theory of circumscription and compromise. Consistent with other developmental theories, Gottfredson acknowledged the cognitive growth and increasing self-concept necessary to navigate vocational decision making (for a detailed explanation, see Gottfredson, 2005). The unique contributions of Gottfredson's theory lie in the role of compromise and circumscription and the resulting zone of acceptable alternatives (Gottfredson, 1981) or self-defined social spaces (Gottfredson, 2005) within the existing cognitive map of occupations.

Circumscription. The process by which an individual eliminates unacceptable occupations from the extensive range of possible careers is termed *circumscription*. Occupations that conflict with self-concept or that are considered socially unacceptable for that particular individual are eliminated as children move through four developmental stages of circumscription. Ultimately, this process will result in the creation of the child's zone of acceptable alternatives (Gottfredson, 1981).

The first developmental stage is *orientation to size and power*, which occurs between the ages of 3 and 5. In this stage, children begin to recognize that there is an adult world, that they will eventually become an adult, and that working at a job will be part of that adult role. The second stage, *orientation to sex roles* occurs approximately between the ages of 6 and 8. Children in this stage develop gender-role boundaries with regard to which occupations are acceptable for each sex. This unique emphasis on gender in early childhood makes Gottfredson's theory instrumental in identifying how gender-role orientation can affect women's views about career choices (Coogan & Chen, 2007). *Orientation to social valuation* is the third stage and occurs approximately between the ages of 9 and 13. By this age, children have become aware of status hierarchies and see occupations not only in terms of sex type but also in terms of prestige level. Children at this stage begin to restrict their zone of acceptable occupations, or social space, to those that are not unacceptably low in social status, or unacceptably difficult. Although this process narrows occupational choice, it also serves to foreclose the experiences necessary to determine whether rejected occupations might actually meet their interests and abilities. The final stage is *orientation to internal, unique self* and occurs at approximately 14 years of

age and older. During this stage, vocational development becomes increasingly conscious and adolescents begin to further explore occupations in their social space for compatibility with their personal interests and values in addition to sex roles, abilities, and social status. It is during this stage that the process of compromise occurs.

Compromise. Gottfredson (1981) defined a small but important difference between choice and compromise. Vocational choice occurs when an individual selects between preferred options. In contrast, *compromise* is the process through which individuals begin to eliminate preferred occupational alternatives for occupations that are less compatible but more accessible (Gottfredson, 2005). Barriers that individuals may see as insurmountable and likely to curtail the vocational decision-making process include familial obligations, the job market, racial and sexual discrimination, and accessibility to training and higher education (Blanchard & Lichtenberg, 2003).

The process of compromise is assumed to be influenced by three factors (Gottfredson, 2005). First, insufficient knowledge of the work world can lead to truncated searches, keeping individuals from exploring an area of work that may be a good match for them. Second, the extent of the investment made in actively exploring options and opportunities will increase the accessibility of a wider range of possible vocational choices. Finally, individuals will settle for a good (or not too bad) vocational choice rather than pursuing their optimal choice if the process of pursuing one's optimal choice is seen as too arduous or inconvenient. When this occurs, individuals will need to identify whether they are more or less willing to compromise on sex type, level, or interest. Generally, Gottfredson (2005) believed that people will relinquish interest first, followed by prestige level, and will violate sex-type boundaries only as a final resort.

Responses to Super's and Gottfredson's Developmental Theories
Critics of established vocational development theories, particularly Super's life-span life-space approach, point to the limited application of advances in developmental theory (Vondracek,

2001) and the limited attention paid to contextual factors in career development (Vondracek & Porfeli, 2002). In a summary critique and call for change, Vondracek et al. (1983) suggested that Super, Gottfredson, and other developmental vocational theorists (a) used key constructs from developmental theory without properly attending to the conceptual, empirical, and methodological problems involved; (b) failed to recognize changes in developmental theory that stress the multidimensional, plastic, contextual, and life-span features of development; (c) failed to design longitudinal research programs that attended adequately to context; and (d) generally misrepresented or ignored developmental research (Vondracek et al., 1983). The authors acknowledged that the type of research they suggested relied on methodologies that would not have been available to Super in the 1950s and 1960s, and they challenged the field to integrate these approaches into contemporary times.

As both awareness of and ability to attend to contextual factors has increased, several theorists have proposed alternatives to or expansions of existing developmental models. Vondracek, Lerner, and Schulenberg (1986) focused on the interaction of the individual and his or her social context over the course of development. Young, Valach, and Collin (2002) and Valach and Young (2004) addressed the issue of career as a function of relationship to a social context. Savickas (2005) expanded Super's model to emphasize the role of meaning making and social construction. Each of these theories is introduced in this section, and the interested reader is referred to the authors' original works for more thorough understanding and information.

Career life-span development model.   Vondracek, Lerner, and Schulenberg (1986) subsequently proposed a career life-span development model that differed from existing models by explicitly examining the interaction of the individual and his or her social context. As noted, a basic assumption of this approach is that the individual and the environment in which he or she exists are viewed as changing *interdependently* over time (Vondracek et al., 1986). Their model is firmly anchored in developmental

psychology theory and strongly asserts the need for rigorous longitudinal research. To the extent that such an agenda can be achieved, a more comprehensive systems perspective of vocational development will emerge (Vondracek, 2007).

Vondracek and colleagues proposed an ambitious approach to understanding the antecedents of vocational behavior and the ongoing interaction of the individual and context that influences vocational decisions throughout the life span. A special section of the *Journal of Vocational Behavior* presented several longitudinal studies that offer empirical support for several components of the developmental–contextual perspective of career development (Vondracek, 2007).

In one longitudinal study of 20,000 individuals born and living in the United Kingdom, the changing sociocultural context was shown to influence career development, along with personal characteristics such as gender, parenting, adolescent aspirations, and level of academic achievement (Schoon, Martin, & Ross, 2007). The authors also concluded that a developmental–contextual paradigm allowed improved understanding of the complex relationships between individual and cultural context, compared with an alternative sociological model. The complex longitudinal analyses supported by these researchers also revealed distinctly more diverse careers held by women than by men (Martin, Schoon, & Ross, 2008), demonstrating the strengths of methodology attached to modern developmental–contextual perspectives. Other studies demonstrated that career development is influenced by part-time work during adolescence, particularly in U.S. samples (Porfeli, 2007); that career preparation contributes to positive adjustment (Skorikov, 2007); and that gender socialization and social policies interact with childhood antisocial behaviors to predict workforce participation in Portugal (Ferreira, Santos, Fonseca, & Haase, 2007).

This impressive array of international and longitudinal research work shows significant promise for the continuing development of a more complex understanding of the interaction of individual and context. As yet, the developmental–contextual approach has not been translated into an applicable or practical approach that can be used directly with clients seeking vocational assistance. The next step in developing this model would be to examine ways in which the developmental–contextual perspective might influence career counseling interventions.

Contextual action theory of career counseling. Also frustrated with what they described as the "shortcomings" (Valach & Young, 2004, p. 62) in career counseling, Young, Valach, and Collin (2002) developed the contextual action theory of career counseling. In contrast to Vondracek et al. (1986), Young and colleagues anchored their basic tenets in cultural and contextual psychology, rather than developmental psychology. This emphasis places the focus of counseling on the actions and relationships of "socially embedded human behavior" (Valach & Young, 2004, p. 76).

In contextual action career counseling, the content of interest may be relevant to developmental approaches, even though the approach is primarily focused on culture and context. For example, the influence of parents and family on adolescents is a topic of significant interest (Young et al., 2001; Young, Ball, Valach, Turkel, & Wong, 2003), but the emphasis of both counseling and research is on the joint actions made by parent–child dyads in relationship to each other and the career-related conversation. This conversation results in the conceptualization of a career "project" that becomes part of the family's larger relationship. This project also informs the way in which participants make meaning of the career conversation and serves as an act of social constructionism (Collin & Young, 2000; Valach & Young, 2004).

Contextual action provides specific guidelines for both research and practice, although the authors are explicit about their belief that "career is first and foremost a practice construct" (Valach & Young, 2004, p. 74). Nonetheless, the relationships and constructs that are emphasized in the practice do provide intriguing areas of inquiry for vocational psychology. Young, Valach, and colleagues have initiated a potentially fruitful line of scholarship that will benefit from replication and expansion. Such research will also support the themes of social construction, meaning making, and relationships that have become incorporated into other vocational theories.

Career construction theory. The career construction theory (Savickas, 2005) also draws from concepts of meaning making and social constructionism. In contrast to the two preceding theories, career construction builds on and expands ideas proposed by Super (1990). In fact, Savickas (2002) has stated that the "psychology of careers must focus on development" (p. 384), and he has fulfilled that call through career construction, with the goal of making Super's essential propositions more applicable to contemporary individuals working within global labor markets (Savickas, 2005).

Philosophically, career construction theory assumes that "individuals construct their careers by imposing meaning on their vocational behavior and occupational experiences" (Savickas, 2005, p. 43). The three major components of career construction theory are vocational personality, career adaptability, and life themes. *Vocational personality* describes the *what* of career and shares common descriptions with the RIASEC model posed by Holland (1997), but herein is conceptualized as socially constructed clusters of skills, interests, and attitudes. This makes personality more useful as a source of possibilities than a prediction of fit and also recognizes that vocational personality is a dynamic rather than stable self-representation (Savickas, 2005).

Career adaptability is emphasized in career construction as a construct necessary for successful navigation of the increasingly volatile labor force and explains the *how* of career (Savickas, 2005). Specifically, it denotes an "individual's readiness and resources for coping with current and imminent vocational development tasks, occupational transitions, and personal traumas" (Savickas, 2005, p. 51). Rather than an end goal of career maturity, career adaptability assumes that the optimal state is to be ready to adapt to changes imposed by social realities. Individuals can foster career adaptability through four dimensions: being concerned about their futures, increasing control over their vocational futures, being curious about possibilities, and having confidence to pursue aspirations. Finally, *life themes* are the narratives or stories individuals use to make meaningful decisions about their career and work roles. The life theme helps the counselor and client understand the *why* of a career (Savickas, 2005).

Career construction theory has been applied primarily to practice situations, and has yet to be the subject of extensive empirical examination. However, Savickas (2005) presented an extensive strategy for interpreting life themes, vocational personality, and adaptability information, which does lend itself to replication and analysis. Scholarship designed to assess the effectiveness of these strategies and to test the added value of career construction propositions beyond those of Super's propositions are warranted to move the theory forward. It would be particularly important to investigate the dimensions and functions of career adaptability, both as they are purported to influence career behaviors and as they compare to extant research on career maturity. Conceptually, career adaptability should vary from career maturity in terms of, for example, readiness for change, but additional research is necessary to verify such differences. A qualitative research agenda that thoroughly explores life themes could make a valuable contribution by illuminating process variables in career decision making. Although other theories focus on antecedents and context of career choice, career construction is uniquely located to examine and understand the complex and interrelated ways in which people make sense of, or process, the numerous variables that come together into a career decision.

SOCIAL LEARNING AND COGNITION THEORIES

Drawing from developmental, trait-and-factor, and learning models established previously, social learning and social cognition theories pay specific attention to the interaction of genetic, learning, and social influences, assuming a dynamic process amenable to intervention at several points in the vocational process. The emphasis on learning experiences, and their subsequent impact on personal characteristics such as approach to tasks, self-efficacy, and outcome expectations, suggest opportunities to control or change vocational outcomes. Yet these theories also recognize that those opportunities are influenced by personal and social characteristics, including genetic and demographic factors, social forces, and cultural context.

Social cognitive career theory (SCCT; Lent, Brown, & Hackett, 1994) has become the most widely adapted and examined contemporary vocational theory, and this theory is explored later in this section after a brief discussion of earlier work in social learning vocational theory. SCCT is inclusive of several components of P-E fit and developmental theories, already presented, as well as earlier work in social learning vocational theory, developed by John Krumboltz (1979).

Social Learning Theory

Krumboltz's (1979) initial vocational social learning theory focused on career decision making. He identified four variables that contributed to identifying vocational goals and making necessary decisions: genetic endowments and special abilities, environmental situations and events, associative and instrumental learning experiences, and task approach skills. The explicit attention to genetic endowments, including sex, race, and special abilities provided a framework for examining differences in vocational attainment across sex, race and ethnicity, and other biologically identified groups of career decision makers. It was the inclusion of social and cultural factors, such as geography, legislation, labor market forces, family factors, and educational settings, that set social learning theory apart from previous vocational theories. It was recognized in social learning theory that individual interests or choices were not the only determinants of vocational attainment.

Krumboltz (1979) included both associative (observation of others) and instrumental (seeing the consequences of one's own actions) learning in his model of career decision making. Together with genetic endowments and the sociocultural situation, learning served as the final antecedent to task approach skills, which were identified as individual work habits, problem-solving skills, and cognitive and emotional responses to work tasks (Krumboltz, 1979). Task approach skills subsequently contributed to the individual's perceptions of his or her own abilities and interests (self-observation generalizations), which led to making a career decision. More recently, in presenting happenstance learning theory, Krumboltz (2009) proposed that "the goal of career counseling is to help clients learn to take actions to achieve more satisfying career and personal lives—not to make a single career decision" (p. 135). This updated goal echoes both the definition of vocational psychology put forth by Walsh and Savickas (2005) and reinforces the centrality of vocational psychology to life satisfaction.

In 1981, Nancy Getz and Gail Hackett applied social learning theory to the examination of women's career development and isolated the role of self-efficacy as a determinant of both outcome expectations and vocational attainment. Their seminal series of work in the 1980s triggered a revolution in examining sex differences in vocational psychology and ultimately led to the development of a theory that arguably has done more to address group differences than any previous vocational theory—that is, SCCT.

Social Cognitive Career Theory

A literature search of SCCT (Lent et al., 1994) revealed that 17 articles examining SCCT were published in 2009 alone, demonstrating the expansive growth and utilization of SCCT in vocational psychology research. SCCT can easily be labeled as one of the most comprehensive and popular theories in the contemporary counseling psychology literature. One reason for SCCT's wide application is its usefulness in guiding inquiry on the career development of women and racial–ethnic minorities (Coogan & Chen, 2007), topics that more traditional career theories developed on the basis of White men's career development fail to adequately address.

SCCT provides a unifying framework for common career-related elements previously identified as important to career development by Super, Holland, Krumboltz, Lofquist, and Dawis (Lent, 2005). Anchored in Bandura's (1986) general social cognitive theory, SCCT integrates the role of environmental influences on the development and pursuit of career and educational interests, choices, and performance. The theory focuses on several cognitive–person variables (self-efficacy expectations, outcome expectations, and goals), and on how these variables interact with other aspects of the person (e.g., gender, ethnicity, ability) and his or her environment (e.g., social supports and barriers) in the formation of career interests and goals.

Major tenets and empirical support of SCCT.
SCCT proposes an understanding of vocational development that includes the interaction of three person variables and three sets of influences or moderating factors to predict outcomes in four segmented models.

SCCT's three person variables. Lent and colleagues (1994) identified three person variables—self-efficacy expectations, outcome expectations, and personal goals—as most important in regulating career-related behavior. *Self-efficacy expectations* are the belief in one's ability to perform specific actions or behaviors, and these expectations are a central mechanism by which career interests are formulated. *Outcome expectations* are an individual's beliefs about the likely consequences of performing specific behaviors or actions. *Personal goals* are the individual's intentions to act to achieve a particular career-related goal.

It is hypothesized that self-efficacy is a precursor of outcome expectations, interests, and goals, and consequently self-efficacy expectations have been the most researched and empirically supported tenant of SCCT. Because of space limitations, this chapter cannot begin to present the mass of empirical support for the concept of self-efficacy in career development. Lent et al. (1994) presented initial meta-analytic correlations of self-efficacy to interests, choice goals, and outcome expectations respectively, of .53, .40, and .49. Rottinghaus, Larson, and Borgen (2003) conducted a more recent meta-analysis of the relationship between self-efficacy and interests and found a correlation of .59 over 60 samples.

Although these findings provide ample evidence that the two constructs are related, they do not address the underlying issue of causality specified by SCCT, that self-efficacy precedes interest development. Research relevant to the directionality of the relationships among the social cognitive variables has provided some evidence for causality (Lent et al., 2008; Silvia, 2003). However, longitudinal evidence has contradictorily indicated that the direction of causality might also be reversed, with interests acting as the precursor to self-efficacy (Nauta, Kahn, Angell, & Cantarelli, 2002; Tracey, 2002). Bonitz, Larson, and Armstrong (2010) conducted an experimental manipulation of interests to evaluate causal links between interests and self-efficacy. They found evidence that changes in interests lead to changes in self-efficacy or choice goals. This evidence has implications for the revision or expansion of the SCCT framework, including the need to focus research more specifically on the recursive relationship between self-efficacy and interests.

SCCT's three sets of influences. SCCT (Lent et al., 1994) also identifies three sets of influences on the basis of aspects of the person and his or her environment that are believed to influence interest formation and the translation of these interests into goals. *Background and proximal contextual influences* include opportunities for task and role model exposure, support for and barriers to engaging in particular activities, and cultural and gender role socialization processes. The second set of influences includes *personal inputs* such as socioeconomic status (SES), gender, ethnicity, and innate abilities. *Learning experiences* are considered the third set of influences and include performance accomplishments, vicarious learning, social persuasion, and physiological arousal. These three sets of influences are thought to affect interest formation as they influence self-efficacy expectations, outcome expectations, and personal goals.

There is a great deal of support for these three sets of theoretical influences proposed by SCCT. Many contextual variables have been empirically explored including parent–teacher support (Gushue & Whiston, 2006), parental involvement (Byars-Winston & Fouad, 2008), Anglo-oriented acculturation, Mexican-oriented acculturation (Flores, Navarro, & DeWitz, 2008), familism, instrumentality, expressivity (Flores, Robitschek, Celebi, Andersen, & Hoang, 2010), perceived occupational barriers (Constantine, Wallace, & Kindaichi, 2005), and environmental supports and barriers (Lent et al., 2003), to name a few. Because of the expansiveness of contextual variables this is an area where much more research is needed.

Support has also been found for the influence of learning experiences on career-related self-efficacy and outcome expectations. Williams and Subich (2006) recently extended this literature by demonstrating moderate to strong association of learning experiences for Holland's (1997) six RIASEC themes to corresponding self-efficacy percepts and outcome expectations. They found that women reported more learning experiences in the social domain, and

men reported more learning experiences in the realistic and investigative domains. Results of their study supported the idea that more reported learning experiences in a given domain relates to higher self-efficacy and outcome expectations in that domain. This highlights the important differences in learning experiences that lead to gender differences in career-related self-efficacy, outcome expectations, and interests. These findings suggest that women's career pursuits can be constricted or expanded by the learning environments to which they are exposed early on and has implications for educational, familial, and counseling interventions.

Tokar, Thompson, Plaufcan, and Williams (2007) more recently sought to examine the potential contribution to learning experiences of three person inputs: personality, gender, and conformity to gender role norms. To build on Williams and Subich's (2006) previous study, they focused on the potential precursors of learning experiences for each of Holland's (1997) RIASEC themes. Their results suggested that both personality and gender play an important role in exposure to vocational learning experiences. Many of the significant relations between basic person inputs and learning experiences, particularly those involving gender, were at least partially accounted for by conformity to gender role norms. Results also suggested that gender role conformity may be most relevant to learning experiences in the realistic and social domains.

SCCT's theoretical framework: Four segmental models. SCCT originally consisted of three conceptually distinct but overlapping segmental models designed to explain the processes through which people form basic academic and career-related interests, make and revise educational and vocational choices, and achieve performances of varying quality in the academic and career domains (Lent et al., 1994). In each of these three models, the basic theoretical elements of self-efficacy, outcome expectations, and goals are seen as operating in concert with other important aspects of the person, their contexts, and learning experiences to shape academic and career development. The *interest model* states that interests (defined as the extent to which an individual enjoys a particular activity, academic subject, college major, or occupation) are jointly predicted by self-efficacy and outcome expectations (Lent et al., 1994). According to the *choice model*, people develop goals to pursue academic and occupational-related activities that are consistent with not only their interests but also their self-efficacy and outcome expectations. Self-efficacy and outcome expectations are hypothesized to affect choice both directly as well as indirectly through interests (Lent et al., 1994). In the *performance model*, educational and vocational performance involves the interplay between people's abilities, self-efficacy, outcome expectations, and performance goals. Ability can affect performance both directly through task knowledge and performance strategies developed over time, and indirectly, by affecting self-efficacy and outcome expectations (Lent et al., 1994). SCCT's interest and choice models are the most empirically tested and supported (Lent et al., 2008; Sheu et al., 2010). Recently, a fourth model, focusing on educational and work satisfaction was introduced (Lent & Brown, 2006). The *satisfaction model* posits that work–educational satisfaction is predicted by five classes of variables: work conditions and outcomes, goal-directed behavior, self-efficacy, goal and efficacy relevant supports and obstacles, and personality and affective traits. Although the satisfaction model is a fairly new addition to SCCT, initial support has been found (Duffy & Lent, 2009).

Contemporary application of SCCT. SCCT research has provided many implications for preventive, developmental, and remedial interventions. Interventions targeting the enhancement of self-efficacy have been linked to positive career development, particularly for women. Readers are referred to an inclusive article by Betz (2007) that thoroughly discusses the extensive research on the applications of Bandura's self-efficacy theory to career theory, assessment, and counseling.

Sullivan and Mahalik (2000) developed a 6-week group intervention for women composed of both didactic and experiential activities and discussion designed to emphasize career choice as a process as well as to increase career decision-making self-efficacy. Results indicated the women in the treatment group improved on career decision-making

self-efficacy and vocational exploration and commitment. In line with SCCT, this study addressed socialization factors that affect self-efficacy for women. Coogan and Chen (2007) have also noted that social and environmental contexts are particularly relevant to women's career needs and experiences.

Initial support for SCCT's satisfaction model provides potential for the theory's application to conceptualizing and organizing methods for promoting work satisfaction. Lent and Brown (2006, 2008) suggested that dissatisfaction may stem from (a) impeded or flat progress toward goals; (b) failure to attain the desired outcomes from work; (c) exposure to unacceptable work conditions; (d) low self-efficacy regarding one's ability to complete work tasks, specific work goals, or cope with negative conditions; or (e) inadequate environmental supports or personal resources. With this in mind, they suggested that it may be useful for counselors or organizational consultants to assess workers along the previously mentioned dimensions to identify individuals who could most benefit from preventative, developmental, or remedial efforts. SCCT's applicability to diverse groups is one of the most currently active and important areas of research. SCCT was originally developed to assist in the understanding of the unique career development needs of individuals on the basis of such factors as sex, race or ethnicity, culture, SES, age, and disability status (Lent, 2005; Lent et al., 1994). SCCT has been extended conceptually and empirically to a number of other client populations, including adults with psychiatric disabilities (Fabian, 2000) and gay and lesbian workers (Morrow, Gore, & Campbell, 1996). The following section will highlight a few of the more recent empirical studies concerning diverse and understudied groups.

Recently a wave of research has been conducted on lower SES Appalachian youth, a typically understudied population (Ali & McWhirter, 2006; Ali, McWhirter, & Chronister, 2005; Ali & Saunders, 2006). Rural Appalachia is characterized by high levels of poverty and unemployment. A recent study indicated that lower SES rural Appalachian high school students might benefit from targeted interventions designed to increase their self-efficacy beliefs or confidence and expectations about their future (Ali & Saunders, 2009). Ali and McWhirter (2006) suggested that vocational psychologists and school counselors working with rural Appalachian high school students may want to design interventions that address student's perceptions of barriers to higher education.

The work of Flores and her colleagues (e.g., Flores et al., 2008; Flores & O'Brien, 2002; Ojeda & Flores, 2008) has focused on Mexican American adolescents because they are an underrepresented population in higher education. Findings that perceived educational barriers significantly predict Mexican American students' educational aspirations (Ojeda & Flores, 2008) and findings that Mexican Americans report higher levels of educational aspirations than educational expectations are disturbing, to say the least. Career counselors working with this population should examine students' beliefs about the resources they need to obtain higher education and help students to develop effective strategies to deal with barriers they encounter or expect to encounter in their educational pursuits. Ojeda and Flores (2008) also warned that practitioners need to be cognizant of Mexican American students' generational level so as not to assume that the student has received the necessary information to successfully navigate the U.S. school system.

A large base of research offers support for many of the theoretical tenants of SCCT. SCCT has the potential to assist in the understanding and career development of a diverse range of individuals, which makes the theory fairly unique. The application of SCCT based interventions appears to be promising on the basis of a few initial theory-based intervention studies (Betz & Schifano, 2000; Luzzo, Hasper, Albert, Bibby, & Martinelli, 1999; Sullivan & Mahalik, 2000). More research is needed, however, to strengthen the empirical base for the practical application of SCCT tenets with clients.

EMERGING VOCATIONAL THEORIES

The rich history of vocational theory has established a tradition of application and empirical support that encourages innovation. It is not surprising, then, that new vocational theories are emerging even as

established theories continue to perform well. Given the attention paid to social justice and social context in vocational psychology, many new theories are directly influenced by changing social norms. In the theories reviewed in this section, the influence of family and relational concerns, socioeconomic factors that limit access to vocational opportunities, and an improved recognition of the role of nonconscious processes in decision making are most apparent. This diverse array of catalysts highlights the relevance of vocation to multiple life domains and vice versa.

The Relational Cultural Paradigm

Established theories such as SCCT (Lent et al., 1994) and developmental–contextualism life-span approach (Vondracek et al., 1986) certainly recognize the role of family and relationships as part of the contextual framework in which vocational behavior evolves. The role of family and parents in vocational behavior has also been the subject of extensive empirical examination (see Whiston & Keller, 2004, for a thorough review).

Explicit attention to the relational nature of work has been put forth in the past decade (Blustein, Schultheiss, & Flum, 2004; Flum, 2001; Schultheiss, 2003) to expand these ideas into a meta-theory that addresses how individuals make meaning of work through relationship (Schultheiss, 2003, 2007). Four essential components of social constructionism (Gergen, 1999) shaped this initial relational paradigm (Blustein et al., 2004): (a) a critical analysis of assumed knowledge; (b) the presumption that an individual's understanding of the world is embedded in culture and history; (c) knowledge is constructed between people and through interactions with others, rather than individual objective observation; and (d) this created knowledge results in social actions, including vocationally relevant behaviors. From this perspective, the self is reconstructed as relationship (Gergen, 1999), and vocational identity is constructed within and across multiple relationships (Collin & Young, 2000; Gergen, 1999) as an integrated part of the self.

In recognition of the integrated and embedded nature of vocational and other aspects of identity, the term *worklife* (Schultheiss, 2007) has been proposed to "represent the nexus of work (unbound by dichotomous distinctions such as labor market and personal work), relationships, and culture (including the cultural construction of gender)" (p. 193). This language provides an inclusive way to refer to the embedded nature of work that is fundamental to the basic tenets of the relational paradigm.

Major tenets of the relational cultural paradigm. Schultheiss (2007) summarized the work of numerous theorists and researchers in identifying four tenets of the relational cultural paradigm. She pointed out that these ideas are not designed to replace other theories but instead are proposed as a meta-theory that will address the role of "meaning and mattering in worklife" (p. 191).

The family as critical to understanding the complexities of vocational development. On the basis of a large extant literature on the role of family (especially parental) relationships in vocational behavior (Whiston & Keller, 2004), the relational paradigm highlights the process and culture of family influences in worklife. The quality and nature of relationships are assumed to provide resources necessary for effective negotiation of work-related tasks as well as to support the ability to create new relationships as an adult.

The psychological experience of work as embedded in relational contexts. This tenet highlights the importance of the relational dimension of embeddedness (Josselson, 1992) to worklife. *Embeddedness* refers to a sense of belonging and assumes a socially and psychologically meaningful network of associations. Work and worklife can meet the needs of belongingness and involvement, and may also be used to avoid feelings of isolation. When work brings feelings of isolation or conflict, it may result in less satisfaction and increased stress. The construct of embeddedness highlights the "artificial" (Schultheiss, 2007, p. 197) boundaries between work and personal life.

The interface of work and family life. Closely related to the idea of embeddedness is the explicit recognition that work and family life influence each other in meaningful ways. The relational paradigm attends to the impact of the changing nature of work on families, the particular needs of families from minority or underrepresented groups, and the expanding definition of families beyond the tradition of a married heterosexual couple with children (Schultheiss, 2007). Schultheiss (2007) called for research that attends to a more inclusive understanding and definition of family.

Relational discourse as a challenge to the cultural script of individualism. In this final tenet, Schultheiss (2007) called for a new language that recognizes the role of relationship and embeddedness in the formation of meaning and representations of the social world. Such a language is critical for the relational paradigm to move forward.

Implications of the cultural relational paradigm. This paradigm is based on sound empirical support for at least two of its major tenets—the role of family in vocational life and the interface of work and family life. Despite several calls to expand research to relational roles beyond parents, other important relationships have not been examined (Motulsky, 2010). The potential for research to examine multiple other relationships—including friendship, sibling relationships (Schultheiss, Kress, Manzi, & Glasscock, 2001), coworkers, and teacher–student—is significant and could add important dimensions to the construct of worklife. In a qualitative study with 13 midcareer women, Motulsky (2010) identified numerous relational connections that influenced career transitions, including parents, partners, extended family, siblings, children, friends, supervisors, colleagues, community members, and professionals such as therapists and clergy. Working from a feminist perspective, Motulsky concluded that both connections and disconnections were important to women's career transitions. These findings both extend the support for relational influence and identify the importance of work relationships, which may contribute to feelings of embeddedness.

The role of embeddedness is theory driven, which provides excellent opportunities for developing empirical support. Several qualitative studies (for summaries, see Blustein et al., 2004; Schultheiss, 2007) have alluded to the value of embeddedness, but explicit examinations, qualitative or quantitative, have not yet been conducted. Nonetheless, the theoretical underpinnings of the embeddedness construct provide a foundation for research questions. It would be interesting, for example, to look at vocational outcome differences among workers who do and do not experience a sense of belongingness in their work environment, or among those who identify a social network among their coworkers. The relationship between antecedents and consequences of embeddedness is also worthy of exploration. For example, it would be interesting to examine whether job satisfaction is correlated with embeddedness once an adequate measurement tool for embeddedness is developed. If such a relationship is found, future research might examine whether a predictive relationship can be identified, to determine whether job satisfaction is a consequence or antecedent of embeddeness, or perhaps to examine whether there is a recursive or other nonlinear relationship between the two. Empirical models that included embeddedness might also be able to identify whether it serves to mediate other work relationships, such as that between job satisfaction and job tenure.

A simultaneous challenge and opportunity for the cultural relational paradigm is posed by the fourth tenet. A meaningful language that effectively communicates the complexity of cultural relational paradigms is necessary for further theory development and empirical support. This is complicated by the fact that the relational language must be broadly accessible to accomplish the goal of the relational cultural paradigm to serve as a complementary metatheory to other vocational theories. Although the authors suggest that the cultural relational paradigm is a rich way to move vocational research forward, that can only be done if the language provides a way to ensure that independent scholars are actually conceptualizing these ideas in a meaningfully similar way. Such a language must capture the meaningfulness of embeddedness and context inherent to the relational cultural paradigm, must remain relevant to theorists and researchers from multiple schools of thought or theoretical perspectives, and must communicate a holistic concept of worklife. Such a task seems daunting, but developing a common and comprehensive language capable of meeting these demands would be a promising and exciting contribution to vocational psychology.

The Psychology of Working

Over the past 2 decades, several theorists have identified limitations to previous definitions of vocational psychology and career, particularly noting that the emphasis on choice and the assumption of lifelong development might ignore the reality of people who do not have the access to resources that might afford such choices (Fouad, 2007; Richardson, 1993). Acknowledging that even the use of the term *career* excludes a significant portion of the global population, Blustein (2006; Blustein, Kenna, Gill, & DeVoy, 2008) proposed the *psychology-of-working* paradigm. Although it has not yet been subject to the empirical examination that will demonstrate its viability as a theory, the constructs within the psychology-of-working paradigm serve as catalysts for some exciting and provocative vocational questions with implications for research, practice, and public policy.

Major tenets of the psychology-of-working paradigm. A basic assumption of the psychology-of-working paradigm is that "working" is a more universal and inclusive experience than "career." *Working* can be defined as the expenditure of energy, activity, and effort to tasks that make a contribution to society, whether they are paid or nonpaid (Blustein, 2006). This definition is therefore inclusive of employment, work in the home, volunteer work, caring for others, and any other activity that contributes meaningfully to society. Importantly, it also includes work that is essential but of less prestige, such as jobs classified as "working class," recognizing that they play a valuable role in the social good. Blustein (2006) further proposed that work fulfills three fundamental needs: survival and power, social connectedness, and self-determination.

Work as a means of survival and power. A basic function of work is to provide people with the food, clothing, shelter, and other resources they need to survive. Blustein (2006) recognized this fundamental need as well as the related need for power, be it economic, social, or psychological. In short, the more of the essential resources a person possesses, the more power he or she is able to accrue.

Despite its essential nature, psychologists have paid minimal attention to survival in the context of vocation and career. Blustein (2006) noted that Smith (1983) is one of the few exceptions to this avoidance of the topic, pointing out that vocational psychologists needed to attend more fully to the survival role of work in 1983. Multicultural critics of vocational psychology (Carter & Cook, 1992; Helms & Cook, 1999) have also pointed out the need to attend to fundamental economic and survival issues. Clearly, vocational psychologists need to address fundamental survival needs to meet the goal of an inclusive and socially just discipline.

The individual who successfully meets and exceeds survival needs begins to be seen as successful and therefore to obtain social power as well as the economic power that comes with adequate resources. Although the accrual of power may be subtle and not even conscious, the social and psychological rewards of it often reinforce working harder and more effectively. Blustein (2006) concluded that "working is integral to the development of power" (p. 75) and that our work culture is increasingly ensuring that the needs for survival and power are closely linked.

Work as a means of social connection. Work has historically been an opportunity for individuals to form connections to others outside of their family, often leading to important relationships including friendships and even intimate partnerships. Blustein (2006) noted that work brings individuals into direct contact with others and also provides them an opportunity to be part of the larger social fabric as they participate in the economic exchange that work and consumerism generates.

As work changes, the nature of these relationships may also change. Blustein (2006) notes that work brings individuals into direct contact with others, and also provides them an opportunity to be part of the larger social fabric as they participate in the economic exchange that work and consumerism generate. When placed in the context of globalization, the potentially competing demands of increased opportunities for global communication or connectedness and increased use of limited resources could either facilitate or impede social connections (Couthino, Dam, & Blustein, 2008). Couthino and colleagues note that vocational counselors can play an important role in helping

individuals seek out opportunities for social connectedness. Blustein (2006) summarized several threads of research that offer empirical support for the use of work as a means of social connectedness. Qualitative work with a variety of populations, including working-class and low-income adolescents and adults (Phillips, Blustein, Jobin-Davis, & White, 2002; Phillips, Christopher-Sisk, & Gravino, 2001; Schultheiss et al., 2001) and American Indians (Juntunen et al., 2001), has demonstrated that connectedness via work is experienced as quite meaningful. Research that examines the relationship between work and caregiving or family roles also suggests that the interface of these relationships is extremely important (Cinamon & Rich, 2010), although this is complicated by the fact that caregiving continues to be undervalued.

Work as a means of self-determination. According to Ryan and Deci (2000), self-determination refers to internalized or intrinsic motivation of human behavior. Self-determination theory (SDT) postulates that social conditions will contribute to whether individuals are engaged and proactive or alienated and passive. Of particular value to vocational psychology, Ryan and Deci (2000) have articulated a continuum of motivation (p. 72), including amotivation, external motivation, and intrinsic motivation, with accompanying regulatory styles and processes that are influenced by social factors and potentially amenable to intervention.

With appropriate support from the social context, individuals can move toward increasingly intrinsic motivation. In the context of the psychology-of-working paradigm, this suggests that satisfaction can be increased when the rewards of work are intrinsic, even if the extrinsic rewards (such as salary and prestige) of specific work are not particularly satisfactory. Contextual social support might include education that increases feelings of competency or counseling to increase awareness of values or increased self-control. Through an intentional process of modifying the social context, individuals can move through different regulatory styles. The *nonregulated* style is associated with a lack of motivation and feelings of incompetency and lack of control. In the context of work, this might be expressed by someone who does not seek work or ends up in a series of jobs with limited volition or belief in their own value to contribute.

Within external motivation, there are four styles that become increasing close to internal motivation; internalization is a process of moving through these four styles, with assistance or in response to changes in the social condition. The first of these is *external regulation*, which is associated with compliance and an orientation toward external rewards and punishments. In the next phase of internalization, *introjected regulation*, there is an increased sense of self-control and some recognition of internal rewards and punishments, but these rewards and punishments are often geared toward feelings of guilt and anxiety at not meeting expectations. The regulatory style becomes more internal in the next phase, *identified regulation*, in which the individual is more likely to engage in tasks because of the value of their outcome. The last internalization style, *integrated regulation*, is recognized by an internal sense of control and a sense of congruence or synthesis with self (Ryan & Deci, 2000). Work may not be inherently interesting, but the individual's perception of his or her own work role is one of being valuable and competent in that role.

If a person does complete the process of internalization, he or she may then be motivated by primarily intrinsic forces, in which activities, including work, are inherently pleasurable or interesting. At this point, the individual is likely to be fully engaged and proactive (Ryan & Deci, 2000). In the context of work, Blustein (2006) acknowledged that internalization is based on the individual's perceptions, and cannot change the work experience itself.

In numerous studies across age-groups and social settings, Ryan, Deci, and their colleagues have found support for the basic tenet that increased internalization contributes to increased well-being and higher performance (summarized in Ryan & Deci, 2000). They have also found that social contexts that support individual autonomy, competence, and relatedness to others are more likely to contribute to well-being and to increased functioning within that context.

As Blustein (2006) discussed in the psychology-of-working paradigm, SDT concepts have significant potential for exploration in the context of vocational psychology. The regulatory processes are amenable to counseling interventions and present excellent opportunities for evidence-supported treatment research. Recognizing the role of the social context in providing essential characteristics of autonomy, competence and relatedness support inquiry that focuses on the work setting rather than continuing to examine only the actions of the individual worker. Such research cannot only move our empirical understanding forward but can also influence policy and practice.

Implications of the psychology-of-working paradigm. The tenets of the psychology-of-working paradigm have yet to be investigated in a holistic way, but Blustein (2006) has outlined an ambitious research agenda that could take vocational psychology in a new direction. At the heart of his proposals is the challenge for vocational psychology to "confront many of the seemingly intractable problems that face workers across the globe" (2006, p. 242). He specifically proposed that social constructionist (Gergen, 1999) and emancipatory communitarian (Prilleltensky, 1997) approaches to scholarship be more fully utilized to expand understanding beyond the current limits imposed by positivistic research paradigms.

The integration of self-determination as a meaningful goal of work provides a strong foundation for theory-driven scholarship, and one that could influence work environments, school reform, and individual counseling practices. Similarly, the role of social connectedness can build on existing research (Flum, 2001; Schultheiss, 2003) and expand the ways in which we think about work in relationships and as relationship. Finally, the reintroduction of the psychological components of power and survival offers the potential to return to the challenge posed by Smith in 1983: "Vocational psychologists need to reexamine the concept of dignity of all work and its corollary that work is central to the lives of all individuals" (p. 187). Given the increasing discussion of the centrality of work, this question may need to be directly addressed; an understanding of the role of work in survival and power can provide a framework from which to do so.

The counseling strategies associated with the psychology-of-working paradigm emphasize increased engagement and increased critical consciousness among previously overlooked populations of clients. These ideas have already been extrapolated into considerations of global need (Coutinho et al., 2008). Two additional strategies, promoting clients' skill building for a changing workforce and providing scaffolding to support volition, have also been introduced (Blustein et al., 2008). An important expansion of traditional vocational counseling is included in the scaffolding strategy, which explicitly advocates for the utilization of multiple resources, including social workers, case management teams, and social advocacy, to support the client in navigating a sometimes-challenging work environment. The potential to apply strategies that can create meaningful change for unemployed, underemployed, and unhappily employed clients is a welcome addition to existing intervention strategies. Blustein also made the very important point that the integration of work as central to the lived experience supports the integration of work as central to the psychotherapy experience and challenges professional as well as vocational psychologists to move toward this integrated service delivery.

Finally, the psychology-of-working principles can inform public policy issues (Blustein, 2006; Blustein et al., 2008), including educational reform, unemployment policies, the role of work in health and mental health policy, work oppression and harassment policies, and employment diversity and cultural knowledge policies. This explicit acknowledgment of the role of vocational psychology in the realm of public policy could significantly influence the development of new ideas. Although Blustein's ideas echo a long history of engagement with social change and reform (Herr, 2001, 2003), they also mark a new intentionality in designing and planning to influence policies that is significantly different from the individual focus of most established theories.

Trilateral Model of Adaptive Career Decision Making

The previous two emerging theories are striving to move vocational psychology into new paradigms by emphasizing the role of context and relationships in the working life of the individual. In contrast, Krieshok, Black, and McKay (2009) have proposed a

model that is focused on increasing our understanding of how individuals respond to a changing context.

Krieshok et al. (2009) began their proposed trilateral model with a common identification of the changing workforce and the need to prepare people for increased adaptability. They then presented a novel model that examines the processes individuals use to make the decisions that will maximize the series of matches that accompany adapting to change over the course of a career.

The trilateral model hinges on the behavior of *occupational engagement*, which is defined as career exploration plus career enrichment, wherein exploration is designed to achieve a career decision and the goal of enrichment is experientially informed decision making that may occur at many varied points in the future. They argued that individuals who are occupationally engaged think about their vocational futures

> even when they are *not* faced with imminent transitions. By behaving in ways that optimize their adaptation to unexpected transitions, they are *engaged* in a process of *enrichment* that can be understood as a subtle, but adaptive preparation for the likelihood of career transition. (Krieshok et al., 2009, p. 285)

They concluded that in vocational counseling, it is important to think of ongoing matching between person and work, rather than *the* match between person and work.

In addition to occupational engagement, the other two sides of the trilateral model involve rational and intuitive decision making. Although most vocational theories, dating back to Parsons (1909), rely on the assumptions of rational decision making, decision-making experts such as Kahneman (2003) recognized that there are boundaries to rational decision-making abilities and that other processes, such as intuition, play a role in most decision-oriented behaviors. The role of intuition in decision making has been further supported by neuroscience research, for example, the observation of the functions of the basal ganglia in implicit learning (Lieberman, 2003) and its subsequent role in decision making.

Initial validation of this model has focused on the role of occupational engagement, including the development of two versions of an occupational engagement scale (Krieshok et al., 2009). Although this model is new, there is some initial evidence that occupational engagement can be both measured and increased (Krieshok et al., 2009). Initial validation of the occupational engagement scale demonstrated that it correlates with vocational identity (Black, 2006; Cox, 2008), with the Openness to Experience, Conscientiousness, and Extraversion factors of the NEO Personality Inventory—Revised (McKay, Kerr, Hansen, & Krieshok, 2008), and with several assessments of well-being and achievement among college students (Cox, 2008). Scott (2006) and Noble (2008) demonstrated that the constructs of job involvement and job curiosity have initial validity in samples of adult workers, supporting the domains of occupational engagement.

To develop this understanding of occupational engagement and readiness to make career decisions, Krieshok et al. (2009) have drawn from an array of disciplines not frequently integrated into vocational psychology: economics, neuroscience, chaos theory, and experimental social psychology. The infusion of ideas from other fields can reinvigorate the study of individual decision-making processes. Most important, Krieshok et al. proposed that the field consider a shift from "a gold-standard outcome of decidedness and commitment to an outcome of engagement and commitment within relativism" (p. 288).

The trilateral model is new, and as such there is limited information to either support or refute many of its claims at present. It is included in this chapter as an example of future-oriented vocational theory that moves beyond maturity and adaptability to consider the active processes of engaging in and anticipating change. In addition, the infusion of the neuroanatomy of decision making into the vocational realm opens up the potential for numerous lines of inquiry and new collaborations with neuroscientists. The ability to bridge disciplines and utilize knowledge from other specialties can expand the impact and reach of vocational psychology, and the trilateral model provides one such perspective on how to achieve that goal.

WHERE DO WE GO FROM HERE?

The diversity of ideas presented in both the established and emerging theories of vocational psychology are inspirational in their scope. Whether the future of the field lies in an increased attention to the larger social context or the inner function of neurotransmitters, or more likely both, vocational psychology will flourish on a solid foundation of thoughtful and empirically supported theory.

The arc along which vocational psychology theory has developed has moved from the goal of replacing random work with rational decision making (Holland, 1997; Parsons, 1909) to establishing orderly and predictable career trajectories (Super, 1990) to recognizing the influence of social context (SCCT, developmental–contextualism) and meaningfulness (psychology-of-working paradigm, relational–cultural) and has come full circle to preparing individuals to be ready for unpredictability and change (career construction, trilateral model of adaptability). This progression reflects an increasing recognition of the complexity involved in vocational decisions and behavior. It also demonstrates that vocational activities are integrated with other domains of human behavior at both the personal and social level.

The task in front of vocational psychology is to assert its centrality to healthy human functioning. All of the theories presented in this chapter have a common emphasis on helping individuals find the optimal work situation, whether to meet the needs of survival, prestige, meaningfulness, satisfaction, or all of the above. Furthermore, most have some, and some have extensive, empirical support to suggest that at least their basic theoretical assumptions are sound. To clearly articulate the value of vocational psychology to policymakers, health care providers, legislators, and other stakeholders, it is incumbent on the field to demonstrate that theory-driven intervention can have a meaningful impact on the lives of individuals. This is particularly important in the 21st century, when global labor market changes and rapidly developing technology makes the workforce a much less safe and predictable place than it once was.

To demonstrate this centrality, vocational psychologists need to take several important steps to move the field past discussion of these issues and into meaningful action. First, we must initiate and sustain working relationships with other scientists from other disciplines, including I-O psychology, economics, neuroscience, and developmental psychology. These relationships will help us to challenge and move past our own assumptions and help us to articulate to new stakeholders why vocational psychology is critical to a healthy society. Second, we must push the current limits of research methodology by asking more complex questions that require more thoughtful analysis and that authentically grapple with the integrative nature of vocational behavior. This challenge also extends to including more underrepresented populations, particularly young children, working adults, older adults, and marginalized groups, in research studies. Third, we must demonstrate that the interventions emerging from vocational psychology theory have a meaningful impact on intended vocational outcomes. Vocational psychology has a rich and valuable empirical history that has established a foundation able to support rigorous clinical trials. Bringing together the science and practice of vocational psychology will make it much more possible to demonstrate the centrality of work to the well-being of society.

References

Ali, S. R., & McWhirter, E. H. (2006). Rural Appalachian youth's vocational/educational postsecondary aspirations: Applying social cognitive career theory. *Journal of Career Development, 33*, 87–111. doi:10.1177/0894845306293347

Ali, S. R., McWhirter, E. H., & Chronister, K. M. (2005). Self-efficacy and vocational outcome expectations for adolescents of lower socioeconomic status: A pilot study. *Journal of Career Assessment, 13*, 40–58. doi:10.1177/1069072704270273

Ali, S. R., & Saunders, J. L. (2006). College expectations of rural Appalachian youth: An exploration of social cognitive career theory factors. *The Career Development Quarterly, 55*, 38–51.

Ali, S. R., & Saunders, J. L. (2009). The career aspirations of rural Appalachian high school students. *Journal of Career Assessment, 17*, 172–188.

Bandura, A. (1986). *Social foundations of thought and action: A social cognitive theory.* Englewood Cliffs, NJ: Prentice-Hall.

Betz, N. E. (2007). Career self-efficacy: Exemplary recent research and emerging directions. *Journal of Career Assessment, 15*, 403–422. doi:10.1177/10690 72707305759

Betz, N. E. (2008). Advances in vocational theories. In R. W. Lent (Ed.), *Handbook of counseling psychology* (4th ed., pp. 357–374). Hoboken, NJ: Wiley.

Betz, N. E., & Schifano, R. S. (2000). Evaluation of an intervention to increase realistic self-efficacy and interests in college women. *Journal of Vocational Behavior, 56*, 35–52. doi:10.1006/jvbe.1999.1690

Black, M. D. (2006). *Reason, intuition, and engagement: A trilateral model of adaptive career decision making.* Unpublished doctoral dissertation, University of Kansas, Lawrence.

Blanchard, C. A., & Lichtenberg, J. W. (2003). Compromise in career decision making: A test of Gottfredson's theory. *Journal of Vocational Behavior, 62*, 250–271. doi:10.1016/S0001-8791(02)00026-X

Blustein, D. L. (2006). *The psychology of working: A new perspective for career development, counseling, and public policy.* Mahwah, NJ: Erlbaum.

Blustein, D. L. (2008). The role of work in psychological health and well-being: A conceptual, historical, and public policy perspective. *American Psychologist, 63*, 228–240. doi:10.1037/0003-066X.63.4.228

Blustein, D. L., Kenna, A., Gill, N., & DeVoy, J. (2008). The psychology of working: A new framework for counseling practice and public policy. *The Career Development Quarterly, 56*, 294–308.

Blustein, D. L., Schultheiss, D. E. P., & Flum, H. (2004). Toward a relational perspective of the psychology of careers and working: A social constructionist analysis. *Journal of Vocational Behavior, 64*, 423–440. doi:10.1016/j.jvb.2003.12.008

Bonitz, V. S., Larson, L. M., & Armstrong, P. I. (2010). Interests, self-efficacy, and choice goals: An experimental manipulation. *Journal of Vocational Behavior, 76*, 223–233. doi:10.1016/j.jvb.2009.09.003

Bronfenbrenner, U. (1977). Toward an experimental ecology of human development. *American Psychologist, 32*, 513–531. doi:10.1037/0003-066X.32.7.513

Brown, S. D., & Krane, N. E. R. (2000). Four (or five) sessions and a cloud of dust: Old assumptions and new observations about career counseling. In R. W. Lent (Ed.), *Handbook of counseling psychology* (3rd ed., pp. 740–766). Hoboken, NJ: Wiley.

Byars-Winston, A. M., & Fouad, N. A. (2008). Math and science social cognitive variables in college students: Contributions of contextual factors in predicting goals. *Journal of Career Assessment, 16*, 425–440. doi:10.1177/1069072708318901

Carter, R. T., & Cook, D. A. (1992). A culturally relevant perspective for understanding the career paths of visible racial/ethnic group people. In H. D. Lea & Z. B. Leibowitz (Eds.), *Adult career development: Concepts, issues and practice* (pp. 192–217). Alexandria, VA: National Career Development Association.

Chartrand, J. M., Dohm, T. E., Dawis, R. V., & Lofquist, L. H. (1987). Estimating occupational prestige. *Journal Of Vocational Behavior, 31,* 14–25. doi:10.1016/0001-8791(87)90031-5

Cinamon, R., & Rich, Y. (2010). Work family relations: Antecedents and outcomes. *Journal of Career Assessment, 18,* 59–70. doi:10.1177/106907270 9340661

Collin, A., & Young, R. A. (Eds.). (2000). *The future of career.* Cambridge, England: Cambridge University Press. doi:10.1017/CBO9780511520853

Constantine, M. G., Wallace, B. C., & Kindaichi, M. M. (2005). Examining contextual factors in the career decision status of African American adolescents. *Journal of Career Assessment, 13,* 307–319. doi:10.1177/1069072705274960

Coogan, P. A., & Chen, C. P. (2007). Career development and counselling for women: Connecting theories to practice. *Counselling Psychology Quarterly, 20,* 191–204. doi:10.1080/09515070701391171

Coutinho, M. T., Dam, U. C., & Blustein, D. L. (2008). The psychology of working and globalisation: A new perspective for a new era. *International Journal for Educational and Vocational Guidance, 8,* 5–18. doi:10.1007/s10775-007-9132-6

Cox, D. W. (2008). *Bringing vocational psychology into the 21st century: The operationalization of occupational engagement and initial validation of the Occupational Engagement Scale for College Students.* Unpublished doctoral dissertation, University of Kansas, Lawrence.

Crites, J. O. (1969). *Vocational psychology: The study of vocational behavior and development.* New York, NY: McGraw-Hill.

Dawis, R. V. (2002). Person-environment-correspondence theory. In D. Brown & Associates, *Career choice and development* (4th ed., pp. 427–464). San Francisco, CA: Jossey-Bass.

Dawis, R. V. (2005). The Minnesota theory of work adjustment. In R. W. Lent (Ed.), *Career development and counseling: Putting theory and research to work* (pp. 3–23). Hoboken, NJ: Wiley.

Dawis, R. V., & Lofquist, L. H. (1976). Personality style and the process of work adjustment. *Journal of Counseling Psychology, 23,* 55–59. doi:10.1037/0022-0167.23.1.55

Dawis, R. V., & Lofquist, L. H. (1984). *A psychological theory of work adjustment.* Minneapolis: University of Minnesota Press.

Day, S. X., & Rounds, J. (1998). Universality of vocational interest structure among racial and ethnic minorities. *American Psychologist, 53,* 728–736. doi:10.1037/0003-066X.53.7.728

Degges-White, S., & Shoffner, M. F. (2002). Career counseling with lesbian clients: Using the theory of work adjustment as a framework. *The Career Development Quarterly, 51,* 87–96.

Dik, B. J., Strife, S., & Hansen, J. C. (2010). The flip side of Holland type congruence: Incongruence and job satisfaction. *The Career Development Quarterly, 58,* 352–358.

Duffy, R. D., & Lent, R. W. (2009). Test of a social cognitive model of work satisfaction in teachers. *Journal of Vocational Behavior, 75,* 212–223. doi:10.1016/j.jvb.2009.06.001

Dumont, F., & Carson, A. D. (1995). Precursors of vocational psychology in ancient civilizations. *Journal of Counseling and Development, 73,* 371–378.

Eggerth, D. E. (2008). From theory of work adjustment to person-environment correspondence counseling: Vocational psychology as positive psychology. *Journal of Career Assessment, 16,* 60–74. doi:10.1177/1069072707305771

Fabian, E. S. (2000). Social cognitive theory of careers and individuals with serious mental health disorders: Implications for psychiatric rehabilitation programs. *Psychiatric Rehabilitation Journal, 23,* 262–269.

Ferreira, J., Santos, E. R., Fonseca, A. C., & Haase, R. F. (2007). Early predictors of career development: A 10-year follow-up study. *Journal of Vocational Behavior, 70,* 61–77.

Flores, L. Y., Navarro, R. L., & DeWitz, S. J. (2008). Mexican American high school students' postsecondary educational goals: Applying social cognitive career theory. *Journal of Career Assessment, 16,* 489–501. doi:10.1177/1069072708318905

Flores, L. Y., & O'Brien, K. M. (2002). The career development of Mexican American adolescent women: A test of social cognitive career theory. *Journal of Counseling Psychology, 49,* 14–27. doi:10.1037/0022-0167.49.1.14

Flores, L. Y., Robitschek, C., Celebi, E., Andersen, C., & Hoang, U. (2010). Social cognitive influences on Mexican Americans' career choices across Holland's themes. *Journal of Vocational Behavior, 76,* 198–210. doi:10.1016/j.jvb.2009.11.002

Flum, H. (2001). Relational dimensions in career development. *Journal of Vocational Behavior, 59,* 1–16. doi:10.1006/jvbe.2000.1786

Fouad, N. A. (2002). Cross-cultural differences in vocational interests: Between-group differences on the strong interest inventory. *Journal of Counseling Psychology, 49,* 283–289. doi:10.1037/0022-0167.49.3.282

Fouad, N. A. (2007). Work and vocational psychology: Theory, research, and applications. *Annual Review of Psychology, 58,* 543–564. doi:10.1146/annurev.psych.58.110405.085713

Fouad, N. A., & Kantamneni, N. (2008). Contextual factors in vocational psychology: Intersections of individual, group, and societal dimensions. In S. D. Brown & R. W. Lent (Eds.), *Handbook of counseling psychology* (4th ed., pp. 408–425). Hoboken, NJ: Wiley.

Friedman, T. L. (2005). *The world is flat: A brief history of the twenty-first century.* New York, NY: Farrar, Straus & Giroux.

Gailbreath, R. D., Wagner, S. L., Moffett, R., & Hein, M. B. (1997). Homogeneity in behavioral preference among U.S. Army leaders. *Group Dynamics: Theory, Research, and Practice, 1,* 222–230. doi:10.1037/1089-2699.1.3.222

Gay, E. G., Weiss, D. J., Hendel, D. D., Dawis, R. V., & Lofquist, L. H. (1971). Manual for the Minnesota Importance Questionnaire. *Minnesota studies in vocational rehabilitation, 28,* 1–83.

Gergen, K. J. (1999). Agency: Social construction and relational action. *Theory and Psychology, 9,* 113–115. doi:10.1177/0959354399091007

Gottfredson, L. S. (1981). Circumscription and compromise: A developmental theory of occupational aspirations. *Journal of Counseling Psychology, 28,* 545–579. doi:10.1037/0022-0167.28.6.545

Gottfredson, L. S. (2005). Applying Gottfredson's theory of circumscription and compromise in career guidance counseling. In D. Brown & R. Lent (Eds.), *Career development and counseling: Putting theory and research to work* (pp. 71–100). Hoboken, NJ: Wiley.

Griffin, B., & Hesketh, B. (2003). Adaptable behaviours for successful work and career adjustment. *Australian Journal of Psychology, 55,* 65–73. doi:10.1080/00049530412331312914

Gushue, G. V., & Whiston, M. L. (2006). The relationship among support, ethnic identity, career decision self-efficacy, and outcome expectations in African American high school students: Applying social cognitive career theory. *Journal of Career Development, 33,* 112–124. doi:10.1177/0894845306293416

Harper, M. C., & Shoffner, M. F. (2004). Counseling for continued career development after retirement: An application of the theory of work adjustment. *The Career Development Quarterly, 52,* 272–284.

Hartung, P. J., Porfeli, E. J., & Vondracek, F. W. (2008). Career adaptability in childhood. *The Career Development Quarterly, 57,* 63–74.

Helms, J. E., & Cook, D. A (1999). *Using race and culture in counseling and psychotherapy: Theory and process.* Boston, MA: Allyn & Bacon.

Herr, E. L. (2001). Career development and its practice: A historical perspective. *The Career Development Quarterly, 49,* 196–211.

Herr, E. L. (2003). The future of career counseling as an instrument of public policy. *The Career Development Quarterly, 52,* 8–17.

Holland, J. L. (1959). A theory of vocational choice. *Journal of Counseling Psychology, 6,* 35–45. doi:10.1037/h0040767

Holland, J. L. (1962). Some explorations of a theory of vocational choice: I. One- and two-year longitudinal studies. *Psychological Monographs: General And Applied, 76,* 1–49. doi:10.1037/h0093823

Holland, J. L. (1985). *Vocational Preference Inventory (VPI): 1985 Edition.* Lutz, FL: Psychological Assessment Resources.

Holland, J. L. (1997). *Making vocational choices: A theory of vocational personalities and work environments* (3rd ed.). Odessa, FL: Psychological Assessment Resources.

Holland, J. L., Daiger, D. C., & Power, P. G. (1980). *My vocational situation.* Palo Alto, CA: Consulting Psychologists Press.

Holland, J. L., Fritzsche, B. A., & Powell, A. B. (1994). *The Self-Directed Search technical manual.* Odessa, FL: Psychological Assessment Resources.

Josselson, R. (1992). *The space between us: Exploring the dimensions of human relationships.* San Francisco, CA: Jossey-Bass.

Juntunen, C. L. (2006). The psychology of working: The clinical context. *Professional Psychology: Research and Practice, 37,* 342–350. doi:10.1037/0735-7028.37.4.342

Juntunen, C. L., Barraclough, D. J., Broneck, C. L., Seibel, G. A., Winrow, S. A., & Morin, P. M. (2001). American Indian perspectives on the career journey. *Journal of Counseling Psychology, 48,* 274–285. doi:10.1037/0022-0167.48.3.274

Kahneman, D. (2003). A perspective on judgment and choice: Mapping bounded rationality. *American Psychologist, 58,* 697–720. doi:10.1037/0003-066X.58.9.697

Krieshok, T. S., Black, M. D., & McKay, R. A. (2009). Career decision making: The limits of rationality and the abundance of non-conscious processes. *Journal of Vocational Behavior, 75,* 275–290. doi:10.1016/j.jvb.2009.04.006

Krumboltz, J. D. (1979). A social learning theory of career decision making. In A. M. Mitchell, G. B. Jones, & J. D. Krumboltz (Eds.), *Social learning and career decision making* (pp. 19–49). Cranston, RI: Carrol Press.

Krumboltz, J. D. (2009). The happenstance learning theory. *Journal of Career Assessment, 17,* 135–154. doi:10.1177/1069072708328861

Lent, R. W. (2005). A social cognitive view of career development and counseling. In R. W. Lent (Ed.), *Career development and counseling: Putting theory and research to work* (pp. 101–127). Hoboken, NJ: Wiley.

Lent, R. W., & Brown, S. D. (2006). Integrating person and situation perspectives on work satisfaction: A social–cognitive view. *Journal of Vocational Behavior, 69*, 236–247. doi:10.1016/j.jvb.2006.02.006

Lent, R. W., & Brown, S. D. (2008). Social cognitive career theory and subjective well-being in the context of work. *Journal of Career Assessment, 16*, 6–21. doi:10.1177/1069072707305769

Lent, R. W., Brown, S. D., & Hackett, G. (1994). Toward a unifying social cognitive theory of career and academic interest, choice, and performance. *Journal of Vocational Behavior, 45*, 79–122. doi:10.1006/jvbe.1994.1027

Lent, R. W., Brown, S. D., Schmidt, J., Brenner, B., Lyons, H., & Treistman, D. (2003). Relation of contextual supports and barriers to choice behavior in engineering majors: Test of alternative social cognitive models. *Journal of Counseling Psychology, 50*, 458–465. doi:10.1037/0022-0167.50.4.458

Lent, R. W., Sheu, H., Singley, D., Schmidt, J. A., Schmidt, L. C., & Gloster, C. S. (2008). Longitudinal relations of self-efficacy to outcome expectations, interests, and major choice goals in engineering students. *Journal of Vocational Behavior, 73*, 328–335. doi:10.1016/j.jvb.2008.07.005

Lieberman, M. D. (2003). Reflective and reflexive judgment processes: A social cognitive neuroscience approach. In J. P. Forgas, K. R.Williams, & W. von Hippel (Eds.), *Social judgments: Implicit and explicit processes* (pp. 44–67). New York, NY: Cambridge University Press.

Lofquist, L. H., & Dawis, R. V. (1991). *Essentials of person-environment-correspondence counseling.* Minneapolis: University of Minnesota Press.

Luzzo, D. A., Hasper, P., Albert, K. A., Bibby, M. A., & Martinelli, E. A., Jr. (1999). Effects of self-efficacy-enhancing interventions on the math/science self-efficacy and career interests, goals, and actions of career undecided college students. *Journal of Counseling Psychology, 46*, 233–243. doi:10.1037/0022-0167.46.2.233

Lyons, H. Z., Brenner, B. R., & Fassinger, R. E. (2005). A multicultural test of the theory of work adjustment: Investigating the role of heterosexism and fit perceptions in the job satisfaction of lesbian, gay, and bisexual employees. *Journal of Counseling Psychology, 52*, 537–548. doi:10.1037/0022-0167.52.4.537

Lyons, H. Z., & O'Brien, K. M. (2006). The role of person-environment fit in the job satisfaction and tenure intentions of African American employees. *Journal of Counseling Psychology, 53*, 387–396. doi:10.1037/0022-0167.53.4.387

Martin, P., Schoon, I., & Ross, A. (2008). Beyond transitions: Applying optimal matching analysis to life course research. *International Journal of Social Research Methodology, 11*, 179–199. doi:10.1080/13645570701622025

McKay, R. A., Kerr, B. A., Hansen, R., & Krieshok, T. S. (2008, August). *Increasing career engagement in creatively gifted students.* Poster presented at the 116th Annual Convention of the American Psychological Association, Boston, MA.

Morrow, S. L., Gore, P. A., Jr., & Campbell, B. W. (1996). The application of a sociocognitive framework to the career development of lesbian women and gay men. *Journal of Vocational Behavior, 48*, 136–148. doi:10.1006/jvbe.1996.0014

Motulsky, S. L. (2010). Relational processes in career transition: Extending theory, research, and practice. *The Counseling Psychologist, 38*, 1078–1114. doi:10.1177/0011000010376415

Nauta, M. M. (2010). The development, evolution, and status of Holland's theory of vocational personalities: Reflections and future directions for counseling psychology. *Journal of Counseling Psychology, 57*, 11–22. doi:10.1037/a0018213

Nauta, M. M., Kahn, J. H., Angell, J. W., & Cantarelli, E. A. (2002). Identifying the antecedent in the relation between career interests and self-efficacy: Is it one, the other, or both? *Journal of Counseling Psychology, 49*, 290–301. doi:10.1037/0022-0167.49.3.290

Nevill, D. D., & Super, D. E. (1988). Career maturity and commitment to work in university students. *Journal of Vocational Behavior, 32*, 139–151. doi:10.1016/0001-8791(88)90011-5

Niles, S. G. (2001). Using super's career development assessment and counselling (C-DAC) model to link theory to practice. *International Journal for Educational and Vocational Guidance, 1*(1–2), 131–139. doi:10.1023/A:1016981000319

Noble, M. S. (2008). *The Occupational Engagement Scale for Employed Adults—Revised (OES-EA-R): Further validation and correlations with personality and Holland code type.* Unpublished doctoral dissertation, University of Kansas, Lawrence.

Ojeda, L., & Flores, L. Y. (2008). The influence of gender, generation level, parent's education level, and perceived barriers on the educational aspirations of Mexican American high school students. *The Career Development Quarterly, 57*, 84–95.

Oliver, L. W., & Spokane, A. R. (1988). Career-intervention outcome: What contributes to client gain? *Journal of Counseling Psychology, 35*, 447–462. doi:10.1037/0022-0167.35.4.447

Parsons, F. (1909). *Choosing a vocation.* Boston, MA: Hougton Mifflin.

Paul, K. I., & Moser, K. (2009). Unemployment impairs mental health: Meta-analyses. *Journal of Vocational Behavior, 74*, 264–282. doi:10.1016/j.jvb.2009.01.001

Phillips, S. D., Blustein, D. L., Jobin-Davis, K., & White, S. (2002). Preparation for the school-to-work transition: The views of high school students. *Journal of Vocational Behavior, 61*, 202–216. doi:10.1006/jvbe.2001.1853

Phillips, S. D., Christopher-Sisk, E. K., & Gravino, K. L. (2001). Making career decisions in a relational context. *The Counseling Psychologist, 29*, 193–213. doi:10.1177/0011000001292002

Porfeli, E. J. (2007). Work values system development during adolescence. *Journal of Vocational Behavior, 70*, 42–60. doi:10.1016/j.jvb.2006.04.005

Porfeli, E. J., Hartung, P. J., & Vondracek, F. W. (2008). Children's vocational development: A research rationale. *The Career Development Quarterly, 57*, 25–37.

Prilleltensky, I. (1997). Values, assumptions, and practices: Assessing the moral implications of psychological discourse and action. *American Psychologist, 52*, 517–535. doi:10.1037/0003-066X.52.5.517

Richardson, M. S. (1993). Work in people's lives: A location for counseling psychologists. *Journal of Counseling Psychology, 40*, 425–433. doi:10.1037/0022-0167.40.4.425

Rottinghaus, P. J., Larson, L. M., & Borgen, F. H. (2003). The relation of self-efficacy and interests: A meta-analysis of 60 samples. *Journal of Vocational Behavior, 62*, 221–236. doi:10.1016/S0001-8791(02)00039-8

Ryan, R. M., & Deci, E. L. (2000). Self-determination theory and the facilitation of intrinsic motivation, social development, and well-being. *American Psychologist, 55*, 68–78. doi:10.1037/0003-066X.55.1.68

Saks, A. M., & Ashforth, B. E. (1997). A longitudinal investigation of the relationships between job information sources, applicant perceptions of fit, and work outcomes. *Personnel Psychology, 50*, 395–426. doi:10.1111/j.1744-6570.1997.tb00913.x

Saks, A. M., & Ashforth, B. E. (2002). Is job search related to employment quality? It all depends on the fit. *Journal of Applied Psychology, 87*, 646–654. doi:10.1037/0021-9010.87.4.646

Savickas, M. L. (2001). A developmental perspective on vocational behaviour: Career patterns, salience, and themes. *International Journal for Educational and Vocational Guidance, 1*(1–2), 49–57. doi:10.1023/A:1016916713523

Savickas, M. L. (2002). Reinvigorating the study of careers. *Journal of Vocational Behavior, 61*, 381–385. doi:10.1006/jvbe.2002.1880

Savickas, M. L. (2005). The theory and practice of career construction. In R. W. Lent (Ed.), *Career development and counseling: Putting theory and research to work* (pp. 42–70). Hoboken, NJ: Wiley.

Schoon, I., Martin, P., & Ross, A. (2007). Career transitions in times of social change: His and her story. *Journal of Vocational Behavior, 70*, 78–96.

Schultheiss, D. E. P. (2003). A relational approach to career counseling: Theoretical integration and practical application. *Journal of Counseling and Development, 81*, 301–310.

Schultheiss, D. E. P. (2007). The emergence of a relational cultural paradigm for vocational psychology. *International Journal for Educational and Vocational Guidance, 7*, 191–201. doi:10.1007/s10775-007-9123-7

Schultheiss, D. E. P., Kress, H. M., Manzi, A. J., & Glasscock, J. (2001). Relational influences in career development: A qualitative inquiry. *The Counseling Psychologist, 29*, 214–239. doi:10.1177/001100000 1292003

Scott, R. T. (2006). *The Occupational Engagement Scale for Employed Adults (ORS EA): Initial validation and development*. Unpublished doctoral dissertation, University of Kansas, Lawrence.

Sheu, H., Lent, R. W., Brown, S. D., Miller, M. J., Hennessy, K. D., & Duffy, R. D. (2010). Testing the choice model of social cognitive career theory across Holland themes: A meta-analytic path analysis. *Journal of Vocational Behavior, 76*, 252–264. doi:10.1016/j.jvb.2009.10.015

Silvia, P. J. (2003). Self-efficacy and interest: Experimental studies of optimal incompetence. *Journal of Vocational Behavior, 62*, 237–249. doi:10.1016/S0001-8791(02)00013-1

Skorikov, V. (2007). Continuity in adolescent career preparation and its effects on adjustment. *Journal of Vocational Behavior, 70*, 8–24. doi:10.1016/j.jvb.2006.04.007

Smith, E. J. (1983). Issues in racial minorities' career behavior. In W. B. Walsh & S. H. Oipow (Eds.), *Handbook of vocational psychology: Vol 1. Foundations* (pp. 161–222). Hillsdale, NJ: Erlbaum.

Spokane, A. R., & Cruza-Guet, M. (2005). Holland's theory of vocational personalities in work environments. In R. W. Lent (Ed.), *Career development and counseling: Putting theory and research to work* (pp. 24–41). Hoboken, NJ: Wiley.

Spokane, A. R., Meir, E. I., & Catalano, M. (2000). Person–environment congruence and Holland's theory: A review and reconsideration. *Journal of Vocational Behavior, 57*, 137–187. doi:10.1006/jvbe.2000.1771

Strauser, D. R., Lustig, D. C., & Çiftçi, A. (2008). Psychological well-being: Its relation to work personality, vocational identity, and career thoughts.

Journal of Psychology: Interdisciplinary and Applied, 142, 21–35. doi:10.3200/JRLP.142.1.21-36

Sullivan, K. R., & Mahalik, J. R. (2000). Increasing career self-efficacy for women: Evaluating a group intervention. *Journal of Counseling and Development, 78*, 54–62.

Super, D. E. (1955). Transition: From vocational guidance to counseling psychology. *Journal of Counseling Psychology, 2*, 3–9. doi:10.1037/h0041630

Super, D. E. (1957). *The psychology of careers: An introduction to vocational development.* Oxford, England: Harper & Bros.

Super, D. E. (1969). Vocational development theory: Persons, positions, and processes. *The Counseling Psychologist, 1*, 2–9. doi:10.1177/001100006900100101

Super, D. E. (1973). The career development inventory. *British Journal of Guidance and Counselling, 1*, 37–50. doi:10.1080/03069887300760201

Super, D. E. (1985). Coming of age in Middletown: Careers in the making. *American Psychologist, 40*, 405–414. doi:10.1037/0003-066X.40.4.405

Super, D. E. (1990). A life-span, life-space approach to career development. In L. Brooks (Ed.), *Career choice and development: Applying contemporary theories to practice* (2nd ed., pp. 197–261). San Francisco, CA: Jossey-Bass.

Super, D. E. (1994). A life span, life space perspective on convergence. In M. L. Savickas & R. W. Lent (Eds.), *Convergence in career development theories: Implications for science and practice* (pp. 63–74). Palo Alto, CA: CPP Books.

Super, D. E., Osborne, W. L., Walsh, D. J., Brown, S. D., & Niles, S. G. (1992). Developmental career assessment and counseling: The C-DAC model. *Journal of Counseling and Development, 71*, 74–80.

Super, D. E., & Šverko, B. (1995). *Life roles, values, and careers: International findings of the work importance study.* San Francisco, CA: Jossey-Bass.

Super, D. E., & Thompson, A. S. (1979). A six-scale, two-factor measure of adolescent career or vocational maturity. *Vocational Guidance Quarterly, 28*, 6–15.

Šverko, B. (2001). Life roles and values in international perspective: Super's contribution through the work importance study. *International Journal for Educational and Vocational Guidance, 1*(1–2), 121–130. doi:10.1023/A:1016929016249

Tokar, D. M., Thompson, M. N., Plaufcan, M. R., & Williams, C. M. (2007). Precursors of learning experiences in social cognitive career theory. *Journal of Vocational Behavior, 71*, 319–339. doi:10.1016/j.jvb.2007.08.002

Tokar, D. M., Withrow, J. R., Hall, R. J., & Moradi, B. (2003). Psychological separation, attachment security, vocational self-concept crystallization, and career indecision: A structural equation analysis. *Journal of Counseling Psychology, 50*, 3–19. doi:10.1037/0022-0167.50.1.3

Tracey, T. J., & Rounds, J. B. (1993). Evaluating Holland's and Gati's vocational-interest models: A structural meta-analysis. *Psychological Bulletin, 113*, 229–246. doi:10.1037/0033-2909.113.2.229

Tracey, T. J. G. (2002). Development of interests and competency beliefs: A 1-year longitudinal study of fifth- to eighth-grade students using the ICA-R and structural equation modeling. *Journal of Counseling Psychology, 49*, 148–163. doi:10.1037/0022-0167.49.2.148

Tsabari, O., Tziner, A., & Meir, E. I. (2005). Updated meta-analysis on the relationship between congruence and satisfaction. *Journal of Career Assessment, 13*, 216–232.

Valach, L., & Young, R. A. (2004). Some cornerstones in the development of a contextual action theory of career and counselling. *International Journal for Educational and Vocational Guidance, 4*, 61–81. doi:10.1023/B:IJVO.0000021138.12299.cf

Vondracek, F. W. (2001). The developmental perspective in vocational psychology. *Journal of Vocational Behavior, 59*, 252–261. doi:10.1006/jvbe.2001.1831

Vondracek, F. W. (2007). Introduction and commentary: Studies of development in context. *Journal of Vocational Behavior, 70*, 1–7. doi:10.1016/j.jvb.2006.04.001

Vondracek, F. W., Lerner, R. M., & Schulenberg, J. E. (1983). The concept of development in vocational theory and intervention. *Journal of Vocational Behavior, 23*, 179–202. doi:10.1016/0001-8791(83)90032-5

Vondracek, F. W., Lerner, R. M., & Schulenberg, J. E. (1986). *Career development: A life-span developmental approach.* Mahwah, NJ: Erlbaum.

Vondracek, F. W., & Porfeli, E. (2002). Integrating person- and function-centered approaches in career development theory and research. *Journal of Vocational Behavior, 61*, 386–397. doi:10.1006/jvbe.2002.1881

Walsh, W. B., & Savickas, M. L. (2005). Current issues and innovations in vocational psychology. In M. L. Savickas (Ed.), *Handbook of vocational psychology: Theory, research, and practice* (3rd ed., pp. 3–11). Mahwah, NJ: Erlbaum.

Weiss, D. J., Dawis, R. V., England, G. W., & Lofquist, L. H. (1967). Manual for the Minnesota Satisfaction Questionnaire. *Minnesota Studies in Vocational Rehabilitation, 22*, 1–119.

Whiston, S. C., & Keller, B. K. (2004). The influences of the family of origin on career development: A review and analysis. *The Counseling Psychologist, 32*, 493–568. doi:10.1177/0011000004265660

Whiston, S. C., Sexton, T. L., & Lasoff, D. L. (1998). Career-intervention outcome: A replication and extension of Oliver and Spokane (1988). *Journal of Counseling Psychology, 45,* 150–165. doi:10.1037/0022-0167.45.2.150

Williams, C. M., & Subich, L. M. (2006). The gendered nature of career related learning experiences: A social cognitive career theory perspective. *Journal of Vocational Behavior, 69,* 262–275. doi:10.1016/j.jvb.2006.02.007

Young, R. A., Ball, J., Valach, L., Turkel, H., & Wong, Y. S. (2003). The family career development project in Chinese Canadian families. *Journal of Vocational Behavior, 62,* 287–304. doi:10.1016/S0001-8791(02)00022-2

Young, R. A., Valach, L., Ball, J., Paseluikho, M. A., Wong, Y. S., DeVries, R. J., . . . Turkel, H. (2001). Career development in adolescence as a family project. *Journal of Counseling Psychology, 48,* 190–202. doi:10.1037/0022-0167.48.2.190

Young, R. A., Valach, L., & Collin, A. (2002). A contextual explanation of career. In D. Brown & Associates, *Career choice and development* (4th ed., pp. 206–250). San Francisco, CA: Jossey-Bass.

CHAPTER 10

RESEARCH IN WORK-RELATED DECISIONS

LaRae M. Jome and Robert P. Carnicella

The landscape of the work world has undergone myriad changes in the past 2 decades, fueled by technological advances and the increasing globalization of the labor market (Blustein, 2006). Recent economic downturns have provided additional elements of instability, and these changes have directly and indirectly influenced the decisions that individuals need to make about their work lives. Work-related transitions and changes have become commonplace experiences for many workers (Clarke, 2007) and individuals often need to make complex decisions about work while navigating a work world that is filled with uncertainty and ambiguity. The past decade has been a time of great change in the work lives of many individuals around the globe. In this chapter, we review research from this time period on work-related decisions across the working life. We evaluate the state of the research literature and examine the kinds of work-related decisions being studied, the types of research questions being asked, and the research methodologies being utilized, and we offer suggestions for future research directions.

The research in work-related decisions is not a cohesive or unified body of literature; rather, research studies come from a variety of disciplines, are focused on various types of decisions or decisional situations, and use samples from a range of populations, countries, and cultural contexts. To provide an organizational structure for the widely varying studies, we broadly categorize studies first by the particular developmental stage of participants or decision point along the work path. From a development perspective (e.g., Super, 1990; Wanberg & Kammeyer-Mueller, 2008), we focus on three broad developmental points along the working life: (a) adolescents and young adults transitioning from school to work, (b) adults in mid–working life, and (c) adults in retirement or transitioning out of paid employment. Within each broad developmental stage, we organize studies by the particular decision or decisional situation of focus in the article.

Following a psychology of working perspective (Blustein, 2006), in our discussion of research in work-related decisions we move away from the term *career* and *career path* and use more inclusive terms, such as *work*, *work path*, and *working life*, to refer to the jobs, positions, and occupations that individuals occupy as they move through their working lives. Current perspectives in vocational psychology point to the importance of examining the totality of work in people's lives, including both paid and unpaid work, and the importance of the contextual factors that influence work choices, recognizing that individuals have varying degrees of volition about their work-related choices (Blustein, 2006; Fouad & Kantamneni, 2008). Our review of the research on work choices within the past decade focuses on the degree to which our research literature is capturing these contextual and volitional perspectives. We do not include research studies on general career development and decision-making processes for adolescents and young adults that were not directly focused on a work decision or a decisional situation related to entrance into employment. Also, we do not address research on work-related decisions for individuals

DOI: 10.1037/13754-010
APA Handbook of Counseling Psychology: Vol. 1. Theories, Research, and Methods, Nadya A. Fouad (Editor-in-Chief)

with developmental or physical disabilities or on vocational rehabilitation for those with work-related injuries. Paralleling the globalization of the work world that has occurred in the past decade, the research literature on work-related decisions spans multiple countries, and we include these international perspectives throughout the chapter.

WORK-RELATED DECISIONS IN ADOLESCENCE AND EARLY ADULTHOOD

One major developmental task in one's work life is to gain entry into and become established within the world of work (Super, 1990), and the transition from the academic environment to the work world arguably involves multiple decisions that are embedded within larger familial, community, and cultural contexts (Fouad & Kantamneni, 2008). We reviewed research on specific decisional situations for adolescents and young adults related to initial workforce entry decisions. As such, we distinguished research on work-related decisions of adolescents and young adults from research on general decision-making processes, career development, and specific factors such as career adaptability and career-related self-efficacy that were not tied to a specific decisional situation. We organized research studies within the past decade on initial work-related decisions of young adults into two broad categories: research on successful workforce entry and research on the school-to-work transition process.

Successful Workforce Entry

One line of inquiry related to the initial work decisions of adolescents has focused on understanding the factors that are predictive of successful workforce entry among young adults, or the degree to which young adults have obtained and maintained full-time employment or are pursuing a college degree. Although these studies do not directly address the individual's decision-making process, they highlight factors that are related to successful outcomes of the work-related decisions.

Predictive factors.   Research studies in this area tend to examine the school-to-work trajectories of groups of young adults over time and identify

childhood and adolescent factors that are predictive of more or less successful entry into the workforce. For example, Wiesner, Vondracek, Capaldi, and Porfeli (2003) followed a group of American, predominantly Caucasian, at-risk boys from age 10 to young adulthood. In general, the more positive academic, parental, and personal factors the men experienced in childhood and adolescence, the more successful their school-to-work transition. Three variables in particular emerged as most important in predicting the degree to which the men achieved stable employment or a college education as young adults: greater academic achievement in childhood and adolescence, fewer arrests during adolescence, and greater mental health. For example, compared with young men with a history of long-term unemployment, men pursuing a college education had been more successful in high school, came from families with higher socioeconomic status, had parents with greater expectations for their success, had fewer conduct problems including fewer arrests, and experienced fewer mental health problems. Similarly, Alon, Donahoe, and Tienda (2001) explored women's school-to-work trajectories and found that the amount and timing of women's early work experiences (i.e., paid employment during high school and college) as well as background factors such as race and ethnicity, family income, mother's education level, and education attainment predicted women's successful transitions from school to stable employment. For example, Black women were more likely to have very high labor force attachment (i.e., stable employment for the past 4 years) compared with White and Hispanic women. Although having more early work experiences was predictive of more stable employment in adulthood in general, education attainment mediated this relationship such that the work experiences obtained after high school or college were more predictive of very high labor force attachment in adulthood. Obtaining a college degree was predictive of stable employment in adulthood, whereas being a high school dropout greatly increased the odds of experiencing unstable employment as an adult.

Related variables.   A number of longitudinal studies with European adolescents have found that successful transition into the workforce was related to a variety of academic, familial, and personal variables. In a sample of German, non-college-bound youth, Pinquart, Juang, and Silbereisen (2003) found that higher academic self-efficacy and grades in high school (ages 12–15) were associated with greater job satisfaction and a lower likelihood of unemployment at age 21. Among samples of Finnish adults, Kokko and Pulkkinen (2000) and Kokko, Pulkkinen, and Puustinen (2000) found that children showing more social aggression, passivity, and anxiety at age 8 had a greater likelihood of experiencing long-term unemployment in adulthood, and Ek, Sovio, Remes, and Järvelin (2005) found that childhood factors (e.g., mothers' attitudes toward work) and psychosocial factors in young adulthood (e.g., low income, poor life satisfaction, and poor subjective health) were related to less successful workforce entry (i.e., longer periods of unemployment during young adulthood).

Another set of studies used a longitudinal design and investigated whether a particular high school career program would be related to more successful workforce entry. Following a diverse sample of high school seniors in the Boston area for 2 years, Gore, Kadish, and Aseltine (2003) found that high school students who were enrolled in a career program that combined both school-based and work-based learning experiences in high school reported a more positive appraisal of their job situation 2 years after graduation, a greater match between their high school training and their current employment, and a more positive outlook on work compared with work-bound students who pursued a more traditional academic curriculum. Utilizing the same sample, Aseltine and Gore (2005) found that young adults who were either working or attending college full time reported better mental health and higher quality of life than those who were employed part time or unemployed.

Although the European studies may not be generalizable to the United States, given the different social structures in place for assisting individuals with the school-to-work transition process, taken together these studies about successful workforce entry highlight the multiple personal, social, familial, and contextual variables that might play a direct or indirect role in an adolescent's decisions about

work. On the basis of these findings, a number of childhood and adolescent factors seem particularly related to successful workforce entry, such as achieving higher grades in school, staying in and graduating from high school, being engaged in one's work path—whether it be school or work—and having greater mental health. Although none of these findings are surprising to psychologists working with adolescents and young adults transitioning to the work world, they underscore the need for programs designed to increase school engagement and improve mental health of adolescents. Although the use of the longitudinal design allows researchers to understand relationships between childhood and adolescent factors and future behavioral outcomes (i.e., obtaining and maintaining employment), these studies do not directly examine the decision-making process of the individual and his or her family and many rely on variables that already exist in a particular data set. A strengths-based focus would be helpful in designing future interventions that include variables related to resilience, coping, and optimism to understand how psychologists can help individuals overcome multiple negative risk factors or lack of external resources and still make a successful entry into the workforce. Finally, it would be helpful to understand the behavioral and psychological pathways by which individuals moved from school to successful or unsuccessful employment.

Obtaining an Apprenticeship

A number of European studies examined successful workforce entry related to the particular decisional situation of searching for and obtaining an apprenticeship among work-bound adolescents. Although the context of the work decision is different from the United States, the studies shed light on the cognitive processes involved in the decisional process and particularly on the strategies that individuals used in working toward the decisional goal. Haase, Heckhausen, and Köller (2008) found that for non-college-bound German adolescent girls, but not boys, greater engagement in the goal of obtaining an apprenticeship was predictive of finding an apprenticeship. Also among non-college-bound German adolescents, Tomasik, Hardy, Haase, and Heckhausen (2009) found that adolescents who were successful in obtaining an apprenticeship within a year after graduating from high school initially reported highly prestigious work aspirations but downgraded those aspirations as their senior year progressed, compared with youth who were unable to secure an apprenticeship. They examined different strategies for approaching the decisional situation, and results revealed that the most adaptive strategy was one in which students focused outward on the environment (i.e., invested time, skills, and energy on the specific goal) rather than focusing on increasing their internal motivation for the goal or disengaging from the pursuit of the goal. Although these findings may have limited generalizability to other cultural contexts, the focus on clarifying the nature of the cognitive process involved in a specific work-related context for adolescents offers promising ideas to pursue in other decisional situations (e.g., decision to go to college).

School-to-Work Transition Experience

Although it is helpful to understand what factors are predictive of successful workforce entry, these studies do not directly identify what decisions individuals need to make or how they make decisions during the school-to-work transition process. There is an emerging body of research on the psychological experience of adolescents and young adults as they transition from school to work, and these studies pay particular attention to contextual factors, such as social class, that influence the transition process. In contrast to the studies predicting work-related outcomes, the majority of studies about the decider's direct experience use qualitative designs with small samples of individuals engaged in a particular decisional situation. For example, Phillips, Blustein, Jobin-Davis, and White (2002) analyzed the narratives of 17 work-bound high school juniors regarding their readiness to transition from school to work. Multiple pathways to a successful transition experience emerged in the data; however, those who were more objectively or externally prepared to enter the adult work world had more work-based learning experiences, received greater support from adults in their environment, and were more oriented to the adult world. The importance of internal psychological resources of the decider such as optimism and resilience emerged in the data, but the pathways

by which these psychological factors might facilitate the transition process were less clear.

Using a similar design but focusing on the role of social class in the work transition process, Blustein et al. (2002) interviewed 10 higher class and 10 lower class working youth. They found that young adults from higher social class backgrounds were able to find jobs that were meaningful and fit with their self-concepts; came from schools with greater resources to help with the transition process; received more help from parents and others in the decision-making process; and showed greater career adaptability, that is, they engaged in more career exploration and were more planful about their careers. In comparison, the lower class youth were less likely to be able to implement their self-concepts within their work, reported fewer educational and relational resources, and reported more relational disruptions (e.g., divorce, family conflict) in their lives.

In directly examining the psychological experience of the decider in a particular decisional situation, these studies offer promising avenues for future inquiry as well as for expanding theoretical perspectives on the transition to work. Although additional studies with broader samples are needed to replicate findings, these studies highlight the importance of preparing adolescents for entering the work world and providing educational, information, and relational resources. The hypotheses generated from these findings about the internal psychological processes that facilitate adaptation and adjustment to the work world could be used to design longitudinal and intervention studies to determine whether these psychological processes can be increased, especially for deciders with few social supports and less readiness for the transition process.

Relational decision making. A number of studies in this area more clearly narrowed in on the role of other people in the school-to-work transition process. For example, Alliman-Brissett, Turner, and Skovolt (2004) found that African American girls who perceived greater emotional support from parents and more parental career modeling reported greater confidence in making the transition from school to work. For African American boys, parental career-related modeling was the main predictor of school-to-work self-efficacy.

Although many studies show significant links between social support from others and positive outcomes, one particular line of inquiry has examined *how* individuals are influential in the decisional process. Schultheiss, Kress, Manzi, and Glasscock (2001) interviewed college students about how others were involved in their career decisions and found that other people provided social support, including emotional support, esteem support, information support, tangible assistance, and social integration. Phillips, Christopher-Sisk, and Gravino (2001) developed a taxonomy of relational decision-making strategies or ways in which other people are involved in the decisional process: (a) Deciders recruit others into the decision-making process, (b) other people involve themselves in the decision, and (c) deciders push people away from being involved in the decision. These studies illuminate possible pathways by which social support is beneficial (or not) to deciders, and future research should seek to replicate these findings with additional samples in order to develop these emerging theoretical models.

Examining relational decision making from an organizational perspective, Tynkkynen, Nurmi, and Salmela-Aro (2010) explored the social ties, or importance of other people, in a sample of Finnish young adults at two points in time. As the young adults aged and transitioned from school to work, they were more likely to mention friends and romantic partners as being important in their career goals, replacing parents and siblings. Tynkkynen et al. found that other variables such as gender, socioeconomic status, family composition, and grade point average were predictive of which specific individuals were mentioned as important career-goal-related social ties. For example, adolescents who mentioned their fathers as a career-goal-related social tie were more likely to enter an academic track, whereas adolescents who named a romantic partner were more likely to enter a vocational track. Although these findings may not be generalizable to U.S. young adults, the study offers an intriguing way to understand how other people—and which people in particular in an individual's environment—are involved in the workforce transition process.

Work mentors.   A couple of studies specifically examined the role of work mentors in the work lives of high school students. Linnehan (2003) found American urban high school students who had mentors in a part-time job had higher self-esteem and perceived greater relevance of school to work compared with students who worked during the school year but did not have a formal or informal mentor. Exploring urban, working adolescents' relationships with work mentors through the lens of social class, Noonan, Hall, and Blustein (2007) noted that supervisors served as role models and encouraged high school students to pursue their dreams, yet there was little recognition by supervisors of the barriers these urban students may face in the pursuit of their dreams, for example, attending college or vocational training. These studies shed light on another potential relational resource for adolescents as they prepare to transition to the work world and offer promising avenues for future intervention studies.

College-to-work transition.   The bulk of the school-to-work transition research is focused on work-bound adolescents; however, some studies focused on the unique aspects of the transition for college-educated young adults entering the workforce. Murphy, Blustein, Bohlig, and Platt (2010) interviewed 10 recent college graduates about their experiences transitioning from college to work. Similar to previous studies, social support played an important role in the transition process, and participants were optimistic about their future work lives. Interestingly, participants' perceptions of the difficulty of their adjustment to the work world were unrelated to their evaluations of their well-being, that is, participants who reported difficult transition experiences also described themselves as positive and satisfied with their lives. Yang and Gysbers (2007) found that college students with lower levels of job search self-efficacy and more psychological distress tended to experience less readiness, confidence, and support in coping with the impending career transition. Wendlandt and Rochlen (2008) developed a theoretical model of the college-to-work transition process. Their three-stage model proposed that college students first anticipate the impending work transition, adjust to the new workplace environment, and finally achieve membership in the organization. Although this model has direct implications for career counselors and college personnel in preparing college students to enter the work world, it also provides a framework for designing future interventions and research studies on the college-to-work transition process.

Summary of Adolescent and Early Adulthood Decisions

There has been much focus on the school-to-work transition process in the research literature in the past decade, with particular attention given to work-bound adolescents as well as contextual factors of race, social class, and family or other relational supports. In this literature, one avenue of inquiry has used longitudinal designs to examine academic and personal factors that are predictive of success in the school-to-work transition process, and another avenue has focused on understanding the experience of making the transition and how contextual factors have influenced the decisional processes. In general, these research findings over the past decade suggest a number of strategies that would be beneficial to adolescents as they transition from school to work, such as increasing their engagement in school and academic achievement, gaining work experiences, becoming oriented to the work world, developing work-related plans and goals, becoming engaged in their work paths (whether they be work-bound or college-bound), seeking out and capitalizing on the resources in their environment (especially using other adults for support), and increasing their psychological health.

More research is needed that explores specific decisional points for adolescents and young adults (e.g., decision to obtain a part-time job, decision to enter a career program in high school, decision to take a particular job) and that describes the decisional pathways for individuals as they move from the academic environment to the world of work. The small sample, qualitative designs offer rich insights into the decision-making experience through the transition process, and future research can build from these studies, develop the constructs identified, and examine antecedents and outcomes of these decisional processes across broader samples. For example, research could study how adolescents and young adults benefit from various forms of relational support when making initial work decisions, and whether particular relational decision-making strategies (Phillips et al., 2001) are related to different psychological and behavioral outcomes.

Given the changes in the work world, especially related to job insecurity and instability, it may be more important to cultivate career adaptability in young adults than a particular decision-making style or particular decision-making skills (van Vianen, De Pater, & Preenen, 2009). There is a burgeoning research literature that identifies aspects of career adaptability that are related to the career development process (e.g., Creed, Fallon, & Hood, 2009; Hirschi, 2009; Kenny & Bledsoe, 2005), and this construct offers much promise in exploring specific decisional points for adolescents and how being more flexible and planful might be helpful in making decisions related to entering work. Additionally, research should explore whether these career adaptability attitudes and skills are related to decisional outcomes such as obtaining more job offers or greater job satisfaction.

WORK-RELATED DECISIONS ACROSS WORKING LIFE IN ADULTHOOD

Mid–working life decisions often involve reevaluation of one's working life. Individuals may make decisions about their work on the basis of their personal lives, their level of satisfaction or dissatisfaction with the job, or the organization in which they work (Wanberg & Kammeyer-Mueller, 2008). The decisions can be related to changing work positions, progression or advancement in work (e.g., accepting or declining a promotion), maintenance (e.g., taking a lateral position), temporarily withdrawing from the workforce, reentry into the workforce, retraining or returning to school, or moving to a second career (Juntunen, Wagner, & Matthews, 2002). The research literature on work-related decisions through the adult working life in the past decade is largely attuned to the changing landscape of the work world, and has examined various work-related decisions and situations that working adults might encounter as they cope with and respond to a continually changing work world.

We have organized the current research studies on work-related decisions across adulthood by the decisional context or type of decision (e.g., work transitions, decisions to leave a work position, decisions related to parenthood), and within each section, we analyze the particular types of research studies conducted. The first section contains a broad array of studies on decisions that reflect work-related transitions or changes the individual is making in his or her work status. Additional sections focus on the decision to leave a position or organization, decisions following job loss, decisions about work related to parenthood, and second careers.

Work Transitions

In this section, we review research studies that have examined decisional situations that reflect a transition or a movement from one status or position to another. This has become a popular area of inquiry as the experience of changing jobs, work positions, or occupational fields has become more commonplace (Clarke, 2007). Within this broad area, we differentiate studies that focused on a specific decisional context (e.g., deciding to advance, become self-employed, or return to school) from those that explored workers' experiences with a work transition process without identifying a specific decisional situation.

The majority of research studies on specific types of work transitions have used qualitative designs; individuals identified as experiencing a particular type of transition were interviewed to explore the reasons why they considered making the transition and to understand their perceptions of the outcome of the decision to make the change. For example, Oplatka (2005) analyzed the narratives of eight Israeli female teachers who made lateral work transitions (i.e., took teaching positions at a different school). This mid-working life transition was perceived as a time of self-renewal, and following the lateral move, the teachers felt more energized, engaged, confident, and innovative. Furbish (2009) explored the decision to take a self-funded leave of absence for 16 university employees in Australia to pursue other life activities (e.g., travel, write a book, fulfill a lifetime goal). Although participants engaged in various types of activities during their leave, they were motivated to take the leave because of the need for personal renewal, to avoid

burnout, to reenergize or reclaim their careers, and to restore work–life balance. These studies increase our understanding of potential motives behind these transition decisions; however, additional research is needed on broader samples and with strong theoretical frameworks to know whether these experiences are unique to a particular sample or type of transition or whether they represent a general reaction to making a work-related change.

Decisions to advance. We found two studies directly related to the decision to seek advancement or promotion in one's work path, and both were focused on the experiences of female faculty as they made decisions about progressing in their academic positions. Reybold and Alamia (2008) studied the work paths of 23 female faculty members and found that although no linear, universal career paths were noted, participants' professional identities tended to be more provisional and transient in the early stages of their work lives as untenured faculty members and became more integrated, stable, and resilient as they progressed in their academic careers. Pruitt, Johnson, Catlin, and Knox (2010) interviewed 10 female associate professors about their reasons for pursuing advancement to full professor as well as factors that might hinder the advancement process. Additionally, they asked participants to relay critical experiences related to the decision to pursue advancement that were both encouraging and discouraging. Although these studies focused on a specific population and the results cannot be generalized beyond female faculty, they are good examples of research that examines the psychological experience of individuals as they actively consider a particular decisional context. Additional research should expand beyond samples of highly educated individuals in professional positions to examine the decisions of workers in factory, middle-management, and service-sector jobs. Decisions related to advancement and progression across different types of work may involve completely different sets of motivations and outcomes for the workers, as the advancement decision may lead to dramatic changes in pay, responsibility, and job tasks.

Decision to return to school. Although it is noted in the popular literature that more adults are deciding to return to school for additional education or training, often following an absence from the paid workforce because of childrearing or unemployment, we found only a few empirical studies on this decisional context. Using a sample of married, heterosexual couples, Hostetler, Sweet, and Moen (2007) found, somewhat unexpectedly, that women and men with the most work and family obligations were more likely to return to school. Women who returned to school after at least a 2-year gap in schooling were more likely to be younger, have married earlier, have made a voluntary job change within the past 4 years, have young children, work long hours, have assistance with child care, and have high personal mastery. Men's return to school was associated with younger age, earlier marriage age, and greater feelings of personal mastery. Sweet and Moen examined perceptions of the outcome of the decision on this same sample and found that married women who had returned to school reported great personal satisfaction with the decision, even though the choice had negative effects on marital satisfaction for those with school-age children. These studies highlight the importance of examining the contextual factors influencing the decision to return to school, although more research is needed to understand the push and pull factors that individuals and their families take into consideration when making these decisions. Returning for additional education as an adult may have unique psychological implications for the individual, and this decision typically requires a significant financial investment. Additional research is needed to examine which individuals are more likely to make the decision to return to school, how they experience the decision and the experience of being a nontraditional adult student, and whether particular internal and external resources seem to facilitate the decision making and are related to positive psychological, family, and work-related outcomes.

Self-employment.   One burgeoning area of study in the past decade is that of the decision to open one's own business, perhaps because of the technological changes that have opened up new possibilities for self-employment. The research spans various countries, and most studies explore individuals' motives in making the decision to become self-employed. Examining overall patterns of employment and self-employment among a database of Canadian workers, Kuhn and Schuetze (2001) concluded that men tended to become self-employed because of unemployment (i.e., moved from paid employment to unemployment to self-employment), whereas women tended to become self-employed because it was now a more feasible and viable employment option. Mallon and Cohen (2001) interviewed 41 women entrepreneurs in the United Kingdom who had moved from traditional careers within organizations to self-employment. The majority of the women left their organizational careers to seek self-employment because of dissatisfaction and disillusionment of the organizational environment, although six of the women were categorized as "entrepreneurs-in-waiting" for whom becoming an entrepreneur was an expected, natural transition. Finally, in a case study of one Finnish woman's career transition to an entrepreneurial career, Sinisalo and Komulainen (2008) noted that family relationships and networks with other entrepreneurs were important in the transition as well as the influence of larger global forces (such as the development of the European Union). Additionally, although her work path was characterized by change, adaptability, and planned happenstance, she created a sense of coherence in her work path. These studies used different methodologies, yet a postmodern theme emerges across these disparate studies emphasizing how workers are taking responsibility for their work paths and seeking to create work lives that fit their values rather than molding their lives around their work. More research is needed to provide a complete picture of this decisional context, such as differentiating types of self-employment, whether gender differences emerge in how the decision unfolds, and to what degree technology is playing a role in those decisions.

General work transitions.   Another line of research on work transitions has focused on the decisional process underlying work transitions in general with less focus on a specific situation or context. In these studies, researchers typically allowed participants to self-identify as having undergone a work or career transition without specifying a particular type of transition. For example, in a qualitative study with employed adults who had made major work-related changes, Amundson, Borgen, Iaquinta, Butterfield, and Koert (2010) found three aspects were important in the decision-making process during the transition: (a) relationships with others both inside and outside of the work context; (b) finding personal meaning in work, either through engagement in the work or in developing one's identity; and (c) the economic reality, which meant individuals needed to make decisions in times of uncertainty, balancing their needs and wants.

Motulsky (2010) interviewed 13 women who underwent some type of career transition at midlife and focused on how relationships with other people—their connections and disconnections—influenced the career transition process. Cabrera (2009) interviewed 25 female business school graduates in mid–working life who had taken time off from work for a variety of reasons (e.g., stay home with children, partner job relocation, burnout) and then returned to work. She found that 17 of these women followed a protean career path when they returned to work, that is, they were self-directed in their work decisions, basing their decisions about reentering the workforce on their personal values, and actively creating a work life that helped them find balance between their work and nonwork lives. Chudzikowski et al. (2009) approached the study of work transitions from a cross-cultural perspective and studied the attributions that individuals in three occupations (businesspeople, nurses, and blue-collar workers) at two different points in the work life (early and later career) and across five countries (United States, Austria, Spain, Serbia, and China) made about the causes of their career transitions. They found that in Europe and the United States the individual was viewed as being the primary source of the career transition (i.e., individuals attributed the career transition to their own initiative), whereas Chinese participants attributed the transition to organizational and macro-level factors.

Qualitative designs with small sample sizes dominate the research literature on work-related transitions, which is not surprising given the recent

transitions of the work world and given that a qualitative methodology allows researchers to paint a rich picture of the psychological experience of a small group of individuals in a relatively new area of inquiry. The major themes emerging from these studies include the role of other people in making the decision and offering support through the decision and the importance that finding or creating meaning in work, as well as personal and cultural values, play in the transition decisions. It is not yet clear whether each particular decisional context is unique or whether there are general decision-making elements, for example, whether individuals voluntarily changing to a new job show a different decisional process compared with downsized workers who return to school for additional training.

As research in this area continues, these initial findings should be used to identify important psychological and work-related constructs and potential theoretical frameworks to guide future inquiries. Theoretical frameworks such as general models of life transitions (e.g., Schlossberg, Waters, & Goodman, 1995) or models specifically of work-related transitions (e.g., Wanberg & Kammeyer-Mueller, 2008) would be beneficial. Additionally, it may be helpful to understand the psychological coping strategies individuals use in the transition process and incorporate measures such as the Career Transitions Inventory (Heppner, Multon, & Johnston, 1994) that assess the internal psychological resources adults possess as they undergo some type of change in their work.

Decisions Related to Leaving a Work Position or Field

The decision to voluntarily leave a particular work position can be fraught with difficulty and ambivalence yet can also be a welcome change, representing the end of a negative experience and hope for a more successful or fulfilling work life. Much of the research in this area has explored this decisional situation from an organizational perspective, examining the degree to which organizational constructs predict employees' turnover intentions in North American and European samples. Studies in the past decade have tended to use large samples of current employees within a company or organization and test theoretical models of the antecedents of the intent to leave or stay. The worker's decision is operationalized differently across studies and includes constructs such as the intent to leave a position, intent to leave a company or organization, intent to stay in a position or company, turnover intentions, and willingness or readiness to change positions. A common theme running through studies on the intent to leave is the focus on workers' perceptions of their adaptability and employability, that is, the degree to which they take responsibility for their work paths.

For example, Ito and Brotheridge (2005) sampled 600 civil servants of the Canadian government and found that workers with greater career adaptability (defined as having engaged in professional development activities as well as attitudes of change or career resilience), less affective commitment to the organization, and less supervisory support reported greater intentions to leave the organization. Cavanaugh and Noe (1999) found that U.S. employees who had experienced an involuntary job loss or downsizing expected less job security from their organization, were more committed to their type of work rather than to the organization, and were more likely to endorse the belief that employees, and not employers, are responsible for their career development. Greater endorsement of these attitudes was related to lower intentions to remain with the organization. Using a sample of public sector employees in Australia, Rafferty and Griffin (2006) found that less psychological uncertainly about one's work position was related to greater job satisfaction and lower turnover intentions. Employees who perceived transformational changes occurring within the organization that drastically changed the values of their units were more likely to be considering voluntarily leaving their jobs. Otto, Dette-Hagenmeyer, and Dalbert (2010) explored the antecedents and behavioral outcomes of the willingness or readiness to change careers in samples of unemployed and employed German workers in various occupations. Person-related characteristics such as self-efficacy for making an occupational change and tolerance for uncertainty were related to greater willingness to change occupations, and work-related attitudes such as work satisfaction, organization

commitment, and work-related worries were negatively related to willingness to change occupations among employed workers. There was a stronger relationship between uncertainty tolerance and willingness to change occupations for those individuals who had made a change in their employment status compared with individuals whose employment status had remained stable over 6 to 9 months. Finally, two studies examined specific predictors of the intention to leave for women. Sexual harassment and gender evaluation (i.e., including gender in employment decisions) predicted turnover intentions in a sample of working Chinese and American women (Shaffer, Joplin, Bell, Lau, & Oguz, 2000), and sexual harassment was related to rates of turnover among military women (Sims, Drasgow, & Fitzgerald, 2005).

A separate line of inquiry into the decisions to leave a work position or occupation has directly asked individuals within a particular occupation what factors were related to their decisions to leave a particular position or field. In one of the few studies to sample individuals who already had made the decision to leave a position, Allen, Armstrong, Riemenschneider, and Reid (2006) found that a number of factors directly and indirectly influenced the decisions of women in information technology positions to voluntarily leave a previous position, including workplace flexibility, barriers to promotion, lack of consistency in the workplace, work stress, managing family responsibilities, and discrimination. Carless and Bernath (2007) sampled Australian psychologists and found that intention to change occupations was related negatively to job satisfaction, career planning, and resilience, suggesting that psychologists who were less satisfied in their jobs, who had not been planful about their work paths, and who found it more difficult to adapt to changing circumstances were more likely to think about finding a new occupation.

One theme emerging from these findings is that person-related characteristics such as being comfortable with uncertainty and change and taking responsibility for one's career path and occupational choices (rather than allowing the organization to guide the career path) seem to be related to a willingness or intention to make employment changes.

Compared with some other decisional contexts, the decision to leave a position or field is a well-developed line of inquiry, with research hypotheses guided by strong theoretical frameworks. The decision of interest (i.e., to leave or stay), however, is conceptualized differently across studies and may not represent interchangeable conceptualizations of the decision. Additionally, some research has examined workers' intentions to leave, but fewer studies have examined whether individuals made the decision, that is, actually left the position or organization. Future studies could follow the example of Otto et al. (2010) and investigate whether workers' intentions or desires translate into behavioral outcomes, such as making a change in employment. Additionally, research could move beyond an organizational lens and include more psychological and contextual variables in the design to further understand what individual or familial factors workers might take into account when making decisions. It could be that family, financial, or other external factors may be more important in predicting the decision or the act of leaving the organization than work-related attitudes or other person factors.

Decisions Following Job Loss

We found a small body of research on the decision to use outplacement career counseling services following job loss. The research tends to be descriptive in nature and explores the types of services chosen, considers group differences in usage of services, and examines whether the choice to engage in particular services is related to reemployment. Gowan and Nassar-McMillan (2001) explored which outplacement program offerings a group of unemployed individuals had participated in, including self-awareness activities (e.g., career assessments, individual or group counseling), action-oriented activities (e.g., job search workshop), and job training (e.g., returning to school). They found that although both men and women participated in self-awareness activities, men were somewhat more likely to engage in action-oriented activities (e.g., attend a job search workshop), whereas women and individuals who were more than 40 years old were more likely to decide to return to school for additional training. No particular outplacement activity

was significantly predictive of reemployment. Westaby (2004) examined displaced managers and executives' use of outplacement services following job loss and found that those who had higher level support programs available to them (i.e., extensive counseling, career assessment, unlimited time to use services) took longer to become reemployed yet reported higher rates of reemployment and higher salaries compared with those who participated in lower support outplacement programs with a 3- or 6-month time limit.

It would be helpful to know more about the timing of the decision to engage in outplacement services, that is, at what point following job loss did individuals decide to engage in the activities and what influenced their decision to use outplacement counseling services. Future research should continue to explore whether particular career counseling activities are related to more positive outcomes. One limitation of these studies is that they only examined individuals who decided to take advantage of outplacement career counseling services that were available to them, so it is not clear whether those who engaged in outplacement counseling showed improved outcomes compared with unemployed workers who did not use these services.

Two studies have examined more directly the psychological experience of the decider in the period following a job loss and the degree to which workers display career adaptability in the face of the loss. Ebberwein, Krieshok, Ulven, and Prosser (2004) interviewed 18 Caucasian American workers who were currently experiencing involuntary job loss. They found that more adaptive responses to job loss include responding quickly to job loss, being planful and preparing for the next career step (even if the next step is not entirely clear), being planful when a job change seems imminent, being thoughtful about whether obtaining stopgap employment is advantageous, and setting realistic career goals. Clarke (2007) examined the decision-making process of 31 Australian workers who had been voluntarily downsized (i.e., who knew their jobs were in danger and who accepted the offer of a severance package from their company). Even though workers were not surprised by the job loss event, most engaged in no future planning or job search activities while they were still employed, yet they remained optimistic and hopeful about their ability to secure another job. Themes of adaptability and planfulness are apparent in these qualitative studies of the psychological experience of moving from unemployment to reemployment. More research on broader samples is needed to more fully understand the decision-making process of individuals following job loss and to determine whether beliefs and perceptions about the importance of being planful and flexible with regard to one's work path translate into more planful and flexible behaviors during the job search process and after the individual transitions into a new job.

Work Decisions Related to Parenthood

Scholars have argued that work-related decisions are embedded within a larger social and cultural context (Blustein, 2006; Cohen et al., 2004; Moen, 2003; Schaeper & Falk, 2003), and there are few work-related decisions in which this larger social context is more evident than those related to pregnancy, childbirth, adoption, and parenting. The myriad decisions parents need to make about their working lives are influenced by cultural norms, national politics, available benefits such as maternity and parental leave, and child care systems (Berggren, 2008; Schaeper & Falk, 2003). The research in this area has focused almost exclusively on the work paths of heterosexual mothers, perhaps because mothers' rates of paid employment have increased steadily in the past few decades; however, the work-related decisions of fathers, adoptive parents, and gay and lesbian parents have been largely neglected.

Patterns of work participation.   Much of the research on decisions related to parenting has examined patterns of workforce behavior—that is, rates of duration of maternity leave, rates at which mothers exit and reenter the workforce following childbirth—and has identified demographic and human capital variables that predict rates of workforce participation. These studies tended to utilize large longitudinal data sets with American, European, or Scandinavian samples, and although they did not directly examine individuals' decisions, the findings highlight factors that are influential in mothers' and fathers' work-related decisions.

In general, these research findings suggest that when working women have children, they tend to temporarily take time off from the paid workforce for maternity leave, reenter the workforce on a part-time basis after having children, and return to the workforce full time once their children get older (Alon et al., 2001; Jenkins, 2006; Stanfors, 2006; Taniguchi & Rosenfeld, 2002). This overall finding can be misleading, however, because more nuanced analyses reveal that a number of different demographic and human capital variables influence the pattern of mothers' workforce participation. For example, the age of the child or children is predictive of workforce participation because mothers with infants and preschool age children are less likely to be employed (Alon et al., 2001; Jenkins, 2006; Park, 2005; Stanfors, 2006). Mothers with higher educational level and professional occupational status are less likely to leave the workforce following childbirth; however, when they do exit the workforce, they are more likely to return on a full-time basis and reenter the workforce more quickly than mothers with lower levels of education (Buchmann, Kriesi, Pfeifer, & Sacchi, 2003; Crosby & Hawkes, 2007; Drobnič, 2003; Jenkins, 2006). Women who are working in the paid workforce before childbirth are more likely return to the workforce after childbirth and also tend to return to work within 3 months postchildbirth (Buchmann et al., 2003; Crosby & Hawkes, 2007; Stanfors, 2006), although women working in part-time jobs before childbirth are less likely to exit their jobs (Buchmann et al., 2003). In addition, studies have found significant differences in rates of mother's workforce participation by race and ethnicity (Crosby & Hawkes, 2007; Park, 2005; Taniguchi & Rosenfeld, 2002) and socioeconomic group (Crosby & Hawkes, 2007; Drobnič, 2003).

This body of research has tended to look at demographic variables, namely, educational level and socioeconomic status, which may influence the degree to which mothers (and other parents) have options about work available to them. Feldman, Sussman, and Zigler (2004) carried out one of the few studies we found that included psychological correlates of workforce behavior. They examined patterns of both maternity and paternity leave following childbirth in a sample of American, Caucasian, upper middle-class, married couples in which the wife returned to work following the birth of their first child. Mothers who took longer maternity leaves (more than 12 weeks) reported less depression, greater preoccupation with their infant, more marital support, and less career centrality. For fathers, longer paternity leave (more than 6.5 days) was predicted by a planned pregnancy, more positive reaction by employer, greater marital support, and higher family salience.

Although these studies provide a picture of the work behavior of mothers and fathers, more research is needed to understand the specific factors that parents take into account when making decisions; the psychological variables that influence the decisional process and outcomes; how the decisions are perceived before, during, and after the decisional situation; and the psychological consequences of the work-related decisions. In addition, research needs to extend beyond heterosexual mothers who have given birth and include adoptive and gay and lesbian parents in research studies.

Mothers' work decisions. We found a few scattered studies that examined the parental decisional context more directly. Moen and Sweet (2003) studied the various strategies that heterosexual, married, dual-career couples with children use to manage family and work obligations. For example, they categorized the majority of the couples in their sample as using a neotraditional strategy in which the wife puts in fewer hours in the paid workforce to take on family obligations. This research offers an interesting theoretical framework and the focus on the family, rather than the individual, as the decisional unit adds an important dimension to the research literature. More research is needed, however, that directly explores how individuals and couples make these decisions, what psychological and human capital variables are related to the decision (such as adherence to gender roles, relationship quality, and pay equity between parents), and what psychological and work-related outcomes there are for all members of the parental unit during and after the decision.

In one of the few studies to focus on the psychological experience of working mothers in mid–working life, Grady and McCarthy (2008)

interviewed 18 Irish women in professional positions who had worked continuously after having children on their perceptions of their work–life integration. The participants actively created meaningful work–life integration that changed over time as their life roles changed; they valued both their motherhood and worker roles, sought flexibility in their working life, and took responsibility for the progression of their work paths. Many of the women noted that they had turned down promotions or advancements in the past that would have taken too much time away from family. More research should explore the ways in which parents make sense of their working decisions and how these decisions change as their parenting roles change.

Valcour and Ladge (2008) examined personal and subjective perceptions of career success among a sample of employed, married women with at least one child. Greater objective success (i.e., having a higher income) was associated with having fewer children, being older at the time of the birth of the first child, having a longer time elapse since the birth of the first child, having fewer interruptions in their career path, not working part time, and having less movement between organizations. Greater subjective perceptions of career success was related to greater career identity and general self-efficacy, greater number of years elapsed since the birth of the first child, having fewer gaps in one's career history, and not placing greater priority on one's husband's career. The study illuminates the importance of focusing on personal definitions of success and recognizing that these perceptions may change as parents make decisions to move in or out of the workforce; however, additional research is needed that examines whether parents take these factors into account when making decisions and whether subjective career success is related to greater life happiness or psychological well-being.

Finally, Bosco and Bianco (2005) examined how college men and women perceive their future or anticipated decisions related to managing work and family roles, and whether the decisional strategies used by their parents would influence these decisions. They found that Generation Y (born in the 1980s and early 1990s) women whose mothers worked full time throughout their childhoods envisioned this same lifestyle choice for themselves in the future. The future lifestyle choices of the men in the sample were not directly influenced by their mother's working patterns; however, the men were more likely to envision a similar work–family pattern for their future wife as their mother had, that is, men whose mothers had remained at home anticipated that their future wife would be a stay-at-home mother, whereas men whose mothers worked full time expected that their future wife would work outside the home after having children. The focus on anticipated decisions in this study provides a unique way of examining work decisions related to parenthood. The gender differences emerging in this study suggest the need for more study on fathers' work-related decisions, as fathers are nearly absent from this research literature.

More research is needed on how mothers and fathers make decisions about their working lives, particularly research that examines the factors individuals consider as they make decisions, how they experience the decisional process during and after the decision, and the psychological and behavioral outcomes of the decision. This research literature also could benefit from theoretical frameworks to guide research questions. Schultheiss (2009) argued that mothering should be viewed as a career choice, yet it has been virtually ignored in the vocational literature and it is clearly absent from career theory. Similarly, Shapiro, Ingols, and Blake-Beard (2008) noted that mothers' decisions surrounding paid work tend to be framed as dichotomous decisions (e.g., a mother either participates in the paid workforce or stays home to raise children) and that mothers are judged against a standard that places paid work as primary in one's life.

One promising avenue for future research is the mother's reentry into the workforce conceptual framework (MoRe Conceptual Framework) developed by Eriksen, Jurgens, Garrett, and Swedburg (2008). They provided a model of the complex decision-making process for women who have left the workforce to take care of children and are making decisions about returning to the workforce. The model articulates driving forces behind the decision (i.e., financial, environmental, self-image, skills and abilities, and interests), filters that may influence the decision (i.e., family demands, social support, educational level, work experience, self-concept, and costs versus benefits of the decision), and outcomes (i.e., deciding to return to work in some capacity, e.g., full or part time, returning to school, delaying the decision).

Decisions Related to Second or Multiple Careers

Unique mid–working life decisions can arise for individuals in certain occupations (such as the military, sports, and physically demanding occupations) or for individuals who for reasons such as injury, economic necessity, or work dissatisfaction decide to enter a new type of work. For individuals with multiple, sequential work paths, the decisions related to ending the first career can parallel many features of a general transition or retirement process, yet they may need or desire to remain in the paid workforce. The research we found related to the decision to begin a second career focused entirely on two specific occupations, sports and military careers. We briefly review the research about the decisional process in these two areas.

Work-related decisions of athletes. Although myriad decisions are involved when an individual embarks on a career as an athlete (e.g., decisions about relocating for training and decisions about joining a new team), a substantial body of research exists exploring the sport retirement decisions of athletes (Alfermann & Stambulova, 2007; Wylleman, Alfermann, & Lavallee, 2004). One line of inquiry is focused on understanding the factors related to the retirement decision, that is, understanding the reasons why athletes retire from sports, especially elite or professional athletes. Findings suggest that athletes typically retire from sports because of age, deselection from competition, injury, and voluntary decisions (e.g., financial concerns, lack of motivation to train, the desire to establish a new career; Kadlcik & Flemr, 2008; Lavallee, Grove, & Gordon, 1997). A recently developed scale, the Athletes' Retirement Decision Inventory (Fernandez, Stephan, & Fouquereau, 2006) shows promise in helping researchers and practitioners measure and understand the reasons behind athletes' retirement from sports.

Other studies have examined the outcomes of the retirement decision and identified factors that hinder the postretirement transition process. Although the vast majority of athletes successfully progress through the transition process, estimates suggest that between 13% and 15% of athletes experience severe negative consequences after retiring (Wylleman et al., 2004). Alfermann, Stambulova, and Zemaityte (2004) studied retired athletes from the Russian Federation, Lithuania, and Germany from a variety of sports and found that athletes with higher levels of athletic identity had more difficulties adjusting to postsport life and had extended periods of transition from sports to a second career. In addition, athletes who planned more for retirement from the sport reported greater life satisfaction and well-being postretirement. In a study with retired professional coaches in the United Kingdom, Lavallee (2006) found that the coaches who had done little career planning before retiring showed little awareness of the transition situation they were experiencing, were unaware of how their personality characteristics influenced the retirement process, and were unaware of their potential needs for social support in that process.

The research has also examined the effectiveness of interventions designed to assist athletes with postsport retirement planning. Lavallee (2005) found that a group of retired athletes who received a life development intervention that included supportive counseling showed significant decreases in their difficulties adjusting to retirement compared with a control group. In general, this body of research on the retirement decisions of athletes serves as a good example of how research can move from asking general questions about the nature of the decision and factors that are predictive of the decision, to understanding the decision-making process and related outcomes to design psychological interventions that facilitate the decision-making process. The research could expand beyond the retirement decision and examine decisions related to sport entry and advancement as well as provide additional evidence for the effectiveness of interventions designed to assist with the transition to a second career.

Work-related decisions of military personnel.
Although the body of research on the retirement

decisions of military personnel is much less extensive than that of athletes, research questions have focused on understanding the reasons behind the decision to retire from the military as well as identifying the factors related to more positive postretirement outcomes. The findings suggest that the retirement decision can be voluntary or involuntary, but it is made primarily on the basis of years of service rather than age and tends to be an abrupt process (Spiegel & Shultz, 2003; Taylor, Shultz, Spiegel, Morrison, & Greene, 2007). Using longitudinal data on the retirement of naval officers in the 1980s, Spiegel and Shultz (2003) found that officers who engaged in more retirement planning and who were able to transfer their military knowledge, skills, and abilities to the new job reported greater life satisfaction and adjustment to civilian life at 6 months, 1 year, and 2 years following military retirement. Utilizing this same data set, Taylor et al. (2007) found that a more positive orientation toward the Navy and more positive experiences in the second career were related to greater postretirement adjustment.

Additional research has examined how individuals go through the retirement decision-making process, incorporating the protean and traditional approaches. Baruch and Quick (2007) found that retired Navy admirals with more protean attitudes about their work lives (i.e., took more individual responsibility for one's work path and progress) found a job more quickly, experienced a positive transition to the second job, and reported greater life and job satisfaction, whereas those taking a more traditional career approach (i.e., looking for job stability in the organization and having the organization define one's career progress) tended to work longer hours in the second career and reported higher salaries and job levels. This research offers promising new avenues for research as scholars can focus on individual differences in the decision-making process and how individuals' values might be especially important to incorporate as they may be related to different life outcomes (i.e., internal feelings of satisfaction vs. external rewards of higher salary).

Summary of Mid–Working Life Decisions
The types of research questions examined across the research studies of the work-related decisions of

adults can be broadly categorized as asking why individuals make particular work-related decisions, what antecedents are predictive of the decision, what group-level patterns of workforce behavior are related to particular work decisions, and how individuals experience the decision and perceive the outcomes of the decision. In general, the research tends to be descriptive, illuminating factors that are predictive of a decision. Although we included studies on a broad array of work-related decisions across the working life, a number of general themes emerge from the studies. First, there is an emphasis on variables related to career adaptability, tolerance for uncertainty, and openness to change, and the findings tentatively suggest that individuals who are more adaptable and flexible might be able to cope more successfully with impending work-related decisions and transitions. Second, another major factor that emerges is the individual's ability to be planful about his or her working life, to take responsibility for his or her work path, and to create a working life that fits with the individual's value system. Individuals who plan for impending work-related decisions and take more responsibility for their working path may be able to navigate the transition process more successfully. In addition, individuals who create working lives that fit with their individual values and lifestyle may experience greater work and life well-being, although there may be trade-offs such as taking a reduction in pay and having fewer advancement opportunities.

Third, researchers are beginning to incorporate more contextual factors, especially related to understanding family and relational influences on work decisions. Gender plays a key role in these studies in that much of the research that examines familial and relational factors have focused on a particular work decisions for women. Fouad et al. (2010) created a scale to measure various ways that family can influence work decisions, and it offers great promise for future research. Finally, much of the research has focused on identifying the reasons individuals make particular work-related decisions and factors that predict the decision. More research is needed that examines the psychological processes underlying the decision, how individuals progress through the decision, and how psychologists can facilitate the decision-making process for clients. Similarly, more longitudinal studies are needed that follow individuals through the decision and identify factors associated with more positive vocational and psychological outcomes. As many of these studies in the past decade on work-related decisions through adulthood represent emerging areas of inquiry, replication of these findings will be vital in forming theoretical frameworks to guide larger experimental and intervention studies.

WORK-RELATED DECISIONS THROUGH RETIREMENT

Retirement is the final phase in an individual's working life, and the retirement process often requires multiple decisions over time as the individual transitions out of the workforce. The traditional conceptualization of retirement, as represented in Super's (1990) theory of career development, views retirement as a process in which workers disengage from the workforce and transition into full-time retirement living. This linear progression from full-time work to full-time retirement, however, has become a less common experience for workers in the past decade. In the contemporary economic climate, many workers are extending their workforce participation by either postponing retirement or working after retirement; workers might formally retire from one position or occupation yet continue to pursue additional full-time or part-time work, sometimes referred to as *bridge employment* (Wang & Shultz, 2010).

Unlike some of the other work-related decisions reviewed thus far, there is a broad body of research on retirement in general, and multiple theoretical perspectives exist to guide the formation of research questions. In sifting through the vast number of studies on retirement, we only included studies that directly explored the decision to retire and thus did not include studies on other aspects of retirement, such as general physical and mental health outcomes. Research on the retirement decision can be broadly categorized into three areas: retirement intentions and planning, retirement decisions and outcomes, and the decision to engage in bridge employment.

Retirement Intentions and Planning

A number of studies investigated the retirement decision by sampling individuals who were in the paid workforce and nearing retirement age (e.g., ages 50–61) and inquiring about their plans or intentions to retire. These studies typically focused on the age at which individuals intended to disengage from their paid employment. Many of these studies identified person- and job-related factors that predict workers' intentions to retire from the workforce early (i.e., before age 62) or to delay their exit from the workforce (i.e., work beyond age 65). For example, using a large national data set, Pienta and Hayward (2002) examined the retirement intentions of husbands and wives between the ages of 51 and 61 who were currently working. In general, characteristics such as having greater household wealth, having lower levels of education, and working in a job with fewer cognitive demands were associated with intentions to retire early. The analyses revealed different patterns of retirement expectations based on gender. For example, being older, in poor health, and not having dependent children were related to husbands' but not wives' intentions to retire early. Using the same data set, Mermin, Johnson, and Murphy (2007) compared two age cohorts of workers (i.e., the pre–World War II generation and early baby boomers) and found that workers' expectations to delay retirement increased over time: Early baby boomers had greater expectations of working past age 65 than did older workers. Particular factors related to the decision to delay retirement included higher levels of education, less access to health benefits, greater expectations of living past age 75, and being self-employed.

We also reviewed two international studies that examined retirement expectations. In a survey of Dutch workers, van Dam, van der Vorst, and van der Heijden (2009) found that employees indicated fewer intentions to retire when they expected their future work to remain challenging and meaningful. In one of the few qualitative studies that emerged in the literature on retirement decisions, Crego, de la Hera, and Martinez-Inigo (2008) found that Spanish employees who anticipated high-quality work conditions were more inclined to postpone retirement.

Finally, in one of the most comprehensive studies to date, Topa, Moriano, Depolo, Alcover, and

Morales (2009) conducted a meta-analysis of studies of retirement planning (and retirement status, which is discussed in the next section). Across the 99 empirical studies included in the analysis, significant antecedents of individuals' expectations to retire included poor health, negative working conditions, a positive attitude toward retirement, less job satisfaction, and less job involvement. They also included studies that examined outcomes of retirement planning and found that retirement planning was related to a higher likelihood of bridge employment as well as increased retirement satisfaction.

Taken together, these studies suggest that a number of person- and work-related characteristics, in particular, health, financial situation, education level, aspects of the job, and workers' attitudes about work and retirement, are related to individuals' expectations or preferences about when they will retire. The gender differences found in the retirement intentions of working men and women, however, suggest that it is important for future research to examine potential moderator variables such as gender, race and ethnicity, social class, and occupation type. For example, workers with lower level jobs who have little or no retirement savings may have very different intentions and expectations regarding retirement compared with higher level workers who have had greater access to financial resources and have been able to plan for retirement financially. Additionally, longitudinal studies that follow individuals from the planning phase to the decision phase and into postretirement living will be beneficial to identify factors that are associated with a successful retirement transition process.

Retirement Decisions and Outcomes

The research studies on retirement expectations capture workers' visions of their ideal retirement decisions, yet workers' intentions may not always match the reality of their retirement decisions. A number of studies have zeroed in on the actual retirement decision, or status of being retired, and have used samples of individuals who were retired. Similar to the research on retirement intentions, these studies focus on the reasons behind the retirement decision or antecedents of the decision; however, because the studies use samples of individuals who have already made the decision to retire, researchers have been able to include psychological and behavioral outcomes of the decision.

Zimmerman, Mitchell, Wister, and Gutman (2000) examined female workers' and female retirees' reasons for retiring. Female retirees listed family caregiving (i.e., providing care for any family member) as a major reason for retiring, whereas female workers did not anticipate that obligations to care for others would influence the retirement decision. Szinovacz and Davey (2005) used data from a large national survey and studied retirees' reasons for retirement and whether they perceived the retirement decision as voluntary or involuntary. The retirement decision was more often perceived as involuntary when the decision to retire was due to physical illness or to provide care for others; however, gender differences emerged such that male retirees characterized the decision to retire to take care of a family member as an involuntary decision, whereas female retirees perceived this as a voluntary decision. In a study examining career success of emergency room physicians, Pachulicz, Schmitt, and Kuljanin (2008) found that physicians who reported a change in income over time were more likely to have retired, that is, those whose salaries were no longer increasing were more likely to retire.

Shultz, Morton, and Weckerle (1998) used data from a large national sample of retired individuals and found that individuals forced or pushed into retirement due to physical illness or injury reported less satisfaction with the retirement decision and less satisfaction with life after retirement compared with participants who cited voluntary reasons (i.e., pull factors) for retiring. Bacharach, Bamberger, Biron, and Horowitz-Rosen (2008) followed a group of blue-collar workers through retirement and found that those who perceived the retirement decision as involuntary tended to have more problematic drinking behavior in retirement compared with retirees who perceived the decision as voluntary.

Results from the Topa et al. (2009) meta-analysis revealed a number of significant antecedents and consequences of the decision to retire or retirement status. Variables that significantly predicted the decision to retire included poor health, negative working conditions, and more positive attitudes toward retirement. In addition, the decision to retire was associated positively with participation in volunteer work, retirement satisfaction, engagement in bridge employment, and life satisfaction. Interestingly, the effect sizes for the relationships of the antecedents and consequences with retirement planning or expectations were larger than those for the retirement decision, suggesting that forces outside of the individual's control might play a large—and unpredictable—role in the behavioral choice to disengage from the paid workforce.

One emerging line of inquiry focuses on the relational context of the retirement decision, especially the marital relationship. Among a sample of retired heterosexual couples, Smith and Moen (1998) examined how much influence an individual's spouse had on the decision to retire. Female retirees perceived their spouses as having more influence on the decision when the spouse was also preparing for his own retirement, whereas male retirees perceived their wives as being influential in their retirement decision, regardless of the spouse's plans for retirement. In a finer tuned analysis, Smith and Moen (2004) studied whether level of agreement of the spousal influence on the retirement decision was correlated with particular outcomes. Gender differences again emerged such that female retirees and their husbands were more likely to report satisfaction with the retirement decision when husbands played no role in the decision. Male retirees and their wives, however, were both more likely to be satisfied with retirement when wives had an influence on the decision to retire.

Taken together, the studies on the retirement decision highlight the importance of differentiating individual's intentions or expectations about retirement from their actual retirement behavior, as individuals may have particular expectations about when they will retire but unforeseen life circumstances such as the need to take care of an aging parent or ill spouse may ultimately be the deciding factors in the retirement decision. Although similar retirement antecedents appear across the studies on retirement intentions and decisions (e.g., poor health, negative work conditions, need to care for others), the studies on the actual retirement decision suggest that individuals' perceptions about the voluntary nature of retirement, that is, whether they felt pushed or pulled into the decision, seem to be related to their psychological and behavioral outcomes postdecision. These studies also illuminate the gendered nature of retirement decisions and outcomes, and future research should continue to examine potential moderators of the retirement decision such as gender and social class. Additional research is needed that goes beyond heterosexual, married couples and includes broader conceptualizations of what constitutes important relationships in workers' lives.

Bridge Employment

One burgeoning area of research that is reflective of changes in the workforce is the decision to engage in bridge employment. Bridge employment "refers to a pattern of employment taken by older-age adults to bridge between their career jobs and full retirement" (Jones & McIntosh, 2010, p. xx). With current economic instability and reduced pension benefits, many workers are relying on bridge employment before full-time retirement (Zhan, Wang, Liu, & Shultz, 2009). The bulk of the research studies we reviewed investigated the antecedents or predictors of the decision to engage in bridge retirement, and they differentiated career bridge employment, that is, working the same field as one held before retirement, and noncareer bridge employment, that is, engaging in postretirement work in a different field than the original work path.

Two studies focused on whether the decisions to fully retire, engage in same-career bridge employment, or seek bridge employment in a different field were differentially predicted by various demographic and work-related characteristics. von Bonsdorff, Shultz, Leskinen, and Tansky (2009) used a database of employees in various branches of the U.S. federal government who planned to retire within the next 5 years and examined their intentions to fully retire or to seek career bridge employment (i.e., continue working in another unit in the government) or noncareer bridge employment (i.e., continue working outside the federal government). They found different antecedents for the three retirement options, although there was less differentiation between the antecedents of engaging in

career versus noncareer bridge employment. Workers who intended to engage in noncareer bridge employment rather than fully retire were more likely to be male, younger, have higher levels of education, perceive the job market positively, desire a better use of their skills, and have more concerns about changes in their benefits. Similarly, workers who intended to engage in career bridge work rather than fully retire tended to be younger, have fewer nonwork interests, desired to earn more money, and desired to put their skills to better use. Similarly, Gobeski and Beehr (2009) examined antecedents of bridge employment and full retirement, but they used a sample of actual retirees from a wide variety of occupations who were engaged in the same-career or noncareer bridge employment or were fully retired. They found that retirees who reported greater job strain in their preretirement work were more likely to be engaged in noncareer bridge employment, whereas those who had more years of experience in their preretirement job and who reported more intrinsic job characteristics of their preretirement job were more likely to be engaged in same-career bridge employment. Predictors of full retirement included higher age and more years of experience in the preretirement career.

Wang, Zhan, Liu, and Shultz (2008) utilized longitudinal data from a national database to examine whether multiple individual, job, retirement planning, and family-related factors were predictive of the decision to engage in bridge employment. In general, they found that physical health, age, satisfaction with preretirement work, and retirement planning tended to be associated with seeking bridge employment versus full-time employment. Using the same data set, Zhan, Wang, Liu, and Shultz (2009) examined physical and mental health outcomes of bridge employment. Individuals in bridge employment had better physical health compared with full-time retirees. Individuals who were engaged in bridge employment within their career field reported greater mental health compared with those whose bridge employment was in a different field or those who were retired.

In a different approach from previous studies, Ulrich and Brott (2005) used a qualitative design and interviewed 24 retirees from a variety of professional, managerial, sales, and administrative support positions about their reasons for engaging in bridge employment following retirement and their perceptions of the outcome of the decision. One of the major reasons participants continued working after retirement was to feel more in control of their work lives. Making the transition to the bridge work was fraught with a number of challenges such as coping with reduced pay, age discrimination, changes in the work environment, and the need for retraining. Despite the challenges, however, workers viewed bridge employment positively and used it to redefine the meaning of retirement for themselves.

Finally, Adams and Rau (2004) moved beyond the reasons behind the decision and applied a model of job seeking to retirees' behaviors related to seeking bridge employment. They used a sample of retirees from a university system, the majority of whom had worked in teaching and managerial positions. In general, there was support for applying a general model of job seeking to retiree's bridge employment–seeking behavior, although not all hypothesized predictors were significantly related to job seeking. Retirees with higher levels of job-seeking behaviors tended to be younger, reported more negative attitudes toward retirement, had higher job-seeking social support, reported more constraints on finding a job because of one's age, reported fewer traditional constraints to job seeking (e.g., health, need for transportation or child care), and reported lower levels of Protestant work ethic attitudes. Interestingly, job-seeking self-efficacy was not related to number of job-seeking behaviors.

The decision to engage in bridge employment is clearly a burgeoning area of research, with the bulk of studies focused on identifying the work- and person-related factors that are predictive of the decision. In general, the findings suggest that individuals near retirement age who are in greater health, are younger, and have more negative attitudes toward retirement would be more likely to engage in bridge employment rather than fully retire. Additionally, there is some tentative evidence that bridge employment is related to more positive psychological outcomes, although finding and obtaining bridge employment may have a unique set of stressors and

challenges. As research in this area continues, it would be helpful to include more contextual variables, such as family, social class, and cultural variables, that may influence the decision, such as examining whether bridge employment is always voluntary and to what degree financial constraints play a role in the decision. Additionally, it would be beneficial to understand whether there are differential outcomes based on type of bridge employment (same career vs. different career), to what degree individuals consider bridge employment as part of their retirement planning, and whether the decision to transition from bridge employment to full-time retirement living represents a unique retirement process.

Summary of Retirement Decisions Research

Compared with the research on other work-related decisions, the research literature in retirement decisions is more cohesive and developed and it is firmly rooted in theoretical models of the retirement process. The studies on the decision itself have largely focused on the reasons why individuals think they will retire, the factors that predict the actual retirement decision, and the factors related to engaging in bridge employment. The findings suggest that age, health, and attitudes about work and retirement are predictive of individual's plans for retirement as well as the decision to retire; however, a number of variables might influence these relationships, particularly gender and family factors. Preparing and planning for retirement also seems to be important in helping workers have a more positive retirement experience; however, despite the workers' best-laid retirement plans, reality can intervene in one's retirement plans such that factors out of the individual's control (e.g., health of self and family members) can play a large role in the decision to retire. A few studies have also examined psychological outcomes of the retirement decision, with some tentative evidence suggesting that individuals who feel more in control of the decision to retire have better psychological outcomes.

Future research in work-related decisions in retirement should examine the psychological experience of workers through the decisional process because the process by which individuals navigate the multiple steps in the retirement decision and what factors are related to a more successful transition process are less clear. In addition, including more psychological and behavioral outcomes of the decision will allow researchers to develop interventions designed to increase the mental health of workers through the retirement process. Given the vast changes in the work world and given that individuals are likely to remain in the workforce longer compared with previous generations, interventions focused on helping individuals be both planful and adaptive in their retirement decisions would greatly contribute to research in this area. Finally, the international studies in this area raise the issue of how social and governmental policies, as well as cultural values about work, may play important roles in individuals' plans for and ultimate decisions regarding retirement.

CONCLUSION

The research in work-related decisions published within the past decade has examined multiple decision points in an individual's working life from entry into the workforce to the decision to retire from the paid workforce. Our review revealed that researchers are attuned to the multiple, ongoing decisions that individuals must make throughout their working lives, and a vast array of studies examine various work-related decisions and decisional situations. One of the strengths of this research area is that it is multidisciplinary, attracting organizational and sociological as well as psychological perspectives; however, a counseling psychology lens, with its focus on assisting individuals with problems of living from a strengths- and prevention-based perspective, is particularly relevant for studying work-related decisions.

The current research in work-related decisions is broad, covering many different types of decisions that workers face across their working life. Despite that breadth, we note a few areas of inquiry missing from this literature, including research on decisions about whether to pursue additional education after high school or to enter the workforce, decisions about promotion and advancement in nonprofessional occupations, decisions about part-time work,

and decisions about engaging in employment considered illegal or paid employment not reported to the government. With a few notable exceptions, studies rely on samples of professional workers with high levels of education who likely have a fair degree of volition about their work decisions. Broader samples are needed, including particularly workers in service and industry positions, part-time workers, and others in jobs with few or no health insurance benefits.

In general, much of the research in work-related decisions focuses on identifying antecedents of the decision, or person-, background-, and work-related variables that pertain to whether individuals pursue a particular type of decision. Although these findings illuminate potential factors of importance in the decision, we know less about which factors deciders pay attention to or deliberately incorporate into their decision-making process. As we go forward, research should explore individuals' perceptions about their decision-making process, and include more postdecision psychological and behavioral outcomes to identify factors related to more positive outcomes. Qualitative studies using small but targeted samples of individuals experiencing a particular work-related decision were prominent in the research within the past decade. These studies provide rich descriptions of the psychological experience of the decision as they navigate a particular decision. Research should expand on these studies, validating findings with additional samples, and clarifying constructs to develop theoretical models to guide future inquiry.

Although the research in work-related decisions is generally more focused on asking theoretical rather than applied questions, some common themes emerge across the disparate studies that offer tentative implications for counseling practice. Qualities that seem to be important in navigating the 21st-century work world include being prepared for and planful about impending work-related decisions, taking an active role in one's work decisions, and remaining adaptable and flexible and able to respond to unexpected changes. Counseling psychologists can cultivate these characteristics in deciders and can help individuals cope with work-related changes in their lives. Another emergent theme across these diverse research studies is that work-related decisions are not made in isolation and that relationships with other people can serve as vital resources in the decisional process. Counseling psychologists can provide relational support for deciders and also assist clients in obtaining and utilizing other people in their environments as they make work-related decisions. Finally, a number of person-related factors, namely, higher education level and higher socioeconomic class, are associated with more positive work-related outcomes and with greater flexibility in and choices about work-related decisions across the working life. These findings point to the need for counseling psychologists to incorporate a context-rich approach in their work with individuals and to understand the familial, sociopolitical, and cultural influences on individuals' work-related decisions.

References

Adams, G., & Rau, B. (2004). Job seeking among retirees seeking bridge employment. *Personnel Psychology, 57*, 719–744. doi:10.1111/j.1744-6570.2004.00005.x

Alfermann, D., & Stambulova, N. (2007). Career transitions and career termination. In G. Tenenbaum & R. C. Eklund (Eds.), *Handbook of sport psychology* (3rd ed., pp. 712–733). Hoboken, NJ: Wiley.

Alfermann, D., Stambulova, N., & Zemaityte, A. (2004). Reactions to sport career termination: A cross-national comparison of German, Lithuanian, and Russian athletes. *Psychology of Sport and Exercise, 5*, 61–75. doi:10.1016/S1469-0292(02)00050-X

Allen, M. W., Armstrong, D. J., Riemenschneider, C. K., & Reid, M. F. (2006). Making sense of the barriers women face in the information technology work force: Standpoint theory, self-disclosure and causal maps. *Sex Roles, 54*, 831–844. doi:10.1007/s11199-006-9049-4

Alliman-Brissett, A., Turner, S. L., & Skovolt, T. M. (2004). Parent support and African American adolescents' career self-efficacy. *Professional School Counseling, 7*, 124–132.

Alon, S., Donahoe, D., & Tienda, M. (2001). The effects of early work experience on young women's labor force attachment. *Social Forces, 79*, 1005–1034. doi:10.1353/sof.2001.0002

Amundson, N. E., Borgen, W. A., Iaquinta, M., Butterfield, L. D., & Koert, E. (2010). Career decisions from the decider's perspective. *The Career Development Quarterly, 58*, 336–351.

Aseltine, R. H., Jr., & Gore, S. (2005). Work, postsecondary education, and psychosocial functioning following the transition from high school. *Journal of Adolescent Research, 20*, 615–639. doi:10.1177/0743558405279360

Bacharach, S., Bamberger, P. A., Biron, M., & Horowitz-Rosen, M. (2008). Perceived agency in retirement and retiree drinking behavior: Job satisfaction as a moderator. *Journal of Vocational Behavior, 73*, 376–386. doi:10.1016/j.jvb.2008.07.007

Baruch, Y., & Quick, J. C. (2007). Understanding second careers: Lessons from a study of U.S. Navy admirals. *Human Resource Management, 46*, 471–491. doi:10.1002/hrm.20178

Berggren, H. M. (2008). U.S. family leave policy: The legacy of "separate spheres." *International Journal of Social Welfare, 17*, 312–323. doi:10.1111/j.1468-2397.2008.00554.x

Blustein, D. L. (2006). *The psychology of working: A new perspective for career development, counseling, and public policy.* Mahwah, NJ: Erlbaum.

Blustein, D. L., Chaves, A. P., Diemer, M. A., Gallagher, L. A., Marshall, K. G., Sirin, S., & Bhati, K. S. (2002). Voices of the forgotten half: The role of social class in the school-to-work transition. *Journal of Counseling Psychology, 49*, 311–323. doi:10.1037/0022-0167.49.3.311

Bosco, S. M., & Bianco, C. A. (2005). Influence of maternal work patterns and socioeconomic status on Gen Y lifestyle choice. *Journal of Career Development, 32*, 165–182. doi:10.1177/0894845305279169

Buchmann, M., Kriesi, I., Pfeifer, A., & Sacchi, S. (2003). Dynamics of women's employment careers: Labor-market opportunities and women's labor-market exit and reentry. In W. R. Heinz & V. W. Marshall (Eds.), *Social dynamics of the lifecourse: Transitions, institutions, and interrelations* (pp. 116–141). New York, NY: Adline de Gruyter.

Cabrera, E. F. (2009). Protean organizations: Reshaping work and careers to retain female talent. *Career Development International, 14*, 186–201. doi:10.1108/13620430910950773

Carless, S. A., & Bernath, L. (2007). Antecedents of intent to change among psychologists. *Journal of Career Development, 33*, 183–200. doi:10.1177/0894845306296646

Cavanaugh, M. A., & Noe, R. A. (1999). Antecedents and consequences of relational components of the new psychological contract. *Journal of Organizational Behavior, 20*, 323–340. doi:10.1002/(SICI)1099-1379(199905)20:3<323::AID-JOB901>3.0.CO;2-M

Chudzikowski, K., Demel, B., Mayrhofer, W., Briscoe, J. P., Unite, J., Milikić, B. B., . . . Zikic, J. (2009). Career transitions and their causes: A country-comparative perspective. *Journal of Occupational and Organizational Psychology, 82*, 825–849. doi:10.1348/096317909X474786

Clarke, M. (2007). Where to from here? Evaluating employability during career transition. *Journal of Management and Organization, 13*, 196–211. doi:10.5172/jmo.2007.13.3.196

Cohen, L., Duberley, J., & Mallon, M. (2004). Social constructionism in the study of career: Accessing the parts that other approaches cannot. *Journal of Vocational Behavior, 64*, 407–422. doi:10.1016/j.jvb.2003.12.007

Creed, P. A., Fallon, T., & Hood, M. (2009). The relationship between career adaptability, person and situation variables, and career concerns in young adults. *Journal of Vocational Behavior, 74*, 219–229. doi:10.1016/j.jvb.2008.12.004

Crego, A., de la Hera, C. A., & Martinez-Inigo, D. (2008). The transition process to post-working life and its psychosocial outcomes: A systematic analysis of Spanish early retirees' discourse. *Career Development International, 13*, 186–204. doi:10.1108/13620430810860576

Crosby, D. A., & Hawkes, D. D. (2007). Cross-national research using contemporary birth cohort studies: A look at early maternal employment in the UK and USA. *International Journal of Social Research Methodology: Theory and Practice, 10*, 379–404. doi:10.1080/13645570701677151

Drobnič, S. (2003). Ties between lives: Dynamics of employment patterns of spouses. In W. R. Heinz & V. W. Marshall (Eds.), *Social dynamics of the life-course: Transitions, institutions, and interrelations* (pp. 259–278). New York, NY: Adline de Gruyter.

Ebberwein, C. A., Krieshok, T. S., Ulven, J. C., & Prosser, E. C. (2004). Voices in transition: Lessons on career adaptability. *The Career Development Quarterly, 52*, 292–308.

Ek, E., Sovio, U., Remes, J., & Järvelin, M. (2005). Social predictors of unsuccessful entrance into the labour market—A socialization process perspective. *Journal of Vocational Behavior, 66*, 471–486. doi:10.1016/j.jvb.2004.02.002

Ericksen, K. S., Jurgens, J. C., Garrett, M. T., & Swedburg, R. B. (2008). Should I stay at home or should I go back to work? Workforce reentry influences on a mother's decision-making process. *Journal of Employment Counseling, 45*, 156–167.

Feldman, R., Sussman, A. L., & Zigler, E. (2004). Parental leave and work adaptation at the transition to parenthood: Individual, marital and social correlates. *Applied Developmental Psychology, 25*, 459–479. doi:10.1016/j.appdev.2004.06.004

Fernandez, A., Stephan, Y., & Fouquereau, E. (2006). Assessing reasons for sport termination: Development of the Athletes' Retirement Decision Inventory (ARDI). *Psychology of Sport and Exercise, 7*, 407–421. doi:10.1016/j.psychsport.2005.11.001

Fouad, N. A., Cotter, E. W., Fitzpatrick, M. E., Kantamneni, N., Carter, L., & Bernfeld, S. (2010). Development and validation of the Family Influences Scale. *Journal of Career Assessment, 18*, 276–291. doi:10.1177/1069072710364793

Fouad, N. A., & Kantamneni, N. (2008). Contextual factors in vocational psychology: Intersections of individual, group, and societal dimensions. In S. D. Brown & R. W. Lent (Eds.), *Handbook of counseling psychology* (4th ed., pp. 408–425). Hoboken, NJ: Wiley.

Furbish, D. S. (2009). Self-funded leave and life role development. *Journal of Employment Counseling, 46*, 38–46.

Gobeski, K. T., & Beehr, T. A. (2009). How retirees work: Predictors of different types of bridge employment. *Journal of Organizational Behavior, 30*, 401–425. doi:10.1002/job.547

Gowan, M. A., & Nassar-McMillan, S. C. (2001). Examination of individual differences in participation in outplacement program activities after a job loss. *Journal of Employment Counseling, 38*, 185–196.

Grady, G., & McCarthy, A. M. (2008). Work-life integration: Experiences of mid-career professional working mothers. *Journal of Managerial Psychology, 23*, 599–622. doi:10.1108/02683940810884559

Haase, C. M., Heckhausen, J., & Köller, O. (2008). Goal engagement during the school-work transition: Beneficial for all, particularly for girls. *Journal of Research on Adolescence, 18*, 671–698. doi:10.1111/j.1532-7795.2008.00576.x

Heppner, M. J., Multon, K. D., & Johnston, J. A. (1994). Assessing psychological resources during career change: Development of the Career Transitions Inventory. *Journal of Vocational Behavior, 44*, 55–74. doi:10.1006/jvbe.1994.1004

Hirschi, A. (2009). Career adaptability development in adolescence: Multiple predictors and effects on sense of power and life satisfaction. *Journal of Vocational Behavior, 74*, 145–155. doi:10.1016/j.jvb.2009.01.002

Hostetler, A. J., Sweet, S., & Moen, P. (2007). Gendered career paths: A life course perspective on returning to school. *Sex Roles, 56*, 85–103. doi:10.1007/s11199-006-9150-8

Ito, J. K., & Brotheridge, C. M. (2005). Does supporting employees' career adaptability lead to commitment, turnover, or both? *Human Resource Management, 44*, 5–19. doi:10.1002/hrm.20037

Jenkins, A. (2006). Women, lifelong learning and transitions into employment. *Work, Employment and Society, 20*, 309–328. doi: 10/1177/0950017006064116

Jones, D. A., & McIntosh, B. R. (2010). Organizational and occupational commitment in relation to bridge employment and retirement intentions. *Journal of Vocational Behavior, 77,* 290–303. doi:10.1016/j.jvb.2010.04.004

Juntunen, C. L., Wagner, K. E., & Matthews, L. G. (2002). Promoting positive career change in midlife. In C. L. Juntunen & D. R. Atkinson (Eds.), *Counseling across the lifespan: Prevention and treatment* (pp. 329–347). Thousand Oaks, CA: Sage.

Kadlcik, J., & Flemr, L. (2008). Athletic career termination model in the Czech Republic: A qualitative exploration. *International Review for the Sociology of Sport, 43,* 251–269. doi: 10.1177/1012690208098544

Kenny, M. E., & Bledsoe, M. (2005). Contributions of the relational context to career adaptability among urban adolescents. *Journal of Vocational Behavior, 66,* 257–272. doi:10.1016/j.jvb.2004.10.002

Kokko, K., & Pulkkinen, L. (2000). Aggression in childhood and long-term unemployment in adulthood: A cycle of maladaptation and some protective factors. *Developmental Psychology, 36,* 463–472. doi:10.1037/0012-1649.36.4.463

Kokko, K., Pulkkinen, L., & Puustinen, M. (2000). Selection into long-term unemployment and its psychological consequences. *International Journal of Behavioral Development, 24,* 310–320. doi:10.1080/01650250050118295

Kuhn, P. J., & Schuetze, H. J. (2001). Self-employment dynamics and self-employment trends: A study of Canadian men and women, 1982–1998. *The Canadian Journal of Economics: Revue Canadienne d'Economique, 34,* 760–784. doi:10.1111/0008-4085.00098

Lavallee, D. (2005). The effect of a life development intervention on sports career transition adjustment. *The Sport Psychologist, 19,* 193–202.

Lavallee, D. (2006). Career awareness, career planning, and career transition needs among sports coaches. *Journal of Career Development, 33,* 66–79. doi:10.1177/0894845306289550

Lavallee, D., Grove, J. R., & Gordon, S. (1997). The causes of career termination from sport and their relationship to post-termination adjust among elite-amateur athletes in Australia. *Australian Psychologist, 32,* 131–135. doi:10.1080/00050069708257366

Linnehan, F. (2003). A longitudinal study of work-based, adult-youth mentoring. *Journal of Vocational Behavior, 63,* 40–54. doi:10.1016/S0001-8791(02)00012-X

Mallon, M., & Cohen, L. (2001). Time for a change? Women's accounts of the move from organizational careers to self-employment. *British Journal of Management, 12,* 217–230. doi:10.1111/1467-8551.00195

Mermin, G. B. T., Johnson, R. W., & Murphy, D. P. (2007). Why do boomers plan to work longer? *The Journals of Gerontology: Series B. Psychological Sciences and Social Sciences, 62B,* S286–S294.

Moen, P. (2003). Linked lives: Dual careers, gender, and the contingent life course. In W. R. Heinz & V. W. Marshall (Eds.), *Social dynamics of the lifecourse: Transitions, institutions, and interrelations* (pp. 237–258). New York, NY: Adline de Gruyter.

Moen, P., & Sweet, S. (2003). Time clocks: Work-hour strategies. In P. Moen (Ed.), *It's about time: Couples and careers* (pp. 17–34). Ithaca, NY: Cornell University Press.

Motulsky, S. L. (2010). Relational processes in career transition: Extending theory, research, and practice. *The Counseling Psychologist, 38,* 1078–1114. doi:10.1177/0011000010376415

Murphy, K. A., Blustein, D. L., Bohlig, A. J., & Platt, M. G. (2010). The college-to-career transition: An exploration of emerging adulthood. *Journal of Counseling and Development, 88*(2), 174–181.

Noonan, A. E., Hall, G., & Blustein, D. L. (2007). Urban adolescents' experience of social class in relationships at work. *Journal of Vocational Behavior, 70,* 542–560. doi:10.1016/j.jvb.2007.01.005

Oplatka, I. (2005). Breaking the routine: Voluntary inter-school transition and women teacher's self-renewal. *Teachers and Teaching: Theory and Practice, 11,* 465–480. doi:10.1080/13540600500238469

Otto, K., Dette-Hagenmeyer, D. E., & Dalbert, C. (2010). Occupational mobility in members of the labor force: Explaining the willingness to change occupations. *Journal of Career Development, 36,* 262–288. doi:10.1177/0894845309345842

Pachulicz, S., Schmitt, N., & Kuljanin, G. (2008). A model of career success: A longitudinal study of emergency physicians. *Journal of Vocational Behavior, 73,* 242–253. doi:10.1016/j.jvb.2008.05.003

Park, J. M. (2005). The roles of living arrangements and household resources in single mothers' employment. *Journal of Social Service Research, 31,* 49–67. doi:10.1300/J079v31n03_03

Phillips, S. D., Blustein, D. L., Jobin-Davis, K., & White, S. K. (2002). Preparation for the school-to-work transition: The views of high school students. *Journal of Vocational Behavior, 61,* 202–216. doi:10.1006/jvbe.2001.1853

Phillips, S. D., Christopher-Sisk, E. K., & Gravino, K. L. (2001). Making career decisions in a relational context. *The Counseling Psychologist, 29,* 193–214. doi:10.1177/0011000001292002

Pienta, A. M., & Hayward, M. D. (2002). Who expects to continue working after age 62? The retirement plans of couples. *Journal of Gerontology: Social Sciences, 57B,* S199–S208. doi:10.1093/geronb/57.4.S199

Pinquart, M., Juang, L. P., & Silbereisen, R. K. (2003). Self-efficacy and successful school-to-work transition: A longitudinal study. *Journal of Vocational Behavior, 63,* 329–346. doi:10.1016/S0001-8791(02)00031-3

Pruitt, N. T., Johnson, A. J., Catlin, L., & Knox, S. (2010). Influences on women counseling psychology associate professors' decisions regarding full professorship pursuit. *The Counseling Psychologist, 38,* 1139–1173. doi:10.1177/0011000010377666

Rafferty, A. E., & Griffin, M. A. (2006). Perceptions of organizational change: A stress and coping perspective. *Journal of Applied Psychology, 91,* 1154–1162. doi:10.1037/0021-9010.91.5.1154

Reybold, L. E., & Alamia, J. J. (2008). Academic transitions in education: A developmental perspective of women faculty experiences. *Journal of Career Development, 35,* 107–128. doi:10.1177/0894845308325644

Schaeper, H., & Falk, S. (2003). Employment trajectories of East and West German mother compared: One nation–one pattern? In W. R. Heinz & V. W. Marshall (Eds.), *Social dynamics of the lifecourse: Transitions, institutions, and interrelations* (pp. 143–163). New York, NY: Adline de Gruyter.

Schlossberg, N. K., Waters, E. B., & Goodman, J. (1995). *Counseling adults in transition: Linking practice with theory* (2nd ed.). New York, NY: Springer.

Schultheiss, D. E. P., Kress, H. M., Manzi, A. J., & Glasscock, J. M. J. (2001). Relationship influences in career development: A qualitative inquiry. *The Counseling Psychologist, 29,* 216–241. doi:10.1177/0011000001292003

Schultheiss, D. P. (2009). To mother or matter: Can women do both? *Journal of Career Development, 36,* 25–48. doi:10.1177/0894845309340795

Shaffer, M. A., Joplin, J. R. W., Bell, M. P., Lau, T., & Oguz, C. (2000). Gender discrimination and job-related outcomes: A cross-cultural comparison of working women in the United States and China. *Journal of Vocational Behavior, 57,* 395–427. doi:10.1006/jvbe.1999.1748

Shapiro, M., Ingols, C., & Blake-Beard, S. (2008). Confronting career double binds: Implications for women, organizations, and career practitioners. *Journal of Career Development, 34,* 309–333. doi:10.1177/0894845307311250

Shultz, K. S., Morton, K. R., & Weckerle, J. R. (1998). The influence of push and pull factors on voluntary and involuntary early retirees' retirement decision and adjustment. *Journal of Vocational Behavior, 53,* 45–57. doi:10.1006/jvbe.1997.1610

Sims, C. S., Drasgow, F., & Fitzgerald, L. F. (2005). The effects of sexual harassment on turnover in the military: Time-dependent modeling. *Journal of Applied Psychology, 90,* 1141–1152. doi:10.1037/0021-9010.90.6.1141

Sinisalo, P., & Komulainen, K. (2008). The creation of coherence in the transitional career: A narrative case study of the woman entrepreneur. *International Journal for Educational and Vocational Guidance, 8,* 35–48. doi:10.1007/s10775-007-9134-4

Smith, D. B., & Moen, P. (1998). Spousal influence on retirement: His, her, and their perceptions. *Journal of Marriage and the Family, 60,* 734–744. doi:10.2307/353542

Smith, D. B., & Moen, P. (2004). Retirement satisfaction for retirees and their spouses: Do gender and the retirement decision-making process matter? *Journal of Family Issues, 25,* 262–285. doi:10.1177/0192513X03257366

Spiegel, P. E., & Shultz, K. S. (2003). The influence of preretirement planning and transferability of skills on naval officers' retirement satisfaction and adjustment. *Military Psychology, 15,* 285–307. doi:10.1207/S15327876MP1504_3

Stanfors, M. A. (2006). Labor force transitions after childbirth among five birth cohorts in Sweden. *Journal of Family and Economic Issues, 27,* 287–309. doi:10.1007/s10834-006-9015-x

Super, D. E. (1990). A life-span, life-space approach to career development. In D. Brown, L. Brooks, & Associates. (Eds.), *Career choice and development: Applying contemporary theories to practice* (2nd ed., pp. 197–261). San Francisco, CA: Jossey-Bass.

Sweet, S., & Moen, P. (2007). Integrating educational careers in work and family. *Community, Work and Family, 10,* 231–250. doi:10.1080/13668800701270166

Szinovacz, M. E., & Davey, A. (2005). Predictors of perceptions of involuntary retirement. *The Gerontologist, 45,* 36–47. doi:10.1093/geront/45.1.36

Taniguchi, H., & Rosenfeld, R. A. (2002). Women's employment exit and reentry: Differences among Whites, Blacks, and Hispanics. *Social Science Research, 31,* 432–471. doi:10.1016/S0049-089X(02)00009-1

Taylor, M. A., Shultz, K. S., Spiegel, P. E., Morrison, R. F., & Greene, J. (2007). Occupational attachment and met expectations as predictors of retirement adjustment of naval offers. *Journal of Applied Social Psychology, 37,* 1697–1725. doi:10.1111/j.1559-1816.2007.00234.x

Tomasik, M., Hardy, S., Haase, C. M., & Heckhausen, J. (2009). Adaptive adjustment of vocational aspirations of German youths during the transition to work. *Journal of Vocational Behavior, 74,* 38–46. doi:10.1016/j.jvb.2008.10.003

Topa, G., Moriano, J. A., Depolo, M., Alcover, C. M., & Morales, J. F. (2009). Antecedents and consequences of retirement planning and decision-making: A meta-analysis and model. *Journal of Vocational Behavior, 75,* 38–55. doi:10.1016/j.jvb.2009.03.002

Tynkkynen, L., Nurmi, J. E., & Salmela-Aro, K. (2010). Career goal-related social ties during two educational transitions: Antecedents and consequences. *Journal of Vocational Behavior, 76,* 448–457. doi:10.1016/j.jvb.2009.12.001

Ulrich, L. B., & Brott, P. E. (2005). Older workers and bridge employment: Redefining retirement. *Journal of Employment Counseling, 42,* 159–170.

Valcour, M., & Ladge, J. J. (2008). Family and career path characteristics as predictors of women's objective and subjective career success: Integrating traditional and protean career explanations. *Journal of Vocational Behavior, 73,* 300–309. doi:10.1016/j.jvb.2008.06.002

van Dam, K., van der Vorst, J. D. M., & van der Heijden, B. I. J. M. (2009). Employees' intentions to retire early: A case of planned behavior and anticipated work conditions. *Journal of Career Development, 35,* 265–289. doi:10.1177/0894845308327274

van Vianen, A. E. M., De Pater, I. E., & Preenen, P. T. Y. (2009). Adaptable careers: Maximizing less and exploring more. *The Career Development Quarterly, 57,* 298–309.

von Bonsdorff, M. E., Shultz, K. S., Leskinen, E., & Tansky, J. (2009). The choice between retirement and bridge employment: A continuity theory and life course perspective. *The International Journal of Aging and Human Development, 69,* 79–100. doi:10.2190/AG.69.2.a

Wanberg, C. R., & Kammeyer-Mueller, J. (2008). A self-regulatory perspective on navigating career transitions. In R. Kanfer, G. Chen, & R. D. Pritchard (Eds.), *Work motivation: Past, present, and future* (pp. 433–469). New York, NY: Routledge.

Wang, M., & Shultz, K. S. (2010). Employee retirement: A review and recommendations for future investigation. *Journal of Management, 36,* 172–206. doi:10.1177/0149206309347957

Wang, M., Zhan, Y., Liu, S., & Shultz, K. S. (2008). Antecedents of bridge employment: A longitudinal investigation. *Journal of Applied Psychology, 93,* 818–830. doi:10.1037/0021-9010.93.4.818

Wendlandt, N. M., & Rochlen, A. B. (2008). Addressing the college-to-work transition: Implications for university career counselors. *Journal of Career Development, 35,* 151–165. doi:10.1177/0894845308325646

Westaby, J. D. (2004). The impact of outplacement programs on reemployment criteria: A longitudinal study of displaced managers and executives. *Journal of Employment Counseling, 41,* 19–28.

Wiesner, M., Vondracek, F. W., Capaldi, D. M., & Porfeli, E. (2003). Childhood and adolescent predictors of early adult career pathways. *Journal of Vocational Behavior, 63,* 305–328. doi:10.1016/S0001-8791(03)00028-9

Wylleman, P., Alfermann, D., & Lavallee, D. (2004). Career transitions in sport: European perspectives. *Psychology of Sport and Exercise, 5,* 7–20. doi:10.1016/S1469-0292(02)00049-3

Yang, E., & Gysbers, N. C. (2007). Career transitions of college seniors. *The Career Development Quarterly, 56,* 157–170.

Zhan, Y., Wang, M., Liu, S., & Shultz, K. S. (2009). Bridge employment and retirees' health: A longitudinal investigation. *Journal of Occupational Health Psychology, 14,* 374–389. doi:10.1037/a0015285

Zimmerman, L., Mitchell, L., Wister, A., & Gutman, G. (2000). Unanticipated consequences: A comparison of expected and actual retirement timing among older women. *Journal of Women and Aging, 12,* 109–128. doi:10.1300/J074v12n01_08

CHAPTER 11

SUPERVISION: RESEARCH, MODELS, AND COMPETENCE

Cal D. Stoltenberg and Brian W. McNeill

Supervision of counseling and psychotherapy has been considered an important area of research and practice in counseling psychology for decades. The breadth and depth of discussion and analysis of issues important to supervision has filled numerous books, so our focus here will be on only certain areas of this rather large literature. In this chapter, we examine some aspects of the "what" and the "how" of supervision. Our discussion is primarily of individual supervision with limited reference to other modalities. Where useful and as guidance for further work, we refer to recent issues in psychotherapy research and their relevance to supervision. We begin by discussing two models of clinical supervision that have been developed by counseling psychologists and provide considerable conceptual depth and detail in addition to being influenced by evidence from supervision research. Consistent with the common factors movement in psychotherapy research and practice, we examine conceptualizations of the supervision process on the basis of similar notions of commonalities among approaches. We also examine the breadth of research that has been conducted relevant to supervision, including the supervision process (relationship issues, conflict, counterproductive events, evaluation, client issues), characteristics of supervisees and supervisors (and clients), multicultural issues, and ethical and legal issues in supervision. We also briefly address the competency movement in professional psychology, particularly as it applies to competence in supervision. We end

the chapter with suggestions for future research and directions for clinical supervision.

CLINICAL EXPERTISE

Clearly the research literature in psychotherapy supervision provides interesting and useful, if tenuous, guidance in avoiding pitfalls and enhancing trainee growth through the supervision process. However, insufficient empirical evidence exists to draw conclusions concerning which models of clinical supervision are most effective (Stoltenberg & Pace, 2008; Westefeld, 2009). In the absence of the confirmed superiority of approaches or techniques of supervision, supervisors are left to rely rather heavily on expertise and clinical judgment in making decisions about the roles, processes, and outcomes of supervision.

Scott, Ingram, Vitanza, and Smith (2000) reported that counseling psychology programs are more likely to offer training and courses in supervision than are clinical psychology programs, even with the American Psychological Association's (APA's; 2002a) Committee on Accreditation guidelines for training in this area. Such training is important as research indicates that similar to other domains of development, experience in conducting supervision alone does not appear to influence supervisor development (Stevens, Goodyear, & Robertson, 1998). Both experience and training are needed to enhance a supervisor's sense of self-efficacy in the supervision process, which has been found to result in a more supportive and less critical or dogmatic approach.

DOI: 10.1037/13754-011
APA Handbook of Counseling Psychology: Vol. 1. Theories, Research, and Methods, Nadya A. Fouad (Editor-in-Chief)

MODELS OF PSYCHOTHERAPY SUPERVISION

We limit our discussion to two models that have made important contributions to counseling psychology, were developed by counseling psychologists, and are intended to be useful across theoretical orientations to counseling and psychotherapy. In order, we briefly discuss Ladany, Friedlander, and Nelson's (2005) interpersonal approach to supervision, which Bernard and Goodyear (2009) classified as a process model within the larger developmental models category, and Stoltenberg and McNeill's (2010) integrative developmental model, which Bernard and Goodyear considered a stage model of development. Both models take a pantheoretical perspective, noting that they are not tied to any particular therapeutic orientation but are applicable to most, if not all, supervision of therapy approaches. In addition, both models are presented based on their book form, which allows for more detail in theory and application than models based on article or chapter formats.

Ladany, Friedlander, and Nelson's Interpersonal Approach

The interpersonal or events-based approach delineated by Ladany et al. (2005) in *Critical Events in Psychotherapy Supervision: An Interpersonal Approach* shines a light on specific events occurring in supervision and provides a framework for working through these events inspired by a task analysis approach to psychotherapy used by Greenberg (1986) and others (e.g., Friedlander, Heatherington, Johnson, & Skowron, 1994; Safran, Crocker, McMain, & Murray, 1990). According to this approach, each event has a *marker*, which can be a supervisee's statement, statements over time, or behavior that serves as an indication for the need for specific help. Once recognized by the supervisor, the marker highlights the need to take action and dictates the type of action to be taken by the supervisor. Similar markers can indicate different problems, whereas different problems can elicit similar markers. Understanding the meaning of the marker sets in motion the interaction sequences (supervisor interventions, strategies; supervisee performances, reactions) that constitute the task environment.

Ladany et al. listed 11 interactional sequences: focus on the supervisory alliance, focus on the therapeutic process, exploration of feelings, focus on countertransference, attend to parallel processes, focus on self-efficacy, normalize experience, focus on skill, assess knowledge, focus on multicultural awareness, and focus on evaluation. They noted that this list is not exhaustive, the sequences are not assumed to be mutually exclusive, and these sequences are thought to be most relevant for events highlighted in the book, whereas other events (not addressed) may suggest other sequences. Ladany et al. noted that each interactional sequence can include various supervisor interventions, which are described in discussing each event and the associated interaction sequences approached chapter by chapter in their book and can be recursive processes. Effective implementation of the appropriate interaction sequences (facilitative interactions between the supervisor and supervisee) results in resolution of the event. Ladany et al., conceptualized *resolutions* in four broad categories with increasing or decreasing self-awareness, knowledge, skills, or effects on the supervisory alliance.

The events-based model posits the supervisory alliance as the foundation of effective supervision, and Ladany et al. (2005) conceptualized it from Bordin's (1983) perspective (agreement on goals and tasks, strong emotional bond) citing the positive influence of a strong versus the negative influence of a weak supervisory alliance. The seven "events" articulated in the events-based model, which can occur within a single session or across sessions, include remediating skill difficulties and deficits, heightening multicultural awareness, negotiating role conflicts, working through countertransference, managing sexual attraction, repairing gender-related misunderstandings, and addressing problematic attitudes and behavior (Ladany et al., 2005, p. 19). They also noted that events can occur within events incorporating more than one type of event into the selection of interactional sequences.

Ladany et al. (2005) noted that their approach is intended to attend primarily to the interpersonal or relational nature of the supervision process in working through critical events. Thus, their focus is more on the specific than on the overall development of the supervisee. They noted, however, that "we emphasize the supervisee's learning, growth, and development over case management" (p. 10), which they did not view as a primary purpose of clinical supervision. They assumed that the focus on critical events should strongly affect supervision outcomes, but they noted that the events-based approach has not been empirically examined and evidence is currently lacking.

Stoltenberg and McNeill's Integrative Developmental Model

Work on this developmental approach to supervision has progressed for nearly 30 years beginning with Stoltenberg's (1981) rather simplistic (through the lens of time) model that posited counselor growth through four stages of professional development. Subsequent books (Stoltenberg & Delworth, 1987; Stoltenberg, McNeill, & Delworth, 1998) significantly expanded this view with the integration of research and constructs from related areas of inquiry. The model is currently articulated in *IDM Supervision: An Integrative Developmental Model for Supervising Counselors and Therapists* (Stoltenberg & McNeill, 2010).

In contrast to the earliest version of the model, which viewed trainees progressing en masse through four stages from neophyte through master counselor, the integrative development model (IDM) posits that professional development occurs in a domain-specific manner, indicated by changes in three overarching structures that serve as markers for development. These changes in self and other awareness, motivation, and autonomy illuminate the developmental progression through three levels across domains of professional activity. Briefly, for the structure of self–other awareness, the trainee begins (Level 1) primarily attending to his or her own thoughts, emotions, and behavior attempting to understand and implement therapeutic processes while dealing with perceptions of low self-efficacy, anxiety, frustration, and hopefulness. Successful negotiation of this level moves the trainee to Level 2 in which the focus moves away from self-consciousness to an increasing focus on the client, or other awareness. This allows for greater learning and understanding of the client's perspective (cognitive and affective) than was

previously possible. This can have both positive (increasing ability to empathize, perspective-taking) as well as negative implications (confusion, emotional contagion, frustration). Movement to Level 3 is marked by more of a balance between a facilitative self-awareness and focus on the client, allowing for the positive impact of empathy and perspective-taking combined with reflection-in-action (Schön, 1987) or a greater ability to reflect on past learning, experiences, one's own thoughts, emotional reactions, and so on, to bring to bear on the counseling process. Similar changes occur for the structures of motivation and autonomy across levels. Motivation moves from global and somewhat extrinsic for Level 1 through variably high and low as it changes from extrinsic to more intrinsic for Level 2 and into a stable, largely intrinsic motivation in Level 3. The autonomy structure changes accordingly, moving from largely dependent in Level 1 through dependency and autonomy vacillation in Level 2 to conditional autonomy in Level 3. In general, trainee development is conceptualized as reflecting quantitative changes within levels and qualitative changes across levels. This is consistent with the developmental framework upon which the IDM is based (Lerner, 1986). The final step, according to the IDM is movement to Level 3i in which the focus becomes more on integration of development across domains.

Differing characteristics and needs at each level of development suggest that the supervision environment should also vary accordingly. In general, the IDM assumes that the amount of structure for the supervision environment provided by the supervisor should be rather high for beginners and reduce over time, moving toward greater supervisee influence on setting the structure for the supervision experience as development continues. Supervision interventions are broadly categorized into facilitative, prescriptive, conceptual, confrontive, and catalytic, which are differentially used across supervisee levels to encourage growth.

An important aspect of the IDM that appears to often be overlooked in critiques and research is that of domain-specific development. Eight domains of professional activity are listed in the IDM, but these are noted as overly broad and as indications of some domains in which the supervisor should attend to differential development among supervisees. The domains are intervention skills competence, assessment techniques, interpersonal assessment, client conceptualization, individual differences, theoretical orientation, treatment plans and goals, and professional ethics. As highlighted by Stoltenberg (2008), however, working with clients from different modalities (i.e., individual and couples counseling) may constitute different domains of development and may require moving between supervision environments appropriate for different levels of development for the same supervisee within a given supervision session as well as across sessions.

The integrative aspect of the IDM includes an examination of theory and research beyond the area of clinical supervision (and psychotherapy) to help illuminate processes held in common with other areas of psychology. Stoltenberg and McNeill (2010) articulated the utility of additional research and conceptualizations in understanding the supervision process, including cognitive models (cognitive and emotional processing; Anderson, 2005; Greenberg, 2002), schema development and refinement (McVee, Dunsmore, & Gavelek, 2005, Schön, 1987), and skill development; development from novice to expert (Anderson, 2005); interpersonal influence (Dixon & Claiborn, 1987; Stoltenberg, McNeill, & Crethar, 1995) and social intelligence (Goleman, 2006); motivation (Petty & Wegener, 1999, Ryan & Deci, 2000); and models of human development (Lerner, 1986).

Is There a Best Model?

Similar to the current state of affairs in psychotherapy research, where there is little evidence for the superiority of any given theoretical orientation over another (Duncan, Miller, Wampold, & Hubble, 2010; Norcross, Beutler, & Levant, 2006), we have little evidence that any specific model of clinical supervision is more adequate or effective than others. Of the two models discussed thus far, the IDM has stimulated the most research (it has also been around the longest) but has been criticized as having not been adequately tested (Ellis, Ladany, Krengel, & Schult, 1996). A more recent review (Inman & Ladany, 2008), however, concluded that "the bulk of the studies suggest some support for a developmental

process operating in supervisees," and "both supervisors and supervisees perceive supervisees differently as supervisees gain experience" (p. 505). The Ladany et al. (2005) model relied on methods and research from task analysis in psychotherapy, suggesting that interactional sequences in supervision surrounding specific events should lead to supervisees' learning and development. As noted by the authors, this model has not been empirically examined and is lacking evidence. Thus, neither model has adequate research support to provide validation, yet both integrate research on supervision into their models.

Both models integrate research on supervision into their descriptions of the process, and they also seek guidance from other literatures (e.g., psychotherapy, learning) to more fully articulate the supervision process. Both models were developed by practicing supervisors who also were involved in research and scholarship in supervision. Given the limitations and challenges associated with research in this area, relying only on empirically supported constructs and interventions to supervise would leave supervisors with inadequate guidance. There is more than one recipe for chili, more than one way to get to the grocery store, no best automobile for all conditions and purposes. Perhaps the utility of a given model of psychotherapy supervision lies in the adequacy with which the model deals with the breadth of possible conceptions of the interactive influences of the therapist, the client, and the therapy context (theoretical orientations) that the supervisor is required to supervise as well as the degree to which the roles and characteristics of supervisors and supervisees and the characteristics and processes of the supervision context are conceptualized. Consistent with Greenberg's (2002) view of psychotherapy integration, each of these models, as well as others not addressed, may affect the supervision process at different points yet produce similar outcomes. This should be examined at the nomothetic and idiographic levels by researchers and practitioners.

The models reviewed here both note that they are intended to be useful across psychotherapy orientations, so they are not tied to any one theory of therapy. They both promote the importance of the supervision relationship, although the focus on aspects of this relationship tends to differ between models. Ladany et al. (2005) highlighted the importance of the supervision relationship, but their frame of reference is less on teaching and learning and more on an extension of the therapeutic working alliance for the supervision context (supervisory alliance). They provided guidance for dealing with specific events viewed as common across supervision dyads with a view of specific interactional sequences that they believe characterize successful resolution of these challenging events. Stoltenberg and McNeill (2010) also noted the importance of the supervision relationship, and although they discussed interpersonal models and the supervisory alliance, they focused more intently on the impact of levels of supervisee professional development on how the supervisory relationship affects trainee growth and skill acquisition for given domains. Their focus tends to extend beyond the particular supervisory relationship and includes a consideration of the trajectory of growth across the training experience and beyond. They also addressed supervisor development and how this might interact with supervisee developmental level.

Ladany et al. (2005) focused on extending the interpersonal psychotherapy approach to the supervision context. Thus, although specific skills are used by the supervisor, conceptualizing the supervision process is linked more directly to interactional sequences that rely heavily on regular attention to the supervisory alliance and relational factors. Although supervisor roles such as teaching, consulting, and collegiality are noted, the interpersonal approach highlights relational aspects of therapy and the supervision process, including the bond, exploration of feelings, focus on countertransference, and attention to parallel processes between therapy and supervision. Thus, the model appears to highlight similar processes for therapy and supervision, assumes critical events will occur in supervision, and focuses less on an educational framework than on processing surrounding these events. Although Stoltenberg and McNeill (2010) noted an overlap in processes between therapy and supervision, they highlighted the educational functions of supervision and how these can be optimized. Rather than positing specific supervisor roles or functions, or interactional sequences believed to be reflective of how supervision is conducted, they focused on supervision environments. These environments are tied to supervisee developmental level for whatever domains are the focus of any given supervision session. The environments vary broadly in terms of the degree of structure provided by the supervisor or supervisee, with increasing responsibility for setting the agenda for supervision assumed by the trainee as she or he develops in a particular area. This translates to broad categories of supervisor interventions used differentially to meet supervisee needs and enhance growth. There appears to be general agreement between the models that, at least implicitly, the roles or functions of the supervisor tend to move from teaching to consultation with support and attention to the supervisory relationship of essential importance. In addition, both models speak to the importance of encouraging supervisee reflection processes as a goal of training as well as focusing on the importance of multicultural issues in supervision and in therapy. Although organized and prioritized differently, both models address similar supervisor behaviors whether they are called *roles, functions, supervision environments, supervisor interventions,* or *interactional sequences.* In addition, they also address similar tasks or foci of training, although the emphasis varies and, sometimes, must be pulled from the narratives of the books rather than brief outlines of the models. Finally, the Stoltenberg and McNeill model deals more directly with institutional influences on the supervision context than the Ladany et al. model.

COMMON FACTORS IN SUPERVISION

The focus on common factors in psychotherapy, although studied for more than 70 years, has recently increased in visibility, given the lack of strong support for the superiority of any given therapeutic orientation (Duncan, Miller, Wampold, & Hubble, 2010; Norcross, Beutler, & Levant, 2006). As with other perspectives first addressed in psychotherapy research and practice, common factors in supervision have emerged as a way to seek a better understanding of the supervision process.

Lampropoulos (2003) has suggested some factors he sees as common across supervision models and promoted an eclectic and prescriptive approach to supervision. Common factors in supervision posited by Lampropoulos include the following: the supervisory relationship (real relationship, working alliance, transference–countertransference); support and relief from tension, anxiety, and distress; instillation of hope and raising of expectations; self-exploration, awareness, and insight; theoretical rationale and ritual for supervision; exposure and confrontation of problems; acquisition and testing of new learning; and mastery of the new knowledge.

From an integrationist perspective, Norcross and Halgin (1997) suggested that supervision (a) be customized to the individual supervisee on the basis of a needs assessment, reflected in specific supervision contracts, utilizing a breadth of supervision methods and clarifying the nature of the supervisory relationship with supervisees; (b) utilize a coherent framework for supervision; (c) alter supervision for specific supervisee variables; (d) take the therapy approach into consideration in deciding how to supervise; (e) attend to the developmental level of the supervisee and his or her cognitive style and personal style; (f) evaluate supervisees' therapeutic skill level; and (g) evaluate the outcomes of supervision. Both the Lampropoulos (2003) and Norcross and Halgin (1997) views provide lists of factors common to different supervision approaches.

Morgan and Sprenkle (2007) introduced a common factors view of supervision aimed primarily at marriage and family therapy training that provides a framework for examining existing models. Their descriptive model lays out two content dimensions (what supervisors do): (a) the *emphasis* dimension reflected as a continuum between emphasizing clinical competence on one pole and professional competence on the other and (b) the *specificity* dimension ranging from idiosyncratic–particular (specific needs of the supervisee and clients) to nomothetic–general standards. A third dimension concerns the supervisory *relationship* (the how of supervision) ranging from collaborative–symmetrical to directive–complementary. Placed on a four-cornered plane with the emphasis and specificity dimensions forming the vertical and horizontal

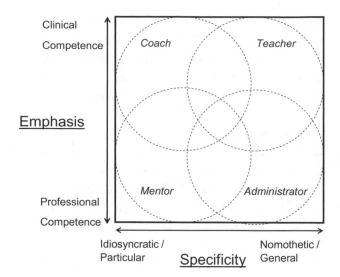

FIGURE 11.1. Supervisory roles as defined by the content dimensions of supervision. From "Toward a Common-Factors Approach to Supervision," by M. Sprenkle, 2007, *Journal of Marital and Family Therapy*, *33*, p. 11. Copyright 2007 by John Wiley & Sons, Inc. Reprinted with permission.

coordinates, the relationship dimension is reflected in four supervision roles (coach, teacher, mentor, administrator), which are described as not mutually exclusive, overlaying the other two dimensions (see Figure 11.1). This model provides a rudimentary framework for conceptualizing and categorizing various supervisory responsibilities, tasks, and roles as well as a mechanism for considering how models of supervision address these dimensions.

As with the psychotherapy literature, common factors perspectives on supervision may prove useful as a mechanism for examining the utility and breadth of supervision models as well as for giving supervisors and supervisees a set of variables to consider in their own supervision experiences. Further development of this frame of reference, through research and examination of relevant theory, might yield a useful lens for evaluating how comprehensive various models of psychotherapy supervision are and point to areas where they may need additional development. An important aspect of the potential benefit of a common factors approach to supervision is the necessity of implementing a coherent framework for supervision (Norcross & Halgin, 1997). Sprenkle and colleagues (Sprenkle & Blow, 2004; Sprenkle, Davis, & Lebow, 2009) have noted that in psychotherapy, common factors work through models that provide the roadmap for the driving force of common factors. It remains to be seen how common factors will influence our understanding of and utilization of supervision models.

Research Evidence

According to Inman and Ladany (2008) in their review of psychotherapy-based supervision research, published studies substantially increased from the 1980s through the 1990s, but the growth has slowed somewhat since 2000, with only a 4% increase in the number of published studies. As we discuss later, the challenges of conducting research on the supervision process, measurement, and methodological issues with this work limit the confidence with which researchers and practitioners can build on or implement the findings from these studies. Although Ellis, D'Iuso, and Ladany (2008) have noted that the quality of evaluation studies in supervision has improved since their earlier reviews (Ellis & Ladany, 1997; Ellis, Ladany, Krengel, & Schult, 1996), it remains difficult to draw substantive conclusions from research when the measurements used suffer from psychometric problems. Indeed, they reported finding only one measure that they can tentatively recommend in its current form (the Evaluation Process Within Supervision Inventory; Lehrman-Waterman & Ladany, 2001). Among challenges for supervision researchers in selecting appropriate measures is the tendency to adapt measures from other domains (e.g., psychotherapy) for use in supervision research, which contributes to psychometric problems (Ellis et al., 2008).

The challenges and complexity faced by psychotherapy researchers in conducting and implementing guidance from research (Duncan, Miller, Wampold, & Hubble, 2010; Norcross, Beutler, & Levant, 2006) are also present in supervision research with the complications of additional roles and functions. In addition to considering the interactive influences of therapist, client, and therapy context, supervision researchers must also consider the roles of supervisor, supervisee, and supervision context as well as training and evaluation functions.

Supervision Process

As with other areas of research in psychotherapy supervision, process research tends to be limited by small sample sizes, which require alternative approaches to research design and statistical methods (Inman & Ladany, 2008) as well as the reliance on correlational studies that suggest associations but cannot determine causal relationships (Castonguay, Boswell, Constantino, Goldfried, & Hill, 2010) and the separation of observations from inferences in assessment (Ellis et al., 2008). Both psychotherapy and clinical supervision processes are relational in nature, so a number of factors influence both processes. In addition, the training function associated with clinical supervision should include, as content and focus, consideration by and education of trainees regarding factors important to the successful implementation of psychotherapy and related activities.

Therapeutic and supervisory relationships. As Stoltenberg and McNeill (2010) have noted, "the supervisory relationship serves as the base of all effective teaching and training" (p. 137). Loganbill, Hardy, and Delworth (1982) posited that the relationship serves a similar essential function in supervision as in psychotherapy, although aspects of the relationships are quite different. As we have previously suggested (Stoltenberg & McNeill, 2010), the focus on relationship dynamics is important for the supervisory relationship and the supervision process, and should enhance the supervisory alliance as well as function as appropriate modeling for the supervisee by the supervisor. As noted by Lambert and Ogles (1997), however, learning interpersonal skills can occur as long as the supervisee perceives the supervisor as invested in being helpful, even when high levels of empathy, genuineness, and unconditional positive regard are absent.

Similar to psychotherapy research, an important factor in supervision process research over the past 20 plus years has been the supervision working alliance (Bordin, 1983). Bahrick's (1990) Supervision Working Alliance Scale (SWAS) assesses the quality of the goals, tasks, and bond dimensions of the supervisory relationship (Inman & Ladany, 2008; Ladany & Inman, 2008). Other studies have used the Supervisory Working Alliance Inventory (Efstation, Patton, & Kardash, 1990). Both instruments have limitations, however, and Ellis (2010) has proposed that the supervisory relationship may be composed of 10 facets rather than the three (goals, tasks, bond) proposed by the supervisory working alliance perspective. Studies using Bahrick's SWAS have indicated that a stronger supervision working alliance is related to goal setting and feedback in supervision (Lehrman-Waterman & Ladany, 2001), supervisee satisfaction (Inman, 2006; Ladany, Ellis, & Friedlander, 1999), greater perceptions of supervisor attractiveness and interpersonal sensitivity (Ladany, Walker, & Melincoff, 2001), matching supervisor and supervisee on stages of racial identity but not on ethnicity (Ladany, Brittan-Powell, & Pannu, 1997), and supervisor self-disclosure (Ladany & Lehrman-Waterman, 1999). Regarding supervisor self-disclosure, Ladany and Lehrman-Waterman (1999) have noted the importance of communicating positive and negative supervisor reactions to the supervisee in supervision as a function of accurate formative or summative feedback. Their work also suggested that supervisor personal issues, supervisor perceptions of their own negative self-efficacy in supervision, and attraction to the supervisee should not be a focus of supervisor self-disclosure in supervision. The supervisory working alliance also seems to mediate burnout and the effects of vicarious traumatization as well as enhance vigor (Deihl & Ellis, 2009; Fama & Ellis, 2005). A weaker supervision working alliance has been found to be related to greater supervisee role conflict and ambiguity (Ladany & Friedlander, 1995), perceptions of poor ethical behavior of the supervisor (Ladany, Lehrman-Waterman, Molinaro, & Wolgast, 1999), and perceptions of lower supervisor multicultural competence (Inman, 2006; see Inman & Ladany, 2008, for review).

Bernard and Goodyear (2009) reviewed research on the supervisory working alliance by examining antecedent factors (supervisor, supervisee, processes) associated with strong alliances and outcomes. For positively contributing supervisor factors, they listed attractive and interpersonally sensitive style (Chen & Bernstein, 2000; Ladany et al., 2001; Spelliscy, Chen, & Zusho, 2007), using expert

and referent power bases (Schultz, Ososkie, Fried, Nelson, & Bardos, 2002), self-disclosure (Ladany & Lehrman-Waterman, 1999), healthy adult attachments (White & Queener, 2003), and effective evaluation practices (Lehrman-Waterman & Ladany, 2001). Supervision processes positively associated with a strong supervisory working alliance include directly discussing racial–ethnicity issues in supervision (Gatmon et al., 2001), and supervisor–supervisee complementarity along power dimensions in interactions (Chen & Bernstein, 2000; Quarto, 2002). Positive outcomes from strong supervisory working alliances noted by Bernard and Goodyear include better adherence to treatment protocols (Patton & Kivlighan, 1997), willingness of supervisees to disclose to supervisors (Ladany et al., 1996; Webb & Wheeler, 1998), clients' perceptions of the therapeutic alliance (Patton & Kivlighan, 1997), reduced role conflict and ambiguity (Ladany & Friedlander, 1995), and satisfaction (Ladany, Ellis, & Friedlander, 1999; Ladany, Lehrman-Waterman, et al., 1999; Son, Ellis, & Yoo, 2009). Although this research is suggestive of the importance of these factors to the supervision relationship, the studies are largely correlational. In addition, the supervision relationship is assessed in various ways and prior critiques of the psychometric properties of these measures remain (Ellis et al., 2008).

The supervisory relationship can be influenced by a number of factors, including characteristics of the participants, demands and constraints of the environment in which supervision is conducted, and the level of relevant professional development of the supervisor and supervisee (Stoltenberg & Pace, 2008). In regards to the latter point, Ramos-Sánchez et al. (2002) found higher developmental levels for supervisees related to stronger supervision working alliance and greater satisfaction with supervision, but some aspects of good or positive supervision experiences appear to be relatively consistent. Good supervisory relationships tend to encompass warmth, acceptance, respect, understanding, and trust (Hutt, Scott, & King, 1983). Supervisors who conduct supervision viewed as good by supervisees tend to appropriately self-disclose, enable an atmosphere of experimentation, and are tolerant of supervisee mistakes (Black, 1988; Hutt et al., 1983;

Nelson, 1978). As perceived by supervisees, good supervisors also show an interest in supervision, are experienced therapists, and have technical or theoretical knowledge to convey (Nelson, 1978). Rabinowitz, Heppner, and Roehlke (1986) found that early clarification of the supervisory relationship (within the first 3 weeks) is valued by supervisees across experience levels. Ellis (1991) examined group supervision of novice supervisors and the individual clinical supervision these students conducted with their supervisees; he found, through critical incidents methodology, that relationship issues were the most frequently identified in both contexts. Similarly, Ramos-Sánchez et al. concluded that the supervisory relationship is one of the most influential factors in trainees' reports of their level of satisfaction with supervision. Ultimately, displayed empathy by the supervisor may be one of the most powerful influences on supervisee satisfaction in supervision (Shanfield, Mohl, Matthews, & Hetherly, 1992). Indeed, Ellis (2010) has suggested that the emotional bond is the most important aspect of the supervisory relationship. Supervisee satisfaction with supervision is not the ultimate measure of the impact of supervision and, as reported, supervisees can learn even in the absence of high levels of perceived empathy on the part of the supervisor.

Qualitative studies on the supervision relationship have yielded results similar to those found in correlational research. Worthen and McNeill (1996) reported a phenomenological investigation of "good" supervision by conducting in-depth interviews with eight intermediate to advanced supervisees. The supervisees reported perceptions of their status at "baseline" from fluctuating to a grounded level of confidence and sense of disillusionment to a sense of efficacy with the therapeutic process. Setting the stage for the good supervision experience was a perceived need although supervisees felt inadequate to do so. There was also an aversion to overt evaluation. Consistent with other studies, the perceived quality of the supervisory relationship was the major component of a good supervision experience. Effective supervisors were described as empathic, nonjudgmental, validating or affirming, and encouraging of supervisee experimentation and

exploration. Perceived support by the supervisor and normalizing the struggles of the supervisee (often through supervisor self-disclosure) were also seen as important. Growth in supervisees was attributed to reduced self-protectiveness in supervision and increased receptivity to supervisory input. Nondefensive analyses, reexamination of assumptions, and development of a meta-perspective were also seen as positive supervisee behaviors. Good supervision was perceived as leading to a stronger supervisory alliance, greater confidence, refined professional identity, greater therapeutic perception, and a better ability to conceptualize and intervene in the therapy process.

Nelson, Barnes, Evans, and Triggiano (2008) also reported the importance of the supervisory relationship as seen by supervisors. Focusing on creating a strong supervisory alliance was viewed by supervisors as essential for effective supervision as well as discussing evaluation early on, providing feedback, modeling openness to dealing with conflict, and engaging in relational processing. These supervisors also reported taking a reflective stance regarding their work in supervision, coaching themselves to empathize with their supervisees, being patient, attending to supervisee strengths, and clarifying the developmental needs of the supervisee.

The supervisory relationship serves as the base of all good therapeutic and professional training (Worthen & McNeill, 1996). Clear communication and respect by the supervisor appear to be more influential in quality supervision than the more structural and didactic components of supervision (Allen, Szollos, & Williams, 1986). Black (1988) noted that the supervisory relationship is the largest factor in determining whether supervision will be effective or ineffective. Central to the development of a positive supervisory relationship is mutual trust between the supervisor and the supervisee. As Bernard and Goodyear (2009) noted, "In general, the higher the supervisee's level of trust in the supervisor, the less he or she will need to exhibit the self-protective behavior that occurs as resistance; and, the less supervisee resistance, the more effective the supervisory relationship" (p. 173). Without trust between the supervisor and supervisee, neither is likely to have the sense of safety that enables open communication and collaboration in the supervision process.

Supervisee anxiety.   Supervisee anxiety is another factor that has been posited as an important and rather pervasive aspect of the supervision process (Bernard & Goodyear, 2009) and has been tied to supervisee level of professional development (Liddle, 1986; Ronnestad & Skovholt, 1993; Stoltenberg, 1981; Stoltenberg & McNeill, 2010). Ellis (2010), however, suggested that a lack of supervisee self-efficacy, competence, or combination of the two may be common issues in supervision, but not anxiety, at least as measured by scales developed for the supervision context by Ellis and colleagues. Perhaps measurement issues are again clouding the view or methodology differences are producing varying results. Interestingly, in their qualitative study examining therapists ranging in experience from graduate school through extensive professional practice, Skovholt and Ronnestad (1992) found higher anxiety during graduate school reported retrospectively by practicing therapists than by current graduate students. This may indicate a possible cohort effect or the impact of time and reflection on perceptions of anxiety, among other possibilities.

Contrary to Ellis's (2010) assertion, Stoltenberg, McNeill, and Delworth (1998) have not described anxiety as always deleterious. Nonetheless, studies have indicated that anxiety (or related constructs, such as insecurity, lacking self-confidence, or self-efficacy) is often present for beginning supervisees (Heppner & Roehlke, 1984; Reising & Daniels, 1983; Worthington, 1984), who note greater concern for supervisor perceptions of their competence than more experienced supervisees (Rabinowitz et al., 1986) and who are more fearful of negative evaluation than more experienced supervisees (Winter & Holloway, 1991). Anxiety also appears to be inversely associated with performance and counselor self-efficacy (Friedlander, Keller, Peca-Baker, & Olk, 1986), is associated with role conflict (Olk & Friedlander, 1992), and (when high) reduces one's capacity to observe (Dombeck & Brody, 1995), but anxiety can be reduced by supervisor-provided structure (Freeman, 1993). As Bernard and

Goodyear (2009) noted, performance suffers with too little or too much anxiety; optimal anxiety (or arousal) enables rather than inhibits better performance. They noted that ambiguity in the supervision context is likely to be the root cause, across levels of supervisee experience, of supervisee anxiety.

Conflict and counterproductivity in supervision.   For the supervision process to be effective and impactful, there needs to be clear, relevant, and open communication between the supervisor and supervisee within professionally appropriate interpersonal boundaries. Supervisors are often limited in their opportunities to directly observe their supervisees' work with clients because of the lack of available technology (one-way mirrors or video). Thus, they may be forced to rely largely on supervisee self-report, case notes, and so on in monitoring and evaluating the effectiveness of the psychotherapy provided by their supervisees. In addition, it is important to access the thoughts and emotions of the supervisee in the therapy context as well as the supervision context. Unfortunately, supervision is not always perceived by supervisees as a safe place to learn. Galante (1988) found that 47% of trainees reported having experienced at least one ineffective supervision relationship. Similarly, in describing a comprehensive survey of nearly 400 supervisees, Ellis (2010) noted that 75% reported receiving inadequate supervision, whereas 51% reported receiving harmful supervision in either current or past supervisory relationships. Ramos-Sánchez et al. (2002) noted that the perceived lack of safety in the supervision relationship can cause psychological harm to supervisees and these perceptions may vary according to the strength of the supervision working alliance and the professional developmental level of the supervisee.

Inman and Ladany (2008) have noted that it is common for supervisees to withhold important information from their supervisors (Ladany, Hill, Corbett, & Nutt, 1996), particularly if supervisees experience shame in supervision related to the fear of negative judgments by the supervisor concerning clinical "mistakes" or in response to negative reactions to the supervisor (Yourman, 2003). If supervisees do not perceive the supervisory relationship as a safe environment in which their relevant thoughts, feelings, and behaviors can be explored and processed in a nonthreatening way, the supervisory working alliance will be negatively influenced (Gray, Ladany, Walker, & Ancis, 2001). This appears to be even more likely in group supervision (with the additional potential for negative evaluation by peers or public shaming) than in individual supervision (Webb & Wheeler, 1998).

Consistent with these perspectives, Magnuson, Wilcoxon, and Norem (2000) reported the results of a qualitative study of poor supervisor behaviors (from the supervisee perspective). They noted that these ineffective supervisor behaviors could be categorized as an imbalance of focus in supervision (lacking sufficient attention to all aspects of supervision), providing developmentally inappropriate interventions, a lack of tolerance of differences, poor modeling of an integration of personal–professional attributes, an inability to manage interpersonal boundaries, and professional apathy.

An examination of conflictual supervision from the perspective of the supervisor was the focus of a study by Nelson, Barnes, Evans, and Triggiano (2008). They identified highly competent supervisors (from peer recommendations) and conducted a qualitative study on conflict in supervision. The participants noted in interviews that conflict in supervision is not inevitable, but when it occurs, effective supervisors are open to exploring the conflict, to interpersonal processing, and to acknowledge their own contributions. These supervisors noted that they are willing to learn from their mistakes and tend to take a developmental orientation to their supervisee's training. When conflicts occur, they view contextualizing the conflicts with regard to supervisee development and environmental factors. They are likely to seek consultation with colleagues, engage in self-coaching, and accentuate the strengths of the supervisee. In addition, there is a willingness to interpret parallel processes between the therapy context and the supervision process and to withdraw from supervisee dynamics when conflicts occur.

Veach (2001) has noted that a necessary component of conflictual supervision relationships is counterproductive events, although not all counterproductive events will result in conflictual supervision relationships. According to Gray et al. (2001), conflictual supervision relationships tend to be characterized by more frequent or repetitive counterproductive events rather than occasional ones. As noted by Veach, perceptions of supervisees and supervisors may lack consistency. Thus, research on supervision processes, including conflict or counterproductive events, would benefit from collecting data from multiple perspectives and not assuming congruence between supervisee and supervisor perceptions of events or processes. Stoltenberg and McNeill (2010) have concluded that "when supervisors attend to supervisee needs and provide the appropriate supervisory environment corresponding to a given developmental level, the supervisory relationship is strengthened and the potential for conflict is reduced" (p. 143).

Therapy process and outcomes. An important indication of effective supervision is client process and outcomes of therapy conducted by supervisees. Inman and Ladany (2008) noted that at least 18 studies of the supervision process examining client outcomes have been conducted since the 1980s. In a review of 10 of these studies, Freitas (2002) observed that although the ultimate benefit of good supervision should be for the clients seen by the supervisees, proving this empirically is complicated. Aspects of the supervision process that may be viewed as positive or that may limit the effectiveness of the supervisee appear to have limited or inconsistent impact on client outcomes. Consistent with other supervision research, Freitas noted a lack of psychometric data reported for the measures used in many studies, failure to control Type I and Type II error, different levels of experience of supervisees as well as lack of uniformity of client populations in the studies, failure to randomize therapist assignment to conditions, lack of multiple measures of client outcome, and lack of control conditions (no supervision). Nonetheless, Inman and Ladany noted that the studies do provide some indication of how the supervision process can affect client outcome.

Supervisees can adjust the way therapy is conducted if they receive ongoing and consistent information (feedback) about client progress, particularly when problems arise (Lambert, Hansen, & Finch, 2001). This produces greater client gains when compared with a no-feedback supervision condition (Reese, Usher, et al., 2009) and increases the likelihood of reliable change in clients in fewer sessions (Reese, Norsworthy, & Rowlands, 2009). Interestingly, in the Reese, Usher et al. (2004) study, receiving regular feedback on client progress did not affect supervisee ratings of the supervisory alliance or satisfaction with supervision. Supervisees in the feedback condition reported a stronger relationship between counselor self-efficacy and client outcome than those in the no-feedback condition.

Conducting supervision sessions close to critical therapy sessions might also be useful (Couchon & Bernard, 1984; Kivlighan, Angelone, & Swafford, 1991), although this might be challenging for scheduling in many sites, particularly with supervisees who are seeing a number of clients. Also, Kivlighan et al. (1991) found that live supervision affected therapist intention more than video-based supervision and was related to a stronger therapeutic alliance. This alliance, however, may have been affected by demand characteristics in that immediate feedback from the supervisor and interruptions in the session could have affected the clients' views of therapy and positively influenced their ratings of outcomes (Freitas, 2002).

Positive results of specific training in supervision on client outcomes were reported by Cukrowicz et al. (2005). They examined changes in client outcome at a university psychology training clinic as a function of moving from treatment and supervision as usual (TAU) to supervision addressing empirically supported treatments. The authors concluded that this change in focus "produced better outcomes, within fewer sessions, among a more symptomatic population of patients experiencing a wide range of psychopathology" (Cukrowicz et al., 2005, p. 334). The additional structure introduced for implementation of treatment as well as clinical supervision may have enhanced outcomes. No measures of satisfaction with supervision were reported. Another psychology training clinic study (Callahan, Almstrom, Swift, Borja, & Heath, 2009) found that supervision accounted for about 16% of the variance in outcome beyond the variance accounted for by the treating

therapist's (supervisee) attributes and the initial client severity level for dyads with congruent trainee–supervisor orientations. Finally, a study of community-based interventions for child neglect also implemented a structured evidence-based practice (EBP) approach in community agencies (Aarons, Sommerfeld, Hecht, Silovsky, & Chaffin, 2009). There was concern that implementing such a structured approach to intervention may have a negative impact on staff retention, so a TAU approach was compared with the EBP approach and for both approaches a fidelity monitoring condition (consultation and supervision) and a condition without fidelity monitoring were compared. The fidelity monitoring consisted of supportive consultation and supervision consistent with the IDM (Stoltenberg, McNeill, & Delworth, 1998). The EBP condition with fidelity monitoring produced the best retention rates for staff over the course of the 29-month study. The authors suggested that supportive consultation–supervision paired with structured interventions enhances retention and reduces the need for regular staff recruitment, increasing program continuity.

Lambert's (2007) program of research on the effects of providing ongoing client progress information to therapists suggested that even rather limited feedback (e.g., "red alarms" for poor response to treatment) may be sufficient to improve outcomes (see Lambert, 2007, for review). Castonguay et al. (2010) noted that feedback measures on the therapeutic alliance, the level of therapist engagement in treatment, and the openness of clients to their experiences are available (Greenberg & Pinsof, 1986; Hill & Lambert, 2004) and may positively affect the therapy process, leading to improved outcomes. Rigidity in psychotherapist application of technique can result in inadequate client assessment with insufficient understanding of client deficits or impairment, client resources, and coping behaviors (see Castonguay et al., 2010 for review). These issues should be salient and amenable to change through the supervision process. Other issues, including assisting clients in replacing ineffective behaviors with more functional ones (not just elimination), are important for supervisees to understand and implement (e.g., Goldfried & Davison, 1994). Finally, optimal exposure duration for some interventions is necessary for client improvement, and suboptimal exposure can contribute to client deterioration (Castonguay et al., 2010). These issues can be dealt with more effectively through ongoing client progress information addressed during the supervision process than through supervision as usual without such assessments.

Although causality has not yet been firmly established, Castonguay et al. (2010) argued that training in skills that enhance the working alliance should be a focus of clinical supervision (for a list of strategies, see Hilsenroth, Ackerman, Clemence, Strassle, & Handler, 2002). Thus, supervisees should become aware of the negative impact on therapy process and outcomes of hostile control, hostile separation, overly complex interpretations, and disaffiliative processes. In addition, Castonguay et al. argued that supervisees should become aware of their own rigid or continued use of some techniques (i.e., cognitive–behavioral interventions, dynamic transference interpretations) when confronted with ruptures in the working alliance, which may lead to further deterioration of the relationship and result in poorer outcomes. They also noted that the focus of supervision should include attention to Lilienfeld's (2007) list of potentially harmful treatments and an awareness that some interventions otherwise viewed as effective may be harmful in certain circumstances, in interaction with certain clients, in particular contexts, when delivered by a given therapist. For example, the ineffective management (or awareness of) countertransference reactions and confrontational self-disclosures may be viewed as noxious by clients (Gelso, Latts, Gomez, & Fassinger, 2002; Hill, Mahalik, & Thompson, 1989). Possible common harmful ingredients in potentially harmful treatments may include the use of pressured confrontation in the presence of intense emotion in the client, inappropriate use of persuasion and suggestion by the therapist, and provocation of strong emotion in the client without concurrently raising awareness or facilitating new meanings.

Castonguay et al. (2010) also noted the importance of training supervisees in the clinically flexible implementation of effective interventions (such as accurate interpretations, homework, and depth of emotional experiencing) and paying attention to timing and contextual issues as well as adequate client assessment. Finally, consistent with conclusions drawn by others (e.g., Goldfried & Davison, 1994), Castonguay et al. noted that empathy, positive regard, and congruence appear not to be associated with negative client outcomes and, therefore, should be a focus of training to enhance the therapeutic working alliance and, subsequently, therapeutic outcomes. Thus, a focus in supervision should include education and training regarding the impact of various supervisee (therapist) skills, rigid versus flexible implementation of interventions, and potentially harmful treatments (or ingredients) on the development of the therapeutic alliance.

The impact of the supervision process appears to vary depending on where one focuses attention. Although concerns about measurement of supervision processes remain, correlational and qualitative studies highlight the importance and positive impact of a strong supervisory relationship. It appears safe to assume that building a strong bond with agreed-on goals and tasks is associated with favorable supervisee perspectives of supervision. Without the trust and safety evident in the effective supervisory alliance, the supervisee openness necessary for the supervisor to monitor trainee competence development and client progress appears to be at risk. Also, the growth of supervisee self-awareness of their own cultural values, attitudes, and impact on clients is likely to be severely limited when supervisees feel inadequate trust in their supervisors and safety in the supervisory context. An open process of self-reflection and discussion of difficult issues appears to be inhibited in poor supervisory relationships. Contributions to facilitative supervisory relationships are made by both the supervisor and the supervisee. Conversely, although the quality of the supervisory relationship may set the stage for important learning on the part of the supervisee, this does not substitute for specific training in interpersonal skills, therapeutic interventions, and client characteristics. Although it is challenging to confirm the impact of supervision, ultimately, positive processes and outcomes of therapy conducted by supervisees remain the primary goal of effective supervision. A singular focus on supervisee satisfaction as an indication of the effectiveness of supervision is likely to tap only a limited number of important influences on supervisee learning and performance. This is highlighted in the studies showing that a greater focus on client feedback, which improves therapy outcomes, does not necessarily result in greater supervisee satisfaction with supervision. Finally, longitudinal studies, although complicated and expensive to conduct, are needed to track short-term and long-term changes in supervision relationships, supervisee therapeutic behavior, and therapy process and outcomes.

Participant Characteristics

Wampold's (2006) work on psychotherapist effects suggests that characteristics of the psychotherapist may be more predictive of outcome in therapy than the working alliance. Correlational studies suggest that therapists with anxious attachment styles may demonstrate less empathy with clients, particularly those with secure or dismissive attachment styles (Beutler, Blatt, Alimohamed, Levy, & Angtuaco, 2006). In addition, therapists who are hostile toward themselves also tend to be hostile toward their clients (Henry, Strupp, Butler, Schacht, & Binder, 1993). This suggests that supervision and training should help supervisees become aware of and understand their own strengths, limitations, interpersonal vulnerabilities, and countertransferential blind spots (Castonguay et al., 2010). Castonguay et al. (2010) suggested that it is also important for trainees to become aware of and monitor how their internal experiences affect the therapeutic relationship, being able to effectively and collaboratively engage their clients while maintaining appropriate distance from client personal and interpersonal dynamics within the therapy relationship. They also recommend that training should specifically assist trainees in understanding that some clients are more challenging to help through therapy than others and some may respond better to some interventions than others.

Bernard and Goodyear (2009) identified other supervisee and supervisor characteristics that have been examined for their impact on the supervision process, including cognitive or learning styles, which have been operationalized as profiles emerging from the Myers-Briggs Type Indicator (MBTI; Myers, 1962; Myers & McCaulley, 1985). Differences in

MBTI profiles have been found between supervisors and supervisees (Carey & Williams, 1986; Craig & Sleight, 1990), and supervisee preference for relationship-oriented versus task-oriented supervision (Lochner & Melchert, 1997), but the MBTI has yielded inconsistent results regarding the effects on supervisee evaluation (Carey & Williams, 1986; Handley, 1982). In addition, some evidence exists for matching effects for theoretical orientation between supervisors and supervisees on the supervisory relationship (Kennard, Stewart, & Gluck, 1987; Ramos-Sánchez et al., 2002) and preference for supervisory style (Lochner & Melchert, 1997) but appears to have less impact than other relationship factors (Schacht, Howe, & Berman, 1989; Wetchler, 1989). Bernard and Goodyear regarded these studies as indications of individual differences in information processing and suggested that supervisors need to develop the ability to flexibly respond to supervisees with differing cognitive or learning styles.

According to Inman and Ladany (2008), supervisee development has received the greatest amount of attention in the supervision literature. Consistent with the views of Stoltenberg (2005) and earlier reviews (Ellis & Ladany, 1997; Holloway, 1982; Stoltenberg, McNeill, & Crethar, 1994; Watkins, 1995; Worthington, 1987), they concluded that the majority of studies conducted examining supervisee development support the relevance of conceptualizing supervision as a developmental process. Bernard and Goodyear (2009) echoed this suggestion and noted that level of supervisee (or psychotherapist) experience is often used as a proxy for professional development (about 20 cited studies) and that support for supervisees at different levels of experience demonstrating different characteristics and abilities emerges from the majority of these studies. They warn, however, that many of these studies confound experience with training (and development) and that there is little evidence that experience without training (including supervision) leads to gains in professional development.

Cognitive complexity (Duys & Hedstrom, 2000; Fong, Borders, Ethington, & Pitts, 1997; Granello, 2002; Stein & Lambert, 1995) is assumed to enhance counseling-related ability, but its impact on cognitive development appears less strong than the impact of supervised experience (Lovell, 1999) and tends to occur mostly in the latter part of the training program (Granello, 2002) and postdegree professional experience (Skovholt & Ronnestad, 1992). Bernard and Goodyear (2009) concluded that supervised experience is associated with supervisee increases in cognitive complexity, which enables them to more adequately analyze and assimilate counseling-relevant information. Indeed, the growing competencies benchmarks literature assumes a developmental process in suggesting guidelines for the acquisition of foundational and functional competencies (Fouad et al., 2009).

Consistent with developmental approaches to supervision (Stoltenberg & McNeill, 2010), studies indicate that supervisees of different levels of professional development require different approaches to supervision that enhance their learning and growth. Bernard and Goodyear (2009) cited more than 20 studies, providing at least partial support for developmental differences in facilitative supervision environments for trainees across levels. Inman and Ladany (2008) summarized this literature as indicating that beginning supervisees require more structured supervision, often including more specific instruction and the supervisor assuming most responsibility for the process of supervision, than advanced supervisees. Also, they noted that evidence exists that supervisee development increases ability to engage in productive reflection and cognitive complexity. Although not totally consistent, supervisors and supervisees tend to view supervisees, and how supervision should be conducted, as varying as a function of experience. Not all investigations, however, have been supportive of matching supervision environment to supervisee level (Ladany, Walker, & Melincoff, 2001; Sumerel & Borders, 1996). Other studies have indicated that additional factors such as supervisee reactance potential and crisis situations (Tracey, Ellickson, & Sherry, 1989) as well as familiarity of the supervisee with particular client issues (child abuse; Leach, Stoltenberg, McNeill, & Eichenfield, 1997) and severity of individual cases (Zarski, Sand-Pringle, Pannell, & Lindon, 1995) may override supervisee developmental-level considerations regarding what supervision environment supervisees prefer. Stoltenberg and colleagues (Stoltenberg &

Delworth, 1987; Stoltenberg & McNeill, 2010; Stoltenberg, McNeill, & Delworth, 1998) suggested that supervisee developmental level and needs, and the associated facilitative supervision environments, will vary by domain and may require differing supervision environments for various client issues within a given supervision session. Thus, more advanced supervisees may reflect a breadth of professional development across domains and, consequently, may require different supervision environments at different points in time depending on the focus in supervision. Stoltenberg (2008) described a supervision case study that exemplified this effect. Also, in a qualitative study on the IDM extending over an academic year (Ashby, Stoltenberg, & Kleine, 2010), the salience for supervisees of issues reflecting different domains of practice were affected by context and also varied somewhat by developmental level.

Developing the ability to augment supervision provided by a supervisor with self-supervision is important, especially because once supervision is no longer required, self-supervision becomes the norm. Some of the skills noted as important for self-supervision are associated with one's ability to self-regulate behavior in the counseling context, including reflection, monitoring, managing, and critiquing one's own behavior and the counseling process (Dennin & Ellis, 2003). Evidence exists that training in self-regulation training (addressing these skills) increases a supervisee's ability to use metaphor but does not affect the use of empathy (Dennin & Ellis, 2003). Conversely, empathy training does appear to be effective in other studies (Crits-Christoph et al., 2006; Hilsenroth et al., 2002), at least in the context of training in fostering the therapeutic alliance. More research is needed to clarify these issues. As with other areas of supervision research, most of the studies examining supervisee development rely heavily on self-report and have significant methodological issues. Additionally, a lack of longitudinal research limits our understanding of these processes.

Multicultural Issues

The *Guidelines on Multicultural Education, Training, Research, Practice, and Organizational Change for Psychologists* (APA, 2002b) serve as the general foundation of training in issues of cultural and individual diversity as well as more recent proposals for developing diversity competencies (e.g., Miville et al., 2009). As previously noted by Ponterotto, Fuertes, and Chen (2000) and Constantine, Miville, and Kindaichi (2008), however, the effectiveness of training in multicultural counseling competencies in regard to client outcome remains unanswered. In contrast, research into perceptions and measurement of multicultural competencies and related cultural issues in supervision has continued. For example, Gloria, Hird, and Tao (2008) assessed the self-reported supervision practices, experiences, and multicultural competence of White intern supervisors. Those who were training directors reported higher self-perceived multicultural supervision competence than staff psychologists. Female supervisors also reported higher multicultural supervision competence and spent more time processing cultural differences with their supervisees than male supervisors. From the trainee perspective, a study by Vereen, Hill, and McNeal (2008) demonstrated a relationship between those receiving clinical supervision related to multicultural issues and conducting counseling with more non-White clients and perceived multicultural competence but not for the number of multicultural courses taken. Again, these findings are based on self-reported multicultural competencies.

Two recent studies investigated the multicultural conceptualization skills of therapists in training. Lee and Tracey (2008) found that the general case conceptualization skills rated by trained raters were affected by clinical training. Multicultural case conceptualization skills were also rated by trained raters, and these ratings were related to training in multicultural counseling. Thus, more advanced trainees showed greater skills (as rated by researchers) than beginning trainees. Results also demonstrated that trainees included more culturally relevant ideas when culture was explicitly stated in case scenarios as a presenting problem versus when culture was implied. No differences in the conceptualizations of White trainees and trainees of color were found. A qualitative study by Neufeldt et al. (2006) in which trainees responded to counseling vignettes that varied along cultural dimensions also indicated that although trainees attended to both aspects of general and multicultural case conceptualization, they varied in their ability to apply diversity factors in their conceptualizations. Trainees of color in this small sample ($N = 17$) also appeared more attentive to cultural issues.

Burkard et al. (2006) found that culturally diverse trainees experienced more incidents of culturally unresponsive supervision in cases in which cultural issues were ignored, actively discounted, or dismissed by supervisors with adverse consequences for the supervisee, the supervisory relationship, or client outcomes than did their European American counterparts. In contrast, in culturally responsive supervision, trainees of all backgrounds felt supported, which positively affected the supervisee, the supervisory relationship, and client outcomes. Evidence presented by Constantine and Sue (2007) also indicated that culturally diverse trainees, in this case African Americans, continue to experience racial microaggressions from White supervisors in the form of invalidating racial–cultural issues, making stereotypic assumptions about Black clients and Black supervisees, and offering culturally insensitive treatment recommendations, again with detrimental effects on the trainee and supervisory relationship. Bhat and Davis (2007) investigated the role of race, racial identity attitudes, and working alliance in a sample of predominantly White supervisors. Results revealed stronger supervisor perceptions of working alliances for supervisory dyads with similar high levels of racial identity development and the weakest working alliance for pairs low in racial identity development.

A recent qualitative investigation by Jernigan et al. (2010) of culturally diverse supervisees' viewpoints in regard to their experiences with their supervisors of color yielded some nuanced descriptions of the nature of their supervisory relationships around dynamics of race and racial identity. In general, supervisees believed that they more often raised the issue of race in supervision and perceived positive responses from their supervisors when they did, describing their supervisors as challenging, encouraging, and enlightening. When they perceived supervisors' responses as unsupportive, trainees felt angry, confused, resentful, and discouraged, resulting in an internalization of self-doubt and incompetence. Another recent qualitative investigation by Verdinelli and Biever (2009) explored Spanish language services supervision experiences of bilingual graduate students and professionals (predominately Latina/o) in a summer training program. Findings indicated that participants felt burdened and stressed by the additional responsibilities of providing services in Spanish and by their sense of obligation to their Spanish-speaking clients. They also reported that they had previous inadequate training or supervision, relying on peer support and networking to cope with such challenges. Conversely, trainees appreciated having supervisors who were culturally competent and open to client's cultural values. These qualitative studies provide rich, detailed descriptions of the phenomena under investigation, providing supervisors with recommendations for working with issues of race in supervision as well as stimulating further research utilizing diverse methodologies.

In a similar vein, a recent special issue of *Training and Education in Professional Psychology* titled *Sharing Wisdom: Ethnic Minority Supervisor Perspectives* provided a number of narrative accounts of culturally diverse supervisors and supervisees from Asian American (Lo, 2010; Murphy-Shigematsu, 2010; Yabusaki, 2010), Latina/o American (Millán, 2010; Reynaga-Abiko, 2010), and African American (Butler-Byrd, 2010) perspectives. Other recent work from a theoretical–conceptual viewpoint has addressed issues of mentoring of culturally diverse students (Alvarez, Blume, Cervantes, & Thomas, 2009), supervision of Latinas from a multicultural developmental perspective (Field, Chavez-Korell, & Domenech Rodríguez, 2010), enhancement of multicultural competence in supervision (Ober, Granello, & Henfield, 2009), supervisee competence in the context of poverty (Smith, 2009), multicultural assessment supervision (Allen, 2007), training in spirituality (Hage, Hopson, Siegel, Payton, & DeFanti, 2006), a social justice approach to supervision (Hernández, 2008), feminist multicultural perspectives on supervision (Nelson et al., 2006), and the integration of multicultural supervision domains with gay and lesbian models of supervision (Singh & Chun, 2010). This recent theoretical, descriptive, and conceptual literature represents a diversity of dynamic, innovative thinking with the potential to generate any number of hypotheses that might generate further empirical scrutiny. Such topics

might include, but are not limited to, the effects of microaggressions, cultural identity, and relational safety on the supervisory process and relationship.

Some issues are emerging in importance in this area. Group supervision in regards to multicultural issues has received some recent attention in the form of models of structured peer group supervision (Lassiter, Napolitano, Culbreth, & Ng, 2008) and the investigation of helpful and hindering multicultural events in group supervision (Kaduvettoor et al., 2009). Helpful events related to supervisee multicultural competence fell into categories of peer vicarious learning, multicultural learning and conceptualization, extragroup events, and supervisor direct influence. Hindering events included indirect discussions and peer multicultural conflicts, supervisor multicultural conflicts, and misapplications of multicultural theory, which were negatively related to supervisee multicultural competence. Riva and Erickson Cornish (2008) surveyed predoctoral internship sites in regards to group supervision practices and multicultural considerations in group supervision and found that 91% of group supervisors indicated that they attended to multicultural issues. These issues ranked second to ethical and legal issues as part of discussions or special topics in group supervision.

Another topic that has received increased attention is the training and supervision of international students. Mori, Inman, and Caskie (2009) found that international student supervisees who had lower acculturation levels but greater cultural discussion in the form of dialogues with their supervisors regarding cultural influences showed more satisfaction with supervision. They also found that cultural discussion partially mediated the relationship between perceived supervisor cultural competence and satisfaction with supervision. Other recent studies have documented the experiences of international students, which reveal adjustment problems, a need for more academic and career support, and increased recognition for their cultural differences (Mittal & Wieling, 2006). Another study documented interestingly different approaches and experiences of Korean clinical supervisors who appear to apply developmental concepts and exploration of trainee's personal issues within a uniquely Korean cultural context (Bang & Park, 2009).

Ethical and Legal Considerations in Supervision

Prior reviews by Werth, Cummings, and Thompson (2008) and Ladany and Inman (2008) addressed ethical and legal issues in supervision, and there continues to be a dearth of empirically based research examining ethical issues and behaviors in supervision. Although Barnett, Cornish, Goodyear, and Lichtenberg (2007) appropriately asserted that modeling ethical and professional behavior with an emphasis on ethical practice in supervision is an essential quality of effective supervisors, Ladany, Lehrman-Waterman, Molinaro, and Wolgast (1999) previously found that 50% of surveyed trainees perceived their supervisors to have engaged in unethical practice during their supervision experience. In addition, Worthington, Tan, and Poulin (2002) found that both supervisors and supervisees reported engaging in various types of ethically questionable behaviors. More recently, a national survey of APA student affiliates by Zakrzewski (2006) presented a somewhat-mixed picture in that 9.2 % of all participants indicated that they had experienced a sexual contact, advance, or both with a psychology educator while they were a student, typically initiated by the educator. In addition, 53% of the students reported that they would not feel safe to pursue appropriate actions if they had firsthand knowledge of a sexual contact occurring. Clearly, more research is needed to determine the effects of the typically mandated ethics training in accredited programs as well as the practices of educators and supervisors.

Conversely, recent theoretical and conceptual literature has addressed issues of multiple relationships in supervision (Gottlieb, Robinson, & Younggren, 2007; Heaton & Black, 2009), the use of contracts in supervision to provide informed consent (Thomas, 2007), and supervision of couples cases (Stratton & Smith, 2006). Handelsman, Gottlieb, and Knapp (2005) presented a conceptualization of ethics training as an acculturation model in which students are confronted with new ethical principles and rules reflective of the culture of psychology, which may be inconsistent with their own moral value traditions. Additionally, Schwartz, Domenech Rodríguez, Santiago-Rivera, Arredondo, and Field (2010) recently opened up a dialogue on the increasingly important ethical considerations regarding the cultural and linguistic competencies in the supervision of culturally diverse trainees and their diverse clientele in languages other than English (e.g., Spanish).

Competence to supervise. As previously noted by Werth et al. (2008), research in regard to the competence of faculty and supervisors is "essentially nonexistent" (p. 8). Stoltenberg and McNeill (2010) reviewed the various sections of the *Ethical Principles of Psychologists and Code of Conduct* (APA, 2010) that address the education and training of students and design of training programs (Standard 7.0), student feedback processes (Standard 7.06), student disclosure of personal information (Standards 7.04–7.05), and sexual relationships between students and supervisors (Standard 7.07) as well as Standard 3.08 prohibiting exploitive relationships and Standard 2.05 regarding delegation of work to others, which are both applicable to supervisees. Stoltenberg and McNeill also noted that there are no explicit guidelines regarding the conduct of supervision, qualifications, or competencies of clinical supervisors.

In contrast, the Association for Counselor Education and Supervision (1993) in its *Ethical Guidelines for Counseling Supervisors* explicitly states that supervisors should have training in supervision. In addition, the Approved Clinical Supervisor credential and the accompanying *Code of Ethics* (Center for Credentialing and Education, 2001) require graduate training or experience in supervision content areas, leading to certification as a clinical supervisor. The current edition of the American Counseling Association (2005) *Code of Ethics* devotes a complete section on supervision, teaching, and training including supervisor preparation. Recent work by Falender et al. (2004) as part of the Association of Psychology Postdoctoral and Internship Centers competencies conference provides supervision competencies, addressing such areas as knowledge, skills, values, and social contexts. Additional competencies address the need to train supervisors via coursework and experience as a supervisor, and assessment of supervisor competence. Although a survey of internship training directors by Rings et al. (2009) indicated agreement on the importance of these competencies, the survey also demonstrated disagreement on the importance of coursework and supervision of supervision as competencies. Participants who had received these types of training experiences were more likely to endorse their importance in training supervisors.

Perhaps the findings of Rings et al. (2009) explain the somewhat-curious situation that the development of supervisor competencies has yet to influence the majority of state boards of psychology, which typically require only that supervisors possess experience as a clinician. Similarly the Association of State and Provincial Psychology Boards (ASPPB) *Guidelines for Practicum Experience* (ASPPB, 2008) assume only that a qualified supervisor is one who is licensed or certified to engage in the practice of psychology and that supervisors have "adequate training, knowledge, and skill to render competently any psychological service which their supervisees undertake" (p. 3). In addition, the ASPPB (2003) *Supervision Guidelines,* while addressing the setting, nature, duration of contact, and necessity to provide feedback, again do not set any qualifications for supervisors beyond experience as a clinician.

Other issues of liability.   In addition to the work on problematic students, previous work by Saccuzzo (2002, 2003), a licensed psychologist and attorney, has provided perhaps the most useful and comprehensive review of liability and standards of care in supervision. More recently, articles by Recupero and Rainey (2007) and Hall, Macvaugh, Merideth, and Montgomery (2007) provided updates and helpful guidelines for risk management for psychotherapy supervision. This work as well as the previously mentioned articles by Elman et al. (1999) and Kaslow et al. (2007) should be considered essential reading for directors of training as well as for university attorneys who are not aware of the issues specific to problematic students in professional psychology programs.

An emerging issue regarding ethics and legal considerations is online supervision. Mallen, Vogel, and Rochlen (2005) provided a comprehensive review of the ethics, training, technology, and competency issues related to online counseling as well as the issues related to supervision of online counseling and provision of online supervision. Certain limitations are apparent, including the establishment of the supervisory relationship with the absence of contextual and nonverbal cues, immediate availability of supervisors for emergency or immediate consultation, and full disclosure of online procedures to clients. Bacigulape (2010) advanced the case for e-supervision, citing the opportunity to work with supervisees at different geographic locations, expanding services to areas of need, and obtaining supervision or consultation from experts in areas of expertise not locally available. Vaccaro and Lambie (2007), however, raised a number of ethical considerations, including confidentiality and security, liability, and technological competence. These authors also noted the lack of procedural and ethical guidelines by most professional organizations regarding computer-based supervision. Additionally, the rapidly evolving nature of online communication technology challenges the most technologically competent supervisor in terms of managing confidentiality, informed consent, jurisdictional, and legal issues.

Attempting to address these issues, the APA Commission on Accreditation (COA; 2009a, 2009b) recently released mandated guidelines on both distance and electronically mediated education in doctoral programs as well as telesupervision, which is defined as "clinical supervision of psychological services through a synchronous audio and video format where the supervisor is not in the same physical facility as the trainee" (2009a, p. 1). Although practicum experiences must be conducted in person and cannot be completed through distance education, a number of guidelines apply to telesupervision. These guidelines include the necessity for a formal policy with an explicit rationale for using telesupervision, how it is consistent with the program's model of training, how and when it is utilized, how it is determined which trainees can participate, and how an off-site supervisor maintains full professional and responsibility for clinical cases. In addition, the formal policy must address how nonscheduled consultation and crisis coverage are managed, assurance of privacy and confidentiality issues for clients and trainees, and the technology, quality, and educational requirements for trainees and supervisors. Finally,

> telesupervision may not account for more than 50% of the total supervision at a given practicum site, and may not be utilized at all until a student has completed his/her first practicum with substantial intervention experience with the doctoral program. (COA, 2009a, p. 1)

In the case of predoctoral internship programs, telesupervision

> may not account for more than one hour (50%) of the minimum required (as defined in the G&P) two weekly hours of individual supervision, and two hours (50%) of the minimum required (as defined in the G&P) four total weekly hours of supervision. (COA, 2009a, p. 1)

Despite these guidelines, the growth of telesupervision appears to be outpacing the ability to generate research to account for its potential strengths, limitations, ethical guidelines, and legalities.

COMPETENCIES

There has been considerable movement over the past few years in the development of competency benchmarks for professional psychology with a focus on health service practice, which includes counseling psychology. Essential resources for exploring the competency framework include the Fouad et al. (2009) article on competency benchmarks and the accompanying article from Kaslow et al. (2009) on the competency assessment tool kit. Additional articles in that issue of *Training and Education in Professional Psychology* highlight strengths and challenges of the identification, assessment, and implementation of the competencies framework. Fouad et al. noted that the benchmarks document is not intended to be prescriptive, but rather to "describe a path to this end as opposed to prescribing what programs need to do" (p. S8). Preliminary to this effort, yet still quite useful, is an outline of competencies for practica offered by Hatcher and Lassiter (2007).

Fouad et al. (2009) presented 15 core competencies, including foundational and functional competencies, each of which is defined with essential components and behavioral anchors for each of three levels of professional development (i.e., readiness for practicum, readiness for internship, readiness for entry into practice). The foundational competencies include professionalism, reflective practice, scientific knowledge and methods, relationships, individual and cultural diversity, ethical and legal standards and policy, and interdisciplinary systems. The functional competencies include assessment, intervention, consultation, research and evaluation, supervision, teaching, administration, and advocacy. Fouad et al. noted that "by examining these descriptors for each competency, one can see the development of knowledge, skill, and attitude expected with the competency area" (p. S8) for each developmental level. A number of the foundational and functional competencies may be addressed in the supervision process, and there is considerable overlap among the areas of focus articulated by various models and discussions of supervision. Attending to these competencies, the associated essential components, and the behavioral anchors may provide useful guidance to supervisors, supervisees, and training programs regarding what should be addressed and evaluated in supervision. The specific functional competency labeled "supervision" reflects the importance of understanding the supervision process, including both the supervisee and supervisor roles at the three levels of professional development (readiness for practicum, internship, entry into practice). These components tap a range of aspects of supervision, including the following essential components: expectations and roles, processes and procedures, skills development, awareness of factors affecting quality, participation process, and ethical and legal issues, which are further refined with behavioral anchors (see Table 11.1).

The article by Kaslow et al. (2009) presented a tool kit that lists specific methods to assess the competencies noted in the benchmarks article, essential components, whether the tool is useful for formative or summative evaluations, and the developmental level for which the method is appropriate. Fifteen assessment methods are offered that are

TABLE 11.1

Supervision: Developmental Level

Readiness for practicum	Readiness for internship	Readiness for entry to practice
A. Expectations and Roles		
Essential Component: **Basic knowledge of expectations for supervision** Behavioral Anchor: ■ Demonstrates knowledge of the process of supervision	Essential Component: **Knowledge of purpose for and roles in supervision.** Behavioral Anchor: ■ Identifies roles and responsibilities of the supervisor and supervisee in the supervision process	Essential Component: **Understands complexity of the supervisor role including ethical, legal, and contextual issues** Behavioral Anchor: ■ Articulates a philosophy or model of supervision and reflects on how this model is applied in practice, including integrated contextual, legal, and ethical perspectives
B. Processes and Procedures		
Essential Component: **Knowledge of supervision models and practice** Behavioral Anchor: ■ Demonstrates basic knowledge of supervision models and practice	Essential Component: **Knowledge of procedures and processes of supervision** Behavioral Anchor: ■ Identifies goals and tasks of supervision related to developmental progression ■ Tracks progress for achieving goals and setting new goals	Essential Component: **Knowledge of procedures and practices of supervision** Behavioral Anchor: ■ Prepares supervision contract ■ Demonstrates knowledge of limits of competency to supervise (assesses metacompetency) ■ Constructs plans to deal with areas of limited competency
C. Skills Development		
Essential Components: **Interpersonal skills of communication and openness to feedback** Behavioral Anchor: ■ Completes self-assessment (e.g., Hatcher & Lassiter, 2006) ■ Integrates faculty/supervisor feedback into self-assessment	Essential Component: **Knowledge of the supervision literature and how clinicians develop into skilled professionals** Behavioral Anchor: ■ Successfully completes coursework on supervision ■ Demonstrates formation of supervisory relationship integrating theory and skills including knowledge of development and educational praxis	Essential Component: **Engages in professional reflection about one's clinical relationships with supervisees as well as supervisees' relationships with their clients** Behavioral Anchor: ■ Clearly articulates how to use supervisory relationships to leverage development of supervisees and their clients
D. Awareness of Factors Affecting Quality		
Essential Component: **Basic knowledge of and sensitivity to issues related to individual and cultural differences (i.e., the APA definition) as they apply to the supervision process and relationships** Behavioral Anchor: ■ Demonstrates basic knowledge of literature on individual and cultural differences and engages in respectful interactions that reflect that knowledge	Essential Component: **Knowledge about the impact of diversity on all professional settings and supervision participants including self as defined by APA policy; beginning knowledge of personal contribution to therapy and to supervision** Behavioral Anchor: ■ Demonstrates knowledge of ICD literature and APA guidelines in supervision practice	Essential component: **Understanding of other individuals and groups and intersection dimensions of diversity in the context of supervision practice; able to engage in reflection on the role of one's self on therapy and in supervision** Behavioral Anchor: ■ Demonstrates integration of diversity and multiple identity aspects in conceptualization of supervision process with all participants (client[s], supervisee, supervisor)

(Continued)

TABLE 11.1   (*Continued*)

Supervision: Developmental Level

	■ Demonstrates awareness of role of oppression and privilege on supervision process	■ Demonstrates adaptation of own professional behavior in a culturally sensitive manner as appropriate to the needs of the supervision context and all parties in it ■ Articulates and uses diversity appropriate repertoire of skills and techniques in supervisory process ■ Identifies impact of aspects of self in therapy and supervision

E. Participation in Supervision Process

Essential Component: **Awareness of need for straightforward, truthful, and respectful communication in supervisory relationship**	Essential Component: **Observation of and participation in supervisory process (e.g., peer supervision)**	Essential Component: **Provide supervision independently to others in routine cases**
Behavioral Anchor: ■ Demonstrates willingness to admit errors, accept feedback	Behavioral Anchor: ■ Reflects on supervision process—areas of strength and those needing improvement ■ Seeks supervision to improve performance by presenting work for feedback and integrating feedback into performance	Behavioral Anchor: ■ Provides supervision to less advanced trainees, peers, or other service providers in typical cases appropriate to the service setting.

F. Ethical and Legal Issues

Essential Component: **Knowledge of principles of ethical practice and basic skills in supervisory ethical decision making; knowledge of legal and regulatory issues in supervision**	Essential Component: **Knowledge of and compliance with ethical/professional codes, standards and guidelines; institutional policies; laws, statutes, rules, regulations, and case law relevant to the practice of psychology and its supervision**	Essential Component: **Command of and application of relevant ethical, legal, and professional standards and guidelines**
Behavioral Anchor: ■ Demonstrates understanding of this knowledge (e.g., APA 2002b ethical principles)	Behavioral Anchor: ■ Behaves ethically ■ Recognizes ethical and legal issues in clinical practice and supervision	Behavioral Anchor: ■ Spontaneously and reliably identifies complex ethical and legal issues in supervision, and analyzes and proactively addresses them ■ Demonstrates awareness of potential conflicts in complex ethical and legal issues in supervision

Note. Supervision and training in the professional knowledge base and of evaluation of the effectiveness of various professional activities. APA = American Psychological Association; ICD = individual and cultural differences. Adapted from "Competency Benchmarks: A Model for Understanding and Measuring Competence in Professional Psychology Across Training Levels," by N. A. Fouad, C. L. Grus, R. L. Hatcher, N. J. Kaslow, P. S. Hutchings, M. B. Madson, F. L. Collins Jr., and R. E. Crossman, 2009, *Training and Education in Professional Psychology, 3,* pp. S21–S23. Copyright 2009 by the American Psychological Association.

identified as very useful, useful, or potentially useful for each essential element of the core competencies. For example, under the supervision functional competency for skills development (an essential element), "very useful" methods include consumer surveys, objective structured clinical examinations, ratings performance, simulations or role plays, and standard patient interviews.

The development of the competencies benchmarks and a competency assessment tool kit is a monumental undertaking reflecting the work of a number of professional psychologists, particularly representatives of the training councils. It also entails a fundamental culture shift from monitoring courses completed, practica hours, and other exposure criteria to behaviorally anchored essential elements across 15 competencies. Although significant progress has been made regarding the delineation of competencies, differences are likely to remain in perceptions of which competencies are important for various specialties (e.g., clinical, counseling, school), different training models (e.g., clinical scientist, scientist-practitioner, scholar-practitioner), therapeutic theoretical orientations, and institutional settings (Lichtenberg et al., 2007). In addition, the competency benchmarks lack empirical validation and it remains to be seen which of the aspects of the approach appear most salient for different constituencies, and how psychometric rigor balances with costs, efficiencies, and informativeness (DeMers, 2009). In discussing the challenges faced by competency assessments in medicine, Schulte and Daly (2009) have noted the relatively poor accuracy, reliability, and validity of the assessments due to the "highly contextualized nature of service delivery" and the ratings of performance dimensions intended "to capture nuanced judgments of trainees" (p. S55). They also noted that these ratings can be easily influenced or distorted by raters, their personal theories, values, and the consequences of evaluation outcomes. A positive attribute of the competency benchmarks document is the provision of a conceptual map, allowing programs and supervisors to consider the breadth of issues relevant to training and suggestions for how to operationalize them for evaluation and decision making.

FUTURE DIRECTIONS

The domain of psychotherapy supervision is alive and well, yet many challenges remain and considerable work is left to be done. We have argued that supervision shares processes in common with psychotherapy, but it is not the same as psychotherapy. Still, the challenges that psychotherapy research and practice face are some of the same challenges encountered by those who engage in supervision. The research through which we understand the supervision process and acquire evidence to support the practice of supervision remains quite limited. Additionally, the quality of the research and the confidence we may have in the conclusions we can draw from this research are also limited.

Ellis, D'Iuso, and Ladany (2008) noted that none of the measures typically used to evaluate supervision have adequate psychometric development regarding reliability and validity. They made specific recommendations for future measures for supervision, including identifying the constructs and contexts of interest; developing item pools, sampling issues, and score stability; using multimethod–multitrait approaches to measurement; and testing inferences. Without sound measures, we lack confidence in how to interpret current supervision research.

Ladany and Inman (2008) offered a number of recommendations for future research and scholarship in supervision, including attention to covert processes (what is *not* said in supervision), supervisee development, parallel processes between therapy and supervision (how they occur, what are the benefits), self-supervision (adequacy and training, the role of reflective processes), supervisor self-disclosure, recording supervisee counseling sessions (although advisable, researching positive and negative implications), supervision ethics (violations by supervisors and implications), supervisor countertransference (how it influences supervision), supervisor training (how it influences supervision), and the impact of supervision on client outcomes, among others.

Work has begun in these areas, but clarification of the influence of these issues across supervisors, supervisees, and supervision contexts is still needed. As suggested by Stoltenberg and McNeill (2010), and consistent with emerging work on competencies benchmarks, examining issues for particular levels of supervisee development is important work that remains to be done. How various issues, characteristics, components, and factors influence the learning process in supervision for trainees at different junctures in their professional growth needs to be examined, domain by domain, in considerably more detail that what we have accomplished. Examining trainee learning and development within specific supervision relationships (often time limited, 3–4 months), across supervision relationships (how does the focus on domains in prior supervision dyads affect the focus and learning in subsequent dyads), and across the training experience (from entry to graduate school to advanced professional status) remains to be accomplished. This necessitates longitudinal studies with all the challenges and expenses associated with this approach. Also, empirical examination of the developmental sequences proposed by Ladany et al. (2005) that are hypothesized to occur within specific supervision dyads is necessary. For example, are the supervision relationships adequately characterized by Bordin's (1983) model, or do they significantly differ from the psychotherapy relationships that formed the basis of this model? How are all of these factors affected by individual characteristics of the supervisor and supervisee, including issues of diversity and cultural influences as well as personal growth and adjustment?

As we have noted, the growth of telesupervision and electronically mediated education appears to be outpacing our understanding, evaluation, and research on the impact of the new technologies. Considerable work remains to examine the possible advantages, disadvantages, ethical challenges, and legal implications of these practices.

The work undertaken on common factors in psychotherapy has stimulated considerable discussion and debate. Is the search for common factors in supervision a productive path toward understanding and optimizing the supervision process? Similarly, the foundational and functional competencies (and associated components and behavioral anchors) of the competencies movement need to be carefully operationalized for various training environments, and the impact of attending to and evaluating these competencies for clinical supervision needs to be assessed. Does engaging in this process produce greater professional development than current supervision-as-usual approaches? Is the "what" that is focused on in supervision and training of primary importance, or is the "how" of supervision more impactful on learning and development? Does the "what" affect the "how," or are supervision processes sufficiently robust across issues, topics, and therapy theoretical orientations?

Wampold (2001, 2006) has challenged the primacy of specific therapy theories and specific techniques in psychotherapy. Does the "dodo bird" (equal effectiveness) hypothesis fly (or, more accurately, not fly) for supervision as for psychotherapy? Are most supervisors doing a good job, or are some excellent and others inadequate? What distinguishes these classifications and to what extent can training impact these effects? We see parallels between Wampold's (2010) recommendations for psychotherapy research and practice and areas where supervision research and practice should focus. Specifically, research should focus primarily on understanding the process of supervision and how outcomes (supervisee and client) can be improved. Although we have little evidence suggesting any approach to supervision is superior to others, we should avoid engaging in "racehorse" (one against another) comparisons or mandating approaches until we know considerably more about the supervision process and how it is affected by supervisor and supervisee characteristics, contexts, and clients. Finally, supervisors should be accountable for the outcomes of supervision, which includes supervisee learning and development and client improvement. To this end, supervisees need access to information about their clients' perceptions of the therapeutic relationship and outcomes, and supervisors need to assess the impact of their supervision sessions on the supervisee and his or her work with clients. Applying Wampold's perspective on psychotherapy to supervision, practice-based evidence may have as much or more impact on the processes and outcomes of supervision than EBP. Although we have rudimentary maps available to organize our efforts, we need to implement, evaluate, and modify them to move forward with a full understanding that the map is not the territory (Korzybski, 1948).

References

Aarons, G. A., Sommerfeld, D. H., Hecht, D. B., Silovsky, J. F., & Chaffin, M. J. (2009). The impact of evidence-based practice implementation and fidelity monitoring on staff turnover: Evidence for a protective effect. *Journal of Consulting and Clinical Psychology, 77*, 270–280. doi:10.1037/a0013223

Allen, G. J., Szollos, S. J., & Williams, B. E. (1986). Doctoral students' comparative evaluations of best and worst psychotherapy supervision. *Professional Psychology: Research and Practice, 17*, 91–99. doi:10.1037/0735-7028.17.2.91

Allen, J. (2007). A multicultural assessment supervision model to guide research and practice. *Professional Psychology: Research and Practice, 38*, 248–258. doi:10.1037/0735-7028.38.3.248

Alvarez, A. N., Blume, A. W., Cervantes, J. M., & Thomas, L. R. (2009). Tapping the wisdom tradition: Essential elements to mentoring students of color. *Professional Psychology: Research and Practice, 40*, 181–188. doi:10.1037/a0012256

American Counseling Association. (2005). *ACA code of ethics.* Alexandria, VA: Author.

American Psychological Association. (2002a). *Book 1: Guidelines and principles for accreditation of programs in professional psychology.* Washington, DC: Office of Program Consultation and Accreditation.

American Psychological Association. (2002b). *Guidelines on multicultural education, training, research, practice, and organizational change for psychologists.* Washington, DC: Author.

American Psychological Association. (2010). *Ethical principles of psychologists and code of conduct (2002, Amended June, 2010).* Retrieved from http://www.apa.org/ethics/code/index.aspx

Anderson, J. R. (2005). *Cognitive psychology and its implications* (6th ed.). New York, NY: Worth.

Ashby, R., Stoltenberg, C. D., & Kleine, P. (2010). A qualitative examination of the IDM. In C. D. Stoltenberg & B. W. McNeill (Eds.), *IDM supervision: An integrative developmental model for supervising counselors and therapists* (3rd ed., pp. 231–261). New York, NY: Routledge.

Association for Counselor Education and Supervision. (1993). *Ethical guidelines for counseling supervisors.* Alexandria, VA: Author. Retrieved from http://www.acesonline.net/ethical_guidelines.asp

Association of State and Provincial Psychology Boards. (2003). *Supervision guidelines.* Montgomery, AL: Author.

Association of State and Provincial Psychology Boards. (2008). *Guidelines for practicum experience.* Montgomery, AL: Author.

Bacigalupe, G. (2010). Supervision 2.0: e-Supervision a decade later. *Family Therapy Magazine, January/February,* 40–41.

Bahrick, A. S. (1990). *Role induction for counselor trainees: Effects on the supervisory working alliance* (Doctoral dissertation). Retrieved from Dissertation Abstracts International, 51(3-b). (Abstract #1991–51645)

Bang, K., & Park, J. (2009). Korean supervisors' experiences in clinical supervision. *The Counseling Psychologist, 37*, 1042–1075. doi:10.1177/0011000009339341

Barnett, J. E., Cornish, J. A. E., Goodyear, R. K., & Lichtenberg, J. W. (2007). Commentaries on the ethical and effective practice of clinical supervision. *Professional Psychology: Research and Practice, 38*, 268–275. doi:10.1037/0735-7028.38.3.268

Bernard, J. M., & Goodyear, R. K. (2009). *Fundamentals of clinical supervision* (4th ed.). Needham Heights, MA: Allyn & Bacon.

Beutler, L. E., Blatt, S. J., Alimohamed, S., Levy, K. M., & Anguaco, L. (2006). Participant factors in treating dyphoric disorders. In L. G. Castonguay & L. E. Beutler (Eds.), *Principles of therapeutic change that work* (pp. 13–63). New York, NY: Wiley.

Bhat, C. S., & Davis, T. E. (2007). Counseling supervisors' assessment of race, racial identity, and working alliance in supervisory dyads. *Journal of Multicultural Counseling and Development, 35*, 80–91.

Black, B. (1988). *Components of effective and ineffective psychotherapy supervision as perceived by supervisees with different levels of clinical experience* (Doctoral dissertation, Columbia University, 1987). Retrieved from Dissertation Abstracts International, 48, 3105B.

Bordin, E. S. (1983). A working alliance model of supervision. *The Counseling Psychologist, 11*, 35–42. doi:10.1177/0011000083111007

Burkard, A. W., Johnson, A. J., Madson, M. B., Pruitt, N. T., Contrearas-Tadych, D. A., Kozlowski, J. M., . . . Knox, S. (2006). Supervisor cultural responsiveness and unresponsiveness in cross-cultural supervision. *Journal of Counseling Psychology, 53*, 288–301. doi:10.1037/0022-0167.53.3.288

Butler-Byrd, N. M. (2010). An African-American supervisor's reflections on multicultural supervision. *Training and Education in Professional Psychology, 4*, 11–15. doi:10.1037/a0018351

Callahan, J. L., Almstrom, C. M., Swift, J. K., Borja, S. E., & Heath, C. J. (2009). Exploring the contribution of supervisors to intervention outcomes. *Training and Education in Professional Psychology, 3*, 72–77. doi:10.1037/a0014294

Carey, J. C., & Williams, D. S. (1986). Cognitive style in counselor education: A comparison of practicum supervisors and counselors in training. *Counselor Education and Supervision, 26*, 128–136.

Castonguay, L. G., Boswell, J. F., Constantino, M. J., Goldfried, M. R., & Hill, C. E. (2010). Training implications of harmful effects of psychological treatments. *American Psychologist, 65*, 34–49. doi:10.1037/a0017330

Center for Credentialing and Education. (2001). *Approved clinical supervisor*. Greensboro, NC: Author.

Chen, E. C., & Bernstein, B. L. (2000). Relations of complementarity and supervisory issues to supervisory working alliance: A comparative analysis of two cases. *Journal of Counseling Psychology, 47*, 485–497. doi:10.1037/0022-0167.47.4.485

Commission on Accreditation. (2009a). *Telesupervision*. Washington, DC: Office of Program Consultation and Accreditation.

Commission on Accreditation. (2009b). *Distance and electronically mediated education in doctoral programs*. Washington, DC: Office of Program Consultation and Accreditation.

Constantine, M. G., & Sue, D. W. (2007). Perceptions of racial microaggressions among Black supervisees in cross-racial dyads. *Journal of Counseling Psychology, 54*, 143–153. doi:10.1037/0022-0167.52.4.490

Constantine, M. G., Miville, M. L., & Kindaichi, M. M. (2008). Multicultural competence in counseling psychology practice and training. In S. D. Brown & R. W. Lent (Eds.), *Handbook of counseling psychology* (pp. 141–158). Hoboken, NJ: Wiley.

Couchon, W. D., & Bernard, J. M. (1984). Effects of timing of supervision on supervisor and counselor performance. *The Clinical Supervisor, 2*, 3–20. doi:10.1300/J001v02n03_02

Craig, C. H., & Sleight, C. C. (1990). Personality relationships between supervisors and students in communication disorders as determined by the Myers-Briggs Type Indicator. *The Clinical Supervisor, 8*, 41–52. doi:10.1300/J001v08n01_04

Crits-Christoph, P., Gibbons, M. B. C., Crits-Christoph, K., Narduci, J., Schamberger, M., & Gallop, R. (2006). Can therapists be trained to improve their alliances? A preliminary study of alliance-fostering psychotherapy. *Psychotherapy Research, 16*, 268–281. doi:10.1080/10503300500268557

Cukrowicz, K. C., White, B. A., Reitzel, L. R., Burns, A. B., Driscoll, K. A., Kemper, T. S., & Joiner, T. E. (2005). Improved treatment outcome associated with the shift to empirically supported treatments in a graduate training clinic. *Professional Psychology: Research and Practice, 36*, 330–337. doi:10.1037/0735-7028.36.3.330

Deihl, L., & Ellis, M. V. (2009, June). *The relevance of the supervisory working alliance in the supervision of residential frontline staff*. Paper presented at the fifth International Interdisciplinary Conference on Clinical Supervision, Buffalo, NY.

DeMers, S. T. (2009). Real progress with significant challenges ahead: Advancing competency assessment in psychology. *Training and Education in Professional Psychology, 3*, S66–S69. doi:10.1037/a0017534

Dennin, M. K., & Ellis, M. V. (2003). Effects of a method of self-supervision for counselor trainees. *Journal of Counseling Psychology, 50*, 69–83. doi:10.1037/0022-0167.50.1.69

Dixon, D. N., & Claiborn, C. D. (1987). A social influence approach to counselor supervision. In J. E. Maddux, C. D. Stoltenberg, & R. Rosenwein (Eds.), *Social processes in clinical and counseling psychology* (pp. 83–93). New York, NY: Springer-Verlag.

Dombeck, M. T., & Brody, S. L. (1995). Clinical supervision: A three-way mirror. *Archives of Psychiatric Nursing, 9*, 3–10. doi:10.1016/S0883-9417(95)80012-3

Duncan, B. L., Miller, S. D., Wampold, B. E., & Hubble, M. A. (Eds.). (2010). *The heart and soul of change: Delivering what works in therapy* (2nd ed.). Washington, DC: American Psychological Association.

Duys, D. K., & Hedstrom, S. M. (2000). Basic counselor skills training and counselor cognitive complexity. *Counselor Education and Supervision, 40*, 8–18.

Efstation, J. F., Patton, M. J., & Kardash, C. M. (1990). Measuring the working alliance in counselor supervision. *Journal of Counseling Psychology, 37*, 322–329. doi:10.1037/0022-0167.37.3.322

Ellis, M. V. (1991). Critical incidents in clinical supervision and in supervisor supervision: Assessing supervisory issue. *Journal of Counseling Psychology, 38*, 342–349. doi:10.1037/0022-0167.38.3.342

Ellis, M. V. (2010). Bridging the science and practice of clinical supervision: Some discoveries, some misconceptions. *The Clinical Supervisor, 29*, 95–116. doi:10.1080/07325221003741910

Ellis, M. V., D'Iuso, N., & Ladany, N. (2008). State of the art in the assessment, measurement, and evaluation of clinical supervision. In C. E. Watkins, Jr. (Ed.), *Handbook of psychotherapy supervision* (pp. 473–507). New York, NY: Wiley.

Ellis, M. V., & Ladany, M. (1997). Inferences concerning supervisees and clients in clinical supervision: An integrative review. In C. E. Watkins, Jr. (Ed.), *Handbook of psychotherapy supervision* (pp. 447–507). New York, NY: Wiley.

Ellis, M. V., Ladany, N., Krengel, M., & Schult, D. (1996). Clinical supervision research from 1981 to 1993: A methodological critique. *Journal of Counseling Psychology, 43*, 35–50. doi:10.1037/0022-0167.43.1.35

Elman, N., Forrest, L., Vacha-Haase, T., & Gizara, S. (1999). A systems perspective on trainee impairment: Continuing the dialogue. *The Counseling Psychologist, 27,* 712–721. doi:10.1177/0011000099275005

Falender, C. A., Cornish, J. A. E., Goodyear, R., Hatcher, R., Kaslow, N. J., Leventhal, G., . . . Grus, C. (2004). Defining competencies in psychology supervision: A consensus statement. *Journal of Clinical Psychology, 60,* 771–785. doi:10.1002/jclp.20013

Fama, L., & Ellis, M. V. (2005, August). *Vicarious traumatization: A concern for doctoral level psychology trainees?* Paper presented at the 113th Annual Convention of the American Psychological Association, Washington, DC.

Field, L. D., Chavez-Korell, S., & Domenech Rodríguez, M. (2010). *No hay rosas sin espinas:* Conceptualizing Latina–Latina supervision from a multicultural developmental supervisory model. *Training and Education in Professional Psychology, 4,* 47–54. doi:10.1037/a0018521

Fong, M. L., Borders, L. D., Ethington, C. A., & Pitts, J. H. (1997). Becoming a counselor: A longitudinal study of student cognitive development. *Counselor Education and Supervision, 37,* 100–114.

Fouad, N. A., Grus, C. L., Hatcher, R. L., Kaslow, N. J., Hutchings, P. S., Madson, M. B., . . . Crossman, R. E. (2009). Competency benchmarks: A model for understanding and measuring competence in professional psychology across training levels. *Training and Education in Professional Psychology, 3,* S5–S26. doi:10.1037/a0015832

Freeman, S. C. (1993). Reiterations on client-centered supervision. *Counselor Education and Supervision, 32,* 213–215.

Freitas, G. J. (2002). The impact of psychotherapy supervision on client outcome: A critical examination of 2 decades of research. *Psychotherapy: Theory, Research, Practice, Training, 39,* 354–367. doi:10.1037/0033-3204.39.4.354

Friedlander, J. L., Heatherington, L., Johnson, B., & Skowron, E. (1994). Sustaining engagement: A change event in family therapy. *Journal of Counseling Psychology, 41,* 438–448. doi:10.1037/0022-0167.41.4.438

Friedlander, M. L., Keller, K. E., Peca-Baker, T. A., & Olk, M. E. (1986). Effects of role conflict on counselor trainees' self-statements, anxiety level, and performance. *Journal of Counseling Psychology, 33,* 73–77. doi:10.1037/0022-0167.33.1.73

Galante, M. (1988). *Trainees' and supervisors' perceptions of effective and ineffective supervisory relationships* (Doctoral dissertation, Memphis State University, 1987). Retrieved from Dissertation Abstracts International, 49, 933B.

Gatmon, D., Jackson, D., Koshkarian, L., Martos-Perry, N., & Rodolfa, E. (2001). Exploring ethnic, gender, and sexual orientation variables in supervision: Do they really matter? *Journal of Multicultural Counseling and Development, 29,* 102–113.

Gelso, C. J., Latts, M. G., Gomez, M. J., & Fassinger, R. E. (2002). Countertransference management and therapy outcome: An initial evaluation. *Journal of Clinical Psychology, 58,* 861–867. doi:10.1002/jclp.2010

Gloria, A. M., Hird, J. S., & Tao, K. W. (2008). Self-reported multicultural supervision competence of White predoctoral intern supervisors. *Teaching and Education in Professional Psychology, 2,* 129–136. doi:10.1037/1931-3918.2.3.129

Goldfried, M. R., & Davison, G. C. (1994). *Clinical behavior therapy* (Expanded ed.). New York, NY: Wiley.

Goleman, D. (2006). *Social intelligence: The new science of human relationships.* New York, NY: Bantam.

Gottlieb, M. C., Robinson, K., & Younggren, J. N. (2007). Multiple relations in supervision: Guidance for administrators, supervisors, and students. *Professional Psychology: Research and Practice, 38,* 241–247. doi:10.1037/0735-7028.38.3.241

Granello, D. H. ((2002). Assessing the cognitive development of counseling students: Changes in epistemological assumptions. *Counselor Education and Supervision, 41,* 279–293.

Gray, L. A., Ladany, N., Walker, J. A., & Ancis, J. R. (2001). Psychotherapy trainees' experience of counterproductive events in supervision. *Journal of Counseling Psychology, 48,* 371–383. doi:10.1037/0022-0167.48.4.371

Greenberg, L. S. (1986). Change process research. *Journal of Consulting and Clinical Psychology, 54,* 4–9. doi:10.1037/0022-006X.54.1.4

Greenberg, L. S. (2002). Integrating an emotion-focused approach to treatment into psychotherapy integration. *Journal of Psychotherapy Integration, 12,* 154–189. doi:10.1037/1053-0479.12.2.154

Greenberg, L. S., & Pinsof, W. M. (Eds.). (1986). *The psychotherapeutic process: A research handbook.* New York, NY: Guilford Press.

Hage, S. W., Hopson, A., Siegel, M., Payton, G., & DeFanti, E. (2006). Multicultural training in spirituality: An interdisciplinary review. *Counseling and Values, 50,* 217–234.

Hall, R. C. W., Macvaugh, G. S., III, Merideth, P., & Montgomery, J. (2007). Commentary: Delving further into liability for psychotherapy supervision. *Journal of the American Academy of Psychiatry and the Law, 35,* 196–199.

Handelsman, M. M., Gottlieb, M. C., & Knapp, S. (2005). Training ethical psychologists: An acculturation model. *Professional Psychology: Research and Practice, 36,* 59–65. doi:10.1037/0735-7028.36.1.59

Handley, P. (1982). Relationship between supervisors' and trainees' cognitive styles and the supervision process. *Journal of Counseling Psychology, 29,* 508–515. doi:10.1037/0022-0167.29.5.508

Hatcher, R. L., & Lassiter, K. D. (2007). Initial training in professional psychology: The practicum competencies outline. *Training and Education in Professional Psychology, 1,* 49–63. doi:10.1037/1931-3918.1.1.49

Heaton, K. J., & Black, L. L. (2009). I knew you when: A case study of managing preexisting nonamorous relationships in counseling. *The Family Journal, 17,* 134–138. doi:10.1177/1066480709332854

Henry, W. P., Strupp, H. H., Butler, S. F., Schacht, T. E., & Binder, J. L. (1993). The effects of training in time-limited dynamic psychotherapy: Changes in therapist behavior. *Journal of Consulting and Clinical Psychology, 61,* 434–440. doi:10.1037/0022-006X.61.3.434

Heppner, P. P., & Roehlke, H. J. (1984). Differences among supervisees at different levels of training: Implications for a developmental model of supervision. *Journal of Counseling Psychology, 31,* 76–90. doi:10.1037/0022-0167.31.1.76

Hernández, P. (2008). The cultural context model in clinical supervision: An illustration of critical psychology in training. *Training and Education in Professional Psychology, 2,* 10–17.

Hill, C. E., & Lambert, M. J. (2004). Methodological issues in studying psychotherapy process and outcomes. In M. J. Lambert (Ed.), *Bergin and Garfield's handbook of psychotherapy and behavior change* (5th ed., pp. 84–135). New York, NY: Wiley.

Hill, C. E., Mahalik, J. R., & Thompson, B. J. (1989). Therapist self-disclosure. *Psychotherapy: Theory, Research, Practice, Training, 26,* 290–295. doi:10.1037/h0085438

Hilsenroth, M. J., Ackerman, S. J., Clemence, A. J., Strassle, C. G., & Handler, L. (2002). Effects of structured clinician training on patient and therapist perspectives of alliance early in psychotherapy. *Psychotherapy: Theory, Research, Practice, Training, 39,* 309–323. doi:10.1037/0033-3204.39.4.309

Holloway, E. L. (1982). Interactional structure of the supervision interview. *Journal of Counseling Psychology, 29,* 309–317. doi:10.1037/0022-0167.29.3.309

Hutt, C. H., Scott, J., & King, M. (1983). A phenomenological study of supervisees' positive and negative experiences in supervision. *Psychotherapy: Theory, Research, and Practice, 20,* 118–123. doi:10.1037/h0088471

Inman, A. G. (2006). Supervisor multicultural competence and its relation to supervisory process and outcome. *Journal of Marital and Family Therapy, 32,* 73–85. doi:10.1111/j.1752-0606.2006.tb01589.x

Inman, A. G., & Ladany, N. (2008). Research: The state of the field. In A. K. Hess, K. D. Hess, & T. H. Hess (Eds.), *Psychotherapy supervision: Theory, research, and practice* (2nd ed., pp. 500–517). Hoboken, NJ: Wiley.

Jernigan, M. M., Green, C. E., Helms, J. E., Perez-Gualdron, L., & Henze, K. (2010). An examination of people of color supervision dyads: Racial identity matters as much as race. *Training and Education in Professional Psychology, 4,* 62–73. doi:10.1037/a0018110

Kaduvettoor, A., O'Shaughnessy, T., Mori, Y., Clyde, B., Weatherford, R. D., & Ladany, N. (2009). Helpful and hindering multicultural events in group supervision: Climate and multicultural competence. *The Counseling Psychologist, 37,* 786–820. doi:10.1177/0011000009333984

Kaslow, N. J., Grus, C. L., Campbell, L. F., Fouad, N. A., Hatcher, R. L., & Rodolfa, E. R. (2009). Competency assessment toolkit for professional psychology. *Training and Education in Professional Psychology, 3,* S27–S45. doi:10.1037/a0015833

Kaslow, N. J., Rubin, N. J., Forrest, L., Elman, N. S., Van Horne, B. A., Jacobs, S. C., . . . Thorn, B. E. (2007). Recognizing, assessing, and intervening with problems of professional competence. *Professional Psychology: Research and Practice, 38,* 479–492. doi:10.1037/0735-7028.38.5.479

Kennard, B. D., Stewart, S. M., & Gluck, M. R. (1987). The supervision relationship: Variables contributing to positive versus negative experiences. *Professional Psychology: Research and Practice, 18,* 172–175. doi:10.1037/0735-7028.18.2.172

Kivlighan, D. M., Jr., Angelone, E. O., & Swafford, K. G. (1991). Live supervision in individual psychotherapy: Effects on therapists' intention use and clients' evaluation of session effect and working alliance. *Journal of Counseling Psychology, 22,* 489–495.

Korzybski, A. (1948). *Science and sanity: An introduction to non-Aristotelian systems and general semantics* (3rd ed.). Lakeville, CT: International Non-Aristotelian Library.

Ladany, N., Brittan-Powell, C. S., & Pannu, R. K. (1997). The influence of supervisory racial identity interaction and racial matching on the supervisory working alliance and supervisee multicultural competence. *Counselor Education and Supervision, 36,* 284–304.

Ladany, N., Ellis, M. V., & Friedlander, M. L. (1999). The supervisory working alliance, trainee self-efficacy, and satisfaction with supervision. *Journal of Counseling and Development, 77,* 447–455.

Ladany, N., & Friedlander, M. J. (1995). The relationship between the supervisory working alliance and trainees' experience of role conflict and role ambiguity. *Counselor Education and Supervision, 34,* 220–231.

Ladany, N., Friedlander, M. L., & Nelson, M. L. (2005). *Critical events in psychotherapy supervision: An interpersonal approach.* Washington, DC: American Psychological Association. doi:10.1037/10958-000

Ladany, N., Hill, C. E., Corbett, M. M., & Nutt, E. A. (1996). Nature, extent, and importance of what psychotherapy trainees do not disclose to their supervisors. *Journal of Counseling Psychology, 43,* 10–24. doi:10.1037/0022-0167.43.1.10

Ladany, N., & Inman, A. G. (2008). Developments in counseling skills training and supervision. In S. D. Brown & R. W. Lent (Eds.), *Handbook of counseling psychology* (4th ed., pp. 338–354). Hoboken, NJ: Wiley.

Ladany, N., & Lehrman-Waterman, D. (1999). The content and frequency of supervisor self-disclosures and their relationship to supervisor style and the supervisory working alliance. *Counselor Education and Supervision, 38,* 143–160.

Ladany, N., Lehrman-Waterman, D., Molinaro, M., & Wolgast, B. (1999). Psychotherapy supervisor ethical practices: Adherence to guidelines, the supervisory working alliance, and supervisee satisfaction. *The Counseling Psychologist, 27,* 443–475. doi:10.1177/0011000099273008

Ladany, N., Walker, J., & Melincoff, D. S. (2001). Supervisee integrative complexity, experience, and preference for supervisor style. *Counselor Education and Supervision, 40,* 203–219.

Lambert, M. J. (2007). Presidential address: What we have learned from a decade of research aimed at improving outcome in routine care. *Psychotherapy Research, 17,* 1–14. doi:10.1080/10503300601032506

Lambert, M. J., Hansen, N. B., & Finch, A. E. (2001). Patent-focused research: Using patient outcome data to enhance treatment effects. *Journal of Consulting and Clinical Psychology, 69,* 159–172. doi:10.1037/0022-006X.69.2.159

Lambert, M. J., & Ogles, B. M. (1997). The effectiveness of psychotherapy supervision. In C. E. Watkins, Jr. (Ed.), *Handbook of psychotherapy supervision* (pp. 421–446). New York, NY: Wiley.

Lampropoulos, G. K. (2003). A common factors view of counseling supervision process. *The Clinical Supervisor, 21,* 77–95. doi:10.1300/J001v21n01_06

Lassiter, P. S., Napolitano, L., Culbreth, J. R., & Ng, K. M. (2008). Developing multicultural competence using the structured peer group supervision model. *Counselor Education and Supervision, 47,* 164–178.

Leach, M. M., Stoltenberg, C. D., McNeill, B. W., & Eichenfield, G. (1997). Self-efficacy and counselor development: Testing the Integrated Developmental Model. *Counselor Education and Supervision, 37,* 115–124.

Lee, D. L., & Tracey, T. J. G. (2008). General and multicultural case conceptualization skills: A cross-sectional analysis of psychotherapy trainees. *Psychotherapy: Theory, Research, Practice, Training, 45,* 507–522. doi:10.1037/a0014336

Lehrman-Waterman, D., & Ladany, N. (2001). Development and validation of the Evaluation Process within Supervision Inventory. *Journal of Counseling Psychology, 48,* 168–177. doi:10.1037/0022-0167.48.2.168

Lerner, R. M. (1986). *Concepts and theories of human development* (2nd ed.). New York, NY: Random House.

Lichtenberg, J., Portnoy, S., Bebeau, M., Leigh, I. W., Nelson, P. D., Rubin, N. J., . . . Kaslow, N. J. (2007). Challenges to the assessment of competence and competencies. *Professional Psychology: Research and Practice, 38,* 474–478. doi:10.1037/0735-7028.38.5.474

Liddle, B. J. (1986). Resistance in supervision: A response to perceived threat. *Counselor Education and Supervision, 26,* 117–127.

Lilienfeld, S. O. (2007). Psychological treatments that cause harm. *Perspectives on Psychological Science, 2,* 53–70. doi:10.1111/j.1745-6916.2007.00029.x

Lo, H. (2010). My racial identity development and supervision: A self-reflection. *Training and Education in Professional Psychology, 4,* 26–28. doi:10.1037/a0017856

Lochner, B. T., & Melchert, T. P. (1997). Relationship of cognitive style and theoretical orientation to psychology interns' preferences for supervision. *Journal of Counseling Psychology, 44,* 256–260. doi:10.1037/0022-0167.44.2.256

Loganbill, C., Hardy, E., & Delworth, U. (1982). Supervision: A conceptual model. *The Counseling Psychologist, 10,* 3–42. doi:10.1177/0011000082101002

Lovell, C. (1999). Supervisee cognitive complexity and the Integrated Developmental Model. *The Clinical Supervisor, 18,* 191–201. doi:10.1300/J001v18n01_12

Magnuson, S., Wilcoxon, S. A., & Norem, K. (2000). A profile of lousy supervision: Experienced counselors' perspectives. *Counselor Education and Supervision, 39,* 189–202.

Mallen, M. J., Vogel, D. L., & Rochlen, A. B. (2005). The practical aspects of online counseling: Ethics, training, technology, and competency. *The Counseling Psychologist, 33,* 776–818.

McVee, M. B., Dunsmore, K., & Gavelek, J. R. (2005). Schema theory revisited. *Review of Educational*

Research, 75, 531–566. doi:10.3102/003465430 75004531

Millán, F. (2010). On supervision: Reflections of a Latino psychologist. *Training and Education in Professional Psychology, 4,* 7–10. doi:10.1037/a0016977

Mittal, M., & Wieling, E. (2006). Training experiences of international doctoral students in marriage and family therapy. *Journal of Marital and Family Therapy, 32,* 369–383. doi:10.1111/j.1752-0606.2006.tb01613.x

Miville, M. L., Duan, C., Nutt, R. L., Waehler, C. A., Suzuki, L., Pistole, M. C., . . . Corpus, M. (2009). Integrating practice guidelines into professional training: Implications for diversity competence. *The Counseling Psychologist, 37,* 519–563. doi:10.1177/0011000008323651

Morgan, M. M., & Sprenkle, D. H. (2007). Toward a common-factors approach to supervision. *Journal of Marital and Family Therapy, 33,* 1–17. doi:10.1111/j.1752-0606.2007.00001.x

Mori, Y., Inman, A. G., & Caskie, G. I. L. (2009). Supervising international students: Relationship between acculturation, supervisor multicultural competence, cultural discussions, and supervision satisfaction. *Training and Education in Professional Psychology, 3,* 10–18. doi:10.1037/a0013072

Murphy-Shigematsu, S. (2010). Microaggressions by supervisors of color. *Training and Education in Professional Psychology, 4,* 16–18. doi:10.1037/a0017472

Myers, I. B. (1962). *The Myers-Briggs Type Indicator.* Palo Alto, CA: Consulting Psychologists Press.

Myers, I. B., & McCaulley, M. H. (1985). *Manual: A guide to the development and use of the Myers-Briggs Type Indicator.* Palo Alto, CA: Consulting Psychologists Press.

Nelson, G. H. (1978). Psychotherapy supervision from the trainee's point of view: A survey of preferences. *Professional Psychology, 9,* 539–550. doi:10.1037/0735-7028.9.4.539

Nelson, M. L., Barnes, K. L., Evans, A. L., & Triggiano, P. J. (2008). Working with conflict in clinical supervision: Wise supervisors perspectives. *Journal of Counseling Psychology, 55,* 172–184. doi:10.1037/0022-0167.55.2.172

Nelson, M. L., Gizara, S., Cromback Hope, A., Phelps, R., Steward, R., & Weitzman, L. (2006). A feminist multicultural perspective on supervision. *Journal of Multicultural Counseling and Development, 34,* 105–115.

Neufeldt, S. A., Pinterits, E. j., Moleiro, C. M., Lee, T. E., Yang, P. H., Brodie, R. E., & Orliss, M. J. (2006). How do graduate student therapists incorporate diversity factors in case conceptualization?

Psychotherapy: Theory, Research, Practice, Training, 43, 464–479. doi:10.1037/0033-3204.43.4.464

Norcross, J. C., Beutler, L. E., & Levant, R. F. (2006). *Evidence-based practices in mental health: Debate and dialogue on the fundamental questions.* Washington, DC: American Psychological Association.

Norcross, J. D., & Halgin, R. P. (1997). Integrative approaches to psychotherapy supervision. In J. C. E. Watkins (Ed.), *Handbook of psychotherapy supervision* (pp. 203–222). New York, NY: Wiley.

Ober, A. M., Granello, D. H., & Henfield, M. S. (2009). A synergistic model to enhance multicultural competence in supervision. *Counselor Education and Supervision, 48,* 204–221.

Olk, M. E., & Friedlander, M. L. (1992). Trainees' experiences of role conflict and role ambiguity in supervisory relationships. *Journal of Counseling Psychology, 39,* 389–397. doi:10.1037/0022-0167.39.3.389

Patton, M. J., & Kivlighan, D. M., Jr. (1997). Relevance of the supervisory alliance to the counseling alliance and to treatment adherence in counselor training. *Journal of Counseling Psychology, 44,* 108–115. doi:10.1037/0022-0167.44.1.108

Petty, R. E., & Wegener, D. T. (1999). The elaboration likelihood model: Current status and controversies. In S. Chaiken & T. Trope (Eds.), *Dual process theories in social psychology* (pp. 37–72). New York, NY: Guilford Press.

Ponterotto, J. G., Fuertes, J. N., & Chen, E. C. (2000). Models of multicultural counseling. In S. D. Brown & R. W. Lent (Eds.), *Handbook of counseling psychology* (3rd ed., pp. 639–669). Hoboken, NJ: Wiley.

Quarto, C. K. (2002). Supervisors' and supervisees' perceptions of control and conflict in counseling supervision. *The Clinical Supervisor, 21,* 21–37. doi:10.1300/J001v21n02_02

Rabinowitz, F. E., Heppner, P. P., & Roehlke, H. J. (1986). Descriptive study of process outcome variables of supervision over time. *Journal of Counseling Psychology, 33,* 292–300. doi:10.1037/0022-0167.33.3.292

Ramos- Sánchez, L., Esnil, E., Goodwin, A., Riggs, S., Touster, L. O., Wright, L. K., . . . Rodolfa, E. (2002). Negative supervisory events: Effects on supervision and supervisory alliance. *Professional Psychology: Research and Practice, 33,* 197–202. doi:10.1037/0735-7028.33.2.197

Recupero, P. R., & Rainey, S. E. (2007). Liability and risk management in outpatient psychotherapy supervision. *Journal of the American Academy of Psychiatry and the Law, 35,* 188–195.

Reese, R. J., Norsworthy, L. A., & Rowlands, S. R. (2009). Does a continuous feedback system improve psychotherapy outcome? *Psychotherapy: Theory, Research,*

Practice, Training, 46, 418–431. doi:10.1037/
a0017901

Reese, R. J., Usher, E. L., Bowman, D. C., Norsworthy, L. A., Halstead, J. L., Rowlands, S. R., & Chisholm, R. R. (2009). Using client feedback in psychotherapy training: An analysis of its influence on supervision and counselor self-efficacy. *Training and Education in Professional Psychology, 3*, 157–168. doi:10.1037/a0015673

Reising, G. N., & Daniels, M. H. (1983). A study of Hogan's model of counselor development and supervision. *Journal of Counseling Psychology, 30*, 235–244. doi:10.1037/0022-0167.30.2.235

Reynaga-Abiko, G. (2010). Opportunity amidst challenge: Reflections of a Latina supervisor. *Training and Education in Professional Psychology, 4*, 19–25. doi:10.1037/a0017052

Rings, J. A., Genuchi, M. C., Hall, M. D., Angelo, M., & Erickson Cornish, J. A. (2009). Is there consensus among predoctoral internship training directors regarding clinical supervision competencies? A descriptive analysis. *Training and Education in Professional Psychology, 3*, 140–147. doi:10.1037/a0015054

Riva, M. T., & Erickson Cornish, J. A. (2008). Group supervision practices at psychology predoctoral internship programs: 15 years later. *Training and Education in Professional Psychology, 2*, 18–25. doi:10.1037/1931-3918.2.1.18

Ronnestad, M. H., & Skovholt, T. M. (1993). Supervision of beginning and advanced graduate students of counseling and psychotherapy. *Journal of Counseling and Development, 71*, 396–405.

Ryan, R. M., & Deci, E. L. (2000). Self-determination theory and the facilitation of intrinsic motivation, social development, and well-being. *American Psychologist, 55*, 68–78. doi:10.1037/0003-066X.55.1.68

Saccuzzo, D. (2002). Liability for failure to supervise adequately: Let the master beware. *The National Register of Health Service Providers in Psychology: The Psychologist's Legal Update, 13*, 1–14.

Saccuzzo, D. (2003). Liability for failure to supervise adequately: Let the master beware. Part 2 ethical basis for standard of care in supervision. *The National Register of Health Service Providers in Psychology: The Psychologist's Legal Update, 13*, 1–20.

Safran, J. D., Crocker, P., McMain, S., & Murray, P. (1990). Therapeutic alliance rupture as a therapy event for empirical investigation. *Psychotherapy: Theory, Research, Practice, Training, 27*, 154–165. doi:10.1037/0033-3204.27.2.154

Schacht, A. J., Howe, H. E., & Berman, J. J. (1989). Supervisor facilitative conditions and effectiveness as perceived by thinking- and feeling-type supervisees.

Psychotherapy: Theory, Research, Practice, Training, 26, 475–483. doi:10.1037/h0085466

Schön, D. A. (1987). *Educating the reflective practitioner.* San Francisco, CA: Jossey-Bass.

Schulte, A. C., & Daly, E. J., III. (2009). Operationalizing and evaluating professional competencies in psychology: Out with the old, in with the new? *Training and Education in Professional Psychology, 3*, S54–S58. doi:10.1037/a0017155

Schultz, J. C., Ososkie, J. N., Fried, J. H., Nelson, R. E., & Bardos, A. N. (2002). Clinical supervision in public rehabilitation counseling settings. *Rehabilitation Counseling Bulletin, 45*, 213–222. doi:10.1177/00343552020450040401

Schwartz, A., Domenech Rodríguez, M. M., Santiago-Rivera, A. L., Arredondo, P., & Field, L. (2010). Cultural and linguistic competence: Welcome challenges from successful diversification. *Professional Psychology: Research and Practice, 41*, 210–220. doi:10.1037/a0019447

Scott, K. J., Ingram, K. M., Vitanza, S. A., & Smith, J. G. (2000). Training in supervision: A survey of current practices. *The Counseling Psychologist, 28*, 403–422. doi:10.1177/0011000000283007

Shanfield, S. B., Mohl, P. C., Matthews, K. L., & Hetherly, V. (1992). Quantitative assessment of the behavior of psychotherapy supervisors. *The American Journal of Psychiatry, 149*, 352–357.

Singh, A., & Chun, K. Y. S. (2010). "From the margins to the center": Moving towards a resilience-based model of supervision for queer people of color supervisors. *Training and Education in Professional Psychology, 4*, 36–46. doi:10.1037/a0017373

Skovholt, T. M., & Ronnestad, M. H. (1992). Themes in therapist and counselor development. *Journal of Counseling and Development, 70*, 505–515.

Smith, L. (2009). Enhancing training and practice in the context of poverty. *Training and Education in Professional Psychology, 3*, 84–93. doi:10.1037/a0014459

Son, E. J., Ellis, M. V., & Yoo, S. K. (2009, August). *Clinical supervision in South Korea and the U.S.: A comparison of supervisees' perceptions.* Paper presented at the 117th Annual Convention of the American Psychological Association, Toronto, Ontario, Canada.

Spelliscy, D., Chen, E. C., & Zusho, A. (2007, August). *Predicting supervisee role conflict and ambiguity: A path analytic model.* Paper presented at the annual meeting of the American Psychological Association, San Francisco, CA.

Sprenkle, D. H., & Blow, A. J. (2004). Common factors are not islands—They work through models: A response to Sexton, Ridley, and Kleiner. *Journal of Marital and Family Therapy, 30*, 151–157. doi:10.1111/j.1752-0606.2004.tb01230.x

Sprenkle, D. H., Davis, S. D., & Lebow, J. L. (2009). *Common factors in couple and family therapy: The overlooked foundation for effective practice.* New York, NY: Guilford Press.

Stein, D. M., & Lambert, M. J. (1995). Graduate training in psychotherapy: Are therapy outcomes enhanced? *Journal of Consulting and Clinical Psychology, 63*, 182–196. doi:10.1037/0022-006X.63.2.182

Stevens, D. T., Goodyear, R. K., & Robertson, P. (1998). Supervisor development: An exploratory study in changes in stance and emphasis. *The Clinical Supervisor, 16*, 73–88. doi:10.1300/J001v16n02_05

Stoltenberg, C. D. (1981). Approaching supervision from a developmental perspective: The counselor complexity model. *Journal of Counseling Psychology, 28*, 59–65. doi:10.1037/0022-0167.28.1.59

Stoltenberg, C. D. (2005). Enhancing professional competence through developmental approaches to supervision. *American Psychologist, 60*, 857–864.

Stoltenberg, C. D. (2008). Developmental approaches to supervision: A case example. In C. A. Falender & E. P. Shafranske (Eds.), *Casebook for clinical supervision: A competency-based approach* (pp. 39–56). Washington, DC: American Psychological Association. doi:10.1037/11792-003

Stoltenberg, C. D., & Delworth, U. (1987). *Supervising counselors and therapists.* San Francisco, CA: Jossey-Bass.

Stoltenberg, C. D., & McNeill, B. W. (2010). *IDM supervision: An integrative developmental model for supervising counselors and therapists* (3rd ed.). New York, NY: Routledge.

Stoltenberg, C. D., McNeill, B. W., & Crethar, H. C. (1994). Changes in supervision as counselors and therapists gain experience: A review. *Professional Psychology: Research and Practice, 25*, 416–449. doi:10.1037/0735-7028.25.4.416

Stoltenberg, C. D., McNeill, B. W., & Crethar, H. C. (1995). Persuasion and development in counselor supervision. *The Counseling Psychologist, 23*, 633–648. doi:10.1177/0011000095234003

Stoltenberg, C. D., McNeill, B. W., & Delworth, U. (1998). *IDM Supervision: An Integrated Developmental Model for supervising counselors and therapists.* San Francisco, CA: Jossey-Bass.

Stoltenberg, C. D., & Pace, T. M. (2008). Science and practice in supervision: An evidence-based practice in psychology approach. In B. W. Walsh (Ed.), *Biennial review of counseling psychology* (pp. 71–95). New York, NY: Routledge.

Stratton, J. S., & Smith, R. D. (2006). Supervision of couples cases. *Psychotherapy: Theory,*

Research, Practice, Training, 43, 337–348. doi:10.1037/0033-3204.43.3.337

Sumerel, M. B., & Borders, L. D. (1996). Addressing personal issues in supervision: Impact of counselor's experience level on various aspects of the supervisory relationship. *Counselor Education and Supervision, 35*, 268–286.

Thomas, J. T. (2007). Informed consent through contracting for supervision: Minimizing risks, enhancing benefits. *Professional Psychology: Research and Practice, 38*, 221–231. doi:10.1037/0735-7028.38.3.221

Tracey, T. J., Ellickson, J. L., & Sherry, P. (1989). Reactance in relation to different supervisory environments and counselor development. *Journal of Counseling Psychology, 36*, 336–344. doi:10.1037/0022-0167.36.3.336

Vaccaro, N., & Lambie, G. W. (2007). Computer-based counselor-in-training supervision: Ethical and practical implications for counselor educators and supervisors. *Counselor Education and Supervision, 47*, 46–57.

Veach, P. (2001). Conflict and counterproductivity in supervision: When relationships are less than ideal: Comment on Nelson and Friedlander (2001) and Gray et al. (2001). *Journal of Counseling Psychology, 48*, 396–400. doi:10.1037/0022-0167.48.4.396

Verdinelli, S., & Biever, J. L. (2009). Experiences of Spanish/English bilingual supervisees. *Psychotherapy: Theory, Research, Practice, Training, 46*, 158–170. doi:10.1037/a0016024

Vereen, L. G., Hill, N. R., & McNeal, D. T. (2008). Perceptions of multicultural counseling competency: Integration of the curricular and the practical. *Journal of Mental Health Counseling, 30*, 226–236.

Wampold, B. E. (2001). *The great psychotherapy debate: Models, methods, and findings.* Mahwah, NJ: Erlbaum.

Wampold, B. E. (2006). Not a scintilla of evidence to support empirically supported treatments as more effective than other treatments. In J. C. Norcross, L. E. Beutler, & R. F. Levant (Eds.), *Evidence-based practices in mental health: Debate and dialogue on the fundamental questions* (pp. 299–308). Washington, DC: American Psychological Association.

Wampold, B. E. (2010). The research evidence for common factors models: A historically situated perspective. In B. L. Duncan, S. D. Miller, B. E. Wampold, & M. A. Hubble (Eds.), *The heart and soul of change: Delivering what works in therapy* (2nd ed., pp. 49–81). Washington, DC: American Psychological Association.

Watkins, C. E. (1995). Researching psychotherapy supervisor development: Four key considerations. *Clinical Psychology Review, 15*, 647–680. doi:10.1016/0272-7358(95)00038-Q

Webb, A., & Wheeler, S. (1998). How honest do counselors dare to be in the supervisory relationship? An exploratory study. *British Journal of Guidance and Counselling, 26,* 509–524.

Werth, J. L., Cummings, D. L., & Thompson, M. N. (2008). *Legal and ethical issues affecting counseling psychologists.* In S. D. Brown & R. W. Lent (eds.), *Handbook of counseling psychology* (pp. 3–20). Hoboken, NJ: Wiley.

Westefeld, J. S. (2009). Supervision of psychotherapy: Models, issues, and recommendations. *The Counseling Psychologist, 37,* 296–316. doi:10.1177/0011000008316657

Wetchler, J. L. (1989). Supervisors' and supervisees' perceptions of the effectiveness of family therapy supervisor interpersonal skills. *American Journal of Family Therapy, 17,* 244–256. doi:10.1080/01926188908250771

White, V. E., & Queener, J. (2003). Supervisor and supervisee attachments and social provisions related to the supervisory working alliance. *Counselor Education and Supervision, 42,* 203–218.

Winter, M., & Holloway, E. L. (1991). Relation of trainee experience, conceptual level, and supervisor approach to selection of audiotaped counseling passages. *The Clinical Supervisor, 9,* 87–103. doi:10.1300/J001v09n02_09

Worthen, J., & McNeill, B. W. (1996). A phenomenological investigation of "good" supervision events. *Journal of Counseling Psychology, 43,* 25–34. doi:10.1037/0022-0167.43.1.25

Worthington, E. L., Jr. (1984). Empirical investigation of supervision of counselors as they gain experience. *Journal of Counseling Psychology, 31,* 63–75. doi:10.1037/0022-0167.31.1.63

Worthington, E. L., Jr. (1987). Changes in supervision as counselors and supervisors gain experience. *Professional Psychology: Research and Practice, 18,* 189–208. doi:10.1037/0735-7028.18.3.189

Worthington, R. L., Tan, J. A., & Poulin, K. (2002). Ethically questionable behaviors among supervisees: An exploratory investigation. *Ethics and Behavior, 12,* 323–351. doi:10.1207/S15327019EB1204_02

Yabusaki, A. S. (2010). Clinical supervision: Dialogues on diversity. *Training and Education in Professional Psychology, 4,* 55–61. doi:10.1037/a0017378

Yourman, D. B. (2003). Trainee disclosure in psychotherapy supervision: The impact of shame. *Journal of Clinical Psychology, 59,* 601–609. doi:10.1002/jclp.10162

Zakrzewski, R. F. (2006). A national survey of American Psychological Association student affiliates' involvement and ethical training in psychology educator-student sexual relationships. *Professional Psychology: Research and Practice, 37,* 724–730. doi:10.1037/0735-7028.37.6.724

Zarski, J. J., Sand-Pringle, C., Pannell, L., & Lindon, C. (1995). Critical issues in supervision: Marital and family violence. *The Family Journal, 3,* 18–26. doi:10.1177/1066480795031004

CHAPTER 12

A CRITICAL REVIEW OF POSITIVE PSYCHOLOGY THEORY AND RESEARCH

Christine Robitschek and Cynthia C. Spering

Counseling psychology is firmly rooted in the premise that we cannot study phenomena in isolation. Instead, it is important to understand how contextual factors have influenced and are currently influencing any phenomenon (cf. Gelso & Fretz, 2001). Therefore, to understand positive psychology theory and research from a counseling psychology perspective, it is necessary to consider the contexts in which the field developed, even if we can consider this only briefly. More complete histories can be found elsewhere (e.g., Diener, 2009; Lopez et al., 2006).

A focus on positive aspects of psychological functioning and human characteristics existed long before counseling psychology was born. It was present in ancient Greek philosophical discourse on hedonic and eudaimonic well-being (Ryan & Deci, 2001); practiced for 2,000 years by Buddhist monks who employed techniques to balance the mind, leading to well-being (Wallace & Shapiro, 2006); and is central to the traditional Navajo (Diné) way of living seeking harmony with the natural world to promote well-being and serve as a protective factor (Johnson, 2008). Within the past hundred years, positive psychology has been approached more directly. For example, Parsons (1909) focused on helping individuals to maximize the potential of their vocational functioning by developing a new method of career counseling. And Maslow (1968) described "growth and self-actualization psychology" (p. 209).

In the latter part of the 20th century, scholars focused on more specific positive aspects of the human condition. For example, scholars examined satisfaction with life (Diener, Emmons, Larsen, & Griffin, 1985), social well-being (Keyes, 1998), happiness (Lyubomirsky, 2001), and dimensions of psychological well-being (Ryff, 1989). Other scholars examined processes of positive functioning. For example, Deci and Ryan (1985) developed self-determination theory to explain the conditions through which our basic psychological needs are fulfilled, which, in turn, leads to well-being. Robitschek (1998, 1999) explored personal growth initiative, the process of intentional self-improvement. And a number of scholars, led by Tedeschi and Calhoun (1995), studied a more specific area of personal growth, identified as *posttraumatic growth*.

In an effort to unify these seemingly disparate lines of inquiry, philosophy, and culturally based prescriptive models of health, the science of positive psychology exploded on the psychological scene in the past 15 years. This largely is due to the American Psychological Association (APA) presidential initiative of Martin Seligman and the strong support of the Gallup Organization, which sponsored annual conferences for positive psychology scholars and practitioners. During these 15 years, a U.S. audience has seen the development of two journals specific to this field, the *Journal of Happiness Studies* and the *Journal of Positive Psychology*, and one international organization, the International Positive Psychology Association. Numerous relevant professional societies and international conferences have sprung up in other countries. As positive psychology continues to grow, the breadth of topics covered in this field is ever widening. For example, Seligman and

DOI: 10.1037/13754-012
APA Handbook of Counseling Psychology: Vol. 1. Theories, Research, and Methods, Nadya A. Fouad (Editor-in-Chief)

Csikszentmihalyi (2000) proposed that we examine positive psychology beyond the individual level, to include communities and institutions.

We note that counseling psychology is one of many contributing specialties within the broad field of positive psychology. Indeed, counseling psychology has played a modest role, at best, in the development of this broad field. Two main factors have contributed to our limited role. First, historically, counseling psychology scholars have published much of our research in journals specific to our field, for example, *The Counseling Psychologist* and *Journal of Counseling Psychology*. This choice has both positive and negative effects. A positive effect is that our scholarship is specifically associated with our field; thus, when scholars from other fields access our literature, they make contact explicitly with counseling psychology. A negative effect, however, is that scholars with greater familiarity in fields outside of counseling psychology may be less inclined to seek out our literature because of a lack of awareness of our field or misconceptions about it. Thus, some of our scholarship might be less well received because it is not in journals most familiar to (and, therefore, respected by) scholars outside of counseling psychology. Second, much of the positive psychology literature in our field has come from vocational psychology (Robitschek & Woodson, 2006). Given vocational psychology's historic struggle to be integrated into other areas of psychology (Robitschek & DeBell, 2002), it is no surprise that positive–vocational psychology scholarship is not yet a central part of the broad field of positive psychology.

CHAPTER GOALS

Given this extensive history and ever-growing field, the task of writing a single short chapter to evaluate positive psychology theory and research and its connection with counseling psychology was daunting. We had to be selective in what we covered and chose material to meet the following goals. First, given counseling psychology's traditional emphasis on improving the individual's well-being (Gelso & Fretz, 2001; Super, 1955), albeit the individual in context (Neufeld et al., 2006), we focus on aspects of positive psychology that share this emphasis, rather than focusing on positive institutions or communities. Second, we illustrate salient current issues in the literature with selected examples of positive psychology theory and research that emphasize the individual's well-being. And, third, we make recommendations for the future of positive psychology theory and research, addressing both counseling psychology specifically and the broader field of positive psychology.

CURRENT ISSUES IN POSITIVE PSYCHOLOGY THEORY AND RESEARCH

Most of positive psychology theory and research can be subsumed under two broad domains of well-being: hedonic and eudaimonic. *Hedonic* well-being is conceptualized as *feeling* well (Ryan & Deci, 2001). There is considerable agreement about operationalizing hedonia as happiness, life satisfaction, and positive affect (Diener et al., 1985; Fredrickson, 2001), that is, positive cognitions and affect about one's life. Some scholars, however, add low levels of negative affect to this definition (e.g., Diener, Suh, Lucas, & Smith, 1999). *Eudaimonic* well-being is conceptualized as functioning well that is, *doing* well in activities of daily life and life roles (Keyes & Annas, 2009; Ryan & Deci, 2001). This has been operationalized broadly, for example, as social (Keyes, 1998), psychological (Ryff, 1989), or vocational (Robitschek & Woodson, 2006) functioning, and narrowly, as focusing on specific functional processes such as intentional personal growth (Robitschek & Keyes, 2009).

The distinctions between hedonic and eudaimonic well-being might appear to be straightforward, but there is considerable variability in how these Greek words are translated into English and operationally defined within psychology. This issue is important to consider because failure to achieve and maintain precise operationalization and distinctions among constructs has trickle-down effects that are harmful to the science of positive psychology in several ways. First, lack of clarity in defining critical constructs threatens the validity of positive psychology theory. This, in turn, makes theoretically based research difficult to implement. Finally, when this problem leads to positive psychology research with widely inconsistent operationalization of basic constructs, it will be impossible to compare findings, including meaningful meta-analyses, or to develop new research that builds on an existing, cohesive body of research.

In the field of positive psychology, however, the importance of distinguishing between eudaimonic and hedonic well-being is not universally supported. Kashdan and colleagues (Kashdan, Biswas-Diener, & King, 2008; Kashdan & Steger, 2007) criticized this distinction, identifying (among other criticisms) a lack of conceptual clarity, particularly for eudaimonia, and conceptual and factorial overlap that might be indicative of synergistic operations between so-called hedonic and eudaimonic well-being. They cited multiple studies identifying considerable statistical overlap in measures of these two purported types of well-being, including research by proponents of the distinction (Compton, Smith, Cornish, & Qualls, 1996; Waterman, 1993). Perhaps Kashdan et al.'s (2008) strongest recommendation was the call for research on more specific aspects of well-being with clear theoretical and operational definitions on which scholars can agree. Proponents of distinguishing between these two types of well-being have responded to the charges, challenging Kashdan et al.'s descriptions of Aristotle's philosophy, linking the distinction between affect and functioning in positive psychology to similar distinctions in psychopathology, and clarifying the nature of the observed relations between hedonic and eudaimonic aspects of well-being (Keyes & Annas, 2009; Waterman, Schwartz, & Conti, 2008).

Although the distinction between these two types of well-being has been delineated by a few counseling psychologists (e.g., Lent, 2004; Robitschek & Keyes, 2009), debate regarding conceptual and operational definitions has occurred almost entirely outside of counseling psychology. We are comfortable with counseling psychology's neglect of this issue because we believe that this debate has hampered forward progress on well-being research by wasting considerable valuable resources. In two volumes of the *Journal of Positive Psychology* (Volumes 3 and 4, spanning 2008 and 2009), 9.9% (7 of 71) of the

"original" and "research" articles focused on this controversy. Is a debate about ancient Greek philosophy really worth almost 10% of a psychology journal's pages for 2 years? Our answer is no. We argue that it does not matter if the concepts of attitude, mood, and functioning map directly onto ancient Greek philosophy. If the words *hedonia* and *eudaimonia* were removed from the debate, would Kashdan et al. actually assert that mood and functioning are not importantly distinct as categories of the human experience? Considerable theory and research on mental disorders has taught us that these categories are importantly distinct, even though they often are correlated (Hirschfeld et al., 2002; Ormel, Oldehinkel, Nolen, & Volleberg, 2004).

We suggest that proponents of the distinction focus their attention on modern implications of this distinction rather than arguing about Greek philosophy as if we were inherently bound to it. It is more important to define mental health to the best of our ability in the 21st century than it is to determine Aristotle's exact meaning for *eudaimonia*. We should draw on philosophy and historical psychological theory only to the extent that these help us build our theories and clarify operational definitions of constructs.

Multidimensional Positive Psychology

Although it may appear that we have more interpretations of some constructs than we need (or can use), several research teams have attempted to identify the breadth of positive psychology individual characteristics. Research has supported two taxonomies as universal across cultures. One taxonomy was developed by the Gallup Organization (Clifton & Anderson, 2002) and consists of 34 *strengths*. For example, people with strong *woo* are good at meeting and greeting new people and establishing connections with others. People who are strong *arrangers* have high, yet balanced, levels of organization and flexibility that enable them to maximize available resources to meet demands of the situation. The second taxonomy consists of 24 *virtues* or *character strengths* (Peterson & Seligman, 2004). For example, people with strength in *bravery and valor* courageously live by their values even in the face of opposition, threat, or pain. People with strength in *perspective (wisdom)* are sought out for advice because their insights help others make sense of the world. Although it is useful to explore the breadth of positive psychological phenomena in a quest for understanding the complexity of this healthy side of the human condition, we urge caution in the development of these lists. The scientific field of positive psychology is still relatively young, particularly in the area of positive functioning (Waterman, 2008). It is premature to believe that we can grasp and sufficiently operationalize the complexity of positive human experiences. For example, neither taxonomy includes intentional personal growth as an important virtue or character strength for human beings. We would argue that the ability to recognize and act on ways to improve the self is a critical element of positive human experience across cultures, with the content of these changes heavily influenced by one's culture (Robitschek, 2003). Therefore, we recommend that positive psychology scholars continue to search for, identify, and understand the breadth and depth of positive human experiences rather than prematurely foreclosing on an already identified list of constructs.

Valence of Well-Being

Perhaps the most fundamental problem in the positive psychology literature, however, is that we have not yet agreed on concepts as basic as the *valence* of well-being (i.e., positive vs. the absence of the negative). This distinction is critically important because resolving distress does not inherently create "health." Instead, research has shown, for example, that even when treatment to alleviate depressive symptoms is successful, psychosocial functioning often remains compromised (Hirschfeld et al., 2002; Ormel et al., 2004). Furthermore, when we compare people with major depressive disorder who also have at least moderate levels of psychological, social, and emotional well-being with people who have no psychiatric disorders but have low levels of well-being, we find something interesting. In a study by Keyes (2003), the groups reported similar levels of at least one type of functioning, specifically, vocational functioning, with 2.2% to 2.5% of group members reporting missing 6 or more work days (out of the past 30 days) due to mental health concerns. These are

examples of the importance of distinguishing theoretically and empirically between the absence of psychological distress and the presence of well-being.

In too much of the literature within and outside of counseling psychology, however, this distinction is blurred. On October 31, 2010, we conducted two online literature searches of the term *psychological well-being*. Our broad search used two databases (MEDLINE and PsycINFO) and yielded more than 11,000 results. We began looking at these results with the most recent entries and quickly realized that the first 10 entries would be sufficient to illustrate our point. Thus, only the 10 most recent entries are described in this chapter, one of which was not applicable, yielding nine entries for review. Our narrow search focused exclusively on the *Journal of Counseling Psychology* (*JCP*) and yielded 28 results, two of which were not applicable. (*The Counseling Psychologist* was excluded because a similar search yielded only four results, at least three of which were not applicable, and none more recent than 1997.) The remaining 26 entries (from *JCP*) are discussed in this chapter, none of which overlap with the nine entries covered in the broad search. In total, 35 entries were reviewed for this analysis of operational definitions of *psychological well-being*.

As we would hope, in both searches psychological well-being was operationalized as a positive construct (e.g., life satisfaction) in a majority of the entries (88.5% and 60.0% of the *JCP* and broad searches, respectively). Much smaller percentages, however, operationalized psychological well-being as *only* a positive construct (53.8% and 22.2% of the *JCP* and broad searches, respectively). Large portions of the entries operationalized psychological well-being at least in part with various types of psychological distress (46.2% and 77.8% of the *JCP* and broad searches, respectively). Of greatest concern, important portions of the entries operationalized psychological well-being *exclusively* as the absence (or low level) of psychological distress (11.5% and 33.3% of the *JCP* and broad searches, respectively). A total of 26 positive constructs, 10 negative constructs, two bipolar (positive–negative) constructs, and one neutral construct were used to operationalize the term *psychological well-being*, and this breadth of operationalization is across only 35 studies.

Examples include absent or low levels of depression (e.g., David, Okazaki, & Saw, 2009; Jalmsell, Kreicbergs, Onelöv, Steineck, & Henter, 2010), anxiety (e.g., David et al., 2009; Jalmsell et al., 2010; Simonsen, Blazina, & Watkins, 2000), and somatization (Ingram, Corning, & Schmidt, 1996). Examples also include high levels of Ryff's (1989) Scales of Psychological Well-Being (e.g., Huppert, Abbott, Ploubidis, Richards, & Kuh, 2010; Iwamoto & Liu, 2010; Robitschek & Keyes, 2009); personal or collective self-esteem (e.g., Cournoyer & Mahalik, 1995; David & Okazaki, 2006; de Niet et al., 2010); satisfaction with life (e.g., Tylka, 2006); and interpersonal constructs, such as interpersonal support and capacity for intimacy (e.g., Cournoyer & Mahalik, 1995; Wright & Heppner, 1993). Making sense of results derived from these disparate operationalizations of a single construct would be difficult, if not impossible.

Given these data, it is tempting to draw the conclusion that counseling psychology may be doing better than other fields in focusing on the "positive" aspects of positive psychology constructs such as psychological well-being (when we do, in fact, focus on these constructs). But we think this would be a misguided interpretation of the data. Instead, the most important information for the field of counseling psychology is that we are still quite confused about what positive psychology is. And we are particularly unclear on the operationalization of specific constructs within positive psychology, such as psychological well-being. Although these problems are not unique to counseling psychology, we are one of few fields to claim that we "focus on people's assets and strengths, and on positive mental health, *regardless* of the degree of disturbance" (Gelso & Fretz, 2001, p. 6). Almost half of the articles published in *JCP* as of October 31, 2010, operationalize psychological well-being, at least in part, as levels of problematic functioning or distress, demonstrating considerable evidence that we are having difficulty distinguishing between Gelso and Fretz's (2001) concepts of "mental health" and "disturbance." Much effort is needed to educate the scientific communities within and outside of counseling psychology about the important qualitative distinctions between mental health and disorder. Agreeing on

the inherently positive (in contrast to the absence of negative) nature of well-being will be an important first step in moving toward clarity and cohesion in the research on positive psychology. A critically important second step will be to agree on more specific definitions of constructs.

Multicultural Issues

Although several positive psychology scholars considered the role of culture in developing theory and conducting research (e.g., Peterson & Seligman, 2004; Robitschek, 2003), to date, the concept of optimal human functioning has been largely culture bound (Lopez et al., 2002). Too frequently optimal human functioning has reflected White Euro-American values of personal control, autonomy, subjective well-being, and self-determination (Sue & Constantine, 2003). Thus, the values of collectivistic cultures, such as self-sacrifice for the group and family honor, as well as certain foci of Asian psychologies, such as enlightenment and higher consciousness, have been largely ignored in contemporary U.S. positive psychology (Sue & Constantine, 2003) but are likely key factors in understanding optimal functioning of certain minority groups in the United States and majority cultures elsewhere in the world.

In addition, struggles with difficult life circumstances, such as oppression, experienced by minority group members may lead to the development of strengths (Hanna, Talley, & Guindon, 2000), and the cultural values of people of color may serve as assets, resources, and protective factors for them (e.g., Lopez et al., 2002). For example, for adolescent African American girls, identifying with Africentric values was predictive of greater levels of perceived social support and self-esteem, which in turn led to high levels of life satisfaction (Constantine Alleyne, Wallace, & Franklin-Jackson, 2006). For African American and Asian American college women, inclusion of relationships with others within their own self-concept predicted life satisfaction (Berkel & Constantine, 2005).

In reality, optimal functioning involves different factors between groups *and* many similar elements across groups of people. Researchers from varied fields need to approach positive psychology theory and research with a complex, multicultural perspective. We recommend that all positive psychology theory and research be grounded in Sue and Sue's (2003) tripartite model of personal identity, in which each person possesses characteristics that are shared with all people, shared with only some people, and unique to the self. Some of this work already exists. Existing taxonomies of *virtues* (Peterson & Seligman, 2004) and *strengths* (Clifton & Anderson, 2002) focus on positive characteristics that are shared with *all* people. Sue and Constantine (2003) focused on positive characteristics that are shared with some people. The majority of positive psychology research, focusing on specific individual characteristics, could be said to operate at this same level of identity, although the vast majority of this research fails to mention culture or take culture into account in research design, making this statement only a conjecture. We are unaware of any positive psychology theory or research that addresses Sue and Sue's third level of identity, that is, the positive characteristics (or patterns of characteristics) that are idiosyncratic to the individual. We also are unaware of theory or research addressing the complex intersection of identity and positive psychology by simultaneously exploring the intersection of all three aspects of identity with personal strengths. Developing theory and expanding research to explain this complex reality for individual human beings would be an important contribution to positive psychology.

On a more basic level, we recommend incorporating more multicultural and person–environment perspectives into positive psychology theory and research. For example, it is critical to operationalize concepts like *happiness* within specific cultural contexts. This is in contrast to assuming that observed differences between Eastern and Western cultures in levels of happiness are real differences even though *happiness* is operationalized in explicitly Western terms (Delle Fave & Bassi, 2009). Consideration of divergent life experiences and how these experiences might differentially affect well-being also is critical to the multicultural study of positive psychology (Constantine & Sue, 2006). For example, experiences as ethnic minority or majority group members might have meaningfully different effects on the development of well-being.

The Gallup Organization, in noteworthy examples of large-scale national and international research that include cultural variables, is conducting unprecedented 100-year longitudinal studies of well-being nationwide (see http://www.well-beingindex.com/default.asp) and worldwide (for a description, see Diener, Ng, Harter, & Arora, 2010), linking these data with social, economic, and political factors. The data gathered from these projects will be useful to psychologists, governments, business leaders, and economists as we gain greater understanding of the interactions of person and environment in promoting or hindering individual and societal well-being. Although the resources needed for this type of research far exceed those available to most researchers, the Gallup Organization's work is an exemplar that can be scaled down for the resources of more typical scholars.

What Determines Who Feels and Functions Well?

The vast majority of positive psychology research has focused on defining and operationalizing feeling and functioning well and identifying typical and exceptional levels of these broad aspects of the human experience. There also has been research examining correlates of feeling and functioning well, most of which assesses outcomes or by-products of feeling and functioning well. Apart from problems operationalizing specific constructs, most of this literature is methodologically strong and readily available using computerized literature searches. Thus, our focus is on a different aspect of the literature, research identifying *who* feels and functions well and *why* they feel and function well.

Predictors and causes of feeling well. Several reviews (Argyle, 2001; Diener et al., 1999; Myers & Diener, 1995; Peterson, 2006) have summarized the research identifying who feels well. These reviews, combined with some additional research (Diener et al., 2010; Emmons, 2003; Hunter & Linn, 1980–1981; Lent, 2004; Morrow-Howell, Hinterlong, Rozario, & Fengyan, 2003; Reis & Gable, 2003; Robitschek & Keyes, 2009; Schwartz, Meisenhelder,

Ma, & Reed, 2003; Steger & Frazier, 2005), have identified predictors that can be categorized as situational, internal, and behavioral. *Situational* predictors include employment status, intimate partner status, and sufficient money for basic needs. *Internal* predictors include extraversion, genetics, self-esteem, meaning in life, optimism, personal growth initiative, physical health, and religiousness or spirituality. *Behavioral* predictors include pursuing personally meaningful and achievable goals, good relationships with other people, leisure activity, and volunteering. The literature also identifies factors that are *not* good predictors of feeling well, including age, education, gender, having more money after basic needs are met, intelligence, minority versus majority ethnicity, or physical beauty. A strength of this research has been the inclusion of diverse and broadly defined samples, for example, age and gender (e.g., Schwartz et al., 2003), ethnicity (e.g., Cacioppo et al., 2008), sexual orientation (e.g., Igreja et al., 2000), and differing abilities (e.g., Pagán-Rodríguez, 2010). Important limitations, however, are that most of this research has not considered cultural factors even when studying diverse samples, and most research has used cross-sectional, correlational methods, which do not address the causes of feeling well. Notable exceptions include the Gallup World and National Polls (see http://www.gallup.com for additional information).

The field of positive psychology has only recently begun to conduct research on the causes of feeling well (Diener et al., 1999); two examples demonstrate current directions in this area. First, within counseling psychology, Lent (2004) proposed a social–cognitive model of life satisfaction. The theory states that when we perceive environments as supporting our goals, we are likely to feel efficacious and have positive outcome expectations about those goal pursuits. In turn, we are likely to pursue goal-directed behavior, resulting in positive situational affect and satisfaction with the relevant life domain. These experiences cause spillover to overall life satisfaction. Also, our personalities and dispositions directly affect how we perceive potential support from our environment, self-efficacy expectations, and satisfaction at both the domain and global levels. Early research (e.g., Lent, do Céu Taveira, Sheu,

& Singley, 2009; Lent et al., 2005; Ojeda, Flores, & Navarro, 2011) generally supports this model across diverse college student samples (including Mexican American, European American, and Portuguese), with minor modifications to the general model. For example, there is little support for direct effects of outcome expectations on goal progress in this social–cognitive model of domain and life satisfaction. Similar research has been conducted predicting life satisfaction with the integration of social–cognitive and other factors. For example, Strachan, Brawley, Spink, and Glazebrook (2010) integrated identity theory (e.g., Stets & Burke, 2003) with social–cognitive theory to predict physical activity and life satisfaction in older adults. Wright and Perrone (2010) combined attachment theory (e.g., Bowlby, 1980) and social–cognitive career theory (Lent, Brown, & Hackett, 1994) to predict life satisfaction. These models provide multiple avenues for intervention when life satisfaction is diminished because of external or internal events (Lent, 2004). For example, family, friends, and professionals can provide a supportive environment, including specific resources. Also, multiple sources can provide assistance with the development of enhanced coping skills (Aspinwall & Taylor, 1997; Heppner, 2008) and resources to improve self-efficacy and outcome expectations. Theory development and research in this area is promising, with recent published research (Lent et al., 2009) incorporating longitudinal designs that can begin to assess causal effects. The addition of experimental designs and increased breadth of life domains are needed to determine the extent to which social–cognitive processes cause domain and life satisfaction across life roles and the life span.

Our second example is the development of interventions to enhance positive human states, which began slowly and recently has accelerated. There are positive psychotherapies that focus clients' attention on building strengths and assets and increasing the frequency of positive experiences. For example, Internet-based activities, such as expressing gratitude, identifying good things that happen each day, and using one's strengths in new ways over the course of a week, have been developed. Research conducted in the United States has shown that these activities increased happiness for up to 6 months (Seligman, Steen, Park, & Peterson, 2005). Another line of research conducted primarily in Italy has studied *well-being therapy* (Fava & Ruini, 2003), which uses cognitive–behavioral techniques to improve psychological well-being as operationalized by Ryff (1989). Clinical research on well-being therapy supports its effectiveness in use with adult clients with generalized anxiety disorder (Fava et al., 2005) and recurrent depression (Fava et al., 2004), with benefits maintained as long as 6 years. Development of interventions to help people feel well is in its infancy compared with interventions to reduce psychological distress and disorder. But most important, this work has begun and will continue to be approached with scientific rigor.

Predictors and causes of functioning well. We have less knowledge about predictors of functioning well in specific domains, and we know very little about predictors of functioning well, in general. The dearth of research in this area could, in part, be due to the difficulties discussed previously with operationalizing eudaimonic well-being. This might indicate that research on functioning well is at an earlier developmental stage than research on feeling well. Much of the research that does exist addressing predictors of functioning well can be organized into three areas: doing well at work or school, doing well after experiencing trauma (e.g., posttraumatic growth), and having high levels of mental functioning, that is, *psychological well-being* as operationalized by Ryff (1989; Ryff & Keyes, 1995). In contrast to emotional well-being, which reflects people's thoughts and feelings about their lives, psychological well-being consists of action-oriented, functional characteristics, specifically, autonomy, environmental mastery, personal growth, purpose in life, positive relations with others, and self-acceptance.

The area about which we know the most is functioning well at school or work. This is a critically important area of functioning because well-being in the work domain has important influences on well-being in other domains (Rath & Harter, 2010). For example, a person's work life often affects other areas of life, such as status, relationships, socioeconomic status, and housing, and consequently, it

appears to be a large component of life satisfaction (Eggerth, 2008). In fact, research has shown that job satisfaction accounts for 18% to 25% of the variance in life satisfaction (Near, Rice, & Hunt, 1987; Tait, Padgett, & Baldwin, 1989). Thus, scholars have argued that vocational psychology should be viewed as central to positive psychology (Eggerth, 2008; Robitschek & Woodson, 2006). Moreover, the goals of vocational psychology are often aligned with positive psychology, namely, increasing well-being and optimizing human potential (Eggerth, 2008). Vocational theories are primarily about human strengths and about utilizing those human strengths to make good decisions about careers (Robitschek, 2003; Robitschek & Woodson, 2006). Good career decisions tend to be associated with higher levels of job and life satisfaction (Robitschek, 2003). Therefore, vocational psychology gives us insight into who feels and functions well.

The many contributions of vocational psychology are well known within the field of counseling psychology. Rather than summarizing these contributions in this chapter, we direct readers to Chapters 9 and 10 of this volume and elsewhere that cover vocational psychology theory and research in depth. And we encourage readers to approach the content of these readings from the perspective of positive psychology and, specifically, the construct of *functioning well* at work or school.

An important strength *and* limitation of counseling psychology's contributions in this area has been our almost exclusive focus on benefiting the individual, with the notable exception of person–environment correspondence theory (Dawis, 2002) and its precursor the theory of work adjustment (Dawis & Lofquist, 1984). We acknowledge that the construct of functioning at work or school appears to be inherently about the individual. But some scholars, primarily outside of counseling psychology, have had a different perspective. They have addressed the interconnected relations of individual functioning with the functioning of workplaces and schools. Indeed, by directly and quantitatively addressing benefit to the organization, these positive psychologists can obtain organizational buy-in for attending to the well-being of the individual worker. Conversely, when organizations attend to individual well-being, this can increase support and commitment to the organization. Therefore, a full consideration of positive psychology as it relates to the individual necessitates some discussion of organizations and work environments.

The Gallup Organization (Buckingham & Clifton, 2001) has focused not only on the importance of identifying and using our strengths to do what we do best in our work and academic settings but also on the benefits to organizations that result from workers using their strengths. Gallup developed the Clifton StrengthsFinder and StrengthsQuest to help people identify strengths such as *activator* (i.e., the ability to take action, even when others are not ready, to evaluate the results of the action, and to learn from the process of taking action), *futuristic* (i.e., the ability to envision a specific, detailed future, and to convey that vision to others such that the vision motivates others), and *strategic* (i.e., the ability to formulate plans, identify possible obstacles, reformulate as needed, and then enact the plan). Gallup (Buckingham & Clifton, 2001) found that using our strengths in academic and work settings leads to increased satisfaction and productivity in school and work environments. As noted, we caution against assuming that the field of positive psychology has identified all possible strengths relevant to work and school environments.

Other research has examined more specific factors predicting functioning well at work. Being a mentor (Liu, Jun, Ho Kwong, & Yina, 2009); having good mentors (Valenčič Zuljan & Vogrinc, 2007); working in situations in which the stated values of the occupation match the actual tasks done by a worker (Gardner, Csikszentmihalyi, & Damon, 2001); and pursuing academic goals that one has chosen freely and that match the person's motives, values, and needs (Sheldon & Houser-Marko, 2001) also predict functioning well at work and school. It remains to be seen, however, how effectively we can predict functioning well at work or school using all existing predictors.

An important subset of the research on functioning well addresses doing so after experiencing trauma, specifically, posttraumatic growth. Although there is considerable research on this topic, only a limited amount addresses predictors of

who is likely to grow after experiencing trauma. Several reviews (Barskova & Oesterreich, 2009; Park, 1998; Tennen & Affleck, 1998) have summarized this scant literature, reporting that cognitive and self-complexity, coping processes, extraversion, hope, intrinsic religiousness or spirituality, optimism, and social support were good predictors of growing after experiencing trauma. A limitation of this literature is that the majority of it uses either retrospective or concurrent methods. Thus, we know little about the characteristics people can develop to optimize posttraumatic growth should they encounter trauma in the future.

Following a similar pattern, there has been extensive research on mental functioning, specifically psychological well-being (Ryff, 1989). But the vast majority of this research has addressed topics other than identifying the characteristics of people with high levels of psychological well-being. The limited relevant research indicates that people who are resilient (Ryff & Singer, 2003); have flexible self-concepts (Kling, Ryff, & Essex, 1997) and productive coping strategies (Kling, Seltzer, & Ryff, 1997); have high levels of personal growth initiative (Robitschek & Keyes, 2009), agreeableness, conscientiousness, and extraversion; have low levels of neuroticism and (for some types of psychological well-being) high levels of openness to experience (Schmutte & Ryff, 1997) tend to have high levels of psychological well-being. Methodological limitations such as cross-sectional, correlational designs indicate that considerably more theory and research are needed to understand the mechanisms involved in developing psychological well-being.

ALTERNATIVE APPROACHES TO POSITIVE PSYCHOLOGY THEORY AND RESEARCH

Many of the identified predictors and causes of feeling and functioning well are relatively stable factors (e.g., extraversion, genetics, and optimism). Other factors, such as employment status and physical health, are more malleable; however, after they are achieved, there is little one can do to use the factor to promote feeling and functioning well. This early focus on stable characteristics and obtainable conditions is reasonable because they are relatively straightforward to conceptualize and operationalize. However, psychological states are limited in that they are mere snapshots of human existence rather than capturing the ongoing complexity and fluidity of human experience from moment to moment, let alone across the life span. More important, the focus on psychological states and status characteristics, to the exclusion of psychological processes, limits our understanding of how these states and statuses develop. This, in turn, limits our ability to develop interventions to enhance feeling and functioning. A minority of identified predictors of feeling and functioning well represent engagement in active processes, such as good relationships, personal growth initiative, and volunteering. If individuals can learn these and other positive psychological processes, they can maximize lifelong well-being and positive functioning. The field of positive psychology can move to a greater emphasis on positive psychological processes by changing research methods and the nature of constructs that are studied.

New Research Methods

Research using experience sampling, which can assess iterative processes as they unfold over time, is an example of how research on states can be transformed into research on processes, determining whether or the extent to which these processes exist. Experience sampling assesses predictor and outcome states over extended time periods and in vivo, and then uses multilevel modeling, time-series analysis, or similar analyses to examine the iterative process over time. For example, despite robust empirical support for an association between positive affect and extraversion (Lucas & Fujita, 2000), competing models have been proposed to explain the process underlying this relation.

One type of model argues for a direct relation and the other type argues for mediation via underlying processes, such as engagement in social activities. Using experience sampling research, Lucas, Le, and Dyrenforth (2008) tested these competing models and found minimal support for underlying processes. Instead, although they found support for extraverts spending more time in social situations than did introverts, this did not account for the relation between extraversion and positive affect.

Instead, even after accounting for possible mediating effects of social activities, the direct effects of extraversion on positive affect were still significant and meaningful. This suggests that rather than underlying mediation or moderation by time spent in social situations, the process underlying the relation between extraversion and positive affect remains unknown and more research is needed to identify the mechanism(s) underlying this relation. Thus, in this example, the use of experience sampling methods was helpful in that it ruled out one of the processes believed to underlie this robust finding.

Studying Positive Processes

An example of a specific process construct contributed by counseling psychology is personal growth initiative (PGI; Robitschek, 1998), which is defined as a person's "active and intentional involvement in the self-change process" (Robitschek, 2003, p. 496). PGI contains both cognitive components, such as identifying what to change and making a plan to change, and behavioral components, such as asking for help and implementing the change (Robitschek, 1998). PGI is not domain specific and can therefore be applied across a number of situations and areas of life. PGI consists of four subdomains: readiness for change, planfulness, using resources, and intentional behavior (Robitschek et al., in press). It does not appear to be limited by age, ethnicity, or gender (Robitschek, 1998, 1999, 2003; Spering, Robitschek, & Hardin, 2010). Culture does appear to play a role, however, in determining the specific areas in which a person chooses to grow (Robitschek, 2003).

A high level of PGI appears to be beneficial to individuals in a number of ways. For example, people with high levels of PGI tend to have high levels of emotional, psychological, and social well-being and low levels of psychological distress (Robitschek & Kashubeck, 1999; Robitschek & Keyes, 2009). Individuals higher in PGI are better able to minimize self-discrepancies, which in turn results in less social anxiety (Hardin, Weigold, Nixon, & Robitschek, 2007). Older adults with high levels of PGI typically have high levels of a reflective dimension of wisdom, which is the ability to take multiple perspectives and to take responsibility for one's circumstances (Spering et al., 2010). Furthermore, PGI appears to be malleable. By teaching people about PGI and its benefits and helping them engage in a small self-change project, PGI can be increased significantly over a 1-week period (Martinez & Robitschek, 2010).

Counseling Psychology's Location in Positive Psychology

Many counseling psychologists have wondered, "Where do we fit in the broad field of positive psychology?" To answer this question, we need to realistically evaluate who we are and what we do, and what the ramifications are of the results of these inquiries for defining counseling psychology as a specialty. In doing this, we run the risk of discovering that perhaps we do not embrace positive psychology as clearly as we profess. Self-examination is inherently risky. But there is much to gain if we are courageous enough to take this risk. Specifically, in efforts to identify ourselves, many have cited Gelso and Fretz (2001) and the second unifying theme of counseling psychology, which is a "focus on people's assets and strengths, and on positive mental health, *regardless* of the degree of disturbance" (p. 6). But in our training programs, we often forget about the last phrase and teach skills from a deficit model, even while we profess the philosophy of a positive psychology (Gerstein, 2006).

There are good examples, however, of counseling psychologists who are implementing a "focus on . . . assets and strengths" (and, therefore, principles of positive psychology) even with populations with severe disturbance. For example, Morgan, Kroner, and Mills (2010) developed and are currently examining a treatment model for incarcerated offenders with severe and chronic mental disorders. The majority of the treatment model uses problem-oriented (in contrast to strengths-oriented) interventions to address such issues as problems in thinking, substance abuse, and criminal attitudes. But it is noteworthy that another aspect of the treatment model is skill development, specifically including vocational and social skills. Development of these aspects of positive functioning (i.e., vocational and social skills) is critical if offenders are going to successfully reintegrate into their communities when released from prison (Travis & Petersilia,

2001). We recommend that counseling psychology training programs become explicit in teaching the application of a positive psychology approach and the attendant skills, including applications for clients with severe pathology or distress.

Counseling psychology can move toward a goal of greater integration with the broad positive psychology community by building on our strengths. We are experts in areas such as vocational psychology, multicultural issues, and health psychology. We could do much more to expand our work in these and other areas if we take an overtly positive psychology approach. For example, counseling psychologists have contributed much research to our understanding of the positive effects of vocational interventions on well-being outside the vocational realm (Oliver & Spokane, 1988; Whiston, Sexton, & Lasoff, 1998). This work could be expanded by building theory and research on how the effects of positive work experiences might spill over into other life domains (Robitschek & Woodson, 2006). And in the arena of health psychology, we can be sure to focus on health (e.g., psychological mechanisms that promote healthy behaviors) and not fall prey to the lure of the money (both federal research and third-party payer dollars) that may seem more readily available when we focus on illness and disease. In addition, we can share our expertise regarding such topics as vocational functioning and cultural influences with the broad field of positive psychology by publishing in journals outside of counseling psychology. These can be overtly positive psychology journals, such as the *Journal of Positive Psychology* and the *Journal of Happiness Studies*, or journals in other specialty areas of psychology and medicine that publish positive psychology articles, such as the *Journal of Personality and Social Psychology*, the *Journal of Personality Assessment*, *Psychological Assessment*, and *Psychological Medicine*. This approach will enrich the broad field's understanding of positive feeling and functioning across a range of populations and life roles.

If we, as an identified specialty, are going to manifest our historic emphasis on human strengths, then we need to embrace the growing body of positive psychology theory and research to inform what we do with people in therapy, schools, families, and communities to enhance the quality of their existence. We also need to embrace the breadth of populations and the depth of human suffering of the people with whom we are working and that we are researching, and apply positive psychology principles to all of our practice and research. Only then can we train ourselves and the next generation of counseling psychologists to help *all* people, through practice and research, to recognize and build on their strengths. This would be a 21st century version of counseling psychology that would be true to our historic roots.

References

Argyle, M. (2001). *The psychology of happiness* (2nd ed.). New York, NY: Routledge.

Aspinwall, L. G., & Taylor, S. E. (1997). A stitch in time: Self-regulation and proactive coping. *Psychological Bulletin, 121*, 417–436. doi:10.1037/0033-2909-.121.3.417

Barskova, T., & Oesterreich, R. (2009). Post-traumatic growth in people living with a serious medical condition and its relations to physical and mental health: A systematic review. *Disability and Rehabilitation: An International, Multidisciplinary Journal, 31*, 1709–1733. doi:10.1080/09638280902738441

Berkel, L. A., & Constantine, M. G. (2005). Relational variables and life satisfaction in African American and Asian American college women. *Journal of College Counseling, 8*, 5–13.

Bowlby, J. (1980). *Attachment and loss: Vol. 3. Loss: Sadness and depression.* New York, NY: Basic Books.

Buckingham, M., & Clifton, D. O. (2001). *Now, discover your strengths.* New York, NY: Free Press.

Cacioppo, J. T., Hawkley, L. C., Kalil, A., Hughes, M. E., Waite, L., & Thisted, R. A. (2008). Happiness and the invisible threads of social connection: The Chicago Health, Aging, and Social Relations Study. In M. Eid & R. J. Larsen (Eds.), *The science of subjective well-being* (pp. 195–219). New York, NY: Guilford Press.

Clifton, D. O., & Anderson, E. C. (2002). *StrengthsQuest: Discover and develop your strengths in academics, career and beyond.* Washington, DC: Gallup Organization.

Compton, W. C., Smith, M. L., Cornish, K. A., & Qualls, D. L. (1996). Factor structure of mental health measures. *Journal of Personality and Social Psychology, 71*, 406–413. doi:10.1037/0022-3514.71.2.406

Constantine, M. G., Alleyne, V. L., Wallace, B. C., & Franklin-Jackson, D. C. (2006). Africentric cultural values: Their relation to positive mental health in African American adolescent girls. *Journal of Black Psychology, 32*, 141–154. doi:10.1177/0095798406286801

Constantine, M. G., & Sue, D. W. (2006). Factors contributing to optimal human functioning in people of color in the United States. *The Counseling Psychologist, 34*, 228–244. doi:10.1177/0011000005281318

Cournoyer, R. J., & Mahalik, J. R. (1995). Cross-sectional study of gender role conflict examining college-aged and middle-aged men. *Journal of Counseling Psychology, 42*, 11–19. doi:10.1037/0022-0167.42.1.11

David, E. J. R., & Okazaki, S. (2006). The Colonial Mentality Scale (CMS) for Filipino Americans: Scale construction and psychological implications. *Journal of Counseling Psychology, 53*, 241–252. doi:10.1037/0022-0167.53.2.241

David, E. J. R., Okazaki, S., & Saw, A. (2009). Bicultural self-efficacy among college students: Initial scale development and mental health correlates. *Journal of Counseling Psychology, 56*, 211–226. doi:10.1037/a0015419

Dawis, R. V. (2002). Person-environment-correspondence theory. In D. Brown (Ed.), *Career choice and development* (4th ed., pp. 427–464). San Francisco, CA: Jossey-Bass.

Dawis, R. V., & Lofquist, L. H. (1984). *A psychological theory of work adjustment.* Minneapolis: University of Minnesota Press.

Deci, E. L., & Ryan, R. M. (1985). *Intrinsic motivation and self-determination in human behavior.* New York, NY: Springer.

Delle Fave, A., & Bassi, M. (2009). The contribution of diversity to happiness research. *The Journal of Positive Psychology, 4*, 205–207. doi:10.1080/17439760902844319

de Niet, J. E., de Koning, C. M., Pastoor, H., Duivenvoorden, H. J., Valkenburg, O., Ramakers, M. J., . . . Laven, J. S. (2010). Psychological well-being and sexarche in women with polycystic ovary syndrome. *Human Reproduction, 25*, 1497–1503. doi:10.1093/humrep/deq068

Diener, E. (2009). Positive psychology: Past, present, and future. In S. J. Lopez & C. R. Snyder (Eds.), *Oxford handbook of positive psychology* (2nd ed., pp. 7–11). New York, NY: Oxford University Press.

Diener, E., Emmons, R. A., Larsen, R. J., & Griffin, S. (1985). The satisfaction with life scale. *Journal of Personality Assessment, 49*, 71–75. doi:10.1207/s15327752jpa4901_13

Diener, E., Ng, W., Harter, J., & Arora, R. (2010). Wealth and happiness across the world: Material prosperity predicts life evaluation, whereas psychosocial prosperity predicts positive feeling. *Journal of Personality and Social Psychology, 99*, 52–61. doi:10.1037/a0018066

Diener, E., Suh, E. M., Lucas, R. E., & Smith, H. L. (1999). Subjective well-being: Three decades of progress. *Psychological Bulletin, 125*, 276–302. doi:10.1037/0033-2909.125.2.276

Eggerth, D. E. (2008). From theory of work adjustment to person-environment correspondence counseling: Vocational psychology as positive psychology. *Journal of Career Assessment, 16*, 60–74. doi:10.1177/1069072707305771

Emmons, R. A. (2003). Personal goals, life meaning, and virtue: Wellsprings of a positive life. In C. L. M. Keyes & J. Haidt (Eds.), *Flourishing: Positive psychology and the life well-lived* (pp. 105–128). Washington, DC: American Psychological Association. doi:10.1037/10594-005

Fava, G. A., & Ruini, C. (2003). Development and characteristics of a well-being enhancing psychotherapeutic strategy: Well-being therapy. *Journal of Behavior Therapy and Experimental Psychiatry, 34*, 45–63. doi:10.1016/S0005-7916(03)00019-3

Fava, G. A., Ruini, C., Rafanelli, C., Finos, L., Conti, S., & Grandi, S. (2004). Six-year outcome of cognitive behavior therapy for prevention of recurrent depression. *The American Journal of Psychiatry, 161*, 1872–1876. doi:10.1176/appi.ajp.161.10.1872

Fava, G. A., Ruini, C., Rafanelli, C., Finos, L., Salmaso, L., Mangelli, L., & Sirigatti, S. (2005). Well-being therapy of generalized anxiety disorder. *Psychotherapy and Psychosomatics, 74*, 26–30. doi:10.1159/000082023

Fredrickson, B. L. (2001). The role of positive emotions in positive psychology: The broaden-and-build theory of positive emotions. *American Psychologist, 56*, 218–226. doi:10.1037/0003-066X.56.3.218

Gardner, H., Csikszentmihalyi, M., & Damon, W. (2001). *Good work: When excellence and ethics meet.* New York, NY: Basic Books.

Gelso, C., & Fretz, B. (2001). *Counseling psychology* (2nd ed.). Fort Worth, TX: Harcourt.

Gerstein, L. H. (2006). Counseling psychology's commitment to strengths: Rhetoric or reality? [Editorial Material]. *The Counseling Psychologist, 34*, 276–292. doi:10.1177/0011000005283518

Hanna, F. J., Talley, W. B., & Guindon, M. H. (2000). The power of perception: Toward a model of cultural oppression and liberation. *Journal of Counseling and Development, 78*, 430–441.

Hardin, E. E., Weigold, I. K., Nixon, A. E., & Robitschek, C. (2007). Self-discrepancy and distress: The role of personal growth initiative [Proceedings Paper]. *Journal of Counseling Psychology, 54*, 86–92. doi:10.1037/0022-0167.54.1.86

Heppner, P. P. (2008). Expanding the conceptualization and measurement of applied problem solving and coping: From stages to dimensions to the almost forgotten cultural context. *American Psychologist, 63*, 805–816. doi:10.1037/0003-066X.63.8.805

Hirschfeld, R. M. A., Dunner, D. L., Keitner, G., Klein, D. N., Koran, L. M., Kornstein, S. G., . . . Martin, B. (2002). Does psychosocial functioning improve independent of depressive symptoms: A comparison of nefazadone, psychotherapy, and their combination. *Biological Psychiatry, 51*, 123–133. doi:10.1016/S0006-3223(01)01291-4

Hunter, K. I., & Linn, M. W. (1980–1981). Psychosocial differences between elderly volunteers and non-volunteers. *The International Journal of Aging and Human Development, 12*, 205–213. doi:10.2190/0H6V-QPPP-7JK4-LR38

Huppert, F. A., Abbott, R. A., Ploubidis, G. B., Richards, M., & Kuh, D. (2010). Parental practices predict psychological well-being in midlife: Life-course associations among women in the 1946 British birth cohort. *Psychological Medicine: A Journal of Research in Psychiatry and the Allied Sciences, 40*, 1507–1518. doi:10.1017/S0033291709991978

Igreja, I., Zuroff, D. C., Koestner, R., Saltaris, C., Brouillette, M. J., & Lalonde, R. (2000). Social motives, social support, and distress in gay men differing in HIV status. *Journal of Research in Personality, 34*, 287–304. doi:10.1006/jrpe.1999.2277

Ingram, K. M., Corning, A. F., & Schmidt, L. D. (1996). The relationship of victimization experiences to psychological well-being among homeless women and low-income housed women. *Journal of Counseling Psychology, 43*, 218–227. doi:10.1037/0022-0167.43.2.218

Iwamoto, D. K., & Liu, W. M. (2010). The impact of racial identity, ethnic identity, Asian values, and race-related stress on Asian Americans and Asian international college students' psychological well-being. *Journal of Counseling Psychology, 57*, 79–91. doi:10.1037/a0017393

Jalmsell, L., Kreicbergs, U., Onelöv, E., Steineck, G., & Henter, J.-I. (2010). Anxiety is contagious-symptoms of anxiety in the terminally ill child affect long-term psychological well-being in bereaved parents. *Pediatric Blood and Cancer, 54*, 751–757.

Johnson, N. K. (2008). Dine College turns 40: Philosophy of Harmony Forms Foundation for nation's first tribal college. *Tribal College Journal of American Indian Higher Education, 19*, 34–36.

Kashdan, T. B., Biswas-Diener, R., & King, L. A. (2008). Reconsidering happiness: The costs of distinguishing between hedonics and eudaimonia. *The Journal of Positive Psychology, 3*, 219–233. doi:10.1080/17439760802303044

Kashdan, T. B., & Steger, M. F. (2007). Curiosity and pathways to well-being and meaning in life: Traits, states, and everyday behaviors. *Motivation and Emotion, 31*, 159–173. doi:10.1007/s11031-007-9068-7

Keyes, C. L. M. (1998). Social well-being. *Social Psychology Quarterly, 61*, 121–140. doi:10.2307/2787065

Keyes, C. L. M. (2003). Complete mental health: An agenda for the 21st century. In C. L. M. Keyes & J. Haidt (Eds.), *Flourishing: Positive psychology and the life well-lived* (pp. 293–312). Washington, DC: American Psychological Association. doi:10.1037/10594-013

Keyes, C. L. M., & Annas, J. (2009). Feeling good and functioning well: Distinctive concepts in ancient philosophy and contemporary science. *The Journal of Positive Psychology, 4*, 197–201. doi:10.1080/17439760902844228

Kling, C., Ryff, C. D., & Essex, M. J. (1997). Adaptive changes in the self-concept during a life transition. *Personality and Social Psychology Bulletin, 23*, 981–990. doi:10.1177/0146167297239008

Kling, K. C., Seltzer, M. M., & Ryff, C. D. (1997). Distinctive late-life challenges: Implications for coping and well-being. *Psychology and Aging, 12*, 288–295. doi:10.1037/0882-7974.12.2.288

Lent, R. W. (2004). Toward a unifying theoretical and practical perspective on well-being and psychosocial adjustment. *Journal of Counseling Psychology, 51*, 482–509. doi:10.1037/0022-0167.51.4.482

Lent, R. W., Brown, S. D., & Hackett, G. (1994). Toward a unifying social cognitive theory of career and academic interest, choice, and performance. *Journal of Vocational Behavior, 45*, 79–122. doi:10.1006/jvbe.1994.1027

Lent, R. W., do Céu Taveira, M., Sheu, H. B., & Singley, D. (2009). Social cognitive predictors of academic adjustment and life satisfaction in Portuguese college students: A longitudinal analysis. *Journal of Vocational Behavior, 74*, 190–198. doi:10.1016/j.jvb.2008.12.006

Lent, R. W., Singley, D., Sheu, H. B., Gainor, K. A., Brenner, B. R., Treistman, D., & Ades, L. (2005). Social cognitive predictors of domain and life satisfaction: Exploring the theoretical precursors of subjective well-being. *Journal of Counseling Psychology, 52*, 429–442. doi:10.1037/0022-0167.52.3.429

Liu, D., Jun, L., Ho Kwong, K., & Yina, M. (2009). What can I gain as a mentor? The effect of mentoring on the job performance and social status of mentors in China. *Journal of Occupational and Organizational Psychology, 82*, 871–895. doi:10.1348/096317908X380664

Lopez, S. J., Magyar-Moe, J. L., Petersen, S. E., Ryder, J. A., Krieshok, T. S., O'Byrne, K. K., . . . Fry, N. A. (2006). Counseling psychology's focus on positive aspects of human functioning. *The Counseling Psychologist, 34*, 205–227. doi:10.1177/0011000005283393

Lopez, S. J., Prosser, E. C., Edwards, L. M., Magyar-Moe, J. L., Neufeld, J. E., & Rasmussen, H. N. (2002). Putting positive psychology in a multicultural context. In C. R. Snyder & S. J. Lopez (Eds.), *Handbook of positive psychology* (pp. 700–714). New York, NY: Oxford University Press.

Lucas, R. E., & Fujita, F. (2000). Factors influencing the relation between extraversion and pleasant affect. *Journal of Personality and Social Psychology, 79*, 1039–1056. doi:10.1037/0022-3514.79.6.1039

Lucas, R. E., Le, K., & Dyrenforth, P. S. (2008). Explaining the extraversion/positive affect relation: Sociability cannot account for extraverts' greater happiness. *Journal of Personality, 76*, 385–414. doi:10.1111/j.1467-6494.2008.00490.x

Lyubomirsky, S. (2001). Why are some people happier than others? The role of cognitive and motivational processes in well-being. *American Psychologist, 56*, 239–249. doi:10.1037/0003-066X.56.3.239

Martinez, M. A., & Robitschek, C. (2010, August). *Increasing personal growth initiative through education and growth activity.* Paper presented at the 118th Annual Convention of the American Psychological Association, San Diego, CA.

Maslow, A. H. (1968). *Toward a psychology of being* (2nd ed.). New York, NY: Wiley.

Morgan, R. D., Kroner, D. G., & Mills, J. F. (2010). *Treating the mentally disordered offender: A model and guide for empirically supported practice.* Manuscript in preparation.

Morrow-Howell, N., Hinterlong, J., Rozario, P. A., & Fengyan, T. (2003). Effects of volunteering on the well-being of older adults. *The Journals of Gerontology: Series B. Psychological Sciences and Social Sciences, 58*, S137–S147. doi:10.1093/geronb/58.3.S137

Myers, D. G., & Diener, E. (1995). Who is happy? *Psychological Science, 6*, 10–19.

Near, J. P., Rice, R. W., & Hunt, R. G. (1987). Job satisfaction and life satisfaction: A profile analysis. *Social Indicators Research, 19*, 383–401. doi:10.1007/BF00300728

Neufeld, J. E., Rasmussen, H. N., Lopez, S. J., Ryder, J. A., Magyar-Moe, J. L., Ford, A. I., . . . Bouwkamp, J. C.

(2006). The engagement model of person-environment interaction. *The Counseling Psychologist, 34,* 245–259. doi:10.1177/0011000005281319

Ojeda, L., Flores, L. Y., & Navarro, R. L. (2011). Social cognitive predictors of Mexican American college students' academic and life satisfaction. *Journal of Counseling Psychology, 58,* 61–71. doi:10.1037/a0021687

Oliver, L. W., & Spokane, A. R. (1988). Career-intervention outcome: What contributes to client gain? *Journal of Counseling Psychology, 35,* 447–462. doi:10.1037/0022-0167.35.4.447

Ormel, J., Oldehinkel, A. J., Nolen, W. A., & Volleberg, W. (2004). Psychosocial disability before, during, and after a major depressive episode: A 3-wave population based study of state, scar and trait effects. *Archives of General Psychiatry, 61,* 387–392. doi:10.1001/archpsyc.61.4.387

Pagán-Rodríguez, R. (2010). Onset of disability and life satisfaction: Evidence from the German socio-economic panel. *The European Journal of Health Economics, 11,* 471–485. doi:10.1007/s10198-009-0184-z

Park, C. L. (1998). Implications of posttraumatic growth for individuals. In R. E. Tedeschi, C. L. Park, & L. G. Calhoun (Eds.), *Posttraumatic growth: Positive changes in the aftermath of crisis* (pp. 153–178). Mahwah, NJ: Erlbaum.

Parsons, F. (1909). *Choosing a vocation.* Boston, MA: Houghton Mifflin.

Peterson, C. (2006). *A primer in positive psychology.* New York, NY: Oxford University Press.

Peterson, C., & Seligman, M. E. P. (2004). *Character strengths and virtues: A handbook and classification.* Washington, DC: American Psychological Association.

Rath, T., & Harter, J. (2010). *Wellbeing: The five essential elements.* New York, NY: Gallup Press.

Reis, H. T., & Gable, S. L. (2003). Toward a positive psychology of relationships. In C. L. M. Keyes & J. Haidt (Eds.), *Flourishing: Positive psychology and the life well-lived* (pp. 129–159). Washington, DC: American Psychological Association. doi:10.1037/10594-006

Robitschek, C. (1998). Personal growth initiative: The construct and its measure. *Measurement and Evaluation in Counseling and Development, 30,* 183–198.

Robitschek, C. (1999). Further validation of the personal growth initiative scale. *Measurement and Evaluation in Counseling and Development, 31,* 197–210.

Robitschek, C. (2003). Validity of Personal Growth Initiative Scale scores with a Mexican American college student population. *Journal of Counseling Psychology, 50,* 496–502. doi:10.1037/0022-0167.50.4.496

Robitschek, C., Ashton, M., Spering, C. C., Geiger, N., Byers, D., Shotts, G. C., & Thoen, M. (in press). Development and psychometric properties of the Personal Growth Initiative Scale–II. *Journal of Counseling Psychology.*

Robitschek, C., & DeBell, C. (2002). The reintegration of vocational psychology and counseling psychology: Training issues for a paradigm shift. *The Counseling Psychologist, 30,* 801–814. doi:10.1177/001100002237755

Robitschek, C., & Kashubeck, S. (1999). A structural model of parental alcoholism, family functioning, and psychological health: The mediating effects of hardiness and personal growth orientation. *Journal of Counseling Psychology, 46,* 159–172. doi:10.1037/0022-0167.46.2.159

Robitschek, C., & Keyes, C. L. M. (2009). Keyes' model of mental health with personal growth initiative as a parsimonious predictor. *Journal of Counseling Psychology, 56,* 321–329. doi:10.1037/a0013954

Robitschek, C., & Woodson, S. J. (2006). Vocational psychology: Using one of counseling psychology's strengths to foster human strength. *The Counseling Psychologist, 34,* 260–275. doi:10.1177/0011000005281321

Ryan, R. M., & Deci, E. L. (2001). On happiness and human potentials: A review of research on hedonic and eudaimonic well-being. *Annual Review of Psychology, 52,* 141–166. doi:10.1146/annurev.psych.52.1.141

Ryff, C. D. (1989). Happiness is everything, or is it? Explorations on the meaning of psychological well-being. *Journal of Personality and Social Psychology, 57,* 1069–1081. doi:10.1037/0022-3514.57.6.1069

Ryff, C. D., & Keyes, C. L. (1995). The structure of psychological well-being revisited. *Journal of Personality and Social Psychology, 69,* 719–727. doi:10.1037/0022-3514.69.4.719

Ryff, C. D., & Singer, B. (2003). Flourishing under fire: Resilience as a prototype of challenged thriving. In C. L. M. Keyes & J. Haidt (Eds.), *Flourishing: Positive psychology and the life well-lived* (pp. 15–36). Washington, DC: American Psychological Association. doi:10.1037/10594-001

Schmutte, P. S., & Ryff, C. D. (1997). Personality and well-being: Reexamining methods and meanings. *Journal of Personality and Social Psychology, 73,* 549–559. doi:10.1037/0022-3514.73.3.549

Schwartz, C., Meisenhelder, J. B., Ma, Y., & Reed, G. (2003). Altruistic social interest behaviors are associated with better mental health. *Psychosomatic Medicine, 65,* 778–785. doi:10.1097/01.PSY.0000079378.39062.D4

Seligman, M. E. P., & Csikszentmihalyi, M. (2000). Positive psychology: An introduction. *American Psychologist, 55*, 5–14. doi:10.1037/0003-066X.55.1.5

Seligman, M. E. P., Steen, T. A., Park, N., & Peterson, C. (2005). Positive psychology progress: Empirical validation of interventions. *American Psychologist, 60*, 410–421. doi:10.1037/0003-066X.60.5.410

Sheldon, K. M., & Houser-Marko, L. (2001). Self-concordance, goal attainment, and the pursuit of happiness: Can there be an upward spiral? *Journal of Personality and Social Psychology, 80*, 152–165. doi:10.1037/0022-3514.80.1.152

Simonsen, G., Blazina, C., & Watkins, C. E., Jr. (2000). Gender role conflict and psychological well-being among gay men. *Journal of Counseling Psychology, 47*, 85–89. doi:10.1037/0022-0167.47.1.85

Spering, C. S., Robitschek, C., & Hardin, E. E. (2010). *Validity of the Personal Growth Initiative Scale in older adults.* Manuscript in preparation.

Steger, M. F., & Frazier, P. (2005). Meaning in life: One link in the chain from religiousness to well-being. *Journal of Counseling Psychology, 52*, 574–582. doi:10.1037/0022-0167.52.4.574

Stets, J. E., & Burke, P. J. (2003). A sociological approach to self and identity. In M. R. Leary & J. P. Tangney (Eds.), *Handbook of self and identity* (pp. 128–152). New York, NY: Guilford Press.

Strachan, S. M., Brawley, L. R., Spink, K., & Glazebrook, K. (2010). Older adults' physically-active identity: Relationships between social cognitions, physical activity and satisfaction with life. *Psychology of Sport and Exercise, 11*, 114–121. doi:10.1016/j.psychsport.2009.09.002

Sue, D. W., & Constantine, M. G. (2003). Optimal human functioning in people of color in the United States. In W. B. Walsh (Ed.), *Counseling psychology and optimal human functioning* (pp. 151–169). Mahwah, NJ: Erlbaum.

Sue, D. W., & Sue, D. (2003). *Counseling the culturally diverse* (4th ed.). Hoboken, NJ: Wiley.

Super, D. E. (1955). Transition: From vocational guidance to counseling psychology. *Journal of Counseling Psychology, 2*, 3–9. doi:10.1037/h0041630

Tait, M., Padgett, M. Y., & Baldwin, T. T. (1989). Job and life satisfaction: A reevaluation of the strength of the relationship and gender effects as a function of the date of the study. *Journal of Applied Psychology, 74*, 502–507. doi:10.1037/0021-9010.74.3.502

Tedeschi, R. G., & Calhoun, L. G. (1995). *Trauma and transformation: Growing in the aftermath of suffering.* Thousand Oaks, CA: Sage.

Tennen, H., & Affleck, G. (1998). Personality and transformation in the face of adversity. In R. G. Tedeschi, C. L. Park, & L. G. Calhoun (Eds.), *Posttraumatic growth: Positive changes in the aftermath of crisis* (pp. 65–98). Mahwah, NJ: Erlbaum.

Travis, J., & Petersilia, J. (2001). Reentry reconsidered: A new look at an old question. *Crime and Delinquency, 47*, 291–313. doi:10.1177/0011128701047003001

Tylka, T. L. (2006). Development and psychometric evaluation of a measure of intuitive eating. *Journal of Counseling Psychology, 53*, 226–240. doi:10.1037/0022-0167.53.2.226

Valenčič Zuljan, M., & Vogrinc, J. (2007). A mentor's aid in developing the competences of teacher trainees. *Educational Studies, 33*, 373–384. doi:10.1080/03055690701423473

Wallace, B. A., & Shapiro, S. L. (2006). Mental balance and well-being: Building bridges between Buddhism and Western psychology. *American Psychologist, 61*, 690–701. doi:10.1037/0003-066X.61.7.690

Waterman, A. S. (1993). Two conceptions of happiness: Contrasts of personal expressiveness (eudaimonia) and hedonic enjoyment. *Journal of Personality and Social Psychology, 64*, 678–691. doi:10.1037/0022-3514.64.4.678

Waterman, A. S. (2008). Reconsidering happiness: A eudaimonist's perspective. *The Journal of Positive Psychology, 3*, 234–252. doi:10.1080/17439760802303002

Waterman, A. S., Schwartz, S. J., & Conti, R. (2008). The implications of two conceptions of happiness (hedonic enjoyment and eudaimonia) for the understanding of intrinsic motivation. *Journal of Happiness Studies, 9*, 41–79. doi:10.1007/s10902-006-9020-7

Whiston, S. C., Sexton, T. L., & Lasoff, D. L. (1998). Career-intervention outcome: A replication and extension of Oliver and Spokane (1988). *Journal of Counseling Psychology, 45*, 150–165. doi:10.1037/0022-0167.45.2.150

Wright, D. M., & Heppner, P. P. (1993). Examining the well-being of nonclinical college students: Is knowledge of the presence of parental alcoholism useful? *Journal of Counseling Psychology, 40*, 324–334. doi:10.1037/0022-0167.40.3.324

Wright, S. L., & Perrone, K. M. (2010). An examination of the role of attachment and efficacy in life satisfaction. *The Counseling Psychologist, 38*, 796–823. doi:10.1177/0011000009359204

PREVENTION IN COUNSELING PSYCHOLOGY: PROMOTING EDUCATION, HEALTH, AND WELL-BEING ACROSS THE LIFE CYCLE

John L. Romano, Julie Koch, and Y. Joel Wong

Prevention has a rich history dating from early years of recorded time. Beliefs and attitudes about preventing illness and natural disasters, and improving the quality of life have been passed down through generations across geographic regions and diverse cultures (Schmolling, Youkeles, & Burger, 1997). Many prevention beliefs are rooted in folklore, for example, "an apple a day keeps the doctor away." In more recent history, research-supported prevention messages have been delivered through an array of institutions across a myriad of topics, dispensing information about how to live healthy and satisfying lives by stopping certain behaviors and starting others.

Prevention is best addressed throughout the life cycle, from initiatives to improve prenatal care (Taylor, Klein, & Hack, 2000) to those that focus on elder care (Goetzel et al., 2007). This chapter reviews several theories and perspectives that inform prevention science and summarize three areas of prevention applications: promoting academic achievement and reducing academic disparities in K–12 settings, preventing racism and racial prejudice, and preventing suicide-related outcomes. Each of these prevention applications has emerged in recent years as important to counseling psychology.

Although people agree that prevention of problem behaviors and the promotion of health-enhancing behaviors are beneficial, certain aspects of the field have been debated in the scientific community. Some of these debates are highlighted in the chapter, including the following: (a) How is prevention defined? (b) What theoretical models or perspectives best inform prevention science? (c) How efficacious are prevention interventions? We begin with a brief history of prevention in counseling psychology.

HISTORY

The history of counseling psychology has been well documented (e.g., Heppner, Casas, Carter, & Stone, 2000; Whiteley, 1984), as has the history of prevention (Conyne, 2004; Cowen, 1996; Romano & Hage, 2000). Therefore, a general history of prevention will not be reviewed. With respect to the history of prevention in counseling psychology, however, it is important to recall that counseling psychology traces its roots to several social justice reforms of the early 20th century, including the vocational guidance, mental hygiene, and social welfare movements (Addams, 1930; Beers, 1908; Parsons, 1909; Richmond, 1922). Early 20th-century reformers advocated for a society that promoted physical, social, and emotional well-being; a society that maximized vocational and career opportunities; and a society that supported social justice for all. Within the context of prevention science, these are important goals. Counseling psychology has maintained these legacies through scientific and applied applications, for example, emphasizing strengths rather than deficits and facilitating life transitions. Therefore, the history of counseling psychology is well aligned with the goals and objectives of prevention science. Despite this legacy, however, some have been

The second and third authors of this chapter are listed alphabetically, contributing equally to the chapter.

DOI: 10.1037/13754-013
APA Handbook of Counseling Psychology: Vol. 1. Theories, Research, and Methods, Nadya A. Fouad (Editor-in-Chief)

critical about counseling psychology's commitment to prevention (Krumboltz, Becker-Haven, & Burnett, 1979; Whiteley, 1984). As such, until more recently, counseling psychology cannot be considered a "trailblazer" among professions promoting and advancing the science and practice of prevention during the 20th century.

A renewed commitment to prevention gained considerable momentum during the early 1990s when American Psychological Association (APA) Division 17 (Society of Counseling Psychology) encouraged members to develop Special Interest Groups (SIG) around themes and areas of practice and research. As a result, the Prevention and Public Interest SIG was organized, and in 2000, the Prevention Section was approved by Division 17. The section was formally called "Prevention: A Section of the Division of Counseling Psychology of the American Psychological Association" ("public interest" was dropped from the official name of the section but remains an important component of the section's mission). As a section, prevention was given greater visibility within Division 17, including guaranteed program time at APA conventions. Allotment of convention program time was important because, historically, prevention scholars in counseling psychology lamented the lack of attention given to prevention in counseling psychology. One specific example was an APA Division 17 convention program proposal on prevention, which despite positive comments by all three reviewers, was rejected because it was deemed of little interest to counseling psychologists (McWhirter, 1993).

During the past 10 years, members of the Prevention Section along with other prevention scholars have forged ahead with annual APA convention programs and scholarly publications (e.g., Conyne, 2010; Kenny, Horne, Orpinas, & Reese, 2009; Reese & Vera, 2007; Romano & Hage, 2000). In her 2001 presidential address, Nadya Fouad encouraged counseling psychologists to embrace prevention science (Fouad, 2002).

A set of Prevention Best Practice Guidelines for Psychologists was first published in *The Counseling Psychologist* (Hage, Romano, Conyne, Kenny, Matthews, et al., 2007). Since then, these guidelines have been revised and currently are under review by APA

committees and boards, with the goal of eventual adoption by the APA Council of Representatives.

The growth of prevention science within counseling psychology parallels the increased visibility and importance of prevention science across many psychological specialties as well throughout the United States and abroad. For example, prevention was highlighted at the 2009 APA Presidential Summit on the Future of Psychology Practice (Martin, 2009) and prevention is emphasized in U.S. health care reforms (see http://www.healthreform.gov). Globally, prevention is emphasized through major international organizations such as the World Health Organization and the United Nations.

Prevention programs and services are delivered in many contexts, including schools (e.g., curricula that teach children about diversity and respect of others), college campuses (e.g., National Depression Screening Day), communities (e.g., psychoeducation groups for women diagnosed with breast cancer), and health care centers (e.g., prevention media messages about healthy lifestyles).

PREVENTION DEFINED

It is important to describe how the definition of prevention has evolved over the past 50 years, especially with respect to scholarship in counseling psychology. The classic definition was popularized by Gerald Caplan (1964) who defined prevention in terms of primary, secondary, and tertiary prevention. Primary prevention is recommended for everyone and reduces the number of new cases of a problem (e.g., flu shots, adolescent pregnancy prevention programs); secondary prevention targets those most at risk or those who show early signs of a problem (e.g., academic tutoring for low-achieving students); and tertiary prevention reduces the impact of an existing condition (e.g., physical exercise for stroke victims).

Although Caplan's (1964) definition was originally conceptualized for the prevention of physical problems and is still widely cited, Romano and Hage (2000) argued that it is difficult to categorize all prevention activities within Caplan's framework. Romano and Hage reasoned that psychological and lifestyle behavior problems do not have easily identified etiologies and, in many settings in which prevention is practiced, such as schools, it is not practical to deliver prevention programs only to those who are at risk for a problem because the at-risk population may be difficult to identify. Romano and Hage also noted that Caplan's definition does not address the promotion of positive behaviors and personal strengths that serve as protections against problems. Furthermore, Caplan's definition does not address the importance of laws (e.g., teenage curfews) and institutional policies (e.g., smoking bans, healthy cafeteria food) that reduce problems and promote healthy behaviors.

Romano and Hage (2000) broadened the definition of prevention to include interventions and activities that are designed to (a) prevent problems from ever occurring; (b) prevent problems with at-risk groups; (c) reduce the impact of an existing problem; (d) promote positive characteristics, strengths, and assets to protect against problem behaviors; and (e) promote public policy and legislative actions to enhance health and well-being systemically across different contexts. Romano and Hage's definition of prevention expands on other definitions of prevention that have a more narrow focus (e.g., Gordon, 1987; Mrazek & Haggerty, 1994). Although protective factors have been added as an important component of prevention by a national government panel of experts, the importance of systemic change in the name of prevention is still lacking (O'Connell, Boat, & Warner, 2009). Romano and Hage's prevention definition is supported by scholarship that focuses on positive human functioning and the promotion of social justice to enhance psychological health and well-being (Lopez & Edwards, 2008; Speight & Vera, 2008).

THEORIES AND PERSPECTIVES THAT INFORM PREVENTION SCIENCE

To facilitate the development of prevention science, it is important that new generations of psychologists receive prevention training, including education about prevention perspectives, theories, research, and applications (Eddy, Smith, Brown, & Reid, 2005). Too often, applied psychology graduate students receive limited exposure to prevention, as

psychopathology and remediation orientations are emphasized, and more balance between prevention and remediation perspectives are needed (Snyder & Elliott, 2005). Areas needing more attentions include theories and perspectives useful in prevention science.

O'Connell et al. (2009) defined prevention research as "the study of the theory and practice related to the prevention of social, physical, and mental health problems, including etiology, epidemiology, and intervention" (p. xxvii). This definition by the Committee on Prevention of Mental Disorders and Substance Abuse (under the auspices of the National Research Council and Institute of Health) recognizes the importance of theory, although the committee does not address prevention theory specifically. Prevention interventions anchored in theory are more likely to provide insight into reasons for the effectiveness, or lack thereof, of an intervention, thus advancing prevention science.

It is beyond the scope of this chapter to provide a summary of all the theories and perspectives that may inform prevention research and practice. Therefore, we focus on four theories and perspectives that have informed prevention science in recent years. These frameworks were selected for specific reasons: (a) They address theoretical constructs important to prevention science, (b) they receive limited exposure in applied psychology graduate programs, (c) they offer examples of empirically based interventions on topics important to counseling psychologists, and (d) they emphasize theoretical perspectives that are strongly associated with counseling psychology. Two theories—the transtheoretical model of change (TTM) and the theory of reasoned action and planned behavior (TRA/PB)—are summarized, followed by two broader conceptualizations that have informed prevention science in recent years: social justice and positive psychology.

Transtheoretical Model of Change

The TTM is a stage-based theory that is widely used to understand the processes of behavioral change (Hoffman & Driscoll, 2000; Painter, Borba, Hynes, Mays, & Glanz, 2008). TTM theorists hypothesize that behavioral change occurs through a series of six stages, although advancement through the stages is not necessarily linear (Prochaska, Johnson, & Lee, 2009). People may be stuck in one stage for a time and may need to revisit an earlier stage to move forward. Because prevention science revolves around behavioral changes to prevent problems or to protect against problems, TTM is well designed to support areas of prevention research and applications important to counseling psychologists. The six TTM stages are described in the following paragraphs.

Precontemplation.   Individuals are not planning to make changes in the near future, usually within the next 6 months. People are not aware that changes are needed and they do not understand the consequences of not making changes. Individuals may avoid thinking about or discussing change and are not motivated to change. Prevention messages are designed to increase awareness and create motivation to change. For example, multicultural scholars have underscored the challenge of antiracism efforts because many people do not view themselves as being capable of perpetuating racism (Sue et al., 2007) or may view racism as a problem that lies outside the scope of their responsibilities (Smith, Constantine, Graham, & Dize, 2008). Accordingly, antiracism prevention messages can help people become aware of their own racist behavior and attitudes and increase their motivation to change.

Contemplation.   In this stage people recognize the benefits of change, and they intend to make changes within the next 6 months. However, they are also aware of disadvantages that may cause them to delay taking action. Prochaska et al. (2009) indicated that people may remain in this stage for long periods as they assess the advantages and disadvantages of change. New Year's resolutions might fall within this stage, as people recognize the need to change but do not follow through. When designing prevention interventions, it is important to balance the positives and negatives that people face with respect to change, appreciating that advantages of existing behaviors may outweigh benefits (at least initially) of new behaviors. For example, strengthening student motivation to engage in school through extracurricula activities may reduce school absences.

Preparation.   People are intending to take action and make changes, usually within 1 month. They have already made some movement toward change, such as joining a fitness center, reading self-help books, or discussing change with a professional and friends. People in this stage are motivated to change. Prevention interventions designed to change behaviors are likely to be most successful if implemented during this stage.

Action.   People have made behavioral changes, usually within the past 6 months. It is easier to measure many physical health related changes in this stage compared with mental health related behaviors. For example, it is easier to measure the amount of physical exercise each week, compared with changes to improve self-esteem.

Maintenance.   The goal of this stage is to prevent relapse. Prochaska et al. (2009) estimated that the maintenance stage can be active from 6 months to 5 years, especially with addictive behaviors. People often remain in the maintenance stage indefinitely (e.g., lifetime commitment to healthy nutrition and physical exercise). Maintaining a lifelong commitment to new behaviors usually requires supportive environments to maintain the behaviors. For example, prevention applications with children and adolescents are most successful if the applications are periodically repeated to booster and reinforce the maintenance of new behaviors.

Termination.   This stage is reached when individuals are convinced that they will not revert to previous behavior and do not need to monitor themselves with respect to the behavior. Practically, this stage is unrealistic for many behavioral changes. In terms of prevention, it is more realistic to consider individuals in the maintenance stage once new a behavior has been established.

TTM offers many applications within the prevention intervention spectrum. Although the largest number of intervention studies have applied TTM to cigarette smoking (Prochaska et al., 2009), TTM also serves as a theoretical framework in other prevention applications, including bullying prevention (Prochaska et al., 2007), stress management (Evers et al., 2006), domestic violence (Levesque, Driskell,

Prochaska, & Prochaska, 2008), and HIV/AIDS prevention (Prochaska et al., 2009). TTM has also been applied to clients in counseling and therapy situations (Koraleski & Larson, 1997; Satterfield, Buelow, Lyddon, & Johnson, 1995; Smith, Subich, & Kalodner, 1995).

Critics of TTM have found methodological flaws in TTM-based studies and limited support for the stages of change (Bridle et al., 2005; van Sluijs, van Poppel, & van Mechelen, 2004). Although continued research may help to refine the theory, TTM is useful to explain how people make changes and to serve as foundation to behavioral interventions. From a prevention perspective, TTM is an attractive theory because it focuses on people's readiness to engage in change, a critical component of prevention work. TTM reminds us that the success of a prevention intervention depends on how closely the intervention is aligned with readiness for change.

Theory of Reasoned Action and Planned Behavior

The TRA was first introduced by Fishbein (1967) to explain the relationship between attitudes and behaviors (Fishbein & Ajzen, 1975). The theory has been used extensively in medicine, public health, and social psychology research to explain motivational factors that drive behavior. The theory has received less attention in applied fields of psychology, including counseling psychology (Romano & Netland, 2008). The theory is based on cognitive principles that are useful in prevention research as it considers attitudes and beliefs about subjective (social) norms and perceived control to initiate new behaviors.

TRA maintains that behavior is a function of behavioral intention, and behavioral intention is related to a person's attitude about a behavior and the subjective norms related to that behavior. Subjective norms refer to the opinions that others, important to the person, have about the behavior. Attitudes and subjective norms can vary tremendously across behaviors and population groups, and therefore, attitudes and subjective norms are important to consider when designing prevention interventions (Romano & Netland, 2008).

The theory of planned behavior (TPB) was added as an extension of TRA by Ajzen (1991) to predict intentions and subsequent behavior when the desired behavior is not completely under the perceived control of the individual. Perceived behavioral control (PBC) was added as a variable that can affect behavioral intentions. PBC can be either internal or external to the person and may be influenced by factors such as self-control beliefs, financial resources, and personal skills. Examples include persons who are restricted from engaging in a behavior (e.g., condom use) because of religious or cultural traditions, or perceived lack of control because of a lack of time to engage in a new behavior (e.g., physical exercise). If PBC is low, intentions to carry out a behavior is also low, thus affecting the desired behavior change strategy. Another example based on this framework is that students who perceive minimal control over academic success and career options may enroll in fewer college preparatory courses and thus limit their postsecondary school options.

One unique contribution of TRA/PB is elicitation research that can identify attitudes, subjective norms, and perceived control of a group that is targeted for a prevention intervention (Ajzen, 2006). Elicitation research provides information about important variables before developing an intervention so that the intervention can take into account salient variables and then tailor the intervention to address those variables. Elicitation research is especially important for interventions with groups for which there is limited knowledge about the attitudes, norms, and perceived control related to the target of behavior change. For example, before embarking on a prevention intervention with a group that includes newly immigrated international students in a junior high school, it behooves the prevention specialist to conduct elicitation research with students to identify important variables before attempting a behavior change application. As another example, before designing an intervention to strengthen school achievement, it is important to conduct elicitation research with boys and girls to identify the most salient variables that will motivate each group to improve academic achievement. Conducting elicitation research before an intervention is a reminder that one-size-fits-all prevention interventions will likely have limited success.

TRA/PB has been used across a large number of problem domains in the health sciences and social psychology (Armitage & Connor, 2001; Cooke & Sheeran, 2004; Montaño & Kasprzyk, 2002; Sutton, 1998). More recently, the theory has been applied in areas of counseling and education. Vogel, Wester, Wei, and Boysen (2005) used TRA/PB to investigate college student intentions to seek counseling services. The study found that positive social norms affected attitudes and intentions to seek counseling. The authors recommended that counseling centers strengthen the social norms associated with seeking counseling to reduce sigma associated with services, especially among students less familiar with them.

In a high school setting, TRA/PB-supported research identified factors that contributed to African American students remaining in high school (Davis, Ajzen, Saunders, & Williams, 2002). The study of African American students examined the TRA/PB variables of attitudes, social norms, and perceived behavioral control on predictors of completing the current academic year and achieving high school graduation. The results showed that intentions to complete the academic year were predicted by attitudes (e.g., short- and long-term consequences), social norms (e.g., expectations of family, friends, and teachers), and perceived behavioral control (e.g., academic skills, school conflicts, and life conditions). Intentions also predicted graduation nearly 3 years later, as did perceived control but to a lesser extent.

TRA/PB can also be applied to other prevention areas that are of interest to counseling psychologists. For instance, there is a need to increase psychological help seeking among suicidal individuals because research has demonstrated that the majority of people who die by suicide did not seek mental health treatment in the preceding 12 months (Luoma, Martin, & Pearson, 2002). In this regard, TRA/PB can be used to identify variables related to help seeking among suicidal individuals.

TRA/PB offers a useful framework for prevention work. Elicitation research provides a process to assess the most salient attitudes, norms, and perceived behavioral control of a group or subgroup that is to receive the intervention. Because prevention interventions are ultimately designed to change

behavior and not only attitudes, however, it is important that longitudinal studies be conducted (e.g., Davis et al., 2002) to thoroughly evaluate the efficacy of TRA/PB to support and maintain behavioral change.

Social Justice Perspective

A social justice perspective with respect to prevention is unlike the previous theories as it is not a theory in the traditional use of the word. The importance of social justice as prevention is important, however, especially to counseling psychology, which has a rich history promoting social justice (Vera, Buhin, & Isacco, 2009). A social justice perspective refers to changing structures of society to eliminate or reduce conditions that negatively influence physical and mental health and that limit possibilities for human development and optimal health. Citing Bell (1997), Speight and Vera (2008) defined the goal of social justice as

> full and equal participation of all groups in a society that is mutually shaped to meet their needs. Social justice includes a vision of society in which the distribution of resources is equitable and all members are physically and psychologically safe and secure. (Bell, 1997, p. 3)

In this context, a social justice perspective refers to the reduction and elimination of societal conditions such as discrimination, neglect, and poverty that are barriers to personal development and full participation in society.

A social justice perspective with respect to prevention considers how societal conditions negatively affect people because poverty, powerlessness, and discrimination are major contributors to problems (Liu & Ali, 2008; U.S. Department of Health and Human Services, 2001). Although legislative actions reduce the impact of negative societal conditions (e.g., laws against discrimination and child abuse), stress and exploitation can also be reduced on smaller scales, such as through schools to promote safe and nurturing environments and in industrial work setting that vigorously enforce employee safety. At individual levels, stress management and wellness skills can be taught as preventive measures, although the overall impact of treating people individually is much lower compared with the macro approaches that effect change across large social systems.

Early 20th century social activists advocated for social reforms to empower and enhance people's lives. In the latter half of the 20th century, George Albee became a major advocate for social justice and used his APA presidency to promote social activism in psychology (Albee, 1986, 2003). Albee was posthumously honored in 2006 with a special award by the Prevention Section of the Society of the Society of Counseling Psychology for his exemplary leadership and historic contributions to prevention and social justice.

Albee's (1986) social justice perspective is focused on themes that address toxic social conditions that create psychological distress and trauma. He has argued that psychology has taken the wrong path with its emphasis on remedial treatments and crisis interventions, writing that no illness has ever been treated out of existence, and prevention is the only way to reduce the incidence of disorders (Albee, 2000). Albee was also critical of psychiatry, government entities, and pharmaceutical companies that place a heavy emphasis on the biological bases of mental disorders, arguing that this emphasis benefits the more powerful and affluent members of society (Albee, 2005; Albee & Joffe, 2004). In Albee's ideal world, nothing short of revolution across many areas of society are needed to reduce the incidence of mental disorders. Societal injustices create human distress and misery and must be replaced by a just society that promotes equality, opportunity, and empowerment (Albee, 1986).

Albee's leadership has encouraged others to carry the social justice as prevention mantle forward (e.g., Kenny et al., 2009; Nelson & Prilleltensky, 2005; Prilleltensky, 2001; Reese & Vera, 2007). Prilleltensky (2001) wrote about "value-based praxis" (p. 747), which promotes the value of social justice and supports collective wellness rather than individual wellness. Like Albee, Prilleltensky expressed the belief that social justice requires changes in the social order, which are difficult to achieve because powerful interests receive benefits from the status quo.

He also acknowledged differences within any population with respect to the value that members of a society place on social justice and social activism. Prilleltensky took the position that the common good underlies collective wellness because a healthy community benefits everyone in the community; similarly, an unhealthy community will negatively affect all members of the community.

Scholars have integrated prevention, social justice, and multiculturalism, especially their importance in implementing culturally competent prevention in ethnic communities (Reese & Vera, 2007; Vera & Speight, 2003). Reese and Vera (2007) recommended that prevention specialists have knowledge of the community in which they work, deliver prevention programs that are valued by the community, and include community members in all phases of a project. Culturally sensitive prevention programs to strengthen personal and academic effectiveness with multiethnic urban youth have been described by Vera et al. (2007) and Rivera-Mosquera, Phillips, Castelino, Martin, and Dobran (2007).

The value of social justice as fundamental to prevention may be debated as people have different values about social activism and advocacy for causes. A social justice perspective must be considered as a viable option to anchor prevention advocacy and practices at the micro and macro levels of society to enhance health and well-being, and to reduce education and health disparities across the population.

Positive Psychology Perspective

Positive psychology has enjoyed immense popularity over the past 15 years. Snyder and Lopez (2007) defined positive psychology as the "scientific and applied approach to uncovering people's strengths and promoting their positive functioning" (p. 3). Positive psychology includes the study of human dimensions such as hope, wisdom, happiness, altruism, courage, and love. Although attention to these attributes has existed throughout history, the recent explosion of psychological study related to positive human characteristics is impressive (Seligman, Steen, Park, & Peterson, 2005). One goal of positive psychology is to bring more balance to psychology, giving increased attention to human assets and strengths while not abandoning the more traditional study of deficits and problems (Seligman & Csikszentmihalyi, 2000).

Positive psychology is strongly associated with prevention (Seligman & Csikszentmihalyi, 2000). Prevention addresses not only the prevention of negative behaviors but also the promotion of positive characteristics that serve as protections from negative emotions and life events. Protective factors, such as resiliency, positive social networks, children supported by caring adults, optimism, hope, and work satisfaction, are important across the life span.

Although the study of concepts under the umbrella of positive psychology has enjoyed a popular resurgence, Donald Clifton, a professor of educational psychology at the University of Nebraska, began his study of positive characteristics of people in the 1950s (Snyder & Lopez, 2007). Clifton was awarded a special commendation by the APA in 2002, honoring him as the Father of Strengths-Based Psychology.

To give structure to a positive psychology framework, several classifications of human strengths and assets will be discussed for readers who may want to apply them for clinical and research purposes. Early on, Clifton and his colleagues developed the classification of human strengths called the Strengths-Finder (Snyder & Lopez, 2007). StrengthsFinder is a web-based inventory that identifies a person's strengths and their relationship to career success. StrengthsFinder is available in adult and youth versions (http://www.strengths.gallup.com). The StrengthsQuest program, and its promotion of student strengths, has been used in career counseling at a number of U.S. colleges.

Another classification, developed by Peterson and Seligman (2004), is called the *character strengths and virtues* (CSV) or *values in action* (VIA; Peterson & Park, 2009). Examples of the six virtues and 24 character strengths that make up the VIA include (a) wisdom and knowledge with character strengths of creativity and curiosity, (b) courage with strengths of authenticity and bravery, and (c) justice with strengths of fairness and leadership. Ongoing study to develop a measure of character strengths has yielded several iterations of the measure called VIA survey of character (or VIA inventory of strengths; see http://www.viacharacter.org; Peterson & Park,

2009; Snyder & Lopez, 2007). Adult and youth versions of VIA are available (Seligman et al., 2005).

The Search Institute in Minneapolis, Minnesota (http://www.search-institute.org) has been a leader in developing a schema of developmental assets of children and adolescents. On the basis of more than 20 years of research, youth assets are important for healthy development and serve as protections against risk behaviors (Benson, 1993). Assets are both external and internal to the person, 20 in each category. Examples of internal assets include motivation and self-esteem, and examples of external assets include positive use of leisure time and supportive environments (Snyder & Lopez, 2007).

Positive psychology offers a viable framework for prevention through the promotion of human strengths, assets, and protective factors. Concepts related to optimal human functioning have been applied to diverse areas, such as the importance of hope in the vocational development of urban youth (Diemer & Blustein, 2007), strengths-based counseling to enhance personal and academic development (Galassi & Akos, 2007; Smith, 2006), assessment of client strengths in clinical settings (Tedeschi & Kilmer, 2005), and employee psychological well-being (Avey, Luthans, Smith, & Palmer, 2010).

Positive psychology enhances prevention research and applications because it offers ways to conceptualize and assess the promotion of human assets, psychological strengths, and protections from risky behaviors (Lopez & Edwards, 2008). A positive psychology perspective has not escaped criticism. For instance, some scholars have cautioned that positive psychological constructs such as well-being and strengths are culture bound and that there is danger that psychologists might pathologize behaviors that do not conform to Western notions of optimal functioning (Constantine & Sue, 2006; Wong, 2006). Accordingly, when using a positive psychology framework, prevention psychologists should critically examine the cultural relevance of strengths and well-being that they endorse in diverse communities.

PREVENTION APPLICATIONS

A special issue of *The Counseling Psychologist* called on the field to "walk the talk" (Hage, Romano,

Conyne, Kenny, Schwartz, & Waldo, 2007). In the spirit of this call to action, examples of prevention applications are highlighted in this chapter. Although any number of applications could be discussed, the applications for this chapter were selected because they represent expertise of the authors, and the topics are increasingly important to counseling psychology in the United States and abroad.

Promoting Academic Success

The promotion of academic achievement in K–12 settings and the reduction of education disparities are highlighted in this section. These topics are extremely important to schools, communities, and the larger society. Quality education supports the social justice perspective that all students deserve the best possible education regardless of socioeconomic status or ethnicity. Applied psychology has an important role to play in supporting and enhancing the very best education opportunities for all youth.

Promoting academic achievement requires prevention efforts that target a number of areas. The achievement gap (sometimes referred to as the *opportunity gap*, see Volume 2, Chapter 2, this handbook) refers to the disparities of academic performance across students from different demographic groups (e.g., boys and girls, urban and suburban, wealthy and impoverished, White and non-White). The achievement gap has been observed in several areas, including student differences in school attendance and grades, enrollment in advanced courses, students who qualify for special education services, standardized test scores, and high school graduate rates (Holcomb-McCoy, 2007). Although the causes of educational disparities are debated, they have been shown to be related to several school components, such as rigor of the curriculum, teacher preparation and experience, teacher attendance, class size, use of technology-assisted instruction, and school safety (Holcomb-McCoy, 2007). Nonschool factors have also been found to be associated with the achievement gap, such as parent involvement and availability, the amount of student mobility, student birthweight, exposure to lead poisoning, poor nutrition and hunger, number of household adults reading to children, and time watching television (Barton, 2003). As protective factors, research has examined concepts from positive psychology, such as students' hopes for the future and school engagement, as contributors to education achievement and school completion rates (Destin & Oyserman, 2010; Kenny, Walsh-Blair, Blustein, Bempachat, & Seltzer, 2010; Kortering & Christenson, 2009; Snyder et al., 2002). Given the number of factors that influence academic achievement, how might schools best promote academic achievement in all students, especially during years of reduced funding for public education?

A number of programs have addressed academic achievement generally (e.g., increasing graduation rates, grade point average [GPA], standardized test scores), some with greater success than others. White and Kelly (2010), in their review of dropout prevention programs, found several strategies that contributed to a decrease in high school dropout rates. The first strategy includes increasing student protective factors such as social support, enhancing positive student monitoring and mentoring, developing student personal and social skills, encouraging parental involvement, and strengthening academic instruction. Examples of student social support include peer mentoring and buddy systems in which socially and academically skilled students coach academically at-risk students. Community-based monitoring and mentoring programs assign volunteer adult community members to at-risk students or to their families to reinforce academic achievement. Developing student personal skills includes strategies that target specific life skills, such as time management and coping with stressful events. Parent involvement programs offer parent training, such as how best to support student reading at home, and match parents with a school partner, such as a staff member. The second strategy addresses academic risk factors, for example, strengthening academic instruction through teacher supports such as the use of paraprofessionals, enhancing teacher skills through regular in-service training, and offering student academic support programs that include after school tutoring and study-skills training. White and Kelly noted that although these strategies have been shown to yield short-term positive results, longitudinal research is needed to assess their long-term impact on school dropout rates.

Klima, Miller, and Nunlist (2009) conducted a meta-analysis of truancy and dropout programs in middle and high schools. They found that only about 10% of the studies were rigorous enough to evaluate because only 22 of 200 studies met their qualifications for rigor. Methodological flaws included lack of a control or comparison group, students not randomly assigned, high attrition rates, and insufficient quantifiable outcome measures. Klima et al. found, however, that some programs specifically targeting student truancy and dropouts had small positive effects on attendance and graduation rates. These programs include those that offer academic remediation and tutoring, career and technical education, case management, contingency management (reward and punishment systems), counseling, mentoring and advocacy, attendance monitoring, and parent outreach. Alternative education programs (i.e., programs with small class sizes, individual instruction, and varied instructional methods) within a traditional school setting were most effective in improving student attendance, achievement, and graduation while also decreasing school dropouts. Student mentoring programs positively affected graduation rates and school attendance, as did behavioral programs that specifically targeted academic behaviors. Programs that did not have a positive effect on attendance, dropouts, achievement, or graduation rates were youth development programs that fostered resilience and competence, academic remediation, and separate alternative schools for alternative-only students. In fact, students enrolled in these alternative schools had higher dropout rates than students in traditional schools (Klima et al., 2009). The reasons are unclear and the authors recommended further research. Students in alternative schools, however, are often more at risk for dropping out to start with, and interventions may not have been sufficiently powerful to keep students in school. Prevatt and Kelly (2003) reviewed intervention programs that addressed dropouts. They utilized Kratochwill and Stoiber's (2000) criteria for empirically supported outcomes, including the use of control–comparison groups and random assignment. Prevatt and Kelly

found few studies, however, that met these criteria. For example, they found only three studies that included random assignment to groups. They concluded that because of a lack of studies that meet criteria for empirically based interventions, there is not one set of best practices or guidelines to prevent school dropouts. They stated that the most promising programs were academically oriented (i.e., focused on academic skills) or had multiple components (e.g., academic achievement and emotional and social skills training).

In addition to promoting academic achievement directly, other prevention applications in education settings have a long history, partly because of available students as well as the beliefs that preventing socioemotional problems, such as alcohol and drug use, will improve academic performance. As identified, school-based prevention programs have increasingly used positive psychology and social justice perspectives to support prevention applications in schools. These include programs that promote character education and prosocial behavior (DeRosier, 2004), career counseling (Lapan, Gysbers, & Petroski, 2001), academic achievement (Bemak, Chung, & Siroskey-Sabdo, 2005; Cohen, Garcia, Apfel, & Master, 2006; Sink & Stroh, 2003), bullying prevention (Black & Jackson, 2007; Espelage & Swearer, 2003; Newman-Carlson & Horne, 2004), conflict resolution (Stevahn, Johnson, Johnson, & Schultz, 2002), suicide prevention (LaFromboise & Howard-Pitney, 1995), and positive school climates (McKown, 2005).

Overall, research in the area of academic achievement has not addressed a number of student and family variables, such as socioeconomic status; geographic region; and differences among urban, suburban, and rural settings. Most research has focused on race and GPA. There is much need for more empirical research on programs that promote academic success and positive career aspirations of all children. More information is needed, for example, to address the low number of girls who take advanced placement math and science courses compared with boys and the low number of White children identified to receive special education services compared with African American children (in some states, as much as 4 times the rate of Whites;

Holcomb-McCoy, 2007). Although the literature is lacking in longitudinal studies, more worrisome is the lack of rigor. Klima et al. (2009) and Prevatt and Kelly (2003) pointed out that few studies related to promotion of academic achievement include control–comparison groups, random assignment of subjects, or specific measurable outcomes.

Example of an application.   One study that addressed academic achievement differences between African American and European American students was conducted by Cohen, Garcia, Apfel, and Master (2006), with follow-up 2 years later (Cohen, Garcia, Purdie-Vaughns, Apfel, & Brzustoski, 2009). The authors hypothesized that African American students who persistently receive messages that they will not achieve at the same levels as their European American peers may have difficulty actually performing because of stereotype pressures and psychological threat. The researchers took a social justice preventive approach by using a self-affirmation intervention designed to heighten African American students' self-worth to investigate its effect on academic achievement.

Cohen et al. (2006) conducted two randomized double-blind field experiments in one middle school. Participants were randomly assigned to either the treatment–affirmation condition or the control condition. The treatment group received an assignment that asked students to reflect on their values. For example, treatment students were asked to write a paragraph about their most important values and why they were important to them. The control students were given a neutral writing exercise (e.g., write about your morning routine).

Cohen et al. (2006) found that African American students in the treatment–affirmation group received higher grades than those in the control group. Overall GPA of the African American treatment group were 0.26 grade points higher in the first year and 0.34 higher in the second year (i.e., the replication study). No academic treatment effects for GPA were found for European American students. The authors also investigated differences between initially low-performing students and initially moderate- and high- performing African American students. The treatment effect was equally strong for low and moderately performing students. The treatment effect was lower (but still significant) for initially higher performing students. The authors reported that these effects transferred to all course areas for treatment condition students, whereas European American students experienced no effect in treatment or control conditions.

The authors concluded that the intervention acted as a buffer for African American students against a downward trend in academic achievement. Although the intervention was small and subtle, even a small increase in academic achievement may have reaffirmed African American students' perceptions of their own abilities and possibly their teachers' perceptions of their abilities, and this affirmed a goal-directed future. The authors stated that this intervention is unique because it targets students most in need while not adversely affecting students who do not receive the intervention.

In a follow-up study, the authors found that the values-affirmative writing exercise closed the achievement gap not only narrowly in the short term but also across four core academic subjects over 2 years. Strengths of this study include the simplicity of the intervention and its promise that the achievement gap between African American and European American students can be addressed successfully. Limitations of this study include its short-term nature and its study of only two racial groups. Further research is needed to explore how to maintain academic achievement beyond the 2 years examined in this study. It would be important to examine how an intervention such as this one could affect other racial or ethnic groups and other student demographics. It also may be useful to consider the variables of social norms, attitudes, and perceived behavioral control (as described in the TRA/PB) and their importance in academic achievement and dropout prevention research.

Prevention of Racism and Racial Prejudice

Racism is a pervasive and oppressive influence in U.S. society and around the world. The deleterious effects of racism on people of color have been well documented by previous research. They include physical and mental health problems (Jackson et al., 1996), poorer academic performance (Cohen

& Steele, 2002), and reduced employment opportunities (Brief, Dietz, Cohen, Pugh, & Vaslow, 2000). Moreover, racism and its negative consequences are manifested in a variety of ways, including individual racism (e.g., brief and subtle interpersonal exchanges that denigrate people of color), institutional racism (e.g., organizational hiring practices that discriminate against people of color), and cultural racism (e.g., cultural norms that emphasize White superiority; Jones, 2002; Sue et al., 2007).

The prevention of racism fits well with the identity of counseling psychology because of its longstanding commitment to multicultural competence (Arredondo, Toporek, Brown, & Jones, 1996; Sue, 2001) and social justice (Vera & Speight, 2003). Counseling psychologists have produced cutting-edge scholarship on racism (e.g., Ridley, 2005; Sue et al., 2007; Utsey & Ponterotto, 1996). These efforts, however, have not included developing and evaluating antiracist preventive interventions in noncounseling settings. Although remedial counseling interventions can empower clients to identify and resist racism, an overemphasis on such interventions may communicate an implicit message that help is justified only after racism has taken its toll (Prilleltensky, 1997). Accordingly, the focus of this application is on preventive interventions of racism in noncounseling settings. Such interventions are congruent with social justice perspectives that locate psychological distress as a consequence of individuals and systems that engender oppression and inequity (Buhin & Vera, 2009; Kenny & Hage, 2009).

Before proceeding, a distinction needs to be made between racism and racial prejudice. Whereas *racism* is defined as "a behavior or pattern of behavior that tends to systematically deny access to opportunities or privileges to members of one racial group" (Ridley, 2005, p. 29), *racial prejudice* refers to negative attitudes toward members of a racial group. Put another way, racial prejudice does not necessarily involve behavior toward members of a racial group. This distinction is important because the overwhelming majority of antiracist preventive interventions focus on preventing racial prejudice rather than on preventing racism.

It is beyond the scope of this chapter to provide a comprehensive review of racism and racial prejudice preventive interventions; instead, we focus on two promising social psychological approaches that have received empirical support from field experimental studies: intergroup contact and the use of social norms. The first approach is premised on intergroup contact. Allport's (1954) contact hypothesis has been one of the most frequently used theoretical basis for racial prejudice and racism preventive interventions. Allport hypothesized that environments that facilitate contact between members of an in-group (e.g., White Americans) and an out-group (e.g., African Americans) result in the reduction of prejudice. Specifically, prejudice is theorized to be reduced under the following optimal conditions: (a) equal status of both groups, (b) shared goals, (c) cooperation rather than competition, and (d) support from institutions or people in authority. Numerous studies have been conducted to test Allport's contact hypothesis. Pettigrew and Tropp's (2008) meta-analysis of 515 studies provided evidence that greater intergroup contact tended to be related to lower levels of intergroup prejudice (mean effect of $r = -.21$).

Closely related to Allport's (1954) contact hypothesis is the concept of cooperative learning (Johnson & Johnson, 1989). This approach to learning involves creating lessons in which students teach and learn from each other. For instance, to promote cooperative learning, a teacher might give each student a portion of the lesson plan, so that successful learning requires students to teach each other their respective portions of the lesson plan. Cooperative learning has been widely applied in school settings. Several studies have shown that this form of learning increased children's engagement in cross-racial friendships (McKown, 2005). Few studies, however, have demonstrated the long-term effects of cooperative learning or its generalizability beyond the specific groups or classrooms to which participants belonged (Paluck & Green, 2009).

The second approach to racism preventive interventions focuses on social norms. Defined as socially shared rules about how people behave and ought to behave, social norms may have an important impact on the reduction of prejudice (Crandall & Stangor,

2005). In one study of Australian secondary school students, the authors found that intergroup contact with Muslims was linked to reduced social distance to Muslims generally and that this association was partially mediated by students' perceived social norms, that is, perceived parental approval of their contact with Muslims (Ata, Bastian, & Lusher, 2009). Antiracist interventions that utilize social norms convey the message that people are engaged in racially inclusive behaviors and that people disapprove of racism. In this regard, the media has been identified as a powerful tool for conveying such social norms. For instance, Paluck and Green (2009) reviewed 17 field experiments on the impact of reading interventions on reducing prejudice among school children. Examples of stories in the interventions include narratives about people of color or about cross-racial friendships. Eleven of these field experiments produced positive results on the basis of self-reported attitudinal outcomes. Perhaps stories are powerful means of communicating social norms about racism because readers are "transported into a narrative world" in which they identify with characters in the stories and they become open to new truths about themselves and the world embedded in those stories (Green, Brock, & Kaufman, 2004, p. 317). Because most media experiments have been conducted in schools, few studies have evaluated the effects of large-scale media campaigns on large audiences (e.g., the effects of radio, television, and Internet programs on a community; Paluck & Green, 2009). Future research should examine the effectiveness of large-scale media campaigns. In this regard, TTM (Prochaska et al., 2009) can be used to identify the most appropriate types of antiracist media campaigns for groups of individuals at different stages of motivation to change their racist attitudes.

The use of social norms in the previous example resembles the variable of subjective norms in TRA/PB to predict behavioral intention. Despite this similarity, we are not aware of any published empirical study that has applied TRA/PB to racism preventive interventions. One potential benefit of TRA/PB is that it may offer a more comprehensive model for developing racism preventive interventions than the more narrow social norms approach. In addition to

social norms, researchers and prevention professionals can address other components of TRA/PB, such as changing individuals' attitudes and perceived behavioral control regarding racism and race relations.

Overall, the body of research on the prevention of racial prejudice and racism is characterized by several limitations. First, antiracist research has largely focused on reducing racial prejudice rather than on racism. In addition, most preventive interventions are evaluated immediately after their conclusion and their long-term effectiveness is unknown. In one study that evaluated the effectiveness of an intervention to improve elementary school children's attitudes toward refugees, the program led to more positive attitudes toward refugees in the short term (1 week posttest) but not longer (7 weeks posttest; Turner & Brown, 2008). In light of these limitations, future studies should focus on the long-term impact of preventive interventions on racism (Paluck & Green, 2009).

Second, despite the proliferation of antiracist preventive interventions (e.g., corporate diversity training programs), many of these interventions are not theoretically grounded (Paluck & Green, 2009). We encourage researchers to draw from diverse theoretical paradigms to develop and evaluate innovative antiracist interventions. For example, drawing from positive psychology and social justice perspectives, interventions can be developed to identify strengths among racially oppressed groups. Such interventions can focus on helping people of color develop positive racial identities and racially critical consciousness as buffers against the pernicious effects of racism (e.g., Watts, Abdul-Adil, & Pratt, 2002). Additionally, TTM and TRA/PB can be applied to identify the most salient variables affecting individuals' willingness to change their racist behaviors and to participate in antiracist training programs (Wiethoff, 2005). In the following section, a mass media preventive intervention that used a social norms approach to reduce racial prejudice in the country of Rwanda is described.

Example of an application.   Paluck (2009) reported the findings of a year-long field experiment that tested the influence of a radio soap opera on intergroup prejudice. The study took place in the African country of Rwanda, where interracial conflict between the Tutsis and Hutus resulted in a genocide that killed hundreds of thousands of people in 1994. Interracial hostilities between the Tutsis and Hutus remained long after the conclusion of the genocide. We focus on this international example because it is a powerful illustration of how a social norms mass media intervention can help reduce deeply entrenched racial prejudice.

Rwandan communities consisting of 480 participants were randomly assigned to listen to one of two radio programs: a reconciliation radio soap opera or an education health soap opera aimed at changing health behavior (the control group). The reconciliation radio soap opera featured a fictional story about two Rwandan communities' struggles with prejudice and violence, an experience that paralleled the history of conflict between the Tutsis and Hutus. The scriptwriters wove into the story educational messages about the sources of intergroup prejudice and violence and the importance of intergroup reconciliation. For example, the program's characters delivered these messages didactically to other characters. Furthermore, the story involved a boy and girl from two different communities who successfully pursue their love for each other despite disapproval from their communities. By portraying the characters as typical Rwandans, the reconciliation radio program aimed to alter listeners' perceptions of social norms. Through focus groups and individual interviews, the authors found that the reconciliation radio program group's perceptions of social norms and behavior changed with regard to some of the critical issues in postconflict Rwanda, such as intermarriage and empathy for other Rwandans. For instance, those exposed to the reconciliation program were more likely to object to prescriptions to marry within one's own group. The strength of this study includes the use of a field experiment; that is, the study combined a randomized controlled design with a real-world intervention in a naturalistic setting. Nonetheless, one limitation of the study is that long-term behavioral changes among participants were not evaluated. Measuring other variables from TRA/PB in addition to social norms may strengthen intervention similar to this one.

Prevention of Suicide-Related Outcomes

In 2006, 33,300 people died by suicide in the United States; put another way, there was an average of 91.2 suicides each day (American Association of Suicidology [AAS], 2009). It is also estimated that for every completed suicide, there are six people who are intimately affected (AAS, 2009). Because of its irreversible nature, suicide inflicts immense emotional pain on suicide survivors. In addition to completed suicides, other suicide-related outcomes (SRO), such as suicide ideation, plans, gestures, and attempts are critical in their own right as indicators of severe psychological distress (Kessler, Berglund, Borges, Nock, & Wang, 2005). Moreover, these and other SRO tend to be more prevalent than completed suicides; one nationally representative study of 9,708 English-speaking adults in the United States found that 3.3% of the sample reported experiencing suicide ideation in the past 12 months (Kessler et al., 2005). Collectively, these findings suggest that SRO are a serious public health problem.

Although it is important to address SRO in clinical settings, it has been estimated that 68% of individuals who die by suicide did not seek mental health treatment in the preceding 12 months (Luoma et al., 2002). Hence, it is imperative that SRO prevention programs encompass a broad range of strategies in addition to counseling and crisis interventions. In line with this notion, the main focus of this application is on the prevention of SRO in noncounseling settings. Such interventions include primary prevention interventions directed toward the population at large or community and secondary prevention interventions aimed at specific groups of individuals who have been identified as high risk for suicide (Joiner, Van Orden, Witte, & Rudd, 2009; Westefeld, Range, Rogers, & Hill, 2008).

Primary prevention efforts include interventions to reduce risk factors and strengthen protective factors associated with SRO. The literature on suicidology, however, tends to emphasize risk factors instead of protective factors (Wingate et al., 2006). Wingate et al. proposed a positive psychological approach to suicide prevention that examines the strengths of people who suffer from multiple suicide risk factors but who, nevertheless, do not engage in SRO. Accordingly, positive psychology prevention interventions focus on enhancing protective factors that buffer the development of SRO. A few SRO prevention interventions have adopted such a strength-based perspective (Davis et al., 2009; Muehlenkamp, Marrone, Gray, & Brown, 2009). For instance, LaFromboise and Howard-Pitney (1995) reported that Zuni adolescents who participated in a school-based, culturally informed curriculum that emphasized the development of life skills (e.g., building self-esteem and problem-solving skills) reported lower levels of suicide probability than a no-intervention control group.

In terms of limitations, research on primary prevention interventions has largely neglected the role of systemic oppressive risk factors implicated in SRO. There is growing scholarly recognition as well as empirical evidence that SRO are associated with oppressive forces, such as racism (Wong & Poon, 2010), poverty (Bernburg, Thorlindsson, & Sigfusdottir, 2009), sexual orientation victimization (Rutter, 2008), and sexual assault victimization (Bryant-Davis, Chung, & Tillman, 2009). In line with social justice perspectives, we recommend that prevention interventions seek to eliminate sources of oppression and inequities (e.g., racism, poverty, and homophobia) that contribute to SRO. For instance, fostering a racially inclusive climate for college students of color on campus is not only consistent with the goals of multiculturalism but also may help undo interpersonal risk factors associated with SROs among students of color (Wong, Koo, Tran, Chiu, & Mok, 2011). Additionally, resources for SRO primary prevention efforts have not always been equitably distributed. Previous SRO primary prevention efforts have focused heavily on adolescents, young adults, and elderly White men (Hu, Wilcox, Wissow, & Baker, 2008). Despite the fact that Asian American women have the highest rate of suicide among women age 65 and above from the major U.S. racial and ethnic groups (U.S. Department of Health and Human Services, 2007), there has been no known evidence-based SRO preventive intervention designed for this population. It is important that more primary prevention resources be directed toward serving communities that have been neglected by previous SRO primary prevention applications and research.

SRO secondary prevention efforts identify and target individuals who are believed to be at risk for suicidal behavior. For instance, in the context of school-based SRO prevention, screening (e.g., through the completion of questionnaires on suicidal behavior) has been proposed as a useful strategy to identify students at risk for SRO (Scott et al., 2009). Such efforts are based on the assumption that many students may be reluctant to reveal information about their suicidality to others, especially in a face-to-face context. A recent study by Scott et al. (2009) highlighted the clinical importance of suicidality screening in schools, as 34% of students with serious mental health problems were identified by screening alone and not by school professionals. One limitation of screening and other efforts to identify at-risk students is that they do not guarantee that identified students would receive follow-up services. Kataoka, Stein, Lieberman, and Wong (2003) found racial disparities in a school-based suicide prevention program, as the prevention program underidentified Latino students who were at high risk for suicide for follow-up services compared with Caucasian students.

In terms of future directions, secondary prevention efforts should include theory-based interventions directed at reducing risk factors among individuals who are at high risk for suicide (Rogers & Lester, 2009). In a study of patients who were admitted to a hospital for parasuicidal behavior, O'Connor, Armitage, and Gray (2006) found that several variables in TRA/PB predicted suicidal thoughts and behavior 3 months later. For example, affective attitude toward deliberate self-harm and self-efficacy in the ability to deliberately harm oneself predicted subsequent suicidal thoughts and behavior. Nevertheless, TRA/PB has yet to be used in research on SRO prevention interventions. In addition to TRA/PB, TTM can also serve as a theoretical basis for the prevention of SROs. In one study, Coombs et al. (2002) applied TTM to explain suicidal behavior among 42 patients who had been hospitalized for suicide ideation or attempts. The authors found that in progressing from an absence of suicide ideation to suicide ideation or suicide attempts, most patients moved through the stages of change predicted by TTM. In addition, all but one change process defined by TTM were used by more than half the sample and were associated with specific stages of change. The authors suggested that future studies investigate whether knowledge of a person's stage of change can be used to create personalized suicidal behavior preventive interventions. The following illustration presents an SRO prevention program that was successful in reducing the number of suicide gestures and attempts among adolescents and young adults in an American Indian reservation.

Example of an application. May, Serna, Hurt, and DeBruyn (2005) evaluated the effectiveness of a 15-year suicidal behavior prevention program among adolescents and young adults in an American Indian tribe located in a New Mexican reservation. In 1988, the tribe had suicide death and attempt rates that were 15 times higher than the national rate and five times higher than the rates for other New Mexico American Indians. Beginning in 1989, the researchers developed a comprehensive, population-based public health strategy for preventing SRO in the tribe. The program focused mainly on 10- to 19-year-olds, a population identified by previous research as being most at risk for suicidal behavior. Suicide education and awareness interventions for young adults in the 20- to 24-year-old age-group were added to the project 5 years later. Although not explicitly discussed, the program had a social justice orientation because of its recognition that suicide cannot be divorced from systemic, oppressive forces, such as unemployment, child abuse, and domestic violence (Smith, Chambers, & Bratini, 2009). The researchers also collaborated with local community members. For example, instead of simply imposing an expert-designed suicidal behavior prevention program on the tribe, the researchers solicited feedback and participation from key constituents of the tribe (e.g., tribal elders, parents, and adolescents) in the development and implementation of the program.

The suicidal behavior prevention program that was created incorporated a comprehensive range of interventions such as (a) outreach to conventional institutions (e.g., health clinics and schools) and unconventional settings (e.g., outdoor venues where alcohol abusers often congregate); (b) school-based prevention programs that focus on life skills;

(c) community education for adults and adolescents; and (d) partnerships between mental health professionals and neighborhood volunteers to provide clinical services in unconventional, nonstigmatizing settings (e.g., outdoors and in cars). After analyzing data from 1988 to 2002, the researchers reported that the annual mean number of self-destructive acts (i.e., suicide gestures, attempts, and completions) dropped from 36 to 14 (61.1%). Further analyses revealed a significant decrease in suicide gestures and attempts but no significant decrease in suicide deaths. A key strength of this study was the use of a long-term, population-based approach to preventing suicidal behavior. One troubling result of the prevention program, however, was that the rate of suicide deaths in the tribe did not decrease during the period in which the program was implemented. Unfortunately, the program did not reach those most at risk for suicide, despite its culturally sensitive and multifaceted design. Further study of systemic social problems across the community that were not addressed by the prevention program may help to explain the number of suicides during the period of the study.

RECOMMENDATIONS

The chapter has summarized literature relevant to prevention science, including history, theories, and applications in areas important to counseling psychology. On the basis of the material presented, the following recommendations are offered to further prevention science in counseling psychology.

■ Advancement of prevention science necessitates the development, implementation, and evaluation of theory and evidence-based prevention interventions. For example, mass persuasion antiracist tactics that rely on simplistic catchphrases and slogans may generate feelings of resentment among people with high levels of racist beliefs (e.g., Duckitt, 2001). It is important that campaign designers give attention to social psychological theories concerning prejudice (e.g., Vrij, Akehurst, & Smith, 2003). Within an education context, programs that promote academic achievement and school completion will yield the most information if they are theory based and employ longitudinal research designs.

■ Engagement in preventive interventions requires counseling psychologists to function in a variety of roles, such as consultant, advocate, and educator. For instance, given the well-documented association between mass media reports of suicide and subsequent increase in suicide rates, counseling psychologists can educate media professionals on the responsible reporting of suicides (e.g., concise and factual descriptions that do not disclose detailed information about suicide methods; Jamieson, Jamieson, & Romer, 2003). Counseling psychologists should strive to overcome the historical controversy associated with school counseling (e.g., Romano & Kachgal, 2004) and take advantage of opportunities to collaborate with school counselors on outcome research related to promotion of academic achievement and school graduation rates.

■ The long-term effectiveness of prevention interventions, despite the inherent difficulties associated with longitudinal research, must be increased across interventions that promote behavior change. Such research is critical in demonstrating the credibility and real-world implications of prevention interventions, where the ultimate goal is sustained change. Cohen et al. (2009) gave a good example of this type of research by including a 2-year follow-up in their study; however, given the young age of the participants, a follow-up study of the students in their senior year of high school would be important to examine long-term effects.

■ Collaboration with community and stakeholders to ensure that prevention programs are culturally relevant to local communities is critically important. For prevention interventions to be culturally relevant, researchers need to spend time gaining familiarity with local communities and involve stakeholders in the design and implementation of the interventions.

CONCLUSION

It is important to acknowledge challenges associated with prevention work. Although prevention science has been advancing, more needs to be accomplished with respect to increasing prevention training in graduate programs, attending to prevention in accreditation and licensing standards, and addressing prevention competencies in the practice of psychology. Additionally, a lack of direct compensation for prevention services has historically been one of the major barriers limiting psychologists' work in prevention because mental health reimbursements are heavily oriented toward crisis intervention and remedial activities. This barrier may be reduced, however, as the 2010 U.S. Patient Protection and Affordable Care Act (http://www.healthcare.gov) includes provisions for prevention services. The impact of financial barriers on prevention work are also mitigated because psychologists are often employed in institutional settings where opportunities to engage in prevention practice and research are complementary to their primary functions. Additionally, prevention research highlighted in this chapter offers potential grant support through government agencies and private foundations.

Prevention science will continue to expand in the 21st century as disciplines and specialty areas come together to address major education, social, vocational, and mental and physical health problems from a prevention perspective. In the years ahead, it is our hope that counseling psychology becomes a leader in promoting a prevention agenda across multiple domains and contexts to enhance life and well-being across the life cycle.

References

Addams, J. (1930). *The second twenty years at Hull-House: September 1909–September 1929*. New York, NY: Macmillan.

Ajzen, I. (1991). The theory of planned behavior. *Organizational Behavior and Human Decision Processes, 50*, 179–211. doi:10.1016/0749-5978(91)90020-T

Ajzen, I. (2006). *Constructing a TpB questionnaire.* Retrieved from http://www.people.umass.edu/aizen/tpb.html

Albee, G. W. (1986). Toward a just society: Lessons from observations on the primary prevention of psychopathology. *American Psychologist, 41*, 891–898. doi:10.1037/0003-066X.41.8.891

Albee, G. W. (2000). Commentary on prevention. *The Counseling Psychologist, 28*, 845–853. doi:10.1177/0011000000286006

Albee, G. W. (2003). The contributions of society, culture, and social class to emotional disorder. In T. P. Guillotta & M. Bloom (Eds.), *Encyclopedia of primary prevention and health promotion* (pp. 97–104). New York, NY: Kluwer.

Albee, G. W. (2005). Call to revolution in the prevention of emotional disorders. *Ethical Human Psychology and Psychiatry, 7*, 37–44.

Albee, G. W., & Joffe, J. M. (2004). Mental illness is NOT "an illness like any other." *The Journal of Primary Prevention, 24*, 419–436. doi:10.1023/B:JOPP.0000024799.04666.8b

Allport, G. (1954). *The nature of prejudice.* Reading, MA: Addison-Wesley.

American Association of Suicidology. (2009). *Suicide in the U.S.* Retrieved from http://www.suicidology.org/c/document_library/get_file?folderId=232&name=DLFE-159.pdf

Armitage, C. J., & Connor, M. (2001). Efficacy of the theory of planned behavior: A meta-analytic review. *British Journal of Social Psychology, 40*, 471–499. doi:10.1348/014466601164939

Arredondo, P., Toporek, R., Brown, S. P., & Jones, J. (1996). Operationalization of the multicultural counseling competencies. *Journal of Multicultural Counseling and Development, 24*, 42–78.

Ata, A., Bastian, B., & Lusher, D. (2009). Intergroup contact in context: The mediating role of social norms and group-based perceptions on the contact–prejudice link. *International Journal of Intercultural Relations, 33*, 498–506. doi:10.1016/j.ijintrel.2009.05.001

Avey, J. B., Luthans, F., Smith, R. M., & Palmer, N. F. (2010). Impact of psychological capital on employee well-being over time. *Journal of Occupational Health Psychology, 15*, 17–28. doi:10.1037/a0016998

Barton, P. E. (2003). *Parsing the achievement gap: Baselines for tracking progress. Policy information report.* Princeton, NJ: Educational Testing Service.

Beers, C. (1908). *A mind that found itself.* Pittsburgh, PA: University of Pittsburgh Press.

Bell, L. A. (1997). Theoretical foundations for social justice education. In M. Adams, L. A. Bell, & P. Griffin (Eds.), *Teaching for diversity and social justice: A sourcebook* (pp. 3–15). New York, NY: Routledge.

Bemak, F., Chung, R. C., & Siroskey-Sabdo, L. A. (2005). Empowerment groups for academic success: An innovative approach to prevent high school failure for at-risk, urban African American girls. *Professional School Counseling, 8*, 377–389.

Benson, P. L. (1993). *Troubled journey: A portrait of 6th-12th grade youth.* Minneapolis, MN: Search Institute.

Bernburg, J. G., Thorlindsson, T., & Sigfusdottir, I. D. (2009). The spreading of suicidal behavior: The contextual effect of community household poverty on adolescent suicidal behavior and the mediating role of suicide suggestion. *Social Science and Medicine, 68*, 380–389. doi:10.1016/j.socscimed.2008.10.020

Black, S. A., & Jackson, E. (2007). Using bullying incident density to evaluate the Olweus Bullying Prevention Programme. *School Psychology International, 28*, 623–638. doi:10.1177/0143034307085662

Bridle, C., Riemsma, P., Pattenden, J., Sowden, A. J., Mather, L., Watt, I. S., & Walker, A. (2005). Systematic review of the effectiveness of health behavior interventions based on the transtheoretical model. *Psychology and Health, 20*, 283–301. doi:10.1080/08870440512331333997

Brief, A. P., Dietz, J., Cohen, R. R., Pugh, S. D., & Vaslow, J. B. (2000). Just doing business: Modern racism and obedience to authority as explanations for employment discrimination. *Organizational Behavior and Human Decision Processes, 81*, 72–97. doi:10.1006/obhd.1999.2867

Bryant-Davis, T., Chung, H., & Tillman, S. (2009). From the margins to the center: Mental health effects of sexual violence in ethnic minority women's lives. *Trauma, Violence, and Abuse, 10*, 330–357. doi:10.1177/1524838009339755

Buhin, L., & Vera, E. M. (2009). Preventing racism and promoting social justice: Person-centered and environment-centered interventions. *The Journal of Primary Prevention, 30*, 43–59. doi:10.1007/s10935-008-0161-9

Caplan, G. (1964). *Principles of preventive psychiatry.* New York, NY: Basic Books.

Cohen, G. L., Garcia, J., Apfel, N., & Master, A. (2006). Reducing the racial achievement gap: A social-psychological intervention. *Science, 313*, 1307–1310. doi:10.1126/science.1128317

Cohen, G. L., Garcia, J., Purdie-Vaughns, V., Apfel, N., & Brzustoski, P. (2009). Recursive processes in self-affirmation: Intervening to close the minority achievement gap. *Science, 324*, 400–403. doi:10.1126/science.1170769

Cohen, G. L., & Steele, C. M. (2002). A barrier of mistrust: How negative stereotypes affect cross-race mentoring. In J. Aaronson (Ed.), *Improving academic achievement: Impact of psychological factors on education* (pp. 303–327). San Diego, CA: Academic Press. doi:10.1016/B978-012064455-1/50018-X

Constantine, M. G., & Sue, D. W. (2006). Factors contributing to optimal human functioning in people of color in the United States. *The Counseling Psychologist, 34*, 228–244. doi:10.1177/0011000005281318

Conyne, R. K. (2004). *Preventive counseling* (2nd ed.). New York, NY: Brunner-Routledge.

Conyne, R. K. (2010). *Prevention program development and evaluation: An incident reduction, culturally relevant approach*. Thousand Oaks, CA: Sage.

Cooke, R., & Sheeran, P. (2004). Moderation of cognition-intention and cognition-behavior: A meta-analysis of properties of variables from the theory of planned behavior. *British Journal of Social Psychology, 43*, 159–186. doi:10.1348/0144666041501688

Coombs, D. W., Fish, L., Grimley, D., Chess, E., Ryan, W., Leeper, J., . . . Willis, S. (2002). The transtheoretical model of change applied to developing suicidal behavior. *Omega: Journal of Death and Dying, 44*, 345–359. doi:10.2190/HG14-V1MX-3LW7-QGF3

Cowen, E. L. (1996). The ontogenesis of primary prevention: Lengthy strides and stubbed toes. *American Journal of Community Psychology, 24*, 235–249. doi:10.1007/BF02510400

Crandall, C. S., & Stangor, C. (2005). Conformity and prejudice. In J. F. Dovidio, P. Glick, & L. A. Rudman, (Eds.), *On the nature of prejudice: Fifty years after Allport* (pp. 295–309). Malden, MA: Blackwell.

Davis, L. E., Ajzen, I., Saunders, J., & Williams, T. (2002). The decision of African-American students to complete high school: An application of the theory of planned behavior. *Journal of Educational Psychology, 94*, 810–819. doi:10.1037/0022-0663.94.4.810

Davis, S. P., Arnette, N. C., Bethea, K. S., Graves, K. N., Rhodes, M. N., Harp, S. E., . . . Kaslow, N. J. (2009). The Grady Nia project: A culturally competent intervention for low-income, abused, and suicidal African American women. *Professional Psychology, Research and Practice, 40*, 141–147. doi:10.1037/a0014566

DeRosier, M. E. (2004). Building relationships and combating bullying: Effectiveness of a school-based social skills group intervention. *Journal of Clinical Child and Adolescent Psychology, 33*, 196–201. doi:10.1207/S15374424JCCP3301_18

Destin, M., & Oyserman, D. (2010). Incentivizing education: Seeing schoolwork as an investment, not a chore. *Journal of Experimental Social Psychology, 46*, 846–849. doi:10.1016/j.jesp.2010.04.004

Diemer, M. A., & Blustein, D. L. (2007). Vocational hope and vocational identity: Urban adolescents' career development. *Journal of Career Assessment, 15*, 98–118. doi:10.1177/1069072706294528

Duckitt, J. (2001). A cognitive-motivational theory of ideology and prejudice. In M. P. Zanna (Ed.), *Advances in experimental social psychology* (Vol. 33, pp. 41–113). San Diego, CA: Academic Press.

Eddy, J. M., Smith, P., Brown, C. H., & Reid, J. B. (2005). A survey of prevention science training: Implications for educating the next generation. *Prevention Science, 6*, 59–71. doi:10.1007/s11121-005-1253-x

Espelage, D. L., & Swearer, S. M. (2003). Research on school bullying and victimization: What have we learned and where do we go from here? *School Psychology Review, 32*, 365–383.

Evers, K. E., Prochaska, J. O., Johnson, J. L., Mauriello, L. M., Padula, J. A., & Prochaska, J. M. (2006). A randomized clinical trial of a population and transtheoretical-based stress management intervention. *Health Psychology, 25*, 521–529. doi:10.1037/0278-6133.25.4.521

Fishbein, M. (Ed.). (1967). *Readings in attitude theory and measurement*. New York, NY: Wiley.

Fishbein, M., & Ajzen, I. (1975). *Belief, attitude, intention, and behavior: An introduction to theory and research*. Reading, MA: Addison-Wesley.

Fouad, N. A. (2002). 2001 presidential address: Dreams for 2010: Making a difference. *The Counseling Psychologist, 30*, 158–166. doi:10.1177/0011000002301014

Galassi, J., & Akos, P. (2007). *Strengths-based counseling: Promoting student development and achievement*. Mahwah, NJ: Erlbaum.

Goetzel, R. Z., Reynolds, K., Breslow, L., Roper, W. L., Shechter, D. C., Stapleton, D. C., . . . McGinnis, J. M. (2007). Health promotion in later life: It's never too late. *American Journal of Health Promotion, 21*, 1–5.

Gordon, R. (1987). An operational definition of disease prevention. In J. A. Sternberg & M. M. Silverman (Eds.), *Preventing mental disorders* (pp. 20–26). Rockville, MD: U.S. Department of Health and Human Services.

Green, M. C., Brock, T. C., & Kaufman, G. F. (2004). Understanding media enjoyment: The role of transportation into narrative worlds. *Communication Theory, 14*, 311–327. doi:10.1111/j.1468-2885.2004.tb00317.x

Hage, S., M., Romano, J. L., Conyne, R. K., Kenny, M., Matthews, C., Schwartz, J. P., & Waldo, M. (2007). Best practice guidelines on prevention practice, research, training, and social advocacy for psychologists. *The Counseling Psychologist, 35*, 493–566. doi:10.1177/0011000006291411

Hage, S. M., Romano, J. L., Conyne, R. K., Kenny, M., Schwartz, J. P., & Waldo, M. (2007). Walking the talk: Implementing the prevention guidelines and transforming the profession of psychology. *The Counseling Psychologist, 35*, 594–604. doi:10.1177/0011000006297158

Heppner, P. P., Casas, J. M., Carter, J., & Stone, G. L. (2000). The maturation of counseling psychology: Multifaceted perspectives, 1978–1998. In S. D. Brown & R. W. Lent (Eds.), *Handbook of counseling psychology* (3rd ed., pp. 3–49). New York, NY: Wiley.

Hoffman, M., & Driscoll, J. M. (2000). Health promotion and disease prevention: A concentric biopsychosocial model of health status. In S. D. Brown & R. W. Lent (Eds.), *Handbook of counseling psychology* (3rd ed., pp. 532–567). New York, NY: Wiley.

Holcomb-McCoy, C. (2007). *School counseling to close the achievement gap.* Thousand Oaks, CA: Corwin Press.

Hu, G., Wilcox, H. C., Wissow, L., & Baker, S. P. (2008). Mid-life suicide: An increasing problem in U.S. Whites, 1999–2005. *American Journal of Preventive Medicine, 35,* 589–593. doi:10.1016/j.amepre.2008.07.005

Jackson, J. S., Brown, T. N., Williams, D. R., Torres, M., Sellers, S. L., & Brown, K. (1996). Racism and the physical and mental health status of African Americans: A thirteen year national panel study. *Ethnicity and Disease, 6,* 132–147.

Jamieson, P., Jamieson, K. H., & Romer, D. (2003). The responsible reporting of suicide in print journalism. *American Behavioral Scientist, 46,* 1643–1660. doi:10.1177/0002764203254620

Johnson, D. W., & Johnson, R. T. (1989). *Cooperation and competition: Theory and research.* Edina, MN: Interaction Book.

Joiner, T. E., Jr., Van Orden, K. A., Witte, T. K., & Rudd, M. D. (2009). *The interpersonal theory of suicide: Guidance for working with suicidal clients.* Washington, DC: American Psychological Association. doi:10.1037/11869-000

Jones, J. M. (2002). Toward a cultural psychology of African Americans. In W. J. Lonner, D. L. Dinnel, S. A. Hayes, & D. N. Sattler (Eds.), *Online readings in psychology and culture.* Bellingham: Center for Cross-Cultural Research, Western Washington University. Retrieved from http://www.ac.wwu.edu/~culture/jones.htm

Kataoka, S. H., Stein, B. D., Lieberman, R., & Wong, M. (2003). Suicide prevention in schools: Are we reaching minority youths? *Psychiatric Services, 54,* 1444. doi:10.1176/appi.ps.54.11.1444

Kenny, M. E., & Hage, S. M. (2009). The next frontier: Prevention as an instrument of social justice. *The Journal of Primary Prevention, 30,* 1–10. doi:10.1007/s10935-008-0163-7

Kenny, M. E., Horne, A. M., Orpinas, P., & Reese, L. E. (Eds.). (2009). *Realizing social justice: The challenge of prevention interventions.* Washington, DC: American Psychological Association. doi:10.1037/11870-000

Kenny, M. E., Walsh-Blair, L. Y., Blustein, D. L., Bempachat, J., & Seltzer, J. (2010). Achievement motivation among urban adolescents: Work hope, autonomy support, and achievement related beliefs. *Journal of Vocational Behavior, 77,* 205–212. doi:10.1016/j.jvb.2010.02.005

Kessler, R. C., Berglund, P., Borges, G., Nock, M., & Wang, P. S. (2005). Trends in suicide ideation, plans, gestures, and attempts in the united states, 1990–1992 to 2001–2003. *Journal of the American Medical Association, 293,* 2487–2495. doi:10.1001/jama.293.20.2487

Klima, T., Miller, M., & Nunlist, C. (2009). *What works? Targeted truancy and dropout programs in middle and high school.* Document No. 09–06-2201. Olympia, WA: Washington State Institute for Public Policy.

Koraleski, S. F., & Larson, L. M. (1997). A partial test of the transtheoretical model in therapy with adult survivors of childhood sexual abuse. *Journal of Counseling Psychology, 44,* 302–306. doi:10.1037/0022-0167.44.3.302

Kortering, L. J., & Christenson, S. (2009). Engaging students in school and learning: The real deal for school completion. *Exceptionality, 17,* 5–15. doi:10.1080/09362830802590102

Kratochwill, T. R., & Stoiber, K. C. (2000). Empirically supported interventions and school psychology: Conceptual and practice issues—Part II. *School Psychology Quarterly, 15,* 233–253. doi:10.1037/h0088786

Krumboltz, J. D., Becker-Haven, J. F., & Burnett, K. F. (1979). Counseling psychology. *Annual Review of Psychology, 30,* 555–602. doi:10.1146/annurev.ps.30.020179.003011

LaFromboise, T. D., & Howard-Pitney, B. (1995). The Zuni Life Skills Development Curriculum: Description and evaluation of a suicide prevention program. *Journal of Counseling Psychology, 42,* 479–486. doi:10.1037/0022-0167.42.4.479

Lapan, R. T., Gysbers, N. C., & Petroski, G. F. (2001). Helping seventh graders be safe and successful: A statewide study of the impact of comprehensive guidance and counseling programs. *Journal of Counseling and Development, 79,* 320–330.

Levesque, D. A., Driskell, M., Prochaska, J. M., & Prochaska, J. O. (2008). Acceptability of a stage-matched expert system intervention for domestic violence offenders. *Violence and Victims, 23,* 432–445. doi:10.1891/0886-6708.23.4.432

Liu, W. M., & Ali, S. R. (2008). Social class and classism: Understanding the psychological impact of poverty and inequality. In S. D. Brown & R. W. Lent (Eds.), *Handbook of counseling psychology* (pp. 159–175). Hoboken, NJ: Wiley.

Lopez, S. J., & Edwards, L. M. (2008). The interface of counseling psychology and positive psychology: Assessing and promoting strengths. In S. D. Brown & R. W. Lent (Eds.), *Handbook of counseling psychology* (pp. 86–99). Hoboken, NJ: Wiley.

Luoma, J. B., Martin, C. E., & Pearson, J. L. (2002). Contact with mental health and primary care providers before suicide: A review of the evidence.

The American Journal of Psychiatry, 159, 909–916. doi:10.1176/appi.ajp.159.6.909

Martin, S. (2009). A new day for practice. *Monitor on Psychology, 40,* 18–21.

May, P. A., Serna, P., Hurt, L., & DeBruyn, L. M. (2005). Outcome evaluation of a public health approach to suicide prevention in an American Indian tribal nation. *American Journal of Public Health, 95,* 1238–1244. doi:10.2105/AJPH.2004.040410

McKown, C. (2005). Applying ecological theory to advance the science and practice of school-based prejudice reduction interventions. *Educational Psychologist, 40,* 177–189. doi:10.1207/s15326985ep4003_4

McWhirter, J. J. (1993). Does prevention have a home in Division 17? *Prevention Special Interest Group Newsletter,* Spring, 2–3.

Montaño, D. E., & Kasprzyk, D. (2002). The theory of reasoned action and the theory of planned behavior. In K. Glanz, B. K. Rimer, & F. M. Lewis (Eds.), *Health behavior and health education: Theory, research, and practice* (pp. 67–98). San Francisco, CA: Jossey-Bass.

Mrazek, P. J., & Haggerty, R. J. (Eds.). (1994). *Reducing risks for mental disorders: Frontiers for preventive intervention research.* Washington, DC: National Academy Press.

Muehlenkamp, J. J., Marrone, S., Gray, J. S., & Brown, D. (2009). A college suicide prevention model for American Indian Students. *Professional Psychology: Research and Practice, 40,* 134–140. doi:10.1037/a0013253

Nelson, G., & Prilleltensky, I. (2005). *Community psychology: In pursuit of liberation and well-being.* New York, NY: Palgrave Macmillan.

Newman-Carlson, D., & Horne, A. M. (2004). Bully busters: A psycho-educational intervention for reducing bullying behavior in middle school students. *Journal of Counseling and Development, 82,* 259–267.

O'Connell, M. E., Boat, T., & Warner, K. E. (Eds.). (2009). *Preventing mental, emotional, and behavioral disorders among young people: Progress and possibilities.* Washington, DC: National Academy Press.

O'Connor, R. C., Armitage, C. J., & Gray, L. (2006). The role of clinical and social cognitive variables in parasuicide. *British Journal of Clinical Psychology, 45,* 465–481. doi:10.1348/014466505X82315

Painter, J. E., Borba, C., Hynes, M., Mays, D., & Glanz, K. (2008). The use of theory in health behavior research from 2000–2005: A systematic review. *Annals of Behavioral Medicine, 35,* 358–362. doi:10.1007/s12160-008-9042-y

Paluck, E. L. (2009). Reducing intergroup prejudice and conflict using the media: A field experiment in Rwanda. *Journal of Personality and Social Psychology, 96,* 574–587. doi:10.1037/a0011989

Paluck, E. L., & Green, D. P. (2009). Prejudice reduction: What works? A critical look at evidence from the field and the laboratory. *Annual Review of Psychology, 60,* 339–367. doi:10.1146/annurev.psych.60.110707.163607

Parsons, F. (1909). *Choosing a vocation.* Boston, MA: Houghton-Mifflin.

Peterson, C., & Park, N. (2009). Classifying and measuring strengths of character. In C. R. Snyder & S. J. Lopez (Eds.), *Oxford handbook of positive psychology* (2nd ed., pp. 25–33). New York, NY: Oxford University Press.

Peterson, C., & Seligman, M. E. P. (2004). *Character strengths and virtues: A handbook and classification.* Washington, DC: American Psychological Association.

Pettigrew, T. F., & Tropp, L. R. (2008). How does intergroup contact reduce prejudice? meta-analytic tests of three mediators. *European Journal of Social Psychology, 38,* 922–934. doi:10.1002/ejsp.504

Prevatt, F. & Kelly, F. D. (2003). Dropping out of school: A review of intervention programs. *Journal of School Psychology, 41,* 377–395.

Prilleltensky, I. (1997). Values, assumptions, and practices: Assessing the moral implications of psychological discourse and action. *American Psychologist, 52,* 517–535. doi:10.1037/0003-066X.52.5.517

Prilleltensky, I. (2001). Value-based praxis in community psychology: Moving toward social justice and social action. *American Journal of Community Psychology, 29,* 747–778. doi:10.1023/A:1010417201918

Prochaska, J. O., Evers, K. E., Prochaska, J. M., Van Marter, D., & Johnson, J. L. (2007). Efficacy and effectiveness trials: Examples from smoking cessation and bullying prevention. *Journal of Health Psychology, 12,* 170–178. doi:10.1177/1359105307071751

Prochaska, J. O., Johnson, S., & Lee, P. (2009). The transtheoretical model of behavior change. In S. A. Shumaker, J. K. Ockene, & K. A. Riekert (Eds.), *The handbook of behavior change* (3rd ed., pp. 59–83). New York, NY: Springer.

Reese, L. E., & Vera, E. M. (2007). Culturally relevant prevention: The scientific and practical considerations of community-based programs. *The Counseling Psychologist, 35,* 763–778. doi:10.1177/0011000007304588

Richmond, M. E. (1922). *What is social casework? An introductory description.* New York, NY: Russell Sage Foundation.

Ridley, C. R. (2005). *Overcoming unintentional racism in counseling and therapy: A practitioner's guide to intentional intervention* (2nd ed.). Thousand Oaks, CA: Sage.

Rivera-Mosquera, E., Phillips, J. C., Castelino, P., Martin, J. K., & Dobran, E. S. M. (2007). Design and implementation of a grassroots precollege program for Latino youth. *The Counseling Psychologist, 35,* 821–839. doi:10.1177/0011000007304593

Rogers, J. R., & Lester, D. (2009). *Understanding suicide: Why we don't and how we might.* Cambridge, MA: Hogrefe.

Romano, J. L., & Hage, S. M. (2000). Prevention and counseling psychology: Revitalizing commitments for the 21st century. *The Counseling Psychologist, 28,* 733–763. doi:10.1177/0011000000286001

Romano, J. L., & Kachgal, M. M. (2004). Counseling psychology and school counseling: An underutilized partnership. *The Counseling Psychologist, 32,* 184–215. doi:10.1177/0011000003261354

Romano, J. L., & Netland, J. D. (2008). The application of the theory of reasoned action and planned behavior to prevention science in counseling psychology. *The Counseling Psychologist, 36,* 777–806. doi:10.1177/0011000007301670

Rutter, P. A. (2008). Suicide protective and risk factors for sexual minority youth: Applying the cumulative factor model. *Journal of LGBT Issues in Counseling, 2,* 81–92.

Satterfield, W. A., Buelow, S. A., Lyddon, W. J., & Johnson, J. T. (1995). Client stages of change and expectations about counseling. *Journal of Counseling Psychology, 42,* 476–478. doi:10.1037/0022-0167.42.4.476

Schmolling, P., Youkeles, M., & Burger, W. R. (1997). *Human services in contemporary America.* Pacific Grove, CA: Brooks Cole.

Scott, M. A., Wilcox, H. C., Schonfeld, I. S., Davies, M., Hicks, R. C., Turner, J. B., & Shaffer, D. (2009). School-based screening to identify at-risk students not already known to school professionals: The Columbia suicide screen. *American Journal of Public Health, 99* 334–339.

Seligman, M. E. P., & Csikszentmihalyi, M. (2000). Positive psychology: An introduction. *American Psychologist, 55,* 5–14. doi:10.1037/0003-066X.55.1.5

Seligman, M. E. P., Steen, T. A., Park, N., & Peterson, C. (2005). Positive psychology progress: Empirical validation of interventions. *American Psychologist, 60,* 410–421. doi:10.1037/0003-066X.60.5.410

Sink, C. A., & Stroh, H. R. (2003). Raising achievement test scores of early elementary school students through comprehensive school counseling programs. *Professional School Counseling, 6,* 350–364.

Smith, E. J. (2006). The strength-based counseling model. *The Counseling Psychologist, 34,* 13–79. doi:10.1177/0011000005277018

Smith, K. J., Subich, L. M., & Kalodner, C. (1995). The transtheoretical model's stages and processes of change and their relation to premature termination. *Journal of Counseling Psychology, 42,* 34–39. doi:10.1037/0022-0167.42.1.34

Smith, L., Chambers, D., & Bratini, L. (2009). When oppression is the pathogen: The participatory development of socially just mental health practice. *American Journal of Orthopsychiatry, 79,* 159–168.

Smith, L., Constantine, M. G., Graham, S. V., & Dize, C. B. (2008). The territory ahead for multicultural competence: The "spinning" of racism. *Professional Psychology: Research and Practice, 39,* 337–345. doi:10.1037/0735-7028.39.3.337

Snyder, C. R., & Elliott, T. R. (2005). Twenty-first century graduate education in clinical psychology: A four level matrix model. *Journal of Clinical Psychology, 61,* 1033–1054. doi:10.1002/jclp.20164

Snyder, C. R., & Lopez, S. J. (2007). *Positive psychology: The scientific and practical explorations of human strengths.* Thousand Oaks, CA: Sage.

Snyder, C. R., Shorey, H. S., Cheavens, J., Pulvers, M. K., Adams, V. H., III, & Wiklund, C. (2002). Hope and academic success. *Journal of Educational Psychology, 94,* 820–826. doi:10.1037/0022-0663.94.4.820

Speight, S. L., & Vera, E. M. (2008). Social justice and counseling psychology: A challenge for the profession. In S. D. Brown & R. W. Lent (Eds.), *Handbook of counseling psychology* (pp. 54–67). Hoboken, NJ: Wiley.

Stevahn, L., Johnson, D. W., Johnson, R. T., & Schultz, R. (2002). Effects of conflict resolution training integrated into a high school social studies curriculum. *The Journal of Social Psychology, 142,* 305–331. doi:10.1080/00224540209603902

Sue, D. W., Capodilupo, C. M., Torino, G. C., Bucceri, J. M., Holder, A. M. B., Nadal, K. L., & Esquilin, M. (2007). Racial microaggressions in everyday life. *American Psychologist, 62,* 271–286. doi:10.1037/0003-066X.62.4.271

Sue, D. W. (2001). Multidimensional facets of cultural competence. *The Counseling Psychologist, 29,* 790–821. doi:10.1177/0011000001296002

Sutton, S. (1998). Predicting and explaining intentions and behavior: How well are we doing? *Journal of Applied Social Psychology, 28,* 1317–1338. doi:10.1111/j.1559-1816.1998.tb01679.x

Taylor, H. G., Klein, N., & Hack, M. (2000). School-age consequences of birth weight less than 750 g: A review and update. *Developmental Neuropsychology, 17,* 289–321. doi:10.1207/S15326942DN1703_2

Tedeschi, R. G., & Kilmer, R. P. (2005). Assessing strengths, resilience, and growth to guide clinical interventions. *Professional Psychology: Research and*

Practice, 36, 230–237. doi:10.1037/0735-7028. 36.3.230

Turner, R. N., & Brown, R. (2008). Improving children's attitudes toward refugees: An evaluation of a school-based multicultural curriculum and an anti-racist intervention. *Journal of Applied Social Psychology, 38*, 1295–1328. doi:10.1111/j.1559-1816. 2008.00349.x

U.S. Department of Health and Human Services. (2001). *Mental health: Culture, Race, and Ethnicity—A supplement to mental health: A report of the Surgeon General.* Rockville, MD: U.S. Department of Health and Human Services, Public Health Service, Office of the Surgeon General.

U.S. Department of Health and Human Services. (2007). *Health, United States, 2007.* Retrieved from http://www.cdc.gov/nchs/data/hus/hus07.pdf

Utsey, S. O., & Ponterotto, J. G. (1996). Development and validation of the Index of Race-Related Stress (IRRS). *Journal of Counseling Psychology, 43*, 490–501. doi:10.1037/0022-0167.43.4.490

van Sluijs, E. M. F., van Poppel, M. N. M., & van Mechelen, W. (2004). Stage-based lifestyle interventions in primary care: Are they effective? *American Journal of Preventive Medicine, 26*, 330–343. doi:10.1016/j.amepre.2003.12.010

Vera, E. M., Buhin, L., & Isacco, A. (2009). The role of prevention in psychology's social justice agenda. In M. E. Kenny, A. M. Horne, P., Orpinas, & L. E. Reese (Eds.), *Realizing social justice: The challenge of prevention interventions* (pp. 79–96). Washington, DC: American Psychological Association.

Vera, E. M., Caldwell, J., Clarke, M., Gonzales, R., Morgan, M., & West, M. (2007). The Choices Program: Multisystemic interventions for enhancing the personal and academic effectiveness of urban adolescents of color. *The Counseling Psychologist, 35*, 779–796. doi:10.1177/0011000007304590

Vera, E. M., & Speight, S. L. (2003). Multicultural competence, social justice, and counseling psychology: Expanding our roles. *The Counseling Psychologist, 31*, 253–272. doi:10.1177/0011000003031003001

Vogel, D. L., Wester, S. R., Wei, M., & Boysen, G. A. (2005). The role of outcome expectations and attitudes on decisions to seek professional help. *Journal of Counseling Psychology, 52*, 459–470. doi:10.1037/0022-0167.52.4.459

Vrij, A., Akehurst, L., & Smith, B. (2003). Reducing ethnic prejudice: An evaluation of seven recommended principles for incorporation in public campaigns. *Journal of Community and Applied Social Psychology, 13*, 284–299. doi:10.1002/casp.736

Watts, R. J., Abdul-Adil, J. K., & Pratt, T. (2002). Enhancing critical consciousness in young African American men: A psychoeducational approach. *Psychology of Men and Masculinity, 3*, 41–50. doi:10.1037/1524-9220.3.1.41

Westefeld, J. S., Range, L., Rogers, J., & Hill, J. (2008). Suicide Prevention. In S. Brown & R. Lent (Eds.), *Handbook of counseling psychology* (pp. 535–551). Hoboken, NJ: Wiley.

White, S. W., & Kelly, D. F. (2010). The school counselor's role in school dropout prevention. *Journal of Counseling and Development, 88*, 227–235.

Whiteley, J. M. (1984). Counseling psychology: A historical perspective. *The Counseling Psychologist, 12*, 3–109. doi:10.1177/0011000084121001

Wiethoff, C. (2004). Motivation to learn and diversity training: Application of the theory of planned behavior. *Human Resource Development Quarterly, 15*, 263–278. doi:10.1002/hrdq.1103

Wingate, L. R., Burns, A., Gordon, K., Perez, M., Walker, R., Williams, F., & Joiner, T. (2006). Suicide and positive cognitions: Positive psychology applied to the understanding and treatment of suicidal behavior. In T. E. Ellis (Ed.), *Cognition and suicide: Theory, research, and therapy* (pp. 261–283). Washington, DC: American Psychological Association. doi:10.1037/11377-012

Wong, Y. J. (2006). Strength-centered therapy: A social constructionist, virtues-based psychotherapy. *Psychotherapy: Theory, Research, Practice, Training, 43*, 133–146. doi:10.1037/0033-3204.43.2.133

Wong, Y. J., Koo, K., Tran, K. K., Chiu, Y.-C., & Mok, Y. (2011). Asian American college students' suicide ideation: A mixed-methods study. *Journal of Counseling Psychology, 58*, 197–209. doi: 10.1037/a0023040

Wong, Y. J., & Poon, M. L. (2010). Counseling Asian American men who demonstrate suicidal behavior. In W. M. Liu, D. Iwamoto, & M. Chae (Eds.), *Culturally responsive counseling with Asian American men* (pp. 279–298). New York, NY: Routledge.

Part III

CONTEXTUAL FACTORS

THE PSYCHOLOGY OF MEN: HISTORICAL DEVELOPMENTS, CURRENT RESEARCH, AND FUTURE DIRECTIONS

Stephen R. Wester and David L. Vogel

Men have been the center of the many of the early developments in both the professional practice of psychology and the exploration of gender. Rather than being a critical analysis, most of this early work involved seeing men as a referent point for other populations (Terman & Miles, 1936). Masculinity was viewed as normative, adaptive, and associated with healthy functioning, whereas deviations from the masculine ideal were identified as problematic (Pleck, 1981). Furthermore, masculinity and the characteristics associated with it was generally considered to be natural, inherent, and biologically based and, therefore, independent of either culture or situational demands (Hare-Mustin & Marecek, 1990). Historically, society considered the "ideal man [as] active, rational, strong, and community-oriented" (Smiler, 2004, p. 17), guided by a "near universal creed linking manhood with the socially necessary activities of protecting, providing, and procreating" (Keen, 1991, p. 27).

The evidence, however, belies the early positive associations regarding the health of men. Men are at the highest risk for alcohol and drug abuse and dependency; between 31% and 47% of all men will develop a substance abuse problem over their lifetimes (e.g., Cochran, 2005), and the lifetime prevalence for alcohol and drug dependency is approximately 30% for men (Robin & Reiger, 1991). Men in the United States die close to 7 years earlier than women (Courtenay, 1998), and for men ages 15 to 24 years, 75% of the annual death rate is from fatal injuries. Men commit suicide 4 to 15 times more often than women (Cochran & Rabinowitz, 2000). Furthermore, even as children boys experience increased health concerns: 16% of school-age boys have been diagnosed with attention deficit disorder (Centers for Disease Control and Prevention, 2005), and 12% of males ages 18 to 24 years are high school dropouts (U.S. Census Bureau, 2005). Eighty percent of boys also report being bullied at least once, and 12% of high school boys report being threatened with a weapon on school property (Centers for Disease Control and Prevention, 2007).

Statistics such as these have led to a reformulation of how masculinity is conceptualized in the extant literature. No longer is masculinity seen in an automatically positive light. Instead, theorists are examining the linkages between masculinity and potential social, physical, and psychological outcomes. Goldberg, for example, with the release of *The Hazards of Being Male: Surviving the Myth of Male Privilege* (1976), was among the first to acknowledge the restrictive roles experienced by men as a result of the male gender role. Society's expectations for men to be rational and strong (Smiler, 2004) as well as protectors and providers, to the exclusion of other endeavors (Keen, 1991), have the potential to limit men's development (Pleck, 1981). As such, Goldberg (1976) called for men to save themselves from the "harness" (p. 1) of traditional masculinity. Similar ideas have been

Special thanks to Lindsay Danforth, Department of Educational Psychology, University of Wisconsin–Milwaukee who assisted in manuscript development, resource compilation, and final editing.

DOI: 10.1037/13754-014

echoed in such writings as the *The Myth of Male Power* (Farrell, 1993) and *Iron John: A Book About Men* (Bly, 1990). The theme of these works is that masculinity both confers significant privilege to some men and contributes to negative outcomes for men, for women, and for society. This led Brooks and Good (2001a) to state, "Contemporary men face opportunities to live lives more richly varied and broadly fulfilling than men in any previous historical era" (p. 4), yet those same men "have been resolutely socialized to limit themselves to narrow and stereotypical roles—warriors, providers, and sexual performers" (p. 10).

Since these early theorists, a strong research base has sprung up within the domains of counseling psychology attempting to articulate the complex nature of masculinity, its impact on men, and its impact on society. The goal of this chapter is to critically review this literature to both conceptualize the current state of the extant literature and also provide a springboard for future work. The magnitude of such a project requires some boundaries, however. First, we focus exclusively on theory and empirical research within the psychology of men (Levant & Pollack, 1995, p. 1) literature as it is operationalized within counseling psychology. Our time frame is set by the genesis of this literature—the late 1970s forward. Masculinity as conceptualized and discussed in literatures such as psychiatry, sociology, archeology, and social work was not the major focus of these narratives. Sociobiological theories (for a review, see Kilmartin & Allison, 2007) were also excluded because of the degree to which they focus on the behavioral manifestations of reproductive actions rather than the psychological underpinnings of masculinity. Because, as of this writing, the majority of the extant literature in this area has emerged from a Caucasian, Euro-American perspective, this chapter largely reflects this worldview, including the notion of hegemonic masculinity—a culturally normative definition of masculinity under which men are expected to align their identities.

This chapter has four sections. The first employs a historical framework to examine the main theoretical threads within the psychology of men and masculinity. The second section examines the current research findings regarding the psychology of men and masculinity, with the goal of critiquing the past and future directions of this area. Our review of this literature suggests that there are two current movements within the psychology of men and masculinity that are guiding empirical developments. On the basis of our assessment, we label these movements the *essentialist* and the *constructivist* movements. Research conducted from an essentialist perspective considers that the characteristics of a group are representative of global traits. Men are universally conceptualized as a set of socialized traits, and it is the enactment of those traits that results in consequences for them, for women, and for society. Research conducted from a constructivist perspective, conversely, is concerned with the context in which a man's definition of masculinity develops as well as the degree to which that definition does or does not fit current situational demands. It is this situational fit, or lack thereof, that determines consequences. It is under these two headings that we outline the empirical findings and offer our critique. The third section consists of counseling implications, and the fourth section briefly discusses possible future directions of inquiry.

THEORETICAL PERSPECTIVES

Some researchers have suggested that men are the way they are because of genetics or evolution (e.g., Buss, 1995). Still others, writing for a more popular rather than scholarly audience, have used the metaphor that men's behavioral styles are due to their planet of origin being Mars rather than Venus (Grey, 2004). Contrary to these perspectives, however, the extant empirical literature largely supports the notion that the majority of behaviors and traits associated with the biological sex male are the result of a social press (see Groeschel, Wester, & Sedivy, 2010) to enact specific values, ideals, and the standards of behavioral practice (see Connell & Messerschmidt, 2005). In the 21st century, this idea is known as the *social construction of gender*, and it extends the foundational work of scholars such as Bem (1974, 1979; see also Spence & Helmreich, 1979, 1981) by suggesting that masculinity is a cohort-specific, learned set of culturally embedded norms defined by society. Specifically, society teaches boys standards of appropriate masculine behavior (Levant, 1995; 2001a, 2001b); adherence to those standards is rewarded, and deviance from those standards is punished.

Among the first prominent writings in this area was by David and Brannon (1976), who asserted that like race or ethnicity, gender was an identity enacted across different spheres of life. This was a key development in the study of men and masculinity because it moved the construct of masculinity away from biology and emphasized the depth to which cultural definitions of masculinity could be internalized. This internalization had the power, therefore, to dramatically shape how men were in the world. David and Brannon developed labels for some of the more prominent masculine identities present in North American culture. These labels such as Sturdy Oak, Big Wheel, No Sissy Stuff, and Give 'Em Hell were some of the first articulations in the psychological literature of the specific expectations that underlie the socialization experiences of men. For example, the Sturdy Oak represented the expectation that individual men were expected to successfully handle the challenges of life independently without complaint, whereas the Big Wheel noted the importance of success and individual achievement. Both of these labels encompassed the degree to which society associated masculinity with individual strength and accomplishment.

These labels were the first attempt to quantify what current scholars have labeled *hegemonic masculinity* (Connell & Messerschmidt, 2005, p. 829; see also O'Neil, 2010)—essentially, the content of what society defines as acceptable masculine values and behaviors under which men are expected to align their identities. Even in the 21st century, men are expected to become successful and important in their lives, and especially in their jobs, as evidence of David and Brannon's (1976) Big Wheel identity. Multicultural research in general, however, has pointed out the importance of also understanding the roles of power and privilege in understanding the enactment of the male gender role. Hence, although David and Brannon mentioned the existence of that privilege, the more current construct of hegemonic masculinity also refers to the degree to which the socialization process assigns power to men as a function of their gender role. Certainly

men in general, and European American men in the United States specifically, have long benefited from the privilege associated with their assigned gender role—a process well documented in the feminist literatures. It is, therefore, important to note that hegemonic masculinity as a construct acknowledges that the socialized male gender role oppresses men as well as women. The male gender role seems to afford men great privilege. But as in the parable of the Sword of Damocles, that privilege has the potential to be costly.

Two theoretical perspectives dominate the research exploring the costs of enacting dominant European American masculinity. The first perspective is that of *social learning* (e.g., Bandura, 1977). Men learn how to be men through the examples of other men; they replicate what they observe, are reinforced for successfully replicating that behavior, and learn to not deviate from the resultant pattern through society's use of consequences as well as punishments. The second theoretical perspective is *social construction* (e.g., Addis, Mansfield, & Syzdek, 2010), which considers the context in which masculinity develops as critical to the construction of a masculine identity. Although social learning stresses the degree to which masculinity is communicated through the generations via observational learning, social construction sees individual men within specific contexts as active agents developing a masculinity designed to meet their needs and the demands of a situation.

Social Learning

One of the first theories that emerged from the perspective of social learning was *gender role strain* (GRS; Pleck, 1981, 1995). GRS theory asserts that men learn a set of societally based proscriptions regarding appropriate masculine behaviors that are maladaptive, problematic, and ultimately unrealistic. No one man can be expected to maintain an iron control of their emotional needs throughout their entire life span, for example. As such, men experience significant psychological distress trying to live up to these unrealistic and often incompatible gender role expectations. Three specific aspects of this stress were identified by GRS theory. The first, *gender role discrepancy*, refers to the idea that a significant portion of males will fail to fulfill the expectations of the traditional male role. Few men can always live up to the unrealistic cultural expectations of *always* being in control, self-sufficient, successful, and independent. As a result, many men experience increased levels of psychological distress because of their perceived failure in meeting these expectations. In other words, differences between the culturally defined male role and one's actual self can lead to undue strain (Pleck, 1981, 1995). The second major concept underlying GRS is *gender role trauma.* According to Pleck (1981, 1995), even if one is successful in meeting all of the expectations all of the time, the very process by which those expectations are socialized is traumatic. Young boys are often shamed into aggressive behaviors, denying their emotionality, and avoiding anything remotely feminine (Brooks, 1990; Levant & Brooks, 1997; Levant & Pollack, 1995). Such experiences can lead some men to feel they are failures if they exhibit these behaviors later in life (for related discussion, see Krugman, 1995; Pollack, 1998). Finally, the third major subtype of GRS is *gender role dysfunction.* In this case, fulfillment of the male gender role expectations can have negative consequences for everyone because the socialized behaviors themselves can be problematic. Examples of these include engaging in aggressive behaviors, distancing themselves from their families, and putting their job above all else (Levant & Pollack, 1995; Pleck, 1995).

Building on the foundation of GRS, O'Neil (e.g., 1987) developed the theory of *gender role conflict* (GRC). Although GRS mostly focuses on the unrealistic expectations of the socialized male gender role and the consequences to men as a result of their attempts to live up to the expectations, GRC (for a review, see O'Neil, 2008) focuses on the degree to which the socialized abilities, behaviors, and values conflict with specific situational demands (e.g., Wester, 2008; Wester & Vogel, 2002) and the problems that arise for men as they inflexibly adhere to their learned gender role. Some men's learned tendency to restrict the public expression of emotion, for example, may be adaptive in situations such as work, school, or interpersonal interactions requiring quick action and response (e.g., in the role of a police officer or soldier; see Brooks, 2001; Wester & Lyubelsky, 2005). At the same time, however, this tendency toward emotional restriction may conflict with the situational demands associated with returning home and being emotionally available to spouses and children.

Four overall patterns of male GRC have been identified (O'Neil, Good, & Holmes, 1995). *Success, power, and competition* (SPC) examines the degree to which men are socialized to focus on "personal achievement . . . obtaining authority . . . or comparing themselves to others" (O'Neil et al., 1995, p. 174). An example of this is some men's desire to excel competitively as opposed to collaboratively. *Restricted emotionality* (RE) discusses the degree to which men are taught to "fear feelings" (O'Neil et al., 1995, p. 176). An example of this includes some men's tendency to avoid the public expression of emotion, despite the fact that their emotional experience is just as intense as that of women (e.g., Wester et al., 2002). *Restricted affectionate behavior between men* (RABBM) explores how men are socialized to have difficulties "expressing [their] feelings and thoughts with other men" (O'Neil et al., 1995, p. 176). An example of this is some men's tendency to avoid verbally expressing their tender feelings for other men. Finally, *conflict between work and family relationships* (CBWFR) discusses the degree to which men struggle with "balancing work, school, and family" (O'Neil et al., 1995, p. 176) because of the competing socialized roles resulting in a tendency to put career ahead of family (Heppner & Heppner, 2001).

Rather than blaming men themselves for the problems they face, GRC theory defines these problems as the result of inflexible application of learned gender role styles in the face of situational demands that are incongruent with one of these four gender socialized patterns. For example, male gender role socialization produces psychological distress only under specific conditions in which the GRCs with the demand of the situation. Examples include when (a) a man is unable to adapt his socialization to a current life situation (i.e., socialized pressure to succeed at work conflicts with interpersonal or family demands) or (b) others are unable to recognize and validate a man's socialized method of expression (e.g., instrumental or action-oriented coping styles; see Heesacker & Bradley, 1997). In the absence of such conditions, however, gender role-related conflict and subsequent psychological distress potentially decreases (see O'Neil, 2008; Wester & Vogel, 2002).

Social Constructivism

Addis and Mahalik (2003) offered a social–constructionist perspective to understand the development of masculinity that incorporates both the importance of socialization while also conceptualizing masculinity as a more fluid, dynamic process. This perspective considers a man's contexts (i.e., the environment) in which he constructs his understanding of what it means to be a man, to be the critical factor. Said another way, "men (and women) learn to enact gender repertoires of behavior to achieve particular social means and ends" (Addis, Mansfield, & Syzdek, 2010, p. 81). Masculinity might be considered as a learned constellation of behaviors but also flexible, responsive to situational demands, and modified as men seek to achieve specific goals deemed critical depending on the context in which the masculine identity developed (Addis & Cohane, 2005). Thus, for some men and under some conditions, certain behaviors—developed to achieve specific social, interpersonal, and individual goals—may be adaptive and appropriate when applied flexibly; however, under different conditions, or for different men, those same behaviors may interfere with functioning. Addis et al. (2010) would call this a pragmatic, functional understanding of masculinity. *Pragmatic* refers to the need to evaluate masculine gender role socialization in light of how adaptive it allows men to be in the world. A *functional* approach, in turn, frames the consequences of masculine gender role socialization in light of both the historical goals of that socialization and the contexts in which those consequences occurred. Said more simply, from this perspective, there are "competing masculinities that are continuously being constructed and contested" (Addis & Cohane, 2005, p. 640) on the basis of an individual context.

Mahalik, Good, and Englar-Carlson (2003) presciently summarized the nature of this construction process into seven masculine scripts—narratives that specify the behaviors, values, and ideals relevant to certain contexts. Mahalik et al. stressed the importance of understanding the meaning an individual man might assign these scripts as well as the goals they seek to accomplish through their enactment as the primary method for understanding the nature of a man's context. For a man developing in a context in which the verbal expression of emotion is not functional, stoicism becomes more important and therefore a significant component of a masculine identity. The "strong and silent" (Mahalik et al., 2003, p. 124) script, for example, stresses the importance of men being stoic and unemotional, lest they be labeled as less manly than their peers. The "tough-guy" (Mahalik et al., 2003 p. 124) builds on this idealized script, stressing both the suppression of emotions so as to be called tough-in-the-face-of-pain while also responding to situations through physical prowess. One example might be a man growing up in an environment in which he must take a taxing job to support his family. He does so because that is what he must do to provide for his family. Emotional expression has little value in this situation, as he must sacrifice himself and his needs to provide for those he loves. Accordingly, this stoicism and work ethic become part of the context in which he and his children develop. They might learn how to cope with disappointment, deal with physical pain, and push themselves toward success in the workplace without revealing one's fears to others to successfully achieve a goal. Later, however, as the situational demands placed on young men change, they might recognize that it is not always in their best interests to remain silent about their emotional needs, in a relationship for example, and that there are situations in which it is appropriate to express one's emotions and meet one's needs.

Summary and Critique

Smiler (2004) has detailed the evolution of the psychology of men as following a path from the unquestioning acceptance of the positive nature of masculinity; through the exploration of masculinity, femininity, and androgyny; to the recognition of the degree to which the socialized male gender role is compatible and incompatible with current situational demands. As mentioned, however, much of the extant literature stems from a Euro-American, Western notion of masculinity. The international applications of this literature need to be fully explored in terms of research, theory, and practice (see Blazina & Shen-Miller, 2011, for a recent exception). Issues of social class have also not been fully integrated into any theory of masculine gender role identity development, and although Hill and Fischer (2001) did explore how men's sense of entitlement mediated the link between masculinity and rape-related variables, there has been little movement exploring the roles played by power and privilege in the psychology of men. Admittedly, there is a growing literature (summarized later in this chapter) aimed at understanding the experiences had by men of color as they navigate the demands of both the dominant culture's socialized male gender role and the gender role expectations of their culture of origin. This work, however, largely relies on definitions and measures developed from a Caucasian, Euro-American perspective; there has not been a ground-up effort to conceptualize, articulate, and operationalize, culturally specific definitions of masculinity despite a growing number of articles using geographically diverse samples of men. Blazina, Pisecco, and O'Neil (2005) pursued research along these lines regarding the GRC experience of Western adolescent boys, reconceptualizing the nature of GRC such that it included a developmental perspective. Something similar is needed with regards to cultural definitions of masculinity.

Furthermore, no single, unifying theory of masculinity has been adopted (e.g., O'Neil, 2010). For example, both social learning and social construction stress the role of society in forming gender. Critics charge that social learning reduces this process to one of an individual responding to observed activities under the influence of rewards and punishments, whereas social construction considers the individual an active agent in the construction of the meaning associated with a masculine identity, the goals that identity is designed to meet, and the situations in which it may (or may not) be adaptive (e.g., Addis & Cohane, 2005). Much more work needs to be done testing these two theories and determining which offers the most useful understanding of masculinity. Indeed, there is also an emerging psychoanalytical understanding of masculine gender role development. The psychoanalytic perspective has its

roots in both object relations (e.g., Fairbairn, 1963) and self-psychology (e.g., Kohut & Wolf, 1978), and as such, they focus on the role played by early interactions, typically with caregivers, in the emotional, interpersonal, and psychological development of boys. Blazina (1997, 2001, 2004) proposed the construct of a "masculine self" to describe how men can, through positive self-object experiences such as adequate mirroring during development and a merging with an idealized other, develop a cohesive sense of themselves as masculine. Krugman (1995), however, argued that young boys were unable to identify with their own sense of shame at not living up to the male gender role ideal and thus sought to avoid such feelings. The subsequent disidentification process—the process through which shame might be processed, understood, and grown from—therefore cannot occur appropriately. Blazina (2001) called this the "fragile masculine self" (p. 50), in that the individual cannot adaptively respond to situations that threaten its masculinity.

This lack of theoretical consensus has led to a dynamic body of scholarship, which shares the goal of understanding the consequences associated with the male gender role. It has also precluded the specific testing of any of these theoretical perspectives. Although the theory of a fragile masculine self is an area of emerging interest, for example, the bulk of the psychology of men scholarship presumes either the social learning or the social construction perspectives. To be fair, this approach has allowed for significant growth in the understanding of how men learn to be men, develop those identities, and refine them on the basis of situational demands. In essence, the profession is now much more able to predict a wide range of social consequences associated with masculinity. At the same time, however, there has been no empirical effort within the psychology of men to link that prediction to the specific components of each theory, thereby disallowing any specific test of the theoretical explanation being employed, a point initially made by Addis et al. (2010):

> And yet, we are neither studying those mechanisms, nor are we operationalizing their effects in ways that are congruent

with our conceptual understanding of them. Without [this], the claims we can make about the nature of gendered social learning will remain of the form, "men who are generally like this, are also generally like that." (p. 81)

RESEARCH

Another consequence of there being no unifying theory of masculinity is that the extant literature on the psychology of men is often organized around the prediction of symptoms and consequences associated with the socialized male gender role (e.g., Nutt & Brooks, 2008). In contrast, and to provide a more critical review, this chapter will utilize as an organizer our assessment of the overarching schools of thought that permeate the psychology of men—categories we label as *essentialist* and *constructivist*. We derived these labels through an assessment of the underlying positions taken by the researchers. The essentialist approach takes the position that characteristics of a group are representative of global traits characteristic of hegemonic masculinity. It is these traits, rather than variations among group members, that are therefore the focus of predictive empirical work. The constructivist perspective, conversely, is more concerned with the context in which a man's definition of masculinity develops (e.g., Addis & Mahalik, 2003; Addis et al., 2010), as well as the situation in which it is currently being enacted (e.g., O'Neil, 2010; Wester, 2008), than with the strict prediction of either positive or negative outcomes. Our hope is that, by using this approach rather than a prediction-based outline, readers will be able to more critically understand both broad conclusions that can be drawn from the extant literature as well as paths that still need exploration.

Essentialist

We see the extant literature in the field of men and masculinity as largely coming from the essentialist approach; men are often described as a set of ingrained socialized traits stemming from the enactment of socially proscribed masculine roles, from which come a largely unavoidable set of consequences.

Said another way, from this perspective, masculinity is seen as a stable construct, enacted on the basis of learned patterns and producing predictable outcomes. This is an important contribution to the psychology of men because it allows for the development of an increased understanding of the social costs associated with masculinity. The focus of much of this research has been in the areas of interpersonal and intrapersonal consequences, and it is therefore those areas under which we organize our review.

Interpersonal consequences. Another large body of research published on men and masculinity has focused on the interpersonal consequences of male gender roles. For example, subscription to the traditional male gender role has been negatively correlated with relationship quality for adult men, including decreased relational intimacy with both the opposite sex (e.g., Cournoyer & Mahalik, 1995; Good et al., 1995, 1996) and the same sex (e.g., Van Hyfte & Rabinowitz, 2001). Historically, Pleck (1995) demonstrated that the low paternal involvement prescribed to men by traditional masculinity is associated with decreased levels of martial success, decreased occupational mobility, and poorer child performance on measures of educational and occupational success. Higher levels of psychological distress (Barnett, Marshall, & Pleck, 1992) and lower levels of well-being (see Pleck, 1995 for review) have also been demonstrated. From these studies, Pleck drew the conclusion that when men conform to this particular male role expectation by being less involved in their family, they pay a severe price over time. At the same time, however, other work suggests that the socially proscribed gender role expectations change as a man ages (e.g., Collison, 1987; Sternbach, 2001) allowing for both increased family involvement and decreased potential for negative consequences the older a man becomes (e.g., Levinson, 1978).

Moore and Stuart (2005) offered a review of the literature on the degree to which subscription to the traditional male gender role predicts partner violence, concluding that across multiple measures of masculinity and with multiple samples of diverse men, increased subscription to the male gender role predicted acceptance of, and in some cases engagement in, intimate partner violence. Cohn and Zeichner (2006), for example, using the response choice aggression paradigm and electric shock delivered under laboratory conditions, demonstrated a similar link between the male gender role and general aggression in collegian males, whereas Moore et al. (2008) showed correlation between the dimensions of gender role stress and partner violence in a clinical sample of violent adult men. More generally, studies have found one or more patterns of GRC or GRS to be significantly related to traditional attitudes toward women as held by both adult and collegian men in the United States (Mintz & Mahalik, 1996; Robinson & Schwartz, 2004) and with U.S. (Hill & Fischer, 2001) and Canadian (Senn et al., 2000) collegian men's interpersonal attitudes or behaviors that imply rape acceptance and violence toward women. These effects were confirmed by Locke and Mahalik (2005), who utilized a sample of 254 U.S. college students to demonstrate that problematic alcohol use and conformity to masculine role norms positively correlated with endorsement of rape myths and sexually aggressive behavior.

Intrapersonal consequences. The majority of research regarding men and masculinity has involved the prediction of intrapersonal outcomes experienced by men as a result of their subscription to the socialized male gender role. In his recent review, for example, O'Neil (2010) noted that across more than 250 empirical studies and a variety of populations published in the psychology of men literature, subscription to the traditionally socialized male gender role in general, and male GRC in particular, significantly predicted negative consequences. These included depression, anxiety, risk-taking behaviors, substance use, higher blood pressure, and increased risk for threats and bullying. For example, one of the most consistent findings is that subscription to the traditionally socialized male gender role is significantly correlated with depressive symptoms, with the GRC pattern of restricted emotionality (i.e., conflict felt as a results of the restricting emotional expression to others) being one of the strongest predictors of that depression (e.g., Blazina & Watkins, 1996; Cournoyer & Mahalik, 1995; Fragoso &

Kashubeck, 2000; Mahalik & Cournoyer, 2000). In turn, all four patterns of GRC regularly correlate with adult men and male collegian anxiety (e.g., Blazina & Watkins, 1996), the psychological distress of adult male medical patients (Mertens, 2001) as well as Australian men (Theodore & Lloyd, 2000), and the low self-esteem of collegians (e.g., Mahalik et al., 2001; Schwartz et al., 1996).

One emerging line of research in this area has been the examination of the degree to which the socialized male gender role leads to engagement in risk-taking behaviors. In a theoretical narrative, Courtenay (1998) outlined how the traditionally socialized male gender role contributes to increased health risks through endorsement of high-risk behaviors. Indeed, endorsement of masculine gender roles has been associated with greater substance abuse (Monk & Ricciardelli, 2003; Pleck, Sonenstein, & Ku, 1993), especially for collegian men (Blazina & Watkins, 1996; Korcuska & Thombs, 2003), risky sexual behavior on the part of both adolescent and college-age men (Pleck et al., 1993), and collegian male aggressive behaviors (Locke & Mahalik, 2005; Mahalik et al., 2003). These links have been shown both within and outside the United States, most notably of late the Russian Federation (e.g., Levant et al., 2003), and have been suggested to account for some of the statistical differences between women and men in regard to life expectancies, dropout rates, and suicide (Courtenay, 1998; Pleck, Sonenstein, & Ku, 1993).

Recent work suggests that the linkage between the male gender role and risky behaviors may be more complex than previously considered. Groeschel, Wester, and Sedivy (2010) demonstrated that with regards to alcohol, GRC, and attitudes toward seeking psychological help, GRC actually mediated the link between male collegians' substance use and attitudes toward seeking psychological help. Their explanation was that for their sample of 399 U.S. college students, the size of any relationship between the male gender role and drinking behavior depended in large measure on the reasons men might be drinking—that is, to live up to the male gender role or to compensate for their not meeting gender role socialized norms. Although Groeschel et al.'s (2010) use of help seeking as an outcome variable means that more work needs to be done to understand the prediction of psychological distress, their explanation suggests that contextual demands might play a role in linking the socialized male gender role and risky behaviors.

Another example of the complexity involved in examining the linkage between socialized masculinity and health behaviors is the recent work demonstrating that subscription to the male gender role also positively correlates with a desire for a muscular body type in the United States (McCreary, Sasse, Saucier, & Dorsch, 2004) and Canada (Morrison, Morrison, Hopkins, & Rowan, 2004), an overall drive for muscularity (Morrison, Morrison, & Hopkins, 2003), and endorsement of the bodybuilding lifestyle in collegian and adult males (e.g., Parish, Baghurst, & Turner, 2010) as well as Israeli men (Rubinstein, 2003) due in large part to the skewed media images presented to men regarding their bodies (e.g., Hobza & Rochlen, 2009). All told, some men who more strongly identify as traditionally masculine structure their lifestyle and health behaviors to obtain the physique considered representative of masculinity (Furnham, Badmin, & Sneade, 2002; Galli & Reel, 2009)—a goal considered by some segments of society as the embodiment of healthy behaviors (King & Schuler, 2003; Schwarzenegger & Dobbins, 1999). For future research, the key might the differentiation between healthy exercise choices and conditions termed body image difficulties (Cafri & Thompson, 2004) or muscle dysmorphia (e.g., Galli & Reel, 2009; Pope, Phillips, & Olivardia, 2000).

Courtenay (1998) noted how masculinity could increase unhealthy risk factors across the life span through its impact on the choice of coping mechanisms to deal with physical and mental health symptoms (e.g., substance use) as well as the avoidance of health care and support systems when problems arise. Consistent with this, a recent trend in the psychology of men literature has involved exploring the degree to which men engage (or do not engage) in the use of health and mental health services (e.g., Boman & Walker, 2010). Berger, Levant, McMillan, Kelleher, and Sellers (2005) linked negative attitudes toward seeking help held by adult men ($N = 155$) to endorsement of the dominant male gender roles and experience of GRC—a relationship

also demonstrated with U.S. collegians (Good, Dell, & Mintz, 1989). Additionally, using a sample of 118 Australian male college students, Boman and Walker (2010) concluded that conformity to male role norms predicted a perception of increased social barriers to seeking health care, an effect moderated in part by their sense of general self-efficacy. To be sure, traditional male gender roles encourage men to be independent, in control, and stoic. Boman and Walker's (2010) explanation for this effect was that the greater a man's sense of his own ability to cope with psychological distress the more likely he was to resist seeking psychological help despite external evidence to the contrary.

Not surprisingly, therefore, men as a group were found to seek professional psychological help less often than women for issues inconsistent with their gender role, such as substance abuse, stress, and depression (Andrews, Issakidis, & Carter, 2001). In fact, Groeschel, Wester, and Sedivy (2010) demonstrated that GRC mediated the linkage between male collegian's alcohol use and their attitudes toward seeking psychological help. The negative correlation between the socialized male gender role and attitudes toward seeking psychological help have been demonstrated even in elderly men (Husaini, Moore, & Cain, 1994), who have been hypothesized as having been given permission by society to move beyond the socialized male gender role (Vacha-Hasse, Wester, & Christianson, 2010). Still, younger males tend to have greater negative attitudes and less willingness toward seeking counseling than their female peers (Gonzalez, Alegria, & Prihoda, 2005); Chandra and Minkovitz (2006) demonstrated this phenomenon as early as the eighth grade. Similarly, subscription to the male gender role has been correlated with psychological defensiveness, treatment fearfulness, and negative perceptions of counselors (e.g., Englar-Carlson & Vandiver, 2001; Schaub & Williams, 2007) as well as the tendency of male college students to avoid discussing distressing emotions (Komiya, Good, & Sherrod, 2000; Vogel & Wester, 2003; Vogel, Wester, Wei, & Boysen, 2005) and their perception of seeing themselves as weak if they were to seek counseling (called *self-stigma*; Vogel, Wade, & Haake, 2006; Vogel, Wade, & Hackler, 2007).

Conclusions regarding how this fear about seeking psychological help can be overcome by counseling psychologists have been mixed. For example, although career counseling has often been suggested as a potential entry point for male clients (e.g., Rochlen, Blazina, & Raghunathan, 2002; Rochlen, Mohr, & Hargrove, 1999; Rochlen & O'Brien, 2002a, 2002b), one that allows men to overcome their reluctance to seek help because of the focus on overt setting of career goals rather than covert emotional analysis, empirical research on the specific mechanisms through which this might occur is sorely lacking. Kantemeni, Smothers, Christianson, and Wester (2011) employed a role induction methodology but concluded that the inclusion of male gender role specific information was no more effective than a general role induction procedure. Hammer and Vogel (2010) used a male-sensitive brochure to advertise counseling services and determined that this method reduced the stigma male collegians associated with seeking psychological help. Wester, Arndt, Sedivy, and Arndt (2010), however, analyzed a sample of 178 male police officers to show that the relationship between male GRC and stigma associated with seeking help is strong enough to persist even when men understand the potential benefits of psychotherapy and counseling.

Summary and critique. Research from an essentialist point of view has greatly increased counseling psychology's understanding of the potential negative consequences associated with the traditionally socialized male gender role. At the same time, some have asserted that there is a negative bias inherent to this body of work. One potential result of this bias is that the focus often becomes one of pathology-based symptomology rather than the more theoretically driven (albeit more complicated) questions of how men learn to be men, how these roles vary across different situational contexts, and in what direction men need to move to lead more fulfilling, productive lives (Addis et al., 2010). One recent exception is the work of Hammer and Good (2010), who ground their efforts in the positive psychology movement (Seligman & Csikszentmihalyi, 2000). They asserted that although it is important to understand deficits, symptoms, and negative consequences associated with the male role, it is also equally important to focus on strengths given that such strengths increase resiliency and adaptive coping. Their study employed a community-based sample of men ranging in age from 18 years to 79 years and demonstrated that conformity to masculine gender roles normed on predicted levels of physical fitness and courage, while also predicting lower levels of resilience and personal control. Their explanation for these findings—that men may be conforming to the expectations of others while simultaneously developing their own masculine identity within the confines of those expectations—certainly requires further study.

Additionally, the extant essentialist literature suffers from an overreliance on samples of convenience, collegian samples, and samples of mostly European American participants of unknown socioeconomic status. Also, much of the published research in this area is survey work; few studies have employed experimental or quasi-experimental designs. Furthermore, although recent work has included more diverse measures such as physiological and behavior observations, the bulk of the literature relies on paper and pencil self-reports. Such instruments are vulnerable to self-presentation variables on the part of respondents, and questions can be raised regarding the degree to which attitudes measured thusly predict behaviors, and how strongly the psychometric data support their use with diverse samples of men. O'Neil (2008), for example, in discussing his own Gender Role Conflict Scale (GRCS), noted the dearth of factorial validity studies on the GRCS, especially as it is experienced by diverse samples of men. The use of the GRCS and other paper-and-pencil measures of subscription to traditionally socialized male gender roles, with men of many different races, classes, nationalities, and ethnic backgrounds, have been increasing, but few of these articles have included psychometric support and factor structure examinations.

Most important, the essentialist perspective—be it focused on either negative or positive outcomes—potentially ignores the situational and cultural variables that may be related to masculinity in its prediction of said outcomes. This runs the risk of placing the psychology of men on a path to be "significantly out of step with current approaches to understanding gender, race, and class" (Addis et al., 2010, p. 81). Other professions, sociology and anthropology, for example, do not consider gender to be a static trait. Rather, gender is understood as a multifaceted set of learned behaviors embedded within both situational contexts and social interactions. Note, for example, that the social conceptions of masculinity change over time. Smiler (2004) explored the evolution of the social construction of masculinity when he cited Stearns (1994), who specifically outlined the transition from emotionally expressive and passionate Victorian masculinity to the more stoic, reserved masculinity of the 20th and 21st centuries. As a result, any understanding of masculinity or its consequences must include situational, contextual, and cultural variables as well as the role these factors play in the lives of men. Some recent research, discussed in the next section, has started to move in this direction but more work is needed.

Constructivist

From this point of view, "immediately observable contextual cues . . . activate corresponding stereotypes and belief systems" (Deaux & Major, 1987, p. 374), which guide a man's construction of his gendered identity. Said another way, "gendered social learning is more flexible and context dependent than one would assume based on the way it has been operationalized in the psychology of men" (Addis et al., 2010, p. 80). Thus, it becomes possible that adhering to the socialized male gender role might be adaptive for some men in some settings but perhaps not for all men in other settings. Although this is a relatively new concept within the psychology of men, some important lines of inquiry have developed, including a few studies that have directly examined the situational context in which masculinity is enacted and a much larger increase in attempts to understand masculinity as it occurs for men of color.

Multicultural masculinity. One of the more significant trends of late in the extant literature has been the integration of variables such as culture

and ethnicity, sexual orientation, and age into an understanding of masculinity (for detailed reviews, see Vacha-Hasse et al., 2010; Wester, 2008). For purposes of this narrative, multicultural masculinity refers to examinations of how multiple aspects of identity, one of which is masculinity, converge to influence an outcome. In essence, it is the interaction of identity variables that is more likely to explain an outcome rather than masculinity independently. Older men, for example, have been demonstrated to struggle with their traditionally socialized male gender role (Drost, 2005) in that as one gets older there is an increasing disconnect between learned behavior style and the demands of an advancing society. The identity they developed as they grew into men and beyond is seen by society as less relevant, potentially leading to a process known as disengagement (Cummings, Henry, & Damianopoulos, 1961). Cummings et al. (1961) originally argued that men have an instrumental role in society that is primarily associated with their employment. When that role changes, older men transition to a period of life associated with less social support (see Hill & Donatelle, 2004) and reduced participatory involvement, despite empirical evidence that as men age, the experience of GRC changes (e.g., Cournoyer & Mahalik, 1995), with older men often experiencing less SPC and CBWFR but similar levels of RE and RABBM. As the disconnect between learned behaviors and the demands of current situations grows to the point of outright conflict, a circular process develops—less involvement means fewer interactions, which both reinforces any maladaptive coping mechanisms and increases the push to disengage.

Recent work (e.g., Carter, Williams, Juby, & Buckley, 2005; Wester, Vogel, Wei, & McLain, 2006) demonstrates that African American male collegians do experience GRC and that this conflict does predict psychological distress affected by racial identity status. As such, the challenge for African American men seems to be to define themselves in light of the masculine gender role demands stemming from both the dominant culture as well as African American culture, while at the same time dealing with racism. Franklin's (1999) construct of *invisibility* is important here; defined as an inner struggle with the recognition that "one's talents, abilities, personality and worth are not valued or recognized because of prejudice and racism" (p. 761), it is a developmental process by which African American men define themselves within the larger context of society and its construction of race as well as gender roles. A vital component to this process is feedback from the African American community at large because they offer a set of rules and values with regards to race that balance those of the dominant culture. The possibility of a paradox exists, however; increased connection with the African American community, despite its many benefits, increases the likelihood that one might violate one of the rules posed by the dominant society. Thus, if they attempt to meet one set of gender roles (i.e., European American) they likely frustrate the other set of gender roles (i.e., African American). Hence, they may find themselves in situations in which they must violate one, fail to meet the other, and experience subsequent psychological distress.

Regarding masculinity as it exists within Latino culture, the construct that most frequently comes to mind is that of machismo—typically defined as an essence of manhood via "physical strength, sexual attractiveness, virtue, and potency" (Ruiz, 1981, p. 191). Fragoso and Kashubeck (2000) examined a sample of 113 Mexican American adult men and determined that GRC and machismo predicted psychological distress. These effects were presciently suggested by Stillson, O'Neil, and Owen (1991) and later supported by Carter et al. (2005), albeit in both cases the research was hampered by small sample sizes. In applying this to contemporary men, Mirandé (2004) explained how *machismo* is actually more of a bipolar construct. One pole consists of an exaggerated masculinity, expressed through economic dominance, violence, and self-centered achievement. The other pole is positive (e.g., Mirandé, 2004). Characteristics here include assertiveness, responsibility, ethics, sincerity, respect, and courage. Unfortunately, the degree to which the dominant culture values the more negative aspects of machismo while closing off the avenues to success potentially produces confusion similar to that faced by more traditionally macho men. Furthermore, the roles played by men outside compared with inside the home differ from the dominant

culture's perception of masculinity. Men are expected to be in charge of their household, and the cultural shifts that occur as a result of exposure to the dominant culture could potentially increase gender role difficulties.

Liu and Iwamoto (2006, 2007) demonstrated that masculine role norms intersect with cultural variables, such as Asian values, coping style, and ethnic identity, to predict various forms of psychological distress (see also Iwamoto, Liao, & Liu, 2010). Chua and Fujino (1999) called it the image of a "model minority" (p. 395) because the dominant culture sees Asian men as being hard-working, economically responsible, and in charge of families who install the dominant cultural values in their children. The perception of Asian men held by the dominant culture in the 21st century serves a twofold purpose: It marginalizes Asian men and simultaneously relies on them to work, contribute to the economy, and raise their families with minimal demands on government services. Liu (2002) seemed to have best captured this contradiction when he wrote how Asian men must strive to occupy a "middle ground . . . [in that] they may need to simultaneously accept and repudiate the White masculine norm in search of alternative definitions of masculinity" (p. 108; see also Chin, 1998). For example, many Asian men perceive themselves as trapped between multiple gender role related demands (e.g., Sue, 2001) and reorganizing their definitions to balance those demands (Chua & Fujino, 1999).

Finally, although the extant literature on men of differing sexual orientations is small, one conclusion that can be drawn is that being either gay or bisexual is a direct violation of the socialized masculine gender role ideal that presumes active heterosexuality (e.g., Schwartzberg & Rosenberg, 1998). All males, regardless of their sexual orientation, grow up being socialized into this presumption (Harrison, 1995). The expression of romantic love and affection for another man might therefore present gay men with significant gender role–related difficulties stemming from an overt violation of gender role expectation. Simonsen, Blazina, and Watkins (2010), for example, linked the experience of GRC to psychological distress for their sample of 117 gay male participants. Indeed, being positioned between two cultures—one of which, the traditional male (i.e., heterosexual) rejects a central aspect of you (i.e., sexual orientation)—is a problematic situation at best. For gay and bisexual men, this places them in an untenable situation because the definitions they incorporate include society's strong homophobic bias (Barber & Mobley, 1999), while they also face significant condemnation for failing to "fulfill the male role and achieve a complete [i.e., heterosexual] male identity" (Harrison, 1995, p. 359). Indeed, Sánchez, Greenberg, Liu, and Vilain (2009) confirmed as much using consensual qualitative methodology and a sample of 547 gay male participants. In another study, however, Sánchez, Bocklandt, and Vilain (2009) suggested that the situation is more complex. Using samples of single and partnered gay men, they determined that GRC occurred differently depending on relationship status, with partnered gay men experiencing more issues stemming from success, power, and competition. Like Wester, Pionke, and Vogel (2005), however, Sánchez et al. (2009) demonstrated that GRC did not predict relationship satisfaction.

Important to the study of multicultural masculinity is the construct of male reference group (Wade, 1998). A *reference group* is that group with which individuals compare themselves, and it is through such comparisons that norms, attitudes, and values develop (for related discussion, see Singer, 1981). The outcome of this experience varies tremendously depending in large part on the makeup of a man's reference group (e.g., Wade, 1998; Wester, 2008), but in general, the identity developed across this experience contains specific skills and values considered important by the cohort. In brief, the more one's reference group is populated exclusively by members of the dominant culture rather than culturally relevant examples, the greater the chance for negative outcomes because the skills and values may include racist, exclusionary values (Wester, 2008). At the same time, Kilianski (2003) recently proposed the idea of an exclusive male identity to explain the potential for a more positive outcome. Drawing on social identity theory (for a review, see Fiske, 1998), and its use of in-group versus out-group perceptions to

explain both the development of a positive self-concept as well as stereotypical beliefs, Kilianski described how some men define themselves as exclusively masculine. In effect, men incorporate society's definition of traditional masculinity, while at the same time rejecting anything that would appear to violate that definition, to maintain their sense of self-esteem and handle the potential racist or homophobic experiences they might encounter.

Careers.   Unfortunately, the empirical research regarding the interaction between masculinity and vocational variables is limited. This is puzzling given the centrality work is to men's identity and self worth (e.g., Fouad & Kantameni, 2008) as well as the fact that GRC seems to be more common, and higher, in adult men within traditionally masculine careers (Jome & Tokar, 1998). Certainly, men have been included in vocation research, usually in an effort to clarify their career choices, their self-efficacy, or the structure of their career interests. In her recent comprehensive review, for example, Betz (2008) detailed how several studies demonstrated that men score higher in Holland's (1962) realistic theme, whereas women score higher on social themes. Research on career self-efficacy, also summarized by Betz, demonstrated similar patterns of differences between men and women: men reported greater access to learning experiences in the realistic and investigative domains, whereas women reported more experiences in social domains (e.g., Williams & Subich, 2006). In neither of these areas, however, and throughout our search of the extant vocational literature in general, was the explanation for these findings grounded in a critical understanding of the male gender role.

This omission stands in sharp contrast to the extensive research regarding women's career development, which has devoted significant effort to understanding the roles played by the female gender role and society such that questions regarding women and vocational variables "continues to be in the forefront of scholarly inquiry" (Swanson & Gore, 2000, p. 248). Admittedly, there has been some foundational work conducted; using a small (N = 212) sample of male collegians, Tokar and Jome (1998) demonstrated that endorsement of traditional masculinity predicted vocational interests but that those same vocational interest fully mediated the link between masculinity and career choice. Contrary to their predictions, however, there was no direct relationship demonstrated between masculinity and career choice. Also, many publications have addressed how to counsel men in vocational settings (e.g., Heppner & Heppner, 2001; Hills, Carlstrom, & Evanow, 2001) because career counseling has often been suggested as a potential entry point for male clients (e.g., Kantemeni et al., 2011; Rochlen, Blazina, & Raghunathan, 2002; Rochlen, Mohr, & Hargrove, 1999; Rochlen, & O'Brien, 2002a, 2002b). But despite some early efforts, research regarding how masculinity might intersect with the psychology of work variables—career choice, vocational barriers, person–environment fit, and vocational satisfaction to name a few—has been lacking.

There have been some initial efforts to understand how masculinity affects the lives of men working in specific career settings, but this has been problematic because it has not integrated vocational theory. Wester et al. (2010) described how the male gender role might, for male police officers, lead to their stigmatizing the very mental health services they require. That same male gender role, however, allowed them to be better police officers—an outcome demonstrated with other groups of men existing in specific career situations (e.g., military veterans; Brooks, 1990). Steinfeldt, Steinfeldt, England, and Speight (2009) explored the gendered experience of 211 male collegiate football players and demonstrated how their male gender role, adaptive though it was on the football field, predicted increased stigma toward mental health services. Rochlen, Good, and Carver (2009), using a sample of 174 male nurses, explored how men who entered nontraditional careers experienced GRC. Interestingly, men employed as nurses reported that despite working in an environment in which they, and their gender role– specific behaviors, were in the minority, they were satisfied with their work, and they reported similar levels of social support and life satisfaction compared with other published samples of men. Work is needed, however, to both verify these findings and link them to the broader vocational psychology literature, as the research questions under study were derived more from a contextualized psychology of men perspective and not a vocational perspective.

Emotions. From some of the earliest writing about men, it has been suggested that men experience pressure to withhold emotional expression (particularly certain emotions such as sadness). In fact, emotional stoicism is one of strongest components of the traditional male gender role socialization (see Wester et al., 2002) held by the public and often generalized to all men by counselors (Vogel, Wester, Heesacker, Boysen, & Seeman, 2006). Indeed, research on the traditionally socialized male gender role demonstrates how boys are discouraged from expressing emotions, with the exceptions of anger and pride (e.g., Levant, 2001b). Levant (1992) even proffered the construct of normative male alexithymia to describe how men's socialization experiences leaves them with an inability to experience or express a sufficiently wide range of emotions. Recent studies have supported a greater occurrence (with consistent effect sizes) of alexithymia in men compared with women (see review by Levant et al., 2006; also Levant, Hall, Williams, & Hasan, 2009).

Other critical reviews, however, focused on both the verbal as well as the nonverbal expression of emotions do not demonstrate a consistent sex-based pattern of results (Wester et al., 2002; Wong & Rochlen, 2005). A potential explanation for these seemingly contradictory findings has been offered by Wong and Rochlen (2005), who detailed how some men translate a covert experience of emotion (e.g., sadness) into both a gender role–specific internal experience of emotion as well as emotional inexpressiveness that might be considered by an external observer to be reflective of alexithymia. Wong and Rochlen therefore asserted that sex differences in emotion may emerge only when individuals experience increased motivation to present themselves in a certain way as a response to normative pressure. In fact, experimental studies have shown that when assigned the task of expressing emotions to one's partner, men and women do not differ in emotional expression (e.g., Ickes et al., 2000; Vogel, Tucker, Wester, & Heesacker, 1999). When the task is manipulated so that emotional expression is viewed as risky, however, men will start to withhold their emotional expression (Vogel, Wester, Heesacker, & Madon, 2003). Thus, the context may interact with the male role to exhibit the behaviors society associates with men's limited range of emotional ability.

Summary and critique. The constructivist approach, despite being relatively new and therefore having received less empirical attention than the essentialist approach, provides an important addition to the extant literature on the psychology of men by pointing out the unique tensions between the socialized male gender role and specific contextual factors. At the same time, much more work is needed to clarify and understand the process of construction. Addis and Mahalik (2003) did put forth the possibility that all situations in which a man exists create interactive processes that need to be understood if we are to truly understand the linkage between masculinity and outcomes (see also Addis et al., 2010). This would advance the profession's understanding of how, specifically, men exist and survive within multiple sets of gender role messages, while at the same time living in a society that often sets impassible barriers to their meeting such expectations. From this point of view, men do not merely behave in ways in which they were taught, but they select from a repertoire of learned behaviors while constructing a masculine identity aimed at meeting their owns needs as well as the demands of their specific contexts. A prominent example is research on men and their emotionality. Although Levant et al. (2009) demonstrated that men consistently score higher on measures of alexithymia than women, they acknowledged that their meta-analysis, despite being well done, "does not tell us anything about the reasons for the observed gender difference" (p. 198). Said another way, the degree to which external variables might be interacting with the socialized male gender role to produce behaviors that are, on the face, suggestive of alexithymia but in reality reflect a more complex dynamic affecting men's emotional expression cannot as yet be ruled out.

At the same time, the constructivist literature suffers from many of the same flaws that plague the

essentialist literature. Most notably, even those studies that incorporate men of color or more diverse samples of men are often of small size collected in convenient settings. Much of the published research in this area continues to be survey work suffering from lower response rates, and few studies have employed experimental or quasi-experimental designs. The bulk of the literature relies on paper and pencil self-reports, and there has been little movement toward incorporating observational, anthropological, or medical techniques. Indeed, when researchers consider a constructivist approach, the relationship between masculinity and predicted outcomes becomes multidimensional. Men are no longer merely collections of learned behaviors that lead to unsurprising consequences; the possibility exists that consequences will differ depending on context. Behaviors could be considered as adaptive in one setting but maladaptive in another setting.

Experimental studies that manipulate contextual demands to explore differential outcomes become critical. From a modeling perspective, tests of moderation and mediation need to be employed rather than more straightforward predictive techniques. Researchers need to consider the use of a more complex interactional model to accurately represent the variables at work. As a field of study, the psychology of men endorses diversity as one of its core values, yet despite the progress that has been made, much of the published research is still based on the assumption of universality. Thus, although researchers usually note the limits to generalization that their mostly European American undergraduate student samples necessitate and call on future research to examine the cross-cultural relevance of the theory under question, this research is rarely done. To be able to increase the cultural relevance, researchers must be willing to test their theories with diverse samples to determine which aspects of a theoretical model have universal utility and which are applicable only to certain groups (Burlew, 2003). This will require a reexamination of the psychometric applicability of the measures being used as well as a potential reconstruction of masculinity as a construct to include variables applicable within and between cultures. Structural invariance analysis is one way to examine the equivalence of theoretical model paths (i.e., hypothesized relationships between variables) across different groups, allowing new cultural data to facilitate theory modification (Miller & Sheu, 2008).

COUNSELING IMPLICATIONS

Although the goal of this chapter was to examine and critique the current state of the extant literature regarding the psychology of men and masculinity, counseling implications from that information also can be addressed. At a minimum, the psychology of men needs to be integrated into multicultural training and coursework in much the same way, and with the same enthusiasm, as the psychology of women has been integrated. Indeed, the previous decade has seen a tremendous increase in the amount of published material available to practitioners working with diverse populations of men in a variety of settings. A working group of the American Psychological Association's Division 51 (Society for the Psychological Study of Men and Masculinity) has been developing practice guidelines for working with boys and men modeled after similar documents aimed at guiding work with girls, people of color, and people of different sexual orientations. Additional published examples include Brooks and Good's (2001b) *The New Handbook of Psychotherapy and Counseling With Men*; Rabinowitz and Cochran's (2002) *Deepening Psychotherapy With Men*; Blazina and Shen-Miller's (2011) *An International Psychology of Men*; Brooks's (2009) *Beyond the Crises of Masculinity: A Transtheoretical Model for Male-Friendly Therapy*; Liu, Iwamoto, and Chae's (2010) *Culturally Responsive Counseling With Asian American Men*; Vacha-Hasse et al.'s (2010) *Psychotherapy With Older Men*; and Kapalka's (2010) *Counseling Boys and Men With ADHD*. Clearly, it is important for those who are training to provide services to male clients to be informed of the extant literature regarding men.

Several overarching themes in these works parallel the content of many multicultural counseling classes. Most notably, the extant literature regarding the provision of service to male clients stresses the importance of working *with* masculine gender role socialization rather than in opposition to it. The goal should not be to condemn or acclaim all socialized masculine behaviors but rather to encourage the development of a wider range of cognitive, affective, and behavioral options. This is consistent with what Kiselica (2006; see also Hammer & Good, 2010) has labeled a "male-friendly" approach to therapy in that men's ways of expressing themselves and experiencing their lives are considered valid. Instrumental expression of emotions is a prominent example, especially when this approach is enacted flexibly. The socialized male ideal of stoicism and restricted emotional expression has been hypothesized to interfere with the development of interpersonal relationships (e.g., Brooks, 2009). Rather than eliminating this aspect of their behavior, with assistance men can learn how to better read the demands of a situation and switch between a stoic demeanor and emotional expression as needed while also addressing the potential stigma associated with this behavior.

Another theme present within the extant literature on counseling men, also parallel to the multicultural counseling literature, is that counseling psychologists need to be aware of their values and ideals regarding masculinity so as to be on guard that those values might disrupt the therapeutic alliance. If one's view of traditionally socialized masculinity is overtly negative, this might interfere with the development of empathy and unconditional positive regard. At the same time, however, if one's view is overtly positive, this might make it hard for a counselor to challenge the maladaptive nature of their client's behaviors. Men must be "challenged to initiate a major reevaluation of their gender role values and assumptions in an effort to bring themselves into harmony with a changing world" (Brooks, 2001, p. 219). Unfortunately, counseling psychology does not have the strongest history of being perceived by men as open to their way of experiencing the world (e.g., Heesacker et al., 1999; Wester et al., 2002). When therapy is packaged and performed in a manner supportive of men and their ways of being men, however, they become more positive in their attitudes toward the process and more likely to consider seeking help (e.g., Rochlen & Hoyer, 2005). The role of the counselor would be to help these men in the journey, support their unique development and process, and learn how to effectively implement this view in the different contexts of their lives. This process of reframing encourages the assignment of new meaning to behaviors as well as the development of new, more adaptive ways of responding to contextual demands.

Counseling psychologists need to help men balance their conflicting gender role messages in addition to social pressures while also overcoming the gender role proscription against psychotherapy (Addis & Mahalik, 2003). This means that counseling psychologists need to be cognizant of the linkages between men's adherence to the socialized male gender role and to interpersonal as well as intrapersonal consequences. Said another way, it is clear from the extant literature that inflexible adherence to hegemonic masculinity leads to myriad psychological symptoms for men as well as for women; counseling psychologists need to become aware of that information. Indeed, masculine gender roles have been associated with risky sexual behavior and greater substance abuse, especially for collegians and young adults (Blazina & Watkins, 1996; Cochran, 2005; Korucuska & Thombs, 2003; Pleck, Sonenstein, & Ku, 1993). Subscription to the traditional male gender role has also been negatively correlated with relationship quality for adult men (e.g., Cournoyer & Mahalik, 1995) and with acceptance of, and in some cases engagement in, intimate partner violence (e.g., Moore & Stuart, 2005). In his recent review, O'Neil (2010) noted that over the past 10 years, research with a multitude of male populations has demonstrated the degree to which subscription to the traditionally socialized male gender role predicts negative consequences, including but not limited to depression, anxiety, risk-taking behaviors, substance use, higher blood pressure, and increased risk for violence.

At the same time, however, those working with male clients need to be aware of how complex those predictions are, as ongoing research is demonstrating the degree to which external variables, such as age, social support, racial identity, personality variables, and situational variables, mediate or moderate (for a review, see Frazier, Tix, & Baron, 2004) what have been traditionally considered two-dimensional predictive relationships (for a review, see O'Neil, 2010). Wester, Christianson, Vogel, and Wei (2007) demonstrated that the degree of social support experienced by collegians fully mediated the linkage between certain aspects of GRC and subsequent psychological distress. Monk and Ricciardelli (2003) suggested that the linkage between the male gender role and risky health behaviors (alcohol consumption, specifically) was mediated by the reasons why collegians drank—compensation, for example. Wester et al. (2010) demonstrated that men's awareness of the benefits of counseling was not enough to overcome their socialized stigma against seeking psychological help, whereas an awareness of the risks of seeking psychological help fully mediated the link between GRC and negative attitudes toward seeking psychological help. Said another way, men's avoidance of counseling may be more due to the risk they run by violating the social stigma attached to such behavior than the socialized male gender role per se.

Furthermore, counseling psychologists should be willing to consider that the socialized male gender role also imparts adaptive attitudes, values, and behaviors to their male clients. The recent work of Hammer and Good (2010), in which they demonstrated that conformity to masculine gender roles norms on predicted levels of physical fitness and on courage, while also predicting lower levels of resilience and personal control, is illustrative of how important it may be to see a man's experience in context to consider both the positive and negative consequences of his subscription to masculine ideology. Levant (1995), for example, detailed several virtues associated with traditionally socialized masculinity, which might be considered positive and, therefore, needing to be encouraged in the form of greater cultural acceptance and tolerance. Chief among those was willingness on the part of men to sacrifice and withstand pain as well as hardship to both protect and provide for their loved ones. More recently, Vacha-Hasse et al. (2010) described how understanding the contextual factors that shaped an older man's sense of his masculinity may allow a counselor to be more responsive to his ways of being and expression, rather than stigmatizing him because his age values no longer fit contemporary society.

FUTURE DIRECTIONS

This is an exciting, dynamic time for the psychology of men because any number of important research questions remain unanswered, including contentious ones regarding the nature of men's emotionality as well as the overall adaptive (or maladaptive) nature of the socialized male gender role. The notable absence of vocational research conducted from a psychology of men perspective needs to be addressed, and the psychology of men needs to be more fully integrated into the broader counseling psychology literature. All told, research methodology needs to become more sophisticated; mediation and moderation techniques, for example, as well as an increased reliance on both experimental design and multitrait–multimethod procedures should be considered. From this follows the need to more fully articulate the linkage between the socialized male gender role, the developmental process of identity construction, and specific outcomes.

First and foremost, however, there needs to be an increased effort to test the theatrical underpinnings of masculinity. For the most part, the extant literature supports the idea that there exists a hegemonic masculinity that imparts specific expectations through the processes of social learning and developmental construction. Although it is not necessary for there to be uniformity, there needs to be a movement beyond using these theories for mere prediction toward testing the specific explanations for observed outcomes. It seems, for example, that there are differential outcomes for men of diverse backgrounds that need to be clarified. How do men of color construct an identity that includes aspects of masculinity drawn from multiple contexts? How does this lead to outcomes? What might their developmental processes tell us about how to better serve male clients? Issues of social class, power, and privilege need to be explored, as do the role of contextual variables on the enactment of masculinity as an identity and its prediction of outcomes.

All exciting, dynamic moments come with challenges, however. For the psychology of men, the need exists to evolve beyond merely understanding the effects of masculine gender role learning on men, women, and society to "promoting a social discourse that is grounded in empirical research and consistent with a priori values and goals" (Addis et al., 2010, p. 78). Addis et al. (2010) have called this a *pragmatic and functional* understanding of masculinity. *Pragmatic* refers to the need to evaluate masculine gender role socialization in light of how adaptive it allows men to be in the world. A *functional* approach, in turn, frames the consequences of masculine gender role socialization in light of both the historical goals of that socialization and the contexts in which those consequences occurred. Understanding these two processes would require increased theoretical specificity and methodological sophistication. For example, such efforts may focus on the nature of the gendered social learning environment for specific groups of men—what are the crucibles in which men forge their definition of masculinity? In essence, Addis et al. are calling for an increased understanding of masculinity that focuses on understanding why men do things through an analysis of not only the consequences of masculinity but also the meaning men assign to the concept of masculinity and the contexts in which said masculinity is enacted. This is a departure from the extant literature in this area because it asserts that the nature of masculinity needs to be understood not just in terms of its consequences but also in the more complicated terms of how men learn to be men, the effects of that learning, and in what direction men need to move to lead more healthy, fulfilling, lives.

It may be the case that the problems men face are not exclusively the result of the socialized male gender role. Rather, the problems seem to stem more from the inflexible adherence to that gender role in the face of situations that demand flexibility. Men of higher socioeconomic status, for example, may not experience the same context as was discussed in this chapter; they might not, accordingly, develop a masculine identity strongly influenced by the "strong and silent" script as their context demanded different values, ideals, and behaviors. Not all scripts are relevant to all men, nor are they adaptive for all situations. Problems therefore stem more from men's inability to respond adaptively in situations that may require flexibility—interpersonal relationships, for example, or team activities at one's workplace. Indeed, Mahalik, Good, and Englar-Carlson (2003) stressed that the psychology of men and masculinity needs to move beyond seeing these scripts as maladaptive or adaptive in and of themselves. Rather, the importance focus should be on altering the perceptions of society so that the scripts can be enacted flexibly, when they are considered contextually valid, without calling a person's masculinity into question. Indeed, the historical evolution of what society considered masculine demonstrates how many of the ideals currently unifying the social construction of masculinity would have been considered dramatically maladaptive at various other points in time (e.g., Vacha-Hasse et al., 2010).

CONCLUSION

This chapter has critically examined the extant literature regarding the psychology of men and masculinity, highlighting the major theories and subsequent empirical findings. The social learning and social construction theoretical perspectives have made significant contributions to understanding the development of masculinity as an identity. The essentialist and constructivist lines of research have furthered our understanding of how that masculinity affects men, women, and society. Recent research also suggests, however, that the direct relationships between the traditionally socialized male gender role and many of the outcome variables studied are more complex than previously thought and that any such relationship may be mediated (or moderated) by contextual variables not yet measured. Indeed, although movement has been made in understanding how masculinity intersects with race, ethnicity, and sexual orientation, more work needs to be done in clarifying how differing groups within these identities differ in reaction to gender role socialization. Characteristics such as social class, cultural affiliation, identity salience, and worldview might affect that intersection, and the current state of research leaves unaddressed the role of such variables as age, education, and even political affiliation. This communicates a vibrant, growing area of work; an extant literature that makes a significant contribution to counseling psychology as well as charts an agenda of research, theory, and practice through the 21st century and beyond.

References

Addis, M. E., & Cohane, G. H. (2005). Social scientific paradigms of masculinity and their implications for research and practice in men's mental health. *Journal of Clinical Psychology, 61,* 633–647. doi:10.1002/jclp.20099

Addis, M. E., & Mahalik, J. (2003). Men, masculinity, and the contexts of help seeking. *American Psychologist, 58,* 5–14. doi:10.1037/0003-066X.58.1.5

Addis, M. E., Mansfield, A. K., & Syzdek, M. R. (2010). Is "masculinity" a problem? Framing the effects of gendered social learning in men. *Psychology of Men and Masculinity, 11,* 77–90. doi:10.1037/a0018602

Andrews, G., Issakidis, C., & Carter, G. (2001). Shortfall in mental health service utilization. *British Journal of Psychiatry, 179,* 417–425. doi:10.1192/bjp.179.5.417

Bandura, A. (1977). *Social learning theory.* Englewood Cliffs, NJ: Prentice-Hall.

Barber, J. S., & Mobley, M. (1999). Counseling gay adolescents. In A. M. Horne & M. S. Kiselica (Eds.), *Handbook of counseling boys and adolescent males: A practitioner's guide* (pp. 161–178). Thousand Oaks, CA: Sage.

Barnett, R. C., Marshall, N. L., & Pleck, J. H. (1992). Men's multiple roles and their relationship to men's psychological distress. *Journal of Marriage and the Family, 54,* 358–367. doi:10.2307/353067

Bem, S. L. (1974). The measurement of psychological androgyny. *Journal of Consulting and Clinical Psychology, 42,* 155–162. doi:10.1037/h0036215

Bem, S. L. (1979). Theory and measurement of androgyny: A reply to the Pedhazur-Tetenbaum and Locksley-Colten critiques. *Journal of Personality and Social Psychology, 37,* 1047–1054. doi:10.1037/0022-3514.37.6.1047

Berger, J., Levant, R., McMillan, K., Kelleher, W., & Sellers, A. (2005). Impact of gender role conflict, traditional masculinity ideology, alexithymia, and age on men's attitudes toward psychological help seeking. *Psychology of Men and Masculinity, 6,* 73–78. doi:10.1037/1524-9220.6.1.73

Betz, N. E. (2008). Advances in vocational theories. In S. D. Brown & R. W. Lent (Eds.), *Handbook of counseling psychology* (4th ed., pp. 357–374). New York, NY: Wiley.

Blazina, C. (2001). Analytic psychology and gender role conflict: The development of the fragile masculine self. *Psychotherapy: Theory, Research, Practice, Training, 38,* 50–59. doi:10.1037/0033-3204.38.1.50

Blazina, C., Pisecco, S., & O'Neil, J. M. (2005). An adaptation of the Gender Role Conflict Scale for adolescents: Psychometric issues and correlates with psychological distress. *Psychology of Men and Masculinity, 6,* 39–45. doi:10.1037/1524-9220.6.1.39

Blazina, C., & Shen-Miller, D. (Eds.). (2011). *An international psychology of men: Theoretical advances, case studies, and clinical innovations.* New York, NY: Routledge.

Blazina, C., & Watkins, C. E. (1996). Masculine gender role conflict: Effects on college men's psychological well-being, chemical substance usage, and attitudes toward help-seeking. *Journal of Counseling Psychology, 43,* 461–465. doi:10.1037/0022-0167.43.4.461

Bly, R. (1990). *Iron John: A book about men.* Reading, MA: Addison Wesley.

Boman, E., & Walker, G. (2010). Predictors of men's health care utilization. *Psychology of Men and Masculinity, 11,* 113–122. doi:10.1037/a0018461

Brooks, G. (2009). *Beyond the crises of masculinity: A transtheoretical model for male-friendly therapy.* Washington, DC: American Psychological Association.

Brooks, G. R. (1990). Post Vietnam gender role strain: A needed concept? *Professional Psychology: Research and Practice, 21,* 18–25. doi:10.1037/0735-7028.21.1.18

Brooks, G. R. (2001). Counseling and psychotherapy for male military veterans. In G. R. Brooks & G. E. Good (Eds.), *A new handbook of counseling and psychotherapy with men* (Vol. 1, pp. 206–225). San Francisco, CA: Jossey-Bass.

Brooks, G. R., & Good, G. E. (2001a). Introduction. In G. R. Brooks & G. E. Good (Eds.), *The new handbook of psychotherapy and counseling with men: A comprehensive guide to settings, problems, and treatment approaches* (Vol. 1, pp. 3–21). San Francisco, CA: Jossey-Bass.

Brooks, G. R., & Good, G. E. (Eds.). (2001b). *The new handbook of psychotherapy and counseling with men: A comprehensive guide to settings, problems, and treatment approaches* (Vols. 1–2). San Francisco, CA: Jossey-Bass.

Burlew, A. K. (2003). Research with ethnic minorities: Conceptual, methodological, and analytical issues. In G. Bernal, J. E. Trimble, A. K. Burlew, & F. T. L. Leong (Eds.), *Handbook of racial and ethnic minority psychology* (pp. 179–197). Thousand Oaks, CA: Sage.

Buss, D. M. (1995). Evolutionary psychology: A new paradigm for psychological science. *Psychological Inquiry, 6,* 1–30. doi:10.1207/s15327965pli0601_1

Cafri, G., & Thompson, J. (2004). Measuring male body image: A review of the current methodology. *Psychology of Men and Masculinity, 5,* 18–29. doi:10.1037/1524-9220.5.1.18

Carter, R. T., Williams, B., Juby, H. L., & Buckley, T. R. (2005). Racial identity as a mediator of the relationship between gender role conflict and the severity of psychological symptoms in Black, Latino, and Asian men. *Sex Roles, 53,* 473–486. doi:10.1007/s11199-005-7135-7

Centers for Disease Control and Prevention. (2005). Mental health in the United States: Prevalence of diagnosis and medication treatment for attention-deficit hyperactivity disorder—United States, 2003. *Morbidity and Mortality Weekly Report, 54,* 842–847.

Centers for Disease Control and Prevention. (2007). *Facts at a glance: Youth violence center for disease control.* Atlanta, GA: Author.

Chandra, A., & Minkovitz, C. (2006). Stigma starts early: Gender differences in teen willingness to use mental health services. *Journal of Adolescent Health, 38,* 754. e1–754.e8. doi:10.1016/j.jadohealth.2005.08.011

Chin, J. (1998). Mental health services and treatment. In L. C. Lee & N. S. Zane (Eds.), *Handbook of Asian American psychology* (pp. 485–504). Thousand Oaks, CA: Sage.

Chua, P., & Fujino, D. C. (1999). Negotiating new Asian-American masculinities: Attitudes and gender expectations. *The Journal of Men's Studies, 7,* 391–413. doi:10.3149/jms.0703.391

Cochran, S. V. (2005). Assessing and treating depression in men. In G. E. Good & G. R. Brooks (Eds.), *The new handbook of psychotherapy and counseling with men: A comprehensive guide to settings, problems, and treatment approaches* (rev. ed., pp. 121–133). San Francisco, CA: Jossey-Bass.

Cochran, S. V., & Rabinowitz, F. (2000). *Men and depression: Clinical and empirical perspectives.* San Diego, CA: Academic Press.

Cohn, A., & Zeichner, A. (2006). Effects of masculine identity and gender role stress on aggression in men. *Psychology of Men and Masculinity, 7,* 179–190. doi:10.1037/1524-9220.7.4.179

Collison, B. (1987). Counseling aging men. In M. Scher, M. Stevens, G. Good, & G. A. Eichenfield (Eds.), *Handbook of counseling and psychotherapy with men* (pp. 165–177). Thousand Oaks, CA: Sage.

Connell, R. W., & Messerschmidt, J. W. (2005). Hegemonic masculinity: Rethinking the concept. *Gender and Society, 19,* 829–859. doi:10.1177/0891243205278639

Cournoyer, R. J., & Mahalik, J. R. (1995). A cross-sectional study of gender role conflict examining college- aged and middle-aged men. *Journal of Counseling Psychology, 42,* 11–19. doi:10.1037/0022-0167.42.1.11

Courtenay, W. H. (1998). College men's health: An overview and a call to action. *Journal of American College Health, 46,* 279–290. doi:10.1080/07448489809596004

Cummings, E., Henry, W. E., & Damianopoulos, E. (1961). A formal statement of disengagement theory. In E. Cumming & W. E. Henry (Eds),

Growing old: The process of disengagement. New York, NY: Basic Books.

David, D., & Brannon, R. (1976). *The forty-nine percent majority: The male sex role*. Reading, MA: Addison-Wesley.

Deaux, K., & Major, B. (1987). Putting gender into context: An interactive model of gender-related behavior. *Psychological Review, 94*, 369–389. doi:10.1037/0033-295X.94.3.369

Drost, C. (2005). *Male gender role conflict in older men* (Doctoral dissertation). Retrieved from Dissertation Abstracts International, 65 (9-B), 4825.

Englar-Carlson, M., & Vandiver, B. (2001, August). Gender role conflict, help seeking, and treatment fearfulness. In J. M. O'Neil & G. E. Good (Chairs), *Gender role conflict research: Testing new constructs and dimensions empirically*. Symposium conducted at the annual meeting of the American psychology Association, San Francisco, CA.

Fairbairn, W. (1963). Synopsis of an object-relations theory of the personality. *The International Journal of Psychoanalysis, 44*, 224–225.

Farrell, W. (1993). *The myth of male power*. New York, NY: Simon and Schuster.

Fiske, S. T. (1998). Stereotyping, prejudice, and discrimination. In D. T. Gilbert, S. T. Fiske, & G. Lindzey (Eds.), *The handbook of social psychology* (4th ed., pp. 357–411). New York, NY: McGraw-Hill.

Fouad, N. F., & Katamneni, N. (2008). Contextual factors in vocational psychology: Intersections of individual, group, and societal dimensions. In S. D. Brown & R. W. Lent (Eds.), *Handbook of counseling psychology* (4th ed., pp. 408–425). New York, NY: Wiley.

Fragoso, J. M., & Kashubeck, S. (2000). Machismo, gender role conflict, and mental health in Mexican American men. *Psychology of Men and Masculinity, 1*, 87–97. doi:10.1037/1524-9220.1.2.87

Frazier, P. A., Tix, A. P., & Baron, K. E. (2004). Testing moderator and mediator effects in counseling psychology research. *Journal of Counseling Psychology, 51*, 115–134. doi:10.1037/0022-0167.51.1.115

Furnham, A., Badmin, N., & Sneade, I. (2002). Body image dissatisfaction: Gender differences in eating attitudes, self-esteem, and reasons for exercise. *Journal of Psychology: Interdisciplinary and Applied, 136*, 581–596. doi:10.1080/00223980209604820

Galli, N., & Reel, J. (2009). Adonis or Hephaestus? Exploring body image in male athletes. *Psychology of Men and Masculinity, 10*, 95–108. doi:10.1037/a0014005

Goldberg, H. (1976). *The hazards of being male: Surviving the myth of male privilege*. New York, NY: Signet.

Gonzalez, J., Alegria, M., & Prihoda, T. (2005). How do attitudes toward mental health treatment vary by age, gender, and ethnicity/race in young adults? *Journal of Community Psychology, 33*, 611–629. doi:10.1002/jcop.20071

Good, G. E., Dell, D. M., & Mintz, L. B. (1989). Male role and gender role conflict: Relations to help seeking in men. *Journal of Counseling Psychology, 36*, 295–300. doi:10.1037/0022-0167.36.3.295

Good, G. E., Robertson, J. M., Fitzgerald, L. F., Stevens, M., & Bartels, K. M. (1996). The relation between masculine role conflict and psychological distress in male university counseling center clients. *Journal of Counseling and Development, 75*, 44–49.

Good, G. E., Robertson, J. M., O'Neil, J. M., Fitzgerald, L. F., Stevens, M., DeBord, K., . . . David, G. (1995). Male gender role conflict: Psychometric issues and relations to psychological distress. *Journal of Counseling Psychology, 42*, 3–10. doi:10.1037/0022-0167.42.1.3

Grey, J. (2004). *Men are from Mars, women are from Venus: The classic guide to understanding the opposite sex*. New York, NY: Harper.

Groeschel, B. L., Wester, S. R., & Sedivy, S. K. (2010). Gender role conflict, alcohol, and help-seeking among college men. *Psychology of Men and Masculinity, 11*, 123–139. doi:10.1037/a0018365

Hammer, J. H., & Good, G. E. (2010). Positive psychology: An empirical examination of beneficial aspects of endorsement of masculine norms. *Psychology of Men and Masculinity, 11*, 303–318.

Hammer, J. H., & Vogel, D. L. (2010). Men's help seeking for depression: The efficacy of a male-sensitive brochure about counseling. *The Counseling Psychologist, 38*, 296–313. doi:10.1177/0011000009351937

Hare-Mustin, R., & Marecek, J. (1990). *Making a difference: Psychology and the construction of gender*. New Haven, CT: Yale University Press.

Harrison, J. (1995). Roles, identities, and sexual orientation: Homosexuality, heterosexuality, and bisexuality. In R. F. Levant & W. S. Pollack (Eds.), *A new psychology of men* (pp. 359–382). New York, NY: Basic Books.

Heesacker, M., & Bradley, M. M. (1997). Beyond feelings: Psychotherapy and emotion. *The Counseling Psychologist, 25*, 201–219. doi:10.1177/0011000097252003

Heesacker, M., Wester, S. R., Vogel, D. C., Wentzel, J. T., Mejia-Millan, C. M., & Goodholm, C. R. (1999). Gender-based emotional stereotyping. *Journal of Counseling Psychology, 46*, 483–495. doi:10.1037/0022-0167.46.4.483

Heppner, M. J., & Heppner, P. P. (2001). Addressing the implications of male socialization for career counseling. In G. E. Good & G. R. Brooks (Eds.), *The new handbook of psychotherapy and counseling with men: A comprehensive guide to settings, problems, and treatment approaches* (Vol. 2, pp. 369–386). San Francisco, CA: Jossey-Bass.

Hill, M. S., & Fischer, A. R. (2001). Does entitlement mediate the link between masculinity and rape-related variables? *Journal of Counseling Psychology, 48,* 39–50. doi:10.1037/0022-0167.48.1.39

Hill, W., & Donatelle, R. (2004). The impact of gender role conflict on multidimensional social support in older men. *International Journal of Men's Health, 4,* 267–276. doi:10.3149/jmh.0403.267

Hills, H., Carlstrom, A., & Evanow, M. (2001). Consulting with men in business and industry. In G. Brooks & G. Good (Eds.), *The new handbook of psychotherapy and counseling with men: A comprehensive guide to settings, problems, and treatment approaches* (Vol. 1, pp. 126–145). San Francisco, CA: Jossey-Bass.

Hobza, C., & Rochlen, A. (2009). Gender role conflict, drive for muscularity, and the impact of ideal media portrayals on men. *Psychology of Men and Masculinity, 10,* 120–130. doi:10.1037/a0015040

Holland, J. L. (1962). Some explorations of a theory of vocational choice: I. One- and two-year longitudinal studies. *Psychological Monographs: General and Applied, 76*(26).

Husaini, B., Moore, S., & Cain, V. (1994). Psychiatric symptoms and help-seeking behavior among the elderly: An analysis of racial and gender differences. *Journal of Gerontological Social Work, 21*(3–4), 177–196. doi:10.1300/J083V21N03_12

Ickes, W., Buysse, A., Pham, H., Rivers, K., Erickson, J., & Hancock, M. (2000). On the difficulty of distinguishing "good" and "poor" perceivers: A social relations analysis of empathic accuracy data. *Personal Relationships, 7,* 219–234. doi:10.1111/j.1475-6811.2000.tb00013.x

Iwamoto, D. K., Liao, L., & Liu, W. M. (2010). Masculine norms, avoidant coping, Asian values, and depression among Asian American men. *Psychology of Men and Masculinity, 11,* 15–24. doi:10.1037/a0017874

Jome, L. M., & Tokar, D. M. (1998). Dimensions of masculinity and major choice traditionality. *Journal of Vocational Behavior, 52,* 120–134.

Kantemeni, N., Smothers, M., Christianson, H. F., & Wester, S. R. (2011). Role induction: A potential method for improving men's perceptions of career counseling. *Career Development Quarterly, 59,* 219–231.

Kapalka, G. (2010). *Counseling boys and men with ADHD.* New York, NY: Routledge.

Keen, S. (1991). *Fire in the belly: On being a man.* New York, NY: Bantam.

Kilmartin, C., & Allison, J. (2007). *Men's violence against women: Theory, research, and activism.* Mahwah, NJ: Erlbaum.

Kilianski, S. E. (2003). Explaining heterosexual men's attitudes toward women and gay men: The theory of exclusively masculine identity. *Psychology of Men and Masculinity, 4,* 37–56. doi:10.1037/1524-9220.4.1.37

King, I., & Schuler, L. (2003). *The book of muscle: The world's most authoritative guide to building your body.* New York, NY: Rodale Books.

Kohut, H., & Wolf, E. (1978). The disorders of the self and their treatment: An outline. *The International Journal of Psychoanalysis, 59,* 413–425.

Komiya, N., Good, G. E., & Sherrod, N. B. (2000). Emotional openness as a predictor of college students' attitudes toward seeking psychological help. *Journal of Counseling Psychology, 47,* 138–143. doi:10.1037/0022-0167.47.1.138

Korcuska, J. S., & Thombs, D. L. (2003). Gender role conflict and sex-specific drinking norms: Relationship to alcohol use in undergraduate women and men. *Journal of College Student Development, 44,* 204–216. doi:10.1353/csd.2003.0017

Krugman, S. (1995). Male development and the transformation of shame. In R. F. Levant & W. S. Pollack (Eds.), *A new psychology of men* (pp. 91–126). New York, NY: Basic Books.

Levant, R. (1992). Toward the reconstruction of masculinity. *Journal of Family Psychology, 5*(3–4), 379–402. doi:10.1037/0893-3200.5.3-4.379

Levant, R. F. (1995). Toward the reconstruction of masculinity. In R. F. Levant & W. S. Pollack (Eds.), *A new psychology of men* (pp. 229–251). New York, NY: Basic Books.

Levant, R. F. (2001a). *The crises of boyhood.* The new handbook of psychotherapy and counseling with men: A comprehensive guide to settings, problems, and treatment approaches (Vol. 2, pp. 355–368). San Francisco, CA: Jossey-Bass.

Levant, R. F. (2001b). Desperately seeking language: Understanding, assessing, and treating normative male alexithymia. In G. Brooks & G. Good (Eds.), *The new handbook of psychotherapy and counseling with men: A comprehensive guide to settings, problems, and treatment approaches* (Vol. 2, pp. 424–443). San Francisco, CA: Jossey-Bass.

Levant, R. F., & Brooks, G. R. (1997). *Men and sex: New psychological perspectives.* New York, NY: Wiley.

Levant, R. F., Cuthbert, A., Richmond, K., Sellers, A., Matveev, A., Mitina, O., . . . Heesacker. M. (2003). Masculinity ideology among Russian and U.S. young men and women and its relationships to unhealthy lifestyles habits among young Russian men. *Psychology of Men and Masculinity, 4,* 26–36. doi:10.1037/1524-9220.4.1.26

Levant, R. F., Good, G., Cook, S., O'Neil, J., Smalley, K., & Owen, K. (2006). The normative male alexithymia scale: Measurement of a gender-linked syndrome. *Psychology of Men and Masculinity, 7*, 212–224. doi:10.1037/1524-9220.7.4.212

Levant, R. F., Hall, R., Williams, C., & Hasan, N. (2009). Gender differences in alexithymia. *Psychology of Men and Masculinity, 10*, 190–203. doi:10.1037/a0015652

Levant, R. F., & Pollack, W. (Eds.). (1995). *A new psychology of men*. New York, NY: Basic Books.

Levinson, D. J. (1978). *The seasons of a man's life*. New York, NY: Knopf.

Liu, W. M. (2002). Exploring the lives of Asian American men: Racial identity, male role norms, gender role conflict, and prejudicial attitudes. *Psychology of Men and Masculinity, 3*, 107–118. doi:10.1037/1524-9220.3.2.107

Liu, W. M., & Iwamoto, D. (2006). Asian American men's gender role conflict: The role of Asian values, self-esteem, and psychological distress. *Psychology of Men and Masculinity, 7*, 153–164. doi:10.1037/1524-9220.7.3.153

Liu, W. M., & Iwamoto, D. (2007). Conformity to masculine norms, Asian values, coping strategies, peer group influences, and substance use among Asian American men. *Psychology of Men and Masculinity, 8*, 25–39. doi:10.1037/1524-9220.8.1.25

Liu, W. M., Iwamoto, D. K., & Chae, M. H. (Eds.). (2010). *Culturally responsive counseling with Asian American men*. New York, NY: Routledge.

Locke, B., & Mahalik, J. (2005). Examining masculinity norms, problem drinking, and athletic involvement as predictors of sexual aggression in college men. *Journal of Counseling Psychology, 52*, 279–283. doi:10.1037/0022-0167.52.3.279

Mahalik, J. R., & Cournoyer, R. J. (2000). Identifying gender role conflict messages that distinguish mildly depressed from non-depressed men. *Psychology of Men and Masculinity, 1*, 109–115. doi:10.1037/1524-9220.1.2.109

Mahalik, J. R., Good, G. E., & Englar-Carlson, M. (2003). Masculinity scripts, presenting concerns, and help seeking: Implications for practice and training. *Professional Psychology: Research and Practice, 34*, 123–131. doi:10.1037/0735-7028.34.2.123

Mahalik, J. R., Locke, B. D., Theordore, H., Cournoyer, R. J., & Lloyd, B. F. (2001). A cross-national and cross-sectional comparison on men's gender role conflict and its relationship to social intimacy and self esteem. *Sex Roles, 45*, 1–14. doi:10.1023/A:1013008800019

McCreary, D., Sasse, D., Saucier, D., & Dorsch, K. (2004). Measuring the drive for muscularity: Factorial validity of the drive for muscularity scale in men and women. *Psychology of Men and Masculinity, 5*, 49–58. doi:10.1037/1524-9220.5.1.49

Mertens, C. E. (2001, August). Male gender role conflict in depressed versus nondepressed medical populations. In J. M. O'Neil & G. E. Good (Chairs), *Gender role conflict research: Testing new constructs and dimensions empirically*. Symposium conducted at the 109th Annual Convention of the American Psychological Association. San Francisco, CA.

Miller, M. J., & Sheu, H. (2008). Conceptual and measurement issues in multicultural psychology research. In S. D. Brown & R. W. Lent (Eds.), *Handbook of counseling psychology* (4th ed., pp. 103–120). New York, NY: Wiley.

Mintz, R., & Mahalik, J. R. (1996). Sex role ideology and gender role conflict as predictors of family roles for men. *Sex Roles, 34*, 805–821. doi:10.1007/BF01544317

Mirandé, A. (2004). "Macho": Contemporary conceptions. In M. S. Kimmel & M. A. Messner (Eds.), *Men's lives* (6th ed., pp. 28–38). Boston, MA: Pearson.

Monk, D., & Ricciardelli, L. (2003). Three dimensions of the male gender role as correlates of alcohol and cannabis involvement in young Australian men. *Psychology of Men and Masculinity, 4*, 57–69. doi:10.1037/1524-9220.4.1.57

Moore, T., & Stuart, G. (2005). A review of the literature on masculinity and partner violence. *Psychology of Men and Masculinity, 6*, 46–61. doi:10.1037/1524-9220.6.1.46

Moore, T., Stuart, G., McNulty, J., Addis, M., Cordova, J., & Temple, J. (2008). Domains of masculine gender role stress and intimate partner violence in a clinical sample of violent men. *Psychology of Men and Masculinity, 9*, 82–89. doi:10.1037/1524-9220.9.2.82

Morrison, T., Morrison, M., & Hopkins, C. (2003). Striving for bodily perfection? An exploration of the drive for muscularity in Canadian men. *Psychology of Men and Masculinity, 4*, 111–120. doi:10.1037/1524-9220.4.2.111

Morrison, T., Morrison, M., Hopkins, C., & Rowan, E. (2004). Muscle mania: Development of new scale examining the drive for muscularity in Canadian males. *Psychology of Men and Masculinity, 5*, 30–39. doi:10.1037/1524-9220.5.1.30

Nutt, R. L., & Brooks, G. R. (2008). Psychology of gender. In S. D. Brown & R. W. Lent (Eds.), *Handbook of counseling psychology* (4th ed., pp. 176–193). New York, NY: Wiley.

O'Neil, J. M. (2008). Summarizing 25 years of research on men's gender role conflict using the Gender Role Conflict Scale: New research paradigms and clinical implications. *The Counseling Psychologist, 36*, 358–445. doi:10.1177/0011000008317057

O'Neil, J. M. (2010). The psychology of men and boys in the year 2010: Theory, research, clinical knowledge, and future directions. In E. Altmaier & J. Hansen (Eds.), *Oxford handbook of counseling psychology* (pp. 375–408). New York, NY: Oxford University Press.

O'Neil, J. M., Good, G. E., & Holmes, S. (1995). Fifteen years of theory and research on men's gender role conflict. In R. F. Levant & W. S. Pollack (Eds.), *The new psychology of men* (pp. 164–206). New York, NY: Basic Books.

Parish, T., Baghurst, T., & Turner, R. (2010). Becoming competitive amateur bodybuilders: Identification of contributors. *Psychology of Men and Masculinity, 11*, 152–159. doi:10.1037/a0018091

Pleck, J. H. (1981). *The myth of masculinity.* Cambridge, MA: MIT Press.

Pleck, J. H. (1995). The gender role strain paradigm: An update. In R. F. Levant & W. S. Pollack (Eds.), *The new psychology of men* (pp. 11–32). New York, NY: Basic Books.

Pleck, J. H., Sonenstein, F. L., & Ku, L. C. (1993). Masculinity ideology and its correlates. In S. Oskamp & M. Costanzo (Eds.), *Gender issues in social psychology* (pp. 85–110). Newbury Park, CA: Sage.

Pollack, W. (1998). The trauma of Oedipus: Toward a new psychoanalytic psychotherapy for men. In W. S. Pollack & R. F. Levant (Eds.), *New psychotherapy for men* (pp. 13–34). New York, NY: Wiley.

Pope, H. G., Phillips, K. A., & Olivardia, R. (2000). *The Adonis complex: How to identify, treat, and prevent body obsession in men and boys.* New York, NY: Touchstone.

Sue, D. W., Ivey, A. E., & Pedersen, P. B. (1996). *A theory of multicultural counseling and therapy.* New York, NY: Brooks/Cole.

Rabinowitz, F. E., & Cochran, S. V. (2002). *Deepening psychotherapy with men.* Washington, DC: American Psychological Association. doi:10.1037/10418-000

Robin, L., & Reiger, D. (1991). *Psychiatric disorders in America.* New York, NY: Free Press.

Robinson, D. T., & Schwartz, J. P. (2004). Relationship between gender role conflict and attitudes toward women and African Americans. *Psychology of Men and Masculinity, 5*, 65–71. doi:10.1037/1524-9220.5.1.65

Rochlen, A., Good, G., & Carver, T. (2009). Predictors of gender-related barriers, work, and life satisfaction among men in nursing. *Psychology of Men and Masculinity, 10*, 44–56. doi:10.1037/a0013291

Rochlen, A. B., Blazina, C., & Raghunathan, R. (2002). Gender role conflict, attitudes toward career counseling, career decision-making, and perceptions of career counseling advertising brochures. *Psychology of Men and Masculinity, 3*, 127–137. doi:10.1037/1524-9220.3.2.127

Rochlen, A. B., & Hoyer, W. D. (2005). Marketing mental health to men: Theoretical and practical consideration. *Journal of Clinical Psychology, 61*, 675–684. doi:10.1002/jclp.20102

Rochlen, A. B., Mohr, J. J., & Hargrove, B. K. (1999). Development of the attitudes toward career counseling scale. *Journal of Counseling Psychology, 46*, 196–206. doi:10.1037/0022-0167.46.2.196

Rochlen, A. B., & O'Brien, K. M. (2002a). Men's reasons for and against seeking help for career-related concerns. *The Journal of Men's Studies, 11*, 55–63. doi:10.3149/jms.1101.55

Rochlen, A. B., & O'Brien, K. M. (2002b). The relation of male gender role conflict and attitudes toward career counseling to interest in and preferences for different career counseling styles. *Psychology of Men and Masculinity, 3*, 9–21. doi:10.1037/1524-9220.3.1.9

Rubinstein, G. (2003). Macho man: Narcissism, homophobia, agency, communion, and authoritarianism–a comparative study among Israeli bodybuilders and a control group. *Psychology of Men and Masculinity, 4*, 100–110. doi:10.1037/1524-9220.4.2.100

Ruiz, R. (1981). Cultural and historical perspective in counseling Hispanics. In D. W. Sue (Ed.), *Counseling the culturally different: Theory and practice* (pp. 186–214). New York, NY: Wiley.

Sánchez, F. J., Bocklandt, S., & Vilain, E. (2009). Gender role conflict, interest in casual sex, and relationship satisfaction among gay men. *Psychology of Men and Masculinity, 10*, 237–243. doi:10.1037/a0016325

Sánchez, F. J., Greenberg, S., Liu, W., & Vilain, E. (2009). Reported effects of masculine ideals on gay men. *Psychology of Men and Masculinity, 10*, 73–87. doi:10.1037/a0013513

Schaub, M., & Williams, C. (2007). Examining the relations between masculine gender role conflict and men's expectations about counseling. *Psychology of Men and Masculinity, 8*, 40–52. doi:10.1037/1524-9220.8.1.40

Schwartz, J., Waldo, M., Bloom-Langell, J., & Merta, R. (1996, August). Gender role conflict: Relationship to spouse abuse, self-esteem, acculturation, and intervention group outcome. In J. M. O'Neil & G. E. Good (Chairs), *Men's gender role conflict: Research advancing the new psychology of men.* Symposium conducted at the 104th Annual Convention of the American Psychological Association, Toronto, Ontario, Canada.

Schwartzberg, S., & Rosenberg, L. G. (1998). Being gay and being male: Psychotherapy with gay and bisexual men. In W. S. Pollack & R. F. Levant (Eds.), *New psychotherapy for men* (pp. 259–281). New York, NY: Wiley.

Schwarzenegger, A., & Dobbins, B. (1999). *The new encyclopedia of modern bodybuilding: The bible of bodybuilding, fully revised and updated.* New York, NY: Simon & Schuster.

Seligman, M. E., & Csikszentmihalyi, M. (2000). Positive psychology: An introduction. *American Psychologist, 55*, 5–14. doi:10.1037/0003-066X.55.1.5

Senn, C. Y., Desmarais, S., Verberg, N., & Wood, E. (2000). Predicting coercive sexual behavior across the lifespan in a random sample of Canadian men. *Journal of Social and Personal Relationships, 17*, 95–113. doi:10.1177/0265407500171005

Simonsen, G., Blazina, C., & Watkins, C. E., Jr. (2000). Gender role conflict and psychological well-being among gay men. *Journal of Counseling Psychology, 47*, 85–89. doi:10.1037/0022-0167.47.1.85

Singer, E. (1981). Reference groups and social evaluations. In M. Rosenberg & R. H. Turner (Eds.), *Social psychology: Sociological perspectives* (pp. 66–93). New York, NY: Basic Books.

Smiler, A. (2004). Thirty years after the discovery of gender: Psychological concepts and measures of masculinity. *Sex Roles, 50(1/2)*, 15–26. doi:10.1023/B:SERS.0000011069.02279.4c

Spence, J., & Helmreich, R. (1979). On assessing androgyny. *Sex Roles, 5*, 721–738. doi:10.1007/BF00287935

Spence, J., & Helmreich, R. (1981). Androgyny versus gender schema: A comment on Bem's gender schema theory. *Psychological Review, 88*, 365–368. doi:10.1037/0033-295X.88.4.365

Stearns, P. N. (1994). *American cool: Constructing a twentieth-century emotional style.* New York, NY: New York University Press.

Steinfeldt, J., Steinfeldt, M., England, B., & Speight, Q. (2009). Gender role conflict and stigma toward help-seeking among college football players. *Psychology of Men and Masculinity, 10*, 261–272. doi:10.1037/a0017223

Sternbach, J. (2001). Psychotherapy with the young older man. In G. R. Brooks & G. E. Good (Eds.), *The new handbook of psychotherapy and counseling with men: A comprehensive guide to settings, problems, and treatment approaches* (Vol. 1, pp. 464–480). San Francisco, CA: Jossey-Bass.

Stillson, R. W., O'Neil, J. M., & Owen, S. V. (1991). Predictors of adult men's gender-role conflict: Race, class, unemployment, age, instrumentality-expressiveness, and personal strain. *Journal of Counseling Psychology, 38*, 458–464. doi:10.1037/0022-0167.38.4.458

Sue, D. (2001). Asian American masculinity and therapy: The concept of masculinity in Asian American males. In G. R. Brooks & G. E. Good (Eds.), *The new handbook of psychotherapy and counseling with men: A comprehensive guide to settings, problems, and treatment approaches* (Vol. 2, pp. 780–795). San Francisco, CA: Jossey-Bass.

Swanson, J. L., & Gore, Jr., P. A. (2000). Advances in vocational psychology theory and research. In S. D. Brown & R. W. Lent (Ed.), *Handbook of counseling psychology* (3rd ed., pp. 233–269). New York, NY: Wiley.

Terman, L., & Miles, C. (1936). *Sex and personality: Studies in masculinity and femininity.* New York, NY: McGraw-Hill.

Theodore, H., & Lloyd, B. F. (2000). Age and gender role conflict: A cross-sectional study of Australian men. *Sex Roles, 42*, 1027–1042. doi:10.1023/A:1007088617819

Tokar, D., & Jome, L. (1998). Masculinity, vocational interests, and career choice traditionality: Evidence for a fully mediated model. *Journal of Counseling Psychology, 45*, 424–435. doi:10.1037/0022-0167.45.4.424

U.S. Census Bureau. (2005). *School enrollment—Social and economic characteristics of students: October, 2003.* Retrieved from http://www.census.gov/prod/2005pubs/p20-554.pdf

Vacha-Hasse, T., Wester, S. R., & Christianson, H. F. (2010). *Psychotherapy with older men.* New York, NY: Routledge.

Van Hyfte, G. J., & Rabinowitz, F. E. (2001). *Men's group affiliation and same-sex intimacy.* Paper presented at the 109th Annual Convention of the American Psychological Association, San Francisco, CA.

Vogel, D. L., Tucker, C., Wester, S., & Heesacker, M. (1999). The impact of sex and situational cues on the endorsement of traditional gender-role attitudes and behaviors in dating couples. *Journal of Social and Personal Relationships, 16*, 459–473. doi:10.1177/0265407599164003

Vogel, D. L., Wade, N. G., & Haake, S. (2006). Measuring the self-stigma associated with seeking psychological help. *Journal of Counseling Psychology, 53*, 325–337. doi:10.1037/0022-0167.53.3.325

Vogel, D. L., Wade, N. G., & Hackler, A. H. (2007). Perceived public stigma and the willingness to seek counseling: The mediating roles of self-stigma and attitudes toward counseling. *Journal of Counseling Psychology, 54*, 40–50. doi:10.1037/0022-0167.54.1.40

Vogel, D. L., & Wester, S. R. (2003). To seek help or not to seek help: The risks of self-disclosure. *Journal of Counseling Psychology, 50*, 351–361. doi:10.1037/0022-0167.50.3.351

Vogel, D. L., Wester, S. R., Heesacker, M., Boysen, G. A., & Seeman, J. (2006). Gender differences in emotional expression: Do mental health trainees overestimate the magnitude? *Journal of Social and Clinical Psychology, 25*, 305–332.

Vogel, D., Wester, S., Heesacker, M., & Madon, S. (2003). Confirming gender stereotypes: A social role perspective. *Sex Roles, 48*(11/12), 519–528. doi:10.1023/A:1023575212526

Vogel, D. L., Wester, S. R., Wei, M., & Boysen, G. A. (2005). The role of outcome expectations and attitudes on decisions to seek professional help. *Journal of Counseling Psychology, 52,* 459–470. doi:10.1037/0022-0167.52.4.459

Wade, J. C. (1998). Male reference group identity dependence: A theory of male identity. *The Counseling Psychologist, 26,* 349–383. doi:10.1177/0011000 098263001

Wester, S. R. (2008). Male gender role conflict and multiculturalism: Implications for counseling psychology. *The Counseling Psychologist, 36,* 294–324. doi:10.1177/0011000006286341

Wester, S. R., Arndt, D., Sedivy, S. K., & Arndt, L. (2010). Male police officers and stigma associated with counseling: The role of anticipated risk, anticipated benefit, and gender role conflict. *Psychology of Men and Masculinity, 11,* 286–302. doi:10.1037/a0019108

Wester, S. R., Christianson, H. F., Vogel, D. L., & Wei, M. (2007). Gender role conflict and psychological distress: The role of social support. *Psychology of Men and Masculinity, 8,* 215–224. doi:10.1037/1524-9220.8.4.215

Wester, S. R., & Lyubelsky, J. (2005). Supporting the thin blue line: Gender sensitive therapy with male police officers. *Professional Psychology: Research and Practice, 36,* 51–58. doi:10.1037/0735-7028.36.1.51

Wester, S. R., Pionke, D., & Vogel, D. L. (2005). Male gender role conflict, gay men, and same-sex romantic relationships. *Psychology of Men and Masculinity, 6,* 195–208. doi:10.1037/1524-9220.6.3.195

Wester, S. R., & Vogel, D. L. (2002). Working with the masculine mystique: Male gender role conflict, counseling self-efficacy, and the training of male psychologists. *Professional Psychology: Research and Practice, 33,* 370–376. doi:10.1037/0735-7028.33.4.370

Wester, S. R., Vogel, D. L., Pressly, P. K., & Heesacker, M. (2002). Sex differences in emotion: A critical review of the literature and implications for counseling psychology. *The Counseling Psychologist, 30,* 630–652. doi:10.1177/00100002030004008

Wester, S. R., Vogel, D. L., Wei, M., & McLain, R. (2006). African-American men, gender role conflict, and psychological distress: The role of racial identity. *Journal of Counseling and Development, 84,* 419–429.

Williams, C. M., & Subich, L. M. (2006). The gendered nature of career related learning experiences: A social cognitive career theory perspective. *Journal of Vocational Behavior, 69,* 262–275. doi:10.1016/j.jvb.2006.02.007

Wong, Y., & Rochlen, A. (2005). Demystifying men's emotional behavior: New directions and implications for counseling and research. *Psychology of Men and Masculinity, 6,* 62–72. doi:10.1037/1524-9220.6.1.62

CHAPTER 15

GENDER: WOMEN—THEORIES AND RESEARCH

Carolyn Zerbe Enns

As early as 1985, Kay Deaux described the literature on gender and sex as extensive, prompting her to state, "This quantity certainly prompts the most dedicated reviewer to cry 'Enough!'" (p. 50). In the 25 years since her review, conceptualizations of gender and sex have continued to increase in complexity and diversity, necessitating a selective review. To that end, this chapter emphasizes recent trends that focus on intersectional perspectives and theories that explore gender and social power (Stewart & McDermott, 2004).

I begin this chapter with a brief historical perspective of 40 years of theory and research about gender that have emerged in the wake of the women's rights and other civil rights movements and then summarize core themes of contemporary gender theory: social constructionism, intersectionality, and social power. I describe four theories that emphasize how power and context inform gender and then summarize approaches to theory and research relevant to sexism and intersecting "isms" as well as social identity development. The chapter concludes with a brief discussion of the implications and challenges of applying intersectional and social constructionist thinking to research and practice.

An assumption that provides a scaffold for this chapter is that individuals "do gender" in biopsychosocial, ecological contexts that encompass (a) the individual's microsystem (familial, spiritual, educational, and other support systems), (b) the mesosystem (interactions among microsystem components), (c) the exosystem (social, governmental, legal, and political institutions and policies that have

an impact on privileges, opportunities, oppression, and general flexibility of movement), and (d) the macrosystem (cultural values, worldviews, ideologies, and global influences; Ballou, Matsumoto, & Wagner, 2002; Bronfenbrenner & Morris, 2006). The manner in which social identities (e.g., race, class, gender, disability) intersect with these systems is crucial to developing an ecologically informed understanding of gender.

A BRIEF HISTORICAL PERSPECTIVE: FROM INDIVIDUAL DIFFERENCES TO A SOCIAL CONTEXTUAL FOCUS

In 1968, Naomi Weisstein criticized psychology for having "nothing" to say about women. She acknowledged that theorists had speculated about women's character and competencies for many years, but they offered no substantive insights because existing theories were not supported by evidence, decontextualized women's lives, or explained gender differences as the consequence of biology and, thus, as indicative women's inferiority. Weisstein's commentary represented a significant catalyst for new and exciting developments in the psychology of women and gender for the past 40 years.

One of the early approaches that moved psychology beyond its "womanless" base can be characterized as the "women as problem" framework (Crawford & Marecek, 1989). This approach focused on exploring women's restrictive socialization experiences and rectifying women's individual skills deficits or problems that were labeled by

DOI: 10.1037/13754-015
APA Handbook of Counseling Psychology: Vol. 1. Theories, Research, and Methods, Nadya A. Fouad (Editor-in-Chief)

phrases such as *fear of success*, the *imposter syndrome*, or the *Cinderella complex*. Although offering options for building individual skills, this approach provided limited insight about social contexts in which problems occur. Androgyny (Bem, 1983) emerged as one potential individual strategy for pursuing individual change and equality. Early research on the popular concept found that androgyny was associated with a broad range of positive mental health behaviors and self-esteem, self-actualization, behavioral flexibility, and nonstereotypic qualities (for a review, see Cook, 1985). Acquiring androgynous behaviors seemed to offer a straightforward path for overcoming constricting gender rules and moving toward equality.

Early optimism was tempered by the realization that social change often fails to follow individual change and that the simplistic assumptions underlying the promise of androgyny did not provide tools for dealing with resistance to individual change (Enns, 1993). By the early 1980s, research revealed that the mental health benefits of androgyny were associated with the masculinity component of androgyny and that expressive traits of femininity did not offer additional mental health benefits (e.g., Bassoff & Glass, 1982). Mednick (1989) labeled androgyny as a "bandwagon" concept, arguing that overemphasis on the prescriptive implications of androgyny deflected attention from social structural aspects of inequality. Bem's (1983) later reformulation of instrumental and expressive behaviors within gender schema theory offered a broader, more complex perspective.

Given early assumptions that gender differences signified women's inferiority (Weisstein, 1968), feminist psychologists also prioritized research that challenged gender myths. Much research about gender similarities and differences was fueled by an "uncomplicated vision" (Eagly, 1995, p. 149) that methodologically sound studies would dispel mythologies about sex and gender. Indeed, Hyde's (2005) extensive review of research on gender similarities and difference in cognitive and social domains provides strong support for a gender similarities hypothesis at the individual level. Her review also concluded that individual gender differences can be removed, minimized, or decreased

substantially through cognitive reframing (e.g., emphasizing women's training and skill relevant to a task) or a shift in context (Hyde, 2005).

Although much of the research of the 1970s and 1980s emphasized individual differences and supported a gender similarities hypothesis, feminist theory about women's "different voice" (Gilligan, 1982, p. 2) competed with gender similarities hypotheses. Gilligan's work pointed out ways in which psychological theory based on white middle-class men's lives tended to overemphasize the importance of autonomy and individualism and contributed to the subtle devaluation of relational roles enacted by many women. By highlighting women's unique identity development and moral decision-making experiences, Gilligan and other relational cultural theorists (e.g., Miller & Stiver, 1997) sought to revalue expressive aspects of women's behavior, and their groundbreaking work informed a variety of other theories that focus on relational approaches to knowing, ethics, conflict management, and other social experiences.

In their evaluation of the gender similarity and gender difference hypotheses of the 1980s, Hare-Mustin and Marecek (1988) identified limitations of each approach. A gender similarities approach may contribute to beta bias or to the minimization of the impact of gender on women's and men's lives; in contrast, a gender differences framework contributes to alpha bias or to the exaggeration of differences between men and women. Marecek (1995) added that both approaches tend to encourage individuals to see gender as lodged within the person rather than as actively created within relationships and social structures. Both alternatives perpetuate beliefs that "the categories of 'man' and 'woman' are natural, self-evident" and unitary (Marecek, 1995, p.162) and may compel individuals to draw conclusions about generic men and women in isolation from other important aspects of social position, social identity, and culture.

As discussions about the strengths and limitations of similarity and difference approaches continued, feminist psychologists increasingly emphasized gender as a social category that is influenced by context (Deaux, 1984; Yoder & Kahn, 2003). For example, social cognitive theory has highlighted gender-related reciprocal interactions between the person and environment, such as the ways in which gender-related experience is shaped by social modeling, direct instruction and guidance about gender-appropriate behavior, and performance experiences that are reinforced by evaluative social reactions and sanctions (Bussey & Bandura, 2004). Gender schema theory (Bem, 1983, 1993) proposes ways in which a culture's gender-related beliefs are internalized, become efficient or automatic, and inform perceptions about the self and others. In addition to guiding personal behaviors, gender-related schemas can contribute to selective attention and recall, and can lead to distorted interpretations of others' behaviors. In contrast to Bem's earlier work, gender schema theory does not prescribe any particular combination of agency and communion (e.g., androgyny) as an ideal model of mental health.

Adding further to an interpersonal emphasis, Deaux and Major's (1987) interactive model has explained gender-related sequences in terms of interactions among (a) a perceiver or expectancy-holder whose gender-related schemas, beliefs, and stereotypes are activated in an interaction; (b) a second, target individual who interacts with the perceiver and who also brings a set of assumptions about gender roles and behaviors to the situation; and (c) the context, which varies with regard to the salience of gender. A fourth, gendered cultures approach (Maccoby, 1998) has explored the ways in which gendered subcultures develop during early childhood and reinforce gender-specific behaviors, rules, and stereotypes. Divergent social interaction styles emerge in childhood social groups rather than at the individual level, and set the stage for gender-related communication dynamics that vary across the life span. These four models each highlight interpersonal aspects of gender and continue to be influential. For example, the interactive model has been expanded and integrated with recent emphases on (a) cultural variations and ways in which gender-related identities and beliefs are associated with historical and social change, (b) themes of intersection and multiplicity, and (c) developmental changes during childhood and adulthood (Deaux & Stewart, 2001).

CONTEMPORARY GENDER THEORIES, SOCIAL CONSTRUCTIONISM, AND INTERSECTIONALITY

Gender is enacted at an individual level, as gender roles and gender-related behavior; at the interpersonal level, as cues that shape reactions and perceptions; and at the social structural level, as a system of power relations (Crawford & Unger, 2004). Whereas most theories and research described in the previous section have placed individual and interpersonal themes in the foreground, recent theories have increasingly emphasized gender as a form of social organization that influences power relationships (Crawford & Marecek, 1989). Underlying these theories is the assumption that it is not possible for men and women to "operate (effortlessly) in a social vacuum where expectations for gender-related behavior . . . are noticeably absent" (Morawski, 1987, p. 55). Gender becomes a verb and encompasses behaviors embedded in interactions and social structures (West & Zimmerman, 1987). In addition, social constructionism, postmodernism, multiplicity, and intersectionality have emerged as tools of analysis. The content that follows builds on multicultural locational approaches to gender that characterize identities as multifaceted and influenced by power structures (American Psychological Association [APA], 2003, 2007; Enns, 2010; Shields, 2008; Stewart & McDermott, 2004).

Social Constructionism and Postmodernism

A social constructionist approach is informed by postmodern and poststructural theory. It is based on the assumption that all knowledge is historically situated, socially negotiated, and embedded in power structures that support communities of knowers and influence the structures of language used to convey knowledge (Marecek, Crawford, & Popp, 2004). Postmodern analyses rely on deconstruction, which encompasses tools that examine hidden meanings underlying suppositions that are often seen as given or inviolable. Deconstruction supports critical thinking and involves teasing apart, and often destabilizing, existing authority and power structures, including underlying assumptions about truth, reality, language, and the self (Flax, 1987). All theory is seen as bound by time, social and power relationships, and context.

When studying gender, relevant deconstructive questions include the following: For which women or men is this theory or "truth" relevant? Who is implicitly and explicitly excluded and included in this analysis? What are the hidden assumptions, implications, strengths, and limitations of the research methods and theoretical perspectives we use? This type of scrutiny is more likely to support modest, moderated, context-specific, and time-specific claims than grand theories that are designed to provide all-encompassing and universal principles (Enns, 2010).

Postmodern deconstruction also reveals how language portrays power relationships, which are often described with bipolar or polarized constructs, such as strong and weak, or masculine and feminine. Bipolar constructions underline our limited ability to think in complex ways or to transcend dichotomous constructs such as heterosexual and homosexual or White and Black. Multiple, nonoppositional, or integrative ways of constructing reality are more elusive and difficult to convey because of the structure of language (Scott, 1988). Social constructionism offers useful tools for (a) critiquing narrow ways of defining and constructing theory and science; (b) supporting reflexive research and applied practices, including continuous self-reflection and nondefensive questioning about the strengths and limitations of our approaches; and (c) underlining the roles of values and language in constructing knowledge (Gergen, 2001).

The influence of social constructionist themes can be seen in evolving definitions of gender and sex. An underlying assumption that guided much research is that "gender is what culture makes out of the 'raw material' of biological sex" (Unger & Crawford, 1992, p. 18). *Sex* was seen as referring to the physiological and biological features of maleness and femaleness, presumed to be stable and similar across cultures (Unger, 1979). In contrast, *gender* was defined as roles related to masculinity and femininity, as malleable, and as modified by social values and cultural variations. More recently, however, queer theorists have proposed that neither sex nor gender is immutable and that both sex and gender are socially constructed, "with the consequence that the distinction between sex and gender turns out to be no distinction at all" (Butler, 1990, p. 346). Butler argued that physical bodies are gendered from birth and that sex does not exist without gender. Marecek et al. (2004) added that "sex, like gender, draws meaning from shifting cultural understandings and ever-changing social practices" (p. 207).

According to queer theorists and other social constructionist perspectives, gender involves performativity, which is scripted, regulated, and inscribed on the body by culture. In addition, queer theorists challenge bipolar categories (e.g., homosexual vs. heterosexual, sex vs. gender) and emphasize fluidity, complexity, and overlapping aspects of identity. Queer theory seeks to create an overarching, inclusive umbrella that encompasses diverse identities associated with gender, race, and sexuality, including bisexual, intersex, transgendered, and "queer heterosexuals" (Jagdose, 1996). Growing awareness of intersexual, transsexual, transgendered, and other nondichotomous identities supports the view that traditional views of sex and gender represent arbitrary methods of placing individuals in dichotomous categories. Consistent with this thinking, Diamond and Butterworth (2008) noted that previous perspectives postulated developmental phases of sexual identity that would result in "a stable, integrated, unambiguous lesbian, gay, or heterosexual identity" (p. 366). Our growing knowledge about the diversity of biological sex has led us to realize that concepts related to both sex and gender are more malleable than previously thought (Riger, 2000).

Multiple Social Identities and Intersectionality

Each person holds multiple social identities, some of which confer privilege and power, and others that are associated with disadvantage or minority status. The terms *social identity* and *collective identity* refer to one's membership in social groups that share specific goals, characteristics, and interests; examples of such social groups include race and ethnicity, socioeconomic class, age, gender, sexual orientation, religious affiliation, geographic identity, and culture (Reid & Deaux, 1996). The importance of a social identity may be influenced by its salience and the degree to which an individual identifies with a specific social group of social location and sees group membership as relevant to self-definition and comparison with others. Salience typically varies across contexts, often depending on the presence or absence of others with a shared social identity and the degree to which a specific identity is part of the foreground or background (e.g., being the only woman in a roomful of men, or participating in a women's-only social function; Deaux & Martin, 2003; Deaux & Stewart, 2001; Stewart & McDermott, 2004). One's social identities may include multiple groups that confer privilege and power (e.g., White, middle-class, male statuses), multiple groups associated with oppression (e.g., African American, female, lesbian), or multiple identifications that confer a mix of privilege and disadvantage (e.g., White, female, lesbian; APA, 2007).

Some social identities are experienced as relatively stable and as providing a sense of continuity and stability to a person's identity; other identities may be experienced as more variable or as relevant only in specific contexts (Shields, 2008). Some social identities are also more visible than are others, and cues related to visibility may include skin color and tone, body size, or gender-related physical characteristics. Cues related to physical characteristics may elicit stereotypes more quickly or automatically than less visible characteristics. Other social identities, such as sexual orientation, are often associated with invisibility. Although invisibility can provide protective effects from immediate oppression (one can "hide" one's identity), invisibility can also contribute to discounting the uniqueness of one's social history, distinctive qualities, or oppressions (Purdie-Vaughns & Eibach, 2008). Such invisibility can delegitimize a collective group's sense of being wronged and the basis from which one seeks social justice.

Gender is a major social identity relevant to women; however, assuming that gender is the most significant or unifying social identity of women glosses over the many differences among groups of women. From an intersectional perspective, gender is inseparable from, or sometimes secondary to, class, age, race, disability, or other important social

identity statuses. Shields (2008) observed that "there is no single identity category that satisfactorily describes how we respond to our social environment or are responded to by others" (p. 403).

Shields (2008) also proposed that various identities "*mutually constitute*" each other (p. 302) such that gender takes on meaning in relationship to other identity categories. In addition, one's self-identification with multiple social groups results in self-concepts and experiences that are "unique, non-additive, and not reducible to the original identities that went into them" (Diamond & Butterworth, 2008, p. 366). A person's multiple identities may also contribute to unique hybrid options that result from living on the boundaries or borders of several identities (Hurtado, 2010). Multiple identities may also result in a variety of context-specific self-definitions marked by fluidity or a refusal to assume an existing, widely shared label (e.g., heterosexual or bisexual). Thus, gender-related identities may be "moving targets, reforming and reshaping themselves across diverse social and interpersonal contexts" (Diamond & Butterworth, 2008, p. 375). This position diverges from earlier models that proposed that oppressions based on multiple marginalized identities were additive or conferred double or triple jeopardy.

Although being female, on average, is associated with lower social status, there are wide variations among those who experience privilege and oppression, and how these experiences affect the person. For example, one social identity such as race or ethnicity may be most relevant for one aspect of experience (e.g., politics), whereas another social identity such as gender may be most relevant for another set of issues (e.g., domestic violence; Stewart & McDermott, 2004). Women of color often observe that racism is frequently experienced as more daily, sustained, toxic, and venomous than sexism. Collins (2000, 2004), a well-known Black feminist theorist, noted that each person participates in a "matrix of domination" (Collins, 2000, p. 18) defined by one's social identities, privileges, and sources of oppression. The interlocking features of these identities are not separable but operate simultaneously and uniquely to shape an individual's experience. Each aspect of identity, such as religion, sexual orientation, or nationality, shapes how other aspects of self are experienced, and the salience of any one dimension may vary across contexts (Hurtado, 2010; Zinn & Dill, 1996). As the foreground and background of various identities shift across contexts, a person may experience privilege in one situation (e.g., because of light skin color, heterosexual orientation, or class status) and discrimination in another setting (e.g., gender-based bias in a setting in which she is the only woman). To gain a complete sense of the complexity of women's lives, multiple chapters in this handbook are relevant, including chapters on men, aging, race and ethnicity, sexual orientation, spirituality, social class, and economic disparities.

Gender, Social Context, and Power

In the section that follows, I summarize four theories that focus on power as an organizing principle. Because power and privilege are typically associated with many social identities, these perspectives can be applied and adapted to intersectional perspectives. Although this section emphasizes theory, illustrative research is also described.

Gender and status. Status theories of gender are built on the assumption that those with greater social power hold substantial control over resources, whereas those who hold less power have limited means for acquiring power. To gain influence, lower status individuals play by the rules established by those in power and exchange something of value with those in more powerful positions. In work situations, for example, individuals with less power may show deference through verbal messages that reinforce lower status and a variety of nonverbal cues such as a softer voice tone, compliant body posture, and tentative word choices (Gerber, 2009).

Expectation states theory, a specific status theory, proposes that gender stereotypes are imbued with widely shared status beliefs that reinforce the notion that men are more competent than women (Ridgeway & Bourg, 2004). These gender stereotypes have an impact on who is perceived to be most capable, who acquires leadership, and who is directed away from positions of influence. Whereas holding higher status and being male are associated with beliefs about competence, having lower status and being female are associated with warmth and responsiveness. For women seeking influence, stepping outside of these gendered expectations can result in negative consequences. More specifically, women who display assertive behaviors (which are associated with competence) without demonstrating accompanying "nice" behaviors are often discounted (Eagly & Carli, 2007).

Status and gender effects are modified by the perceptions of the actor, situational interactions and group composition, and the societal context (Sell & Kuipers, 2009; Webster & Rashotte, 2009). Sell and Kuipers (2009) noted that social identities such as gender are made salient when their numbers are small (e.g., token status) or when the demands of an environment, such as competitive norms, are consistent with gendered expectations. For example, a study of responses to social dilemmas found that in contrast to occasions in which group members were aware of the gender of members, behavioral gender differences were not observed when group members were unaware of the gender of other members (Sell, Chen, Hunter-Holmes, & Johansson, 2002). Women have also been found to show similar competitive behaviors as men when women are competing with other women (Gneezy, Niederle, & Rustichini, 2003).

Persons of both genders with higher status are typically perceived as and perceive themselves as displaying higher levels of instrumental–assertive behaviors, whereas persons with lower status are seen as showing more accommodating, expressive traits (Gerber, 2009). Expressive roles, often associated with lower status, can serve the function of appeasement and can reinforce existing power differentials but also can augment power of lower status persons. For example, a status disclaimer or self-effacement may simultaneously acknowledge one's lower power while also allowing one to use manipulation as a power tactic. Complaining behaviors can involve efforts to influence while also acknowledging that the person with higher status can choose to ignore or accept the influence.

Status differences are often reinforced through gendered nonverbal mechanisms, including women's greater sensitivity to nonverbal cues and greater accuracy in decoding nonverbal language, and men's greater likelihood to use interruption and silence to control discussion and to take up more personal space (Gilbert & Scher, 1999; LaFrance & Henley, 1997). Compared with high-status persons, persons with lower status often exhibit greater interpersonal sensitivity and accuracy about the perceptions of higher status persons (Kenny, Snook, Boucher, & Hancock, 2010), suggesting that lower status persons enhance their coping and survival by being able to discern the desires and intentions of those with greater power.

Social role and structural theory. Social role or social structural theory proposes that individuals enact roles, behaviors, and personal traits that optimize their ability to fulfill assigned social functions (Eagly & Wood, 1999; Wood & Eagly, 2002). According to this theory, the social roles of women and men are influenced by (a) a variety of complex cultural beliefs and mandates, including economic and structural aspects of societies, and (b) the biological and physiological characteristics of women and men. At the cultural level, societies create gender-related rules about economic practices and division of labor, which represent the engine that places constraints on men's and women's degree of flexibility. Cultural beliefs and rules interact with physical differences relevant to women's childbearing and nursing capacities as well as men's greater average strength and size. When physical strength and strenuous activity are crucial to survival, physical attributes become important factors in role assignment.

Social role theory posits that at early phases of societal formation, women's involvement in caregiving and men's participation in physically demanding activities offered an efficient, cooperative division of labor. As cultures evolved, greater power and status were accorded to roles that men typically fulfilled, and this status contributed to men's dominance behaviors, agentic and assertive roles, and the roles of providing food and economic resources. In contrast, women's caregiving roles were equated with less power and required women to assume more subordinate, domestic, relationally oriented behaviors (Wood & Eagly, 2002). Although physiological

gender differences offer few survival advantages in the 21st century, gender-related power structures are highly resistant to change. They take on a "life of their own" and are reinforced through a variety of gender-related biases. Gender role expectations and traits are reproduced through enduring socialization and power structures, and women continue to be seen as valuing relational and expressive qualities and men as valuing instrumental qualities (Rudman & Glick, 2008).

Social structural theory was proposed, at least in part, as an alternative explanation to the gender-related differences approach proposed by evolutionary psychologists (Katz-Wise, Priess, Hyde, 2010; Wood & Eagly, 2002). Evolutionary psychologists have argued that men and women acquired different behaviors in response to evolutionary adaptive requirements and survival risks. Men adopted dominance behaviors, at least in part, in response to their need to compete with other men for sexual partners, whereas women developed relational qualities that supported caregiving and ensured the long-term faithfulness of men who would provide the necessary means of physical and economic survival (Buss & Kenrick, 1998; Wood & Eagly, 2002). In contrast to evolutionary theorists, social structural theorists have argued that gender differences emerge in response to social structural roles as well as men's greater social power.

Social dominance theory. Social dominance theory (Pratto & Walker, 2004; Sidanius & Pratto, 1999) offers insights about the development and maintenance of inequities in societies, including gender inequities. Social dominance theory posits that societies are characterized by the two universal hierarchies of gender and age as well as other hierarchies (which vary across cultures) based on religion, ethnicity, nationality, sexual orientation, and other social statuses. Various "isms" such as sexism and racism emerge as a consequence of these hierarchies. At the top of social hierarchies, hegemonic groups, often consisting of older White males, hold high social status and work to maintain dominance.

A variety of legitimizing myths justify and reinforce social dominance and include paternalistic myths (e.g., "the more powerful care for those who are weak and dependent"), reciprocal myths (e.g., "socially dominant groups and groups with lower power are actually equal"), and sacred myths (e.g., beliefs about who should govern, which are determined on the basis of religion or other value systems). These myths justify existing structures and can be identified in the attitudes, beliefs, values, stereotypes, and cultural ideologies of people within a culture. Social comparisons provide a foundation for individual discrimination, and discriminatory behaviors increase the self-esteem of actors.

Pratto and Walker (2004) identified four bases of gendered power: (a) force, which includes various forms of violence and abuse against women; (b) men's greater control over resources, such as health, jobs, and institutional influence; (c) social obligations, which include the caregiving and nurturing expectations that reinforce women's lower level of power; and (d) consensual ideologies, such as beliefs, stereotypes, and norms relevant to gender roles. Recently, social dominance theory has been useful for conceptualizing research findings relevant to ambivalent sexism (e.g., Fowers & Fowers, 2010; Sibley, Overall, & Duckitt, 2007).

Rosenthal and Levy (2010) also used social dominance theory as an integrative framework for understanding women's risk for HIV infection. For example, rape and sexual assault, emotional and physical abuse in relationships, and women's economic dependency on men (resource control differences) contribute to women's direct risk of infection as well as women's decreased ability to assertively initiate safe-sex practices. Women's sense of obligation to satisfy a partner and commitment to a long-term relationship as well as consensual ideologies such as "women should be faithful in spite of infidelity" pose additional risks.

System justification theory.   System justification theory proposes that people hold psychological and social motivations to view existing, status quo power arrangements as legitimate, fair, and desirable. This theory explains the wide range of rationalizations designed to support the validity or justness of existing economic, political, and social arrangements. In addition to shaping the perspectives of individuals in dominant groups, system justification

thinking can be absorbed by members of disadvantaged groups, including women, and can contribute to internalized beliefs about personal inferiority (Jost & Banaji, 1994; Jost, Banaji, & Nosek, 2004). People may not be aware of their motivations to support status quo arrangements as these motivations often operate at unconscious levels. Endorsing ideologies that support the status quo can also have palliative functions, which can result in decreased negative emotion and increased positive emotion and satisfaction (Napier & Jost, 2008).

System justification theory offers a potential framework for understanding research on men's elevated entitlement beliefs and women's lack of grievance in spite of gender inequality. For example, Major (1993) noted that employed women in heterosexual marriages used a variety of explanations that justified status quo household arrangements and often incorporated an "economy of gratitude" (p. 151) for any assistance, however incomplete, received from spouses. Rather than comparing themselves with their husbands, working women tended to use exacting normative standards that focused on comparing their household task performance with that of their mothers or nonemployed married women. Justifications also included making self-comparisons about women's household contributions pre- and postemployment ("I'm working less at home now"), identifying housework as more relevant to women's identities, believing that women had fewer psychological needs than spouses (hence needing less downtime), and expressing gratitude that spouses "heard" women's frustrations about inequities and empathized with them. A recent study reveals that women continue to expect that they will carry more responsibility for household labor than their male partners (Askari, Liss, Erchull, Staebell, & Axelson, 2010).

Gender differences in entitlement beliefs are also evident in research about gender wage gaps, and women's tendency to compare their salaries to the earnings of other women rather than men has been defined as the depressed entitlement effect (e.g., Jost, 1997). This system-justifying rationale, when internalized by women or other lower status persons, can contribute to beliefs that they deserve less pay than persons of higher status. Although gender gaps in pay expectations continue, recent findings have revealed that women who expected to hold positions in male-dominated careers held higher pay expectations than those who planned to pursue female-dominated careers (Hogue, DuBois, & Fox-Cardamone, 2010). Hogue and Yoder (2003) also found that when women's status was elevated with a statement about women's cognitive strengths (a gender-legitimizing rationale) or their advanced educational status (status enhanced condition), depressed entitlement effects disappeared. Another study found that when men were informed that women typically outperform men on a specific task, men responded with heightened perceptions about their own competence and awarded themselves "resistant high self-pay" (Hogue, Yoder, & Singleton, 2007, p. 573). Authors concluded that these men were "unwilling to forego the privilege of high reward that accompanies that position when that privilege is openly threatened" (p. 577).

Hogue and Yoder (2003) criticized the characterization of gender-related cognitions about wage gaps as women's "depressed entitlement" (p. 330) and suggested that emphasizing the internalization of inequality can detract attention from objective inequities, contribute to victim blaming, or reinforce "man is the norm" thinking (Tavris, 1993, p. 150). Labeling men's wage-entitlement beliefs as "elevated wage entitlement" (Hogue et al., 2007, p. 573) may reframe issues so that victim blaming is not reinforced. Recent research (Moss-Racusin & Rudman, 2010) also has revealed that women limit their self-promotion and requests for equality as part of their efforts to avoid backlash, a finding that provides a more complete view of women's behavior.

Summary and commentary. The theories described in this section hold much in common, but differences among these theories are also noteworthy. Social structural theory identifies specific biological differences that contribute to social roles; social dominance theory identifies interlocking social systems that provide a foundation for dominance; and system justification theory emphasizes motivational and cognitive factors, such as how and why individuals need to see the status quo as just, and how persons in lower status groups internalize

beliefs that condone or reinforce subordination. The fourth theory, status theory, focuses on how status differences are maintained. Much past research on gender has been atheoretical, and these theories offer a way of organizing and studying complex social identities that are imbued with privilege or oppression. Because the theories described in this section share an emphasis on how systems of dominance and power emerge and are reinforced, future efforts to integrate these models will be useful. Alternatively, research studies that test the potential advantages of one of these approaches over another are likely to advance our understanding.

Although the theories described in this section can support an intersectional perspective and the examination of various social identities through the lens of power, much of the existing research (e.g., social role theory, entitlement beliefs, and social justification theory) has focused primarily on gender-related questions. Theoretically grounded research that explores multiple intersecting identities through the lens of power will be important in the future. The theories described in this section have also supported intriguing conceptual models that have not yet been adequately linked to research. For example, research that builds on Rosenthal and Levy's (2010) conceptualization of social dominance theory and women's HIV infection is needed to gain additional understanding of this crucial issue. In addition, future research should explore how social contexts imbued with power interact with individual differences and microsystemic aspects of experience. A biopsychosocial ecological model of gender will be enhanced by efforts that examine the complexity of individual variables as well as macrosystemic factors associated with power and cultural values.

Gender Bias and Sexism

During the 1990s, researchers noted that blatant or explicit forms of prejudice and discrimination had decreased (e.g., Campbell, Schellenberg, & Senn, 1997) and that contemporary forms of sexism, racism, and related biases had taken on more subtle or clandestine forms referred to as *modern racism* or sexism, or *unintentional* or *symbolic racism* and sexism (e.g., Dovidio, Gaertner, Kawakami, &

Hodson, 2002; Swim, Aikin, Hall, & Hunter, 1995). This section provides a brief overview of those models that have relevance to gender-related "isms" and can lend themselves to an intersectional approach.

Modern sexism and neosexism.   *Modern sexism* is described as consisting of three components: (a) the denial that discrimination continues in the present, (b) antagonism toward women's expectations and demands for equity, and (c) resentment about women who expect "special favors" or preferential treatment (Swim et al., 1995). Modern sexism can include unintentional and unconscious attitudes, and entails the veiled expression of prejudice, in part because individuals are attentive to societal pressures to express politically correct attitudes (Barreto & Ellemers, 2005). Modern sexist statements may be voiced as opposition to progressive policies or may express the view that reverse discrimination is an outcome of social policies. Individuals who convey modern sexist views make efforts to support any statements with a rationale that cannot be construed as prejudiced.

Another closely related conceptual framework is referred to as *neosexism*, which is defined as an expression of the conflict between stated egalitarian values and "residual negative feelings about women" (Tougas, Brown, Beaton, & Joly, 1995, p. 843). The modern sexism and neosexism frameworks appear to highlight different facets of contemporary prejudice, with modern sexism emphasizing personal denial of discrimination and neosexism emphasizing antagonism toward women's demands and resentment of women (Campbell et al., 1997; Swim, Becker, Lee, & Pruitt, 2010). Research reveals that individuals are less likely to perceive modern and benevolent sexist behaviors as sexism, providing support for the notion that these forms of bias are subtle (Swim, Mallett, Russo-Devosa, & Stangor, 2005). Modern sexism is also associated with the lack of awareness of subtle sexism in sexist language and the lower likelihood of using nonsexist language (Swim, Mallett, & Stangor, 2004).

Ambivalent sexism.   Theory and research on ambivalent sexism (Glick & Fiske, 2001) and ambivalence toward men (Glick & Fiske, 1999) explore the combination of subjectively positive and subjectively negative attitudes toward men and women that reinforce sexism and male dominance and system-justifying arguments (Sibley, Overall, & Duckitt, 2007). Thus, theory and research on ambivalent sexism can be integrated with social dominance theory or system justification theory. In general, hostile forms of sexism are directed at women who challenge existing power structures and refuse to "stay in their place" (e.g., career women or feminists). Benevolent sexism represents a more subtle form of sexism that consists of warmth, praise, or patronizing and protective behaviors toward women who fulfill traditional communal feminine roles (e.g., as homemakers and caregivers), and thus, do not challenge existing power structures. Specifically, benevolent sexism consists of (a) protective paternalism, such as protective attitudes toward women; (b) complementary gender differentiation, such as notions that men's and women's roles should differ and that women are more pure or refined than men; and (c) heterosexual intimacy, or the notion that a man is incomplete without a woman.

In response to their limited social power, women may experience ambivalence toward men in the forms of both hostility and benevolence (Glick & Fiske, 1999; Lee, Fiske, & Glick, 2010). Benevolence toward men involves respect for men's status and is characterized by the three themes of (a) maternalism, which involves the need to nurture and protect men because of their weaknesses related to caregiving, domestic, and other relational roles; (b) gender differentiation, which conveys appreciation for men's roles as protectors and providers as well as their willingness to take risks or place themselves in danger; and (c) heterosexual intimacy, or beliefs about the need to be cherished by a man or experience completion through a romantic intimate relationship with a men. Hostility toward men reflects frustration about men's more dominant status and is displayed through (a) resentment of paternalism, or negative reactions in response to men's dominating behaviors; (b) compensatory gender differentiation, which involves criticizing men for "male" behaviors, such as arrogance or competitiveness but without challenging men's dominance; and (c) heterosexual hostility, which entails viewing men as potential predators or as likely to abuse power.

During the past decade, the consequences of being the target of ambivalent sexism have received growing attention. Researchers and theorists conclude that benevolent sexist attitudes and behaviors are not easily recognized as sexist but may be seen as signs of respectful chivalry or minimized as the outgrowth of old-fashioned but harmless, and perhaps even refreshing, traditional attitudes. Compared with hostile sexism, benevolent sexism often remains unchallenged and may contribute to increased justification of restrictive gender relations (Barreto & Ellemers, 2005; Jost & Kay, 2005). Benevolent sexism can also become incorporated with self-protective or defensive strategies used by women who encounter other person's negative attitudes about women. In other words, endorsing benevolent sexist beliefs (e.g., that women should be cherished by men or are morally superior to men) allows women to maintain a level of self-esteem in the face of restrictive attitudes (Fischer, 2006).

Because the cues associated with benevolent sexism are ambiguous, the target person may feel that she is seen as having limited competence in a male domain, but it is difficult for her to determine whether the benevolent behaviors she is experiencing are markers of sexism or politeness. Research findings have revealed that in work performance situations, benevolent sexism appears to operate through the mechanisms of self-doubt, mental intrusions, and self-questioning about one's performance (Dardenne, Dumont, & Bollier, 2007; Dumont, Sarlet, & Dardenne, 2010). Women exposed to benevolent sexism have been found to have greater access to autobiographical memories about incompetence, show slower responses to task performance demands (Dumont et al., 2010), and have greater access to relational self-descriptors than task-related skills or self-descriptors (Barreto, Ellemers, Piebinga, & Moya, 2010).

According to a study by Vescio, Gervais, Snyder, and Hoover (2005), although both men and women experienced anger in response to a patronizing condition that involved being placed in a devalued position while also being praised, women were more

likely than men to perform worse. Patronizing behaviors, a form of benevolent sexism, may be more likely to contribute to internalized negative social stereotypes in women than men, and women's performance may be differentially affected by these internalized stereotypes. The potentially insidious effects of benevolent sexism may be related to that fact that whereas individuals expect others to experience negative reactions to hostile attitudes and "isms," the impact of benevolent sexism can be underestimated (Bosson, Pinel, & Vandello, 2010). When a target of benevolent sexism discloses frustration, members of her social network may have difficulty understanding why patronizing types of events are upsetting, which leads to greater isolation for the targeted person.

Research on ambivalent sexism includes the exploration of ambivalent attitudes toward women and men in multiple cultures (Glick et al., 2000, 2004; Glick & Fiske, 2001) and shows that the highest levels of both hostile and benevolent sexism are found in countries characterized by lower levels of gender equality. Across cultures, women are less likely than men to endorse sexist views, especially hostile sexism (Napier, Thorisdottir, & Jost, 2010). Napier et al. (2010) proposed that benevolent sexism provides a palliative function or "system-justifying buffer," especially in countries characterized by lower levels of gender inequality, and "complementary justifications of traditional gender roles can help to mask the inequality that exists" (p. 416). Although measures of ambivalent sexism have been translated with care, more efforts to conceptualize culture-specific aspects of ambivalent sexism will be important in the future. For example, whereas beliefs that support gender differentiation are defined as benevolent sexism within the West, some cultures view gender differentiation as compatible with gender equality, and these themes are incorporated within feminist thought (e.g., Japan; see Enns, 2004).

Stereotype threat. The concept of stereotype threat has been useful for studying how the internalization of stereotypes about a marginalized identity (e.g., race and ethnicity or gender) poses risks to individuals in the form of anxiety, working memory, and performance decrements in specific contexts

(Cohen & Garcia, 2008; Steele, 1997). *Stereotype threat* is defined as the fear of substantiating or backing up a stereotype and is thought to operate by increasing a person's performance-interfering stress and cognitive load. It is situational and triggered by specific achievement or work situations, and it is most likely to occur when a task is difficult (e.g., advanced math), the individual has significant skill in the domain, and the task is relevant to the individual's identity. Specific circumstances (e.g., token status) can increase one's visibility and exacerbate the effects of stereotype threat (Roberson & Kulik, 2007). Cues that elicit stereotype threat can be explicit or subtle (Nguyen & Ryan, 2008); for example, a preperformance demographic questionnaire can make a specific social identity more accessible and contribute to stereotype threat (e.g., Danaher & Crandall, 2008; Rydell, McConnell, & Beilock, 2009).

Recent efforts have turned toward identifying and implementing interventions that decrease or eliminate stereotype threat, thus building on resilience and resistance skills of individuals. Promising interventions include increasing access to positive role models (e.g., Huguet & Régner, 2007), reframing threats as challenges (e.g., Alter, Aronson, Darley, Rodriguez, & Ruble, 2010), reminding women of academic characteristics or skills they share with men (e.g., Rosenthal, Crisp, & Suen, 2007), teaching research participants about stereotype threat and clarifying its potential impact on performance (e.g., Johns, Schmader, & Martens, 2005), using same-sex testing or work environments (Huguet & Régner, 2007), heightening awareness of a social identity that is not associated with stereotype threat (e.g., college student), and employing self-affirmation strategies that remind individuals of their larger values and purpose that transcend the threatened social identity (Cohen & Garcia, 2008).

Differences in how stereotype threat may operate in various domains and social identity groups have also been detected (Nguyen & Ryan, 2008). For example, meta-analysis revealed that among women, subtle cues resulted in the largest effects; for members of racial and ethnic minority groups, however, moderately explicit stereotype-inducing cues resulted in the largest effects or decrements.

In addition, multiple identities can have varied impacts on stereotype threat. When Asian women were reminded of their Asian status rather than their female status, their math performances were stronger (Shih, Pittinsky, & Ambady, 1999). Rydell and Boucher (2010) found that increasing women's awareness of their social identities as college students provided a buffer against stereotype threats associated with comparisons to men.

Sexism and body objectification. Discrimination and its negative effects have been linked to mental health problems, interpersonal discrimination, workplace events, violence, and sexual objectification (for a review, see Moradi & Yoder, 2012). As an example, body and sexual objectification have received substantial attention during the past decades. In daily diary studies, sexual objectification, along with gender role stereotyping and demeaning experiences, is identified as a major form of everyday sexism (Brinkman & Rickard, 2009; Swim, Hyers, Cohen, & Ferguson, 2001). Objectification theory (Fredrickson & Roberts, 1997) proposes that as a consequence of routine, ubiquitous exposure to objectification, women take on an observer's perspective when viewing their own bodies, and this process leads to self-objectification.

The internalization of pervasively displayed perfect body images can lead to habitual body monitoring or surveillance, which contributes to women's shame and anxiety, the reduction of peak motivational states or flow, and decreased awareness of internal signals of hunger and satiation. Self-objectification has been linked to a variety of problems such as body image and unhealthy eating practices, performance problems, body shame, depressive symptoms, and disconnection from specific body functions (for a review, see Moradi & Huang, 2008). Recent research has demonstrated the relevance of self-objectification to women over age 25 (e.g., Augustus-Horvath & Tylka, 2009), lesbians (e.g., Hill & Fischer, 2008), and African American women (e.g., Buchanan, Fischer, Tokar, & Yoder, 2007).

Collins (2004) argued that hegemonic or dominant femininity, which includes beauty practices and appearance-related ideals, becomes a gendered power structure and yardstick for all women. Women of color are particularly vulnerable to being devalued for not meeting White standards of beauty (Cole & Zucker, 2007). Building on this observation, Buchanan et al.'s (2007) study of African American women revealed that higher levels of skin-tone surveillance were related to skin-tone dissatisfaction and body shame. Additional studies that expand on and examine such concepts as body objectification from an intersectional perspective will become increasingly important for extending our knowledge of gender-related effects.

Gendered racism.   In addition to appearance-related beauty standards, Collins (2004) proposed four additional elements of hegemonic femininity: expectations about womanly demeanor or deportment, prescriptions about traditional marriage and family arrangements, sexuality, and White race. Although some White middle-class women are sometimes able to achieve these standards, women of color are especially vulnerable to social devaluation. The concept of gendered racism offers an intersectional perspective to oppression, showing how gender and race shape experience simultaneously and cannot be parceled out or understood simply as "double jeopardy" (Thomas, Witherspoon, & Speight, 2008, p. 307).

Moradi and Subich's (2003) quantitative study of African American women, which used separate assessments of perceived racist and sexist events, found that both sexist and racist events were associated with psychological distress, but that racist and sexist events did not interact to predict distress. Similarly, Szymanski and Stewart's (2010) study of African American women found that both perceived racism and sexism were related to higher levels of psychological distress, but when examined concomitantly, only perceived sexism was associated with distress. Recently, after examining perceived racism and sexism (via separate instruments) in African American women, DeBlaere and Moradi (2008) suggested that racism may be experienced as a more global or omnipresent than sexism, which may be more context specific, such as in interpersonal contexts or public domains.

King's (2005) quantitative study used the term *ethgender* to conceptualize the interaction of gender and race; she concluded that for African American women, it is important to consider the combination of racism and sexism when conceptualizing stress-related reactions and coping. Using a revised version of a sexism inventory that assessed the fusion of sexism and racism, Thomas et al. (2008) found that interpersonal situations represented the greatest source of gendered racism and were associated with substantial psychological distress. These interpersonal situations included interactions with service professionals, employers, supervisors, fellow students or coworkers, strangers, teachers, and helping professionals. The most common forms of coping involved cognitive–emotional processing that involved minimizing or avoiding thoughts about discrimination.

Qualitative studies can also provide rich data about gendered racism, including several studies of African American and White women firefighters that revealed the intertwining of race and gender in patterns of subordination (Yoder & Berendsen, 2001). For example, whereas White women were more likely to experience paternalistic overprotection associated with images of fragility, African American women were more likely to report being treated as welfare recipients or "beasts of burden" who were expected to carry heavy loads. African American women reported being consistently aware of the "omnirelevance" (Yoder & Berendsen, 2001, p. 27) of race. Another qualitative study found that controlling cultural images framed the differential forms of gendered racism that professional Black men and women encountered (Wingfield, 2007). Whereas men's experiences of gendered racism were shaped as "angry Black man" images, women were more likely to be exploited via "modern Mammy" stereotypes of Black women as willing to sacrifice their personal lives and show "unshakeable loyalty" (Wingfield, 2007, p. 202) to the boss. These women were expected to silently accept exploitation marked by disrespectful and disparaging treatment, unreasonable expectations, and condescending attitudes.

Summary and commentary.   The theories and research described in this section provide insight about the consequences of gender bias and how these forms of bias can be internalized and have detrimental effects. Although concepts such as ambivalent sexism and stereotype threat were built on adaptations of research and theory on ambivalent and modern racism (e.g., Katz, & Hass, 1988; McConahay, 1986) and race-based stereotype threat (e.g., Steele, 1997), efforts to integrate and examine the intersections of constructs such as modern and ambivalent racism with modern and ambivalent sexism are limited. To date, for example, ambivalent sexism is examined as a worldwide phenomenon, but it has not been explored in interaction with other marginalized identities, such as race and ethnicity. In the future, the concomitant exploration of multiple and subtle "isms" through the use of multiple research methods (e.g., quantitative and qualitative) will be important for understanding the dynamics of intersectionality.

During the past decade, a variety of studies have explored and found links between perceived sexist, racist, and heterosexist experiences and psychological distress (e.g., Klonoff, Landrine, & Campbell, 2000; Moradi & DeBlaere, 2010; Moradi & Funderburk, 2006; Moradi & Subich, 2003; Szymanski, 2005). A growing number of quantitative studies have focused on examining interactions among multiple internalized oppressions and distress in lesbians (e.g., Szymanski, 2005); lesbian, gay, bisexual, and questioning persons of color (Szymanski & Gupta, 2009a, 2009b); and women of color (Szymanski & Stewart, 2010). Additional quantitative studies that examine multiple internalized "isms" in diverse groups of women will add to our knowledge base. Shields (2008) noted, however, that most statistical analyses are built on the assumption that social identities such as race, gender, class, and sexual orientation are independent of each other, and they do not provide necessary options for examining the complexity of multiple identities or the ways in which constructs such as race and gender are fused, modify each other, or are inseparable. In keeping with the assumption that bias and privilege are often bound by context, it is not only important to explore whether "isms" have detrimental effects but also to examine when and where biases and oppressions operate (Hurtado, 2010).

Promising developments include the extension and elaboration of theories, such as body objectification theory for specific groups of women, an approach that facilitates an intersectional perspective (Buchanan et al., 2008; Hill & Fischer, 2008). Concepts such as gendered racism represent an important development, but the literature on this topic remains small and needs to be extended to additional groups of women with multiple identities. Recent approaches to gendered racism (e.g., King, 2005; Thomas et al., 2008) have moved beyond double or triple jeopardy approaches to oppression and are consistent with the most recent assumptions about intersectionality. Additional refinement and understanding of how gendered racism operates in multiple and diverse groups of women and men through both qualitative and quantitative research methods have the potential to offer valuable new insights. Reid's (2002) proposed "complexity paradigm" includes important suggestions for furthering the intersectional study of ethgender and gendered racism, including recommendations to be attentive to heterogeneity within all communities of people.

The research and theory described in this section speaks primarily to negative outcomes related to gendered oppressions. In the future, research that explores resilience and positive coping methods in the face of oppression will become increasingly important (APA, 2007). Research on stereotype threat has identified ways in which the strategic use of specific cognitive skills or an emphasis on social identities can be used to enhance performance and confidence. Extending this approach to areas such as the prevention of and coping with ambivalent sexism and racism, body objectification, and gendered racism will provide additional intervention tools for psychologists who work in clinical, education, and community settings.

Social Identity Development

A variety of social identities contribute to women's relative social privilege or social disadvantage. Women's social identities that are most likely to contribute to privilege and power include White racial or ethnic identification, middle- or upper class status, or advanced education credentials. Disadvantage and oppression are more likely associated with minority racial or ethnic status, older age, or sexual minority identities. From an intersectional paradigm, these identities or social locations interact in unique ways, depending on their salience within multiple contexts. In this section, examples of three types of social identifications are used to illustrate identity developmental processes: feminist, womanist, lesbian, and sexual minority identities.

Feminist and womanist identity. Downing and Roush's (1985) feminist identity model, which was inspired by Cross's (1971) model of African American identity development, identifies developmental phases that begin with denial of discrimination and a passive acceptance of society's attitudes toward women. Passive acceptance of the status quo typically comes to an end when a person encounters a series of inequities, which leads to an unsettling awareness of sexism and other forms of injustice. This awareness, often accompanied by crisis or anger, unfolds into a phase of prioritizing intensive communication and connections with other feminists as well as learning more about the strengths, values, and competencies of this chosen reference group. The feminist development process culminates in the emergence of an integrated consciousness and active commitment to social change.

Women of color and global feminists have sometimes preferred the term *womanist* instead of *feminist* to reflect their commitments to the "survival and wholeness of an entire people, male and female" (Walker, 1983, p. xii). Womanist identity development (Ossana, Helms, & Leonard, 1992) emphasizes tasks that may be shared by diverse groups of women and is based on the assumption that healthy identity development may or may not be related to the endorsement of feminism or activism. Womanist identity is seen as an integrated identity that transcends sexist norms as well as politically oriented tenets of feminism (Parks, Carter, & Gushue, 1996). Boisnier's (2003) study concluded that although feminist and womanist identity models hold much in common, a womanist identity model may offer a better fit for conceptualizing Black women's experiences.

Phases of feminist identity development have been associated with attitudes and behaviors such as awareness or perceptions of sexism (e.g., Fischer et al., 2000; Moradi & Subich, 2002), egalitarianism (e.g., Fischer & Good, 1994; Yoder, Perry, & Saal, 2007), and satisfaction and psychological well-being (e.g., Saunders & Kashubeck-West, 2006; Yakushko, 2007). Initial phases of feminist identity, which trigger a heightened awareness of sexism, are also associated with symptoms of psychological distress or lower levels of mental health (Moradi & Subich, 2002; Peterson, Grippo, & Tantleff-Dunn, 2008; Saunders & Kashubeck-West, 2006) and reflect the disorienting effects of facing bias. Studies have also identified associations between feminist self-identification and collective action (Nelson et al., 2008; Zucker, 2004).

Research with diverse groups of women also supports the relevance of feminist identity for women of color (Boisnier, 2003; Flores, Carrubba, & Good, 2006; Myaskovsky & Wittig, 1997; White, Strube, & Fisher, 1998) and sexual minority women (e.g., Liss & Erchull, 2010; Szymanski, 2004). Szymanski's (2004) study of lesbian and bisexual women found significant negative relationships between heterosexism and feminist identity, suggesting that a feminist perspective facilitates sexual minority women's ability to cope with heterosexist biases.

A question raised by a variety of theorists and researchers is whether concepts of feminism or womanism that emerged out of the zeitgeist of earlier waves of activism are relevant to 21st-century identities (Liss & Erchull, 2010). For example, recent research studies (Erchull et al., 2009; Liss & Erchull, 2010; Yakushko, 2007) indicated that one of the later phases of development, labeled *synthesis*, may not be uniquely related to feminist identification or awareness of gender injustice. Synthesis, which is hypothesized to reflect the integration of new understandings about gender with positive self-perceptions and personal strengths, may also be characterized by the confident attitudes held by many younger women who take the products of recent social changes for granted, are unaware of remaining inequities, and do not identify themselves as feminist. These women "feel empowered but remain unaware of social injustice" (Liss & Erchull, 2010, p. 93). Recent findings suggest that it is important to revisit and revise feminist identity development models.

Lesbian and sexual minority identity development. Lesbian identity formation has been the focus of extensive exploration within the psychology of women and merits at least brief attention. McCarn and Fassinger's (1996) model of lesbian identity proposed that developmental processes related to personal identification and public identification as a lesbian may or may not be linked. For example, contextual factors such as discrimination in the workplace, place of worship, or family may decrease the likelihood of public identification despite an individual's clarity and fulfillment with regard to sexual identity. More recently, Fassinger and Arseneau (2007) have written about the multidimensionality of "gender transgressive" (p. 22) sexual minority development, which requires negotiating interactions of gender orientation, sexual orientation, and cultural orientation (including race, ethnicity, social class, disability, and religion). Individual differences and developmental experiences related to personal health, interpersonal relationships, education and work, and legal and political rights also contribute to complex intersectional identities.

In general, recent theory and research show that the identity development and sexual attraction patterns of sexual minority women are marked by substantial variability and fluidity (Diamond, 2005; Diamond & Savin-Williams, 2000; Fassinger & Israel, 2010). During earlier phases of development (e.g., adolescence and early adulthood), changes in identifications may be more common than stability, leading Diamond (2006, 2008) to argue that the notion that sexual identity development involves a one-time-only sequence of phases is flawed and that adopting a lesbian or bisexual label often involves revisiting and reworking identity questions. Queer theory and the increased attention given to transgender identities contribute additional questions about the degree to which categories associated with sex and gender are stable.

Growing knowledge about diversity among women and sexual minorities led Fassinger and Israel (2010) to question whether self-identification

with a specific sexual minority identity is necessarily or consistently the healthiest expression of same-sex intimacy. They recommended exploring the myriad intimate connections between diverse women of many social identities, and revisioning sexual identity formation and health. These observations are consistent with the work of Rich (1989), who conceptualized lesbian experience as a continuum, which can include various forms of "primary intensity between and among women, including the sharing of a rich inner life, the bonding against male tyranny, and the giving and receiving of practical and political support" (p. 129).

The future of identity development models. In light of growing knowledge of the complexity of social identity, models of social identity development have been modified to reflect the multidimensional nature of social identity with regard to such themes as the complexity and variability of identity (e.g., Fassinger & Arseneau, 2007) or the salience and centrality of racial identity to self-concept (e.g., Sellers, Smith, Shelton, Rowley, & Chavous, 1998). Most theories, however, continue to focus on multidimensional aspects of a single social identity (e.g., racial and ethnic or feminist identity). Additional research and theory that explore the intersections and intertwining of these social identities are needed.

As noted in this section, a social identity such as feminist self-identification often interacts with other social identities, such as lesbian, racial or ethnic, womanist, and social class identities (Hoffman, 2006; Ossana, Helms, & Leonard, 1992; Parks et al., 1996; Reynolds & Pope, 1991). Identity development is likely to be associated with the implications and challenges associated with juggling multiple identities, such as the degree to which various identities are related or easily integrated, a person's life events and transitions, the salience and visibility of identity domains, the relevance of these identities to current developmental experiences, the extent to which identities are associated with oppression or privilege, and family or cultural background (Stewart & McDermott, 2004). Qualitative research approaches, such as the phenomenological methods used to explore the complexity of multiracial identity development (Miville, Constantine, Baysden, & So-Lloyd, 2005), hold promise for examining the complex intersections of gender with other social identities.

An intersectional perspective on identity development is also likely to be facilitated by such models as optimal theory, which represents an option for integrating identity in response to a "pervasive number of 'isms'" (Myers et al., 1991, p. 54). This approach posits that marginalization contributes to dissonance and self-questioning about identity. To move forward, marginalized individuals focus their energy on "people like me" (Myers et al., 1991, p. 59), which allows for immersion in activities and people associated with devalued social identities as well as for the development of feelings of self-worth. An optimal, holistic identity and inner security emerge from the integration of new, positive views of devalued identities with other aspects of self-identity and worldview. The process is not linear but unfolds as an "expanding spiral" (Myers et al., 1991, p. 59).

As another alternative, Reynolds and Pope's (1991) multidimensional identity model describes four ways in which multiple identities may be negotiated, including identification with (a) one aspect of identity in a passive manner, (b) one aspect of identity through conscious identification, (c) multiple aspects of the self in a segmented fashion, and (d) combined aspects of the self through identity intersection. This model is consistent with the recognition that the salience of specific identities varies within individuals as well as across contexts.

Finally, theories of multiracial identity development (e.g., Rockquemore, Brunsma, & Delgado, 2009; Suyemoto & Tawa, 2009) and multicultural feminist theory (e.g., Hurtado, 2010) can be used to enhance intersectional perspectives that explore possibilities for mixed social identities, new multi-category or hybrid identities, or border identities in which multiple identities intersect. An ecological approach to multiracial identity avoids foregrounding or privileging any one social identity over another, does not envision an optimal endpoint or predictable developmental phases, and instead focuses on how individuals construct different identities in response to specific contexts (Rockquemore et al., 2009). These models hold potential for supporting productive

theory development and research regarding gender and intersections.

CONCLUSIONS AND IMPLICATIONS: TOWARD FURTHER TRANSFORMATION

During the past 40 years, psychologists committed to social justice and a "transformation framework" (Crawford & Marecek, 1989, p. 147) have sought to develop theories that contextualize "doing" gender and to conceptualize the biases and power differences that affect human development. Feminist social constructionist perspectives, which emphasize situated knowledge and the questioning of dominant versions of truth and knowledge (Riger, 2000), have provided the necessary tools for moving this transformation project forward. Social constructionism also allows for the integration of feminist empiricism or for the rigorous study of gender through the application of traditional scientific research methods and feminist standpoint perspectives, which feature efforts to centralize the knowledge of persons and groups whose experiences have been marginalized or discounted. More specifically, social constructionism supports the integration of (a) a pragmatic empiricism, or the recognition that psychological findings cannot be generalized beyond a specific social group, location, and time; (b) the in-depth exploration of human experience through the use of qualitative methods; (c) the building of bridges to other disciplines that share postmodern assumptions; and (d) critical reflection about how knowledge is created within psychology (Marecek et al., 2004). Each of these themes requires ongoing self-reflection, and the creation of modest theories that are open to modification. As knowledge about gender has evolved, intersectionality and integration efforts are becoming increasingly important. The following sections summarize the implications and challenges of intersectionality for theory, practice, and research.

Intersectionality and Research

The level of complexity associated with intersectionality is difficult to address with traditional social science methods (Shields, 2008; Warner, 2008). Cole (2009) proposed, however, that it is unwise to assume that the research challenges are insurmountable and identified three basic questions or themes that can help psychologists attend to intersectionality. First, for any group studied, researchers should seek to prioritize the diversities that are present within a category. More specifically, counseling psychologists should continue to study neglected groups within the general category of gender and explore the experiences of these group members without comparing their experiences to the normative standard of dominant group members (e.g., White women). Placing women of color and women with other diversities (e.g., older women, sexual minorities, economically disadvantaged women) at the center of inquiry is a consistent reminder of the complexity and multiplicity of identity and also helps to further transform psychology. Second, psychologists should explore the role that inequality and power differences play. Throughout the research process (e.g., conceptualization as well as interpretation), it is important to consider how the structural positions of group members who are studied are relevant to their differences from dominant groups (see also Warner, 2008). Theories that focus on gender and power offer useful frameworks for framing research about gender in a social structural framework. Third, researchers can consider ways in which members of diverse groups are similar. For example, research participants from two rather different cultures may share class-related characteristics and immigration status. How might these similarities affect members of diverse groups in similar as well as different ways? While noting similarities, highlighting "nuanced variations" (Cole, 2009, p. 172) remains crucial. Recent research on the concept of gendered racism (e.g., Cole & Zucker, 2007) represents one effort to implement these practices.

Warner (2008) noted the importance of being especially thoughtful about research decisions and choices, noting that "although researchers do not need to examine every social identity, we need to be aware of which ones we choose and why" (p. 455). Given the fact that specific social identities may "mutually constitute" (Shields, 2008, p. 302) each other, tools such as analysis of variance cannot be used to neatly parcel out the specific effects related to such variables as age, race, or gender. Factorial designs, however, can be reconceptualized so that

specific factors reflect an intersectional category (e.g., Black male, Black female), thus avoiding assumptions about "master categories" such as gender (Warner, 2008). Qualitative methods, which are becoming increasingly influential in counseling psychology, also provide significant promise for teasing out the "particular, partial, and emergent nature of meaning" (Warner, 2008, p. 461). Finally, all data need to be interpreted in light of the social structural environment.

Intersectionality and Practice

Formal diagnostic practices facilitate the diagnosis of specific symptom patterns but offer few tools for understanding the complexity of a person and her or his social identities and locations. In keeping with an intersectional perspective, psychologists are encouraged to think of traditional assessment and diagnosis as starting points that can be expanded and deepened through the use of ecologically sound inquiries about a client's multiple identities as well as his or her life contexts, barriers, and experiences with power dynamics.

To ensure that assessment practices are relevant to intersectional aspects of identity, psychologists are encouraged to incorporate tools that facilitate attentiveness to multiple social identities (for a list of alternatives, see Enns, 2010). APA's (2007) *Guidelines for Psychological Practice With Girls and Women* offer suggestions for implementing practices that attend to diversity, multiple identities, and ecological contexts in which individuals live. Hays's (2008) *Addressing Cultural Complexities in Practice: Assessment, Diagnosis, and Therapy* offers a useful framework for guiding the assessment of identities associated with age, disability, religion, ethnicity or race, social class, sexual orientation, indigenous origins, national origin, and gender. In addition, it is important to assess which identities are more salient and important to the individual, how various identities may be fused or overlap, as well as when and how these identities are associated with privilege and marginalization. An intersectional analysis facilitates an understanding of a person's complexity, pain, and distress as well as sources of strength and resilience, which can be used to help individuals transcend symptoms and build on strengths (Brown, 2009).

The feminist therapy tool of power analysis (Worell & Remer, 2003) allows for the organization and understanding of experiences associated with empowerment and loss of power. The four theories described in this review and other theories that emphasize the relevance of power to identity can be helpful to psychologists and clients as they consider why individual and social structural change are difficult and what change strategies can offer tools for resistance.

Toward Integration

Although gender can be described as a "master category" that has an impact on humans from cradle to grave, gender has many social meanings and is modified by one's opportunities and membership in various communities and cultures. This review has emphasized theories and research that can inform an integrated, intersectional perspective on gender. It is time for counseling psychologists to examine, even more completely than in the past, how findings about various identity models and dominant and subordinate statuses can be integrated and inform each other. Exploring concepts such as gendered racism and stereotype threat as they are associated with multiple identities represent examples of the types of future explorations that will further our understanding of gender. Placing findings within explanatory frameworks that are attentive to social power and cultural variations and considering life-long developmental changes in the experience of gender also remain major priorities.

Absent from this review is any substantive discussion of biological sex differences or cultural variations in gender roles. Although biology is an important component of an integrative biopsychosocial, ecological perspective, recent books such as *The Female Brain* (Brizendine, 2006) and *The Male Brain* (Brizendine, 2010) have contributed to a preoccupation with biological difference and oversimplification of gender-related behavior. This chapters has emphasized the ways in which gender is informed by social structural realities and learned behaviors. In addition, space limitations have not permitted the exploration of cross-cultural variations of gender; however, as global travel and global identities become more common in the 21st century, attentiveness to gender in cultural context will become increasingly important. Counseling psychologists have excellent training for exploring the "doing" of gender in multiple cultural contexts, including how gender is influenced by cultural values, public policy, and social institutions. Gaining more knowledge about cultural variations will also contribute to more complex and complete frameworks for understanding Western concepts of gender.

References

Alter, A. L., Aronson, J., Darley, J., Rodriguez, D., & Ruble, D. (2010). Rising to the threat: Reducing stereotype threat by reframing the threat as a challenge. *Journal of Experimental Social Psychology, 46,* 166–171. doi:10.1016/j.jesp.2009.09.014

American Psychological Association. (2003). Guidelines on multicultural education, training, research, practice, and organizational change for psychologists. *American Psychologist, 58,* 377–402. doi:10.1037/0003-066X.58.5.377

American Psychological Association. (2007). Guidelines for psychological practice with girls and women. *American Psychologist, 62,* 949–979. doi:10.1037/0003-066X.62.9.949

Askari, S. F., Liss, M., Erchull, M. J., Staebell, S. E., & Axelson, S. J. (2010). Men want equality, but women don't expect it: Young adults' expectations for participation in household and child care chores. *Psychology of Women Quarterly, 34,* 243–252. doi:10.1111/j.1471-6402.2010.01565.x

Augustus-Horvath, C. L., & Tylka, T. L. (2009). A test and extension of objectification theory as it predicts disorders eating: Does women's age matter? *Journal of Counseling Psychology, 56,* 253–265. doi:10.1037/a0014637

Ballou, M., Matsumoto, A., & Wagner, M. (2002). Toward a feminist ecological theory of human nature: Theory building in response to real-world dynamics. In M. Ballou & L. S. Brown (Eds.), *Rethinking mental health and disorder: Feminist perspectives* (pp. 99–141). New York, NY: Guilford Press.

Barreto, M., & Ellemers, N. (2005). The burden of benevolent sexism: How it contributes to the maintenance of gender inequalities. *European Journal of Social Psychology, 35,* 633–642. doi:10.1002/ejsp.270

Barreto, M., Ellemers, N., Piebinga, L., & Moya, M. (2010). How nice of us and how dumb of me: The effect of exposure to benevolent sexism on women's task and relational self-descriptions. *Sex Roles, 62,* 532–544. doi:10.1007/s11199-009-9699-0

Bassoff, E. S., & Glass, G. V. (1982). The relationship between sex roles and mental health: A meta-analysis of twenty-sex studies. *The Counseling Psychologist, 10*, 105–112. doi:10.1177/0011000082104019

Bem, S. L. (1983). Gender schema theory and its implications for child development: Raising gender-aschematic children in a gender-schematic society. *Sign, 8*, 598–616. doi:10.1086/493998

Bem, S. L. (1993). *The lenses of gender: Transforming the debate on sexual inequality.* New Haven, CT: Yale University Press.

Boisnier, A. D. (2003). Race and women's identity development: Distinguishing between feminism and womanism among Black and White women. *Sex Roles, 49*, 211–218. doi:10.1023/A:1024696022407

Bosson, J. K., Pinel, E. C., & Vandello, J. A. (2010). The emotional impact of ambivalent sexism: Forecasts versus real experiences. *Sex Roles, 62*, 520–531.

Brinkman, B. G., & Rickard, K. M. (2009). College students' descriptions of everyday gender prejudice. *Sex Roles, 61*, 461–475. doi:10.1007/s11199-009-9643-3

Brizendine, L. (2006). *The female brain.* New York, NY: Broadway Books.

Brizendine, L. (2010). *The male brain.* New York, NY: Broadway Books.

Bronfenbrenner, U., & Morris, P. A. (2006). The bioecological model of human development. In R. M. Lerner (Ed.), *Handbook of child psychology: Vol. 1. Theoretical models of human development* (6th ed., pp. 793–828). Hoboken, NJ: Wiley.

Brown, L. S. (2009). Cultural competence: A new way of thinking about integration in therapy. *Journal of Psychotherapy Integration, 19*, 340–353. doi:10.1037/a0017967

Buchanan, T. S., Fischer, A. R., Tokar, D. M., & Yoder, J. D. (2007). Testing a culture-specific extension of objectification theory regarding African American women's body image. *The Counseling Psychologist, 36*, 697–718. doi:10.1177/0011000008316322

Buss, D. M., & Kenrick, D. T. (1998). Evolutionary social psychology. In D. T. Gilbert, S. T. Fiske, & G. Lindzey (Eds.), *The handbook of social psychology* (4th ed., Vol. 2, pp. 982–1026). Boston, MA: McGraw-Hill.

Bussey, K., & Bandura, A. (2004). Social cognitive theory of gender development and functioning. In A. H. Eagly, A. E. Beall, & R. J. Sternberg (Eds.), *The psychology of gender* (2nd ed., pp. 92–119). New York, NY: Guilford Press.

Butler, J. (1990). *Gender trouble.* New York, NY: Routledge.

Campbell, B., Schellenberg, E. G., & Senn, C. Y. (1997). Evaluating measures of contemporary sexism. *Psychology of Women Quarterly, 21*, 89–101. doi:10.1111/j.1471-6402.1997.tb00102.x

Cohen, G. L., & Garcia, J. (2008). Identity, belonging and achievement: A model, interventions, implications. *Current Directions in Psychological Science, 17*, 365–369. doi:10.1111/j.1467-8721.2008.00607.x

Cole, E. R. (2009). Intersectionality and research in psychology. *American Psychologist, 64*, 170–180. doi:10.1037/a0014564

Cole, E. R., & Zucker, A. N. (2007). Black and White women's perspectives on femininity. *Cultural Diversity and Ethnic Minority Psychology, 13*, 1–9. doi:10.1037/1099-9809.13.1.1

Collins, P. H. (2000). *Black feminist thought: Knowledge, consciousness, and the politics of empowerment* (2nd ed.). New York, NY: Routledge.

Collins, P. H. (2004). *Black sexual politics: African Americans, gender, and the new racism.* New York, NY: Routledge. doi:10.4324/9780203309506

Cook, E. P. (1985). *Psychological androgyny.* New York, NY: Pergamon.

Crawford, M., & Marecek, J. (1989). Psychology reconstructs the female: 1968–1988. *Psychology of Women Quarterly, 13*, 147–165. doi:10.1111/j.1471-6402.1989.tb00993.x

Crawford, M., & Unger, R. (2004). *Women and gender: A feminist psychology* (4th ed.). Boston, MA: McGraw-Hill.

Cross, W. E., Jr. (1971). The Negro-to-Black conversion experience. *Black World, 20*(9), 13–27.

Danaher, K., & Crandall, C. S. (2008). Stereotype threat in applied settings re-examined. *Journal of Applied Social Psychology, 38*, 1639–1655. doi:10.1111/j.1559-1816.2008.00362.x

Dardenne, B., Dumont, M., & Bollier, T. (2007). Insidious dangers of benevolent sexism: Consequences for women's performance. *Journal of Personality and Social Psychology, 93*, 764–779. doi:10.1037/0022-3514.93.5.764

Deaux, K. (1984). From individual differences to social categories: Analysis of a decades' research on gender. *American Psychologist, 39*, 105–116. doi:10.1037/0003-066X.39.2.105

Deaux, K. (1985). Sex and gender. *Annual Review of Psychology, 36*, 49–81. doi:10.1146/annurev.ps.36.020185.000405

Deaux, K., & Major, B. (1987). Putting gender into context: An interactive model of gender-related behavior. *Psychological Review, 94*, 369–389. doi:10.1037/0033-295X.94.3.369

Deaux, K., & Martin, D. (2003). Interpersonal networks and social categories: Specifying levels of context in identity processes. *Social Psychology Quarterly, 66,* 101–117. doi:10.2307/1519842

Deaux, K., & Stewart, A. (2001). Framing gendered identities. In R. K. Unger (Ed.), *Handbook of the psychology of women and gender* (pp. 84–97). New York, NY: Wiley.

DeBlaere, C., & Moradi, B. (2008). Structures of the schedules of racism and sexist events: Confirmatory factor analyses of African American women's responses. *Psychology of Women Quarterly, 32,* 83–94. doi:10.1111/j.1471-6402.2007.00409.x

Diamond, L. M. (2005). A new view of lesbian subtypes: Stable versus fluid identity trajectories over an 8-year period. *Psychology of Women Quarterly, 29,* 119–128. doi:10.1111/j.1471-6402.2005.00174.x

Diamond, L. M. (2006). What we got wrong about sexual identity development: Unexpected findings from a longitudinal study of young women. In A. M. Omoto & H. S. Kurtzman (Eds.), *Sexual orientation and mental health: Examining identity and development in lesbian, gay, and bisexual people* (pp. 73–94). Washington, DC: American Psychological Association. doi:10.1037/11261-004

Diamond, L. M. (2008). Female bisexuality from adolescence to adulthood: Results from a 10-year longitudinal study. *Developmental Psychology, 44,* 5–14. doi:10.1037/0012-1649.44.1.5

Diamond, L. M., & Butterworth, M. (2008). Questioning gender and sexual identity: Dynamic links over time. *Sex Roles, 59,* 365–376. doi:10.1007/s11199-008-9425-3

Diamond, L. M., & Savin-Williams, R. C. (2000). Explaining diversity in the development of same-sex sexuality among young women. *Journal of Social Issues, 56,* 297–313. doi:10.1111/0022-4537.00167

Dovidio, J. F., Gaertner, S. L., Kawakami, K., & Hodson, G. (2002). Why can't we just get along? Interpersonal biases and interracial distrust. *Cultural Diversity and Ethnic Minority Psychology, 8,* 88–102. doi:10.1037/1099-9809.8.2.88

Downing, N. E., & Roush, K. L. (1985). From passive acceptance to active commitment: A model of feminist identity development for women. *The Counseling Psychologist, 13,* 695–709. doi:10.1177/0011000085134013

Dumont, M., Sarlet, M., & Dardenne, B. (2010). Be too kind to a woman, she'll feel incompetent: Benevolent sexism shifts self-construal and autobiographical memories toward incompetence. *Sex Roles, 62,* 545–553. doi:10.1007/s11199-008-9582-4

Eagly, A. H. (1995). The science and politics of comparing women and men. *American Psychologist, 50,* 145–158. doi:10.1037/0003-066X.50.3.145

Eagly, A. H., & Carli, L. L. (2007). *Through the labyrinth: The truth about how women become leaders.* Boston, MA: Harvard Business School Press.

Eagly, A. H., & Wood, W. (1999). The origins of sex differences inhuman behavior: Evolved dispositions versus social roles. *American Psychologist, 54,* 408–423. doi:10.1037/0003-066X.54.6.408

Enns, C. Z. (1993). Twenty years of feminist counseling and therapy: From naming biases to implementing multifaceted practice. *The Counseling Psychologist, 21,* 3–87. doi:10.1177/0011000093211001

Enns, C. Z. (2004). *Feminist theories and feminist psychotherapies: Origins, themes, and diversity* (2nd ed.). New York, NY: Haworth Press.

Enns, C. Z. (2010). Locational feminisms and feminist social identity analysis. *Professional Psychology: Research and Practice, 41,* 333–339. doi:10.1037/a0020260

Erchull, M. J., Liss, M., Wilson, K. A., Bateman, L., Peterson, A., & Sanchez, C. E. (2009). The feminist identity development model: Relevant for young women today? *Sex Roles, 60,* 832–842. doi:10.1007/s11199-009-9588-6

Fassinger, R. E., & Arseneau, J. R. (2007). "I'd rather get wet than be under that umbrella": Differentiating the experiences and identities of lesbian, gay, bisexual, and transgender people. In K. J. Bieschke, R. M. Perez, & K. A. DeBord (Eds.), *Handbook of counseling and psychotherapy with lesbian, gay, bisexual, and transgender clients* (pp. 19–49). Washington, DC: American Psychological Association. doi:10.1037/11482-001

Fassinger, R. E., & Israel, T. (2010). Sanctioning sexuality within cultural contexts: Same-sex relationships for women of color. In H. Landrine & N. F. Russo (Eds.), *Handbook of diversity in feminist psychology* (pp. 211–231). New York, NY: Springer.

Fischer, A. R. (2006). Women's benevolent sexism as reaction to hostility. *Psychology of Women Quarterly, 30,* 410–416. doi:10.1111/j.1471-6402.2006.00316.x

Fischer, A. R., & Good, G. E. (1994). Gender, self, and others: Perceptions of the campus environment. *Journal of Counseling Psychology, 41,* 343–355. doi:10.1037/0022-0167.41.3.343

Fischer, A. R., Tokar, D. M., Mergl, M. M., Good, G. E., Hill, M. S., & Blum, S. A. (2000). Assessing women's feminist identity development: Studies of convergent, discriminant, and structural validity. *Psychology of Women Quarterly, 24,* 15–29. doi:10.1111/j.1471-6402.2000.tb01018.x

Flax, J. (1987). Postmodernism and gender relations in feminist theory. *Signs, 12,* 621–643. doi:10.1086/494359

Flores, L. Y., Carrubba, M. D., & Good, G. E. (2006). Feminism and Mexican American adolescent women: Examining the psychometric properties of two measures. *Hispanic Journal of Behavioral Sciences, 28*, 48–64. doi:10.1177/0739986305283222

Fowers, A., & Fowers, B. (2010). Social dominance and sexual self-schema as moderators of sexist reactions to female subtypes. *Sex Roles, 62*, 468–480. doi:10.1007/s11199-009-9607-7

Fredrickson, B. L., & Roberts, T. A. (1997). Objectification theory: Toward understanding women's lived experiences and mental health risks. *Psychology of Women Quarterly, 21*, 173–206.

Gerber, G. L. (2009). Status and the gender stereotyped personality traits: Toward an integration. *Sex Roles, 61*, 297–316. doi:10.1007/s11199-008-9529-9

Gergen, M. (2001). *Feminist reconstructions in psychology.* Thousand Oaks, CA: Sage.

Gilbert, L. A., & Scher, M. (1999). *Gender and sex in counseling and psychotherapy.* Boston, MA: Allyn & Bacon.

Gilligan, C. (1982). *In a different voice.* Cambridge, MA: Harvard University Press.

Glick, P., Fiske, S.T., Mladinic, A., Saiz, J. L., Abrams, D., Masser, B., . . . López, W. (2000). Beyond prejudice as simple antipathy: Hostile and benevolent sexism across cultures. *Journal of Personality and Social Psychology, 79*, 763–775. doi:10.1037/0022-3514.79.5.763

Glick, P., Lameiras, M., Fiske, S. T., Eckes, T., Masser, B., Volpatto, C., . . . Wells, R. (2004). Bad but bold: Ambivalent attitudes toward predict gender inequality in 16 nations. *Journal of Personality and Social Psychology, 86*, 713–728. doi:10.1037/0022-3514.86.5.713

Glick, P., & Fiske, S. T. (1999). The ambivalence toward men inventory: Differentiating hostile and benevolent beliefs about men. *Psychology of Women Quarterly, 23*, 519–536. doi:10.1111/j.1471-6402.1999.tb00379.x

Glick, P., & Fiske, S. T. (2001). An ambivalent alliance: Hostile and benevolent sexism as complementary justifications for gender inequality. *American Psychologist, 56*, 109–118. doi:10.1037/0003-066X.56.2.109

Gneezy, U., Niederle, M., & Rustichini, A. (2003). Performance in competitive environments: Gender differences. *The Quarterly Journal of Economics, 118*, 1049–1074. doi:10.1162/00335530360698496

Hare-Mustin, R. T., & Marecek, J. (1988). The meaning of difference: Gender theory, postmodernism, and psychology. *American Psychologist, 43*, 455–464. doi:10.1037/0003-066X.43.6.455

Hays, P. A. (2008). *Addressing cultural complexities in practice: Assessment, diagnosis, and therapy* (2nd ed.). Washington, DC: American Psychological Association. doi:10.1037/11650-000

Hill, M. S., & Fischer, A. R. (2008). Examining objectification theory: Lesbian and heterosexual women's experiences with sexual- and self-objectification. *The Counseling Psychologist, 36*, 745–776. doi:10.1177/0011000007301669

Hoffman, R. M. (2006). Gender self-definition and gender self-acceptance in women: Intersections with feminist, womanist, and ethnic identities. *Journal of Counseling and Development, 84*, 358–372.

Hogue, M., DuBois, C. L. Z., & Fox-Cardamone, L. (2010). Gender differences in pay expectations: The roles of job intention and self-view. *Psychology of Women Quarterly, 34*, 215–227. doi:10.1111/j.1471-6402.2010.01563.x

Hogue, M., & Yoder, J. D. (2003). The role of status in producing depressed entitlement in women's and men's pay allocations. *Psychology of Women Quarterly, 27*, 330–337. doi:10.1111/1471-6402.00113

Hogue, M., Yoder, J. D., & Singleton, S. B. (2007). The gender wage gap: An explanation of men's elevated wage entitlement. *Sex Roles, 56*, 573–579. doi:10.1007/s11199-007-9199-z

Huguet, P., & Régner, I. (2007). Stereotype threat among schoolgirls in quasi-ordinary classroom circumstances. *Journal of Educational Psychology, 99*, 545–560. doi:10.1037/0022-0663.99.3.545

Hurtado, A. (2010). Multiple lenses: Multicultural feminist theory. In H. Landrine & N. F. Russo (Eds.), *Handbook of diversity in feminist psychology* (pp. 29–54). New York, NY: Springer.

Hyde, J. S. (2005). The gender similarities hypothesis. *American Psychologist, 60*, 581–592. doi:10.1037/0003-066X.60.6.581

Jagdose, A. (1996). *Queer theory: An introduction.* New York: New York University Press.

Johns, M., Schmader, T., & Martens, A. (2005). Knowing is half the battle: Teaching stereotype threat as a means of improving women's math performance. *Psychological Science, 16*, 175–179. doi:10.1111/j.0956-7976.2005.00799.x

Jost, J. T. (1997). An experimental replication of the depressed-entitlement effect among women. *Psychology of Women Quarterly, 21*, 387–393. doi:10.1111/j.1471-6402.1997.tb00120.x

Jost, J. T., & Banaji, M. R. (1994). The role of stereotyping in system-justification and the production of false consciousness. *British Journal of Social Psychology, 33*, 1–27. doi:10.1111/j.2044-8309.1994.tb01008.x

Jost, J. T., Banaji, M. R., & Nosek, B. A. (2004). A decade of system justification theory: Accumulated evidence of conscious and unconscious bolstering of the status quo. *Political Psychology, 25,* 881–919. doi:10.1111/j.1467-9221.2004.00402.x

Jost, J. T., & Kay, A. C. (2005). Exposure to benevolent sexism and complementary gender stereotypes: Consequences for specific and diffuse forms of system justification. *Journal of Personality and Social Psychology, 88,* 498–509. doi:10.1037/0022-3514-.88.3.498

Katz, I., & Hass, R. G. (1988). Racial ambivalence and American value conflict: Correlational and priming studies of dual cognitive structures. *Journal of Personality and Social Psychology, 55,* 893–905. doi:10.1037/0022-3514.55.6.893

Katz-Wise, S. L., Priess, H. A., & Hyde, J. S. (2010). Gender-role attitudes and behavior across the transition to parenthood. *Developmental Psychology, 46,* 18–28. doi:10.1037/a0017820

Kenny, D. A., Snook, A., Boucher, E. M., & Hancock, J. T. (2010). Interpersonal sensitivity, status, and stereotype accuracy. *Psychological Science, 21,* 1735–1739.

King, K. R. (2005). Why is discrimination stressful? The mediating role of cognitive appraisal. *Cultural Diversity and Ethnic Minority Psychology, 11,* 202–212. doi:10.1037/1099-9809.11.3.202

Klonoff, E. A., Landrine, H., & Campbell, R. (2000). Sexist discrimination may account for well-known gender differences in psychiatric symptoms. *Psychology of Women Quarterly, 24,* 93–99. doi:10.1111/j.1471-6402.2000.tb01025.x

LaFrance, M., & Henley, N. M. (1997). On oppressive hypotheses: Or differences in nonverbal sensitivity revisited. In M. R. Walsh (Ed.), *Women, men, and gender: Ongoing debates* (pp. 104–119). New Haven, CT: Yale University Press.

Lee, T. L., Fiske, S. T., & Glick, P. (2010). Next gen ambivalent sexism: Converging correlated, causality in context, and converse causality, an introduction to the special issue. *Sex Roles, 62,* 395–404. doi:10.1007/s11199-010-9747-9

Liss, M., & Erchull, M. J. (2010). Everyone feels empowered: Understanding feminist self-labeling. *Psychology of Women Quarterly, 34,* 85–96. doi:10.1111/j.1471-6402.2009.01544.x

Maccoby, E. E. (1998). *The two sexes: Growing up apart, coming together.* Cambridge, MA: Belknap Press of Harvard University Press.

Major, B. (1993). Gender, entitlement, and the distribution of family labor. *Journal of Social Issues, 49,* 141–159. doi:10.1111/j.1540-4560.1993.tb01173.x

Marecek, J., Crawford, M., & Popp, D. (2004). On the construction of gender, sex, and sexualities. In A. H. Eagly, A. E. Beall, & R. J. Sternberg (Eds.), *The psychology of gender* (2nd ed., pp. 192–216). New York, NY: Guilford Press.

Marecek, J. (1995). Gender, politics, and psychology's ways of knowing. *American Psychologist, 50,* 162–163. doi:10.1037/0003-066X.50.3.162

McCarn, S. R., & Fassinger, R. E. (1996). Revisioning sexual minority identity formation: A new model of lesbian identity and its implications for counseling and research. *The Counseling Psychologist, 24,* 508–534. doi:10.1177/0011000096243011

McConahay, J. B. (1986). Modern racism, ambivalence, and the modern racism scale. In J. F. Dovidio & S. L. Gaertner (Eds.), *Prejudice, discrimination, and racism* (pp. 91–125). New York, NY: Academic Press.

Mednick, M. T. (1989). On the politics of psychological constructs: Stop the bandwagon, I want to get off. *American Psychologist, 44,* 1118–1123. doi:10.1037/0003-066X.44.8.1118

Miller, J. B., & Stiver, I. (1997). *The healing connection: How women form relationships in therapy and in life.* Boston, MA: Beacon Press.

Miville, M. L., Constantine, M. G., Baysden, M. F., & So-Lloyd, G. (2005). Chameleoun changes: An exploration of racial identity themes of multiracial people. *Journal of Counseling Psychology, 52,* 507–516. doi:10.1037/0022-0167.52.4.507

Moradi, B., & De Blaere, C. (2010). Women's experiences of sexist discrimination: Review of research and directions for centralizing race, ethnicity, and culture. In H. Landrine & N. F. Russo (Eds.), *Handbook of diversity in feminist psychology* (pp. 173–210). New York, NY: Springer.

Moradi, B., & Huang, Y. (2008). Objectification theory and psychology of women: A decade of advances and future directions. *Psychology of Women Quarterly, 32,* 377–398. doi:10.1111/j.1471-6402.2008.00452.x

Moradi, B., & Subich, L. M. (2002). Perceived sexist events and feminist identity development attitudes: Links to women's psychological distress. *The Counseling Psychologist, 30,* 44–65. doi:10.1177/0011000002301003

Moradi, B., & Subich, L. M. (2003). A concomitant examination of the relations of perceived racist and sexist events to psychological distress for African American women. *The Counseling Psychologist, 31,* 451–469. doi:10.1177/0011000003031004007

Moradi, B., & Yoder, J. D. (2012). Women. In E. Altmaier & J. Hansen (Eds.), *Oxford handbook of counseling psychology* (pp. 346–374). New York, NY: Oxford University Press.

Moradi, G., & Funderburk, J. R. (2006). Roles of perceived sexist events and perceived social support in the mental health of women seeking counseling.

Journal of Counseling Psychology, 53, 464–473. doi:10.1037/0022-0167.53.4.464

Morawski, J. G. (1987). The troubled quest for masculinity, femininity, and androgyny. In P. Shaver & C. Hendrick (Eds.), *Sex and gender* (pp. 44–69). Newbury Park, CA: Sage.

Moss-Racusin, C. A., & Rudman, L. A. (2010). Disruptions in women's self-promotion: The backlash avoidance model. *Psychology of Women Quarterly, 34,* 186–202. doi:10.1111/j.1471-6402.2010.01561.x

Myaskovsky, L., & Wittig, M. A. (1997). Predictors of feminist social identity among college women. *Sex Roles, 37,* 861–883. doi:10.1007/BF02936344

Myers, L. J., Speight, S. L., Highlen, P. S., Cox, C. I., Reynolds, A. L., Adams, E. M., & Hanley, C. P. (1991). Identity development and worldview: Toward an optimal conceptualization. *Journal of Counseling and Development, 70,* 54–63.

Napier, J. L., & Jost, J. T. (2008). Why are conservatives happier than liberals? *Psychological Science, 19,* 565–572. doi:10.1111/j.1467-9280.2008.02124.x

Napier, J. L., Thorisdottir, H., & Jost, J. T. (2010). The joy of sexism? A multinational investigation of hostile and benevolent justifications for gender inequality and their relations to subjective well-being. *Sex Roles, 62,* 405–419. doi:10.1007/s11199-009-9712-7

Nelson, J. A., Liss, M., Erchull, M. J., Hurt, M. M., Ramsey, L. R., Turner, D. L., & Haines, M. E. (2008). Identity in action: Predictors of feminist self-identification and collective action. *Sex Roles, 58,* 721–728. doi:10.1007/s11199-007-9384-0

Nguyen, H. D., & Ryan, A. M. (2008). Does stereotype threat affect test performance of minorities and women? A meta-analysis of experimental evidence. *Journal of Applied Psychology, 93,* 1314–1334. doi:10.1037/a0012702

Ossana, S. M., Helms, J. E., & Leonard, M. M. (1992). Do "womanist" identity attitudes influence college women's self-esteem and perceptions of environmental bias? *Journal of Counseling and Development, 70,* 402–408.

Parks, E. E., Carter, R. T., & Gushue, G. V. (1996). At the crossroads: Racial and womanist identity development in Black and White women. *Journal of Counseling and Development, 74,* 624–631.

Peterson, R. D., Grippo, K. P., & Tantleff-Dunn, S. (2008). Empowerment and powerlessness: A closer look at the relationship between feminism, body image, and eating disturbance. *Sex Roles, 58,* 639–648. doi:10.1007/s11199-007-9377-z

Pratto, F., & Walker, A. (2004). The bases of gendered power. In A. H. Eagly, A. E. Beall, & R. J. Sternberg (Eds.), *The psychology of gender* (2nd ed., pp. 242–268). New York, NY: Guilford Press.

Purdie-Vaughns, V., & Eibach, R. P. (2008). Intersectional invisibility: The distinctive advantages and disadvantages of multiple subordinate-group identities. *Sex Roles, 59,* 377–391. doi:10.1007/s11199-008-9424-4

Reid, A., & Deaux, K. (1996). Relationship between social and personal identities: Segregation or integration? *Journal of Personality and Social Psychology, 71,* 1084–1091. doi:10.1037/0022-3514.71.6.1084

Reid, P. T. (2002). Multicultural psychology: Bringing together gender and ethnicity. *Cultural Diversity and Ethnic Minority Psychology, 8,* 103–114. doi:10.1037/1099-9809.8.2.103

Reynolds, A. L., & Pope, R. L. (1991). The complexities of diversity: Exploring multiple oppressions. *Journal of Counseling and Development, 70,* 174–180.

Rich, A. (1989). Compulsory heterosexuality and lesbian existence. In L. Richardson & V. Taylor (Eds.), *Feminist frontiers II* (pp. 120–141). New York, NY: McGraw-Hill.

Ridgeway, C. L., & Bourg, C. (2004). Gender as status: An expectation states theory approach. In A. H. Eagly, A. E. Beall, & R. J. Sternberg (Eds.), *The psychology of gender* (2nd ed., pp. 217–241). New York, NY: Guilford Press.

Riger, S. (2000). *Transforming psychology: Gender in theory and practice.* New York, NY: Oxford University Press.

Roberson, L., & Kulik, C. T. (2007). Stereotype threat at work. *The Academy of Management Perspectives, 21,* 24–40. doi:10.5465/AMP.2007.25356510

Rockquemore, K. A., Brunsma, D. L., & Delgado, D. J. (2009). Racing to theory or retheorizing race? Understanding the struggle to build a multiracial identity theory. *Journal of Social Issues, 65,* 13–34. doi:10.1111/j.1540-4560.2008.01585.x

Rosenthal, H. E. S., Crisp, R. J., & Suen, M. (2007). Improving performance expectancies in stereotypic domains: Task relevance and the reduction of stereotype threat. *European Journal of Social Psychology, 37,* 586–597. doi:10.1002/ejsp.379

Rosenthal, L., & Levy, S. (2010). Understanding women's risk for HIV infection using social dominance theory and the four bases of gendered power. *Psychology of Women Quarterly, 34,* 21–35. doi:10.1111/j.1471-6402.2009.01538.x

Rudman, L. A., & Glick, P. (2008). *The social psychology of gender: How power and intimacy shape gender relations.* New York, NY: Guilford Press.

Rydell, R. J., & Boucher, K. L. (2010). Capitalizing on multiple socialidentities to prevent stereotype threat:

The moderating role of self-esteem. *Personality and Social Psychology Bulletin, 36*, 239–250. doi:10.1177/0146167209355062

Rydell, R. J., McConnell, A. R., & Beilock, S. L. (2009). Multiple social identities and stereotype threat: Imbalance, accessibility, and working memory. *Journal of Personality and Social Psychology, 96*, 949–966. doi:10.1037/a0014846

Saunders, K. J., & Kashubeck-West, S. (2006). The relations among feminist identity development, gender-role orientation, and psychological well-being in women. *Psychology of Women Quarterly, 30*, 199–211. doi:10.1111/j.1471-6402.2006.00282.x

Scott, J. W. (1988). Deconstructing equality-versus-difference: Or, the uses of poststructuralist theory for feminism. *Feminist Studies, 14*, 32–50. doi:10.2307/3177997

Sell, J., Chen, Z. Y., Hunter-Holmes, P., & Johansson, A. (2002). A cross-cultural comparison of resource goods and public goods. *Social Psychology Quarterly, 65*, 285–297. doi:10.2307/3090124

Sell, J., & Kuipers, K. J. (2009). A structural social psychological view of gender differences in cooperation. *Sex Roles, 61*, 317–324. doi:10.1007/s11199-009-9597-5

Sellers, R. M., Smith, M. A., Shelton, J. N., Rowley, S. A. J., & Chavous, T. M. (1998). The multidimensional model of racial identity: A reconceptualization of African American racial identity. *Personality and Social Psychology Review, 2*, 18–39. doi:10.1207/s15327957pspr0201_2

Shields, S. A. (2008). Gender: An intersectionality perspective. *Sex Roles, 59*, 301–311. doi:10.1007/s11199-008-9501-8

Shih, M., Pittinsky, T. L., & Ambady, N. (1999). Stereotype susceptibility: Identity salience and shifts in quantitative performance. *Psychological Science, 10*, 80–83. doi:10.1111/1467-9280.00111

Sibley, C. G., Overall, N. C., & Duckitt, J. (2007). When women become more hostilely sexist toward their gender: The system-justifying effect of benevolent sexism. *Sex Roles, 57*, 743–754. doi:10.1007/s11199-007-9306-1

Sidanius, J., & Pratto, F. (1999). *Social dominance: An intergroup theory of social hierarchy and oppression.* New York, NY: Cambridge University Press.

Steele, C. M. (1997). A threat in the air: How stereotypes shape intellectual identity and performance. *American Psychologist, 52*, 613–629. doi:10.1037/0003-066X.52.6.613

Stewart, A. J., & McDermott, C. (2004). Gender in psychology. *Annual Review of Psychology, 55*, 519–544. doi:10.1146/annurev.psych.55.090902.141537

Suyemoto, K. L., & Tawa, J. (2009). Multiracial Asian Americans. In N. Tewari & A. N. Alvarez (Eds.), *Asian American psychology: Current perspectives* (pp. 381–398). New York, NY: Psychology Press.

Swim, J. K., Aikin, K. J., Hall, W. S., & Hunter, B. A. (1995). Sexism and racism: Old fashioned and modern prejudices. *Journal of Personality and Social Psychology, 68*, 199–214. doi:10.1037/0022-3514.68.2.199

Swim, J. K., Becker, J. C., Lee, E., & Pruitt, E. (2010). Sexism reloaded: Worldwide evidence for its endorsement, expression, and emergence in multiple contexts. In H. Landrine & N. F. Russo (Eds.), *Handbook of diversity in feminist psychology* (pp. 137–171). New York, NY: Springer.

Swim, J. K., Hyers, L. L., Cohen, L. L., & Ferguson, M. J. (2001). Everyday sexism: Evidence for its incidence, nature, and psychological impact from three daily diary studies. *Journal of Social Issues, 57*, 31–53. doi:10.1111/0022-4537.00200

Swim, J. K., Mallett, R., Russo-Devosa, Y., & Stangor, C. (2005). Judgments of sexism: A comparison of the subtlety of sexism measures and sources of variability in judgments of sexism. *Psychology of Women Quarterly, 29*, 406–411.

Swim, J. K., Mallett, R., & Stangor, C. (2004). Understanding subtle sexism: Detection and use of sexist language. *Sex Roles, 51*, 117–128.

Szymanski, D. M. (2004). Relations among dimensions of feminism and internalized heterosexism in lesbians and bisexual women. *Sex Roles, 51*, 145–159. doi:10.1023/B:SERS.0000037759.33014.55

Szymanski, D. M. (2005). Heterosexism and sexism as correlates of psychological distress in lesbians. *Journal of Counseling and Development, 83*, 355–360.

Szymanski, D. M., & Gupta, A. (2009a). Examining the relationship between multiple internalized oppressions and African American lesbian, gay, bisexual, and questioning persons' self-esteem and psychological distress. *Journal of Counseling Psychology, 56*, 110–118. doi:10.1037/a0013317

Szymanski, D. M., & Gupta, A. (2009b). Examining the relationships between multiple oppressions and Asian American sexual minority persons' psychological distress. *Journal of Gay and Lesbian Social Services: Issues in Practice, Policy and Research, 21*, 267–281. doi:10.1080/10538720902772212

Szymanski, D. M., & Stewart, D. N. (2010). Racism and sexism as correlates of African American women's psychological distress. *Sex Roles, 63*, 226–238. doi:10.1007/s11199-010-9788-0

Tavris, C. (1993). The mismeasure of woman. *Feminism and Psychology, 3*, 149–168. doi:10.1177/0959353593032002

Thomas, A. J., Witherspoon, K. M., & Speight, S. L. (2008). Gendered racism, psychological distress, and coping styles of African American women. *Cultural Diversity and Ethnic Minority Psychology, 14*, 307–314. doi:10.1037/1099-9809.14.4.307

Tougas, F., Brown, R., Beaton, A. M., & Joly, S. (1995). Neosexism: Plus ca change, plus c'est pareil. *Personality and Social Psychology Bulletin, 21*, 842–849. doi:10.1177/0146167295218007

Unger, R. K. (1979). Toward a redefinition of sex and gender. *American Psychologist, 34*, 1085–1094. doi:10.1037/0003-066X.34.11.1085

Unger, R. K., & Crawford, M. E. (1992). *Women and gender: A feminist psychology*. New York, NY: McGraw-Hill.

Vescio, T. K., Gervais, S. J., Snyder, M., & Hoover, A. (2005). Power and the creation of patronizing environments: The stereotype-based behaviors of the powerful and their effects on female performance in masculine domains. *Journal of Personality and Social Psychology, 88*, 658–672. doi:10.1037/0022-3514.88.4.658

Walker, A. (1983). *In search of our mothers' gardens: Womanist prose*. New York, NY: Harcourt, Brace, Jovanovich.

Warner, L. R. (2008). A best practices guide to intersectional approaches to psychological research. *Sex Roles, 59*, 454–463. doi:10.1007/s11199-008-9504-5

Webster, M., & Rashotte, L. S. (2009). Fixed roles and situated actions. *Sex Roles, 61*, 325–327. doi:10.1007/s11199-009-9606-8

Weisstein, N. (1968). *Kinder, kirche, kuche as scientific law: Psychology constructs the female*. Boston, MA: New England Free Press.

West, C., & Zimmerman, D. G. (1987). Doing gender. *Gender and Society, 1*, 125–151. doi:10.1177/0891243287001002002

White, A. M., Strube, M. J., & Fisher, S. (1998). A black feminist model of rape myth acceptance. *Psychology of Women Quarterly, 22*, 157–175. doi:10.1111/j.1471-6402.1998.tb00148.x

Wingfield, A. H. (2007). The modern Mammy and the angry Black man: African American professionals' experiences with gendered racism in the workplace. *Race, Gender and Class, 14*, 196–212.

Wood, W., & Eagly, A. H. (2002). A cross-cultural analysis of the behavior of women and men: Implications for the origins of sex differences. *Psychological Bulletin, 128*, 699–727. doi:10.1037/0033-2909.128.5.699

Worell, J., & Remer, P. (2003). *Feminist perspectives in therapy: Empowering diverse women* (2nd ed.). New York, NY: Wiley.

Yakushko, O. (2007). Do feminist women feel better about their lives? Examining patterns of feminist identity development and women's subjective well-being. *Sex Roles, 57*, 223–234. doi:10.1007/s11199-007-9249-6

Yoder, J. D., & Berendsen, L. L. (2001). "Outsider within" the firehouse: African American and White women firefighters. *Psychology of Women Quarterly, 25*, 27–36. doi:10.1111/1471-6402.00004

Yoder, J. D., & Kahn, A. S. (2003). Making gender comparisons more meaningful: A call for more attention to social context. *Psychology of Women Quarterly, 27*, 281–290. doi:10.1111/1471-6402.00108

Yoder, J. D., Perry, R. L., & Saal, E. I. (2007). What good is a feminist identity? Women's feminist identification and role expectations for intimate and sexual relationships. *Sex Roles, 57*, 365–372. doi:10.1007/s11199-007-9269-2

Zinn, M. B., & Dill, B. T. (1996). Theorizing difference from multiracial feminism. *Feminist Studies, 22*, 321–331. doi:10.2307/3178416

Zucker, A. N. (2004). Disavowing social identities: What it means when women say, "I'm not a feminist, but . . . ." *Psychology of Women Quarterly, 28*, 423–435. doi:10.1111/j.1471-6402.2004.00159.x

CHAPTER 16

SEXUAL ORIENTATION AND SEXUAL IDENTITY: THEORY, RESEARCH, AND PRACTICE

Y. Barry Chung, Dawn M. Szymanski, and Elizabeth Markle

Over the past 3 decades, a significant body of literature has emerged in counseling psychology that deals with sexual orientation and sexual identity issues. From being marginalized to mainstreamed, scholarship on lesbian, gay, bisexual, and transgender (LGBT) issues has become increasingly accepted and valued. This body of work is now taught in counseling psychology training programs, researched by scholars of various sexual orientations and cultural backgrounds, incorporated in counseling practice, and used for social advocacy by psychologists. We identified two books that provide comprehensive coverage of counseling and psychotherapy issues with LGBT clients (Bieschke, Perez, & DeBord, 2007; Ritter & Terndrup, 2002). For a more concise review, Croteau, Bieschke, Fassinger, and Manning (2008) wrote a book chapter with an excellent synthesis of this literature. They specifically selected the following topics as their focus of analysis: history and current status of LGBT affirmative perspectives, sexual and gender identity theories, vocational development, education and training, and counseling practice.

Our chapter builds upon Croteau et al.'s (2008) work by focusing on the following aspects: (a) social and political context of LGBT issues, (b) nature of sexual orientation and recent advances on the understanding of conversion therapy, (c) special issues such as LGB parenting and LGB youth, (d) diversity and cultural issues, and (e) implications for counseling psychology. The rationales for such emphases are discussed in relevant sections of this chapter. Limited by space, we discuss other key topics briefly (e.g., sexual identity development; discrimination and oppression; well-being, mental health, and coping; vocational development) because they are well covered in Croteau et al.'s review and in Volume 2, Chapter 15, this handbook.

Our chapter's focus is sexual orientation and sexual identity, but we include transgender issues whenever appropriate or relevant. Although transgenderism has to do with gender identity and expression, we include transgender issues as much as we can because of the overlapping history and similarities in experience between LGB and transgender persons, unless the original work we reviewed did not include transgender persons in its sample.

SOCIAL AND POLITICAL CONTEXT

We approach LGBT issues from a social justice perspective, and consider the social and political context as core to the understanding of LGBT issues. Research shows that homosexuality per se does not cause mental health dysfunction or behavioral disorders (American Psychological Association [APA], 1998, 2009; Division 44/Committee on Lesbian, Gay, and Bisexual Concerns Joint Task Force, 2000). Rather, it is societal disapproval and deprivation of fundamental human rights that cause concerns to LGBT persons (Meyer, 2003; Volume 2, Chapter 15, this handbook). This perspective is parallel to the approach that considers *barriers in the environment* as contributors to a person's disability

DOI: 10.1037/13754-016
APA Handbook of Counseling Psychology: Vol. 1. Theories, Research, and Methods, Nadya A. Fouad (Editor-in-Chief)

status rather than *deficits in the person* (Fabian & Liesener, 2005). Therefore, LGBT issues cannot be adequately addressed without the examination of the social and political context. In this section, we first discuss social and political issues in the general public, followed by attitudes and positions of mental health professionals.

Public Attitudes and Policies

According to Gallup polls in the late 1970s, 56% of Americans favored equal rights in job opportunities for LGB people, versus 85% in 2001 (Patterson, 2007). In the 1980s, only 34% of Americans thought that homosexuality was an acceptable alternative lifestyle, compared with 54% in 2003 (Patterson, 2007). Sodomy laws were in effect in many states as a convenient means to imprison LGB persons. These laws were finally overturned in 2003 by the U.S. Supreme Court (Stevenson, 2007). It seems that America has become increasingly more liberal on sexual orientation issues over the past few decades, although the public is still more conservative when it comes to marriage and parenting rights. With regard to marriage rights for same-sex couples, the following countries have legalized same-sex marriage since 2001: Netherlands, 2001; Belgium, 2003; Spain, 2005; Canada, 2005; South Africa, 2006; Israel, 2006; Norway, 2008; Sweden, 2009; Buenos Aires, 2009; Portugal, 2010; Iceland, 2010; and Argentina, 2010. Unfortunately, the United States lags behind this movement. There is currently no U.S. federal recognition of same-sex relationships. Only nine members of the federal union have legalized same-sex marriage, including Massachusetts, 2004; Connecticut, 2008; Iowa, 2009; Vermont, 2009; New Hampshire, 2010; the District of Columbia, 2010; New York, 2011; Washington, 2012; and Maryland, 2012. Four states provide spousal-equivalent benefits to same-sex couples (California, Nevada, New Jersey, and Oregon), whereas four other states provide partial rights (Colorado, Hawaii, Maine, and Wisconsin). In June 2008, California was allowed to grant same-sex marriage licenses, but the state endured a major setback with the passing of Proposition 8

in November 2008 to amend the state's constitution to limit marriage to between a man and a woman. In February 2012, the 9th Circuit Court at Appeals panel ruled that Proposition 8 is unconstitutional.

Most states allow adoption by a single LGB person, except Florida. In September 2010, the Florida intermediate appellate court ruled to overturn the adoption ban. The finalizing of this ruling awaits further legal hearing procedures. Regarding the right of same-sex couples to jointly adopt children, five states prohibit such actions (Arkansas, Florida, Michigan, Mississippi, and Utah). Four states (Arkansas, Florida, Nebraska, and Utah) prohibit *second-parent adoption* (i.e., for a same-sex coparent to adopt his or her partner's child).

The small number of victories on the international and domestic scenes cannot overshadow the fact that a majority of LGBT people in the world and the United States are denied their fundamental human rights. In fact, the recent LGBT movement has sparked severe measures by fundamentalists in attempts to change state and federal constitutions to defend what they believe is the true meaning of marriage—between a man and a woman (Levitt et al., 2009). Existing research shows that same-sex and heterosexual couples have the same dimensions of psychosocial relationships and parenting abilities and that marriage recognition contributes to positive psychological, relational, social, health, and financial benefits (Herek, 2006). For example, Balsam, Beauchaine, Rothblum, and Solomon (2008) found that same-sex couples in civil unions or heterosexual married couples were more likely to stay together during the 3-year duration of their study than same-sex couples not in civil unions. Furthermore, empirical data suggest that living in states without legal protection for sexual minorities is related to more psychosocial distress (i.e., more stress, depressive symptoms, internalized heterosexism, and less meaning in one's life; Riggle, Rostosky, & Horne, 2010) and increased risks for psychiatric disorders among LGB persons (e.g., anxiety disorders, posttraumatic stress disorder, dysthymia; Hatzenbuehler, Keyes, & Hasin, 2009).

Mental Health Professionals

Within mental health professions, positions on LGBT issues have come a long way. In 1952, homosexuality was officially classified as a mental illness in the first edition of the *Diagnostic and Statistical Manual of Mental Disorders* (*DSM*). This classification was removed in 1973 from the second edition (*DSM–II*), and the APA endorsed the same position in 1975 (Ritter & Terndrup, 2002). See Morgan and Nerison (1993), for a historical review of this movement.

APA has adopted a number of policy statements on LGBT concerns, such as opposing discrimination against homosexuals (Conger, 1975); sexual orientation, parents, and children (Paige, 2005); hate crimes (Paige, 2005); sexual orientation and military service (Paige, 2005); sexual orientation and marriage (Paige, 2005); opposing discriminatory legislation and initiatives aimed at LGB persons (Anton, 2008); transgender, gender identity, and gender expression nondiscrimination (Anton, 2009); and appropriate affirmative responses to sexual orientation distress and change efforts (Anton, 2010). These statements can all be found on APA's website (http://www.apa.org/pi/lgbt/resources/policy/index.aspx). APA continues to advocate for public policy and judicial decision making related to the rights of LGBT persons by providing evidence from psychological science (Bersoff & Ogden, 1991).

Despite these policy changes and data suggesting that the number of psychologists having an LGB affirmative view and approach toward counseling with LGB clients has increased over the past 2 decades (Kilgore, Sideman, Amin, Baca, & Bohanske, 2005), heterosexist bias continues to be present and has been shown to negatively influence counseling practice with LGB clients. Mental health professionals' nonaffirmative attitudes toward LGB persons and therapy with LGB clients are associated with being male, being older, frequency of church attendance, being a member of the Republican political party, not having a gay or lesbian friend or personal acquaintance, not having participated in training about LGB issues in the past year, and not having worked with a gay or lesbian client (Kilgore et al., 2005; Liddle, 1996; Satcher & Leggett, 2007; Satcher & Schumacker, 2009). In addition, negative views of homosexuality are related to low willingness to work with LGB clients, more negative perceptions of LGB clients, inaccurate information processing, cognitive errors, and verbal avoidance behaviors that discouraged or inhibited LGB clients from expressing or exploring sexual orientation themes during counseling sessions (Gelso, Fassinger, Gomez, & Latts, 1995; Hayes & Erkis, 2000; Hayes & Gelso, 1993).

Liddle (1996) found that the following therapist practices were important predictors of helpfulness ratings by LGB clients and termination after first session: assuming client is heterosexual, negative beliefs about LGB identities, pressuring client to renounce sexual orientation, appropriate or inappropriate problem attribution to sexual orientation, therapist initiating termination after client disclosure, lack of LGB knowledge, not valuing same-sex relationships, lack of understanding of societal prejudice or internalized heterosexism, knowledge about LGB community and resources, openness to dealing with sexual orientation issues, and promotion of client self-acceptance. Similarly, Dorland and Fischer's (2001) analogue study found that LGB participants exposed to a counseling vignette that was free from heterosexist language bias were more likely to express a higher likelihood of returning to see the counselor, to perceive the counselor as more credible, to indicate greater willingness to disclose personal information in counseling, and to express greater comfort in disclosing their sexual orientation to the counselor than participants exposed to a similar counseling vignette that contained heterosexist language.

Given the infancy of this area of research, there are many avenues in which to develop theory-driven programmatic research. For example, given the lack of attention to transgender persons and to subgroups of sexual minority persons (e.g., lesbians, bisexual men, bisexual women), future research may explore attitudes toward these subgroups, and such attitudes' relation to various outcome variables. In addition to attitudes, more research is needed to examine the impact of therapists' heterosexist bias and behaviors on LGB clients. For example, drawing from recent research on therapists' microaggressions toward female clients (Owen, Tao, & Rodolfa, 2010), future efforts might examine LGB clients' perceptions of heterosexist bias in therapy and how these perceptions may negatively affect working alliance and clinical outcomes. In addition, future research might assess therapist perceptions of their cultural competency with sexual minority clients, and how these perceptions may relate to psychotherapy outcomes. Research using both retrospective and prospective longitudinal designs would add to the mostly analogue design studies used thus far.

SEXUAL ORIENTATION AND SEXUAL IDENTITY

We define *sexual orientation* as a person's affective or emotional and physical or sexual attractions toward males and females. These attractions can be described using multidimensional continua, namely a 2 × 2 model, including affective or emotional attractions and physical or sexual attractions as well as attractions toward males and females (see Chung & Kataymaya, 1996; Chung, Szymanski, & Amadio, 2006). From this multidimensional perspective, it will be overly simplistic to describe a person's sexual orientation using categories such as heterosexual, homosexual (gay or lesbian), or bisexual. We acknowledge that the definition of sexual orientation and its assessment are complicated issues in LGB literature without any consensus (Chung & Kataymaya, 1996; Klein, Sepekoff, & Wolf, 1985; Sell, 1997; Shively, Jones, & De Cecco, 1983–1984). For example, conceptualization of sexual orientation may involve dimensions of domains (social behavior, sexual behavior, affective preference, and physical or sexual preference) and time (past, present, and ideal). Discussion of these complications is beyond the scope of this chapter. Readers are referred to the aforementioned citations for more in-depth analyses.

We define *sexual identity* as how a person identifies him- or herself in reference to his or her sexual orientation (e.g., heterosexual, homosexual, lesbian, gay, bisexual, queer, questioning, asexual). Sexual identity tends to be a simplified representation of oneself and is derived from one's sexual orientation and its interaction with one's experience in the social context. Like all other identities, sexual identity is socially constructed. The fluidity of sexual

identity is the core of most sexual identity development models. Although most people have some degree of bisexuality in terms of sexual orientation, those who self-identify as bisexual may differ from lesbian or gay-identified persons in some significant ways. Herek, Norton, Allen, and Sims's (2010) study of a national probability sample found that the majority of coupled bisexuals were in a heterosexual relationship, whereas lesbian and gay persons reported stronger commitment to a sexual minority identity, greater community identification and involvement, and greater disclosure of their sexual orientation to others. Worthington and Reynolds's (2009) study suggested distinct subgroups of bisexual men, bisexual women, gay men, and heterosexual women. The aforementioned findings signify the importance of sexual identity as well as between-group and within-group differences among persons of various sexual identities.

Nature of Sexual Orientation

What determines a person's sexual orientation? Can sexual orientation be changed? Biological and social scientists have been studying these questions for many years (e.g., Bailey, Bobrow, Wolfe, & Mikach, 1995; Bailey et al., 1999; Bem, 2000; Camperio-Ciani, Corna, & Capiluppi, 2004; Ellis & Ames, 1987; Golombok & Tasker, 1996; Kirk, Bailey, Dunne, & Martin, 2000), yet no one can give definite answers (Bailey & Dawood, 1998). According to Ritter and Terndrup (2002), the two most supported theories of sexual orientation formation are (a) prenatal hormone development and genetic inheritance and (b) family and psychosocial factors (e.g., family composition, family dynamics, early sexual experience, gender nonconformity). The current dominant theory, called *interaction* theory, proposes that sexual orientation results from both biological and psychosocial input variables (Blackwell, 2008).

The search for determinants of sexual orientation is not solely a matter of scientific interest, but it serves the purposes of different political agendas. Evidence of biological causes may be used by antigay activists to justify calling homosexuality a sickness, but paradoxically this same evidence may be used by gay activists to justify that sexual orientation is not a choice. In either case, a major interest in uncovering determinants of sexual orientation is to support whether sexual orientation can be changed, and how it should be changed. In the following section, we discuss recent developments in examining the evidence regarding conversion therapy.

Conversion Therapy

Conversion or *reparative* therapy refers to interventions aimed at changing clients' sexual orientation or behavior from homosexual to heterosexual. Such therapy may use methods such as electric shock to the hands or genitals, nausea-inducing drugs, masturbatory reconditioning, visualization and social skills training, prayer, and group support or pressure (Haldeman, 2002). Some psychologists argue for the merit of conversion therapy (e.g., Throckmorton & Welton, 2005). Faerden, Smith, and King's (2009) survey of 1,328 mental health professionals in the United Kingdom suggested that 17% of these respondents had assisted at least one client in trying to change the client's same-sex orientation.

Although reparative therapists reported success rates ranging from 11% to 37%, there is no conclusive evidence to support that conversion therapy is beneficial to clients (Hein & Matthews, 2010). Critiques of conversion therapy research include sampling bias, response bias, and lack of follow-up studies (Haldeman, 2002). Existing follow-up studies only targeted control of same-sex behavior, rather than same-sex attraction, calling into question whether conversion therapy actually changed clients' sexual orientation (Hein & Matthews, 2010). Bieschke, Paul, and Blasko's (2007) review of empirical literature suggested that religious beliefs tend to be a motive for seeking conversion therapy, with highly motivated clients more likely to report changes in sexual behavior (vs. sexual orientation) after conversion therapy. In addition, Tozer and Hayes (2004) found that internalized heterosexism fully mediated the relationship between religiosity and propensity to seek conversion therapy. That is, individuals who saw religion as a central organizing principle in their lives were more likely to internalize negative attitudes toward homosexuality, which in turn led to an increased propensity to seek

conversion therapy. R. J. Cramer, Golom, LoPresto, and Kirkley (2008) reviewed existing conversion therapy literature using established empirical and ethical criteria for therapeutic interventions. They concluded that this literature fails to support conversion therapy, and questioned the ethical rationale for such clinical practice.

In addition to a lack of scientific evidence for the efficacy of conversation therapy, existing data also show that clients ultimately consider conversion therapy harmful (Bieschke, Paul, & Blasko, 2007). Blackwell's (2008) review suggested that reparative therapy may cause psychological, social, and interpersonal harm to LGB persons. Haldeman's (1991, 1994, 1999, 2002) publications demonstrated that conversion therapy not only does not achieve its purpose but instead results in long-term sexual dysfunction (e.g., decreased sexual arousal), chronic depression, lower self-esteem, difficulty sustaining relationships, loss of family ties and religiosity, and elevated anxiety. Similarly, Beckstead and Morrow (2004) suggested that conversion therapy results in self-hatred, denial, emotional turmoil, depression, suicidality, and anger at parents.

In response to ongoing conversion therapy practices, the APA appointed a task force to review available research on conversion therapy and to provide recommendations to the association. The task force critically reviewed more than 80 studies in this area and came to similar conclusions as the reviews described thus far. The task force produced a comprehensive report, and the APA Council of Representatives adopted a Resolution on Appropriate Therapeutic Responses to Sexual Orientation Distress and Change Efforts in 2009. This resolution, which is based on an accumulated body of research on this topic, is a much stronger statement than the one adopted in 1997. Given the lack of evidence concerning the efficacy of conversion therapy and the potential harm to clients undergoing such therapy, the statement clearly states that psychologists should not tell clients that they can change their sexual orientation through therapy or other means. In addition, it encourages the public to avoid sexual orientation treatments that portray homosexuality as a developmental disorder or mental illness and to seek treatments and services that (a) provide accurate information about homosexuality; (b) increase social support; and (c) reduce rejection, bias, and discrimination of sexual minority persons.

Sexual Identity Development

Sexual identity development refers to the process and experience of how a person becomes aware of his or her sexual orientation, makes connections with others of similar sexual orientations, deals with self-acceptance, discloses one's sexual orientation to others and deals with disclosure consequences, embraces a sexual identity, and integrates one's sexual identity with other aspects of life. Theoretically, sexual identity development applies to people of all sexual orientations, including heterosexual persons. The scholarly work on sexual identity development is reviewed below in two sections: coming out experience and theories of sexual identity formation.

Experience of coming out. *Coming out* refers to stepping out of the closet—going from keeping one's sexual orientation hidden to disclosing that information to others. Scholars on LGB issues often think of coming out as a dual process—coming out to oneself (self-awareness and acceptance) and coming out to others (intentional disclosure to others about one's sexual orientation). These two processes operate in an interactive manner. Increased self-acceptance prepares oneself for disclosure to others; experience with disclosure to others influences one's self-acceptance. As more is revealed about coming out, psychologists realize the complexity of this process.

D'Augelli's (2006) research showed that LGB youths reported awareness of same-sex feelings at about age 10, whereas self-labeling as LGB occurred about 5 years later. On average, it took 5 years for boys to progress from initial awareness to their first same-sex sexual experience, whereas for girls it took 4 years. First disclosure of sexual identity occurred at about age 17, with wide variations. Existing data also show that the younger generations are coming out at earlier ages than their older cohorts (Grov, Bimbi, Nanín, & Parsons, 2006). Ethnic differences in patterns of coming out have also been reported, with ethnic minority adolescents and adults being less likely to disclose their sexual orientation to

others than their White counterparts (Grov et al., 2006; Moradi et al., 2010; Rosario, Schrimshaw, & Hunter, 2004). In addition, Rosario et al. (2004) found that Black youths reported less involvement in gay-related social activities and more negative attitudes toward their sexual identity than White youths. Over time, however, Black youths became more comfortable with their sexual identity, having greater increases in positive attitudes toward their sexual identity than White youths. In another study, Parks, Hughes, and Matthews (2004) found that lesbians of color, compared with White lesbians, were younger at first awareness of their same-sex orientation and took more time to come out to themselves, but they disclosed their sexual identity more quickly. Taken together, these research findings suggest that cultural factors may delay rather than impede on LGB youths' coming out process (Rosario et al., 2004).

In reviewing the aforementioned research findings, it is important to attend to possible cultural differences in the concept of forming an LGB identity. Because formation of an LGB identity is socially constructed, certain cultural groups may not endorse such ideology of LGB identity construction. Walters and Old Person (2008) suggested that self-labeling as LGBT may not be embraced by LGBT people of color and that nonverbal disclosure may be more salient than verbal disclosure among these people. Other scholars cautioned against pushing LGB people of color to achieve complete disclosure of their sexual orientation to all people, incorrectly assuming that it is the only way to achieve integrated and healthy sexual identities. It is possible that LGB people of color choose different levels of disclosure to different groups (e.g., family, friends, and coworkers), yet they are able to achieve harmony with themselves and with various communities.

Savin-Williams (1998) suggested that coming out to parents often is the most difficult process for LGB youths. He found that parents may react by verbal or physical assaults, with more girls than boys being physically assaulted. In an older study, D. W. Cramer and Roach (1988) found that most parents initially react negatively to their gay sons' disclosure but become more positive over time. The gay sons also had closer relationships with their mothers, both before and after coming out. Similarly, newer data suggest that LGB adolescents seem to be more likely to disclose to mothers than fathers, and mothers seem to respond more positively than fathers (D'Augelli, 2006; Savin-Williams, 1998).

With the advancement of recent media and computer technology, one would expect that technology will dramatically change the coming out experience of LGB youths and young adults. Using retrospective surveys of LGB college students regarding their coming experience, Bond, Hefner, and Drogos (2009) found that the Internet played a major role in the development of these students' LGB identities. Although the use of Internet was not related to loneliness or self-esteem, frequent users of the Internet while coming out were less likely to openly communicate with their families at the time of the survey. The authors explained that these frequent Internet users may be reluctant to be open with their family members regarding their sexuality and preferred the safety and support from their online relationships with other LGB persons. Last, a growing body of research has examined the use of identity labels (such as *lesbian* or *bisexual*) and found that some individuals are choosing to eschew them altogether, finding these labels unnecessary, potentially stigmatizing, and restricting of a broader understanding of identity (Diamond, 2003; Savin-Williams, 2005).

Sexual identity formation theories. Theoretical frameworks have been proposed in the past three decades to delineate the process of sexual identity formation (e.g., Cass, 1979, 1984; Coleman, 1981–1982; McCarn & Fassinger, 1996; Mohr & Fassinger, 2000; Rosario, Hunter, Maguen, Gwadz, & Smith, 2001; Troiden, 1979, 1989). Early theoretical models of homosexual identity formation (e.g., Cass, 1979, 1984; Coleman, 1982–1982; Troiden, 1979, 1989) share major commonalities that are summarized by Chung and Singh (2009) as a linear progression in a two-dimensional model: (a) initial assumption of a heterosexual orientation because of socialization (positive attitudes toward heterosexuality and negative attitudes toward homosexuality); (b) awareness of same-sex attraction, confusion, and exploration (negative attitudes

toward both heterosexuality and homosexuality); (c) identify affirmation and pride (positive attitudes toward homosexuality and negative attitudes toward heterosexuality); and (d) integrated identity (positive attitudes toward both heterosexuality and homosexuality).

Diamond (2006) questioned the validity of early models of sexual identity development, citing problems of using retrospective data and using primarily gay male samples that are exclusively attracted to the same sex. From the outcome of a longitudinal study of 89 women over 8 years, Diamond suggested the following mistaken assumptions in early sexual identity development models: (a) that sexual minorities are exclusively attracted to the same sex, (b) that sexual identity development follows a linear progression, and (c) that adoption of an LGB label is the healthy outcome for all.

Liddle (2007) discussed the process of lesbian identity development from a more contemporary perspective, focusing on the relevance of community and cultural factors. Fassinger and Arseneau (2007) also discussed the social construction process of sexual orientation as an identity. Their identity enactment model of gender-transgressive sexual minorities includes gender orientation, sexual orientation, and cultural orientation, together intersecting with individual differences in a developmental trajectory in four arenas: (a) personal arena of health, (b) interpersonal arena of relationships and families, (c) social arena of education and work, and (d) sociopolitical arena of legal and political rights.

Weinberg, Williams, and Pryor (1994) proposed the first bisexual identity development model, followed by Collins (2000), Brown (2002), and Bradford (2004). See Potozniak (2007) for a comparison and synthesis of these models. Potozniak (2007) suggested multiple types of bisexual identities that are "multifaceted, multidimensional, dynamic, and individualized" (p. 129).

Although transgender identity technically does not fall under sexual identity development, we do want to mention Lev's (2007) model that describes six developmental stages that transgender people may experience while going through the sex-reassignment decision-making process: (a) awareness of desire to change, (b) seeking information and reaching out, (c) disclosure to significant others, (d) exploration—identity and self-labeling, (e) exploration—transition issues and possible body modification, and (f) integration—acceptance and dealing with posttransition issues.

To summarize, models of sexual identity development have come a long way, from linear stagewise progression models primarily based on gay male experiences, to lesbian identity development theories that acknowledge the significance of social and relational aspects, to bisexual identity development for men and women, and finally to fluid multidimensional models that incorporate the complexities of individuality and social–cultural factors. More empirical work is needed to examine these evolving theoretical models and their practical implications for counseling psychology.

DISCRIMINATION AND OPPRESSION

According to Herek, Gillis, and Cogan (2009), *sexual stigma* refers to "negative regard, inferior status, and relative powerlessness that society collectively accords anyone associated with non-heterosexual behaviors, identity, relationships, or communities" (p. 33). Furthermore, sexual stigma can manifest on institutional or cultural levels as well as on the individual level. Sexual stigma at the individual level includes (a) enacted sexual stigma (overt negative actions against sexual minorities, such as hate crimes and heterosexist prejudice, rejection, and discrimination), (b) felt sexual stigma (expectations about circumstances in which sexual stigma will be enacted), and (c) internalized sexual stigma (personal acceptance of sexual stigma as part of one's value system and self-concept).

Among heterosexual persons, felt stigma often manifests in behaviors that support one's heterosexual identity such as public disclosures of one's sexual orientation and avoiding gender nonconformity and same-sex physical contact, whereas internalized stigma presents in negative attitudes toward homosexuality and LGB persons. Among sexual minority persons, felt stigma typically manifests in hiding one's LGB identity, whereas internalized stigma (also known as internalized homophobia, internalized heterosexism, or internalized homonegativity)

presents in negative attitudes toward oneself as an LGB person, other LGB persons, or homosexuality in general. For a review of the psychosocial correlates of heterosexual persons' negative attitudes and behaviors toward LGB persons, and LGB persons' experiences of sexual stigma, see Volume 2, Chapter 15, this handbook.

WELL-BEING, MENTAL HEALTH, AND COPING

Although it has been well-established that homosexuality per se is not a mental health disorder, research consistently shows that LGB persons are at higher risk than their heterosexual counterparts on several mental and physical health variables because of their experience with external and internalized heterosexism (Volume 2, Chapter 15, this handbook). Effects of heterosexism on LGB persons may include (a) social withdrawal and passivity; (b) anxiety, suspicion, and insecurity; (c) denial of one's minority group membership; and (d) self-hatred and low self-esteem (Ritter & Terndrup, 2002). Research in the past few decades has revealed that LGB adolescents are at higher risk than their heterosexual peers for health risk behaviors, mental health problems, depression and anxiety, lower levels of self-esteem, suicidal thoughts and attempts, and use and abuse of alcohol and drugs (e.g., marijuana, cocaine, tobacco; Russell, 2006). Cochran and Mays (2006) found that men who had sex with men (MSM) were more likely than heterosexual men to meet diagnostic criteria for lifetime prevalence of recurrent depression and to have significantly greater prevalence of suicide attempts (five times as likely), especially among younger age groups. They further reported that MSM were more likely than heterosexual men to meet criteria for 1-year prevalence of major depression and panic attack, whereas lesbians were more likely than heterosexual women to evidence drug and alcohol dependence. Russell (2006) also found that bisexual girls were at risk for substance use and abuse, whereas same-sex relationships may be protective against alcohol abuse for boys. Finally, closeted gay men may have an increased risk of certain disease outcomes such as upper respiratory infection and accelerated HIV disease progression (Cole, 2006).

King et al.'s (2008) meta-analyses involving 214,344 heterosexual and 11,971 LGB people suggested that LGB persons were at higher risk than heterosexual persons on the following: (a) a twofold excess in suicide attempts, (b) 1.5 times higher rate in depression and anxiety disorders, and (c) 1.5 times higher rate of alcohol and other substance dependence. These results were similar in both sexes, although lesbian and bisexual women were particularly at risk of alcohol and drug dependence, whereas gay and bisexual men had higher lifetime prevalence of suicide attempt. Cochran and Mays (2009) cautioned that health risk comparisons should take into account confounding or moderating factors such as gender, sexual orientation (vs. sexual identity), and HIV status. Their study with 2,272 participants showed that heterosexually identified men who were MSM had greater risks for psychological morbidity compared with men with a heterosexual orientation. Bisexual women seemed to be particularly vulnerable among women with a minority sexual orientation. Finally, among gay and bisexual men, much of the increased health risk was related to concurrent HIV infection.

On the basis of existing literature, we make the following observations. First, LGB persons as a group tend to have higher risks than heterosexual persons on (a) self-denial and lower self-esteem; (b) social withdrawal; (c) depression, anxiety, and suicide attempts; and (d) alcohol and substance abuse. Second, understanding of these differences can be enhanced by taking into account moderator variables such as gender, sexual orientation, outness, and HIV status. For example, gay and bisexual men tend to be more vulnerable to depression, anxiety, and suicide attempts, whereas lesbian and bisexual women are at greater risk for alcohol and substance abuse. Sexual orientation seems to be a better indicator of health risk than self-reported sexual identity. Closeted gay men are more at risk for physical symptoms such as respiratory infection and accelerated HIV progression. And finally, HIV positive status could be a source for other health risks.

Meyer (1995, 2003) explained the higher prevalence of mental disorders of LGB persons using the theory of minority stress, which posits that stigma, prejudice, and discrimination create a hostile and stressful social environment that causes mental health problems. This model describes how environmental circumstances and minority statuses and identities affect general stressors and distal or proximal minority stress processes, which in turn influence mental health outcomes as moderated by coping, social support, and characteristics of minority identity. Readers may refer to Meyer's articles for an in-depth discussion of the model and its empirical support. We agree that the minority stress model holds promise for understanding the effects of heterosexism and the coping of LGB persons, especially for LGB persons with multiple minority statuses, such as racial or ethnic minorities, women, and persons with disabilities.

Addressing sources of stress, Iwasaki and Ristock (2007) identified the following stressors from their focus group study with 30 lesbians and gay men: (a) the coming-out process, (b) family relations and intimate relationships, (c) societal heterosexism, and (d) financial and work-related issues. These stressors can fit under general stressors and minority stress processes in the minority stress model. In addition, Szymanski and Moffitt (Volume 2, Chapter 15, this handbook) have identified various ways that LGB persons cope with these minority stressors, such as building social support systems, engaging or disengaging from minority stressors, viewing heterosexist stressors from a sociopolitical rather than individual lens, relying on internal resources, and engaging in collective action aimed at eradicating heterosexism and improving the lives of LGB persons and communities.

SPECIAL ISSUES

We discuss the following special issues to address some of the most vibrant LGBT topics in counseling psychology and to complement recent reviews in other volumes.

Vocational Development

Chung (2003) suggested that literature on LGB vocational behavior is one of the most significant recent advancements in vocational psychology. Croteau, Anderson, Distefano, and Kampa-Kokesch (2000) identified five major areas of inquiry in this literature: (a) discrimination and workplace climate, (b) sexual identity management, (c) LGB identity development and career development, (d) career interests and choices, and (e) career interventions. Only the first two areas, however, have received sustained scholarly attention (Croteau et al., 2008). In the following paragraphs, we discuss literature on discrimination and workplace climate for LGBT persons, sexual identity management, and other recent advances in this literature.

Chung (2001) proposed theoretical frameworks for conceptualizing (a) work discrimination and climate, (b) sexual identity management, and (c) discrimination management. These frameworks seem to be the only theoretical work available to date for delineating the dynamics of workplace climate for LGB persons (Croteau et al., 2008). Although these theoretical frameworks were derived from career counseling literature and have influenced subsequent work, direct empirical test and revision of these models were provided only recently by Chung, Williams, and Dispenza (2009).

Chung's (2001) work discrimination and climate model specifies three dimensions of discrimination: perceived (based on perception) versus real (based on reality), potential (possible discrimination should a person's LGB identity be known or assumed) versus encountered (discrimination encountered by LGB persons), and formal (institutional policies and decisions on employee work status and assignments) versus informal (work climate and interpersonal relationships). These three dimensions result in eight forms of work discrimination or climate (e.g., perceived-potential-formal discrimination, real-encountered-informal discrimination). This model may be used by counseling psychologists to differentiate the nature and dynamics of various forms of discrimination and climate and to examine how LGB persons cope with these various forms of discrimination and climate.

Many scholars have documented the existence of work discrimination and its profound effects on the well-being of LGB persons (Croteau, 1996; Croteau & Hedstrom, 1993; Driscoll, Kelley, & Fassinger, 1996; Elliott, 1993; Fassinger, 1995, 1996; Griffin, 1992; Hetherington, Hillerbrand, & Etringer, 1989; Levine & Leonard, 1984; Morgan & Brown, 1991;

Orzek, 1992; Pope, 1995, 1996; Worthington, McCrary, & Howard, 1998). Waldo (1999) developed the Workplace Heterosexism Experiences Questionnaire to assess LGB workers' perception of harassment and discrimination on the basis of their sexual orientation. Liddle, Luzzo, Hauenstein, and Schuck (2004) also created the Lesbian, Gay, Bisexual, and Transgendered Climate Inventory for assessing positive and negative aspects of the workplace climate for LGBT persons. Both instruments seem to have good psychometric qualities.

More recently, researchers have focused on the relation between work climate, worker perceptions, identity disclosure, coping, and vocational outcome variables. In one study of work discrimination and climate, both organizational policies and practices were found to be strongly related to perceived discrimination (Ragins & Cornwell, 2001). Rostosky and Riggle (2002) also found that having a nondiscrimination policy at work and a lower level of internalized heterosexism were predictive of being more out at work. Smith and Ingram (2004) found that experiences with heterosexism and unsupportive social interactions (negative responses from others concerning one's experience of heterosexism) were related to depression and distress among LGB employees. Finally, Huffman, Watrous-Rodriguez, and King's (2008) survey of LGB workers suggested that support is needed from supervisor, coworker, and organization for LGB employees. Supervisor support was related to job satisfaction; coworker support was related to life satisfaction; and organizational support was related to outness at work.

Sexual identity management refers to strategies LGB persons use to manage the disclosure of their sexual identity at work. Chung's (2001) model of sexual identity management was adapted from the work of Griffin (1992), and includes fives strategies: (a) acting (engaging in a heterosexual relationship to make believe that one is heterosexual), (b) passing (fabricating information to convey that one is heterosexual), (c) covering (omitting or censuring information that may reveal one's LGB identity), (d) implicitly out (behaving honestly without labeling oneself as LGB), and (e) explicitly out (openly stating that one is LGB). These five strategies lie on a continuum from being most discreet and somewhat deceiving to the most transparent and honest. These strategies may be used by any LGB person in different situations, however, depending on the person's assessment of risk and his or her sexual identity development and efficacy in dealing with potential consequences.

M. Z. Anderson, Croteau, Chung, and Distefano (2001) developed a measure of sexual identity management on the basis of Griffin's (1992) model. Their factor analysis suggested the combination of passing and covering scales. The measure was recently revised by Lance, Anderson, and Croteau (2010). Although psychometric improvements were achieved, there was still concern about the passing scale. In a related study about sexual identity management, Button (2004) identified three strategies used by lesbians and gay men to manage their identity: counterfeiting a heterosexual identity, appearing asexual by avoiding the topic of sexuality, and integrating a gay or lesbian identity into an organizational setting. These strategies seem to overlap with Griffin's (1992) or Chung's (2001) model.

More recently, scholars have applied psychological theories to examine how LGB persons make decisions on their sexual identity management. On the basis of social cognitive career theory, Lidderdale, Croteau, Anderson, Tovar-Murray, and Davis (2007) proposed a model depicting how LGB workers choose sexual identity management strategies. The model remains to be tested empirically. Ragins, Singh, and Cornwell (2007) used stigma theory to study the role of fear in the disclosure of LGB identities. Their results suggested that working in a group perceived to be supportive and sharing their stigma was related to less fear and more disclosure.

Revised from Chung's (2001) model using data from qualitative interviews with LGB workers who had encountered work discrimination, Chung et al. (2009) identified three categories of coping strategies for managing discrimination: (a) nonassertive coping (quitting, silence, avoidance, self-talk, overcompensation), (b) social support from one's partner, friends, family, coworkers, or mental health professionals; and (c) confrontation (directed to the offender, supervisor, or human resources; or taking legal action, using publicity and media, or circumventing policies). Less is known about discrimination management strategies, such as how LGBT persons decide on which strategies to use and the effectiveness of such strategies.

Chung (2003) called for more scholarly work on the vocational behaviors of lesbian, bisexual, and transgender persons because gay men have been the main focus in existing research. Recent studies seem to be more inclusive of lesbian and bisexual persons, but few specifically target their unique career concerns. The exploration of transgender career development has just begun. O'Neil, McWhirter, and Cerezo (2008) provided a good discussion of vocational and workplace issues for transgender persons, and offered recommendations for practice, advocacy, and research. Dispenza, Watson, Chung and Brack (in press) conducted qualitative analyses of transgender persons' identity and career development. Their findings highlight the importance of family and educational experiences.

LGB Parenting

Examining the experiences of LGB persons in families from an ecological perspective (Bronfenbrenner, 1986) requires that attention be given to multiple realms, contexts, and levels of influence that affect both adults and children in society. This section presents information from research that has been done recently on LGB parenting. An excellent resource on this topic is Goldberg's (2010) *Lesbian and Gay Parents and Their Children: Research on the Family Life Cycle,* which comprehensively summarizes research on lesbian and gay families, including an extensive discussion of issues related to parenting.

Changes in the legal, political, and social climate over the past 30 years have created an environment in which LGB persons are increasingly willing and able to choose to become parents. However, the experience of same-sex couples who become parents remains in many ways different from that of heterosexual couples. Several models of parental identity development specific to same-sex couples have been proposed, and they offer frameworks for understanding the personal, familial, and social–contextual experience of choosing parenthood by LGB persons. J. D. Matthews and Cramer (2006) provided useful suggestions for adoption professionals working with LGB persons during the three phases of adoption process: preplacement, placement, and postplacement. Brinamen and Mitchell (2008) conducted in-depth interviews with gay men who became fathers and proposed a six-stage process of considering and integrating the role of parenthood in conjunction with a gay identity. Gianino (2008) discussed internalized heterosexism as a significant and persistent challenge facing same-sex couples who desire to become parents, citing negative societal notions about lesbian and gay families' abilities to successfully raise children as a major barrier to choosing parenthood. Countering this hurdle and providing couples with the inspiration, conviction, and courage to seek parenthood are factors including developing connections with other LGB parents and meeting a partner who is equally committed to becoming a parent (Berkowitz & Marsiglio, 2007).

Having made the decision to become parents, same-sex couples are faced with a number of options, including (but not limited to) adoption, alternative insemination, and surrogacy. Although advances in medical technology have made a number of these options possible, each choice carries its own costs in terms of finance, time, and legal complexities. Similarly, although some states have made advances in making adoption a viable and accessible option for same-sex couples, other states continue to discriminate against nontraditional families.

Lesbian and gay persons who become parents continue to face challenges related to parenting in a heterosexist society. Many lesbian and gay parents fear that their children will face stigmatization, teasing, and social victimization because of their nontraditional family structure, and have forged a variety of strategies for defining and communicating their family status to their communities (Goldberg, 2010). When supporting and advocating for their children in the school context, LGB parents have experienced a variety of both supportive and discriminatory responses to their LGB family identity. LGB families are challenged to define and develop their roles as parents, dividing child care, housework, and paid work between the two parents. Research suggests that same-sex couples tend to share the burdens of paid and unpaid work more equally than heterosexual couples (e.g., Fulcher, Sutfin, Chan, Scheib, &

Patterson, 2006). Equal division of labor was found to be related to mother satisfaction and better child adjustment (Patterson, 1995). Goldberg (2010) argued that lesbian and gay parents have been "blending mother and father roles such that they created new, hybrid, degendered parenting roles" (p. 103). The construction and maintenance of these roles often involve complex negotiation and are influenced both by contextual factors and the intentional desires of the two parents.

The issue of social and family support for LGB parents is one that has recently attracted attention in research. Social support has long been understood to be a factor in parental adjustment, and research suggests that lesbian and gay parents may receive less support from both family members and friends than do heterosexual couples (DeMino, Appleby, & Fisk, 2007; Kindle & Erich, 2005; Mallon, 2004; C. R. Matthews & Lease, 2000).

Conservative laws and policy makers have attempted to ban LGB persons from parenting rights by arguing that (a) LGB persons are not capable of becoming good parents; (b) children of LGB parents may be molested or are disadvantaged, endangered, or oppressed because of being raised by homosexual parents; and (c) children will become homosexual if raised by homosexual parents (Falk, 1989; Wardle, 1997). On the contrary, empirical literature suggests that children of lesbian and gay parents are as psychologically healthy as their peers with heterosexual parents (Adams, Jaques, & May, 2004; Bos, Gartrell, Peyser, & van Balen, 2008; Lambert, 2005). Whether using convenience samples, samples drawn from known populations (e.g., the Sperm Bank of California), or national representative samples, studies conducted both in the United States and abroad have consistently shown that children of lesbian and gay parents demonstrate appropriate social and personality development, cognitive and behavioral functioning, quality of peer relationships, and overall psychological adjustment on par with those of heterosexual parents (Fulcher et al., 2006; Gartrell, Deck, Rodas, Peyser, & Banks, 2005; Golombok et al., 2003; MacCallum & Golombok, 2004; Patterson, 2006, 2009; Rivers, Poteat, & Noret, 2008). In addition, evidence indicates that family process variables (e.g., attitudes and behaviors) and the quality of family relationships, rather than sexual orientation or gender of parents, are the important predictors of parenting outcomes (Patterson, 2006, 2009).

Although evidence does exist that children of LGB parents are more likely to be teased specifically about their parents' sexuality or their own presumed sexuality (Bos & van Balen, 2008; Tasker & Golombok, 1997), studies suggest that the overall quantity of teasing, bullying, or social victimization that these children experience is no greater than that experienced by children of heterosexual parents (Vanfraussen, Ponjaert-Kristoffersen, & Brewaeys, 2002). Schools that offer a specific LGBT-awareness curriculum seem to be successful in protecting children against the negative impact of heterosexism on childhood psychological adjustment (Bos et al., 2008).

Studies of gender role identity and behavior have generally found that children of lesbian and gay parents do not differ significantly from children of heterosexual parents (Fulcher, Sutfin, & Patterson, 2008). Some studies have indicated, however, that children of lesbian and gay parents may possess greater flexibility in their interests and activities or espouse more androgynous values, possibly attributable to less rigid gender stereotypes and conformity to traditional gender roles modeled by their parents (Kweskin & Cook, 1982). Finally, research suggests that children of lesbian and gay parents are no more likely than children of heterosexual parents to later identify as LGB (Bailey et al., 1995; Golombok & Tasker, 1996; Tasker & Golombok, 1997).

In sum, research has begun to closely examine the experiences of LGB families and has started to elucidate the complex identities and sociopolitical factors involved in navigating the path to parenthood. In addition, the psychological and social health of children raised by LGB parents has been examined, with results consistently suggesting that these children develop normally and have similar developmental paths and social relationships to their peers with heterosexual parents. Despite the progress made, there is still much work to be done to provide psychologists and policy makers with the information they need to design standards of practice and legislation that best support LGB persons in their experiences of forming families and raising children. For example, future research is needed about the process of family formation among LGB persons and family transitions that occur over time among families formed through surrogacy, adoption, foster care, birth from donor insemination, or birth from previous heterosexual relationships. In addition, research is needed to examine how LGB parents and their children cope with and resist interpersonal, institutional, and cultural heterosexist prejudice and discrimination in their lives. Increasing the diversity of methods used to study LGB families, such as the use of daily diary studies, longitudinal designs, and behavioral observation, is also warranted (Patterson, 2009).

LGB Youth

Over the past 50 years, researchers have paid increasing attention to the experience of LGB youth, addressing questions related to sexual, social, and psychological development; physical and psychological health; and the practice of psychotherapy with this population. In addition to recent trends in identity development and adoption of identity labels described earlier in this chapter, experiences of abuse and victimization related to sexuality have been studied as the corollaries to societal heterosexism. This section briefly summarizes these research findings, and makes suggestions for ethical and effective practice with LGB youth.

Much concern and numerous studies have focused on the social, verbal, physical, and sexual victimization of LGB youths by their peers (D'Augelli, 2006; D'Augelli, Grossman, & Starks, 2006; D'Augelli, Pilkington, & Hershberger, 2002). For example, D'Augelli (2006) reported that 81% of LGB youths experienced verbal abuse, 38% were threatened with physical attacks, 22% had objects thrown at them, 15% were physically assaulted, 6% were assaulted with a weapon, and 16% were sexually assaulted. Furthermore, males were more often threatened with violence than females. Berlan, Corliss, Field, Goodman, and Austin (2010) studied a large sample of adolescents, and found that LGB males and females were more likely to have experienced bullying than their heterosexual peers and were less likely to report having engaged in bullying themselves.

With experience of victimization, together with stressors associated with adolescence and coming out, LGB youth may encounter issues such as emotional problems, suicide, physical and sexual abuse, homelessness, prostitution, substance abuse, and dating challenges (Kruks, 1991; Ritter & Terndrup, 2002). LGB youths are more likely to display several health risk behaviors (including substance use, sexual risk behaviors, and suicidal ideation and attempts) and to have initiated these risk behaviors at earlier ages than their heterosexual peers (Garofalo, Wolf, Kessel, Palfrey, & DuRant, 1998). Eisenberg and Resnick (2006) studied sexually active high school students, and found that more than half of LGB students had thought about suicide and more than 37% had attempted suicide; these figures dramatically exceed estimates for heterosexual youth. Furthermore, these researchers found that family connectedness, teacher caring, caring by other adults, and school safety emerged as protective factors that reduce suicidal risk.

Literature on the well-being of LGB youths has focused on their safety and comfort in school, examining variables that relate to the perceived hostility of school environments. Kosciw, Greytak, and Diaz (2009) found that rural communities and those with lower adult education attainment were more likely to have hostile school environments, with greater frequency of victimization on the basis of sexual orientation and gender expression. Other studies attempted to identity strengths and facilitative factors for LGB youth, such as internal locus of control, positive self-esteem, and social and family support (e.g., A. L. Anderson, 1998).

In sum, research on LGB youth has explored different dimensions of risk, health, identity, and development—within individual, family, and broader sociocultural contexts. It offers insight into the complex experience of growing up in a heterosexist society and helps psychologists understand the risk factors, needs, and challenges faced by sexual minority youth, enabling psychologists to shape their clinical and education practices to best support LGB youth. In contrast to pathologizing or conversion therapy, researchers and practitioners from psychology and social work have put forth recommendations for gay-affirmative practice, some

specifically for working with youth that suggests a context-sensitive, culturally competent, and strength-based perspective (Crisp & McCave, 2007).

DIVERSITY AND CULTURAL ISSUES

Literature on LGBT issues has just begun in the past 15 years or so to acknowledge and examine cultural diversity within this population as well as the complexity of interaction between multiple cultural identities. Most of this emerging scholarly work addresses racial and ethnic issues among LGBT persons. Some attention is also given to gender, age, religion, and disability. Clarke and Peel (2007) discussed an inclusive approach to deal with diversity in LGBT populations, focusing on contextual factors (e.g., social class, gender, race/ethnicity, disability). In this section, we discuss preliminary theoretical and empirical work on these topics.

Race and Ethnicity

Greene's (1997) edited book, *Ethnic and Cultural Diversity Among Lesbians and Gay Men,* was the first significant contribution to the study of racial and ethnic diversity of lesbian and gay persons. Authors of the book chapters addressed specific cultural issues for the major ethnic minority and gender groups, which set the foundation for future empirical work. Readers may also refer to Greene's (1998) discussion of language, family, and gender roles as cultural factors in the lives of LGB people of color.

LGBT people of color experience racism in the LGBT communities as well as heterosexism in communities of color (Ibañez, Van Oss Marin, Flores, Millett, & Diaz, 2009; Walters & Old Person, 2008). This marginalizing experience with both LGBT and communities of color creates unique minority stress processes for the dual-identity development of LGBT people of color. Chung and Szymanski (2006) found some empirical support for Chung and Katayama's (1998) theoretical model depicting the racial and sexual identity development of Asian American gay men. According to this model, the interaction between the two minority identities can be represented by the sexual identity progression in a 2 × 2 grid of positive and negative attitudes toward one's own ethnic group and the majority ethnic group (Berry, 1980). Asian American gay men who have the most negative attitudes about their sexual identity (i.e., high internalized heterosexism) tend to endorse positive attitudes toward the majority ethnic group and negative attitudes toward their own ethnic group (i.e., *assimilationist*). This typically occurs at the beginning stage of coming out. As these gay men continue to come out and become more positive about their sexual identity, they also experience racism in the gay community, and their racial identity attitudes become negative toward both majority group and their own cultural group (*marginalist*). Forming community with other Asian American gay men helps strengthen one's sexual identity, resulting in *separationist* racial identity attitudes (positive attitudes toward one's own cultural group, but negative attitudes toward the majority group). Finally, Asian American gay men achieve the most positive sexual identity attitudes when they have a better understanding of and coping system with heterosexism and racism, resulting in *integrationist* racial identity attitudes (positive attitudes toward both the majority group and one's own cultural group). Chung and Szymanski's (2006) validation study of the model involved a very small sample size. Replications using larger samples are needed, and the model's applicability to other racial and ethnic groups may be examined.

Jamil, Harper, and Fernandez (2009) conducted a qualitative study with 22 gay, bisexual, and questioning Latino and African American male adolescents. They concluded that the development of sexual and ethnic identities occurred simultaneously but involved different and independent processes. Several factors may be considered for the difference between Jamil et al.'s findings and those of Chung and Szymanski (2006), such as ethnic background, age of participants, and the social context of the participations growing up with different generations. Much more empirical work is needed to understand the relation between sexual and ethnic identities for different cultural groups.

Several studies examined racial and ethnic differences in heterosexism and internalized heterosexism. Negy and Eisenman (2005) found that African American college students had higher heterosexism scores than White college students, although such differences could be statistically accounted for by church attendance, religious commitment, and socioeconomic status. Regarding internalized heterosexism, Ross, Rosser, and Neumaier (2008) found that African American gay male respondents tended to have more internalized heterosexism than White and Hispanic gay men. The relatively higher level of internalized heterosexism among African American LGB persons is alarming because it is found to be related to psychological distress and lower self-esteem among African Americans (Szymanski & Gupta, 2009). Bowleg, Craig, and Burkholder's (2004) study suggested that Black lesbians' active coping was predicted by internal (self-esteem, race and lesbian identity) and external factors (social support, perceived availability of LGB resources). Finally, Díaz, Bein, and Ayala (2006), in a study of Latino gay men, found a high frequency of distress symptoms resulting from participants' sexual orientation, ethnicity, and poverty status.

Given the paucity of research on racial and ethnic minority LGBT persons, much work needs to be done. For example, much of the empirical literature on LGB persons of color, particularly related to group comparisons, has been atheoretical. Thus, much attention needs to be directed toward strengthening the theory base about LGB persons of color. Reliable and valid measures need to be developed for studying the unique experiences of LGB persons of color. In addition, more research is needed to examine how cultural factors affect dimensions of sexual identity experience among LGB people of color. For example, how does adherence to traditional Asian values, the process of acculturation, and experiences with both racism and heterosexism influence psychological, social, and sexual identities among Asian American LGB persons?

Gender

Recent research on gender issues has focused on unique issues related to being a sexual minority male or female, and how these issues relate to aspects of sexual identity and psychosocial health. Among gay and bisexual men, research has addressed how adoption of traditional cultural values such as masculinity and aesthetic standards affect well-being. Hamilton and Mahalik (2009) studied 315 gay male participants and found that gay men who adopted traditional ideology of masculinity were more likely to engage in risky health practices (e.g., substance use, unsafe sex practices). Similarly, both Szymanski and Carr (2008) and Sánchez, Westefeld, Liu, and Vilain (2010) found that gender role conflict (i.e., when the internalization of rigid, sexist, and restrictive cultural messages about what it means to be a man results in personal restriction, devaluation, or violation of self and others) is related to more internalized heterosexism. Furthermore, Szymanski and Carr (2008) found support for a mediated model in which gender role conflict was both directly and indirectly (through negative attitudes about being gay or bisexual) related to lower self-esteem, and lower self-esteem was directly and indirectly (through avoidant coping) related to psychological distress. This suggests that how a gay or bisexual male constructs his notion of being a man is likely to influence his sexual identity development and his attitudes and feelings about being a sexual minority man, which in turn can negatively influence mental health. Finally, Wiseman and Moradi's (2010) study with 231 sexual minority men (gay, bisexual, and transgender) found that internalizing traditional cultural standards of attractiveness was related to body image problems and eating disorder symptoms.

Paralleling the research on masculinity and sexual minority men, recent research on lesbians and bisexual women has explored how negative attitudes and feelings about being a sexual minority female are related to endorsement of traditional cultural values concerning femininity and women's roles. For example, negative attitudes and feelings about being lesbian or bisexual are positively related to sexual minority women's passive acceptance of traditional gender roles and unawareness or denial of cultural, institutional, and individual sexism (Szymanski, 2004); devaluation and distrust of women as well as a belief in male superiority (Szymanski & Kashubeck-West, 2008); and self-objectification or the internalization of sexually objectifying experiences that manifests in how frequently a woman watches her appearance and experiences her body

according to how it looks (Haines et al., 2008). In addition, having less negative feelings about being a sexual minority woman is related to self-identification as a feminist, favorable attitudes toward feminism, involvement in feminist activities, greater feminist identity development, and greater endorsement of the tenets of various feminist theories (Szymanski, 2004). These findings suggest that feminism may promote acceptance of one's sexual identity, perhaps by providing (a) tools to critique the institutions of patriarchy and heterosexuality, (b) strategies for confronting and dealing with oppressive environments, and (c) bridges to supportive communities. Finally, as reviewed by Szymanski and Moffitt (Chapter 15 of this volume), sexual minority women's experiences of oppression, on the basis of sexual orientation and gender, have direct effects that jointly affect mental health.

In sum, recent research indicates the important role that social constructions of gender can have on LGB persons' sexual identity development as well as on their psychosocial well-being. In addition, it illustrates how oppression associated with multiple identities can compound to influence mental health. Future research is needed to examine mediators and moderates in the gender role ideology, sexual identity development, and psychosocial health links. Investigations are needed to examine culture-specific gender role norms (e.g., traditional *machismo* and *caballerismo* among Latino gay or bisexual men, *marianismo* among Latina lesbian or bisexual women) and their influence on the sexual identity and psychosocial health of LGB people of color.

Age

Age is another diversity factor that has just begun to receive attention in LGBT psychology. Kimmel (2002) contended that LGBT persons over age 65 have experienced a lot of repressive actions against them (e.g., being fired for their sexual orientation, being treated for pathology by psychologists and psychiatrists). Older LGBT persons have witnessed the 1970s gay and feminist movement as well as the AIDS epidemic in the 1980s (Kimmel, 2002). Thus, it is important to acknowledge generational and cohort differences as well as the current and past social context when working with elderly LGBT persons. Research shows that older LGBT persons are coping relatively well and may have developed crisis competence from their life experience. Such findings, however, need to be considered with the possible effects of sample selection (e.g., those coping less well are not included in research or are no longer available; Kimmel, 2002).

LGBT persons face additional heterosexist stressors as they age, such as invisibility within the mainstream aging community, insensitive and biased health care, discrimination from retirement communities and senior centers, and economic discrimination from denial of a partner's social security and pension benefits (Grossman, D'Augelli, & O'Connell, 2002; Haber, 2009; Kimmel, Rose, & David, 2006). Social support, especially from friends, is an important predictor of psychosocial health and well-being among elderly LGBT person (Masini & Barrett, 2007). Grossman and colleagues (Grossman, D'Augelli, & Hershberger, 2000; Grossman et al., 2002) found that the most important factor contributing to LGBT older adults' satisfaction with their social support was their social support system members' knowledge of their sexual orientation. Older LGBT persons typically build support systems that differ from the traditional ones often established in heterosexual communities. For example, LGBT persons are more likely to participate in LGBT social groups than in a local senior center (Quam & Whitford, 1992), and LGBT persons' social support systems most often include same-sex close friends (Grossman et al., 2000, 2002). Finally, both care-giving and care-receiving can be complicated when encountering heterosexism and when elderly LGBT persons have not disclosed their sexual orientation to their parents or children (Fredriksen-Goldsen, Kim, Muraco, & Mincer, 2009; Grossman, D'Augelli, & Dragowski, 2005).

IMPLICATIONS FOR COUNSELING PSYCHOLOGY

In this section, we discuss implications for counseling psychology along four domains: education and training, practice, research, and advocacy.

Education and Training

Pilkington and Cantor (1996) surveyed professional psychology students' perception of heterosexism in their training programs. They found instances of heterosexism in the following areas: (a) textbooks and course materials, (b) instructor comments, (c) research supervision, (d) practica and internships, (e) interactions with program administrators and faculty, (f) teaching assistantships, and (g) course content. More recently, Burkard, Knox, Hess, and Schultz's (2009) qualitative study explored LGB supervisees' experience of LGB nonaffirming and LGB affirmative supervision. They found that supervisors' biased and oppressive attitudes and practices concerning sexual orientation negatively affected LGB supervisees, the supervisory relationship, and perceived client outcomes. In addition to heterosexist bias, research also shows that students of professional psychology programs report receiving inadequate training on LGBT issues (Allison, Crawford, Echemendia, Robinson, & Knepp, 1994; Buhrke, 1989). Among practicing psychologists, formal education about LGB issues is related to sexual orientation, gender, and age, with LGB psychologists reporting more education than heterosexual psychologists (32% compared with 13%, respectively), females reporting more education than males (19% compared with 10%), and younger psychologists reporting more education than older psychologists (32% for those 30–39 years old compared with 9% 60–69 years old; Kilgore et al., 2005).

Israel and Hackett's (2004) experiment compared the effects of four training conditions: an information-based intervention, an attitude-exploration based intervention, a combined treatment intervention (both information and attitude exploration), and a placebo control condition. They found that counselor trainees' knowledge of LGB issues benefited from an information-based intervention; however, their attitude-based intervention resulted in more negative attitudes toward LGB issues. The authors attributed the latter finding to increased awareness of one's heterosexism because of the attitude intervention. Finally, Halpert, Reinhardt, and Toohey (2007) proposed the integrative affirmative supervision model, which was derived from four other models of training (Buhrke, 1989; Holloway, 1995; Pett, 2000; Stoltenberg & Delworth, 1987).

Taken together, existing data suggest the need to continue infusing LGB issues into counseling psychology education and training. Chung and Brack (2005) discussed methods for enhancing LGB-affirmative training in academic and clinical settings. For academic training, they described (a) three ways to infuse LGB training in all academic courses; (b) recruitment and retention of LGB and LGB-affirmative faculty, staff, and students; (c) the establishment of LGB-affirmative training climate; (d) research and publication on LGB issues; and (e) advocacy and community outreach efforts. For clinical training, they proposed a three-level LGB-affirmative training: (a) didactic learning, (b) encouragement of trainee independence, and (c) learning to use self as an instrument. Research is needed to provide an updated view of current implementation of LGBT-affirmative training as well as the effectiveness of such efforts.

Practice

Scholarship in the area of practice has focused mainly on developing guidelines or suggestions for providing competent and affirmative LGB therapy. For example, in 1998, the APA endorsed a resolution on appropriate therapeutic responses to sexual orientation and provided guidelines for psychotherapy with LGB clients (Division 44/Committee on Lesbian, Gay, and Bisexual Concerns Joint Task Force, 2000). In February 2011, the APA Council of Representative adopted a revision of these practice guidelines. Greene (2007) emphasized that therapists need to deal with personal beliefs and potential heterosexist bias and to obtain competence to deal with diverse LGB clients. Pachankis and Goldfried (2004) identified knowledge in the following areas as important for affirmative psychotherapy with LGB clients: sexual identity development, couple relationships and parenting, LGB persons as members of families, legal and workplace issues, and LGB subgroups that are underrepresented in LGB literature (e.g., older adults, racial and ethnic minorities, religious persons, bisexual men and women). Bidell (2005) developed the Sexual Orientation Counselor

Competency Scale for assessing attitudes, skills, and knowledge of counselors working with LGB clients, with appropriate psychometric properties. Finally, Morrow (1996) found that a lesbian-affirmative 10-week group intervention that addressed culturally sensitive issues (e.g., lesbian identity development, heterosexism, religion, career, family, sexism, racism, and assertiveness skills development) resulted in participant gains in ego development, lesbian identity, empowerment, and sexual orientation disclosure to others.

Korell and Lorah (2007) identified the following important issues for counseling transgender clients: support systems, family issues, social and emotional stressors, medical issues, career concerns, and assessment and diagnostic issues. Bess and Stabb's (2009) qualitative study with seven transgender clients (five male to female and two female to male) showed that these clients reported supportive and affirming relationships with their therapists. Psychologists who work with clients seeking sex-reassignment surgery should be familiar with the Standards of Care established by the World Professional Association of Transgender Health (Bess & Stabb, 2009). Finally, Jeltova and Fish (2005) provided suggestions on how to conduct systemic consultation to promote LGBT-friendly environments in schools. Clearly, the development and promotion of suggestions for providing competent and affirmative LGBT therapy are important; however, evaluating the effectiveness of such interventions continues to be an important and needed direction within this area.

Research

Moradi, Mohr, Worthington, and Fassinger (2009) discussed several conceptual and methodological issues in sexual minority research, including (a) construct definition and assessment (e.g., nature and scope of construct, level of analysis), (b) population studied (e.g., relevance to research question, defining dimensions of sexual minority status, within-group differences), (c) internal validity (e.g., use of experimental, repeated measure, and longitudinal designs), (d) external and ecological validity (e.g., sampling and recruitment methods, generalizability to actual phenomena), (e) measurement (e.g., appropriate instrument and strategy for construct and population of interest, psychometric properties of new or adapted instruments, routine assessment of sexual orientation or gender identity), (f) procedural issues (e.g., use of pilot studies, possible negative procedural effects, giving back to the community studied), and (g) professional writing (e.g., literature review, clarity, rationale for design, sample description, biased language, limitations of study). Researchers are encouraged to consider these issues in research design, implementation, and report and application of findings.

In addition to addressing the aforementioned conceptual and methodological issues, future research is needed to strengthen the theory base behind many constructs in LGB psychology as well as relationships between constructs. Research also needs to move away from convenience samples that are primarily White, middle-class, well-educated, urban, and open about their sexual orientation. Given the dearth of empirical research on the unique experiences and issues of transgender, bisexual, racial and ethnic minority, working class, and poor sexual minority persons, more attention to diversity within the LGBT community is clearly needed. Expanding the type of methodologies used to examine the lives and experiences of LGBT persons, beyond cross-sectional and qualitative designs, is also needed.

Advocacy

Given the prevalence of heterosexist oppression in U.S. culture and its negative impact on the lives of LGBT persons, scholars have recently emphasized for the need for psychologists to infuse social justice advocacy interventions into counseling psychology practice (cf. Kashubeck-West, Szymanski, & Meyer, 2008; Toporek, Gerstein, Fouad, Roysircar, & Israel, 2006; Volume 2, Chapter 15, this handbook). As such, Lewis, Arnold, House, and Toporek (2002) developed the Advocacy Competencies to assist psychologists in developing and implementing social justice advocacy interventions into their work. These competencies were highlighted and illustrated with case examples in a special section of the *Journal of Counseling and Development* on Advocacy Competence (Goodman, 2009).

Applying Lewis et al.'s (2002) model to work with LGBT issues, interventions can emphasize advocacy with or advocacy on behalf of sexual minority clients across three levels: client, community, and public arena. The client level of advocacy uses direct counseling interventions to empower LGBT clients (e.g., exploring with LGBT clients how their presenting problems may stem from external and internalized heterosexism, teaching LGBT clients skills to deal with heterosexist bias) and to advocate on their behalf (e.g., connecting a client in the early phases of coming out with an LGBT community support group, consulting with teachers on how to address antigay bullying in the schools). The community level of advocacy focuses on community collaboration (e.g., developing alliances with groups working to reduce heterosexism and to improve LGBT persons' lives) and systems advocacy (e.g., providing research data on the negative effects of antigay bullying to administrators, teachers, and students in the schools; providing training on LGBT issues in the workplace). The public arena level of advocacy emphasizes informing the public about heterosexism and LGBT issues (e.g., using a variety of media to educate the public about the negative effects of anti-LGB initiatives, such as the Defense of Marriage Act, on same-sex couples and families) and shaping public policy (e.g., campaigning for the passage of sexual orientation nondiscrimination laws). Similar to research on education and training and on practice, future research is needed to document the types and extent to which counseling psychologists engage in advocacy efforts and to evaluate the effectiveness of such interventions.

Counseling psychologists have made important advances to our understanding of LGBT person's lives and the unique issues they face as a result of living in a heterosexist society. In addition, counseling psychologists are in a unique position to deliver culturally competent education, practice, research, and advocacy for the advancement of LGBT persons struggling with issues resulting from an oppressive social environment.

References

Adams, J. L., Jaques, J. D., & May, K. M. (2004). Counseling gay and lesbian families: Theoretical considerations. *The Family Journal, 12*, 40–42. doi:10.1177/1066480703258693

Allison, K. W., Crawford, I., Echemendia, R., Robinson, L. V., & Knepp, D. (1994). Human diversity and professional competence: Training in clinical and counseling psychology revisited. *American Psychologist, 49*, 792–796. doi:10.1037/0003-066X.49.9.792

American Psychological Association. (1998). Resolution on appropriate therapeutic responses to sexual orientation. *American Psychologist, 53*, 782–783.

American Psychological Association. (2009). *Report of the task force on appropriate therapeutic responses to sexual orientation.* Washington, DC: Author.

Anderson, A. L. (1998). Strengths of gay male youth: An untold story. *Child and Adolescent Social Work Journal, 15*, 55–71. doi:10.1023/A:1022245504871

Anderson, M. Z., Croteau, J. M., Chung, Y. B., & Distefano, T. M. (2001). Developing an assessment of sexual identity management for lesbian and gay workers. *Journal of Career Assessment, 9*, 243–260. doi:10.1177/106907270100900303

Anton, B. S. (2008). Proceedings of the American Psychological Association, Incorporated, for the legislative year 2007: Minutes of the annual meeting of the Council of Representatives. *American Psychologist, 63*, 360–442. doi:10.1037/0003-066X.63.5.360

Anton, B. S. (2009). Proceedings of the American Psychological Association for the legislative year 2008: Minutes of the annual meeting of the Council of Representatives. *American Psychologist, 64*, 372–453. doi:10.1037/a0015932

Anton, B. S. (2010). Proceedings of the American Psychological Association for the legislative year 2009: Minutes of the annual meeting of the Council of Representatives and minutes of the meetings of the Board of Directors. *American Psychologist, 65*, 385–475. doi:10.1037/a0019553

Bailey, J. M., Bobrow, D., Wolfe, M., & Mikach, S. (1995). Sexual orientation of adult sons of gay fathers. *Developmental Psychology, 31*, 124–129. doi:10.1037/0012-1649.31.1.124

Bailey, J. M., & Dawood, K. (1998). Behavioral genetics, sexual orientation, and the family. In C. J. Patterson & A. R. D'Augelli (Eds.), *Lesbian, gay, and bisexual identities in families: Psychological perspectives* (pp. 3–18). New York, NY: Oxford University Press.

Bailey, J. M., Pillard, R. C., Dawood, K., Miller, M. B., Farrer, L. A., Trivedi, S., & Murphy, R. L. (1999). A family history study of male sexual orientation using three independent samples. *Behavior Genetics, 29*, 79–86. doi:10.1023/A:1021652204405

Balsam, K. F., Beauchaine, T. P., Rothblum, E. D., & Solomon, S. E. (2008). Three-year follow-up of same-sex couples who had civil unions in Vermont, same-sex couples not in civil unions, and heterosexual married couples. *Developmental Psychology, 44*, 102–116. doi:10.1037/0012-1649.44.1.102

Beckstead, A. L., & Morrow, S. L. (2004). Mormon clients' experiences of conversion therapy: The need for a new approach for treatment. *The Counseling Psychologist, 32*, 651–690. doi:10.1177/0011000004267555

Bem, D. J. (2000). Exotic becomes erotic: Interpreting the biological correlates of sexual orientation. *Archives of Sexual Behavior, 29*, 531–548. doi:10.1023/A:1002050303320

Berkowitz, D., & Marsiglio, W. (2007). Gay men: Negotiating procreative, father, and family identities. *Journal of Marriage and Family, 69*, 366–381. doi:10.1111/j.1741-3737.2007.00371.x

Berlan, E. D., Corliss, H. L., Field, A. E., Goodman, E., & Austin, S. B. (2010). Sexual orientation and bullying among adolescents in the Growing Up Today Study. *Journal of Adolescent Health, 46*, 366–371. doi:10.1016/j.jadohealth.2009.10.015

Berry, J. W. (1980). Acculturation as varieties of adaptation. In A. M. Padilla (Ed.), *Acculturation: Theory, models and some new findings* (pp. 9–25). Boulder, CO: Westview Press.

Bersoff, D. N., & Ogden, D. W. (1991). APA Amicus curiae briefs: Furthering lesbian and gay male civil rights. *American Psychologist, 46*, 950–956. doi:10.1037/0003-066X.46.9.950

Bess, J. A., & Stabb, S. D. (2009). The experiences of transgendered persons in psychotherapy: Voices and recommendations. *Journal of Mental Health Counseling, 31*, 264–282.

Bidell, M. P. (2005). The Sexual Orientation Counselor Competency Scale: Assessing attitudes, skills, and knowledge of counselors working with lesbian, gay, and bisexual clients. *Counselor Education and Supervision, 44*, 267–279.

Bieschke, K. J., Paul, P. L., & Blasko, K. A. (2007). Review of empirical research focused on the experience of lesbian, gay, and bisexual clients in counseling and psychotherapy. In K. J. Bieschke, R. M. Perez, & K. A. DeBord (Eds.), *Handbook of counseling and psychotherapy with lesbian, gay, bisexual, and transgender clients* (2nd ed., pp. 293–315). Washington, DC: American Psychological Association. doi:10.1037/11482-012

Bieschke, K. J., Perez, R. M., & DeBord, K. A. (Eds.). (2007). *Handbook of counseling and psychotherapy with lesbian, gay, bisexual, and transgender clients* (2nd ed.). Washington, DC: American Psychological Association. doi:10.1037/11482-000

Blackwell, C. W. (2008). Nursing implications in the application of conversion therapies on gay, lesbian, bisexual, and transgender clients. *Issues in Mental Health Nursing, 29*, 651–665. doi:10.1080/01612840802048915

Bond, B. J., Hefner, V., & Drogos, K. L. (2009). Information-seeking practices during the sexual development of lesbian, gay, and bisexual individuals: The influence and effects of coming out in a mediated environment. *Sexuality and Culture: An Interdisciplinary Quarterly, 13*, 32–50. doi:10.1007/s12119-008-9041-y

Bos, H. M. W., Gartrell, N. K., Peyser, H., & van Balen, F. (2008). The USA National Longitudinal Lesbian Family Study (NLLFS): Homophobia, psychological adjustment, and protective factors. *Journal of Lesbian Studies, 12*, 455–471. doi:10.1080/10894160802278630

Bos, H. M. W., & van Balen, F. (2008). Children in planned lesbian families: Stigmatisation, psychological adjustment and protective factors. *Culture, Health and Sexuality, 10*, 221–236. doi:10.1080/13691050701601702

Bowleg, L., Craig, M. L., & Burkholder, G. (2004). Rising and surviving: A conceptual model of active coping among Black lesbians. *Cultural Diversity and Ethnic Minority Psychology, 10*, 229–240. doi:10.1037/1099-9809.10.3.229

Bradford, M. (2004). The bisexual experience: Living in a dichotomous culture. *Journal of Bisexuality, 4*(1–2), 7–23. doi:10.1300/J159v04n01_02

Brinamen, C. F., & Mitchell, V. (2008). Gay men becoming fathers: A model of identity expansion. *Journal of GLBT Family Studies, 4*, 521–541. doi:10.1080/15504280802191772

Bronfenbrenner, U. (1986). Ecology of the family as a context for human development: Research perspectives. *Developmental Psychology, 22*, 723–742. doi:10.1037/0012-1649.22.6.723

Brown, T. (2002). A proposed model of bisexual identity development that elaborates on experiential differences of women and men. *Journal of Bisexuality, 2*(4), 67–91. doi:10.1300/J159v02n04_05

Buhrke, R. A. (1989). Female student perspectives on training in lesbian and gay issues. *The Counseling Psychologist, 17*, 629–636. doi:10.1177/0011000089174006

Burkard, A. W., Knox, S., Hess, S. A., & Schultz, J. (2009). Lesbian, gay, and bisexual supervisees' experiences of LGB-affirmative and nonaffirmative supervision. *Journal of Counseling Psychology, 56*, 176–188. doi:10.1037/0022-0167.56.1.176

Button, S. B. (2004). Identity management strategies utilized by lesbian and gay employees: A quantitative investigation. *Group and Organization Management, 29*, 470–494. doi:10.1177/1059601103257417

Camperio-Ciani, A., Corna, F., & Capiluppi, C. (2004). Evidence for maternally inherited factors favouring male homosexuality and promoting female fecundity. *Proceedings: Biological Sciences/The Royal Society, 271*, 2217–2221. doi:10.1098/rspb.2004.2872

Cass, V. C. (1979). Homosexuality identity formation: A theoretical model. *Journal of Homosexuality, 4*, 219–235. doi:10.1300/J082v04n03_01

Cass, V. C. (1984). Homosexual identity formation: Testing a theoretical model. *Journal of Sex Research, 20*, 143–167. doi:10.1080/00224498409551214

Chung, Y. B. (2001). Work discrimination and coping strategies: Conceptual frameworks for counseling lesbian, gay, and bisexual clients. *The Career Development Quarterly, 50*, 33–44.

Chung, Y. B. (2003). Career counseling with lesbian, gay, bisexual, and transgendered persons: The next decade. *The Career Development Quarterly, 52*, 78–85.

Chung, Y. B., & Brack, C. J. (2005). Those who care, teach: Toward sexual orientation equity in academic and clinical training. In J. M. Croteau, J. S. Lark, M. A. Lidderdale, & Y. B. Chung (Eds.), *Deconstructing heterosexism in the counseling professions: A narrative approach* (pp. 211–228). Thousand Oaks, CA: Sage.

Chung, Y. B., & Katayama, M. (1996). Assessment of sexual orientation in lesbian/gay/bisexual studies. *Journal of Homosexuality, 30*(4), 49–62. doi:10.1300/J082v30n04_03

Chung, Y. B., & Katayama, M. (1998). Ethnic and sexual identity development of Asian-American lesbian and gay adolescents. *Professional School Counseling, 1*(3), 21–25.

Chung, Y. B., & Singh, A. A. (2009). Lesbian, gay, bisexual, and transgender Asian Americans. In N. Tewari & A. N. Alvarez (Eds.), *Asian American psychology: Current perspectives* (pp. 233–246). New York, NY: Psychology Press.

Chung, Y. B., & Szymanski, D. M. (2006). Racial and sexual identities of Asian American gay men. *Journal of LGBT Issues in Counseling, 1*(2), 67–93. doi:10.1300/J462v01n02_05

Chung, Y. B., Szymanski, D. M., & Amadio, D. M. (2006). Empirical validations of a multidimensional model for assessing sexual orientation. *Journal of LGBT Issues in Counseling, 1*(3), 3–13. doi:10.1300/J462v01n03_02

Chung, Y. B., Williams, W., & Dispenza, F. (2009). Validating work discrimination and coping strategy models for sexual minorities. *The Career Development Quarterly, 58*, 162–170.

Clarke, V., & Peel, E. (2007). From lesbian and gay psychology to LGBTQ psychologies: A journey into the unknown (or unknowable)? In V. Clarke & E. Peel (Eds.), *Out in psychology: Lesbian, gay, bisexual, trans and queer perspectives* (pp. 11–35). West Sussex, England: Wiley.

Cochran, S. D., & Mays, V. M. (2006). Estimating prevalence of mental and substance-using disorders among lesbians and gay men from existing national health data. In A. M. Omoto & H. S. Kurtzman (Eds.), *Sexual orientation and mental health: Examining identity and development in lesbian, gay, and bisexual people* (pp. 143–165). Washington, DC: American Psychological Association. doi:10.1037/11261-007

Cochran, S. D., & Mays, V. M. (2009). Burden of psychiatric morbidity among lesbian, gay, and bisexual individuals in the California Quality of Life Survey. *Journal of Abnormal Psychology, 118*, 647–658. doi:10.1037/a0016501

Cole, S. W. (2006). Social threat, personal identity, and physical health in closeted gay men. In A. M. Omoto & H. S. Kurtzman (Eds.), *Sexual orientation and mental health: Examining identity and development in lesbian, gay, and bisexual people* (pp. 245–267). Washington, DC: American Psychological Association. doi:10.1037/11261-012

Coleman, E. (1981–1982). Developmental stages of the coming out process. *Journal of Homosexuality, 7(2–3)*, 31–43. doi:10.1300/J082v07n02_06

Collins, J. F. (2000). Biracial-bisexual individuals: Identity coming of age. *International Journal of Sexuality and Gender Studies, 5*, 221–253. doi:10.1023/A:1010137025394

Conger, J. J. (1975). Proceedings of the American Psychological Association, Incorporated, for the year 1974: Minutes of the annual meeting of the Council of Representatives. *American Psychologist, 30*, 620–651. doi:10.1037/h0078455

Cramer, D. W., & Roach, A. J. (1988). Coming out to mom and dad: A study of gay males and their relationships with their parents. *Journal of Homosexuality, 15(3–4)*, 79–92. doi:10.1300/J082v15n03_04

Cramer, R. J., Golom, F. D., LoPresto, C. T., & Kirkley, S. M. (2008). Weighing the evidence: Empirical assessment and ethical implications of conversion therapy. *Ethics and Behavior, 18*, 93–114. doi:10.1080/10508420701713014

Crisp, C., & McCave, E. L. (2007). Gay affirmative practice: A model for social work practice with gay, lesbian, and bisexual youth. *Child and Adolescent Social Work Journal, 24*, 403–421. doi:10.1007/s10560-007-0091-z

Croteau, J. M. (1996). Research on the work experiences of lesbian, gay and bisexual people: An integrative review of methodology and findings. *Journal of Vocational Behavior, 48*, 195–209. doi:10.1006/jvbe.1996.0018

Croteau, J. M., Anderson, M. Z., Distefano, T. M., & Kampa-Kokesch, S. (2000). Lesbian, gay, and bisexual vocational psychology: Reviewing foundations and planning construction. In R. M. Perez, K. A. DeBord, & K. J. Bieschke (Eds.), *Handbook of counseling and psychotherapy with lesbian, gay, and bisexual clients* (pp. 383–408). Washington, DC: American Psychological Association. doi:10.1037/10339-016

Croteau, J. M., Bieschke, K. J., Fassinger, R. E., & Manning, J. L. (2008). Counseling psychology and sexual orientation: History, selective trends, and future directions. In S. D. Brown & R. W. Lent (Eds.), *Handbook of counseling psychology* (4th ed., pp. 194–211). Hoboken, NJ: Wiley.

Croteau, J. M., & Hedstrom, S. M. (1993). Integrating commonality and difference: The key to career counseling with lesbian women and gay men. *The Career Development Quarterly, 41*, 201–209.

D'Augelli, A. R. (2006). Developmental and contextual factors and mental health among lesbian, gay, and bisexual youths. In A. M. Omoto & H. S. Kurtzman (Eds.), *Sexual orientation and mental health: Examining identity and development in lesbian, gay, and bisexual people* (pp. 37–53). Washington, DC: American Psychological Association. doi:10.1037/11261-002

D'Augelli, A. R., Grossman, A., & Starks, M. (2006). Childhood gender atypicality, victimization, and PTSD among lesbian, gay, and bisexual youth. *Journal of Interpersonal Violence, 21*, 1462–1482. doi:10.1177/0886260506293482

D'Augelli, A. R., Pilkington, N. W., & Hershberger, S. L. (2002). Incidence and mental health impact of sexual orientation victimization of lesbian, gay, and bisexual youths in high school. *School Psychology Quarterly, 17*, 148–167. doi:10.1521/scpq.17.2.148.20854

DeMino, K. A., Appleby, G., & Fisk, D. (2007). Lesbian mothers with planned families: A comparative study of internalized homophobia and social support. *American Journal of Orthopsychiatry, 77*, 165–173. doi:10.1037/0002-9432.77.1.165

Diamond, L. M. (2003). Was it a phase? Young women's relinquishment of lesbian/bisexual identities over a 5-year period. *Journal of Personality and Social Psychology, 84*, 352–364. doi:10.1037/0022-3514.84.2.352

Diamond, L. M. (2006). What we got wrong about sexual identity development: Unexpected findings from a longitudinal study of young women. In A. M. Omoto & H. S. Kurtzman (Eds.), *Sexual orientation and mental health: Examining identity and development in lesbian, gay, and bisexual people* (pp. 73–94). Washington, DC: American Psychological Association. doi:10.1037/11261-004

Díaz, R. M., Bein, E., & Ayala, G. (2006). Homophobia, poverty, and racism: Triple oppression and mental health outcomes in Latino gay men. In A. M. Omoto & H. S. Kurtzman (Eds.), *Sexual orientation and mental health: Examining identity and development in lesbian, gay, and bisexual people* (pp. 207–224). Washington, DC: American Psychological Association. doi:10.1037/11261-010

Dispenza, F., Watson, L. B., Chung, Y. B., & Brack, G. (in press). Experience of career-related discrimination for female-to-male (FTM) transgender persons: A qualitative study. *The Career Development Quarterly*.

Division 44/Committee on Lesbian, Gay, and Bisexual Concerns Joint Task Force. (2000). Guidelines for psychotherapy with lesbian, gay, and bisexual clients. *American Psychologist, 55*, 1440–1451. doi:10.1037/0003-066X.55.12.1440

Dorland, J. M., & Fischer, A. R. (2001). Gay, lesbian, and bisexual individuals' perceptions: An analogue study. *The Counseling Psychologist, 29*, 532–547. doi:10.1177/0011000001294004

Driscoll, J. M., Kelley, F. A., & Fassinger, R. E. (1996). Lesbian identity and disclosure in the workplace: Relation to occupational stress and satisfaction. *Journal of Vocational Behavior, 48*, 229–242. doi:10.1006/jvbe.1996.0020

Eisenberg, M. E., & Resnick, M. D. (2006). Suicidality among gay, lesbian and bisexual youth: The role of protective factors. *Journal of Adolescent Health, 39*, 662–668. doi:10.1016/j.jadohealth.2006.04.024

Elliott, J. E. (1993). Career development with lesbian and gay clients. *The Career Development Quarterly, 41*, 210–226.

Ellis, L., & Ames, M. A. (1987). Neurohormonal functioning and sexual orientation: A theory of homosexuality-heterosexuality. *Psychological Bulletin, 101*, 233–258. doi:10.1037/0033-2909.101.2.233

Fabian, E. S., & Liesener, J. J. (2005). Promoting the career potential of youth with disabilities. In S. D. Brown & R. W. Lent (Eds.), *Career development and counseling: Putting theory and research to work* (pp. 551–572). Hoboken, NJ: Wiley.

Faerden, A., Smith, G., & King, M. (2009). The response of mental health professionals to clients seeking help to change or redirect same-sex sexual orientation. *BMC Psychiatry, 9*(11), 1–8. doi:10.1186/1471-244X-9-11

Falk, P. J. (1989). Lesbian mothers: Psychosocial assumptions in family law. *American Psychologist, 44*, 941–947. doi:10.1037/0003-066X.44.6.941

Fassinger, R. E. (1995). From invisibility to integration: Lesbian identity in the workplace. *The Career Development Quarterly, 44*, 148–167.

Fassinger, R. E. (1996). Notes from the margins: Integrating lesbian experience into the vocational psychology of women. *Journal of Vocational Behavior, 48*, 160–175. doi:10.1006/jvbe.1996.0016

Fassinger, R. E., & Arseneau, J. R. (2007). "I'd rather get wet than be under that umbrella": Differentiating the experiences and identities of lesbian, gay, bisexual, and transgender people. In K. J. Bieschke, R. M. Perez, & K. A. DeBord (Eds.), *Handbook of counseling and psychotherapy with lesbian, gay, bisexual, and transgender clients* (2nd ed., pp. 19–49). Washington, DC: American Psychological Association. doi:10.1037/11482-001

Fredriksen-Goldsen, K. I., Kim, H., Muraco, A., & Mincer, S. (2009). Chronically ill midlife and older lesbians, gay men, and bisexuals and their informal caregivers: The impact of the social context. *Sexuality Research and Social Policy: A Journal of the NSRC, 6*, 52–64. doi:10.1525/srsp.2009.6.4.52

Fulcher, M., Sutfin, E. L., Chan, R. W., Scheib, J. E., & Patterson, C. J. (2006). Lesbian mothers and their children: Findings from the contemporary families study. In A. M. Omoto & H. S. Kurtzman (Eds.), *Sexual orientation and mental health: Examining identity and development in lesbian, gay, and bisexual people* (pp. 281–299). Washington, DC: American Psychological Association. doi:10.1037/11261-014

Fulcher, M., Sutfin, E. L., & Patterson, C. J. (2008). Individual differences in gender development: Associations with parental sexual orientation, attitudes, and division of labor. *Sex Roles, 58*, 330–341. doi:10.1007/s11199-007-9348-4

Garofalo, R., Wolf, R. C., Kessel, S., Palfrey, J., & DuRant, R. H. (1998). The association between health risk behaviors and sexual orientation among a school-based sample of adolescents. *Pediatrics, 101*, 895–902. doi:10.1542/peds.101.5.895

Gartrell, N., Deck, A., Rodas, C., Peyser, H., & Banks, A. (2005). The National Lesbian Family Study 4: Interviews with the 10-year-old children. *American Journal of Orthopsychiatry, 75*, 518–524. doi:10.1037/0002-9432.75.4.518

Gelso, C. J., Fassinger, R., Gomez, M. J., & Latts, M. G. (1995). Countertransference reactions to lesbian clients: The role of homophobia, counselor gender, and countertransference management. *Journal of Counseling Psychology, 42*, 356–364. doi:10.1037/0022-0167.42.3.356

Gianino, M. (2008). Adaptation and transformation: The transition to adoptive parenthood for gay male couples. *Journal of GLBT Family Studies, 4*, 205–243. doi:10.1080/15504280802096872

Goldberg, A. E. (2010). *Lesbian and gay parents and their children: Research on the family life cycle.* Washington, DC: American Psychological Association. doi:10.1037/12055-000

Golombok, S., Perry, B., Burston, A., Murray, C., Mooney-Somers, J., Stevens, M., & Golding, J. (2003). Children with lesbian parents: A community study. *Developmental Psychology, 39*, 20–33. doi:10.1037/0012-1649.39.1.20

Golombok, S., & Tasker, F. (1996). Do parents influence the sexual orientation of their children? Findings from a longitudinal study of lesbian families. *Developmental Psychology, 32*, 3–11. doi:10.1037/0012-1649.32.1.3

Goodman, J. (2009). Special section: Advocacy competence. *Journal of Counseling and Development, 87*, 259.

Greene, B. (1998). Family, ethnic identity, and sexual orientation: African-American lesbians and gay men. In C. J. Patterson & A. R. D'Augelli (Eds.), *Lesbian, gay, and bisexual identities in families: Psychological perspectives* (pp. 40–52). New York, NY: Oxford University Press.

Greene, B. (2007). Delivering ethical psychological services to lesbian, gay, and bisexual clients. In K. J. Bieschke, R. M. Perez, & K. A. DeBord (Eds.), *Handbook of counseling and psychotherapy with lesbian, gay, bisexual, and transgender clients* (2nd ed., pp. 181–199). Washington, DC: American Psychological Association. doi:10.1037/11482-007

Greene, B. (Ed.). (1997). *Ethnic and cultural diversity among lesbians and gay men.* Thousand Oaks, CA: Sage.

Griffin, P. (1992). From hiding out to coming out: Empowering lesbian and gay educators. In K. M. Harbeck (Ed.), *Coming out of the classroom closet* (pp. 167–196). Binghamton, NY: Harrington Park.

Grossman, A. H., D'Augelli, A. R., & Dragowski, E. A. (2005). Caregiving and care receiving among older lesbian, gay, and bisexual adults. *Journal of Gay and Lesbian Social Services: Issues in Practice, Policy and Research, 18*, 15–38.

Grossman, A. H., D'Augelli, A. R., & Hershberger, S. L. (2000). Social support networks of lesbian, gay, and bisexual adults 60 years of age and older. *The Journals of Gerontology. Series B: Psychological Sciences and Social Sciences, 55*, 171–179. doi:10.1093/geronb/55.3.P171

Grossman, A. H., D'Augelli, A. R., & O'Connell, T. (2002). Being lesbian, gay, bisexual and 60 or older in North America. *Journal of Gay and Lesbian Social Services: Issues in Practice, Policy and Research, 13*, 23–40. doi:10.1300/J041v13n04_05

Grov, C., Bimbi, D. S., Nanín, J. E., & Parsons, J. T. (2006). Race, ethnicity, gender, and generational factors associated with the coming-out process among gay, lesbian, and bisexual individuals. *Journal of Sex Research, 43*(2), 115–121. doi:10.1080/00224490609552306

Haber, D. (2009). Gay aging. *Gerontology and Geriatrics Education, 30*, 267–280. doi:10.1080/02701960903133554

Haines, M. E., Erchull, M. J., Liss, M., Turner, D. L., Nelson, J. A., Ramsey, L. R., & Hurt, M. M. (2008). Predictors and effects of self-objectification in lesbians. *Psychology of Women Quarterly, 32*, 181–187. doi:10.1111/j.1471-6402.2008.00422.x

Haldeman, D. C. (1991). Sexual orientation conversion therapy: A scientific examination. In J. Gonsiorek & J. Wienreich (Eds.), *Homosexuality: Research implications for public policy* (pp. 149–160). Newbury Park, CA: Sage.

Haldeman, D. C. (1994). The practice and ethics of sexual orientation conversion therapy. *Journal of Consulting and Clinical Psychology, 62*, 221–227. doi:10.1037/0022-006X.62.2.221

Haldeman, D. C. (1999). The pseudo-science of sexual orientation conversion therapy. *Angles, 4*, 1–4.

Haldeman, D. C. (2002). Gay rights, patient rights: The implications of sexual orientation conversion therapy. *Professional Psychology: Research and Practice, 33*, 260–264. doi:10.1037/0735-7028.33.3.260

Halpert, S. C., Reinhardt, B., & Toohey, M. J. (2007). Affirmative clinical supervision. In K. J. Bieschke, R. M. Perez, & K. A. DeBord (Eds.), *Handbook of counseling and psychotherapy with lesbian, gay, bisexual, and transgender clients* (2nd ed., pp. 341–358). Washington, DC: American Psychological Association. doi:10.1037/11482-014

Hamilton, C. J., & Mahalik, J. R. (2009). Minority stress, masculinity, and social norms predicting gay men's health risk behaviors. *Journal of Counseling Psychology, 56*, 132–141. doi:10.1037/a0014440

Hatzenbuehler, M. L., Keyes, K. M., & Hasin, D. S. (2009). State-level policies and psychiatric morbidity in lesbian, gay, and bisexual populations. *American Journal of Public Health, 99*, 2275–2281. doi:10.2105/AJPH.2008.153510

Hayes, J. A., & Erkis, A. J. (2000). Counselor homophobia, client sexual orientation, and source of client HIV infection as predictors of counselor reactions to clients with HIV. *Journal of Counseling Psychology, 47*, 71–78. doi:10.1037/0022-0167.47.1.71

Hayes, J. A., & Gelso, C. J. (1993). Male counselors' discomfort with gay and HIV-infected clients. *Journal of Counseling Psychology, 40*, 86–93. doi:10.1037/0022-0167.40.1.86

Hein, L. C., & Matthews, A. K. (2010). Reparative therapy: The adolescent, the psych nurse, and the issues. *Journal of Child and Adolescent Psychiatric Nursing, 23*, 29–35. doi:10.1111/j.1744-6171.2009.00214.x

Herek, G. M. (2006). Legal recognition of same-sex relationships in the United States: A social science perspective. *American Psychologist, 61*, 607–621. doi:10.1037/0003-066X.61.6.607

Herek, G. M., Gillis, J. R., & Cogan, J. C. (2009). Internalized stigma among sexual minority adults: Insights from a social psychological perspective. *Journal of Counseling Psychology, 56*, 32–43. doi:10.1037/a0014672

Herek, G. M., Norton, A. T., Allen, T. J., & Sims, C. L. (2010). Demographic, psychological, and social characteristics of self-identified lesbian, gay, and bisexual adults in a US probability sample. *Sexuality Research and Social Policy, 7*(3), 176–200. doi:10.1007/s13178-010-0017-y

Hetherington, C., Hillerbrand, E., & Etringer, B. (1989). Career counseling with gay men: Issues and recommendations for research. *Journal of Counseling and Development, 67*, 452–454.

Holloway, E. L. (1995). *Clinical supervision: A systems approach.* Thousand Oaks, CA: Sage.

Huffman, A. H., Watrous-Rodriguez, K. M., & King, E. B. (2008). Supporting a diverse workforce: What type of support is most meaningful for lesbian and gay employees? *Human Resource Management, 47*, 237–253. doi:10.1002/hrm.20210

Ibañez, G. E., Van Oss Marin, B., Flores, S. A., Millett, G., & Diaz, R. M. (2009). General and gay-related racism experienced by Latino gay men. *Cultural Diversity and Ethnic Minority Psychology, 15*, 215–222. doi:10.1037/a0014613

Israel, T., & Hackett, G. (2004). Counselor education on lesbian, gay, and bisexual issues: Comparing information and attitude exploration. *Counselor Education and Supervision, 43*, 179–191.

Iwasaki, Y., & Ristock, J. L. (2007). The nature of stress experienced by lesbians and gay men. *Anxiety, Stress and Coping: An International Journal, 20*, 299–319. doi:10.1080/10615800701303264

Jamil, O. B., Harper, G. W., & Fernandez, M. I. (2009). Sexual and ethnic identity development among gay-bisexual-questioning (GBQ) male ethnic minority adolescents. *Cultural Diversity and Ethnic Minority Psychology, 15*, 203–214. doi:10.1037/a0014795

Jeltova, I., & Fish, M. C. (2005). Creating school environments response to gay, lesbian, bisexual, and transgender families: Traditional and systemic approaches for consultation. *Journal of Educational and Psychological Consultation, 16*(1–2), 17–33. doi:10.1207/s1532768xjepc161&2_2

Kashubeck-West, S., Szymanski, D. M., & Meyer, J. (2008). Internalized heterosexism: Clinical implications and training considerations. *The Counseling Psychologist, 36*, 615–630. doi:10.1177/0011000007309634

Kilgore, H., Sideman, L., Amin, K., Baca, L., & Bohanske, B. (2005). Psychologists' attitudes and therapeutic approaches toward gay, lesbian, and bisexual issues continue to improve: An update. *Psychotherapy: Theory, Research, and Practice, 42*, 395–400. doi:10.1037/0033-3204.42.3.395

Kimmel, D. C. (2002). Aging and sexual orientation. In B. E. Jones & M. J. Hill (Eds.), *Mental health issues in lesbian, gay, bisexual, and transgender communities* (pp. 17–36). Washington, DC: American Psychiatric Publishing.

Kimmel, D., Rose, T., & David, S. (Eds.). (2006). *Lesbian, gay, bisexual and transgender aging: Research and clinical perspectives.* New York, NY: Columbia University Press.

Kindle, P., & Erich, S. (2005). Perceptions of social support among heterosexual and homosexual adopters. *Families in Society, 86*, 541–546. doi:10.1606/1044-3894.3459

King, M., Semlyen, J., Tai, S. S., Killaspy, H., Osborn, D., Popelyuk, D., & Nazareth, I. (2008). A systematic review of mental disorder, suicide, and deliberate self harm in lesbian, gay and bisexual people. *BMC Psychiatry, 8*(70), 1–17. doi:10.1186/1471-244X-8-70

Kirk, K. M., Bailey, J. M., Dunne, M. P., & Martin, N. G. (2000). Measurement models for sexual orientation in a community twin sample. *Behavior Genetics, 30*, 345–356. doi:10.1023/A:1026557719181

Klein, F., Sepekoff, B., & Wolf, T. J. (1985). Sexual orientation: A multi-variable dynamic process. *Journal of Homosexuality, 11*(1–2), 35–49. doi:10.1300/J082v11n01_04

Korell, S. C., & Lorah, P. (2007). An overview of affirmative psychotherapy and counseling with transgender clients. In K. J. Bieschke, R. M. Perez, & K. A. DeBord (Eds.), *Handbook of counseling and psychotherapy with lesbian, gay, bisexual, and transgender clients* (2nd ed., pp. 271–288). Washington, DC: American Psychological Association. doi:10.1037/11482-011

Kosciw, J. G., Greytak, E., & Diaz, E. (2009). Who, what, where, when, and why: Demographic and ecological factors contributing to hostile school climate for lesbian, gay, bisexual, and transgender youth. *Journal of Youth and Adolescence, 38*, 976–988. doi:10.1007/s10964-009-9412-1

Kruks, G. (1991). Gay and lesbian homeless/street youth: Special issues and concerns. *Journal of Adolescent Health, 12*, 515–518. doi:10.1016/0197-0070(91)90080-6

Kweskin, S. L., & Cook, A. S. (1982). Heterosexual and homosexual mothers' self-described sex-role behavior and ideal sex-role behavior in children. *Sex Roles, 8*, 967–975. doi:10.1007/BF00290021

Lambert, S. (2005). Gay and lesbian families: What we know and where to go from here. *The Family Journal, 13*, 43–51. doi:10.1177/1066480704270150

Lance, T. S., Anderson, M. Z., & Croteau, J. M. (2010). Improving measurement of workplace sexual identity management. *The Career Development Quarterly, 59*, 19–26.

Lev, A. I. (2007). Transgender communities: Developing identity through connection. In K. J. Bieschke, R. M. Perez, & K. A. DeBord (Eds.), *Handbook of counseling and psychotherapy with lesbian, gay, bisexual, and transgender clients* (2nd ed., pp. 147–175). Washington, DC: American Psychological Association. doi:10.1037/11482-006

Levine, M. P., & Leonard, R. (1984). Discrimination against lesbians in the work force. *Signs, 9*, 700–710. doi:10.1086/494094

Levitt, H. M., Ovrebo, E., Anderson-Cleveland, M. B., Leone, C., Jae, Jeong, Y., Arm, J. R., . . . Horne, S. G. (2009). Balancing dangers: GLBT experience in a time of anti-GLBT legislation. *Journal of Counseling Psychology, 56*, 67–81. doi:10.1037/a0012988

Lewis, J., Arnold, M. S., House, R., & Toporek, R. (2002). *Advocacy competencies*. Retrieved from http://www.counseling.org/Resources/Competencies/Advocacy_Competencies.pdf

Lidderdale, M. A., Croteau, J. M., Anderson, M. Z., Tovar-Murray, D., & Davis, J. M. (2007). Building lesbian, gay, and bisexual vocational psychology: A theoretical model of workplace sexual identity management. In K. J. Bieschke, R. M. Perez, & K. A. DeBord (Eds.), *Handbook of counseling and psychotherapy with lesbian, gay, bisexual, and transgender clients* (2nd ed., pp. 245–270). Washington, DC: American Psychological Association. doi:10.1037/11482-010

Liddle, B. J. (1996). Therapist sexual orientation, gender, and counseling practices as they relate to ratings of helpfulness by gay and lesbian clients. *Journal of Counseling Psychology, 43*, 394–401. doi:10.1037/0022-0167.43.4.394

Liddle, B. J. (2007). Mutual bonds: Lesbian women's lives and communities. In K. J. Bieschke, R. M. Perez, & K. A. DeBord (Eds.), *Handbook of counseling and psychotherapy with lesbian, gay, bisexual, and transgender clients* (2nd ed., pp. 51–69). Washington, DC: American Psychological Association. doi:10.1037/11482-002

Liddle, B. J., Luzzo, D. A., Hauenstein, A. L., & Schuck, K. (2004). Construction and validation of the Lesbian, Gay, Bisexual, and Transgendered Climate Inventory. *Journal of Career Assessment, 12*, 33–50. doi:10.1177/1069072703257722

MacCallum, F., & Golombok, S. (2004). Children raised in fatherless families from infancy: A follow-up of children of lesbian and single heterosexual mothers at early adolescence. *Journal of Child Psychology and Psychiatry, 45*, 1407–1419. doi:10.1111/j.1469-7610.2004.00324.x

Mallon, G. P. (2004). *Gay men choosing parenthood*. New York, NY: Columbia University Press.

Masini, B. E., & Barrett, H. A. (2007). Social support as a predictor of psychological and physical well-being and lifestyle in lesbian, gay, and bisexual adults aged 50 and over. *Journal of Gay and Lesbian Social Services: Issues in Practice, Policy and Research, 20*, 91–110.

Matthews, C. R., & Lease, S. H. (2000). Focus on lesbian, gay, and bisexual families. In R. M. Perez, K. A. DeBord, & K. J. Bieschke (Eds.), *Handbook of counseling and psychotherapy with lesbian, gay, and bisexual clients* (pp. 249–273). Washington, DC: American Psychological Association. doi:10.1037/10339-011

Matthews, J. D., & Cramer, E. P. (2006). Envisaging the adoption process to strengthen gay- and lesbian-headed families: Recommendations for adoption professionals. *Child Welfare: Journal of Policy, Practice, and Program, 85*, 317–340.

McCarn, S. R., & Fassinger, R. E. (1996). Revisioning sexual minority identity formation: A new model of lesbian identity and its implications for counseling and research. *The Counseling Psychologist, 24*, 508–534. doi:10.1177/0011000096243011

Meyer, I. H. (1995). Minority stress and mental health in gay men. *Journal of Health and Social Behavior, 36*, 38–56. doi:10.2307/2137286

Meyer, I. H. (2003). Prejudice, social stress, and mental health in lesbian, gay, and bisexual populations: Conceptual issues and research evidence. *Psychological Bulletin, 129*, 674–697. doi:10.1037/0033-2909.129.5.674

Mohr, J., & Fassinger, R. (2000). Measuring dimensions of lesbian and gay male experience. *Measurement and Evaluation in Counseling and Development, 33*, 66–90.

Moradi, B., Mohr, J. J., Worthington, R. L., & Fassinger, R. E. (2009). Counseling psychology research on sexual (orientation) minority issues: Conceptual and methodological challenges and opportunities. *Journal of Counseling Psychology, 56*, 5–22. doi:10.1037/a0014572

Moradi, B., Wiseman, M. C., DeBlaere, C., Goodman, M. B., Sarkees, A., Brewster, M. E., & Huang, Y. (2010). LGB of color and White individuals' perceptions of heterosexist stigma, internalized homophobia, and outness: Comparisons of levels and links. *The Counseling Psychologist, 38*, 397–424. doi:10.1177/0011000009335263

Morgan, K. S., & Brown, L. S. (1991). Lesbian career development, work behavior, and vocational counseling. *The Counseling Psychologist, 19*, 273–291. doi:10.1177/0011000091192013

Morgan, K. S., & Nerison, R. M. (1993). Homosexuality and psychopolitics: An historical overview. *Psychotherapy: Theory, Research, Practice, Training, 30*, 133–140. doi:10.1037/0033-3204.30.1.133

Morrow, D. F. (1996). Coming-out issues for adult lesbians: A group intervention. *Social Work, 41*, 647–656.

Negy, C., & Eisenman, R. (2005). A comparison of African American and White college students' affective and attitudinal reactions to lesbian, gay, and bisexual individuals: An exploratory study. *Journal of Sex Research, 42*, 291–298. doi:10.1080/00224490509552284

O'Neil, M. E., McWhirter, E. H., & Cerezo, A. (2008). Transgender identities and gender variance in vocational psychology: Recommendations for practice, social advocacy, and research. *Journal of Career Development, 34*, 286–308. doi:10.1177/0894845307311251

Orzek, A. M. (1992). Career counseling for the gay and lesbian community. In S. Dworkin & F. Gutierrez (Eds.), *Counseling gay men and lesbians: Journey to the end of the rainbow* (pp. 23–34). Alexandria, VA: American Counseling Association.

Owen, J., Tao, K., & Rodolfa, E. (2010). Microaggressions and women in short-term psychotherapy: Initial evidence. *The Counseling Psychologist, 38*, 923–946. doi:10.1177/0011000010376093

Pachankis, J. E., & Goldfried, M. R. (2004). Clinical issues in working with lesbian, gay, and bisexual clients. *Psychotherapy: Theory, Research, Practice, Training, 41*, 227–246. doi:10.1037/0033-3204.41.3.227

Paige, R. U. (2005). Proceedings of the American Psychological Association, Incorporated for the legislative year 2004: Minutes of the annual meeting of the Council of Representatives. *American Psychologist, 60*, 436–511. doi:10.1037/0003-066X.60.5.436

Parks, C. A., Hughes, T. L., & Matthews, A. K. (2004). Race/ethnicity and sexual orientation: Intersecting identities. *Cultural Diversity and Ethnic Minority Psychology, 10*, 241–254. doi:10.1037/1099-9809.10.3.241

Patterson, C. J. (1995). Families of the lesbian baby boom: Parents' division of labor and children's adjustment. *Developmental Psychology, 31*, 115–123. doi:10.1037/0012-1649.31.1.115

Patterson, C. J. (2006). Children of lesbian and gay parents. *Current Directions in Psychological Science, 15*, 241–244. doi:10.1111/j.1467-8721.2006.00444.x

Patterson, C. J. (2007). Lesbian and gay family issues in the context of changing legal and social policy environments. In K. J. Bieschke, R. M. Perez, & K. A. DeBord (Eds.), *Handbook of counseling and psychotherapy with lesbian, gay, bisexual, and transgender clients* (2nd ed., pp. 359–377). Washington, DC: American Psychological Association. doi:10.1037/11482-015

Patterson, C. J. (2009). Lesbian and gay parents and their children. A social science perspective. In D. A. Hope (Ed.), *Contemporary perspectives on lesbian, gay, and bisexual identities* (pp. 141–182). New York, NY: Springer. doi:10.1007/978-0-387-09556-1_6

Pett, J. (2000). Gay, lesbian and bisexual therapy and its supervision. In D. Dominic & C. Neal (Eds.), *Therapeutic perspectives on working with lesbian, gay and bisexual clients* (pp. 54–72). Buckingham, England: Open University Press.

Pilkington, N. W., & Cantor, J. M. (1996). Perceptions of heterosexual bias in professional psychology programs: A survey of graduate students. *Professional Psychology: Research and Practice, 27*, 604–612. doi:10.1037/0735-7028.27.6.604

Pope, M. (1995). Career interventions for gay and lesbian clients: A synopsis of practice knowledge and research needs. *The Career Development Quarterly, 44*, 191–203.

Pope, M. (1996). Gay and lesbian career counseling: Special career counseling issues. *Journal of Gay and Lesbian Social Services, 4*, 91–106. doi:10.1300/J041v04n04_06

Potoczniak, D. J. (2007). Development of bisexual men's identities and relationships. In K. J. Bieschke, R. M. Perez, & K. A. DeBord (Eds.), *Handbook of counseling and psychotherapy with lesbian, gay, bisexual, and transgender clients* (2nd ed., pp. 119–145). Washington, DC: American Psychological Association. doi:10.1037/11482-005

Quam, J. K., & Whitford, G. S. (1992). Adaptation and age-related expectations among older gay and lesbian adults. *The Gerontologist, 32*, 367–374. doi:10.1093/geront/32.3.367

Ragins, B. R., & Cornwell, J. M. (2001). Pink triangles: Antecedents and consequences of perceived workplace discrimination against gay and lesbian employees. *Journal of Applied Psychology, 86*, 1244–1261. doi:10.1037/0021-9010.86.6.1244

Ragins, B. R., Singh, R., & Cornwell, J. M. (2007). Making the invisible visible: Fear and disclosure of sexual orientation at work. *Journal of Applied Psychology, 92*, 1103–1118. doi:10.1037/0021-9010.92.4.1103

Riggle, E. D. B., Rostosky, S. S., & Horne, S. G. (2010). Psychological distress, well-being, and legal recognition in same-sex couple relationships. *Journal of Family Psychology, 24*, 82–86. doi:10.1037/a0017942

Ritter, K. Y., & Terndrup, A. I. (2002). *Handbook of affirmative psychotherapy with lesbians and gay men*. New York, NY: Guilford Press.

Rivers, I., Poteat, V., & Noret, N. (2008). Victimization, social support, and psychosocial functioning among children of same-sex and opposite-sex couples in the United Kingdom. *Developmental Psychology, 44,* 127–134. doi:10.1037/0012-1649.44.1.127

Rosario, M., Hunter, J., Maguen, S., Gwadz, M., & Smith, R. (2001). The coming-out process and its adaptational and health-related associations among gay, lesbian, and bisexual youths: Stipulations and exploration of a model. *American Journal of Community Psychology, 29,* 113–160. doi:10.1023/A:1005205630978

Rosario, M., Schrimshaw, E. W., & Hunter, J. (2004). Ethnic/racial differences in the coming-out process of lesbian, gay, and bisexual youths: A comparison of sexual identity development over time. *Cultural Diversity and Ethnic Minority Psychology, 10,* 215–228. doi:10.1037/1099-9809.10.3.215

Ross, M. W., Rosser, B. R. S., & Neumaier, E. R. (2008). The relationship of internalized homonegativity to unsafe sexual behavior in HIV-seropositive men who have sex with men. *AIDS Education and Prevention, 20,* 547–557. doi:10.1521/aeap.2008.20.6.547

Rostosky, S. S., & Riggle, E. D. B. (2002). "Out" at work: The relation of actor and partner workplace policy and internalized homophobia to disclosure status. *Journal of Counseling Psychology, 49,* 411–419. doi:10.1037/0022-0167.49.4.411

Russell, S. T. (2006). Substance use and abuse and mental health among sexual-minority youths: Evidence from Add Health. In A. M. Omoto & H. S. Kurtzman (Eds.), *Sexual orientation and mental health: Examining identity and development in lesbian, gay, and bisexual people* (pp. 13–35). Washington, DC: American Psychological Association. doi:10.1037/11261-001

Sánchez, F. J., Westefeld, J. S., Liu, W. M., & Vilain, E. (2010). Masculine gender role conflict and negative feelings about being gay. *Professional Psychology: Research and Practice, 41,* 104–111. doi:10.1037/a0015805

Satcher, J., & Leggett, M. (2007). Homonegativity among professional school counselors: An exploratory study. *Professional School Counseling, 11,* 10–16. doi:10.5330/PSC.n.2010-11.10

Satcher, J., & Schumacker, R. (2009). Predictors of modern homonegativity among professional counselors. *Journal of LGBT Issues in Counseling, 3*(1), 21–36. doi:10.1080/15538600902754452

Savin-Williams, R. C. (1998). Lesbian, gay, and bisexual youths' relationships with their parents. In C. J.

Patterson & A. R. D'Augelli (Eds.), *Lesbian, gay, and bisexual identities in families: Psychological perspectives* (pp. 75–98). New York, NY: Oxford University Press.

Savin-Williams, R. C. (2005). *The new gay teenager.* Cambridge, MA: Harvard University Press.

Sell, R. L. (1997). Defining and measuring sexual orientation: A review. *Archives of Sexual Behavior, 26,* 643–658. doi:10.1023/A:1024528427013

Shively, M. G., Jones, C., & De Cecco, J. P. (1983–1984). Research on sexual orientation: Definitions and methods. *Journal of Homosexuality, 9*(2–3), 127–136. doi:10.1300/J082v09n02_08

Smith, N. G., & Ingram, K. M. (2004). Workplace heterosexism and adjustment among lesbian, gay, and bisexual individuals: The role of unsupportive social interactions. *Journal of Counseling Psychology, 51,* 57–67. doi:10.1037/0022-0167.51.1.57

Stevenson, M. R. (2007). Public policy, mental health, and lesbian, gay, bisexual, and transgender clients. In K. J. Bieschke, R. M. Perez, & K. A. DeBord (Eds.), *Handbook of counseling and psychotherapy with lesbian, gay, bisexual, and transgender clients* (2nd ed., pp. 379–397). Washington, DC: American Psychological Association. doi:10.1037/11482-016

Stoltenberg, C., & Delworth, U. (1987). *Supervising counselors and therapists.* San Francisco, CA: Jossey-Bass.

Szymanski, D. M. (2004). Relations among dimensions of feminism and internalized heterosexism in lesbians and bisexual women. *Sex Roles, 51*(3–4), 145–159. doi:10.1023/B:SERS.0000037759.33014.55

Szymanski, D. M., & Carr, E. R. (2008). The roles of gender role conflict and internalized heterosexism in gay and bisexual men's psychological distress: Testing two mediation models. *Psychology of Men and Masculinity, 9,* 40–54. doi:10.1037/1524-9220.9.1.40

Szymanski, D. M., & Gupta, A. (2009). Examining the relationship between multiple internalized oppressions and African American lesbian, gay, bisexual, and questioning persons' self-esteem and psychological distress. *Journal of Counseling Psychology, 56,* 110–118. doi:10.1037/a0013317

Szymanski, D. M., & Kashubeck-West, S. (2008). Mediators of the relationship between internalized oppressions and lesbian and bisexual women's psychological distress. *The Counseling Psychologist, 36,* 575–594. doi:10.1177/0011000007309490

Tasker, F., & Golombok, S. (1997). *Growing up in a lesbian family: Effects on child development.* New York, NY: Guilford Press.

Throckmorton, W., & Welton, G. (2005). Counseling practices as they relate to ratings of helpfulness by consumers of sexual reorientation therapy. *Journal of Psychology and Christianity, 24,* 332–342.

Toporek, R. L., Gerstein, L. H., Fouad, N. A., Roysircar, G., & Israel, T. (2006). *Handbook for social justice in counseling psychology: Leadership, vision, and action.* Thousand Oaks, CA: Sage.

Tozer, E. E., & Hayes, J. A. (2004). Why do individuals seek conversion therapy? The role of religiosity, internalized homonegativity, and identity development. *The Counseling Psychologist, 32,* 716–740. doi:10.1177/0011000004267563

Troiden, R. R. (1979). Becoming homosexual: A model of gay identity acquisition. *Psychiatry: Journal for the Study of Interpersonal Processes, 42,* 362–373.

Troiden, R. R. (1989). The formation of homosexual identities. *Journal of Homosexuality, 17*(1–2), 43–73. doi:10.1300/J082v17n01_02

Vanfraussen, K., Ponjaert-Kristoffersen, I., & Brewaeys, A. (2002). What does it mean for youngsters to grow up in a lesbian family created by means of donor insemination? *Journal of Reproductive and Infant Psychology, 20,* 237–252. doi:10.1080/0264683021000033165

Waldo, C. R. (1999). Working in a majority context: A structural model of heterosexism as minority stress in the workplace. *Journal of Counseling Psychology, 46,* 218–232. doi:10.1037/0022-0167.46.2.218

Walters, K. L., & Old Person, R. L. (2008). Lesbians, gays, bisexuals, and transgender people of color: Reconciling divided selves and communities. In G. P. Mallon (Ed.), *Social work practice with lesbian, gay, bisexual, and transgender people* (2nd ed., pp. 41–68). New York, NY: Routledge.

Wardle, L. D. (1997). The potential impact of homosexual parenting of children. *University of Illinois Law Review, 833,* 1–9.

Weinberg, M. S., Williams, C. J., & Pryor, D. W. (1994). *Dual attraction: Understanding bisexuality.* New York, NY: Oxford University Press.

Wiseman, M. C., & Moradi, B. (2010). Body image and eating disorder symptoms in sexual minority men: A test and extension of objectification theory. *Journal of Counseling Psychology, 57,* 154–166. doi:10.1037/a0018937

Worthington, R. L., McCrary, S. I., & Howard, K. A. (1998). Becoming an LGBT affirmative career adviser: Guidelines for faculty, staff, and administrators. In R. Sanlo (Ed.), *Working with lesbian, gay, bisexual, and transgender college students: A handbook for faculty and administrators* (pp. 135–143). Westport, CT: Greenwood.

Worthington, R. L., & Reynolds, A. L. (2009). Within-group differences in sexual orientation and identity. *Journal of Counseling Psychology, 56,* 44–55. doi:10.1037/a0013498

COUNSELING PSYCHOLOGY THEORY AND RESEARCH ON RACE AND ETHNICITY: IMPLICATIONS FOR A PSYCHOLOGICAL SCIENCE OF DIVERSITY

Stephen M. Quintana, Aaronson Chew, and Gwynneth Schell

Research and theory about race and ethnicity are central to the field of counseling psychology. The profession is known for its visionary scholars being among the first to theorize in a systematic way about the psychological implications of race and ethnicity. This chapter provides a synthesis of recent research, articulating a framework for understanding the nature of this work. As is customary, we begin with definitions of key terms. Next, we identify some critical dimensions that underlie much of the counseling psychology theory and research on race and ethnicity. Like the common factors approach to psychotherapy research, we identify common underlying factors associated with theories about race and ethnicity. These broad principles form the basis for a psychological science of diversity.

RACE VERSUS ETHNICITY: OVERLAP AND DISTINCTIVENESS

Much ado has been made in counseling psychology about the differences between ethnicity and race, but much of the debate has focused on definitional issues, or how the terms *race* and *ethnicity* should be defined, and thereby trespasses into allied disciplines of sociology and anthropology. Although these academic debates are engaging, our concern is that they distract from issues that psychologists, especially counseling psychologists, are trained to examine. Phinney (1996) sought to clarify the two terms by defining *race and racial groups* to be a

subset of *ethnicity and ethnic groups* and suggesting ethnic groupings would represent cultural features, identification with an ethnic group, and experiences with a minority status. Helms and Talleyrand (1997) rejected Phinney's definition, suggesting that race and ethnicity should be considered different categories and recommending that the minority group component be taken out of the definition of ethnicity, leaving it restricted to cultural features and immigrant status. They recommended an alternative definitional scheme in which the overlap between race and ethnicity would be eliminated by removing from ethnicity the connotations associated with minority status; consequently, only racial groups would involve some social stigmatization. Despite these attempts to provide explicit definitions, ongoing concern with counseling psychology researchers' use of these terms led to a special issue of the *Journal of Counseling Psychology* (Ponterotto & Mallinckrodt, 2007). Within official policy of the American Psychological Association (APA; 2003), *race* is explicitly defined as a socially constructed construct based on how others classify a group of persons on the basis of racial phenotypes, whereas *ethnicity* is defined by how members of the group consider themselves and their acceptance of and affiliation with cultural traditions, values, and practices. Consequently, there seems to be overlap among these terms when a group that has been racially stigmatized comes to identify with being a member of the stigmatized group, develops a sense

DOI: 10.1037/13754-017
APA Handbook of Counseling Psychology: Vol. 1. Theories, Research, and Methods, Nadya A. Fouad (Editor-in-Chief)

of belonging to the group, and affiliates with the cultural traditions of the group. The attempts within counseling psychology and, to some extent, within psychology to separate these terms ignores the larger context, particularly given that the U.S. government directs specific definitions be employed and used for census purposes (e.g., Office of Management and Budget, 1997). The United Nations has also formulated definitions associated with race and ethnicity (United Nations Education, Scientific, and Cultural Organization, 1952), stating that *ethnicity* should be used broadly to refer to the groups we consider ethnic and racial groups. Similarly, the official statement by the American Anthropological Association (1997) recommends that the term *race* be removed from official descriptions of persons and that *ethnicity* or *ethnic groups* be used instead to refer more generally to groups. The American Sociological Association's (2003) official statement suggested that it may be valuable to classify and collect data by putative racial groups, but it tended to use the two terms as having similar connotations related to stigmatization and status within society.

Counseling psychology has less professional standing, relative to these organizations, to assert and implement alternative definitions of race and ethnicity. Nonetheless, as psychologists, we may have an important perspective to share with other organizations if our research could demonstrate that there are important differences in psychological functioning between race and ethnicity. That is, moving beyond definitional issues, does extant research identify important differences in the psychological sequelae associated with race when compared with ethnicity? Alternatively, does identification with a racial group involve different psychological processes than identification with an ethnic group? As another example, does discrimination on the basis of racial prejudice have a different effect than discrimination on the basis of ethnic prejudice? In other words, are there some essential differences between ethnic and racial phenomena in the psychological processes associated with these phenomena? By essential differences, we mean that there would be psychological implications for racial differences that would not be involved in ethnic differences. If

research detects that different psychological functioning is associated with racial groups that are not present for ethnic groups, then counseling psychology may have a stronger position with which to lobby for particular definitions. Fortunately, the field has amassed considerable data to answer these questions.

To begin, research suggests considerable overlap between ethnic and racial groups using a number of sociological indexes. For example, on the basis of U.S. Census Bureau (2011) data, although there are significant differences in education attainment in the United States between some racial groups (e.g., White vs. African American), the difference between other racial groups (White vs. Asian American) is smaller than differences between some ethnic groups (Anglos vs. Latinos), and the academic attainment rate for a racial group (African Americans) is comparable to that for an ethnic group (Latinos). Similar patterns can be observed on the basis of other sociological markers, such as health disparities (U.S. Department of Health and Human Services, 2003) or incarceration rates (Bureau of Justice Statistics, 2009), which reflect similar trends in the magnitude of differences associated with race versus ethnicity.

Consequently, there is considerable overlap, using sociological indexes, between ethnic and racial groups. These patterns are better understood as reflecting sociological processes rather than some essential difference between ethnic and racial groups. Critical sociological processes include the social distance between racial or ethnic groups in a society, which are partly responsible for racial and ethnic disparities in educational achievement (White, Kim, & Glick, 2005). Considering the psychological implications of some of these sociological processes, we find considerable overlap. Moreover, even when there is evidence for differences associated with racial differences relative to ethnic differences, research suggests that the differences are in magnitude not in different kinds of psychological function. For example, in comparable contexts, African Americans perceive more discrimination than Latinos, but the relationship between perceived discrimination and ethnic or racial identity development was not different: For both groups, the amount of discrimination, whether it was racial or ethnic, predicted similar trends in racial or ethnic identity development (Pahl & Way, 2006). Furthermore, considerable psychological research indicates there is similarity in psychological processes associated with identification with racial group and with ethnic groups. To illustrate, research with Phinney's (1992) multigroup ethnic identity measure (MEIM) allows participants to respond to items on the basis of their membership in ethnic or racial groups or even on the basis of what would be considered cultural groups. Data from the MEIM are combined across scores reflecting ethnic identity and racial identity—when group differences are observed, the differences are mean differences in the identification with a group, but the relationships between the MEIM scores and criterion variables such as self-esteem tend to be similar across ethnic and racial groups, with the exception of White groups (Smith & Silva, 2011). Similarly, Fuligni, Witkow, and Garcia (2005) showed that the psychological investment in identifying with an ethnic or racial label was more important than if the labels were ethnic or racial in nature when predicting psychological adjustment.

Hence, empirical research suggests considerable overlap among ethnic and racial groups and among the psychological implications of processes, such as discrimination, when the process is focused on ethnic or racial issues (e.g., racial discrimination or ethnic discrimination). When differences between race and ethnicity manifest, they tend to be associated with differences in magnitude related to underlying processes (e.g., social distance, investment in a group identification) but not with differences in the functioning of psychological processes. Consequently, although there are important differences between ethnic and racial groups on the basis of demographic considerations (e.g., racial or national region), there is considerable overlap in sociological processes associated with race and ethnicity, and these differences are often not associated with differences in the kind of psychological functioning associated with ethnic versus racial group differences.

The consensus of major theoreticians is moving toward integrating ethnicity and race. Like many researchers in developmental psychology, Phinney

(1996) has long held that racial groups are a subset of the larger category of ethnic groups, and her most recent writings do not appear to have significantly modified that position. Helms and Talleyrand (1997) suggested coining a new term, *sociorace*, to refer to all those groups that experience ethnic or racial stigmatization. Cross and Cross (2008) suggested that theoreticians and researchers appear to be imposing categorical differences onto race and ethnicity that do not fit participants' subjective experiences of their sociocultural identifications. Instead, Cross and Cross advised the field to investigate cultural-ethnic-racial identities rather than racial identities.

When attempting to understand the psychological implications of racial group or ethnic group membership, we need to focus not on the demographic nature of the groups per se, but on the critical sociological processes that are associated with the specific ethnic and racial groups of interest. The field would be more productive in examining the underlying psychological factors associated with race and ethnicity than attempting to redefine concepts that have been clearly defined by those professions more closely focused on those concepts.

Consequently, we use ethnicity and race to refer to demographic markers, reflecting racial or national origin, to correspond to the how the data are tracked by the U.S. Census and to be generally consistent with how those terms are used in official statements proffered by the disciplines of anthropology and sociology. We recognize that on the basis of sociological and psychological processes, the terms could be used somewhat interchangeably given the overlap in functioning for ethnic and racial groups.

DIMENSIONS UNDERLYING RACE AND ETHNICITY

The foregoing discussion highlights the value of identifying dimensions that underlie demographic, sociological, and psychological constructs. To illustrate, when conceptualizing observed differences in, for example, rates of utilization for counseling services between White and African Americans, it is important to understand which underlying dimensions are responsible for differences in utilization rates. We posit two critical dimensions as underlying much of the counseling research on race and ethnicity: cultural orientations and racialization processes. By *cultural orientations*, we refer to enculturation to heritage culture, acculturation to other cultural groups, and identifications with cultural groups. By *racialization*, we refer to those processes that reflect and maintain the racial stratification of a society, which includes bias, stigmatization, and discrimination and can include intergroup relations (e.g., discrimination) and intragroup or intrapsychic dynamics (e.g., internalized racism) and can refer to the process of imposing disadvantage onto a group (e.g., stigmatization or discrimination) or assuming advantage or privilege that legitimize inequities across groups. Importantly, both cultural orientation and racialization processes influence the psychological functioning of all racial and ethnic groups such that differences between ethnic groups reflect both racialization and cultural orientations; analogously, differences between racial groups also reflect different cultural orientations and racialization processes.

To illustrate, in the previous example, African Americans may underutilize counseling services, relative to Whites, on the basis of cultural orientations related to differences in levels of cultural congruity with extant counseling services. Alternatively, the legacy of racial oppression as well as contemporary racial microaggressions (D. W. Sue, 2010) may manifest in counseling services (e.g., racial attitudes of counselors) and pose a barrier to fuller utilization of counseling by African Americans. By probing the underlying dimensions of racial and ethnic groups, we can build a more explanatory, less descriptive science of ethnic and racial diversity and also implicate important practices, such as modifying counseling to be more culturally congruent or reducing African Americans' exposure to microaggressions during counseling. Our review focuses, where possible, on the relative contribution of these underlying dimensions to the observed patterns associated with ethnic or racial groups.

To elaborate on the brief definition, by *cultural orientations* we refer broadly to the sequelae of acculturation and enculturation processes, with *acculturation* being associated with exposure to and socialization by a different cultural orientation and *enculturation* being associated with socialization within a cultural group (i.e., by members of one's own cultural differences). A person's cultural socialization represents a complex mix of acculturation and enculturation processes and results in a confluence of multiple cultural orientations. The dimensions underlying these cultural orientations can be divided further into cultural practices, values, and identification (Schwartz, Unger, Zamboanga, & Szapocznik, 2010). Gross differences in cultural orientations are sometimes drawn between collectivism and individualism, and there are measures dedicated to index Asian (Asian Cultural Values; B. K. Kim, Atkinson, & Yang, 1999), Latino (Acculturation Rating Scale for Mexican Americans–II [ARSMA-II]; Cuéllar, Arnold, & Maldonado, 1995), African American (Measurement of Acculturation Strategies for People of African Descent [MASPAD]; Obasi & Leong, 2010) and American Indian (Living in Two Worlds; LaFromboise, 1999) cultural orientations, which are differentiated from the cultural orientations associated with Caucasian, Anglo, White, or European Americans (European American Values Scale for Asian Americans–Revised [EAVS-AA]; Wolfe, Yang, Wong, & Atkinson, 2001).

Fascinating research suggests that there are different neural processes associated with different cultural orientations. For example, Telzer, Masten, Berkman, Lieberman, and Fuligni (2010) found different levels of neural activity associated with pleasure for Latino children who sacrificed individual reward for the good of the family, whereas White children evidenced greater pleasure when they chose personal reward over sacrificing for their families. Kitayama and Tompson (2010) have provided a broader review of the neurological foundation for different cultural orientations.

Cultural orientations are an important underlying factor in research on ethnicity and race because of the cultural embedding of dominant culture into psychological services and contexts (e.g., schools, work settings). Ethnic and racial minority groups may react to the level of cultural incongruity for them in counseling services and in their adjustment to their sociocultural contexts. Some of the variations reflecting different cultural orientations, such as the education needs of Latino university students (e.g., Gloria & Hird, 1999), may be inconsistent with dominant values within predominately White institutions. A pernicious challenge in the field of counseling psychology is the embedding of dominant cultural values and orientations into psychological theories. To understand the functioning of the ethnic and racial groups of interest often requires examining alternatives to these mainstream theories.

Importantly, many of the variations in cultural orientations reflect the sequelae of second culture acquisition processes or the consequences of being exposed to cultural orientations that are different from their culture of origin (see also LaFromboise, Coleman, & Gerton, 1993). There are several variations in how intercultural contact leads to second culture acquisition. For example, Portes and Rumbaut (2006) described Latinos' reactions to pressure to assimilate by developing a reactive identification with one's own ethnic group, in which there is a particularly strong ethnic identification in responses to cultural pressures to assimilate.

The second underlying dimension critical to understanding research on race and ethnicity is the racialization process. By racialization processes, we note that the ethnic and racial groups are not only marked by differences in cultural orientations but also by the psychological implications of ethnic and racial stigmatization associated with ethnic or racial group membership. These processes include the ethnic or racial discrimination they experience (D. W. Sue, 2010) as well as social identity processes (Tajfel & Turner, 1986) associated with identification with a socially stigmatized group. African, Asian, Latino, and Native American groups in the United States are subject to prejudice, discrimination, and bias. Social psychological theory and research demonstrate that being stigmatized has important implications for psychological functioning, ranging from behavioral reactions to the health consequences of stress that result from the stigmatization (Carter, 2007). In addition to the direct impact of discrimination, there are important psychological consequences of identifying with a stigmatized ethnic or racial group (Tajfel & Turner, 1986). These consequences include the potential costs to the person's personal

and collective self-esteem (e.g., Crocker & Major, 1989). Social psychological principles applied to the racialization of groups imply that there are critical variables regarding the way in which the person identifies with the stigmatized group. These variables include the salience and centrality of group membership (Sellers et al., 1998) and intensification of attitudes toward in-group and out-group members (e.g., Cross, 1995). Racial identity models (Cross, 1971; Helms, 1995) have articulated several of the important consequences of identifying with a group that is racially stigmatized.

We next review counseling psychology research associated with race and ethnicity and attempt to identify which underlying processes may mediate the effect of differences in ethnic and racial group membership on psychological outcomes. First, however, we need to consider some critical confounds in research putatively investigating race and ethnicity. The most critical confounds include social class and immigrant status. Racial and ethnic groups differ on the basis of the cultural and racialization processes described thus far but also on the basis of social class and immigrant status. Differences among ethnic or racial groups may be due to their group membership or related to the confounding of ethnic and racial status with social class or immigrant status. Hence, many ethnic or racial differences observed in psychological research may reflect differences in social class more so than in cultural characteristics or in experience of racial oppression. We attempt to identify the factors responsible for ethnic or racial differences that are associated with social class differences and separate those from the effects associated more closely with ethnic or racial identifications or cultural orientations.

Finally, immigrant status is often confounded with ethnic and racial status. Some processes attributed to ethnic groups may be associated with immigrant status or generational level. For example, valuing of education, commitment to familism, and other dimensions vary across race and ethnicity, but when immigrant status is controlled, some ethnic and racial differences disappear (e.g., Tseng, 2006). That is, Tseng found strong generation status effects (first vs. second vs. third generation) across African,

Latino, and Asian descent groups in preferring math and science content. Elsewhere, Tseng (2004) found that generation and immigrant status mediated many of the observed ethnic differences in academic motivation and family independence among Asian, African, and Latino descent college students. There may be protective factors associated specifically with immigrant status leading to an *immigrant paradox* (Schwartz et al., 2010). That is, immigrants may have better health outcomes despite being exposed to mundane stressors as well as to acculturative stress, and this should be considered when attempting to account for ethnic and racial group differences, particularly when ethnic group is confounded with immigrant status. Again, we work to identify the role of immigrant status, the immigrant paradox, and the more general role of generational status in accounting for ethnic and racial group differences.

ETHNIC AND RACIAL IDENTITY THEORY AND RESEARCH

Counseling psychologists and those closely aligned with the field have made seminal contributions to the field of psychology through their scholarship on racial identity. The genius underlying racial identity theory is that it provided one of the first means to explore within-group variability for racial minorities (Cross, 1971; Thomas, 1971). Previously, the literature treated ethnic and racial minority groups as if they were monolithic, implicitly assuming that members within each group had similar attitudes, values, and other psychological characteristics. Conversely, racial identity models provided heuristics for examining psychological processes that underlie demographic status, which is a critical milestone in the development of a diversity science within counseling psychology. To explain using Bronfenbrenner's (1979) ecological model, racial identity models provided a more proximal explanation of the distal factor of racial group membership in accounting for racial differences as well as differences within race. That is, racial identity dimensions are believed to mediate the effect of racial group membership on psychological characteristics such as attitudes toward help seeking. To better understand the mechanisms by which racial identity variables

influence adjustment, it is instructional to survey the dimensions underlying different models of racial and ethnic identity.

Cross's (1971) and Helms's (1995) versions of racial identity were focused on African Americans and articulated originally a model of development that progressed toward increasing (a) awareness and then critical consciousness of race and racism, (b) personal identification with a racial reference group, (c) positive orientation toward racial group membership, and (d) resolution of racial identity exploration. The racial identity models were anchored by a putative progression trajectory of racial ideologies ranging from assimilation to White orientations to internalizations involving Black nationalism or multicultural inclusiveness (Vandiver, Cross, Worrell, & Fhagen-Smith, 2002). These models and the development of respective instrumentation illustrate the evolution of diversity science progressing through theory creation, instrumentation, pruning of measures, and a reconceptualization of old theories to engender new theories.

For example, Phinney (1989, 1992) proposed her model of ethnic identity, which focused on (a) sense of attachment, affiliation, and belongingness to an ethnic culture and (b) searching for and a commitment to ethnic identity. In contrast, Cross's (1971) and Helms's (1995) models were explicitly focused on the sequelae of racialization processes (exposure to racism, identification with a stigmatized in-group) but included components of enculturation in African cultural orientations and acculturation to White norms. Furthermore, as Helms has pointed out, Phinney's ethnic identity measure does not address directly the stigmatization or racialization of ethnic groups. Intriguingly, despite the absence of content in Phinney's measure of ethnic identity focused on discrimination or bias, research finds that ethnic identity exploration is stimulated by exposure to discrimination (for review, see Quintana, 2007). The finding that ethnic identity, measured without reference to specific racialization processes, is empirically associated with discrimination further reinforces our point regarding the inability to separate into distinct domains racial from ethnic identity.

Along similar lines, Quintana (1998) has proposed and evaluated a model of ethnic perspective-taking that identifies the cognition that underlies ethnic and racial identity development. His model charts development from early childhood through adolescence and is compatible with the major features of ethnic and racial identity development models. Phinney's (1989) and Quintana's (1998) models are grounded in theories of normative development, and these models provide important linkage between normative development and development that occurs in response to cultural socialization and racialization processes. The nature and rhythm of development for children's perspective-taking ability follows the same pattern across ethnic and racial groups, further reinforcing our notion that similar psychological processes underlie demographic differences associated with ethnic and racial status.

The trend in recent research on ethnic and racial identity has been to expand the number of underlying dimensions. For example, Umaña-Taylor and Fine (2004) proposed a model specific to Latinos that replicated and extended Phinney's (1989) model with separate dimensions of ethnic identity affirmation, exploration, and commitment. Sellers, Smith, Shelton, Rowley, and Chavous (1998) proposed the Multidimensional Inventory of Black Identity, which articulates four dimensions within African American racial identity: salience, centrality, regard (i.e., public and private), and ideology (i.e., nationalist, oppressed minority, assimilationist, or humanist)—we believe that these dimensions appear to be underlying most forms of ethnic and racial identity.

First, most models of ethnic or racial identity involve dimensions of affective orientation (Umaña-Taylor & Fine, 2004), ranging from an internalization or acceptance of negative ethnic stereotypes (e.g., preencounter, negative private regard) to a positive reorientation toward the stigmatized ethnic or racial group (e.g., positive private regard, affirmation, immersion). The affective dimension is consistent with social identity theory (Tajfel & Turner, 1986), which focuses on the connection between individual and collective self-esteem on the basis of one's identification with an ethnic or racial group

and that group's relative status in society and personally. Although racial identity theorists had supposed that those in early stages of racial identity development, before their developing critical consciousness about their stigmatization, would be self-hating and self-loathing, these predictions have been contradicted by empirical research (e.g., Crocker & Major, 1989; Cross, 1995; Oyserman, Coon, & Kemmelmeier, 2002).

Intriguingly, research seems to suggest that children of color may be relatively aschematic with respect to socially identifying with their ethnic or racial status, whereas White children appear to have cognitive schemas for race. That is, young White children appear to identify socially with their racial group, as evidenced by their elevated levels, relative to children of color, of (a) ethnocentrism, (b) negative evaluation of members of other racial groups and generally, and (c) positive bias toward other White children. In contrast, young children of color appear to lack this ethnocentric bias (for a review, see Quintana & Chavez, in press). This pattern contradicts prevalent notions that Whites are unaware of their racial status. Although rarely does anyone ask, "why are all the White kids sitting together in the cafeteria," White children tend to be more socially segregated, reflecting self-segregation in elementary school, whereas children from other racial groups are more egalitarian in the social relations and attitudes (for a review relative to Latino children see Quintana, 2010). Banks (1976) noted in reinterpreting the famous Clark and Clark (1939) doll study that the findings indicated not that the Black children had a negative view toward their own racial group but that White children's racial self-esteem seemed to be particularly elevated or positive.

Later in childhood and early adolescence, children of color develop more explicitly positive identifications and affiliations toward their ethnic or racial group and seem to develop positive bias toward their own reference group orientation, which in effect, closes the gap between their own racial attitudes and the racial attitudes of White children. Hence, the socialization of young White children provides ample support for developing affective schema about their racial group but not for most children of color raised in U.S. society. Clearly, the affective dimension is critical to development of racial identifications and, later in childhood, to racial identity.

The second dimension underlying most models of ethnic and racial identity is the development of psychological and interpersonal connections (e.g., immersion, belongingness) to the person's ethnic or racial reference group, which is consistent with sociological processes associated with the tendency for members of ethnic or racial groups to affiliate socially with each other. That is, one of the strongest predictors of acculturation status is the social affiliation with same race and other race persons (see Cuéllar et al., 1995). Ethnic and racial identity models reflect the outcome of enculturation or socialization processes cultivating strong attachments to an in-group, relative to out-group affiliations. Umaña-Taylor, Alfaro, Bámaca, and Guimond (2009) found that familial ethnic socialization, the type of socialization that encourages the learning of the values and behaviors of one's cultural heritage, was positively related to ethnic identity achievement as well as predicted future levels of ethnic identity exploration, resolution, and affirmation (Umaña-Taylor & Fine, 2004; Umaña-Taylor & Guimond, 2010). Other findings have demonstrated a positive connection between parents' ethnic socialization practices and youth's ethnic identities (Hughes et al., 2008; Knight et al., 1993; Umaña-Taylor, Alfaro, et al., 2009). The prevalent socialization strategy used across ethnic and racial groups is socialization toward equality, instilling the belief that everyone, regardless of ethnic or racial group should be treated equally, relative to other groups (Hughes et al., 2008). Cultural socialization, instilling pride in one's ethnic culture, was reported more frequently than parents' preparing children for discrimination or promoting mistrust in other ethnic groups. Interestingly, in their sample, Hughes et al. (2008) found that Chinese parents promoted more cultural mistrust in children than parents of other children, suggesting the Chinese parents socialize their children more strongly regarding with whom their children should connect and whom to avoid.

Contextual factors also account for the development of psychological and social connections to adolescents' ethnic and racial group, probably because of the relative exposure to enculturation and acculturation that occurs in sociocultural contexts. Some scholars identify multicultural communities as encouraging ethnic identification because interethnic contact encourages reflection on one's own ethnicity (e.g., Matsunaga et al., 2010) and creates salience and meaning of one's ethnic identity (Umaña-Taylor & Shin, 2007). Furthermore, an increase in the proportion of same-ethnic peers was also related to ethnic exploration as ethnic group exploration is a joint process that occurs in relationships (Kiang, Witkow, Baldelomar, & Fuligni, 2010; Kiang, Yip, Gonzales-Backen, Witkow, & Fuligni, 2006). Thus, a greater proportion of same-ethnic peer relationships is predictive of ethnic identity development. Ethnic identity exploration may be stimulated during immigration because of the youth being labeled by the host culture as a racial minority (Roehling, Jarvis, Sprik, & Campbell, 2010). This suggests that ethnic identity develops in the context of others' cultural and social orientations toward the immigrant's heritage culture (Matsunaga et al., 2010). Taken together, ethnic and racial identity develops in response to important sociological features of the interpersonal context of socialization.

The third main dimension of ethnic and racial identity models involves exploration and commitment to racial and ethnic groups, which parallels developmental models of identity formation (e.g., Erikson, 1968; Marcia, 1966). Quintana (2007) reviewed the research evaluating the developmental assumptions underlying ethnic and racial identity models. In regards to the development of racial and ethnic identity, researchers have found an increase in racial and ethnic identity searching during middle adolescence (French, Seidman, Allen, & Aber, 2000, 2006), noting that many encounter experiences occur during this developmental period (Umaña-Taylor & Guimond, 2010). Moreover, there is a normative increase in ethnic identity exploration—although not the expected crisis in identity—through early to mid-adolescence, and there is a normative progression toward identity achievement through adolescence and early adulthood (see Quintana, 2007). Charmaraman and Grossman (2010) found high levels of pride, positive regard, and appreciation for one's racial or ethnic group in a sample of 923 high school students; however, by college, Syed, Azmitia, and Phinney (2007) found no significant changes in ethnic identity across the span of a year, suggesting that normative development of ethnic and racial identity peaks in middle adolescence and plateaus in late adolescence. Hence, ethnic and racial identity involves the confluence of social psychological, sociological, and developmental processes.

An explicit dimension of racial identity models, but not most ethnic identity models, is the role of discrimination in identity development. The variations in sociocultural contexts described above reflect different levels of acculturation and enculturation but when the cultural groups represent different statuses in society, ethnic or racial bias and discrimination may manifest. Indeed, early models indicated that racial identity development is stimulated by encounter experiences (Cross, 1971, 1995; Helms, 1995). D. W. Sue (2010) used the term *microaggressions* to label and investigate these subtle, pernicious assertions of ethnic or racial dominance on racial and ethnic minority groups. Quintana's (2007) review of the literature found support for the expectation (e.g., Cross, 1971) that discrimination triggers ethnic and racial identity exploration and that advanced levels of racial identity development were associated with greater self-reports of racism. Importantly, the connection between discrimination and later racial identity scores was stronger than the reverse, suggesting that discrimination promotes racial identity exploration and that racial identity development increases sensitivity toward racism, but that the connection between racism and later identity development is stronger than vice versa (Pahl & Way, 2006). Consequently, it seems as if adolescence is a time for racial identity development to be elicited by exposure to inter-racial conflict.

How should we understand these normative increases in ethnic and racial identity development during adolescence? These developmental trends seem to be connected to two other normative forms of development. First, peer group dynamics and cliques are known to form and intensify during this same developmental epoch, with strong in-group

and out-group dynamics (see Selman, 1979). These changes in ethnic and racial identity development mirror this intensification of identification with an in-group and stigmatization of out-groups. Furthermore, formation of peer groups along ethnic and racial lines increases. Consequently, to some extent, adolescents appear to recreate and, sometimes, exaggerate the social divisions reflective of adult society. Hence, the intensification of peer dynamics typical of adolescence corresponds to the growth in ethnic and racial identity exploration and commitment.

A second normative process during adolescence that corresponds to this increased exploration and commitment to ethnic and racial identity is adolescents' social cognitive development. Quintana (1998) has shown that the main areas of expansion in adolescents' ethnic cognition are (a) understanding and detecting social discrimination and (b) formation of peer groups and dynamics among groups (Quintana, 1998). These advances in ethnic cognition allow the youth to construe psychologically the pervasiveness of how stigmatization is personally relevant. That is, youths become more conscious of group-based forms of stigmatization in which they need not be the direct target of stigmatization. Stigmatization that targets their ethnic group is now understood by adolescents as having personal relevance for them as individual members of that ethnic group. Moreover, there is a merging of the personal sense of self with the ethnic group, as described by Cross (1995). These forms of ethnic cognition have been empirically connected to ethnic identity development (Quintana et al., 1999). When taken together, the research suggests that the racialization process, or the ethnic and racial stigmatization, of adolescents seems to trigger the growth in ethnic and racial identity during mid-adolescence. If stigmatization promotes the exploration and growth of ethnic and racial identity during mid-adolescence, then we would not expect those who do not experience the same stigmatization to develop their identity along similar lines, such as White or other youth who are members of ethnic or racial groups that have higher social status in larger society.

We have discussed the precursors and nature of ethnic and racial identity formation. The raison d'être for our field's focus on ethnic and racial identities is their implications for psychological development and adjustment. Extensive research has indicated that having high scores on ethnic or racial identity measures is associated with psychological adjustment (e.g., Phinney, 1992; Quintana, 2007; Seaton et al., 2006; Yip et al., 2006). Thus, pride and regard for one's cultural heritage have been associated with psychological adjustment (Settles, Navarrete, Pagano, Abdou, & Sidanius, 2010; Utsey, Hook, Fischer, & Belvet, 2008). Research has shown that having more positive ethnic or racial identity or demonstrating high levels of ethnic or racial identity development is associated with positive adjustment. For example, Smith and Silva (2011) conducted a meta-analysis of 184 studies investigating ethnic identity research and indexes of well-being, self-esteem, and psychological distress and found a modest relationship for ethnic identity. The effect sizes were larger when examining well-being than when examining indexes of distress, but they were not different across social class, racial or ethnic group, or gender; however, they were stronger for adolescents than for adults over 40 years of age.

One of two main benefits of ethnic identity development for adjustment is that ethnic identity is an important form of normative development for stigmatized youth. For nonstigmatized youth, development of positive self-concepts and ego identity are seen as the major developmental task for adolescence (Erikson, 1968). Analogously, for youth who are ethnically or racially stigmatized, the development of positive ethnic self-concepts and ethnic identity is a major developmental task for these subgroups of adolescents (Phinney, 1989; Quintana, 1998). Counseling research over the past decades confirms that high levels of development for ethnic identity are associated with adjustment for ethnic and racial minority youth (e.g., Smith & Silva, 2011).

Original models of racial identity marked the development from self-hating toward positive notions of one's racial and ethnic groups (e.g., Cross, 1971). Although the negative self-esteem that was expected for children of color was not confirmed, research has confirmed the strong connection between self-esteem and positive forms of

ethnic and racial identity (e.g., Cross, 1991). Consequently, considerable research supports the prediction that the formation of positive and strong ethnic and racial identity represents the culmination of normative development for ethnic and racial minority children and adolescents. Despite stigmatization, ethnic and racial minority youth develop positive notions of ethnic self-concepts and ethnic or racial identity (Quintana, Segura-Herrera, & Nelson, 2010).

A more critical theoretical expectation for ethnic and racial identity is whether it moderates or buffers against the deleterious effects of discrimination on, for example, self-esteem or positive self-concepts. Racial discrimination was associated with adolescents' less positive view of themselves and of their racial background (Lee, 2005; Seaton, Yip, & Sellers, 2009). Research on internalized racism and heterosexism has found that multiple internalized oppressors act additively on psychological health, resulting in lower self-esteem (Szymanski & Gupta, 2009). Clearly, stigmatization can undermine positive views toward the self.

These findings on ethnic identity parallel results conducted with parents whose socialization practices help prepare their children and youth for discrimination. For adolescents in the context of high levels of ethnic discrimination, parental preparation for discrimination buffered against the negative effects of racial discrimination (Neblett et al., 2008). In that same sample, youths in contexts of low levels of discrimination had lower levels of adjustment when parents prepared them for discrimination at high levels.

Recent research has examined the connection between ethnic and racial identity and views toward the self (Smith & Silva, 2011). Unfortunately, most of this research has been cross-sectional (Smith & Silva, 2011) and, consequently, provides little useful information in determining the sequencing of influence among discrimination, ethnic or racial identity, and self-esteem. Is ethnic or racial identity merely a consequence and extension of the process of developing esteem about one's self, or does ethnic or racial identity buffer against ethnic stigmatization and thereby allow youth to maintain self-esteem in the face of discrimination? Longitudinal research is beginning to tease out the direction of influence.

Umaña-Taylor, Vargas-Chanes, Garcia, and Gonzales-Backen (2008) replicated the strong concurrent relationship between self-esteem and ethnic identity, but found no prospective relationship between ethnic identity and later self-esteem. Moreover, they found that self-esteem, not ethnic identity, was prospectively related to coping with discrimination. Although there is little doubt that ethnic identity is connected to self-esteem, there is little research suggesting that ethnic identity leads prospectively to enhancements in self-esteem and, more critically, the evidence is, at best, mixed regarding whether strong ethnic identity buffers against ethnic or racial discrimination. Counseling research needs to address these basic questions about the role of ethnic and racial identity on adjustment for children, youth, and young adults.

Interestingly, perceived discrimination is associated with an increase in ethnic identity affirmation and exploration among adolescents (Umaña-Taylor & Guimond, 2010), which suggests the possibility that ethnic group exploration and membership provide a healthy form of coping. Recent research on ethnic identity has found a link between ethnic identity and positive psychosocial outcomes (see review by Quintana, 2007). For example, higher levels of self-esteem (Umaña-Taylor, Gonzales-Backen, & Guimond, 2009), academic achievement (Costigan, Koryzma, Hua, & Chance, 2010), and subjective well-being (Rivas-Drake, Hughes, & Way, 2009) among ethnic minority adolescents were correlated with higher scores on ethnic identity measures. In addition, ethnic identity has been shown to possibly have protective measures against delinquency (Bruce & Waelde, 2008), drug and alcohol use (Marsiglia, Kulis, Hecht, & Sills, 2004), sexual risk-taking (Beadnell et al., 2003), and other harmful coping methods (Schwartz et al., 2010; Yoo & Lee, 2005). Multiple racial groups have been found to have high levels of ethnic identity (e.g., African American, Latino, Asian, and multiethnic), and the most positive adjustment resulted when individuals focused on the positive aspects of their ethnic group (Quintana, 2007).

Intriguingly, several studies have identified ethnic identity as a possible risk factor. In a sample of Asian American students, Yoo and Lee (2008) found that ethnic identity actually exacerbated the effects of racial discrimination on negative affect. In another study, with Black Canadian students, Outten, Guiguère, Schmitt, and Lalonde (2010) discovered that adherence to racial beliefs that emphasized the Black experience was associated with greater perceived discrimination. There are important implications for ethnic and racial identity theory in these empirical trends. Greater centrality of and stronger identifications with ethnic and racial identity seem to be associated with psychological well-being for ethnic and racial minority youth, but there are some contexts—namely, those involving high levels of discrimination—in which there are costs associated with identifying strongly with the ethnic and racial identity.

Two pernicious issues, however, plague much of the ethnic and racial identity research. First, there is a proliferation of identity dimensions, and to some extent measures of ethnic and racial identity. Some theorists have suggested that these identity dimensions are relatively orthogonal and may operate somewhat independently (Sellers et al., 1998; Umaña-Taylor & Fine, 2004), whereas other models suggest that an interconnectedness of the dimensions challenges whether it is sufficiently meaningful to isolate some dimensions from the other dimensions (e.g., Cross & Cross, 2008; Quintana, 1998). There is, to some degree, inconsistency across studies regarding which dimensions are significant predictors of various criterion variables, signaling perhaps that separating dimensions of ethnic identity may be a trivialization of more complex, irreducible processes. Future research and theory need to tackle the proliferation of ethnic identity dimensions and conduct critical tests of whether our knowledge of ethnic and racial identity is enhanced or further obfuscated by the acceleration of ethnic identity measures.

The second pernicious problem is the proliferation of cross-sectional, observational investigations into ethnic identity formation. There is a long-standing expectation that ethnic identity would be connected to personal identity and sense of self (e.g., Phinney, 1989). We do not know, however, whether a strong ethnic identity—high scores on ethnic identity measures—produces (causes), is a reflection of (is caused by), or has a spurious relationship with self-esteem, with both being influenced by other psychological process (e.g., ego development). A recent meta-analysis demonstrated the significant connection between self-esteem and ethnic identity (Smith & Silva, 2011). A series of cross-sectional and longitudinal studies by Umaña-Taylor et al. (2008) using their measure of ethnic identity is instructional. That is, like the meta-analysis, they found significant correlational relationships in cross-sectional designed research but found, at best, weak prospective relationships predicting later self-esteem from ethnic identity. Importantly, they found that self-esteem, not ethnic identity, was a significant predictor of coping with discrimination, the raison d'être for ethnic identity. Hence, ethnic identity may be a consequence of a strong sense of self, but it may have limited independent value, which has significant implications for practice and counseling theory.

One potential reason that ethnic identity was not more strongly associated with buffering against racial stress is the failure to differentiate between process and content in ethnic identity formation. Most measures of ethnic identity confound process, such as the process of ethnic identity formation with the content of ethnic identity, such as the ethnic labels. Quintana, Segura-Herrera, and Nelson (2010) drew parallels between formation of ego and self-identity and formation of ethnic identity. Erikson (1968) differentiated between ego identity (formation of identity) and self-identity (including self-concepts). Analogously, Quintana et al. differentiated between ethnic identity, analogous to Erikson's description of ego identity, and ethnic self-concepts, analogous to self-identity in Erikson's theory. In Quintana et al.'s model, ethnic self-concepts, which included ethnic labels with which they identified, were the outcomes of ethnic identity filtering and synthesizing. Quintana et al. suggested that ethnic identity processes function to buffer and integrate ethnic or racial experiences that result in ethnic self-concepts and in orientations toward interethnic and intraethnic experiences. Hence,

confusing ethnic identity processes with ethnic self-concepts would undermine our ability to demonstrate the connection between ethnic identity and protecting against the deleterious effects of ethnic and racial stigmatization. More research is needed into the processes through which ethnic identity buffers and filters inter- and intraethnic experiences to protect against ethnic discrimination.

To reiterate, ethnic and racial identity processes are related to the racialization processes described thus far. Racial and ethnic stigmatization promotes the need for the targets of that discrimination to cope psychologically. Important social identity processes unfold from the need to maintain a positive sense of self in the context of identifying with a stigmatized group. Ethnic and racial identity formation represents a psychological response to that discrimination as it is stimulated by exposure to and encounters with discrimination. Research documents among adolescents a growing ethnic and racial affiliation and identification with their ethnic or racial group. Research supports the connection between strong ethnic identification and positive adjustment and self-esteem. Ethnic and racial identities are believed to promote adjustment by serving protective or buffering roles in response to discrimination. Research is emerging, however, that strong ethnic or racial identification in the context of high levels of discrimination may be associated with lower levels of adjustment. Although research supports the connection between ethnic identity and self-esteem, results from early longitudinal studies call into question whether ethnic and racial identity promotes later self-esteem.

ETHNIC AND RACIAL DISCRIMINATION

We have considered racialization processes in the context of racial and ethnic identity. Other important counseling psychological research examines more general coping and deleterious effects of discrimination. Carter (2007) has provided the most authoritative overview of exposure to and coping with racism for ethnic and racial minority groups. Carter reiterated Jones's (1997) identification of different forms of discrimination: individual, institutional, and cultural forms. Individual forms of racism occur in interpersonal interactions between individuals; institutional racism is perpetuated by practices and policies by institutions (e.g., schools, criminal justice systems) that unfairly discriminate against ethnic and racial minority groups; cultural racism is expressed as hostility toward the cultural characteristics or values of a racial group. Carter reviewed research examining the incidence of racism across various contexts. Latino and African American youth experience a higher incidence of racism, particularly institutional forms perpetuated within schools, when compared with White and Asian American youth, and the latter group experienced elevated levels of individual racism from their peers (Rosenbloom & Way, 2004). Researchers have consistently found a link between reports of racism and mental health symptoms, such as depression and anxiety (for a review, see Carter, 2007). Researchers found that nearly all of their participants of color from university and community contexts experienced discrimination during the past year (Landrine & Klonoff, 1996). Across the studies reviewed, Carter found that between 40% and 98% of the participants of color experienced racism, usually within the past year.

Quintana and McKown (2008) delineated multiple pathways by which ethnic and racial minority children and adolescents experience the deleterious effects of racism. Most research focuses on direct effects of racism in which the child is the target of racism, usually of individual forms of racism. This focus on direct effects of racism underestimates the effect of racism because it ignores other forms. That is, Quintana and McKown identified vicarious exposure to racism in which a child witnesses another member of his or her ethnic or racial minority group being the target of racism. Quintana's (1998) interviews with ethnic and racial minority children revealed that more children were witnesses to racism targeting their peers than were direct recipients of racism—and these children reported being influenced by these vicarious exposures to racism. A particularly important exposure to racism is indirect (Quintana & McKown, 2008), in which the child or adolescent need not be present when the racism is perpetuated but is still influenced by the act of racism. For example, children whose parents

experienced racism when they were in school may pass onto the children their racial mistrust for educators. As another example, parents' health status may be negatively affected by institutional forms of racism (Carter, 2007) and their compromised health status, in turn, likely affects their children's physical and psychological well-being. Children are likely to be relatively unaware of the extent to which their lives are negatively influenced by their indirect exposure to racism. Hence, there are multiply pathways by which children are exposed to the deleterious effects of racism, but empirical research focuses primarily on the direct exposure to racism, even though those effects may not be the most deleterious in influencing children's lives.

Carter's (2007) review examined the psychological effects of racism and found that racism has negative effects on self-esteem and quality of life and contributes to symptoms of depression, anxiety, and other forms of emotional distress. When gender differences were reported, men tended to have higher exposure to racism and greater negative effects of reported racism. Racial differences tended to demonstrate that African Americans and Latinos reported higher levels of racism and greater psychological costs.

To potentially minimize the negative effects of racism, the target must find effective ways of coping (Carter, 2007). To understand coping with racism, Slavin, Rainer, McCreary, and Gowda (1991) adapted Lazarus and Folkman's (1984) model of coping. As with Lazarus and Folkman's model, Slavin et al.'s multicultural stress model (MSM) emphasizes the role of the appraisal of a stressful event and of possible coping responses. The MSM, unlike Lazarus and Folkman's model, focuses on cultural aspects involved in coping, particularly with racism and cultural stressors. That is, the primary appraisal within the MSM focuses on interpreting the significance of the racist event for the target's psychological functioning. A highly threatening incident would elicit an intense psychological reaction or stress response. Carter (2007) suggested that the racism could be traumatizing, depending on the intensity of the threat and whatever control the target may or may not have over the event. Although clinical definitions of traumatic events require exposure to physical, life-threatening violence, three components that could lead to racialized trauma have been identified: (a) Subjective experience of the event is intense and leads to avoidance or re-experiencing of the traumatizing events through, for example, intrusive memories; (b) the racist event occurs unexpectedly or unpredictably; and (c) the event is uncontrollable. Quintana (2008) suggested that racism that occurs in forms that overwhelm the child's ability to comprehend its occurrence would be experienced as traumatizing. Each of these forms of primary appraisal of racialized stress could be traumatizing.

The secondary appraisal within the MSM focuses on possible responses to the racist event (Slavin, Rainer, McCreary, & Gowda, 1991). Targets of racism assess whether they have an effective response within their repertoire or whether they should withdraw and seek assistance. Responses that are active and focused on problem solving are considered and have been empirically found to be adaptive. Conversely, responses that are avoidant or passive tend to be associated with problematic adjustment. The final and third phase of MSM involves the cultural or racial expression of stress. Slavin et al. (1991) noted that expression of stress will vary across cultural, ethnic, and racial groups. Subsequent to the expression of stress, the individual coping may turn to various cultural, ethnic, or racial sources of assistance. The extent to which the larger dominant ethnic or racial group is held responsible for the experience of racism may undermine the individual's willingness to seek formal or professional services from agencies and institutions in which the dominant culture and racial group is well entrenched.

Research on discrimination is plagued by self-report methodology and cross-sectional research, making the directions of influence difficult to discern. One longitudinal research study (Brody et al., 2006), however, indicated that although the exposure to discrimination was associated with developing later symptoms associated with behavior disorders and the development of behavior disorders was associated with later forms of discrimination, the former pathway was stronger than the latter pathway. In other words, in this case, discrimination is a stronger cause than effect of behavior problems. We need more longitudinal research that examines pathways of direction.

ACCULTURATION PROCESSES

Acculturation theory (e.g., Sam & Berry, 2010) is foundational to much of the counseling psychology research investigating ethnicity and race. Acculturation theory describes processes that result when two cultural groups come into contact. The term *acculturation* is used to describe the sequelae of this cultural contact as well as to describe the more specific process of acquiring cultural characteristics from the dominant group (Sam & Berry, 2010), in which case a cultural minority group is thought to acculturate to a host cultural group by adopting some of the culture of the host society. The complement to the process of adjusting to contact with a different cultural group is the process of enculturation, which is socialization within a cultural group. Consequently, the theory of acculturation is also focused on enculturation processes, which refer specifically to the socialization within a cultural heritage in-group (B. K. Kim, 2007; Park, Kim, Chiang, & Ju, 2010). Multicultural principles (Arredondo & Perez, 2006) emphasize the benefits of enculturation and retaining cultural characteristics from the culture of origin. Together acculturation and enculturation processes constitute the major processes within acculturation theory. Individuals can experience acculturation and enculturation on multiple levels: geographically (e.g., new neighborhood), biologically (e.g., new foods, diseases), culturally (e.g., new political, economic, or religious systems), and socially (e.g., change in psychological orientation toward ethnic groups). As a result, acculturation processes are marked along a number of dimensions, including linguistic (e.g., linguistic patterns), demographic (e.g., country of origin, place of birth, years in the United States), sociocultural (e.g., values, attitudes, beliefs, behaviors, social relations among ethnic groups), and psychological (e.g., personality, identity, ethnic identity; Bornstein & Cote, 2006; Sam & Berry, 2010).

Originally developed in anthropological and sociological contexts in which cultural groups acculturate in response to contact, Berry (1997; Sam & Berry, 2010) was one of the first to apply the principles of acculturation to the psychological processes associated with the sequelae of cultural contact (Graves, 1967). Individuals who are highly acculturated adopt cultural practices of the dominant culture and those who are considered less acculturated retain many of the traditions practiced in their former country (Hwang & Ting, 2008). Berry identified four orientations within the cultural adaptation process: assimilation (identification mostly with the receiving culture), integration (high identification with both cultures, also known as *biculturalism*), separation (identification mostly with the culture of origin), or marginalization (low identification with both cultures). These acculturative orientations are also connected with adjustment. Integration is the most psychologically healthy for individuals as it allows for them to hold cultural values that are functional in both cultural contexts (Benet-Martínez & Haritatos, 2005; Matsunaga, Hecht, Elek, & Ndiaye, 2010). Integrated or bicultural individuals are considered to be better adjusted across cultural contexts (Chen, Benet-Martínez, & Bond, 2008; Schwartz, Zamboanga, & Jarvis, 2007). Assimilation allows individuals to function in European American–dominated cultural contexts but may lead to difficulties in intraethnic relations and culture of origin contexts. Separation allows individuals to function in their culture of origin contexts but may be associated with problems (e.g., discrimination, alienation) in European American cultural contexts. Marginalization is the considered least adaptive of all orientations.

Berry (1997) considered acculturation orientations as a means of accessing resources from the dominant and culture-of-origin communities, with adopting dominant cultural values and behaviors acting as a means of accessing resources within the ethnically or racially dominant groups, such as the education system or employment. Berry also considered the retention of culture-of-origin skills and values as a means of maintaining resources from the culture of origin, such as social and psychological support. Early research identified the benefits and incentives for minority ethnic groups to assimilate to dominant cultural norms; there was less

appreciation and recognition of the important sociological and psychological benefits that would be lost if assimilation meant giving up or losing culture-of-origin resources. A fundamental principle and goal of multiculturalism (D. W. Sue & Sue, 2003) was to recognize the value of retaining multiple cultural orientations to counter assimilation policies within U.S. society that threatened the maintenance of minority cultural orientations.

Research within and outside of counseling psychology has been successful in documenting the importance, with respect to psychological health and adjustment, of maintaining culture-of-origin characteristics and resisting assimilation for ethnic and racial minority populations. Overwhelming research continues to mount regarding the importance of maintaining cultural values, behaviors, and orientations for the adjustment and success of children (see Ponterotto, Suzuki, Casas, & Alexander, 2010). The principle of maintaining culture-of-origin skills is probably no better illustrated than in the research investigating bilingual education in which, somewhat counterintuitively, more comprehensive bilingual programs in which there is "late exit" from instruction taught in a language minority child's native tongue was associated with better academic achievement, even when the achievement was tested in English (e.g., Willig, 1985). The research on ethnic identity formation summarized previously further reinforces the tenets of multiculturalism in the value of retaining multiple cultural orientations, skills, and traditions and resisting cultural homogenization through assimilation.

Although the fundamental concepts of acculturation theory are clearly defined, the empirical relationships among the constructs are complex. That is, in some contexts, high levels of acculturation may be associated with negative predictors of adjustment or health, but in other contexts, they predict higher levels of adjustment. That is, the process of adjusting to a new cultural context, in which new cultural patterns may be adopted while some cultural traditions are challenged or stigmatized, can lead to acculturative stress (Berry & Annis, 1988). Despite the stressful nature of immigrating to a new cultural context and acculturating sufficiently to access the resources available in the new context, there is an interesting "immigration paradox" in which immigrant groups tend to have higher levels of education ambition and health status than those who are second or third generation (see Schwartz et al., 2010; Tseng, 2006).

Acculturative Stress and Immigrant Paradox

The immigrant paradox is most easily described in the context of health status. The epidemiological literature suggests that the more acculturated immigrants, who are defined as those who stay longer in the United States and have more generations living in the United States, have a higher risk for developing mental illnesses (Hwang & Ting, 2008). The idea behind this finding is that the longer individuals are in the United States, the greater their exposure to acculturative stressors, which are associated with a higher risk of psychopathology, as compared with their risk for psychopathology living in their native country (Escobar, 1998). Consequently, more recent immigrants would have had less exposure to acculturative stress than those who had immigrated sooner. For example, Asian Americans who are less acculturated, recently immigrated, or foreign born are at lower risk for psychological maladjustment than those who are more acculturated (Yip, Gee, & Takeuchi, 2008). On the other hand, the more recently arrived immigrants and generations are more likely to be affected by the greater differences between their culture of origin and the new cultural context and, therefore, find the cultural discordance to be particularly stressful, whereas those who have accommodated the dominant culture experience less cultural discordance, resulting in less intense acculturative stress.

To make sense out of the apparently contradictory predictions requires differentiating acculturation stress and culture-specific stress. The latter refers to stress that is inherent within a cultural group and not a by-product of intercultural contact. Conversely, acculturative stress involves the stress of being exposed to or immersed in a cultural context that is different from one's culture of origin. Researchers define acculturative stress as the subjective experience of stress that results from acculturation (see Sam & Berry, 2010). Several studies have found a positive correlation between levels of acculturative stress and mental health outcomes; specifically, acculturative stress is associated with lower levels of mental health (e.g., confusion, anxiety, depression), feelings of marginality and alienation, heightened psychosomatic symptom level, and identity confusion (Castillo, Cano, Chen, Blucker, & Olds, 2008). Wang and Mallinckrodt (2006) found greater distress for those Chinese students who were low in acculturation. Additionally, Moyerman and Forman (1992) conducted a meta-analytic study involving 49 studies of adaptation and adjustment and found that acculturative stress was positively correlated with psychosocial and health problems. In a more recent study, Hwang and Ting (2008) found that acculturative stress is significantly related to psychological distress and clinical depression.

Acculturative stress is usually understood as a result of the acculturation process, but acculturative stress can also be experienced as a result of tensions within an ethnic group (Castillo, Conoley, Brossart, & Quiros, 2007) due to a conflict in values. For example, second-generation children born and raised in the United States who have adopted more U.S. cultural values may experience family conflict on the basis of a difference in values orientation from their parents (Lee, Choe, Kim, & Ngo, 2000), and this has proven to be detrimental to the acculturating individual's psychological health. Furthermore, some research has examined intragroup marginalization, which examines the interpersonal distancing that occurs when an acculturating individual is believed to exhibit behaviors, values, and beliefs that are outside the heritage culture's group norms (Castillo, Conoley, Brossart, & Quiros, 2007). This intragroup marginalization is not only negatively associated with psychological well-being (Rodriguez, Myers, Morris, & Cardoza, 2000) but also provides a lens for viewing how individuals in the same ethnic or racial group may differ on the basis of behaviors and values. As a result, cultural values and behaviors also have distinct important considerations because cultural values affect individuals on multiple levels, some of which have been described in the form of ethnic or racial identity, acculturation, and enculturation.

Conversely, there is culture-specific stress that involves the stress that is intrinsic to a cultural orientation. For example, functioning in an urban context in which individualism is emphasized can be inherently stressful. Native members of such cultural contexts tend to have elevated levels of stress as well as the sequelae of the deleterious effects of this stress, such as high blood pressure and increased rates of alcoholism and drug addiction (e.g., Steffen, Smith, Larson, & Butler, 2006; Suinn, 2010). Hahm, Lahiff, and Guterman (2004) found that binge drinking occurred more frequently for those scoring high, compared with those scoring low, on acculturation. Hence, as an ethnic group takes on some of the cultural characteristics of a dominant ethnic group, they will experience many of the same problems that are an inherent aspect of that cultural orientation. The immigrant paradox results from immigrants, despite experiencing considerable acculturative stress, having better health outcomes than their more acculturated peers. Schwartz et al. (2010) identified the health-related markers of this immigrant paradox: lower drug and alcohol usage, greater physical activity, lower consumption of fast food, and adherence to health regimens (e.g., for diabetes).

Moving beyond some of these specific health markers, the relationship between acculturation and adjustment is complex. For example, B. S. K. Kim and Omizo (2005, 2006) found that cognitive flexibility and self-efficacy were associated with acculturation to European American culture but were not associated with enculturation to Asian cultural values. B. S. K. Kim and Omizo (2006) found that Asian cultural values were negatively associated with flexibility and not with self-efficacy. Similarly, Yoon, Lee, and Goh (2008) found a significant relationship between acculturation and satisfaction with life and positive affect, whereas enculturation to Korean communities was not positively related to these indexes of adjustment. Glass and Owen (2010) found that Latino fathers' adherence to traditional macho attitudes was negatively associated with paternal involvement, but enculturation into Latino culture was positively associated with paternal involvement in child rearing. Similarly, males' endorsement of Mexican values was associated with

more traditional masculine gender roles (Ojeda, Rosales, & Good, 2008). Conversely, women's endorsement of Anglo acculturation was significantly related to career self-efficacy (Rivera et al., 2007). Shim and Schwartz (2008) found that acculturation was negatively associated with psychological distress, whereas adherence to Asian values was not significantly related. At other times, high levels of enculturation within one's own native culture is associated with adjustment, at other times it is not. For example, Bettendorf and Fischer (2009) found that enculturation and specifically enculturation into familism values were negatively associated with symptoms of eating disorders, whereas acculturation was either positively related or unrelated to these symptoms of eating disorders.

To understand these patterns, it is important to differentiate the contexts in which these cultural orientations are being evaluated. When the criterion variable is related to success in White or Anglo cultures, then enculturation values tend to disadvantage participants, whereas acculturation advantages the participants. For example, eating disorders tend to occur more often in Anglo than in other cultures—consequently, enculturation into, for example, Latino culture, provides some protection against developing eating disorders. Smoking, alcoholism, and drug use tend to be higher in Anglo and White culture than in Latino cultures, and consequently, enculturation would be a protective factor and acculturation would be a risk factor for developing these addictions. Alternatively, when the criterion variables are associated with individualistic cultural values, such as self-esteem, then acculturation to Anglo norms often provides important benefits. Similarly, collective self-esteem is associated with minority cultural values and, consequently, ethnic identification with and enculturation into minority cultures are associated with higher scores on collective self-esteem (e.g., B. S. K. Kim & Omizo, 2005). Conversely, Schwartz et al. (2010) noted that individualistic attitudes and values may place ethnic and racial minority persons at risk for health-compromising behaviors, whereas collectivistic attitudes and values may be protective. Hence, the acculturation process is met with many struggles and possible psychological risks.

As mentioned, immigrant and ethnic minority groups' adherence to their culture-of-origin values are associated, in some contexts, with adjustment problems. Schwartz et al. (2010) identified several group-specific values that help to understand various cultural values orientations. These values include communalism in some African-descent groups (Boykin, Jagers, Ellison, & Albury, 1997); *familismo* (family), *machismo* (masculinity), *marianismo* (femininity), *respeto* (respect), *simpatia* (community), and *confianza* (trust) in many Latino contexts (Garza & Watts, 2010); and filial piety, conformity, family recognition, emotional self-control, and humility in many Asian contexts (Park & Kim, 2008). Recently, Arciniega, Anderson, Tovar-Blank, and Tracey (2008) have investigated differences in Latino masculine gender roles by differentiating traditional *machismo* from *caballerismo*, with the former associated with more stereotypical form of hypermasculinity and the latter associated with Latino values related to men who emphasize responsibility and emotional connectedness to family. As expected, traditional machismo was associated with problems with adjustment and delinquency, whereas caballerismo was associated with positive forms of problem solving and ethnic identity. Interestingly, both traditional machismo and caballerismo were negatively associated with acculturation (Arciniega et al., 2008). This pattern suggests that some forms of enculturation into Mexican culture, those that promote traditional forms of machismo, are associated with problems in adjustment, whereas other forms of enculturation, those that promote Caballerismo, are associated with positive adjustment. Arciniega et al.'s research indicates that the field needs to examine the forms of adaptation that are endogenous to a cultural group and avoid equating culture with problematic dimensions (e.g., machismo).

Similarly, there has been important research into Asian American's adjustment, and researchers have found that various aspects of Asian Americans culture (i.e., interdependence, perfectionism, internalization of stress, intergenerational conflict, model minority myth) and immigrant-related factors are correlated with poor mental health outcomes (Chan & Mendoza-Denton, 2008; Hwang & Goto, 2008).

Yoon and Lau (2008) revealed that interdependence, maladaptive perfectionism, and parent-driven perfectionism were associated with depressive symptoms for Asian Americans. Moreover, S. Sue et al. (1995) suggested that Asian Americans are less likely than the general population to use mental health services, which is understood to be linked to Asian American cultural values of perfectionism, internalization of stress, and interdependence.

This pattern of results reinforces the notion that in some contexts acculturation is adaptive and in other contexts enculturation is more adaptive. Over the past several decades, much of the counseling research has been concerned with demonstrating that pressures to assimilate may pose psychological disadvantage to ethnic minority groups. In contrast, counseling psychology research has been relatively uninterested in investigating biculturalism, with a few exceptions (e.g., LaFromboise et al., 1993). Although early in its development, Phinney's (1992) MEIM included an interest in other ethnic groups scale, but there was relatively little research into this subscale, and in more recent versions, the subscale was excluded in typical scoring. Moreover, early instrumentation for acculturation (e.g., Cuéllar, Harris, & Jasso, 1980) was based on a unidimensional model in which participants would manifest either acculturation or enculturation orientations. Unidimensional models articulate acculturation processes on a single continuum, such that as an individual acculturates and adopts more of the mainstream culture with respect to values, attitudes, and behaviors, the individual moves away from their culture of origin (see Schwartz et al., 2010).

More recent literature suggests that the acculturation process is better represented as multidimensional in which immigrant groups demonstrate biculturalism by maintaining adherence to their cultural heritage as well as adopting mainstream cultural values, behaviors, and attitudes (B. S. K. Kim & Omizo, 2006). Miller (2010) described how over the past two decades the common conceptualization of acculturation has been bilinear, but the most common empirical representations of it (i.e., measurement strategy) have been unidimensional.

Recently developed instrumentation assesses for a dominant cultural orientation separately from a culture-of-origin orientation (e.g., Cuéllar et al., 1995). Multidimensional measures of acculturation, also called *orthogonal models*, demonstrate that individuals can adhere to more than one culture independently (Cuéllar et al., 1995; LaFromboise et al., 1993; Oetting & Beauvais, 1990). In two recent studies, Miller (2007, 2010) found that Asian Americans can maintain two cultural orientations concurrently as a high level of engagement in one orientation does not necessarily determine a level of engagement in the other. Schwartz, Zamboanga, and Jarvis (2007) found that U.S. and Hispanic orientations together predict positive behavioral adjustment for Hispanic youth. In a later study, Schwartz et al. (2011) found that ethnic and racial minority college students' adherence to collectivistic values was associated with health benefits, whereas their acculturation to individualistic values also put them at greater risk for health problems. Interestingly, adherence to heritage cultural values by Hispanics is associated with elevated levels of engaging in risky sexual behavior. Most collectivistic values seem to provide benefits, but the fatalism attitudes held by Hispanic college students may put them at greater risk in protecting themselves against sexually risky behavior (Schwartz et al., 2011).

Importantly, researchers have developed instrumentation that specifically defines bicultural orientations in ethnic and racial identity instrumentation. For example, the Cross Racial Identity Scale model of racial identity development defines an internalization–multicultural orientation in which there is bridging with other oppressed groups, although there is not a multicultural identity that involves an integration of Black and White orientations. Cokley (2005) found convergence around a nonracialized ethnic identity in which African American students had Afrocentric values and strong ethnic identification and identified with the struggle of other ethnic groups, which was differentiated from a racialized identity that involved rejection of other groups, including Whites and ethnic minorities. Cokley's identity consolidation of a nonracialized identity seems consistent bi- or multicultural identification. Others, however, have identified forms of cross-ethnic competence and orientation. For example, Oyserman, Kemmelmeier, Fryberg,

Brosh, and Hart-Johnson (2003) described several variants of bicultural racial identities. Importantly, David, Okazaki, and Saw (2009) have developed an instrument specifically representing bicultural competence, drawn from LaFromboise et al.'s (1993) notions of biculturalism. This scale was strongly related to life satisfaction, academic and general self-efficacy, low levels of depressive symptoms, and positive in-group identification. The David et al. scale has important implications for future research in being able to investigate bicultural competence and identifications.

Thus, the field has been consumed with demonstrating the value of resisting assimilation pressures, but it has not focused sufficient attention on the benefits of biculturalism. Recent instrumentation provides empirical representations of biculturalism and identifications with multiple ethnic orientations to match conceptual models of biculturalism (e.g., LaFromboise et al., 1993). There seems to be much promise in these investigations into the adaptation associated with biculturalism, which could clarify more complex trends related to acculturation and enculturation.

COUNSELING IMPLICATIONS OF ETHNICITY AND RACE

Because counseling is based on individualistic, Western values, and modes of services, there are critical challenges in providing services to those clients who are from alternative cultural, ethnic, and racial backgrounds (see Wrenn, 1962). Research has documented that ethnic and racial minority populations are underserved, relative to nonminority populations, based on utilization rates (Neighbors et al., 2007) and number of sessions completed (e.g., Kearney, Draper, & Barón, 2005). Evidence is mixed regarding if, once counseling has begun, minority clients are underserved or less effectively served in traditional counseling, relative to their White peers. In attempting to understand the implications of race and ethnicity for counseling, the field has focused on several issues—primarily client and counselor characteristics—but there has been nearly unquestioned faith that counseling would be effective for ethnic and racial minority clients, if only administered by multiculturally competent counselors. The extant counseling psychology research in exploring why ethnic and racial minority clients may be underserved has focused on (a) clients' attitudes toward counseling as barriers to entering counseling and (b) counseling outcomes to identify ways to increase effectiveness of counseling.

Attitudes Toward Counseling

Research has investigated the challenges for clients and potential clients in seeking and receiving counseling. Much of this research has investigated the implication of acculturation for clients seeking and receiving counseling services. Research on ethnicity and race has investigated the barriers that clients of color face when seeking counseling as well as the adaptations to counseling services to minimize premature termination, increase satisfaction, and improve the effectiveness of services.

Considerable counseling research has examined attitudes toward seeking services by potential clients from ethnic and racial minority backgrounds to understand which factors predict favorable attitudes toward counseling. Interestingly, much of this research seems to have an uncritical assumption that counseling services would be beneficial for clients of color. That is, counseling research has focused on identifying client variables associated with attitudes toward counseling but has provided relatively little examination of which aspects of counseling potential clients find culturally incongruent.

Researchers find that more acculturated clients and potential clients have more open attitudes toward counseling, relative to those who are less acculturated (e.g., B. S. K. Kim, Ng, & Ahn, 2005; Miville & Constantine, 2007; Obasi & Leong, 2009). Wallace and Constantine (2005) found that African Americans' adherence to Africentric values was associated with the stigma they associated with receiving help and with self-concealment, but stigma and self-concealment were associated with attitudes toward receiving psychological services only for men. Conversely, Gloria, Castellanos, Park, and Kim (2008) found that Asian values negatively predicted help seeking attitude, but only for women. Liao, Rounds, and Klein (2005) found that Asian and Asian American students had less positive attitudes

toward counseling the stronger their adherence to Asian values, the lower their acculturation to Western values, and the greater their predispositions to conceal private information from others. Interestingly, the greater the severity of personal concerns, the less positive were their attitudes toward counseling and the greater the disposition toward self-concealment. Obasi and Leong (2009) also found that the greater African American students' distress was, the worse were their attitudes toward counseling. Miville and Constantine (2007) found that adherence to Asian cultural values was associated with perceived stigma about seeking counseling, and both were predictive of lower levels of intentions to seek counseling.

Perceived stigma is considered a mediator or explanation for why acculturation or enculturation variables influence attitudes toward counseling (Miville & Constantine, 2007). P. K. Kim and Park (2009) found that subjective norms associated with seeking counseling (e.g., perceived social norms regarding the use of counseling) mediated the effects of adherence to Asian values on attitudes and willingness to seek counseling. Interestingly, much of the prior research was conducted with the intention of identifying mediators that explain why higher levels of enculturation were associated with less positive attitudes toward counseling or seeking counseling, but only stigma was identified with much consistency as a mediator. Other variables appear to be independent of acculturation in predicting intentions to seek counseling. For example, self-concealment was associated with cultural values, but its effect in predicting attitudes toward counseling was independent of variance associated with cultural values. Another interesting trend is that although greater levels of distress increase the tendency to seek counseling in White clients, the level of distress was negatively associated with attitudes toward seeking counseling for African American (Obasi & Leong, 2009) and Asian American clients (Miville & Constantine, 2007)—those potential clients who seem to be in greater need for counseling may feel uncomfortable seeking counseling.

As mentioned, attitudes toward counseling were implicitly assumed to reflect cultural characteristics of ethnic and racial minority groups. For example, their negative attitudes are attributed to stigma, which assumes that these clients are misperceiving the potential benefits of counseling. It appears as if ethnic minority clients may be more willing to seek counseling for academic, career or other issues that may not involve high levels of personal disclosure. The reservations from students of color in seeking more personal forms of counseling, particularly when distress may be somewhat elevated suggests that their reservations about counseling are deeper than merely the stigma associated with seeking counseling. The implicit conclusion from this research is that many ethnic and racial minority clients appear ill-suited for counseling, in part, because of their bias about counseling. There is less research into how traditional counseling may be ill-suited for more traditional, less acculturated clients.

Research using real or analogue clients observing or participating in counseling sessions provides more insight into how race and ethnicity have implications for counseling. Bryan Kim and colleagues have systematically investigated how Asian Americans react to counseling, either by surveying clients or investigating students' preference in analogue counseling settings. B. K. Kim et al. (2003) found that although clients' adherence to Asian values did not predict outcome, when counselors disclosed their strategy for counseling, rather than more personal or social attitudes (e.g., approval, self-disclosure), the interactions within sessions were more productive. Li, Kim, and O'Brien (2007) found that although ratings of counselor credibility were not different whether or not they articulated their congruity with Asian values, there was a difference in counselor credibility when, in the condition of cultural incongruity, the counselor commented on racial difference. These findings suggest that counselor's openness to understanding cultural differences may have been more important than whether the counselor has similar cultural values with the client. In a third analogue study, Wang and Kim (2010) found Asian American students rated therapists who demonstrated multicultural competence higher than those who did not demonstrate multicultural competence. Those participants in the

analogue study who were higher on emotional self-control rated the therapist lower than those who were lower on self-control. These three analogue studies taken together suggest that Asian American clients' comfort with counseling may be increased with a more explicit focus on treatment strategies, openness to acknowledging racial differences between counselor and client, and greater demonstration of multicultural competence.

Working with volunteer clients, B. S. K. Kim and Atkinson (2002) found that those who adhered more to Asian cultural values rated empathy higher for an Asian American compared with a Caucasian counselor, but those low in Asian cultural values rated a Caucasian counselor's empathy higher. B. S. K. Kim et al. (2005) found that when volunteer clients' were matched with a counselor who had a similar worldview, clients rated their therapist higher and the working alliance stronger. Additionally, B. S. K. Kim et al. (2005) found that those clients who had high expectations for counseling and identified with European American values perceived that the counselor demonstrated high levels of empathy. Finally, B. S. K. Kim et al. (2009) examined clients who were seeking counseling services and found that when matched on beliefs about problem etiology, clients rated their counselors higher in empathy and cross-cultural competence and perceived a stronger working alliance and greater session depth. Mallinckrodt, Shigeoka, and Suzuki (2005) examined the etiological beliefs of Asian American students. They found that more acculturated students were more consistent with counselors' beliefs about etiology. Interestingly, there was a tendency for those who had lower levels of acculturation to cite internal reasons for personal problems (e.g., weak mind, sins, brain dysfunction) more often than counselors, whereas counselors were more likely to cite other interpersonal problems or change in life circumstances as the etiology of problems. This research suggests that counselors should attend more closely to matching clients on their problem etiology and that cultural differences could be overcome with counselor openness to discussing racial differences and demonstrating multicultural competence.

Counseling Outcomes for Ethnic and Racial Minority Clients

Three large-scale studies of ethnic and racial minorities in counseling are informative of the extent to which clients of color can benefit from traditional counseling. First, Kearney, Draper, and Barón (2005) investigated 666 college students of color compared with 301 White clients receiving services, and despite the large sample size and statistical power, they found no ethnic differences in outcome and no differences in outcome for ethnically matched versus unmatched counselor–client pairings. The main racial difference was that White clients, on average, had attended nearly twice as many sessions as clients of color. Comparisons of initial level of distress indicated that Asian American clients scored higher than White and African American clients, but no other ethnic differences were detected by Kearney et al. These findings suggest two possible conclusions. First, it may be that once in counseling, ethnic and racial minority college students benefit as much as White clients. Second, it may be that college students of color who seek counseling have been acculturated to a sufficient degree to benefit from counseling. The Kearney et al. study does not address those potential clients of color who may not have acculturated to a sufficient degree to benefit from counseling.

In a second large-scale study of substance abuse counseling for adolescents, Wintersteen, Mensinger, and Diamond (2005) found that ethnic and racial minority clients and White clients stayed in therapy longer when they had same race counselor and that girls and boys stayed in treatment longer when they received a same gender counselor. Interestingly, in mixed racial pairings, only counselors reported lower levels of therapeutic alliance relative to matched race pairings. Clients did not rate therapeutic alliance lower in mixed-race pairings, relative to same-race pairings.

In an important meta-analysis, Griner and Smith (2006) found that cultural adaptations made to therapy were associated with larger effect sizes, when compared with therapy services that were not adapted. They found that matching client and therapist on native language was a particularly important cultural adaptation, whereas matching on race was

only modestly associated with larger effect sizes. Interestingly, when cultural adaptations were made specific to an ethnic group, that is, when the sample was homogeneous, larger effect sizes were detected compared with studies in which adaptations were made across multiple racial or ethnic groups. Newell (2005) also found that effect sizes were higher when the sample was either predominately White or Black for behavioral interventions for school-age children. Consequently, extant evidence reveals that ethnic and racial minority clients are able to benefit from counseling, and they seem to benefit as much or nearly as much as White clients. Benish, Quintana, and Wampold (2011) replicated Griner and Smith's meta-analysis and found the strongest evidence for cultural adaptations in which there was a therapist–client match in etiological explanations of psychological problems and rationale for treatments. That is, Benish et al. found that when the counselor's approach matched the client's worldview with respect to why the client was in counseling and the ways in which the problem should be addressed in counseling, it was associated with larger effect sizes. These findings reinforce the direction of research for B. S. K. Kim et al. (2005) in studying match for etiological explanations for Asian and Asian American clients.

TRAINING OF ETHNIC AND RACIAL MINORITY COUNSELORS

Although the purpose of this chapter is not to review multicultural theory and research, there is some intriguing preliminary evidence challenging extant practices for training ethnic and racial minority counseling students. That is, there are some indicators suggesting that multicultural training may be relatively ineffective for ethnic and racial minority trainees, compared with their White peers. First, Chao, Wei, Good, and Flores (2011) found that whereas multicultural training was associated with higher levels of multicultural competence for White trainees, there were no differences for ethnic and racial minority trainees. Second, Bellini (2003) investigated rehabilitation counseling and found that high levels of counselor multicultural competence were associated with better outcome only when the counselor was White, compared with ethnic and racial minority counselors. Conversely, greater levels of multicultural competence were associated with lower levels of outcome for ethnic and racial minority counselors. These results are too preliminary to make conclusions, but more research into how ethnic and racial minority counselors develop their multicultural competence when working with White clients is an area of research that is conspicuous by its absence.

Taken together, these results suggest that local adaptations of counseling are associated with client outcome, but the current research provides more limited support for the role of generic adaptations in promoting client outcome. Until more evidence is generated, counseling psychologists should look to cultural adaptations tailored to specific ethnic or racial groups, particularly in the etiological beliefs of clients to make therapy more effective. Although there are relatively small, if any, benefits for matching the race of client and counselor, larger effect sizes are associated with cultural adaptations in the etiological explanations and rationale for treatment. Counseling psychologists should attend to treatment acceptability of services, given that some clients of color, particularly some Asian American clients, may find high levels of personal disclosure to be less acceptable forms of treatment than White or Caucasian clients. We need to avoid assuming that clients are ill-suited and distorted in their attitudes toward counseling and instead consider how counseling may be ill-suited for some clients and how counseling could be better suited to those clients.

ENDEMIC CHALLENGES TO A SCIENCE OF DIVERSITY IN COUNSELING PSYCHOLOGY

Several challenges endemic to research into ethnic and racial diversity stem from using ethnic or racial groups as a main unit of analysis. The emphasis and articulation of the perspectives of racial or ethnic groups requires the assumption of sufficient homogeneity within each ethnic and racial group to justify making generalizations across groups as well as the assumption of sufficient heterogeneity between groups to justify classifying persons into those groupings.

Understandably, however, there has been some overreaching within diversity theories that can be traced to foundational assumptions. Research and theory in counseling psychology concerning race ethnicity assume that persons should be nested under their racial or ethnic groupings. This approach is analogous to taking the unit of analysis as an ethnic or racial group, which has provided insights into a person's psychological functioning as evidenced by the importance of racial identity theory. This approach in research, however, leads to some challenges in creating a balanced psychological science of diversity. Specifically, there has been some overemphasis of the role of ethnic or racial group membership in psychological functioning. To illustrate, early versions of racial identity theory overemphasized the role of racial identity development in psychological adaptation (e.g., Cross, 1971; Helms, 1995). That is, African American children, youth, and some adults who had not progressed through racial identity stages or statuses were considered psychologically unhealthy and believed to have internalized the society's racism which, in turn, resulted in being self-hating. Research on children and adolescents contradicted this assumption, however, and found that African American children were not self-hating (Cross, 1995) but rather had higher self-esteem than White children (Crocker & Major, 1989). Cross's (1991) review of extant evidence led him to revise his model and challenge the assumption that all those in lower stages of racial identity would be self-hating. A second example of the overemphasis of racial group membership within theories of diversity is that racial identity stages have been considered reflective of developmental movement with the higher stages being equated with more mature functioning and those remaining in lower stages being developmentally immature. The not-so-subtle message is clear: Any person who does not demonstrate putatively advanced forms of racial identity should be considered immature. Quintana's (2007) review of extant research challenged the notion that higher racial identity stages represented normatively mature levels of functioning.

A third example of some overreaching is the view that ethnic and racial socialization or enculturation is critical to the adaptation and adjustment of children and adolescents of color. Although much research supports this proposition (Hughes et al., 2008), research also suggests some important exceptions or limitations to this assumption (Caughy, Nettles, O'Campo, & Lohrfink, 2006; McHale et al., 2006). That is, racial socialization or preparation for racism is associated with adjustment in contexts in which youth experience high levels of discrimination, but it is associated with lower forms of adjustment in contexts in which discrimination is infrequent. Similarly, enculturation into an ethnic or racial group is not associated with positive adjustment in some contexts, such as predominately White universities and colleges—instead, levels of acculturation or adjustment to dominant culture are associated with adjustment in these contexts (e.g., Gloria & Hird, 1999). A fourth, albeit related, example in which there are important exceptions to the role of ethnic or racial group membership in healthy functioning is the notion that identification with one's ethnic group is adaptive (Phinney, 1989). Again, research supports this conclusion in many contexts (Smith & Silva, 2011) but also suggests some important exceptions. Namely, as reviewed, those who have somewhat diffuse identifications with a stigmatized ethnic or racial group tend to be less distressed by racial or ethnic bias compared with those whose ethnic or racial identity is central (Sellers et al., 1998). In this case, there are situations in which strong ethnic or racial identifications may be counterproductive.

An additional challenge for the way in which counseling psychology research examines ethnic and racial population is the apparent tendency to adopt a monoracial bias. That is, multicultural theories and research are often designed to account for the psychological functioning of monoracial persons. Essentially, by focusing on monoracial persons and failing to consider bi- and multiracial persons, these theories become grounded in artificial dichotomies and, thereby, tend to overestimate between-group heterogeneity and within-group homogeneity. One example of this monoracial bias is the tendency for items in racial or ethnic identity instruments to be grounded in a monoracial perspective, such as Phinney's (1992) item: "I feel a strong attachment to my ethnic group." The items tend to reflect the

assumption that participants have membership in only one reference group, making it difficult for those belonging to two or more reference groups to respond meaningfully. Another apparent reflection of monoracial bias is the assumption that racial identities need to be stable to be adaptive, which is in contrast to the fluidity of expressions and experiences of racial identifications for bi- and multiracial persons (Yip et al., 2006).

The extent to which monoracial bias influences counseling theory on ethnicity and race will, of course, limit the theories' applicability to bi- and multiracial populations, which are growing populations. The monoracial bias, however, may even distort the theoretical representations of monoracial persons' psychological functioning. For example, the assumption that identity stability reflects adjustment has been challenged by research with monoracial participants who have been found to cycle through racial identity statuses or stages through adulthood (Parham, 1989). As mentioned, recent samplings of racial identity salience and experiences show considerable variability within a short period of time and across contexts for monoracial persons and show that particular variations in the salience and experiences of racial identity are associated with adjustment (Yip et al., 2006). Hence, there are important exceptions to the value of a stable racial identity for adaptation even for monoracial persons. Consequently, addressing monoracial bias in extant psychological theories of diversity has implications for applying these theories to multiracial or multiethnic persons and, importantly, may also redress some of the inherent limitations with a monoracial perspective for theory and research on monoracial persons.

Several important principles can be abstracted from the way in which empirical research has provided a check on the validity of psychological theories of diversity to redress some inherent bias within counseling psychology. First, the finding of limitations and exceptions to psychological principles of diversity does not undermine the foundation of these theories. Instead, these expansions and subsequent contractions of the extension of psychological theory reflect the healthy winnowing of ideas that is the foundation for scholarly inquiry. Consequently, empirical research provides invaluable opportunities to evaluate, test, and refine our multicultural theories.

Second, empirical evaluation's reining in of some predictions that are grounded in psychological principles of diversity provides insight into the mechanisms by which multicultural processes operate. To illustrate, finding that fluidity of racial identity seems adaptive implies that racial identity functions to negotiate variations within interracial and intraracial social landscapes. As another example, finding that the benefits of parental socialization to prepare minority children and youth for discrimination is limited to those contexts in which discrimination is prevalent provides insight into why certain types of racial socialization are adaptive. This pattern of findings reinforces the notion that these racial socialization practices help youth navigate discrimination in their social environments. Alternatively, finding that the effects of these racial socialization were unrelated to level of discrimination experienced would require us to reconsider the conceptual foundation for why this kind of parental socialization was adaptive. To reiterate, identifying limits and exceptions to the benefits of multicultural processes informs psychological theory in critical ways and can facilitate the accurate application of psychological principles of diversity.

HORIZONTAL GROWTH AND NAIVE EMPIRICISM

The previous section has described several inherent challenges within a science of diversity that have been identified and redressed, largely through empirical evaluation. There are, however, several inherent challenges that have not been sufficiently recognized and, consequently, limit the usefulness of the science of diversity in counseling psychology. First, much of the focus of diversity research in counseling psychology is horizontal in nature. *Horizontal growth* in research refers to the applying of either mainstream or multicultural theoretical constructs to new samples, typically ethnic or racial groups or subgroups thereof to which the constructs had not been applied. In short, horizontal research refers to the research that addresses the external

validity of the theory by extending it to a new population or subpopulation.

The horizontal growth of diversity research is contrasted with a vertical expansion that involves probing the theoretical foundations of psychological processes underlying diversity. The distinction between vertical and horizontal is made on the basis of the extent to which the study design addresses theoretical principles or the participant sampling addresses external validity. *Vertical growth* refers to research that evaluates critical theoretical principles. There are several critical limitations to the horizontal approach to expanding multicultural psychology. First, all too often, there are critical threats to the external validity of studies and, consequently, the results have limited ability to fulfill the studies' purposes. Rarely does any psychological research involve random selection from a broad population, which is required for the logic of statistical inference. The lack of random selection is as serious of a threat to external validity as the lack of random assignment is to internal validity. There are, however, serious threats to external validity in those studies in which samples of convenience are surveyed rather than random sampling. The reasons why a sample is convenient to researchers are often the reasons that make the samples unrepresentative of the populations of interest.

Given that these threats to external validity are not unique to our research, should we be concerned about these threats for research on ethnicity and race? Several differences between mainstream and psychological research on diversity are important to note. First, because as S. Sue (2003) noted, mainstream research is not particularly concerned with external validity, the standards for external validity in mainstream research are not ones that researchers of diversity necessarily want to emulate. Second, mainstream research does not justify its research on the basis of external validity to the same extent as research on diversity.

Moreover, because much of diversity research is investigating minority populations, threats to external validity may be more common to research on diversity, relative to mainstream research. That is, when needing to recruit samples from minority populations, researchers may need to stray farther from random selection, using, for example, snowball sampling, to secure samples of sufficient size for statistical analysis. To recruit a sufficiently large sample, multicultural researchers in counseling psychology frequently need to identify contexts in which desired participants are prevalent, which often involve multicultural organizations or courses that are focused on matters of interest to ethnic and racial minority groups (e.g., ethnic organizations, ethnic studies courses). Of concern for external validity, these organizations and courses tend to attract participants with particular characteristics and lead to biased sampling. That these particular characteristics (e.g., interest in ethnic and racial issues) have a connection to the constructs being investigated (e.g., ethnic or racial identity) increases the likelihood that the obtained results may be idiosyncratic to the subgroup represented in the sample and unrepresentative of the larger population of interest.

Despite their prevalence and severity, these threats to external validity are rarely seriously considered or integrated into discussion of results. These threats to external validity seriously undermine the case that these research studies can make a significant contribution to the literature on the basis of external validity. The consequence of disregarding these serious threats to external validity is that a body of literature evolves in which we do not know to what extent the patterns of findings are due to artifacts of the recruitment strategies, the characteristics of the idiosyncratic samples that were obtained, or the psychological characteristics of meaningful populations of interest. In short and somewhat ironically, compared with mainstream research, external validity may be, in some ways, more compromised in research on diversity, which has prided itself on its contributions to external validity.

Even if these logistic challenges of recruiting representative samples of populations of interest could be overcome, there is a second fundamental challenge to the horizontal approach to developing a psychology of diversity. Specifically, there appears to be an implicit assumption underlying this approach to research: Knowledge about each of the racial or ethnic groups is constructed separately.

A logical extension of this assumption leads to the view that each measure, theory, model, and principle should be validated on a population before being applied or generalized to that population, which is a version of *naive empiricism*—the idea that science moves forward by the sheer accumulation of empirical findings with minimal inference or, as in the case with some diversity research, science progresses by evaluating theories on new populations. Considering the multiplicity of racial, ethnic, and cultural groups, the many different subgroups within those groups as well as the intersections of different group statuses (e.g., sex, social class, sexual orientation, to name a few), we quickly realize that this horizontal approach to growing diversity research is impractical. Consequently, rational inferences and interpretations about the applicability of research for various populations become necessary to move beyond strict statistical inference associated with random sampling of populations.

There is a third fundamental problem associated with the horizontal approach to building a psychological science of diversity. This horizontal approach is a natural extension of our researchers' focus on populations that are defined in demographic terms. That is, ethnic and racial minority groups are defined by demographic characteristics. There are important consequences of this focus on demographic groups. First, with a focus on demographic characteristics, knowledge generated from an accumulation of research findings tends to be more segmented than continuous. That is, to generalize across different demographic groups requires some basis for combining or pooling groups. Indeed, as long as groups of interest are defined by demographic characteristics, it is difficult to develop a heuristic that would justify combining or generalizing across groups, unless there are some demographic similarities. For example, it seems more acceptable to combine across different Latino subgroups than to generalize across different racial groups. Additionally, it seems more acceptable to generalize across different racial groups (e.g., Latino, Asian Americans, American Indians) when these groups are contrasted with a group that is perceived to have different demographic origins (e.g., Caucasians). The more the groups are seen as different demographic categories, the greater the perceived need to conduct research separately on each group rather than pooling across groups. This focus on demographic categories seems to reflect the tendency to accentuate intergroup differences and intragroup similarities.

Another consequence of this focus on demographic characteristics is that diversity research tends to be descriptive rather than explanatory in nature. It is difficult to provide an explanatory link between demographic characteristics and psychological processes being investigated because racial or ethnic status does not, per se, cause the characteristics associated with racial status (e.g., educational disparities). That is, research focused on demographic characteristics may be able to predict or describe who is, for example, at some academic risk, but may have difficulty providing an explanation for why they are at risk. Conversely, focusing on the sociological and psychological characteristics associated with the demographic groups would facilitate the specification of psychological explanations for why ethnic and racial groups psychologically function as they do. To become a psychological science of diversity, we need to focus our theories on the underlying psychological processes. In other words, instead of focusing on describing the characteristics that are associated with various groups of interest, a psychological science of diversity could identify relevant psychological dynamics that explain or account for patterns we observe.

VERTICAL GROWTH OF PSYCHOLOGICAL SCIENCE OF DIVERSITY

In contrast to the horizontal expansion, vertical growth of a psychological science of diversity involves specifying and testing theoretical principles about the processes that underlie the psychological functioning of diverse groups. This vertical growth allows for greater depth of understanding into the underlying psychological processes associated with multicultural groups. Moreover, vertical growth allows for the refinement of theoretical constructs associated with processes associated with diversity. Populations to be sampled are chosen less by their demographic status per se and more by the

intriguing psychological characteristics they bring that provide for a probing investigation of theoretical principles. Hence, groups to be sampled would be selected strategically so that they represent critical psychological processes to provide an evaluation of theoretical principles related to diversity.

Herman's (2008, 2009) research on multiracial populations provides a compelling example of a strategy for stimulating vertical growth of psychological science of diversity. To illustrate, Herman (2008) has conducted interesting research with biracial populations that helps to tease out the sequelae of psychologically identifying with a racial group from the sociological processes associated with being identified with a racial group on the basis of phenotype. She found that phenotype influenced persons' racial identification but that there were education outcomes that appeared to reflect the persons' psychological identification with a racial group that was independent of racial phenotype and a range of other variables for which she controlled. This research provides insight into the process of identifying with a racial group that could not be examined in monoracial populations. An important development in the process of vertical development is the extent to which particular processes can be abstracted from specific contexts. Herman (2009) later examined the academic performance of biracial populations to test three theories attempting to explain education disparities, which could be evaluated in a way that was not possible with monoracial youth. This research illustrated how it is possible to examine particular psychological processes that can abstracted from specific contexts and thereby provide an important innovative way of testing psychological theories of diversity.

Additionally, this differentiation of horizontal and vertical expansions of multicultural theory and research parallels two different ways of expanding monocultural constructs in which the phenomenon had been previously defined in the context of only a single cultural context. The first way of expanding a monocultural construct is to define it in the context of a second cultural group by translating from one cultural context into the second cultural context. In this regard, there is no attempt to decontextualize the phenomenon for the particular cultural contexts.

The second approach attempts to define the phenomenon so that it is not embedded in only one cultural context by either (a) focusing on the underlying psychologically processes or (b) focusing on the similarities of the phenomenon across cultural contexts. Another component of decontextualization involves viewing a phenomenon from multiple cultural perspectives and abstracting the common features of the phenomenon—which would seem particularly consistent with a multicultural perspective. The astute reader may recognize that the first way of expanding monocultural constructs in which the construct is embedded in a second cultural context may be a first step in the processes of understanding a construct from multiple cultural perspectives. An important consideration, however, is that the multiple cultural perspectives should represent strategic or critical multiplism and not reflect naïve multiplism. That is, the different cultural perspectives should be chosen to represent compelling perspectives. For example, understanding acculturation from the perspective of three different Latino subgroups may not be as helpful as understanding acculturation from three other groups, such as Latin American, Asian, and African origin groups. Hence, trying to understand a phenomenon is enhanced with strategic or critical forms of multiplism in cultural perspectives. To develop a multicultural perspective, it is necessary to first understand a different cultural perspective; the next step is to further decontextualize it from a particular context. Consequently, the main difference between the horizontal and vertical approaches is that for the former, the main goal is to understand the phenomenon in a particular cultural context. For the latter, the main goal is to understand the phenomenon across cultures and to understand the theoretical principles and dynamics at work by selecting groups that provide a strategic and critical evaluation of the underlying theoretical principles.

Fortunately, several important examples of research provide a vertical expansion of multicultural psychology. Research into racial identity has uncovered important insights into multicultural processes. Although originally descriptive of nigrescence for African Americans, racial identity theory has been applied to numerous racial groups and

ethnic subgroups (Atkinson, Morten, & Sue, 1999). Despite differences in demographic characteristics, racial and ethnic identity processes are similar for Latino and African American youth. Investigations reveal that across these two groups, exposure to discrimination triggers increases in identity exploration, and their developmental trajectory for racial identity development is remarkably similar (Pahl & Way, 2006). This research provides insight into the psychological mechanisms associated with racial identity development and implicates a potential explanation for why racial identity develops. That is, because racial identity develops, in part, in reaction to exposure to discrimination, one of its main psychological purposes or teleological goals seems to be to cope with discrimination. Research on yet another group, Asian Americans, confirms that racial identity processes can facilitate coping with racial stress (Yoo & Lee, 2008). This series of research studies demonstrates that the foundation of generalizing multicultural research need not be by demographic representation, per se. Additionally, research that is focused on the underlying psychological characteristics provides more valuable insight into processes and constructs than research that uses demographic status as proxies for various psychological processes.

Researchers have strategically selected demographic groups to tease out the implications of different psychological processes. Research on monoracial persons is limited because many underlying processes are confounded. To illustrate, Tajfel and Turner's (1986) social identity theory and social categorization theory emphasize the importance of psychologically identifying with a racial group, but other more sociological theories emphasize the consequences of phenotypical characteristics for how members of a racial group are treated in a particular society. Although it is possible in monoracial populations to investigate outcomes associated with variability in phenotype (e.g., variations in skin coloration), it is more difficult to investigate variations in which racial groups persons identify, given that most monoracial persons only identify with the racial group corresponding to their phenotype. As illustrated, research on biracial populations may provide important insights into psychological processes underlying monoracial populations.

CONCLUSION

In this chapter, we have proposed a structure for the psychological science of diversity related to race and ethnicity such that the focus is on translating the implications of race and ethnicity for psychological functioning. We believe unnecessary attention within counseling psychology is devoted to definitional issues when there are government agencies and allied disciplines that have more authority on the concepts of race and ethnicity. As psychologists, our discipline should focus on research that investigates the psychological implications of racial and ethnic group membership.

We propose two major pillars of a science of diversity: acculturation and racialization processes. Within acculturation, there are two complementary processes, including enculturation within an ethnic or racial group and socialization to a difference ethnic or racial group. In more extreme forms, intense enculturation could lead to separation or segregation, whereas restrictive socialization to dominant culture could lead to assimilation to dominant culture. Multicultural research has effectively challenged assimilation policies that sought to acculturate diverse groups to dominant cultural norms. Indeed, important benefits are derived from maintaining heritage culture traditions and language. On the other hand, research has identified some challenges with adherence to traditional cultural in contexts or institutions that are predominately White. To date, relatively little research has been conducted into the psychological benefits of acquiring a second culture or becoming bicultural. Recent instrumentation on biculturalism is a promising area of research.

Similarly, much is known about racialization processes in which ethnic or racial discrimination fosters identity exploration and formation for many ethnic and racial groups that are stigmatized. There are significant costs to exposure to discrimination and multiple pathways by which discrimination can influence psychological adjustment, including direct, indirect, and vicarious exposures to racism

and ethnic discrimination. A purportedly main function for ethnic and racial identity is to provide protection against the deleterious effects of discrimination. Although considerable cross-sectional research demonstrates that a strong identity is associated with psychological adjustment, initial longitudinal research challenges whether ethnic and racial identity leads to psychological adjustment or whether psychological adjustment (e.g., self-esteem) leads to strong ethnic or racial identity. Additionally, research has shown that having a more centralized racial or ethnic identity can be associated with lower levels of adjustment in the context of high levels of discrimination. Ethnic and racial identity needs to be, consequently, tailored to the nature of the intergroup context to be most adaptive.

In this chapter, we make a case that the important contribution of research on diversity is not based on its external validity but rather in the way in which different populations can be sampled to provide alternative perspectives on key issues associated with ethnicity and race. Herman's (2008) research into multiracial populations was offered as an example of research that investigates identity formation in a novel manner. More generally, we suggest that forms of critical multiplism can be applied to examine the cultural expressions of various principles of diversity in different ethnic and racial contexts and thereby make important contributions to a science of diversity. Finally, a psychological science of diversity is promoted through the winnowing of theoretical principles that have been evaluated using empirical research.

References

American Anthropological Association. (1997). *Response to OMB directive 15: Race and ethnic standards for federal statistics and administrative reporting.* Retrieved from http://www.aaanet.org/gvt/ombdraft.htm

American Psychological Association. (2003). Guidelines on multicultural education, training, research, practice, and organizational change for psychologists. *American Psychologist, 58,* 377–402. doi:10.1037/0003-066X.58.5.377

American Sociological Association. (2003). *Statement of the American Sociological Association on the importance of collecting data and doing scientific research on race.* Retrieved from http://www2.asanet.org/media/asa_race_statement.pdf

Arciniega, G. M., Anderson, T. C., Tovar-Blank, Z., & Tracey, T. J. G. (2008). Toward a fuller conception of machismo: Development of a traditional machismo and caballerismo scale. *Journal of Counseling Psychology, 55,* 19–33. doi:10.1037/0022-0167.55.1.19

Arredondo, P., & Perez, P. (2006). Historical perspectives on the multicultural guidelines and contemporary applications. *Professional Psychology: Research and Practice, 37,* 1–5. doi:10.1037/0735-7028.37.1.1

Atkinson, D., Morten, G., & Sue, D. (1999). Counseling American minorities: A cross cultural perspective. Dubuque, IA: Brown.

Banks, W. (1976). White preference in Blacks: A paradigm in search of a phenomenon. *Psychological Bulletin, 83,* 1179–1186. doi:10.1037/0033-2909.83.6.1179

Beadnell, B. B., Stielstra, S. S., Baker, S. S., Morrison, D. M., Knox, K. K., Gutierrez, L. L., & Doyle, A. A. (2003). Ethnic identity and sexual risk-taking among African-American women enrolled in an HIV/STD prevention intervention. *Psychology Health and Medicine, 8,* 187–198. doi:10.1080/1354850031000087564

Bellini, J. (2003). Counselors' multicultural competencies and vocational rehabilitation outcomes in the context of counselor-client racial similarity and difference. *Rehabilitation Counseling Bulletin, 46,* 164–173.

Benet-Martínez, V., & Haritatos, J. (2005). Bicultural Identity Integration (BII): Components and psychosocial antecedents. *Journal of Personality, 73,* 1015–1049. doi:10.1111/j.1467-6494.2005.00337.x

Benish, S. G., Quintana, S. M., & Wampold, B. (2011). Culturally adapted psychotherapy and the legitimacy of myth: A director comparison meta-analysis. *Journal of Counseling Psychology, 58,* 279–289.

Berry, J. W. (1997). Constructing and expanding a framework: Opportunities for developing acculturation research. *Applied Psychology: An International Review, 46,* 62–68. doi:10.1080/026999497378548

Berry, J. W., & Annis, R. (1988), *Ethnic psychology: Research and practice with immigrants, refugees, native peoples, ethnic groups, and sojourners.* Lisse, Netherlands: Swets & Zeitlinger.

Bettendorf, S. K., & Fischer, A. R. (2009). Cultural strengths as moderators of the relationship between acculturation to the mainstream U.S. society and eating- and body-related concerns among Mexican American women. *Journal of Counseling Psychology, 56,* 430–440. doi:10.1037/a0016382

Bornstein, M., & Cote, L. (Eds.). (2006). *Acculturation and parent-child relationships: Measurement and development.* Mahwah, NJ: Erlbaum.

Boykin, A., Jagers, R. J., Ellison, C. M., & Albury, A. (1997). Communalism: Conceptualization and measurement of an Afrocultural social orientation. *Journal of Black Studies, 27,* 409–418. doi:10.1177/002193479702700308

Brody, G. H., Chen, Y., Murry, V. M., Ge, X., Simons, R. L., Gibbons, F. X., . . . Cutrona, C. E. (2006). Perceived discrimination and the adjustment of African American youths: A five-year longitudinal analysis with contextual moderation effects. *Child Development, 77,* 1170–1189. doi:10.1111/j.1467-8624.2006.00927.x

Bronfenbrenner, U. (1979). Contexts of child rearing: Problems and prospects. *American Psychologist, 34,* 844–850. doi:10.1037/0003-066X.34.10.844

Bruce, E., & Waelde, L. C. (2008). Relationships of ethnicity, ethnic identity, and trauma symptoms to delinquency. *Journal of Loss and Trauma, 13,* 395–405. doi:10.1080/15325020802171326

Bureau of Justice Statistics. (2009). *Growth in prison and jail populations slowing.* Retrieved from http://bjs.ojp.usdoj.gov/content/pub/press/pimjim08stpr.cfm

Carter, R. T. (2007). Racism and psychological and emotional injury: Recognizing and assessing race-based traumatic stress. *The Counseling Psychologist, 35,* 13–105. doi:10.1177/0011000006292033

Castillo, L. G., Cano, M. A., Chen, S. W., Blucker, R. T., & Olds, T. S. (2008). Family conflict and intragroup marginalization as predictors of acculturative stress in Latino college students. *International Journal of Stress Management, 15,* 43–52. doi:10.1037/1072-5245.15.1.43

Castillo, L. G., Conoley, C. W., Brossart, D. F., & Quiros, A. E. (2007). Construction and validation of the Intragroup Marginalization Inventory. *Cultural Diversity and Ethnic Minority Psychology, 13,* 232–240. doi:10.1037/1099-9809.13.3.232

Caughy, M. O., Nettles, S., O'Campo, P., & Lohrfink, K. (2006). Neighborhood matters: Racial socialization of African American children. *Child Development, 77,* 1220–1236. doi:10.1111/j.1467-8624.2006.00930.x

Chan, W., & Mendoza-Denton, R. (2008). Status-based rejection sensitivity among Asian Americans: Implications for psychological distress. *Journal of Personality, 76,* 1317–1346. doi:10.1111/j.1467-6494.2008.00522.x

Chao, R., Wei, M., Good, G. E., & Flores, L. Y. (2011). Race/ethnicity, color-blind racial attitudes, and multicultural counseling competence: The moderating effects of multicultural counseling training. *Journal of Counseling Psychology, 58,* 72–82. doi:10.1037/a0022091

Charmaraman, L., & Grossman, J. M. (2010). Importance of race and ethnicity: An exploration of Asian, Black,

Latino, and multiracial adolescent identity. *Cultural Diversity and Ethnic Minority Psychology, 16,* 144–151. doi:10.1037/a0018668

Chen, S. X., Benet-Martínez, V., & Bond, M. (2008). Bicultural identity, bilingualism, and psychological adjustment in multicultural societies: Immigration-based and globalization-based acculturation. *Journal of Personality, 76,* 803–838. doi:10.1111/j.1467-6494.2008.00505.x

Clark, K. B., & Clark, M. P. (1939). Segregation as a factor in the racial identification of Negro preschool children. *Journal of Experimental Education, 8,* 161–163.

Cokley, K. O. (2005). Racial(ized) identity, ethnic identity, and Afrocentric values: Conceptual and methodological challenges in understanding African American identity. *Journal of Counseling Psychology, 52,* 517–526. doi:10.1037/0022-0167.52.4.517

Costigan, C. L., Koryzma, C., Hua, J. M., & Chance, L. J. (2010). Ethnic identity, achievement, and psychological adjustment: Examining risk and resilience among youth from immigrant Chinese families in Canada. *Cultural Diversity and Ethnic Minority Psychology, 16,* 264–273. doi:10.1037/a0017275

Crocker, J., & Major, B. (1989). Social stigma and self-esteem: The self-protective properties of stigma. *Psychological Review, 96,* 608–630. doi:10.1037/0033-295X.96.4.608

Cross, W. E., Jr. (1971). The Negro to Black conversion experience. *Black World, 20,* 13–27.

Cross, W. E., Jr. (1991). *Shades of black: Diversity in African-American identity.* Philadelphia, PA: Temple University Press.

Cross, W. E., Jr. (1995). The psychology of nigrescence: Revising the Cross model. In J. G. Ponterotto, J. M. Casas, L. A. Suzuki, & C. M. Alexander (Eds.), *Handbook of multicultural counseling* (pp. 93–122). Thousand Oaks, CA: Sage.

Cross, W. E., Jr., & Cross, T. B. (2008). Theory, Research, and Models. In S. M. Quintana & C. McKown (Eds.), *Race, racism and developing child* (pp. 154–181). New York, NY: Wiley.

Cuéllar, I., Arnold, B., & Maldonado, R. (1995). Acculturation Rating Scale for Mexican Americans-II: A revision of the original ARSMA Scale. *Hispanic Journal of Behavioral Sciences, 17,* 275–304. doi:10.1177/07399863950173001

Cuéllar, I., Harris, L. C., & Jasso, R. (1980). An acculturation scale for Mexican American normal and clinical populations. *Hispanic Journal of Behavioral Sciences, 2,* 199–217.

David, E. R., Okazaki, S., & Saw, A. (2009). Bicultural self-efficacy among college students: Initial scale development and mental health correlates. *Journal*

of *Counseling Psychology, 56,* 211–226. doi:10.1037/a0015419

Erikson, E. H. (1968). *Identity: Youth and crisis.* Oxford, England: Norton.

Escobar, J. I. (1998). Immigration and mental health: Why are immigrants better off? *Archives of General Psychiatry, 55,* 781–782. doi:10.1001/arch-psyc.55.9.781

French, S., Seidman, E., Allen, L., & Aber, J. (2000). Racial/ethnic identity, congruence with the social context, and the transition to high school. *Journal of Adolescent Research, 15,* 587–602.

French, S. E., Seidman, E., Allen, L., & Aber, J. L. (2006). The development of ethnic identity during adolescence. *Developmental Psychology, 42,* 1–10. doi:10.1037/0012-1649.42.1.1

Fuligni, A. J., Witkow, M., & Garcia, C. (2005). Ethnic identity and the academic adjustment of adolescents from Mexican, Chinese, and European backgrounds. *Developmental Psychology, 41,* 799–811. doi:10.1037/0012-1649.41.5.799

Garza, Y., & Watts, R. E. (2010). Filial therapy and Hispanic values: Common ground for culturally sensitive helping. *Journal of Counseling and Development, 88,* 108–113.

Glass, J., & Owen, J. (2010). Latino fathers: The relationship among machismo, acculturation, ethnic identity, and paternal involvement. *Psychology of Men and Masculinity, 11,* 251–261. doi:10.1037/a0021477

Gloria, A. M., Castellanos, J., Park, Y., & Kim, D. (2008). Adherence to Asian cultural values and cultural fit in Korean American undergraduates' help-seeking attitudes. *Journal of Counseling and Development, 86,* 419–428.

Gloria, A. M., & Hird, J. S. (1999). Influences of ethnic and nonethnic variables on the career decision-making self-efficacy of college students. *The Career Development Quarterly, 48,* 157–174.

Graves, T. D. (1967). Acculturation, access, alcohol in a tri-ethnic country. *American Anthropologist, 59,* 306–321.

Griner, D., & Smith, T. B. (2006). Culturally adapted mental health intervention: A meta-analytic review. *Psychotherapy: Theory, Research, Practice, Training, 43,* 531–548. doi:10.1037/0033-3204.43.4.531

Hahm, H. C., Lahiff, M., & Guterman, N. B. (2004). Asian American Adolescents' Acculturation, Binge Drinking, and Alcohol- and Tobacco-Using Peers. *Journal of Community Psychology, 32,* 295–308. doi:10.1002/jcop.20002

Helms, J. E. (1995). An update of Helms' White and people of color racial identity models. In J. G. Ponterotto, J. M. Casas, L. A. Suzuki, & C. M. Alexander (Eds.),

Handbook of multicultural counseling (pp. 181–198). Thousand Oaks, CA: Sage.

Helms, J. E., & Talleyrand, R. (1997). Race is not ethnicity. *American Psychologist, 52*, 1246–1247. doi:10.1037/0003-066X.52.11.1246

Herman, M. R. (2008). Racial identification among multiracial youth: Implications for adjustment. In S. M. Quintana, C. McKown, S. M. Quintana, & C. McKown (Eds.), *Handbook of race, racism, and the developing child* (pp. 203–225). Hoboken, NJ: Wiley.

Herman, M. R. (2009). The Black-White-other achievement gap: Testing theories of academic performance among multiracial and monoracial adolescents. *Sociology of Education, 82*, 20–46. doi:10.1177/003804070908200102

Hughes, D., Rivas, D., Foust, M., Hagelskamp, C., Gersick, S., & Way, N. (2008). How to catch a moonbeam: A mixed-methods approach to understanding ethnic socialization processes in ethnically diverse families. In S. M. Quintana & C. McKown (Eds.), *Handbook of race, racism, and the developing child* (pp. 226–277). Hoboken, NJ: Wiley.

Hwang, W. C., & Goto, S. (2008). The impact of perceived racial discrimination on the mental health of Asian American and Latino college students. *Cultural Diversity and Ethnic Minority Psychology, 14*, 326–335. doi:10.1037/1099-9809.14.4.326

Hwang, W. C., & Ting, J. Y. (2008). Disaggregating the effects of acculturation and acculturative stress on the mental health of Asian Americans. *Cultural Diversity and Ethnic Minority Psychology, 14*, 147–154. doi:10.1037/1099-9809.14.2.147

Jones, J. M. (1997). *Prejudice and racism* (2nd ed.). New York, NY: McGraw-Hill.

Kearney, L. K., Draper, M., & Barón, A. (2005). Counseling utilization by ethnic minority college students. *Cultural Diversity and Ethnic Minority Psychology, 11*, 272–285. doi:10.1037/1099-9809.11.3.272

Kiang, L., Witkow, M. R., Baldelomar, O. A., & Fuligni, A. J. (2010). Change in ethnic identity across the high school years among adolescents with Latin American, Asian, and European backgrounds. *Journal of Youth and Adolescence, 39*, 683–693. doi:10.1007/s10964-009-9429-5

Kiang, L., Yip, T., Gonzales-Backen, M., Witkow, M., & Fuligni, A. (2006). Ethnic identity and the daily psychological well-being of adolescents from Mexican and Chinese backgrounds. *Child Development, 77*, 1338–1350. doi:10.1111/j.1467-8624.2006.00938.x

Kim, B. K. (2007). Adherence to Asian and European American cultural values and attitudes toward seeking professional psychological help among Asian American college students. *Journal of Counseling Psychology, 54*, 474–480. doi:10.1037/0022-0167.54.4.474

Kim, B. K., Atkinson, D. R., & Yang, P. H. (1999). The Asian Values Scale: Development, factor analysis, validation, and reliability. *Journal of Counseling Psychology, 46*, 342–352. doi:10.1037/0022-0167.46.3.342

Kim, B. K., Hill, C. E., Gelso, C. J., Goates, M. K., Asay, P. A., & Harbin, J. M. (2003). Counselor self-disclosure, East Asian American client adherence to Asian cultural values, and counseling process. *Journal of Counseling Psychology, 50*, 324–332. doi:10.1037/0022-0167.50.3.324

Kim, B. S. K., & Atkinson, D. R. (2002). Asian American client adherence to Asian cultural values, counselor expression of cultural values, counselor ethnicity, and career counseling process. *Journal of Counseling Psychology, 49*, 3–13. doi:10.1037/0022-0167.49.1.3

Kim, B. S. K., Ng, G. F., & Ahn, A. J. (2005). Effects of client expectation for counseling success, client-counselor worldview match, and client adherence to Asian and European American cultural values on counseling process with Asian Americans. *Journal of Counseling Psychology, 52*, 67–76. doi:10.1037/0022-0167.52.1.67

Kim, B. S. K., Ng, G. F., & Ahn, A. J. (2009). Client adherence to Asian cultural values, common factors in counseling, and session outcome with Asian American clients at a university counseling center. *Journal of Counseling and Development, 87*, 131–142.

Kim, B. S. K., & Omizo, M. M. (2005). Asian and European American cultural values, collective self-esteem, acculturative stress, cognitive flexibility, and general self-efficacy among Asian American college students. *Journal of Counseling Psychology, 52*, 412–419. doi:10.1037/0022-0167.52.3.412

Kim, B. S. K., & Omizo, M. M. (2006). Behavioral acculturation and enculturation and psychological functioning among Asian American college students. *Cultural Diversity and Ethnic Minority Psychology, 12*, 245–258. doi:10.1037/1099-9809.12.2.245

Kim, P. Y., & Park, I. J. K. (2009). Testing a multiple mediation model of Asian American college students' willingness to see a counselor. *Cultural Diversity and Ethnic Minority Psychology, 15*, 295–302. doi:10.1037/a0014396

Kitayama, S., & Tompson, S. (2010). Envisioning the future of cultural neuroscience. *Asian Journal of Social Psychology, 13*, 92–101. doi:10.1111/j.1467-839X.2010.01304.x

Knight, G. P., Bernal, M. E., Garza, C. A., Cota, M. K., & Ocampo, K. A. (1993). Family socialization and the ethnic identity of Mexican-American children. *Journal of Cross-Cultural Psychology, 24*, 99–114. doi:10.1177/0022022193241007

LaFromboise, T. D. (1999). *The Living in Two Worlds Survey*. (Unpublished test instrument). Stanford University, Stanford, CA.

LaFromboise, T. D., Coleman, H. L., & Gerton, J. (1993). Psychological impact of biculturalism: Evidence and theory. *Psychological Bulletin, 114,* 395–412. doi:10.1037/0033-2909.114.3.395

Landrine, H., & Klonoff, E. A. (1996). The schedule of racist events: A measure of racial discrimination and a study of its negative physical and mental health consequences. *Journal of Black Psychology, 22,* 144–168. doi:10.1177/00957984960222002

Lazarus, R.S., & Folkman, S. (1984). *Stress, appraisal and coping*. New York, NY: Springer.

Lee, R. M. (2005). Resilience against discrimination: Ethnic identity and other-group orientation as protective factors for Korean Americans. *Journal of Counseling Psychology, 52,* 36–44. doi:10.1037/0022-0167.52.1.36

Lee, R. M., Choe, J., Kim, G., & Ngo, V. (2000). Construction of the Asian American Family Conflicts Scale. *Journal of Counseling Psychology, 47,* 211–222. doi:10.1037/0022-0167.47.2.211

Li, L. C., Kim, B. S. K., & O'Brien, K. M. (2007). An analogue study of the effects of Asian cultural values and counselor multicultural competence on counseling process. *Psychotherapy: Theory, Research, Practice, Training, 44,* 90–95. doi:10.1037/0033-3204.44.1.90

Liao, H., Rounds, J., & Klein, A. G. (2005). A test of Cramer's (1999). Help-seeking model and acculturation effects with Asian and Asian American college students. *Journal of Counseling Psychology, 52,* 400–411. doi:10.1037/0022-0167.52.3.400

Mallinckrodt, B., Shigeoka, S., & Suzuki, L. A. (2005). Asian and pacific island American students' acculturation and etiology beliefs about typical counseling presenting problems. *Cultural Diversity and Ethnic Minority Psychology, 11,* 227–238. doi:10.1037/1099-9809.11.3.2272

Marcia, J. E. (1966). Development and validation of ego-identity status. *Journal of Personality and Social Psychology, 3,* 551–558. doi:10.1037/h0023281

Marsiglia, F. F., Kulis, S., Hecht, M. L., & Sills, S. (2004). Ethnicity and ethnic identity as predictors of drug norms and drug use among preadolescents in the US Southwest. *Substance Use and Misuse, 39,* 1061–1094. doi:10.1081/JA-120038030

Matsunaga, M., Hecht, M. L., Elek, E., & Ndiaye, K. (2010). Ethnic identity development and acculturation; A longitudinal analysis of Mexican-heritage youth in the southwest United States. *Journal of Cross-Cultural Psychology, 41,* 410–427. doi:10.1177/0022022109359689

McHale, S. M., Crouter, A. C., Kim, J., Burton, L. M., Davis, K. D., Dotterer, A. M., & Swanson, D. P. (2006). Mothers' and fathers' racial socialization in African American families: Implications for youth. *Child Development, 77,* 1387–1402. doi:10.1111/j.1467-8624.2006.00942.x

Miller, M. J. (2007). A bilinear multidimensional measurement model of Asian American acculturation and enculturation: Implications for counseling interventions. *Journal of Counseling Psychology, 54,* 118–131. doi:10.1037/0022-0167.54.2.118

Miller, M. J. (2010). Testing a bilinear domain-specific model of acculturation and enculturation across generational status. *Journal of Counseling Psychology, 57,* 179–186. doi:10.1037/a0019089

Miville, M. L., & Constantine, M. G. (2007). Cultural values, counseling stigma, and intentions to seek counseling among Asian American college women. *Counseling and Values, 52,* 2–11.

Moyerman, D. R., & Forman, B. D. (1992). Acculturation and adjustment: A meta-analytic study. *Hispanic Journal of Behavioral Sciences, 14,* 163–200. doi:10.1177/07399863920142001

Neblett, E. W., Jr., White, R. L., Ford, K. R., Philip, C. L., Nguyên, H. X., & Sellers, R. M. (2008). Patterns of racial socialization and psychological adjustment: Can parental communications about race reduce the impact of racial discrimination? *Journal of Research on Adolescence, 18,* 477–515. doi:10.1111/j.1532-7795.2008.00568.x

Neighbors, H. W., Caldwell, C., Williams, D. R., Nesse, R., Taylor, R., Bullard, K., & Jackson, J. S. (2007). Race, ethnicity, and the use of services for mental disorders: Results from the National Survey of American Life. *Archives of General Psychiatry, 64,* 485–494. doi:10.1001/archpsyc.64.4.485

Newell, M. (2005). *African Americans and aggressive behaviors: Situating intervention effectiveness within the context of discursive formations*. Unpublished master's thesis.

Obasi, E. M., & Leong, F. L. (2010). Construction and validation of the Measurement of Acculturation Strategies for People of African Descent (MASPAD). *Cultural Diversity and Ethnic Minority Psychology, 16,* 526–539. doi:10.1037/a0021374

Obasi, E. M., & Leong, F. T. L. (2009). Psychological distress, acculturation, and mental health-seeking attitudes among people of African descent in the united states: A preliminary investigation. *Journal of Counseling Psychology, 56,* 227–238. doi:10.1037/a0014865

Oetting, G. R., & Beauvais, F. (1990). Orthogonal cultural identification theory: The cultural identification of minority adolescents. *International*

Journal of the Addictions, 25, 655–685. doi:10.3109/10826089109077265

Office of Management and Budget. (1997). *1997 North American industry classification system—1987 standard industrial classification replacement. Federal Register, 62,* 17288–17478.

Ojeda, L., Rosales, R., & Good, G. E. (2008). Socioeconomic status and cultural predictors of male role attitudes among Mexican American men: Son más machos? *Psychology of Men and Masculinity, 9,* 133–138. doi:10.1037/1524-9220.9.3.133

Outten, H., Giguère, B., Schmitt, M. T., & Lalonde, R. N. (2010). Racial identity, racial context, and ingroup status: Implications for attributions to discrimination among Black Canadians. *Journal of Black Psychology, 36,* 172–196. doi:10.1177/0095798409344083

Oyserman, D., Coon, H., & Kemmelmeier, M. (2002). Rethinking individualism and collectivism: Evaluation of theoretical assumptions and meta-analyses. *Psychological Bulletin, 128,* 3–72. doi:10.1037/0033-2909.128.1.3

Oyserman, D., Kemmelmeier, M., Fryberg, S., Brosh, H., & Hart-Johnson, T. (2003). Racial-ethnic self-schemas. *Social Psychology Quarterly, 66,* 333–347. doi:10.2307/1519833

Pahl, K., & Way, N. (2006). Longitudinal trajectories of ethnic identity among urban Black and Latino adolescents. *Child Development, 77,* 1403–1415. doi:10.1111/j.1467-8624.2006.00943.x

Parham, T. A. (1989). Cycles of psychological Nigrescence. *The Counseling Psychologist, 17,* 187–226. doi:10.1177/0011000089172001

Park, Y. S., & Kim, B. S. K. (2008). Asian and European American cultural values and communication styles among Asian American and European American college students. *Cultural Diversity and Ethnic Minority Psychology, 14,* 47–56. doi:10.1037/1099-9809.14.1.47

Park, Y. S., Kim, B. S. K., Chiang, J., & Ju, C. M. (2010). Acculturation, enculturation, parental adherence to Asian cultural values, parenting styles, and family conflict among Asian American college students. *Asian American Journal of Psychology, 1,* 67–79. doi:10.1037/a0018961

Phinney, J. (1989). Stages of ethnic identity development in minority group adolescents. *The Journal of Early Adolescence, 9*(1–2), 34–49. doi:10.1177/0272431689091004

Phinney, J. (1992). The multigroup ethnic identity measure: A new scale for use with diverse groups. *Journal of Adolescent Research, 7,* 156–176. doi:10.1177/074355489272003

Phinney, J. (1996). When we talk about American ethnic groups, what do we mean? *American Psychologist, 51,* 918–927. doi:10.1037/0003-066X.51.9.918

Ponterotto, J. G., & Mallinckrodt, B. (2007). Introduction to the special section on racial and ethnic identity in counseling psychology: Conceptual and methodological challenges and proposed solutions. *Journal of Counseling Psychology, 54,* 219–223. doi:10.1037/0022-0167.54.3.219

Ponterotto, J. G., Suzuki, L., Casas, M., & Alexander, C. (2010). *Handbook of multicultural counseling* (3rd ed.). Thousand Oaks, CA: Sage.

Portes, A., & Rumbaut, R. G. (2006). *Immigrant America: A portrait* (3rd ed.). Berkeley: University of California Press.

Quintana, S. M. (1998). Development of children's understanding of ethnicity and race. *Applied and Preventive Psychology: Current Scientific Perspectives, 7,* 27–45.

Quintana, S. M. (2007). Racial and ethnic identity: Developmental perspectives and research. *Journal of Counseling Psychology, 54,* 259–270. doi:10.1037/0022-0167.54.3.259

Quintana, S. M. (2008). Children's racial perspective-taking ability. In S. M. Quintana & C. McKown (Eds.), *Handbook of race, racism, and the developing child* (pp. 16–36). Hoboken, NJ: Wiley.

Quintana, S. M. (2010). Ethnicity, race and children's social development. In P. K. Smith & C. H. Hart (Eds.), *Wiley-Blackwell handbook of childhood social development* (pp. 299–316). Oxford, England: Wiley-Blackwell.

Quintana, S. M., Castañeda-English, P., & Ybarra, V. C. (1999). Role of perspective-taking ability and ethnic socialization in the development of adolescent ethnic identity. *Journal of Research on Adolescence, 9,* 161–184. doi:10.1207/s15327795jra0902_3

Quintana, S. M., & Chavez, T. (in press). Mexican American children's ethnic identity. In D. Rejos-Castillo & Y. Caldera (Eds.), *Understanding Mexican-American children and families: Multi-disciplinary perspectives.* Philadelphia, PA: Psychology Press.

Quintana, S. M., & McKown, C. (2008). Introduction: Race, racism, and the developing child. In S. M. Quintana, C. McKown, S. M. Quintana, & C. McKown (Eds.), *Handbook of race, racism, and the developing child* (pp. 1–15). Hoboken, NJ: Wiley.

Quintana, S. M., Segura-Herrera, T., & Nelson, M. L. (2010). Mexican American high school students' ethnic self-concepts and identity. *Journal of Social Issues, 66,* 11–28. doi:10.1111/j.1540-4560.2009.01630.x

Rivas-Drake, D., Hughes, D., & Way, N. (2009). A preliminary analysis of associations among ethnic racial socialization, ethnic discrimination, and ethnic identity among urban sixth graders. *Journal of Research on Adolescence, 19,* 558–584. doi:10.1111/j.1532-7795.2009.00607.x

Rivera, L. M., Chen, E. C., Flores, L. Y., Blumberg, F., & Ponterotto, J. G. (2007). The effects of perceived barriers, role models, and acculturation on the career self-efficacy and career consideration of Hispanic women. *The Career Development Quarterly, 56,* 47–61.

Rodriguez, N., Myers, H. F., Morris, J. K., & Cardoza, D. (2000). Latino college student adjustment: Does an increased presence offset minority-status and acculturative stresses? *Journal of Applied Social Psychology, 30,* 1523–1550. doi:10.1111/j.1559-1816.2000.tb02534.x

Roehling, P. V., Jarvis, L., Sprik, J. M., & Campbell, P. H. (2010). The immigration debate and its relationship to the ethnic identity development and well-being of Latino and White youth. *Hispanic Journal of Behavioral Sciences, 32,* 292–308. doi:10.1177/0739986310366458

Rosenbloom, S., & Way, N. (2004). Experiences of discrimination among African American, Asian American, and Latino Adolescents in an urban high school. *Youth and Society, 35,* 420–451. doi:10.1177/0044118X03261479

Sam, D. L., & Berry, J. W. (2010). Acculturation: When individuals and groups of different cultural backgrounds meet. *Perspectives on Psychological Science, 5,* 472–481. doi:10.1177/1745691610373075

Schwartz, S. J., Unger, J. B., Zamboanga, B. L., & Szapocznik, J. (2010). Rethinking the concept of acculturation: Implications for theory and research. *American Psychologist, 65,* 237–251. doi:10.1037/a0019330

Schwartz, S. J., Weisskirch, R. S., Zamboanga, B. L., Castillo, L. G., Ham, L. S., Huynh, Q., . . . Ham, L. S. (2011). Dimensions of acculturation: Associations with health risk behaviors among college students from immigrant families. *Journal of Counseling Psychology, 58,* 27–41. doi:10.1037/a0021356

Schwartz, S. J., Zamboanga, B. L., & Jarvis, L. H. (2007). Ethnic identity and acculturation in Hispanic early adolescents: Mediated relationships to academic grades, prosocial behaviors, and externalizing symptoms. *Cultural Diversity and Ethnic Minority Psychology, 13,* 364–373. doi:10.1037/1099-9809.13.4.364

Seaton, E. K., Scottham, K., & Sellers, R. (2006). The status model of racial identity development in African American adolescents: Evidence of structure, trajectories, and well-being. *Child Development, 77,* 1416–1426. doi:10.1111/j.1467-8624.2006.00944.x

Seaton, E. K., Yip, T., & Sellers, R. M. (2009). A longitudinal examination of racial identity and racial discrimination among African American adolescents. *Child Development, 80,* 406–417. doi:10.1111/j.1467-8624.2009.01268.x

Sellers, R. M., Smith, M. A., Shelton, J. N., Rowley, S. A. J., & Chavous, T. M. (1998). Multidimensional model of racial identity: A reconceptualization of African American racial identity. *Personality and Social Psychology Review, 2,* 18–39. doi:10.1207/s15327957pspr0201_2

Selman, R. L. (1979). *Assessing interpersonal understanding: An interview and scoring manual in five parts constructed by the Harvard-Judge Backer Social Reasoning Project.* Boston, MA: Harvard-Judge Baker Social Reasoning Project.

Settles, I. H., Navarrete, C. D., Pagano, S. J., Abdou, C. M., & Sidanius, J. (2010). Racial identity and depression among African American women. *Cultural Diversity and Ethnic Minority Psychology, 16,* 248–255. doi:10.1037/a0016442

Shim, Y. R., & Schwartz, R. C. (2008). Degree of acculturation and adherence to Asian values as correlates of psychological distress among Korean immigrants. *Journal of Mental Health, 17,* 607–617. doi:10.1080/09638230701506838

Slavin, L. A., Rainer, K. L., McCreary, M. L., & Gowda, K. K. (1991). Toward a multicultural model of the stress process. *Journal of Counseling and Development, 70,* 156–163.

Smith, T. B., & Silva, L. (2011). Ethnic identity and personal well-being of people of color: A meta-analysis. *Journal of Counseling Psychology, 58,* 42–60. doi:10.1037/a0021528

Steffen, P. R., Smith, T. B., Larson, M., & Butler, L. (2006). Acculturation to Western society as a risk factor for high blood pressure: A meta-analytic review. *Psychosomatic Medicine, 68,* 386–397. doi:10.1097/01.psy.0000221255.48190.32

Sue, D. W. (2010). *Microaggressions in everyday life: Race, gender, and sexual orientation.* Hoboken, NJ: Wiley.

Sue, D. W., & Sue, D. (2003). *Counseling the culturally diverse: Theory and practice* (4th ed.). Hoboken, NJ: Wiley.

Sue, S. (2003). Science, ethnicity, and bias: Where have we gone wrong? In A. E. Kazdin & A. E. Kazdin (Eds.), *Methodological issues and strategies in clinical research* (3rd ed., pp. 173–188). Washington, DC: American Psychological Association.

Sue, S., Sue, D. W., Sue, L., & Takeuchi, D. T. (1995). Psychopathology among Asian Americans: A model minority? *Cultural Diversity and Mental Health, 1,* 39–51.

Suinn, R. M. (2010). Reviewing acculturation and Asian Americans: How acculturation affects health, adjustment, school achievement, and counseling. *Asian American Journal of Psychology, 1,* 5–17. doi:10.1037/a0018798

Syed, M., Azmitia, M., & Phinney, J. S. (2007). Stability and change in ethnic identity among Latino emerging adults in two contexts. *Identity: An International*

Journal of Theory and Research, 7, 155–178. doi:10.1080/15283480701326117

Szymanski, D. M., & Gupta, A. (2009). Examining the relationships between multiple oppressions and Asian American sexual minority persons' psychological distress. *Journal of Gay and Lesbian Social Services: Issues in Practice, Policy and Research, 21* (2–3), 267–281. doi:10.1080/10538720902772212

Tajfel, H., & Turner, J. (1986). The social identity theory of intergroup behavior. In S. Worchel & W. Austin (Eds.), *Psychology of intergroup relations* (pp. 7–24). Chicago, IL: Nelson-Hall.

Telzer, E. H., Masten, C. L., Berkman, E. T., Lieberman, M. D., & Fuligni, A. J. (2010). Gaining while giving: An fMRI study of the rewards of family assistance among White and Latino youth. *Social Neuroscience, 5*(5–6), 508–518. doi:10.1080/17470911003687913

Thomas, C. (1971). *Boys no more: A black psychologist's view of community.* Oxford, England: Glencoe.

Tseng, V. (2004). Family interdependence and academic adjustment in college: Youth from immigrant and U.S.-born families. *Child Development, 75*, 966–983. doi:10.1111/j.1467-8624.2004.00717.x

Tseng, V. (2006). Unpacking immigration in youths' academic and occupational pathways. *Child Development, 77*, 1434–1445. doi:10.1111/j.1467-8624.2006.00946.x

Umaña-Taylor, A. J., Alfaro, E. C., Bámaca, M. Y., & Guimond, A. B. (2009). The central role of familial ethnic socialization in Latino adolescents' cultural orientation. *Journal of Marriage and Family, 71*, 46–60. doi:10.1111/j.1741-3737.2008.00579.x

Umaña-Taylor, A. J., & Fine, M. A. (2004). Examining ethnic identity among Mexican-origin adolescents living in the United States. *Hispanic Journal of Behavioral Sciences, 26*, 36–59. doi:10.1177/0739986303262143

Umaña-Taylor, A. J., Gonzales-Backen, M. A., & Guimond, A. B. (2009). Latino adolescents' ethnic identity: Is there a developmental progression and does growth in ethnic identity predict growth in self-esteem? *Child Development, 80*, 391–405.

Umaña-Taylor, A. J., & Guimond, A. B. (2010). A longitudinal examination of parenting behaviors and perceived discrimination predicting Latino adolescents' ethnic identity. *Developmental Psychology, 46*, 636–650. doi:10.1037/a0019376

Umaña-Taylor, A. J., & Shin, N. (2007). An examination of ethnic identity and self-esteem with diverse populations: Exploring variation by ethnicity and geography. *Cultural Diversity and Ethnic Minority Psychology, 13*, 178–186. doi:10.1037/1099-9809.13.2.178

Umaña-Taylor, A. J., Vargas-Chanes, D., Garcia, C. D., & Gonzales-Backen, M. (2008). A longitudinal examination of Latino adolescents' ethnic identity, coping with discrimination, and self-esteem. *The Journal of Early Adolescence, 28*, 16–50. doi:10.1177/0272431607308666

United Nations Educational, Scientific, and Cultural Organization. (1952). *The race question in modern science: Results of an inquiry.* Paris, France: Imprimeri des Arts et Manufactures.

U.S. Census Bureau. (2011). *Statistical abstract of the United States, Table 225. Educational attainment by race and Hispanic origin 1970–2009.* Retrieved from http://www.census.gov/compendia/statab/2011/tables/11s0225.pdf

U.S. Department of Health and Human Services. (2003). *National healthcare disparities report.* Retrieved from http://www.ahrq.gov/qual/nhdr03/nhdrsum03.htm

Utsey, S. O., Hook, J. N., Fischer, N., & Belvet, B. (2008). Cultural orientation, ego resilience, and optimism as predictors of subjective well-being in African Americans. *The Journal of Positive Psychology, 3*, 202–210. doi:10.1080/17439760801999610

Vandiver, B. J., Cross, W. E., Jr., Worrell, F. C., & Fhagen-Smith, P. E. (2002). Validating the Cross Racial Identity Scale. *Journal of Counseling Psychology, 49*, 71–85. doi:10.1037/0022-0167.49.1.71

Wallace, B. C., & Constantine, M. G. (2005). Africentric cultural values, psychological help-seeking attitudes, and self-concealment in African American college students. *Journal of Black Psychology, 31*, 369–385. doi:10.1177/0095798405281025

Wang, C., & Mallinckrodt, B. (2006). Acculturation, attachment, and psychosocial adjustment of Chinese/Taiwanese international students. *Journal of Counseling Psychology, 53*, 422–433. doi:10.1037/0022-0167.53.4.422

Wang, S., & Kim, B. S. K. (2010). Therapist multicultural competence, Asian American participants' cultural values, and counseling process. *Journal of Counseling Psychology, 57*, 394–401. doi:10.1037/a0020359

White, M., Kim, A. H., & Glick, J. E. (2005). Mapping social distance: Ethnic residential segregation in a multiethnic metro. *Sociological Methods and Research, 34*, 173–203. doi:10.1177/0049124105280198

Willig, A. C. (1985). A meta-analysis of selected studies on the effectiveness of bilingual education. *Review of Educational Research, 55*, 269–317. doi:10.2307/1170389

Wintersteen, M. B., Mensinger, J. L., & Diamond, G. S. (2005). Do gender and racial differences between patient and therapist affect therapeutic alliance and treatment retention in adolescents? *Professional*

Psychology: Research and Practice, 36, 400–408. doi:10.1037/0735-7028.36.4.400

Wolfe, M. M., Yang, P. H., Wong, E. C., & Atkinson, D. R. (2001). Design and development of the European American values scale for Asian Americans. *Cultural Diversity and Ethnic Minority Psychology, 7,* 274–283. doi:10.1037/1099-9809.7.3.274

Wrenn, C. (1962). The culturally encapsulated counselor. *Harvard Educational Review, 32,* 444–449.

Yip, T., Gee, G. C., & Takeuchi, D. T. (2008). Racial discrimination and psychological distress: The impact of ethnic identity and age among immigrant and United States-born Asian adults. *Developmental Psychology, 44,* 787–800. doi:10.1037/0012-1649.44.3.787

Yip, T., Seaton, E., & Sellers, R. (2006). African American racial identity across the lifespan: Identity status, identity content, and depressive symptoms. *Child Development, 77,* 1504–1517. doi:10.1111/j.1467-8624.2006.00950.x

Yoo, H. C., & Lee, R. M. (2005). Ethnic identity and approach-type coping as moderators of the racial discrimination/well-being relation in Asian Americans. *Journal of Counseling Psychology, 52,* 497–506. doi:10.1037/0022-0167.52.4.497

Yoo, H. C., & Lee, R. M. (2008). Does ethnic identity buffer or exacerbate the effects of frequent racial discrimination on situational well-being of Asian Americans? *Journal of Counseling Psychology, 55,* 63–74. doi:10.1037/0022-0167.55.1.63

Yoon, E., Lee, R. M., & Goh, M. (2008). Acculturation, social connectedness, and subjective well-being. *Cultural Diversity and Ethnic Minority Psychology, 14,* 246–255. doi:10.1037/1099-9809.14.3.246

Yoon, J., & Lau, A. S. (2008). Maladaptive perfectionism and depressive symptoms among Asian American college students: Contributions of interdependence and parental relations. *Cultural Diversity and Ethnic Minority Psychology, 14,* 92–101.

CHAPTER 18

AGING THEORY AND RESEARCH

Tammi Vacha-Haase, Robert D. Hill, and Douglas W. Bermingham

Society is aging, with many living into their advanced years. For the 38 million Americans over age 65 (U.S. Census Bureau, 2008), almost 6 million have celebrated their 85th birthday, with estimates of more than 100,000 centenarians living in the nation. The most recent actualized data places average life expectancy for men at 75 and women at 80 (U.S. Census Bureau, 2008).

As people live longer, the nature of aging and how it is perceived by the individual as well as others also change. Such evolution is mirrored in evolving theories and accumulating research of how, why, and what it means to grow old. Counseling psychology can play a significant role in this progression by offering contributions to the expansion of meaningful theory in the aging process on the basis of the profession's core values of affirmative adaptation and social inclusiveness.

Counseling psychology has an affirmative approach to life-span adaptation (Lopez et al., 2006), with specific focus on strengths-based counseling as well as research and theory development in positive social change (Magyar-Moe & Lopez, 2008) and multicultural inclusivity (Baker & Subich, 2008; Constantine, Fuertes, Roysircar, & Kindaichi, 2008). The profession emphasizes people's assets and strengths, with an essential commitment and valuing of the integration of individual and cultural diversity and the vital importance of multiculturalism within the changing U.S. society (Gelso & Fretz, 1992).

Within these traditional values and beliefs lies the framework for understanding older adults

through a combination of a strengths-based approach, with a recognition of individual characteristics or identity (e.g., gender, cohort, race or ethnicity), and developmental age-related challenges. As Lopez et al. (2006) summarized, "Over the course of its development as a specialty, counseling psychology has held to a philosophical focus and a professional emphasis on identifying and developing personal and social resources and on helping individuals more effectively use these resources" (p. 206). This could not be more relevant than for those in their later years of life.

The present chapter begins with a brief identification of emergent definitions of aging, followed by a more extensive review of multiple theories of strengths-based aging, including Erikson's (1963, 1968) psychosocial model of development, continuity theory, selective optimization with compensation (SOC), and positive aging. Focus is then given to a growing literature examining identity intersection and linking aspects of traditional theories with aging and the multicultural movement. Guided by the profession's values, theoretical and empirical expansion in conceptualizing those in their later years through their intersecting identities is further explored. The final section suggests that in addition to applying the profession's value of diversity to aging theory, counseling psychology's historical traditions in career education and counseling can be utilized to expand vocational psychology to those in their later years, including areas such as late-stage work life, recareering, and retirement planning.

DOI: 10.1037/13754-018
APA Handbook of Counseling Psychology: Vol. 1. Theories, Research, and Methods, Nadya A. Fouad (Editor-in-Chief)

AGING DEFINITIONS: PAST TO PRESENT

Across disciplines, early definitions characterized human aging as a biological process gone awry, akin to chronic disease; that is, aging (like disease) was viewed in the 1960s and 1970s as time related, irreversible, and deleterious to health (Palmore, 1970). Although arguably simplistic, this definition mirrored the powerlessness that individuals felt in adapting to the vicissitudes of aging.

A later proposed alternative to this early disease-based paradigm of aging-as-disease was proposed by Shock et al. (1984), employing data from the Baltimore Longitudinal Study of Aging (BLSA). The BLSA followed multiple cohorts of adults throughout their life span and data from this study suggested that aging could be defined by its heterogeneity—that is, although biological decline is a given part of human aging, aging is not disease per se. Rather, unlike disease, the nature and rate of decline in normal aging varies substantially among and within individuals. This concept of intra- and interindividual variability within the larger human aging process was given the formal label *normal aging,* and more recent research has suggested that normal aging does indeed capture the phenomenology of change in later life (Lövdén, Bergman, Adolfsson, Linderberger, & Nilsson, 2005). A critical distinction of the normal aging (vs. disease) processes is the presence or absence of a diagnosable disease condition. When disease is present, the rate of decline that an individual experiences is always steeper and more uniform within and across individuals than nondiseased or normal aging.

Several years after Shock et al. (1984) proposed the normal aging paradigm as a kind of senescence (or biological degradation) that was absent of disease, Rowe and Kahn (1987) articulated what they called *successful aging*—that is, the process of aging could be captured under more optimal conditions. They juxtaposed *usual* with *successful* aging by suggesting that *usual aging* was the "avoidance of disease and disability," and *successful aging* was "maintenance of high physical and cognitive function, and sustained engagement in social and productive activities" (Rowe & Kahn, 1998, p. 439). In other words, successful aging described a subset of

persons who were not only disease free but who also were fully intact cognitively and were socially engaged. This optimistic view of aging, along with findings from the McArthur Longitudinal Studies of Successful Aging (Berkman et al., 1993), culminated in the general definition of successful aging based on three underlying postulates: Successful agers were characterized by (a) active engagement with life, (b) absence or avoidance of disease or risk factors for disease, and (c) maintenance of high levels of physical and cognitive functioning (Depp & Jeste, 2006; Rowe & Kahn, 1998).

Although currently no single definition of successful aging has been unanimously accepted, consensus is emerging that successful aging is a multidimensional construct and that longevity is necessary but insufficient to capture it. Rather, successful aging also includes a sense of personal well-being and a minimum of disability (Depp, Vahia, & Jeste, 2010).

There is no doubt that the notion of successful aging offered by Rowe and Kahn (1987) greatly influenced the public view of the human aging process. Quantitative studies, however, indicate that few older adults actually meet the Rowe and Kahn (1998) criteria for successful aging, with estimates that only 11.9% (McLaughlin, Connell, Heeringa, Li, & Roberts, 2010) to 18.8% (Strawbridge, Wallhagen, & Cohen, 2002) of older adults could be characterized as successful agers by these criteria. In contrast, however, research has found that when asked, most older adults *believe* they are aging successfully even though their health, cognitive, and social circumstances do not objectively warrant this label (Depp et al., 2010). The discrepancy between older adults' self-appraisal of their own aging and that of objective reality may be due to the fact that most people desire to age successfully. In other words, most people want to view their own aging from an affirmative mind-set. Research to date argues for the necessity of continued exploration and most likely modification of the successful aging concept so that it encompasses personal beliefs about one's own aging experience (McLaughlin et al., 2010).

Contemporary views of the nature of human aging (e.g., Charles & Carstensen, 2010) tend to focus on the positive aspects of growing old in terms of maturity and adaptation versus the deteriorative aspects of aging that are embedded in the disease model. That is, present-day theories of aging and adult life-span development highlight older adult capabilities (rather than deficits) in terms of maturational processes and the capacity for adaptation to life transitions that are a predictable part of the aging process. In this view, adapting optimally to a life transition requires understanding the nature of the individual (individual characteristics), the context in which the individual is embedded (one's community or the larger society), and the viewpoint of the individual who is making the transition (an optimistic vs. pessimistic viewpoint). This line of reasoning opens the door for understanding the nature of human aging through concepts akin to person–environment fit (Fry, 1990) and a facilitation perspective, with the goal of finding optimal outcomes in later life even in the presence of age-related decline (Hill, 2005).

AGING THEORIES REFLECTING COUNSELING PSYCHOLOGY VALUES

Developmental theory has long been integrated into models of counseling psychology (Blocher, 2000). Traditional theoretical constructs that tend to employ counseling psychology's strengths-based perspective can be found in three well-established developmental models: (a) Erikson's (1963, 1968) psychosocial model of development, (b) continuity theory, and (c) SOC. "Positive aging" (Hill, 2005), a relatively newer perspective of aging, includes a conceptual reconstruction and synthesis of these theories. In this theory, Hill (2005) attempted to integrate selected components of continuity theory and the SOC model around meaning-centered concepts associated with affirmative (or resource-based) adaptation skills. Employing concepts embedded within the positive psychology movement (see Seligman & Csikszentmihalyi, 2000), the central thesis of a positive aging framework is that all people have strengths (Hill, 2005).

Erikson's Psychosocial Life-Span Development Model
Erikson's (1963, 1968) psychosocial model of development, rooted in psychoanalytic theory, provides a

useful foundation with its rich descriptive quality. Representing an early description of the strengths-based maturational framework that emerged from a traditional viewpoint of life-span development that was previously restricted to childhood, this psychosocial development model has continued to support the idea that the processes of growing old involve bringing resources and adaptive facilitation to negotiate the late-life developmental experience.

Erikson (1963, 1968) based his stage model of life-span development on data from the Berkeley Guidance Study, a longitudinal investigation that consisted of interview data collected from 248 older participants in Berkeley, California, in the late 1920s (Erikson, Erikson, & Kivnick, 1986). This study relied primarily on qualitative data that encompassed health, behavioral, and personality questions that were both retrospective and prospective, beginning by querying participants' recollections of their early years of life and continuing through anticipatory future events in old age (e.g., planning for retirement and one's own death), focusing on exploring early behaviors and emotions and how these evolved over the life span. It was Erikson's view that maturation occurred over the entire life span and progressed through stages characterized by a critical juncture or crisis point and that the change process was not only biologically determined but also involved social and psychological factors. In many respects, Erikson's model of development was the first epigenetic framework for understanding the full extent of human aging that also incorporated the concept or utilizing personal resources to negotiate the maturation process. Erikson's model employs a now well-known eight-stage taxonomy, described in the following paragraphs, that describes how a typical individual becomes increasingly more sensitive to social, biological, and psychological forces that shape awareness, relationship quality, and life choices over time.

The earliest stage, trust versus mistrust, occurs during infancy and is successfully resolved by the individual with the emergence of the maturational quality of *hope* as the developmental consequence. Following this stage, the early childhood years progress through the stages of autonomy versus shame and doubt and initiative versus guilt, which, when successfully resolved, result in the mature qualities of *will* and *purpose*, respectively. Adolescents and young adults must navigate the stages of industry versus inferiority and identity versus role confusion, with the mature resolutions of these stages producing the qualities of *personal competence* and *fidelity* In the adult years, the focus shifts to the challenge of intimacy versus isolation with the emergence of developing *love* as a product of successful stage resolution during this time frame. The stages most often associated with adult aging are generativity versus self-absorption, in which concerns of establishing and guiding the next generation arise, and ego integrity versus despair, which requires asking, "Have I lived a full life?" These, when resolved successfully, yield the mature qualities or capabilities of the capacity to *care* for others and the development of the ultimate manifestation of maturity, namely, *wisdom*.

Erikson (1963, 1968) created what most researchers believe were arbitrary age confidence intervals within which a person typically encounters these psychosocial development periods, although recent studies have suggested that it is likely that individuals recycle through stages during the life course; that is, a person may reexperience unresolved or incompletely negotiated transitions that occurred at earlier points in the life span (Whitbourne & Waterman, 1979; Whitbourne, Zuschlag, Elliot, & Waterman, 1992). For instance, an older adult may need to renegotiate earlier stages of development beyond generativity and integrity. This could happen, for example, with the death of an intimate loved one, which then creates the tensions or conflicts around intimacy associated with re-establishing one's close social network.

Erikson (1963) summarized individual identity development across the life span by simply highlighting the question, "Who am I?" Extending Erikson's work, Marcia (1966) defined identity in terms of identity statuses, suggesting that identity is determined largely by the choices and commitments made regarding personal and social traits. Marcia viewed identity through a lens of life domains, including gender and religion. Applying this notion to adulthood, identity process theory (Whitbourne, 2002) is parallel in form to Erikson's model of psychosocial development, emphasizing the role of

personal identity consolidation as a conduit for accommodating or adapting to new life experiences as these are encountered in one's later years. Whitbourne, Sneed, and Skultety (2002) conceptualized identity for the older adult as "a broad biopsychosocial self-definition" (p. 30) that among other areas, included the individual's self-representation of largely defined social roles. Although relatively new and limited in replication, research on this concept (e.g., Sneed & Whitbourne, 2003; Whitbourne, Sneed, & Sayer, 2009) has yielded results that support the identity process theory, suggesting that "by defining successful aging as the ability to adapt flexibly to age-related changes without relinquishing central components of self-definition, identity process theory places the theoretical focus of understanding psychological development in adulthood squarely in the realm of the self" (Sneed & Whitbourne, 2003, p. 318).

Continuity Theory

Continuity theory is based on the premise that in normal aging individuals engage in behaviors and patterns of thought with the goal of preserving intra- and interpersonal stability. Atchley (1989, 1999) initially articulated continuity theory as a challenge to historical theories of aging, such as disengagement theory (Cumming & Henry, 1961) and activity theory (Havighurst, 1961), which argues that people's response to growing old is either to disengage from society or to stave off aging through increased social activity. Atchley, through the development of the Ohio Long-Term Care Research Project (Atchley, 1999), argued from his qualitative data of participant interviews that older adults were more committed to preserving personal consistency in later life. The main proposition of continuity theory is that in normal aging, persons make adaptive choices to preserve internal and external structures to maintain a sense of personal stability through the life span to maintain life satisfaction for as long as possible (Atchley, 1989).

In preserving internal structures, Atchley (1989) focused on an individual's identity and values. The preservation of internal continuity occurs as a person lives consistently within his or her values structure. Similarly, the preservation of external structures such as the person's social roles and living environment is part of external continuity. It was Atchley's (1989) view that the aging person uses familiar strategies to accommodate to change that takes place as one grows old, and thereby internal and external continuity is achieved. Changes, particularly sudden and traumatic ones, can cause disruptions—or discontinuities—to one's internal and external stability perceptions. These, even when they are positive, can produce substantial disruption. Atchley (1999) suggested that the process of resolving discontinuities across the life span not only was associated with greater perceived life satisfaction but also produced maturity and wisdom as a consequence.

Although a review of the empirically based literature suggests that general support for this theory remains fairly absent, continuity theory has been advanced through methodologically strong research, utilizing both qualitative and quantitative approaches, and across a variety of topics to explain behaviors that persons engage in during the later years to maintain well-being. Career and vocational specialties within the field of counseling psychology have benefited from continuity theory. For instance, bridge employment, or employment postretirement, has made use of continuity theory. Within this framework, the older adult is envisioned to have the same likes and dislikes, inclinations, desires, and interests as they did when they were younger (Atchley, 1989, 1999). Similar research has employed continuity theory to predict in which types of bridge jobs retirees engage (Gobeski & Beehr, 2009) and how bridge employment is related to long-term physical health (Zhan, Wang, Liu, & Shultz, 2009). Possibly one of the most elegant examples of how continuity theory manifests in the lived experiences of older adults comes from a qualitative study exploring meaning in old age (Fischer, Nordberg, & Lundman, 2008). In this study, a continuity theory congruent theme in older person's reports of aging emerged: "It seems important to be as one used to be, unchanged, and yet to be changed: embracing being changed and feeling the same" (Fischer et al., 2008, p. 268).

Selective Optimization With Compensation

In contrast to the psychosocial model and continuity theory, SOC emerged from the successful aging

paradigm and described a tripartite behavioral repertoire that an individual can employ to mediate the inevitable deficits that are due to the biology of age-related decline. In SOC, these behaviors are defined as sociocultural supports. SOC is a process-based construal of adaptation that was developed with older adults' issues in mind and is embedded within the larger framework of successful aging (P. B. Baltes, 1997). SOC is particularly important for counseling psychology because it is based on a positive resource framework; that is, older persons can act on the aging process to offset deficits. In this model, age-related decline in functional capacity is explicitly acknowledged and its consequences are construed as a dynamic interplay between biological processes inherent in human aging and the adaptive potential of the human organism through sociocultural mechanisms.

In brief, *S* represents selectivity, referring to the restriction of any given life domain to fewer areas of function, most often those that are declining because of aging-related losses in functionality (P. Baltes & Baltes, 1990). Selectively concentrating on those areas that are of highest priority is an adaptation that allows for success in those areas of greatest importance. Selectivity also describes the nature of adjustment that individuals make around personal expectations. In doing so, the individual may be able to reconstrue a sense of subjective well-being, enjoyment of life, and personal control even when these are only partially achievable (e.g., as is the case for functionality in advanced age). P. B. Baltes's (1997) example of selectivity is the pianist Arthur Rubenstein, who in later life eliminated pieces from his professional performance repertoire as these became too difficult to play when he was in his 80s. This allowed him to continue to play professionally into his 8th decade of life.

O, or optimization, refers to engaging in behaviors that maximize an individual's ability to maintain those areas of function that remain in the presence of advanced aging. Optimization also improves and increases reserve capacity, which P. Baltes and Baltes (1990) described as latent potentiality that could be accessed even in old age through training and practice. Optimization has been used extensively to improve memory through the use of strategic memory techniques, such as mnemonic training, to offset age-related deficits in memory function (Kliegl, Smith, & Baltes, 1989, 1990).

Compensation, the *C*, involves the use of the culturally grounded adaptation processes or devices (including those embedded in assistive technology) to reduce or eliminate age-related deficits (P. B. Baltes, 1997; P. Baltes & Baltes, 1990). For example, the use of a wheelchair, which is a culturally generated device, to facilitate continued mobility when ambulating with one's legs is no longer possible is an example of compensation. Atchley (1999) poignantly described how one of the subjects in the Ohio Long-Term Care Research Project employed the element of compensation to maintain stability (and subsequently preserve life satisfaction) even in the presence of substantial age-related deterioration. This individual was very active, but as physical problems magnified her activity deficits, she altered her expectations and began watching more television and using assistive devices to help her maintain functionality within her increasingly limited living situation.

M. M. Baltes and Lang (1997) argued that those with more resources are able to make more frequent use of the processes of selection, optimization, and compensation and subsequently delay aging declines. A follow-up study (Lang, Rieckmann, & Baltes, 2002) supported these results and interpretation. In particular, the authors suggested that those people with more resources select activities that are most rewarding, optimize their enjoyment by spending more time with family members, increase the variability of time investments, and engage in more compensatory strategies such as taking more naps.

In a more recent review, Ouwehand, de Ridder, and Bensing (2007) indicated that although SOC is a leading model in successful aging, to date, the empirical support is somewhat limited. The authors concluded, however, that empirical studies suggest that the SOC model is a promising model of successful aging with the potential to be useful in explaining successful aging, in general, as well as the adaptation needed for age-related challenges.

Positive Aging

In applying principles of positive psychology to age-related coping, Hill (2005) characterized the positive ager as possessing four characteristics: (a) the ability to mobilize latent resources or reserve capacity to cope with age-related decline; (b) the making of lifestyle choices to preserve well-being even in situations of irretrievable loss (e.g., the death of a spouse; age-related memory decline); (c) the cultivation of flexibility, both in action and in thought, to adapt to change; and (d) as in positive psychology, maintaining an optimistic perspective even with respect to the inevitabilities associated with decline in old age. If available resources are diminished as a consequence of age-related decline, latent resources can be employed to sustain psychological well-being in the face of progressive decline.

In positive aging, the preservation of a perceived sense of well-being and life satisfaction is central to this coping framework. Strategies that engage psychological reserves to preserve the consistency (or continuity) of life routines by allowing one's self to be assisted by others when one's own ability is insufficient to engage a life routine is a concrete example of the reserve capacity construct in operation. This idea is also captured in continuity theory about which Atchley (1999) noted, "Despite significant changes in health, functioning, and social circumstances, a large proportion of older adults show considerable consistency over time in their patterns of thinking, activity profiles, living arrangements, and social relationships" (p. 1).

Flexibility refers to a person's capacity to invoke novel strategies of behaving or thinking to promote better adaptation. Schaie (2005) defined *cognitive flexibility* as an approach to cognitive problem solving that involves the dynamic manipulation of multiple solution sets to yield the best outcome in the shortest amount of time. Flexibility in this definition is also skills based and is associated with specific behavioral outcomes.

Decisional ability involves options or alternatives confronting older adults on a daily basis, ranging from the simple to the complex. Patterns of choices undergird even established life routines. Decision making is skill based, and those who are better at evaluating choices and making decisions adapt better to their environment. Through active engagement in this process, decisions are made that lead to adaptive as well as maladaptive consequences for well-being and life satisfaction. As a positive aging characteristic, optimal decision making occurs when the balance of decisions made across the life span weigh in favor of those for which the consequences promote personal well-being and happiness. The focus of decision making as a positive aging characteristic is on establishing a plan to address a goal that is an outcome or a consequence of age-related decline.

Another central characteristic of positive aging is the cultivation of an optimistic worldview. By definition, an optimistic worldview describes an affirmative approach to life that is exemplified by a striving for happiness versus a focus on alleviating symptoms of distress. In this scheme, a person's pursuit of better health would be considered "flourishing" (a positive valence) if she or he possessed high levels of positive emotion, including active social engagement, the cultivation of meaningful personal relationships, and a positive future outlook.

The research support for successful aging is wide-ranging, with an extensive array of methodological approaches (Hill, 2005) and with many researchers focusing on discrete groups of older persons with specific patterns of decline, such as optimal aging (e.g., Newman et al., 2003), normal aging (e.g., Rowe & Kahn, 1987), and diseased or accelerated aging (e.g., Mitnitski, Graham, Mogliner, & Rockwood, 1999). Support is found for this model across multiple levels of functioning, such as physical, cognitive, and emotional (Hill, 2005). In addition, the literature is full of well-known scientific longitudinal studies such as the MacArthur Studies of Successful Aging (Berkman et al., 1993; Rowe & Kahn, 1998) and the BLAS (e.g., Shock et al., 1984) as well as shorter and more specifically targeted longitudinal studies such as the 8-year Cardiovascular Health Study with 3,000 adults who, being free of cardiovascular disease, were identified as successfully aging (e.g., Newman et al., 2003).

EXPANDING ON TRADITIONAL MODELS

The theories reviewed thus far embrace the strength-based view of aging; however, they may not fully acknowledge counseling psychology's value for diversity and individual differences. That is, recognition is needed that the definition of successful aging may be culture dependent (Torres, 1999), and future theory and research may need to be more fully explored as a social construct and within the context of individual differences. Thus, older adults may be best conceptualized through recognition of their "intersecting identities."

Intersecting Identities of Older Adults

The "fourth force" in psychology (i.e., the multicultural movement; Pedersen, 1998), supported by contemporary thinking of feminists who have called for flexibility in approaching differences among individuals (Friedman, 1999), has given rise to the belief that "differences among people due to gender, race, ethnicity, age, and sexual orientation are the starting point for theory building" (Enns, 2010, p. 338). Honoring the intertwining or intersection of diverse social identities, Cole (2009) identified that theory and research "may be understood within the rubric of *intersectionality*" to best "consider the meaning and consequences of multiple categories of social group membership" (p. 170).

Although the concept of intersecting identities may have existed for centuries (Cole, 2009), King (1988) is credited with promoting concerns regarding the lack of intersection among race, gender, and class. Individual characteristics, such as gender or race, are sources of how individuals perceive themselves and how others perceive them. Identity is characterized as a complex interaction of biological, psychological, and social factors and is simultaneously deeply personal and embedded in sociopolitical processes (Howard, 2000) as well as in religion and spirituality (Atchley, 2009).

Notably, age is missing within many of the significant contributions surrounding the issues identified thus far as well as throughout the intersectionality literature. Exceptions are beginning to emerge, however, as aging theory is increasingly being linked with feminist ideology (Allen &

Walker, 2009) and key feminist concepts (Calasanti, 2009). In the recent revision of the *Handbook of Theories of Aging*, the editors argued that "a focus on intersecting inequalities is critical to understanding those experiences of aging and that feminist gerontology is uniquely able to offer scholars a lens through which to view these intersections" (Bengtson, Silverstein, Putney, & Gans, 2009, p. 16). Furthering Whitbourne et al.'s (2002) understanding of identity in later years as being a broad, biopsychosocial concept including self-image and societal views—similar to Atchley's (1989) focus on individual values and social roles—intersecting identities celebrate the complexity of the individual rather than reducing the identity of older adults to only their age, gender, ethnicity, sexual orientation, religion, or functional ability.

The fundamental intent of intersecting identities correlates well with core counseling psychology values of understanding strengths within a social and cultural context (Gelso & Fretz, 1992) and can increasingly be identified in the profession's contemporary literature. For example, in the *Biennial Review of Counseling Psychology* (Walsh, 2008), intersecting identities were highlighted in the lesbian, gay, bisexual, transgender, and queer theory and research, with indications that the field was experiencing a paradigm shift with increased inclusion of "a multiplicity of experiences and contexts" (Bieschke, Hardy, Fassinger, & Croteau, 2008, p. 177). Bieschke et al. (2008) focused on the intersection of cultural location with sexual orientation to foster understanding of how cultural context influences the personal, interpersonal, social, and sociopolitical experience of sexual minorities. Focus on "a multiplicity of experiences and contexts" can easily be applied to older adults and provides an encompassing theoretical framework for understanding those in their later years. Currently, and certainly in the future, aging is likely to be best understood using a multifaceted lens of intersecting identities, incorporating culture within age.

Further Exploring the Multifaceted Aspects of Later Life

Identity of older adults, then, can be characterized as a broad, biopsychosocial concept with

self-definition as well as a larger societal-defined role or representation (Whitbourne et al., 2002). Gilleard and Higgs (2005) may have been the first to directly address the issues of class, cohort, and community as reference points in describing the aging population and current society. With respect to demographic characteristics, the nature of these age cohorts represents a special class of diversity considering that each of these age groupings is embedded in social ideas and viewpoints about the world that are influenced by substantial events that occurred during the time periods in which they lived.

Adding individual factors to age and cohort greatly increases the complexity of theoretical information as well as research that has a bearing on late-life development. This may be one reason to explain the limited research and theory that is available for those older individuals of minority status; this is especially true for sexual orientation, which has been practically invisible (Shankle, Maxwell, Katzman, & Landers, 2003). Although current aging theory and research has included such issues as gender, ethnicity or race, socioeconomic status (SES), and health, much work is needed across all aspects of diversity and individual differences within the aging research and theory.

Gender.   Gender is just one example, as the literature has not kept pace with the need. Age must be included as an important mediating variable in the development of any gender theory because "gender is increasingly understood as defining a system of power relations embedded in other power relations" (Stewart & McDermott, 2004, p. 519). Applegate (1997) highlighted "a blind spot" (p. 2) in the aging literature, capturing the significant omission of older men. Even though there were more than 16 million men in the United States age 65 or older in 2008 (U.S. Census Bureau, 2008), older men are relatively invisible in aging research and theory. This continues, even though being an older man in today's society brings about loss of independence and power, social isolation, and increased emotional distress with a higher likelihood of suicide completion (e.g., Vacha-Haase, Wester, & Christianson, 2010).

It is true that women over the age of 65 outnumber men of similar age by almost two to one (U.S. Census Bureau, 2008). Even though the older woman may be in the majority group within her own cohort, she remains a minority when one considers the broader picture. Although recent history has witnessed an extension of the social context and psychology of women, research and theory on aging from a feminist perspective have only just emerged, particularly within the field of counseling psychology (Calasanti & Slevin, 2006). With feminist theory consistently focusing on issues regarding women in the workplace as well as their roles as wife and mother, much that matters to an aging woman has virtually been ignored (Hooyman, Browne, Ray, & Richardson, 2002). Social issues that are most likely to be experienced by older women include the increased likelihood of being poor compared with older men (Wu, 2007), living alone (Cameron, Song, Manheim, & Dunlop, 2010), and experiencing some form of disability while outliving their partners (Crose, 1999). Thus, although older women undoubtedly benefited and may continue to gain from advances in the areas of education, reproduction rights, and employment opportunities, the unique needs of this group appear to move beyond any singular focus of younger women (Antonucci, Blieszner, & Denmark, 2010).

Differences in late-life decline. Related to gender as well as other individual differences is the heterogeneity of the trajectory of late-life decline (Lövdén et al., 2005). There are some individuals who decline very rapidly at the latter end of the life cycle as opposed to individuals whose trajectory of decline is relatively flat followed by a precipitous decline just before the end of life. Factors that explain this form of diversity are complex and include biological and genetic factors, disease, lifestyle variables, and even geographic region where one resides.

Recent epidemiological surveys have indicated that more than 85% of persons 80 years and older have at least one chronic health condition and many (62%) have more than one (Anderson & Horvath, 2004). In contrast to previous research focusing on cognitive and physical decline, a review of the current research focusing on emotional aging suggested a positive trajectory for age-related changes in emotional well-being (Scheibe & Carstensen, 2010).

The fact is, however, that the nature of aging is perceived differently when one is progressing along a rapid trajectory versus a slow trajectory of age-related decline, cognitively, emotionally, or physically. Intertwined with this unique characteristic of late-life development is the access to, and use of, health care. And not surprisingly, differences across all groups within the older adult population have been a long-standing concern.

For example, older women more frequently report functional limitations and disability, have fewer physician visits, and are less likely to have hospital stays when compared with men with similar health profiles (Cameron, Song, Manheim, & Dunlop, 2010). Although these authors suggested economics may not be the driving force of these differences, across gender, older individuals of lower SES have increased mortality rates (Bassuk, Berkman, & Amick, 2002), higher stroke incidence (Avendano et al., 2006), higher incidence of progressive chronic kidney disease (Merkin et al., 2007), lower health-related quality of life (Huguet, Kaplan, & Feeny, 2008), increased depression (APA, 2003), and higher rates of dementia (Fratiglioni, Winblad, & von Strauss, 2007). Thus, given the lack of clear trends, reasons contributing to health disparities and access to care across genders, as well as SES, merit further exploration.

Racial and ethnic differences. Some consensus is obtained when exploring racial and ethnic differences within the older adult population. Research (e.g., Hummer, Benjamins, & Rogers, 2004; Rooks & Whitfield, 2004) has consistently suggested that non-White older adults experience higher rates of poor physical and mental health conditions than do their White peers. Discrepancies by ethnicity in access to or use of health care has been documented, with race being associated with less preventative health care (McBean & Gornick, 1994), less in-patient health care (Lee, Gehlbach, Hosmer, Reti, & Baker, 1997), and less home health care (Davitt & Kaye, 2010). In a recent study with a nationally representative sample, Weinick et al. (2011) ruled out the contention that differing racial groups have varying expectations of health care treatment, concluding that discrepancies in health care were not due to a difference of expectations or approach to questionnaire items for participants' from diverse backgrounds but reflected actual differences in experiences. Additional research is clearly needed to further identify and understand these differences, their causes, and approaches for improvement of access and care.

FUTURE DIRECTIONS FOR AGING AND INTERSECTING IDENTITY WITHIN COUNSELING PSYCHOLOGY

As the number of older adults increases, so too does the opportunity for future research and theory development in counseling psychology through areas of diversity and individual differences in this population. The combination of an individual's multiple dimensions and experiences shapes one's identity, with aging adults being a uniquely heterogeneous population (Nelson & Dannefer, 1992). Perhaps no other group demonstrates intersecting identities as do that of people over the age of 65, experiencing "double jeopardy" as they potentially internalize ageism as well as other self-defining characteristics.

Unfortunately, *ageism*, "the systematic stereotyping of, and discrimination against people, simply because of their age" (Butler, 1975), appears to have existed throughout history, dominating almost every society (Wade, 2001) through political, economic, and social values. Current trends in research identify ageism as the most commonly experienced form of prejudice (Bousfield & Hutchison, 2010). Many in their later years resist identification with the older adult identity (Minichiello, Browne, & Kendig, 2000) or change their physical appearance (Jones & Pugh, 2005) to maintain a sense of culturally relevant personal identity and competence. According to Levy, "At the point that age stereotypes are directed at oneself in old age, they can be classified as self-perceptions of aging" (p. 332). Women in particular are at risk for experiencing a broader range of negative psychological experiences with aging because of a specific form of gender-based ageism (Hatch, 2005). Yang and Levkoff (2005) noted that "internalized ageism among older minorities is pernicious, undermining both their self-worth and the importance of their existence" (p. 43), yet this undoubtedly increases in complexity when aspects of sexism and other prejudices are factored in. The 75-year-old Hispanic lesbian woman may face "triple or quadruple jeopardy" as individual differences encompassing multiple aspects of diversity emerge, with increased inherent challenges when issues of privilege, inequality, and interdependence are acknowledged. Thus, counseling psychology can extend the developmental framework and values of inclusivity to a comprehensive theory of aging. As Cole (2009) called for, "Intersectional analysis requires a conceptual shift, even a paradigm shift" (p. 178).

Counseling psychology may help to combat ageism by consistently including diverse older adults in its research and theory development and engaging in policy change and advocacy. This could come in many forms, including a focus on health care as well as theory and research about meaningful approaches to long-term care, possibly through such programs as the Program of All-inclusive Care for the Elderly and through focusing on such issues as older adult sexuality or decision making and subjective well-being at the end of life.

Aging Theory and Research for Counseling Psychology

To date, published literature in the profession's prominent journals may have offered only limited additions to aging theory (Werth et al., 2003). Counseling psychology's well-established values of multicultural differences, however, does provide a strong paradigm from which to continue to develop the concept of intersecting identities of older adults. In addition, given the profession's historical focus on career development education and counseling, an area ripe for expansion is vocational psychology, through the inclusion of work life at the later end of the life span. Current theories could be stretched to include the concept of recareering and modern-day retirement, embracing the trends of older adults who reinvent themselves during this developmental stage of life.

Expanding vocational psychology to later years of life. Approximately 16% of Americans 65 and older are currently in the labor force (see data at http://factfinder.census.gov/). The number of workers over the age of 55 is projected to grow by 46.7%, compared with the 8.5% growth projected for the overall labor force; and by 2016, nearly one in four American workers will be over the age of 55 (Bureau of Labor Statistics, 2009). Thus, given the changing and diverse nature of the workplace, counseling psychology is well positioned to further research and theory of aging within the work context. Areas of focus might include concerns that arise for older adults in the workplace, including cohort differences, ageism, and other stage of life barriers, such as physical changes and role transitions.

Much promise also lies in further exploration of the process of moving out of the workplace, a part-time second career, volunteer work, or bridge employment, a relatively new concept (Wang & Shultz, 2010) to explain the pattern of labor force participation exhibited by older workers as they leave their career jobs and move toward complete labor force (Shultz, 2003). Incorporating a person–environment (PE) fit framework (e.g., Ostroff & Schulte, 2007) in studying retirement choices, outcomes, and bridge employment decisions folds seamlessly into the expansion of the PE interaction paradigm.

Retirement: Age-related transition. Retirement has often been understood using continuity theory, assuming that maintaining patterns of preferred levels of central voluntary activities established earlier in life helps older people to maintain psychological well-being (Atchley, 1989, 1999). Research has supported this theory, with results suggesting that higher activity levels during retirement lead to happiness (e.g., Menec, 2003; Tkach & Lyubomirsky, 2006; Pushkar et al., 2010).

Although a major baby boomer retirement is projected (U.S. Census Bureau, 2008), relatively little attention has been given to the concept of *planned retirement*. Utilizing two general theoretical conceptualizations that appear to have shaped the literature over the past 20 years—that is, retirement as an adjustment process and retirement as a career development stage (Wang & Shultz, 2010)—counseling psychology' extensive history makes it well positioned to promote continued theory and research in this late-life stage. For example, counseling

psychologists may help to further explore the adjustment process of retirement. Although a majority of retirees will adapt well to their new lifestyle, much more is needed to understand the trajectories of adjustment to retirement, particularly given that approximately 10% will experience a sense of role loss when they retire, and almost 15% will experience a slight increase in life satisfaction, followed by despair, and then a subsequent leveling of satisfaction (Pinquart & Schindler, 2007). Better understanding of these trajectories as well as helping older adults to prepare for the developmental transitions is easily within the profession's expertise.

CONCLUSION

This chapter has explored aging research and theory within a counseling psychology perspective, focusing on the profession's core values of strengths-based approaches and value of individual differences in the area of aging. The new century has brought an increasingly expanding and diverse older population, and with this, opportunities and challenges for counseling psychology to rethink and expand current theories and research in the area of diversity as well as vocational psychology.

References

Allen, K. R., & Walker, A. J. (2009). Theorizing about families and aging from a feminist perspective. In V. L. Bengtson, D. Gans, D. N. M. Pulney, & M. Silverstein (Eds.), *Handbook of theories of aging* (2nd ed., pp. 517–528). New York, NY: Springer.

American Psychological Association. (2003). *Fact sheet: Facts about depression in older adults.* Washington, DC: Author.

Anderson, G. F., & Horvath, J. (2004). The growing burden of chronic disease in America. *Public Health Reports, 119*, 263–270. doi:10.1016/j.phr.2004.04.005

Antonucci, T. C., Blieszner, R., & Denmark, F. L. (2010). Psychological perspective on older women. In H. Landrine & N. Russo (Eds.), *Handbook of diversity in feminist psychology* (pp. 233–257). New York, NY: Springer.

Applegate, J. S. (1997). Theorizing older men. In J. I. Kosberg & L. W. Kaye (Eds.), *Elderly men: Special problems and professional challenges* (pp. 1–15). New York, NY: Springer.

Atchley, R. C. (1989). A continuity theory of normal aging. *The Gerontologist, 29,* 183–190. doi:10.1093/geront/29.2.183

Atchley, R. C. (1999). *Continuity and adaptation in aging: Creating positive experiences.* Baltimore, MD: Johns Hopkins University Press.

Atchley, R. C. (Ed.). (2009). *Spirituality and aging.* Baltimore, MD: Johns Hopkins University Press.

Avendano, M., Kawachi, I., Van Lenthe, F., Boshuizen, H. C., Mackenbach, J. P., Van den Bos, G. A. M., . . . Berkman, L. F. (2006). Socioeconomic status and stroke incidence in the U.S. elderly: The role of risk factors in the EPESE study. *Stroke, 37,* 1368–1373.

Baker, D. B., & Subich, L. M. (2008). Counseling psychology: Historical perspectives. In W. B. Walsh (Ed.), *Biennial review of counseling psychology* (Vol. 1, pp. 1–26). New York, NY: Routledge.

Baltes, M. M., & Lang, F. (1997). Everyday functioning and successful aging: The impact of resources. *Psychology and Aging, 12,* 433–443. doi:10.1037/0882-7974.12.3.433

Baltes, P. B. (1997). On the incomplete architecture of human ontogeny: Selection, optimization, and compensation as foundation of developmental theory. *American Psychologist, 52,* 366–380. doi:10.1037/0003-066X.52.4.366

Baltes, P., & Baltes, M. (1990). Plasticity and variability in psychology: Methodological and theoretical issues. In G. E. Gurski (Ed.), *Determining the effects of aging on the central nervous system* (pp. 41–66). Berlin, Germany: Schering.

Bassuk, S. S., Berkman, L. F., & Amick, B. C. (2002). Socioeconomic status and mortality among the elderly: Findings from four U.S. communities. *American Journal of Epidemiology, 155,* 520–533. doi:10.1093/aje/155.6.520

Bengtson, V. L., Silverstein, M., Putney, N. M., & Gans, D. (Eds.). (2009). *Handbook of theories of aging* (2nd ed.). New York, NY: Springer.

Berkman, L. F., Seeman, T. E., Albert, M. S., Blazer, D., Kahn, R., Mohs, R., Finch, C., . . . Nesselroade, J. (1993). Successful, usual and impaired functioning in community dwelling elderly: McArthur Successful Aging Field Studies. *Journal of Clinical Epidemiology, 46,* 1129–1140. doi:10.1016/0895-4356(93)90112-E

Bieschke, K. J., Hardy, J. A., Fassinger, R. E., & Croteau, J. M. (2008). Intersecting identities of gender-transgressive sexual minorities: Toward a new paradigm of affirmative psychology. In W. B. Walsh (Ed.), *Biennial review of counseling psychology* (Vol. 1, pp. 177–207). New York, NY: Routledge.

Blocher, D. H. (2000). *The evolution of counseling psychology.* New York, NY: Springer.

Bousfield, C., & Hutchison, P. (2010). Contact, anxiety, and young people's attitudes and behavioral intentions towards the elderly. *Educational Gerontology, 36,* 451–466. doi:10.1080/03601270903324362

Bureau of Labor Statistics. (2009). *Economic and employment projections.* Retrieved from http://www.bls.gov/news.release/ecopro.toc.htm

Butler, R. (1975). *Why survive being old in America?* New York, NY: Harper & Row.

Calasanti, T. (2009). Theorizing feminist gerontology, sexuality, and beyond: An intersectional approach. In V. L. Bengtson, D. Gans, N. M. Pulney, M. Norella, & M. Silverstein (Eds.), *Handbook of theories of aging* (2nd ed., pp. 471–485). New York, NY: Springer.

Calasanti, T. M., & Slevin, K. F. (Eds.). (2006). *Age matters: Realigning feminist thinking.* New York, NY: Routledge.

Cameron, K. A., Song, J., Manheim, L. M., & Dunlop, D. D. (2010). Gender disparities in health and healthcare use among older adults. *Journal of Women's Health, 19,* 1643–1650. doi:10.1089/jwh.2009.1701

Charles, S. T., & Carstensen, L. L. (2010). Social emotional aging. *Annual Review of Psychology, 61,* 383–409. doi:10.1146/annurev.psych.093008.100448

Cole, E. R. (2009). Intersectionality and research in psychology. *American Psychologist, 64,* 170–180. doi:10.1037/a0014564

Constantine, M. G., Fuertes, J. N., Roysircar, G., & Kindaichi, M. M. (2008). Multicultural competence: Clinical practice, training and supervision, and research. In W. B. Walsh (Ed.), *Biennial review of counseling psychology* (Vol. 1, pp. 97–127). New York, NY: Routledge.

Crose, R. G. (1999). Addressing late life developmental issues for women: Body image, sexuality, and intimacy. In M. Duffy (Ed.), *Handbook of counseling and psychotherapy with older adults* (pp. 57–76). Hoboken, NJ: Wiley.

Cumming, E., & Henry, W. (1961). *Growing old: The process of disengagement.* New York, NY: Basic Books.

Davitt, J. K., & Kaye, L. W. (2010). Racial/ethnic disparities in access to Medicare home health care: The disparate impact of policy. *Journal of Gerontological Social Work, 53,* 591–612. doi:10.1080/01634372.2010.503984

Depp, C., Vahia, I., & Jeste, D. (2010). Successful aging: Focus on cognitive and emotional health. *Annual Review of Clinical Psychology, 6,* 527–550. doi:10.1146/annurev.clinpsy.121208.131449

Depp, C. A., & Jeste, D. V. (2006). Definitions and predictors of successful aging: A comprehensive review of larger quantitative studies. *The American Journal of Geriatric Psychiatry, 14,* 6–20. doi:10.1097/01.JGP.0000192501.03069.bc

Enns, C. Z. (2010). Locational feminisms and feminist social identity analysis. *Professional Psychology: Research and Practice, 41*, 333–339. doi:10.1037/a0020260

Erikson, E. (1963). *Childhood and society.* New York, NY: Norton.

Erikson, E. (1968). *Identity youth and crisis.* New York, NY: Norton.

Erikson, E., Erikson, J., & Kivnick, H. (1986). *Vital involvement in old age.* New York, NY: Norton.

Fischer, R., Nordberg, A., & Lundman, B. (2008). Embracing opposites: Meanings of growing old as narrated by people aged 85. *The International Journal of Aging and Human Development, 67*, 259–271. doi:10.2190/AG.67.3.d

Fratiglioni, L., Winblad, B., & von Strauss, E. (2007). Prevention of Alzheimer's disease and dementia: Major findings from the Kungsholmen Project. *Physiology and Behavior, 92*, 98–104.

Friedman, L. J. (1999). *Identity's architect: A biography of Erik H. Erikson.* New York, NY: Simon & Schuster.

Fry, P. (1990). The person-environment congruence model: Implications and applications for adjustment counselling with older adults. *International Journal for the Advancement of Counselling, 13*, 87–106. doi:10.1007/BF00115705

Gelso, C., & Fretz, B. (1992). *Counseling psychology.* New York, NY: Harcourt Brace.

Gilleard, C., & Higgs, P. (2005). *Contexts of ageing: Class, cohort and community.* Malden, MA: Polity Press.

Gobeski, K., & Beehr, T. (2009). How retirees work: Predictors of different types of bridge employment. *Journal of Organizational Behavior, 30*, 401–425. doi:10.1002/job.547

Hatch, R. L. (2005). Gender and ageism. *Generations, 29*, 19–25.

Havighurst, R. J. (1961). Successful aging. *The Gerontologist, 1*, 8–13. doi:10.1093/geront/1.1.8

Hill, R. (2005). *Positive aging: A guide for mental health professionals and consumers.* New York, NY: Norton.

Hooyman, N., Browne, C. V., Ray, R., & Richardson, V. (2002). Feminist gerontology and the life course. *Gerontology and Geriatrics Education, 22*, 3–26. doi:10.1300/J021v22n04_02

Howard, G. S. (2000). Adapting human lifestyles for the 21st century. *American Psychologist, 55*, 509–515. doi:10.1037/0003-066X.55.5.509

Huguet, N., Kaplan, M. S., & Feeny, D. (2008). Socioeconomic status and health- related quality of life among elderly people. *Social Science and Medicine, 66*, 803–810. doi:10.1016/j.socscimed.2007.11.011

Hummer, R. A., Benjamins, M. R., & Rogers, R. G. (2004). Racial and ethnic disparities in health and mortality among the U.S. elderly population. In N. B. Anderson, R. A. Bulatao, & B. Cohen, (Eds.), *Critical perspectives on racial and ethnic differences in health in late life* (pp. 53–94). Washington, DC: National Academies Press.

Jones, J., & Pugh, S. (2005). Aging gay men: Lessons from the sociology of embodiment. *Men and Masculinities, 7*, 248–260. doi:10.1177/1097184X04265990

King, D. K. (1988). Multiple jeopardy, multiple consciousnesses: The context of a Black feminist ideology. *Signs, 14*, 42–72. doi:10.1086/494491

Kliegl, R., Smith, J., & Baltes, P. B. (1989). Testing-the-limits and the study of adult age differences in cognitive plasticity of a mnemonic skill. *Developmental Psychology, 25*, 247–256. doi:10.1037/0012-1649.25.2.247

Kliegl, R., Smith, J., & Baltes, P. B. (1990). On the locus and process of magnification of age differences during mnemonic training. *Developmental Psychology, 26*, 894–904. doi:10.1037/0012-1649.26.6.894

Lang, F. R., Rieckmann, N., & Baltes, M. (2002). Adapting to aging losses: Do resources facilitate strategies of selection, compensation, and optimization in everyday functioning? *The Journals of Gerontology: Series B. Psychological Sciences and Social Sciences, 57*, P501–P509. doi:10.1093/geronb/57.6.P501

Lee, A. J., Gehlbach, S., Hosmer, D., Reti, M., & Baker, C. (1997). Medicare treatment differences for Blacks and Whites. *Medical Care, 35*, 1173–1189. doi:10.1097/00005650-199712000-00002

Levy, B. (2009). Stereotype embodiment: A psychosocial approach to aging. *Current Directions in Psychological Science, 18*, 332–336. doi:10.1111/j.1467-8721.2009.01662.x

Lopez, S. J., Magyar-Moe, J. L., Petersen, S. E., Ryder, J. A., Krieshok, T. S., O'Byrne, K. K., . . . Fry, N. A. (2006). Counseling psychology's focus on positive aspects of human functioning. *The Counseling Psychologist, 34*, 205–227. doi:10.1177/0011000005283393

Lövdén, M., Bergman, L., Adolfsson, R., Linderberger, U., & Nilsson, L. (2005). Studying individual aging in an interindividual context: Typical paths of age-related, dementia-related, and mortality-related cognitive development in old age. *Psychology and Aging, 20*, 303–316. doi:10.1037/0882-7974.20.2.303

Magyar-Moe, J. L., & Lopez, S. J. (2008). Human agency, strengths-based development, and well-being. In W. B. Walsh (Ed.), *Biennial review of counseling psychology* (Vol. 1, pp. 157–175). New York, NY: Routledge.

Marcia, J. E. (1966). Development and validation of ego identity status. *Journal of Personality and Social Psychology, 3*, 551–558. doi:10.1037/h0023281

McBean, A. M., & Gornick, M. (1994). Differences by race in the rates of procedures performed in hospitals for Medicare beneficiaries. *Health Care Financing Review, 15*(4), 77–90.

McLaughlin, S. J., Connell, C. M., Heeringa, S. G., Li, L. W., & Roberts, J. S. (2010). Successful aging in the United States: Prevalence estimates from a national sample of older adults. *The Journals of Gerontology: Series B. Psychological Sciences and Social Sciences, 65B*(2), 216–226. doi:10.1093/geronb/gbp101

Menec, V. H. (2003). The relationship between everyday activities and successful aging. *The Journals of Gerontology. Series B. Psychological Sciences and Social Sciences, 58*, S74–S82. doi:10.1093/geronb/58.2.S74

Merkin, S. S., Diez Roux, A.V., Coresha, J., Fried, L. F., Jackson, S. A., & Powe, N. R. (2007). Individual and neighborhood socioeconomic status and progressive chronic kidney disease in an elderly population: The Cardiovascular Health Study. *Social Science and Medicine, 65*, 809–821. doi:10.1016/j.socscimed.2007.04.011

Minichiello, V., Browne, J., & Kendig, H. (2000). Perceptions and consequences of ageism: Views from older persons. *Ageing and Society, 20*, 253–278. doi:10.1017/S0144686X99007710

Mitnitski, A. B., Graham, J. E., Mogliner, A. J., & Rockwood, K. (1999). The rate of decline in function in Alzheimer's disease and other dementias. *The Journals of Gerontology: Series A. Biological and Medical Sciences, 54*, 65–69.

Nelson, E. A., & Dannefer, D. (1992). Age heterogeneity: Fact or fiction? The fact of diversity in gerontological research. *The Gerontologist, 32*, 17–23. doi:10.1093/geront/32.1.17

Newman, A. B., Arnold, A. M., Naydeck, B. L., Fried, L. P., Burke, G. L., Enright, P., . . . Tracy, R. (2003). "Successful aging": Effect of subclinical cardiovascular disease. *Archives of Internal Medicine, 163*, 2315–2322. doi:10.1001/archinte.163.19.2315

Ostroff, C., & Schulte, M. (2007). Multiple perspectives of fit in organizations across levels of analysis. In C. Ostroff & T. Judge (Eds.), *Perspectives on organizational fit* (pp. 3–69). New York, NY: Erlbaum.

Ouwehand, C., de Ridder, D. T. D., & Bensing, J. M. (2007). A review of successful aging models: Proposing proactive coping as an important additional strategy. *Clinical Psychology Review, 27*, 873–884. doi:10.1016/j.cpr.2006.11.003

Palmore, E. (1970). *Normal aging.* Oxford, England: Duke University Press.

Pedersen, P. B. (1998). *Multiculturalism as a fourth force.* Philadelphia, PA: Bruner-Mazel.

Pinquart, M., & Schindler, I. (2007). Changes of life satisfaction in the transition to retirement. *Psychology and Aging, 22*, 442–455. doi:10.1037/0882-7974.22.3.442

Pushkar, D., Chaikelson, J., Conway, M., Etezadi, J., Giannopolous, C., Li, K., & Wrosch, C. (2010). Testing continuity and activity variables as predictors of positive and negative affect in retirement. *The Journals of Gerontology: Series B. Psychological Sciences and Social Sciences, 65B*(1), 42–49. doi:10.1093/geronb/gbp079

Rooks, R., & Whitfield, K. (2004). Health disparities among African Americans: Past, present, and future perspectives. In K. Whitfield (Ed.), *Closing the gap: Improving the health of minority elders in the new millennium* (pp. 45–54). Washington, DC: The Gerontological Society of America.

Rowe, J. W., & Kahn, R. L. (1987). Human aging: Usual and successful. *Science, 237*, 143–149. doi:10.1126/science.3299702

Rowe, J. W., & Kahn, R. L. (1998). *Successful aging.* New York, NY: Pantheon Books.

Schaie, K. W. (2005). What can we learn from longitudinal studies of adult development? *Research in Human Development, 2*, 133–158. doi:10.1207/s15427617rhd0203_4

Scheibe, S., & Carstensen, L. L. (2010). Emotional aging: Recent findings and future trends. *The Journals of Gerontology: Series B. Psychological Sciences and Social Sciences, 65B*(2), 135–144. doi:10.1093/geronb/gbp132

Seligman, M. E., & Csikszentmihalyi, M. (2000). Positive psychology: An introduction. *American Psychologist, 55*, 5–14. doi:10.1037/0003-066X.55.1.5

Shankle, M. D., Maxwell, C. A., Katzman, E. S., & Landers, J. D. (2003). An invisible population: Older lesbian, gay, bisexual, and transgender individuals. *Clinical Research and Regulatory Affairs, 20*, 159–182. doi:10.1081/CRP-120021079

Shock, N. S., Greulich, R. C., Andres, R., Arenberg, D., Costa, P. T., Lakatta, E. G., . . . Tobin, J. D. (1984). *Normal human aging: The Baltimore Longitudinal Study of Aging* (No. 84–2450). Washington, DC: National Institutes of Health.

Shultz, K. S. (2003). Bridge employment: Work after retirement. In G. A. Adams & T. A. Beehr (Eds.), *Retirement: Reasons, processes, and results* (pp. 214–241). New York, NY: Springer.

Sneed, J. R., & Whitbourne, S. K. (2003). Identity processing and self-consciousness in middle and later adulthood. *Journal of Gerontology: Series B. Psychological Sciences and Social Sciences, 58B*, 313–319.

Stewart, A. J., & McDermott, C. (2004). Gender in psychology. *Annual Review of Psychology, 55,* 519–544. doi:10.1146/annurev.psych.55.090902.141537

Strawbridge, W. J., Wallhagen, M. I., & Cohen, R. D. (2002). Successful aging and well-being: Self-rated compared with Rowe and Kahn. *The Gerontologist, 42,* 727–733. doi:10.1093/geront/42.6.727

Tkach, C., & Lyubomirsky, S. (2006). How do people pursue happiness? *Journal of Happiness Studies, 7,* 183–225. doi:10.1007/s10902-005-4754-1

Torres, S. (1999). A culturally-relevant theoretical framework for the study of successful aging. *Ageing and Society, 19,* 33–51. doi:10.1017/S0144686X99007242

U.S. Census Bureau. (2008, August 14). *U.S. Census Bureau news: An older and more diverse nation by midcentury.*Washington, DC: U.S. Government Public Information Office.

Vacha-Haase, T., Wester, S. R., & Christianson, H. (2010). *Psychotherapy with older men.* New York, NY: Routledge.

Wade, S. (2001). Combating ageism: An imperative for contemporary health care. *Reviews in Clinical Gerontology, 11,* 285–294. doi:10.1017/S095925980101139X

Walsh, W. B. (Ed.). (2008). *Biennial review of counseling psychology.* New York, NY: Routledge.

Wang, M., & Shultz, K. S. (2010). Employee retirement: A review and recommendations for future investigation. *Journal of Management, 36,* 172–206. doi:10.1177/0149206309347957

Weinick, R. M., Elliott, M. N., Volandes, A. E., Lopez, L., Burkhart, Q., & Schlesinger, M. (2011). Using standardized encounters to understand reported racial/ethnic disparities in patient experiences with care. *Health Services Research, 46,* 491–509. doi:10.1111/j.1475-6773.2010.01214.x

Werth, J. L., Kopera-Frye, K., Blevins, D., & Bossick, B. (2003). Older adult representation in the counseling psychology literature. *The Counseling Psychologist, 31,* 789–814. doi:10.1177/0011000003258391

Whitbourne, S. K. (2002). *The aging individual: Physical and psychological perspectives* (2nd ed.). New York, NY: Springer.

Whitbourne, S. K., Sneed, J. R., & Sayer, A. (2009). Psychosocial development form college through midlife: A 34-year sequential study. *Developmental Psychology, 45,* 1328–1340. doi:10.1037/a0016550

Whitbourne, S. K., Sneed, J. R., & Skultety, K. M. (2002). Identity processes in adulthood: Theoretical and methodological challenges. *Identify: An International Journal of Theory and Research, 2,* 29–45. doi:10.1207/S1532706XID0201_03

Whitbourne, S., & Waterman, A. (1979). Psychosocial development in young adulthood: Age and cohort comparisons. *Developmental Psychology, 15,* 373–378.

Whitbourne, S. K., Zuschlag, M., Elliot, L., & Waterman, A. (1992). Psychosocial development in adulthood: A 22-year sequential study. *Journal of Personality and Social Psychology, 63,* 260–271. doi:10.1037/0022-3514.63.2.260

Wu, K. B. (2007). *Sources of income for women age 65 and older.* Washington, DC: AARP Public Policy Institute. Retrieved from http://assets.aarp.org/rgcenter/econ/dd161_income.pdf

Yang, F. M., & Levkoff, S. E. (2005). Ageism and minority populations: Strengths in the face of challenge. *Generations,* 42–48.

Zhan, Y., Wang, M., Liu, S., & Shultz, K. (2009). Bridge employment and retirees' health: A longitudinal investigation. *Journal of Occupational Health Psychology, 14,* 374–389. doi:10.1037/a0015285

RELIGION AND SPIRITUALITY: THEORIES AND RESEARCH

Stephen W. Cook, Lance S. Dixon, and Petra J. McGuire

Surveys estimate that approximately 85% of the world population (see http://www.adherents.com/Religions_By_Adherents.html) and 80% of the U.S. population (Kosmin & Keysar, 2009) claim at least some identification with some form of religion. Also, approximately 81% of Americans consider religion to be at least a fairly important part of their lives (Gallup, Inc., 2010), and 50% to 85% of people experiencing difficult situations report using religion and spirituality to cope (Pargament, 1997). One of the early pioneers in the psychological study of religion, William James (1902/1961), described the nature of religion as "the feelings, acts, and experiences of individual [people] in their solitude, so far as they apprehend themselves to stand in relation to whatever they may consider the divine" (p. 42). Examining the experiences, thoughts, feelings, and behaviors associated with religiousness and spirituality is important for counseling psychologists, as well as for social scientists more generally, to obtain a more accurate understanding of people.

This chapter begins by critically analyzing definition and measurement issues that have served as the focus of substantial research and theoretical developments in this area of study during recent years. Next, several content domains in the psychological study of religiousness are summarized and critiqued to provide counseling psychologists with a useful introduction to this area.

DEFINITION AND MEASUREMENT ISSUES

One area that typically causes problems in scientific writing focused on religiousness and spirituality is how these two terms are defined, and more particularly, how they are to be distinguished, if at all. We prefer the definitions offered by Pargament from Zinnbauer and Pargament (2005) that define *spirituality* as "a search for the sacred" (p. 36) and *religiousness* as "a search for significance in ways related to the sacred" (p. 36). This conceptualization places spirituality within a broader construct of religiousness, acknowledging that spirituality serves as the core of religiousness, with religiousness including a wider range of behaviors than often considered when referring to spirituality.

Zinnbauer and Pargament (2005) described how psychologists have traditionally agreed that both religiousness and spirituality are multidimensional concepts and how both terms have often been used interchangeably. Since the 1980s, however, the concept of spirituality has emerged as more distinct from religiousness. With this change, a polarization of spirituality and religion began to emerge (Zinnbauer & Pargament, 2005; see Table 19.1). Several researchers have criticized this move toward polarization (e.g., Hill & Pargament, 2003). For example, most every religious social institution is concerned with individual aspects of belief, spiritual practices, and personalized experience, and even the most individual forms of spirituality cannot be found outside of a cultural or social context. Also, in contrast to the polarizing view that religiousness denotes maladaptive aspects and spirituality denotes adaptive aspects of a faith perspective, most researchers in this area currently acknowledge that it is important to base evaluations of religiousness and spirituality on an

DOI: 10.1037/13754-019
APA Handbook of Counseling Psychology: Vol. 1. Theories, Research, and Methods, Nadya A. Fouad (Editor-in-Chief)
Copyright © 2012 by the American Psychological Association. All rights reserved.

507

TABLE 19.1

Polarized Definitions of Religion and Spirituality

Religion	Spirituality
Substantive	Functional
Static	Dynamic
Institutional and objective	Personal and subjective
Belief based	Emotional or experiential based
Negative	Positive

Note. Summarized from Zinnbauer and Pargament (2005).

accumulation of empirical findings, rather than a priori judgments (Cook, Borman, Moore, & Kunkel, 2000; Hood, Hill, & Spilka, 2009; Pargament, 1999). Much research has been invested in the past 2 decades attempting to untangle these definition issues, resulting in a renewed commitment to base psychologists' understanding of religiousness and spirituality on an empirical foundation.

Similar to problems with defining religiousness and spirituality, the tackling of measurement issues in this area has been difficult. Hill (2005) echoed Gorsuch's (1984) concerns about researchers having an overemphasis on developing effective measurement in the psychological study of religiousness rather than focusing on the psychological study of religiousness itself. The development of effective ways to assess primary variables in this domain has been necessary for the study of religiousness and spirituality to progress. Along with the increasing recognition of religion and spirituality as one aspect of culture (e.g., American Psychological Association [APA], 1992; Fukuyama & Sevig, 1999; Sue, Bingham, Porche-Burke, & Vasquez, 1999) has come an increasing responsibility to assess religiousness and spirituality as one of various demographic variables that should be assessed to accurately describe our research samples.

For several years, members of Stephen W. Cook's research group have considered various strategies to collect efficient and accurate demographic information regarding religiousness. The group recommended employing three different methods as a quick way to assess core aspects of this construct: affiliation, importance, and behavior frequency. At

the most basic level, the group assesses research participants' current religious affiliation (sometimes referred to as religious preference or religious identification). Participants are provided with response options listing the most prevalent religious affiliations for the research populations' geographic area (for survey information describing religious affiliation in specific geographic areas, see the website of the Association of Religious Data Archives at http://www.thearda.com/). Response options describing possible religious affiliations include options for both atheist and agnostic designations as well as an open-ended "Other" response option that participants can complete if their self-described religious affiliation does not match any of the response options provided.

The research group also assesses a second level of religiousness for demographic purposes regarding the importance of religion and spirituality to research participants. The group assesses this dimension by asking two questions (one for religiousness and one for spirituality) with a multiple-choice response format—that is, "How religious [or spiritual] do you consider yourself?" Finally, the group includes single items that assess both self-reported frequency of religious service attendance and frequency of prayer. Assessment of these three domains is an efficient method of providing baseline demographic information to describe participant religiousness for any research study. Beyond assessing religiousness more simply as a demographic variable, there has also been recognition that religiousness and spirituality are complex constructs that require assessment along a variety of dimensions for effective research and theoretical development. Hill and colleagues (e.g., Hill, 2005; Hill & Pargament, 2003) have summarized efforts to capture empirically sound operationalizations of the various aspects of religiousness. For example, Hill and Hood (1999) provided descriptions and critiques of more than 100 measures of religiousness and related constructs. This text, organized into 17 major domains of religiously oriented constructs, is a useful resource for researchers. Similarly, the Fetzer Institute/National Institute on Aging Working Group (1999; see also Idler et al., 2003) developed measures of 12 "health-relevant domains of religiousness and spirituality as they are broadly understood" (p. 3). The items and scales developed by this effort represent an important step in capturing a broad-based assessment of many aspects of religiousness and spirituality considered to be relevant to health outcomes. The reliability and validity evidence for some of the scale scores is lacking, however. Additional summaries of measures of religiousness and spirituality can be obtained by consulting the useful reviews by Hill (2005); Hill and Pargament (2003); Sherman and Simonton (2001); and Koenig, McCullough, and Larson (2001, Chapter 13).

Many aspects of religiousness and spirituality can be considered relevant to the work of counseling psychologists. The remaining part of this chapter will focus on summarizing research and theoretical developments in several areas that provide a useful perspective on understanding the human experience.

MODELS OF RELIGIOUS AND SPIRITUAL DEVELOPMENT

Religion and spirituality have been reported as important aspects in the lives of adolescents as well as middle-aged and older adults (Cobb, 2001; Schaie, Krause, & Booth, 2004), so gaining insight into religious and spiritual development can contribute to a more complete understanding of overall human development. Many models of religious and spiritual development are stage models that focus on processes taking place in childhood. Elkind's (1970) model parallels Piaget's (1954/1937) stages of cognitive development by proposing that children move from a concrete way of thinking about religion when they are younger to a more abstract way of thinking as they approach adolescence. In a series of three studies, Elkind (1961, 1962, 1963) asked questions containing religious ideas to Catholic, Jewish, and Protestant children. Children in similar age groups demonstrated similar cognitive processes such that they moved from concrete to more abstract thinking with age. Goldman (1964) found similar results when he asked questions of 5- to 15-year-old children about religious pictures and Bible stories. The work of Elkind and Goldman indicated that the development of religious thinking may be

productively conceptualized utilizing a Piagetian model (Hood et al., 2009), providing a useful framework for counseling psychologists working with children and adolescents.

Fowler (1981) developed a stage-oriented model of faith development that applies to the entire life span of religious development. It is notable that Fowler (1981) defined *faith* broadly in his model as a "way of discerning and committing ourselves to centers of value and power that exert ordering force in our lives" (pp. 24–25). Although Fowler contended that his theory provides a helpful framework for understanding faith development, there are criticisms of his approach. An assumption of his theory is that a person must pass through acceptance of relativism to move to the highest level of faith development. This assumption has been critiqued because many complex systems of belief would not allow for acceptance of relativism, and Fowler's theory suggests that anyone in those systems could not develop a fully mature faith (Levenson, Aldwin, & D'Mello, 2005). Fowler's theory has also been critiqued for focusing too much on cognitive development and neglecting unique aspects of the individual's experience, such as religious language or stories and socialization (Day, 2001; McDargh, 2001).

Another important stage theory that focuses on the development of religious judgment was formulated by Oser and colleagues (Oser, 1991; Oser & Gmünder, 1991). This model is based on seven dimensions of apparent "tensions" that Oser (1991) asserted are essential in confronting when making religious judgments. These tensions include seemingly opposing values, such as freedom versus dependence on God and feeling faith versus feeling fear in a situation. How people think about and reconcile these tensions determines in which of five stages of religious judgment they are engaged. Oser and Gmünder (1991) posited that people in the earlier stages tend to resolve these tensions by considering these values as opposites and choosing one over the other. In contrast, people in the last stage of religious judgment recognize the ability for seemingly opposite values to exist simultaneously.

Oser's theory has an intuitive appeal for many psychologists as well religious experts, serving to describe the different and near-universal task across various faith orientations of wrestling with apparent inconsistencies between particular ideals or between a particular ideal and reality. This theory has also received several criticisms, however. Oser himself noted a lack of substantial empirical support for any stage theory of religious judgment (Oser & Reich, 1996). Levenson et al. (2005) noted that the oldest participant in Oser's (1991) study was 25, which does not provide data for religious judgment throughout the life span as the model claims. Levenson et al. also noted that the stages of religious judgment illustrate "a number of well-established attitudes toward the divine, but it is not at all clear how these attitudes constitute developmental stages" (p. 154). It seems this theory, along with those mentioned previously, can serve as guides to enhance counseling psychologists' thinking about religious or spiritual development; however, it is also clear that it is difficult to provide a model that encompasses all of the various components that are essential in different faith perspectives.

Recently, researchers have argued that conceptualizing religious and spiritual development as a continuous process, rather than as a stage process, may be more accurate (Hood et al., 2009; Streib, 2001). Other researchers have suggested that models of faith need to leave the confines of cognitive-stage models and allow for more individually focused approaches that speak to the particular experiences of each person (Day, 2001; McDargh, 2001). Boyatzis (2005) expressed concern that too many theories address cognitive aspects of religious development and recommended considering social, cultural, and historical contexts when conceptualizing religious and spiritual development.

GOD CONCEPT OR IMAGE AND ATTACHMENT TO GOD

A significant component in the beliefs of many spiritual and religious people is the idea of a supreme or transcendent being, such as Allah or God. In this chapter, the term *God* is utilized to refer to the notion of a person's understanding of a divine being, higher power, or transcendent force that is the focus in her or his particular religious or spiritual

orientation. For researchers in the psychological study of religion, this concept of a transcendent being leads to questions about how people form their understanding of God and whether particular ideas about God are more adaptive than others. This area of research is important because it can add to our understanding of how and why people experience religion very differently, and in turn, behave differently. For example, if an individual feels God is loving, involved, and concerned during a crisis, that person may experience and cope with the crisis differently than a person who understands God as less loving and uninvolved.

The notion of God image as a psychological construct was introduced by Rizzuto (1979) who, hypothesizing from an object relations perspective, believed a person's image of God is formed on the basis of relationships with early caregivers, mainly the mother, and this image serves as a transitional object. Such a transitional object is of utmost importance because it provides people with a source of comfort and security they can depend on while navigating stressful life situations during various developmental stages—relevant to counseling psychologists' traditional emphasis on both developmental perspectives and a focus on normality rather than pathology (Gelso & Fretz, 2001). Most transitional objects are no longer needed as people move to higher levels of development, but Rizzuto posited that a unique aspect of the God image is its ability to serve as a transitional object throughout the life span.

On the basis of Rizzuto's (1979) suggestion that parents or early caregivers are the prototypes for children's images of God, there has been a great deal of research examining the relationships between the two. Specifically, a number of studies have examined the associations between people's mother images or father images and their images of God, and findings have been mixed (e.g., Hertel & Donahue, 1995; Roof & Roof, 1984). Research suggests that additional factors need to be considered as influences on God images, including the effect of parents' images of God on children's images of God (Dickie, Ajega, Kobylak, & Nixon, 2006) as well as the association of parents' religious practices and education level with children's images of God

(Potvin, 1977). Religious clients can benefit from working with therapists to understand the factors that may have influenced their images of God. This process may allow clients to appreciate how their images of God may be associated with how they perceive themselves and the world as well as how they may relate to other people.

Several aspects of quality of life have been found to be related to particular images of God. Rejecting and nonloving images of God were found to be associated with low self-esteem, whereas loving images of God were associated with higher levels of self-esteem (P. Benson & Spilka, 1973). Francis, Gibson, and Robbins (2001) found a positive relationship between loving and forgiving images of God and self-worth as well as a negative relationship between punishing and cruel images of God and self-worth. People who reported higher levels of depression also reported images of God that were more alienating (Exline, Yali, & Sanderson, 2000). Higher levels of religious behaviors and practices were found to be positively related to images of God as more accepting, available, and challenging (Buchko & Witzig, 2003). Overall, research indicates images of God that are positive, such as more loving and forgiving, were highly associated with positive variables such as self-esteem and self-worth. However, these studies operationalized God images differently (i.e., card sorts, single vs. multiple item measures); therefore, it is difficult to be certain the same constructs were being assessed when comparing results.

Attachment theory researchers have also suggested that images of God may be related to people's experiences in relationships. These researchers extended Bowlby's (1969) emphasis on the importance of parent–child attachments and studied its potential impact on images of God. Research on attachment and God image has led to different ideas about how these may be associated. The "compensation" hypothesis suggests that people may develop loving and available images of God to serve as the ideal attachment figure and make up for the lack of this relationship with early caregivers (e.g., Granqvist, 2002). Alternatively, the "correspondence" hypothesis suggests a person's attachment style in relationships may be similar to how they perceive

God (e.g., Kirkpatrick & Shaver, 1992). Although both theories show how images of God can be influenced by relationships, they do not explain why individuals from similar environments and experiences may develop entirely different images of God. Although more research in this area is needed, the current research indicates that God images play an important role in the lives of religious and spiritual people.

RELIGIOUSNESS, SPIRITUALITY, AND HEALTH

The research investigations of relationships between religion or spirituality and health are numerous. Hood et al. (2009) listed several reviews of these studies that although criticisms exist (e.g., Sloan & Bagiella, 2002), generally indicate associations between increased religiousness and better health, particularly in terms of mental health. Hood et al. stated, however, that "it is an overgeneralization to say that religion is necessarily good or bad for one's health" (p. 445). Some important preliminary interpretations may be drawn from these attempts to clarify the links that religion and spirituality may have with both physical and mental health outcomes.

Physical Health

One physical health outcome that has been frequently investigated in the religion and health literature is that of mortality. In an often-cited meta-analysis, McCullough, Hoyt, Larson, Koenig, and Thoresen (2000), examined 42 independent samples that included more than 125,000 people. Controlling for 10 possible confounding variables, results indicated that religious involvement was associated with a 25% reduction in the average mortality rate. More specifically, research has widely demonstrated that religious service attendance is associated with a decreased risk for all-cause mortality (e.g., Cohen & Koenig, 2003; Musick, Traphagan, Koenig, & Larson, 2000; Pargament, Koenig, Tarakeshwar, & Hahn, 2001), with one review reporting an average 30% reduction in mortality risk, even when accounting for the effects of demographic, socioeconomic, and health-related variables

(Powell, Shahabi, & Thoresen, 2003). Religious variables have been linked with better cardiovascular health, including a lower occurrence of high blood pressure and reduced hypertension (Musick et al., 2000). Finally, the frequency of religious service attendance has been correlated with engaging in and maintaining healthier behaviors, a speedier recovery from surgery (Larson & Larson, 2003), and improved functional health in older adults (e.g., Koenig, George, & Titus, 2004; Musick et al., 2000). Although simply whether or not one participates in organized religion seems to be a relevant predictor of physical health outcomes, other associations suggest that the quality of one's experiences with religion may also be an important consideration in understanding religion's associations with health. For example, among those people who report attending religious services, those who feel as if they belong in their religious community report greater satisfaction with their own physical health status (Krause & Wulff, 2005).

Mental Health

Research has demonstrated relationships between religiousness and both the prevalence and severity of mental illness. General psychological distress ratings are often lower among religious individuals (Hackney & Sanders, 2003), particularly among those who frequently attend religious services (Ellison, Boardman, Williams, & Jackson, 2001). Research suggests a link between religiousness or spirituality and lower rates of depression, fewer depressive symptoms, and lower rates of suicidality (e.g., Larson & Larson, 2003; Smith, McCullough, & Poll, 2003), Mixed findings exist regarding the relationship between religiousness and anxiety with some suggesting that religiousness predicts less concurrent and prospective anxiety (Koenig & Larson, 2001) and others finding positive associations between these variables (e.g., Miller & Kelley, 2005). Finally, religious involvement has been linked to lower rates of drug and alcohol abuse (Chatters, 2000; Koenig & Larson, 2001) with religious service attendance predicting a lower likelihood of smoking, and religiously affiliated smokers tending to smoke significantly less than nonaffiliated smokers (Larson & Larson, 2003).

Religiousness has been linked to positive aspects of psychological adjustment as well (Hood et al., 2009; Miller & Kelley, 2005). Psychological well-being has been significantly associated with religious involvement (e.g., Ellison et al., 2001). Individuals who participate in religious activities have been shown to have higher rates of happiness (Cohen & Koenig, 2003) and greater life satisfaction (e.g., Hackney & Sanders, 2003; Larson & Larson, 2003). Feeling that their spiritual needs are being supported by a religious community has also been found to predict better quality of life ratings among cancer patients (Balboni et al., 2007).

Religious and Spiritual Struggles

Although associations between religiousness and better health outcomes have been reported in many research studies, several studies have been unable to provide evidence that support such associations. In addition, some aspects of the religious experience have demonstrated associations with poorer health outcomes. For example, religious struggles, that is, the difficulties that may arise in an individual's religious experiences, have been linked to a greater risk of mortality among hospitalized older adults (Pargament et al., 2001), worsened functional abilities during medical rehabilitation (Powell et al., 2003), and a greater likelihood of depression (Edmondson, Park, Chaudoir, & Wortmann, 2008).

Some religious struggles are intrapersonal in nature, including such phenomena as religious doubts, anger at God, and feeling alienated from God. Religious doubting involves the questioning of one's own religious beliefs, and this doubt has been associated with higher rates of depression (e.g., Krause & Wulff, 2004) and lower life satisfaction (Gauthier, Christopher, Walter, Mourad, & Marek, 2006). Anger at God is another type of religious struggle, with 63% of the participants in a U.S. sample reporting sometimes feeling angry at God (Exline, 2006). This anger has been linked with depression, low self-esteem, and an increased likelihood of leaving a religious affiliation (Exline, 2006). Associations between a sense of alienation from God and depression as well as between fear and guilt related to religion and suicidality have been reported, even when accounting for the comfort derived from religious involvement (Exline et al., 2000).

In contrast to religious struggles that can occur within an individual, there also exists the possibility for conflicts to occur between individuals in a religious setting or centering on religious issues. The experience of interpersonal religious conflicts has been associated with greater anxiety among religious group members as well as with more negative mood and less spiritual growth among a college student sample (Pargament, Zinnbauer, et al., 1998). Interpersonal conflicts related to religion have been be linked to more depressive symptoms, even after accounting for one's degree of religious involvement and the comfort derived from it (Exline et al., 2000). Interpersonal religious struggles include conflicts among congregation members, conflicts between congregation members and clergy, and conflicts over religious teaching (Krause, Chatters, Meltzer, and Morgan, 2000).

To the extent that religious struggles have been found to be negatively associated with physical and mental health, there seem to be significant implications for counseling psychologists. These data suggest that the nature of one's religious experiences, in addition to the extent of one's religious participation, is an important consideration in research aimed at exploring the associations between religion and mental health. Given the prevalence of data generally interpreted as providing support for the benefits of religiousness, it may be tempting for counseling psychologists to assume that clients describing religious involvement or affiliation bring associated strengths to the therapeutic exchange. Research findings also indicate, however, that negative associations exist between health and aspects of religiousness, including interpersonal religious struggles, which should serve as a reminder of the importance of thoroughly exploring various aspects of a person's religious experience.

Possible Mediating Variables

Even as the relationships between religion and health remain complex and at times ambiguous, researchers have begun to look for potential explanations for why these relationships may exist. Several reviews are available that discuss the

mechanisms by which religion may be related to health outcomes (e.g., George, Ellison, & Larson, 2002; Hood et al., 2009). Generally, these reviews have proposed explanations (i.e., mediating variables) for why positive associations between religiousness and health may exist; however, it is important to note that research exploring such possible mediating variables is limited or, in the case of some explanations, virtually nonexistent (Thoresen & Harris, 2002). Because these mediators remain largely hypothetical to date, one potentially important area of future research in religion and health involves empirical investigations of these proposed mediational associations.

Reviews in this area have commonly described the emphasis many religious orientations place on healthy lifestyles and behaviors as potential mediating variables for any positive relationships between religiousness and health. This has been emphasized by some religious groups through general suggestions to care for the body "as a temple" and, by some, through more specific guidelines or prohibitions of such activities as substance use or abuse, sex outside the confines of a marriage relationship, and so on (Chatters, 2000; George et al., 2002).

Another mediating variable that has been proposed involves the claim that religious individuals may have access to psychosocial resources unavailable to those who are nonreligious. It has been proposed that religious individuals may make use of coping strategies unique to religiousness such as prayer, collaborating with one's higher power to solve life's problems, and so on (Pargament, 1997). The suggestion, then, is that religious individuals may have a wider range of possible coping strategies than their nonreligious peers (Pargament, Koenig, Tarakeshwar, & Hahn, 2004). Others have suggested that religiousness may promote a belief system that encourages positive attitudes, positive emotional states, and a greater sense of meaning or purpose in life, which has been hypothesized to contribute to improved mental health (George et al., 2002; Steger & Frazier, 2005).

Perhaps the most widely proposed explanation for the relationships between religiousness and health is the notion that positive effects on health are related to the social support a religious person can derive from his or her religious community members and leaders (e.g., Lim & Putnam, 2010). Significant positive relationships between social support and health have been widely demonstrated, and on the basis of this, researchers have proposed that religious individuals have a somewhat unique opportunity to connect with a group of people with whom they share a belief system. This increased interaction may serve to increase the extent to which individuals feel supported by others in their religious groups (Chatters, 2000; George et al., 2002).

Evaluating Religion and Health Literature
In addition to examining the role of possible mediating variables underlying the positive associations found between religiousness and health, some researchers have pointed out methodological concerns regarding the evidence for these associations. For example, Sloan and Bagiella (2002) noted that some articles included in reviews or meta-analyses have introduced issues of multiple comparisons and inattention to potential confounds. Others have discussed the importance of introducing research methods designed to address issues of causality in religion and health literature. Research efforts to understand the relationships between religiousness and health would benefit from prospective and longitudinal studies, as much of the work to date has involved cross-sectional research designs (Chatters, 2000; George et al., 2002; Thoresen & Harris, 2002). Also, very rarely has this area been explored using an experimental research design, relying nearly entirely on correlational data thus far. An additional methodological concern in the religion and health literature to date involves the relatively common practice of operationally defining religiousness in an overly simplistic manner—for example, a single-item measure of religious service attendance. This seems likely to limit the ability to understand the complexity of diverse religious experience. It has been suggested that utilizing measures of various aspects of religiousness may offer a clearer understanding of the religious nuances that do and do not have associations with health outcomes (Thoresen & Harris, 2002).

Finally, research studies demonstrating positive associations between religiousness and health are generally conducted only with individuals currently identifying as religious. Although this seems the obvious population of interest in such research, excluding individuals who do not currently identify with religion may introduce a selection bias in research outcomes. It seems likely that these data are incapable of accounting for individuals who have had difficult or particularly negative experiences with religion, contributing to a decision to discontinue their religious affiliation.

RELIGIOUS COPING
As noted, one of the mechanisms that may explain the positive associations between religiousness and health is using religious strategies to cope with difficulties. An extensive body of research regarding religious coping has been developed by Pargament and others since the late 1980s. Building on the psychology of stress and coping (e.g., Lazarus & Folkman, 1984), Pargament (1997) broadly categorized coping, including religious coping, using a functional perspective, as either focusing toward the conservation of significance or the transformation of significance. Even though many social scientists have seen religious coping for the purpose of conservation of significance as one of the primary, if not exclusive, functions of religion (e.g., Freud, 1927/1961), empirical evidence suggests that religiousness serves purposes beyond this, being associated not only with simple tension reduction but also with actively oriented types of coping and processing of stressful events (Pargament, 1997; Pargament, Ano, & Wachholtz, 2005). Thus, religious coping for the purpose of transforming significance (e.g., forgiving an offender) can create dramatic changes in a person's life in response to a stressful event, can often be painful, and can result in a significant change of values, meaning, and direction in a person's life. Summaries of research on religious coping (see Hood et al., 2009, Chapter 13; Pargament et al., 2005) indicate that various aspects of religious coping can be adaptive or maladaptive, religious coping strategies contribute to psychological outcomes beyond the effects of nonreligious types of coping, and specific variables are being

identified (e.g., religious affiliation, level of religiousness, severity of the stressful event) that seem to moderate the associations between religious coping and important outcomes.

Pargament and various colleagues developed several measures of religious coping. The most comprehensive measure, the 100-item RCOPE (Pargament et al., 2000), offers a broad-based measure of coping that assesses a wide variety of religious coping and appraisal strategies. The individual scales of the RCOPE can be administered separately, allowing for an efficient assessment of only those aspects of religious coping that are considered relevant (K. I. Pargament, personal communication, July 20, 2007). Pargament et al. (2000) provided some psychometric evidence regarding the stability of the RCOPE factor structure, but additional support for this would be useful. Also, Pargament has categorized various religious coping items or scales as assessing strategies that are generally considered adaptive or maladaptive (Pargament et al., 2000; Pargament, Smith, et al., 1998). Even though some research supports such an organization, this type of categorization seems premature pending further examination of these different religious coping strategies in a wider variety of settings and populations.

PRAYER

Along with forgiveness, Hood et al. (2009) concluded that prayer is one of two aspects of religious coping that deserve special consideration. Hood et al. described prayer as occupying a "central and significant role in the lives of most people" (p. 465). Spilka (2005) described prayer as being at the core of religious practice. Prayer is often an important means for some people to communicate and interact with something transcendent or superempirical (McCullough & Larson, 1999). James (1902/1961) referred to prayer as "the very soul and essence of religion" (p. 361). A 1999 survey in the United States found that 75% of participants report praying on a daily basis, and most believed their prayers were heard by God (Gallup, 1999). Although people pray for a variety of reasons, many pray to cope with problems they encounter in their lives (Pargament, 1997). People utilize prayer for coping with illness, psychological distress, and persistent problems that

seem out of the individual's control (e.g., Laird et al., 2004; McCaffrey, Eisenberg, Legedza, Davis, & Phillips, 2004; McCullough, 1995). As such, prayer would often seem to be used by people seeking counseling who are struggling with personal difficulties. Indeed, prayer for one's self and prayer for others were among the top two forms of alternative therapies reportedly used by older adults (Barnes, Powell-Griner, McFann, & Nahin, 2002). Considering the importance of prayer to those who utilize it, and the frequency in which it is reportedly engaged, it is likely prayer will continue to be an important resource utilized by many people (Masters & Spielmans, 2007) and therefore a subject of interest to counseling psychologists.

Research suggests that prayer is a complicated and multidimensional construct that cannot be measured with a single item or question (Bade & Cook, 2008; Ladd & Spilka, 2002; Laird et al., 2004). Using measures that better account for an individual's thoughts and experiences during prayer (e.g., Cook & Bade, 1998; Ladd & Spilka, 2006) can provide counseling psychologists with a better understanding of prayer as it functions in peoples' lives. Many types of prayer have been described from a theological perspective (e.g., Foster, 1992), and efforts to describe the multidimensionality of prayer from a social science perspective have also emerged. Ladd and Spilka (2002, 2006) identified three primary aspects of prayer that are directed inward, toward other people, and toward the divine. Poloma and Pendleton (1991) developed a measure of prayer that assessed meditative (focusing on God's presence), ritualistic (memorized or learned prayers), petitionary (requesting things for self or others), and colloquial (conversational, seeking guidance or forgiveness) types of prayer.

Types of prayer have been associated with various psychological outcomes: meditative prayer was positively correlated with existential and religious well-being, colloquial prayer was positively associated with happiness, and ritualistic prayer was positively correlated with negative affect (Poloma & Pendleton, 1991). However, other studies examining the association between health outcomes and prayer have yielded mixed results (e.g., Bradshaw, Ellison, & Flannelly, 2008; Hackney & Sanders,

2003). For instance, frequency of prayer and mystical experiences during prayer have been found to be significant predictors of well-being and positive religious coping (e.g., McCullough, 1995; Nooney & Woodrum, 2002). Alternatively, many studies have suggested that there is not a significant positive association between prayer and health (e.g., H. Benson et al., 2006; Masters & Spielmans, 2007).

One concern regarding research on the associations between prayer and psychological outcomes is whether the most salient aspects of prayer are being assessed. Frequency of prayer has been utilized as a measure of prayer in multiple studies, and some researchers question whether it is able to explain the complex associations between prayer and various outcomes (Poloma & Pendleton, 1991). A recent development in prayer research has been the development of the Prayer Functions Scale (Cook & Bade, 1998), which measures the ways that prayer is used to deal with personal problems. People facing difficult situations may utilize prayer for a variety of reasons—for example, to provide them with acceptance, calm and focus, and assistance, or to defer responsibility to God (Bade & Cook, 2008). Prayer functions have predicted levels of trait anxiety and posttraumatic growth (Harris, Schoneman, & Carrera, 2002, 2005) as well as positive affect and satisfaction with life (Dixon & Cook, 2010). Examining the function that prayer serves as a coping strategy may help researchers gain new insights into the effectiveness, or lack of effectiveness, of various prayer types. In conclusion, prayer is an important component in the lives of many people, it is often used to cope with difficult situations, and some evidence indicates that it is related to important psychological outcomes. The work of counseling psychologists will benefit from an increased understanding of the various roles that prayer may serve in peoples' lives.

CONCLUSION

This chapter has provided a summary of issues and contents areas that are important to the theoretical and empirical foundation of the psychological study of religion. There are several other areas that hold great promise in the near future for important research and theoretical contributions to counseling psychology. Many counseling psychologists (e.g., Wade, Worthington, & Haake, 2009; Worthington, 2006; Worthington, Witvliet, Pietrini, & Miller, 2007) are making significant empirical and theoretical developments in the area of forgiveness, often closely associated with religiousness. Scholarly work providing neurophysiological (e.g., Inzlicht & Tullett, 2010; Newberg & Newberg, 2006), cognitive (e.g., Bering, 2006), and evolutionary (e.g., Kirkpatrick, 2005; Shariff & Norenzayan, 2007) perspectives is challenging theoretical understandings of the role that religiousness plays in people's lives. New areas of research particularly relevant for counseling psychologists include examinations of the role of religiousness in one's vocation or workplace (e.g., Duffy, 2006; Giacalone & Jurkiewicz, 2003). Similarly, the role of religiousness in social justice movements and conflict resolution and, alternatively, as a motivation toward violence and terrorism (see Silberman, 2005) holds strong potential for future productive contributions to our field. On the basis of the current state of the scholarly literature regarding religion and spirituality, several recommendations can be made regarding important next steps:

1. There is a need for an increased emphasis on diverse (i.e., non-Christian) religious and spiritual orientations. The majority of psychological research on religiousness has used Christian samples. Fortunately, several counseling psychologists are currently leading research efforts with non-Christian samples (e.g., Fukuyama & Sevig, 1999; Jana-Masri & Priester, 2007; Schlosser, Ali, Ackerman, & Dewey, 2009).

2. There is a need to incorporate religiousness more consistently into the areas of cultural diversity and cultural competency. For example, even though spirituality was acknowledged as an important aspect of the human condition by leaders in the first National Multicultural Conference Summit (NMCS; Sue et al., 1999), religiousness is not currently included as one of the several aspects of multiculturalism in the NMCS mission statement (see http://www.multiculturalsummit.org). Evidence also indicates that religious issues are not adequately addressed in the training of

counseling psychologists (Hage, 2006). APA (2007) recently passed a *Resolution on Religious, Religion-Based, and/or Religion-Derived Prejudice* that makes a positive statement about the importance of the respectful consideration of religiousness in a variety of ways, including "the dissemination of relevant empirical findings about the psychological correlates of religious/spiritual beliefs, attitudes, and behaviors to concerned stakeholders with full sensitivity to the profound differences between psychology and religion/spirituality" (p. 3).

3. There is a need to expand the types of research designs used to study religiousness to capture the diversity and the complexity of this aspect of experience. This means employing both qualitative and quantitative research strategies as well as using descriptive, experimental, and longitudinal designs (Hood et al., 2009, Chapter 2; Park & Paloutzian, 2005). APA Division 36 (Psychology of Religion) recently established a journal entitled *Psychology of Religion and Spirituality*, which provides an increased opportunity to publish a wide variety of research in this area.

4. There is a need to move beyond an unbalanced focus on measurement issues toward more theory-based research. As noted, several researchers have called for an end to what could be seen as a prevailing "measurement paradigm" in order to develop research that more directly examines the way that religiousness is involved in people's lives (Gorsuch, 1984; Hill, 2005). For this to happen, not only must sound theoretical approaches to the psychological study of religiousness be developed (e.g., Spilka & McIntosh, 1997) but also better translation between these theoretical approaches and empirically based research should ensue (Nelson, 2009; Park & Paloutzian, 2005). For example, after reviewing existing research regarding religious and spiritual development, P. L. Benson (2006) developed a comprehensive theory or architecture of spiritual development that incorporates recent developments within various subfields of psychology, such as developmental psychology and personality psychology.

5. There is a need to broaden the types of criterion variables examined in research to constructs that are more relevant to religiously oriented individuals. It is quite conceivable that people who consider religiousness an important and salient dimension of their lives would value other types of outcomes besides mental and physical health outcomes typically assessed in research (Hill & Pargament, 2003; Pargament, 2002). Such criterion variables might include spiritually oriented constructs related to issues involved in pursuing truth, life purpose, or meaning (Exline, 2002) or feeling accepted within a religious community or close to a deity (Pargament, 2002). Discovery-oriented research approaches should be used to understand what types of outcomes are most relevant to religiously oriented people, and these outcomes should be incorporated into research and theory.

6. There is a need to foster constructive dialogue between the fields of psychology and religion. Jones (1994) described the relatively rare and lop-sided manner of how psychology interacted with religion, outlined areas of common ground between the two disciplines and described ways that both disciplines could be enhanced by better interaction between the two. Since that time, researchers have made progress integrating psychology and religion in applied psychological work such as psychotherapy (e.g., Aten, McMinn, & Worthington, 2011; Richards & Bergin, 2005). It could be argued, however, that less progress has been made on developing helpful communication among experts in both psychology and religion in ways that serve to enhance both fields.

In general, the psychological study of religiousness provides a rich opportunity to understand an important aspect of many people's lives. An improved understanding in this area will help counseling psychologists provide better assistance to the various groups that we serve. For further information in this area, we refer readers to recent comprehensive summaries of theory and research in the psychological study of religion for a more thorough examination of these issues (see Hood et al., 2009; Paloutzian & Park, 2005; Plante & Sherman, 2001).

References

American Psychological Association. (1992). Ethical principles of psychologists and code of conduct. *American Psychologist, 47,* 1597–1611. doi:10.1037/0 003-066X.47.12.1597

American Psychological Association. (2007). *Resolution on religious, religion-based and/or religion-derived prejudice.* Retrieved from http://www.apa.org/about/governance/council/policy/religious-discrimination.pdf

Aten, J. D., McMinn, M. R., & Worthington, E. L., Jr. (2011). *Spiritually oriented interventions for counseling and psychotherapy.* Washington, DC: American Psychological Association. doi:10.1037/12313-000

Bade, M. K., & Cook, S. W. (2008). Functions of Christian prayer in the coping process. *Journal for the Scientific Study of Religion, 47,* 123–133. doi:10.1111/j.1468-5906.2008.00396.x

Balboni, T. A., Vanderwerker, L. C., Block, S. D., Paulk, M. E., Lathan, C. S., Peteet, J. R., & Prigerson, H. G. (2007). Religiousness and spiritual support among advanced cancer patients and associations with end-of-life treatment preferences and quality of life. *Journal of Clinical Oncology, 25,* 555–560. doi:10.1200/JCO.2006.07.9046

Barnes, P., Powell-Griner, E., McFann, K., & Nahin, R. (2002). *CDC advance data report #343: Complementary and alternative medicine use among adults: United States, 2002.* Washington, DC: National Center for Complementary and Alternative Medicine.

Benson, H., Dusek, J. A., Sherwood, J. B., Lam, P., Bethea, C. F., Carpenter, W., . . . Hibberd, P. L. (2006). Study of the therapeutic effects of intercessory prayer (STEP) in cardiac bypass patients: A multicenter randomized trial of uncertainty and certainty of receiving intercessory prayer. *American Heart Journal, 151,* 934–942. doi:10.1016/j.ahj.2005.05.028

Benson, P., & Spilka, B. (1973). God image as a function of self-esteem and locus of control. *Journal for the Scientific Study of Religion, 12,* 297–310. doi:10.2307/1384430

Benson, P. L. (2006). The science of child and adolescent spiritual development: Definitional, theoretical, and field-building challenges. In E. C. Roehlkepartain, P. E. King, L. Wagener, & P. L. Benson (Eds.), *The handbook of spiritual development in childhood and adolescence* (pp. 484–497). Thousand Oaks, CA: Sage.

Bering, J. (2006). The cognitive psychology of belief in the supernatural. *American Scientist, 94,* 142–149. doi:10.1511/2006.2.142

Bowlby, J. (1969). *Attachment and Loss: Vol. 1. Attachment.* New York, NY: Basic Books.

Boyatzis, C. J. (2005). Religious and spiritual development in childhood. In R. F. Paloutzian & C. L. Park (Eds.), *Handbook of the psychology of religion and spirituality* (pp. 123–143). New York, NY: Guilford Press.

Bradshaw, M., Ellison, C. G., & Flannelly, K. J. (2008). Prayer, God imagery, and symptoms of psychopathology. *Journal for the Scientific Study of Religion, 47,* 644–659. doi:10.1111/j.1468-5906.2008.00432.x

Buchko, K. J., & Witzig, T. (2003). Relationship between God-image and religious behaviors. *Psychological Reports, 93,* 1141–1148. doi:10.2466/PR0.93.8.1141-1148

Chatters, L. M. (2000). Religion and health: Public Health research and practice. *Annual Review of Public Health, 21,* 335–367. doi:10.1146/annurev.publhealth.21.1.335

Cobb, N. J. (2001). *Adolescence: Continuity, change and diversity* (4th ed.). Mountain View, CA: Mayfield.

Cohen, A. B., & Koenig, H. G. (2003). Religion, religiosity, and spirituality in the biopsychosocial model of health and ageing. *Ageing International, 28,* 215–241. doi:10.1007/s12126-002-1005-1

Cook, S. W., & Bade, M. K. (1998, August). *Reliability and validity information for the Prayer Functions Scale.* Paper presented at the 106th Annual Covention of the American Psychological Association, San Francisco, CA.

Cook, S. W., Borman, P. D., Moore, M. A., & Kunkel, M. A. (2000). College students' perceptions of spiritual people and religious people. *Journal of Psychology and Theology, 28,* 125–137.

Day, J. M. (2001). From structuralism to eternity? Re-imagining the psychology of religious development after the cognitive-developmental paradigm. *International Journal for the Psychology of Religion, 11,* 173–183. doi:10.1207/S15327582IJPR1103_04

Dickie, J. R., Ajega, L. V., Kobylak, J. R., & Nixon, K. M. (2006). Mother, father and self: Sources of young adults' God concepts. *Journal for the Scientific Study of Religion, 45,* 57–71. doi:10.1111/j.1468-5906.2006.00005.x

Dixon, L. S., & Cook, S. W. (2010). *God image and prayer functions: Relations with well-being and distress.* Unpublished manuscript, Department of Psychology, Texas Tech University, Lubbock.

Duffy, R. D. (2006). Spirituality, religion, and career development: Current status and future directions. *The Career Development Quarterly, 55,* 52–63.

Edmondson, D., Park, C. L., Chaudoir, S. R., & Wortmann, J. F. (2008). Death without God: Religious struggle, death concerns, and depression in the terminally ill. *Psychological Science, 19,* 754–758. doi:10.1111/j.1467-9280.2008.02152.x

Elkind, D. (1961). The child's concept of his religious denomination: I. The Jewish child. *The Journal of Genetic Psychology: Research and Theory on Human Development, 99*, 209–225. doi:10.1016/S0001-6918(61)80057-7

Elkind, D. (1962). The child's concept of his religious denomination: II. The Catholic child. *The Journal of Genetic Psychology: Research and Theory on Human Development, 101*, 185–193.

Elkind, D. (1963). The child's concept of his religious denomination: III. The Protestant child. *The Journal of Genetic Psychology, 103*, 291–304.

Elkind, D. (1970). The origins of religion in the child. *Review of Religious Research, 12*, 35–42. doi:10.2307/3510932

Ellison, C. G., Boardman, J. D., Williams, D. R., & Jackson, J. S. (2001). Religious involvement, stress, and mental health: Findings from the 1995 Detroit area study. *Social Forces, 80*, 215–249. doi:10.1353/sof.2001.0063

Exline, J. J. (2002). The picture is getting clearer, but is the scope too limited? Three overlooked questions in the psychology of religion. *Psychological Inquiry, 13*, 245–247. doi:10.1207/S15327965PLI1303_07

Exline, J. J. (2006, March). *Emotional atheism and anger toward god.* Invited address at the Mid-Year Research Conference on Religion and Spirituality, Baltimore, MD.

Exline, J. J., Yali, A. M., & Sanderson, W. C. (2000). Guilt, discord, and alienation: The role of religious strain in depression and suicidality. *Journal of Clinical Psychology, 56*, 1481–1496. doi:10.1002/1097-4679(200012)56:12<1481::AID-1>3.0.CO;2-A

Fetzer Institute/National Institute on Aging Working Group. (1999). *Multidimensional measurement of religiousness/spirituality for use in health research: A report of the Fetzer Institute/National Institute on Aging Working Group.* Kalamazoo, MI: Fetzer Institute.

Foster, R. J. (1992). *Prayer: Finding the heart's true home.* New York, NY: Harper Collins.

Fowler, J. W. (1981). *Stages of faith: The psychology of human development and the quest for meaning.* San Francisco, CA: Harper & Row.

Francis, L. J., Gibson, H. M., & Robbins, M. (2001). God images and self-worth among adolescents in Scotland. *Mental Health, Religion and Culture, 4*, 103–108. doi:10.1080/13674670110048327

Freud, S. (1961). *Future of an illusion* (J. Strachey, Trans.). New York, NY: Norton. (Original work published 1927)

Fukuyama, M. A., & Sevig, T. D. (1999). *Integrating spirituality into multicultural counseling.* Thousand Oaks, CA: Sage.

Gallup, G., Jr. (1999, May 6). *As nation observes national day of prayer, 9 in 10 pray—3 in 4 daily.* Retrieved from http://www.gallup.com/poll/3874/Nation-Observes-National-Day-Prayer-Pray-Daily.aspx

Gallup, Inc. (2010). *Religion.* Retrieved from http://www.gallup.com/poll/1690/Religion.aspx

Gauthier, K. J., Christopher, A. N., Walter, M. I., Mourad, R., & Marek, P. (2006). Religiosity, religious doubt, and the need for cognition: Their interactive relationship with life satisfaction. *Journal of Happiness Studies, 7*, 139–154. doi:10.1007/s10902-005-1916-0

Gelso, C. J., & Fretz, B. R. (2001). *Counseling psychology* (2nd ed.). Ft. Worth, TX: Harcourt College.

George, L. K., Ellison, C. G., & Larson, D. B. (2002). Explaining the relationships between religious involvement and health. *Psychological Inquiry, 13*, 190–200. doi:10.1207/S15327965PLI1303_04

Giacalone, R. A., & Jurkiewicz, C. L. (Eds.). (2003). *Handbook of workplace spirituality and organizational performance.* Armonk, NY: Sharpe.

Goldman, R. (1964). *Religious thinking from childhood to adolescence.* New York, NY: Seabury Press.

Gorsuch, R. L. (1984). Measurement: The boon and bane of investigating religion. *American Psychologist, 39*, 228–236. doi:10.1037/0003-066X.39.3.228

Granqvist, P. (2002). Attachment and religiosity in adolescents: Cross sectional and longitudinal evaluations. *Personality and Social Psychology Bulletin, 28*, 260–270. doi:10.1177/0146167202282011

Hackney, C. H., & Sanders, G. S. (2003). Religiosity and mental health: A meta-analysis of recent studies. *Journal for the Scientific Study of Religion, 42*, 43–55. doi:10.1111/1468-5906.t01-1-00160

Hage, S. M. (2006). A closer look at the role of spirituality in psychology training programs. *Professional Psychology: Research and Practice, 37*, 303–310. doi:10.1037/0735-7028.37.3.303

Harris, J. I., Schoneman, S. W., & Carrera, S. R. (2002). Approaches to religiosity related to anxiety among college students. *Mental Health, Religion and Culture, 5*, 253–265. doi:10.1080/13674670110112730

Harris, J. I., Schoneman, S. W., & Carrera, S. R. (2005). Preferred prayer styles and anxiety control. *Journal of Religion and Health, 44*, 403–412. doi:10.1007/s10943-005-7179-6

Hertel, B. R., & Donahue, M. J. (1995). Parental influences on God images among children: Testing Durkheim's parallelism. *Journal for the Scientific Study of Religion, 34*, 186–199. doi:10.2307/1386764

Hill, P. C. (2005). Measurement in the psychology of religion and spirituality: Current status and evaluation. In R. F. Paloutzian & C. L. Park (Eds.), *Handbook of the psychology of religion and spirituality* (pp. 43–61). New York, NY: Guilford Press.

Hill, P. C., & Hood, R. W., Jr., (Eds.). (1999). *Measures of religiosity*. Birmingham, AL: Religious Education Press.

Hill, P. C., & Pargament, K. I. (2003). Advances in the conceptualization and measurement of religion and spirituality: Implications for physical and mental health research. *American Psychologist, 58*, 64–74. doi:10.1037/0003-066X.58.1.64

Hood, R. W., Jr., Hill, P. C., & Spilka, B. (2009). *The psychology of religion: An empirical approach* (4th ed.). New York, NY: Guilford Press.

Idler, E. L., Musick, M. A., Ellison, C. G., George, L. K., Krause, N., Ory, M. G., . . . Williams, D. R. (2003). Measuring multiple dimensions of religion and spirituality for health research: Conceptual background and findings from the 1998 General Social Survey. *Research on Aging, 25*, 327–365. doi:10.1177/0164027503025004001

Inzlicht, M., & Tullett, A. M. (2010). Reflecting on God: Religious primes can reduce neurophysiological response to errors. *Psychological Science, 21*, 1184–1190. doi:10.1177/0956797610375451

James, W. (1961). *The varieties of religious experience: A study in human nature.* New York, NY: Collier Books. (Original work published 1902)

Jana-Masri, A., & Priester, P. E. (2007). The development and validation of a Qur'an-based instrument to assess Islamic religiosity: The Religiosity of Islam Scale. *Journal of Muslim Mental Health, 2*, 177–188. doi:10.1080/15564900701624436

Jones, S. L. (1994). A constructive relationship for religion with the science and profession of psychology: Perhaps the boldest model yet. *American Psychologist, 49*, 184–199. doi:10.1037/0003-066X.49.3.184

Kirkpatrick, L. A. (2005). *Attachment, evolution, and the psychology of religion.* New York, NY: Guilford Press.

Kirkpatrick, L. A., & Shaver, P. R. (1992). An attachment-theoretical approach to romantic love and religious belief. *Personality and Social Psychology Bulletin, 18*, 266–275. doi:10.1177/0146167292183002

Koenig, H. G., George, L. K., & Titus, P. (2004). Religion, spirituality, and health in medically ill hospitalized older patients. *Journal of the American Geriatrics Society, 52*, 554–562. doi:10.1111/j.1532-5415.2004.52161.x

Koenig, H. G., & Larson, D. B. (2001). Religion & mental health: Evidence for an association. *International Review of Psychiatry, 13*, 67–78. doi:10.1080/09540260124661

Koenig, H. G., McCullough, M. E., & Larson, D. B. (2001). *Handbook of religion and health.* New York, NY: Oxford University Press.

Kosmin, B. A., & Keysar, A. (2009, March). *American Religious Identification Survey* [ARIS 2008]: Summary Report. Retrieved from http://www.americanreligion-survey-aris.org/reports/ARIS_Report_2008.pdf

Krause, N., Chatters, L., Meltzer, T., & Morgan, D.L. (2000). Negative interaction in the church: Insights from focus groups with older adults. *Review of Religious Research, 41*, 510–533. doi:10.2307/3512318

Krause, N., & Wulff, K. M. (2004). Religious doubt and health: Exploring the potential dark side of religion. *Sociology of Religion, 65*, 35–56. doi:10.2307/3712506

Krause, N., & Wulff, K. M. (2005). Church-based social ties, a sense of belonging in a congregation, and physical health status. *International Journal for the Psychology of Religion, 15*, 73–93. doi:10.1207/s15327582ijpr1501_6

Ladd, K. L., & Spilka, B. (2002). Inward, outward, and upward: Cognitive aspects of prayer. *Journal for the Scientific Study of Religion, 41*, 475–484. doi:10.1111/1468-5906.00131

Ladd, K. L., & Spilka, B. (2006). Inward, outward, upward prayer: Scale reliability and validation. *Journal for the Scientific Study of Religion, 45*, 233–251. doi:10.1111/j.1468-5906.2006.00303.x

Laird, S. P., Snyder, C. R., Rapoff, M. A., & Green, S. (2004). Measuring private prayer: Development, validation, and clinical application of the multidimensional prayer inventory. *International Journal for the Psychology of Religion, 14*, 251–272. doi:10.1207/s15327582ijpr1404_2

Larson, D. B., & Larson, S. S. (2003). Spirituality's potential relevance to physical and emotional health: A brief review of quantitative research. *Journal of Psychology and Theology, 31*, 37–51.

Lazarus, R. S., & Folkman, S. (1984). *Stress, appraisal, and coping.* New York, NY: Springer.

Levenson, M. R., Aldwin, C. M., & D'Mello, M. (2005). Religious development from adolescence to middle adulthood. In R. F. Paloutzian & C. L. Park (Eds.), *Handbook of the psychology of religion and spirituality* (pp. 144–161). New York, NY: Guilford Press.

Lim, C., & Putnam, R. D. (2010). Religion, social networks, and life satisfaction. *American Sociological Review, 75*, 914–933. doi:10.1177/0003122410386686

Masters, K. S., & Spielmans, G. I. (2007). Prayer and health: Review, meta-analysis, and research agenda. *Journal of Behavioral Medicine, 30*, 329–338. doi:10.1007/s10865-007-9106-7

McCaffrey, A. M., Eisenberg, D. M., Legedza, A. T. R., Davis, R. B., & Phillips, R. S. (2004). Prayer for health concerns: Results of a national survey on prevalence and patterns of use. *Archives of Internal Medicine, 164,* 858–862. doi:10.1001/archinte.164.8.858

McCullough, M. E. (1995). Prayer and health: Conceptual issues, research review, and research agenda. *Journal of Psychology and Theology, 23,* 15–29.

McCullough, M. E., Hoyt, W. T., Larson, D. B., Koenig, H. G., & Thoresen, C. E. (2000). Religious involvement and mortality: A meta-analytic review. *Health Psychology, 19,* 211–222. doi:10.1037/0278-6133.19.3.211

McCullough, M. E., & Larson, D. B. (1999). Prayer. In W. R. Miller (Ed.), *Integrating spirituality into treatment* (pp. 85–110). Washington, DC: American Psychological Association.

McDargh, J. (2001). Faith development theory and the postmodern problem of foundations. *International Journal for the Psychology of Religion, 11,* 185–199. doi:10.1207/S15327582IJPR1103_05

Miller, L., & Kelley, B. S. (2005). Relationships of religiosity and spirituality with mental health and psychopathology. In R. F. Paloutzian & C. L. Park (Eds.), *Handbook of the psychology of religion and spirituality* (pp. 460–478). New York, NY: Guilford Press.

Musick, M. A., Traphagan, J. W., Koenig, H. G., & Larson, D. B. (2000). Spirituality in physical health and aging. *Journal of Adult Development, 7,* 73–86. doi:10.1023/A:1009523722920

Nelson, J. M. (2009). *Psychology, religion, and spirituality.* New York, NY: Springer.

Newberg, A. B., & Newberg, S. K. (2006). A neuropsychological perspective on spiritual development. In E. C. Roehlkepartain, P. E. King, L. Wagener, & P. L. Benson (Eds.), *The handbook of spiritual development in childhood and adolescence* (pp. 183–196). Thousand Oaks, CA: Sage.

Nooney, J., & Woodrum, E. (2002). Religious coping and church-based support as predictors of mental health outcomes: Testing a conceptual model. *Journal for the Scientific Study of Religion, 41,* 359–368. doi:10.1111/1468-5906.00122

Oser, F. (1991). The development of religious judgment. In F. K. Ower & W. G. Scarlett (Eds.), *Religious development in childhood and adolescence* (pp. 5–25). San Francisco, CA: Jossey-Bass.

Oser, F., & Gmünder, P. (1991). *Religious judgment: A developmental perspective.* Birmingham, AL: Religious Education Press.

Oser, F. K., & Reich, K. H. (1996). Psychological perspectives on religious development. *World Psychology, 2,* 365–396.

Paloutzian, R. F., & Park, C. L. (Eds.). (2005). *Handbook of the psychology of religion and spirituality.* New York, NY: Guilford Press.

Pargament, K. I. (1997). *The psychology of religion and coping: Theory, research, practice.* New York, NY: Guilford Press.

Pargament, K. I. (1999). The psychology of religion and spirituality? Yes and no. *International Journal for the Psychology of Religion, 9,* 3–16. doi:10.1207/s15327582ijpr0901_2

Pargament, K. I. (2002). The bitter and the sweet: An evaluation of the costs and benefits of religiousness. *Psychological Inquiry, 13,* 168–181. doi:10.1207/S15327965PLI1303_02

Pargament, K. I., Ano, G. G., & Wachholtz, A. B. (2005). The religious dimension of coping: Advances in theory, research, and practice. In R. F. Paloutzian & C. L. Park (Eds.), *Handbook of the psychology of religion and spirituality* (pp. 479–495). New York, NY: Guilford Press.

Pargament, K. I., Koenig, H. G., & Perez, L. M. (2000). The many methods of religious coping: Development and initial validation of the RCOPE. *Journal of Clinical Psychology, 56,* 519–543. doi:10.1002/(SICI)1097-4679(200004)56:4<519::AID-JCLP6>3.0.CO;2-1

Pargament, K. I., Koenig, H. G., Tarakeshwar, N., & Hahn, J. (2001). Religious struggle as predictor of mortality among medically ill elderly patients. *Archives of Internal Medicine, 161,* 1881–1885. doi:10.1001/archinte.161.15.1881

Pargament, K. I., Koenig, H. G., Tarakeshwar, N., & Hahn, J. (2004). Religious coping methods as predictors of psychological, physical, and spiritual outcomes among medically ill elderly patients: A two-year longitudinal study. *Journal of Health Psychology, 9,* 713–730. doi:10.1177/1359105304045366

Pargament, K. I., Smith, B. W., Koenig, H. G., & Perez, L. (1998). Patterns of positive and negative religious coping with major life stressors. *Journal for the Scientific Study of Religion, 37,* 710–724. doi:10.2307/1388152

Pargament, K. I., Zinnbauer, B. J., Scott, A. B., Butter, E. M., Zerowin, J., & Stanik, P. (1998). Red flags and religious coping: Identifying some religious warning signs among people in crisis. *Journal of Clinical Psychology, 54,* 77–89. doi:10.1002/(SICI)1097-4679(199801)54:1<77::AID-JCLP9>3.0.CO;2-R

Park, C. L., & Paloutzian, R. F. (2005). One step toward integration and an expansive future. In R. F. Paloutzian & C. L. Park (Eds.), *Handbook of the psychology of religion and spirituality* (pp. 550–564). New York, NY: Guilford Press.

Piaget, J. (1954). *The construction of reality in the child* (M. Cook, Trans.). New York, NY: Basic Books. (Original work published 1937)

Plante, T. G., & Sherman, A. C. (Eds.). (2001). *Faith and health: Psychological perspectives*. New York, NY: Guilford Press.

Poloma, M. M., & Pendleton, B. F. (1991). The effects of prayer and prayer experiences on measures of general well-being. *Journal of Psychology and Theology, 19*, 71–83.

Potvin, R. H. (1977). Adolescent God images. *Review of Religious Research, 19*, 43–53. doi:10.2307/3509579

Powell, L. H., Shahabi, L., & Thoresen, C. E. (2003). Religion and spirituality: Linkages to physical health. *American Psychologist, 58*, 36–52. doi:10.1037/0003-066X.58.1.36

Richards, P. S., & Bergin, A. E. (2005). *A spiritual strategy for counseling and psychotherapy* (2nd ed.). Washington, DC: American Psychological Association.

Rizzuto, A. M. (1979). *The birth of the living god*. Chicago, IL: University of Chicago Press.

Roof, W. C., & Roof, J. L. (1984). Review of the polls: Images of God among Americans. *Journal for the Scientific Study of Religion, 23*, 201–205. doi:10.2307/1386110

Schaie, K. W., Krause, N., & Booth, A. (Eds.). (2004). *Religious influences on health and well-being in the elderly*. New York, NY: Springer.

Schlosser, L. Z., Ali, S. R., Ackerman, S. R., & Dewey, J. J. H. (2009). Religion, ethnicity, culture, way of life: Jews, Muslims, and multicultural counseling. *Counseling and Values, 54*, 48–64.

Shariff, A. F., & Norenzayan, A. (2007). God is watching you: Priming God concepts increases prosocial behavior in an anonymous economic game. *Psychological Science, 18*, 803–809. doi:10.1111/j.1467-9280.2007.01983.x

Sherman, A. C., & Simonton, S. (2001). Assessment of religiousness and spirituality in health research. In T. G. Plante & A. C. Sherman (Eds.), *Faith and health: Psychological perspectives* (pp. 139–163). New York, NY: Guilford Press.

Silberman, I. (2005). Religious violence, terrorism, and peace. In R. F. Paloutzian & C. L. Park (Eds.), *Handbook of the psychology of religion and spirituality* (pp. 529–549). New York, NY: Guilford Press.

Sloan, R. P., & Bagiella, E. (2002). Claims about religious involvement and health outcomes. *Annals of Behavioral Medicine, 24*, 14–21. doi:10.1207/S15324796ABM2401_03

Smith, T. B., McCullough, M. E., & Poll, J. (2003). Religiousness and depression: Evidence for a main effect and the moderating influence of stressful life events. *Psychological Bulletin, 129*, 614–636. doi:10.1037/0033-2909.129.4.614

Spilka, B. (2005). Religious practice, ritual, and prayer. In R. F. Paloutzian & C. L. Park (Eds.), *Handbook of the psychology of religion and spirituality* (pp. 365–377). New York, NY: Guilford Press.

Spilka, B., & McIntosh, D. H. (Eds.). (1997). *The psychology of religion: Theoretical approaches*. Boulder, CO: Westview Press.

Steger, M. F., & Frazier, P. (2005). Meaning in life: One link in the chain from religiousness to well-being. *Journal of Counseling Psychology, 52*, 574–582. doi:10.1037/0022-0167.52.4.574

Streib, H. (2001). Faith development theory revisited: The religious styles perspective. *International Journal for the Psychology of Religion, 11*, 143–158. doi:10.1207/S15327582IJPR1103_02

Sue, D. W., Bingham, R. P., Porche-Burke, L., & Vasquez, M. (1999). The diversification of psychology: A multicultural revolution. *American Psychologist, 54*, 1061–1069. doi:10.1037/0003-066X.54.12.1061

Thoresen, C. E., & Harris, A. H. S. (2002). Spirituality and health: What's the evidence and what's needed? *Annals of Behavioral Medicine, 24*, 3–13. doi:10.1207/S15324796ABM2401_02

Wade, N. G., Worthington, E. L., Jr., & Haake, S. (2009). Comparison of explicit forgiveness interventions with an alternative treatment: A randomized clinical trial. *Journal of Counseling and Development, 87*, 143–151.

Worthington, E. L., Jr. (2006). *Forgiveness and reconciliation: Theory and application*. New York, NY: Brunner-Routledge.

Worthington, E. L., Jr., Witvliet, C. V. O., Pietrini, P., & Miller, A. J. (2007). Forgiveness, health, and well-being: A review of evidence for emotional versus decisional forgiveness, dispositional forgivingness, and reduced unforgiveness. *Journal of Behavioral Medicine, 30*, 291–302. doi:10.1007/s10865-007-9105-8

Zinnbauer, B. J., & Pargament, K. I. (2005). Religiousness and spirituality. In R. F. Paloutzian & C. L. Park (Eds.), *Handbook of the psychology of religion and spirituality* (pp. 21–42). New York, NY: Guilford Press.

CHAPTER 20

SOCIAL CLASS AND PSYCHOLOGY

Laura Smith and Susan Mao

Social class has important implications for psychological theory, research, and practice—especially within counseling psychology, a specialty that has increasingly embraced social justice commitments as central to its professional identity. In this chapter, we outline these considerations by beginning with an overview of social class stratification theory. We profile social class as a phenomenon in U.S. society, and in so doing, our framework positions social class as part of the social justice spectrum—a conceptualization within which societal ideologies, policies, and procedures are understood to systematically operate to the advantage of some groups as they disadvantage others. We take care to differentiate social class from the proxies for social class that psychologists most frequently employ. Within the context of social class stratification, we define classism as the operant form of oppression and present examples of classism at work in everyday life. We describe the relationships between social class and emotional and physical well-being as well as how social class interfaces with psychological service provision as it is conventionally delivered. Finally, we present social exclusion theory as a social class orientation that crystallizes many of the implications of class stratification for psychology and then conclude the chapter by suggesting future directions for researchers.

SOCIAL CLASS AND CLASSISM: AN OVERVIEW

Given that Americans tend to think of themselves as members of a classless society (Zweig, 2000), it is perhaps not surprising that social class constitutes a little-studied aspect of sociocultural identity within counseling psychology research (Liu et al., 2004). Not only is social class rarely a primary object of study, but psychologists who address it often target its corollaries, including (a) numerical proxies for social class, such as income level or one of various formulas for socioeconomic status (SES); or (b) people's attitudes and beliefs regarding social class. Of course, each of these subjects *is* highly relevant to social class. Income levels and SES calculations are, in large part, correlated with social class stratification, and useful information can be gathered on this basis—in fact, many such studies will be reported in the course of the present discussion. Nevertheless, these related areas of examination are to be differentiated from consideration of social class itself, the study of which has a long, distinguished history in other social sciences. Psychologists need not seek to reproduce those efforts, but we can learn from them in service of improving our own attention to the psychological sequelae of social class stratification (L. Smith, 2010).

The Basics of Social Class Stratification

Societies can be understood to be *stratified*—or composed of an array of different groups or strata—along a number of dimensions. One reason for addressing the existence of such social strata is that it allows for consideration of the distribution of power and the dynamics of inequity in society—an issue of interest to psychologists who are interested in multicultural and social justice approaches

DOI: 10.1037/13754-020
APA Handbook of Counseling Psychology: Vol. 1. Theories, Research, and Methods, Nadya A. Fouad (Editor-in-Chief)

(L. Smith, 2007). Along these lines, multicultural psychologists have made significant progress over the past few decades in exploring the dynamics of racial stratification and racism, thereby contributing theories of racial identity (e.g., Carter, 1995; Helms, 1990), racism-related trauma (Bryant-Davis & Ocampo, 2005), racial microaggressions (Sue et al., 2007), and approaches to psychotherapy that incorporate all of these (Sue & Sue, 2007). The psychological implications of gender stratification and sexism have been explicated similarly by feminist psychologists (e.g., Enns, 2004; Miller & Stiver, 1997). Just as race and gender represent dimensions of stratification along which power and oppression can be examined and addressed, social class represents another such dimension of sociocultural identity—and one that is often missing from social justice analyses.

As mentioned, one of the hindrances to our consideration of social class may be that our national identity is to some extent premised on the idea that class differences do not exist in the United States. In addition, ideological beliefs relating to meritocracy and upward mobility lie close to the heart of the "American dream" (Zweig, 2000). Certainly, hard work and talent *are* undeniable parts of the success stories of many Americans; meritocratic worldviews, however, generalize this statement in such a way that sociocultural systems of privilege and oppression may be excluded from the equation. Wealth, accordingly, may be represented primarily or solely as the result of individual characteristics such as ambition and intelligence, whereas poverty is cast as the result of personal failures. Ryan (1971/2007) conceptualized the coinciding tendency to pathologize the poor as an example of "blaming the victim" (p. 689), whereby the consequences of poverty and injustice are attributed to defects of the individual and the contributions of social forces are ignored. Such explanations deflect our attention away from the complexities of social class dynamics and also support class-privileged people in preserving a sense of having more because they deserve more.

The need to part aside the conceptual clouds that obscure our vision of social class is critical. The full consideration of social class within psychology's social justice spectrum adds a missing piece to our understanding of the dynamics of privilege and oppression. Moreover, this is a time in our nation's history during which the gap between the circumstances of society's haves and have-nots has widened prodigiously—a gulf to which Collins and Yeskel (2005) referred in the title of their book *Economic Apartheid in America*. Whereas households across the class spectrum experienced proportionate patterns of economic growth during the first 3 decades following World War II, something very different began to occur during the 1970s: The accumulation of wealth by people in the most privileged social classes began to escalate dramatically, while the poorest Americans became proportionately poorer. Between 1979 and 2003, the people in the highest income quintile (i.e., the highest 20% of U.S. earners) saw their earnings grow by 51%; the income of the highest 5% skyrocketed by 75%. Meanwhile, in the bottom quintile, incomes actually dropped by 2%, and in the second-to-lowest quintile, incomes grew by only 8%. Collins and Yeskel provided another window into this trend with an example of the widening gap between the highest paid worker and the average worker in U.S. firms. In 1975, the ratio was 41 to 1; by 2003, it was 301 to 1. The steady upward trickle of the nation's wealth has continued even throughout the global economic recession that began in 2008. In fact, 2009 saw the number of millionaires grow by 17% to 10 million, while their collective wealth increased by 19% to $39 trillion (Giannone, 2010).

When we do initiate a focus on social class dynamics, we are faced with another challenge: how to understand what the different classes are and what to call them. Class stratification models represent systematic attempts to answer these questions. Sociologist Gilbert (2008) proposed that class stratification models generally take shape from theorists' answers to basic questions that arise in three broad areas:

1. Economic basis: How do class distinctions arise from economic distinctions? And how, in particular, does economic change transform the class system?
2. Social basis: How are economic class distinctions reflected in social distinctions and social behavior?

3. Political implications: How does the class system affect the political system? How do economically dominant classes interact politically with the other classes in a society? (p. 10)

Theorists' answers, according to Gilbert (2008), call into play four economic variables (*occupation, wealth, income,* and *poverty*), four social variables (*prestige, association, socialization,* and *social mobility*), and two political variables (*power* and *class consciousness*). Grusky and Ku (2008) suggested that social class groups that emerge from the interplay of these variables will be distinguished by particular, characteristic "reward packages" (p. 5) of socially valued goods, which may include assets of the following types:

1. Economic (money, property)
2. Power (whether in the political sphere or in the workplace)
3. Cultural (knowledge, "good" manners)
4. Social (social associations, informal networks)
5. Honorific (merit-based or occupational honors and titles)
6. Civil (such as access to due process)
7. Human (education, training, experience)
8. Physical (such as enhanced physical and emotional well-being)

This concept of characteristic packages of social class assets is important to understanding why proxies for social class—such as income—do not accurately capture the nature of the social class hierarchy. Income levels can be described by a smooth numerical distribution, and using income as an indicator of social class implies that people whose incomes place them higher in the distribution also rank higher on the social class spectrum, and therefore they enjoy relatively more class-related advantages than people at lower points. This happens to coincide with reality for some examples but not for others. For example, the average construction site equipment operator earned $46,580 in 2009 (U.S. Department of Labor, 2010), which is slightly more than the average university mathematics instructor at $42,782 (Chronicle of Higher Education, 2010). An advantage in purchasing power undoubtedly accrues to the construction worker, yet many additional socially valued assets are part of the mathematics instructor's social class package of goods, which is likely to include cultural assets like prestige, respected educational credentials, social mobility, "refined" tastes and manners, and a less physically risky workplace environment. These sociocultural assets protect and enhance the life chances of people in more privileged social classes in many ways, such as widening the scope of their opportunities, enhancing the favorable attitudes that greet them in society at large, and lengthening their lives.

A TYPOLOGY FOR SOCIAL CLASS

If we accept, then, the notion of stratified social class groups with different packages of assets, the question remains: What is their structure and what do we call them? Many different, complex social class models have been created as sociological theorists grappled with these questions (for a comprehensive introduction, see Grusky, 2008), and there is no one right model. Rather, the choice of which model is most useful will vary according to different subjects of inquiry. Psychologists who are interested in understanding social class from a social justice perspective, for example, will need a model that facilitates the analysis of sociocultural power and oppression. This is the approach that informs the suggestion of the basic social class typology presented here. This typology combines the work of Betsy Leondar-Wright (2005), a class activist, and Michael Zweig (2000), a professor of economics, whose formulations are quite similar to each other. Each preserves the essential class distinctions proposed by many theorists regarding (a) the sources of socioeconomic power in the ownership of wealth and property and (b) the operations of socioeconomic power in regard to the process of economic production:

1. *Poverty:* Predominantly describes working-class people who, because of unemployment, low-wage jobs, health problems, or other crises, are without enough income to support their families' basic needs.
2. *Working class:* People who have little power or authority in the workplace, little control over the

availability or content of jobs, and little say in the decisions that affect their access to health care, education, and housing. They tend to have lower levels of income, net worth, and formal education than more powerful classes.

3. *Middle class*: Professionals, managers, small business owners, often college educated and salaried. Middle-class people have more autonomy and control in the workplace than working-class people, and more economic security; however, they rely on earnings from work to support themselves.

4. *Owning class*: People who own enough wealth and property that they do not need to work to support themselves (although they may choose to); people who own and control the resources by which other people earn a living. The owning class includes people who, as a result of their economic power, also have significant social, cultural, and political power relative to other classes.

This hierarchy places people living in poverty at the bottom of the social class hierarchy, with the other three positions having relatively more power and privilege than the ones below it. Poverty carries with it, therefore, not only the obvious deprivations associated with a lack of purchasing power but also a relative lack of other socially sanctioned assets, along with the discriminatory attitudes that accompany that position. This typology, like all social class models, is not without gray areas and ambiguities—which, incidentally, is also true of every other aspect of socioculturally constructed identity that is studied by psychologists. For example, the racial categories recognized by social scientists (as well as the U.S. Census Bureau) have varied widely over the years, and the simplistic nature of traditional binary gender constructions is being challenged as our understanding of sexuality and transgenderism evolves. Our conceptualizations and language, therefore, must be acknowledged as works in progress—vehicles that provide a useful (if qualified) starting point for our attempts to understand systems of oppression. That is the spirit behind the proposal of the framework described in this chapter. Although this is our suggested framework for

conceptualizing class membership, we also will use other terminology at various points in keeping with the language used by the authors we cite.

CLASSISM

As mentioned, social justice approaches to psychological theory and practice are concerned with power and oppression as they exist along various identity-related dimensions. Oppression associated with race is, of course, referred to as *racism*, and the analogous form of oppression associated with social class is called *classism*. Classism has been explicated by social psychologists Lott and Bullock (2007) as composing two general forms. *Institutional classism* refers to the practices, attitudes, assumptions, behaviors, and policies through which social institutions function to perpetuate the deprivation and low status of poor people. *Interpersonal classism* is characterized by prejudice, stereotyping, and discrimination.

Like all forms of oppression, some forms of classism are easy to spot, whereas others are nuanced and hidden within everyday interactions. They include the negative attitudes toward the poor that have been revealed by social psychologists like Cozzarelli, Wilkinson, and Tagler (2001), in whose study undergraduate participants assigned traits such as *lazy, stupid, dirty*, and *immoral* more often to poor people than to middle-class people. Lott and Saxon (2002) presented their mostly undergraduate participants with information about a hypothetical target woman and found that regardless of their ethnicities, working-class mothers were judged to be less suitable as potential officers in a parent-teacher organization and were more often described as *crude* and *irresponsible* than were middle-class women. An online study of adult participants from across the United States suggested that crimes and infractions that could ostensibly be committed by anyone—such as painting graffiti or not bathing enough—were more likely to be attributed to poor people than to people of other social class groups (L. Smith, Allen, & Bowen, 2010). These negative attitudes reveal themselves within ordinary interpersonal interactions through *classist microaggressions* (L. Smith & Redington, in press), the commonplace indignities and slights that are analogous to the racial microaggressions explicated by Sue et al. (2007). Classist microaggressions include the negatively valenced use of descriptors like *low rent* and *low class* as well as the frequent portrayal of poor people in mainstream media as lazy, dysfunctional, and drug-abusing (Bullock, Wyche, & Williams, 2001).

In addition to its interpersonal ramifications, classism is revealed through a wide variety of inequities that call to mind the asset packages described by Grusky and Ku (2008). These inequities are present within our public educational system, through which we provide children in poor communities with fewer books, computers, and teachers than we do in more affluent communities (Kozol, 2005). As a result of classist and racist environmental injustice, the communities of poor people and people of color tend to become waste-dumping grounds for the rest of society (Bullard, 2000). Our nation's acceptance of the continuing low level of the minimum wage is also meaningful in the context of classism. The current federal minimum wage of $7.25 is not a *living* wage, which has been defined as the amount necessary to bring a family of four at least to the poverty line (Economic Policy Institute, 2007)— or as the Penn State Living Wage Project explains it, the wage rate required to meet minimum standards of living for low-wage earners and their families according to basic food, child care, medical, housing, and transportation requirements. Their Living Wage Calculator, which can be found online at http://www.livingwage.geog.psu.edu, places a living wage for a family of one adult and one child in Raleigh, North Carolina, at $16.59 an hour. (Even one adult *alone* requires $9.00 an hour to support basic living requirements.) In Topeka, Kansas, the living wage is $15.21 an hour. In Los Angeles, California, it is $19.96 an hour. Given that we depend on the labor of low-wage workers to support our families' everyday lives, the lack of national concern about the fact that they cannot earn enough to lift their own families out of poverty is meaningful.

With regard to emotional and physical well-being, poor people face "elevated rates of threatening and uncontrollable life events, noxious life conditions, marital dissolution, infant mortality, many diseases, violent crime, homicide, accidents, and deaths from all causes" (Belle et al., 2000, p. 1160), and their access to medical care, the quality of care they receive, and their relationships with their doctors is reduced relative to other citizens (Scott, 2005). In the section that follows, we take up these aspects of social class stratification that interface directly with psychological practice.

SOCIAL CLASS STRATIFICATION AND WELL-BEING

In a sense, the psychological literature on emotional and physical well-being is primarily the study of the well-being of particular social class groups, those being middle-class and owning-class people. This point parallels Guthrie's (1976) analysis of the field's traditional, unexamined Eurocentric focus, and Miller's (1976) deconstruction of the patriarchal underpinnings of conventional psychotherapeutic theory: Much of our field's received knowledge about psychological development, well-being, and disorder is rooted in perspectives that derive from the experiences of class-privileged people and exclude the realities of life in an oppressed social class location.

In fact, that oppressed location seems to have a characteristic pathogenic effect on the mental and physical health of the people who occupy it (L. Smith, Chambers, & Bratini, 2009). Research on the relationship between social class and well-being has consistently found that people at the bottom of the social class hierarchy—those living in poverty— experience poorer psychological and physical health outcomes across literally countless dimensions (Adler & Snibbe, 2003; Seeman et al., 2004). As Seeman et al. (2004) summarized, "an individual's socioeconomic status represents one of the most enduring of all risk factors" (p. 1985). Poverty has been linked with high rates of innumerable physical illnesses such as cardiovascular disease, arthritis, diabetes, chronic respiratory diseases, and cervical cancer (Adler & Snibbe, 2003; Seeman et al., 2004) as well as a greater overall vulnerability to morbidity and mortality (Adler et al., 1994; Belle, 1990; Gallo, Bogart, Vranceanu, & Matthews, 2005). Researchers have emphasized that the association of social class and health outcomes does not exclusively occur under conditions of poverty; rather, gradations of this effect appear to correspond to the entire social class hierarchy so that those at every level experience better health than those below them (Adler et al., 1994; Correspondents of the New York Times, 2005).

With regard to emotional distress, the epidemiological correlation between social class and the prevalence of psychological symptoms has been so thoroughly documented that researchers of past decades considered this relationship to be a "given" (Allen & Britt, 1983, p. 149). The linkages between SES and depressive symptoms have been especially well studied (e.g., Blazer, Kessler, McGonagle, & Schwartz, 1994; Bruce, Takeuchi, & Leaf, 1991; Siefert, Bowman, Heflin, Danziger, & Williams, 2000). Lorant et al. (2003) conducted a meta-analysis of socioeconomic inequality and depression, and found SES to be a moderate to strong correlate for depression across 51 prevalence studies, five incidence studies, and four persistence studies published in the fields of psychiatry, psychology, sociology, medicine, and economics. Results of the analysis indicated that as SES decreased, the risk for episode onset and the risk for persistence of depression increased steadily. The incidence of other psychological disorders has also been found to be greater among individuals of lower SES (Bradley & Corwyn, 2002; Bruce, Takeuchi, & Leaf, 1991). Bruce et al. (1991) conducted a longitudinal examination of the affect of poverty on psychiatric status. The analyses conducted in this study concerned eight disorders from the third edition of *Diagnostic and Statistical Manual of Mental Disorders* (American Psychiatric Association, 1980): alcohol abuse or dependence, bipolar disorder or mania, drug abuse or dependence, major depressive disorder, obsessive–compulsive disorder, panic disorder, phobia, and schizophrenic disorders. A comparison of the rates of each outcome variable stratified by poverty status indicated that poor participants were at greater risk for every assessed disorder with the exception of panic disorder (Bruce et al., 1991).

The impact of social class on the psychological development of children and adolescents has received special focus within research on class-related well-being (e.g., Evans, 2004; Leventhal & Brooks-Gunn, 2000). Leventhal and Brooks-Gunn (2000) conducted a comprehensive review of research on neighborhood characteristics and child outcomes and found that children living in higher SES neighborhoods exhibited higher levels adjustment in terms of school readiness, school achievement, intelligence quotient scores, and education attainment. Low SES elementary and high school students were found to have more behavioral problems than students from more affluent families on the basis of the number and severity of disciplinary referrals (Boroughs, Massey, & Armstrong, 2006), and lower social class children tend to experience lowered teacher expectations (McLoyd, 1998). Children living in poverty have demonstrated more symptoms of psychiatric disturbance and maladaptive social functioning (Bradley & Corwyn, 2002), and the physical health disparities associated with poverty have been found to begin even before birth. Low-SES children are more likely to experience in utero growth retardation and inadequate neurobehavioral development, premature birth, birth defects, AIDS, respiratory illnesses, and injuries and death. Additionally, when low-SES children experience such health problems, they often sustain more severe consequences than do their more affluent counterparts (Bradley & Corwyn, 2002). The stunning "natural experiment" presented by Costello, Compton, Keeler, and Angold (2003, p. 2023) is a notable example within this category of research. The authors compared children's psychiatric assessments conducted before and after a casino was built on an American Indian federal reservation, after which the income level of the entire community was raised. The findings supported a social causation (as opposed to a social selection) theory of the correlation between SES and emotional well-being in children.

To create an integrative approach to understanding socioeconomic health disparities and associated emotional factors Gallo and Matthews (2003) developed the *reserve capacity model*. According to this model, lower SES environments expose inhabitants of such environments to greater amounts of stress that elicit more negative emotions and less positive emotions. Lower SES environments, therefore, are associated with greater use and depletion of psychosocial resources and fewer opportunities to develop resource reserves (Gallo et al., 2005). Therefore, according to this framework, living in poverty requires a greater amount of resources to survive in a context in which fewer resources are available. This discrepancy leads to greater emotional distress, which ultimately contributes to negative health outcomes (Gallo et al., 2005).

LIMITATIONS OF THE LITERATURE ON POVERTY: THE OTHER SIDE OF THE COIN

Research on the physical and emotional correlates of a life in poverty, therefore, has established convincingly the damage that results to poor adults, children, and families. The conclusiveness of these results must be considered as a strength of this literature. Clinicians, social service professionals, policy makers, and others will find ample data to support advocacy on behalf of the poor. Nevertheless, on the other side of this same coin is a limitation of this literature: Psychologists and others who address the poor predominantly from this perspective end up positioning them primarily as a population with a characteristic illness profile. Having identified the diagnoses and deficiencies that accompany a life in poverty, the logical conclusion of such examinations often centers on the proposal of professional treatments and services of which the poor may be in need.

Such professional propositions are not a problem per se, and when poor people can benefit from treatment of their depression, or when poor children can benefit from remediative educational services, then proposing and supplying these treatments is important and useful. The problem is that, in the process, this literature conveys a restricted, "medical model" conception of poverty that disregards what epidemiologist Marmot called "the causes of the causes" (Marmot & Wilkinson, 2006, p. 2): that is, the social forces that contribute to the life circumstances that create the symptoms. These forces are manifestations of the broad social class system discussed previously, and which privileges researchers and clinicians as it simultaneously disadvantages the objects of their investigations into the effects of

poverty. Remediating these effects can undeniably be helpful; what might be even more helpful in the long term (and more consistent with a social justice framework) is if psychologists were to direct their talents toward elucidating and remediating social class inequity in the first place.

SOCIAL CLASS STRATIFICATION AS PATHOGEN

How *can* psychologists orient their work more directly toward economic injustice itself? Former American Psychological Association (APA) president George Albee offered such a perspective on the impact of poverty upon the physical and emotional health of poor families. "It is not necessary to search the scientific literature for evidence that water runs downhill," he observed, going on to explain that we do not "require elaborate epidemiological studies to validate the observation that economically exploited groups are regarded as inferior, even subhuman, by the exploiters. And it is clear that these groups have higher rates of both physical illness and mental/emotional disorders" (Albee, 1996, p. 1132). Recognizing that people are both social and biological beings, Krieger's (2005) work elaborated on this line of thought in a specific, concrete fashion: She suggested that social power differentials are displayed in the conditions of human beings' physical bodies, a phenomenon that she referred to as *embodiment*. Rather than focusing on decontextualized elements of disease and well-being, Krieger investigated bodily clues related to the impact of dynamic social, material, and ecological contexts:

> Consider only: food insecurity and fast food profiteering; inadequate sanitation and lack of potable water; economic and social deprivation and discrimination; physical and sexual abuse; ergonomic strain and toxic exposure; and inadequate health care—all leave their marks on the body. As do their converse: the security of a living wage, pensions for old age, and societal support for childcare; universal sanitation and sustainable development; safe workplaces and healthy cities; universal

health care and immunisations; and the protection and promotion of human rights—economic, social, political, civil, and cultural. (p. 350)

In this spirit, Belle and Doucet (2003) considered the unequivocal findings regarding the relationship between poverty and women's mental health. Describing the chronic deprivation, inadequate housing, dangerous communities, overwhelming responsibilities, social stigma, and scarce resources that often characterize life in poverty, Belle and Doucet articulated the no-win situation often faced by poor women doing their best to cope:

> Poor women are often so powerless in their dealings with employers, landlords, and government bureaucracies that their coping strategies are severely constrained and unsuccessful. . . . One of Wasyl-ishyn and Johnson's (1998) respondents actually defined poverty as "having no options" (p. 978). Repeated coping failures may then lead to the belief that stress factors cannot be overcome, leading women to palliative coping strategies such as self-medication with drugs or alcohol, overeating, sleeping during the day, and repressing thoughts of the problem. (p. 104)

Belle and Doucet (2003) concluded that poverty itself must be understood to be broadly "depressogenic" (p. 109). An analogy from public health helps make their point: With all the spectacular advances that have been made in the medical, surgical, and pharmacological treatment of diseases over the past century, by far the greatest reductions in U.S. mortality came about through the introduction of modern municipal water filtration and chlorination systems (Cutler & Miller, 2005)—an intervention, in other words, that targeted the source of illness and distress rather than those who were already suffering from its effects. In the same way, counseling psychologists can work to orient their theory, research, and practice toward the analysis of classism and the eradication of poverty—in addition to proposing and offering treatments for the emotional

damage that it causes. In the following section, we take up the question of psychological practice in the context of social class oppression.

SOCIAL CLASS STRATIFICATION AND PSYCHOLOGICAL SERVICE PROVISION

Javier and Herron (2002) described the culture of the psychologist's office as the culture of Whiteness and class privilege. This assertion lends context to the fact that the availability and adequacy of psychological services for people living in poverty does not correspond to their relatively high level of vulnerability to psychological distress—psychology's attention to the provision of competent services for the poor has been inconsistent at best (L. Smith, 2005, 2010). The community mental health center movement of the 1970s represented an exception to this statement, in that federal support and professional sentiments came together in the promise of new clinics aimed specifically to serve the needs of poor communities. Most of these clinics were never built, however, and the initiative faded away in the 1980s, when psychology returned largely to its position of benign neglect regarding psychological attention to clients living in poverty (Albee & Gulotta, 1997). This is not to suggest that psychologists were unsympathetic to the plight of the poor; rather, psychologists simply pursued theory and practice that did not incorporate consideration of poverty or social class stratification, resulting in approaches that were not always relevant or useful in the context of poverty.

Counseling psychologists can contribute to the reversal of these trends by understanding potential obstacles to optimal services for the poor, which begin at the level of our own biases and attitudes. Even given their specialized training with regard to the potential impact of therapist countertransference, multicultural psychological research has made it clear that psychologists are not immune to the influence of societal biases within their work with clients from marginalized groups. For example, with regard to research on more commonly studied aspects of identity, researchers have shed light on the potential for attitudes related to clients' race (Barnes, 2004; Pavkov, Lewis, & Lyons, 1989), gender (Heesacker et al., 1999), and sexual orientation (Mohr, Israel, & Sedlacek, 2001) to distort the therapeutic alliance along with therapists' early diagnostic impressions. The limited results that exist with regard to the impact of clients' social class point to a similar effect. Presenting their participants with audiotaped interviews with hypothetical clients, both Lee and Temerlin (1970) and di Nardo (1975) found that when clients were described as having lower SES, they were more likely to be evaluated as being mentally ill or dysfunctional than clients described as having higher SES even though the symptom profiles were the same. Stein, Green, and Stone (1972) and L. Smith, Mao, Perkins, and Ampuero (in press) both used written case vignettes to reveal that lower SES clients were furthermore considered by practitioner trainees to be less appealing to work with than higher SES clients. Given that such predispositions may be present in the minds of therapists from the time of their first encounters with clients, they can only serve to undermine the development of a solid therapeutic alliance with these clients. Moreover, the biased diagnoses that may result from therapists' preconceptions have the potential to dramatically affect subsequent referrals or service delivery.

Beyond the impact of unexamined classist attitudes on elements of the therapeutic process, conventional psychological practice is rooted in normative assumptions that largely exclude the experiences of class-oppressed people. Not only has psychotherapeutic theory been described as a depiction of the developmental experiences of middle-class Western European American culture (Javier & Herron, 2002), but also the landscape of poverty, with its survival-related vicissitudes and daily indignities, is often alien and disorienting for therapists (L. Smith, 2010). These encounters can force therapists to bump up against common mistaken assumptions about poverty as well as the discomfort of confronting the disparities between their lives and their clients' circumstances (L. Smith, 2005, 2010). Psychologists' lack of preparation can create anxiety for their clients as well: Chalifoux (1996), who interviewed six working-class women about their therapeutic experiences, challenged the lack of attention to issues of class and poverty within the

psychotherapeutic process. Her participants reported how uncomfortable they became upon observing their *therapists'* anxiety whenever the subject of money was raised, prompting Chalifoux to suggest that "not acknowledging class perpetuates shame and secrecy, keeping the client disempowered and making the therapeutic encounter oppressive" (p. 26). Such in-depth qualitative inquiries hold promise for enriching our understanding of the exclusionary messages that are encoded within conventional psychological practices, yet the small number of participants in such studies must be borne in mind as a limitation.

Therapists' attempts to press their clients into a conventional modality that does not fit their stories or their lives can result in therapeutic failures that are often attributed to clients' "resistance" or general unsuitability for therapy (Dumont, 1992; J. M. Smith, 2000). Schnitzer (1996) wrote of her experiences as part of a team of practitioners and trainees working in a clinic in a poor urban community and analyzed the common, unexamined narratives that emerged within her colleagues' comments about their clients from the community, such as "They're so disorganized," and "They don't come in" (pp. 574–575). Schnitzer noted that these offhand comments about poor clients' compliance failures were typically made with no understanding of the effort that poor families must exert simply to survive: "There is no overestimating the depletion of time, energy, and spirit involved in managing health, cleanliness, safety, and the search for a way out if you are poor" (p. 574). The constraints of poverty that interfaced with clients' therapeutic experiences were often misinterpreted (or missed entirely) by their therapists:

> A social worker reports a story about a mother who waited four hours with her children for a clinic appointment, and then finally acceded to the demands of her youngest for a snack. When the doctor eventually appeared, the mother hadn't yet returned and her absence was taken as a sign of irresponsibility. Filing for neglect was initiated. (Schnitzer, 1996, p. 574)

A White doctor had asked [a Black female staff member] to comment as a Black woman on how a poor Black man and his family had responded to the diagnosis of HIV. They hadn't seemed upset enough, the doctor thought, not to the degree he'd expected, not in the manner he was used to. When the doctor said, "They don't seem to care," she had tried to explain, "You don't understand. It's just one more thing." (Schnitzer, 1996, p. 575)

How can counseling psychologists work to enhance the class-related competence of their practice? Guidelines for multicultural counseling competence, which were developed to guide practitioner practice with regard to diverse populations (Sue, Arredondo, & McDavis, 1992), provide a strong foundation for this endeavor, and, as a group, vocational psychologists are leading the field in its implementation with regard to social class (e.g., Fouad & Brown, 2000; Thompson & Subich, 2006). Blustein et al. (2002), for example, developed a thoroughgoing integration of social class considerations within vocational counseling, highlighting the voices of working-class people as those of "the forgotten half" (p. 311). Blustein, McWhirter, and Perry (2005) noted that if social inequity goes unchallenged by vocational psychologists, the preventative impact of their work will be substantially undermined:

Vocational psychology can be described as maintaining a concerted investment in the prevention of problems, including unrealized aspirations, job dissatisfaction, glass ceilings, and unemployment. If we accept the social structures that guarantee, sustain, and promote these problems as unchangeable or the responsibility of someone else (especially in the working lives of poor and working-class people), then the term prevention has little meaning. (p. 170)

With regard to counseling and psychotherapy, Liu et al. (2004) have been in the forefront of applied psychologists bringing attention to social class. Liu et al. were instrumental in alerting the field to its neglect of social class as a variable and proposed a social class worldview approach as an "intrapsychic framework (i.e., lens)" (p. 10) by which psychologists can conceptualize the subjective aspects of people's understanding of social class. Within this framework, "social class [is] considered to be a descriptor of a psychological process such as a worldview" (Liu et al., 2004, p. 14), and therefore, multiple economic cultural experiences are understood to be possible. Liu (2002) provided case vignettes to show how this model could be applied within counseling work with male clients who may be experiencing class-related pressures. Liu, Pickett, and Ivey (2007) worked from McIntosh's (1988) explication of White privilege to develop a list of self-statements corresponding to White middle-class privilege. These statements included "I can be assured that I have adequate housing for myself and my family" (Liu et al., 2007, p. 205), and the authors emphasized that clients' expectations in association with these privileges can be important influences on behavior.

The creation of innovative practices such as these will be facilitated as psychologists sharpen their attention to social class awareness in the training of new practitioners (L. Smith, Foley, & Chaney, 2008). The APA Task Force on Resources for the Inclusion of Social Class in Psychology Curricula (APA, 2008), an outstanding resource for supervisors and educators, contains listings and descriptions of class-related course syllabi, classroom exercises, scholarly books and articles, popular media, and websites. Working from such materials, clinical supervisors can take action within supervisory sessions to highlight issues of classism by implementing such strategies as helping trainees to consider the impact of their own social class privilege, discussing the impact of structural influences on case material and its interpretation, and supporting flexible approaches to treatment (L. Smith, 2009).

With regard to flexible, appropriate practice in poor communities (and in the context of oppression more generally), psychologists should consider modifications of the conventional professional roles and practices that have emerged from (and that support) the sociocultural status quo (Prilleltensky, 1989).

Conventional expert-driven helping paradigms can, in effect, reproduce socially sanctioned power differentials between class-privileged therapists and their poor clients. Moreover, when this transaction occurs with no acknowledgment of oppression, it corresponds to what Freire (1970) called *false generosity*. Psychologists' alternatives to this paradigm can be described as a continuum of interventions (L. Smith, 2010) that begin with socially just *transformed psychotherapy* modalities, such as relational cultural therapy (RCT; Miller & Stiver, 1997). RCT refers to a feminist psychotherapeutic orientation that is enacted within a traditional dyad configuration but that is based in a nontraditional set of assumptions. These include the conceptualization of mutuality and affiliation as healthy modes of living (rather than privileging Western values such as autonomy) and the explicit affirmation that, in the best psychotherapy, the therapist also changes and grows as a result of the encounter (Jordan, 2000). Further down the continuum and less similar to conventional modalities are *cocreated therapeutic interventions*, through which practitioners partner with community members to create interventions that represent the optimal combination of professional skills and local needs and wisdom. For example, L. Smith, et al. (2009) described a group modality based on poetry and spoken-word performance that was cocreated with adolescent community members and that was considered to be therapeutic although *not* therapy. Finally, through *community praxis* involvements, psychologists can work collaboratively with communities to create programming for well-being that actually incorporates collective prosocial action. Examples of such collaborations include participatory action research projects (L. Smith & Romero, 2010) and the ROAD (Reaching Out About Depression) project, through which counselors and law students partnered with women in a poor urban community to create systems of support against the depressogenic effects of poverty in their lives (Goodman et al., 2007).

SOCIAL EXCLUSION THEORY

A theoretical angle on social class stratification that pulls together much of the foregoing discussion is *social exclusion theory*, which considers people's degree of inclusion with regard to ordinary societal resources and opportunities. Social exclusion has been defined as a process by which people are "systematically blocked from access to the rights, resources, and opportunities that are normally available to members of the society in which they reside" (Todman et al., 2009, p. 330). People with relatively more class privilege, therefore, have a greater degree of access to such helpful resources as clean neighborhoods, safe housing, high-quality education resources, health care, and legal representation. The privileges of citizenship are relatively more open and available to the privileged, including everything from the most mundane (such as occupying public spaces) all the way to the more specialized (such as the opportunity to officially represent one's municipality at the local, state, or federal levels). People nearer the bottom of the social class spectrum are, by contrast, largely excluded from many of these opportunities. For example, public schools provided for children in poor communities lack the education resources provided in more affluent neighborhoods (Kozol, 2005), and the U.S. legal system does not actually provide representation for everyone who cannot afford it (Rhode, 2004), despite assurances to the contrary on television police dramas. Even the occupation of public spaces cannot be taken for granted: Local ordinances are passed with regularity that not only discourage the presence of the poor in public spaces but also criminalize it, such as Santa Cruz's "sleeping ban" (Steinvick, 2010), through which homeless people are subject to arrest if they sleep in public spaces or even in their own cars, and Seattle's "sitting ban" (Knight, 2010), which accomplishes the same thing among people who are awake.

The relative exclusion of poor people from full participation in mainstream social experiences may, therefore, be understood as a consequence of poverty or alternatively as a defining feature of poverty in and of itself, a perspective that is developed within social exclusion theory. According to Silver (1994), discourse relating to social exclusion originated in France during the 1960s and has since been a growing focus of social and political attention among various countries throughout Europe and the

United Kingdom. Silver and Miller (2002, as cited in Todman et al., 2009) suggested that social exclusion is characterized by five key attributes:

1. It is *relational*, primarily concerned with the nature of relations among social groups in society.
2. It is *dynamic*, characterized by cumulative processes in which past conditions and experiences shape current experiences and conditions, which, in turn, shape future conditions and experiences.
3. It is *relative*, defined and measured in terms of societal norms that prevail at a particular place and time.
4. It is *multidimensional*, characterized by economic, political, civic, cultural, geographic, and judicial dimensions along which people may be excluded.
5. It is *active* in the sense that the consequences of the (non-)decisions and (in-)actions of agents (e.g., people, institutions, and processes) other than the excluded generally lay beyond the control of the excluded. (pp. 330–331)

A social exclusion perspective on poverty, then, is a relational perspective. In other words, instead of casting poverty as a situation facing *them*, it is a perspective that encompasses all of *us* in portraying poverty as more than the absence of purchasing power. Rather, poverty is an excluded (and thereby, oppressed) social location that exists as a function of the decisions, actions, and practices that characterize a dynamic, interrelated social class system—decisions, actions, and practices that systematically benefit people in some social class groups as they exclude people in others.

According to social exclusion theory, the social boundaries between the "ins" and "outs" are reinforced through the repeated action of social distancing over time (Silver, 1994). This notion dovetails with Lott's (2002) social psychological theorizing, within which the concept of distancing is used similarly to describe the mechanism underlying classism and the creation of classist barriers in the United States. Lott referred to cognitive and behavioral distancing as "the dominant response to poor people on the part of those who are not poor" (p. 100) and

explained that "distancing, separation, exclusion, and devaluing operationally define discrimination" (p. 100). Lott described interpersonal distancing in particular as an "issue focused on poor people's daily experiences of exclusion, of being demeaned and discounted" (p. 107), and she explained how human service professionals may unintentionally engage in psychological and physical distancing by holding assumptions about the inferiority and deviance of poor people.

The harmful effects of social exclusion on individual well-being are more than theoretical—they have been demonstrated in the laboratory in a series of social psychological studies (e.g., Baumeister, DeWall, Twenge, & Ciarocco, 2005; Twenge, Baumeister, DeWall, Ciarocco, & Bartels, 2007). For example, Baumeister et al. (2005) created experimental paradigms in which experiences of exclusion or rejection were found to be associated with reductions in self-regulation, such as participants' decreased ability to drink a healthy (but bad-tasting) beverage, being more prone to eat unhealthy foods, being more prone to give up on a puzzle task, and being less able to avoid distractions (Baumeister et al., 2005). These exclusion experiences took the form, for example, of bogus feedback to participants on the basis of a personality inventory score that they would likely be all alone later in life (as opposed to receiving predictions that they would experience other unfavorable outcomes such as physical injury). Social exclusion was also found to decrease participants' prosocial behavior; when participants were told that they would end up alone or that other participants had rejected them, they tended to donate less money to a student fund, were less willing to volunteer for additional lab experiments, were less helpful after a mishap, and were less cooperative in a game with another student (Twenge et al., 2007). Social exclusion was even found to affect cognitive processes and intelligent thought (Baumeister, Twenge, & Nuss, 2002).

A two-phase study utilizing both qualitative and quantitative methods offered similar support for the differential experiences of isolation and belonging on the basis of social class (Stewart et al., 2009). Working with participants from two large Canadian cities, the authors interviewed 59 participants individually and another 34 in group formats. They established income threshold divisions among participants according to Canada's calculation of low-income cutoff criteria and found that higher income participants reported a generally higher sense of community belonging, greater perceptions of acceptance, and a greater sense of connection to institutions, places, and groups with similar interests. These participants reported that their everyday lives included a variety of invitations for inclusion: Schools, for example,

> enabled parents to connect with other parents and facilitated participation in varied social activities, [such as] "socializing with the parents . . . going for walks with another family . . . going skating . . . having play dates for [their] kids where [they] end up doing stuff together."
> (Stewart et al., 2009, p. 182)

The same communities were experienced very differently by lower income participants, who reported a higher likelihood of feeling isolated by structural (e.g., lack of resources, education opportunities, transportation) and interpersonal factors (e.g., stereotyping and discrimination). Lott's (2002) equation of classism with cognitive distancing is recalled by the reports of lower income participants that the predominant interpersonal factor influencing their isolation was social distancing. One described this phenomenon as "an ignoring, exclusion kind of thing" (Stewart et al., 2009, p. 185), while another commented, "They regard you as . . . a loser" (p. 185). Stewart et al. (2009) pointed out that the limitations of their study included the fact that they did not include non-English-speaking participants, which prevented them from assessing such factors as the intersections of poverty and ethnicity.

EVOLVING AREAS FOR PRACTICE, RESEARCH, AND THEORY

Perhaps the most obvious but also the most important comment that we can offer regarding the psychological literature on social class and poverty is that we need more of it. Recalling our earlier critique of the existing research on poverty, this is not a call for more research to document the unfavorable psychological sequelae of poverty—like Allen and Britt (1983), we feel that that ground has been well covered. Rather, psychologists could help illuminate social class stratification, economic injustice, and classism by addressing the following five suggestions for action:

1. Incorporate considerations of class stratification and social exclusion into applied psychological theory, research, and practice. Important strides have been made by the counseling psychologists mentioned in this chapter, and future efforts in this direction should find a natural context within the specialty's emphasis on social justice and multicultural approaches.

2. Develop class stratification models that lend themselves to the work of counseling psychologists. In this chapter, we provided a cursory overview of social class theorizing and offered a basic typology as an example. Yet, many of us who have taken even one sociology course know that elaborate, complex social class models have been proposed by a variety of theorists throughout the century, and there is no reason that counseling psychologists cannot learn from, adapt, or build on that work. In so doing, we can address one of the issues that can make psychological work in this area cumbersome: Psychologists are largely without shared, clear, user-friendly language for speaking about social class. We look forward to learning from our colleagues' ideas in addressing these gaps.

3. Develop an approach to the assessment of social class membership. It is one thing to accept that social class extends beyond variables like income and SES to encompass differentials of socioeconomic power; it is quite another to assess that construct in such a way that we can incorporate it within research. Krieger, Williams, and Moss (1997) have written about this dilemma, suggesting that instruments that capture elements of individuals' access to socioeconomic power, such as participation in (or exclusion from) workplace decision making, may be part of the solution.

4. Investigate the experiences of poor clients with mental health service providers. Psychologists

currently know little about the experiences of poor and working-class men and women in psychotherapy. The little research that does exist (e.g., Chalifoux, 1996) suggests that counselors may not be meeting the needs of poor clients and that they may be unaware of the ways in which classist attitudes influence their relationships with these clients.

5. Develop innovative, socially just practices for use in poor communities. Even when psychologists sincerely embrace social justice principles, it can be challenging to change established practices in service of social justice goals, especially at the community level. The ROAD project (Goodman et al., 2007) is an example of a multifaceted programmatic intervention that literally and tangibly combines counseling practice with action to fight the impact of structural oppression. Such practices will take counseling psychologists into territory far beyond the 50-minute talk therapy hour and also offer great promise in truly merging emotional support and growth with prosocial movement.

CONCLUSION

A social exclusion perspective on poverty underscores a foundational assumption within social class theory: that social class stratification is a relational phenomenon. According to this perspective, the circumstances of people living in poverty cannot be understood apart from the decisions and actions (or lack thereof) of the rest of society throughout the social class hierarchy. Similarly, people who enjoy great privilege did not create and do not maintain their advantageous positions within a vacuum; rather, in addition to their own effort, their accumulation of wealth is supported by the contributions of low-wage workers around the world as well as the U.S. economic system and tax structure (L. Smith, 2010). This realization brings with it a new kind of accountability with regard to the poor and calls for a new kind of help that goes beyond remediation of the psychological harm exacted by poverty and beyond sympathy and charity. It is the kind of help that Freire (1970) called "true generosity" (p. 29):

addressing ourselves to the inequities that are causing the damage in the first place. Counseling psychologists have led the field in directing their theory, research, and practice toward the eradication of oppression (e.g., Toporek, Gerstein, Fouad, Roysicar, & Israel, 2006), and these efforts can only be enhanced through the full incorporation of issues of social class and poverty. Albee (1996) put it simply: "Eliminate poverty and help achieve equality for all, and mental disorders will decline. . . . Building stronger, more secure, and more optimistic people makes them resistant across the board" (p. 1130).

References

Adler, N. E., Boyce, T., Chesney, M. A., Cohen, S., Folkman, S., Kahn, R. L., & Syme, S. L. (1994). Socioeconomic status and health. *American Psychologist, 49*, 15–24. doi:10.1037/0003-066X.49.1.15

Adler, N. E., & Snibbe, A. C. (2003). The role of psychosocial processes in explaining the gradient between socioeconomic status and health. *Current Directions in Psychological Science, 12*, 119–123. doi:10.1111/1467-8721.01245

Albee, G. W. (1996). Revolutions and counterrevolutions in prevention. *American Psychologist, 51*, 1130–1133. doi:10.1037/0003-066X.51.11.1130

Albee, G. W., & Gulotta, T. P. (1997). Primary prevention's evolution. In G. Albee & T. Gulotta (Eds.), *Primary prevention works* (pp. 3–22). Thousand Oaks, CA: Sage.

Allen, L., & Britt, D. (1983). Social class, mental health, and mental illness. In R. Felner, L. Jason, J. Moritsugu, & S. Farber (Eds.), *Preventative psychology: Theory, research, and practice* (pp. 149–160). New York, NY: Pergamon.

American Psychiatric Association. (1980). *Diagnostic and statistical manual of mental disorders* (3rd ed.). Washington, DC: Author.

American Psychological Association. (2008). *Report of the Task Force on Resources for the Inclusion of Social Class in Psychology Curricula*. Retrieved from http://www.apa.org/pi/ses/

Barnes, A. (2004). Race, schizophrenia, and admission to state psychiatric hospitals. *Administration and Policy in Mental Health, 31*, 241–252.

Baumeister, R. F., DeWall, C. N., Twenge, J. M., & Ciarocco, N. J. (2005). Social exclusion impairs self-regulation. *Journal of Personality and Social Psychology, 88*, 589–604. doi:10.1037/0022-3514.88.4.589

Baumeister, R. F., Twenge, J. M., & Nuss, C. K. (2002). Effects of social exclusion on cognitive processing. *Journal of Personality and Social Psychology, 83,* 817–827. doi:10.1037/0022-3514.83.4.817

Belle, D. (1990). Poverty and women's mental health. *American Psychologist, 45,* 385–389. doi:10.1037/0003-066X.45.3.385

Belle, D., & Doucet, J. (2003) Poverty, inequality and discrimination as sources of depression among women. *Psychology of Women Quarterly, 27,* 101–113. doi:10.1111/1471-6402.00090

Belle, D., Doucet, J., Harris, J., Miller, J., & Tan, E. (2000). Who is rich? Who is happy? *American Psychologist, 55,* 1160–1161. doi:10.1037/0003-066X.55.10.1160

Blazer, D. G., Kessler, R. C., McGonagle, K. A., & Schwartz, M. S. (1994). The prevalence and distribution in a national community sample: The National Comorbidity Survey. *The American Journal of Psychiatry, 151,* 979–989.

Blustein, D. L., Chaves, A. P., Diemer, M. A., Gallagher, L. A., Marshall, K. G., Sirin, S., & Bhati, K. S. (2002). Voices of the forgotten half: The role of social class in the school-to-work transition. *Journal of Counseling Psychology, 49,* 311–323. doi:10.1037/0022-0167.49.3.311

Blustein, D. L., McWhirter, E. H., & Perry, J. C. (2005). An emancipatory communitarian approach to vocational development theory, research, and practice. *The Counseling Psychologist, 33,* 141–179. doi:10.1177/0011000004272268

Boroughs, M., Massey, O. T., & Armstrong, K. H. (2006). Socioeconomic status and behavior problems. *Journal of School Violence, 4,* 31–46. doi:10.1300/J202v04n04_03

Bradley, R. H., & Corwyn, R. F. (2002). Socioeconomic status and child development. *Annual Review of Psychology, 53,* 371–399. doi:10.1146/annurev.psych.53.100901.135233

Bruce, M. L., Takeuchi, D. T., & Leaf, P. J. (1991). Poverty and psychiatric status. *Archives of General Psychiatry, 48,* 470–474.

Bryant-Davis, T., & Ocampo, C. (2005). Racist incident-based trauma. *The Counseling Psychologist, 33,* 479–500. doi:10.1177/0011000005276465

Bullard, R. D. (2000). *Dumping in Dixie.* Boulder, CO: Westview Press.

Bullock, H. E., Wyche, K. F., & Williams, W. R. (2001). Media images of the poor. *Journal of Social Issues, 57,* 229–246. doi:10.1111/0022-4537.00210

Carter, R. T. (1995). *The influence of race and racial identity in psychotherapy: Toward a racially inclusive model.* New York, NY: Wiley.

Chalifoux, B. (1996). Speaking up: White, working class women in therapy. *Women and Therapy, 18*(3–4), 25–34. doi:10.1300/J015v18n03_04

Chronicle of Higher Education (2010). *Average faculty salaries by field and rank at 4-year colleges and universities, 2009–10.* Retrieved from http://chronicle.com/article/Chart-Average-Faculty/64500/

Collins, C., & Yeskel, F. (2005). *Economic apartheid in America.* New York, NY: New Press.

Correspondents of the New York Times. (2005). *Class matters.* New York, NY: Henry Holt.

Costello, E. J., Compton, S. N., Keeler, G., & Angold, A. (2003). Relationships between poverty and psychopathology: A natural experiment. *JAMA, 290,* 2023–2029. doi:10.1001/jama.290.15.2023

Cozzarelli, C., Wilkinson, A. V., & Tagler, M. J. (2001). Attitudes toward the poor and attributions for poverty. *Journal of Social Issues, 57,* 207–227. doi:10.1111/0022-4537.00209

Cutler, D., & Miller, G. (2005). The role of public health improvements in health advances. *Demography, 42,* 1–22. doi:10.1353/dem.2005.0002

di Nardo, P. A. (1975). Social class and diagnostic suggestion as variables in clinical judgment. *Journal of Consulting and Clinical Psychology, 43,* 363–368. doi:10.1037/h0076728

Dumont, M. P. (1992). *Treating the poor.* Belmont, MA: Dymphna Press.

Economic Policy Institute (EPI). (2007). *Living wage facts.* Retrieved from http://www.epinet.org/content.cfm/issueguides_livingwage_livingwagefacts.

Enns, C. Z. (2004). *Feminist theories and feminist psychotherapies.* New York, NY: Taylor & Francis.

Evans, G. W. (2004). The environment of childhood poverty. *American Psychologist, 59,* 77–92. doi:10.1037/0003-066X.59.2.77

Fouad, N. A., & Brown, M. T. (2000). The role of race and class in development. In S. D. Brown & R. W. Lent (Eds.), *Handbook of counseling psychology* (3rd ed., pp. 379–408). New York, NY: Wiley.

Freire, P. (1970). *The pedagogy of the oppressed.* New York, NY: Continuum.

Gallo, L. C., Bogart, L. M., Vranceanu, A. M., & Matthews, K. A. (2005). Socioeconomic status, resources, psychological experiences, and emotional responses. *Journal of Personality and Social Psychology, 88,* 386–399. doi:10.1037/0022-3514.88.2.386

Gallo, L. C., & Matthews, K. A. (2003). Understanding the association between socioeconomic status and physical health. *Psychological Bulletin, 129,* 10–51. doi:10.1037/0033-2909.129.1.10

Giannone, J. (2010). *World's rich got richer in 2009*. Retrieved from http://www.msnbc.msn.com/id/37846803/ns/business-personal_finance/

Gilbert, D. (2008). *The American class structure in an age of growing inequality*. Los Angeles, CA: Pine Forge Press.

Goodman, L. A., Litwin, A., Bohlig, A., Weintraub, S. R., Green, A., Walker, J., . . . Ryan, N. (2007). Applying feminist theory to community practice: A multilevel empowerment intervention for low-income women with depression. In E. Aldarondo (Ed.), *Advancing social justice through clinical practice* (pp. 265–290). Mahwah, NJ: Erlbaum.

Grusky, D. B. (Ed.). (2008). *Social stratification*. Philadelphia, PA: Westview Press.

Grusky, D. B., & Ku, M. C. (2008). Gloom, doom, and inequality. In D. B. Grusky (Ed.), *Social stratification* (pp. 2–28). Philadelphia, PA: Westview Press.

Guthrie, R. V. (1976). *Even the rat was White*. Needham Heights, MA: Allyn & Bacon.

Heesacker, M., Wester, S. R., Vogel, D. L., Wentzel, J. T., Mejia-Millan, C. M., & Goodholm, C. R. (1999). Gender-based emotional stereotyping. *Journal of Counseling Psychology, 46*, 483–495. doi:10.1037/0022-0167.46.4.483

Helms, J. (Ed.). (1990). *Black and White racial identity*. Westport, CT: Greenwood.

Javier, R. A., & Herron, W. G. (2002). Psychoanalysis and the disenfranchised: Countertransference issues. *Psychoanalytic Psychology, 19*, 149–166. doi:10.1037/0736-9735.19.1.149

Jordan, J. V. (2000). The role of mutual empathy in relational/cultural therapy [from the PsycARTICLES database]. *Journal of Clinical Psychology, 56*, 1005–1016. doi:10.1002/1097-4679(200008)56:8<1005:AID-JCLP2>3.0.CO;2-L

Knight, H. (2010). *San Francisco looks to Seattle: Did sidewalk sitting ban help?* Retrieved from http://www.seattlepi.com/local/417578_sit30.html

Kozol, J. (2005). *The shame of the nation*. New York, NY: Crown.

Krieger, N. (2005). Embodiment: A conceptual glossary for epidemiology. *Journal of Epidemiology and Community Health, 59*, 350–355. doi:10.1136/jech.2004.024562

Krieger, N., Williams, D. R., & Moss, N. E. (1997). Measuring social class in U.S. Public Health. *Annual Review of Public Health, 18*, 341–378. doi:10.1146/annurev.publhealth.18.1.341

Lee, S. D., & Temerlin, M. K. (1970). Social class, diagnosis, and prognosis for psychotherapy. *Psychotherapy: Theory, Research and Practice, 7*, 181–185. doi:10.1037/h0086584

Leondar-Wright, B. (2005). *Class matters*. Gabriola Island, British Columbia, Canada: New Society.

Leventhal, T., & Brooks-Gunn, J. (2000). The neighborhoods they live in: The effect of neighborhood residence on child and adolescent outcomes. *Psychological Bulletin, 126*, 309–337. doi:10.1037/0033-2909.126.2.309

Liu, W. M. (2002). The social class–related experience of men: Integrating theory and practice. *Professional Psychology: Research and Practice, 33*, 355–360. doi:10.1037/0735-7028.33.4.355

Liu, W. M., Ali, S. R., Soleck, G., Hopps, J., Dunston, K., & Pickett, T., Jr. (2004). Using social class in counseling psychology research. *Journal of Counseling Psychology, 51*, 3–18. doi:10.1037/0022-0167.51.1.3

Liu, W. M., Pickett, T., & Ivey, A. E. (2007). White middle-class privilege: Social class bias and implications for training and practice. *Journal of Multicultural Counseling and Development, 35*, 194–206.

Lorant, V., Deliege, D., Eaton, W., Robert, A., Philippot, P., & Ansseau, M. (2003). Socioeconomic inequalities in depression: A meta-analysis. *American Journal of Epidemiology, 157*, 98–112. doi:10.1093/aje/kwf182

Lott, B. (2002). Cognitive and behavioral distancing from the poor. *American Psychologist, 57*, 100–110. doi:10.1037/0003-066X.57.2.100

Lott, B., & Bullock, H. E. (2007). *Psychology and economic injustice: Personal, professional, and political intersections*. Washington, DC: American Psychological Association.

Lott, B., & Saxon, S. (2002). The influence of ethnicity, social class, and context on judgments about U.S. women. *The Journal of Social Psychology, 142*, 481–499. doi:10.1080/00224540209603913

Marmot, M., & Wilkinson, R. G. (Eds.). (2006). *The social determinants of health*. Oxford, England: Oxford University Press.

McIntosh, P. (1988). *White privilege and male privilege: A personal account of coming to see correspondences through work in women's studies*. Wellesley, MA: Working Paper Series, Wellesley College.

McLoyd, V. C. (1998). Socioeconomic disadvantage and child development. *American Psychologist, 53*, 185–204. doi:10.1037/0003-066X.53.2.185

Miller, J. B. (1976). *Toward a new psychology of women*. Boston, MA: Beacon Press.

Miller, J. B., & Stiver, I. P. (1997). *The healing connection*. Boston, MA: Beacon Press.

Mohr, J., Israel, T., & Sedlacek, W. E. (2001). Counselors' attitudes regarding bisexuality as predictors of counselors' clinical responses. *Journal of Counseling Psychology, 48*, 212–222. doi:10.1037/0022-0167.48.2.212

Pavkov, T. W., Lewis, D. A., & Lyons, J. S. (1989). Psychiatric diagnoses and racial bias. *Professional Psychology: Research and Practice, 20*, 364–368. doi:10.1037/0735-7028.20.6.364

Prilleltensky, I. (1989). Psychology and the status quo. *American Psychologist, 44*, 795–802. doi:10.1037/0003-066X.44.5.795

Rhode, D. (2004). Access to justice: Connecting principles to practice. *The Georgetown Journal of Legal Ethics, 17*, 369–422.

Ryan, W. (2007). Blaming the victim. In P. S. Rothenberg (Ed.), *Race, class, and gender in the United States* (pp. 688–717). New York, NY: Worth. (Original work published in 1971)

Schnitzer, P. K. (1996). "They don't come in!" Stories told, lessons taught about poor families in therapy. *American Journal of Orthopsychiatry, 66*, 572–582. doi:10.1037/h0080206

Scott, J. (2005). Life at the top in America isn't just better, it's longer. In Correspondents of the New York Times, *Class matters* (pp. 27–50). New York, NY: Times Books.

Seeman, T. E., Crimmins, E., Huang, M. H., Singer, B., Bucur, A., Gruenwald, T., . . . Reuben, D. B. (2004). Cumulative biological risk and socioeconomic differences in mortality. *Social Science and Medicine, 58*, 1985–1997. doi:10.1016/S0277-9536(03)00402-7

Siefert, K., Bowman, P. J., Heflin, C. M., Danziger, S. H., & Williams, D. R. (2000). Social and environmental predictors of maternal depression in current and recent welfare recipients. *American Journal of Orthopsychiatry, 70*, 510–522. doi:10.1037/h0087688

Silver, H. (1994). Social exclusion and social solidarity: Three paradigms. *International Labour Review, 133*, 531–578.

Smith, J. M. (2000). Psychotherapy with people stressed by poverty. In A. N. Sabo & L. Havens (Eds.), *Real world guide to psychotherapy practice* (pp. 71–92). Cambridge, MA: Harvard University Press.

Smith, L. (2005). Classism, psychotherapy, and the poor: Conspicuous by their absence. *American Psychologist, 60*, 687–696. doi:10.1037/0003-066X.60.7.687

Smith, L. (2007). Positioning classism within counseling psychology's social justice agenda. *The Counseling Psychologist, 36*, 895–924. doi:10.1177/0011000007309861

Smith, L. (2009). Enhancing training and practice in the context of poverty. *Training and Education in Professional Psychology, 3*, 84–93. doi:10.1037/a0014459

Smith, L. (2010). *Psychology, poverty, and the end of social exclusion*. New York, NY: Teachers College Press.

Smith, L., Allen, A., & Bowen, R. (2010). Expecting the worst: Exploring the associations between poverty and misbehavior. *Journal of Poverty, 14*, 33–54.

Smith, L., Chambers, D. A., & Bratini, L. (2009). When oppression is the pathogen: The participatory development of socially-just mental health practice. *American Journal of Orthopsychiatry, 79*, 159–168. doi:10.1037/a0015353

Smith, L., Foley, P. F., & Chaney, M. P. (2008). Addressing classism, ableism, and heterosexism within multicultural-social justice training. *Journal of Counseling and Development, 86*, 303–309.

Smith, L., Mao, S., Perkins, S., & Ampuero, M. (in press). The relationship of clients' social class to early therapeutic impressions. *Counselling Psychology Quarterly*.

Smith, L., & Redington, R. (in press). Class dismissed: Making the case for the study of classist microaggressions. In D. W. Sue (Ed.), *Microaggressions and marginalized groups in society: Race, gender, sexual orientation, class and religious manifestations*. New York, NY: Wiley.

Smith, L., & Romero, L. (2010). Psychological interventions in the context of poverty: Participatory action research as practice. *American Journal of Orthopsychiatry, 80*, 12–25. doi:10.1111/j.1939-0025.2010.01003.x

Stein, L. S., Green, B. L., & Stone, W. N. (1972). Therapist attitudes as influenced by A-B therapist type, patient diagnosis, and social class. *Journal of Consulting and Clinical Psychology, 39*, 301–307. doi:10.1037/h0033427

Steinvick, B. (2010). *How do you sleep at night?* Retrieved from http://www.cityonahillpress.com/2010/06/03/how-do-you-sleep-at-night/

Stewart, M. J., Makwarimba, E., Reutter, L. I., Veenstra, G., Raphael, D., & Love, R. (2009). Poverty, sense of belonging and experiences of social isolation. *Journal of Poverty, 13*, 173–195. doi:10.1080/10875540902841762

Sue, D. W., Arredondo, P., & McDavis, R. J. (1992). Multicultural competencies/standards: A call to the profession. *Journal of Counseling and Development, 70*, 477–486.

Sue, D. W., Capodilupo, C. M., Torino, G. C., Bucceri, J. M., Holder, A. M., Nadal, K. L., & Esquilin, M. (2007). Racial microaggressions in everyday life: Implications for clinical practice. *American Psychologist, 62*, 271–286. doi:10.1037/0003-066X.62.4.271

Sue, D. W., & Sue, S. (2007). *Counseling the culturally diverse*. New York, NY: Wiley

Thompson, M. N., & Subich, L. M. (2006). The relation of social status to the career decision-making process. *Journal of Vocational Behavior, 69*, 289–301. doi:10.1016/j.jvb.2006.04.008

Todman, L. C., Taylor, S., Cochrane, K., Arbaugh-Korotko, J., Berger, J., Burt, E., . . . Mandeleew, D. (2009). Social exclusion indicators for the United States. *Journal of Individual Psychology, 65,* 330–359.

Toporek, R. L., Gerstein, L. H., Fouad, N. A., Roysicar, G., & Israel, T. (2006). *The handbook for social justice in counseling psychology.* Thousand Oaks, CA: Sage.

Twenge, J. M., Baumeister, R. F., DeWall, C. N., Ciarocco, N. J., & Bartels, J. M. (2007). Social exclusion decreases prosocial behavior. *Journal of Personality and Social Psychology, 92,* 56–66. doi:10.1037/0022-3514.92.1.56

U.S. Department of Labor. (2010). *Industries at a glance: Construction.* Retrieved from http://www.bls.gov/iag/tgs/iag23.htm

Zweig, M. (2000). *The working class majority.* Ithaca, NY: Cornell University Press.